# Teacher's Wraparound Edition

Glencoe

# Economics

## Today and Tomorrow

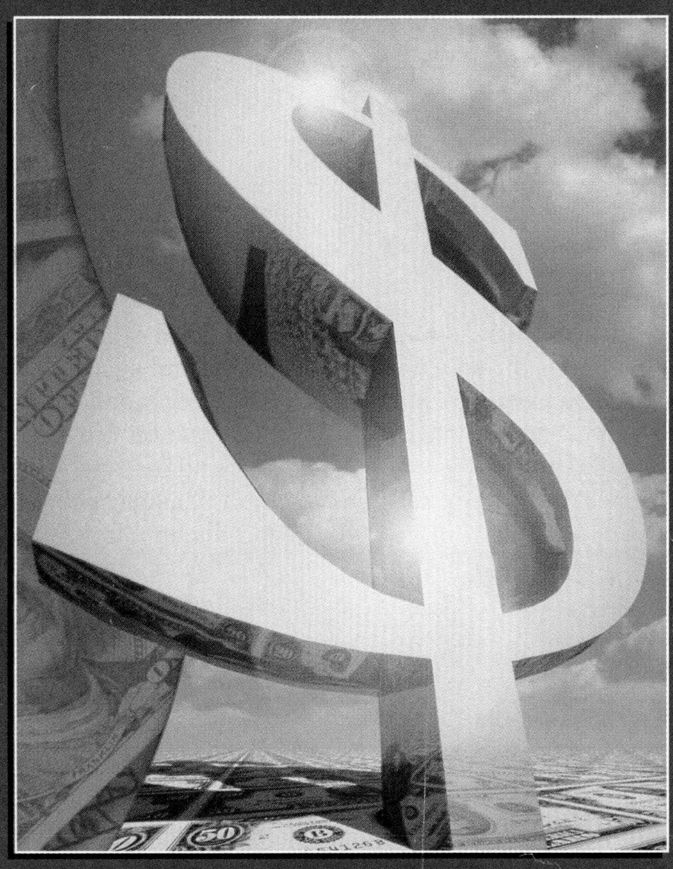

Roger LeRoy Miller, Ph.D.

With Features From

BusinessWeek

STANDARD & POOR'S

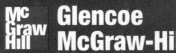

Mc Graw Hill Glencoe McGraw-Hill

New York, New York Columbus, Ohio Woodland Hills, California Peoria, Illinois

# About the Author

**Roger Leroy Miller** graduated Phi Beta Kappa from the University of California at Berkeley, where he also won the Department Prize in Economics. He was a Woodrow Wilson Honor Fellow, National Science Foundation Fellow, and Lilly Honor Fellow at the University of Chicago, where he received his Ph.D. in economics in 1968. Now at the Institute for University Studies in Arlington, Texas, Dr. Miller has taught at the University of Washington, the University of Miami, Clemson University, and the University of Texas. He has also taught methodology to teachers of high school economics for the National Council on Economic Education. Among the more than 200 books he has written or co-authored are works on economics, statistics, law, consumer finance, and government. Dr. Miller also has operated several retail and Internet businesses and served as a consultant to government agencies, private corporations, and law firms.

# Contributors

***Business Week*** is the most widely read business publication in the world and is the only weekly business news publication in existence. *Business Week* provides incisive and comprehensive interpretation of events by evaluating the news and its implications for the United States, regional, and world economies.

STANDARD & POOR'S

**Standard & Poor's** is a leading source of data, news, and analyses on regional, national, and global economic developments. Standard & Poor's information is used by industrial firms, financial institutions, and government agencies for setting policy, managing financial positions, planning production, formulating marketing strategies, and a range of similar activities. Standard & Poor's data services represent the single most sophisticated source of information for organizations that need to understand the impact of the path of economic growth and of government fiscal and monetary policies on their activities.

***Glencoe/McGraw-Hill***
*A Division of The McGraw-Hill Companies*



Send all inquiries to:
Glencoe/McGraw-Hill
8787 Orion Place
Columbus, OH 43240

Student Edition ISBN: 0-07-820489-5
Teacher's Wraparound Edition ISBN: 0-07-820490-9

2 3 4 5 6 7 8 9 10 071/043 08 07 06 05 04 03 02 01

# REVIEWERS

## ACADEMIC CONSULTANTS

**Candace Allen**
Economics Education Consultant
Tucson, Arizona

**Ryan C. Amacher**
Professor of Economics
University of Texas
Arlington, Texas

**David M. Blitzer**
Vice President & Chief Economist
Standard & Poor's
New York, New York

**Roger E. Meiners**
Professor of Economics
University of Texas
Arlington, Texas

**Joe Mullin**
Professor of Economics
Columbus State Community College
Columbus, Ohio

**Harold S. Stovall**
Senior Investment Strategist
Standard & Poor's
New York, New York

## EDUCATIONAL REVIEWERS

**Joanna Ackley**
John F. Kennedy High School
Taylor, Michigan

**Eleanor Allen**
Foothill High School
Sacramento, California

**Lourdes Rayneri Barrenechea**
LaSalle High School
Miami, Florida

**Charles E. Cleveland**
Belen Jesuit Preparatory School
Miami, Florida

**Charles Erlandson**
All Saints Episcopal School
Tyler, Texas

**Jeff Harris**
Dinuba High School
Dinuba, California

**Denny C. Jackson**
Switzerland County High School
Vevay, Indiana

**Rick Johnson**
New Harmony Public School
New Harmony, Indiana

**Richard P. Joyce**
Wilmington High School
Wilmington, Illinois

**Hal Kraynek**
Valley High School
Santa Ana, California

**Roger C. Lyder**
Pelham High School
Pelham, New Hampshire

**Howard D. Merrick, Jr.**
Pottsville Area High School
Pottsville, Pennsylvania

**Bill Nichols**
The Lovett School
Atlanta, Georgia

**Greg Parsley**
Roncalli High School
Indianapolis, Indiana

**Nancy Peterson**
Gilbert Junior–Senior High School
Gilbert, Iowa

**Brian M. Sage**
Niagara Falls High School
Niagara Falls, New York

**Ann Tapp**
Southern Baptist Educational Center
Olive Branch, Mississippi

**Douglas J. Woods**
Washington High School
Cherokee, Iowa

**Christopher S. Ziller**
Tecumseh Junior–Senior High School
Lynnville, Indiana

Photo Credits:
**T4–5** Horizons [Companies]; **T11** (t)KS Studio, (b)Geoff Butler; **T12** (t)Russ Einhorn/Liaison Agency, (tc)CORBIS/Bettmann, (tr)Mark Scott/FPG, (bl)Matt Mendolson/CORBIS, (br)Jonathon Kirn/Liaison Agency; **T13** Guy Crittendon; **T14** (l) Doug Martin, (c)CORBIS, (r)Hulton Getty Picture Library/Liaison Agency; **T24** Walter Hodges/Stone; **T25** (l)Geoff Butler, (r)Securities Industry Foundation for Economic Education; **T26 T26–27** Martucci Studio; **T28–29 T30–31 T32** Geoff Butler.

Glencoe

# Economics

## Today and Tomorrow

# You Demanded It! Glencoe Supplied It!

*A Truly Readable Economics Text*

*Dynamic Classroom Resources*

*Integrated Technology*

# Introducing the *Economics Today and* Integrated Internet Support

**Economics Online** boxes at point of use in the chapter direct students to use Web curriculum as part of an integrated study of economics.

**You Need:** Current Content
✓ **We Provide:** Updated Information via the Web

**You Need:** Help with Assessment
✓ **We Provide:** Self-Check Quizzes and Interactive Puzzles

**You Need:** Integration of Web Resources into Your Lessons
✓ **We Provide:** Complete Student Activities, Teacher Strategies, and Additional Links

Use our Web site for additional resources. All essential content is covered in the Student Edition.

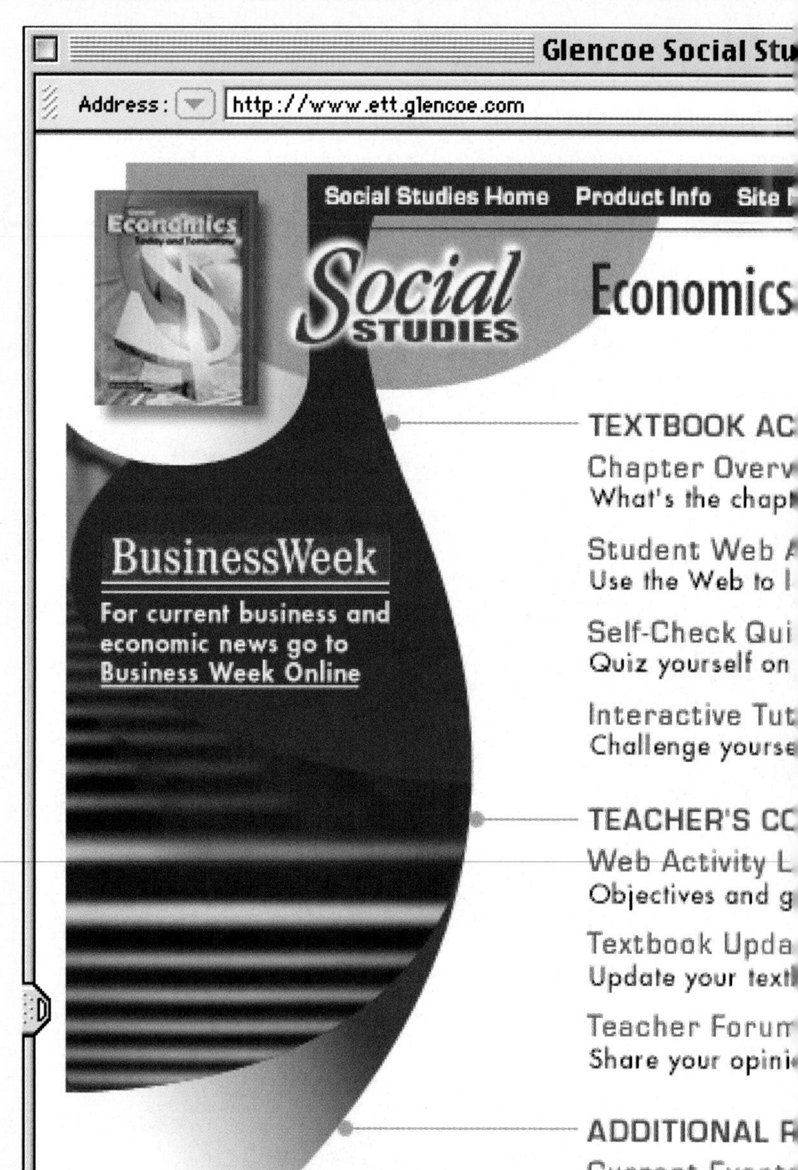


### Our Pledge to You

Glencoe is committed to providing textbooks that are as error free and as accurate as possible. As part of this commitment, we will be updating critical time-sensitive data such as charts, graphs, and statistics along with the latest information in the field of economics on our Web site. In this way, you and your students will always have access to the most accurate information possible.

# *Tomorrow* Web Site: ett.glencoe.com
## for Your Student Edition

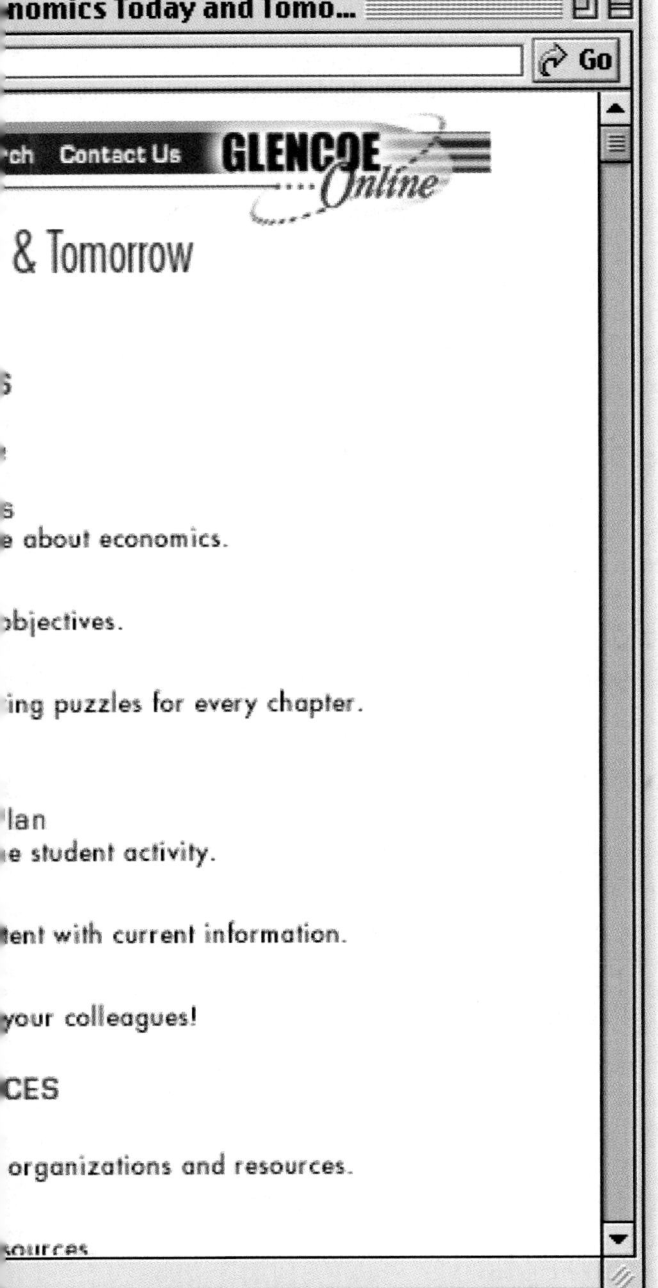


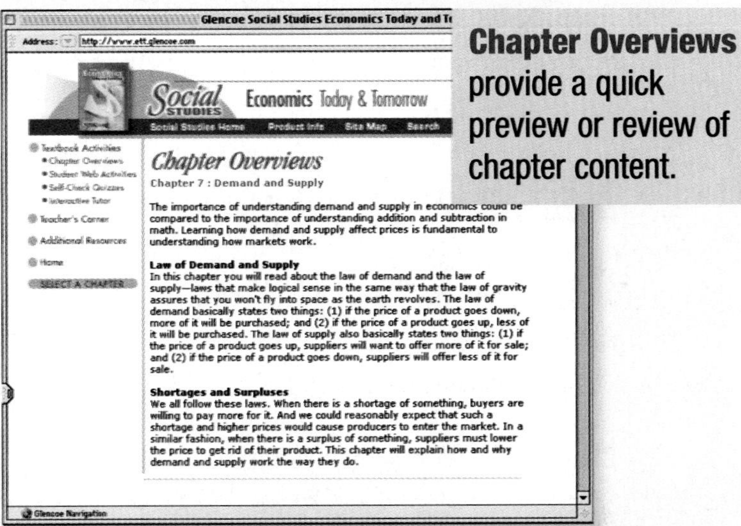


**Chapter Overviews** provide a quick preview or review of chapter content.

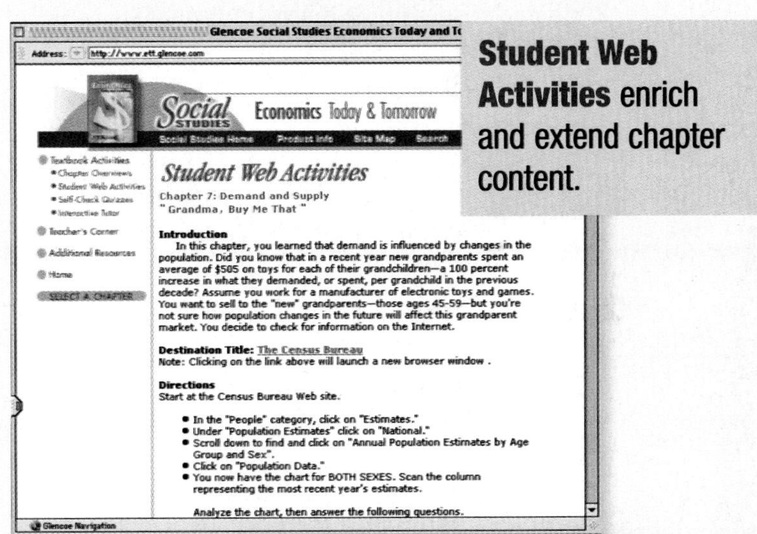


**Student Web Activities** enrich and extend chapter content.

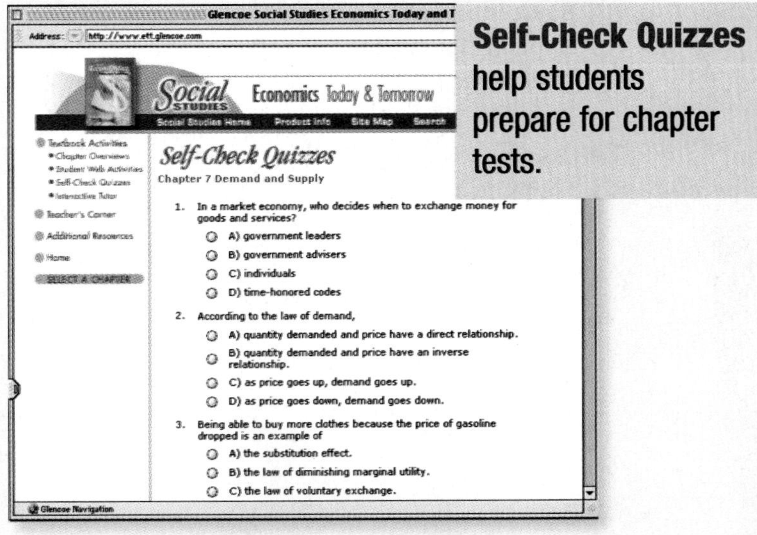


**Self-Check Quizzes** help students prepare for chapter tests.

# CONTENTS

# ett.glencoe.com

**Visit the** *Economics Today and Tomorrow* **Web site!**

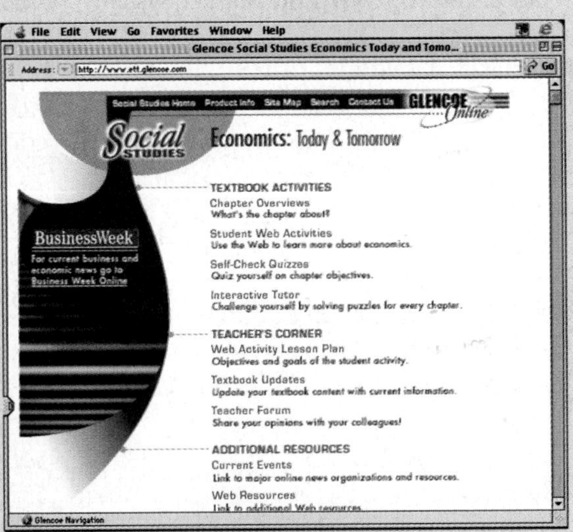


- **Chapter Overviews** provide you with a quick preview or review of the chapter.
- **Student Web Activities** take you into the real world of economics.
- **Self-Check Quizzes** help you prepare for the Chapter Test.

*Use our Web site for additional resources. All essential content is covered in the Student Edition.*

# BusinessWeek

## Spotlight on the Economy

## Focus on Free Enterprise

## Economics Lab

## Global Economy

# FEATURES

## People & Perspectives

## CAREERS

# Skills

## Economic Handbook

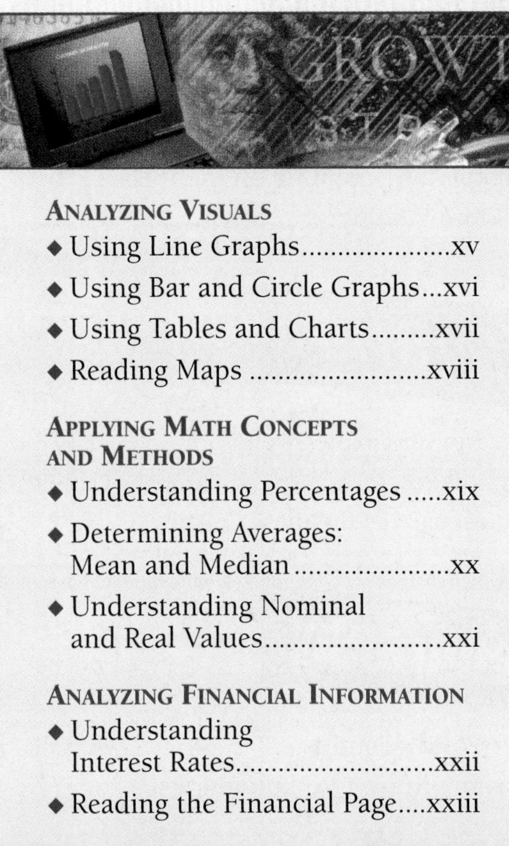

### Analyzing Visuals



### Applying Math Concepts and Methods



### Analyzing Financial Information



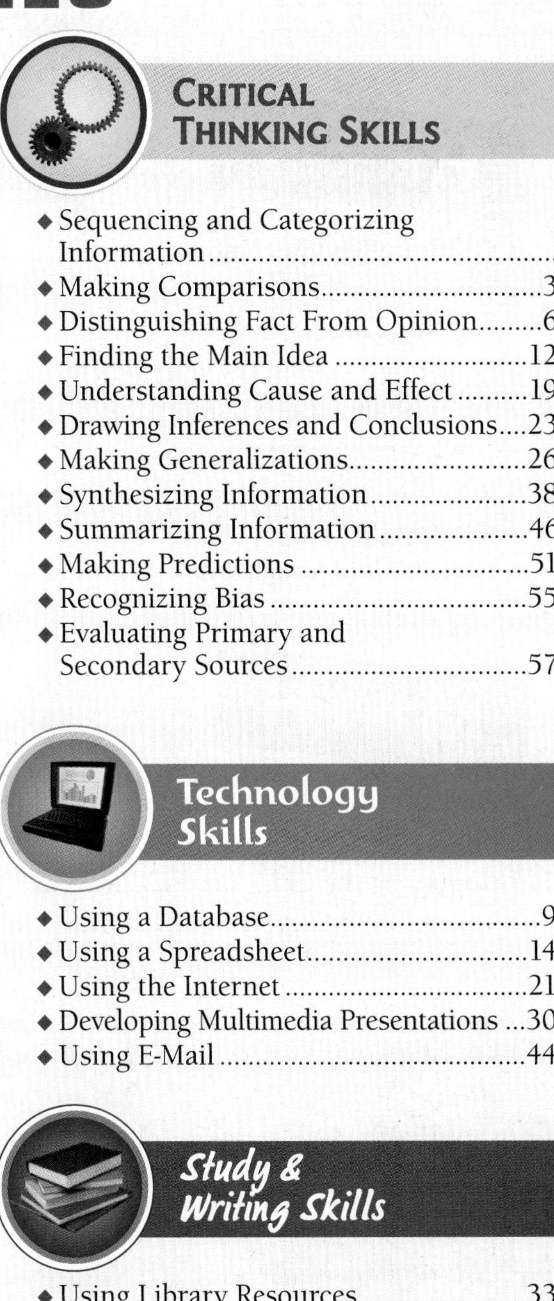

## Critical Thinking Skills



## Technology Skills



## Study & Writing Skills

# Economic Connection to...

## History



## Math



## Technology



## Literature



## Geography

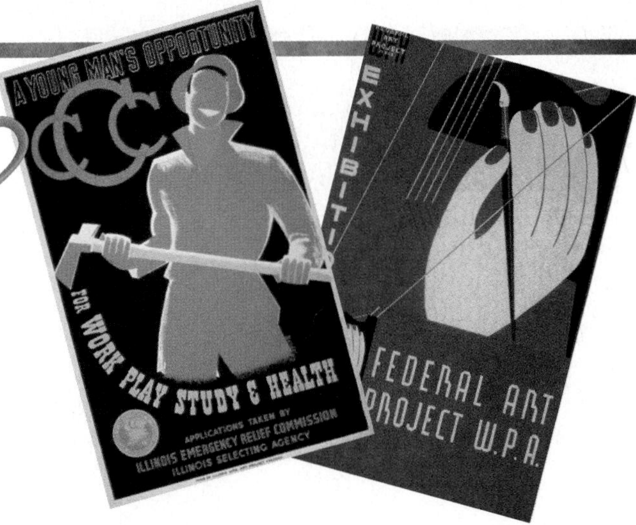

# GRAPHS, CHARTS, & TABLES

## Graphs



*Credit Card Charge of $200 at 10% Interest*

| | | |
|---|---|---|
| Amount Charged | $200.00 | $200.00 |
| Interest at 10% | $20.00 | $20.00 |
| Annual Membership Fee | none | $5.00 |
| APR | 10% | 12.5% |



## Charts and Tables

# GRAPHS, CHARTS, & TABLES

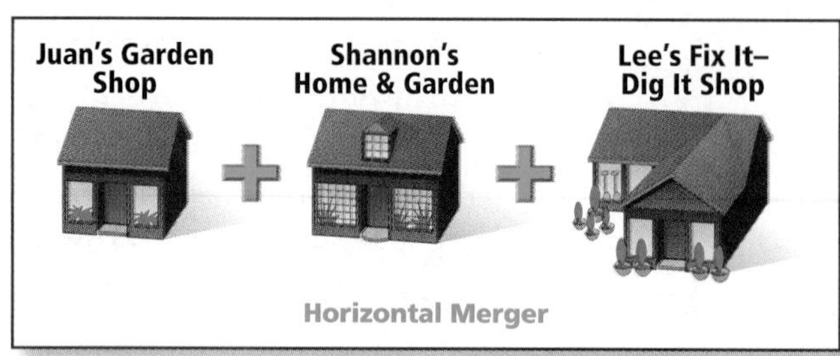
Juan's Garden Shop
Shannon's Home & Garden
Lee's Fix It–Dig It Shop
Horizontal Merger

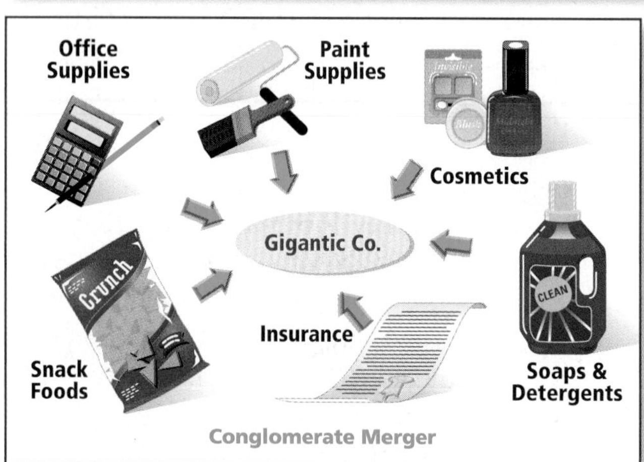
Office Supplies
Paint Supplies
Cosmetics
Gigantic Co.
Snack Foods
Insurance
Soaps & Detergents
Conglomerate Merger

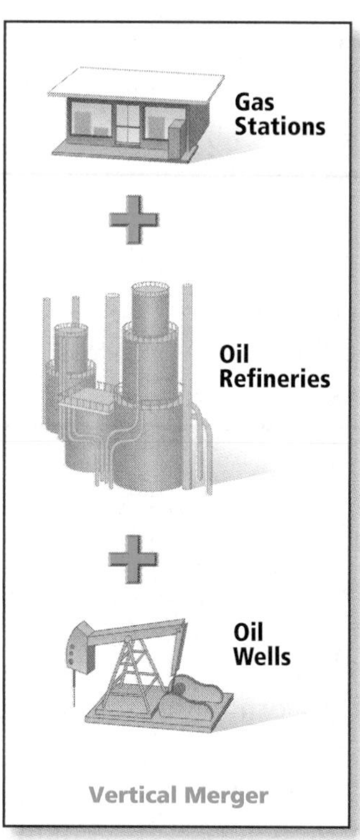
Gas Stations
Oil Refineries
Oil Wells
Vertical Merger

## Maps



## Checklists



NATIONAL GEOGRAPHIC SOCIETY

## Reference Atlas



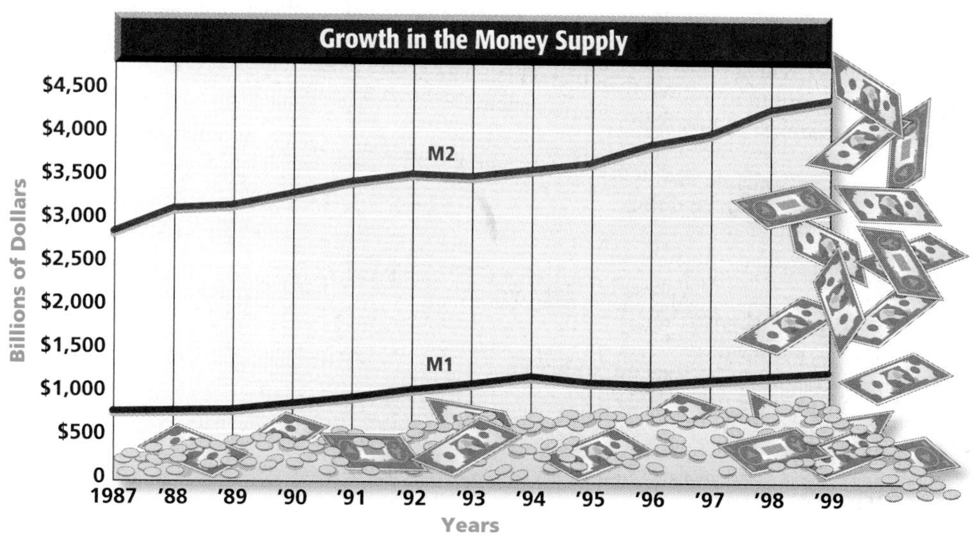

**National Council on Economic Education**

THE **Economics**America AND **Economics**International PROGRAMS

January 21, 2000
*In Our 51st Year of Leadership and Service as the Nation's Premier Economic Education Organization*

Dear Educator,

We commend this textbook to teachers. The Principles and Practices of sound, standards-based Economics are needed for our students and our society, now, more than ever. These lessons are correlated with the Voluntary National Content Standards in Economics written and published by the National Council on Economic Education.

Economics is no longer (if it ever was) the "dismal science." It is an essential set of reasoning and decision-making skills for surviving, let alone thriving, in a changing, competitive global economy.

As we confront the issues of the increasing number of personal bankruptcies, uncontrolled credit card debt, ignorance of the value of saving and investing, and the inability of many of our students and their families to grasp the repercussions of international trade, these public concerns magnify the need for increasing economic literacy in our young adults and for enhancing economic education in our nation's schools.

The challenge was expressed over fifty years ago in the founding of the National Council on Economic Education (NCEE): "There is no aspect of education more important than that which makes all our citizens intelligent and truly informed about the economic system in which they live and work."

In principle and in practice, teaching standards-based economics is an excellent thing to be doing.

Respectfully,

Robert Duvall

Robert F. Duvall
President & Chief Executive Officer

*The Campaign for Economic Literacy*

1140 Avenue of the Americas, New York, NY 10036 212.730.7007 fax 212.730.1793 ncee@eaglobal.org

# Voluntary National Content Standards in Economics

In 1994 the United States Congress designated economics as one of the nine core subjects to be taught in America's schools. As a result, the National Council on Economic Education developed the *Voluntary National Content Standards in Economics* for use in economics curricula.

*Economics Today and Tomorrow* provides extensive coverage for the 20 voluntary content standards. For a complete discussion of the standards, you can reach the National Council on Economic Education through the Internet at www.nationalcouncil.org, or at 1-800-338-1192.

| For each standard, students will understand that: | *Economics Today and Tomorrow* Chapter and Section Coverage |
|---|---|
|  Productive resources are limited. Therefore, people cannot have all the goods and services they want; as a result, they must choose some things and give up others. | **Chapter 1 What Is Economics?**<br>**Section 1:** The Basic Problem in Economics<br>**Section 2:** Trade-Offs<br>**Chapter 3 Your Role as a Consumer**<br>**Section 1:** Consumption, Income, and Decision Making<br>**Section 2:** Buying Principles or Strategies<br>**Chapter 5 Buying the Necessities**<br>**Section 1:** Shopping for Food<br>**Section 2:** Clothing Choices<br>**Section 3:** To Rent or to Buy |
|  Effective decision making requires comparing the additional costs of alternatives with the additional benefits. Most choices involve doing a little more or a little less of something; few choices are all-or-nothing decisions. | **Chapter 1 What Is Economics?**<br>**Section 2:** Trade-Offs<br>**Chapter 3 Your Role as a Consumer**<br>**Section 1:** Consumption, Income, and Decision Making<br>**Section 2:** Buying Principles, or Strategies<br>**Chapter 5 Buy the Necessities**<br>**Section 1:** Shopping for Food<br>**Section 2:** Clothing Choices<br>**Section 3:** To Rent or to Buy<br>**Section 4:** Buying and Operating a Vehicle |
|  Different methods can be used to allocate goods and services. People, acting individually or collectively through government, must choose which methods to use to allocate different kinds of goods and services. | **Chapter 2 Economic Systems and the American Economy**<br>**Section 1:** Economic Systems<br>**Chapter 19 Converging Economic Systems**<br>**Section 1:** Comparing Capitalism and Socialism<br>**Section 2:** Changing Authoritarian Socialism—The Case of China<br>**Section 3:** Nations Move Toward the Market System |

| will understand that: | Chapter and Section Coverage |
|---|---|
| **4** People respond predictably to positive and negative incentives. | **Chapter 2** Economic Systems and the American Economy<br>Section 1: Economic Systems<br>Section 2: Characteristics of the American Economy<br>Section 3: The Goals of the Nation<br>**Chapter 11** Marketing and Distribution<br>Section 1: The Changing Role of Marketing<br>Section 2: The Marketing Mix<br>Section 3: Distribution Channels |
| **5** Voluntary exchange occurs only when all participating parties expect to gain. This is true for trade among individuals or organizations within a nation, and among individuals or organizations in different nations. | **Chapter 3** Your Role as a Consumer<br>Section 1: Consumption, Income, and Decision Making<br>**Chapter 18** Trading With Other Nations<br>Section 1: The Benefits of World Trade<br>Section 2: Financing World Trade<br>Section 3: Restrictions on World Trade |
| **6** When individuals, regions, and nations specialize in what they can produce at the lowest cost and then trade with others, both production and consumption increase. | **Chapter 18** Trading With Other Nations<br>Section 1: The Benefits of World Trade<br>Section 2: Financing World Trade<br>Section 3: Restrictions on World Trade<br>**Chapter 20** Economic Growth in Developing Nations<br>Section 2: The Process of Economic Development<br>Section 3: Obstacles to Growth in Developing Nations<br>**Chapter 21** The Global Economy<br>Section 1: Reasons for and Results of Global Integration<br>Section 2: Direct Foreign Investment—Should We Be Worried?<br>Section 3: Multinationals and Economic Competition |
| **7** Markets exist when buyers and sellers interact. This interaction determines market prices and thereby allocates scarce goods and services. | **Chapter 7** Demand and Supply<br>Section 1: Demand<br>Section 2: The Demand Curve and Elasticity of Demand<br>Section 3: The Law of Supply and the Supply Curve<br>Section 4: Putting Supply and Demand Together |
| **8** Prices send signals and provide incentives to buyers and sellers. When supply or demand changes, market prices adjust, affecting incentives. | **Chapter 7** Demand and Supply<br>Section 1: Demand<br>Section 2: The Demand Curve and Elasticity of Demand<br>Section 3: The Law of Supply and the Supply Curve<br>Section 4: Putting Supply and Demand Together<br>**Chapter 11** Marketing and Distribution<br>Section 1: The Changing Role of Marketing<br>Section 2: The Marketing Mix |

| For each standard, students will understand that: | *Economics Today and Tomorrow* Chapter and Section Coverage |
|---|---|
|  Competition among sellers lowers costs and prices, and encourages producers to produce more of what consumers are willing and able to buy. Competition among buyers increases prices and allocates goods and services to those people who are willing and able to pay the most for them. | **Chapter 9 Competition and Monopolies**<br>**Section 1:** Perfect Competition<br>**Section 2:** Monopoly, Oligopoly, Monopolistic Competition<br>**Section 3:** Government Policies Toward Competition |
|  Institutions evolve in market economies to help individuals and groups accomplish their goals. Banks, labor unions, corporations, legal systems, and not-for-profit organizations are examples of important institutions. A different kind of institution, clearly defined and well enforced property rights, is essential to a market economy. | **Chapter 4 Going Into Debt**<br>**Section 2:** Sources of Loans and Credit<br>**Section 3:** Applying for Credit<br>**Section 4:** Government Regulation of Credit<br>**Chapter 6 Saving and Investing**<br>**Section 1:** Why Save?<br>**Section 2:** Investing: Taking Risks With Your Savings<br>**Section 3:** Special Savings Plans and Goals<br>**Chapter 8 Business Organizations**<br>**Section 1:** Starting a Business<br>**Section 2:** Sole Proprietorships and Partnerships<br>**Section 3:** The Corporate World and Franchises<br>**Chapter 10 Financing and Producing Goods**<br>**Section 1:** Investing in the Free Enterprise System<br>**Chapter 12 The American Labor Force**<br>**Section 1:** Americans at Work<br>**Section 2:** Organized Labor<br>**Section 3:** Collective Bargaining<br>**Chapter 14 Money and Banking**<br>**Section 2:** History of American Money and Banking |
|  Money makes it easier to trade, borrow, save, invest, and compare the value of goods and services. | **Chapter 14 Money and Banking**<br>**Section 1:** The Functions and Characteristics of Money<br>**Section 2:** History of American Money and Banking<br>**Section 3:** Types of Money in the United States<br>**Chapter 15 The Federal Reserve System and Monetary Policy**<br>**Section 2:** Money Supply and the Economy |
|  Interest rates, adjusted for inflation, rise and fall to balance the amount saved with the amount borrowed, thus affecting the allocation of scarce resources between present and future uses. | **Chapter 4 Going Into Debt**<br>**Section 1:** Americans and Credit<br>**Section 2:** Sources of Loans and Credit<br>**Section 3:** Applying for Credit<br>**Section 4:** Government Regulation of Credit<br>**Chapter 6 Saving and Investing**<br>**Section 1:** Why Save?<br>**Section 2:** Investing: Taking Risks With Your Savings<br>**Section 3:** Special Savings Plans and Goals |

| will understand that: | Chapter and Section Coverage |
|---|---|
|  Income for most people is determined by the market value of the productive resources they sell. What workers earn depends, primarily, on the market value of what they produce and how productive they are. | **Chapter 12 The American Labor Force**<br>Section 1: Americans at Work<br>Section 2: Organized Labor<br>Section 3: Collective Bargaining |
|  Entrepreneurs are people who take the risks of organizing productive resources to make goods and services. Profit is an important incentive that leads entrepreneurs to accept the risks of business failure. | **Chapter 8 Business Organizations**<br>Section 1: Starting a Business<br>Section 2: Sole Proprietorships and Partnerships<br>Section 3: The Corporate World and Franchises<br>**Chapter 21 The Global Economy**<br>Section 1: Reasons for and Results of Global Integration<br>**Chapter 22 Cybernomics**<br>Section 1: The Growth of E-Commerce<br>Section 2: A New Economy? |
|  Investment in factories, machinery, new technology, and the health, education, and training of people can raise future standards of living. | **Chapter 10 Financing and Producing Goods**<br>Section 1: Investing in the Free Enterprise System<br>Section 2: Types of Financing for Business Operations<br>Section 3: The Production Process<br>**Chapter 20 Economic Growth in Developing Nations**<br>Section 2: The Process of Economic Development<br>Section 3: Obstacles to Growth in Developing Nations<br>**Chapter 22 Cybernomics**<br>Section 1: The Growth of E-Commerce<br>Section 2: A New Economy? |
|  There is an economic role for government to play in a market economy whenever the benefits of a government policy outweigh its costs. Governments often provide for national defense, address environmental concerns, define and protect property rights, and attempt to make markets more competitive. Most government policies also redistribute income. | **Chapter 2 Economic Systems and the American Economy**<br>Section 2: Characteristics of the American Economy<br>Section 3: The Goals of the Nation<br>**Chapter 9 Competition and Monopolies**<br>Section 3: Government Policies Toward Competition<br>**Chapter 16 Government Spends, Collects, and Owes**<br>Section 1: Growth in the Size of Government<br>Section 2: The Functions of Government<br>Section 3: The Federal Budget and the National Debt<br>Section 4: Taxation |

| For each standard, students will understand that: | *Economics Today and Tomorrow* Chapter and Section Coverage |
|---|---|
|  Costs of government policies sometimes exceed benefits. This may occur because of incentives facing voters, government officials, and government employees, because of actions by special interest groups that can impose costs on the general public, or because social goals other than economic efficiency are being pursued. | **Chapter 7 Demand and Supply**<br>Section 4: Putting Supply and Demand Together<br>**Chapter 16 Government Spends, Collects, and Owes**<br>Section 1: Growth in the Size of Government<br>Section 2: The Functions of Government<br>Section 3: The Federal Budget and the National Debt<br>**Chapter 18 Trading With Other Nations**<br>Section 3: Restrictions on World Trade<br>**Chapter 20 Economic Growth in Developing Nations**<br>Section 3: Obstacles to Growth in Developing Nations |
|  A nation's overall levels of income, employment, and prices are determined by the interaction of spending and production decisions made by all households, firms, government agencies, and others in the economy. | **Chapter 13 Measuring the Economy's Performance**<br>Section 1: National Income Accounting<br>Section 2: Correcting Statistics for Inflation<br>Section 3: Aggregate Demand and Supply<br>Section 4: Business Fluctuations<br>Section 5: Causes and Indicators of Business Fluctuations<br>**Chapter 20 Economic Growth in Developing Nations**<br>Section 1: Characteristics of Developing Nations<br>Section 2: The Process of Economic Development<br>Section 3: Obstacles to Growth in Developing Nations<br>Section 4: Industrialization and the Future |
|  Unemployment imposes costs on individuals and nations. Unexpected inflation imposes costs on many people and benefits some others because it arbitrarily redistributes purchasing power. Inflation can reduce the rate of growth of national living standards, because individuals and organizations use resources to protect themselves against the uncertainty of future prices. | **Chapter 13 Measuring the Economy's Performance**<br>Section 2: Correcting Statistics for Inflation<br>Section 4: Business Fluctuations<br>Section 5: Causes and Indicators of Business Fluctuations<br>**Chapter 17 Stabilizing the National Economy**<br>Section 1: Unemployment and Inflation |
|  Federal government budgetary policy and the Federal Reserve System's monetary policy influence the overall levels of employment, output, and prices. | **Chapter 15 The Federal Reserve System and Monetary Policy**<br>Section 1: Organization and Functions of the Federal Reserve System<br>Section 2: Money Supply and the Economy<br>Section 3: Regulating the Money Supply<br>**Chapter 16 Government Spends, Collects, and Owes**<br>Section 3: The Federal Budget and the National Debt<br>**Chapter 17 Stabilizing the National Economy**<br>Section 1: Unemployment and Inflation<br>Section 2: The Fiscal Policy Approach to Stabilization<br>Section 3: Monetarism and the Economy |

# THE STOCK MARKET GAME™

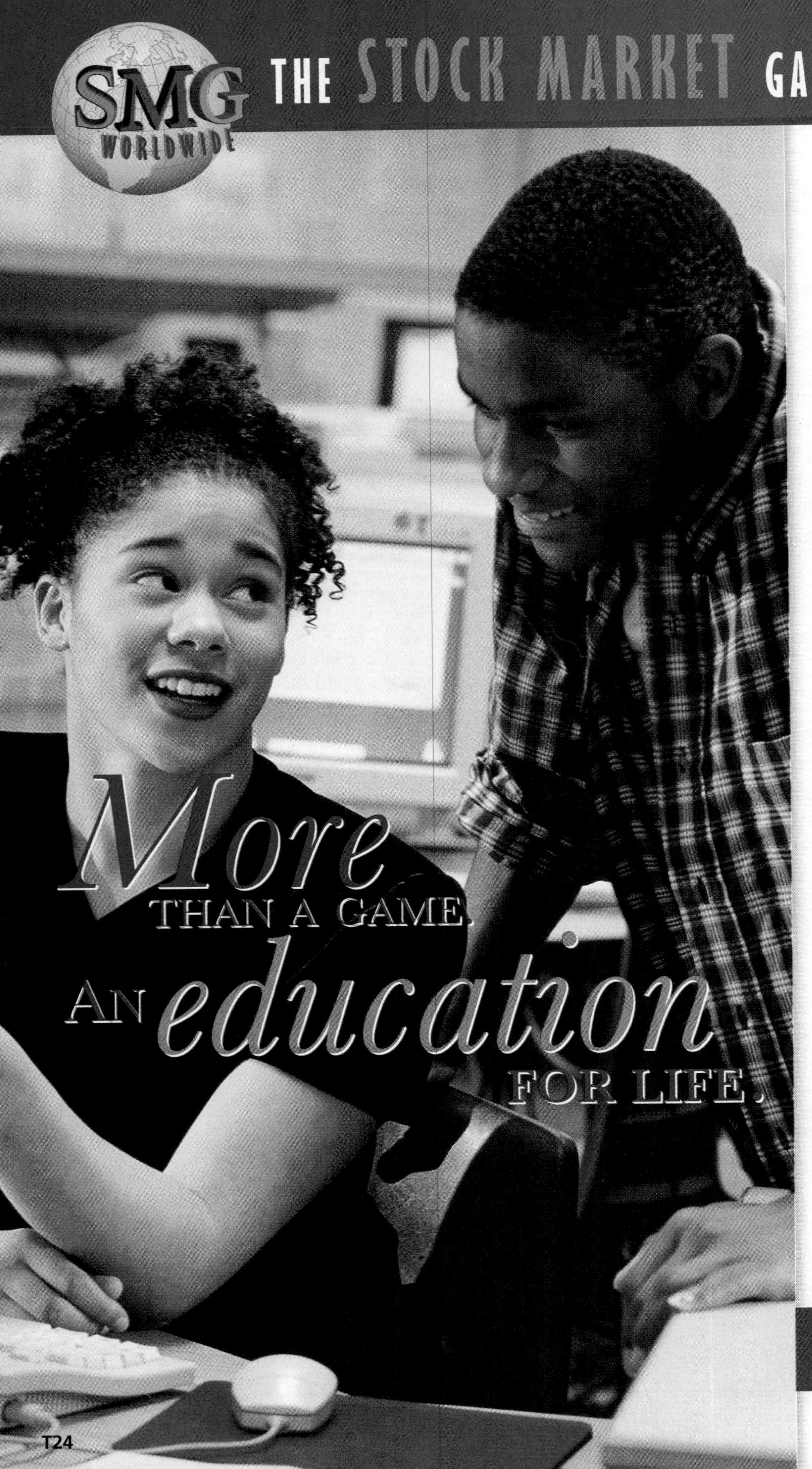
SMG
WORLDWIDE
More
THAN A GAME.
AN education
FOR LIFE.

## What is the Stock Market Game?

**The Stock Market Game** (SMG) is an educational simulation that teaches about the stock markets, the American economic system, and the global economy.

Participants develop skills in math, language arts, research and critical thinking, while building and maintaining a stock portfolio.

SMG is used in grades 4–12, college courses, and by those who seek to learn more about investing.

Since 1977, over 8 million students have participated in this national program.

## How does it work?

Teams of three to five students invest a hypothetical $100,000 in a portfolio of common stocks listed on the New York and American stock exchanges and the NASDAQ stock market.

Most teams use the Internet to follow their portfolios, research stocks, enter trades at end-of-day prices, and see their weekly division ranking.

Those without Internet access use a paper-based version of SMG. These team portfolios are updated and mailed back once a week.

In each state, the program is administered by an SMG Coordinator who provides introductory workshops, training and on-going support.

## How do I get more information?

Contact your local SMG Coordinator by visiting our Web site www.smgww.org or by calling the **Securities Industry Foundation for Economic Education** at (212) 618-0519.

## Are curriculum materials provided?

Lesson plans, curriculum guides, teacher resources and videos for all grade and ability levels are available through the SMG Coordinator. Additional materials are available on the Web site to participants.

## What's the cost?

The small registration fee varies from state to state. Internet access costs are determined by local Internet providers.

## Who sponsors The SMG Program?

The Stock Market Game is a trademarked program of the Securities Industry Foundation for Economic Education (SIFEE), an affiliate of the Securities Industry Association (SIA). SMG is supported nationally and locally by securities industry firms, SIA Districts, the National Council on Economic Education, Newspapers in Education, and other organizations involved in economic and financial literacy education.

**Securities Industry Foundation for Economic Education**
120 Broadway, 35th Floor,
New York, NY 10271-0080
212-618-0519 212-791-5020 fax
sifee@sia.com

# Participating in the Fed Challenge

## *The Challenge*

The Federal Reserve Banks invite high school teams to enter the Fed Challenge. This multi-level national competition is designed to bring real-world economics into the classroom.

## *Goals*

- To increase understanding of the Federal Reserve's role in setting U.S. Monetary Policy
- To develop students' research, cooperation, presentation, and critical-thinking skills
- To promote interest in economics, not only as a subject for undergraduate and postgraduate study, but as the basis for a career
- To foster a closer relationship between schools and participating Federal Reserve Banks

## *How It Works: Presentations and Judges' Q&A*

The Fed Challenge is a **25-minute performance-based assessment** conducted at participating Federal Reserve Banks and Branches. Each performance consists of two parts: a **15-minute presentation**—inspired by the work of the Federal Open Market Committee (FOMC)—and a **10-minute question-and-answer session.**

High School teams (only one per school), made up of five students each, gather research to make a presentation including:

- An analysis of economic and financial conditions (as of the day of the presentation)
- A forecast of economic, financial, and international conditions, for the near-term, of critical importance in developing monetary policy (e.g., unemployment, inflation, output, etc.)
- Identification of pressing economic, financial, and international issues that should be of special concern for monetary policy-makers
- A recommendation to increase, decrease, or leave unchanged the level of short-term interest rates

Following the presentation, a panel of judges, typically made up of Federal Reserve staff members, financial professionals, and educators, question the team about its analysis, forecast, recommendation, and the Federal Reserve's role in developing and implementing monetary policy.

## *Scoring*

Judges will score teams based on five criteria:

1. Knowledge of the Federal Reserve's role in developing and implementing monetary policy
2. Responses to judge's questions
3. Quality of the presentation
4. Quality of the research and analysis
5. Evidence of teamwork and cooperation

All rounds of the Fed Challenge—from district competitions to NATIONAL championship—use the same scoring rubric and adhere to the following rules: Students may refer to, but not read from, notes or scripts. Each team member must play a substantial role in making the presentation. More than one team member may answer a judge's question. While huddling to formulate a response to a judge's question is permitted, teams are cautioned that lengthy and excessive huddling will result in points being deducted, to the extent that it significantly limits the number of questions posed.

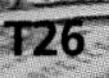

## *Awards, Prizes and Endorsements*

Citibank has established the **Citibank Scholarships and Grants for the Fed Challenge**. As a result, the team that wins the National Championship will be awarded $100,000, comprised of $50,000 in scholarships ($10,000 per team member), a $10,000 achievement award (for the teacher), and a $40,000 grant to set up an in-school economics laboratory.

Each of the other national finalist teams will take home a total of $35,000, comprised of $20,000 in scholarship money ($4,000 per student), a $4,000 achievement award (for the teacher), and an $11,000 grant to set up an in-school economics laboratory.

The **McGraw-Hill Companies** will sponsor a reception in Washington, D.C., for all students and teachers of Federal Reserve District champions.

## *Registration and More Information*

- Outside the 212 area code, call toll free: 1-877-FED-CHLG (1-877-333-2454)
- In area codes 212, 718, 516 and 914, call: 212-720-1836

## *Sample Fed Challenge Questions*

Questions from Fed Challenge judges generally are from the following categories:

- Questions based upon the presentation
- Interpretive questions
- Hypothetical questions
- Program learning or evaluative questions

The following questions from previous competitions provide examples of these types of questions.

1. On the fiscal policy side, how would the passage of a federal balanced budget measure affect the Fed's monetary policy decisions? Do you think balancing the federal budget is an important goal?
2. What is the impact of the nation's trade deficit on U.S. growth prospects?
3. What did you learn from participating in the Fed Challenge?
4. What is the primary goal of monetary policy? What do you think the goal(s) should be?
5. In your own words, explain the Phillips Curve. What is it and what does it show? Why do some economists question the validity of the Phillips Curve? Is there any justification to question its validity?
6. The CPI (consumer price index) and PPI (producer price index) are recognized measures of inflation. Why in your presentation did you include capacity utilization as a measure of inflation?
7. How would movement in the unemployment rate, wages, salaries, benefits, and total compensation figure into your analysis of an inflationary trend? Are you worried about recent gas and food price movements? Explain the concept of Core CPI and why it is important.
8. Should all FOMC (Federal Open Market Committee) members be appointed by the U.S. President and confirmed by the U.S. Senate?
9. Talk about the issues involved in trying to balance inflation and unemployment in the short-run and in the long-run.
10. The most recent rate hike resulted in letters of protest from several members of Congress. How would you respond to criticism that the Fed is not considering the consequences of unemployment, which may arise from rate hikes?

# Alternate Course Outlines

*Economics Today and Tomorrow* is organized so that it can be adjusted easily for alternative lengths or varied course emphases. The models on the following pages are based on the basic concepts listed below, which are provided in "A Framework for Teaching Basic Economic Concepts," written by the National Council on Economic Education (NCEE).

## NCEE Basic Concepts

### Fundamental Economic Concepts

- Scarcity and Choice
- Opportunity Cost and Trade-Offs
- Productivity
- Economic Systems
- Economic Institutions and Incentives
- Exchange, Money, and Interdependence

### Macroeconomic Concepts

- Gross Domestic Product
- Aggregate Supply and Aggregate Demand
- Unemployment
- Inflation and Deflation
- Monetary Policy
- Fiscal Policy

### Microeconomic Concepts

- Markets and Prices
- Supply and Demand
- Competition and Market Structures
- Income Distribution
- Market Failures
- The Role of Government

### International Economic Concepts

- Absolute and Comparative Advantage and Barriers to Trade
- Exchange Rates and the Balance of Payments
- International Aspects of Growth and Stability

### Measurement Concepts and Methods

- Tables
- Charts and Graphs
- Ratios and Percentages
- Index Numbers
- Real vs. Nominal Values
- Averages and Distributions Around the Average

### Broad Social Goals

- Economic Freedom
- Economic Efficiency
- Economic Equity
- Economic Security
- Full Employment
- Price Stability
- Economic Growth
- Other Goals

## Course Length: 9 Weeks
## Emphasis on Microeconomic Concepts

| Chapter or Section | Basic Concepts | Length of Study in Days |
|---|---|---|
| **Economic Handbook** | • Measurement Concepts and Methods | 3 |
| **Chapter 1** What Is Economics? | • Fundamental Economic Concepts | 4 |
| **Chapter 2** Economic Systems and the American Economy | • Fundamental Economic Concepts<br>• Broad Social Goals | 5 |
| **Chapter 3, Section 3** Consumerism | • Microeconomic Concepts | 2 |
| **Chapter 4, Section 4** Government Regulation of Credit | • Microeconomic Concepts | 2 |
| **Chapter 7** Demand and Supply | • Microeconomic Concepts | 6 |
| **Chapter 8** Business Organizations | • Fundamental Economic Concepts | 4 |
| **Chapter 9** Competition and Monopolies | • Microeconomic Concepts | 4 |
| **Chapter 10** Financing and Producing Goods | • Fundamental Economic Concepts<br>• Microeconomic Concepts | 4 |
| **Chapter 11** Marketing and Distribution | • Microeconomic Concepts | 4 |
| **Chapter 14, Section 3** Types of Money in the United States | • Microeconomic Concepts<br>• Fundamental Economic Concepts | 2 |
| **Chapter 22** Cybernomics | • Microeconomic Concepts<br>• International Economic Concepts | 4 |
| | **Total Days:** | **44** |

# Alternate Course Outlines

## Course Length: 12 Weeks
## Emphasis on Macroeconomic Concepts

| Chapter or Section | Basic Concepts | Length of Study in Days |
|---|---|---|
| **Economic Handbook** | • Measurement Concepts and Methods | 3 |
| **Chapter 1** What Is Economics? | • Fundamental Economic Concepts | 6 |
| **Chapter 2** Economic Systems and the American Economy | • Fundamental Economic Concepts<br>• Broad Social Goals | 6 |
| **Chapter 12, Section 1** Americans at Work | • Macroeconomic Concepts | 2 |
| **Chapter 13** Measuring the Economy's Performance | • Macroeconomic Concepts | 8 |
| **Chapter 14** Money and Banking | • Macroeconomic Concepts<br>• Fundamental Economic Concepts | 6 |
| **Chapter 15** The Federal Reserve System and Monetary Policy | • Macroeconomic Concepts | 8 |
| **Chapter 16** Government Spends, Collects, and Owes | • Macroeconomic Concepts<br>• Broad Social Goals | 7 |
| **Chapter 17** Stabilizing the National Economy | • Macroeconomic Concepts | 6 |
| **Chapter 21** The Global Economy | • Macroeconomic Concepts<br>• International Economic Concepts | 6 |
| | **Total Days:** | **58** |

## Course Length: 18 Weeks

### Emphasis on Fundamental, Macroeconomic, and International Economic Concepts

| Chapter or Section | Basic Concepts | Length of Study in Days |
|---|---|---|
| **Economic Handbook** | • Measurement Concepts and Methods | 3 |
| **Chapter 1** What Is Economics? | • Fundamental Economic Concepts | 5 |
| **Chapter 2** Economic Systems and the American Economy | • Fundamental Economic Concepts<br>• Broad Social Goals | 6 |
| **Chapter 7** Demand and Supply | • Microeconomic Concepts | 6 |
| **Chapter 8** Business Organizations | • Fundamental Economic Concepts | 5 |
| **Chapter 13** Measuring the Economy's Performance | • Macroeconomic Concepts | 7 |
| **Chapter 14** Money and Banking | • Fundamental Economic Concepts<br>• Macroeconomic Concepts | 6 |
| **Chapter 15** The Federal Reserve and Monetary Policy | • Macroeconomic Concepts | 7 |
| **Chapter 16** Government Spends, Collects, and Owes | • Macroeconomic Concepts<br>• Broad Social Goals | 6 |
| **Chapter 17** Stabilizing the National Economy | • Macroeconomic Concepts | 6 |
| **Chapter 18** Trading With Other Nations | • International Economic Concepts | 5 |
| **Chapter 19** Converging Economic Systems | • International Economic Concepts<br>• Fundamental Economic Concepts | 5 |
| **Chapter 20** Economic Growth In Developing Nations | • International Economic Concepts | 5 |
| **Chapter 21** The Global Economy | • International Economic Concepts | 5 |
| **Chapter 22** Cybernomics | • International Economic Concepts | 5 |
| | **Total Days:** | **82** |

# Alternate Course Outlines

## Course Length: 18 Weeks

### Emphasis on Fundamental and Microeconomic Concepts

| Chapter or Section | Basic Concepts | Length of Study in Days |
|---|---|---|
| **Economic Handbook** | • Measurement Concepts and Methods | 3 |
| **Chapter 1** What Is Economics? | • Fundamental Economic Concepts | 6 |
| **Chapter 2** Economic Systems and the American Economy | • Fundamental Economic Concepts<br>• Broad Social Goals | 7 |
| **Chapter 3** Your Role as a Consumer | • Fundamental Economic Concepts | 5 |
| **Chapter 4** Going Into Debt | • Fundamental Economic Concepts<br>• Microeconomic Concepts | 5 |
| **Chapter 5** Buying the Necessities | • Fundamental Economic Concepts<br>• Microeconomic Concepts | 5 |
| **Chapter 6** Saving and Investing | • Fundamental Economic Concepts<br>• Broad Social Goals | 6 |
| **Chapter 7** Demand and Supply | • Microeconomic Concepts | 8 |
| **Chapter 8** Business Organizations | • Fundamental Economic Concepts | 5 |
| **Chapter 9** Competition and Monopolies | • Microeconomic Concepts | 6 |
| **Chapter 10** Financing and Producing Goods | • Microeconomic Concepts | 5 |
| **Chapter 11** Marketing and Distribution | • Microeconomic Concepts | 5 |
| **Chapter 12** The American Labor Force | • Fundamental Economic Concepts | 5 |
| **Chapter 14** Money and Banking | • Fundamental Economic Concepts | 5 |
| **Chapter 19** Converging Economic Systems | • Fundamental Economic Concepts<br>• International Economic Concepts | 6 |
| | **Total Days:** | **82** |

# Internet Resources

The economics information available on the Internet is staggering in both volume and variety—not to mention the speed with which it changes. Throughout the pages of this Teacher's Wraparound Edition, you'll find Web addresses that will help your students narrow their search for information. Those sites and more are listed here to provide you with a handy reference tool for finding economics-related Internet information.

**AFL-CIO**
www.aflcio.org

**Antitrust Division of the Department of Justice**
www.usdoj.gov/atr/index.html

**Bureau of Labor Statistics**
www.bls.gov

**Census Bureau**
www.census.gov

**CIA's World Fact Book**
www.odci.gov/cia/publications/pubs.html

**Department of Commerce**
www.doc.gov

**European Union**
www.europa.eu.int

**Federal Communications Commission (FCC)**
www.fcc.gov

**Federal Reserve banks:**
Atlanta: www.frbatlanta.org/
Boston: www.bos.frb.org
Chicago: www.frbchi.org
Cleveland: www.clev.frb.org
Dallas: www.dallasfed.org
Kansas City: www.frbkc.org/contents.htm
Minneapolis: woodrow.mpls.frb.fed.us/
New York: www.ny.frb.org
Philadelphia: www.phil.frb.org
Richmond: www.Rich.FRB.org/
St. Louis: www.stls.frb.org/
San Francisco: www.frbsf.org/index2.html

**Federal Trade Commission (FTC)**
www.ftc.gov

**Fed Stats**
www.Fedstats.gov

**Government Printing Office (for federal budget)**
www.access.gpo.gov/usbudget/index.html

**Handbook of International Economic Statistics**
gopher://gopher.umsl.edu/11/library/govdocs/crpt

**International Monetary Fund**
www.imf.org

**NASDAQ**
www.nasdaq.com

**New York Stock Exchange**
www.nyse.com

**Organization for Economic Cooperation and Development (OECD)**
www.oecd.org

**Securities and Exchange Commission**
www.sec.gov

**Social Security Administration**
www.ssa.gov/

**United States Treasury**
www.ustreas.gov

**The White House, Council of Economic Advisers**
www.whitehouse.gov/WH/EOP/CEA/html/CEA.html

**The White House, Economic Statistics Briefing Room**
www.whitehouse.gov/fsbr/esbr.html

**World Bank**
www.worldbank.org

**World Confederation of Labor**
www.cmt-wcl.org/

**World Trade Organization (WTO)**
www.wto.org

## Teach

Discuss with students any difficulties they have in understanding economic statistics and graphic information. Point out that the steps described in this Handbook will help them simplify the task of learning economics. The Handbook will also give them tools they need to analyze and understand other forces shaping their lives–figuring sales tax, averaging their semester grade, and figuring how much interest their savings account will earn, for example.

Each skill in this Handbook is accompanied by a reproducible master in the **Reinforcing Economic Skills** booklet in the Teacher's Classroom Resource package.

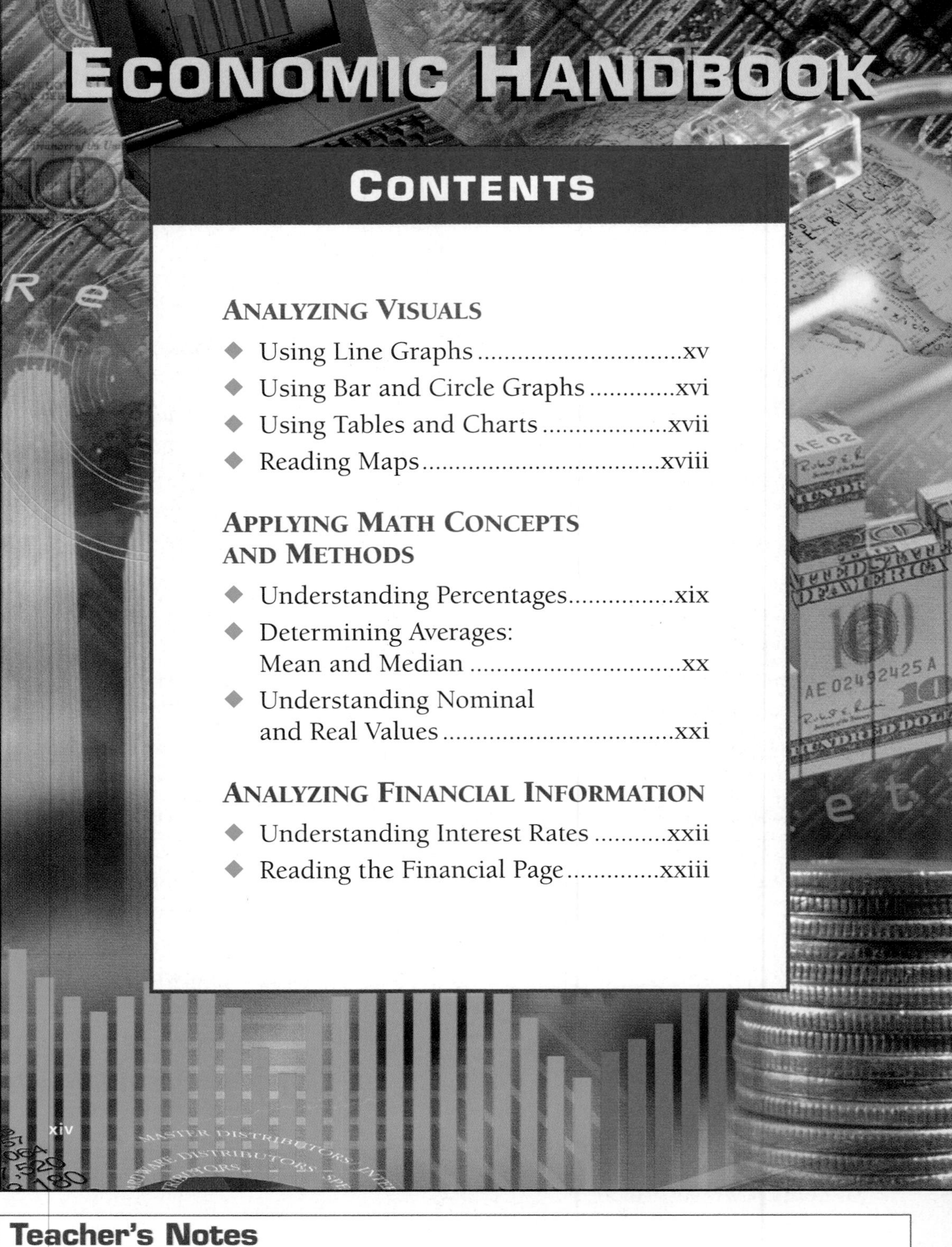

# Economic Handbook

## Contents





### Teacher's Notes

# Using Line Graphs

A graph, like a picture, may present information in a more concise way than words. Line graphs are drawings that compare numerical values. They often are used to compare changes over time or differences between places, groups of items, or other related events.

## LEARNING THE SKILL

Follow these steps to learn how to understand and use line graphs. Then answer the questions below.

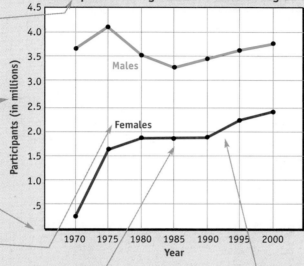

**Participation in High School Athletic Programs**

Participants (in millions): 4.5, 4.0, 3.5, 3.0, 2.5, 2.0, 1.5, 1.0, .5

Year: 1970, 1975, 1980, 1985, 1990, 1995, 2000

Males

Females

**1.** Read the title of the graph. This should tell you what to expect or look for.

**2.** Note the information on the left side of the graph—the vertical axis. The information being compared usually appears on this axis.

**3.** Note the information along the bottom of the graph—the horizontal axis. Time often appears along this axis.

**4.** Determine what the line(s) or curve(s) symbolizes.

**5.** Select a point on the line, then note the date below this point on the horizontal axis and the quantity measured on the vertical axis.

**6.** Analyze the movement of the line (whether increasing or decreasing over time) or compare lines (if more than one are on the graph) to determine the point being made.

## PRACTICING THE SKILL

1. About how many males participated in high school athletic programs in 1970? In 1997?
2. About how many females participated in high school athletic programs in 1970? In 1997?

## Applying the Skill to Economics

1. What trends are shown on the graph?
2. How do you think these trends affected the manufacture and sale of sports-related products from the early to late 1990s?





# Teach

## Using Line Graphs

Tell students that graphs are a good way to present data in a way that readers can grasp easily and quickly. Inform them that graphs come in many forms—line graphs, bar graphs, and circle graphs are the most common. (How to use bar graphs and circle graphs is explained on page xvi.)

Each type of graph has a different way of displaying information. Line graphs show data and how they have changed over time, which is good for showing trends and predictions. Remind students to familiarize themselves with the label on the vertical axis. This label tells what is being compared—often quantities or percentages. The label along the horizontal axis is usually time-related—years, months, and so on.

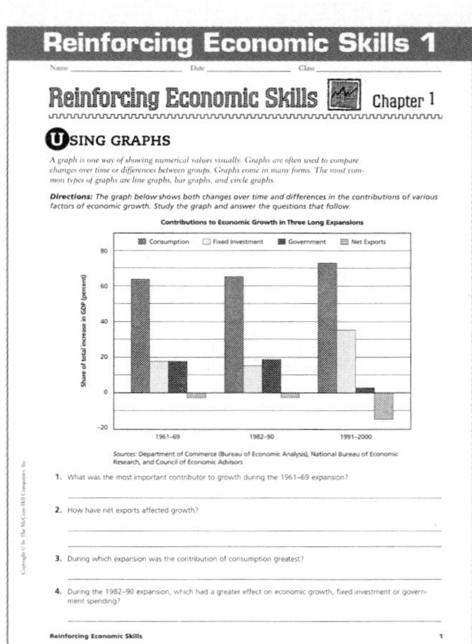

**Reinforcing Economic Skills 1**

Name ______ Date ______ Class ______

**Reinforcing Economic Skills** Chapter 1

**USING GRAPHS**

*A graph is one way of showing numerical values visually. Graphs are often used to compare changes over time or differences between groups. Graphs come in many forms. The most common types of graphs are line graphs, bar graphs, and circle graphs.*

***Directions:*** *The graph below shows both changes over time and differences in the contributions of various factors of economic growth. Study the graph and answer the questions that follow.*



Sources: Department of Commerce (Bureau of Economic Analysis), National Bureau of Economic Research, and Council of Economic Advisors

1. What was the most important contributor to growth during the 1961–69 expansion?
2. How have net exports affected growth?
3. During which expansion was the contribution of consumption greatest?
4. During the 1982–90 expansion, which had a greater effect on economic growth, fixed investment or government spending?



Reinforcing Economic Skills 1

## Answers to PRACTICING THE SKILL

1. about 3.6 million; about the same number
2. about 250,000; about 2.3 million

## Answers to Applying the Skill to Economics

1. Answers may note that the number of males participating in high school athletic programs peaked around 1975, then decreased and is slowly increasing again. The number of females in high school athletic programs increased dramatically from 1970 to 1975, and has been increasing slowly since then.
2. Answers may note that manufacturers of sports-related products for both males and females experienced increased sales from the early to late 1990s.

# Teach

## Using Bar and Circle Graphs

Unlike line graphs, which usually show how data change over time, bar graphs show data in relation to a fixed scale, which is good for comparing items to each other. Have students sit in five rows. Direct each row of students to total the number of pets they have. Note the totals on the board. Then have students present the information on the board in the form of a bar graph.

Explain to students that a circle graph is like a sliced pie; often, it is even called a pie chart. Circle graphs show proportions rather than absolute amounts. They often are used when the information being compared totals 100 percent.

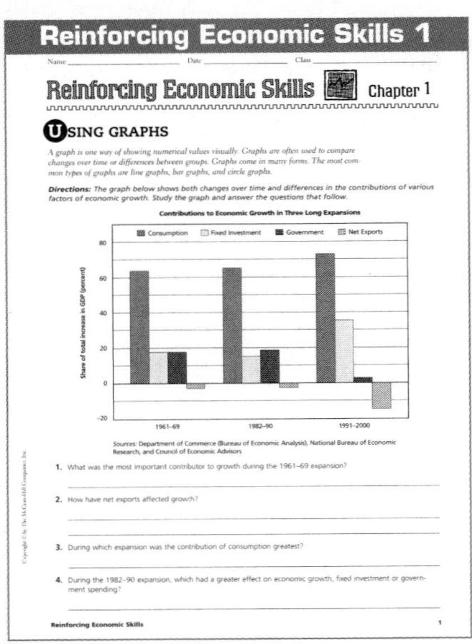

**Reinforcing Economic Skills 1**

Name ______ Date ______ Class ______

**Reinforcing Economic Skills** Chapter 1

**USING GRAPHS**

*A graph is one way of showing numerical values visually. Graphs are often used to compare changes over time or differences between groups. Graphs come in many forms. The most common types of graphs are line graphs, bar graphs, and circle graphs.*

***Directions:*** *The graph below shows both changes over time and differences in the contributions of various factors of economic growth. Study the graph and answer the questions that follow.*

Contributions to Economic Growth in Three Long Expansions
Consumption
Fixed Investment
Government
Net Exports
Share of total increase in GDP (percent)
80
60
40
20
0
-20
1961–69
1982–90
1991–2000

*Sources:* Department of Commerce (Bureau of Economic Analysis), National Bureau of Economic Research, and Council of Economic Advisors

1. What was the most important contributor to growth during the 1961–69 expansion?
2. How have net exports affected growth?
3. During which expansion was the contribution of consumption greatest?
4. During the 1982–90 expansion, which had a greater effect on economic growth, fixed investment or government spending?

Reinforcing Economic Skills 1

# Using Bar Graphs

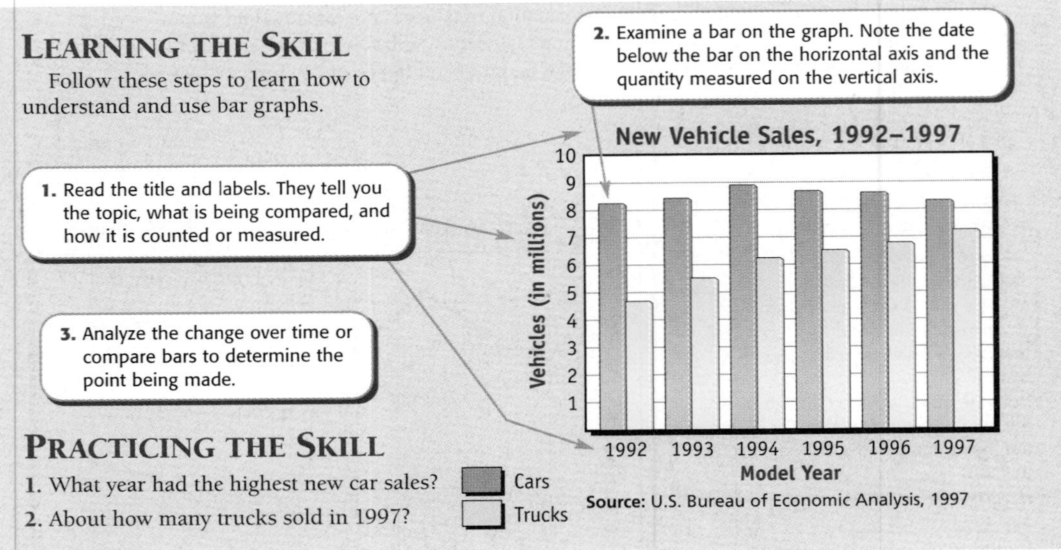

### LEARNING THE SKILL

Follow these steps to learn how to understand and use bar graphs.

1. Read the title and labels. They tell you the topic, what is being compared, and how it is counted or measured.
2. Examine a bar on the graph. Note the date below the bar on the horizontal axis and the quantity measured on the vertical axis.
3. Analyze the change over time or compare bars to determine the point being made.
New Vehicle Sales, 1992–1997
Vehicles (in millions)
10
9
8
7
6
5
4
3
2
1
1992
1993
1994
1995
1996
1997
Model Year
Cars
Trucks

**Source:** U.S. Bureau of Economic Analysis, 1997

### PRACTICING THE SKILL

1. What year had the highest new car sales?
2. About how many trucks sold in 1997?

# Using Circle Graphs

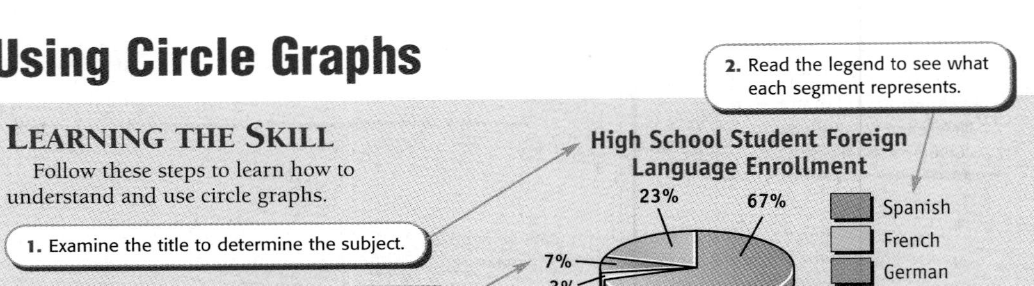

### LEARNING THE SKILL

Follow these steps to learn how to understand and use circle graphs.

1. Examine the title to determine the subject.
2. Read the legend to see what each segment represents.
3. Compare the relative sizes of the circle segments, thus analyzing the relationship of the parts to the whole.
High School Student Foreign Language Enrollment
23%
67%
7%
3%
Spanish
French
German
Other

**Source:** *Statistical Abstract of the United States*, 1998

### PRACTICING THE SKILL

1. What percent of foreign language students are studying German?
2. What foreign language has the greatest student enrollment?

### Applying the Skill to Economics

1. Using the bar graph, what projection could you make about the future of new car sales?
2. Based on the circle graph, which foreign language textbooks probably have the greatest sales volume?

## Answers to Practicing the Skill

**Using Bar Graphs**

1. 1994
2. about 7 million

**Using Circle Graphs**

1. 7 percent
2. Spanish

## Answers to Applying the Skill to Economics

1. Answers will vary, but students should infer that new car sales are declining slightly each year.
2. Spanish

# Using Tables and Charts

Tables and charts are often used to show comparisons between similar categories of information. Tables usually compare statistical or numerical data. Tabular data is presented in columns and rows. Charts often show a wider variety of information than tables.

## LEARNING THE SKILL

Follow these steps to learn how to understand and use tables. Then answer the questions below.

1. Read the title of the table to learn what content is being presented.
2. Read the headings in the top row. They define the groups or categories of information to be compared.
3. Examine the labels in the left-hand column. They describe ranges or subgroups, and are often organized chronologically or alphabetically.
4. Note the source of the data. It may tell you about the reliability of the table.
5. Compare the data presented in the other columns. This is the body of the table.

**Average Earnings of Full-Time Workers by Age and Education, 1996**

| Age and Sex | All Workers | Some High School | High School Graduate | Four-Year College Degree |
|---|---|---|---|---|
| **Male** | **$42,077** | **$25,283** | **$32,521** | **$63,127** |
| 18–24 | 18,856 | 15,478 | 18,779 | 27,257 |
| 25–34 | 33,055 | 19,910 | 27,349 | 44,355 |
| 35–44 | 45,840 | 26,116 | 35,138 | 70,035 |
| 45–54 | 51,705 | 34,527 | 39,178 | 72,461 |
| 55–64 | 49,916 | 32,926 | 38,032 | 71,070 |
| **Female** | **$28,363** | **$17,313** | **$21,893** | **$41,339** |
| 18–24 | 17,002 | 12,512 | 15,219 | 24,980 |
| 25–34 | 26,119 | 16,826 | 19,526 | 34,132 |
| 35–44 | 30,879 | 18,261 | 23,134 | 46,923 |
| 45–54 | 31,222 | 18,007 | 23,833 | 45,012 |
| 55–64 | 27,629 | 19,039 | 23,179 | 41,342 |

**Source:** U.S. Bureau of the Census

## PRACTICING THE SKILL

1. What are the average earnings for 25- to 34-year-old women with college degrees?
2. What are the average earnings for 18- to 24-year-old males without high school diplomas?

## Applying the Skill to Economics

1. What age-related trends do you notice?
2. What conclusions could you draw from this data about the economic effect of education on earnings?





# Teach

## Using Tables and Charts

Ask how many students have after-school jobs. How many play on a sports team? Then tell them that statistics like these could be explained in text form, but a table or a chart would present the information in a more concise and easily interpreted format.

Have students analyze the information in the table on this page. ASK: What information is being compared? *(average full-time worker earnings for gender and age groups, based on education level)* How is the information grouped into categories? *(by gender and age and by education level)*

**Reinforcing Economic Skills 2**

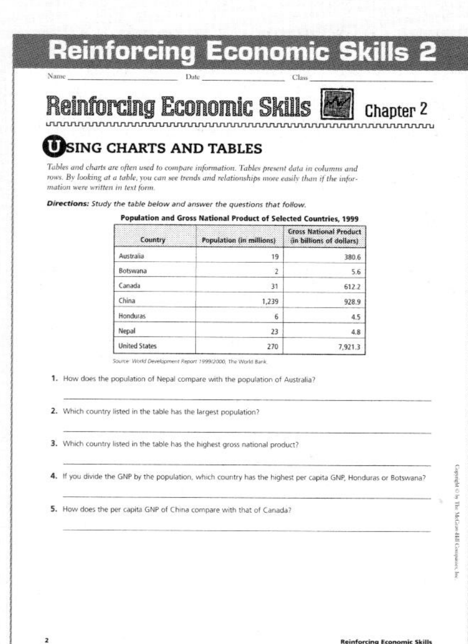
Name ____ Date ____ Class ____

Reinforcing Economic Skills Chapter 2

USING CHARTS AND TABLES

*Tables and charts are often used to compare information. Tables present data in columns and rows. By looking at a table, you can see trends and relationships more easily than if the information were written in text form.*

**Directions:** *Study the table below and answer the questions that follow.*

**Population and Gross National Product of Selected Countries, 1999**

| Country | Population (in millions) | Gross National Product (in billions of dollars) |
|---|---|---|
| Australia | 19 | 380.6 |
| Botswana | 2 | 5.6 |
| Canada | 31 | 612.2 |
| China | 1,239 | 928.9 |
| Honduras | 6 | 4.5 |
| Nepal | 23 | 4.8 |
| United States | 270 | 7,921.3 |

Source: *World Development Report 1999/2000*, The World Bank

1. How does the population of Nepal compare with the population of Australia?
2. Which country listed in the table has the largest population?
3. Which country listed in the table has the highest gross national product?
4. If you divide the GNP by the population, which country has the highest per capita GNP, Honduras or Botswana?
5. How does the per capita GNP of China compare with that of Canada?



2 Reinforcing Economic Skills

### Answers to PRACTICING THE SKILL

1. $34,132
2. $15,478

### Answers to Applying the Skill to Economics

1. Answers will vary, but students should infer that for men and women of all education levels, average earnings rise through the 40s or 50s and then decline.
2. Answers will vary, but students should infer that the higher the education level, the greater the earnings.

# Teach

## Reading Maps

Discuss with students their use of maps. Most have probably used a map to locate a particular geographic region or land feature. In addition, most have probably used a map to help them navigate from one place to another. Have students study the map on this page. ASK: In what part of the country are the most manufacturing areas? *(the northeast and around the Great Lakes)* What does the color green on the map represent? *(commercial farming)*

Have students draw their own maps showing the route they use to come to school. They should incorporate symbols representing buildings, vegetation, and unusual items. Ask them to include a compass rose, a map scale, and a key on their maps. If possible, also have them indicate at what latitude and longitude their location is.

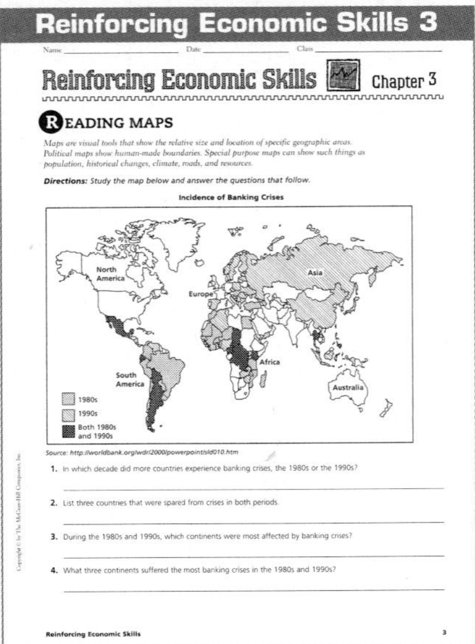

**Reinforcing Economic Skills 3**

Name ______ Date ______ Class ______

**Reinforcing Economic Skills** Chapter 3

**READING MAPS**

*Maps are visual tools that show the relative size and location of specific geographic areas. Political maps show human-made boundaries. Special purpose maps can show such things as population, historical changes, climate, roads, and resources.*

***Directions:*** *Study the map below and answer the questions that follow.*

**Incidence of Banking Crises**



*Source: http://worldbank.org/wdr/2000/powerpoint/sld010.htm*

1. In which decade did more countries experience banking crises, the 1980s or the 1990s?
2. List three countries that were spared from crises in both periods.
3. During the 1980s and 1990s, which continents were most affected by banking crises?
4. What three continents suffered the most banking crises in the 1980s and 1990s?



Reinforcing Economic Skills 3



# Reading Maps

Maps are visual tools that show to scale the relative size and location of specific geographic areas. There are political maps, which show human-made boundaries. There are physical maps, which show physical features of an area. There are also special purpose maps that can show historical change, cultural features, population, climate, land use, or resources. Regardless of type, all maps use symbols to convey information.

## LEARNING THE SKILL

Follow these steps to learn how to understand and use maps. Then answer the questions below.

## PRACTICING THE SKILL

1. What is the primary content shown on this map?
2. Which region of the United States has the heaviest concentration of manufacturing areas?

### Applying the Skill to Economics

1. How could this map be a helpful reference if you were planning to buy ranch land to raise cattle?
2. What generalizations could you draw from this map about energy resources in the United States?



## Answers to PRACTICING THE SKILL

1. land use and resources in the United States
2. the Northeast

## Answers to Applying the Skill to Economics

1. Answers will vary, but students should infer that the map shows where ranch land is located.
2. Answers will vary, but students should infer that the map shows abundant petroleum and coal resources, as well as some natural gas and forest resources.

# Understanding Percentages

If you shop, you probably like seeing the word *percent.* Stores often advertise sale prices as a percent of regular price. *Percent* means "parts per hundred." So, 30 percent means the same thing as 30/100 or 0.30. Expressing change as a percentage allows you to analyze the relative size of the change.

## LEARNING THE SKILL

Follow these steps to learn how to calculate and use percentages. Then answer the questions below.

**1.** Suppose a pair of shoes is on sale for 30 percent off the regular price. Calculate the discount by multiplying the original price by the sale percentage. Change percent to a decimal before you multiply.

**2.** Find the sale price by subtracting the discount from the regular price.

**3.** Or, figure the sale price by multiplying the regular price by the percent you *will* pay. (Subtract the sale percentage from 100 to get the percent you will pay.) Change percent to a decimal before you multiply.

**Calculating Percent**

| | | | | | |
|---|---|---|---|---|---|
| Regular price of shoes | $57.00 | Regular price | $57.00 | | $57.00 |
| 30% | × .30 | Discount | −17.10 | OR | × .70 |
| Discount | $17.10 | Sale price | $39.90 | | $39.90 |

**4.** Calculate an increase in sales by subtracting the quantity sold last year from the quantity sold this year.

**5.** Determine the percentage change by dividing the arithmetic difference by the original quantity. Multiply by 100 to change the decimal to percent.

**Arithmetic Change vs. Percentage Change**

Arithmetic change
  1.6 billion pounds of butter sold this year
−1.5 billion pounds of butter sold last year
  .1 billion pounds

Percentage change $\frac{0.1}{1.5} = .067 \times 100 = 6.7$ percent

## PRACTICING THE SKILL

1. A store advertises a shirt at 25 percent off the original price of $44. What is the sale price?
2. What is the percentage increase in high school enrollment from 1,165 students to 1,320?

**Applying the Skill to Economics**

In 1997 about 32 percent of all music recordings sold were classified as rock music. That year about $12 billion was spent on all recordings. How much was spent on rock music?



**Answers to** PRACTICING THE SKILL

1. $33.00
2. 13.3 percent

**Answers to Applying the Skill to Economics**

$3.84 billion



# Teach

## Understanding Percentages

Empty two rolls of pennies (100 coins) into a container. Remove five pennies and ask students what percentage of the total number of pennies the five represent. Write the decimal .05 on the board. Tell students that *percent* means parts per hundred, just as cents are a portion or percentage of a dollar.

Call on a student to determine the sales tax on an item that sells for $10.00 if the tax rate is 4 percent. Have the student write the calculation on the board.
*(.04 × $10.00 = $.40)*

**Reinforcing Economic Skills 4**

Name ______ Date ______ Class ______

**Reinforcing Economic Skills** Chapter 4

**UNDERSTANDING PRECENTAGES**

*Understanding percentages is very important in business and economics. Discounts, taxes, price changes, and inflation rates are all given in percentages. A percentage is a figure expressed in hundredths. The figure 2 percent is equal to the fraction 2/100 or the decimal 0.02. For example, to figure out how much 2 percent of 250 is, state the percentage as a decimal and multiply the decimal times 250 (.02 × 250 = 5).*

***Directions:** Read the following paragraph, and then answer the questions that follow.*

You order 12 cartons of notebooks at $50 a carton. Because you ordered a dozen cartons, you receive a quantity discount of 10 percent. You also purchase 50 pens that are on sale for 20 percent of the regular price of $.69 apiece. Finally, you purchase a package of copier paper priced at $8.99 instead of the regular price of $9.99. The tax in your state is 5 percent.

1. How much did you pay for the 12 cartons of notebooks? How did you figure it out?
2. How much would you have paid for the 50 pens you purchased if they had not been on sale?
3. How much did you pay for the pens? How did you figure it out?
4. By what percentage was the price of the copier paper you purchased reduced? How did you figure it out?
5. How much tax did you pay on your purchase? How did you figure it out?

# Teach

## Determining Averages: Mean and Median

*Mean* and *median* are used often in economics to summarize information. They are particularly useful for comparing data over time or among different categories, such as showing an increase or a decrease in average wages in manufacturing over five years.

Make sure students understand the difference between mean and median. Have them go through the steps and calculations several times to be certain they know how to determine both measures.

Have students read steps 1–3. ASK: What is the primary reason for the difference between the mean ($60) and the median ($41) in this example? *Students should infer that one student earns more than twice as much ($175) as any other student. This high salary skews the mean, which makes the median the more useful statistic in this case.*

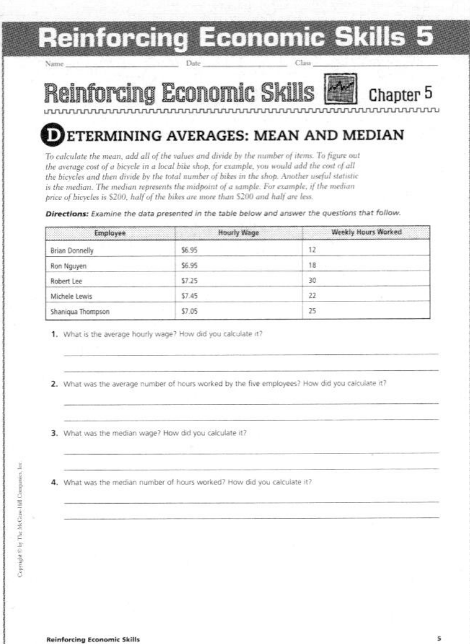

**Reinforcing Economic Skills 5**

Name ______ Date ______ Class ______

**Reinforcing Economic Skills** Chapter 5

**DETERMINING AVERAGES: MEAN AND MEDIAN**

*To calculate the mean, add all of the values and divide by the number of items. To figure out the average cost of a bicycle in a local bike shop, for example, you would add the cost of all the bicycles and then divide by the total number of bikes in the shop. Another useful statistic is the median. The median represents the midpoint of a sample. For example, if the median price of bicycles is $200, half of the bikes are more than $200 and half are less.*

***Directions:*** *Examine the data presented in the table below and answer the questions that follow.*

| Employee | Hourly Wage | Weekly Hours Worked |
|---|---|---|
| Brian Donnelly | $6.95 | 12 |
| Ron Nguyen | $6.95 | 18 |
| Robert Lee | $7.25 | 30 |
| Michele Lewis | $7.45 | 22 |
| Shaniqua Thompson | $7.05 | 25 |

1. What is the average hourly wage? How did you calculate it?
2. What was the average number of hours worked by the five employees? How did you calculate it?
3. What was the median wage? How did you calculate it?
4. What was the median number of hours worked? How did you calculate it?

Reinforcing Economic Skills



# Determining Averages: Mean and Median

The most commonly used summary statistic is the average. There are two ways to compute the average: by using the mean or the median. The *mean* is the average of a series of items. When your teacher computes the class average, he or she is really computing the mean. Sometimes using the mean to interpret statistics is misleading, however. This is especially true if one or two numbers in the series are much higher or lower than the others. The median can be more accurate. The *median* is the midpoint in any series of numbers arranged in order.

## Learning the Skill

Follow these steps to learn how to determine and use averages. Then answer the questions below.

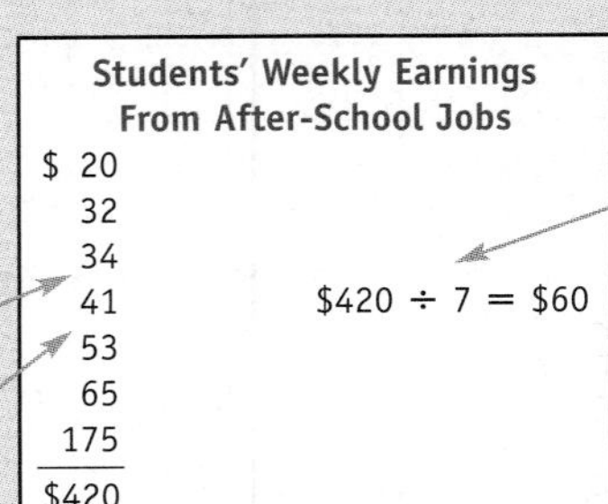

**Students' Weekly Earnings From After-School Jobs**

| |
|---|
| $ 20 |
| 32 |
| 34 |
| 41 |
| 53 |
| 65 |
| 175 |
| $420 |

$420 ÷ 7 = $60

**1.** Suppose you want to find the mean weekly salary for a group of teenagers. First, add all the earnings together.

**2.** Divide the sum by the number of students to find the mean.

**3.** Locate the median by finding the midpoint in the series ($41). Compare the mean with the median. Determine which is the more useful statistic.

**Median Weekly Income of the Four Highest-Paid Students**

| | | |
|---|---|---|
| $ 41 | $ 53 | |
| 53 | + 65 | |
| 65 | $118 | $118 ÷ 2 = $59 |
| 175 | | |

**4.** Suppose you want to calculate the median for the four highest-paid students. First, arrange the numbers in order.

**5.** When an even number of figures is in the series, the median is the mean of the two middle numbers. Follow steps 1 and 2 to find the mean.

## Practicing the Skill

1. What is the median salary for all seven students?
2. What is the median salary for the four lowest-paid students?

## Applying the Skill to Economics

**Average Monthly Rent: 2-Bedroom Apartment**

| City | Rent | City | Rent |
|---|---|---|---|
| Atlanta, GA | $688 | Dallas, TX | $ 718 |
| Boston, MA | $906 | San Jose, CA | $1,139 |

**1.** What is the mean monthly rent for these four cities?

**2.** What is the median monthly rent?



## Answers to Practicing the Skill

1. $41
2. $33

## Answers to Applying the Skill to Economics

1. $862.75
2. $812

# Understanding Nominal and Real Values

The rise in the economy's average price level is called inflation. To make comparisons between the prices of things in the past and those of today, you have to make the distinction between *nominal,* or current, and *real,* or adjusted for inflation, values. You can use the consumer price index (CPI), an index of average prices for consumer goods, to calculate real values. Then you can *accurately* compare changes in income and prices over time.

## LEARNING THE SKILL

Follow these steps to learn how to understand and calculate nominal and real values. Then answer the questions below.

**1.** Suppose a family sells a house after living there for 10 years. To calculate whether they made any profit from the sale, they need to know the real sale price of their house. First, find the nominal price increase.

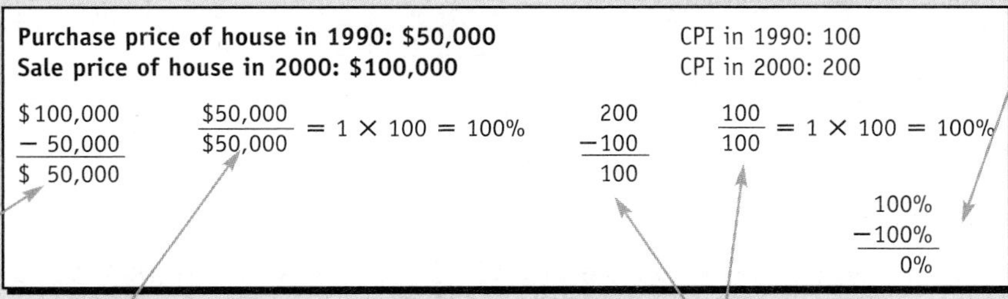

Purchase price of house in 1990: $50,000
Sale price of house in 2000: $100,000
CPI in 1990: 100
CPI in 2000: 200
$100,000
− 50,000
$ 50,000
$50,000 / $50,000 = 1 × 100 = 100%
200
−100
100
100 / 100 = 1 × 100 = 100%
100%
−100%
0%


**2.** Calculate the nominal percentage increase in price. Divide the amount of increase by the original price and multiply by 100 to express the answer as a percent.

**3.** Determine the percentage increase in the consumer price index. First find the actual change in CPI. Then divide the amount of increase by the original CPI and multiply by 100.

**4.** Determine the percentage increase in real price. Subtract the percentage increase in CPI from the percentage increase in nominal price. Evaluate the sale in real values.

**5.** Suppose that last year you earned $10 per hour. You receive a 5 percent raise. The CPI is 3 percent higher than last year's CPI, which means there is a 3 percent inflation rate.

Earnings: $10 per hour
Raise: 5%
Inflation Rate: 3%

5%
−3%
2%

**6.** Calculate the real salary increase by subtracting the inflation rate from the nominal raise.

## PRACTICING THE SKILL

1. What was the nominal price increase on the sale of the house?
2. How much money, in real dollars, was made on the house?
3. How much was the real value of the raise?

### Applying the Skill to Economics

Between 1980 and 1997, the amount spent on advertising in the United States increased by 240 percent. How could you adjust this figure for inflation?



### Answers to PRACTICING THE SKILL

1. $50,000
2. none
3. 2 percent

### Answers to Applying the Skill to Economics

You must subtract the inflation rate for the same time period from the increase in advertising expenditures.

# Teach

## Understanding Nominal and Real Values

Discuss with students whether they have ever heard their parents, grandparents, or other older friend or relative talk about how much things cost when they were teenagers. Throughout the history of the United States, prices have tended to increase over time. This phenomenon is called inflation, and students must take current, inflated prices into account when comparing them against prices of the past.

Remind students that to calculate nominal versus real prices, they must know four figures: the price in the original year, the price today, the consumer price index in the original year, and the consumer price index today.

ASK: To receive a real 5 percent raise in a year with 3 percent inflation, what would the nominal raise need to be? *8 percent*

### Reinforcing Economic Skills 6

Name ______ Date ______ Class ______

**Reinforcing Economic Skills** Chapter 6

**UNDERSTANDING REAL AND NOMINAL VALUES**

*A house may have cost just $20,000 in 1960, but $20,000 then was worth a lot more than it is today. To make an accurate comparison between the price of goods today and the price of goods in the past, you need to compare the real value of those goods, not the nominal value. Nominal values are values given in the currency at the time. To convert that value into a real value, you need to multiply it by the change in the overall price index.*

***Directions:*** *The table below shows the consumer price index (CPI) for 1991–98. This index allows you to express all nominal values as real values. The time used as the index for the CPI is 1982–84. This means that all nominal values can be expressed as real values in 1982–84 dollars. For example, the index for 1991 was 136.2, or 1.362 times greater than the base index of 100 (136.2/100). This number indicates that goods in 1991 cost 1.362 times as much as they did in 1982–84. To convert a 1991 nominal price into a real price, you will need to divide the nominal price by this factor. The real value of a poster that cost $15.00 in 1991 is thus $11.01 ($15.00/1.362).*

**Consumer Price Index, 1991–98**
**(1982 − 84 = 100)**

| Year | Index |
|---|---|
| 1991 | 136.2 |
| 1992 | 140.3 |
| 1993 | 144.5 |
| 1994 | 148.2 |
| 1995 | 152.4 |
| 1996 | 156.9 |
| 1997 | 160.5 |
| 1998 | 163.0 |

Source: U.S. Department of Commerce

1. What is the real cost of a watch that cost $45.00 in 1995?
2. How much did a movie that cost $7.50 in 1998 cost in 1982–84?
3. If the going rate for babysitting was $4.50 in 1996 and $5.50 in 1998, in which year did babysitters earn a higher real wage?
4. What was the real cost of a CD that cost $13.99 in 1998? If the nominal cost of the same CD was $12.99 in 1993, in which year was the real cost lower?



6 Reinforcing Economic Skills

# Teach

## Understanding Interest Rates

Use the following activity to guide students through the mathematics for calculating simple and compound interest. Have students imagine that they have $100 to deposit in a savings account. They can place the money in an account that pays 5 percent compound interest or an account that pays 6 percent simple interest.

Lead them through the steps of calculating the total savings per year at 5 percent interest on $100 compounded annually for eight years: $105, $110.25, $115.76, $121.55, $127.63, $134.01, $140.71, $147.75.

Then guide students to calculate that 6 percent simple interest over eight years would amount to $48, for a total savings of $148. Help students conclude that the first account would be more profitable for long-term savings, and the second would be more profitable for short-term savings.

**Reinforcing Economic Skills 7**

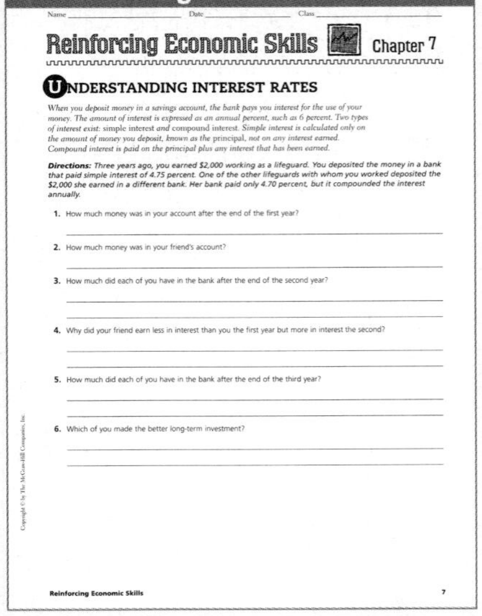

Name ____________ Date ____________ Class ____________

**Reinforcing Economic Skills** Chapter 7

**UNDERSTANDING INTEREST RATES**

*When you deposit money in a savings account, the bank pays you interest for the use of your money. The amount of interest is expressed as an annual percent, such as 6 percent. Two types of interest exist:* simple interest *and* compound interest. *Simple interest is calculated only on the amount of money you deposit, known as the* principal, *not on any interest earned. Compound interest is paid on the principal plus any interest that has been earned.*

***Directions:** Three years ago, you earned $2,000 working as a lifeguard. You deposited the money in a bank that paid simple interest of 4.75 percent. One of the other lifeguards with whom you worked deposited the $2,000 she earned in a different bank. Her bank paid only 4.70 percent, but it compounded the interest annually.*

1. How much money was in your account after the end of the first year?
2. How much money was in your friend's account?
3. How much did each of you have in the bank after the end of the second year?
4. Why did your friend earn less in interest than you the first year but more in interest the second?
5. How much did each of you have in the bank after the end of the third year?
6. Which of you made the better long-term investment?



Reinforcing Economic Skills 7



# Understanding Interest Rates

When you deposit money in a savings account, the bank pays you interest for the use of your money. The amount of interest is expressed as a percent, such as 6 percent, for a time period, such as per year. Two types of interest exist: simple and compound. *Simple interest* is figured only on the principal, or original deposit, not on any interest earned. *Compound interest* is paid on the principal plus any interest that has been earned. Over time, there is a significant difference in earnings between simple and compound interest.

## Learning the Skill

Follow these steps to learn how to understand and calculate interest rates. Then answer the questions below.

**1.** Suppose you deposit $100 in a savings account that earns 6 percent simple interest per year. Get ready to figure your earnings by converting 6 percent to a decimal.

**2.** To calculate the simple interest earned, multiply the principal by the interest rate.

**3.** Calculate the account balance for the first two years, assuming the bank pays the same interest rate each year. Add the principal, the first year's interest, and the second year's interest.

**Simple Interest**

| | | |
|---|---|---|
| 6% = .06 | $ 100 | $100 |
| | × .06 | + 6 |
| | $6.00 | 6 |
| | | $112 |

**4.** Suppose you deposit $100 in a savings account that earns 6 percent compound interest per year. Calculate the interest earned the first year.

**5.** Find the bank balance for the end of the first year. Add the principal and first year's interest.

**6.** Determine the interest earned in the second year. Multiply the new balance by the interest rate.

**7.** Figure the total bank balance after two years. Add the second year's interest to the first year's balance.

**Compound Interest**

| | | | |
|---|---|---|---|
| $ 100 | $100 | $ 106 | $106.00 |
| × .06 | + 6 | × .06 | + 6.36 |
| $6.00 | $106 | $6.36 | $112.36 |

## Practicing the Skill

1. What would be the difference in earnings between simple and compound interest if your initial balance was $1,000 rather than $100?
2. What would be the difference in earnings between simple and compound interest on your $100 savings after five years?

### Applying the Skill to Economics

1. What would be the impact of compounding interest on a daily basis rather than an annual basis?
2. Banks often pay higher rates of interest on money you agree to keep in the bank for longer periods of time. Explain why this might be.



## Answers to Practicing the Skill

1. $3.60
2. $3.82

## Answers to Applying the Skill to Economics

1. You would earn more interest.
2. Answers will vary, but students should infer that the bank benefits by having longer use of your money, so the bank is willing to pay more for that benefit.

# Reading the Financial Page

A stock market report alphabetically lists stocks and provides information about stock prices and trades. Every business day, shares of stock are bought and sold. At the beginning of each trading day, stocks open at the same prices they closed at the day before. Prices generally go up and down throughout the day as the conditions of supply and demand change. At the end of the day, each stock's closing price is recorded.

## Learning the Skill

Follow these steps to learn how to understand and use the financial page. Then answer the questions below.

1. Locate the stock in the alphabetical list. Names are abbreviated.
2. Examine the stock's history over the last 52 weeks. The high and low prices for one share of stock appear.
3. Note the ticker symbol, or computer code, for the stock.
4. Evaluate the annual dividend. Stockholders receive this dividend, or payment, for each share of stock they own.
5. Review the yield. The yield is the return on investment per share of stock. It is calculated by dividing the dividend by the closing price.
6. Read the price/earnings ratio. Lower price/earnings ratios generally mean more earnings per share.
7. Note the volume, or number of shares of stock, traded that day. The number given represents hundreds of shares.
8. Examine the day's high, low, and closing stock price.
9. Examine how the day's closing stock price compares with the prior business day's closing price. Positive numbers indicate a price increase. Negative numbers mean a price drop.

**Stock Quotations**

| 52 Weeks Hi | 52 Weeks Lo | Stock | Sym | Div | Yld % | PE | Vol 100s | Hi | Lo | Close | Net Chg |
|---|---|---|---|---|---|---|---|---|---|---|---|
| 94.15 | 29.25 | TxInstr | TXN | .17 | .2 | 57 | 39008 | 80.80 | 77.55 | 79.60 | +1.5 |
| 59.50 | 41 | TexPacTr | TPL | .40 | .9 | 28 | 23 | 44.25 | 43.85 | 44.25 | + .15 |
| 48 | 35.50 | TX Util | TXU | 2.30 | 6.2 | 13 | 17307 | 37.20 | 36.45 | 36.80 | − .15 |

## Practicing the Skill

1. How many shares of Texas Instruments stock were traded on the day shown?
2. What was the day's highest price for a share of Texas Utilities stock?
3. Which stock had the greatest increase in closing price from the previous day?

### Applying the Skill to Economics

If you had purchased 100 shares of Texas Instruments stock at its lowest 52-week price and sold it at this day's closing price, how much money would you earn?



**Answers to Practicing the Skill**

1. 3,900,800
2. $37.20
3. Texas Instruments

**Answers to Applying the Skill to Economics**

$5,035.00

ECONOMIC HANDBOOK

# Teach

## Reading the Financial Page

Because so much information is provided on page xxiii, it might be useful to have students read aloud the explanations for each entry. To show students how this format is used in the everyday financial world, display the New York Stock Exchange (NYSE) list from a current newspaper. A stock market report from *The Wall Street Journal,* like the one shown here, provides a complete listing of information. Your local newspaper, however, may delete some of the information to save space.

Tell students that the NYSE now uses decimals rather than the centuries-old tradition of quoting price changes in fractions of a dollar. Most non-U.S. equities markets trade in decimals.

**Reinforcing Economic Skills 8**

Name ______ Date ______ Class ______

Reinforcing Economic Skills Chapter 8

READING THE FINANCIAL PAGE

*To find information about stock prices and trades, you can read the stock market report on the financial page of the newspaper. Every business day, shares of stock are bought and sold. At the beginning of each trading day, stocks are bought and sold at the same prices at which they closed the day before. At the end of the day, each stock's closing price is recorded. People read the financial page to follow the prices of stocks they own or are thinking of purchasing and to monitor the strength of the country's business economy.*

***Directions:*** *Study the stock market information below and answer the questions that follow.*

| 52-week High | Net Low | Stock | Div | Yld % | P/E | Sales 100s | High | Low | Last | Chg |
|---|---|---|---|---|---|---|---|---|---|---|
| 63 9/16 | 32 1/16 | BankOne | 1.68 | 4.8 | 13 | 46648 | 35 3/8 | 33 15/16 | 35 15/16 | +1 3/8 |
| 76 3/8 | 48 1/16 | Bk of Am | 1.80 | 2.9 | 15 | 55925 | 61 1/16 | 58 1/16 | 61 1/16 | +2 3/4 |

Source: New York Times, October 28, 1999

1. At what price did BankOne shares close October 27, 1999?
2. What is the price/earnings (P/E) ratio of Bank of America?
3. What is the difference between the high and low values of a BankOne share on October 27?
4. What was the lowest price at which Bank of America shares traded in the previous 52 weeks?
5. What was the highest price at which BankOne shares traded in the previous 52 weeks?
6. How many shares of Bank of America were traded October 27?



8 Reinforcing Economic Skills

# Reading for Information

Think about your textbook as a tool that helps you learn more about the world around you. It is an example of nonfiction writing—it describes real-life events, people, ideas, and places. Here is a menu of reading strategies that will help you become a better textbook reader. As you come to passages in your textbook that you don't understand, refer to these reading strategies for help.

## BEFORE YOU READ

### Set a Purpose

- Why are you reading the textbook?
- How does the subject relate to your life?
- How might you be able to use what you learn in your own life?

### Preview

- Read the chapter title to find what the topic will be.
- Read the subtitles to see what you will learn about the topic.
- Skim the photos, charts, graphs, or maps. How do they support the topic?
- Look for vocabulary words that are boldfaced. How are they defined?

### Draw From Your Own Background

- What have you read or heard about concerning new information on the topic?
- How is the new information different from what you already know?
- How will the information that you already know help you understand the new information?

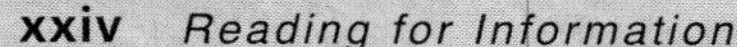

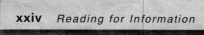

## AS YOU READ

**Question**

- What is the main idea?
- How do the photos, charts, graphs, and maps support the main idea?

**Connect**

- Think about people, places, and events in your own life. Are there any similarities with those in your textbook?
- Can you relate the textbook information to other areas of your life?

**Predict**

- Predict events or outcomes by using clues and information that you already know.
- Change your predictions as you read and gather new information.

**Visualize**

- Pay careful attention to details and descriptions.
- Create graphic organizers to show relationships that you find in the information.

### LOOK FOR CLUES AS YOU READ

- **Comparison-and-Contrast Sentences:**

  Look for clue words and phrases that signal comparison, such as *similarly, just as, both, in common, also,* and *too.*

  Look for clue words and phrases that signal contrast, such as *on the other hand, in contrast to, however, different, instead of, rather than, but,* and *unlike.*

- **Cause-and-Effect Sentences:**

  Look for clue words and phrases such as *because, as a result, therefore, that is why, since, so, for this reason,* and *consequently.*

- **Chronological Sentences:**

  Look for clue words and phrases such as *after, before, first, next, last, during, finally, earlier, later, since,* and *then.*

## AFTER YOU READ

**Summarize**

- Describe the main idea and how the details support it.
- Use your own words to explain what you have read.

**Assess**

- What was the main idea?
- Did the text clearly support the main idea?
- Did you learn anything new from the material?
- Can you use this new information in other school subjects or at home?
- What other sources could you use to find more information about the topic?



xxv

# Basic Concepts in Economics

*Economics Today and Tomorrow* incorporates the 21 basic concepts established in *A Framework for Teaching Basic Economic Concepts,* published by the National Council on Economic Education.

## FUNDAMENTAL ECONOMIC CONCEPTS

1. **Scarcity and Choice** *Scarcity* is the universal problem that faces all societies because there are not enough resources to produce everything people want. Scarcity requires people to make *choices* about the goods and services they use.
2. **Opportunity Cost and Trade-Offs** *Opportunity cost* is the foregone benefit of the next best alternative when scarce resources are used for one purpose rather than another. *Trade-offs* involve choosing less of one thing to get more of something else.
3. **Productivity** *Productivity* is a measure of the amount of output (goods and services) produced per unit of input (productive resources) used.
4. **Economic Systems** *Economic systems* are the ways in which people organize economic life to deal with the basic economic problem of scarcity.
5. **Economic Institutions and Incentives** *Economic institutions* include households and families and formal organizations such as corporations, government agencies, banks, labor unions, and cooperatives. *Incentives* are factors that motivate and influence human behavior.
6. **Exchange, Money, and Interdependence** *Exchange* is a voluntary transaction between buyers and sellers. It is the trading of a good or service for another good or service, or for money. *Money* is anything that is generally accepted as final payment for goods and services, and thus serves as a medium of exchange. *Interdependence* means that decisions or events in one part of the world or in one sector of the economy affect decisions and events in other parts of the world or sectors of the economy.

## MICROECONOMIC CONCEPTS

7. **Markets and Prices** *Markets* are arrangements that enable buyers and sellers to exchange goods and services. *Prices* are the amounts of money that people pay for a unit of a particular good or service.
8. **Supply and Demand** *Supply* is defined as the different quantities of a resource, good, or service that will be offered for sale at various possible prices during a specific time period. *Demand* is defined as the different quantities of a resource, good, or service that will be purchased at various possible prices during a specific time period.
9. **Competition and Market Structure** *Competition* is the struggle between businesses that strive for the same customer or market. Competition depends on *market structure*–the number of buyers and sellers, the extent to which firms can control price, the nature of the product, the accuracy and timeliness of information, and the ease with which firms can enter and exit the market.
10. **Income Distribution** *Income distribution* refers to the way the nation's income is distributed by function–to those who provide productive resources–and by recipient, primarily individuals and families.

**11. Market Failures** *Market failures* occur when there is inadequate competition, lack of access to reliable information, resource immobility, externalities, and the need for public goods.

**12. The Role of Government** *The role of government* includes establishing a framework of law and order in which a market economy functions. The government plays a direct and an indirect role in the economy as both a producer and a consumer of goods and services.

## MACROECONOMIC CONCEPTS

**13. Gross Domestic Product** *Gross Domestic Product (GDP)* is defined as the market value of the total output of all final goods and services produced within a country's boundaries during one year.

**14. Aggregate Supply and Aggregate Demand** *Aggregate supply* is the total amount of goods and services produced by the economy during a period of time. *Aggregate demand* is the total amount of spending on goods and services in the economy during a period of time.

**15. Unemployment** *Unemployment* is defined as the number of people without jobs who are actively seeking work. This is also expressed as a rate when the number of unemployed is divided by the number of people in the labor force.

**16. Inflation and Deflation** *Inflation* is a sustained increase in the average price level of the entire economy. *Deflation* is a sustained decrease in the average price level of an entire economy.

**17. Monetary Policy** *Monetary policy* consists of actions initiated by a nation's central bank that affect the amount of money available in the economy and its cost (interest rates).

**18. Fiscal Policy** *Fiscal policy* consists of changes in taxes, in government expenditures on goods and services, and in transfer payments that are designed to affect the level of aggregate demand in the economy.

## INTERNATIONAL ECONOMIC CONCEPTS

**19. Absolute and Comparative Advantage and Barriers to Trade** *Absolute advantage* and *comparative advantage* are concepts that are used to explain why trade takes place. *Barriers to trade* include tariffs, quotas, import licenses, and cartels.

**20. Exchange Rates and the Balance of Payments** An *exchange rate* is the price of one nation's currency in terms of another nation's currency. The *balance of payments* of a country is a statistical accounting that records, for a given period, all payments that the residents, businesses, and governments of one country make to the rest of the world as well as the receipts that they receive from the rest of the world.

**21. International Aspects of Growth and Stability** *International aspects of growth and stability* are more important today than in the past because all nations are much more interdependent.

# UNIT 1 Resource Manager

The following transparencies may be used at any time during Unit 1.

## Economic Forms and Financial Pages Transparencies

Transparency 4

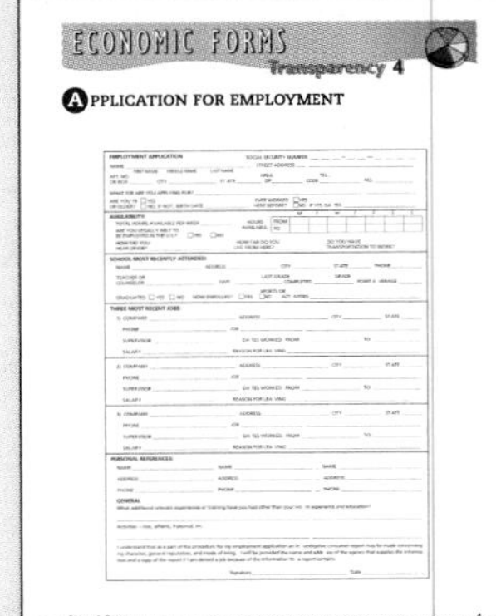


Transparency 5

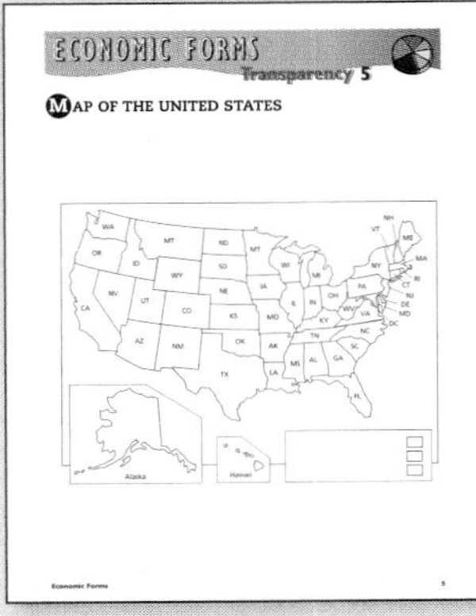


Transparency 6

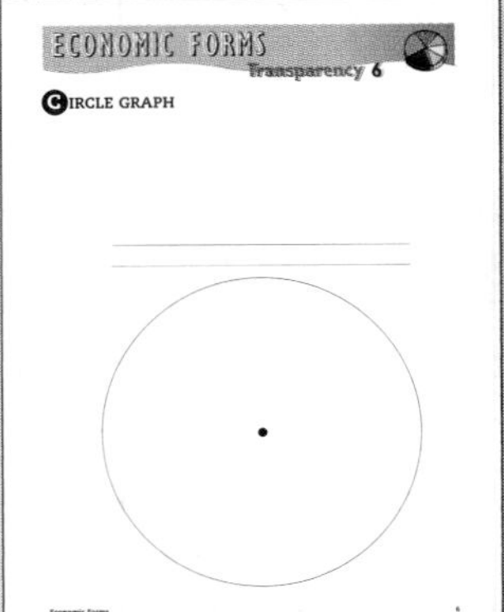


## Economic Concepts Transparencies

Transparency 1

Transparency 2

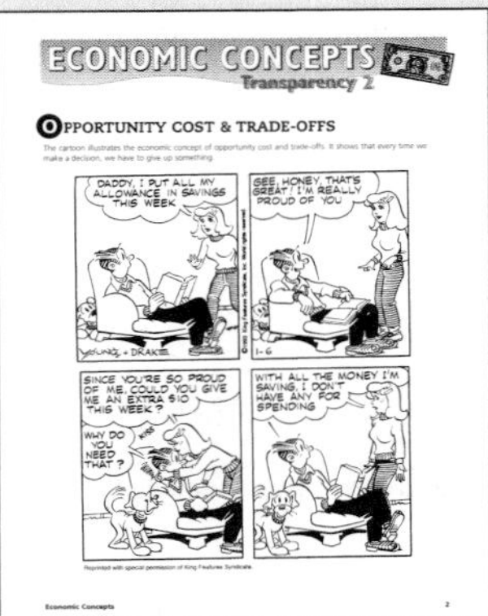


Transparency 4

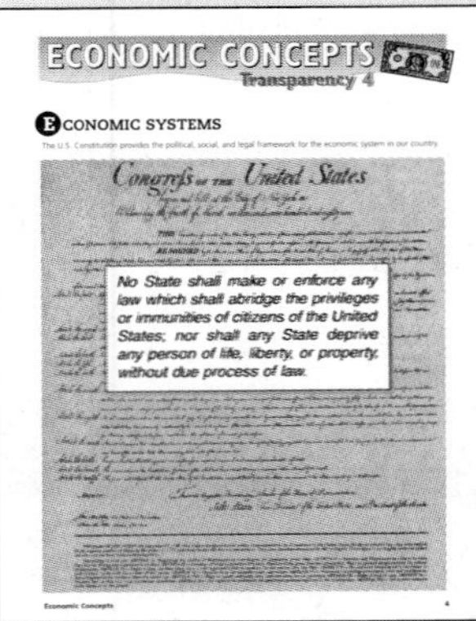


## Real-World Economics

Have your students learn about investing and managing their financial futures by participating in the exciting simulation **The Stock Market Game**™. See page T24 for more information.

Strengthen students' research, cooperation, presentation, and critical thinking skills by having them compete in the **Fed Challenge**. See page T26 for further information.

## Additional Glencoe Resources for This Unit

- Nightly Business Report *Economics & You* Video Program
- Economic Survival: A Financial Simulation
- Interactive Economics! Software

# UNIT 1 Resource Manager

## Assessment and Evaluation

Unit 1 Test Form A

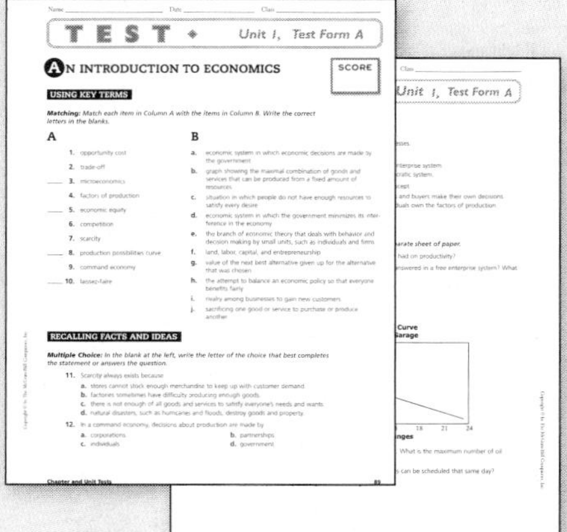

Unit 1 Test Form B

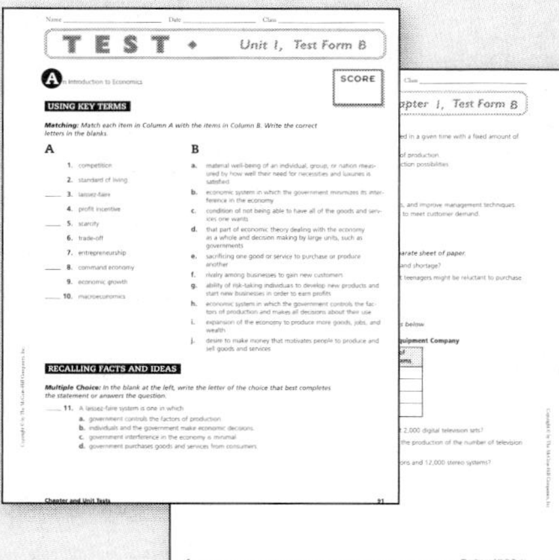

**Use the following tools to easily assess student learning:**

- Performance Assessment Strategies and Activities
- Section Quizzes
- Chapter and Unit Tests
- ExamView® Pro Testmaker
- Interactive Tutor Self-Assessment Software
- SAT I/II Test Practice
- MindJogger Videoquiz
- ett.glencoe.com

## Application and Enrichment

Economics Laboratory 1

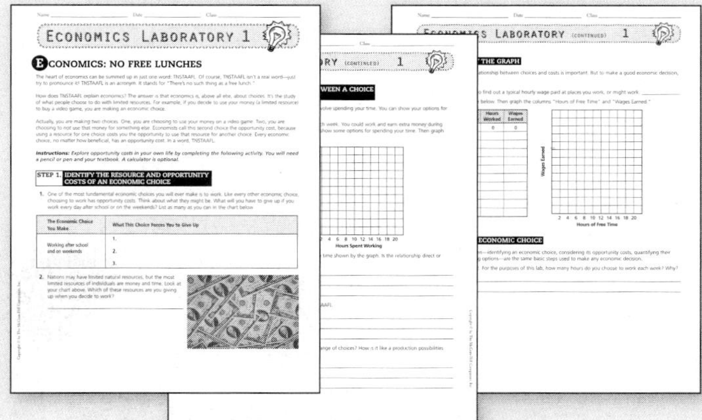

*Business Week* Focus on the New Economy

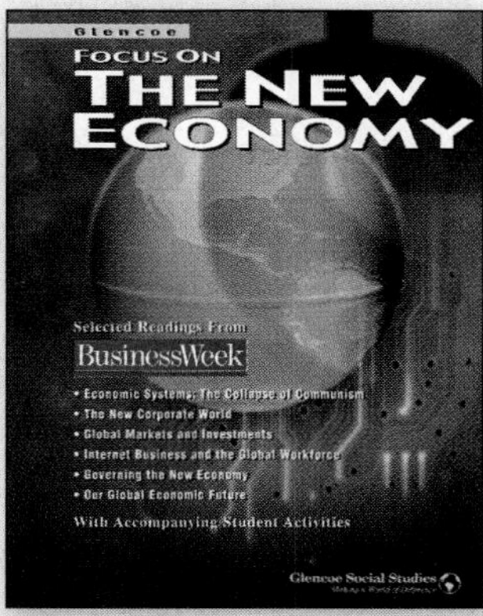


## ECONOMICS Online

*Glencoe's Web sites provide additional resources. All essential content is covered in the Student Edition.*

ett.glencoe.com

Visit the **Economics Today and Tomorrow** Web site for Chapter Overviews, Textbook Updates, Student Web Activities, Web Activity Lesson Plans, and Self-Check Quizzes.

socialstudies.glencoe.com

Visit the **Glencoe Social Studies** Web site for additional social studies activities, updates, and links to other sites.

**Glencoe's *Guide to Using the Internet*** provides an introduction to many of the current Internet technologies, social studies and professional resources, and teaching strategies.

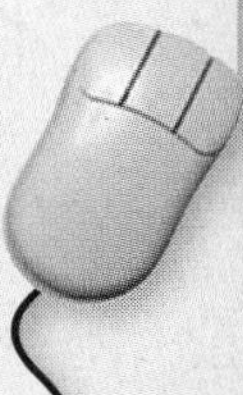

## Unit Objectives

After studying this unit, students will be able to:

- **Define** economics and outline the basic principles of economic systems.
- **Compare** the ways traditional, command, market, and mixed economies answer the basic economic questions.
- **Characterize** the American free enterprise system.

## Unit Overview

The two chapters that comprise **Unit 1** provide an introduction to economics.

**Chapter 1** explains or describes economics, the major economic principles, the use of economic models, and why studying economics is important.

**Chapter 2** explains how various economic systems address the four basic economic questions.

### 00:00 Out of Time?

If time does not permit teaching each chapter in this unit, you may use the **Audio Program** that includes a 1-page activity and a 1-page test for each chapter.

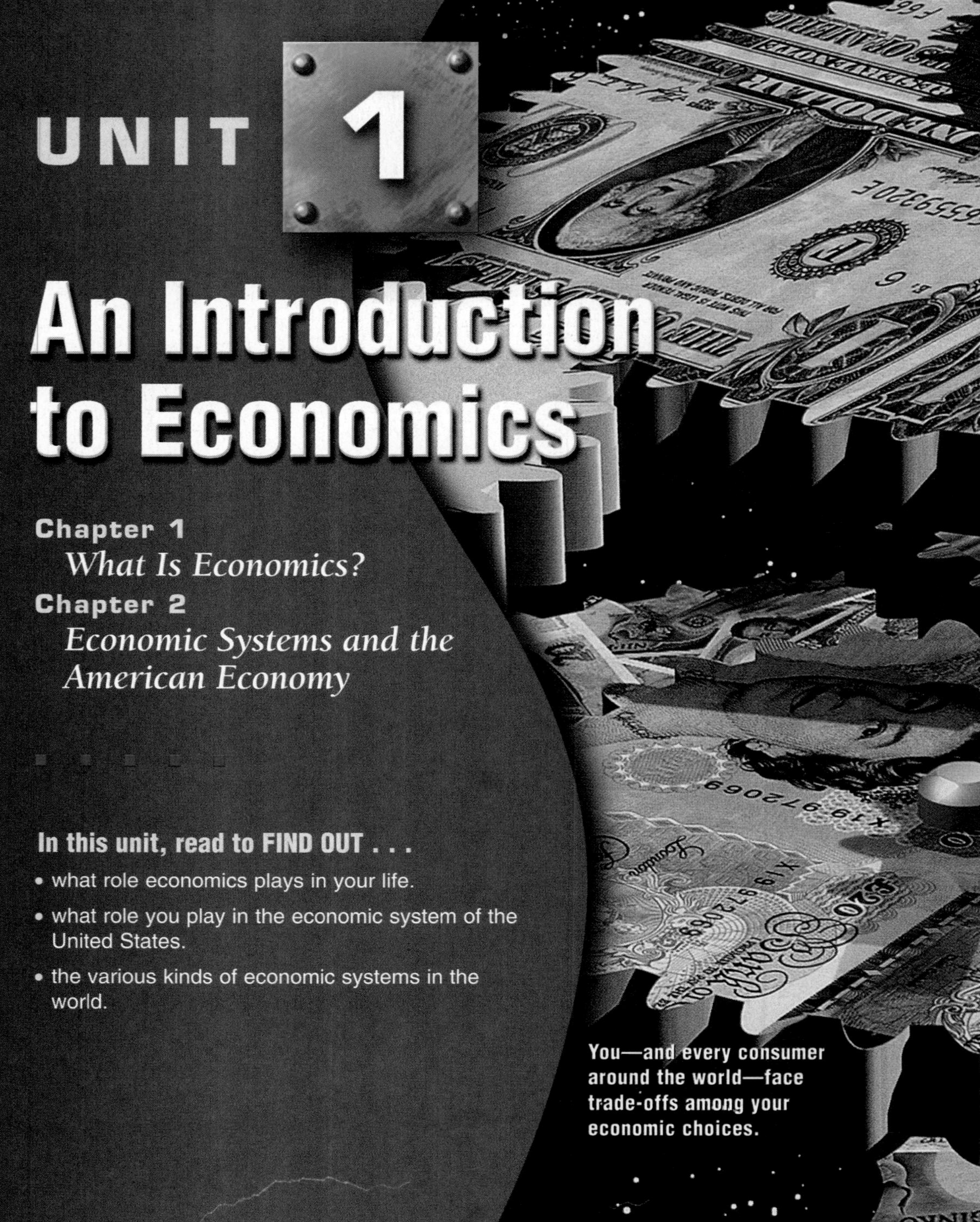

# UNIT 1

# An Introduction to Economics



**In this unit, read to FIND OUT . . .**

- what role economics plays in your life.
- what role you play in the economic system of the United States.
- the various kinds of economic systems in the world.

You—and every consumer around the world—face trade-offs among your economic choices.

## ECONOMIC SIMULATION

**Trade-Offs** Have the class assume the role of a government committee charged with hearing arguments for and against increasing the amount of timber that can be cut in Tongass National Forest, Alaska. Select six students to research the subject: three to speak for a timber company, and three to speak as environmentalists. Have the six students present their arguments to the class. Then ask the class to discuss the issue to reach a consensus. In a follow-up discussion, ask students to explain how the concept of trade-offs played a role in their decision.

Your decisions as a consumer determine how many goods and services will be produced.

The United States and Japan have market economies—also known as free enterprise.

The "gears" that run every nation's economy are the factors of production—land, labor, capital, and entrepreneurship.

The basic problem facing every type of economy is the presence of scarcity.

1

Introducing UNIT 1

## Making It Relevant

ASK: What role does economics play in your life? Remind students that many of them receive payment for part-time jobs or chores. Also, they regularly make purchases—clothes, books, CDs, and so on. Then point out that when they agree to a particular payment for the jobs or chores they do or decide to make a purchase, they are making *economic* decisions.

### BusinessWeek ONLINE

To find up-to-date news and analysis on the economy, business, technology, markets, entrepreneurs, investments, and finance, have students search feature articles and special reports on the *Business Week* Web site. www.businessweek.com

### EXTRA CREDIT PROJECT

Ask students to watch the local and national television news broadcasts for one week. Have them note the number of news items on each broadcast that deal with economic issues. Suggest that they record the economic issue addressed in each item, and the time given to each item. Encourage students to present the data they collect in chart form.

# CHAPTER 1 Resource Manager

## Teaching Transparencies

### Economic Concepts Transparency 1

ECONOMIC CONCEPTS Transparency 1

SCARCITY

Calvin and Hobbes by Bill Watterson

### Economic Concepts Transparency 2

ECONOMIC CONCEPTS Transparency 2

OPPORTUNITY COST & TRADE-OFFS



## Application and Enrichment

### Enrichment Activity 1

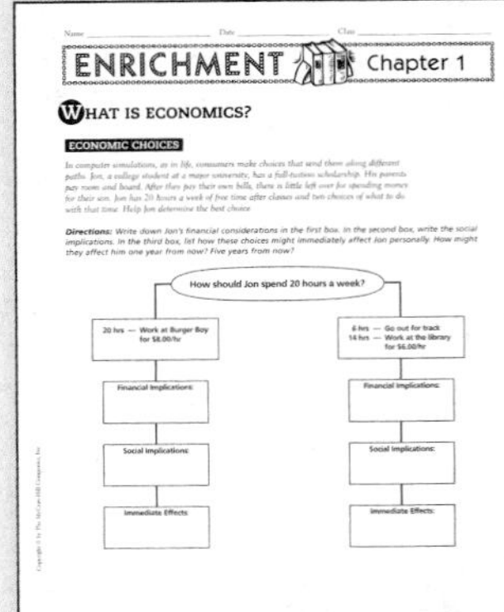
ENRICHMENT Chapter 1

WHAT IS ECONOMICS?

How should Jon spend 20 hours a week?

### Consumer Applications Activity 1

Con$umer Applications Activity 1

MAKING ECONOMIC DECISIONS

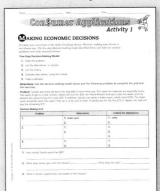

## Application and Enrichment

### Free Enterprise Activity 1

FREE ENTERPRISE ACTIVITY 1

PRODUCTIVE RESOURCES

### Cooperative Learning Simulations and Problems 1

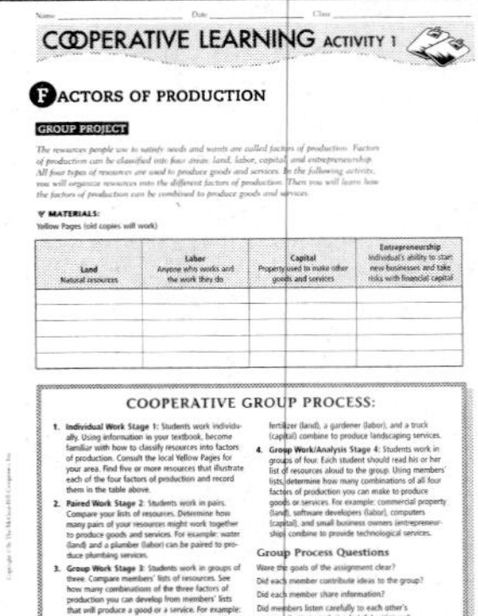
COOPERATIVE LEARNING ACTIVITY 1

FACTORS OF PRODUCTION

COOPERATIVE GROUP PROCESS:

### Primary and Secondary Source Reading 1

PRIMARY & SECONDARY SOURCES Reading 1

GETTING AND SPENDING

### Math Practice for Economics Activity 1

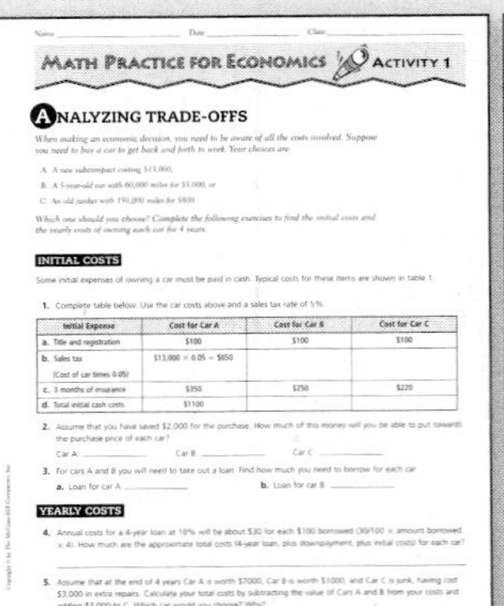
MATH PRACTICE FOR ECONOMICS ACTIVITY 1

ANALYZING TRADE-OFFS

### Economic Cartoons Activity 1

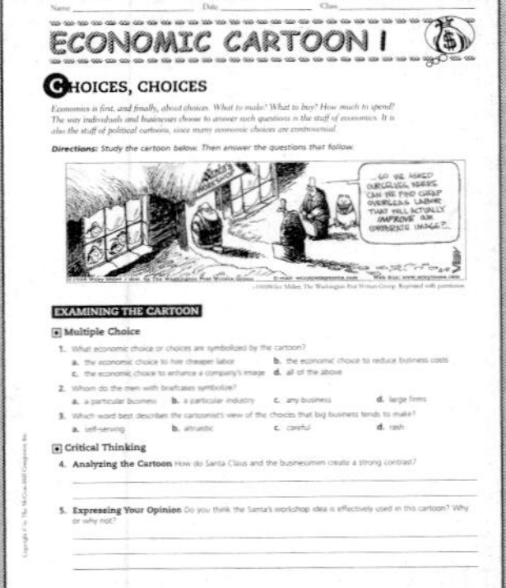
ECONOMIC CARTOON 1

CHOICES, CHOICES

## Review and Reinforcement

### Critical Thinking Activity 1

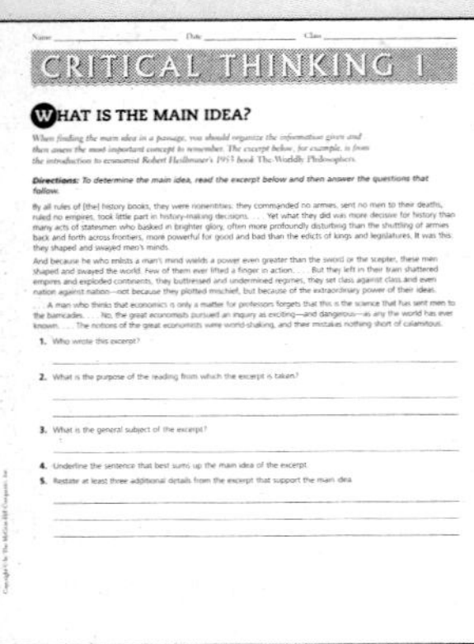
CRITICAL THINKING 1

WHAT IS THE MAIN IDEA?

### Reteaching Activity 1

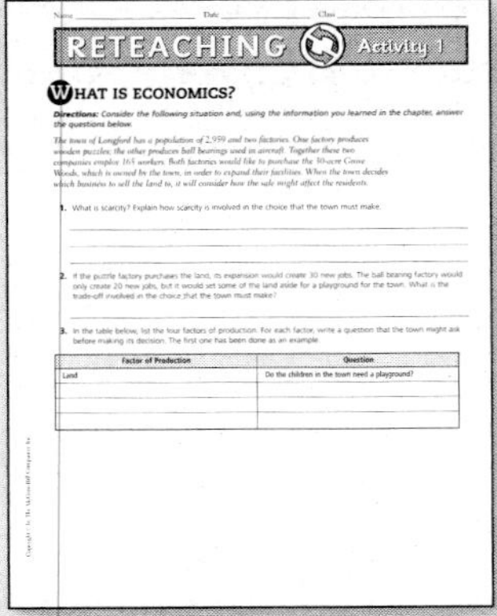
RETEACHING Activity 1

WHAT IS ECONOMICS?

### Economic Vocabulary Activity 1

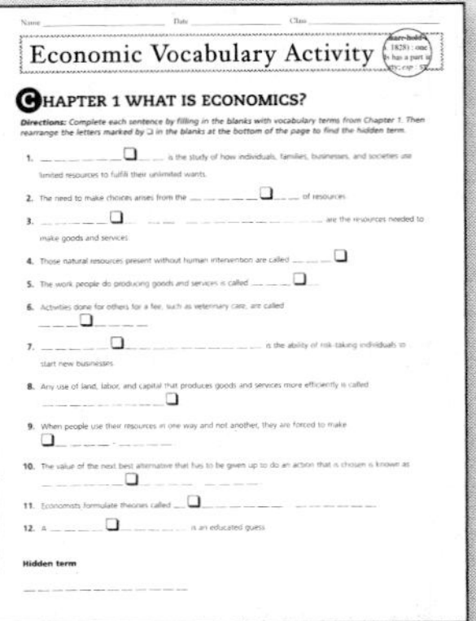
Economic Vocabulary Activity

CHAPTER 1 WHAT IS ECONOMICS?

### Reinforcing Economic Skills 9

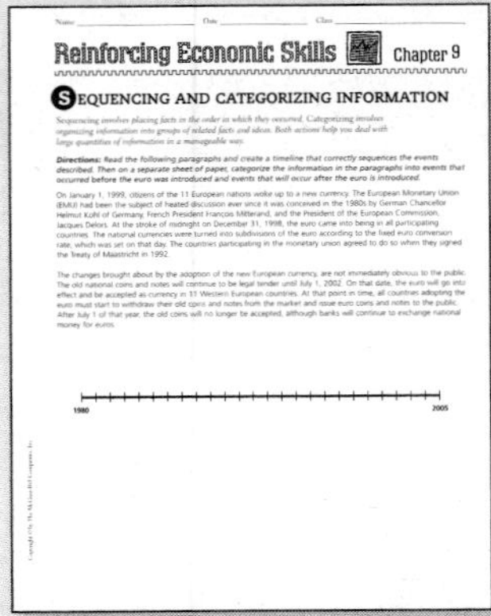
Reinforcing Economic Skills Chapter 9

SEQUENCING AND CATEGORIZING INFORMATION

# CHAPTER 1 Resource Manager

## Assessment and Evaluation

Chapter 1 Test Form A

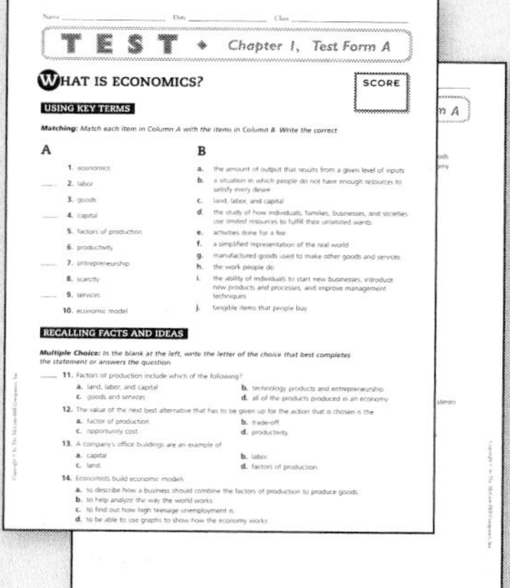
TEST ◆ Chapter 1, Test Form A

WHAT IS ECONOMICS?

SCORE

USING KEY TERMS

RECALLING FACTS AND IDEAS

Chapter 1 Test Form B

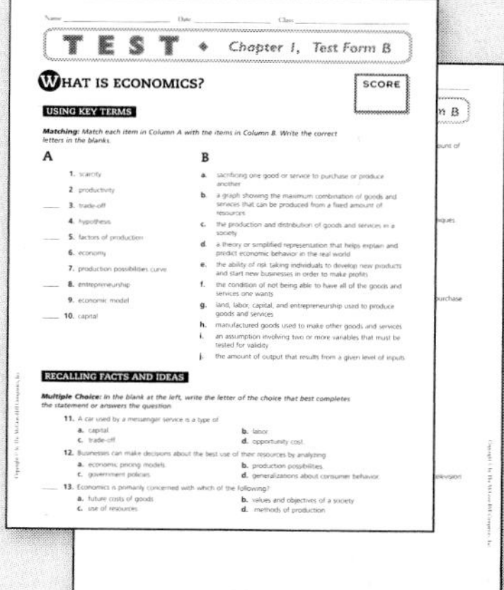
TEST ◆ Chapter 1, Test Form B

WHAT IS ECONOMICS?

SCORE

USING KEY TERMS

RECALLING FACTS AND IDEAS

Performance Assessment Activity 1

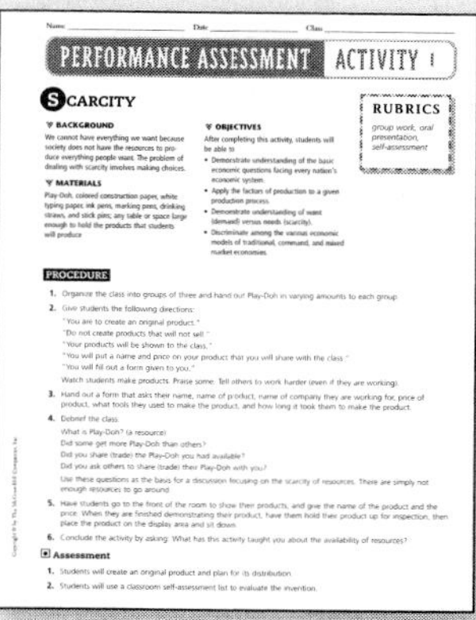
PERFORMANCE ASSESSMENT ACTIVITY 1

SCARCITY

RUBRICS

PROCEDURE

ExamView® Pro Testmaker

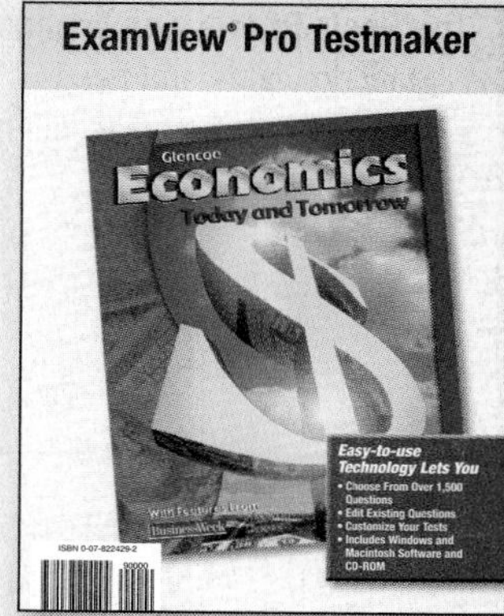


## Technology and Multimedia

 Vocabulary PuzzleMaker Software

 Interactive Tutor Self-Assessment Software

 ExamView® Pro Testmaker

 NBR *Economics & You* Video Program (English/Spanish)

 Presentation Plus!

 Glencoe Skillbuilder Interactive Workbook CD-ROM, Level 2

 Interactive Lesson Planner

 MindJogger Videoquiz

 Interactive Economics! CD-ROM

Audio Program (English/Spanish)

You and your students can visit ett.glencoe.com—the Web site companion to **Economics Today and Tomorrow.** This innovative integration of electronic and print media offers your students a wealth of opportunities. The student text directs students to the Web site for the following options:

- **Chapter Overviews**
- **Self-Check Quizzes**
- **Student Web Activities**
- **Textbook Updates**

Answers are provided for you in the **Web Activity Lesson Plan.** Additional Web resources and Interactive Puzzles are also available.

Use the Glencoe Web site for additional resources. All essential content is covered in the Student Edition.

## Spanish Resources

 Spanish Economic Concepts Transparency 1

 Spanish Vocabulary Activity 1

 Spanish Reteaching Activity 1

Spanish Section Quizzes for Chapter 1

 Spanish Chapter 1 Audio Program, Activity, and Test

## Additional Resources

### Reading for the Student

Eggert, James. *What Is Economics?* 4th ed. Mountain View, CA: Mayfield Publishing, 1997. Explains basic concepts of economics with real-world examples.

### Reading for the Teacher

Heilbroner, Robert L., and Lester C. Thurow. *Economics Explained*, 4th ed. New York: Simon & Schuster, 1998. An authoritative review of the fundamentals of economics.

# CHAPTER 1 Resource Manager

## Section Resources

| Reading Objectives | Reproducible Resources | Technology/Multimedia Resources |
|---|---|---|
| **Section 1**<br>**The Basic Problem in Economics**<br>• How do wants and needs differ?<br>• Why does scarcity face all people at all times?<br>• What are the four factors of production? | Reproducible Lesson Plan 1-1<br>Daily Lecture Notes 1-1<br>Guided Reading Activity 1-1<br>Reading Essentials and Study Guide 1-1<br>Daily Focus Activity 1<br>Section Quiz 1-1*<br>Reinforcing Economic Skills 9 | Daily Focus Transparency 1<br>Economic Concepts Transparency 1<br>Vocabulary PuzzleMaker<br>Interactive Tutor Self-Assessment Software<br>MindJogger Videoquiz<br>NBR's *Economics & You**<br>Presentation Plus!<br>ExamView® Pro Testmaker |
| **Section 2**<br>**Trade-Offs**<br>• How are trade-offs and opportunity costs related?<br>• How can society's trade-offs be shown on a production possibilities curve? | Reproducible Lesson Plan 1-2<br>Daily Lecture Notes 1-2<br>Guided Reading Activity 1-2<br>Reading Essentials and Study Guide 1-2<br>Daily Focus Activity 2<br>Section Quiz 1-2* | Daily Focus Transparency 2<br>Economic Concepts Transparency 2<br>Vocabulary PuzzleMaker<br>Interactive Tutor Self-Assessment Software<br>MindJogger Videoquiz<br>Interactive Economics!<br>Presentation Plus!<br>ExamView® Pro Testmaker |
| **Section 3**<br>**What Do Economists Do?**<br>• How do economists use models to study the real world?<br>• Why are there different schools of economic thought? | Reproducible Lesson Plan 1-3<br>Daily Lecture Notes 1-3<br>Guided Reading Activity 1-3<br>Reading Essentials and Study Guide 1-3<br>Daily Focus Activity 3<br>Section Quiz 1-3* | Daily Focus Transparency 3<br>Vocabulary PuzzleMaker<br>Interactive Tutor Self-Assessment Software<br>MindJogger Videoquiz<br>Presentation Plus!<br>ExamView® Pro Testmaker |

*Also available in Spanish

Blackline Master
Transparency

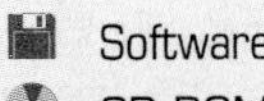
Software
CD-ROM

Videodisc
Audiocassette

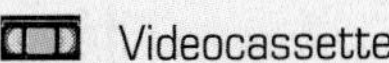
Videocassette

# CHAPTER 1 Resource Manager

## ACTIVITY From the Classroom of

**Charles Erlandson**
**All Saints Episcopal School**
**Tyler, Texas**

### The Scarcity of Time

Time is a very precious resource. To help students grasp the concept of time as a scarce resource, have them keep a one-week log of how all their hours (168) are spent in one week. Ask students to divide these hours into categories such as sleep, school, studying, eating, entertainment, travel, preparation, shopping, and so on. Then have students enter the information in a database and convert it into a circle graph. Students should compare their graphs.

## Easy Planning and Preparation!

Use Glencoe's **Presentation Plus!**, a Microsoft PowerPoint® application, to teach **What Is Economics?**. With this multimedia teacher tool, you can customize ready-made presentations. At your fingertips are interactive transparencies, on-screen lecture notes, audio-visual presentations, and links to the Internet and to other Glencoe multimedia.

### Interactive Lesson Planner

Planning has never been easier! Organize your week, month, semester, or year with all the lesson helps you need to make teaching creative, timely, and relevant—the way it is meant to be. The Interactive Lesson Planner opens Glencoe's **Chapter 1** resources, helps you build your schedule, and tracks your progress.

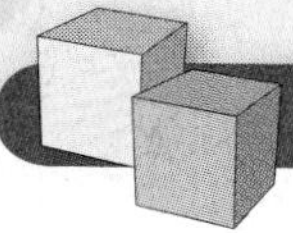

## Block Schedule

Activities that are particularly suited to use within the block scheduling framework are identified throughout this chapter by the following designation: BLOCK SCHEDULING

## Key to Ability Levels

**Teaching strategies have been coded for varying learning styles and abilities.**

L1 BASIC activities for all students
L2 AVERAGE activities for average to above-average students
L3 CHALLENGING activities for above-average students
ELL ENGLISH LANGUAGE LEARNER activities

## National Council on Economic Education

## THE EconomicsAmerica AND EconomicsInternational PROGRAMS

### Voluntary Standards Emphasized in Chapter 1

**Content Standard 1** Students will understand that productive resources are limited. Therefore, people cannot have all the goods and services they want; as a result, they must choose some things and give up others.

**Content Standard 2** Students will understand that effective decision making requires comparing the additional costs of alternatives with the additional benefits. Most choices involve doing a little more or a little less of something; few choices are all-or-nothing decisions.

### Resources Available from NCEE

- *Capstone: The Nation's High School Economics Course*
- *MCG–Economics and Entrepreneurship*
- *Focus: High School Economics*
- *Personal Decision Making: Focus on Economics*

To order these materials, or to contact your State Council on Economic Education about workshops and programs, call 1-800-338-1192 or visit the NCEE Web site at http://www.nationalcouncil.org

ECONOMICS & YOU

What Is Economics?

Chapter 2
Disc 1, Side 1

ASK: If an item that everyone needs is scarce, how can it be allocated? *Answers may include through rationing programs.*

Also available in VHS.

## Chapter Overview

Economics is the study of how individuals and nations make choices about how to fulfill their wants. **Chapter 1** explains or describes scarcity, the four factors of production, the relationship between trade-offs and opportunity costs, and how economists use economic data to test the economic models they formulate.

### GLENCOE TECHNOLOGY

Use **MindJogger Videoquiz** VHS to preview Chapter 1 content.

Introduce students to chapter content and key terms by having them access **Chapter 1—Chapter Overviews** at *ett.glencoe.com*

# CHAPTER 1

# What Is Economics?

### Why It's Important

*How do scarce resources—including time—affect you and everyone around you? How do economists simplify the world to help us better understand it? This chapter will explain what economics is, and how it is part of your daily life.*

*To learn more about scarcity and how it forces you to make choices, view the* **Economics & You** *Chapter 2 video lesson:* **What Is Economics?**

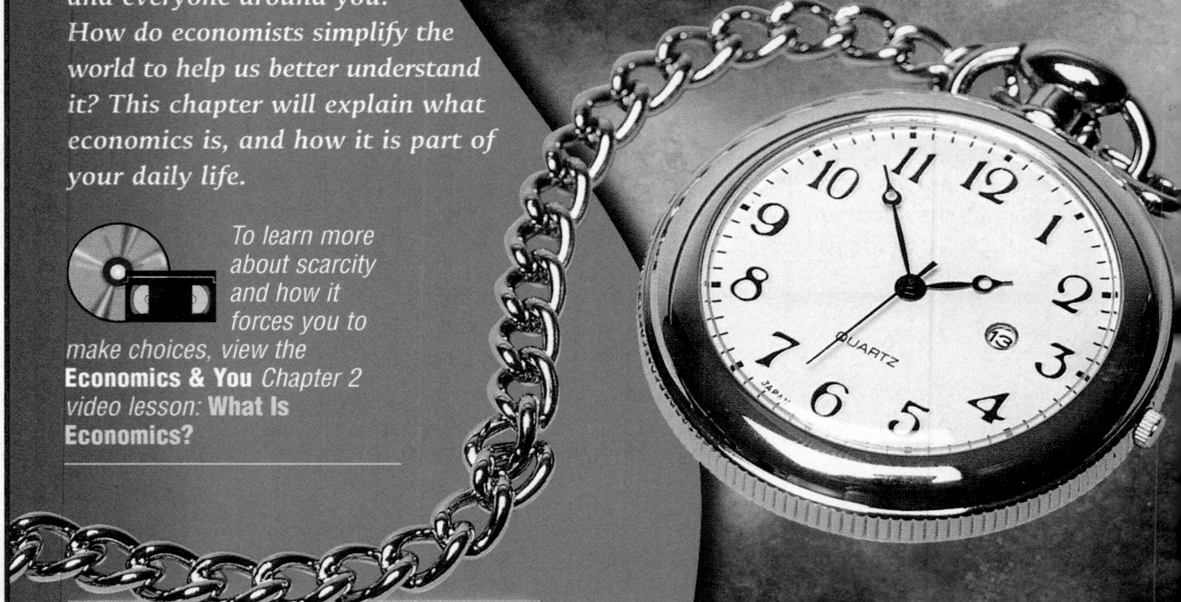

ECONOMICS Online

**Chapter Overview** Visit the *Economics Today and Tomorrow* Web site at ett.glencoe.com and click on ***Chapter 1—Chapter Overviews*** to preview chapter information.

## CHAPTER LAUNCH ACTIVITY

Ask students to imagine that they have $100 to spend. Have them make a list of the items they would like to buy and the approximate price of each. Have them add up the prices and, if the total exceeds $100, remove items so that they do not exceed their budget. Lead students in a discussion of their choices and the thought process that led them to those choices. Conclude by pointing out that *choice* is a key concept in economics.

SECTION 1

# The Basic Problem in Economics

## Cover Story

*The Columbus Dispatch*, March 23, 1999

When 5-year-old Michael Badurina spied a classmate wearing *Blue's Clues* clothes, he implored a higher power, "Mommy, I want some of those! I *need* some of those!"

. . . For the uninitiated, *Blue's Clues* is the most-watched preschool TV program in the United States, with 14 million viewers each week.

### Reader's Guide

**Terms to Know**

- economics
- scarcity
- factors of production
- land
- labor
- goods
- services
- capital
- productivity
- entrepreneurship
- technology

**Reading Objectives**

1. How do wants and needs differ?
2. Why does scarcity face all people at all times?
3. What are the four factors of production?

Starting at a very young age, many Americans use the words *want* and *need* interchangeably. How often do you think about what you "want"? How many times have you said that you "need" something? When you say, "I need some new clothes," are you stating a want, or a real need? As you read this section, you'll find that economics deals with questions such as these.

What, exactly, is economics? **Economics** is the study of how individuals, families, businesses, and societies use limited resources to fulfill their unlimited wants.

**economics:** *the study of how individuals and societies make choices about ways to use scarce resources to fulfill their needs and wants*



## Section 1 Resource Manager

**Reproducible Masters**

- Reproducible Lesson Plan 1–1
- Reading Essentials and Study Guide 1–1
- Guided Reading Activity 1–1
- Section Quiz 1–1
- Daily Focus Activity 1
- Daily Lecture Notes 1–1

**Multimedia**

- Daily Focus Transparency 1
- Economic Concepts Transparency 1
- Vocabulary PuzzleMaker
- Interactive Tutor Self-Assessment Software
- ExamView® Pro Testmaker
- MindJogger Videoquiz
- NBR's *Economics & You*
- Presentation Plus!



# 1 Focus

## Overview

Section 1 explains or describes the importance of economics, the relationship of scarcity to unlimited wants, and the four factors of production.

### Bellringer

**Motivational Activity**

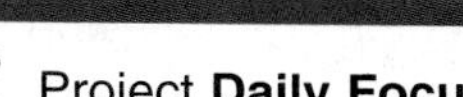

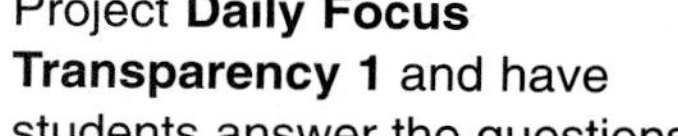

Project **Daily Focus Transparency 1** and have students answer the questions.

This activity is also available as a blackline master.

**Daily Focus Transparency 1**

FOCUS ACTIVITIES Transparency 1

THE BASIC ECONOMIC PROBLEM: SCARCITY

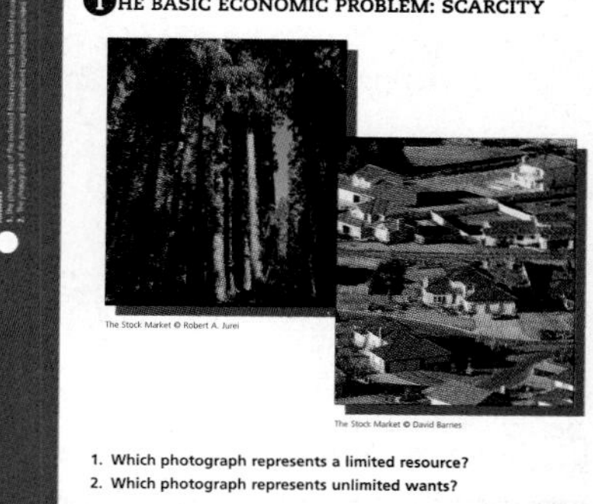

1. Which photograph represents a limited resource?
2. Which photograph represents unlimited wants?

### Reader's Guide

Answers to the **Reading Objectives** questions are on page 8.

**Preteaching Vocabulary**

Ask students to make crossword puzzles using the **Terms to Know.** Then pair students and have partners exchange puzzles.

**Vocabulary PuzzleMaker**

# 2 Teach

## Guided Practice

**L1 Understanding Ideas** Write the following statements on the board for students to complete:

"Things I need to live include..."

"Things I want to have include..."

Call on volunteers to read their completed statements to the class. Then have students discuss how they distinguished between what they need and what they want. Conclude by having students consider how their views on needs and wants compare with those of economists.

**Daily Lecture Notes 1-1**

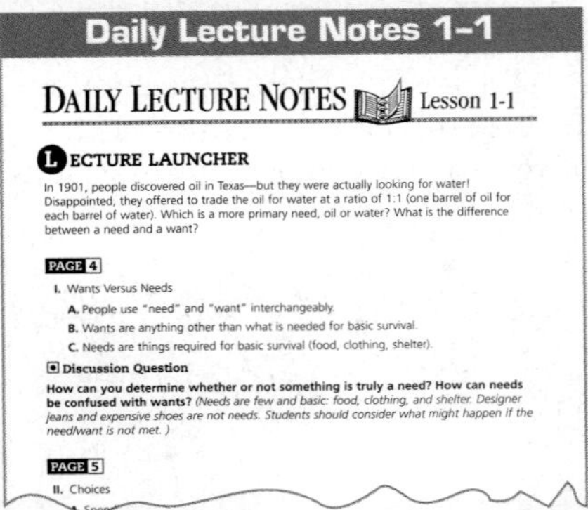

DAILY LECTURE NOTES Lesson 1-1

**LECTURE LAUNCHER**

In 1901, people discovered oil in Texas—but they were actually looking for water! Disappointed, they offered to trade the oil for water at a ratio of 1:1 (one barrel of oil for each barrel of water). Which is a more primary need, oil or water? What is the difference between a need and a want?

PAGE 4

I. Wants Versus Needs

A. People use "need" and "want" interchangeably.

B. Wants are anything other than what is needed for basic survival.

C. Needs are things required for basic survival (food, clothing, shelter).

**Discussion Question**

**How can you determine whether or not something is truly a need? How can needs be confused with wants?** *(Needs are few and basic: food, clothing, and shelter. Designer jeans and expensive shoes are not needs. Students should consider what might happen if the need/want is not met.)*

PAGE 5

II. Choices

**Visual Instruction FIGURE 1.1**

**Answer:** *by making choices*

**Visual Instruction FIGURE 1.2**

**Answer:** *scarcity*

ZITS

FIGURE  1.1

**Wants Versus Needs**
Luxuries such as concert tickets often become necessities in the eyes of consumers. ***How do consumers satisfy their seemingly unlimited wants?***

## Wants Versus Needs

Typically the term *need* is used very casually. When most people use the word, as shown in **Figure 1.1,** they really mean that they want something they do not have. Obviously, everyone needs certain things to survive—food, clothing, and shelter. Americans also consider education and health care as needs.

To economists, however, everything other than basic survival needs is considered a *want.* People want such items as new cars and personal computers. What begins as a luxury, or want, becomes to many people a necessity.

So how do individuals satisfy their unlimited wants in a world of limited resources? They must do this by making choices.

FIGURE  1.2

**Economic Choices**
Everyone, including governments, must make choices in a world of limited resources. If the government allocates funds to build Stealth bombers, then funds for higher education could be limited. ***What is the basic economic problem that makes choices necessary?***

**Meeting Special Needs** 

**Reading Disability** Students with various reading and information organization difficulties may have problems relating pictures, captions, and the main text. Before they read the text in Section 1, ask students to look at the pictures and read the captions. Have students discuss what the pictures illustrate. Then have students read Section 1. Ask them to explain again what the pictures illustrate and have them suggest why they think the pictures were included in this section.

Refer to *Inclusion for the Social Studies Classroom Strategies and Activities* for students with different learning styles.

## Choices

As a student, you probably have a small income from an allowance or a part-time job. As a result, you have to make choices about its use. Whenever you make such a spending decision, each available choice competes with every other available choice. Suppose you have $20.00 to spend. When you decide whether to spend your money on lunch or clothes or a new CD, you are making an economic choice.

Like individuals, businesses must also make choices. Businesspeople make decisions daily about what to produce now, what to produce later, and what to stop producing. These decisions in turn affect workers' incomes and people's ability to buy. Societies, too, face choices about how to utilize their resources in the production of goods and services. As shown in **Figure 1.2**, elected government representatives in the United States must decide how much to spend on defense versus higher education, for example. How people and societies make these choices is the focus of economics.

## The Problem of Scarcity

The need to make choices arises because everything that exists is limited, although some items (such as fresh water or labor) may appear to be in abundant supply. At any single moment, a fixed amount of resources is available. At the same time, people have competing uses for these resources. This situation results in scarcity—the basic problem of economics.

**Scarcity** means that people do not have and cannot have enough income, time, and other resources to satisfy their every want. What you buy as a student is limited by the amount of income you have. In this case, your income is the scarce resource. Even if everyone in the world were rich, however, scarcity would continue to exist—in the form of goods and services NOT available because no one would want to work!

It is important not to confuse scarcity with *shortages.* Scarcity always exists because of competing alternative uses for resources, whereas shortages are temporary. Shortages often occur, for example, after hurricanes or floods destroy goods and property.

*__scarcity:__ condition of not being able to have all of the goods and services one wants, because wants exceed what can be made from all available resources at any given time*

## Factors of Production

When economists talk about scarce resources, they are referring to the **factors of production,** or resources needed to produce goods and services. Traditionally, economists have classified

*__factors of production:__ resources of land, labor, capital, and entrepreneurship used to produce goods and services*





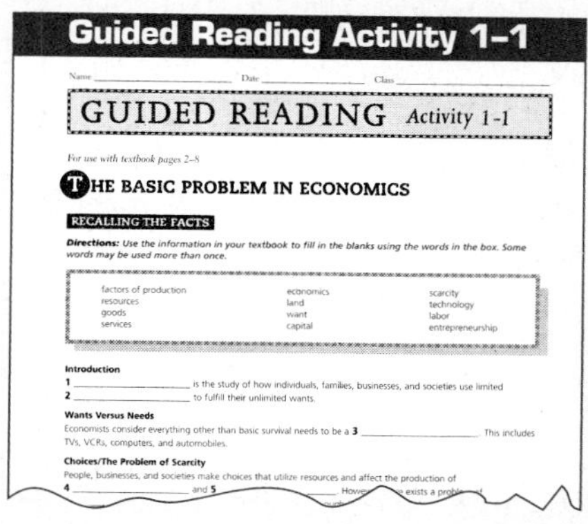
**Guided Reading Activity 1-1**

GUIDED READING Activity 1-1

THE BASIC PROBLEM IN ECONOMICS

RECALLING THE FACTS

Directions: Use the information in your textbook to fill in the blanks using the words in the box. Some words may be used more than once.

| factors of production | economics | scarcity |
|---|---|---|
| resources | land | technology |
| goods | want | labor |
| services | capital | entrepreneurship |

Introduction

1 ________ is the study of how individuals, families, businesses, and societies use limited
2 ________ to fulfill their unlimited wants.

Wants Versus Needs

Economists consider everything other than basic survival needs to be a 3 ________. This includes TVs, VCRs, computers, and automobiles.

Choices/The Problem of Scarcity

People, businesses, and societies make choices that utilize resources and affect the production of
4 ________ and 5 ________.

**L2 Analyzing Ideas** Lead the class in a discussion of what life would be like if no economic scarcity existed. Note ideas on the board as students offer them. Then ask students to use the information on the board to write a paragraph that begins: "If there were no economic scarcity..."

Project **Economic Concepts Transparency 1** and have students discuss the accompanying questions.

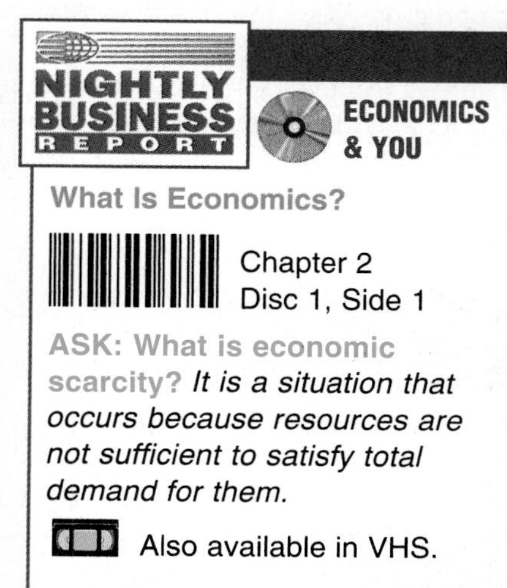

NIGHTLY BUSINESS REPORT
ECONOMICS & YOU
What Is Economics?
Chapter 2
Disc 1, Side 1
ASK: What is economic scarcity? It is a situation that occurs because resources are not sufficient to satisfy total demand for them.
Also available in VHS.


### Cooperative Learning

Organize students into small groups, and ask groups to create storyboards for a short television commercial designed to encourage the study of economics in schools. Mention that in their commercials, groups should explain what economics is, demonstrate the subject's relevance to everyday life, and explain how knowledge of the subject might help people. Encourage groups to share their storyboards with the rest of the class. If video equipment is available, some groups may wish to "shoot" their commercials.

BLOCK SCHEDULING

## Independent Practice

**L1 Creating Posters** Ask each student to select one of the following subjects: Economic Needs/Economic Wants, Scarcity, or Factors of Production. Then ask students to create a poster for their selected subject. Tell students that their posters should be designed as visual aids for teaching the content of Section 1. Display finished posters around the classroom. BLOCK SCHEDULING

## Global Economy

### Factors of Production

Economic development in developing countries, as in developed countries, is linked to the factors of production. Many economists believe that the biggest obstacle to economic growth in developing countries is the quality of labor. With low literacy rates and poor health conditions, labor forces in developing countries do not have the skills needed to keep up with modern technology.

## Visual Instruction FIGURE 1.3

Have students study Figure 1.3. Then have them consider which, if any, of the four factors of production is the most important. Ask students to explain their answers.

these productive resources as land, labor, capital, and entrepreneurship. **Figure 1.3** shows you the four factors of production.

**land:** *natural resources and surface land and water*

**Land** As an economic term, **land** refers to natural resources present without human intervention. "Land" includes actual surface land and water, as well as fish, animals, forests, mineral deposits, and other "gifts of nature."

**labor:** *human effort directed toward producing goods and services*

**goods:** *tangible objects that can satisfy people's wants*

**services:** *actions that can satisfy people's wants*

**Labor** The work people do is **labor**—which is often called a human resource. Labor includes anyone who works to produce goods and services. As you know, economic **goods** are tangible items that people buy, such as pharmaceuticals, shampoo, or computers. **Services** are activities done for others for a fee. Doctors, hair stylists, and Web-page designers all sell their services.

**capital:** *previously manufactured goods used to make other goods and services*

**Capital** Another factor of production is **capital**—the manufactured goods used to make other goods and services. The machines, buildings, and tools used to assemble automobiles, for example, are *capital goods*. The newly assembled goods are not considered capital unless they, in turn, produce other goods and services, such as an automobile performing services as a taxicab.

**FIGURE 1.3**

**The Four Factors of Production** The four general categories of resources needed in the production of all goods and services include land, labor, capital, and entrepreneurship.

**A** Land
*Natural resources, such as timber, are all the things found in nature—on or in water and the earth.*

**B** Labor
*This child-care worker falls under the category of* labor*—she is performing a service for a fee.*

6

## Free Enterprise Activity

**Goods and Services** Organize students into several small groups, and assign each group the category of *goods* or *services*. Ask groups to locate a business in their community that provides their category. Then have them research examples of the four factors of production used by their selected business. Have groups present their findings in chart form. BLOCK SCHEDULING

When capital is combined with land and labor, the value of all three factors of production increases. Think about the following situation. If you combine an uncut diamond (land), a diamond cutter (labor), and a diamond-cutting machine (capital), you end up with a highly valued gem.

Capital also increases **productivity**—the ability to produce greater quantities of goods and services in better and faster ways. Consider how much faster a mechanical reaper—a capital good—can harvest grain than a person clearing the field with a scythe.

*__productivity:__ the amount of output (goods and services) that results from a given level of inputs (land, labor, capital)*

**Entrepreneurship** The fourth factor of production is **entrepreneurship.** This refers to the ability of individuals to start new businesses, to introduce new products and processes, and to improve management techniques. Entrepreneurship involves initiative and willingness to take risks in order to reap profits.

*__entrepreneurship:__ ability of risk-taking individuals to develop new products and start new businesses in order to make profits*

Entrepreneurs must also incur the costs of failed efforts. About 30 percent of new business enterprises fail. Of the 70 percent that do survive, only a few become wildly successful businesses such as Microsoft, The Limited, or Blockbuster Video.

**Technology** Some economists add technology to the list of factors of production. In the past, **technology** included any use of land, labor, and capital that produced goods and services more efficiently. For example, a computer keyboard was a technological advance over the typewriter.

*__technology:__ advance in knowledge leading to new and improved goods and services and better ways of producing them*

**C** Capital
*Capital goods, such as these robots, are unique in that they are the result of previous manufacturing.*

**D** Entrepreneurship
*These entrepreneurs are taking a financial risk to make a profit for themselves and to bring innovative products and services to consumers.*

## Critical Thinking Activity

**Analyzing Information** Organize students into several small groups. Have group members brainstorm a list of the activities they pursue after school—including homework—in a typical week. Then ask them to create a five-day schedule for six hours of activities after school. Have group representatives present and explain their schedules to the class. Conclude by asking students to discuss the problems they faced in developing their schedules and how those problems are similar to the economic problems of scarcity.



# 3 Assess

## Meeting Lesson Objectives

Assign Section 1 Assessment as homework or an in-class activity.

Use **Interactive Tutor Self-Assessment Software** to review Section 1.

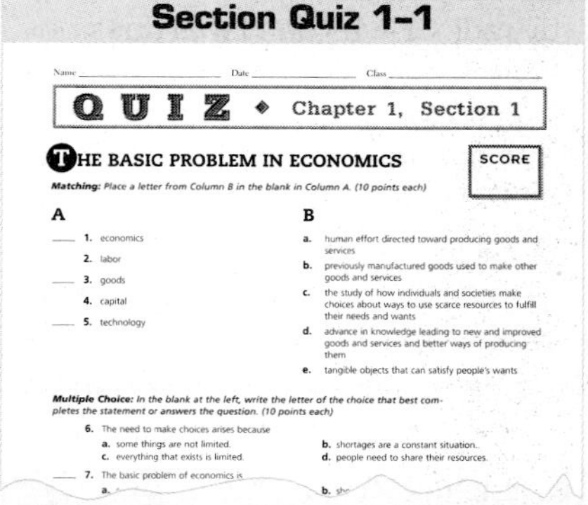

**Section Quiz 1-1**

Name ______ Date ______ Class ______

**QUIZ ◆ Chapter 1, Section 1**

**THE BASIC PROBLEM IN ECONOMICS** SCORE

***Matching:*** *Place a letter from Column B in the blank in Column A. (10 points each)*

| A | B |
|---|---|
| ___ 1. economics | a. human effort directed toward producing goods and services |
| ___ 2. labor | b. previously manufactured goods used to make other goods and services |
| ___ 3. goods | c. the study of how individuals and societies make choices about ways to use scarce resources to fulfill their needs and wants |
| ___ 4. capital | d. advance in knowledge leading to new and improved goods and services and better ways of producing them |
| ___ 5. technology | e. tangible objects that can satisfy people's wants |

***Multiple Choice:*** *In the blank at the left, write the letter of the choice that best completes the statement or answers the question. (10 points each)*

___ 6. The need to make choices arises because
a. some things are not limited.
b. shortages are a constant situation.
c. everything that exists is limited.
d. people need to share their resources.

___ 7. The basic problem of economics is

## Reteach

Have students copy the headings in Section 1 as the main headings of an outline. Then ask them to complete the outline by adding secondary headings and details.

## Economic Connection to... Technology

"Smart labels" may one day, replace the bar codes that you see on items you buy at the store. These labels contain a computer chip, which can carry a wealth of information. And new data can be added even after the label has been attached to a package. Also, because the chip communicates by radio waves, the label does not have to be held directly in front of a scanner to be read. The radio waves can even penetrate dirt or other grime that might cover the label. The one disadvantage to this new technology is cost—about 30¢ per label.

**Reading Essentials and Study Guide 1-1**

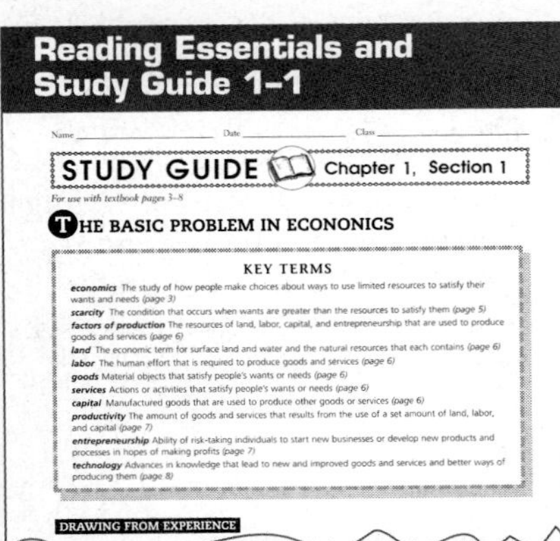
Name ______ Date ______ Class ______

STUDY GUIDE Chapter 1, Section 1

*For use with textbook pages 3–8*

THE BASIC PROBLEM IN ECONONICS

KEY TERMS

***economics*** The study of how people make choices about ways to use limited resources to satisfy their wants and needs *(page 3)*
***scarcity*** The condition that occurs when wants are greater than the resources to satisfy them *(page 5)*
***factors of production*** The resources of land, labor, capital, and entrepreneurship that are used to produce goods and services *(page 6)*
***land*** The economic term for surface land and water and the natural resources that each contains *(page 6)*
***labor*** The human effort that is required to produce goods and services *(page 6)*
***goods*** Material objects that satisfy people's wants or needs *(page 6)*
***services*** Actions or activities that satisfy people's wants or needs *(page 6)*
***capital*** Manufactured goods that are used to produce other goods or services *(page 6)*
***productivity*** The amount of goods and services that results from the use of a set amount of land, labor, and capital *(page 7)*
***entrepreneurship*** Ability of risk-taking individuals to start new businesses or develop new products and processes in hopes of making profits *(page 7)*
***technology*** Advances in knowledge that lead to new and improved goods and services and better ways of producing them *(page 8)*

DRAWING FROM EXPERIENCE

# 4 Close

Have students write a paragraph using the following as a topic sentence: Everyone makes economic choices.

## Economic Connection to... Technology

### Technology Saves You a Trip to the Store

Only a few years ago, computers were as big as refrigerators. Now, Frigidaire Home Products has unveiled a fridge that contains a computer. The computer has a touch-screen monitor and a bar code scanner mounted on the freezer door. There's even a jack for an Internet connection. After emptying a carton of milk, you could swipe the carton past the bar code scanner, tap a couple of buttons on the screen, and the fridge would order replacements from an online grocery store. ■

Today, technology usually describes the use of science to develop new products and new methods for producing and distributing goods and services. Without satellite technology, for example, it would be impossible for you to see real-time events happening on the other side of the world. Without Internet technology, you could not e-mail a friend 8,000 miles away for the price of a local phone call.

**Practice** and **assess** key skills with ***Skillbuilder Interactive Workbook, Level 2.***

## SECTION 1 Assessment

### Understanding Key Terms

1. **Define** economics, scarcity, factors of production, land, labor, goods, services, capital, productivity, entrepreneurship, technology.

### Reviewing Objectives

2. What is the difference between wants and needs?
3. Why does scarcity exist?
4. **Graphic Organizer** Create a chart like the one shown in the next column, then list the four factors of production and provide two examples of each.

| Factor of Production | Example 1 | Example 2 |
|---|---|---|
| | | |
| | | |

### Applying Economic Concepts

5. **Factors of Production** Provide an example in which a capital good has improved your personal productivity.

### Critical Thinking Activity

6. **Summarizing Information** Use a search engine to help you research an entrepreneur. Explain what benefits were brought to society by his or her risk-taking entrepreneurship.



## SECTION 1 Assessment Answers

1. All definitions can be found in the Glossary.
2. Needs are basic to survival. Wants are things other than these basic needs.
3. Scarcity exists because there are not enough resources to satisfy everyone's wants.
4. Answers may include: Land—water, fish, animals, forests, mineral deposits, etc.; Labor—factory worker, painter, bus driver, plumber, doctor, lawyer, hair stylist, etc.; Capital—assembly lines, factories, wrenches, hammers, etc.; Entrepreneurship—managers, business owners who organize factors of production, etc.
5. Examples should explain how a capital good has improved students' productivity.
6. Answers should reflect an entrepreneur and benefits that he or she brought to society.

## CRITICAL THINKING SKILLS

# Sequencing and Categorizing Information

Sequencing *involves placing facts in the order in which they occurred.* Categorizing *entails organizing information into groups of related facts and ideas. Both actions help you deal with large quantities of information in an understandable way.*

- Look for dates or clue words that provide you with a chronological order: *in 2004, the late 1990s, first, then, finally, after the Great Depression,* and so on.
- If the information you're studying did not happen in a sequential order, you may categorize it instead. To do so, look for information with similar characteristics.
- List these characteristics, or categories, as the headings on a chart.
- As you read, fill in details under the proper category on the chart.

### LEARNING THE SKILL

To learn sequencing and categorizing skills, follow the steps listed on the left.

### PRACTICING THE SKILL

Read the passage below, then answer the questions that follow.

> "*Twinkies were invented in 1930 by James A. Dewar, a plant manager for Continental Baking Company. Faced with economic hardship, it didn't make sense to Dewar that the bakery had lots of expensive pans dedicated to a product called Little Short Cake Fingers that was baked only six weeks a year–during strawberry season. Dewar thought the little cakes could sell year-round if the company came up with something to replace the strawberry cream placed inside. He mixed up a banana-flavored 'crème' and figured out a way to inject it into the shortcake using three syringe-like injection tubes.*"
>
> –Adapted from Jack Mingo's *How the Cadillac Got Its Fins,* HarperCollins, ©1994

1. How can the facts here be organized sequentially?
2. Now organize the facts under the categories of *Land, Labor, Capital,* and *Entrepreneurship.*

**Practice** and **assess** key skills with *Skillbuilder Interactive Workbook, Level 2.*

### APPLICATION ACTIVITY

Find a newspaper or magazine article about a local business. Sequence or categorize the information in a chart.



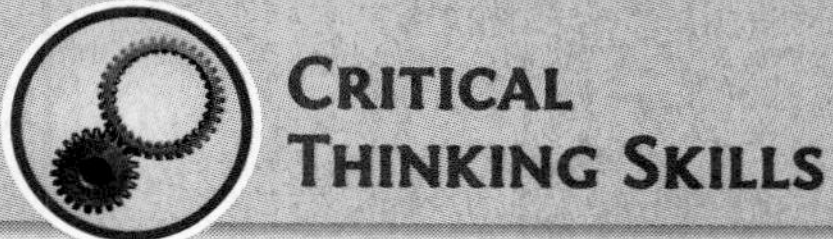


### Sequencing and Categorizing Information

Discuss the guidelines for sequencing and categorizing noted in the **Learning the Skill** section. Then point out that the following simple equation will help students distinguish between the two skills:

Sequence = Time
Category = Similar Ideas and Facts

On the left side of the board, under the heading "Sequence," list the numbers 1 though 4. On the right side of the board, under the heading "Categorize," create a chart with "Land," "Labor," "Capital," and "Entrepreneurship" as column headings. Call on volunteers to complete the list and chart.

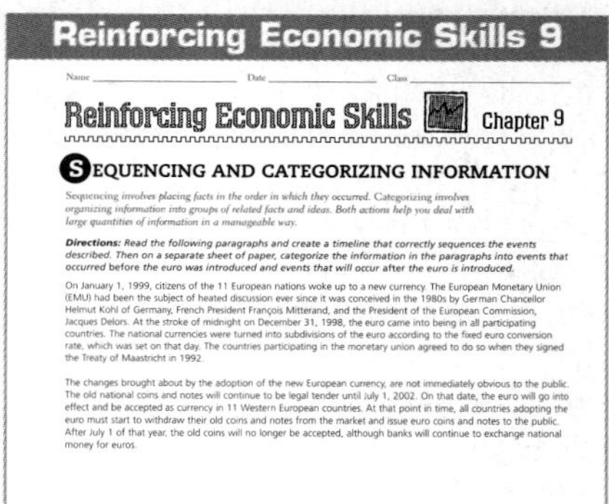

**Reinforcing Economic Skills 9**

Name ______ Date ______ Class ______

**Reinforcing Economic Skills** Chapter 9

**SEQUENCING AND CATEGORIZING INFORMATION**

Sequencing *involves placing facts in the order in which they occurred.* Categorizing *involves organizing information into groups of related facts and ideas. Both actions help you deal with large quantities of information in a manageable way.*

***Directions:*** *Read the following paragraphs and create a timeline that correctly sequences the events described. Then on a separate sheet of paper, categorize the information in the paragraphs into events that occurred before the euro was introduced and events that will occur after the euro is introduced.*

On January 1, 1999, citizens of the 11 European nations woke up to a new currency. The European Monetary Union (EMU) had been the subject of heated discussion ever since it was conceived in the 1980s by German Chancellor Helmut Kohl of Germany, French President François Mitterand, and the President of the European Commission, Jacques Delors. At the stroke of midnight on December 31, 1998, the euro came into being in all participating countries. The national currencies were turned into subdivisions of the euro according to the fixed euro conversion rate, which was set on that day. The countries participating in the monetary union agreed to do so when they signed the Treaty of Maastricht in 1992.

The changes brought about by the adoption of the new European currency, are not immediately obvious to the public. The old national coins and notes will continue to be legal tender until July 1, 2002. On that date, the euro will go into effect and be accepted as currency in 11 Western European countries. At that point in time, all countries adopting the euro must start to withdraw their old coins and notes from the market and issue euro coins and notes to the public. After July 1 of that year, the old coins will no longer be accepted, although banks will continue to exchange national money for euros.

**GLENCOE TECHNOLOGY**

**Glencoe Skillbuilder Interactive Workbook, Level 2**

This interactive CD-ROM reinforces student mastery of essential social studies skills.

### Answers to PRACTICING THE SKILL

1. Answers may be similar to the following: (1) Twinkies invented in 1930. (2) Dewar thought it wasteful to use expensive shortcake pans for only 6 weeks during the strawberry season. (3) Decided to utilize cake pans for another type of cake. (4) Dewar developed a banana filling and worked out a way to inject it into the cakes.

2\.

| Land | Labor | Capital | Entrepreneurship |
|---|---|---|---|
| strawberries, bananas | plant manager | bakery; expensive cake pans; syringe-like injection tubes | Dewar's decision to find a way to use the expensive cake tins all year round; the switch from strawberry filling to banana filling |

**APPLICATION ACTIVITY** Note cards or charts will vary.

# 1 Focus

Hold up a pencil and tell students the following points:

- Americans use about 2.8 billion pencils every year.
- The average pencil can draw a line 35 miles long or write about 45,000 words.

Then point out that in this feature, students will discover that this simple writing tool is a little more complex than they think.

# 2 Teach

Before students read this feature, ask them to identify the materials that are used to make pencils. List student responses on the board. When they think they have named all the materials, draw a line under the list. Then have students identify the countries of origin of these pencil components. List the appropriate country next to each pencil component. Ask students to copy these lists into their notebooks. As they read the feature, ask students to add to or subtract from these original lists.

## ? Did You Know

The island nation of Sri Lanka, located just off the southeastern coast of India, is the world's leading producer of graphite.

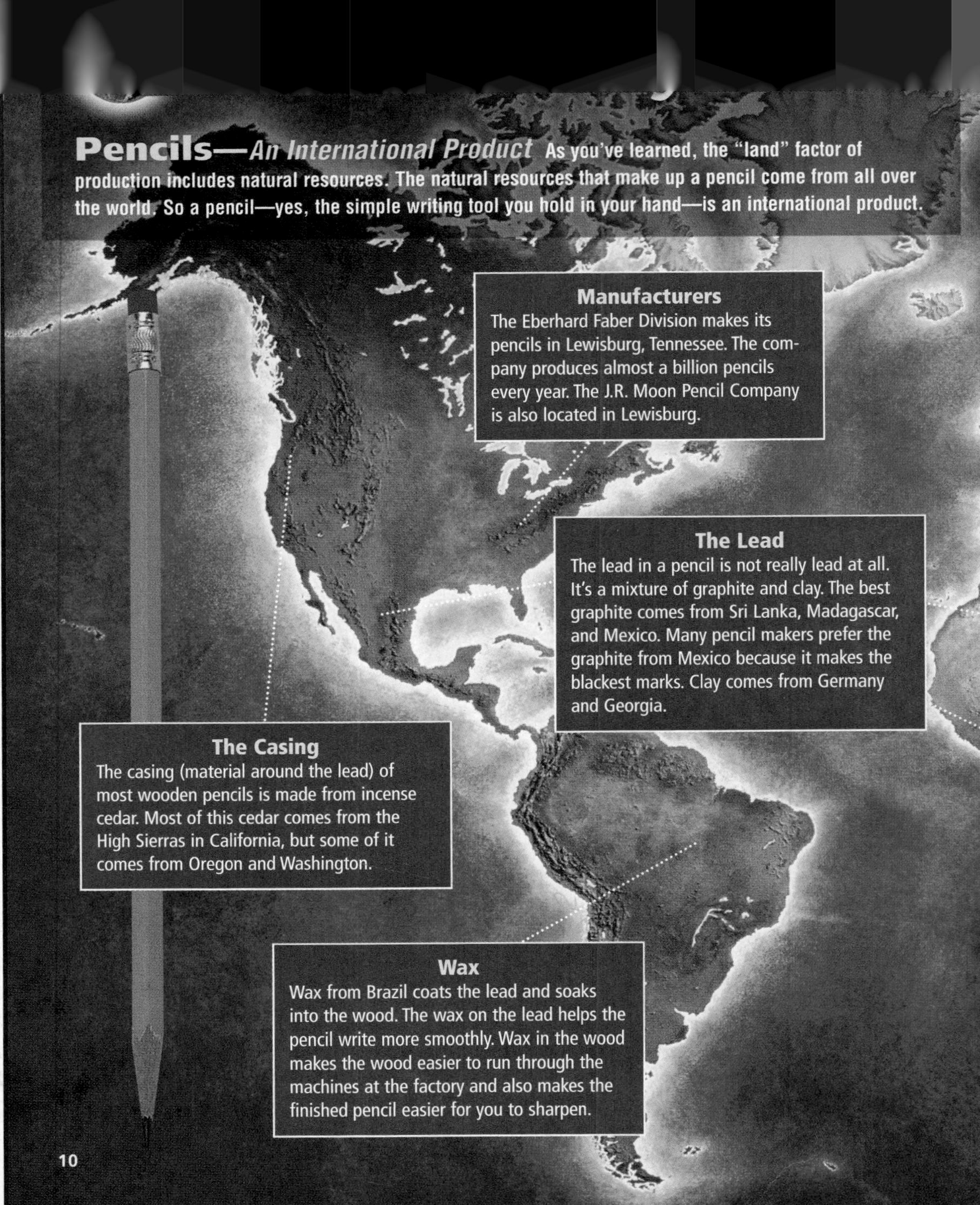

**Pencils**—*An International Product* As you've learned, the "land" factor of production includes natural resources. The natural resources that make up a pencil come from all over the world. So a pencil—yes, the simple writing tool you hold in your hand—is an international product.
**Manufacturers**
The Eberhard Faber Division makes its pencils in Lewisburg, Tennessee. The company produces almost a billion pencils every year. The J.R. Moon Pencil Company is also located in Lewisburg.
**The Lead**
The lead in a pencil is not really lead at all. It's a mixture of graphite and clay. The best graphite comes from Sri Lanka, Madagascar, and Mexico. Many pencil makers prefer the graphite from Mexico because it makes the blackest marks. Clay comes from Germany and Georgia.
**The Casing**
The casing (material around the lead) of most wooden pencils is made from incense cedar. Most of this cedar comes from the High Sierras in California, but some of it comes from Oregon and Washington.
**Wax**
Wax from Brazil coats the lead and soaks into the wood. The wax on the lead helps the pencil write more smoothly. Wax in the wood makes the wood easier to run through the machines at the factory and also makes the finished pencil easier for you to sharpen.
10


## Extending the Content

**The Incense Cedar** California incense cedar is the favorite wood of pencil makers all over the world. How do timber companies in the United States ensure that there will be a steady supply of wood for pencils? They cut the incense cedar on a sustained-yield basis. This means that the annual growth of the incense cedar forests is greater than the amount the timber companies cut.

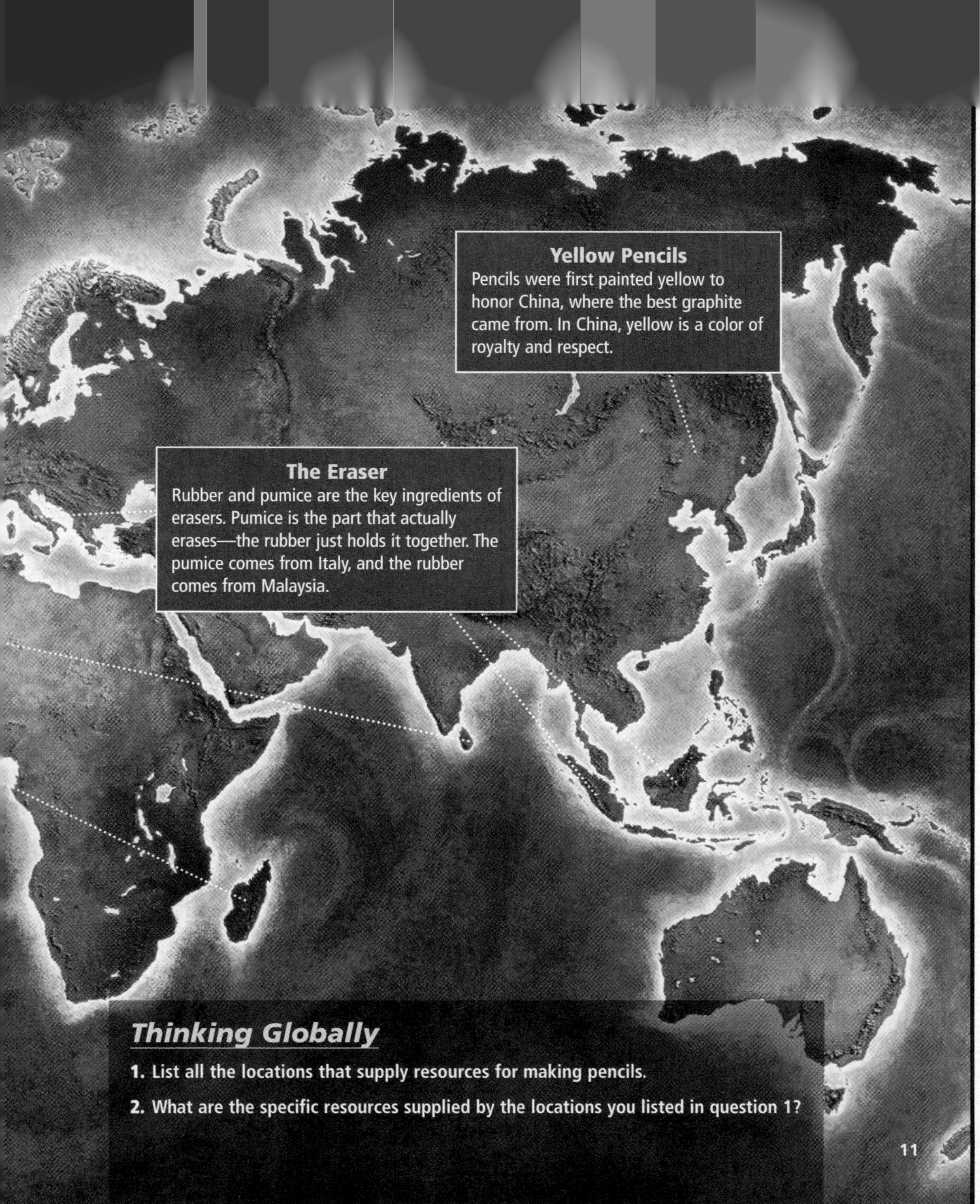

Yellow Pencils
Pencils were first painted yellow to honor China, where the best graphite came from. In China, yellow is a color of royalty and respect.
The Eraser
Rubber and pumice are the key ingredients of erasers. Pumice is the part that actually erases—the rubber just holds it together. The pumice comes from Italy, and the rubber comes from Malaysia.
Thinking Globally
1. List all the locations that supply resources for making pencils.
2. What are the specific resources supplied by the locations you listed in question 1?
11

## Answers to *Thinking Globally*

1. Mexico; Sri Lanka; Madagascar; Germany; Brazil; Italy; Malaysia; Georgia, California, Washington, and Oregon, United States
2. Mexico, Sri Lanka, Madagascar–graphite; Germany, Georgia–clay; California, Washington, Oregon–wood casing; Brazil–wax; Italy–pumice; Malaysia–rubber

# 3 Assess

Have students answer the **Thinking Globally** questions.

# 4 Close

Mention that the pencil is not the only everyday item that provides an illustration of the global economy. Encourage students to research the origins of the materials used in another everyday item–gym shoes, for example.

### Economic Connection to... *Literature*

American author John Steinbeck, who wrote *Grapes of Wrath*—the classic study of life in the United States during the Great Depression—used as many as 60 pencils a day.

### Did You Know

The first rubber eraser was made in 1770. Up until that time, the most common type of eraser was bread crumbs. The first pencil with an attached eraser was made in 1858.

# 1 Focus

## Overview

Section 2 explains how the concept of trade-offs is related to opportunity costs and the production possibilities curve.

**BELLRINGER**
**Motivational Activity**

Project **Daily Focus Transparency 2** and have students answer the questions.

This activity is also available as a blackline master.

**Daily Focus Transparency 2**

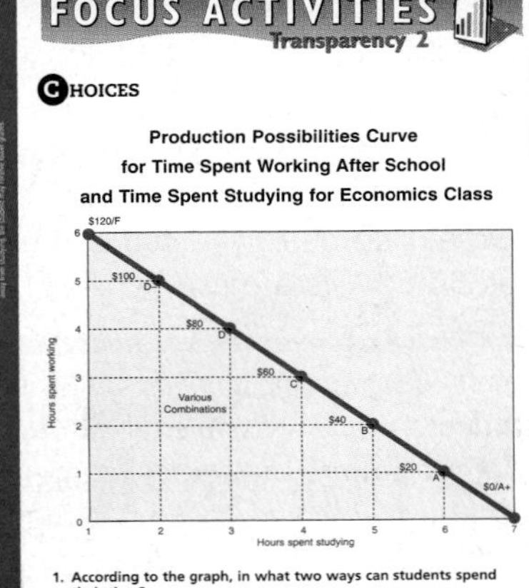
FOCUS ACTIVITIES
Transparency 2
CHOICES
Production Possibilities Curve
for Time Spent Working After School
and Time Spent Studying for Economics Class
Hours spent working
Hours spent studying
1. According to the graph, in what two ways can students spend their time?
2. How would students benefit from spending time on each of these activities? How would they lose?

**READER'S GUIDE**

Answers to the **Reading Objectives** questions are on page 16.

**Preteaching Vocabulary**

Call on volunteers to suggest what each of the **Terms to Know** means. Have students check these definitions by finding the terms in the Glossary.

Vocabulary PuzzleMaker

# SECTION 2 Trade-Offs

**READER'S GUIDE**

**Terms to Know**

- trade-off
- opportunity cost
- production possibilities curve

**Reading Objectives**

1. How are trade-offs and opportunity costs related?
2. How can society's trade-offs be shown on a production possibilities curve?

## COVER STORY

*BUSINESS WEEK*, FEBRUARY 15, 1999

If education is the key to America's future and the well-being of its individual citizens, the nation's youth—and particularly young females—seem to have gotten the right message. Over 70% of female high-school grads are enrolled in college, far more than the 63.5% of their male counterparts who did so.

As you learned in Section 1, scarcity forces people to make choices about how they will use their resources. In this section you'll learn that the effects of these choices may be long-lasting. For example, you may go to college or work full-time after graduating from high school. This decision affects not only your life now, but also what you'll earn in the future.

### Trade-Offs

The economic choices people make involve exchanging one good or service for another. If you choose to buy a DVD player, you are exchanging your money for the right to own the DVD. Exchanging one thing for the use of another is called a **trade-off.**

**trade-off:** *sacrificing one good or service to purchase or produce another*

Individuals, families, businesses, and societies are forced to make trade-offs every time they use their resources in one way and not another. **Figure 1.4** shows a trade-off common to growing communities.

**The Cost of Trade-Offs** The result of a trade-off is what you give up in order to get or do something else. Time, for example, is

**SECTION 2 RESOURCE MANAGER**

**Reproducible Masters**

- Reproducible Lesson Plan 1–2
- Reading Essentials and Study Guide 1–2
- Guided Reading Activity 1–2
- Section Quiz 1–2
- Daily Focus Activity 2
- Daily Lecture Notes 1–2

**Multimedia**

- Daily Focus Transparency 2
- Economic Concepts Transparency 2
- Vocabulary PuzzleMaker
- Interactive Tutor Self-Assessment Software
- ExamView® Pro Testmaker
- MindJogger Videoquiz
- Interactive Economics!
- Presentation Plus!

**FIGURE 1.4**

**Trade-Offs** The trade-off of maintaining a historical community is the convenience that modern roads would provide. ***How can a trade-off you make today affect your future?***

a scarce resource—there are only so many hours in a day—so you must choose how to use it. When you decide to study economics for an hour, you are giving up any other activities you could have chosen to do during that time.

In other words, there is a cost involved in time spent studying this book. Economists call it an **opportunity cost**—the value of the next best alternative that had to be given up to do the action that *was* chosen. You may have many trade-offs when you study—connecting to your favorite Web site, going to the mall, or practicing the guitar, for example. But whatever you consider the *single next best alternative* is the opportunity cost of your studying economics for one hour.

**opportunity cost:** *value of the next best alternative given up for the alternative that was chosen*

A good way to think about opportunity cost is to realize that when you make a trade-off (and you *always* make trade-offs), you lose. What do you lose? You lose the ability to engage in your next highest valued alternative, as shown in **Figure 1.5** on page 14. In economics, therefore, opportunity cost is always an opportunity that is given up.

### Considering Opportunity Costs

Being aware of trade-offs and their resulting opportunity costs is vital in

## Global *Economy*

### Rain Forest Trade-Offs

How do trade-offs of resources affect our future? The Amazon River Basin in Brazil is the world's largest tropical rain forest and river system. But within the Basin an area equal to 5,000 soccer fields is being destroyed every day. Farmers burn the forests to gain farmland for other profitable crops. Loggers cut and export the fine hardwoods for a profit. And people have penetrated the forests to strip the Amazon of its curative and medicinal plants.

What are the trade-offs for the future? Many scientists believe the destruction of the forest will speed up global warming. Rain forests supply one-fifth of the world's oxygen supply, as well as trap poisonous carbon compounds. If the area is destroyed, its untold medicinal secrets also will be lost forever. ■





# 2 Teach

## Guided Practice

**L1 Applying Ideas** Ask students to list recreational or purchasing choices they have made recently. Then ask them to identify the opportunity cost for each of these choices. Encourage students to share and compare their lists.

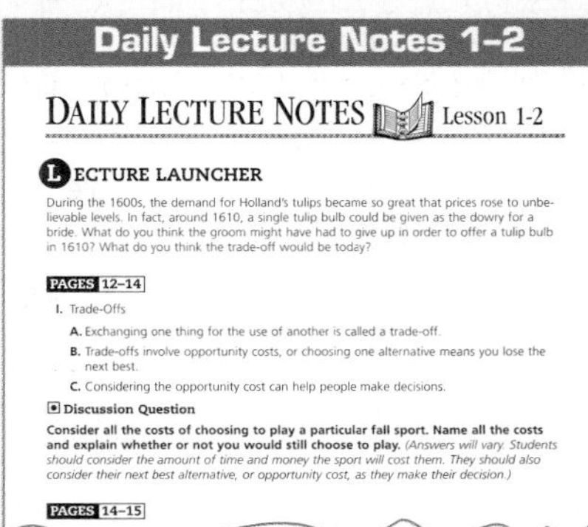

**Daily Lecture Notes 1–2**

DAILY LECTURE NOTES Lesson 1-2

**LECTURE LAUNCHER**

During the 1600s, the demand for Holland's tulips became so great that prices rose to unbelievable levels. In fact, around 1610, a single tulip bulb could be given as the dowry for a bride. What do you think the groom might have had to give up in order to offer a tulip bulb in 1610? What do you think the trade-off would be today?

PAGES 12–14

I. Trade-Offs

A. Exchanging one thing for the use of another is called a trade-off.

B. Trade-offs involve opportunity costs, or choosing one alternative means you lose the next best.

C. Considering the opportunity cost can help people make decisions.

**Discussion Question**

**Consider all the costs of choosing to play a particular fall sport. Name all the costs and explain whether or not you would still choose to play.** *(Answers will vary. Students should consider the amount of time and money the sport will cost them. They should also consider their next best alternative, or opportunity cost, as they make their decision.)*

PAGES 14–15

### Visual Instruction FIGURE 1.4

**Answer:** *Answers may vary. Most students probably will suggest that going to college instead of taking a job immediately after graduating from high school may affect future earning potential.*

### Meeting Special Needs

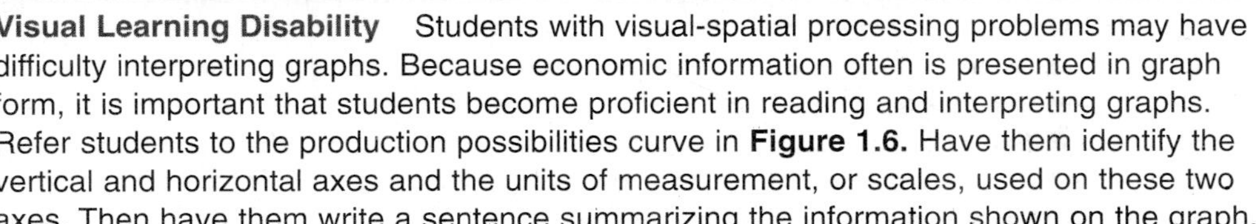

**Visual Learning Disability** Students with visual-spatial processing problems may have difficulty interpreting graphs. Because economic information often is presented in graph form, it is important that students become proficient in reading and interpreting graphs. Refer students to the production possibilities curve in **Figure 1.6.** Have them identify the vertical and horizontal axes and the units of measurement, or scales, used on these two axes. Then have them write a sentence summarizing the information shown on the graph.

 Refer to *Inclusion for the Social Studies Classroom Strategies and Activities* for students with different learning styles.

### Visual Instruction FIGURE 1.5

**Answer:** *A trade-off is the choice a person makes between alternatives. Opportunity cost is the next best alternative that is given up when making that choice.*

### Guided Reading Activity 1-2

GUIDED READING Activity 1-2

For use with textbook pages 12–16

TRADE-OFFS

RECALLING THE FACTS

*Directions: Use the information in your text book to answer the questions.*

1. What is a trade-off?
2. What kinds of trade-offs do you make as a student?
3. What does an opportunity cost cause a person to lose?
4. What is important to know before one makes a decision related to their available resources?

**Production Possibilities Curve**

5. What is a production possibilities curve?

Project **Economic Concepts Transparency 2** and have students discuss the accompanying questions.

### INTERACTIVE ECONOMICS!

**LESSON 1: OPPORTUNITY COSTS**

Have students complete the "Economics Lab" and "Math Practice" sections of the lesson on opportunity costs. Students will determine whether firms have an absolute advantage or a comparative advantage in producing certain goods. Based on this information, students will decide which goods the firms should produce.

Supplied in both CD-ROM and disk formats.

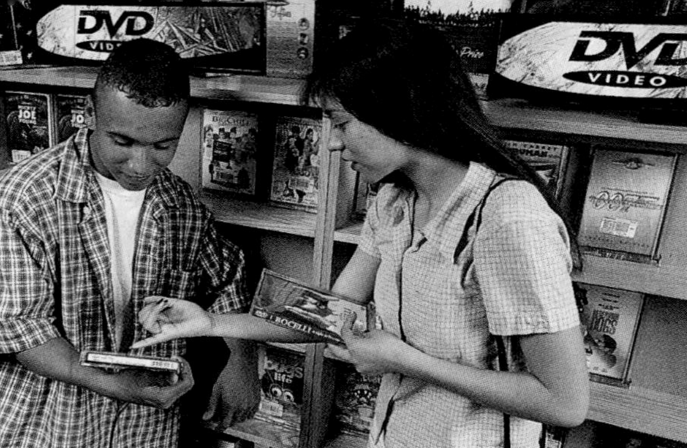


**FIGURE 1.5**

**Opportunity Cost** Any time you pay money to purchase a good or service, you lose the opportunity to purchase your next best alternative. ***How do trade-offs and opportunity costs differ?***

making economic decisions at all levels. Businesses must consider trade-offs and opportunity costs when they choose to invest money or hire workers to produce one good rather than another.

Consider an example at the national level. Suppose Congress votes $220 billion to finance needed highways. Congress could have voted for increased spending on new schools. The opportunity cost of building new highways, then, is fewer new schools.

## Production Possibilities Curve

Obviously, many businesses produce more than one type of product. An automobile company, for example, may manufacture several makes of cars per plant in a given year. Does this mean that the company makes no trade-offs? No, what this means is that the company produces combinations of goods—which still results in an opportunity cost.

**production possibilities curve:** *graph showing the maximum combinations of goods and services that can be produced from a fixed amount of resources in a given period of time*

Economists use a model called the **production possibilities curve** to show the maximum combinations of goods and services that can be produced from a fixed amount of resources in a given period of time. This curve can help people and businesses determine how much of each item to produce, thus revealing the trade-offs and opportunity costs involved in each decision.

Imagine that you run a jewelry-making business. Working 20 hours a week, you have enough resources to make either 10 bracelets or 5 pairs of earrings. If you want to make some of both, **Figure 1.6** shows your production possibilities.

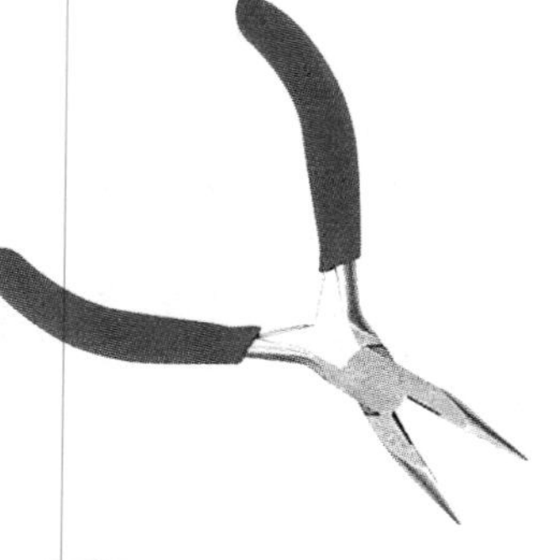

**The Classic Example** The classic example for explaining production possibilities in economics is the trade-off between military defense and civilian goods, sometimes referred to as *guns* versus *butter*. The extremes for a



### Cooperative Learning

Organize students into small groups to search through recent newspapers and magazines to find articles that discuss economic decisions. Ask groups to list these economic decisions. Then, for each decision, have group members indicate whether an individual or group (a corporation or government, for example) made the decision, the opportunity costs of the decision, and the economic benefits expected from each decision. Call on groups to present their findings to the class in an illustrated report. BLOCK SCHEDULING nation would be using all its resources to produce only one or the other.

Look at **Figure 1.7** on page 16. Point A on the graph represents all resources being used to produce only guns (military defense). Point E represents the other extreme—all resources being used to produce only butter (civilian goods). The amount of military goods given up in the year is the opportunity cost for increasing civilian goods production. Members of the federal government determine where on the curve the nation will be.

The real world and our graphs are not always quite the same, however. In the real world, it takes time to move from point A to point B. The important point is that by using a production possibilities curve, a nation, business, or individual can decide how best to use its resources.

**FIGURE 1.6** **Production Possibilities for Jewelry** The curve here represents the production possibilities between bracelets and pairs of earrings during a 20-hour workweek. Note that if you make 10 bracelets (point A on the curve), you have no resources or time to make earrings. If you make only 6 bracelets (point B on the curve), you have enough resources and time to also make 2 pairs of earrings. Therefore, the opportunity cost of making 2 pairs of earrings is the 4 bracelets not made. Although you are making both bracelets and earrings, you—and businesses and nations—cannot produce more of one thing without giving up something else.

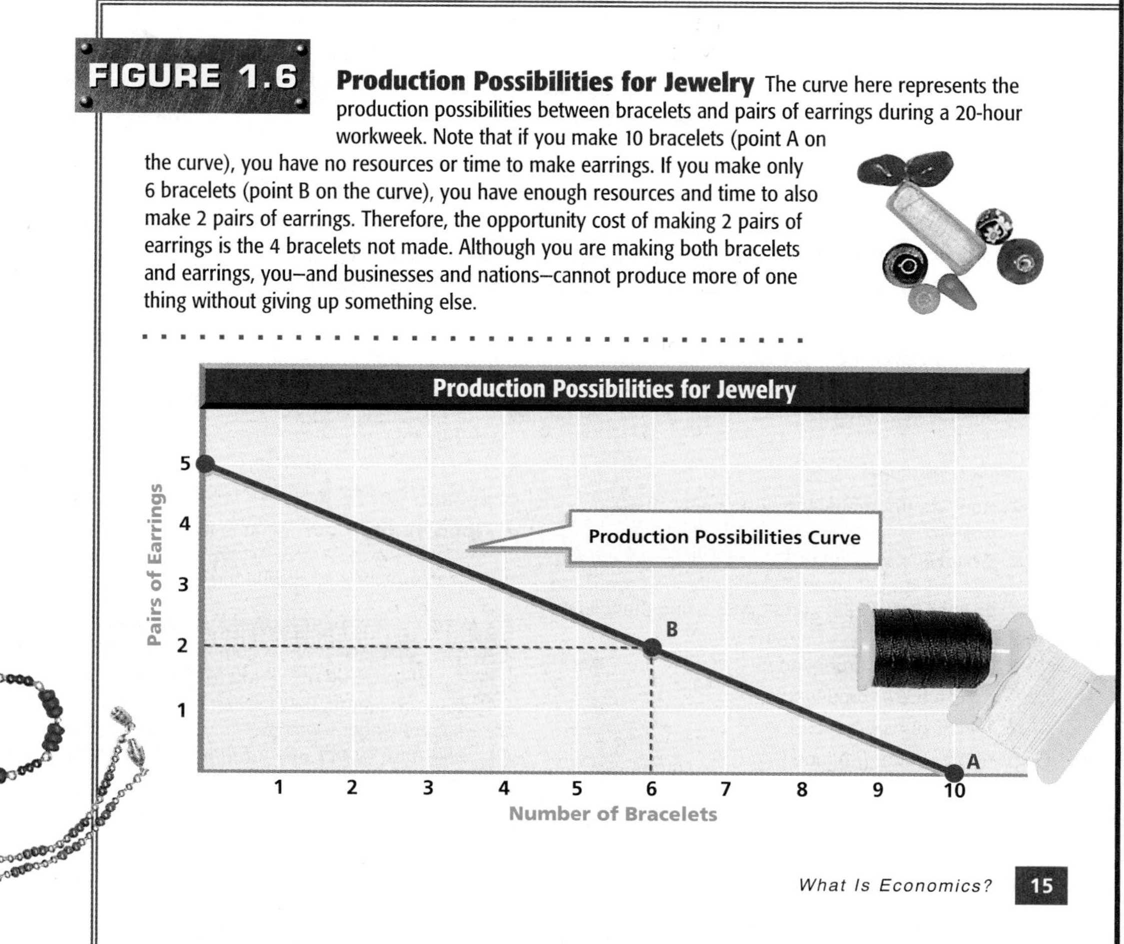




## Extending the Content

**Guns *and* Butter?** Is it economically possible to have more guns *and* more butter? The economists' answer is, "Yes, but . . ." First, if resources are not being used to their full potential, the level of production would fall inside the production possibilities curve. Using resources efficiently would increase the production of both guns and butter. Second, sustained economic growth over a lengthy period of time would push the production possibilities curve outward. Again, more of both guns and butter would be produced. Even so, in both cases scarcity would still exist. The economy could not produce all the guns and butter to fulfill people's wants.



### Independent Practice

L2 **Creating Cartoons** Have students create cartoons illustrating the concept of opportunity cost. Call on volunteers to display and explain their cartoons.

ELL BLOCK SCHEDULING

## 3 Assess

### Meeting Lesson Objectives

Assign Section 2 Assessment as homework or an in-class activity.

Use **Interactive Tutor Self-Assessment Software** to review Section 2.

### Visual Instruction FIGURE 1.6

Direct students to study **Figure 1.6.** ASK: How do the numbers of bracelets and earrings for each marked point on the curve illustrate trade-offs and opportunity costs? The numbers of earrings and bracelets at each marked point illustrate trade-offs in that they show the choices made among alternative uses of resources. The numbers illustrate opportunity costs because they show the alternatives that were given up in making those choices.

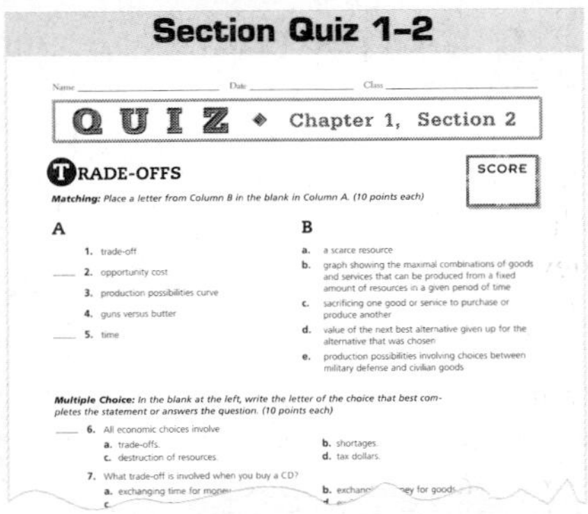
**Section Quiz 1-2**

Name ______ Date ______ Class ______

QUIZ ◆ Chapter 1, Section 2

TRADE-OFFS

SCORE

*Matching:* Place a letter from Column B in the blank in Column A. (10 points each)

| A | B |
|---|---|
| ___ 1. trade-off | a. a scarce resource |
| ___ 2. opportunity cost | b. graph showing the maximal combinations of goods and services that can be produced from a fixed amount of resources in a given period of time |
| ___ 3. production possibilities curve | c. sacrificing one good or service to purchase or produce another |
| ___ 4. guns versus butter | d. value of the next best alternative given up for the alternative that was chosen |
| ___ 5. time | e. production possibilities involving choices between military defense and civilian goods |

*Multiple Choice:* In the blank at the left, write the letter of the choice that best completes the statement or answers the question. (10 points each)

___ 6. All economic choices involve
a. trade-offs. b. shortages.
c. destruction of resources. d. tax dollars.

7. What trade-off is involved when you buy a CD?
a. exchanging time for mone b. exchan ey for goods

## Reteach

Have students write five questions for each of the two subsections of Section 2. Pair students and have partners use their questions to quiz each other on the section content.

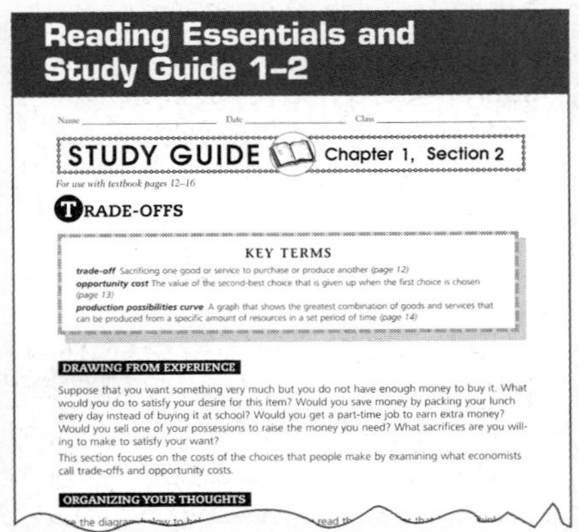
**Reading Essentials and Study Guide 1-2**

Name ______ Date ______ Class ______

STUDY GUIDE Chapter 1, Section 2

*For use with textbook pages 12–16*

TRADE-OFFS

KEY TERMS

***trade-off*** Sacrificing one good or service to purchase or produce another *(page 12)*

***opportunity cost*** The value of the second-best choice that is given up when the first choice is chosen *(page 13)*

***production possibilities curve*** A graph that shows the greatest combination of goods and services that can be produced from a specific amount of resources in a set period of time *(page 14)*

DRAWING FROM EXPERIENCE

Suppose that you want something very much but you do not have enough money to buy it. What would you do to satisfy your desire for this item? Would you save money by packing your lunch every day instead of buying it at school? Would you get a part-time job to earn extra money? Would you sell one of your possessions to raise the money you need? What sacrifices are you willing to make to satisfy your want?

This section focuses on the costs of the choices that people make by examining what economists call trade-offs and opportunity costs.

ORGANIZING YOUR THOUGHTS

## 4 Close

Discuss with students how using a production possibilities curve enables a business to use its resources in an economically efficient manner.

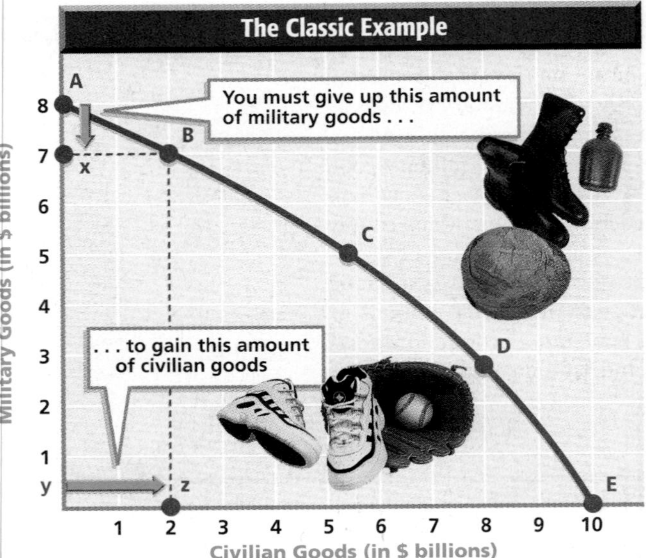


FIGURE  1.7

**Production Possibilities—Military Goods Versus Civilian Goods** Nations produce combinations, or mixes, of goods. If the nation starts with all gun production and no butter production (point A), it can only get to some butter production (point B) by giving up some gun production. In other words, the price of having some civilian goods (represented by the horizontal distance from y to point z) is giving up some military goods (represented by the vertical distance from point A to point x).

**Practice** and **assess** key skills with ***Skillbuilder Interactive Workbook, Level 2.***

# SECTION 2 Assessment

### Understanding Key Terms

1. **Define** trade-off, opportunity cost, production possibilities curve.

### Reviewing Objectives

2. How are trade-offs and opportunity costs related?
3. **Graphic Organizer** Create a diagram like the one in the next column to identify the production possibilities of guns and butter using the following actions:
   - 100% guns produced
   - 70% butter produced
   - 40% guns produced
   - 25% butter produced

| Action | → | Result |
|---|---|---|
| 1. | → | |
| 2. | → | |

### Economic Concepts

4. **Opportunity Cost** What is the opportunity cost of going to a university for four years after high school instead of working?

### Critical Thinking Activity

5. **Synthesizing Information** Build your own production possibilities curve with "Hours Spent Watching TV" on the horizontal axis and "Hours Spent Studying Economics" on the vertical axis. Write a caption explaining the opportunity cost of each activity.

16 CHAPTER 1

## SECTION 2 Assessment Answers

1. All definitions can be found in the Glossary.
2. Every trade-off involves an opportunity cost.
3. 100% guns produced → No butter produced;
   70% butter produced → 30% guns produced;
   40% guns produced → 60% butter produced;
   25% butter produced → 75% guns produced
4. the potential earnings from having had a job
5. Students' production possibilities curves will vary.

# BusinessWeek

# Spotlight on the Economy

## Coasters Find a Whole New Way to Roll

**Check It Out! In this chapter you learned about the factors of production—land, labor, capital, and entrepreneurship. In the following article, read to learn how traditional roller coasters are being modernized, keeping in mind the factors of production needed to perform this modernization.**

Hold on tight. The Joker's Jinx, a new roller coaster at the Six Flags America theme park in Largo, Maryland, will make its debut this coming May. And its trick piece of technology, the linear induction motor (LIM), is helping redefine the way roller coasters roll. The new beasts are faster, smoother, and scarier than their wooden predecessors.

So far, Premier Rides of Maryland, the roller coaster manufacturer that helped develop the technology, has launched seven LIM coasters. Three more, including The Joker's Jinx, will follow this year. Conventional roller coasters are dragged by chains or cables–clank, clank, clank–to the top of the first hill. Then gravity causes the cars to accelerate. In contrast, Premier Rides' coasters slingshot passengers out of the loading station, accelerating from zero to 70 miles per hour in less than four seconds. The secret is the high-tech motors, about 200 of which are used in each coaster. When juiced with an alternating current, the motors create an electromagnetic force that accelerates the coaster over the first 200 feet of the ride.

–Reprinted from April 12, 1999 issue of *Business Week* by special permission, copyright © 1999 by The McGraw-Hill Companies, Inc.

### *Think About It*

1. **Provide two examples of each factor of production that went into developing the new coasters.**
2. **What is the opportunity cost of spending a day at an amusement park?**

17

### Answers to *Think About It*

1. Examples may include: Land–raw materials to make steel for rails, waiting platform; Labor–workers who manufactured new motors and constructed the new roller coaster; Capital–electricity that produces electromagnetic force, computers and robots that built linear induction motor; Entrepreneurship–Premier Rides of Maryland developed new technology, Six Flags America introduced new ride to the public
2. the next best alternative given up to go to the amusement park

BusinessWeek Spotlight

## Teach

As students read the article, have them note the role that technology played in the development of the new roller coasters. ASK: How is the Joker's Jinx different from conventional roller coasters? *It is powered by linear induction motors, which slingshot it out of the station. In contrast, conventional coasters are dragged by chains or cable.*

### BusinessWeek ONLINE

To find up-to-date news and analysis on the economy, business, technology, markets, entrepreneurs, investments, and finance, have students search feature articles and special reports on the *Business Week* Web site. *www.businessweek.com*

### Sidelight

Medusa was another new roller coaster introduced by the Six Flags group in 1999. It was the world's first "heartline" roller coaster. In a heartline, riders feel as if there is nothing above or below them. On Medusa, passengers' feet dangle without touching anything below. And the tilt of the seats gives riders the impression that they are completely open to the sky above.

# 1 Focus

## Overview

Section 3 describes and explains the use of economic models by economists.

**BELLRINGER**
**Motivational Activity**

Project **Daily Focus Transparency 3** and have students answer the questions.

This activity is also available as a blackline master.

**Daily Focus Transparency 3**

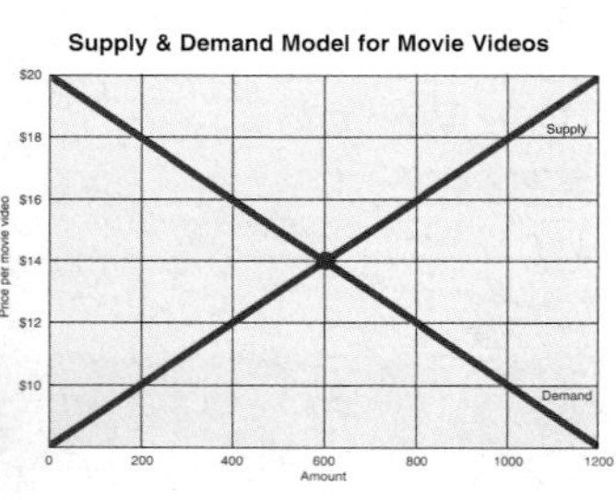


1. As the price of movie videos goes up, what happens to the amount producers are willing to supply?
2. As the price of movie videos goes up, what happens to the amount consumers will demand, or want to purchase?

### Reader's Guide

Answers to the **Reading Objectives** questions are on page 23.

**Preteaching Vocabulary**

Have students show how the **Terms to Know** are related by using them together in sentences. Call on volunteers to share their sentences with the rest of the class.

Vocabulary PuzzleMaker

SECTION 

# What Do Economists Do?

### Reader's Guide

**Terms to Know**

- microeconomics
- macroeconomics
- economy
- economic model
- hypothesis

**Reading Objectives**

1. How do economists use models to study the real world?
2. Why are there different schools of economic thought?

## Cover Story

*Business Week*, February 15, 1999

Are Americans in the grip of a luxury fever? It would seem so. The $5,000-a-night suites at Aspen's Little Nell hotel are booked up months in advance, as are all 84 spots on World Tours' $38,000-a-head round-the-world excursions. Yacht makers are so backlogged that used boats sell for close to their original prices. Vacation houses are booming, as is everything from cosmetic surgery to expensive cigars and wines.

But are Americans happy?

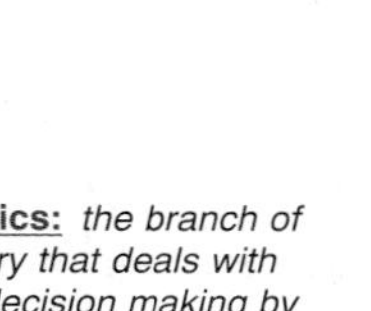

As you've learned, economics is a social science concerned with the ways individuals and nations choose to use their scarce resources. Economists might analyze how the super-rich spend their money, for example, and the effect this spending has on the economy. As you read this section, you'll find that something economists *don't* do, however, is judge whether there *should be* a social strata of the super-rich. They leave value judgments up to other social scientists.

Another thing to keep in mind as you read this textbook is that economics is divided into two parts. **Microeconomics** is the branch of economic theory that deals with behavior and decision making by small units such as individuals and firms. **Macroeconomics** is that branch of economic theory dealing

__microeconomics:__ *the branch of economic theory that deals with behavior and decision making by small units such as individuals and firms*

__macroeconomics:__ *the branch of economic theory dealing with the economy as a whole and decision making by large units such as governments*

## SECTION 3 RESOURCE MANAGER

**Reproducible Masters**
- Reproducible Lesson Plan 1–3
- Reading Essentials and Study Guide 1–3
- Guided Reading Activity 1–3
- Section Quiz 1–3
- Daily Focus Activity 3
- Daily Lecture Notes 1–3

**Multimedia**
- Daily Focus Transparency 3
- Vocabulary PuzzleMaker
- Interactive Tutor Self-Assessment Software
- ExamView® Pro Testmaker
- MindJogger Videoquiz
- Presentation Plus!

with the economy as a whole and decision making by large units such as governments.

## Economic Models

To economists, the word ***economy*** means all the activity in a nation that together affects the production, distribution, and use of goods and services. When studying a specific part of the economy—rising teenage unemployment, for example—economists often formulate theories and gather data. See **Figure 1.8.** The theories that economists use in their work are called **economic models,** which are simplified representations of the real world. Solutions that emerge from testing economic models often become the basis for actual decisions by private businesses or government agencies.

**What Models Show** Physicists, chemists, biologists, and other scientists use models to understand in simple terms the complex workings of the world. Similarly, the purpose of economic models is to show visual representations of consumer, business, or other economic behavior. The production possibilities curve that you learned about in Section 2 is an economic model that reveals opportunity cost. The most common economic model is a line graph explaining how

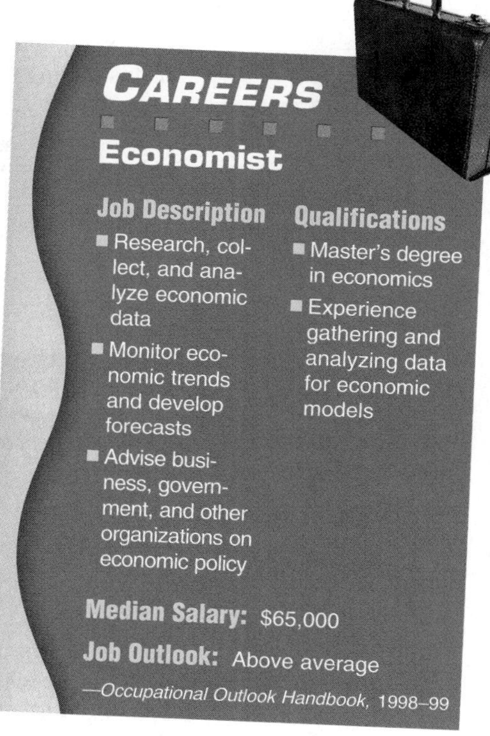

### Careers

**Economist**

**Job Description**
- Research, collect, and analyze economic data
- Monitor economic trends and develop forecasts
- Advise business, government, and other organizations on economic policy

**Qualifications**
- Master's degree in economics
- Experience gathering and analyzing data for economic models

**Median Salary:** $65,000

**Job Outlook:** Above average

—*Occupational Outlook Handbook*, 1998–99

economy: *the production and distribution of goods and services in a society*

economic model: *a theory or simplified representation that helps explain and predict economic behavior in the real world*

**FIGURE 1.8**

**Help Wanted** Economic models are developed to help solve problems such as teenage unemployment. ***What is the purpose of economic models?***



# 2 Teach

## Guided Practice

**L3 Synthesizing** Read through the information in **Figure 1.9** with students. Next, have them study **Figure 1.10** and the text related to it. Then ask students to use the information they have gathered to develop and test a hypothesis on teenage unemployment and the minimum wage.

**Daily Lecture Notes 1–3**

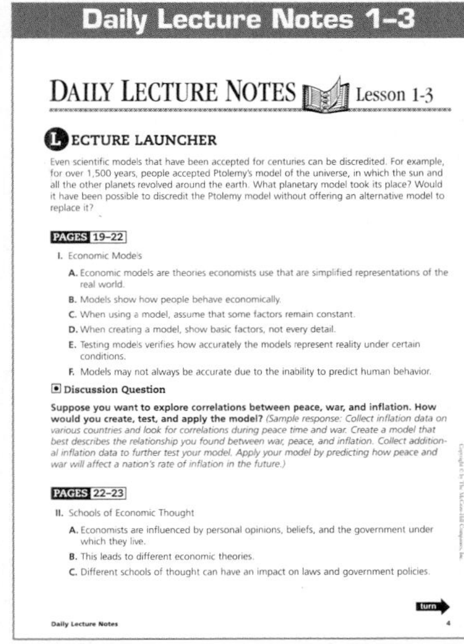

DAILY LECTURE NOTES Lesson 1-3

**LECTURE LAUNCHER**

Even scientific models that have been accepted for centuries can be discredited. For example, for over 1,500 years, people accepted Ptolemy's model of the universe, in which the sun and all the other planets revolved around the earth. What planetary model took its place? Would it have been possible to discredit the Ptolemy model without offering an alternative model to replace it?

PAGES 19–22

I. Economic Models
   - **A.** Economic models are theories economists use that are simplified representations of the real world.
   - **B.** Models show how people behave economically.
   - **C.** When using a model, assume that some factors remain constant.
   - **D.** When creating a model, show basic factors, not every detail.
   - **E.** Testing models verifies how accurately the models represent reality under certain conditions.
   - **F.** Models may not always be accurate due to the inability to predict human behavior.

**Discussion Question**

**Suppose you want to explore correlations between peace, war, and inflation. How would you create, test, and apply the model?** *(Sample response: Collect inflation data on various countries and look for correlations during peace time and war. Create a model that best describes the relationship you found between war, peace, and inflation. Collect additional inflation data to further test your model. Apply your model by predicting how peace and war will affect a nation's rate of inflation in the future.)*

PAGES 22–23

II. Schools of Economic Thought
   - **A.** Economists are influenced by personal opinions, beliefs, and the government under which they live.
   - **B.** This leads to different economic theories.
   - **C.** Different schools of thought can have an impact on laws and government policies.

turn

Daily Lecture Notes 4



**Visual Instruction FIGURE 1.8**

**Answer:** *to show visual representations of consumer, business, or other economic behavior*

## Meeting Special Needs

**Language Disability** Practice is an important part of learning. Those with weaker reading skills need guided practice, which may be phased out as mastery of the skill develops. Have students restate sentences in Section 3, using common language. Listen to students' sentences to be sure they understand that you are not asking simply for a rearrangement of words, but for them to state the idea of the sentence in their own words. ELL

Refer to *Inclusion for the Social Studies Classroom Strategies and Activities* for students with different learning styles.

## Visual Instruction FIGURE 1.9

Discuss the content of **Figure 1.9** with students. Then ask students to recast this information in the form of a flow chart.

## Guided Reading Activity 1-3

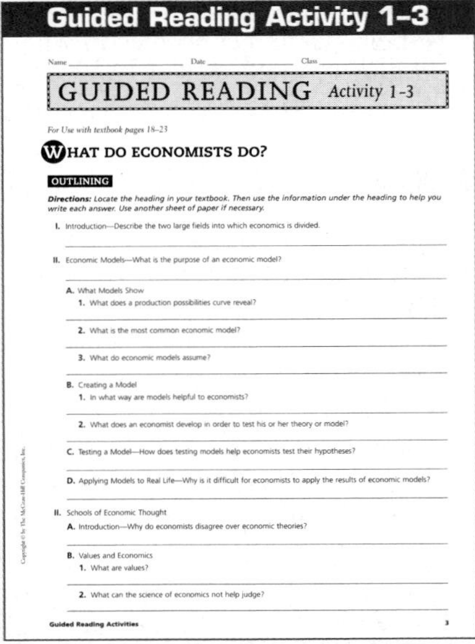

Name ____ Date ____ Class ____

GUIDED READING Activity 1-3

*For Use with textbook pages 18–23*

**WHAT DO ECONOMISTS DO?**

**OUTLINING**

***Directions:*** *Locate the heading in your textbook. Then use the information under the heading to help you write each answer. Use another sheet of paper if necessary.*

**I.** Introduction—Describe the two large fields into which economics is divided.

**II.** Economic Models—What is the purpose of an economic model?

**A.** What Models Show
**1.** What does a production possibilities curve reveal?
**2.** What is the most common economic model?
**3.** What do economic models assume?

**B.** Creating a Model
**1.** In what way are models helpful to economists?
**2.** What does an economist develop in order to test his or her theory or model?

**C.** Testing a Model—How does testing models help economists test their hypotheses?

**D.** Applying Models to Real Life—Why is it difficult for economists to apply the results of economic models?

**II.** Schools of Economic Thought
**A.** Introduction—Why do economists disagree over economic theories?
**B.** Values and Economics
**1.** What are values?
**2.** What can the science of economics not help judge?



**Guided Reading Activities** 3

## Independent Practice

**L1 Creating Posters** Refer students to the definition of the term *economy* on page 19. Then have students work in small groups to create a poster illustrating that definition. Tell groups that their posters should be designed as teaching aids for an economics class. Display finished posters around the classroom. **ELL**

BLOCK SCHEDULING

consumers react to changes in the prices of goods and services. You'll learn about this model in Chapter 7.

Economic models assume that some factors remain constant. In studying the production possibilities curve for making jewelry in Section 2, for example, we assumed that the price of inputs (beads, wire, and so on) would not increase. We also assumed that inclement weather would not close schools for a day, which would have enabled you to work more than 20 hours a week on jewelry.

**hypothesis:** *an assumption involving two or more variables that must be tested for validity*

Why are these constant-factor assumptions important? Economists realize that, in the real world, several things may be changing at once. Using a model holds everything steady except the variables assumed to be related. In the same way that a map does not show every alley and building in a given location, economic models do not record every detail and relationship that exists about a problem to be studied. A model will show only the basic factors needed to analyze the problem at hand.

### FIGURE 1.9

## Using a Hypothesis

**The list below reviews the steps involved in making and testing hypotheses. In working with models, economists use these same steps.**

1. Define the problem.
2. From the possible alternatives, state a hypothesis that appears to offer the best solution to a problem or explanation of an event.
3. Gather data to test the hypothesis. Besides using facts from the real world, an economist must identify economic principles involved.
4. Evaluate the data and discard any that are not relevant, or related to the immediate situation, or that are not based on fact.
5. Make sure there are enough data to test the hypothesis thoroughly.
6. Develop a conclusion based on the data. To do this, an economist evaluates whether the alternative is the best, in view of its consequences and trade-offs.
7. If the hypothesis appears to be valid, retest it with new data to see if the same results can be obtained again.
8. If the hypothesis still appears to be valid, form a generalization that can be applied to other cases. A *generalization* pulls together common ideas among facts and is true in most cases. For an economist, this step involves developing an economic policy based on the best alternative.

**Creating a Model** Models are useful if they help us analyze the way the real world works. An economist begins with some idea about the way things work, then collects facts and discards those that are not relevant. Let's assume that an economist wants to find out why teenage unemployment rises periodically. Perhaps this unemployment occurs when the federal minimum wage goes up, thereby forcing employers to pay their teenage workers more or to lay some workers off. The economist can test this theory, or model, in the same way that other scientists test a **hypothesis**—an educated guess or prediction. **Figure 1.9** explains how hypotheses are used as the starting point for investigations.

**Testing a Model** Testing a model, or hypothesis, allows economists to see if the model represents reality under certain



## Cooperative Learning

Organize the class into groups of three or four. Direct groups to locate economic models in recent editions of newspapers and magazines. Encourage groups to record the economic issue addressed by each model and whether it is presented in text form, in visual form, or as a mathematical equation. Have groups present their findings in the form of an annotated graph. BLOCK SCHEDULING conditions. Suppose an economist has developed the model shown in *Graph A* of **Figure 1.10.** The economist would collect data on the amount of teenage unemployment every year for the last 30 years. He or she would also gather 30 years of information on federal legislation that increased the legal minimum wage paid to teenagers.

The economist can be fairly satisfied with the model if teenage unemployment rose every time the minimum wage rate increased. But suppose that the data instead resulted in *Graph B* of **Figure 1.10,** which does not show a relationship between teenage unemployment and increases in the legal minimum wage. The economist then will have to develop another model to explain changes in teenage unemployment.

**Applying Models to Real Life** Much of the work of economists involves predicting how people will react in a particular situation. Individual human behavior is not always predictable, though. As a result, an economist's predictive model may not apply under different conditions.

## FIGURE 1.10

**Economic Models** The purpose of economic models is to show visual representations of consumer, business, or other economic behavior. Economic models, however, must be tested to see if they represent reality. Graph A supports the theory that a direct relationship exists between increases in the minimum wage rate and increases in teenage unemployment. Graph B does not support that theory.

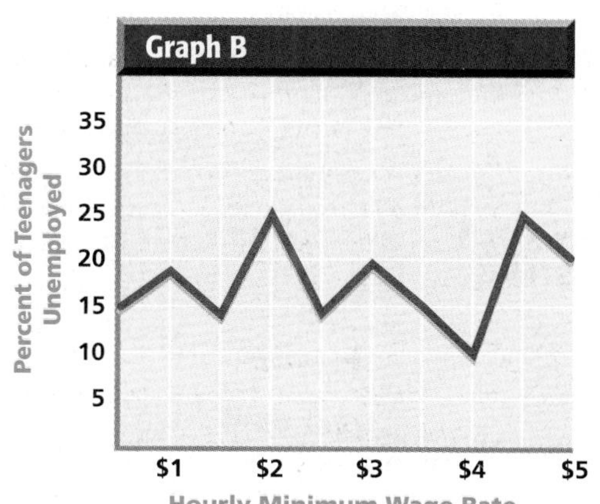




## Relevant Issues in Economics

**Economic Models and Accuracy** Economic models do not always accurately predict economic behavior. For example, economists in the 1970s were surprised when the traditional methods of fighting inflation—reducing the money supply and raising taxes—failed to bring prices under control. Even more surprising, the high inflation was accompanied by an economic slowdown. This situation was so unusual that economists had to create a new term—stagflation—to describe it.



### Did You Know

The area of economics that uses mathematical models to analyze, interpret, and predict economic behavior is known as *econometrics*. Economists Ragnar Frisch of Norway and Jan Tinbergen of Holland developed this approach in the 1930s. They won the 1969 Nobel Prize in economics for their groundbreaking work.

**L3 Debating** To provide an example of differing opinions on economic issues, organize the class to debate the following: Resolved—The government should spend more money on education, even if it requires raising taxes.

After the debate, ask students to analyze the differences in values that the debate illustrates.

### Visual Instruction FIGURE 1.10

As students review the information in **Figure 1.10**, point out that whenever an increase in the minimum wage is debated, a major argument against an increase is that it will cause unemployment.

See the **Web Activity Lesson Plan** at *ett.glencoe.com* for an introduction, lesson description, and answers to the **Student Web Activity** for this chapter.

# 3 Assess

## Meeting Lesson Objectives

Assign Section 3 Assessment as homework or an in-class activity.

Use **Interactive Tutor Self-Assessment Software** to review Section 3.

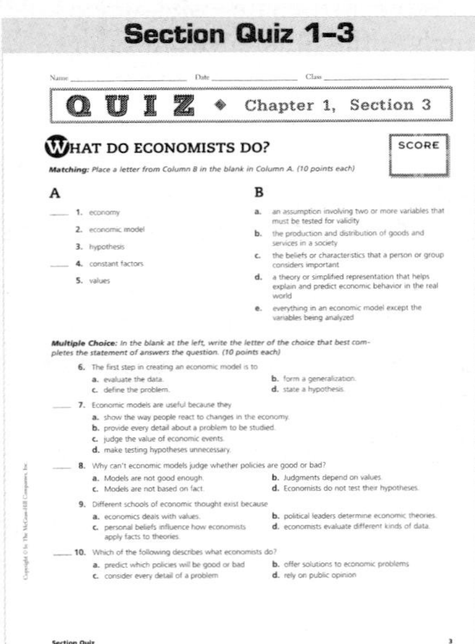

**Section Quiz 1–3**

Name ____________ Date ____________ Class ____________

**QUIZ** ◆ Chapter 1, Section 3

**WHAT DO ECONOMISTS DO?**

SCORE

***Matching:*** *Place a letter from Column B in the blank in Column A. (10 points each)*

**A**

____ 1. economy
____ 2. economic model
____ 3. hypothesis
____ 4. constant factors
____ 5. values

**B**

a. an assumption involving two or more variables that must be tested for validity
b. the production and distribution of goods and services in a society
c. the beliefs or characteristics that a person or group considers important
d. a theory or simplified representation that helps explain and predict economic behavior in the real world
e. everything in an economic model except the variables being analyzed

***Multiple Choice:*** *In the blank at the left, write the letter of the choice that best completes the statement of answers the question. (10 points each)*

____ 6. The first step in creating an economic model is to
a. evaluate the data.
b. form a generalization.
c. define the problem.
d. state a hypothesis.

____ 7. Economic models are useful because they
a. show the way people react to changes in the economy.
b. provide every detail about a problem to be studied.
c. judge the value of economic events.
d. make testing hypotheses unnecessary.

____ 8. Why can't economic models judge whether policies are good or bad?
a. Models are not good enough.
b. Judgments depend on values.
c. Models are not based on fact.
d. Economists do not test their hypotheses.

____ 9. Different schools of economic thought exist because
a. economics deals with values.
b. political leaders determine economic theories.
c. personal beliefs influence how economists apply facts to theories.
d. economists evaluate different kinds of data.

____ 10. Which of the following describes what economists do?
a. predict which policies will be good or bad
b. offer solutions to economic problems
c. consider every detail of a problem
d. rely on public opinion

Section Quiz 3

**Student Web Activity** Visit the *Economics Today and Tomorrow* Web site at ett.glencoe.com and click on ***Chapter 1—Student Web Activities*** to learn about famous economists and their contributions.

For example, some economists believe that to stimulate the economy, taxes should be cut and government spending increased. Cutting taxes, these economists believe, may put more money into consumers' pockets, which will increase personal spending and increase total production. However, some people's fears concerning possible higher taxes in the future might cause them to save the extra income rather than spend it. As this example illustrates, economists cannot take into account all of the factors that may influence people's behavior.

## Schools of Economic Thought

Economists deal with facts. Their personal opinions and beliefs may nonetheless influence how they view those facts and fit them to theories. The government under which an economist lives also shapes how he or she views the world. As a result, all economists will not agree that a particular theory offers the best solution to a problem. Often, economists from competing schools of thought claim that their theories are better in predicting a certain result than are others' theories. See **Figure 1.11.**

During a given period of time, a nation's political leaders may agree with one school of economic thought and develop policies based on it. Later, leaders may agree with another group of economists. Throughout American history, many economists have stressed the importance of government maintaining "hands off" in business and consumer affairs as a method of preventing increased unemployment and inflation. Other influential economists have proposed that the federal government should intervene in the economy to reduce unemployment and prevent inflation.

**Economic Information**
Economists analyze events and their effects on the economy.

### Free Enterprise Activity

Point out that in a free enterprise system, the emphasis is on the individual. Identify some roles the individual may play in a free enterprise system, including consumer, producer, owner of factors of production, voting citizen, investor, and saver. Next, have students assume each role, explaining why their assigned role is important in a free enterprise economy and illustrating how their role is interdependent with others. Direct the rest of the class to discuss and add to the students' descriptions.

**Values and Economics** Learning about economics will help you predict what may happen if certain events occur or certain policies are followed. But economics will *not* tell you whether the result will be good or bad. Judgments about results depend on a person's values.

*Values* are the beliefs or characteristics that a person or group considers important, such as religious freedom, equal opportunity, individual initiative, freedom from want, and so on. Even having the same values does not mean that people will agree about solutions to problems, strategies, or interpretation of data, however.

For example, those in favor of decreasing teenage unemployment in order to bring about economic opportunity may disagree about the best way to solve this problem. If you were a legislator, you might show your commitment to this value by introducing a bill to decrease teenage unemployment. The economists who help you research the causes of teenage unemployment will tell you, based on their expertise, whether the proposed solution will actually reduce teenage unemployment.

Remember, however, that the science of economics is not used to judge whether a certain policy is good or bad. Economists only inform us as to likely short-term and long-term outcomes of these policies.

**Practice** and **assess** key skills with ***Skillbuilder Interactive Workbook, Level 2.***

## SECTION 3 Assessment

### Understanding Key Terms

1. **Define** microeconomics, macroeconomics, economy, economic model, hypothesis.

### Reviewing Objectives

2. **Graphic Organizer** Create a diagram like the one below to show how economists use models to study the real world.

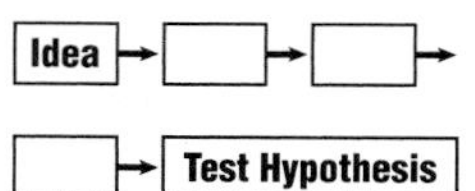


3. Why are there different schools of economic thought?

### Applying Economic Concepts

4. **Economic Models** If you were to make a model showing the effect of hiring senior citizens into previously-held teenage job markets, what factors would you analyze?

### Critical Thinking Activity

5. **Distinguishing Fact From Opinion** Write three "headlines" about the economy that reveal a value judgment. Then rewrite the headlines to omit the value judgment.





## Reteach

Have students write two brief paragraphs summarizing the main ideas in each of the two main section subheads.

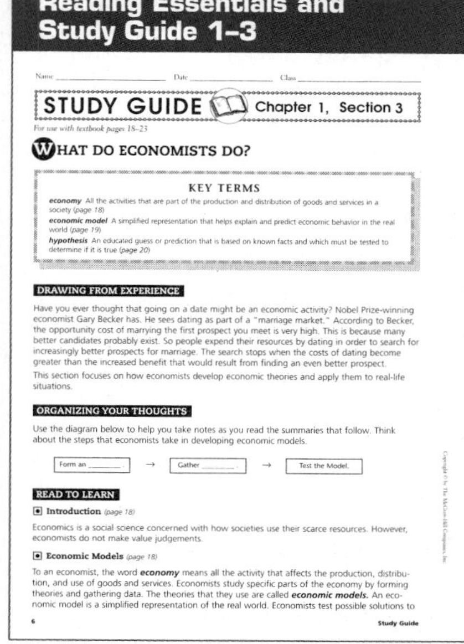

**Reading Essentials and Study Guide 1-3**

Name ______ Date ______ Class ______

STUDY GUIDE Chapter 1, Section 3

*For use with textbook pages 18–23*

WHAT DO ECONOMISTS DO?

KEY TERMS

***economy*** All the activities that are part of the production and distribution of goods and services in a society *(page 18)*

***economic model*** A simplified representation that helps explain and predict economic behavior in the real world *(page 19)*

***hypothesis*** An educated guess or prediction that is based on known facts and which must be tested to determine if it is true *(page 20)*

DRAWING FROM EXPERIENCE

Have you ever thought that going on a date might be an economic activity? Nobel Prize-winning economist Gary Becker has. He sees dating as part of a "marriage market." According to Becker, the opportunity cost of marrying the first prospect you meet is very high. This is because many better candidates probably exist. So people expend their resources by dating in order to search for increasingly better prospects for marriage. The search stops when the costs of dating become greater than the increased benefit that would result from finding an even better prospect.

This section focuses on how economists develop economic theories and apply them to real-life situations.

ORGANIZING YOUR THOUGHTS

Use the diagram below to help you take notes as you read the summaries that follow. Think about the steps that economists take in developing economic models.

Form an ______. → Gather ______. → Test the Model.

READ TO LEARN

**Introduction** *(page 18)*

Economics is a social science concerned with how societies use their scarce resources. However, economists do not make value judgements.

**Economic Models** *(page 18)*

To an economist, the word ***economy*** means all the activity that affects the production, distribution, and use of goods and services. Economists study specific parts of the economy by forming theories and gathering data. The theories that they use are called ***economic models.*** An economic model is a simplified representation of the real world. Economists test possible solutions to

6 Study Guide



# 4 Close

Lead students in a discussion of the following question: How can an understanding of basic economic principles help people become more effective citizens?

## SECTION 3 Assessment Answers

1. All definitions can be found in the Glossary.
2. Idea ⇒ Gather Data ⇒ Evaluate Data ⇒ Draw Conclusion ⇒ Test Hypothesis
3. Economists' personal opinions and beliefs may influence how they view facts and fit them to theories. The government under which economists live also shapes how they view the world.
4. changes in employment among senior citizens and changes in unemployment levels among teenagers
5. Newspaper headlines will vary.

## Background

During his studies at Harvard University and the New School for Social Research, Robert Heilbroner became fascinated with the economic theories of Adam Smith, Karl Marx, John Stuart Mill, and other classical economists. This fascination led him to write *The Worldly Philosophers*. When the book was first published in 1953, sales were slow. Over time, however, it became a mainstay of college economics courses. By the late 1990s, sales had passed the two million mark. Heilbroner's success as an author lies in his ability to convey to readers his feelings about economics—that it is a dynamic and exciting subject.

# Teach

Call on volunteers to read aloud the quoted excerpts from *The Worldly Philosophers*. Then have students paraphrase each excerpt to gain a better understanding of Heilbroner's ideas. Finally, ask students to complete the **Checking for Understanding** questions.

Interested students may wish to review Heilbroner's book *Teachings from the Worldly Philosophy* (1996), a collection of readings from the "worldly philosophers" themselves.

# People & Perspectives

## Robert L. Heilbroner

*ECONOMIST (1919–)*

- **Attended Harvard University and the New School for Social Research in New York City**
- **Has taught at the New School for Social Research since 1972**
- **Published *The Worldly Philosophers* (1953), *The Future as History* (1960), *Visions of the Future* (1995), and *The Crisis of Vision in Modern Economic Thought* (1996)**

Robert L. Heilbroner's book *The Worldly Philosophers* gives a unique and insightful look into the lives and works of the great economists of the past. In his introduction, Heilbroner explains the importance of these great economists to history:

*"By all rules of schoolboy history books, they were nonentities: they commanded no armies, sent no men to their deaths, ruled no empires, took little part in history-making decisions. . . . Yet what they did was more decisive for history than many acts of statesmen who basked in brighter glory, often more profoundly disturbing than the shuttling of armies back and forth across frontiers, more powerful for good and bad than the edicts of kings and legislatures. It was this: they shaped and swayed men's minds."*

Heilbroner expresses his belief that economists have a major impact on the world. He disagrees with the perception that the work of economists is dull and boring:

*". . . A man who thinks that economics is only a matter for professors forgets that this is the science that has sent men to the barricades. . . . No, the great economists pursued an inquiry as exciting–and dangerous–as any the world has ever known. . . . The notions of the great economists were world-shaking, and their mistakes nothing short of calamitous."*

### *Checking for Understanding*

1. **Why is it important to study the great economists of the past?**
2. **Have economists made a real difference in the world? Explain your answer.**

24

### Answers to *Checking for Understanding*

1. Answers will vary but should indicate that it is important to study the great economists because their ideas had historical implications.
2. Answers will vary but should indicate that economists made a difference in that their ideas shaped economic policies and practices.

# CHAPTER  Summary

**Chapter Overview** Visit the *Economics Today and Tomorrow* Web site at ett.glencoe.com and click on ***Chapter 1—Chapter Overviews*** to review chapter information.

## SECTION 1 The Basic Problem in Economics

- **Economics** is the study of how individuals, families, businesses, and societies use limited resources to fulfill their unlimited wants.
- Individuals satisfy their unlimited wants in a world of limited resources by making choices.
- The need to make choices arises because of **scarcity,** the basic problem of economics.
- The resources needed to make goods and services are known as the **factors of production.**
- The four factors of production include **land,** or natural resources; **labor,** also known as human resources; **capital,** the manufactured goods used to make other goods and services; and **entrepreneurship,** the ability of risk-taking individuals to start new businesses and introduce new products and processes.
- Some economists add **technology** to the list of factors of production.

## SECTION 2 Trade-Offs

- People are forced to make **trade-offs** every time they use their resources in one way and not another.
- The cost of making a trade-off is known as **opportunity cost**—the value of the next best alternative that had to be given up to do the action that was chosen.
- A **production possibilities curve** is a graph that shows the maximum combinations of goods and services that can be produced from a fixed amount of resources in a given period of time.
- The classic example for explaining production possibilities in economics is the trade-off between guns (military defense) and butter (civilian goods).

## SECTION 3 What Do Economists Do?

- Economists study the **economy**—all the activity in a nation that together affects the production, distribution, and use of goods and services.
- Economists also formulate theories called **economic models,** which are simplified representations of the real world.
- Economists test their models in the same way that other scientists test **hypotheses,** or educated guesses.
- Economists deal with facts, although their personal opinions may sway their theories.
- Economists offer solutions to economic problems, but they do not put value judgments on those solutions.



## Economics Journal

**Opportunity Cost** Have students start an Economics Portfolio in which they store the Economics Journal writing activities for this and subsequent chapters. Ask students to keep track of all the economic decisions they make during a set time period—one week, perhaps. Remind students that they should record the money they spend, the items they purchase, and the choices they make. Also suggest that they note the reasons for these various choices. Direct students to complete their journal entries by writing a brief explanation of how their growing knowledge of economics helped them become better decision makers.

**ECONOMICS & YOU**

**What Is Economics?**

Chapter 2
Disc 1, Side 1

If you do not have access to a videodisc player, the ***Economics & You*** programs are also available in VHS.

Use the **Chapter 1 Summary** to preview, review, condense, or reteach the chapter.

## Preview/Review

**Vocabulary PuzzleMaker Software** reinforces the key terms used in Chapter 1.

**Interactive Tutor Self-Assessment Software** allows students to review Chapter 1 content.

## Condense

Have students listen to the Chapter 1 **Audio Program** (also available in Spanish) in the TCR. Assign the Chapter 1 Audio Program Activity and give students the Chapter 1 Audio Program Test.

## Reteach

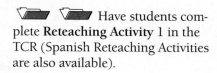

Have students complete **Reteaching Activity** 1 in the TCR (Spanish Reteaching Activities are also available).

Have students visit the *Economics Today and Tomorrow* Web site at ett.glencoe.com to review Chapter 1 and take the Self-Check Quiz.

**GLENCOE TECHNOLOGY**

**MindJogger Videoquiz**

Use MindJogger to review Chapter 1 content.

## Identifying Key Terms

Paragraphs will vary.

## Recalling Facts and Ideas

1. scarcity
2. Scarcity refers to the fixed, or set, amount of resources available to fulfill unlimited wants. Shortages refer to situations where items are temporarily in short supply.
3. Answers may vary. However, most students will note that it would be a need if the clothes were an absolute necessity; it would be a want if a simple desire for more clothes was being expressed.
4. land, labor, capital, entrepreneurship
5. to exchange one thing for the use of another
6. opportunity cost
7. a foregone opportunity
8. a graph showing the combination of goods and services that can be produced with a fixed amount of resources in a given period of time
9. as the basis for testing theories that explain an event or offer a solution to a problem
10. an economic model
11. if it provides useful material for analyzing the way the real world works

## Thinking Critically

1. Answers will vary. Some students may agree, pointing out that people do not have to give up anything of value to breathe the air. Others might disagree, noting that because of pollution, an economic cost is paid to clean up the air and to cover the medical expenses of those made sick by the pollution.



CHAPTER 1

# Assessment and Activities

**ECONOMICS Online**

**Self-Check Quiz** Visit the *Economics Today and Tomorrow* Web site at ett.glencoe.com and click on ***Chapter 1—Self-Check Quizzes*** to prepare for the Chapter Test.

## Identifying Key Terms

*Write a short paragraph about the factors of production in the United States using all of the following terms.*

- scarcity
- factors of production
- entrepreneurship
- technology
- trade-off
- land
- labor
- capital
- goods
- services

## Recalling Facts and Ideas

**Section 1**

1. What is the condition that results because wants are unlimited?
2. What is the difference between scarcity and shortages?
3. Your friend says, "I need some new clothes." Under what conditions would this be expressing a need? A want?
4. What are the four factors of production?

**Section 2**

5. What does making a trade-off require you to do?
6. What do economists call the next best alternative that had to be given up for the one chosen?
7. In economics, what is cost?
8. What does a production possibilities curve show?

**Section 3**

9. For what purposes do economists use real-world data in building models?
10. An economic theory is another name for what?
11. When does an economist consider an economic model useful?

## Thinking Critically

1. **Drawing Inferences and Conclusions** Some people argue that air is not an economic good. Explain why you agree or disagree with this statement.
2. **Categorizing Information** Create three diagrams like the one below and label the center oval with one of the following services: providing financial advice, teaching economics, producing a movie. Fill in examples of each factor of production that went into developing these services.

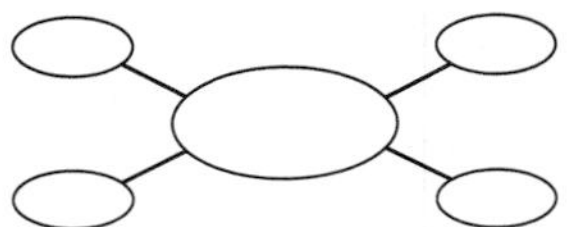

3. **Summarizing Information** Why will studying economics not tell you whether a possible solution to a problem is either good or bad?

## Applying Economic Concepts

**Trade-Offs and Opportunity Costs** Because your time is scarce, you are constantly facing trade-offs. Make a list of the trade-offs you have made in choosing how you used your time during a one-week period. What activities did you choose to do? What were the opportunity costs involved in your choices?

## Cooperative Learning Project

Working in groups of four, choose a consumer product such as a DVD player, a pair of sunglasses, or an automobile. Determine and list the elements of each of the four factors of production that went into making that consumer product. Discuss your lists with the rest of the class.

## Technology Activity

**Using the Internet** Each time you access the Internet you see advertising–banners, buttons, keywords, click-on ads, and other promotions. Home pages of popular Web search engines like Yahoo! face an opportunity cost: any screen space that a site uses to promote its own services cannot be sold to advertisers.

Design a home page for your own Web site. Assume that you can sell some screen space to advertisers, but be aware that too many ads will cause users to switch to a less cluttered site. Consider every square inch on your home page as having an opportunity cost.

## Reviewing Skills

**Sequencing and Categorizing Information** In this chapter you learned that some economists add technology as a fifth factor of production. *Technology,* as you recall, is an advance in knowledge leading to new and improved goods and services and better ways of producing them. This includes any use of land, labor, capital, and entrepreneurship that produces goods and services more efficiently.

Choose a product or service, and then research the technology that went into developing it. Construct a diagram like the one below that displays in sequential order the technology involved in preparing the factors of production that ultimately create your good or service. Share your diagram with the rest of the class.

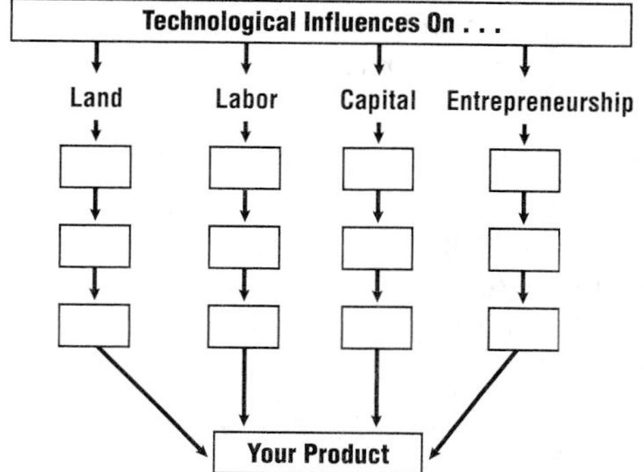


## Analyzing the Global Economy

Watch television news reports and read newspapers and/or news magazines every day for one week. Make a list of proposed actions on the part of international governments that involve trade-offs and opportunity costs. Report your findings to the class.



# CHAPTER 1 Assessment and Activities

## Applying Economic Concepts

Answers will vary. Students should make sure that the opportunity cost includes only the next-highest ranked alternative.

## Cooperative Learning Project

Students might present their information in the form of a diagram.

## Technology Activity

Home page designs will vary.

## Reviewing Skills

Diagrams will vary.

## Analyzing the Global Economy

Reports will vary.

### Chapter Bonus Test Question

**ASK: When is an automobile considered a capital good?** *when it is used to produce a service, such as pizza delivery*

2. Diagrams will vary. Possible examples: Providing financial advice–land: timber and steel for office buildings; labor: financial officer, clerks; capital: office buildings, telephone, computers; entrepreneurship: officer's ideas on financial issues. Teaching economics–land: raw materials used to build school buildings; labor: teacher; capital: school buildings, textbooks; entrepreneurship: teacher's approach to teaching the subject. Producing a movie–land: raw materials to build movie sets; labor: actors, scriptwriters; capital: movie cameras, costumes; entrepreneurship: ideas of director and producer.
3. Economists describe or predict behavior–the way people react. They are not concerned with value judgments and do not try to suggest what people should think about a decision.

CASE STUDY **Focus on Free Enterprise**

# 1 Focus

Call on students who have made a purchase on the Internet to raise their hands. Ask them why they made the purchase by e-commerce rather than through the traditional approach of going to a store. Then have them identify what they feel are the advantages and disadvantages of e-commerce. List their responses on the board. Conclude by mentioning that this feature provides information on one of the leaders in e-commerce–Amazon.com.

# 2 Teach

Guide students through the text, having them note how Amazon.com compares with conventional bookstores. Then refer students to the list on the board of advantages and disadvantages of e-commerce. Call on volunteers to suggest which of the listed advantages and disadvantages apply to Amazon.com.

## ? Did You Know ?

Amazon.com's sales topped $1.4 billion in 1999.

CASE STUDY **Focus on Free Enterprise**

# Amazon.com

***In 1994 30-year-old Jeff Bezos, a Princeton summa cum laude graduate, noticed that this newfangled thing called the World Wide Web was growing by 2,300 percent a year. He wanted in by the smartest available route. Methodically, he drew up a list of products that could be sold on the Internet, including computers, software, music, videos, and clothing.***

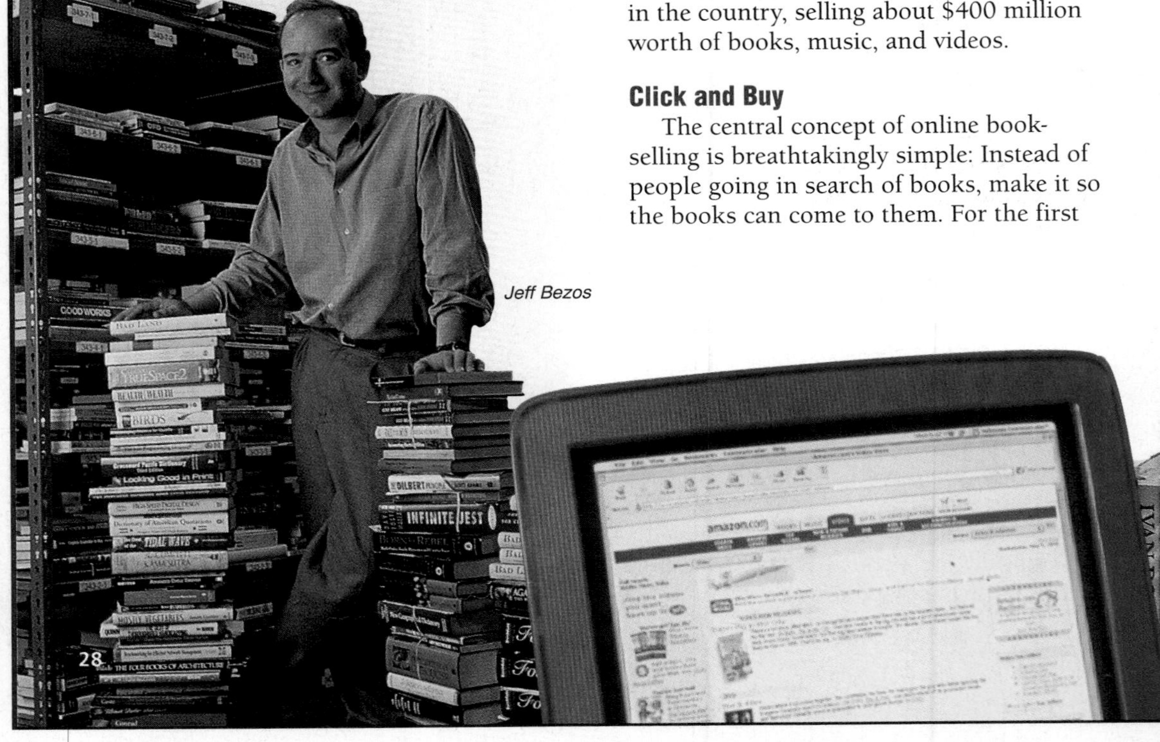
Jeff Bezos

### Curling Up With a Good Book

He finally decided on books because of the variety of product (more than a million titles in print), because no single merchandisers dominated the market, and because computer search engines could be very useful in helping customers find hazily remembered volumes.

Jeff Bezos, founder of Amazon.com, wasn't the first to see that the Internet offered a useful way to match up people and books, but he has pushed the concept harder and faster. Three years after making its first sale, Amazon.com is the third-largest bookseller in the country, selling about $400 million worth of books, music, and videos.

### Click and Buy

The central concept of online bookselling is breathtakingly simple: Instead of people going in search of books, make it so the books can come to them. For the first



**Teacher's Notes**

time, nearly any book is only a mouse click and a few days away from any reader in the country.

In a business using the most sophisticated technology, Bezos's whole purpose is to retrieve something that thrived in the past. "I want to transport online bookselling," he says, "back to the days of the small bookseller who got to know you very well."

Once the customer has made his choice, a premium is put on speed. Customer service workers at Amazon.com take the orders and pass them along to a wholesale book company, which ships the books immediately. Most books arrive at the customer's front door only a few days after the order is sent—so quickly, so painlessly that the buyer is supposed to lose interest in going to the library or superstore. "I abide by the theory that says in the late 20th century, the scarcest resource is time," Bezos says. "If you can save people money and time, they'll like that."

#### Virtual Overhead

Since Amazon.com is virtual, it doesn't have many of the fixed costs for real estate and employees that real-world bookstores do. As a company, Amazon.com owns almost nothing—no buildings, no factories, nothing that qualifies as equity in the traditional sense. It also takes advantage of its medium to allow its customers to post their own book reviews online—which costs nothing, yet bonds its readers into a community.

Another advantage is that it doesn't have to order most books from publishers or wholesalers until a customer actually wants them. A bookstore in the real world has to do things the opposite way: It orders a stack of books and hopes customers will want them.

#### Cyber Irony

Only a few years ago, futurists were predicting that the digital age would be the death of conventional publishing. Instead, the hottest business on the burgeoning Internet is selling old-fashioned books.

—Excerpted from *The Washington Post National Weekly Edition*, July 20–27, 1998.

> ***Free Enterprise in Action***
>
> **1. What is the basic concept of online bookselling?**
>
> **2. Why does Amazon.com have lower fixed costs than regular bookstores?**

## Answers to *Free Enterprise In Action*

1. Instead of people going in search of books, online book-selling makes it so the books can come to them.
2. It does not have many of the fixed costs for real estate and employees that traditional bookstores do. Also, it does not have to order most books from publishers or wholesalers until a customer actually wants them.

# 3 Assess

Have students answer the **Free Enterprise in Action** questions.

# 4 Close

Remind students that Jeff Bezos feels that, with Amazon.com, he is returning "to the days of the small bookseller, who got to know you very well." Then point out that other people suggest that Amazon.com is helping to destroy the small, independent bookseller. Have students debate both views.

### Did You Know

Amazon.com has steadily added to its product line. By 2000, as well as books it was selling greeting cards, CDs and audiotapes, videos, computer software, toys, electrical appliances, and home-improvement products. Amazon.com also offered online auction services.

# CHAPTER 2 Resource Manager

## Teaching Transparency

### Economic Concepts Transparency 4

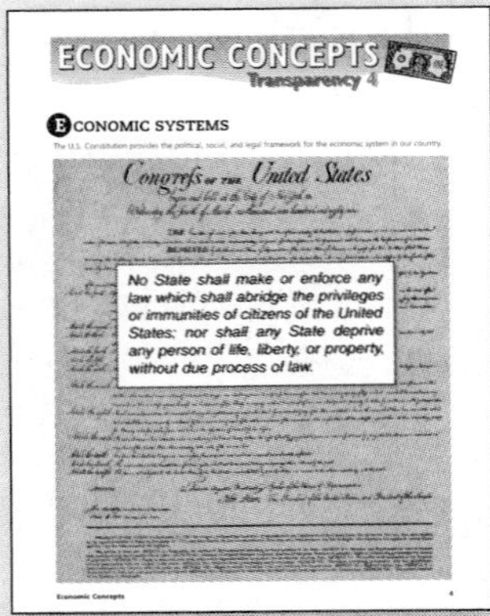
ECONOMIC CONCEPTS Transparency 4

ECONOMIC SYSTEMS

No State shall make or enforce any law which shall abridge the privileges or immunities of citizens of the United States; nor shall any State deprive any person of life, liberty, or property, without due process of law.

## Application and Enrichment

### Enrichment Activity 2

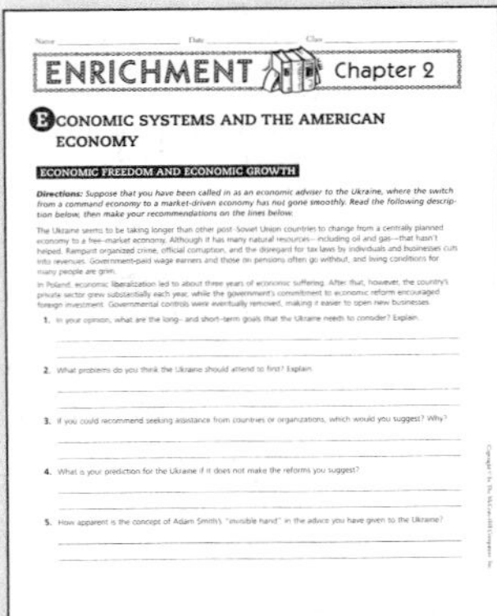
ENRICHMENT Chapter 2

ECONOMIC SYSTEMS AND THE AMERICAN ECONOMY

ECONOMIC FREEDOM AND ECONOMIC GROWTH

### Consumer Applications Activity 2

Con$umer Applications Activity 2

THE JOB MARKET

### Free Enterprise Activity 2

FREE ENTERPRISE ACTIVITY 2

BUSINESS AND GOVERNMENT

## Application and Enrichment

### Cooperative Learning Simulations and Problems 2

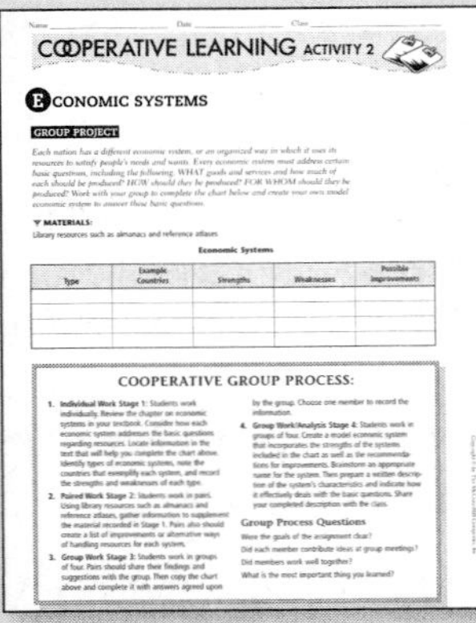
COOPERATIVE LEARNING ACTIVITY 2

ECONOMIC SYSTEMS

GROUP PROJECT

COOPERATIVE GROUP PROCESS:

### Primary and Secondary Source Reading 2

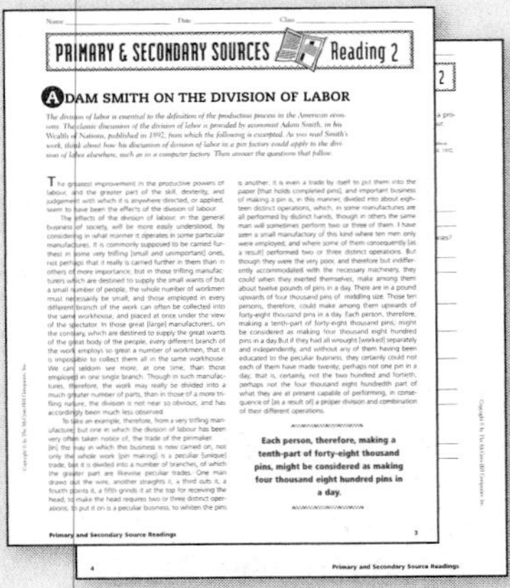
PRIMARY & SECONDARY SOURCES Reading 2

ADAM SMITH ON THE DIVISION OF LABOR

Each person, therefore, making a tenth part of forty-eight thousand pins, might be considered as making four thousand eight hundred pins in a day.

### Math Practice for Economics Activity 2

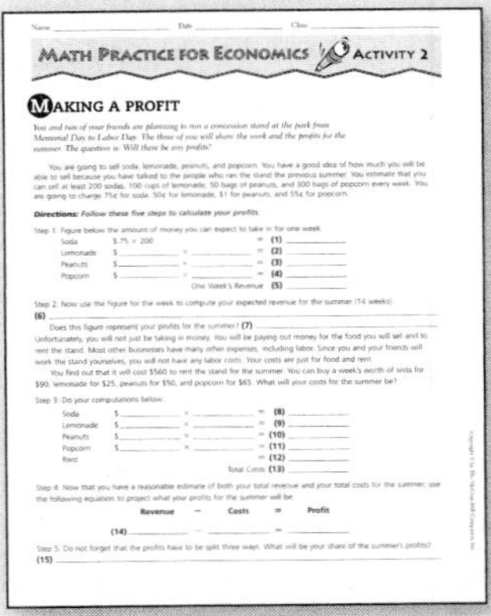
MATH PRACTICE FOR ECONOMICS ACTIVITY 2

MAKING A PROFIT

### Economic Cartoons Activity 2

ECONOMIC CARTOON 2

WHO GETS THE CREDIT? WHO TAKES THE BLAME?

## Review and Reinforcement

### Critical Thinking Activity 2

CRITICAL THINKING 2

CAUSE AND EFFECT IN A MARKET ECONOMY

### Reteaching Activity 2

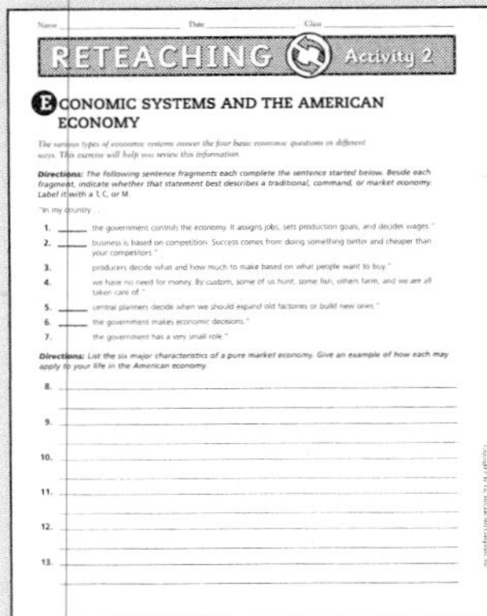
RETEACHING Activity 2

ECONOMIC SYSTEMS AND THE AMERICAN ECONOMY

### Economic Vocabulary Activity 2

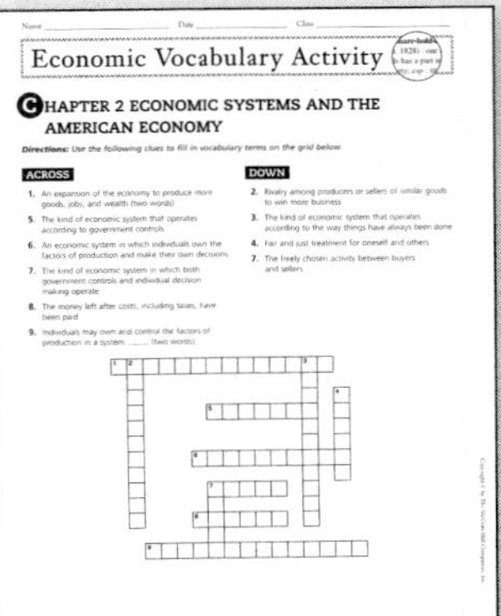
Economic Vocabulary Activity

CHAPTER 2 ECONOMIC SYSTEMS AND THE AMERICAN ECONOMY

ACROSS

DOWN

### Reinforcing Economic Skills 11

Reinforcing Economic Skills Chapter 11

MAKING COMPARISONS

# CHAPTER 2 Resource Manager

## Assessment and Evaluation

Chapter 2 Test Form A

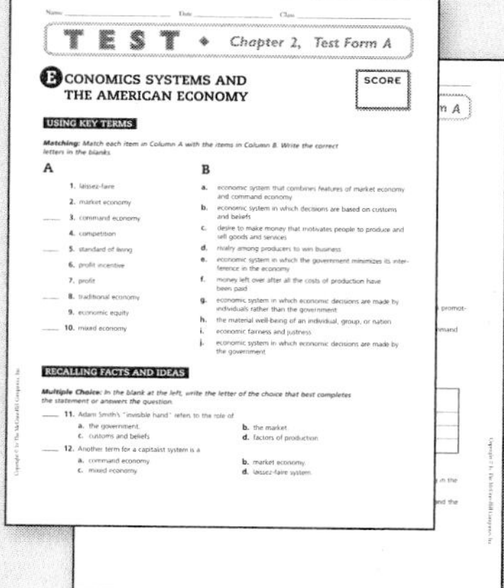

Chapter 2 Test Form B

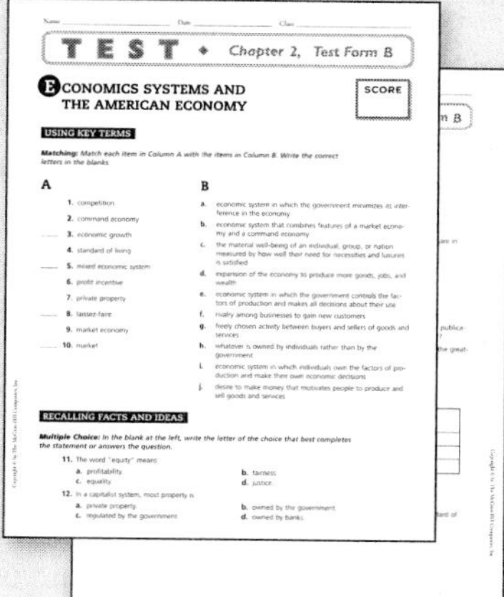

Performance Assessment Activity 2

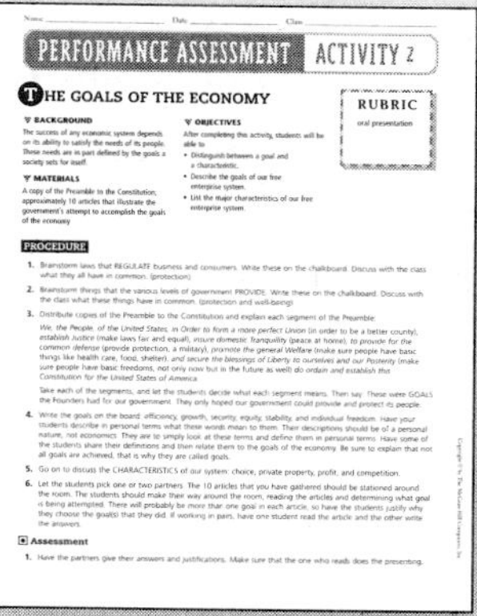

ExamView® Pro Testmaker

## Technology and Multimedia

 Vocabulary PuzzleMaker Software

 Interactive Tutor Self-Assessment Software

 ExamView® Pro Testmaker

 NBR *Economics & You* Video Program (English/Spanish)

 Presentation Plus!

 Glencoe Skillbuilder Interactive Workbook CD-ROM, Level 2

 Interactive Lesson Planner

 MindJogger Videoquiz

 Interactive Economics! CD-ROM

Audio Program (English or Spanish)

## ECONOMICS Online

You and your students can visit ett.glencoe.com—the Web site companion to **Economics Today and Tomorrow.** This innovative integration of electronic and print media offers your students a wealth of opportunities. The student text directs students to the Web site for the following options:

- **Chapter Overviews**
- **Self-Check Quizzes**
- **Student Web Activities**
- **Textbook Updates**

Answers are provided for you in the **Web Activity Lesson Plan.** Additional Web resources and Interactive Puzzles are also available.

Use the Glencoe Web site for additional resources. All essential content is covered in the Student Edition.

## Spanish Resources

 Spanish Economic Concepts Transparency 4

 Spanish Vocabulary Activity 1

 Spanish Reteaching Activity 1

 Spanish Section Quizzes for Chapter 2

 Spanish Chapter 2 Audio Program, Activity, and Test

## Additional Resources

### Reading for the Student

Stein, Herbert, and Murray Foss. *The New Illustrated Guide to the American Economy.* Washington, D.C.: American Enterprise Institute, 1995.

### Multimedia Material

*Economics in a Changing World: Where Do I Fit In?* Churchill Media, 1995. VHS. First video in series covers the basic tools of economics.

# CHAPTER 2 Resource Manager

## Section Resources

| Reading Objectives | Reproducible Resources | Technology/Multimedia Resources |
|---|---|---|
| **Section 1**<br>**Economic Systems**<br>• What three questions must all economic systems answer?<br>• What are the major types of economic systems and their differences? | Reproducible Lesson Plan 2-1<br>Daily Lecture Notes 2-1<br>Guided Reading Activity 2-1<br>Reading Essentials and Study Guide 2-1<br>Daily Focus Activity 6<br>Section Quiz 2-1*<br>Reinforcing Economic Skills 11 | Daily Focus Transparency 6<br>Economic Concepts Transparency 4<br>Vocabulary PuzzleMaker<br>Interactive Tutor Self-Assessment Software<br>MindJogger Videoquiz<br>NBR's *Economics & You**<br>Interactive Economics!<br>Presentation Plus!<br>ExamView® Pro Testmaker |
| **Section 2**<br>**Characteristics of the American Economy**<br>• What is the role of government in our free enterprise economy?<br>• How do freedom of enterprise and freedom of choice apply to the American economy?<br>• What roles do private property, the profit incentive, and competition play in the American economy? | Reproducible Lesson Plan 2-2<br>Daily Lecture Notes 2-2<br>Guided Reading Activity 2-2<br>Reading Essentials and Study Guide 2-2<br>Daily Focus Activity 7<br>Section Quiz 2-2* | Daily Focus Transparency 7<br>Vocabulary PuzzleMaker<br>Interactive Tutor Self-Assessment Software<br>MindJogger Videoquiz<br>Presentation Plus!<br>ExamView® Pro Testmaker |
| **Section 3**<br>**The Goals of the Nation**<br>• What are the major goals of a market economy?<br>• How can people balance economic rights with economic responsibilities? | Reproducible Lesson Plan 2-3<br>Daily Lecture Notes 2-3<br>Guided Reading Activity 2-3<br>Reading Essentials and Study Guide 2-3<br>Daily Focus Activity 8<br>Section Quiz 2-3* | Daily Focus Transparency 8<br>Vocabulary PuzzleMaker<br>Interactive Tutor Self-Assessment Software<br>MindJogger Videoquiz<br>Presentation Plus!<br>ExamView® Pro Testmaker |

*Also available in Spanish

Blackline Master
Transparency

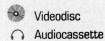

Software
CD-ROM

Videodisc
Audiocassette

Videocassette

# CHAPTER 2 Resource Manager

## ACTIVITY From the Classroom of

**Mark Ward**
**Owego Free Academy**
**Owego, New York**

### Local Economics

Have students become familiar with their community's economy. The entire class will analyze a map of the community and divide it into six smaller regions. Then, in small groups, students will research one of these economic regions. Have groups investigate their area by interviewing shopkeepers and consumers. Find out local history about the area and what the future holds. After each group gathers information, come together as a class. Design and produce booklets about the local economy.

## Easy Planning and Preparation!

Use Glencoe's **Presentation Plus!**, a Microsoft PowerPoint® application, to teach **Economic Systems and the American Economy.** With this multimedia teacher tool, you can customize ready-made presentations. At your fingertips are interactive transparencies, on-screen lecture notes, audiovisual presentations, and links to the Internet and to other Glencoe multimedia.

**Interactive Lesson Planner**
Planning has never been easier! Organize your week, month, semester, or year with all the lesson helps you need to make teaching creative, timely, and relevant—the way it is meant to be. The Interactive Lesson Planner opens Glencoe's **Chapter 2** resources, helps you build your schedule, and tracks your progress.

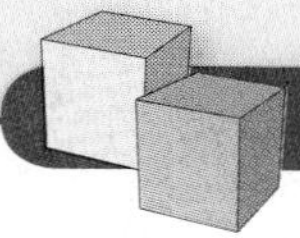

## Block Schedule

Activities that are particularly suited to use within the block scheduling framework are identified throughout this chapter by the following designation: BLOCK SCHEDULING

## Key to Ability Levels

**Teaching strategies have been coded for varying learning styles and abilities.**

L1 BASIC activities for all students
L2 AVERAGE activities for average to above-average students
L3 CHALLENGING activities for above-average students
ELL ENGLISH LANGUAGE LEARNER activities

## National Council on Economic Education

## THE EconomicsAmerica AND EconomicsInternational PROGRAMS

### Voluntary Standards Emphasized in Chapter 2

**Content Standard 3** Students will understand that different methods can be used to allocate goods and services. People, acting individually or collectively through government, must choose which methods to use to allocate different kinds of goods and services.

**Content Standard 16** Students will understand that there is an economic role for government to play in a market economy whenever the benefits of a government policy outweigh its costs.

### Resources Available from NCEE

- *Capstone: The Nation's High School Economics Course*
- *Focus: High School Economics*
- *Civics and Government: Focus on Economics*
- *Economics in Transition: Command to Market*

**To order these materials, or to contact your State Council on Economic Education about workshops and programs, call 1-800-338-1192 or visit the NCEE Web site at http://www.nationalcouncil.org**

# Introducing CHAPTER 2

ECONOMICS & YOU

Economic Systems and the American Economy

Chapter 3
Disc 1, Side 1

ASK: What are some examples of government's role in the American economy? *Answers may include requiring businesses to pay workers a minimum wage and requiring them to meet environmental standards.*

Also available in VHS.

## Chapter Overview

**Chapter 2** explains or describes how economic systems answer basic questions about production and distribution of goods and services; how economic systems differ; and what constitutes the major characteristics of the United States market economy.

### GLENCOE TECHNOLOGY

Use **MindJogger Videoquiz** VHS to preview Chapter 2 content.

Introduce students to chapter content and key terms by having them access **Chapter 2—Chapter Overviews** at *ett.glencoe.com*

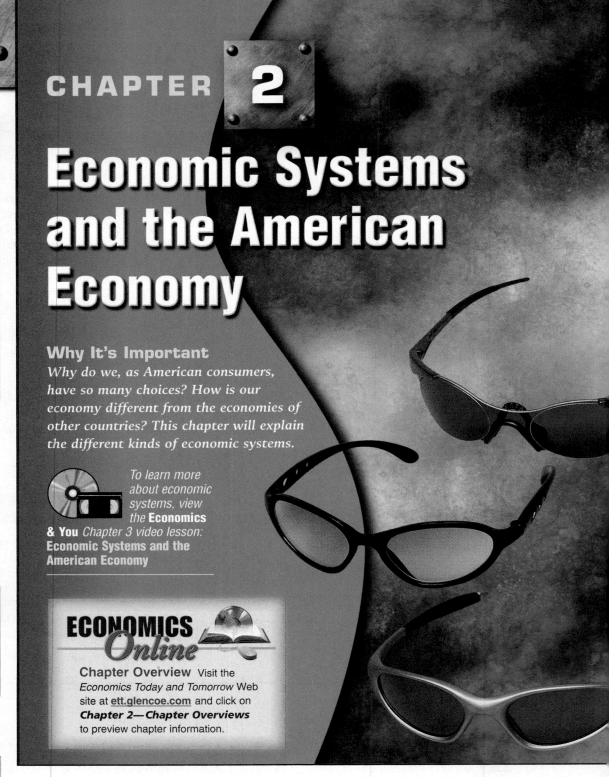

# CHAPTER 2

# Economic Systems and the American Economy

### Why It's Important

*Why do we, as American consumers, have so many choices? How is our economy different from the economies of other countries? This chapter will explain the different kinds of economic systems.*

*To learn more about economic systems, view the* **Economics & You** *Chapter 3 video lesson:* **Economic Systems and the American Economy**

ECONOMICS Online

**Chapter Overview** Visit the *Economics Today and Tomorrow* Web site at ett.glencoe.com and click on ***Chapter 2—Chapter Overviews*** to preview chapter information.

### CHAPTER LAUNCH ACTIVITY

Call on students to identify the characteristics of the American economic system. If students have difficulty, provide clues that might lead them to correct answers. For example, to elicit the response "freedom of choice," you might say: "When you go to the store to buy breakfast cereal, are there many kinds or just one? If there are many, you have ___________." Note responses on the board. Then underline the terms *choice* and *competition*, and point out that in this chapter students will learn that these are major characteristics of the American economy.

SECTION 1

# Economic Systems

## COVER STORY

*WE LIVE IN ARGENTINA*, BY ALEX HUBER

Diaguita Indians have lived in this region for generations. . . . We grow beans, corn and potatoes on the mountain slopes. To irrigate these crops, we still use the channels built centuries ago by our ancestors. We also breed llamas. . . . In our community, the more llamas you own, the richer you are. . . . You can tell to which community someone belongs by the way they dress, the color of their clothes, and the hairstyle of the women.

### READER'S GUIDE

**Terms to Know**

- economic system
- traditional economy
- command economy
- market economy
- market
- circular flow of economic activity
- mixed economy

**Reading Objectives**

1. What three questions must all economic systems answer?
2. What are the major types of economic systems and their differences?

You probably have set some goals for your life, such as going to college, learning a trade, or opening a business. If you were to compare your personal goals to the goals of a Diaguita living in Argentina or to a North Korean teenager, the lists might vary widely. One of the reasons for this variance is that each of these persons lives in a community or nation with a different **economic system,** or way of determining how to use resources to satisfy people's wants and needs. In this section, you'll learn about the different kinds of economic systems in the world.

economic system: *way in which a nation uses its resources to satisfy its people's needs and wants*

## Three Basic Questions

Although nations will have different economic systems, each system is faced with answering the same three basic questions:





# 1 Focus

## Overview

Section 1 explains or describes the three basic questions that define the major economic systems, and the concepts of traditional, command, market, and mixed economies.

**BELLRINGER**
**Motivational Activity**

Project **Daily Focus Transparency 6** and have students answer the questions.

This activity is also available as a blackline master.

**Daily Focus Transparency 6**

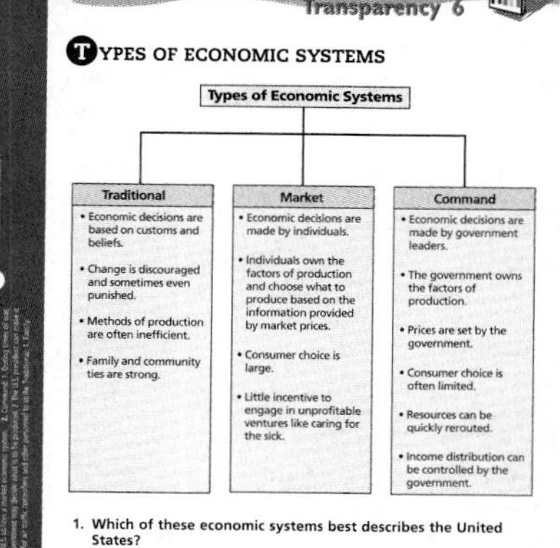

FOCUS ACTIVITIES
Transparency 6

TYPES OF ECONOMIC SYSTEMS

Types of Economic Systems

| Traditional | Market | Command |
|---|---|---|
| • Economic decisions are based on customs and beliefs.<br>• Change is discouraged and sometimes even punished.<br>• Methods of production are often inefficient.<br>• Family and community ties are strong. | • Economic decisions are made by individuals.<br>• Individuals own the factors of production and choose what to produce based on the information provided by market prices.<br>• Consumer choice is large.<br>• Little incentive to engage in unprofitable ventures like caring for the sick. | • Economic decisions are made by government leaders.<br>• The government owns the factors of production.<br>• Prices are set by the government.<br>• Consumer choice is often limited.<br>• Resources can be quickly rerouted.<br>• Income distribution can be controlled by the government. |

1. Which of these economic systems best describes the United States?
2. Give examples of when the other two systems have been (or might be) utilized by the United States for making economic decisions.

Daily Focus Transparencies

### READER'S GUIDE

Answers to the **Reading Objectives** questions are on page 38.

**Preteaching Vocabulary**

Write the **Terms to Know** on the board. Invite volunteers to come to the board and write what they think the terms mean. Have students check these definitions against the definitions in the Glossary.

**Vocabulary PuzzleMaker**

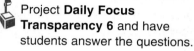

## SECTION 1 RESOURCE MANAGER

**Reproducible Masters**

- Reproducible Lesson Plan 2–1
- Reading Essentials and Study Guide 2–1
- Guided Reading Activity 2–1
- Section Quiz 2–1
- Daily Focus Activity 6
- Daily Lecture Notes 2–1

**Multimedia**

- Daily Focus Transparency 6
- Economic Concepts Transparency 4
- Vocabulary PuzzleMaker
- Interactive Tutor Self-Assessment Software
- ExamView® Pro Testmaker
- MindJogger Videoquiz
- NBR's *Economics & You*
- Interactive Economics!

# 2 Teach

## Guided Practice

**L1 Constructing a Chart** Call on students to identify how each of the economic systems answers the basic economic questions. Note responses on the board. Then have students use the information on the board to construct a chart titled "Comparing Economic Systems—the Basic Economic Questions."

### Visual Instruction FIGURE 2.1

**Answer:** *because economics is ruled by scarcity and trade-offs—if more of one particular item is produced, then less of something else will be produced*

### Daily Lecture Notes 2-1

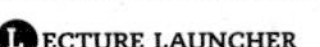

DAILY LECTURE NOTES Lesson 2-1

**LECTURE LAUNCHER**

In 1953, China began to force its farmers into cooperatives of 20 to 30 households. The farmer would own his house, a garden plot, and his personal savings. Just three years later, over 88 percent of China's peasants lived in cooperatives. If you had to make economic decisions cooperatively with a dozen of your classmates, how might your economic activities be changed?

PAGES 31–33

I. Three Basic Questions
   A. What goods and services should be produced?
   B. How should they be produced?
   C. Who will get the goods and how will they be distributed?

**Discussion Question**

**Think of a good or service in your school or community that is offered on a first-come-first-served basis. Why do you think it is distributed in this manner? Do you agree with this method of distribution?** *(Answers will vary. Students should be able to consider the merits of this form of distribution and compare it with other methods. Price, lotteries, and first-in-line policies are all methods for rationing goods.)*

II. Types of Economic Systems

### Visual Instruction FIGURE 2.2

**Answer:** *how the combination of available resources will get the job done for the least cost*

What goods and services should be produced? How should they be produced? Who should share in what is produced?

**What Should Be Produced?** As you've learned, we live in a world of scarcity and trade-offs. If more of one particular item is produced, then less of something else will be produced. If the government decides to use resources to build new roads, then fewer resources are available to maintain national parks. If a city decides to hire more police officers, fewer funds are available to add teachers to classrooms. Similarly, as shown in **Figure 2.1,** an automobile manufacturer must decide whether to produce pickup trucks, minivans, all-terrain vehicles, or luxury cars—and how much of each.

**FIGURE 2.1**

**What to Produce?** An automobile manufacturer must decide how to use its limited supplies of labor, steel, rubber, and so on. ***Why can't businesses or nations produce as much as they want?***

**How Should It Be Produced?** After deciding what to produce, an economic system must then decide *how* those goods and services will be produced. Will more laborers be hired? Will skilled laborers or unskilled laborers do the work? Will capital goods be used to manufacture the products, thereby reducing the number of laborers needed? As shown in **Figure 2.2,** a decision must be made as to how the combination of available inputs will get the job done for the least cost.

**FIGURE 2.2**

**How to Produce?** Trade-offs exist among the available factors of production. A farmer could use a horse-drawn plow to prepare a field for planting, or instead use modern equipment. ***What factors must be considered when deciding how to produce a good or service?***

### Meeting Special Needs

**Reading Disability** To increase text comprehension, tell students to scan the **Reader's Guide** before reading the entire section. Knowing what to look for before reading helps students who have difficulty focusing attention to gain direction.

Refer to *Inclusion for the Social Studies Classroom Strategies and Activities* for students with different learning styles.

**HAGAR THE HORRIBLE**

IS THERE MUCH MONEY IN BEING A DOCTOR?
WELL, I'M NOT RICH...

© 1999 by King Features Syndicate, Inc. World rights reserved.

Reprinted with special permission of King Features Syndicate.

**FIGURE** 

**For Whom to Produce?**
In the United States economy, people's career choices determine their level of income, which in turn affects their ability to purchase produced items. ***Do you think goods and services should be distributed in a way other than based on income? Explain.***

**For Whom Should It Be Produced?** After goods or services are produced, the type of economic system under which people live determines how the goods and services will be distributed among its members. See **Figure 2.3.** Who receives the new cars? Who benefits from a new city school? Who lives in new apartment buildings? As you will read, most goods and services in the United States are distributed to individuals and businesses through a price system. Other economies may distribute products through majority rule, a lottery, on a first-come-first-served basis, by sharing equally, by military force, and in a variety of other ways.

## Types of Economic Systems

Economists have identified four types of economic systems. They differ from one another based on how they answer the three basic questions of what, how, and for whom to produce. The four types of economic systems are traditional, command (or controlled), market (or capitalist), and mixed. Keep in mind that the four systems described here are theoretical representations of economies found throughout the world. No "pure" systems really exist—they are all mixed economies to some degree.

**Traditional System** A pure **traditional economy** answers the three basic questions according to tradition. In such a system, things are done "the way they have always been done." Economic decisions are based on customs and beliefs—often religious—handed down from generation to generation.

*traditional economy: system in which economic decisions are based on customs and beliefs that have been handed down from generation to generation*

If you lived in a traditional economic system, your parents would teach you to perform the same tasks that they learned from their parents. As a male, for example, if your father was a fisherman, you would become a fisherman. You would learn to





**Visual Instruction FIGURE 2.3**

**Answer:** *Answers will vary. Encourage students to provide reasons for their answers.*

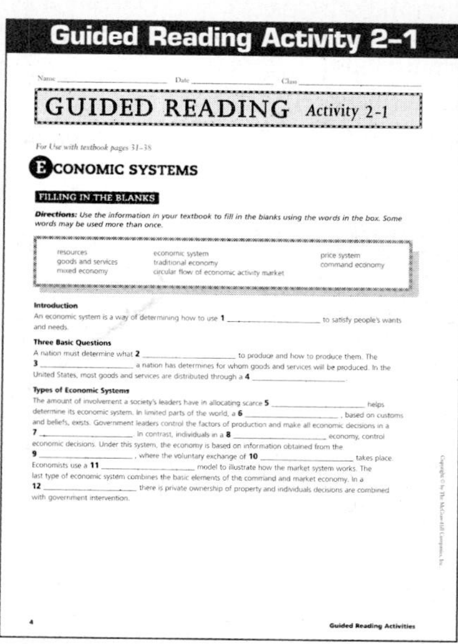

**Guided Reading Activity 2-1**

Name ____________ Date ____________ Class ____________

GUIDED READING *Activity 2-1*

*For Use with textbook pages 31–38*

ECONOMIC SYSTEMS

FILLING IN THE BLANKS

***Directions:*** *Use the information in your textbook to fill in the blanks using the words in the box. Some words may be used more than once.*

resources
goods and services
mixed economy
economic system
traditional economy
circular flow of economic activity market
price system
command economy

**Introduction**
An economic system is a way of determining how to use **1** ____________ to satisfy people's wants and needs.

**Three Basic Questions**
A nation must determine what **2** ____________ to produce and how to produce them. The **3** ____________ a nation has determines for whom goods and services will be produced. In the United States, most goods and services are distributed through a **4** ____________.

**Types of Economic Systems**
The amount of involvement a society's leaders have in allocating scarce **5** ____________ helps determine its economic system. In limited parts of the world, a **6** ____________, based on customs and beliefs, exists. Government leaders control the factors of production and make all economic decisions in a **7** ____________. In contrast, individuals in a **8** ____________ economy, control economic decisions. Under this system, the economy is based on information obtained from the **9** ____________, where the voluntary exchange of **10** ____________ takes place. Economists use a **11** ____________ model to illustrate how the market system works. The last type of economic system combines the basic elements of the command and market economy. In a **12** ____________ there is private ownership of property and individuals decisions are combined with government intervention.

Copyright © by The McGraw-Hill Companies, Inc.

4 **Guided Reading Activities**

**L2 Applying Ideas** Review the information on the three economic systems with students. Then ask students to consider the following question: How might each of the three economic systems respond to the introduction of new technology? Assist students by suggesting that they look at how each economic system views new ideas.

Project **Economic Concepts Transparency 4** and have students discuss the accompanying questions.

## Cooperative Learning

List the advantages and disadvantages of the market economic system on a sheet of paper. Organize students into several groups, and give each group a copy of the list. Ask groups to search newspapers and magazines and to watch television news programs to locate examples of each of the listed advantages and disadvantages. Suggest that groups present their findings in a pictorial essay titled "Market Economies: Advantages and Disadvantages." Call on group representatives to share their essays with the class.

BLOCK SCHEDULING

## Independent Practice

**L1** Creating a Bulletin-Board Display Have students work in small groups to collect images from newspapers and magazines that illustrate aspects of the three economic systems. Direct groups to use their visual materials to create a bulletin-board display titled "Illustrating the Three Economic Systems." ELL

## Did You Know

An element of the traditional economic system persists in the United States—barter. This involves the exchange of goods and services. According to the National Association of Trade Exchanges, there are 350,000 to 400,000 businesses in the United States and Canada conducting about $4.3 billion in barter trade a year.

make fishing nets the same way he was taught. And you would distribute your catch in the manner that it had always been done.

An advantage of living in a traditional economy is that you know what is expected of you. In addition, family and community ties are usually very strong. Disadvantages include an economy in which change is discouraged and perhaps even punished, and one in which the methods of production are often inefficient. Consequently, choices among consumer goods are rare.

As *Part C* of **Figure 2.4** shows, traditional economies exist to some extent in very limited parts of the world today. The Inuit of North America, the San of the Kalahari in Africa, and the Aborigines of Australia are organized into traditional economic systems.

**command economy:** *system in which the government controls the factors of production and makes all decisions about their use*

### Command System

The pure **command economy** is somewhat similar to the traditional economy in that the individual has little, if any, influence over how the basic economic questions are answered. In a command or controlled system, however, government leaders—not tradition—control the factors of production and, therefore, make all decisions about their use.

The government may be one person, a small group of leaders, or a group of central planners in an agency. These people choose what is to be produced and how resources are to be used at each stage in production. They also decide how goods and services will be distributed. If you lived in a command economy, you would be paid according to what the central planners decide, and you might even lose your ability to make a career choice. Through a series of regulations about the kinds and amounts of available education, the government guides people into certain jobs.

An advantage of a controlled economy is the speed with which resources can be rerouted. If war is likely, the central planning agency can halt all manufacturing of civilian goods and channel the factors of production into making strictly military goods. Disadvantages include a lack of incentives to work hard or to show inventiveness, as well as a lack of consumer choices. Because the government sets workers' salaries, there is no reason to work efficiently or smartly.

Only a few countries in the world today still have much of a command economy. North Korea and the People's Republic of China are the two main examples because so much economic activity there is government-planned. See *Part B* of **Figure 2.4.**



## Free Enterprise Activity

Have students work individually or in groups to study a local business. Monitor students' choices to ensure that both manufacturing and service-oriented businesses are covered. Ask students to find recent decisions and actions taken by their selected businesses that were influenced by the three basic economic questions. Have students present their findings in a brief oral report. BLOCK SCHEDULING

**FIGURE 2.4**

**Types of Economic Systems** The types of economic systems differ from one another based on how they answer the three basic questions of what, how, and for whom to produce.

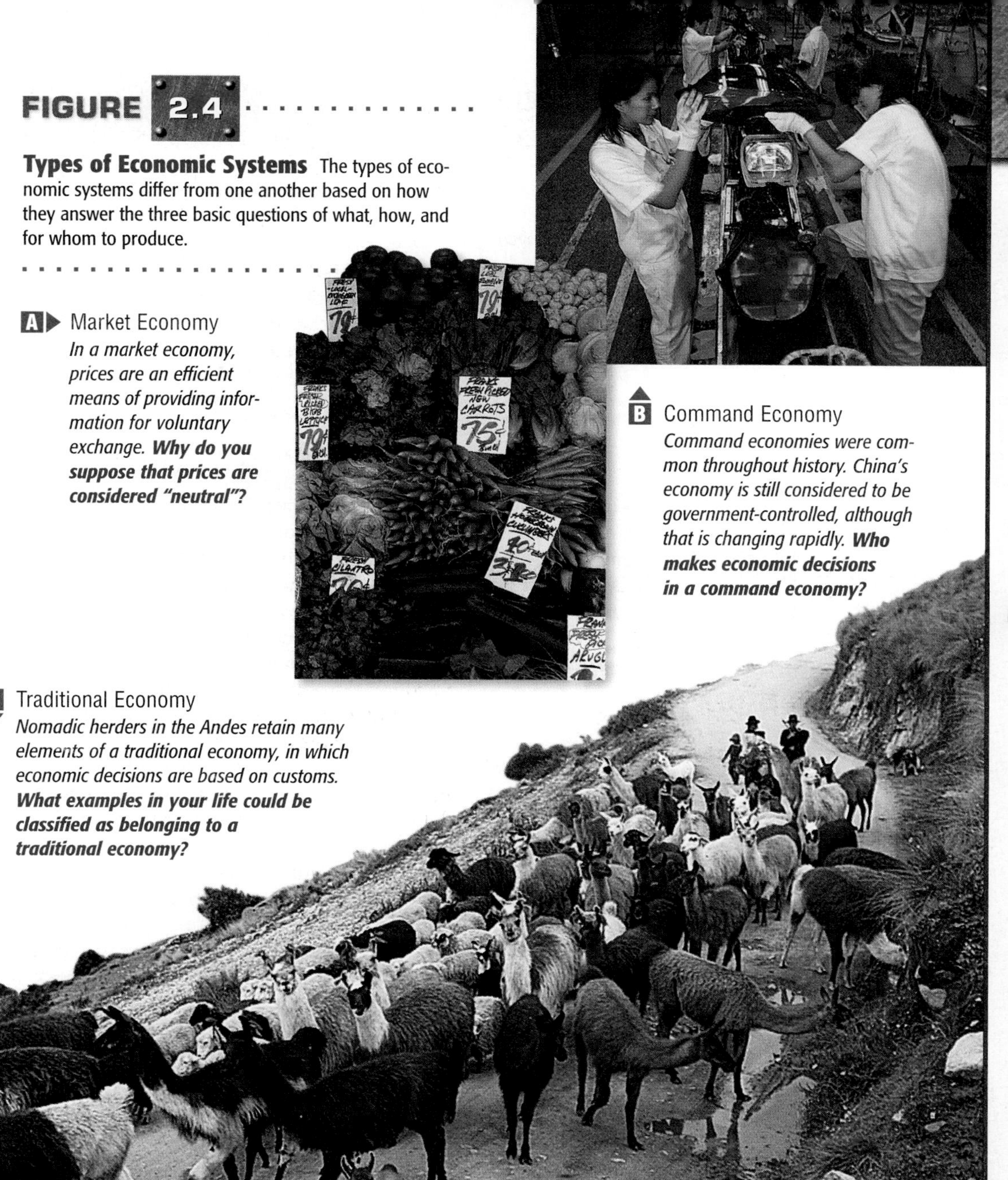

**A** Market Economy
*In a market economy, prices are an efficient means of providing information for voluntary exchange.* ***Why do you suppose that prices are considered "neutral"?***

**B** Command Economy
*Command economies were common throughout history. China's economy is still considered to be government-controlled, although that is changing rapidly.* ***Who makes economic decisions in a command economy?***

**C** Traditional Economy
*Nomadic herders in the Andes retain many elements of a traditional economy, in which economic decisions are based on customs.* ***What examples in your life could be classified as belonging to a traditional economy?***

## Extending the Content

**Ideal Types** To make the study and analysis of social phenomena easier, social scientists often use ideal types. An ideal type is a simplified description of a particular phenomenon that focuses on the common attributes of that phenomenon. In other words, it offers a picture of that phenomenon's essential nature. The three kinds of economic systems discussed in this section are ideal types.

### Visual Instruction FIGURE 2.4

You might ask students to summarize each economic system in a one-word summary.
**Answer:** PART A: *because they are free to rise and fall*
PART B: *government leaders*
PART C: *Answers will vary. Encourage students to explain their answers.*

## Global Economy

### China and Free Enterprise

In 1999 China changed its constitution to allow the private sector to become an important part of the economy. However, the constitution still refers to the Chinese economic system as "socialist."

**L2 Applying Ideas** Organize students into several groups, and tell groups to imagine that they work for an advertising company. They have been given the task of "selling" each of the three economic systems to the public. Direct groups to develop an advertising slogan for each system that focuses on its advantages. Call on group representatives to present their slogans to the class. Encourage class members to act as a focus group and critique the slogans.
BLOCK SCHEDULING

ECONOMICS & YOU

Economic Systems and the American Economy

Chapter 3
Disc 1, Side 1

ASK: What are some examples of government's role in the American economy? *The government regulates business by requiring businesses to pay workers a minimum wage and by requiring them to meet environmental standards. It also provides services such as health care to the elderly.*

 Also available in VHS.

ECONOMICS Online

See the **Web Activity Lesson Plan** at ett.glencoe.com for an introduction, lesson description, and answers to the **Student Web Activity** for this chapter.

## Economic Connection to... History

# The Soviet Union's Quota System

In the former Soviet Union, workers often used resources inefficiently or completely wasted them when trying to fill government production quotas. For example, after the central planning committee ordered a quota for glass based on the number of panes, workers made *many* panes of glass—each paper-thin and shattering easily! When the production quota was changed to be based on the weight of the panes, workers made the glass panes so thick that they were useless. ■

**market economy:** *system in which individuals own the factors of production and make economic decisions through free interaction while looking out for their own and their families' best interests*

**market:** *freely chosen activity between buyers and sellers of goods and services*

**Market System** The opposite of a pure command economy is a pure **market economy**—also called capitalism. In a market system, economic decisions are not made by government, but by individuals looking out for their own and their families' best interests. A limited government makes it possible for individuals to decide for themselves the answers to the three basic questions. Individuals own the factors of production, and therefore choose what to produce and how to produce it. Individuals also choose what to buy with the income received from selling their labor and other resources. All of these choices are guided not by tradition or a central planning agency, but by information in the form of market prices.

A **market** is not necessarily a place. Rather, it is the *voluntary exchange* of goods and services between buyers and sellers. This exchange may take place in a worldwide market for a good such as crude oil. It may also take place in a neighborhood market for services such as paper delivery, snow shoveling, and baby-sitting.

ECONOMICS Online

**Student Web Activity** Visit the *Economics Today and Tomorrow* Web site at ett.glencoe.com and click on ***Chapter 2—Student Web Activities*** to learn more about the command economy of the former Soviet Union.

As shown in *Part A* of **Figure 2.4** on page 35, prices in a market coordinate the interaction between buyers and sellers. As prices change, they act as signals to everyone within the system as to what should be bought and what should be produced. A high price for a good generally means that it is relatively scarce. A low price suggests that it is relatively abundant. The freedom of prices to rise and fall results in a neutral, self-organizing, incentive-driven system.



## Critical Thinking Activity

**Applying Ideas** Ask students to consider the role that they play in the American economy. Suggest that they think of and list the consumer purchases they have made and the jobs they have held. Encourage them to write a brief paragraph on how their economic decisions and actions influence the American market economic system.

The flow of resources, goods and services, and money in a market system is actually circular, as shown in **Figure 2.5.** Economists use this model, called a **circular flow of economic activity,** to illustrate how the market system works. Note how dollars flow from businesses to individuals and back to businesses again. The factors of production flow from individuals to businesses, which use them to produce goods and services that flow back to individuals. The circular flow works because the information needed for its operation is scattered among all participants in the economy.

**circular flow of economic activity:** *economic model that pictures income as flowing continuously between businesses and consumers*

The advantages of a pure market system are many. People have freedoms–to choose a career, to spend or not spend their income how they wish, to own private property, to take risks and earn profits. In addition, the existence of competition provides consumers in a market economy with a wide array of goods and services from which to choose, as well as an efficient system of determining how much they cost. One disadvantage of a pure market system involves concern about those too young, too old,

**FIGURE 2.5**

**Circular Flow** The inside arrows on the graph show individuals selling the factors of production to businesses, who use them to produce goods and services. The outside of the graph shows the flow of money income from businesses to individuals in the form of rents, wages, interest, and profits; and the return of money to businesses as consumer spending. ***What underlying factor makes this circular flow work?***

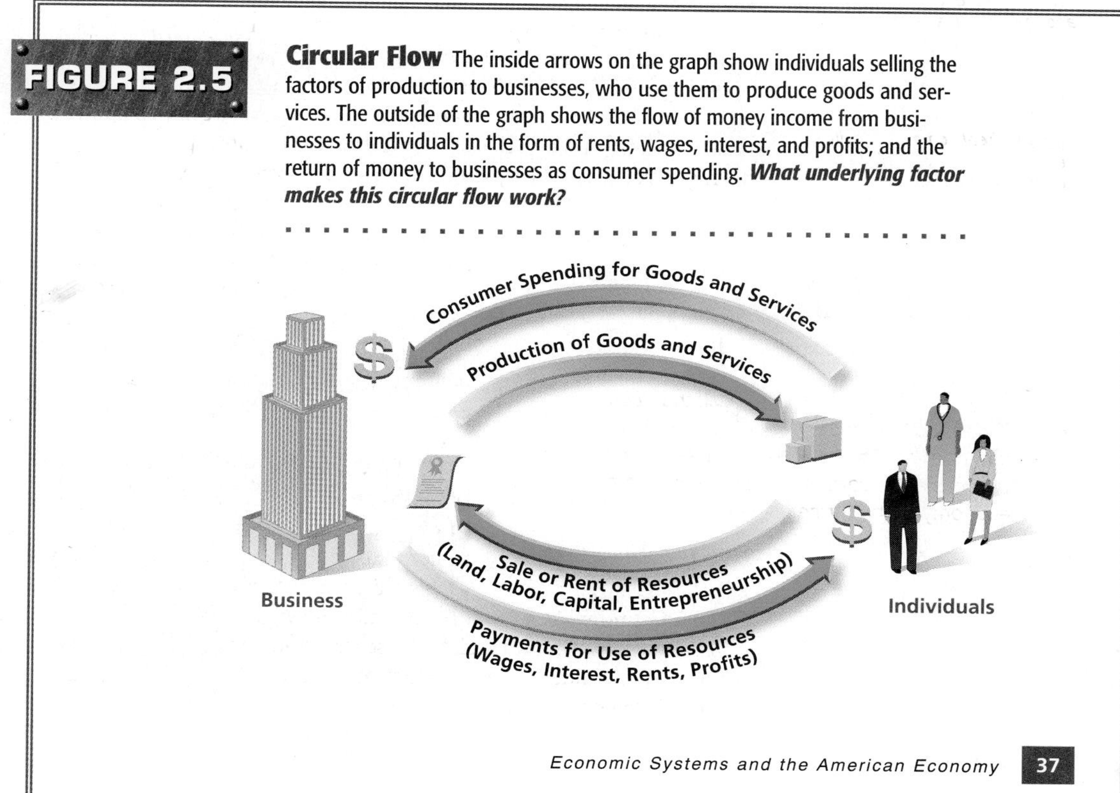




## Visual Learning Activity

**Graphic Organizer** Ask students to copy this diagram into their notebooks. Then have them complete the diagram by listing in the appropriate boxes the advantages and disadvantages of each economic system.

| System | Advantages | Disadvantages |
|---|---|---|
| | | |
| | | |
| | | |



INTERACTIVE ECONOMICS!

**LESSON 2: CIRCULAR FLOWS**

Have students study the Lesson 2 "Tutorial," which focuses on circular flows. Students will see how the basic two-sector model works. After students read the "Tutorial," have them attempt to complete the "Economics Lab" dealing with circular flows. The lab includes the third sector—government—in the circular flow, so have students click and drag the correct terms to only the outer circular flow dealing with the business and household sectors.

Supplied in both CD-ROM and disk formats.

# 3 Assess

## Meeting Lesson Objectives

Assign Section 1 Assessment as homework or an in-class activity.

Use **Interactive Tutor Self-Assessment Software** to review Section 1.

**Visual Instruction FIGURE 2.5**

**Answer:** *The circular flow works because the information needed for its operation is scattered among all participants in the economy.*

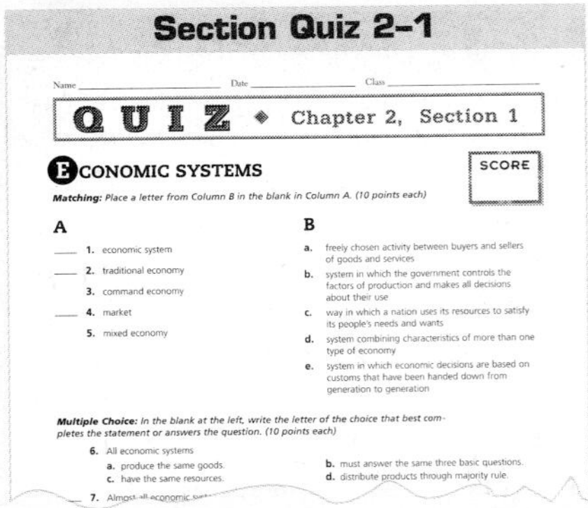

Section Quiz 2-1

Name ______ Date ______ Class ______

**QUIZ ◆ Chapter 2, Section 1**

ECONOMIC SYSTEMS

SCORE

***Matching:*** *Place a letter from Column B in the blank in Column A. (10 points each)*

| A | B |
|---|---|
| ____ 1. economic system | a. freely chosen activity between buyers and sellers of goods and services |
| ____ 2. traditional economy | b. system in which the government controls the factors of production and makes all decisions about their use |
| 3. command economy | c. way in which a nation uses its resources to satisfy its people's needs and wants |
| ____ 4. market | d. system combining characteristics of more than one type of economy |
| 5. mixed economy | e. system in which economic decisions are based on customs that have been handed down from generation to generation |

***Multiple Choice:*** *In the blank at the left, write the letter of the choice that best completes the statement or answers the question. (10 points each)*

6. All economic systems
   a. produce the same goods.
   b. must answer the same three basic questions.
   c. have the same resources.
   d. distribute products through majority rule.

____ 7. Almost all economic sys...

## Reteach

Have students write two summary paragraphs–one on the basic economic questions and one on the types of economic systems.

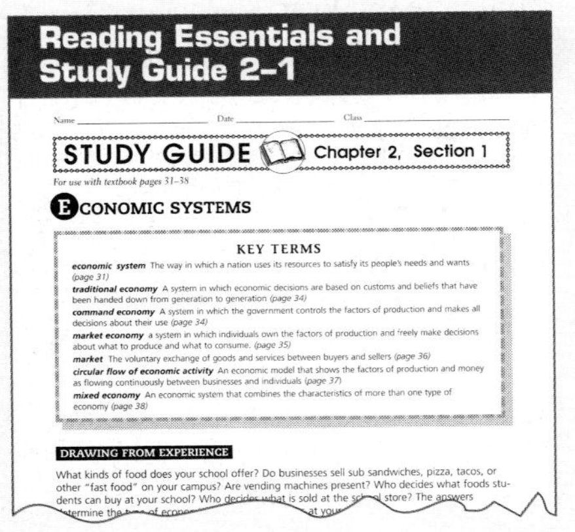

Reading Essentials and Study Guide 2-1

Name ______ Date ______ Class ______

**STUDY GUIDE** Chapter 2, Section 1

*For use with textbook pages 31–38*

ECONOMIC SYSTEMS

KEY TERMS

***economic system*** The way in which a nation uses its resources to satisfy its people's needs and wants *(page 31)*

***traditional economy*** A system in which economic decisions are based on customs and beliefs that have been handed down from generation to generation *(page 34)*

***command economy*** A system in which the government controls the factors of production and makes all decisions about their use *(page 34)*

***market economy*** a system in which individuals own the factors of production and freely make decisions about what to produce and what to consume. *(page 35)*

***market*** The voluntary exchange of goods and services between buyers and sellers *(page 36)*

***circular flow of economic activity*** An economic model that shows the factors of production and money as flowing continuously between businesses and individuals *(page 37)*

***mixed economy*** An economic system that combines the characteristics of more than one type of economy *(page 38)*

DRAWING FROM EXPERIENCE

What kinds of food does your school offer? Do businesses sell sub sandwiches, pizza, tacos, or other "fast food" on your campus? Are vending machines present? Who decides what foods students can buy at your school? Who decides what is sold at the school store? The answers determine the ...

## 4 Close

Have students prepare a two-minute oral report on which of the economic systems they would like to live in and why.

or too sick to work. Many fear that survival for these people would be difficult unless the government, churches, family members, or other organizations stepped in to provide goods and services.

__mixed economy:__ *system combining characteristics of more than one type of economy*

**Mixed System** A **mixed economy** combines basic elements of a pure market economy and a command economy. Most countries of the world have a mixed economy in which private ownership of property and individual decision making are combined with government intervention and regulations. In the United States, most decisions are made by individuals reacting as participants within the market. However, federal, state, and local governments make laws protecting private property and regulating certain areas of business. In Section 2, you'll learn more about the United States's mixed economy, and the role of government in it.

To summarize, consider why a society has one type of economic system and not another. The goals that individuals set for their society help determine their economic system. The amount of government involvement in allocating scarce resources also determines a society's economic system.

**Practice** and **assess** key skills with ***Skillbuilder Interactive Workbook, Level 2.***

## SECTION 1 Assessment

### Understanding Key Terms

1. **Define** economic system, traditional economy, command economy, market economy, market, circular flow of economic activity, mixed economy.

### Reviewing Objectives

2. What three questions must all economic systems answer?
3. **Graphic Organizer** In a chart like the one below, list the major types of economic systems and their differences.

| Type of System | Who Answers 3 Basic Questions? | Advantages | Disadvantages |
|---|---|---|---|
| | | | |
| | | | |

### Applying Economic Concepts

4. **Economic Systems** Identify and describe at least two instances in American history when the economy was predominantly a traditional system. Then identify and describe an instance in American history when the economy could have been labeled a command system.

### Critical Thinking Activity

5. **Synthesizing Information** Using **Figure 2.5** as a base, make a circular flow of economic activity reflecting your own life. Replace the general information shown on **Figure 2.5** with detailed specifics about your income, items you purchase, and so on. *For help in using graphs, see page xvi in the Economic Handbook.*



## SECTION 1 Assessment Answers

1. All definitions can be found in the Glossary.
2. What should be produced? How should it be produced? For whom should it be produced?
3. Traditional—Tradition answers questions; Adv: individuals know what is expected, strong family ties; Disadv: change is discouraged, inefficient production, few consumer choices. Command—Government leaders answer questions; Adv: resources rerouted quickly; Disadv: lack of incentives to work hard, lack of consumer choices. Market—Individuals answer questions; Adv: many economic freedoms, many consumer choices; Disadv: some people are not cared for
4. Traditional: period prior to the arrival of Europeans and the early colonial period; Command: the economy during World War II
5. Circular flow diagrams will differ.

## Critical Thinking Skills

# Making Comparisons

*When you make comparisons, you determine similarities and differences among ideas, objects, or events. Making comparisons is an important skill because it helps you choose among alternatives.*

- Identify or decide what will be compared.
- Determine a common area or areas in which comparisons can be drawn.
- Look for similarities and differences within these areas.

### Learning the Skill

To learn how to make comparisons, follow the steps listed on the left.

### Practicing the Skill

Read the passages below, then answer the questions.

> "*So long as mankind lived by raising crops and herding animals, there was not much need for measuring small units of time. The seasons were all important—to know when to expect the rain, the snow, the sun, the cold. Why bother with hours and minutes? Daylight was the only important time, the only time when men could work.*"
>
> —From Daniel J. Boorstin's *The Discoverers: A History of Man's Search to Know His World and Himself*, 1985

> "*Getting workers to work at the appointed clock hours was a recurring problem. In industrial cities, a steam whistle would blow at five in the morning to wrest people from their sleep. If that proved insufficient, employers would hire 'knockers,' men who went from flat to flat 'rapping on bedroom windows with long poles.' Sometimes the knockers even pulled on strings 'dangling from a window and attached to a worker's toe.'*"
>
> —From Jeremy Rifkin's *Time Wars: The Primary Conflict in Human History*, 1987

1. What is the topic of these passages?
2. How are the passages similar? Different?

### Application Activity

Survey your classmates about an issue in the news. Summarize the opinions and write a paragraph comparing the different opinions.

**Practice** and **assess** key skills with ***Skillbuilder Interactive Workbook, Level 2.***



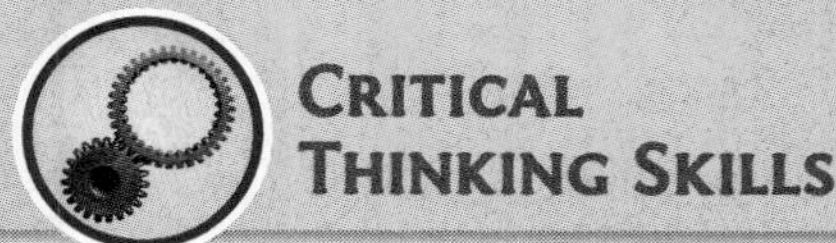


## Making Comparisons

Work through the **Learning the Skill** steps with students. Then practice the skill by applying it to the text on traditional, command, and market economic systems on pages 33–38. ASK: What will be compared? *(three economic systems)* In which common area can comparisons be drawn? *(how the economic systems answer the basic economic questions)* What similarities or differences can be seen in this common area? *The three economic systems answer the basic questions differently: traditional—through traditions; command—by government leaders; market—by individuals.* Conclude by asking students to complete the **Practicing the Skill** and **Application Activity** questions.

**Reinforcing Economic Skills 11**

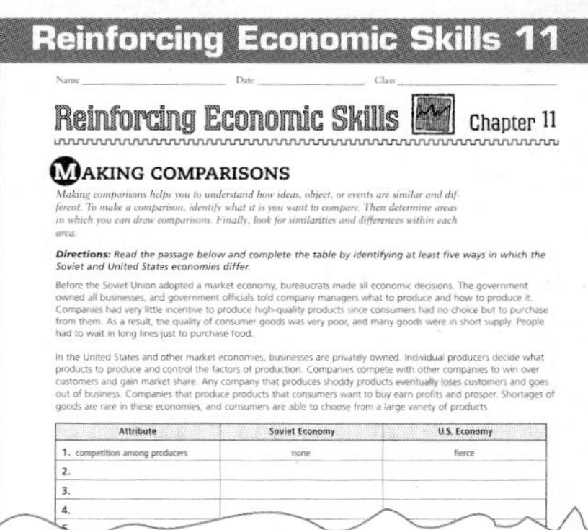

Name ______ Date ______ Class ______

Reinforcing Economic Skills Chapter 11

MAKING COMPARISONS

*Making comparisons helps you to understand how ideas, object, or events are similar and different. To make a comparison, identify what it is you want to compare. Then determine areas in which you can draw comparisons. Finally, look for similarities and differences within each area.*

***Directions:*** *Read the passage below and complete the table by identifying at least five ways in which the Soviet and United States economies differ.*

Before the Soviet Union adopted a market economy, bureaucrats made all economic decisions. The government owned all businesses, and government officials told company managers what to produce and how to produce it. Companies had very little incentive to produce high-quality products since consumers had no choice but to purchase from them. As a result, the quality of consumer goods was very poor, and many goods were in short supply. People had to wait in long lines just to purchase food.

In the United States and other market economies, businesses are privately owned. Individual producers decide what products to produce and control the factors of production. Companies compete with other companies to win over customers and gain market share. Any company that produces shoddy products eventually loses customers and goes out of business. Companies that produce products that consumers want to buy earn profits and prosper. Shortages of goods are rare in these economies, and consumers are able to choose from a large variety of products.

| Attribute | Soviet Economy | U.S. Economy |
|---|---|---|
| 1. competition among producers | none | fierce |
| 2. | | |
| 3. | | |
| 4. | | |

**GLENCOE TECHNOLOGY**

**Glencoe Skillbuilder Interactive Workbook, Level 2**

This interactive CD-ROM reinforces student mastery of essential social studies skills.

### Answers to Practicing the Skill

1. the relationship between time and work
2. Both excerpts talk about time. The first mentions that the sun was the chief measure of time when work was predominantly agricultural. The second talks about the methods used to get workers to work on time in industrial cities.

**Application Activity** Paragraphs will vary. Encourage students to accompany their paragraphs with a table showing survey results.

# 1 Focus

## Overview

Section 2 explains or describes the major components of a market economic system and how they apply to the American free enterprise system.

### BELLRINGER
**Motivational Activity**

Project **Daily Focus Transparency 7** and have students answer the questions.

This activity is also available as a blackline master.

**Daily Focus Transparency 7**

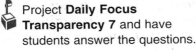

FOCUS ACTIVITIES
Transparency 7

THE MARKET ECONOMY

1. How many different businesses can you identify in this photograph? Who do you think owns them?
2. How would the local economy be affected if another appliance store opened across the street?

Daily Focus Transparencies

### Reader's Guide

Answers to the **Reading Objectives** questions are on page 44.

**Preteaching Vocabulary**

Read aloud the Glossary definitions of the **Terms to Know.** After reading each definition, call on volunteers to identify the term that was defined.

**Vocabulary PuzzleMaker**

SECTION 2

# Characteristics of the American Economy

## Reader's Guide

**Terms to Know**

- capitalism
- laissez-faire
- free enterprise system
- profit
- profit incentive
- private property
- competition

**Reading Objectives**

1. What is the role of government in our free enterprise economy?
2. How do freedom of enterprise and freedom of choice apply to the American economy?
3. What roles do private property, the profit incentive, and competition play in the American economy?

## Cover Story

*Business Week*, March 22, 1999

Ready to take the next step beyond Coke and Pepsi, orange and grape, tea and fruit drinks? Then how about some Wisdom or maybe a little Eros? Those aren't metaphysical thirst quenchers, but the real thing, examples of the latest trend in soft drinks: mystery concoctions that give little or no hint of what flavor is in the bottle.

Perhaps you wouldn't buy a soft drink called "Wisdom," but someone will. That's one of the characteristics of a market economy–freedom of choice. A seller can choose to make or not make a product, and you can choose to buy it or not.

In this section you'll learn that a pure market economic system has six major characteristics: (1) little or no government control, (2) freedom of enterprise, (3) freedom of choice, (4) private property, (5) the profit incentive, and (6) competition. These characteristics are interrelated, and all are present in the American economy to varying degrees.

### SECTION 2 RESOURCE MANAGER

**Reproducible Masters**

- Reproducible Lesson Plan 2–2
- Reading Essentials and Study Guide 2–2
- Guided Reading Activity 2–2
- Section Quiz 2–2
- Daily Focus Activity 7
- Daily Lecture Notes 2–2

**Multimedia**

- Daily Focus Transparency 7
- Vocabulary PuzzleMaker
- Interactive Tutor Self-Assessment Software
- ExamView® Pro Testmaker
- MindJogger Videoquiz
- Presentation Plus!

## Limited Role of Government

In his book *An Inquiry into the Nature and Causes of the Wealth of Nations*, economist Adam Smith in 1776 described a system in which government has little to do with a nation's economic activity. He said that individuals left on their own would work for their own self-interest. In doing so, they would be guided as if by an "invisible hand" to use resources efficiently and thus achieve the maximum good for society.

CAREERS
Environmental Health Inspector
Job Description
■ Ensures that food, water, and air meet government standards
■ Checks cleanliness and safety of food and beverages
Qualifications
■ Bachelor's degree in environmental health or biological sciences
■ Licensed by examining boards
Average Yearly Salary: $52,940
Job Outlook: Below average
—Occupational Outlook Handbook, 1998–99

Smith's version of the ideal economic system is called **capitalism,** another name for the market system. Pure capitalism has also been called a **laissez-faire** system. The French term means "let [people] do as they choose." A pure capitalist system is one in which the government lets people and businesses make their own economic decisions without government constraints. Capitalism as practiced in the United States today would be best defined as an economic system in which private individuals own the factors of production, but decide how to use them within legislated limits. See **Figure 2.6.**

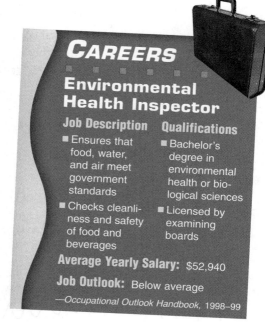

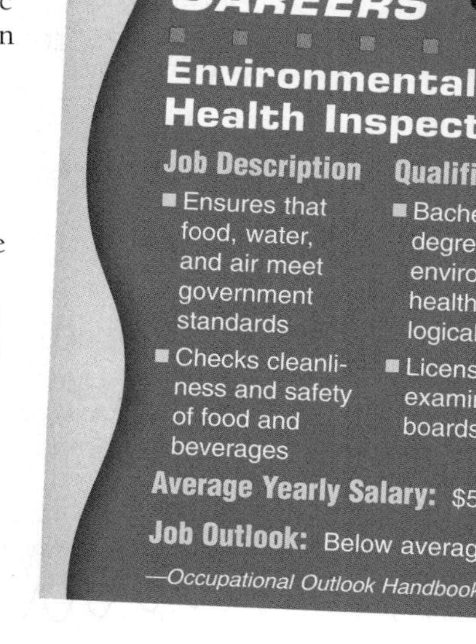


**capitalism:** *economic system in which private individuals own the factors of production and decide how to use them within legislated limits*

**laissez-faire:** *economic system in which the government minimizes its interference with the economy*

**FIGURE 2.6**

**Role of Government** The government acts as a provider of public services, such as maintaining our national parks. It also acts as protector in the form of food and drug inspection. ***List three more examples of how the government is involved in our economy.***

### Meeting Special Needs

**Attention Disorders** To help students grasp the main idea, have them create a word web as they read the section. Direct students to write the section title as the center of the web and to include important ideas in ovals around the center. Mention that supporting details for main ideas should be included in ovals connected to main idea ovals. By taking small pieces of information at a time and analyzing their importance, students with attention problems are better able to stay focused.

Refer to *Inclusion for the Social Studies Classroom Strategies and Activities* for students with different learning styles.



# 2 Teach

## Guided Practice

**L2 Understanding Ideas** Write the following on the board: "Freedom of Enterprise," "Freedom of Choice," "Private Property," "Profit Incentive," and "Competition." Call on volunteers to explain how government limits each of these in the American free enterprise system. Note responses under the appropriate heading. Then ask students to use the information to write a brief essay titled "Government Involvement in the American Economy."

### Daily Lecture Notes 2-2

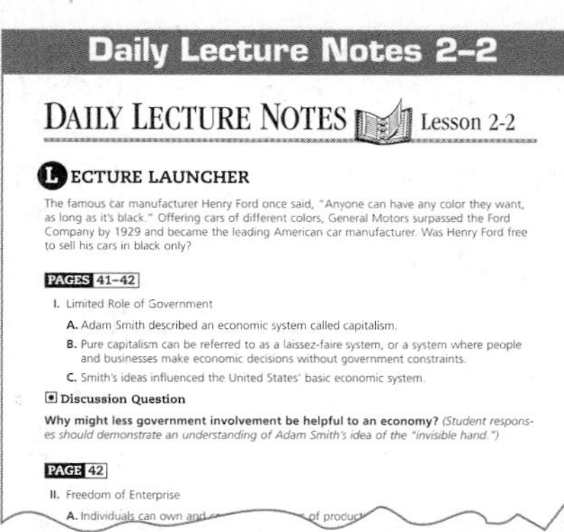
DAILY LECTURE NOTES Lesson 2-2

LECTURE LAUNCHER

The famous car manufacturer Henry Ford once said, "Anyone can have any color they want, as long as it's black." Offering cars of different colors, General Motors surpassed the Ford Company by 1929 and became the leading American car manufacturer. Was Henry Ford free to sell his cars in black only?

PAGES 41–42

I. Limited Role of Government

A. Adam Smith described an economic system called capitalism.

B. Pure capitalism can be referred to as a laissez-faire system, or a system where people and businesses make economic decisions without government constraints.

C. Smith's ideas influenced the United States' basic economic system.

**Discussion Question**

**Why might less government involvement be helpful to an economy?** *(Student responses should demonstrate an understanding of Adam Smith's idea of the "invisible hand.")*

PAGE 42

II. Freedom of Enterprise

A. Individuals can own and ... of produc...

### Visual Instruction FIGURE 2.6

**Answer:** *Answers may vary, but typical responses could include: Federal government regulates nation's money and banking system, workplace safety, and environmental pollution. It also provides social programs such as Social Security and Medicare. State and local governments play a role in education, job training, recreation, support for arts, care for elderly.*

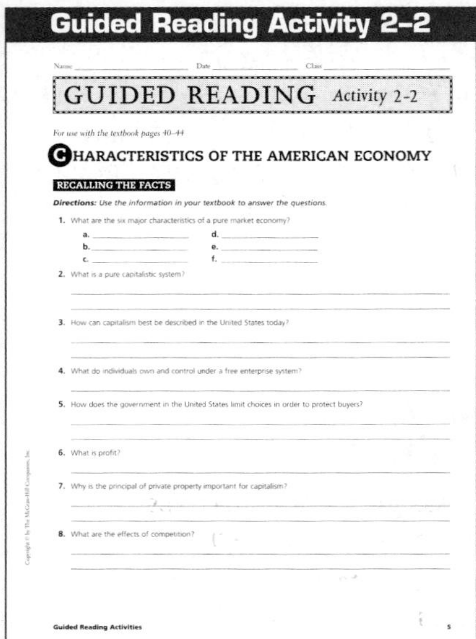

Guided Reading Activity 2-2

Name ______ Date ______ Class ______

GUIDED READING Activity 2-2

*For use with the textbook pages 40–44*

CHARACTERISTICS OF THE AMERICAN ECONOMY

RECALLING THE FACTS

***Directions:*** *Use the information in your textbook to answer the questions.*

1. What are the six major characteristics of a pure market economy?
   a. ______ d. ______
   b. ______ e. ______
   c. ______ f. ______
2. What is a pure capitalistic system?
3. How can capitalism best be described in the United States today?
4. What do individuals own and control under a free enterprise system?
5. How does the government in the United States limit choices in order to protect buyers?
6. What is profit?
7. Why is the principal of private property important for capitalism?
8. What are the effects of competition?

Copyright © by The McGraw-Hill Companies, Inc.

Guided Reading Activities 5

## Independent Practice

**L2 Writing Editorials** Ask students to write a newspaper editorial supporting or opposing the following statement: The government should play a greater role in the American economy.

Select students to read their editorials to the class. Use these readings as the starting point for a class discussion on the role of government in American free enterprise.

Smith's ideas influenced the Founders of the United States, who limited the role of government mainly to national defense and keeping the peace. Since the 1880s, however, the role of government—federal, state, and local—has increased significantly. Among other things, federal agencies regulate the quality of various foods and drugs, watch over the nation's money and banking system, inspect workplaces for hazardous conditions, and guard against damage to the environment. The federal government also uses tax money to provide social programs such as Social Security and Medicare. State and local governments have expanded their roles in such areas as education, job training, recreation, and care for the elderly.

**free enterprise system:** *economic system in which individuals own the factors of production and decide how to use them within legal limits; same as* capitalism

## Freedom of Enterprise

As well as *capitalist,* the American economy is also called a **free enterprise system.** This term emphasizes that individuals are free to own and control the factors of production. If you go into business for yourself, you may become rich selling your product. However, you may instead lose money, because you—or any entrepreneur—have no guarantee of success.

The government places certain legal restrictions on freedom of enterprise. For instance, just because you know how to fix cars does not mean that you can set up an automobile-repair business in your backyard. Zoning regulations, child-labor laws, hazardous waste disposal, and other regulations limit free enterprise to protect you *and* your neighbors.

## Freedom of Choice

Freedom of choice is the other side of freedom of enterprise. It means that buyers, not sellers, make the decisions about what should be produced. The success or failure of a good or service in the marketplace depends on individuals freely choosing what they want to buy. If a music company releases a new CD, but few people buy it, the music company most likely will not sign that particular group again. Buyers have signaled that they do not like that group.

Although buyers are free to make choices, the marketplace has become increasingly complex. The government has intervened in various areas of the economy to protect buyers. As shown in **Figure 2.7,** laws set safety standards for such things as toys, electric appliances, and automobiles. In industries dominated by just a few companies—such as public utilities selling natural gas or electricity—the government regulates the prices they may charge.



## Cooperative Learning

Organize students into groups to conduct a survey. Have groups interview fellow students, friends, neighbors, local business leaders, shoppers at a local mall, and so on to discover what the term *free enterprise* means to them. Have each group collate its findings and present them in an oral report to the class. Use the presentations as a starting point for a class discussion on why people might have different views of free enterprise.

 BLOCK SCHEDULING

**FIGURE 2.7**

**Freedom of Choice** Consumers in a market economy have the advantage of being able to choose among products. Laws require producers to make sure that the products consumers choose are safe ones. ***How do consumers' choices determine what will be produced?***

## Profit Incentive

When a person invests time, know-how, money, and other capital resources in a business, that investment is made with the idea of making a profit. **Profit** is the money left after all the costs of production have been paid, including wages, rents, interest, and taxes. The desire to make a profit is called the **profit incentive.** It is mainly this desire that motivates entrepreneurs to establish new businesses and produce new kinds of goods and services.

The risk of failing is also part of the free enterprise system. What happens when profits are *not* realized–when businesses fail? Losses are a signal to move resources elsewhere. Thus, the interaction of both profits and losses leads to an economy that is more efficient, adaptable to change, and continuously growing.

profit: *money left after all the costs of production—wages, rents, interest, and taxes—have been paid*

profit incentive: *desire to make money that motivates people to produce and sell goods and services*

## Private Property

One of the most important characteristics of capitalism is the existence of **private property,** or property that is held by individuals or groups rather than by the federal, state, or local governments. You as an individual are free to buy whatever you can afford, whether it is land, a business, an automobile, or baseball cards. You can also control how, when, and by whom your property is used. What are called the rights of property, however, are actually the rights of humans to risk investment, own productive assets, learn new ways of producing, and then to enjoy the benefits if these choices reap profits.

private property: *whatever is owned by individuals rather than by government*

The Founders of the United States recognized that such rights must not be violated, because these rights are the invisible engine for creating wealth and prosperity for all. The Constitution guarantees an owner's right to private property and its use. Thus, in principle, no level of government in the United States can seize or use private property, at least not without paying the owners.

## Extending the Content

**The Origins of Laissez-Faire** The economy most closely linked with the term *laissez-faire* is that of the United States. However, the term was first used by a group of French economists, known as the physiocrats, in the 1700s. They believed in free trade, and their slogan was *laissez-faire, laissez passez,* which, loosely translated, means "let us alone, let us pass unhindered." The term came to mean government noninterference in economic affairs through the writings of British economist Adam Smith.



### Visual Instruction FIGURE 2.7

**Answer:** *By making purchasing choices, consumers signal what they will or will not buy.*

## 3 Assess

### Meeting Lesson Objectives

Assign Section 2 Assessment as homework or an in-class activity.

Use **Interactive Tutor Self-Assessment** Software to review Section 2.

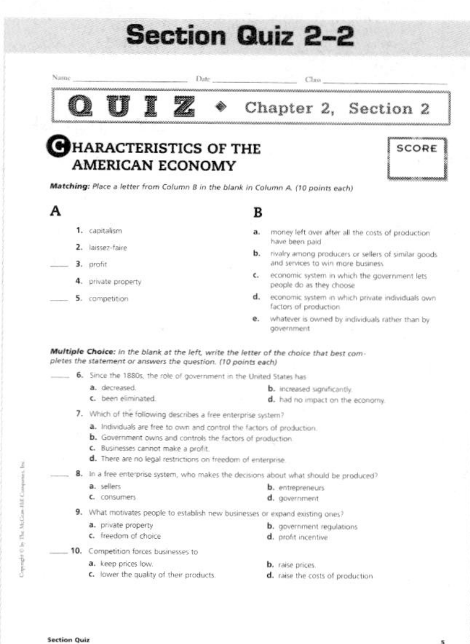

**Section Quiz 2-2**

Name ______ Date ______ Class ______

**QUIZ** ◆ Chapter 2, Section 2

**CHARACTERISTICS OF THE AMERICAN ECONOMY**

SCORE

***Matching:*** *Place a letter from Column B in the blank in Column A. (10 points each)*

**A**

**1.** capitalism
**2.** laissez-faire
____ **3.** profit
**4.** private property
____ **5.** competition

**B**

**a.** money left over after all the costs of production have been paid
**b.** rivalry among producers or sellers of similar goods and services to win more business
**c.** economic system in which the government lets people do as they choose
**d.** economic system in which private individuals own factors of production
**e.** whatever is owned by individuals rather than by government

***Multiple Choice:*** *In the blank at the left, write the letter of the choice that best completes the statement or answers the question. (10 points each)*

____ **6.** Since the 1880s, the role of government in the United States has
**a.** decreased. **b.** increased significantly.
**c.** been eliminated. **d.** had no impact on the economy.

**7.** Which of the following describes a free enterprise system?
**a.** Individuals are free to own and control the factors of production.
**b.** Government owns and controls the factors of production.
**c.** Businesses cannot make a profit.
**d.** There are no legal restrictions on freedom of enterprise.

____ **8.** In a free enterprise system, who makes the decisions about what should be produced?
**a.** sellers **b.** entrepreneurs
**c.** consumers **d.** government

**9.** What motivates people to establish new businesses or expand existing ones?
**a.** private property **b.** government regulations
**c.** freedom of choice **d.** profit incentive

____ **10.** Competition forces businesses to
**a.** keep prices low. **b.** raise prices.
**c.** lower the quality of their products. **d.** raise the costs of production

**Section Quiz** 5

# CHAPTER 2

SECTION 2, Pages 40–44

## Reteach

Ask students to imagine they have a friend in the People's Republic of China. Ask them to write a letter to their friend explaining the six characteristics of a market economy and how these characteristics relate to the American free enterprise system.

### Reading Essentials and Study Guide 2-2

Name ____________ Date ____________ Class ____________

**STUDY GUIDE** Chapter 2, Section 2

*For use with textbook pages 40–44*

**CHARACTERISTICS OF THE AMERICAN ECONOMY**

**KEY TERMS**

***capitalism*** An economic system in which private individuals own the factors of production and decide how to use them within certain legal limits *(page 41)*

***laissez-faire*** A system in which government lets people and businesses make their own decisions without putting controls and restrictions on them *(page 41)*

***free enterprise system*** System in which individuals are free to own the factors of production and decide how to use them within certain legal limits set by government; another name for capitalism *(page 42)*

***profit*** The money left after all the costs of production have been paid *(page 43)*

***profit incentive*** The desire to make a profit, which motivates business owners to produce and sell goods and services *(page 43)*

***private property*** Whatever is owned by individuals or groups rather than by government *(page 43)*

***competition*** Rivalry among producers or sellers of similar products to win more business *(page 44)*

**DRAWING FROM EXPERIENCE**

If you wanted to start your own business, what would it be? Would you hire some school friends and paint houses during summer vacation. Could you bake cookies in your kitchen at home and sell them to a local store? Perhaps you already are in business, cutting lawns or shoveling snow from driveways or parking lots. Your ability to make these choices is a result of the American free enterprise system.

This section focuses on the six characteristics of a pure market system and shows how they are present in the American economy.

**ORGANIZING YOUR THOUGHTS**

Use the diagram below to help you take notes as you read the summaries that follow. Think about the six characteristics of capitalism.

Limited ________.
Free ________ System
Freedom of ________.
Capitalism
________ Incentive
________ Incentive
Competition



Study Guide 11

# 4 Close

Ask students to discuss the following question: What makes the free enterprise system unique?

## Competition

**competition:** *rivalry among producers or sellers of similar goods and services to win more business*

In a free enterprise system, the lure of profits encourages **competition**—the rivalry among producers of similar products to win more business by offering the lowest prices or better quality. Effective competition requires a large number of independent sellers, which means that no single company can noticeably affect the price of a particular product or service. If one company raises its prices, potential customers can simply go to other sellers.

Competition leads to an efficient use of resources. How so? Businesses have to keep prices low enough to attract buyers, yet high enough to make a profit. This forces businesses to keep their costs of production as low as possible.

For competition to exist, barriers to enter and exit from industries must be weak. Businesses must be free to expand into other industries. For the most part, the United States has weak barriers to entry and exit. Yet some industries have tougher barriers to entry. For example, a person cannot become a physician until he or she has received a license from a state government.

**Practice** and **assess** key skills with ***Skillbuilder Interactive Workbook, Level 2.***

## SECTION 2 Assessment

### Understanding Key Terms

1. **Define** capitalism, laissez-faire, free enterprise system, profit, profit incentive, private property, competition.

### Reviewing Objectives

2. What is the role of government in our free enterprise economy?
3. How do freedom of enterprise and freedom of choice apply to the American economy?
4. **Graphic Organizer** Create a chart like the one in the next column to summarize the roles that profit incentive, private property, and competition play in the American economy.

| Characteristic | Definition | Role in Capitalism |
|---|---|---|
| | | |

### Applying Economic Concepts

5. **Competition** Describe a situation in which a lack of competition caused you to pay more for a good or service.

### Critical Thinking Activity

6. **Synthesizing Information** Shoe Store A offers a pair of high-top sneakers for $48, whereas a competitor—Shoe Store B—offers the same shoe at 25 percent off their regular price of $62. From which store should you buy the shoes? *For help in understanding percentages, see page xix in the Economic Handbook.*



## SECTION 2 Assessment Answers

1. All definitions can be found in the Glossary.
2. Government plays a limited role.
3. Freedom of enterprise: Americans may establish businesses, decide production methods and levels, and take risks in seeking profits. Freedom of choice: American consumers are free to make choices and, therefore, they—not sellers—make the ultimate decisions about what should be produced.
4. Profit Incentive: motivates entrepreneurs to establish new businesses, expand existing ones, and change kinds of goods and services produced; Private Property: individuals free to buy whatever they can afford; also control how, when, and by whom property is used; Competition: leads to an efficient use of resources
5. Answers will vary.
6. from Shoe Store B, because 25 percent off $62 ($46.50) is cheaper than $48

# People & Perspectives

- Born in Kirkaldy, County Fife, Scotland
- Called the founder of modern economics
- Teacher at the University of Glasgow
- Lectured and wrote on moral philosophy
- Wrote *An Inquiry into the Nature and Causes of the Wealth of Nations* (1776)

## Adam Smith

*ECONOMIST (1723–1790)*

In *An Inquiry into the Nature and Causes of the Wealth of Nations,* Adam Smith argues against government interference in the marketplace. He believed that individuals, seeking profit, end up benefiting society as a whole.

*"[E]very individual, therefore, endeavours as much as he can [to direct his resources toward his own business] so that its produce may be of the greatest value; every individual . . . neither intends to promote the public interest, nor knows how much he is promoting it. . . . He intends only his own gain, and he is in this, as in many other cases, led by an invisible hand to promote an end which was no part of his intention. . . . By pursuing his own interest he frequently promotes that of the society more effectually than when he really intends to promote it."*

Smith criticized government officials who had "the folly" to attempt to direct people in what they should produce. He believed that no single person could direct resources more efficiently than individuals watching out for their own self-interest.

*"It is the maxim of every prudent master of a family, never to attempt to make at home what it will cost him more to make than to buy. The ta[i]lor does not attempt to make his own shoes, but buys them of the shoemaker. The shoemaker does not attempt to make his own clothes, but employs a ta[i]lor. The farmer attempts to make neither the one nor the other, but employs those different [craftsmen]. All of them find it [in their best interests] to employ their whole industry in a way in which they have some advantage over their neighbours, and to purchase . . . whatever else they have occasion for."*

### *Checking for Understanding*

1. **How does an "invisible hand" directing an individual's economic choices benefit society as a whole?**
2. **In Smith's opinion, why should people not attempt to "employ their resources" in many industries?**

45



## Background

While working as a professor in Scotland, Adam Smith developed a close friendship with the Scottish philosopher David Hume. Hume's ideas greatly influenced Smith's thinking on philosophy and economics. The work of the French economists known as the physiocrats also contributed greatly to Smith's ideas on economics.

# Teach

As students read the excerpts from *The Wealth of Nations,* have them note how Smith suggests that the "invisible hand" of self-interest benefits not only the individual, but also society at large. Then point out that Smith's ideas still wield considerable influence among economists today.

## Did You Know

Adam Smith was very impressed with the American colonies. He wrote that they seemed "very likely to become one of the most formidable [nations] that ever was in the world."

## Answers to *Checking for Understanding*

1. Smith suggests that the invisible hand of self-interest often promotes the good of society.
2. Smith notes that it is in individuals' best interests to put all their resources into what they are best at and, with the profits that they make, buy the things they cannot make.

# 1 Focus

## Overview

**Section 3** explains or describes the major goals of the United States economy and the benefits and responsibilities of individuals in a free enterprise system.

**BELLRINGER**
**Motivational Activity**

Project **Daily Focus Transparency 8** and have students answer the questions.

This activity is also available as a blackline master.

**Daily Focus Transparency 8**

FOCUS ACTIVITIES
Transparency 8

NATIONAL ECONOMIC GOALS

*We, the People of the United States, in order to form a more perfect Union, establish justice, insure domestic tranquility, provide for the common defense, promote the general welfare, and secure the blessings of liberty to ourselves and our posterity, do ordain and establish this Constitution for the United States of America.*

*—the Preamble to the Constitution of the United States*

1. Which goal or goals in the Preamble do you think include economic goals?
2. How might the economic goal of economic growth be related to the use of the word "posterity" in the Preamble?

Daily Focus Transparencies

### Reader's Guide

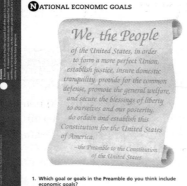

Answers to the **Reading Objectives** questions are on page 49.

**Preteaching Vocabulary**

Ask students to use the Glossary to find definitions of the **Terms to Know.** Then have them use the terms correctly in sentences.

**Vocabulary PuzzleMaker**

SECTION 3

# The Goals of the Nation

### Reader's Guide

**Terms to Know**
- economic efficiency
- economic equity
- standard of living
- economic growth

**Reading Objectives**
1. What are the major goals of a market economy?
2. How can people balance economic rights with economic responsibilities?

## Cover Story

**Preamble to the Constitution of the United States**

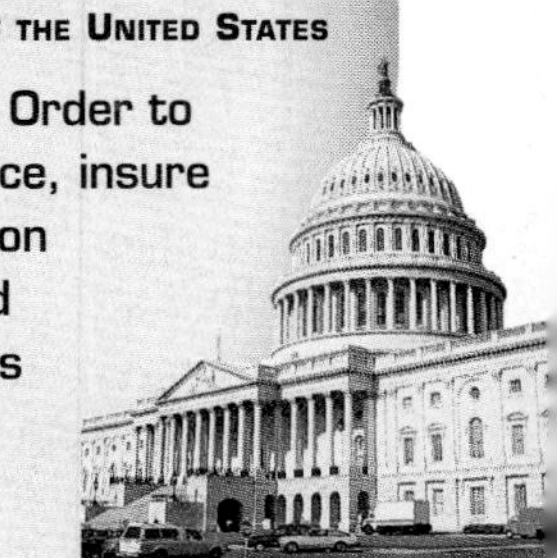

**We, the people of the United States, in Order to form a more perfect Union, establish Justice, insure domestic Tranquility, provide for the common defense, promote the general Welfare, and secure the Blessings of Liberty to ourselves and our Posterity, do ordain and establish this Constitution for the United States.**

Nations have values, and they set goals for themselves based on those values. The United States is no exception. Its goals are evident in the law of the land—the Constitution of the United States—as well as in its government policies and in the actions of people like you. In this section you'll learn how the American economy strives to "promote the general Welfare."

## Goals of Free Enterprise

The United States has a free enterprise, or capitalist, system. Therefore, the major characteristics of a market economy should be evident in its goals. Among the national goals of Americans are freedom, efficiency, equity, security, stability, and growth. Although these goals have ethical, social, and religious elements, let's focus on their economic implications instead.

**Economic Freedom** The goal of economic freedom is to allow each member of society to make choices. Americans have the highest degree of freedom in the world to start their own businesses, to own private property, to make decisions in the marketplace,

## SECTION 3 RESOURCE MANAGER

**Reproducible Masters**
- Reproducible Lesson Plan 2–3
- Reading Essentials and Study Guide 2–3
- Guided Reading Activity 2–3
- Section Quiz 2–3
- Daily Focus Activity 8
- Daily Lecture Notes 2–3

**Multimedia**
- Daily Focus Transparency 8
- Vocabulary PuzzleMaker
- Interactive Tutor Self-Assessment Software
- ExamView® Pro Testmaker
- MindJogger Videoquiz
- Presentation Plus!

## STEP C Creating an Economic Model

Use the results of your tests to draw a graph (bar, circle, or line) visually showing which item came out ahead of the others. Draw your graph(s) on poster board to use in a presentation to the rest of the class.

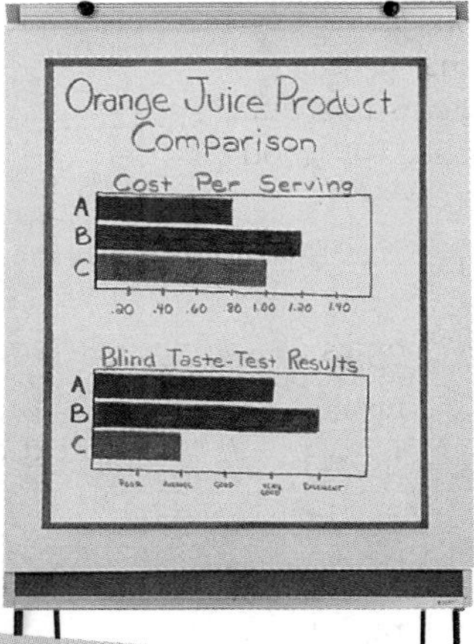


4. Now you'll devise a product-comparison test to use on the three versions of each item. Scan copies of *Consumer Reports* tests to get an idea of what categories to use in your tests—cost per unit, durability, flavor, aftertaste, ease of use, reliability, overall score, and so on.

5. Within your group, perform the product-comparison tests. You may want to include the rest of the class in a blind test to get a larger response.

## STEP D Lab Report Analysis

Study the graph that you created in step C, then answer the questions below.

1. How wide was the price difference among competing brands of resources?
2. What other factors influenced your choice of items to use in your product?
3. Were you surprised by the results of your tests? Explain.

# 3 Assess

Have students answer the **Lab Report Analysis** questions in Step D.

# 4 Close

Have students discuss how the exercise conducted in the Economics Lab might help business efficiency and profit-making potential.

### ? Did You Know

After businesses have decided on the materials to use in their products, they then test consumer responses to those products. Business representatives randomly select people for focus groups. These groups then take part in blind tastings or surveys. Finally, the business representatives collate results to evaluate consumer response.

### Answers to Lab Report Analysis

Answers will vary. In a review session of this Economics Lab, have students compare and discuss their responses.

# UNIT 2 Resource Manager

The following transparencies may be used at any time during Unit 2.

## Economic Forms and Financial Pages Transparencies

### Transparency 10

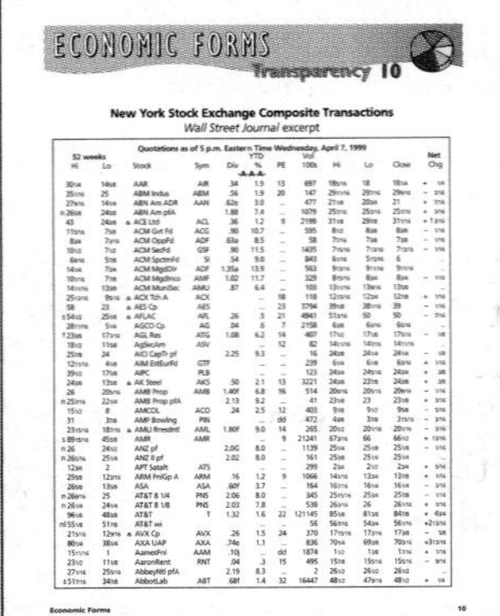

ECONOMIC FORMS
Transparency 10

New York Stock Exchange Composite Transactions
*Wall Street Journal excerpt*

### Transparency 11

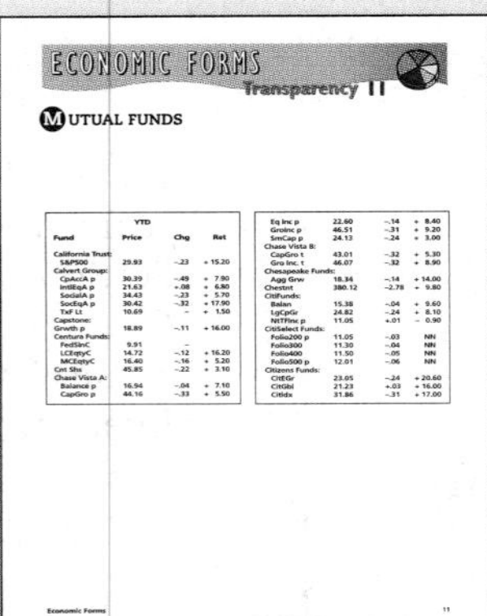

ECONOMIC FORMS
Transparency 11

MUTUAL FUNDS

### Transparency 12

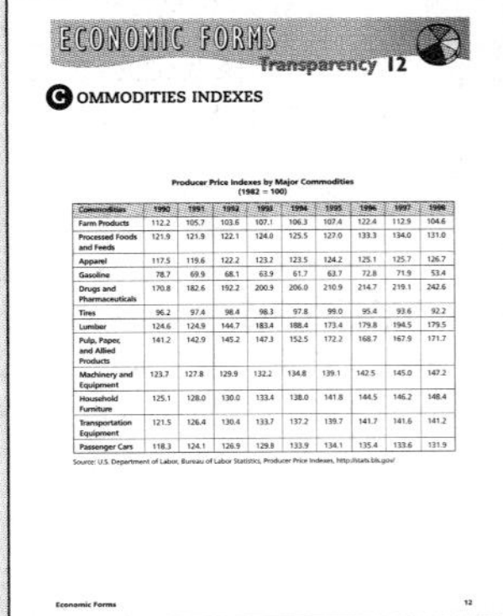

ECONOMIC FORMS
Transparency 12

COMMODITIES INDEXES

### Transparency 15

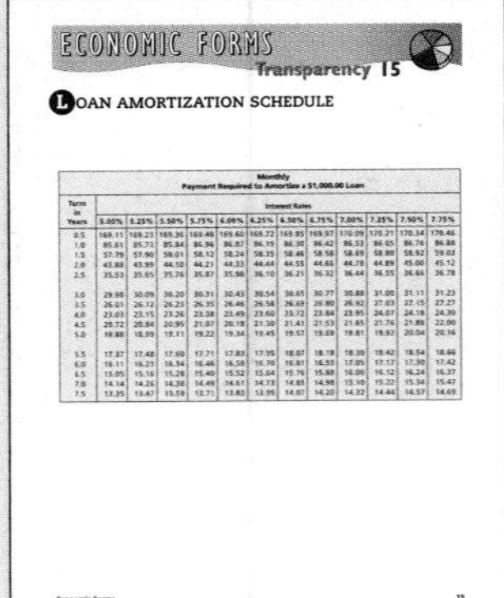

ECONOMIC FORMS
Transparency 15

LOAN AMORTIZATION SCHEDULE

## Economic Concepts Transparencies

### Transparency 2

ECONOMIC CONCEPTS
Transparency 2

OPPORTUNITY COST & TRADE-OFFS



### Transparency 6

ECONOMIC CONCEPTS
Transparency 6

EXCHANGE, MONEY, AND INTERDEPENDENCE



### Transparency 10

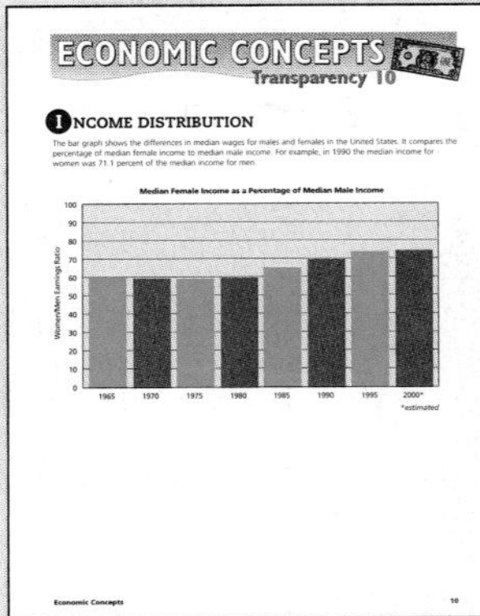

ECONOMIC CONCEPTS
Transparency 10

INCOME DISTRIBUTION



### Transparency 12

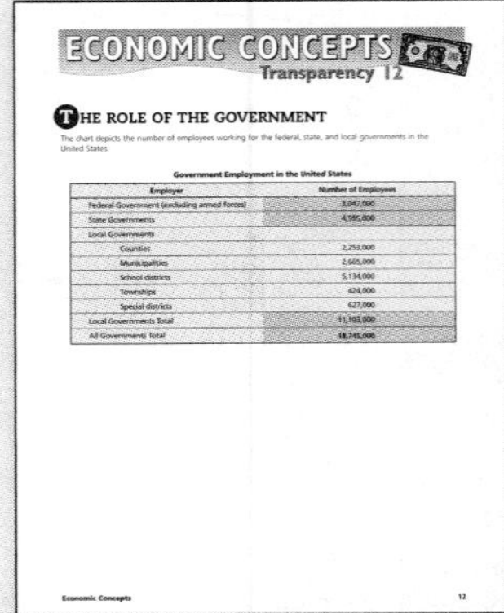

ECONOMIC CONCEPTS
Transparency 12

THE ROLE OF THE GOVERNMENT

Government Employment in the United States

## Real-World Economics

Have your students learn about investing and managing their financial futures by participating in the exciting simulation **The Stock Market Game**™. See page T24 for more information.

Strengthen students' research, cooperation, presentation, and critical thinking skills by having them compete in the **Fed Challenge**. See page T26 for further information.

## Additional Glencoe Resources for This Unit

- Nightly Business Report *Economics & You* Video Program
- Economic Survival: A Financial Simulation
- Interactive Economics! Software

# UNIT 2 Resource Manager

## Assessment and Evaluation

Unit 2 Test Form A

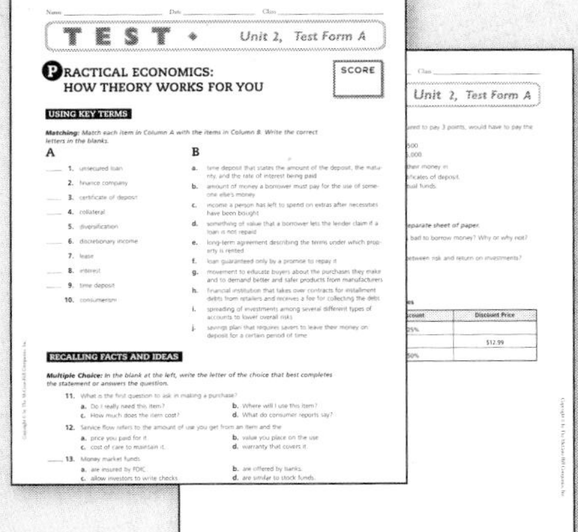

Unit 2 Test Form B

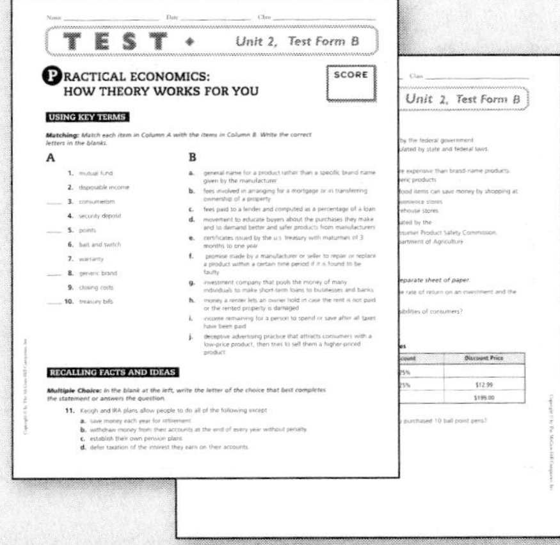

**Use the following tools to easily assess student learning:**

- Performance Assessment Strategies and Activities
- Section Quizzes
- Chapter and Unit Tests
- ExamView® Pro Testmaker
- Interactive Tutor Self-Assessment Software
- SAT I/II Test Practice
- MindJogger Videoquiz
- ett.glencoe.com

## Application and Enrichment

Economics Laboratory 3

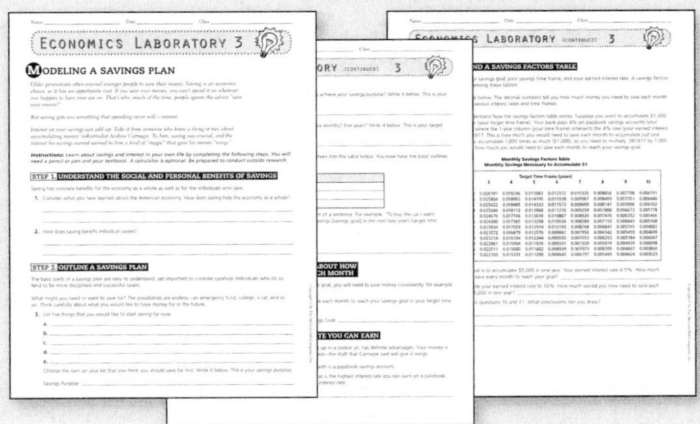

*Business Week* Focus on the New Economy

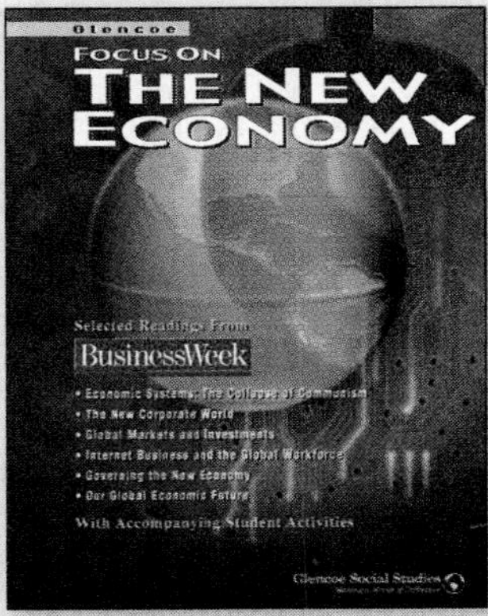

## ECONOMICS Online

*Glencoe's Web sites provide additional resources. All essential content is covered in the Student Edition.*

*ett.glencoe.com*

Visit the **Economics Today and Tomorrow** Web site for Chapter Overviews, Textbook Updates, Student Web Activities, Web Activity Lesson Plans, and Self-Check Quizzes.

*socialstudies.glencoe.com*

Visit the **Glencoe Social Studies** Web site for additional social studies activities, updates, and links to other sites.

**Glencoe's *Guide to Using the Internet*** provides an introduction to many of the current Internet technologies, social studies and professional resources, and teaching strategies.

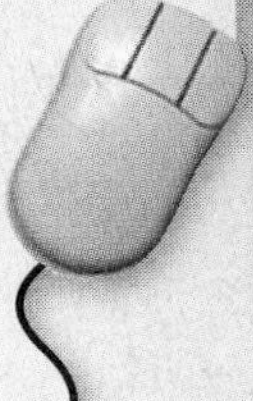

## Unit Objectives

After studying this unit, students will be able to:

- **Evaluate** the individual role of the consumer.
- **Analyze** buying decisions.
- **Understand** how to balance a budget.
- **Learn** the value of saving and investing money.

## Unit Overview

The four chapters in **Unit 2** address how economic theory applies to everyday buying and budgeting.

**Chapter 3** explains disposable and discretionary income, the role of advertising, and consumers' rights.

**Chapter 4** explains what causes families to go into debt and how to manage debt wisely.

**Chapter 5** discusses responsible budgeting for food, clothing, housing, and transportation.

**Chapter 6** describes options for saving and investing.

### 00:00 Out of Time?

If time does not permit teaching each chapter in this unit, you may use the **Audio Program** that includes a 1-page activity and a 1-page test for each chapter.

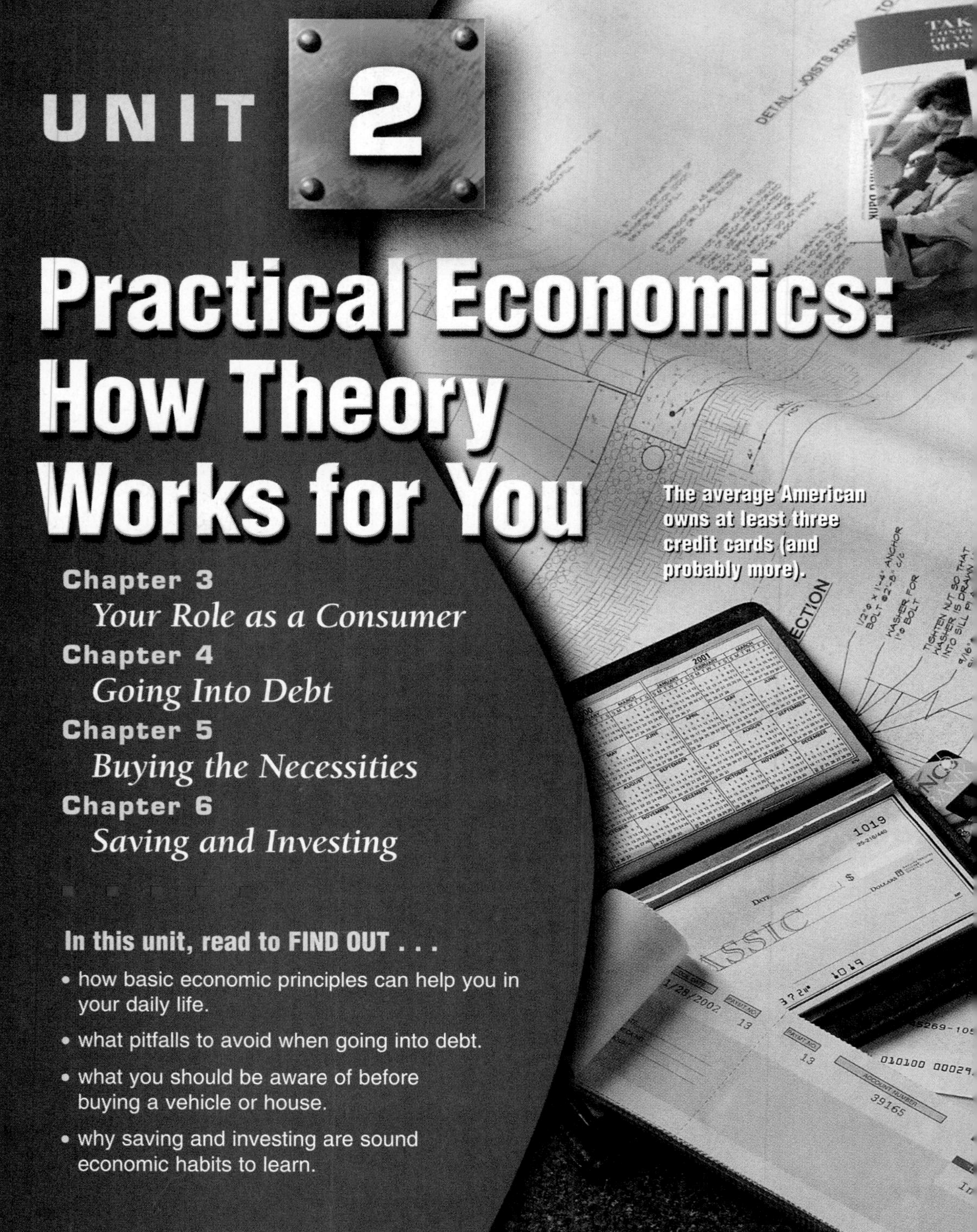

# UNIT 2

# Practical Economics: How Theory Works for You

The average American owns at least three credit cards (and probably more).



**In this unit, read to FIND OUT . . .**

- how basic economic principles can help you in your daily life.
- what pitfalls to avoid when going into debt.
- what you should be aware of before buying a vehicle or house.
- why saving and investing are sound economic habits to learn.

## ECONOMIC SIMULATION

**Grocery Purchasing Options** Encourage students to imagine that they live in a community that has no grocery supermarket. Then organize students into several groups. Ask groups to research traditional grocery supermarkets, consumer food cooperatives, supermarkets that specialize in organic foods, and a computerized grocery delivery service—Peapod®, for example. Have groups use their findings to write a report recommending a grocery service that suits the needs of their community.

## *Introducing* UNIT 2

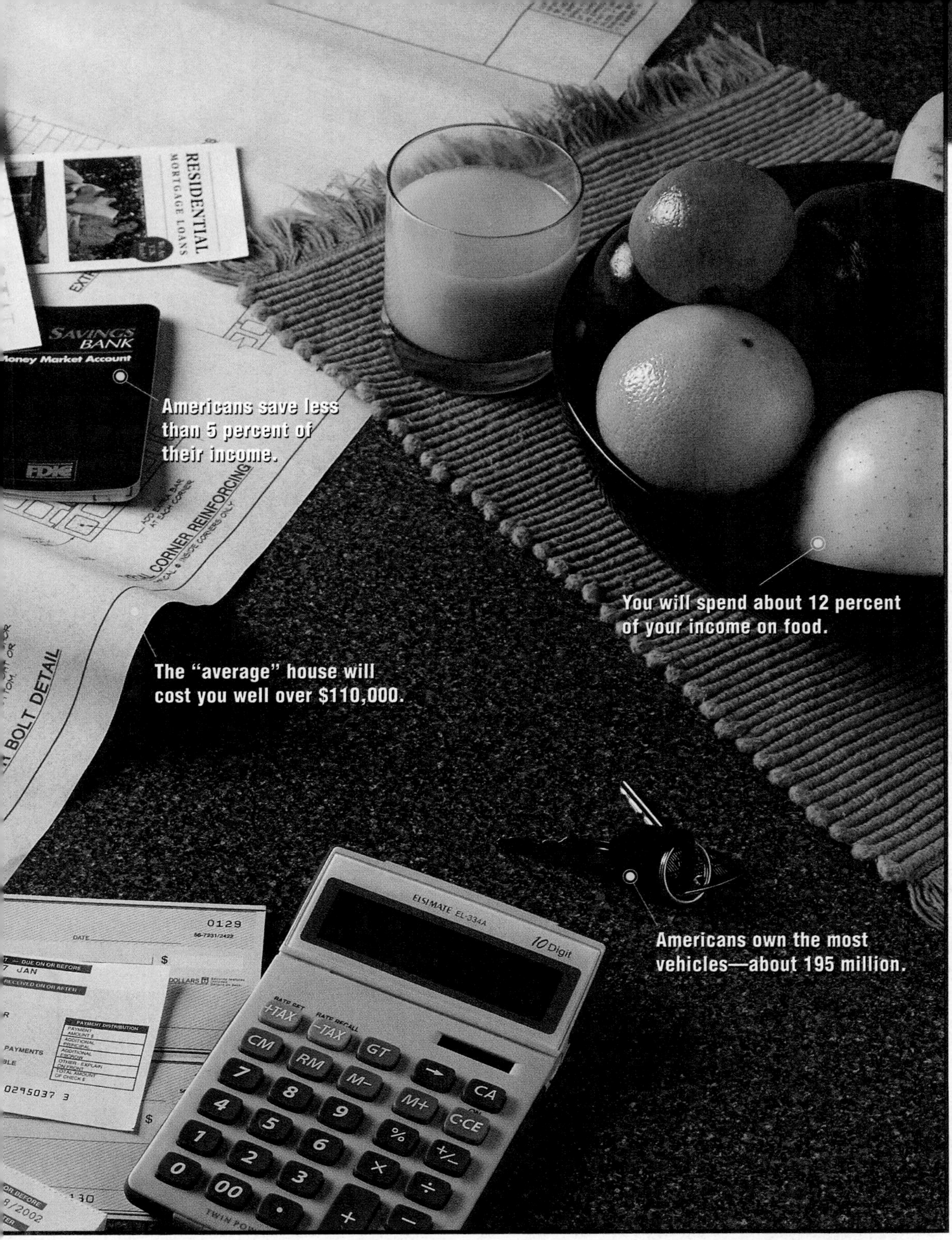
Americans save less than 5 percent of their income.
You will spend about 12 percent of your income on food.
The "average" house will cost you well over $110,000.
Americans own the most vehicles—about 195 million.
RESIDENTIAL MORTGAGE LOANS
SAVINGS BANK
Money Market Account

### Making It Relevant

Briefly discuss each of the following questions with students: How much do you think the average family spends on groceries each week? How many credit cards do you think the average American holds? How many cars does the average American family own? Do you compare prices when you shop? Do factors other than price influence your buying choices? How much of your income do you save?

Conclude the discussion by mentioning that while these questions may not seem connected, they all address some aspect of consumer behavior—the topic of Unit 2.

### BusinessWeek ONLINE

To find up-to-date news and analysis on the economy, business, technology, markets, entrepreneurs, investments, and finance, have students search feature articles and special reports on the *Business Week* Web site. www.businessweek.com

### EXTRA CREDIT PROJECT

Have students work in small groups to conduct research on advertising. Encourage each group to research a different aspect of this topic—the history of advertising in the United States, the history of advertising in Europe, the history of print advertising, techniques in television advertising, new developments in advertising, and so on. Suggest that groups present their findings in an illustrated report.

# CHAPTER 3 Resource Manager

## Teaching Transparency

### Economic Concepts Transparency 12

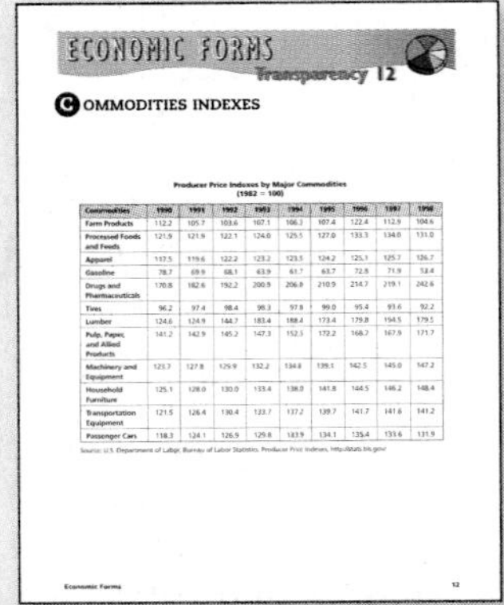

ECONOMIC FORMS Transparency 12

COMMODITIES INDEXES

Producer Price Indexes by Major Commodities

## Application and Enrichment

### Enrichment Activity 3

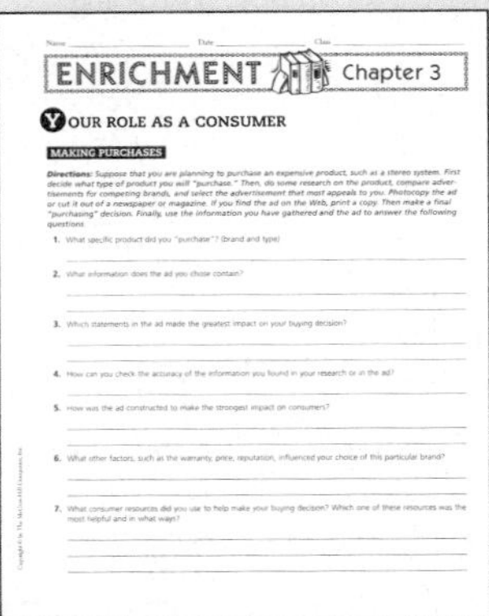

ENRICHMENT Chapter 3

YOUR ROLE AS A CONSUMER

MAKING PURCHASES

### Consumer Applications Activity 3

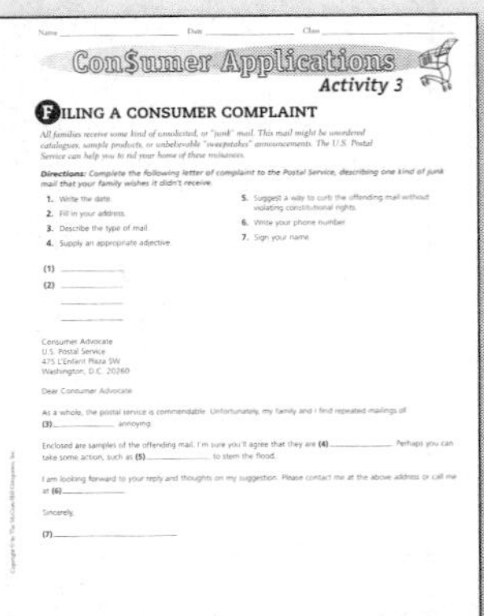

Con$umer Applications Activity 3

FILING A CONSUMER COMPLAINT

### Free Enterprise Activity 5

FREE ENTERPRISE ACTIVITY 5

NEEDS, WANTS, MARKETERS

## Application and Enrichment

### Cooperative Learning Simulations and Problems 9

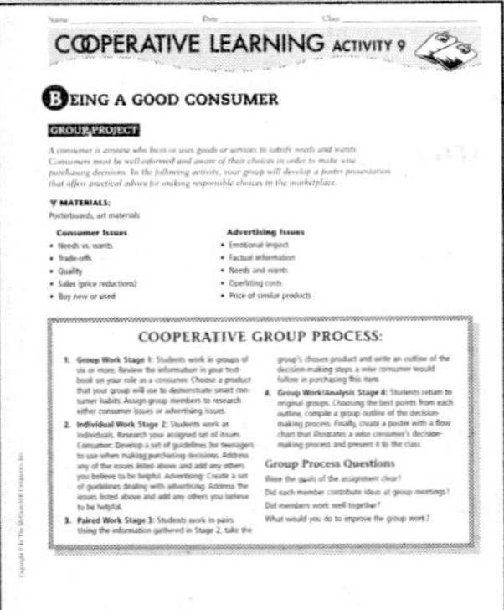

COOPERATIVE LEARNING ACTIVITY 9

BEING A GOOD CONSUMER

COOPERATIVE GROUP PROCESS:

### Primary and Secondary Source Reading 3

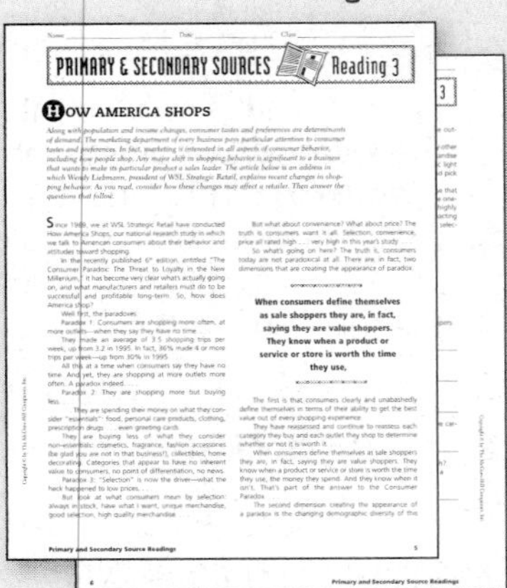

PRIMARY & SECONDARY SOURCES Reading 3

HOW AMERICA SHOPS

### Math Practice for Economics Activity 9

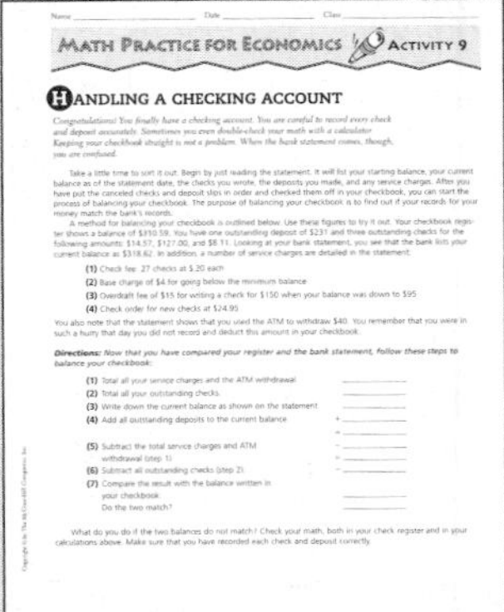

MATH PRACTICE FOR ECONOMICS ACTIVITY 9

HANDLING A CHECKING ACCOUNT

### Economic Cartoons Activity 7

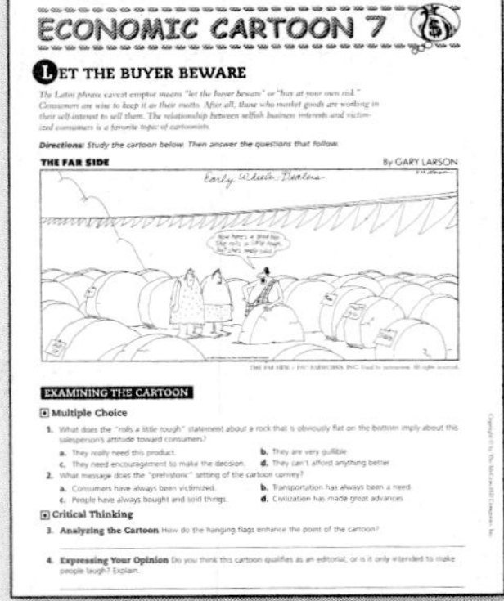

ECONOMIC CARTOON 7

LET THE BUYER BEWARE

## Review and Reinforcement

### Critical Thinking Activity 3

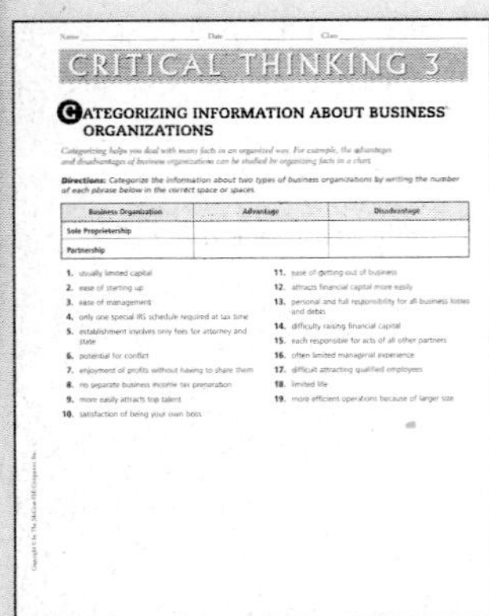

CRITICAL THINKING 3

CATEGORIZING INFORMATION ABOUT BUSINESS ORGANIZATIONS

### Reteaching Activity 3

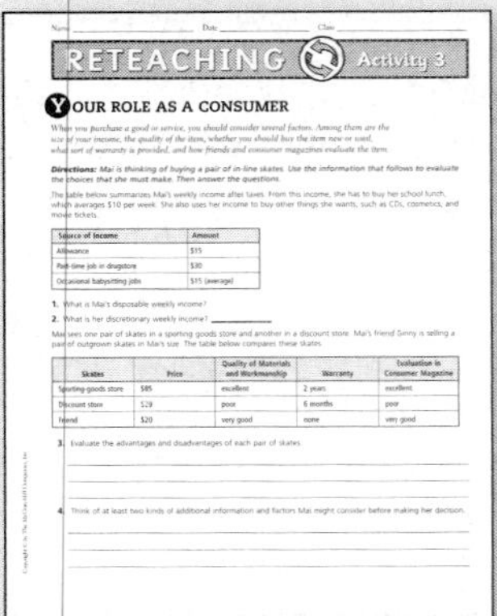

RETEACHING Activity 3

YOUR ROLE AS A CONSUMER

### Economic Vocabulary Activity 3

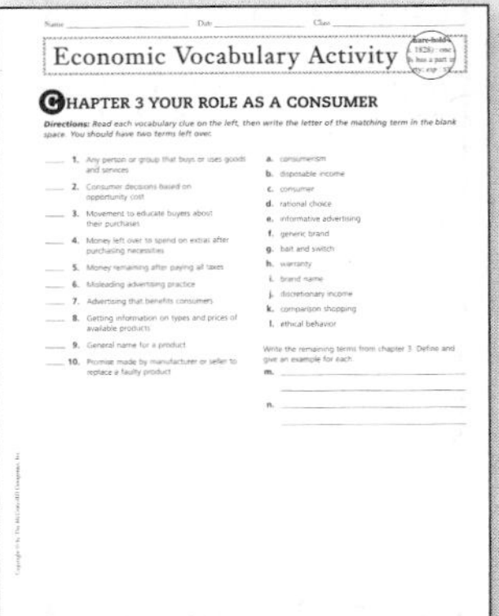

Economic Vocabulary Activity

CHAPTER 3 YOUR ROLE AS A CONSUMER

### Reinforcing Economic Skills 18

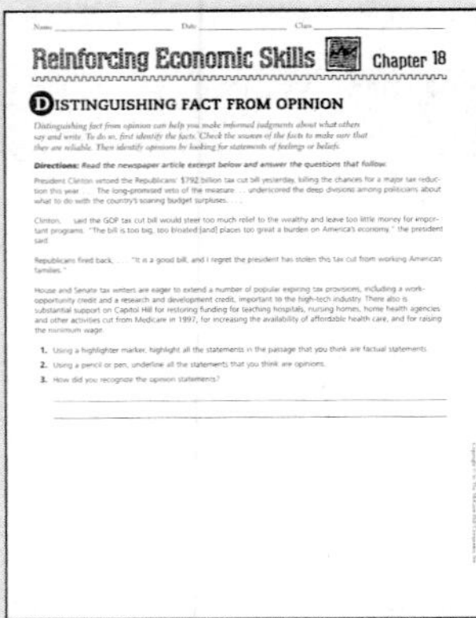

Reinforcing Economic Skills Chapter 18

DISTINGUISHING FACT FROM OPINION

# CHAPTER 3 Resource Manager

## Assessment and Evaluation

Chapter 3 Test Form A

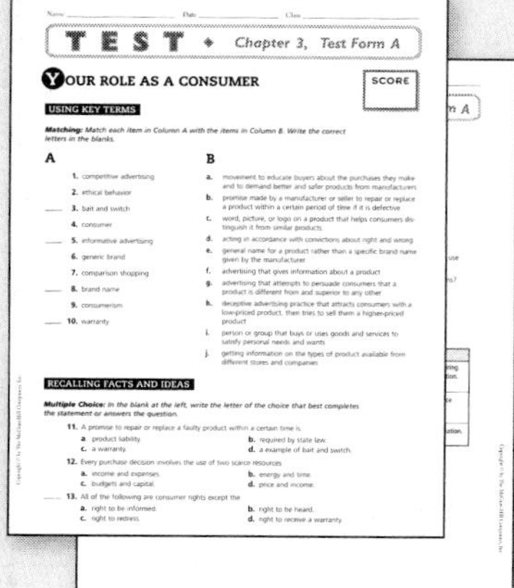
TEST ◆ Chapter 3, Test Form A

YOUR ROLE AS A CONSUMER

Chapter 3 Test Form B

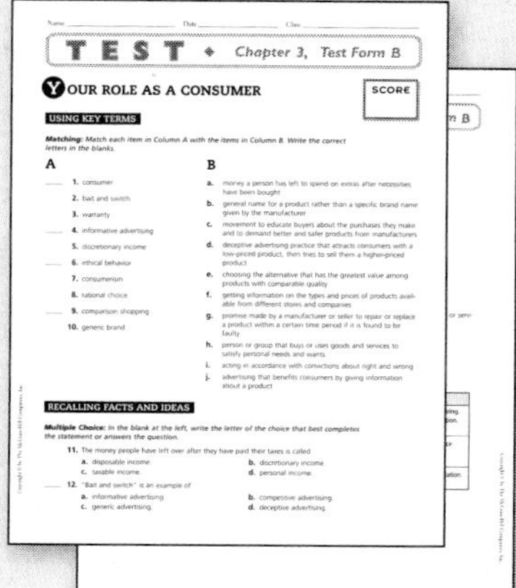
TEST ◆ Chapter 3, Test Form B

YOUR ROLE AS A CONSUMER

Performance Assessment Activity 6

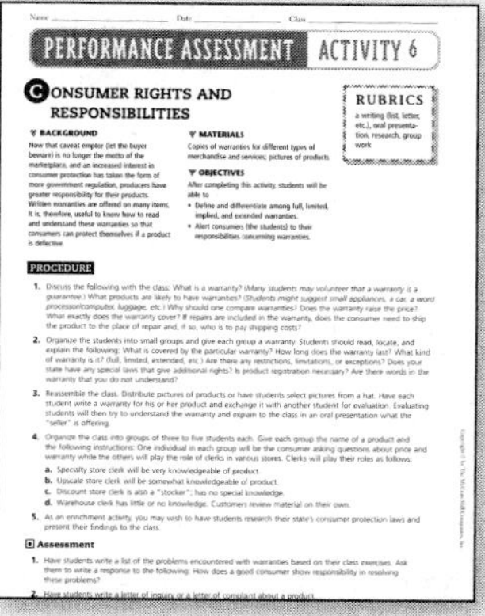
PERFORMANCE ASSESSMENT ACTIVITY 6

CONSUMER RIGHTS AND RESPONSIBILITIES

ExamView® Pro Testmaker

## Technology and Multimedia

Vocabulary PuzzleMaker Software

Interactive Tutor Self-Assessment Software

ExamView® Pro Testmaker

NBR *Economics & You* Video Program (English/Spanish)

Presentation Plus!

Glencoe Skillbuilder Interactive Workbook CD-ROM, Level 2

Interactive Lesson Planner

MindJogger Videoquiz

Interactive Economics! CD-ROM

Audio Program (English or Spanish)

You and your students can visit ett.glencoe.com—the Web site companion to **Economics Today and Tomorrow.** This innovative integration of electronic and print media offers your students a wealth of opportunities. The student text directs students to the Web site for the following options:

- **Chapter Overviews**
- **Student Web Activities**
- **Self-Check Quizzes**
- **Textbook Updates**

Answers are provided for you in the **Web Activity Lesson Plan.** Additional Web resources and Interactive Puzzles are also available.

Use the Glencoe Web site for additional resources. All essential content is covered in the Student Edition.

## Spanish Resources

Spanish Economic Concepts Transparency 12

Spanish Vocabulary Activity 3

Spanish Reteaching Activity 3

Spanish Section Quizzes for Chapter 3

Spanish Chapter 3 Audio Program, Activity, and Test

## Additional Resources

### Reading for the Student

Day, Nancy. *Advertising: Information or Manipulation?* Berkeley Heights, NJ: Enslow Publishers, 1999. Analysis of the methods used to persuade consumers to buy.

### Multimedia Material

*Your Consumer Rights,* 1996. Learning Seed, 330 Telser Road, Lake Zurich, IL 60047. VHS. Explains how consumers' rights are protected in the marketplace.

# CHAPTER 3 Resource Manager

## Section Resources

| Reading Objectives | Reproducible Resources | Technology/Multimedia Resources |
|---|---|---|
| **Section 1**<br>**Consumption, Income, and Decision Making**<br>• What is the difference between disposable and discretionary income?<br>• What three considerations should govern your decision making as a consumer? | Reproducible Lesson Plan 3-1<br>Daily Lecture Notes 3-1<br>Guided Reading Activity 3-1<br>Reading Essentials and Study Guide 3-1<br>Daily Focus Activity 27<br>Section Quiz 3-1*<br>Reinforcing Economic Skills 18 | Daily Focus Transparency 27<br>Vocabulary PuzzleMaker<br>Interactive Tutor Self-Assessment Software<br>MindJogger Videoquiz<br>NBR's *Economics & You**<br>Presentation Plus!<br>ExamView® Pro Testmaker |
| **Section 2**<br>**Buying Principles or Strategies**<br>• What trade-offs occur when you are gathering information?<br>• What forms of advertising exist?<br>• How can you learn to practice comparison shopping? | Reproducible Lesson Plan 3-2<br>Daily Lecture Notes 3-2<br>Guided Reading Activity 3-2<br>Reading Essentials and Study Guide 3-2<br>Daily Focus Activity 28<br>Section Quiz 3-2* | Daily Focus Transparency 28<br>Vocabulary PuzzleMaker<br>Interactive Tutor Self-Assessment Software<br>MindJogger Videoquiz<br>Presentation Plus!<br>ExamView® Pro Testmaker |
| **Section 3**<br>**Consumerism**<br>• What are your rights as a consumer?<br>• What private and federal help can you receive as a consumer?<br>• What are your responsibilities as a consumer? | Reproducible Lesson Plan 3-3<br>Daily Lecture Notes 3-3<br>Guided Reading Activity 3-3<br>Reading Essentials and Study Guide 3-3<br>Daily Focus Activity 29<br>Section Quiz 3-3* | Daily Focus Transparency 29<br>Vocabulary PuzzleMaker<br>Interactive Tutor Self-Assessment Software<br>MindJogger Videoquiz<br>Presentation Plus!<br>ExamView® Pro Testmaker |

*Also available in Spanish

Blackline Master
Transparency

Software
CD-ROM

Videodisc
Audiocassette

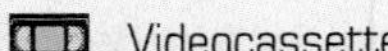
Videocassette

# CHAPTER 3 Resource Manager

## ACTIVITY From the Classroom of

**Greg Parsley**
**Roncalli High School**
**Indianapolis, Indiana**

### Mission: Smart Shopping

Have students read aloud the information listed in **Figure 3.4** on page 63 (Checklist for Consumer Decision Making) and **Figure 3.7** on page 68 (Checklist for Analyzing Ads). Students are then required to make one purchase based upon the information presented in these charts and the rest of Chapter 3. Students must give an in-class presentation with their purchased product in hand. They must explain the reasoning behind the purchase, including advertising, cost, appeal, and so on.

## Easy Planning and Preparation!

Use Glencoe's **Presentation Plus!**, a Microsoft PowerPoint® application, to teach **Your Role as a Consumer.** With this multimedia teacher tool, you can customize ready-made presentations. At your fingertips are interactive transparencies, on-screen lecture notes, audiovisual presentations, and links to the Internet and to other Glencoe multimedia.

### Interactive Lesson Planner

Planning has never been easier! Organize your week, month, semester, or year with all the lesson helps you need to make teaching creative, timely, and relevant—the way it is meant to be. The Interactive Lesson Planner opens Glencoe's **Chapter 3** resources, helps you build your schedule, and tracks your progress.

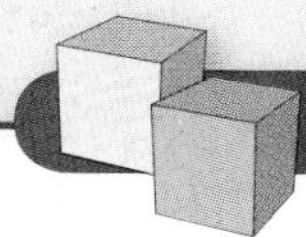

## Block Schedule

Activities that are particularly suited to use within the block scheduling framework are identified throughout this chapter by the following designation: BLOCK SCHEDULING

## Key to Ability Levels

**Teaching strategies have been coded for varying learning styles and abilities.**

L1 BASIC activities for all students
L2 AVERAGE activities for average to above-average students
L3 CHALLENGING activities for above-average students
ELL ENGLISH LANGUAGE LEARNER activities

## National Council on Economic Education

## THE EconomicsAmerica AND EconomicsInternational PROGRAMS

### Voluntary Standards Emphasized in Chapter 3

**Content Standard 1** Students will understand that productive resources are limited. Therefore, people cannot have all the goods and services they want; as a result, they must choose some things and give up others.

**Content Standard 2** Students will understand that effective decision making requires comparing the additional costs of alternatives with the additional benefits. Most choices involve doing a little more or a little less of something; few choices are all-or-nothing decisions.

### Resources Available from NCEE

- *Capstone: The Nation's High School Economics Course*
- *Civics and Government: Focus on Economics*
- *Personal Finance Economics: Wallet Wisdom*
- *Personal Decision Making: Focus on Economics*

To order these materials, or to contact your State Council on Economic Education about workshops and programs, call 1-800-338-1192 or visit the NCEE Web site at http://www.nationalcouncil.org

ECONOMICS & YOU

Your Role as a Consumer

Chapter 9
Disc 1, Side 1

ASK: What is a consumer? *A consumer is a person who purchases goods and services.*

 Also available in VHS.

## Chapter Overview

**Chapter 3** explains the difference between disposable and discretionary income and examines how each is spent. Chapter 3 also explores the role of advertising and reviews the rights and responsibilities of consumers.

### GLENCOE TECHNOLOGY

Use **MindJogger Videoquiz** VHS to preview Chapter 3 content.

### ECONOMICS Online

Introduce students to chapter content and key terms by having them access **Chapter 3—Chapter Overviews** at *ett.glencoe.com*

# CHAPTER 3

# Your Role as a Consumer

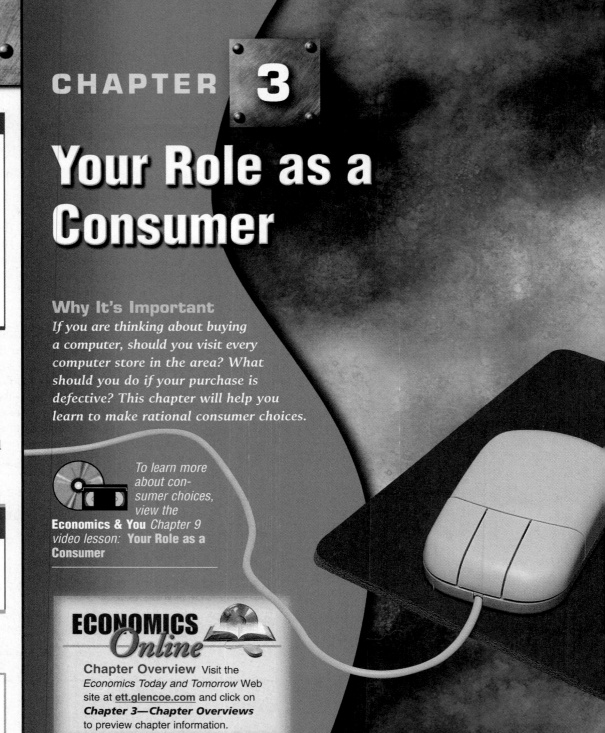

### Why It's Important

*If you are thinking about buying a computer, should you visit every computer store in the area? What should you do if your purchase is defective? This chapter will help you learn to make rational consumer choices.*

*To learn more about consumer choices, view the* **Economics & You** *Chapter 9 video lesson:* **Your Role as a Consumer**

### ECONOMICS Online

**Chapter Overview** Visit the *Economics Today and Tomorrow* Web site at ett.glencoe.com and click on ***Chapter 3—Chapter Overviews*** to preview chapter information.

### CHAPTER LAUNCH ACTIVITY

Ask students to identify a product they have recently purchased. Then ask them to write answers to the following questions: Before making your purchase, what questions did you ask yourself and others, and what information did you look for? Why did you buy this particular item and not another? Do you think you acted wisely in making your purchase? Why or why not? Call on volunteers to share their responses with the class. Then point out that by asking questions and seeking information before making purchases, students are developing buying strategies that will help them act wisely as consumers.

SECTION 1

# Consumption, Income, and Decision Making

## Cover Story

*Kiplinger's Personal Finance Magazine*, October 1998

Worried about being kidnapped by aliens? We didn't really think so. But fears of alien abduction plague enough people that at least one insurance company offers a policy that will pay if little green men come to take you away. You can also buy coverage against being injured by a ghost, eaten (as opposed to abducted) by an alien, or hit by an asteroid (hey, it could happen).

Who buys this stuff? "Normally, they're feeble-minded," explains Simon Burgess, who is managing director of the London insurance brokerage that has tapped the Twilight Zone market.

### Reader's Guide

**Terms to Know**
- consumer
- disposable income
- discretionary income
- rational choice

**Reading Objectives**
1. What is the difference between disposable and discretionary income?
2. What three considerations should govern your decision making as a consumer?

You and everyone around you are consumers and, as such, play an important role in the economic system. A **consumer** is any person or group that buys or uses goods and services to satisfy personal needs and wants. Consumers buy a wide variety of things—food, clothing, automobiles, movie tickets, and, as noted in the *Cover Story* above, even insurance against alien abductions. In this section you'll learn how to spend—or *not* spend—your income wisely.

consumer: *any person or group that buys or uses goods and services to satisfy personal needs and wants*



## 1 Focus

### Overview

**Section 1** explains the difference between disposable and discretionary income and describes five considerations in consumer decision making.

### BELLRINGER
**Motivational Activity**

Project **Daily Focus Transparency 27** and have students answer the questions.

This activity is also available as a blackline master.

**Daily Focus Transparency 27**

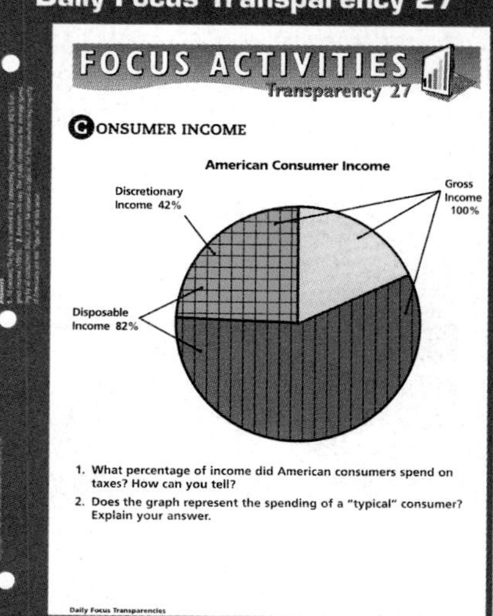


### Reader's Guide

Answers to the **Reading Objectives** questions are on page 64.

**Preteaching Vocabulary**

Instruct students to locate definitions of the **Terms to Know** in the Glossary. Then ask students to use each term correctly in a sentence.

**Vocabulary PuzzleMaker**

## SECTION 1 RESOURCE MANAGER

**Reproducible Masters**
- Reproducible Lesson Plan 3–1
- Reading Essentials and Study Guide 3–1
- Guided Reading Activity 3–1
- Section Quiz 3–1
- Daily Focus Activity 27
- Daily Lecture Notes 3–1

**Multimedia**
- Daily Focus Transparency 27
- Vocabulary PuzzleMaker
- Interactive Tutor Self-Assessment Software
- ExamView® Pro Testmaker
- MindJogger Videoquiz
- NBR's *Economics & You*
- Presentation Plus!

# 2 Teach

## Guided Practice

**L1** Writing Generalizations Ask students to consider the following individuals:

1. a farm laborer with no high school certificate living in rural Texas
2. a computer engineer with a graduate degree living in Austin, the state capital of Texas

Have students write a generalization that compares these individuals' discretionary spending.

### Daily Lecture Notes 3–1

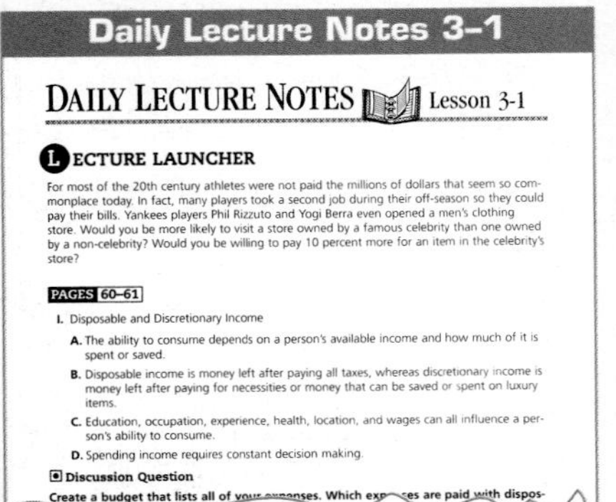

DAILY LECTURE NOTES Lesson 3-1

**LECTURE LAUNCHER**

For most of the 20th century athletes were not paid the millions of dollars that seem so commonplace today. In fact, many players took a second job during their off-season so they could pay their bills. Yankees players Phil Rizzuto and Yogi Berra even opened a men's clothing store. Would you be more likely to visit a store owned by a famous celebrity than one owned by a non-celebrity? Would you be willing to pay 10 percent more for an item in the celebrity's store?

PAGES 60–61

I. Disposable and Discretionary Income
   - A. The ability to consume depends on a person's available income and how much of it is spent or saved.
   - B. Disposable income is money left after paying all taxes, whereas discretionary income is money left after paying for necessities or money that can be saved or spent on luxury items.
   - C. Education, occupation, experience, health, location, and wages can all influence a person's ability to consume.
   - D. Spending income requires constant decision making.

**Discussion Question**

**Create a budget that lists all of your expenses. Which expenses are paid with dispos-**

### Visual Instruction FIGURE 3.1

Review **Figure 3.1** with students. Then refer them to the **Global Economy** feature on page 62. Encourage them to create a circle graph for consumer spending in Canada.

**Answer:** *Housing and Household Operation, Transportation, Taxes and Social Security*

## Disposable and Discretionary Income

A person's role as a consumer depends on his or her ability to consume. This ability to consume, in turn, depends on available income and how much of it a person chooses to spend now or save for future spending. **Figure 3.1** shows how typical American consumers spend their money income.

Income can be both disposable and discretionary. **Disposable income** is the money income a person has left after all taxes have been paid. People spend their disposable income on many kinds of goods and services. First, they buy the necessities: food, clothing, and housing. Any leftover income, which can be saved or spent on extras such as luxury items or entertainment, is called **discretionary income.** See **Figure 3.2.**

**disposable income:** *income remaining for a person to spend or save after all taxes have been paid*

**discretionary income:** *money income a person has left to spend on extras after necessities have been bought*

Education, occupation, experience, and health can all make differences in a person's earning power and thus in his or her ability to consume. **Figure 3.3** shows how much more you could earn with a four-year college degree. Where a person lives can also influence how much he or she earns. City dwellers tend to earn more than those who live in rural areas. Wages in some regions of the country tend to be higher than in other regions.

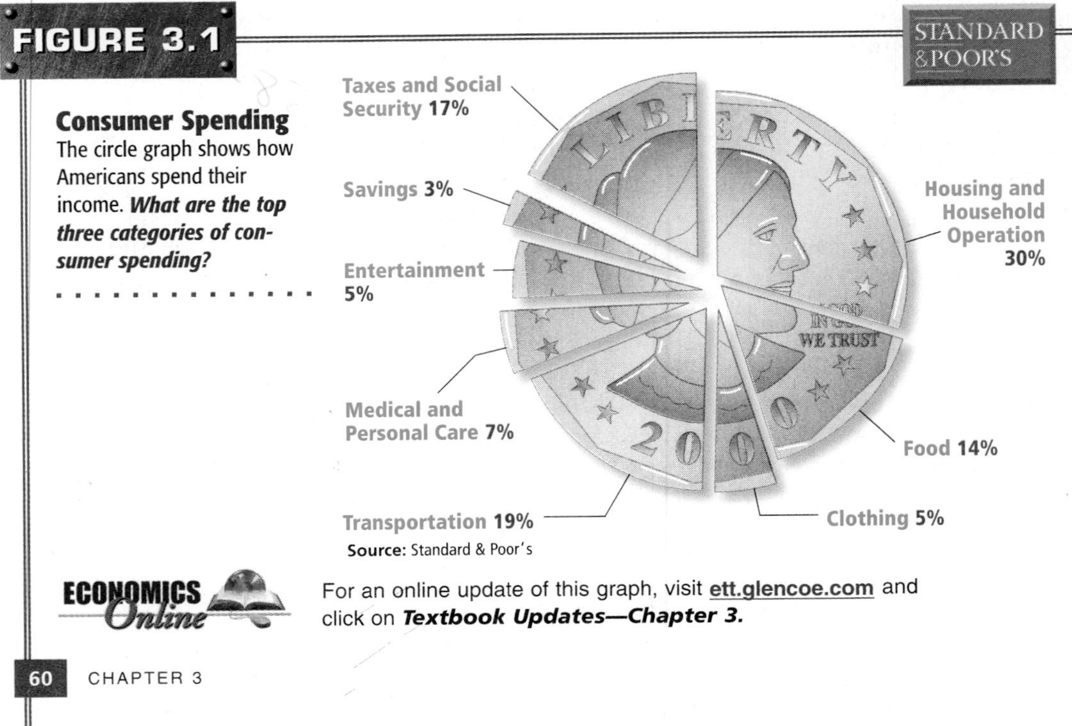


**Consumer Spending** The circle graph shows how Americans spend their income. ***What are the top three categories of consumer spending?***

**Source:** Standard & Poor's

ECONOMICS Online For an online update of this graph, visit ett.glencoe.com and click on ***Textbook Updates—Chapter 3.***



### Meeting Special Needs

**Reading Disability** Allow students who have difficulty with reading comprehension to read aloud with a partner. Have readers stop at the end of each page and discuss what they have read. Encourage them to note definitions and important facts. The auditory cues of reading aloud and discussing the material should increase comprehension.

Refer to *Inclusion for the Social Studies Classroom Strategies and Activities* for students with different learning styles.

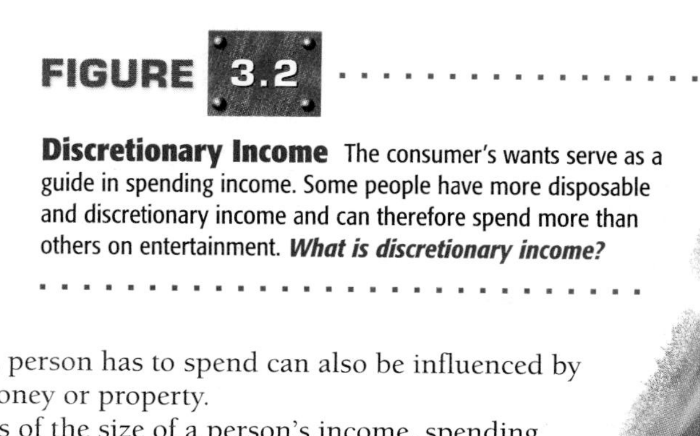

FIGURE 3.2

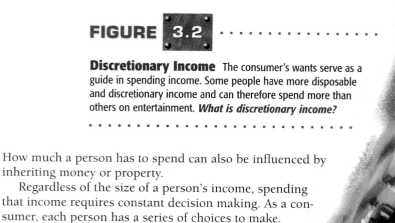

**Discretionary Income** The consumer's wants serve as a guide in spending income. Some people have more disposable and discretionary income and can therefore spend more than others on entertainment. ***What is discretionary income?***

How much a person has to spend can also be influenced by inheriting money or property.

Regardless of the size of a person's income, spending that income requires constant decision making. As a consumer, each person has a series of choices to make.

## Decision Making as a Consumer

The first decision a consumer must make is whether to buy an item or not. This may sound so basic as to be unnecessary to mention, but how many times do you actually think about the reasons for the purchase you are about to make? Do you think about whether you really need the item? Do you consider the trade-offs involved?

FIGURE 3.3

**Earning Power** The number of years you are educated has a direct effect on your income. ***How much can you expect to make per year if you do not graduate from high school? If you graduate from college with a bachelor's degree?***

**How Education Affects Income**

| Amount of Education | Median Income for Males | Median Income for Females |
|---|---|---|
| Not a High School Graduate | $19,575 | $10,725 |
| High School Graduate | $28,307 | $16,906 |
| Some College | $32,641 | $19,856 |
| Bachelor's Degree | $50,056 | $30,119 |
| Advanced Degree | $78,032 | $42,744 |

**Source:** Bureau of the Census

For an online update of this graph, visit ett.glencoe.com and click on ***Textbook Updates—Chapter 3.***



### Visual Instruction FIGURE 3.2

Ask students to identify discretionary purchases they have made recently.
**Answer:** *any leftover income after necessities have been purchased, which can be saved or spent on extras such as luxury items or entertainment*

### Guided Reading Activity 3-1

Name ______ Date ______ Class ______

GUIDED READING Activity 3-1

*For Use with textbook pages 59–64*

**CONSUMPTION, INCOME, AND DECISION MAKING**

**RECALLING THE FACTS**

***Directions:*** *Use the information in your textbook to answer the questions.*

1. What are the characteristics of a consumer?

**Disposable and Discretionary Income**

2. What are the two types of income?
   a. ______ income
   b. ______ income
3. How are the two types of income different from one another?
4. What factors help determine a person's potential earning power?

**Decision Making as a Consumer**

5. What are the three decisions

### Visual Instruction FIGURE 3.3

One generalization that can be drawn from the chart is that income increases as level of education rises. ASK: What is another generalization you can draw from this chart? *Men receive higher incomes than women at all levels of education.*
**Answer:** *Males–$19,575, Females–$10,725; Males–$50,056, Females–$30,119*

### Cooperative Learning

Organize students into several groups, and ask groups to carefully study **Figure 3.4** on page 63. Then tell groups their task is to prepare a script for a 5- to 10-minute television documentary titled *Consumer Decision Making.* Inform groups that their documentary materials should include a brief synopsis of the program, a detailed script, and several storyboards illustrating scenes from the program. Call on groups to present their documentary materials to the rest of the class. If audiovisual equipment is available, some groups may wish to "shoot" their documentaries. BLOCK SCHEDULING

# CHAPTER 3
SECTION 1, Pages 59–64

## Independent Practice

**L2 Applying Ideas** Have students imagine they are thinking of making a major purchase—a new stereo system, perhaps. Ask students to write a description of the decision-making process for this purchase, using the guidelines set out in **Figure 3.4** on page 63. Encourage students to share and discuss their descriptions.

**Your Role as a Consumer**

Chapter 9
Disc 1, Side 1

**ASK: What is the difference between disposable income and discretionary income?** *Disposable income is the money left after taxes that is spent on such basics as food, clothing, and housing. Discretionary income is the money that is left over for things that are not considered essential, such as CDs or jewelry.*

 Also available in VHS.

Making consumer decisions involves three parts, each including several steps. **Figure 3.4** can help guide you through the entire process. The steps in *Part A* of **Figure 3.4** will help you analyze the first consumer decision—whether to buy an item in the first place.

## Global Economy

### Consumers in Canada

How do our neighbors to the north spend their money? According to Statistics Canada—the Canadian equivalent of the U.S. Bureau of the Census—Canadian consumers spend each dollar as follows:

| | |
|---|---|
| • Housing and Household Operation | $.24 |
| • Personal Income Taxes | .21 |
| • Transportation | .12 |
| • Food | .11 |
| • Insurance Payments and Pension Contributions | .06 |
| • Recreation | .06 |
| • Clothing | .05 |
| • Health and Personal Care | .04 |
| • Other | .11 |

**Scarce Resources** After you have decided to make a purchase, at least two scarce resources are involved—income and time. Before you spend your money income, you need to invest time in obtaining information about the product you wish to buy. Suppose you decide to buy a mountain bike. The time spent visiting stores checking models and prices is a cost to you. This time cannot be used for anything else.

**Opportunity Cost** Virtually all of the steps in consumer decision making involve an opportunity cost. Remember that opportunity cost is the value of your highest alternative choice that you did not make. In step 1 of *Part B* of **Figure 3.4,** for example, your choice between a low-, medium-, or high-quality product involves an opportunity cost.

In general, a high-quality product costs more than a low-quality product. For example, suppose that you are trying to decide between new cross-training shoes. One model has a pump system that allows you to get a closer fit on your ankle. The other model does not. The pump system model costs $80 more than the other model. If you choose the higher-priced pump system shoe, you will sacrifice $80. The opportunity cost of the pump model over the lesser-quality model shoe is therefore $80, or what you could have bought with that $80. See **Figure 3.5** on page 64.

**Rational Choice** When you make consumer decisions based on opportunity cost, you are engaging in **rational choice.** Economists define rational choice as the alternative that has the greatest perceived value.

<u>rational choice:</u> *choosing the alternative that has the greatest value from among comparable-quality products*

Rational choice involves choosing the best-quality item that is the least expensive from among comparable-quality products. As a consumer, you will make rational choices when you purchase the goods and services you believe can best satisfy your wants.

## Free Enterprise Activity

Organize the class into several small groups to conduct a survey on how consumers decide to make purchases. Have groups create a questionnaire based on the information in **Figure 3.4** on page 63. Next, have groups use their questionnaires to survey consumers in their community. Then have groups use their findings to create a report on consumer decision-making behavior. Call on groups to present their reports to the class.

 BLOCK SCHEDULING

# FIGURE 3.4 Checklist for Consumer Decision Making

**Part A. Deciding to Spend Your Money**
Before you buy anything, you should ask yourself:

1. Do I really require this item? Why? Real needs are few, but wants are unlimited.
2. Is this good or service worth the time I spent earning the income to pay for it?
3. Is there any better use for my income now? Should I save instead for future needs?

**Part B. Deciding on the Right Purchase**
After you have made up your mind to buy a good or service, you are faced with more questions:

1. Do I want high, medium, or low quality? *Quality* refers to appearance, materials used, and the length of time a product will last. For a higher price, you can usually get higher quality. For a lower price, you can usually expect a product that may not be so attractive or as long lasting. At times, such a purchase may suit your needs very well, however.
2. If I am buying an appliance or a car, do I want one that will be the most efficient to operate each year? The answer will probably involve a trade-off. A small automobile, for example, may use less gasoline than a larger one, but it provides less protection in an accident.
3. Does this particular item—a Brand Y laptop, for example—require more service than Brands A, B, and C? If so, do I want this additional problem and expense?
4. Should I wait until there is a sale on the item I want? Sales of certain items are seasonal. For example, winter clothes are on sale after Christmas and summer clothes in August.
5. If I am looking for an expensive item, should I buy it new or used? What things are better to buy new than used? How can I protect myself if I buy a used item?
6. Should I choose a product with a well-known brand name even though it costs more than a similar product without a brand name? Are there any benefits to buying a brand-name product? What are they?
7. Does anyone I know own this product so that I can get a firsthand opinion?
8. Is the warranty on this particular product comparable to warranties on similar items?
9. Is the return or exchange policy of the store where I am thinking of buying a product comparable to the policies of other stores selling similar items?
10. What do consumer magazines say about the product?

**Part C. Deciding How to Use Your Purchase**
Once you own something—whether it is clothing, a DVD player, or an automobile—you must decide:

1. How much time and effort should I spend personally repairing and maintaining the product?
2. How much should I spend on repairs and maintenance?
3. At what point should I replace this item? Why? (This brings you back to Part A.)



**CHAPTER 3**
**SECTION 1, Pages 59–64**

# 3 Assess

## Meeting Lesson Objectives

Assign Section 1 Assessment as homework or an in-class activity.

Use **Interactive Tutor Self-Assessment Software** to review Section 1.

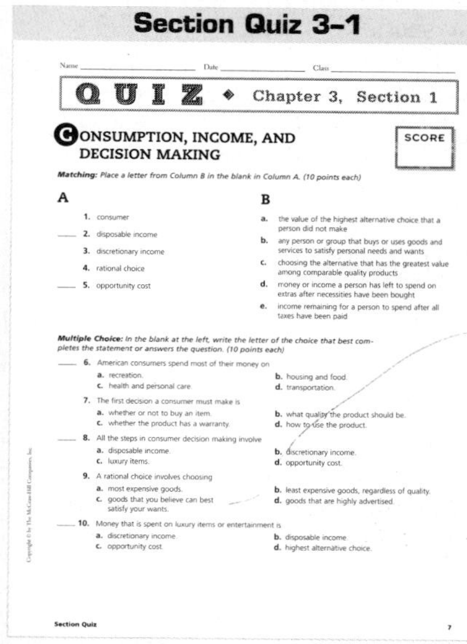

**Section Quiz 3-1**

Name ______ Date ______ Class ______

**QUIZ ◆ Chapter 3, Section 1**

**CONSUMPTION, INCOME, AND DECISION MAKING** SCORE

***Matching:*** *Place a letter from Column B in the blank in Column A. (10 points each)*

| A | B |
|---|---|
| 1. consumer | a. the value of the highest alternative choice that a person did not make |
| ___ 2. disposable income | b. any person or group that buys or uses goods and services to satisfy personal needs and wants |
| 3. discretionary income | c. choosing the alternative that has the greatest value among comparable quality products |
| 4. rational choice | d. money or income a person has left to spend on extras after necessities have been bought |
| ___ 5. opportunity cost | e. income remaining for a person to spend after all taxes have been paid |

***Multiple Choice:*** *In the blank at the left, write the letter of the choice that best completes the statement or answers the question. (10 points each)*

___ 6. American consumers spend most of their money on
a. recreation. b. housing and food.
c. health and personal care. d. transportation.

7. The first decision a consumer must make is
a. whether or not to buy an item. b. what quality the product should be.
c. whether the product has a warranty. d. how to use the product.

___ 8. All the steps in consumer decision making involve
a. disposable income. b. discretionary income.
c. luxury items. d. opportunity cost.

9. A rational choice involves choosing
a. most expensive goods. b. least expensive goods, regardless of quality.
c. goods that you believe can best satisfy your wants. d. goods that are highly advertised.

___ 10. Money that is spent on luxury items or entertainment is
a. discretionary income. b. disposable income.
c. opportunity cost. d. highest alternative choice.



Section Quiz 7

## Visual Learning Activity

**Graphic Organizer** Copy the following diagram on the board:

| Disposable Income | – | Expenses | = | Discretionary Income |
|---|---|---|---|---|

Have students use upward, downward, or horizontal arrows to show what would happen to the size of the boxes in these situations:

**a.** You receive a pay raise. (*Disposable Income↑, Expenses→, Discretionary Income↑*)
**b.** You cut energy expenses. (*Disposable Income→, Expenses↓, Discretionary Income↑*)
**c.** Wanting to graduate from college sooner rather than later, you leave your full-time job for a lower-paid part-time position. (*Disposable Income↓, Expenses→, Discretionary Income↓*)

# CHAPTER 3

SECTION 1, Pages 59–64

### Visual Instruction FIGURE 3.5

**Answer:** *income and time*

## Reteach

Have students create a flowchart, starting with "Consumer" and ending with "Rational Choice," to illustrate the main points discussed in the section.

### Reading Essentials and Study Guide 3-1

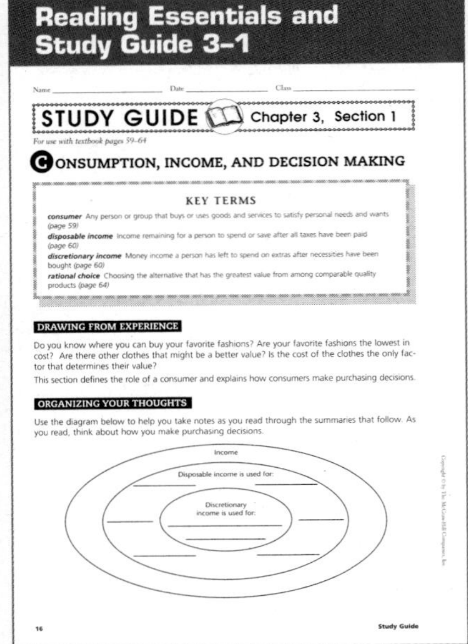
Name ______ Date ______ Class ______

**STUDY GUIDE** Chapter 3, Section 1

*For use with textbook pages 59–64*

**CONSUMPTION, INCOME, AND DECISION MAKING**

**KEY TERMS**

***consumer*** Any person or group that buys or uses goods and services to satisfy personal needs and wants *(page 59)*

***disposable income*** Income remaining for a person to spend or save after all taxes have been paid *(page 60)*

***discretionary income*** Money income a person has left to spend on extras after necessities have been bought *(page 60)*

***rational choice*** Choosing the alternative that has the greatest value from among comparable quality products *(page 64)*

**DRAWING FROM EXPERIENCE**

Do you know where you can buy your favorite fashions? Are your favorite fashions the lowest in cost? Are there other clothes that might be a better value? Is the cost of the clothes the only factor that determines their value?

This section defines the role of a consumer and explains how consumers make purchasing decisions.

**ORGANIZING YOUR THOUGHTS**

Use the diagram below to help you take notes as you read through the summaries that follow. As you read, think about how you make purchasing decisions.

Income

Disposable income is used for:

Discretionary income is used for:



16 Study Guide

## 4 Close

Have students discuss the following: You are thinking of hiring a disc jockey for a school dance. What would you consider in making this hiring decision?

Do not get the impression that wise consumers will all make the same choices. Remember the definition: A rational choice is one that generates the greatest perceived value for any given expenditure. Rational choices that are based on careful consumer decision making will still lead to billions of different consumer choices yearly.

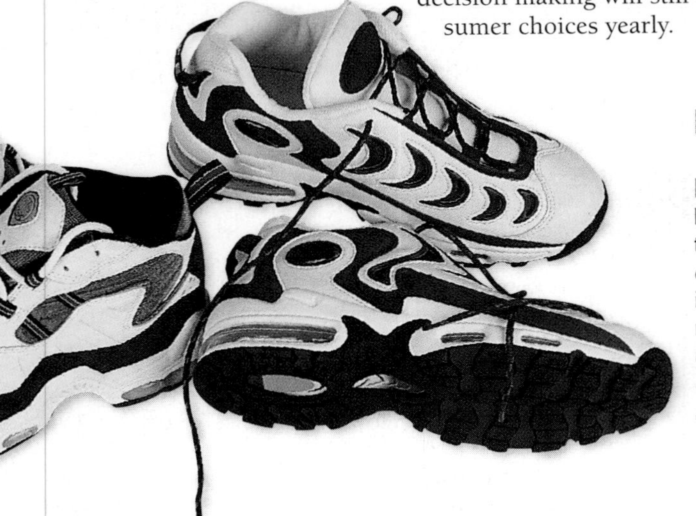

**FIGURE 3.5**

**Buying Decisions** If you choose the higher-priced product, you must believe that the opportunity cost for the higher quality is worth the higher price—that nothing else at that instant will give you as much value. ***What two scarce resources are involved in every consumer purchase you make?***

**Practice** and **assess** key skills with *Skillbuilder Interactive Workbook, Level 2.*

# SECTION 1 Assessment

### Understanding Key Terms

1. **Define** consumer, disposable income, discretionary income, rational choice.

### Reviewing Objectives

2. What kinds of products are purchased with discretionary income?
3. **Graphic Organizer** Create a diagram like the one below to describe three things a consumer should consider before deciding to make a purchase.

**Decision to Spend Your $**

3. ______
2. ______
1. ______

### Applying Economic Concepts

4. **Rational Choice** List three major purchases you've made in the past month. Explain why you think you did or did not apply rational choice when making the purchases.

### Critical Thinking Activity

5. **Categorizing Information** Draw a circle graph like **Figure 3.1**—Consumer Spending—on page 60. Develop your own categories that reflect how you spend your income. Then calculate the amount you spend in each category. Transpose this amount into a percentage to show your personal consumer spending as a circle graph. *For help in using circle graphs, see page xvi in the Economic Handbook.*



## SECTION 1 Assessment Answers

1. All definitions can be found in the Glossary.
2. extras such as luxury items or entertainment
3. **1.** Do I really require this item? **2.** Is this good or service worth the time I spent earning the income to pay for it? **3.** Is there any better use for my income now?
4. Answers will vary.
5. Circle graphs will vary. Encourage students to share and compare their graphs.

## Critical Thinking Skills

# Distinguishing Fact From Opinion

*Distinguishing fact from opinion can help you make reasonable judgments about what others say and write. Facts can be proved by evidence such as records, documents, or historical sources. Opinions are based on people's differing values and beliefs.*

- Read or listen to the information carefully. Identify the facts. Ask: Can these statements be proved? Where would I find information to verify them?
- If a statement can be proved, it is factual. Check the sources for the facts. Often statistics sound impressive, but they may come from an unreliable source.
- Identify opinions by looking for statements of feelings or beliefs. The statements may contain words like *should, would, could, best, greatest, all, every,* or *always.*

### Learning the Skill

To learn how to identify facts and opinions, follow the steps listed on the left.

### Practicing the Skill

Read the excerpt below, then answer the questions.

> *"Sony's Digital Creatures Laboratory [has] introduced what is almost certainly the world's most sophisticated entertainment robot. Priced at $2,000, it's called AIBO, a Japanese word for 'companion' that's also short for Artificial Intelligence Robot. And yes, AIBO is a robotic dog. This puppy is not ready to bring you your slippers, but in sheer brain power, he puts your basic Furby to shame.*
>
> *Sony hopes AIBO is just the first in a whole menagerie of artificial dogs, cats, monkeys, and creatures yet to be imagined. . . . Indeed, AIBO is just smart enough not to fall off the edge of a table. But within a few years, such companions could be running errands, helping with household chores, and assisting the handicapped."*
>
> –*Business Week,* May 24, 1999

1. What are three factual statements in the passage?
2. Which statements are opinions? Explain.

### Application Activity

Record a television interview. List three facts and three opinions that were stated.

**Practice** and **assess** key skills with ***Skillbuilder Interactive Workbook, Level 2.***



### Answers to Practicing the Skill

1. The robot is priced at $2,000; it is called AIBO; *aibo* is a Japanese word for "companion;" AIBO is also short for Artificial Intelligence Robot; AIBO is a robotic dog.
2. almost certainly the world's most sophisticated entertainment robot; AIBO is just smart enough not to fall off the edge of a table; such companions could be running errands, helping with household chores, and assisting the handicapped. Phrases such as "almost certainly," "most sophisticated," "just smart enough," and "could be" act as signals for opinions.

**Application Activity** Answers should include both facts and opinions.

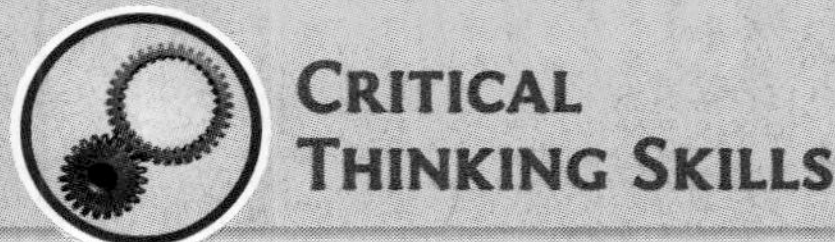

## Critical Thinking Skills

### Distinguishing Fact From Opinion

Help students distinguish between facts and opinions by offering the following examples:

1. In 1998 the population of the United States was about 270 million.
2. In the third quarter of 1999, consumer spending increased at an annual rate of 4.3 percent.
3. There are too many people living in the United States.
4. Consumers waste most of their money.

Point out that 1. and 2. are factual statements–they can be proven by statistics. Statements 3. and 4., however, cannot be proven.

Have students demonstrate that they understand this difference by writing several facts and opinions.

**Reinforcing Economic Skills 18**

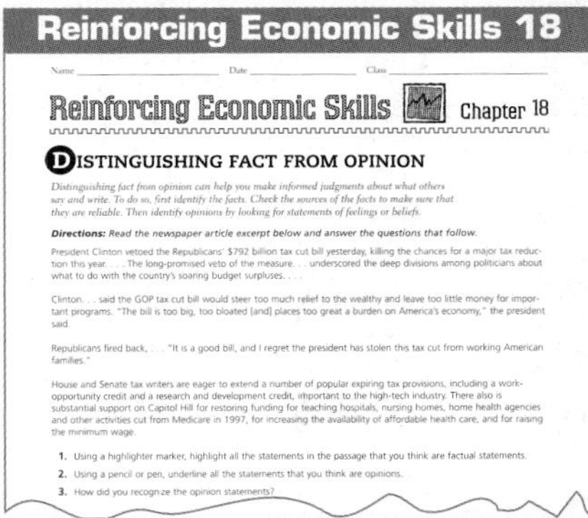

Name ______ Date ______ Class ______

**Reinforcing Economic Skills** Chapter 18

**DISTINGUISHING FACT FROM OPINION**

*Distinguishing fact from opinion can help you make informed judgments about what others say and write. To do so, first identify the facts. Check the sources of the facts to make sure that they are reliable. Then identify opinions by looking for statements of feelings or beliefs.*

**Directions:** *Read the newspaper article excerpt below and answer the questions that follow.*

President Clinton vetoed the Republicans' $792 billion tax cut bill yesterday, killing the chances for a major tax reduction this year. . . . The long-promised veto of the measure. . . underscored the deep divisions among politicians about what to do with the country's soaring budget surpluses. . . .

Clinton. . . said the GOP tax cut bill would steer too much relief to the wealthy and leave too little money for important programs. "The bill is too big, too bloated [and] places too great a burden on America's economy," the president said.

Republicans fired back, . . . "It is a good bill, and I regret the president has stolen this tax cut from working American families."

House and Senate tax writers are eager to extend a number of popular expiring tax provisions, including a work-opportunity credit and a research and development credit, important to the high-tech industry. There also is substantial support on Capitol Hill for restoring funding for teaching hospitals, nursing homes, home health agencies and other activities cut from Medicare in 1997, for increasing the availability of affordable health care, and for raising the minimum wage.

1. Using a highlighter marker, highlight all the statements in the passage that you think are factual statements.
2. Using a pencil or pen, underline all the statements that you think are opinions.
3. How did you recognize the opinion statements?

**GLENCOE TECHNOLOGY**

**Glencoe Skillbuilder Interactive Workbook, Level 2**

This interactive CD-ROM reinforces student mastery of essential social studies skills.

# 1 Focus

## Overview

Section 2 explains or describes the trade-offs required in gathering buying information, various forms of advertising, and how consumers practice comparison shopping.

### BELLRINGER
**Motivational Activity**

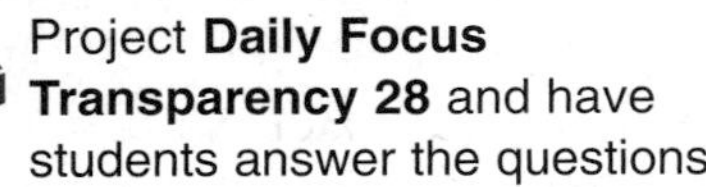

Project **Daily Focus Transparency 28** and have students answer the questions.

This activity is also available as a blackline master.

**Daily Focus Transparency 28**

CONSUMERS AND ADVERTISING

1. What do you find appealing about this advertisement? Does it make you want to buy a watch?
2. What did you learn about the product from reading the advertisement?

Daily Focus Transparencies

### Reader's Guide

Answers to the **Reading Objectives** questions are on page 70.

**Preteaching Vocabulary**

Have students work in small groups to brainstorm definitions of the **Terms to Know**. Call on volunteers to give definitions and write them on the board. Then ask students to compare Glossary definitions with those on the board.

Vocabulary PuzzleMaker

SECTION 2

# Buying Principles or Strategies

### Reader's Guide

**Terms to Know**

- competitive advertising
- informative advertising
- bait and switch
- comparison shopping
- warranty
- brand name
- generic brand

**Reading Objectives**

1. What trade-offs occur when you are gathering information?
2. What forms of advertising exist?
3. How can you learn to practice comparison shopping?

### Cover Story

*Business Week*, February 8, 1999

You know it's Super Bowl season in Hollywood. Top talent is switching focus from movies to 30- and 60-second ads that dazzle, that wow, and that keep millions of sports fans glued to their sets during the commercial breaks.

Companies that advertise on the championship telecast pay dearly for it—$3 million for one half-minute—but are rewarded with a domestic audience that is expected to exceed 140 million.

The goal of advertisements is to win your consumer dollars, and advertisers are willing to spend millions of dollars to attract your attention to their products. Because of the problems of scarce income and time, however, *your* goal should be to obtain the most satisfaction from your limited income and time. In this section, you'll learn about three basic buying principles that can help you and all consumers achieve this goal. They are: (1) gathering information; (2) using advertising wisely; and (3) comparison shopping.

## Gathering Information

Suppose that you want to buy a mountain bike. After you have made this decision, you must select a brand and a model. How



### SECTION 2 RESOURCE MANAGER

**Reproducible Masters**

- Reproducible Lesson Plan 3–2
- Reading Essentials and Study Guide 3–2
- Guided Reading Activity 3–2
- Section Quiz 3–2
- Daily Focus Activity 28
- Daily Lecture Notes 3–2

**Multimedia**

- Daily Focus Transparency 28
- Vocabulary PuzzleMaker
- Interactive Tutor Self-Assessment Software
- ExamView® Pro Testmaker
- MindJogger Videoquiz
- Presentation Plus!

should you go about doing this? First, you have to obtain information about mountain bikes. You can spend time testing out friends' mountain bikes. As **Figure 3.6** shows, you could also go to different stores and discuss the good and bad points of various brands and models with salespeople. Actually, as a wise consumer, you would do both.

**How Much Information Do You Need?** Information is costly because obtaining it involves your time. You are faced with the problem of deciding how much information to obtain. In the case of the mountain bike, the buying principle to follow is: Obtain only as much information as is worthwhile. What, however, does *worthwhile* mean? The value of your time and effort spent gathering information should not be greater than the value you receive from making the best choice of product for yourself.

**Developing a Consumer Knowledge Base** As you shop for different products, you will begin to develop a consumer knowledge base. Information you obtain looking for a mountain bike might help you someday to make decisions about choosing a car or a computer. Simply getting salespeople to give you accurate information is a skill that you can acquire and sharpen over time while you shop for other products.

One relatively easy way to obtain much information in a short amount of time is to go to the Internet. Use a standard search engine to look up information on a product you wish to buy. Also, visit the numerous sites that offer such products for sale.

FIGURE 3.6

**Gathering Information** When shopping for a product, obtain only as much information as is worthwhile. You would not, for example, want to go to every bike store in your town or city and spend two hours with every salesperson discussing every model. In contrast, you would probably want to spend more than two minutes reading one advertisement about one model.

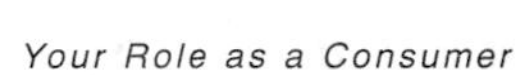





# 2 Teach

## Guided Practice

**L1 Categorizing Information** Have students create a two-column table showing the pros and cons of advertising. Call on volunteers to share their tables with the class. Then lead the class in a discussion of the following question: What are the advantages of advertising for me as a consumer?

**Daily Lecture Notes 3-2**

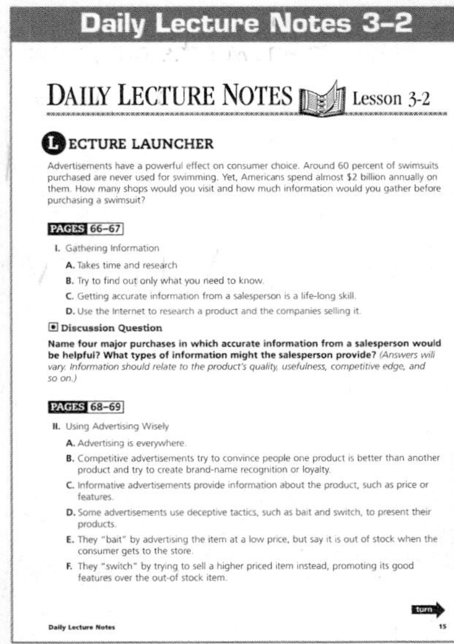

DAILY LECTURE NOTES Lesson 3-2

**LECTURE LAUNCHER**

Advertisements have a powerful effect on consumer choice. Around 60 percent of swimsuits purchased are never used for swimming. Yet, Americans spend almost $2 billion annually on them. How many shops would you visit and how much information would you gather before purchasing a swimsuit?

PAGES 66–67

I. Gathering Information
   A. Takes time and research
   B. Try to find out only what you need to know.
   C. Getting accurate information from a salesperson is a life-long skill.
   D. Use the Internet to research a product and the companies selling it.

**Discussion Question**

**Name four major purchases in which accurate information from a salesperson would be helpful? What types of information might the salesperson provide?** *(Answers will vary. Information should relate to the product's quality, usefulness, competitive edge, and so on.)*

PAGES 68–69

II. Using Advertising Wisely
   A. Advertising is everywhere.
   B. Competitive advertisements try to convince people one product is better than another product and try to create brand-name recognition or loyalty.
   C. Informative advertisements provide information about the product, such as price or features.
   D. Some advertisements use deceptive tactics, such as bait and switch, to present their products.
   E. They "bait" by advertising the item at a low price, but say it is out of stock when the consumer gets to the store.
   F. They "switch" by trying to sell a higher priced item instead, promoting its good features over the out-of stock item.

turn



**Visual Instruction FIGURE 3.6**

Ask students what steps they would follow to gather useful information when purchasing a mountain bike.

**Meeting Special Needs**

**Auditory Learning Disability** Some students are unable to recall words they have heard. To develop a facility with important terms, create sentence completion exercises on a tape recorder. Record the definition for each term in a partial sentence. Leave a pause where the student is to complete the sentence. The student might record the answers on the tape recorder for independent practice, review answers with the teacher or a partner, or write the answers in his or her notebook.

Refer to *Inclusion for the Social Studies Classroom Strategies and Activities* for students with different learning styles.

**Guided Reading Activity 3-2**

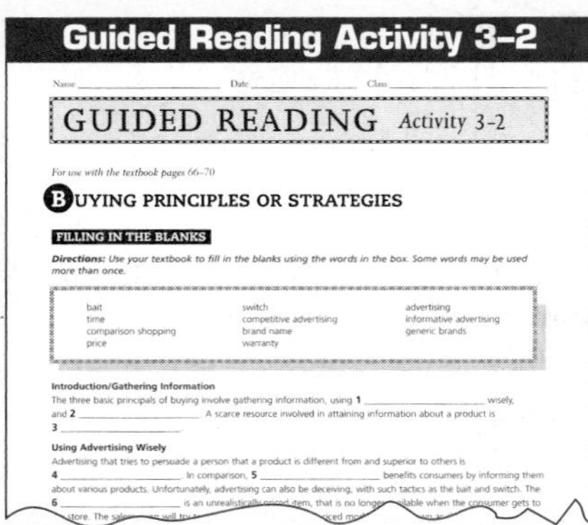
Name ______ Date ______ Class ______

GUIDED READING Activity 3-2

*For use with the textbook pages 66–70*

BUYING PRINCIPLES OR STRATEGIES

FILLING IN THE BLANKS

***Directions:*** *Use your textbook to fill in the blanks using the words in the box. Some words may be used more than once.*

| | | |
|---|---|---|
| bait | switch | advertising |
| time | competitive advertising | informative advertising |
| comparison shopping | brand name | generic brands |
| price | warranty | |

**Introduction/Gathering Information**

The three basic principals of buying involve gathering information, using **1** ______ wisely, and **2** ______. A scarce resource involved in attaining information about a product is **3** ______.

**Using Advertising Wisely**

Advertising that tries to persuade a person that a product is different from and superior to others is **4** ______. In comparison, **5** ______ benefits consumers by informing them about various products. Unfortunately, advertising can also be deceiving, with such tactics as the bait and switch. The **6** ______ is an unrealistically priced item, that is no longer available when the consumer gets to

## Independent Practice

**L3 Analyzing Information** Direct students to clip several advertisements from used magazines and newspapers. Ask them to write a brief analysis of each advertisement, noting whether its main appeal is to the reader's intelligence or emotions. Pair students and have partners compare and discuss their advertisements and analyses.

BLOCK SCHEDULING

**Visual Instruction FIGURE 3.8**

Call on volunteers to give examples of competitive and informative advertisements they have seen on television or heard on the radio.

**FIGURE 3.7 Checklist for Analyzing Ads**

**As you read advertisements, ask yourself:**

1. Does the ad only appeal to my emotions or does it provide facts?
2. What are the special features of the product? Do I need any of these features?
3. Does the ad tell me anything about operating costs?
4. Does the ad tell me anything about a product's durability, or ability to last?
5. Does the advertised price compare favorably with the price of similar products?
6. Is the advertised price the entire price, or are there extra costs in small print?

## Using Advertising Wisely

Advertising is all around you. Whenever you turn on the radio or television or log on to the Internet, you will more than likely hear or see a commercial. You also read advertising on billboards, on posters, on buses, and so on. **Figure 3.7** gives you some tips for reading these ads, which can generally be classified as competitive or informative.

**Competitive Advertising** Advertising that attempts to persuade consumers that a product is different from and superior to any other is **competitive advertising.** Its purpose may be to take customers away from competitors or to keep competitors from taking away customers. Ads for well-established brand names and products, such as Dell computers and Nike shoes, are often of this type. As shown in *Part A* of **Figure 3.8,** competitive ads also appeal to people's emotions.

**competitive advertising:** *advertising that attempts to persuade consumers that a product is different from and superior to any other*

**informative advertising:** *advertising that benefits consumers by giving information about a product*

**Informative Advertising** **Informative advertising** benefits consumers by giving information about a product. From such ads, you can learn about the existence, price, quality, and special features of products without spending much time or effort. See *Part B* of **Figure 3.8.** Informative advertising may also be competitive in nature.

**FIGURE 3.8**

**Advertising** Competitive ads often strive to evoke an emotional attachment to a product, whereas the purpose of informative ads is to provide data on a product.

◀A Competitive Advertisement

B▶ Informative Advertisement

**Free Enterprise Activity**

Organize students into groups, and have groups develop lists of 10 common household items. Then have groups visit at least three stores where these items are available and price items by store and brand. Have groups include store brand and generic product prices where applicable. Have groups organize their data into tables. Then have them compare their tables to see which is the "best buy" for each item. BLOCK SCHEDULING

**Bait and Switch** Some advertisers use deceptive, or false, advertising. Sellers may misrepresent the quality, features, or the true price of goods.

One of the most widely used methods of deceptive advertising is **bait and switch.** The bait is an advertised item at an unrealistically low price. When the consumer gets to the store, the item is no longer available, or the salesperson points out all the bad features of the advertised item. The salesperson then shows the customer higher-priced models and points out all their good features—the switch. This practice is both deceptive and illegal.

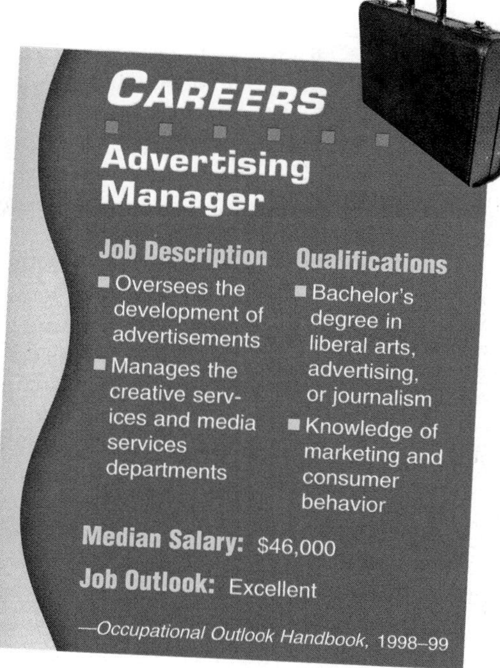

CAREERS
Advertising Manager
Job Description
■ Oversees the development of advertisements
■ Manages the creative services and media services departments
Qualifications
■ Bachelor's degree in liberal arts, advertising, or journalism
■ Knowledge of marketing and consumer behavior
Median Salary: $46,000
Job Outlook: Excellent
—Occupational Outlook Handbook, 1998–99


## Comparison Shopping

After you have gathered the information about the make and model of the product you want, you must decide *where* to buy it. It is generally worthwhile to get information on the types and prices of products available from different stores or companies. This process is known as **comparison shopping.**

To efficiently comparison shop, read newspaper advertisements, make telephone calls, browse the Web, and visit different stores. Armed with prices that you obtain from the Web, negotiate with local merchants to get them to match (or come close to) the lowest price.

<u>bait and switch:</u> *ad that attracts consumers with a low-priced product, then tries to sell them a higher-priced product*

<u>comparison shopping:</u> *getting information on the types and prices of products available from different stores and companies*

**Economic Connection to... Technology**

## Comparison Shopping on the Web

The Internet makes price comparisons easy. Type *comparison shopping* into your search engine. You will come up with dozens of Web sites that allow you to easily comparison shop when you know a specific brand and model of an item you wish to buy. You can also use an intelligent shopping agent, a program that continually searches the Web to find the best price for the item you wish to buy. ■





# 3 Assess

## Meeting Lesson Objectives

Assign Section 2 Assessment as homework or an in-class activity.

Use **Interactive Tutor Self-Assessment Software** to review Section 2.

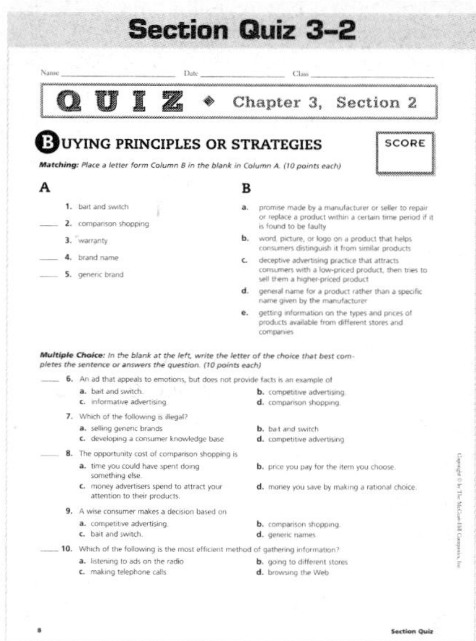

**Section Quiz 3-2**

Name ______ Date ______ Class ______

**QUIZ ◆ Chapter 3, Section 2**

**BUYING PRINCIPLES OR STRATEGIES** SCORE

***Matching:*** *Place a letter form Column B in the blank in Column A. (10 points each)*

**A**

1. bait and switch
2. comparison shopping
3. warranty
4. brand name
5. generic brand

**B**

a. promise made by a manufacturer or seller to repair or replace a product within a certain time period if it is found to be faulty
b. word, picture, or logo on a product that helps consumers distinguish it from similar products
c. deceptive advertising practice that attracts consumers with a low-priced product, then tries to sell them a higher-priced product
d. general name for a product rather than a specific name given by the manufacturer
e. getting information on the types and prices of products available from different stores and companies

***Multiple Choice:*** *In the blank at the left, write the letter of the choice that best completes the sentence or answers the question. (10 points each)*

6. An ad that appeals to emotions, but does not provide facts is an example of
   a. bait and switch. b. competitive advertising. c. informative advertising d. comparison shopping.
7. Which of the following is illegal?
   a. selling generic brands b. bait and switch c. developing a consumer knowledge base d. competitive advertising
8. The opportunity cost of comparison shopping is
   a. time you could have spent doing something else. b. price you pay for the item you choose. c. money advertisers spend to attract your attention to their products. d. money you save by making a rational choice.
9. A wise consumer makes a decision based on
   a. competitive advertising. b. comparison shopping. c. bait and switch. d. generic names
10. Which of the following is the most efficient method of gathering information?
   a. listening to ads on the radio b. going to different stores c. making telephone calls d. browsing the Web



8 Section Quiz

## Reteach

Organize students into small groups and have groups think up phrases, sayings, proverbs, jingles, or symbols that summarize the main ideas in each of the three subheads: Gathering Information, Using Advertising Wisely, and Comparison Shopping.

## Cooperative Learning

Organize students into several small groups and tell groups that they work for an advertising agency. Direct them to create either a competitive advertisement or an informative advertisement for one of the following products: mountain bike, glow-in-the-dark socks, a portable CD player, the latest model of cross-training shoe, or a new snack food. Advertisements may be for the print media, television, or radio. Groups that select print media should create a mock-up of the advertisement itself. Groups that select television should write a script and create storyboards, while groups that select radio should write a script. Have students display or present their advertisements for the class. BLOCK SCHEDULING

## Did You Know

Studies reveal that Americans are bombarded with 3,000 to 5,000 advertising messages a day. The assault is so overwhelming that people scarcely notice most of these messages.

**Reading Essentials and Study Guide 3–2**

Name ________ Date ________ Class ________

STUDY GUIDE Chapter 3, Section 2

*For use with textbook pages 66–70*

BUYING PRINCIPLES OR STRATEGIES

KEY TERMS

***competitive advertising*** Advertising that attempts to persuade consumers that a product is different from and superior to any other *(page 68)*

***informative advertising*** Advertising that benefits consumers by giving information about a product *(page 68)*

***bait and switch*** Deceptive advertising practice that attracts consumers with a low-priced product, then tries to sell them a higher-priced product *(page 69)*

***comparison shopping*** Getting information on the types and prices of products available from different stores and companies *(page 69)*

***warranty*** Promise made by a manufacturer or a seller to repair or replace a product within a certain time period if it is found to be faulty *(page 70)*

***brand name*** Word, picture, or logo on a product that helps consumers distinguish it from similar products *(page 70)*

***generic brands*** General name for a product rather than a specific brand name given by the manufacturer *(page 70)*

DRAWING FROM EXPERIENCE

Think about the last major item you purchased. How much information did you gather before deciding to purchase? Did advertise... plenty of inf...ion? Did yo...ck different

## 4 Close

Ask students to outline the buying strategies they would follow when buying a television.

**warranty:** *promise made by a manufacturer or a seller to repair or replace a product within a certain time period if it is found to be faulty*

**Warranties** When you comparison shop, the most obvious influence on your decision will be the price you have to pay for the product. However, don't forget to find out which store offers the best **warranty,** or the promise made by a manufacturer or seller to repair or replace a product if it is found to be faulty within a certain period of time.

**brand name:** *word, picture, or logo on a product that helps consumers distinguish it from similar products*

**generic brand:** *general name for a product rather than a specific brand name given by the manufacturer*

**Brand-Name or Generic Products** Another consumer choice is between buying brand-name and generic products. A **brand name** is a word, picture, or logo on a product that helps consumers distinguish it from similar products. Brand-name products are usually sold nationwide and are backed by major companies.

Some companies produce and sell **generic brands,** which means there is no brand name at all. The word *generic* means "pertaining to a general class." It is difficult to know who produced the product. Brand-name products versus generic products will be further discussed in Chapter 5.

**Practice** and **assess** key skills with ***Skillbuilder Interactive Workbook, Level 2.***

## SECTION 2 Assessment

### Understanding Key Terms

1. **Define** competitive advertising, informative advertising, bait and switch, comparison shopping, warranty, brand name, generic brand.

### Reviewing Objectives

2. What trade-offs occur when you are gathering information?
3. **Graphic Organizer** Create a chart like the one below to analyze and label at least 10 advertisements as to whether they are competitive or informative.

| Ad Description | Type | Explain |
|---|---|---|
| 1. | | |

4. How can you learn to practice comparison shopping?

### Applying Economic Concepts

5. **Advertising** Think of an advertisement you've seen in the past week. Analyze the ad by applying it to the six points in **Figure 3.7** on page 68. Was the ad successful in influencing your consumer behavior? Why or why not?

**Critical Thinking Activity**

6. **Making Comparisons** Select a product that you use every day: a hair dryer or television, for example. Do some comparison shopping by finding at least five separate locations that sell this product. What were the differences in price for the product?



## SECTION 2 Assessment Answers

1. All definitions can be found in the Glossary.
2. Consumers trade time and effort when gathering information. For some consumers, time may also represent money.
3. Charts will vary. Ensure that charts indicate an understanding of the difference between informative and competitive advertising.
4. by gathering information on the types and prices of products available from different stores or companies
5. Answers will vary. Ensure that students fully explain if and why they were influenced by each advertisement.
6. Answers will vary. Encourage students to present their results in chart form.

# BusinessWeek

# Spotlight on the Economy

## Grab Some Cash, Check Out a Flick

**Check It Out!** In this chapter you have learned about various forms of advertising. In the following article, read to learn how advertising is popping up in some unusual places.

Is it advertising run amok? Movie trailers have come to your ATM. And more may be on the way. Full-motion video ads are now running on the screens of automated teller machines at some 7-Eleven stores in New York, Chicago, San Diego, and, naturally, Los Angeles. Customers have already seen coming attractions for some films at the convenience store, and who knows, you may yet see that *Star Wars* trailer at your local S&L.

Trailers are a natural choice for showing off the video capabilities of new, sophisticated ATMs, says Cassie Metzger, a marketing manager at Diebold, a big ATM maker. And since people often stop to pick up cash before seeing a flick, she says, a 15- or 30-second trailer, with sound, could influence what they see. The ads don't lengthen transaction time. They play while the ATM is already processing.

Banks, such as Union Federal Savings in Indiana, are still conservative. So far, they've run only bank ads. But other advertisers are expected. After all, it's a marketer's dream: Customers can't change channels and they can't walk away—at least not without leaving their cash.



### Think About It

1. **Where has advertising now appeared?**
2. **Do you think this type of advertising would have an effect on your consumer decisions? Why or why not?**



### Answers to *Think About It*

1. on the screens of ATMs
2. Answers will vary. Some students will say that this kind of advertising might affect them because they have no choice but to watch it. Others may say that they will not be influenced and simply will ignore the ATM screen while they wait for their cash to be dispensed.

BusinessWeek **Spotlight**

## Teach

Point out that some ATMs offer another way of grabbing consumers' attention—coupons. As well as making withdrawals from and deposits to their accounts, ATM users also can opt to receive coupons. These coupons offer everything from a few cents off a soft drink at a fast-food restaurant to free movie tickets. The coupons are dispensed with the transaction receipt.

### BusinessWeek ONLINE

To find up-to-date news and analysis on the economy, business, technology, markets, entrepreneurs, investments, and finance, have students search feature articles and special reports on the *Business Week* Web site. www.businessweek.com

### Sidelight

The ATM at the Rock and Roll Hall of fame in Cleveland, Ohio, plays music, not advertisements. Shaped like a jukebox, the ATM blasts snippets of rock songs while it dispenses cash. Banks are not rushing to install musical cash machines, however. The jukebox model costs about $37,000 to manufacture.

# 1 Focus

## Overview

Section 3 explains or describes consumer rights, private and government agencies that protect and enforce those rights, and the relationship between consumer responsibilities and ethical behavior.

**BELLRINGER**
**Motivational Activity**

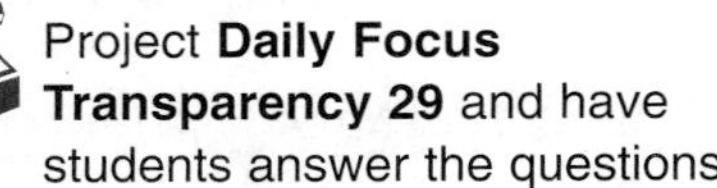

Project **Daily Focus Transparency 29** and have students answer the questions.

This activity is also available as a blackline master.

**Daily Focus Transparency 29**

FOCUS ACTIVITIES
Transparency 29

CONSUMER RIGHTS AND RESPONSIBILITIES

**Consumer Rights**
- The Right to Safety
- The Right to Choose
- The Right to be Informed
- The Right to be Heard

**Consumer Responsibilities**

Learning as much as possible about the product or service in order to purchase the best product at the best price

1. Give an example of an occasion when you felt that your consumer rights were violated.
2. When you purchase goods and services, do you always act as a responsible consumer? Explain your answer.

Daily Focus Transparencies

## Reader's Guide

Answers to the **Reading Objectives** questions are on page 75.

**Preteaching Vocabulary**

Have students check the Glossary to find the definitions of the **Terms to Know**. Then point out that people may have different interpretations of what kinds of behavior are ethical.

Vocabulary PuzzleMaker

# SECTION 3 Consumerism

## Reader's Guide

**Terms to Know**
- consumerism
- ethical behavior

**Reading Objectives**
1. What are your rights as a consumer?
2. What private and federal help can you receive as a consumer?
3. What are your responsibilities as a consumer?

## Cover Story

*The Columbus Dispatch*, May 20, 1999

A consumer-protection bill for new-car buyers passed in the Ohio House of Representatives. Existing law requires the manufacturer to buy back a lemon [chronically-defective new car] after three attempts to fix the same defect, eight attempts to fix a variety of defects, or a total of 30 days in the repair shop. The bill extends the lemon law to leased vehicles and applies up to five years after delivery of the vehicle.

If a manufacturer tries to resell a car it has had to repurchase, the title must identify the car as a "buyback." Consumer groups wanted the title to say "lemon."

Most Americans are concerned with the reliability of the products and services they use. Many private groups and government actions, like the "lemon law" in the *Cover Story* above, work to ensure the well-being of consumers. Consumers themselves, however, must be proactive in their buying habits. In this section, you'll learn how **consumerism,** a movement to educate buyers about the purchases they make and to demand better and safer products from manufacturers, affects you personally.

**consumerism:** *movement to educate buyers about the purchases they make and to demand better and safer products from manufacturers*

## Consumer Rights

Since the early 1960s, consumerism has grown steadily. Businesses can no longer assume it is the buyer's responsibility to know whether a product is safe, food is healthful, or advertising is accurate. See **Figure 3.9.**

## SECTION 3 RESOURCE MANAGER

**Reproducible Masters**
- Reproducible Lesson Plan 3–3
- Reading Essentials and Study Guide 3–3
- Guided Reading Activity 3–3
- Section Quiz 3–3
- Daily Focus Activity 29
- Daily Lecture Notes 3–3

**Multimedia**
- Daily Focus Transparency 29
- Vocabulary PuzzleMaker
- Interactive Tutor Self-Assessment Software
- ExamView® Pro Testmaker
- MindJogger Videoquiz
- Presentation Plus!

In 1962 President John F. Kennedy sent the first consumer protection message to Congress. He stated four consumer rights:

- the right to safety—protection against goods that are dangerous to life or health.
- the right to be informed—information for use not only as protection against fraud but also as the basis for reasoned choices.
- the right to choose—the need for markets to be competitive (have many firms) and for government to protect consumers in markets where competition does not exist, such as electric service.
- the right to be heard—the guarantee that consumer interests will be listened to when laws are being written.

President Richard Nixon later added a fifth right:

- the right to redress—the ability to obtain from the manufacturers adequate payment in money or goods for financial or physical damages caused by their products.

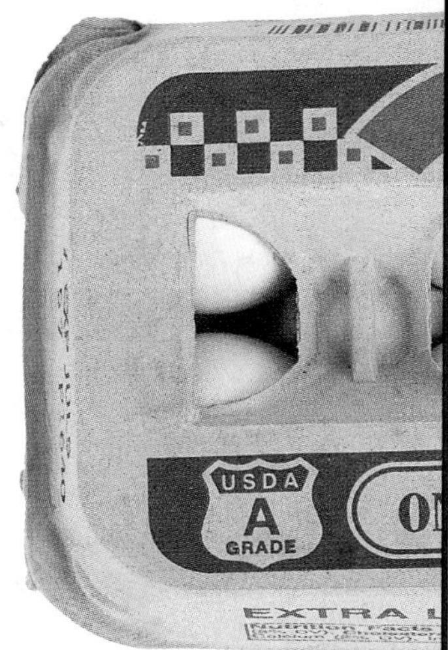


## Help for Consumers

Using President Kennedy's list, Congress passed consumer-protection legislation. Today, consumers dissatisfied with a specific product can complain to the store manager or write to the manufacturer. They also may take the case to small claims court or hire a lawyer. In addition, many private and government agencies are available to help consumers.

Among the private groups that aid consumers are local citizens' action groups and local chapters of the Better Business Bureau. Many major cities and some smaller ones have Better Business Bureaus. The bureaus give consumers information on products and selling practices and help settle disagreements between buyers and sellers.

Numerous federal agencies also have programs to aid consumers. **Figure 3.10** on page 74 lists these agencies and what they do. States also have consumer affairs councils or agencies.

## Consumer Responsibilities

You have consumer responsibilities as well as rights. If a product or service is faulty, it is the consumer's responsibility to initiate the problem-solving process. The Office of Consumer Affairs suggests that you do the following:

**(1)** Report the problem immediately. Do not try to fix a product yourself, because doing so may cancel the warranty.

**(2)** State the problem and suggest a fair and just solution—replacement, refund, etc.

**FIGURE** 

**Consumer Protection**
Government laws require the inspection of many products in order to protect consumers' health and safety and to raise quality standards. ***What four consumer rights did President Kennedy believe in?***

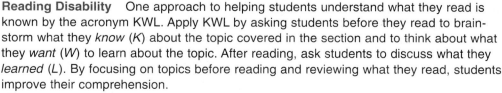

## Meeting Special Needs

**Reading Disability** One approach to helping students understand what they read is known by the acronym KWL. Apply KWL by asking students before they read to brainstorm what they *know* (*K*) about the topic covered in the section and to think about what they *want* (*W*) to learn about the topic. After reading, ask students to discuss what they *learned* (*L*). By focusing on topics before reading and reviewing what they read, students improve their comprehension.

Refer to *Inclusion for the Social Studies Classroom Strategies and Activities* for students with different learning styles.



# 2 Teach

## Guided Practice

**L1** Applying Ideas Have students create a two-column chart with the headings "Consumer Rights" and "Examples." In the first column, have students enter the five consumer rights discussed in Section 3. In the second column, ask students to list two instances where they might have to assert each right.

### Daily Lecture Notes 3-3

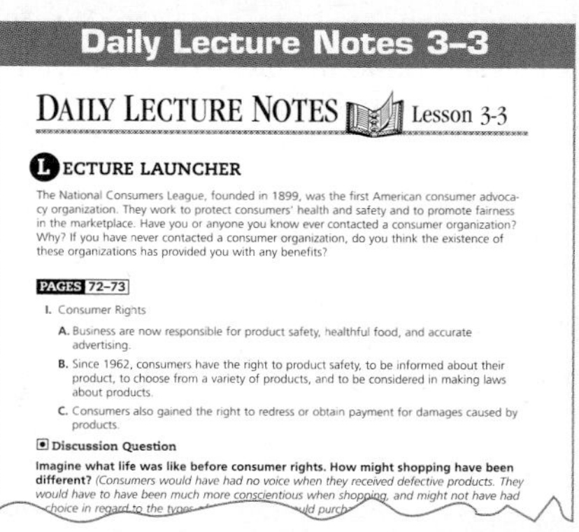

DAILY LECTURE NOTES Lesson 3-3

LECTURE LAUNCHER

The National Consumers League, founded in 1899, was the first American consumer advocacy organization. They work to protect consumers' health and safety and to promote fairness in the marketplace. Have you or anyone you know ever contacted a consumer organization? Why? If you have never contacted a consumer organization, do you think the existence of these organizations has provided you with any benefits?

PAGES 72–73

I. Consumer Rights
   A. Business are now responsible for product safety, healthful food, and accurate advertising.
   B. Since 1962, consumers have the right to product safety, to be informed about their product, to choose from a variety of products, and to be considered in making laws about products.
   C. Consumers also gained the right to redress or obtain payment for damages caused by products.

**Discussion Question**

**Imagine what life was like before consumer rights. How might shopping have been different?** *(Consumers would have had no voice when they received defective products. They would have to have been much more conscientious when shopping, and might not have had*

### Visual Instruction FIGURE 3.9

**Answer:** *the right to safety, the right to be informed, the right to choose, the right to be heard*

### Guided Reading Activity 3-3

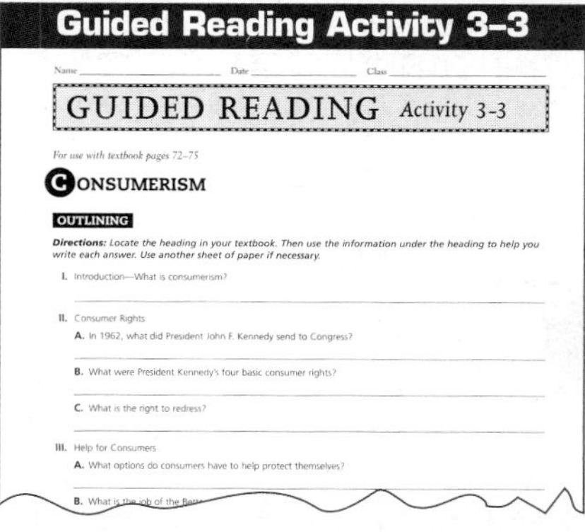

Name ____ Date ____ Class ____

GUIDED READING Activity 3-3

*For use with textbook pages 72–75*

CONSUMERISM

OUTLINING

***Directions:*** *Locate the heading in your textbook. Then use the information under the heading to help you write each answer. Use another sheet of paper if necessary.*

I. Introduction—What is consumerism?

II. Consumer Rights
   A. In 1962, what did President John F. Kennedy send to Congress?
   B. What were President Kennedy's four basic consumer rights?
   C. What is the right to redress?

III. Help for Consumers
   A. What options do consumers have to help protect themselves?

## Independent Practice

**L2** Consumer Information File Mention to students that most state and local governments have offices that offer advice on or protection of consumer rights. Have students work in groups to research the location of these offices in their state and community. Then have group representatives write letters to these offices requesting information on the services they offer. Suggest that groups combine the materials they receive in a class "Consumer Information File." BLOCK SCHEDULING

# 3 Assess

## Meeting Lesson Objectives

Assign Section 3 Assessment as homework or an in-class activity.

Use **Interactive Tutor Self-Assessment Software** to review Section 3.

Section Quiz 3-3

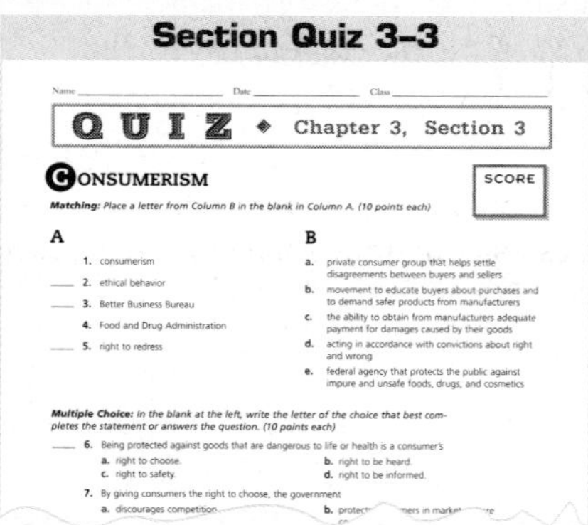

Name ______ Date ______ Class ______

QUIZ ◆ Chapter 3, Section 3

CONSUMERISM

SCORE

*Matching: Place a letter from Column B in the blank in Column A. (10 points each)*

A

1. consumerism
2. ethical behavior
3. Better Business Bureau
4. Food and Drug Administration
5. right to redress

B

a. private consumer group that helps settle disagreements between buyers and sellers
b. movement to educate buyers about purchases and to demand safer products from manufacturers
c. the ability to obtain from manufacturers adequate payment for damages caused by their goods
d. acting in accordance with convictions about right and wrong
e. federal agency that protects the public against impure and unsafe foods, drugs, and cosmetics

*Multiple Choice: In the blank at the left, write the letter of the choice that best completes the statement or answers the question. (10 points each)*

6. Being protected against goods that are dangerous to life or health is a consumer's
   a. right to choose. b. right to be heard.
   c. right to safety. d. right to be informed.

7. By giving consumers the right to choose, the government
   a. discourages competition. b. protect...

## FIGURE 3.10 Federal Agencies and Consumerism

| Agency | How It Helps the Consumer |
|---|---|
| **Consumer Information Center Program** | Provides free catalog of government publications on consumer topics. |
| **Federal Trade Commission** | Promotes competition by enforcing laws against monopolies, price fixing, false advertising, and other illegal business practices; regulates labeling of products and protects the public against violations of consumer credit laws. |
| **Consumer Product Safety Commission** | Protects the public against unreasonable risk of injury from consumer products; sets product safety requirements, forbids the production and sale of dangerous consumer products, and conducts research and education programs on safety concerns for industry and the public. |
| **Government Printing Office** | Sells more than 15,000 government publications on a wide variety of topics; lists those of interest to consumers in a free booklet, *Consumer Information Subject Bibliography.* |
| **U.S. Postal Service** | Through its Inspection Services, protects public from mail fraud and other violations of postal laws; through Consumer Advocate's office, acts on complaints and provides information on schemes used to cheat the public. |
| **U.S. Department of Agriculture** | Inspects and grades meat, fish, poultry, dairy products, and fruits and vegetables through the department's Food Safety and Quality Service; ensures that food production is sanitary and that products are labeled truthfully. |
| **U.S. Office of Consumer Affairs (Department of Health and Human Services)** | Coordinates all federal activities on behalf of consumers, advises President on consumer affairs, and works for and testifies on behalf of consumer legislation; the Complaint Coordination Center helps solve consumer problems. |
| **Food and Drug Administration (Department of Health and Human Services)** | Protects the public against impure and unsafe foods, drugs, and cosmetics; researches and tests new products in these areas and ensures accurate labeling; publishes *FDA Consumer* magazine and maintains regional consumer affairs offices. |
| **National Highway Traffic Safety Administration (Department of Transportation)** | Sets requirements for automobile safety, maintenance, and fuel economy; tests products for compliance; researches ways to save fuel and make highways safer; investigates complaints from consumers about vehicle safety. |



## Cooperative Learning

Organize students into five groups, and tell groups they are developing a pamphlet titled "The Cartoon Guide to Consumer Rights." Assign one of the following consumer rights to each group: the right to safety, the right to be informed, the right to choose, the right to be heard, the right to redress. Ask groups to create several cartoons that illustrate some aspect of their assigned topic. Call on groups to display their finished cartoons around the classroom. ELL BLOCK SCHEDULING

**(3)** Include important details and copies of receipts, guarantees, and contracts to support your case.

**(4)** Describe any action you have taken to try to correct the problem.

**(5)** Keep an accurate record of your efforts to get the problem solved. Include the names of people you speak or write to and the dates on which you communicated.

**(6)** Allow each person reasonable time, such as three weeks, to solve the problem before contacting another source.

**(7)** If you need to contact the manufacturer in writing, type your letter or send an E-mail directly. Keep a copy.

**(8)** Keep cool. The person who will help you solve your problem is probably not responsible for the problem.

Another responsibility of consumers is to exhibit **ethical behavior** by respecting the rights of producers and sellers. For example, a responsible consumer will not try to return a used item because it has been advertised elsewhere for a lower price.

**Student Web Activity** Visit the *Economics Today and Tomorrow* Web site at ett.glencoe.com and click on ***Chapter 3—Student Web Activities*** to learn more about the Office of Consumer Affairs.

__ethical behavior:__ *acting in accordance with moral and ethical convictions about right and wrong*

**Practice** and **assess** key skills with ***Skillbuilder Interactive Workbook, Level 2.***

## SECTION 3 Assessment

### Understanding Key Terms

1. **Define** consumerism, ethical behavior.

### Reviewing Objectives

2. **Graphic Organizer** Create a diagram like the one below to list your rights as a consumer.

3. What private and federal help can you receive as a consumer?

4. What are your consumer responsibilities?

### Applying Economic Concepts

5. **Consumerism** Describe two examples of how you educated yourself about a product before buying it.

### Critical Thinking Activity

6. **Summarizing Information** Prepare a video or multimedia presentation for middle school students that demonstrates ethical and unethical consumer behavior. Conclude the presentation with a creative explanation of consumer rights and responsibilities. Share the presentation with the other members of your class.



## SECTION 3 Assessment Answers

1. All definitions can be found in the Glossary.
2. In the outer ovals, students should write "safety," "to be informed," "choice," "to be heard," and "redress."
3. Private organizations give consumers information on products and selling practices; some help settle disagreements between buyers and sellers. Federal agencies set health and safety requirements, inspect products, promote free and fair competition, and provide a great deal of consumer information.
4. to learn as much as possible about the product the consumer wishes to buy; to initiate the problem-solving process if a product is faulty; to behave ethically in dealing with producers and sellers
5. Examples will vary.
6. Videos will vary. Encourage students to show their finished videos to younger school members.

See the **Web Activity Lesson Plan** at *ett.glencoe.com* for an introduction, lesson description, and answers to the **Student Web Activity** for this chapter.

## Reteach

Have students create an outline showing the section's main ideas and supporting details.

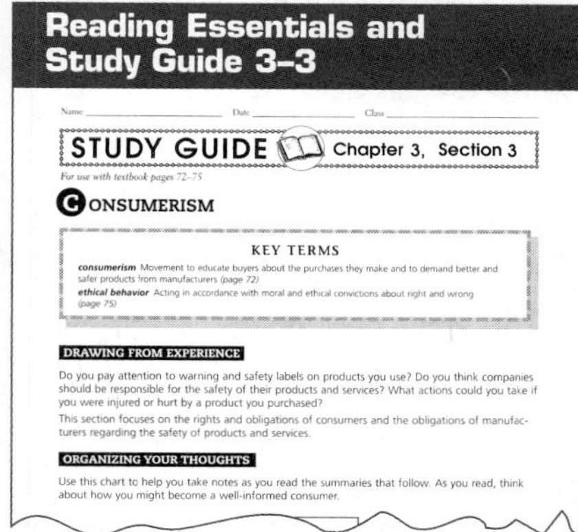
**Reading Essentials and Study Guide 3–3**

Name ______ Date ______ Class ______

STUDY GUIDE Chapter 3, Section 3

*For use with textbook pages 72–75*

CONSUMERISM

KEY TERMS

***consumerism*** Movement to educate buyers about the purchases they make and to demand better and safer products from manufacturers *(page 72)*

***ethical behavior*** Acting in accordance with moral and ethical convictions about right and wrong *(page 75)*

DRAWING FROM EXPERIENCE

Do you pay attention to warning and safety labels on products you use? Do you think companies should be responsible for the safety of their products and services? What actions could you take if you were injured or hurt by a product you purchased?

This section focuses on the rights and obligations of consumers and the obligations of manufacturers regarding the safety of products and services.

ORGANIZING YOUR THOUGHTS

Use this chart to help you take notes as you read the summaries that follow. As you read, think about how you might become a well-informed consumer.

## 4 Close

Have students write a paragraph on how knowing their responsibilities as consumers makes them better citizens.

## Background

Point out that all of the publicity that surrounds Oprah Winfrey's life has made her an easily recognizable celebrity. However, she has strong views on celebrity status:

"I don't think you should be considered a celebrity just because you can catch a ball, throw a ball, sing, talk, but because of what you have done in your life to better somebody else's."

Ask students to discuss whether or not they agree with Winfrey's view of celebrity.

# Teach

Organize students into several small groups. Ask groups to use library resources and the Internet to find information about Oprah Winfrey's philanthropic programs. Call on groups to present their findings to the class. Use these presentations to begin a class discussion on social responsibility.

### Sidelight

In the fall of 1999, Winfrey took on another job—as a college professor. She taught a class titled "Dynamics of Leadership" at the J.J. Kellogg School of Management, the business school of Northwestern University.

# People & Perspectives

## Oprah Winfrey

*ENTREPRENEUR (1954–)*

- **Chairperson of HARPO Entertainment Group, a media empire**
- **Recipient of the 1996 George Foster Peabody Individual Achievement Award and the 1998 National Academy of Television Arts & Sciences' Lifetime Achievement Award**
- **One of the 100 most influential people of the 20th century (*Time,* 1998)**
- **The second most powerful woman in business (*Fortune Magazine,* 1998)**

Oprah Winfrey emerged from an underprivileged and abusive childhood in rural Mississippi to become one of the wealthiest and most powerful women in the United States. Today, she heads the HARPO Entertainment Group–a movie, television, and video production company headquartered in Chicago. Winfrey also hosts the widely acclaimed *The Oprah Winfrey Show,* the number-one television talk show in the world for more than 12 years. It is seen by 33 million viewers weekly in the United States and is broadcast in 135 countries.

Oprah believes that her success can be attributed, in part, to her philosophy of helping others:

> *"As a rule, we are a society that has based our lives and importance in our lives on how much we can accomplish through material goods. In the end what matters is how were you able to serve and who were you able to love."*

She fulfills this ideal through generous donations to charities. For example, she has given millions of dollars to universities, such as Morehouse College, Spelman College, and Tennessee State University. She uses her show to encourage her viewers to "practice random acts of kindness" to make the world a better place:

> *"This show's still the thing for me. It gives me the platform to try to figure out how do you get people to lead better lives? How do you get fathers to spend more time with their children?"*

### *Checking for Understanding*

1. **What corporation does Oprah head?**
2. **In what ways does Oprah try to help others?**



### Answers to *Checking for Understanding*

1. HARPO Entertainment Group
2. She makes generous donations to charities and encourages her viewers to "practice random acts of kindness."

# CHAPTER 3 Summary

**Chapter Overview** Visit the *Economics Today and Tomorrow* Web site at ett.glencoe.com and click on ***Chapter 3—Chapter Overviews*** to review chapter information.

## SECTION 1 Consumption, Income, and Decision Making

- A **consumer** is any person or group that buys or uses goods and services to satisfy personal wants.
- Income can be both **disposable** and **discretionary.**
- Education, occupation, experience, and health can all make differences in a person's earning power and thus in his or her ability to consume.
- Making consumer decisions involves three parts: (1) deciding to spend your money; (2) deciding on the right purchase; and (3) deciding how to use your purchase.
- When you make consumer decisions based on opportunity cost, you are engaging in **rational choice.**

## SECTION 2 Buying Principles or Strategies

- Three basic buying principles that can help you obtain the most satisfaction from your limited income and time are gathering information, using advertising wisely, and comparison shopping.
- The value of your time and effort spent gathering information should not be greater than the value you receive from making the best choice of product.
- Most advertising falls under one of two types: **competitive advertising** or **informative advertising.** Be aware of deceptive advertising, which includes **bait and switch.**
- To efficiently **comparison shop,** read newspaper advertisements, make telephone calls, surf the Internet, and visit different stores. Also consider the product's **warranty,** and **brand-name** versus **generic** manufacturers.

## SECTION 3 Consumerism

- **Consumerism** is a movement to educate buyers about the purchases they make and to demand better and safer products from manufacturers.
- Consumer advocates promote the following consumer rights: the right to safety, to be informed, to choose, to be heard, and to redress.
- Private groups that aid consumers include local citizens' action groups and the Better Business Bureau.
- Numerous federal agencies have programs to aid consumers, including the Consumer Product Safety Commission and the Food and Drug Administration.
- Consumers' responsibilities include reading contracts and warranties, following directions for proper use of the product, initiating the problem-solving process, and exhibiting **ethical behavior.**



CHAPTER 3 Summary

**ECONOMICS & YOU**

**Your Role as a Consumer**

Chapter 9
Disc 1, Side 1

If you do not have access to a videodisc player, the ***Economics & You*** programs are available in VHS.

Use the **Chapter 3 Summary** to preview, review, condense, or reteach the chapter.

## Preview/Review

**Vocabulary PuzzleMaker Software** reinforces the key terms used in Chapter 3.

**Interactive Tutor Self-Assessment Software** allows students to review Chapter 3 content.

## Condense

Have students listen to the Chapter 3 **Audio Program** (also available in Spanish) in the TCR. Assign the Chapter 3 Audio Program Activity and give students the Chapter 3 Audio Program Test.

## Reteach

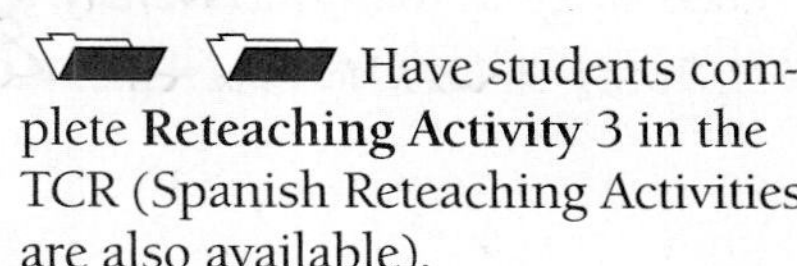

Have students complete **Reteaching Activity** 3 in the TCR (Spanish Reteaching Activities are also available).

## Economics Journal

**Buying Strategies** Have students identify the steps they, or someone they know, took in buying a small appliance. Encourage them to list alternative items and alternative stores explored before the final purchase was made. Also, have them explain why these alternatives were explored and why they were rejected.

# CHAPTER 3
## Assessment and Activities

**ECONOMICS Online**

Have students visit the *Economics Today and Tomorrow* Web site at ett.glencoe.com to review Chapter 3 and take the Self-Check Quiz.

**GLENCOE TECHNOLOGY**

**MindJogger Videoquiz**

Use MindJogger to review Chapter 3 content.

### Identifying Key Terms

1. d
2. f
3. a
4. b
5. e
6. h
7. c
8. j
9. g
10. i

### Recalling Facts and Ideas

1. Do I really need this? Is it worth the time? Is there any better use for my money?
2. No. People disagree about what generates the greatest value for any expenditure.
3. gathering information, using advertising wisely, comparison shopping
4. competitive advertising and informative advertising
5. enough to make an informed choice
6. the rights to safety, to be informed, to choose, and to be heard
7. Answers may vary but may include: to learn as much as they can about a product before buying, to respect the rights of producers and sellers, and to practice ethical behavior.

# CHAPTER 3 Assessment and Activities

**Self-Check Quiz** Visit the *Economics Today and Tomorrow* Web site at ett.glencoe.com and click on ***Chapter 3—Self-Check Quizzes*** to prepare for the Chapter Test.

## Identifying Key Terms

*Write the letter of the definition in Column B that correctly defines each term in Column A.*

**Column A**

1. disposable income
2. warranty
3. bait and switch
4. comparison shopping
5. competitive advertising
6. informative advertising
7. generic brand
8. consumer
9. discretionary income
10. brand name

**Column B**

a. deceptive advertising
b. getting information about similar types of products and prices
c. "pertaining to a general class"
d. money income left after paying taxes
e. attempts to persuade consumers that certain products are superior to others
f. written guarantee of a product
g. income left after buying necessities
h. provides information about the price, quality, and features of products
i. logo on a product
j. person or group that buys or uses goods and services to satisfy personal wants

## Recalling Facts and Ideas

**Section 1**

1. Before you buy anything, what three questions should you ask yourself?
2. Do all rational consumers think alike? Why or why not?

**Section 2**

3. What are three important buying principles?
4. What are two types of advertising?
5. How much information should you obtain before you make a purchase?

**Section 3**

6. What are the four consumer rights that President John F. Kennedy stated?
7. What are two consumer responsibilities?

## Thinking Critically

1. **Understanding Cause and Effect** Create a diagram like the one below to explain how education, occupation, and location make a difference in a person's earning power.

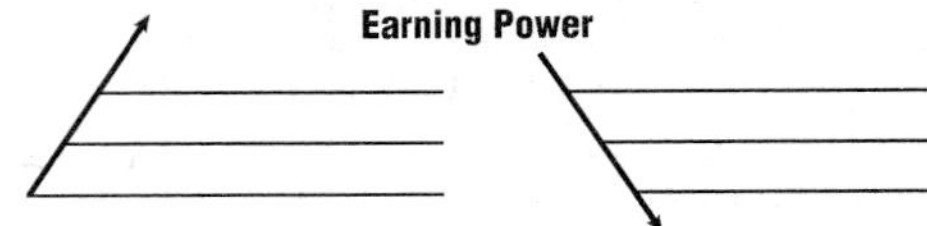


2. **Making Generalizations** Why do some people buy brand-name products and other people buy generic products? What are the trade-offs involved in this decision?



### Thinking Critically

1. Better education, higher-paying occupation, and city location lead to higher earning power. Lower levels of education, lower-paying occupation, and rural location lead to reduced earning power.
2. Answers may vary but might include: brand-name products ensure more consistent quality and reliability; generic products offer cost savings.

### Applying Economic Concepts

Answers will vary. Ensure that students analyze advertisements according to the points noted on the checklist.

## Applying Economic Concepts

**Competition and Market Structure** Design a print advertisement for a product of your choosing. After you complete the ad, use the checklist on page 68 to analyze it. Write a sentence to answer each of the questions on the checklist. Do you think it is a competitive ad, an informative ad, or both? Explain.

## Cooperative Learning Project

Working in groups of four, take a copy of the checklist on page 63 and shop for one of the following: DVD player, portable CD player, or personal computer. Each of you should keep a record of the steps you take and the information you gather using a table like the one below. Compare your information with what others in the class found.

| Checklist Number | Step | Information |
|---|---|---|
| 1. | | |
| 2. | | |
| 3. | | |

## Reviewing Skills

**Distinguishing Fact From Opinion** Analyze the advertisement below, then answer the questions that follow.

1. Which of the statements in the ad are based on facts? Explain.
2. Which of the statements are based on opinion? Explain.

**WE DELIVER!**

**Air freight. Ocean services. Less-than-truckload. Full truckload. Nationally. Globally.**

**We're a group of market-leading businesses that deliver in a "need-it-now" world.**

**We're a $5 billion company, with 33,000 people, 25,000 pieces of equipment, up to 100 jet freighters, and the industry's most advanced information systems.**

## Technology Activity

**Using E-Mail** Many consumers will complain about a defective product or lousy service to friends and family members. Learn to address a problem purchase with someone who can solve it—the manufacturer. Think of a product or service you were dissatisfied with after purchasing it. Practice writing an E-mail to the manufacturer using the outline below.

Your Address
City, State, Zip Code
Phone
Date

Customer Service Department
Company Name
Street Address
City, State, Zip Code

Dear Customer Service Representative:

I bought a (product name, serial no., model no.) at (location and date of purchase). Unfortunately, (state problem, history of problem, and efforts to solve it).

I would appreciate your (state specific actions to be taken). Enclosed are copies of the following records: (list and enclose all documents connected with the problem).

I am looking forward to your reply and resolution of my problem and will wait (state reasonable time period) before seeking third party assistance. Please contact me at the above address or by phone.

Sincerely,

## Analyzing the Global Economy

Research how consumers in other countries resolve unsatisfactory purchases. Use the Internet to find government agencies in foreign nations that have duties similar to the United States Department of Commerce.



# CHAPTER 3
## Assessment and Activities

### Cooperative Learning Project

Tables may vary. Tables should represent a detailed account of the shopping process for the selected item.

### Reviewing Skills

1. The following phrases are based on facts: "Air freight. Ocean services. Less-than-truckload. Full truckload. Nationally. Globally"; "We're a $5 billion company, with 33,000 people, 25,000 pieces of equipment, up to 100 jet freighters." They can be checked by looking at statistics available in company and industry records.
2. "market-leading businesses" and "industry's most advanced information systems"; They are value judgments.

### Technology Activity

E-mail letters will vary. Encourage students to share and compare their letters.

### Analyzing the Global Economy

Research findings may vary. Ask students to present their findings in a brief written report.

### Chapter Bonus Test Question

ASK: What manufacturer's agreement allows you to return a watch for free repair during a stated period? *warranty*

CASE STUDY **Focus on Free Enterprise**

# 1 Focus

You might introduce this feature by mentioning that Michael Dell is just one of several young American entrepreneurs who used their knowledge of computers and computing to create successful businesses. Call on volunteers to identify others. *Students' suggestions might include: Bill Gates, founder of Microsoft; Steve Jobs and Steve Wozniak, founders of Apple; Jeff Bezos, founder of Amazon.com.*

# 2 Teach

Review with students Dell's direct marketing methods. Next, ask students to identify the advantages of such a marketing approach in the computer industry. *Student responses may vary. A typical response might be that the computer industry is prone to rapid technological change. By not carrying a large inventory of assembled computers, Dell is able to add the latest technology as soon as it becomes available.* Then ask students what the disadvantages of Dell's approach might be. *Most students will point out that if there were shortages of particular computer components, Dell would have difficulty filling its orders.*

CASE STUDY **Focus on Free Enterprise**

# Dell Computer Corporation

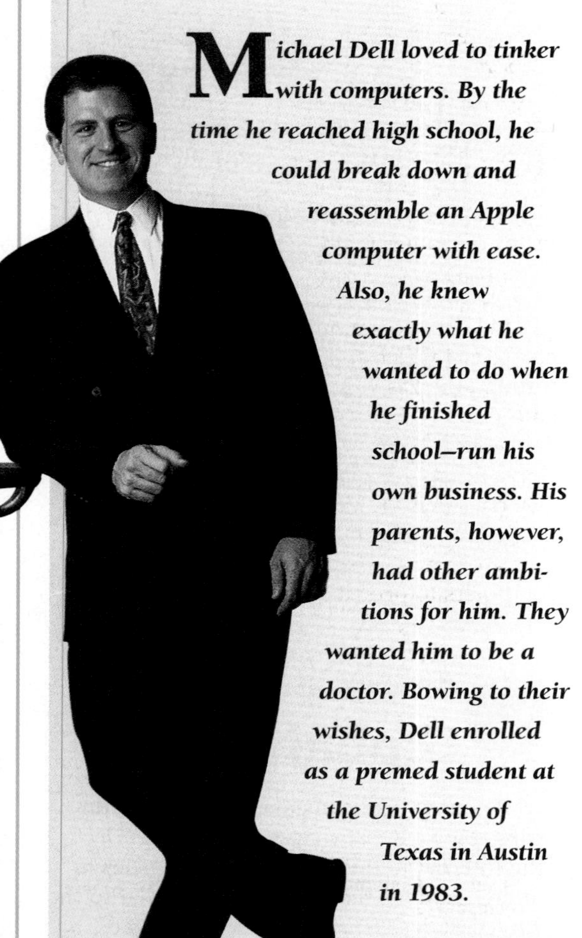

***Michael Dell loved to tinker with computers. By the time he reached high school, he could break down and reassemble an Apple computer with ease. Also, he knew exactly what he wanted to do when he finished school—run his own business. His parents, however, had other ambitions for him. They wanted him to be a doctor. Bowing to their wishes, Dell enrolled as a premed student at the University of Texas in Austin in 1983.***

### Student Entrepreneur

Many students take on part-time jobs to help pay their college expenses. Dell was no exception, although the job he took was rather exceptional. He ran his own computer company! Dell bought outdated PCs from local computer stores and upgraded them with the latest technology. At first, he sold the refurbished PCs to university students. Then he started selling them by mail order.

As the business became more successful, Dell's dorm room started to look like a warehouse. PCs and computer parts occupied every free inch of space. He even used the bathtub as a storage area! Of course, running the business left him little time for his studies. When his parents discovered this, they were furious. They told him to focus on his schoolwork. Dell reluctantly agreed, promising to limit his business activities to the summer vacation.

Dell's business boomed that summer. In the last month of the vacation, he recorded $180,000 in sales. He never returned for his

### Extending the Content

**More About Michael Dell** Michael Dell used his expertise with computers to achieve business success—selling newspaper subscriptions—even before he graduated from high school. He realized that people setting up new households—newlyweds and people moving into the area, for example—would be the most likely to want newspaper subscriptions. So he obtained marriage-license and property tax lists from local government offices. He then used his computer to generate letters to the thousands of names on these lists. With the money he made from subscription sales, Dell bought himself a car—a BMW!

sophomore year at the University of Texas. Instead, he went into the computer business full time, setting up Dell Computer Corporation in Austin. Rather than upgrade old computers, Dell Computer built new ones from scratch. The results were the same. The company consistently racked up impressive sales figures.

### Dell Direct

Dell Computer Corporation's success is a result of its business approach—the direct business model. Rather than sell computers through dealers, Dell sells directly to consumers. Instead of having huge warehouses stacked with ready-made computers, Dell makes computers to customer specifications. Fast delivery—within two weeks of ordering—and excellent technical service are also part of Dell's direct business model. This approach results in cheaper, more up-to-date computers for consumers.

At first, customers ordered computers from Dell by mail or telephone. After the introduction of the Internet, Dell also offered an online ordering service. Michael Dell immediately saw the potential of the Internet: "[Y]ou could order anything [online]—including a computer. And the great thing was, you needed a computer to do this! I couldn't imagine a more powerful creation for extending our business."

Dell's view proved correct. Today, the Dell Computer Corporation Web site logs about 2 million visitors a week. It generates $14 million in sales per day, making Dell one of the leading companies in Internet commerce.

### An Industry Leader

From its beginnings as a one-person, dorm-room operation in 1983, Dell Computer has grown into a multinational corporation. It maintains manufacturing centers and sales offices in several countries, and employs more than 24,000 people. With yearly revenues in the billions of dollars, Dell is the world's second-largest—only Compaq is bigger—and fastest-growing major computer manufacturer.

### Future Plans

Michael Dell's immediate plans for his company involve continuing growth through increased Internet sales. To this end, Dell launched a new Web site—Gigabuys.com—in 1999. The Dell Computer Corporation's original Web site sells only Dell computers and various accessories needed to run them. Gigabuys, however, sells an array of products—everything from computers to printer paper. Introducing consumers to his services, Dell hopes, will help achieve his long-term goal—for everyone to own a Dell computer!

#### *Free Enterprise in Action*

1. **What is the Dell direct business model?**
2. **Why did Michael Dell feel that the development of the Internet was important for his company?**



# 3 Assess

Have students answer the **Free Enterprise in Action** questions.

# 4 Close

Lead students in a discussion of why they think Michael Dell was able to achieve business success.

## ? Did You Know

In 1999 Dell Computer was ranked 78th among the Fortune 500 companies and 210th in the Fortune Global 500 listings.

### Answers to *Free Enterprise In Action*

1. Rather than sell computers through dealers, Dell sells directly to consumers. Instead of having huge warehouses stacked with ready-made computers, Dell makes computers to customer specifications.
2. because you could buy anything on the Internet—including computers, and you needed a computer for access to the Internet

# CHAPTER 4 Resource Manager

## Teaching Transparency

### Economic Concepts Transparency 6

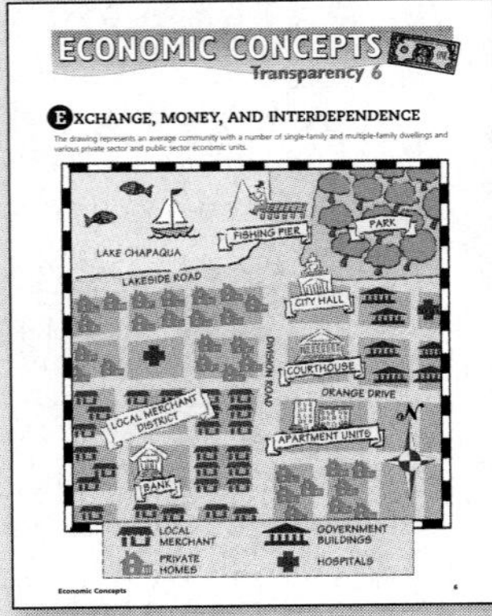

## Application and Enrichment

### Enrichment Activity 4

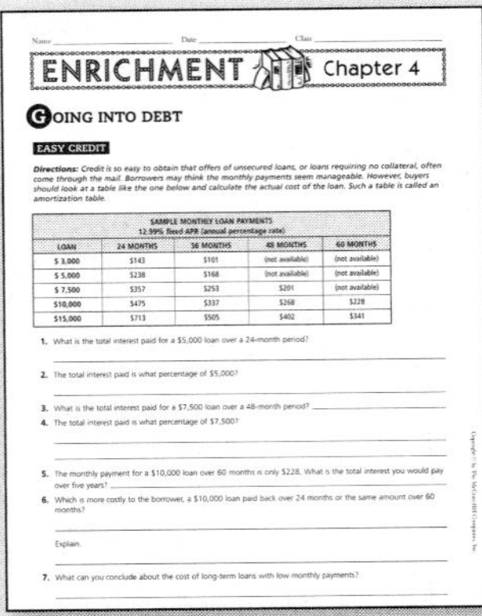

### Consumer Applications Activity 10

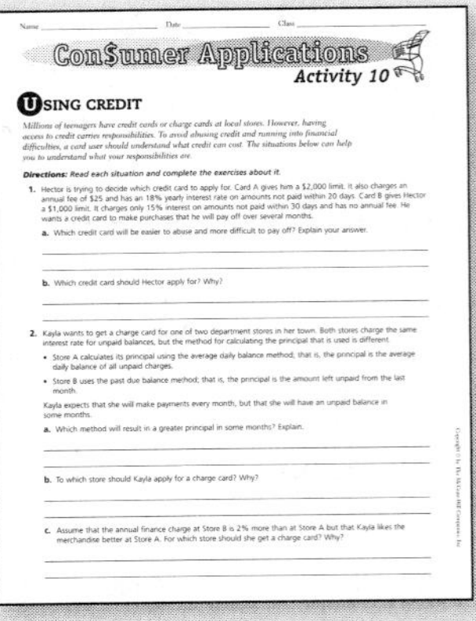

### Free Enterprise Activity 10

## Application and Enrichment

### Cooperative Learning Simulations and Problems 10

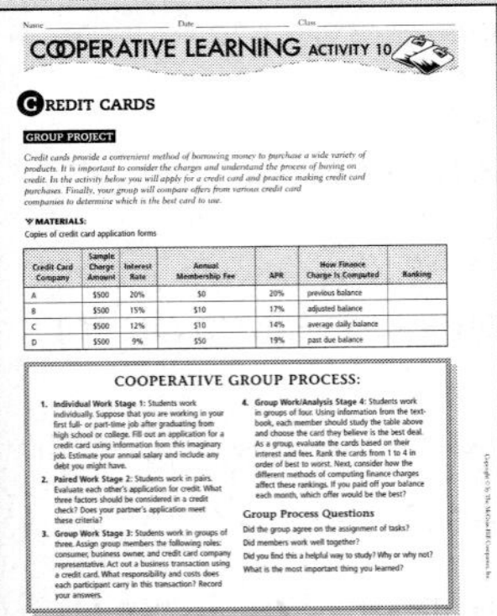

### Primary and Secondary Source Reading 10

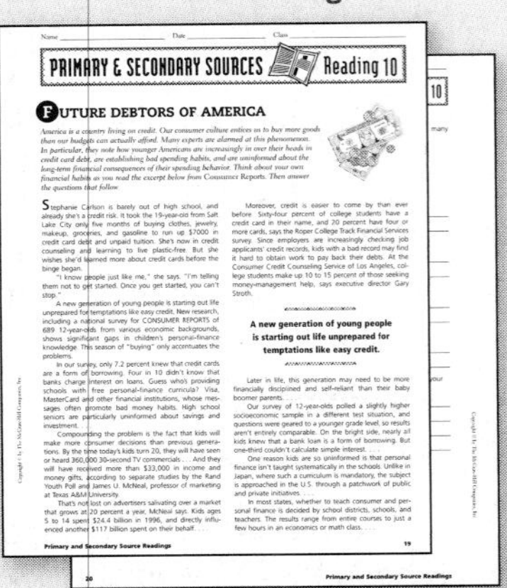

### Math Practice for Economics Activity 10

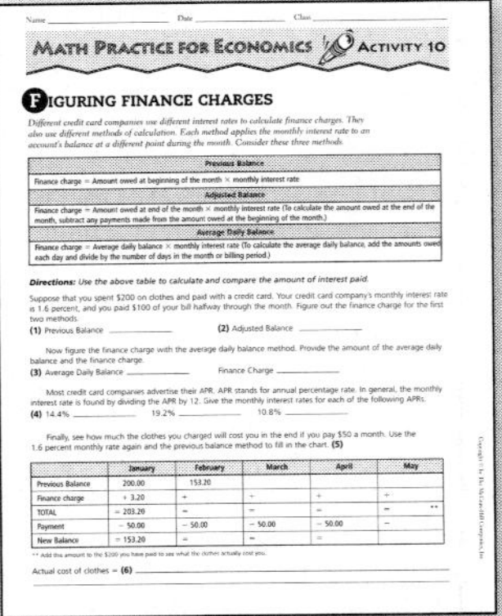

### Economic Cartoons Activity 10

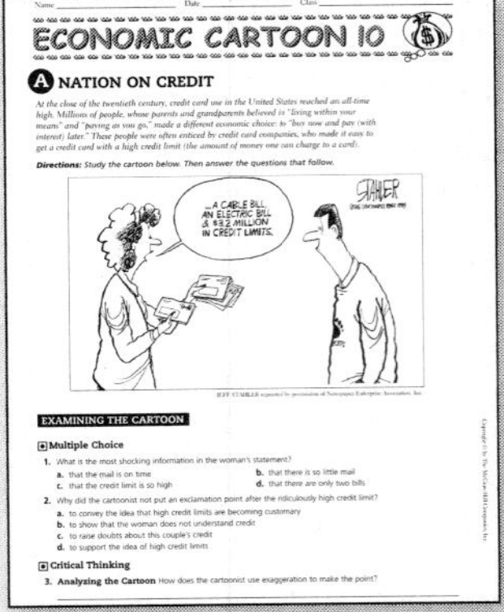

## Review and Reinforcement

### Critical Thinking Activity 10

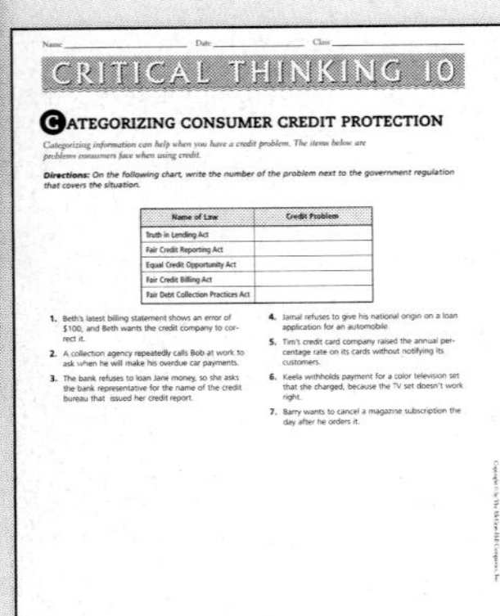

### Reteaching Activity 4

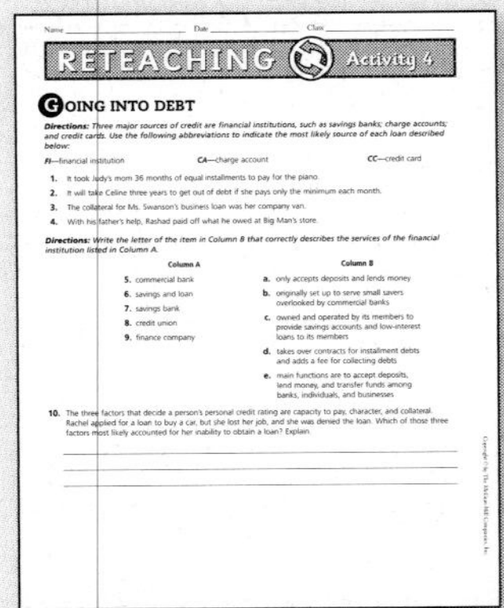

### Economic Vocabulary Activity 4

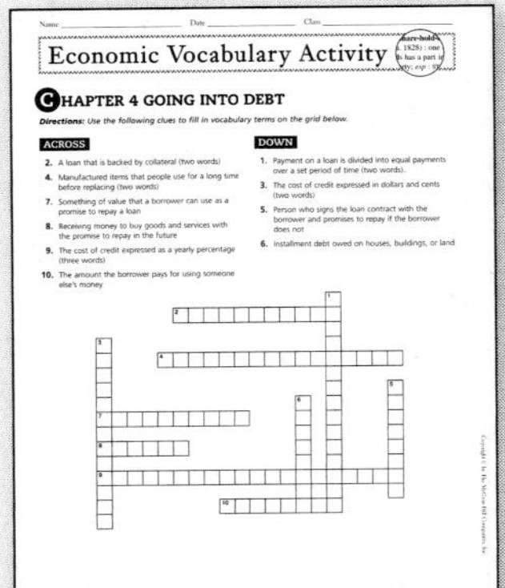

### Reinforcing Economic Skills 23

# CHAPTER 4 Resource Manager

## Assessment and Evaluation

Chapter 4 Test Form A

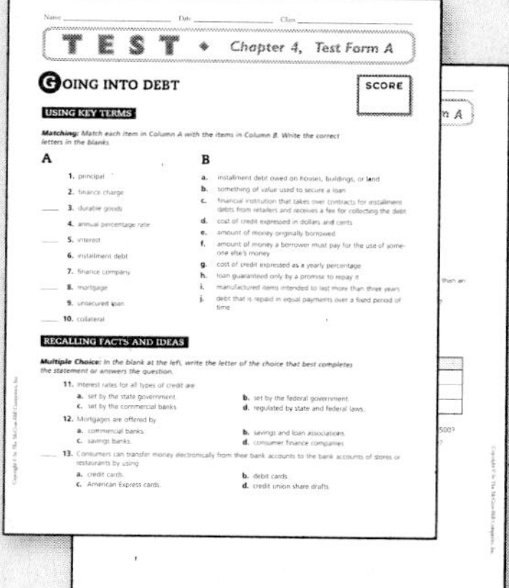
TEST ◆ Chapter 4, Test Form A

GOING INTO DEBT

SCORE

USING KEY TERMS

RECALLING FACTS AND IDEAS

Chapter 4 Test Form B

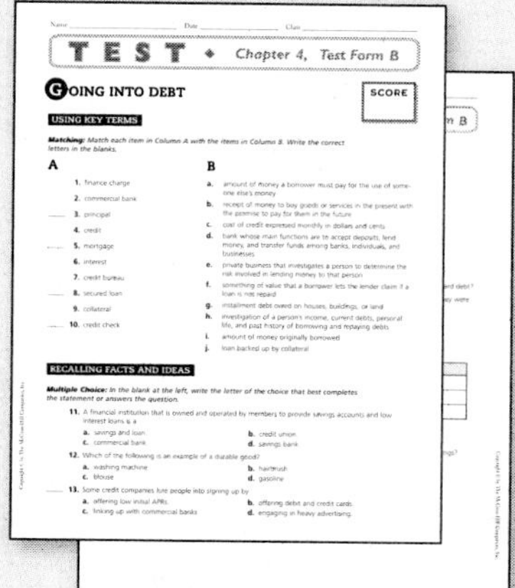
TEST ◆ Chapter 4, Test Form B

GOING INTO DEBT

SCORE

USING KEY TERMS

RECALLING FACTS AND IDEAS

Performance Assessment Activity 10

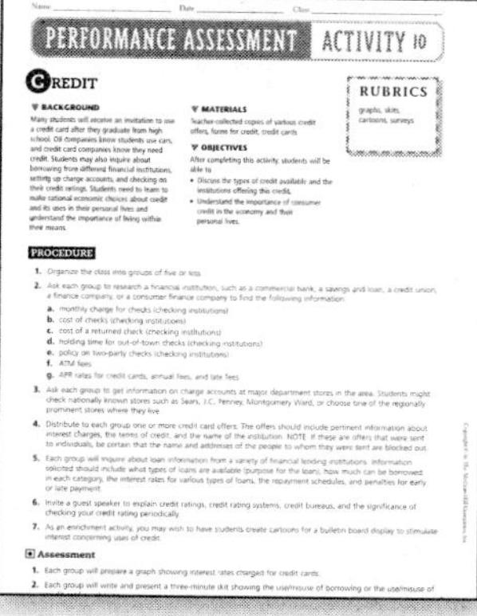
PERFORMANCE ASSESSMENT ACTIVITY 10

CREDIT

RUBRICS

PROCEDURE

ExamView® Pro Testmaker

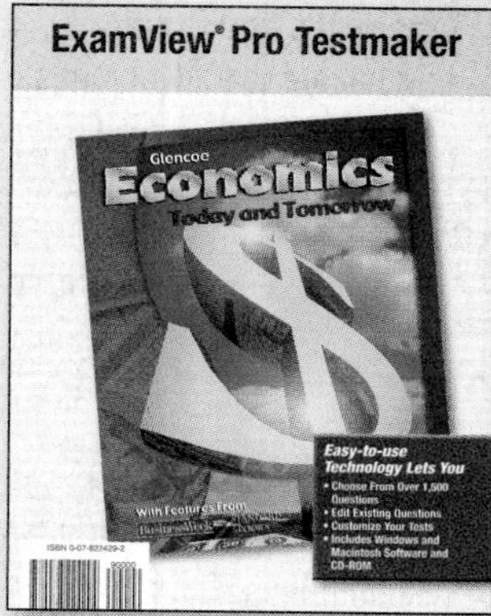


## Technology and Multimedia

 Vocabulary PuzzleMaker Software

 Interactive Tutor Self-Assessment Software

 ExamView® Pro Testmaker

 NBR *Economics & You* Video Program (English/Spanish)

 Presentation Plus!

 Glencoe Skillbuilder Interactive Workbook CD-ROM, Level 2

 Interactive Lesson Planner

 MindJogger Videoquiz

 Interactive Economics! CD-ROM

Audio Program (English or Spanish)

## ECONOMICS Online

You and your students can visit ett.glencoe.com—the Web site companion to **Economics Today and Tomorrow.** This innovative integration of electronic and print media offers your students a wealth of opportunities. The student text directs students to the Web site for the following options:

- **Chapter Overviews**
- **Self-Check Quizzes**
- **Student Web Activities**
- **Textbook Updates**

Answers are provided for you in the **Web Activity Lesson Plan.** Additional Web resources and Interactive Puzzles are also available.

Use the Glencoe Web site for additional resources. All essential content is covered in the Student Edition.

## Spanish Resources

 Spanish Economic Concepts Transparency 6

 Spanish Vocabulary Activity 4

 Spanish Reteaching Activity 4

 Spanish Section Quizzes for Chapter 4

 Spanish Chapter 4 Audio Program, Activity, and Test

## Additional Resources

### Reading for the Student

Solomon, Michael R. *Consumer Behavior: Buying, Having, and Being,* 4th ed. New York: Prentice Hall, 1998. A detailed discussion of the buying behavior of consumers.

### Multimedia Material

*User Friendly Budgeting,* 1998. Learning Seed, 330 Telser Road, Lake Zurich, IL 60047. VHS. Newly graduated students show that independent living requires budgeting.

# CHAPTER 4 Resource Manager

## Section Resources

| Reading Objectives | Reproducible Resources | Technology/Multimedia Resources |
|---|---|---|
| **Section 1**<br>**Americans and Credit**<br>• What are the advantages of repaying installment debt over a long period?<br>• Why do people go into debt?<br>• What factors should you consider when deciding whether or not to use credit? | Reproducible Lesson Plan 4-1<br>Daily Lecture Notes 4-1<br>Guided Reading Activity 4-1<br>Reading Essentials and Study Guide 4-1<br>Daily Focus Activity 30<br>Section Quiz 4-1* | Daily Focus Transparency 30<br>Vocabulary PuzzleMaker<br>Interactive Tutor Self-Assessment Software<br>MindJogger Videoquiz<br>Presentation Plus!<br>ExamView® Pro Testmaker |
| **Section 2**<br>**Sources of Loans and Credit**<br>• What are six types of financial institutions?<br>• What three kinds of charge accounts are available from stores?<br>• How are credit cards used?<br>• How do a finance charge and an annual percentage rate differ? | Reproducible Lesson Plan 4-2<br>Daily Lecture Notes 4-2<br>Guided Reading Activity 4-2<br>Reading Essentials and Study Guide 4-2<br>Daily Focus Activity 31<br>Section Quiz 4-2*<br>Reinforcing Economic Skills 23 | Daily Focus Transparency 31<br>Economic Concepts Transparency 6<br>Vocabulary PuzzleMaker<br>Interactive Tutor Self-Assessment Software<br>MindJogger Videoquiz<br>NBR's *Economics & You**<br>Presentation Plus!<br>ExamView® Pro Testmaker |
| **Section 3**<br>**Applying for Credit**<br>• What four factors determine a person's credit rating?<br>• What are your responsibilities as a borrower? | Reproducible Lesson Plan 4-3<br>Daily Lecture Notes 4-3<br>Guided Reading Activity 4-3<br>Reading Essentials and Study Guide 4-3<br>Daily Focus Activity 32<br>Section Quiz 4-3* | Daily Focus Transparency 32<br>Vocabulary PuzzleMaker<br>Interactive Tutor Self-Assessment Software<br>MindJogger Videoquiz<br>Presentation Plus!<br>ExamView® Pro Testmaker |
| **Section 4**<br>**Government Regulation of Credit**<br>• How has the Equal Credit Opportunity Act affected consumer credit?<br>• What are state usury laws?<br>• Why might a person declare personal bankruptcy? | Reproducible Lesson Plan 4-4<br>Daily Lecture Notes 4-4<br>Guided Reading Activity 4-4<br>Reading Essentials and Study Guide 4-4<br>Daily Focus Activity 33<br>Section Quiz 4-4* | Daily Focus Transparency 33<br>Vocabulary PuzzleMaker<br>Interactive Tutor Self-Assessment Software<br>MindJogger Videoquiz<br>Presentation Plus!<br>ExamView® Pro Testmaker |

*Also available in Spanish

Blackline Master
Transparency

Software
CD-ROM

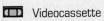

Videodisc
Audiocassette

Videocassette

# CHAPTER 4 Resource Manager

## ACTIVITY From the Classroom of

**Hal Kraynek**
**Valley High School**
**Santa Ana, California**

### Buying a Home

In this activity, students research to find out what is involved in purchasing a home. They need to contact a local title agency or real estate agent, or use the Internet, to find information about the following:

- Time spent in escrow
- Fees and charges
- Interest rates for 15-, 20-, and 30-year mortgages
- Payment rates
- Types of homeowners' insurance
- Buying a new versus a used home
- Landscape expenditures
- Repair expenditures
- Location near schools and shopping

Students may work with a partner and present their findings in an oral report to the class.

## Easy Planning and Preparation!

Use Glencoe's **Presentation Plus!**, a Microsoft PowerPoint® application, to teach **Going Into Debt.** With this multimedia teacher tool, you can customize ready-made presentations. At your fingertips are interactive transparencies, on-screen lecture notes, audiovisual presentations, and links to the Internet and to other Glencoe multimedia.

### Interactive Lesson Planner

Planning has never been easier! Organize your week, month, semester, or year with all the lesson helps you need to make teaching creative, timely, and relevant—the way it is meant to be. The Interactive Lesson Planner opens Glencoe's **Chapter 4** resources, helps you build your schedule, and tracks your progress.

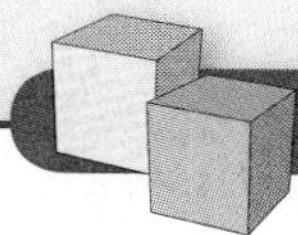

## Block Schedule

Activities that are particularly suited to use within the block scheduling framework are identified throughout this chapter by the following designation: BLOCK SCHEDULING

## Key to Ability Levels

**Teaching strategies have been coded for varying learning styles and abilities.**

L1 BASIC activities for all students
L2 AVERAGE activities for average to above-average students
L3 CHALLENGING activities for above-average students
ELL ENGLISH LANGUAGE LEARNER activities

## National Council on Economic Education

### THE EconomicsAmerica AND EconomicsInternational PROGRAMS

#### Voluntary Standards Emphasized in Chapter 4

**Content Standard 12** Students will understand that interest rates, adjusted for inflation, rise and fall to balance the amount saved with the amount borrowed, thus affecting the allocation of scarce resources between present and future uses.

**Content Standard 10** Students will understand that institutions evolve in market economies to help individuals and groups accomplish their goals

#### Resources Available from NCEE

- *Capstone: The Nation's High School Economics Course*
- *Personal Decision Making: Focus on Economics*
- *Personal Finance Economics: Wallet Wisdom*
- *MCG–Economics and Entrepreneurship*

To order these materials, or to contact your State Council on Economic Education about workshops and programs, call 1-800-338-1192 or visit the NCEE Web site at http://www.nationalcouncil.org

ECONOMICS & YOU

Going Into Debt

Chapter 10
Disc 1, Side 1

ASK: What is the difference between a secured and an unsecured loan? *A secured loan is backed with collateral. If the loan is not paid back, the bank can claim the collateral. An unsecured loan is issued on the basis of a person's reputation and does not require collateral.*

Also available in VHS.

## Chapter Overview

Chapter 4 explains the advantages of buying items on credit and why people decide to use credit; six types of lending institutions; how credit ratings are determined; and borrowers' responsibilities.

## GLENCOE TECHNOLOGY

Use **MindJogger Videoquiz** VHS to preview Chapter 4 content.

Introduce students to chapter content and key terms by having them access **Chapter 4—Chapter Overviews** at ett.glencoe.com

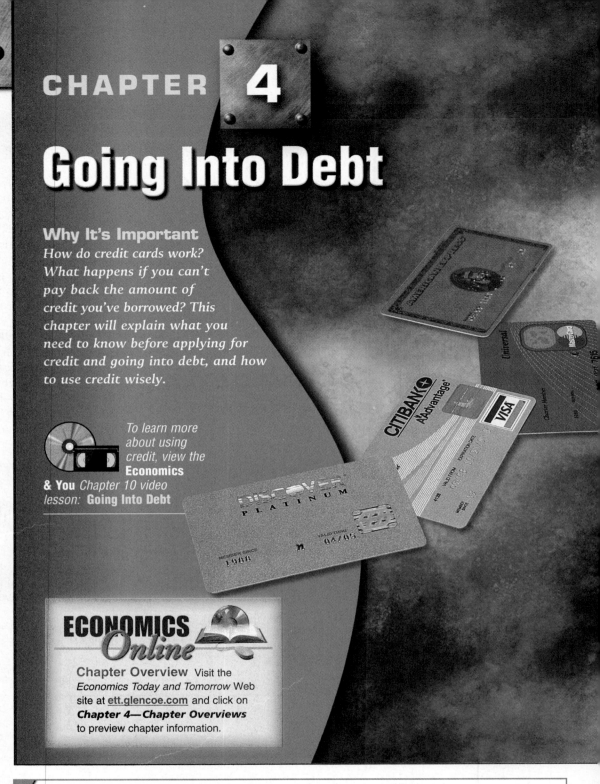

# CHAPTER 4
# Going Into Debt

### Why It's Important

*How do credit cards work? What happens if you can't pay back the amount of credit you've borrowed? This chapter will explain what you need to know before applying for credit and going into debt, and how to use credit wisely.*

*To learn more about using credit, view the* **Economics & You** *Chapter 10 video lesson:* **Going Into Debt**

ECONOMICS Online

**Chapter Overview** Visit the *Economics Today and Tomorrow* Web site at ett.glencoe.com and click on ***Chapter 4—Chapter Overviews*** to preview chapter information.

## CHAPTER LAUNCH ACTIVITY

Offer students the following scenario: Two friends have offered to lend you $1,000 to buy whatever you want. The first friend would like you to refund the money within the year, but for every month that goes by without repayment, he or she will charge you $10 interest. The second friend places no time limit on repayment, but will charge you $5 interest for every month that goes by without repayment. Ask students, from which friend, if either, they would borrow the $1,000. Steer students toward such topics as the financial cost and opportunity cost of borrowing money. Close the discussion by pointing out that in Chapter 4 they will learn about credit and debt.

SECTION 1

# Americans and Credit

## COVER STORY

*THE WASHINGTON POST,* MAY 10, 1999

Debt is not itself a bad thing. Used properly, credit allows young families to buy their own homes and acquire other trappings of middle-class life without waiting until middle age. Homeownership, in turn, gives these families a stake in their communities and encourages them to take an active role in keeping it a good place to live.

But easy credit—and plainly credit is very easy today—creates a temptation to push the envelope, to live at a higher level than the borrower can safely afford.

### READER'S GUIDE

**Terms to Know**

- credit
- principal
- interest
- installment debt
- durable goods
- mortgage

**Reading Objectives**

1. What are the advantages of repaying installment debt over a long period?
2. Why do people go into debt?
3. What factors should you consider when deciding whether or not to use credit?

Americans use credit to make many purchases. The total amount of funds borrowed and lent each year is enormous. In addition to individuals borrowing funds, the federal, state, and local governments all borrow funds, too. The nation's economy, in fact, depends on individuals and groups being able to buy and borrow on credit. In this section, you'll learn what credit is and why people use it.

## What Is Credit?

**Credit** is the receiving of funds either directly or indirectly to buy goods and services today with the promise to pay for them in the future. The amount owed–the debt–is equal to the principal

**credit:** *receipt of money either directly or indirectly to buy goods and services in the present with the promise to pay for them in the future*

## SECTION 1 RESOURCE MANAGER

**Reproducible Masters**

- Reproducible Lesson Plan 4–1
- Reading Essentials and Study Guide 4–1
- Guided Reading Activity 4–1
- Section Quiz 4–1
- Daily Focus Activity 30
- Daily Lecture Notes 4–1

**Multimedia**

- Daily Focus Transparency 30
- Vocabulary PuzzleMaker
- Interactive Tutor Self-Assessment Software
- ExamView® Pro Testmaker
- MindJogger Videoquiz
- Presentation Plus!



# 1 Focus

## Overview

Section 1 explains or describes the importance and uses of consumer credit and loans in the economy, the advantages of repaying loans over the long term, and why and how consumers decide to use credit.

### BELLRINGER
**Motivational Activity**

Project **Daily Focus Transparency 30** and have students answer the questions.

This activity is also available as a blackline master.

**Daily Focus Transparency 30**

USING CREDIT

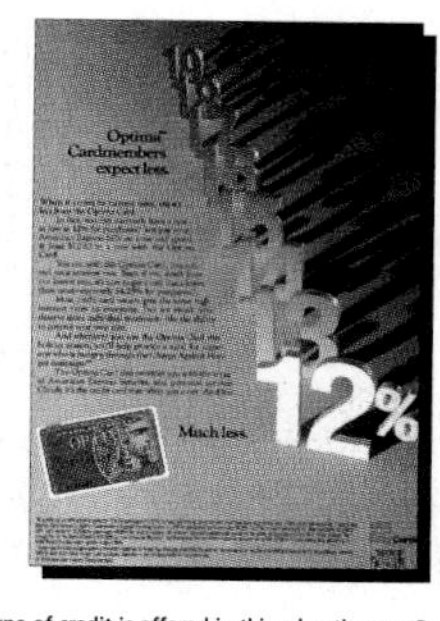


1. What type of credit is offered in this advertisement?
2. What important consumer information is supplied in this advertisement?

Daily Focus Transparencies

### READER'S GUIDE

Answers to the **Reading Objectives** questions are on page 87.

**Preteaching Vocabulary**

Have students write sentences using the **Terms to Know**—one term per sentence. Then have them rewrite the sentences on a separate sheet of paper, replacing the terms with blanks. Pair students and have partners exchange and complete the sentence sheets.

**Vocabulary PuzzleMaker**

# CHAPTER 4

SECTION 1, Pages 83–87

# 2 Teach

## Guided Practice

L2 Applying Ideas Help students understand the importance of credit in the economy by asking them to discuss what life would be like if all purchases had to be paid for with cash. Begin the discussion by listing on the board purchases people often make with credit–houses, automobiles, home improvement, college tuition, and vacations, for example. Have students use the point developed in the discussion to write a brief essay titled "Life Without Credit."

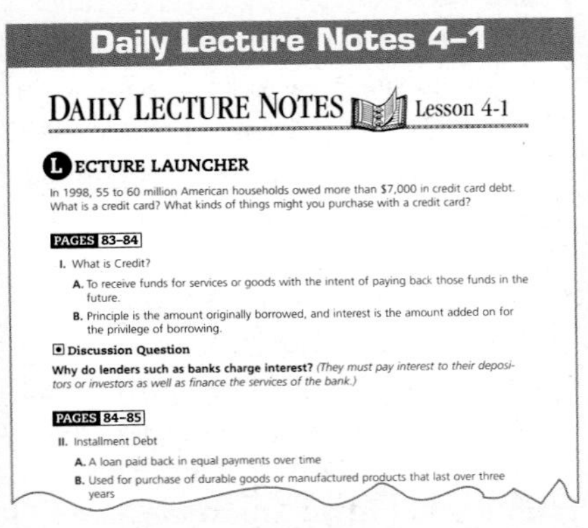
Daily Lecture Notes 4–1

DAILY LECTURE NOTES Lesson 4-1

LECTURE LAUNCHER

In 1998, 55 to 60 million American households owed more than $7,000 in credit card debt. What is a credit card? What kinds of things might you purchase with a credit card?

PAGES 83–84

I. What is Credit?

A. To receive funds for services or goods with the intent of paying back those funds in the future.

B. Principle is the amount originally borrowed, and interest is the amount added on for the privilege of borrowing.

Discussion Question

**Why do lenders such as banks charge interest?** *(They must pay interest to their depositors or investors as well as finance the services of the bank.)*

PAGES 84–85

II. Installment Debt

A. A loan paid back in equal payments over time

B. Used for purchase of durable goods or manufactured products that last over three years

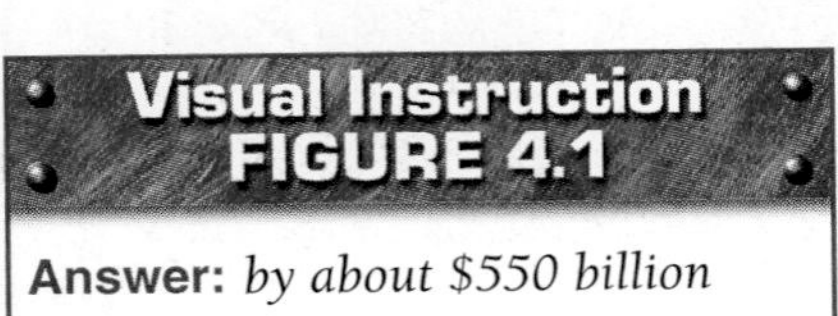


**Answer:** *by about $550 billion*

**principal:** *amount of money originally borrowed in a loan*

**interest:** *amount of money the borrower must pay for the use of someone else's money*

plus interest. The **principal** is the amount originally borrowed. The **interest** is the amount the borrower must pay for the use of someone else's money. That "someone else" may be a bank, a credit card company, or a store.

Any time you receive credit, you are borrowing funds and going into debt. Taking out a loan is the same as buying an item on credit. In both cases, you must pay interest for the use of someone else's purchasing power.

**installment debt:** *type of loan repaid with equal payments, or installments, over a specific period of time*

**durable goods:** *manufactured items that have a life span longer than three years*

## Installment Debt

One of the most common types of debt is **installment debt.** Consumers repay this type of loan with equal payments, or installments, over a period of time; for example, 36 equal payments over 36 months. Many people buy **durable goods,** or manufactured items that last longer than three years, on an installment plan. Automobiles, refrigerators, washers, and other appliances are

**FIGURE 4.1**

**Increase in Borrowing** More and more Americans are choosing to buy durable goods on credit. ***By how much did consumer debt increase between 1990 and 2000?***

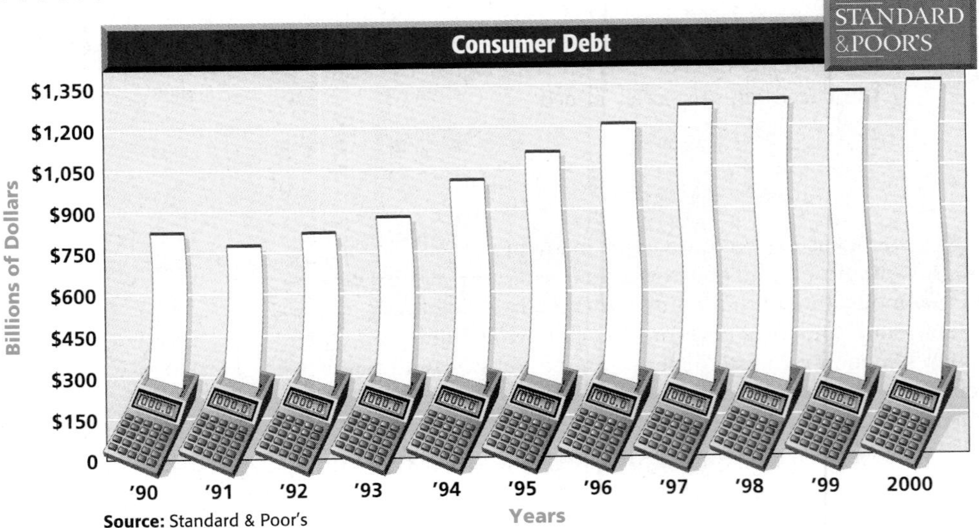


ECONOMICS Online For an online update of this graph, visit ett.glencoe.com and click on ***Textbook Updates—Chapter 4.***



## Meeting Special Needs

**Reading Disability** Students with reading or organizational difficulties may not readily comprehend that installment debt can be both a benefit and a liability. Discuss the material in this section to show students how installment debt can be a liability if the value of the purchased item goes down over the term of the loan. Then point out that, in contrast, an installment debt can be a benefit if the monthly payments match more closely the value of the consumer's use of the item.

Refer to *Inclusion for the Social Studies Classroom Strategies and Activities* for students with different learning styles.

considered durable goods. People can also borrow cash and pay it back in installments. **Figure 4.1** shows how installment debt owed each year in the United States has steadily increased.

The length of the installment period is important in determining the size of the borrower's monthly payments and the total amount of interest he or she must pay. A longer repayment period results in a smaller monthly payment. For example, **Figure 4.2** shows that if the repayment of a loan is spread over three years, the monthly payments will be smaller than if the loan were repaid in two years. There is a trade-off, however. The longer it takes to repay an installment loan, the greater the total interest the lender charges.

The largest form of installment debt in this country is the money people owe on mortgages. A **mortgage** is an installment debt owed on real property—houses, buildings, or land. See **Figure 4.3.** Interestingly, most people who owe a mortgage on their home do not consider themselves deeply in debt. Because people must have housing, they think of a mortgage as being a necessary monthly payment not similar to other kinds of debt. A mortgage is a debt, however, because somebody has provided the owner with funds to purchase property. In return, the owner must repay the loan with interest in installments over a number of years.

**FIGURE 4.3**

**Installment Debt** Mortgages make up the largest form of installment debt in the country. Most mortgages are repaid in monthly installments for 15 to 30 years.

**mortgage:** *installment debt owed on houses, buildings, or land*

**FIGURE 4.2**

**Pay Now or Pay Later?** Your monthly payment is lower if you choose the 36-month loan. ***How much more interest will you pay, however, if you spread the loan payment over 36 months rather than 24 months?***

**$1,000 Installment Loan at 9% Interest**

| Term of Loan | 24 Months | 36 Months |
|---|---|---|
| Monthly Payments | $45.69 | $31.80 |
| Total Interest | $96.56 | $114.80 |
| Total Payments | $1,096.56 | $1,144.80 |

## CHAPTER 4
SECTION 1, Pages 83–87

### Visual Instruction FIGURE 4.2

**Answer:** *$18.24*

### Guided Reading Activity 4–1

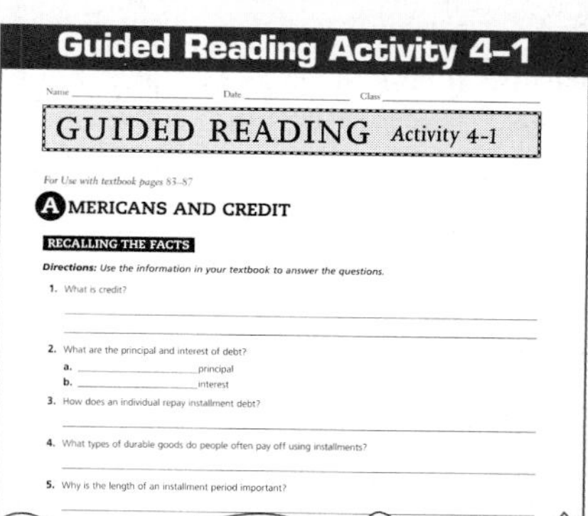

Name ______ Date ______ Class ______

GUIDED READING Activity 4-1

*For Use with textbook pages 83–87*

AMERICANS AND CREDIT

RECALLING THE FACTS

***Directions:*** *Use the information in your textbook to answer the questions.*

1. What is credit?
2. What are the principal and interest of debt?
   a. ______ principal
   b. ______ interest
3. How does an individual repay installment debt?
4. What types of durable goods do people often pay off using installments?
5. Why is the length of an installment period important?

### ? Did You Know

The Federal National Mortgage Association, or Fannie Mae, is the nation's largest provider of funds for home mortgages. Fannie Mae does not lend money directly to home buyers. Rather, it purchases mortgages from lending institutions. These lenders then use the money to provide mortgages to home buyers. Since it became a private company in 1968, Fannie Mae has helped more than 30 million American families to buy homes.

### Cooperative Learning

Organize students into small groups. Tell groups to imagine that they work for an advertising agency and have been asked to work on a radio campaign designed to inform people about the questions they should ask before buying on credit. Direct groups to write five jingles for the campaign one for each of the questions listed in **Figure 4.5** on page 87. Call on groups to broadcast their jingles for the rest of the class. BLOCK SCHEDULING

## Independent Practice

**L1 Illustrating Ideas** Have students work in small groups to collect newspaper and magazine advertisements, flyers, and direct mailings promoting various forms of credit in the United States. Direct groups to use the materials they collected to create a collage titled "Credit and Americans." Encourage groups to display their collages around the classroom.

ELL BLOCK SCHEDULING

### Visual Instruction FIGURE 4.4

Have students read the caption of **Figure 4.4**. Then call on volunteers to answer the following: What choice would you make and why?

## 3 Assess

### Meeting Lesson Objectives

Assign Section 1 Assessment as homework or an in-class activity.

Use **Interactive Tutor Self-Assessment Software** to review Section 1.

## Why People Use Credit

In a sense, people feel forced to buy items on credit because they believe they require these items immediately. They do not want to wait. Of course, consumers are not really "forced" to buy most goods and services on credit. They could decide instead to save the funds needed to make their purchases.

Some might say that you would be better off saving and waiting to buy a pickup truck. During the years you are saving for the truck, however, you forgo the pleasure of driving it. Many people do not want to postpone purchasing an important durable good. They would rather buy on credit and enjoy the use of the item now rather than later. See **Figure 4.4.**

Another reason for going into debt is to spread the payments over the life of the item being purchased. For example, people do not buy a truck or car to have it sit in the garage. What they buy is the availability of the vehicle each day, week, month, and year that they own it.

**FIGURE 4.4**

**Spreading Payments**
Suppose you want to buy a pickup truck that costs $15,000. You have a choice. You could borrow $15,000 right now and buy the truck, but you would have to make interest payments on the borrowed funds for three to five years. However, you can also enjoy using it at the same time you are paying for it. Alternatively, you could start saving now, earn interest on your savings, and pay cash for the truck in several years.

Suppose you buy the pickup truck for $15,000 and plan to keep it for five years. At the end of that time, it will be worth only $5,000. Over that five-year period, however, you will get approximately $2,000 worth of use per year, or $166 per month. By buying on the installment plan, a person makes monthly payments that more or less correspond to the value of the use he or she receives from the product.

## Deciding to Use Credit

The decision to borrow or use credit involves whether the satisfaction the borrower gets from the purchases is greater than the interest payments. It is basically a question of comparing costs and benefits. The benefit of borrowing is being able to buy and enjoy the good or service now rather than later. The cost is whatever the borrower must pay in interest or lost opportunities to buy other items.

The benefit of borrowing is something only you can decide for yourself. You and every other borrower, however, should be aware of the costs involved. **Figure 4.5** can help you decide when to use credit. It can also help you avoid the improper use of credit by overspending.



### Free Enterprise Activity

Remind students that just as financial institutions do not necessarily pay savers the same rate of interest, neither do they charge the same rate of interest on loans. Organize students into groups, and have them use library resources and the Internet to research mortgage rates charged by banks, savings and loan associations, and other financial institutions that provide mortgages. Have groups present their findings in chart form. In a follow-up discussion, ask students to suggest why mortgage rates might differ among lenders. BLOCK SCHEDULING

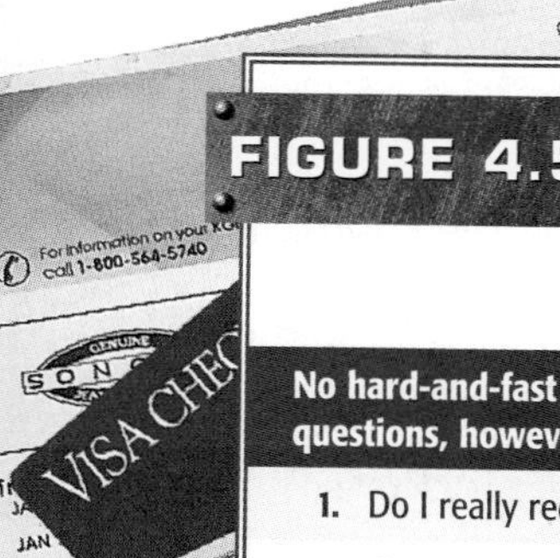

## FIGURE 4.5 Checklist for Buying on Credit

**No hard-and-fast rules can tell you whether or not to buy on credit. The following list of questions, however, can help you determine if you are making a wise decision.**

1. Do I really require this item? Can I postpone purchasing the item until later?
2. If I pay cash, what will I be giving up that I could buy with this money? This is an opportunity cost.
3. If I borrow or use credit, will the satisfaction I get from the item I buy be greater than the interest I must pay? This is also an opportunity cost.
4. Have I done comparison shopping for credit? In other words, after you have determined that you are not going to pay cash for something, you should look for the best loan or credit deal, including the lowest interest rate and other conditions of repayment.
5. Can I afford to borrow or use credit now?

**Practice** and **assess** key skills with *Skillbuilder Interactive Workbook, Level 2.*

## SECTION 1 Assessment

### Understanding Key Terms

1. **Define** credit, principal, interest, installment debt, durable goods, mortgage.

### Reviewing Objectives

2. What are the advantages of repaying installment debt over a long period?
3. Why do people go into debt?
4. **Graphic Organizer** Create a diagram like the one below to list the factors you should consider when deciding whether to use credit.

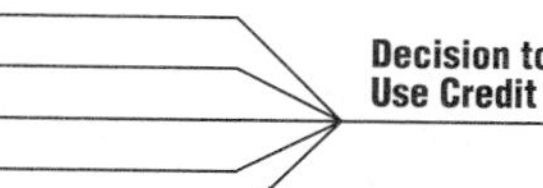


### Applying Economic Concepts

5. **Opportunity Cost** Think of an item that you have been saving for. How long will it take you to save the funds needed to purchase this item? What are you giving up buying in the meantime?

### Critical Thinking Activity

6. **Synthesizing Information** Imagine that you are shopping for a used car. If you borrow $10,000 to buy a used car, and the simple interest rate on the loan is 11 percent, what will your total payment be at the end of 24 months? At the end of 36 months? *For help in understanding interest rates, see page xxii in the Economic Handbook.*



## SECTION 1 Assessment Answers

1. All definitions can be found in the Glossary.
2. It allows people to buy and use durable goods, paying in small monthly payments rather than with a large lump sum that they may not have. Also, it allows people to borrow cash for immediate needs and pay back the debt in installments.
3. They feel they must purchase certain items right away, to spread the payments over the life of the item being purchased.
4. Answers will vary but may include: Do I really require this item? If I pay cash, what will I be giving up that I could buy with this money? Will the satisfaction I get from the item I buy be greater than the interest I must pay? Have I done comparison shopping for credit? Can I afford to borrow or use credit now?
5. Answers will vary.
6. $12,200; $13,300



### Section Quiz 4-1

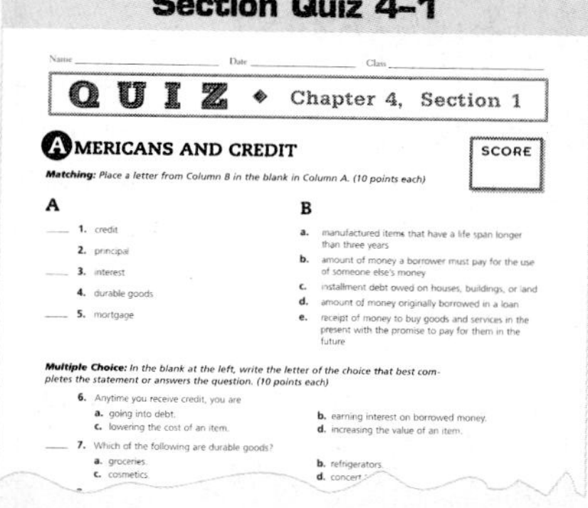

QUIZ ◆ Chapter 4, Section 1

AMERICANS AND CREDIT

SCORE

*Matching: Place a letter from Column B in the blank in Column A. (10 points each)*

| A | B |
|---|---|
| ___ 1. credit | a. manufactured items that have a life span longer than three years |
| ___ 2. principal | b. amount of money a borrower must pay for the use of someone else's money |
| ___ 3. interest | c. installment debt owed on houses, buildings, or land |
| ___ 4. durable goods | d. amount of money originally borrowed in a loan |
| ___ 5. mortgage | e. receipt of money to buy goods and services in the present with the promise to pay for them in the future |

*Multiple Choice: In the blank at the left, write the letter of the choice that best completes the statement or answers the question. (10 points each)*

___ 6. Anytime you receive credit, you are
a. going into debt. b. earning interest on borrowed money.
c. lowering the cost of an item. d. increasing the value of an item.

___ 7. Which of the following are durable goods?
a. groceries b. refrigerators
c. cosmetics d. concert

### Reteach

Have students write a summary outlining the main points of Section 1. Encourage students to share and compare their summaries.

### Reading Essentials and Study Guide 4-1

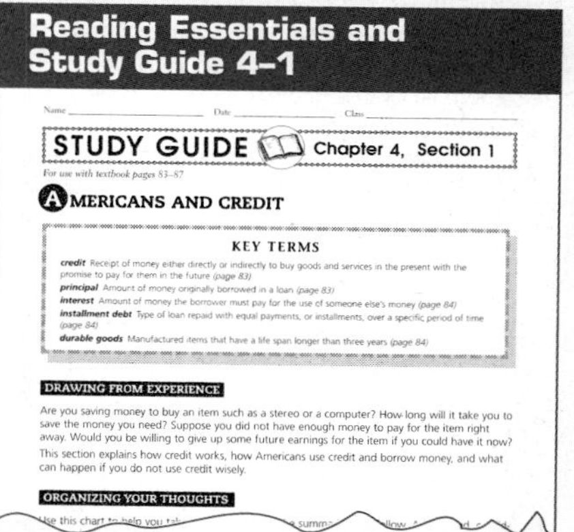

STUDY GUIDE Chapter 4, Section 1

AMERICANS AND CREDIT

KEY TERMS

**credit** Receipt of money either directly or indirectly to buy goods and services in the present with the promise to pay for them in the future (page 83)
**principal** Amount of money originally borrowed in a loan (page 83)
**interest** Amount of money the borrower must pay for the use of someone else's money (page 84)
**installment debt** Type of loan repaid with equal payments, or installments, over a specific period of time (page 84)
**durable goods** Manufactured items that have a life span longer than three years (page 84)

DRAWING FROM EXPERIENCE

Are you saving money to buy an item such as a stereo or a computer? How long will it take you to save the money you need? Suppose you did not have enough money to pay for the item right away. Would you be willing to give up some future earnings for the item if you could have it now? This section explains how credit works, how Americans use credit and borrow money, and what can happen if you do not use credit wisely.

ORGANIZING YOUR THOUGHTS

## 4 Close

Tell students that they have been invited to write an article, titled "How I Make Wise Credit Choices," for a consumer magazine. Then ask students to develop an outline for this article.

# 1 Focus

## Overview

Section 2 describes the credit choices available to consumers, and how to calculate annual percentage rates and finance charges.

### BELLRINGER
**Motivational Activity**

Project **Daily Focus Transparency 31** and have students answer the questions.

This activity is also available as a blackline master.

**Daily Focus Transparency 31**

FOCUS ACTIVITIES Transparency 31

FINANCIAL INSTITUTIONS

Financial Institutions in the United States (selected types)

| Type | Number of Establishments (in thousands) |
|---|---|
| Commercial banks | 65.8 |
| Savings institutions | 17.9 |
| Credit unions | 15.1 |
| Consumer finance institutions | 16.8 |
| Mortgage finance institutions | 20.1 |

Source: Statistical Abstract of the United States

1. What is the most common type of financial institution listed in the table?
2. What conclusions can you draw from the table?

Daily Focus Transparencies

### READER'S GUIDE

Answers to the **Reading Objectives** questions are on page 94.

**Preteaching Vocabulary**

Provide pairs of students with 18 index cards. One partner writes each of the **Terms to Know** on a card. The other partner writes each definition on a card. Have the first player lay down a term card and the second player define the term by laying the correct definition card.

**Vocabulary PuzzleMaker**

SECTION 2

# Sources of Loans and Credit

### READER'S GUIDE

**Terms to Know**

- commercial bank
- savings and loan association
- savings bank
- credit union
- finance company
- charge account
- credit card
- finance charge
- annual percentage rate (APR)

**Reading Objectives**

1. What are six types of financial institutions?
2. What three kinds of charge accounts are available from stores?
3. How are credit cards used?
4. How do a finance charge and an annual percentage rate differ?

### COVER STORY

KIPLINGER'S PERSONAL FINANCE MAGAZINE, DECEMBER 1998

Capital One and First USA deserve high marks for helping credit card customers jump off the teaser-rate merry-go-round. Both issuers began offering a platinum Visa with a 9.9% fixed interest rate and no annual fee.

But First USA loses points for jumping on the spank-the-cardholder bandwagon. The bargain rate jumps to 19.99% if you miss the payment-due date twice in six months. And in its fine print, Capital One reserves the right to change the rate if your credit rating slips.

There are two major types of credit—using credit cards and borrowing money directly from a financial institution. Although lending institutions differ in their services, they all charge interest on the funds they lend. In this section, you'll learn what those financial institutions are. You'll also learn about charge accounts and credit cards—and why you should be aware of the high interest rates they charge.

## Types of Financial Institutions

You should comparison shop when you have decided to apply for a loan. See **Figure 4.6.** To gather information, check various lending agencies in person, over the phone, or at their Web sites.



### SECTION 2 RESOURCE MANAGER

**Reproducible Masters**

- Reproducible Lesson Plan 4–2
- Reading Essentials and Study Guide 4–2
- Guided Reading Activity 4–2
- Section Quiz 4–2
- Daily Focus Activity 31
- Daily Lecture Notes 4–2

**Multimedia**

- Daily Focus Transparency 31
- Economic Concepts Transparency 6
- Vocabulary PuzzleMaker
- Interactive Tutor Self-Assessment Software
- ExamView® Pro Testmaker
- MindJogger Videoquiz
- NBR's *Economics & You*
- Presentation Plus!

**Commercial Banks** The first place you might think to go for a loan is a **commercial bank.** Commercial banks today control the largest amount of money and offer the widest range of services. These services include offering checking and savings accounts and loans to individuals. They also transfer funds among banks, individuals, and businesses.

**Savings and Loan Associations** A **savings and loan association (S&L),** like a commercial bank, accepts deposits and lends funds. S&Ls make many single-family and multi-family mortgage loans. They also finance commercial mortgages and auto loans. Their interest rates for loans are often slightly less than those for commercial banks.

**Savings Banks** **Saving banks** were first set up to serve the small savers who were overlooked by the large commercial banks. Most savings banks, like S&Ls, lend funds for home mortgages, although they do make personal and auto loans. Since 1980, savings banks, like commercial banks, have also been able to offer services similar to checking accounts.

**Credit Unions** Union members and employees of many companies often have a credit union. A **credit union** is owned and operated by its members to provide savings accounts and low-interest loans only to its members. Credit unions primarily make personal, auto, and home improvement loans, although larger

**commercial bank:** *bank whose main functions are to accept deposits, lend money, and transfer funds among banks, individuals, and businesses*

**savings and loan association (S&L):** *depository institution that accepts deposits and lends money*

**savings bank:** *depository institution originally set up to serve small savers overlooked by commercial banks*

**credit union:** *depository institution owned and operated by its members to provide savings accounts and low-interest loans only to its members*

B Finance Company

**Financial Institutions** Financial institutions differ in several factors, including differences in interest rates and loan repayment terms.

**Meeting Special Needs**

**Poor Math Skills** Calculating interest and finance charges can be difficult for students whose math skills are below average. Ensure that students know how to use the formulas for determining the cost of credit. Have them work through an exercise in which they intend to make an imaginary credit purchase and must calculate and compare the costs under different charge accounts. Explain that knowing how to find the best credit bargain can save hundreds—even thousands—of dollars.

Refer to *Inclusion for the Social Studies Classroom Strategies and Activities* for students with different learning styles.



# 2 Teach

## Guided Practice

**L1 Making Comparisons** Ask students to create two tables–one titled "Financial Institutions" and the other titled "Charge Accounts." In the former, have students compare and contrast the services offered by the different types of financial institutions. In the latter, have students compare and contrast the three types of charge accounts. Encourage students to display and discuss their tables.

**Daily Lecture Notes 4–2**

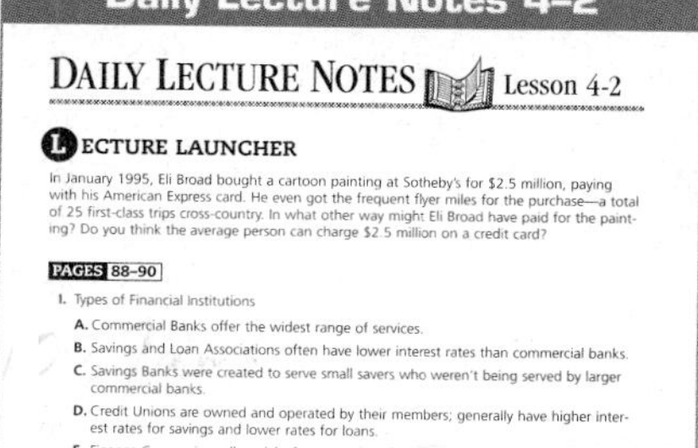
DAILY LECTURE NOTES Lesson 4-2

**LECTURE LAUNCHER**

In January 1995, Eli Broad bought a cartoon painting at Sotheby's for $2.5 million, paying with his American Express card. He even got the frequent flyer miles for the purchase—a total of 25 first-class trips cross-country. In what other way might Eli Broad have paid for the painting? Do you think the average person can charge $2.5 million on a credit card?

PAGES 88–90

I. Types of Financial Institutions
   - A. Commercial Banks offer the widest range of services.
   - B. Savings and Loan Associations often have lower interest rates than commercial banks.
   - C. Savings Banks were created to serve small savers who weren't being served by larger commercial banks.
   - D. Credit Unions are owned and operated by their members; generally have higher interest rates for savings and lower rates for loans.
   - E. Finance Companies collect debt for stores' installment loans; generally have very high interest for loans.

**Discussion Question**

**Compare two of the types of financial institutions. Which would offer better service for a corporation? a young student who is trying to save money?** *(The corporation*

**Visual Instruction FIGURE 4.6**

After students have viewed **Figure 4.6**, point out that the differences among financial institutions in terms of services provided have lessened since the 1980s. Financial experts predict this trend to continue in the next few years.

Guided Reading Activity 4-2

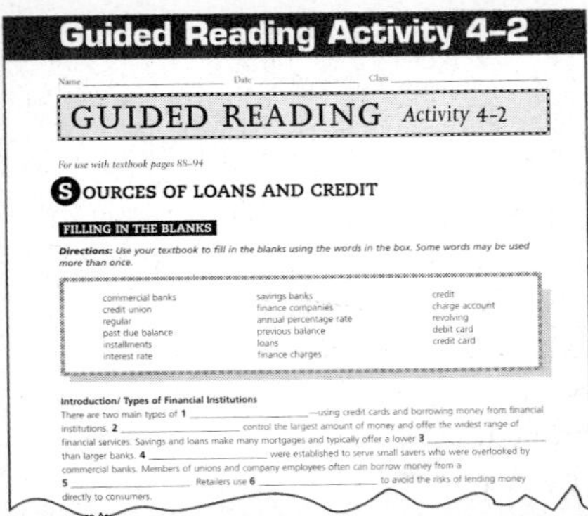
Name ____ Date ____ Class ____

GUIDED READING Activity 4-2

*For use with textbook pages 88–94*

**SOURCES OF LOANS AND CREDIT**

**FILLING IN THE BLANKS**

***Directions:*** *Use your textbook to fill in the blanks using the words in the box. Some words may be used more than once.*

| | | |
|---|---|---|
| commercial banks | savings banks | credit |
| credit union | finance companies | charge account |
| regular | annual percentage rate | revolving |
| past due balance | previous balance | debit card |
| installments | loans | credit card |
| interest rate | finance charges | |

**Introduction/ Types of Financial Institutions**

There are two main types of **1** ____—using credit cards and borrowing money from financial institutions. **2** ____ control the largest amount of money and offer the widest range of financial services. Savings and loans make many mortgages and typically offer a lower **3** ____ than larger banks. **4** ____ were established to serve small savers who were overlooked by commercial banks. Members of unions and company employees often can borrow money from a **5** ____. Retailers use **6** ____ to avoid the risks of lending money directly to consumers.

Project **Economic Concepts Transparency** 6 and have students discuss the accompanying questions.

**L2 Practicing Skills** Give students practice in computing finance charges by adjusting the monthly interest rate in the example in **Figure** 4.9 on page 93. Give students the following three monthly interest rates: 0.5, 1.0, and 2.0. For each of these interest rates, have students calculate the finance charge and the balance for all four computing methods. Encourage students to compare their results.

**Economic Connection to... History**

**Savings and Loans** Oxford Provident Building Association, founded in Frankfort, Pennsylvania, in 1831, was the first savings and loan association in the U.S. At that time, American commercial banks, for the most part, dealt only with businesses. Oxford Provident, however, provided a place for ordinary individuals to invest and borrow.

credit unions offer home mortgages as well. In general, credit unions offer higher interest rates on savings and charge lower interest rates on loans than other financial institutions.

**finance company:** *company that takes over contracts for installment debts from stores and adds a fee for collecting the debt; a consumer finance company makes loans directly to consumers at high rates of interest*

**Finance Companies** A **finance company** takes over contracts for installment debts from stores and adds a fee for collecting the debt. The consumer pays the fee in the form of slightly higher interest than he or she would pay to the retailer. Retailers use this method to avoid the risks involved in lending money to consumers.

A *consumer finance company* makes loans directly to consumers at relatively high rates of interest—often more than 20 percent a year. The people who use consumer finance companies are usually unable to borrow from other sources with lower rates because they have not repaid loans in the past or have an uneven employment record.

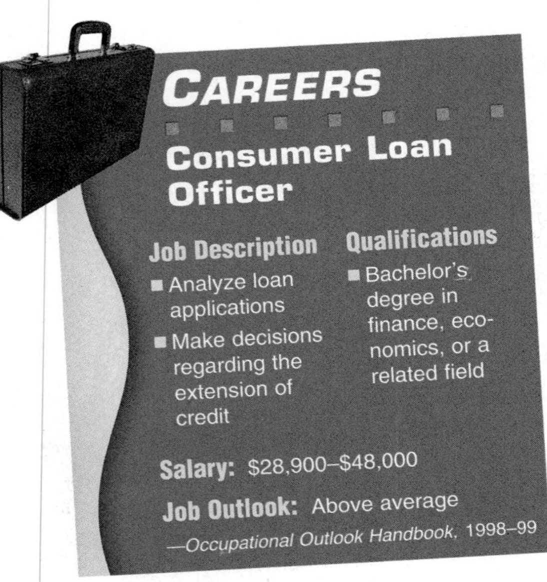

CAREERS
Consumer Loan Officer
Job Description
■ Analyze loan applications
■ Make decisions regarding the extension of credit
Qualifications
■ Bachelor's degree in finance, economics, or a related field
Salary: $28,900–$48,000
Job Outlook: Above average
—Occupational Outlook Handbook, 1998–99


## Charge Accounts

A second major type of credit is extended directly to an individual, without that person having to borrow money first. This credit may be in the form of a charge account or a credit card. As shown in **Figure 4.7,** a **charge account** allows a customer to buy goods or services from a particular company and pay for them later. Department stores, for example, offer three types of charge accounts: regular, revolving, or installment.

**charge account:** *credit extended to a consumer allowing the consumer to buy goods or services from a particular company and to pay for them later*

**Regular Charge Accounts** A *regular charge account,* also known as a 30-day charge, has a credit limit such as $500 or $1,000. A *credit limit* is the maximum amount of goods or services a person or business can buy on the promise to pay in the future. At the end of every 30-day period, the store sends a bill for the entire amount. No interest is charged, but the entire bill must be paid at that time. If it is not, interest is charged on the unpaid amount.

**Revolving Charge Accounts** A *revolving charge account* allows you to make additional purchases from the same store even if you have not paid the previous month's bill in full. Usually you must pay a certain portion of your balance each



**Cooperative Learning**

Organize students into several small groups. Ask groups to create some form of visual advertisement that encourages people to borrow from one of the financial institutions discussed in this section. Inform groups that their advertisements might take the form of posters, billboards, bumper stickers, buttons, or T-shirt designs. Have groups use their finished products to create an "advertisement corner" in the classroom.

 ELL  BLOCK SCHEDULING

## FIGURE 4.7

**Charge Accounts** Many stores issue their own charge cards, which consumers may use to purchase goods in their stores. ***What is a credit limit?***

month—one-fifth of the amount due, for example. Interest is charged on the amount you do not pay. Of course, if you pay everything you owe each month, no interest is charged. This type of account also has a credit limit.

**Installment Charge Accounts** Major items such as sofas, televisions, and refrigerators are often purchased through an *installment charge account*. The items are purchased and paid for through equal payments spread over a period of time. Part of the amount paid each month is applied to the interest, and part is applied to the principal. At the end of the payment period, the borrower owns the item he or she has made payments on.

*credit card: credit device that allows a person to make purchases at many kinds of stores, restaurants, and other businesses without paying cash*

## Credit Cards

A **credit card,** like a charge account, allows a person to make purchases without paying cash. The difference is that credit cards can be used at many kinds of stores, restaurants, hotels, and other businesses throughout the United States and even foreign countries. As shown in **Figure 4.8,** Visa, MasterCard, and others issue cards through banks. These cards can be used to purchase items in stores that accept them, or they may be used to borrow funds up to a certain limit. This gives consumers access to loans at all times without having to apply for them.

## FIGURE 4.8

**Credit Card Trade-Off**
Although using credit cards is convenient, it is also costly. Stores must pay a certain percentage of credit purchases to the company that issued the card. The stores include this cost in the prices they charge customers, making prices higher for everyone. ***What is the difference between a credit card and a charge account?***

## Finance Charges and Annual Percentage Rates

The terms *finance charge* and *annual percentage rate* tell the consumer the same thing—the cost of credit. Each, however, is expressed in a different way.



### Extending the Content

**Savings and Loan Associations** Most of the early savings and loan associations were what is known as "terminating institutions." Such institutions were set up with one aim in mind—to enable members to buy a home. Members made regular monthly deposits and, in turn, took out loans to buy homes. Members then paid off their mortgages in monthly installments. Once all members had purchased homes and paid off their loans, the savings and loan association was terminated.



### Visual Instruction FIGURE 4.7

**Answer:** *the maximum dollar value of goods or services a person or business can buy on the promise to pay in the future*

## Independent Practice

**L2 Conducting a Survey** Organize students into groups to conduct a survey on attitudes about consumer credit and debt. Suggest that groups develop a short questionnaire on these issues. Encourage groups to conduct the survey at various locations to obtain as varied a sampling as possible. Suggest that groups present their survey results in tables or charts accompanied by any necessary explanatory notes. Discuss results of the survey with the class.
BLOCK SCHEDULING

### Visual Instruction FIGURE 4.8

**Answer:** *A credit card can be used at many kinds of stores, restaurants, hotels, and other businesses. Charge accounts allow people to buy on credit only at a particular company.*

**L2 Conducting Research** Have students conduct research into regulations established by their state government regarding fees and interest rates charged by credit card companies. Ask students to present their findings in a written report that explains why these regulations were originally enacted.

## ? Did You Know

Many credit card issuers try to attract customers by offering affinity cards. These are regular credit cards that are issued under the name of an organization—a charity, educational institution, or professional body, for example. The issuing companies assume that people with ties to—or an *affinity* with—these organizations will take one of the cards. In return, the issuing companies make small donations to the organizations whenever the cards are used for transactions.

**finance charge:** *cost of credit expressed monthly in dollars and cents*

**Finance Charges** The **finance charge** is the cost of credit expressed in dollars and cents. It must take into account interest costs plus any other charges connected with credit. For example, yearly membership fees for the use of a credit card are included in the finance charge.

The way finance charges are computed is an important factor in determining the cost of credit. Store charge accounts and credit cards use one of four methods to determine how much people will pay for credit: previous balance, average daily balance, adjusted balance, or past due balance. Each method applies the interest rate to an account's balance at a different point during the month. The different methods can result in widely varying finance charges. See **Figure 4.9.**

**annual percentage rate (APR):** *cost of credit expressed as a yearly percentage*

**Annual Percentage Rates** The **annual percentage rate (APR)** is the cost of credit expressed as a yearly percentage. Like the finance charge, the APR must take into account any noninterest costs of credit such as a membership fee. **Figure 4.10** on page 94 shows how a sample APR affects the cost of credit.

Knowing which creditor is charging the most for credit would be very difficult without some guide for comparison. The APR provides that guide by allowing consumers to compare costs regardless of the dollar amount of those costs or the length of the credit agreement. Suppose creditor A is charging an APR of 16 percent, while creditor B is charging 17 percent, and creditor C is charging 18½ percent. On a yearly basis, creditor C is charging the most for credit and creditor A the least.

## Economic Connection to... History

### The First Credit Card

In 1958 the Bank of America mailed 60,000 BankAmericards to customers in Fresno, California. Each card had a credit line of $300 to $500 and could be used at 300 stores in the area. The next year, the bank mailed out 2 million cards and persuaded 20,000 stores to accept them.

Initially, BankAmericard proved a financial disaster. Unpaid accounts ran above 20 percent, and credit-card fraud was rampant. By early 1960, the losses on BankAmericard approached $9 million. The bank quickly addressed these problems, and within a year BankAmericard was turning a profit. ■



## Free Enterprise Activity

Have students work in groups to create a board game titled "Credit Crunch!". Indicate that the object of the game is to go into debt and then pay it off. Point out that lucky breaks (a pay raise or a contest cash prize, for example) and bad breaks (rising energy costs or unexpected repair bills, for example) might advance or stall a player's progress. Note that the first player to retire his or her debt wins the game. Suggest that groups research various board games to help them create their own. BLOCK SCHEDULING

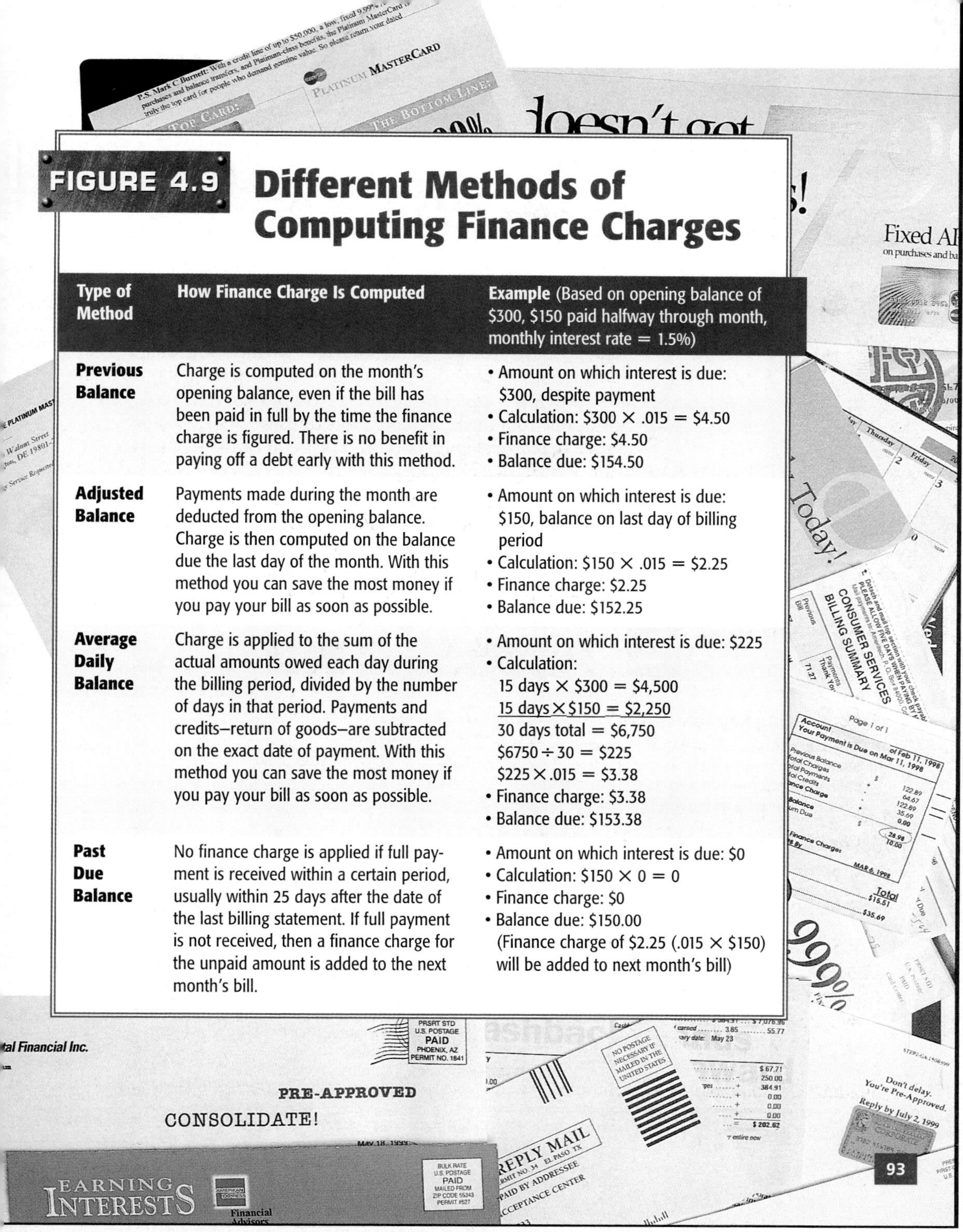

## FIGURE 4.9 Different Methods of Computing Finance Charges

| Type of Method | How Finance Charge Is Computed | Example (Based on opening balance of $300, $150 paid halfway through month, monthly interest rate = 1.5%) |
|---|---|---|
| **Previous Balance** | Charge is computed on the month's opening balance, even if the bill has been paid in full by the time the finance charge is figured. There is no benefit in paying off a debt early with this method. | • Amount on which interest is due: $300, despite payment<br>• Calculation: $300 × .015 = $4.50<br>• Finance charge: $4.50<br>• Balance due: $154.50 |
| **Adjusted Balance** | Payments made during the month are deducted from the opening balance. Charge is then computed on the balance due the last day of the month. With this method you can save the most money if you pay your bill as soon as possible. | • Amount on which interest is due: $150, balance on last day of billing period<br>• Calculation: $150 × .015 = $2.25<br>• Finance charge: $2.25<br>• Balance due: $152.25 |
| **Average Daily Balance** | Charge is applied to the sum of the actual amounts owed each day during the billing period, divided by the number of days in that period. Payments and credits—return of goods—are subtracted on the exact date of payment. With this method you can save the most money if you pay your bill as soon as possible. | • Amount on which interest is due: $225<br>• Calculation:<br>15 days × $300 = $4,500<br>15 days × $150 = $2,250<br>30 days total = $6,750<br>$6750 ÷ 30 = $225<br>$225 × .015 = $3.38<br>• Finance charge: $3.38<br>• Balance due: $153.38 |
| **Past Due Balance** | No finance charge is applied if full payment is received within a certain period, usually within 25 days after the date of the last billing statement. If full payment is not received, then a finance charge for the unpaid amount is added to the next month's bill. | • Amount on which interest is due: $0<br>• Calculation: $150 × 0 = 0<br>• Finance charge: $0<br>• Balance due: $150.00<br>(Finance charge of $2.25 (.015 × $150) will be added to next month's bill) |

**ECONOMICS & YOU**

**Going Into Debt**

Chapter 10
Disc 1, Side 1

**ASK: How does a credit card work?** *When a credit card is used for a purchase, the owner receives a monthly statement. If the entire bill is paid immediately, no interest is charged. If the bill is not paid in full, interest charges begin to accumulate on the balance.*

Also available in VHS.

# 3 Assess

## Meeting Lesson Objectives

Assign Section 2 Assessment as homework or an in-class activity.

Use **Interactive Tutor Self-Assessment Software** to review Section 2.

**Section Quiz 4–2**

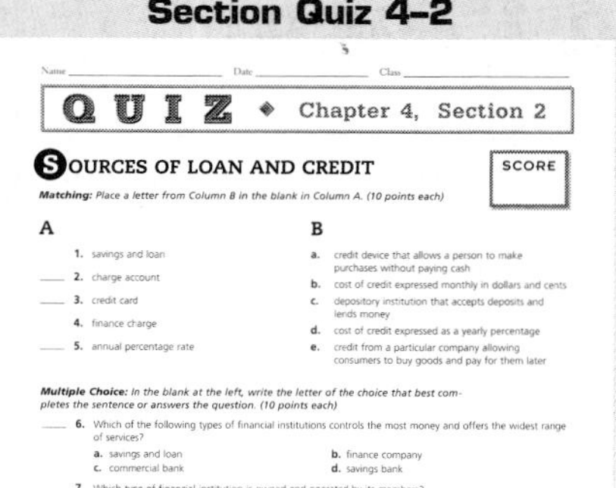

## Relevant Issues in Economics

**Payday Loans** The payday loan service is one of the fastest-growing segments of the consumer credit industry, totaling about $1 billion in business a year. Payday lenders advance cash against a borrower's next paycheck. In the typical payday loan transaction, the borrower writes a postdated check for the amount plus a loan fee. The lender then deposits the check on the posted date, normally the day the borrower gets paid. Payday loans are quite small—usually between $100 and $200—and short term—rarely more than two weeks. However, when the fees charged on the loans are translated into APRs, they run anywhere from 250 to 800 percent!

## Did You Know

There are nearly 68 million debit card holders in the United States. Debit card transactions total about $100 billion a year.

## Reteach

Ask students to write 5 to 10 questions on the content of Section 2. Pair students and have partners exchange and answer their questions.

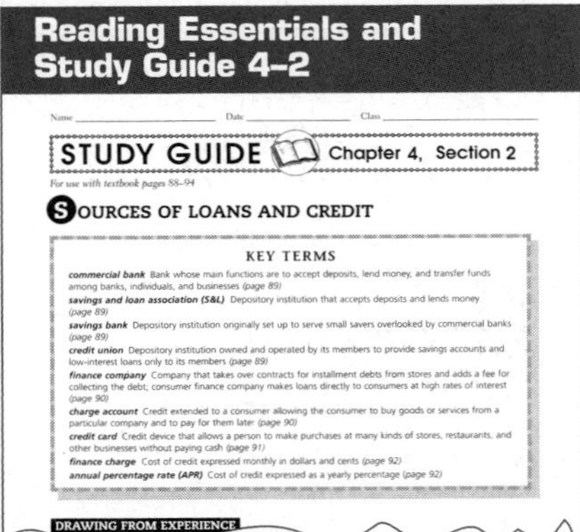

**Reading Essentials and Study Guide 4–2**

Name ______ Date ______ Class ______

STUDY GUIDE Chapter 4, Section 2

*For use with textbook pages 88–94*

SOURCES OF LOANS AND CREDIT

KEY TERMS

***commercial bank*** Bank whose main functions are to accept deposits, lend money, and transfer funds among banks, individuals, and businesses *(page 89)*

***savings and loan association (S&L)*** Depository institution that accepts deposits and lends money *(page 89)*

***savings bank*** Depository institution originally set up to serve small savers overlooked by commercial banks *(page 89)*

***credit union*** Depository institution owned and operated by its members to provide savings accounts and low-interest loans only to its members *(page 89)*

***finance company*** Company that takes over contracts for installment debts from stores and adds a fee for collecting the debt; consumer finance company makes loans directly to consumers at high rates of interest *(page 90)*

***charge account*** Credit extended to a consumer allowing the consumer to buy goods or services from a particular company and to pay for them later *(page 90)*

***credit card*** Credit device that allows a person to make purchases at many kinds of stores, restaurants, and other businesses without paying cash *(page 91)*

***finance charge*** Cost of credit expressed monthly in dollars and cents *(page 92)*

***annual percentage rate (APR)*** Cost of credit expressed as a yearly percentage *(page 92)*

DRAWING FROM EXPERIENCE

## 4 Close

Lead students in a discussion of the importance of having a choice of lending institutions and knowing the cost of credit.

**FIGURE 4.10**

**Computing APR** Suppose that you charge $200 worth of clothes. The interest rate charged to you, let's say, is 10 percent, but the annual fee for the credit card is $5. Your APR will be $20 of interest plus the $5 fee, or 12½ percent. The APR is normally larger than the interest rate because it includes the noninterest cost of extending credit.

*Credit Card Charge of $200 at 10% Interest*

| | | |
|---|---|---|
| Amount Charged | $200.00 | $200.00 |
| Interest at 10% | $20.00 | $20.00 |
| Annual Membership Fee | none | $5.00 |
| APR | 10% | 12.5% |

## Debit Cards

You may have heard about a method of payment known as a debit card. A *debit card* does not provide a loan. Instead, it makes cashless purchases easier by enabling customers to transfer funds electronically from their bank accounts directly to the store or restaurant where they purchased goods. Debit cards were first available in the 1970s but did not catch on with the public until the 1990s. At that time, banks combined credit cards with their debit cards.

**Practice** and **assess** key skills with ***Skillbuilder Interactive Workbook, Level 2.***

## SECTION 2 Assessment

### Understanding Key Terms

1. **Define** commercial bank, savings and loan association, savings bank, credit union, finance company, charge account, credit card, finance charge, annual percentage rate (APR).

### Reviewing Objectives

2. **Graphic Organizer** Create a diagram like the one below to list the six types of financial institutions and describe their main services.

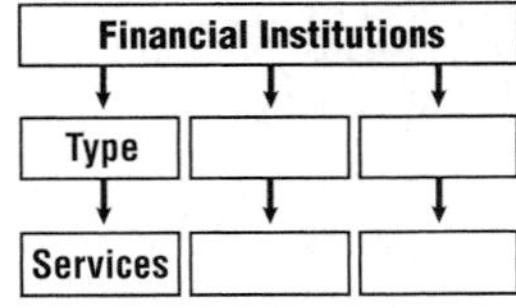


3. What three kinds of charge accounts are available from stores?
4. How are credit cards used?
5. How do a finance charge and an annual percentage rate differ?

### Applying Economic Concepts

6. **Annual Percentage Rates** What would be the APR if you charged $1,000 on a credit card whose interest rate was 20 percent with an annual fee of $30?

### Critical Thinking Activity

7. **Making Generalizations** Poll five adult family members. Ask: (1) Do you own a credit card? (2) Have you used an installment charge account? (3) Do you own a debit card? Tally your results, then write a generalization about the use of credit.



## SECTION 2 Assessment Answers

1. All definitions can be found in the Glossary.
2. Commercial bank—checking, savings and loans, transfers funds. S&L—accepts deposits and lends funds, finances mortgages and auto loans. Savings bank—home mortgages, personal and auto loans, checking accounts. Credit union—savings accounts and low-interest loans only to members. Finance company—takes over contracts for installment debts from stores. Consumer finance company—high-interest loans directly to consumers.
3. regular, revolving, and installment charge accounts
4. They allow a person to make purchases at many kinds of businesses without paying cash.
5. finance charge is cost of credit expressed in dollars and cents; APR is cost of credit expressed as a yearly percentage
6. 23 percent
7. Generalizations will vary.

## Technology Skills

# Using a Database

*A computerized database program can help you organize and manage a large amount of information. After entering data in a database table, you can quickly locate the information according to keywords.*

1. Determine what facts you want to include in your database—names, addresses, and phone numbers, for example—and research to collect that information.
2. Follow the instructions in the DBMS that you're using to set up fields. Then enter each item of data in its assigned field.
3. Determine how you want to organize the facts in the database—chronologically by the date, alphabetically, or by some other category.
4. Follow the instructions in your computer program to sort the information in order of importance.
5. Evaluate that all the information in your database is correct. If necessary, add, delete, or change information or fields.

### Learning the Skill

An electronic database is a collection of facts that are stored in a file on the computer. The information is organized into categories called *fields*. For example, one field may be the names of your clients. Another field may be the street addresses of your clients. All the related fields make up a *record*. Together, all the records make up the database.

A database can be organized and reorganized in any way that is useful to you. By using a database management system (DBMS)—or special software developed for record keeping—you can easily add, delete, change, or update information. When you want to retrieve information, the computer searches through the files, finds the information, and displays it on the screen.

### Practicing the Skill

Follow the steps listed on the left to build a database that organizes information about your friends.

Using a database can help organize population statistics, clients' names and addresses, and even baseball card collections.

### Application Activity

Research and build a database on types and services of financial institutions. Explain why the database is organized the way it is and how it might be used in this class.



## Technology Skills

### Using a Database

In discussing the construction of a database, give some examples of *fields*—the year that an event took place, the name of the event, or people connected with the event, for example. Then point out that all of the data fields related to the same subject make up a *record*, and that a collection of records is a *data file*. Finally, if possible, show students examples of a database management system, data files, records, and fields on a computer.

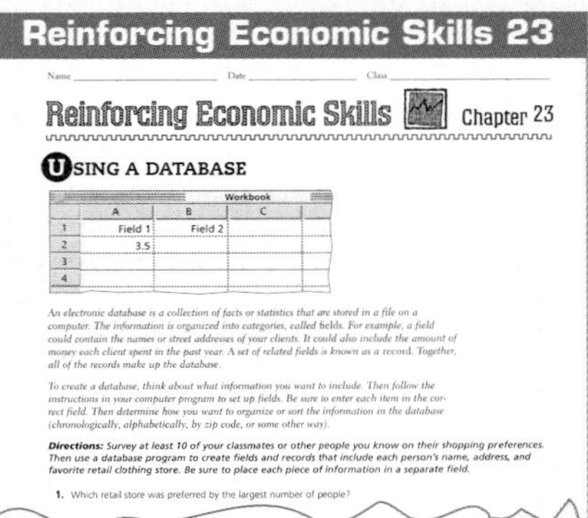

Reinforcing Economic Skills 23

Name ______ Date ______ Class ______

Reinforcing Economic Skills Chapter 23

USING A DATABASE

Workbook

| | A | B | C |
|---|---|---|---|
| 1 | Field 1 | Field 2 | |
| 2 | 3.5 | | |
| 3 | | | |
| 4 | | | |

*An electronic database is a collection of facts or statistics that are stored in a file on a computer. The information is organized into categories, called fields. For example, a field could contain the names or street addresses of your clients. It could also include the amount of money each client spent in the past year. A set of related fields is known as a record. Together, all of the records make up the database.*

*To create a database, think about what information you want to include. Then follow the instructions in your computer program to set up fields. Be sure to enter each item in the correct field. Then determine how you want to organize or sort the information in the database (chronologically, alphabetically, by zip code, or some other way).*

***Directions:*** *Survey at least 10 of your classmates or other people you know on their shopping preferences. Then use a database program to create fields and records that include each person's name, address, and favorite retail clothing store. Be sure to place each piece of information in a separate field.*

1. Which retail store was preferred by the largest number of people?

**GLENCOE TECHNOLOGY**

**Glencoe Skillbuilder Interactive Workbook, Level 2**

This interactive CD-ROM reinforces student mastery of essential social studies skills.

### Answers to Practicing the Skill

Databases will vary. Ask students to explain why they chose their particular method of organizing information.

**Application Activity** Databases will vary. Have students compare their databases to note similarities and differences.

# 1 Focus

## Overview

**Section 3** explains or describes the factors that establish a person's credit rating, the difference between a secured loan and an unsecured loan, and the responsibilities a borrower assumes on taking out a loan.

### BELLRINGER
**Motivational Activity**

Project **Daily Focus Transparency 32** and have students answer the questions.

This activity is also available as a blackline master.

**Daily Focus Transparency 32**

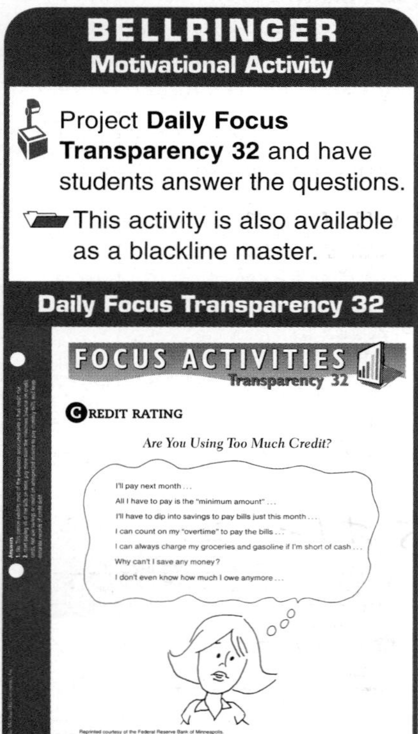

FOCUS ACTIVITIES
Transparency 32

CREDIT RATING

*Are You Using Too Much Credit?*

I'll pay next month . . .
All I have to pay is the "minimum amount" . . .
I'll have to dip into savings to pay bills just this month . . .
I can count on my "overtime" to pay the bills . . .
I can always charge my groceries and gasoline if I'm short of cash . . .
Why can't I save any money?
I don't even know how much I owe anymore . . .



Reprinted courtesy of the Federal Reserve Bank of Minneapolis.

1. Is it likely that the person in the cartoon has a good credit rating? Why?
2. What changes should she make to improve her credit rating?

Daily Focus Transparencies

### READER'S GUIDE

Answers to the **Reading Objectives** questions are on page 99.

**Preteaching Vocabulary**

Ask students to write two notes to a friend. In the first note they should explain how the terms *credit bureau, credit check,* and *credit rating* are related. In the second note, they should explain the difference between secured loans and unsecured loans.

Vocabulary PuzzleMaker

SECTION  3

# Applying for Credit

### READER'S GUIDE

**Terms to Know**
- credit bureau
- credit check
- credit rating
- collateral
- secured loan
- unsecured loan

**Reading Objectives**
1. What four factors determine a person's credit rating?
2. What are your responsibilities as a borrower?

### COVER STORY

*BUSINESS WEEK*, MARCH 15, 1999

Jason Britton, now 21 and a senior at Georgetown University in Washington, racked up $21,000 in debt over four years on 16 [credit] cards. "When I first started, my attitude was: 'I'll get a job after college to pay off all my debt,'" he says. He realized he dug himself into a hole when he couldn't meet the minimum monthly payments. Now, he works three part-time jobs. His parents are helping pay his tuition and loans.

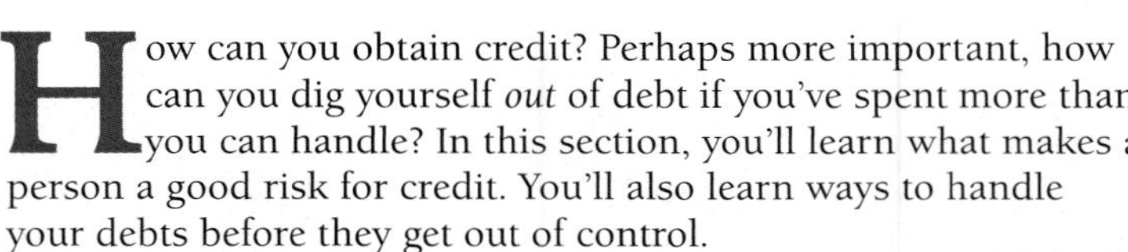

How can you obtain credit? Perhaps more important, how can you dig yourself *out* of debt if you've spent more than you can handle? In this section, you'll learn what makes a person a good risk for credit. You'll also learn ways to handle your debts before they get out of control.

## Creditworthiness

Several factors determine a person's creditworthiness. When you apply for credit, you usually will be asked to fill out a credit application. After you have filled out the application, the store, bank, or other lending agency will hire a **credit bureau**, a private business, to do a **credit check.** This investigation will

**credit bureau:** *private business that investigates a person to determine the risk involved in lending money to that person*

**credit check:** *investigation of a person's income, current debts, personal life, and past history of borrowing and repaying debts*

 SECTION 3 RESOURCE MANAGER

**Reproducible Masters**
- Reproducible Lesson Plan 4–3
- Reading Essentials and Study Guide 4–3
- Guided Reading Activity 4–3
- Section Quiz 4–3
- Daily Focus Activity 32
- Daily Lecture Notes 4–3

**Multimedia**
- Daily Focus Transparency 32
- Vocabulary PuzzleMaker
- Interactive Tutor Self-Assessment Software
- ExamView® Pro Testmaker
- MindJogger Videoquiz
- Presentation Plus!

reveal your income, any current debts, details about your personal life, and how well you have repaid debts in the past.

## The Credit Rating

The information supplied by the credit bureau provides the creditor with a **credit rating** for you. This is a rating of the risk—good, average, or poor—involved in lending funds to a specific person or business. If you have a history of poor credit use—usually late in paying debts—you will receive a poor credit rating. The creditor reviewing the credit check will be less willing to lend you money.

*credit rating: rating of the risk involved in lending money to a specific person or business*

Though past history of credit use is important in deciding a person's creditworthiness, the creditor also looks at three other factors that a credit check reveals. These are your capacity to pay, your character, and any collateral you may have. See **Figure 4.11.**

**Capacity to Pay** *Capacity to pay* is related to income and debt. If your employment has been spotty, your capacity to pay will be considered questionable. The amount of debt that you are already carrying is also a factor. If your debts are large, creditors will be reluctant to loan you more.

**FIGURE 4.11**

**Creditworthiness** When a creditor looks at your creditworthiness, three factors are considered: your ability to hold a steady job, your character, and any collateral you have that may secure a loan.





# 2 Teach

## Guided Practice

**L1 Understanding Ideas** On the board, draw a table with "Capacity to Pay," "Character," and "Collateral" as horizontal column headings, and "Good Risk" and "Bad Risk" as vertical column headings. Call on students to come to the board and enter examples of good risks and bad risks in the appropriate spaces.

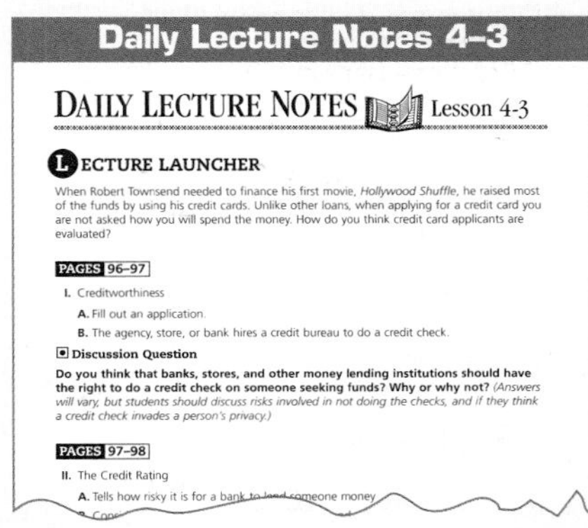

**Daily Lecture Notes 4–3**

DAILY LECTURE NOTES Lesson 4-3

**LECTURE LAUNCHER**

When Robert Townsend needed to finance his first movie, *Hollywood Shuffle*, he raised most of the funds by using his credit cards. Unlike other loans, when applying for a credit card you are not asked how you will spend the money. How do you think credit card applicants are evaluated?

PAGES 96–97

I. Creditworthiness
   A. Fill out an application.
   B. The agency, store, or bank hires a credit bureau to do a credit check.

**Discussion Question**

**Do you think that banks, stores, and other money lending institutions should have the right to do a credit check on someone seeking funds? Why or why not?** *(Answers will vary, but students should discuss risks involved in not doing the checks, and if they think a credit check invades a person's privacy.)*

PAGES 97–98

II. The Credit Rating
   A. Tells how risky it is for a bank to lend someone money

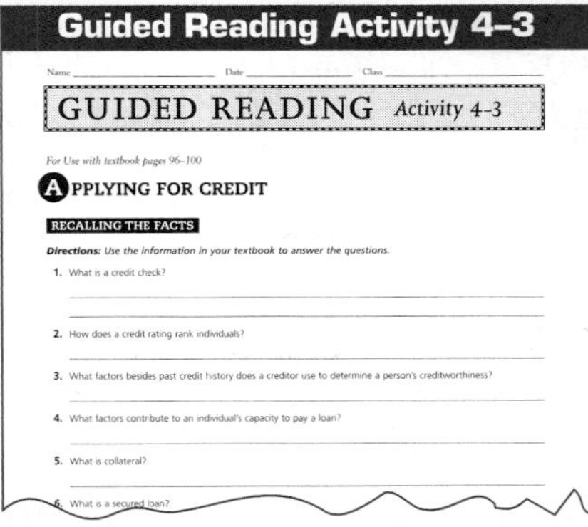

**Guided Reading Activity 4–3**

Name ______ Date ______ Class ______

GUIDED READING Activity 4-3

*For Use with textbook pages 96–100*

**APPLYING FOR CREDIT**

RECALLING THE FACTS

***Directions:*** *Use the information in your textbook to answer the questions.*

1. What is a credit check?
2. How does a credit rating rank individuals?
3. What factors besides past credit history does a creditor use to determine a person's creditworthiness?
4. What factors contribute to an individual's capacity to pay a loan?
5. What is collateral?
6. What is a secured loan?

## Meeting Special Needs

**Analyzing Cause and Effect** Some students may not fully appreciate how actions taken today can have an impact on creditworthiness. To help students see the connection, provide the following example. If a person is chronically late with payments, defaults on a credit card account, or fails to fulfill other credit obligations, such facts will be reported on his or her credit history. Several years later, potential lenders may read this history and turn down that person s request for a loan or a credit card. Then ask students to offer ideas on how the person in the example might have kept his or her credit history sound.

Refer to *Inclusion for the Social Studies Classroom Strategies and Activities.*

**Visual Instruction FIGURE 4.12**

**Answer:** *when a person has not had enough experience with borrowing and repaying money to build up a financial reputation*

## Independent Practice

**L2 Applying Ideas** Ask students to imagine they have been asked to cosign a loan. Have them list reasons why they would or would not be willing to be a cosigner. Then ask students to write a paragraph comparing how the borrower, the lender, and the cosigner might view cosigning.

# 3 Assess

## Meeting Lesson Objectives

Assign Section 3 Assessment as homework or an in-class activity.

Use **Interactive Tutor Self-Assessment Software** to review Section 3.

**FIGURE 4.12**

**Cosigning a Loan**
If someone you know asks you to cosign a loan, think carefully. If he or she does not make payments, you are responsible for the debt. ***When is a cosigner needed?***

**Character** *Character* refers to a person's reputation as a reliable and trustworthy person. The creditor may look at your educational background, whether or not you have had any problems with the law, and any other factors that might indicate your strength of character.

**Collateral** Lenders also consider **collateral,** or the size of your capital or personal wealth. Collateral is important because it indicates your past ability to save and accumulate. It also indicates your present ability to pay off a loan, even if you lose your job, because you could sell some of your belongings in order to make the payments.

**Secured Loans** Usually when a financial institution makes a loan, it will ask for collateral from the borrower. The collateral may be the item purchased with the loan money, such as a house or car. It may be something of value the borrower already owns. The borrower then signs a legal agreement allowing the lender to claim the collateral if the loan is not repaid. A loan that is backed up with collateral in this way is called a **secured loan.**

**Unsecured Loans** Usually a young adult will have little to offer as collateral. When dealing with a trusted customer, financial institutions will sometimes lend funds on the person's reputation alone. Such a loan is called an **unsecured loan.** It is not guaranteed by anything other than a promise to repay it.

A bank will sometimes lend funds to a person without a financial reputation if he or she has a cosigner. As shown in **Figure 4.12,** a *cosigner* is a person who signs a loan contract along with the borrower and promises to repay the loan if the borrower does not.

**collateral:** *something of value that a borrower lets the lender claim if a loan is not repaid*

**secured loan:** *loan that is backed up by collateral*

**unsecured loan:** *loan guaranteed only by a promise to repay it*

## Responsibilities as a Borrower

After you have applied for credit and obtained it, you have taken on certain responsibilities. After all, the businesses that gave you credit expect to earn a profit.

If you do not pay your debts on time, the business that lends you funds may have to hire a collection agency to help get back the money loaned to you. If you never pay off your debt, the



**Free Enterprise Activity**

Organize students into six groups, and assign each group one of the six financial institutions discussed in Section 2. Have groups interview loan officers at their assigned financial institution to discover the methods used to establish borrowers' creditworthiness and to deal with borrowers who fall behind on payments or default on their loans. Have groups present their findings to the class in a brief written report. BLOCK SCHEDULING lending institution has to write it off and take a loss. These costs are passed on to all consumers in the form of higher interest rates charged.

Another negative thing happens when you do not pay your debts: you get a bad credit history. You may then have a difficult or impossible time when you really need credit for something else—to purchase a house, for example.

Another responsibility as a borrower is to keep a complete record of all the charges you have made. You also must notify the credit-card issuer immediately if your card is lost or stolen.

What if you've lost control of your debt? Financial planners advise you to make a list of everything you owe, what the interest rate is, and what the payments are. Concentrate on paying the high-interest credit cards first, and pay more than the minimum payment, or it will take you years to reduce the debt.

### Loans for the Poor

In the mid-1970s, Muhammad Yunus, an economics professor, took a trip through Bangladesh. He saw a woman weaving bamboo chairs but earning only a few pennies a day, most of which went to pay the high interest rates on loans she took out to buy raw materials.

Yunus realized that if the woman could get loans at reasonable interest rates, she could make a living wage. So, Yunus started his own bank, the Grameen—or "Village"—Bank. Today, with more than 1,000 branch offices throughout Bangladesh, it has lent money to more than 2 million people, most of whom are women. Each loan averages $160, and 97 percent of these loans have been repaid on time. ■

**Practice** and **assess** key skills with *Skillbuilder Interactive Workbook, Level 2.*

## SECTION 3 Assessment

### Understanding Key Terms

1. **Define** credit bureau, credit check, credit rating, collateral, secured loan, unsecured loan.

### Reviewing Objectives

2. **Graphic Organizer** Create a diagram like the one below to describe the four factors that determine a person's credit rating.

3. What are your responsibilities as a borrower?

### Applying Economic Concepts

4. **Creditworthiness** Which of the four factors determining a person's credit rating do you think is most important in deciding whether a person is creditworthy? Explain.

### Critical Thinking Activity

5. **Finding the Main Idea** What is the main idea of the following excerpt?

*Banks now assign point values to each item on a credit application, such as how much debt you owe, how much credit you have available, your repayment history, and your age. Your total score will determine whether you're approved.*



## SECTION 3 Assessment Answers

1. All definitions can be found in the Glossary.
2. The following should appear in the outer ovals: Credit History, Capacity to Pay, Character, Collateral.
3. to pay debts on time, to keep complete records of all credit charges made, and to notify card issuers immediately if cards are lost or stolen
4. Answers will vary. Ensure that students offer a full explanation of their response.
5. Today it is more likely that a computer, rather than a human, will establish a borrower's credit rating.



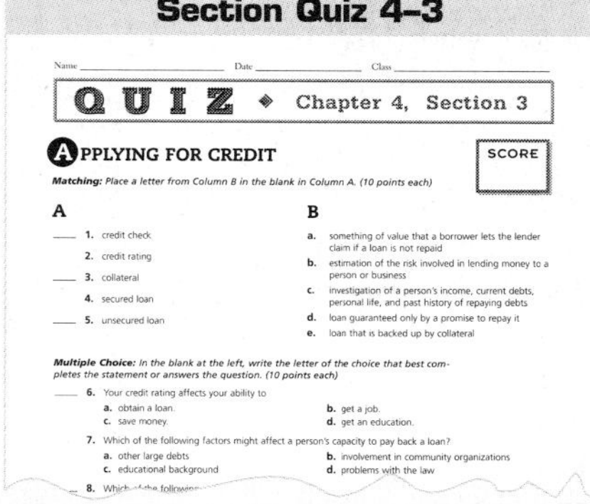
Section Quiz 4-3

Name ______ Date ______ Class ______

QUIZ ◆ Chapter 4, Section 3

APPLYING FOR CREDIT

SCORE

*Matching: Place a letter from Column B in the blank in Column A. (10 points each)*

A

____ 1. credit check
2. credit rating
____ 3. collateral
4. secured loan
____ 5. unsecured loan

B

a. something of value that a borrower lets the lender claim if a loan is not repaid
b. estimation of the risk involved in lending money to a person or business
c. investigation of a person's income, current debts, personal life, and past history of repaying debts
d. loan guaranteed only by a promise to repay it
e. loan that is backed up by collateral

*Multiple Choice: In the blank at the left, write the letter of the choice that best completes the statement or answers the question. (10 points each)*

____ 6. Your credit rating affects your ability to
a. obtain a loan. b. get a job.
c. save money. d. get an education.

7. Which of the following factors might affect a person's capacity to pay back a loan?
a. other large debts b. involvement in community organizations
c. educational background d. problems with the law

8. Which of the following

## Reteach

Ask students to outline Section 3, using section subheadings as main ideas.

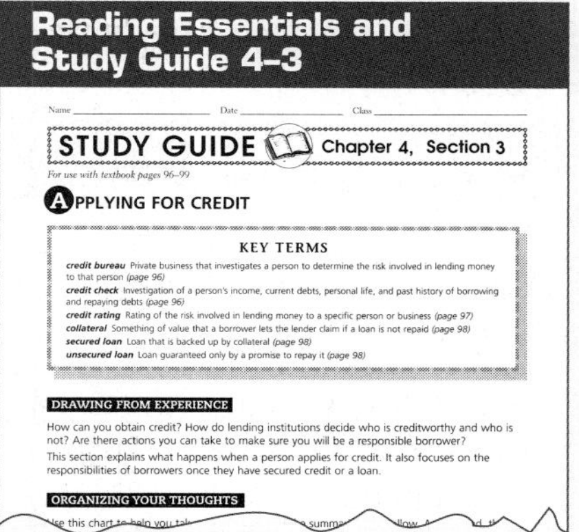
Reading Essentials and Study Guide 4-3

Name ______ Date ______ Class ______

STUDY GUIDE Chapter 4, Section 3

*For use with textbook pages 96–99*

APPLYING FOR CREDIT

KEY TERMS

***credit bureau*** Private business that investigates a person to determine the risk involved in lending money to that person *(page 96)*
***credit check*** Investigation of a person's income, current debts, personal life, and past history of borrowing and repaying debts *(page 96)*
***credit rating*** Rating of the risk involved in lending money to a specific person or business *(page 97)*
***collateral*** Something of value that a borrower lets the lender claim if a loan is not repaid *(page 98)*
***secured loan*** Loan that is backed up by collateral *(page 98)*
***unsecured loan*** Loan guaranteed only by a promise to repay it *(page 98)*

DRAWING FROM EXPERIENCE

How can you obtain credit? How do lending institutions decide who is creditworthy and who is not? Are there actions you can take to make sure you will be a responsible borrower?

This section explains what happens when a person applies for credit. It also focuses on the responsibilities of borrowers once they have secured credit or a loan.

ORGANIZING YOUR THOUGHTS

## 4 Close

Ask students to suggest a slogan for a campaign encouraging consumers to be responsible borrowers.

BusinessWeek

Spotlight

# Teach

Point out that one recent study estimated that the average college student carries $1,843 in credit card debt. Another study estimated that about 20 percent have credit card debt of $10,000 or more.

Inform students that colleges are taking steps to bring the student debt problem under control. Nearly 450 colleges and universities have forbidden credit card companies to market their wares on campus. In addition, legislators have drafted bills to control the distribution of credit cards to young people. ASK: What do you think should be done to bring this problem under control?

**BusinessWeek ONLINE**

To find up-to-date news and analysis on the economy, business, technology, markets, entrepreneurs, investments, and finance, have students search feature articles and special reports on the *Business Week* Web site. www.businessweek.com

**Sidelight**

Approximately 75 percent of college students carry and use at least one credit card. And 25 percent of these students reported that they obtained their first card while still in high school.

# BusinessWeek

## Spotlight on the Economy

## A Hard Lesson on Credit Cards

**Check It Out!** In this chapter you've learned about your responsibilities as a borrower. In this article, read to learn what pitfalls to avoid when applying for credit cards.

The moment college students step on campus, they become highly sought-after credit-card customers. To establish relationships card marketers hope will extend well beyond the college years, they are offering students everything from free T-shirts to chances to win airline tickets as enticements to sign up. As a result, college students now have heavy card debts.

As long as they are over 18, students can get a card without asking mom or dad to co-sign. Since card issuers' pitches may be confusing, experts dish out this advice:

- *Beware of teaser rates.* Credit-card marketers may advertise a low annual percentage rate (APR), but it often jumps substantially after three to nine months.
- *Pay on time.* Because students move often and may not get their mail forwarded quickly, bills can get lost. Then the students fall prey to late-payment fees. If one or two payments are overdue, many cards bump interest rates up as well.
- *Shun cash advances.* Students are often unaware that rates on cash advances are much higher than those on card balances.
- *Don't ask for extra credit.* Instead, find a card that has a restrictive credit line. Another option: Get a secured credit card. Its credit limit depends on your savings at the issuing bank.

Debt advisers say students should hold only a credit card on which they can carry a small balance and a charge card they must pay off monthly. They should pay more than the minimum on credit cards. And they should not charge purchases they can pay for in cash, such as pizza and gas.



### Think About It

1. How are students enticed to get credit cards?
2. Describe six ways to avoid credit card debt.

### Answers to *Think About It*

1. from free T-shirts to chances to win airline tickets
2. Avoid cards with low initial APRs; pay on time; do not use the card for cash advances; do not ask for a higher line of credit; get a credit card that allows only a small monthly balance and a charge card that must be paid off monthly; pay cash for everyday items, such as gasoline and pizza.

# SECTION 4

# Government Regulation of Credit

## COVER STORY

*KIPLINGER'S PERSONAL FINANCE MAGAZINE*, DECEMBER 1998

| RS | 0, TOTAL FIRST CARD DOLLARS | 33 | |
|---|---|---|---|
| ance | Finance Charge Balance** | Minimum Payment Due | Annual Percentage Rate |
| .10 | 46.43 | 20.00 | 17.31% |
| | | | Corresponding Finance Charge Balance |

Lawmakers are at odds over a bill that would require credit card issuers to disclose more information to consumers. Among other things, the statement would show how long it would take to pay off your balance if you made only the minimum payment. For example, at 21% interest, it would take nearly four years to pay off a $1,000 balance if you paid $35 a month.

Card issuers say such a disclosure would be burdensome and costly.

### READER'S GUIDE

**Terms to Know**
- usury law
- bankruptcy

**Reading Objectives**
1. How has the Equal Credit Opportunity Act affected consumer credit?
2. What are state usury laws?
3. Why might a person declare personal bankruptcy?

To protect consumers, the federal and state governments regulate the credit industry. Some states have set a maximum on the interest rates charged for certain types of credit. The federal government has also passed laws designed to increase the flow of credit information to consumers. In this section, you'll learn about these laws and how they protect consumers from unfair credit practices.



## SECTION 4 RESOURCE MANAGER

**Reproducible Masters**
- Reproducible Lesson Plan 4–4
- Reading Essentials and Study Guide 4–4
- Guided Reading Activity 4–4
- Section Quiz 4–4
- Daily Focus Activity 33
- Daily Lecture Notes 4–4

**Multimedia**
- Daily Focus Transparency 33
- Vocabulary PuzzleMaker
- Interactive Tutor Self-Assessment Software
- ExamView® Pro Testmaker
- MindJogger Videoquiz
- Presentation Plus!

# 1 Focus

## Overview

**Section 4** describes state usury laws and federal laws that regulate the credit industry and explains why a person who cannot repay debts might file for bankruptcy.

### BELLRINGER
**Motivational Activity**

Project **Daily Focus Transparency 33** and have students answer the questions.

This activity is also available as a blackline master.

**Daily Focus Transparency 33**

FOCUS ACTIVITIES
Transparency 33

ROLE OF GOVERNMENT IN CONSUMER CREDIT

| Major Consumer Credit Laws | |
|---|---|
| *WHAT* They Are | • Federal laws |
| *WHO* They Affect | • Financial institutions that extend credit and consumers who seek or have credit |
| *WHEN* They Were Enacted | • Most were passed in the 1970s |
| *WHERE* They are in Force | • Throughout the United States |
| *WHY* They Were Enacted | • Primarily to protect consumers, to ensure they have full information, privacy, equal treatment, and are not abused |
| *HOW* They Function | • Financial institutions must follow the laws or face the threat of criminal and civil actions |

1. Why were consumer credit laws enacted?
2. What can you infer from the table about consumer credit in the United States in the 1960s?

Daily Focus Transparencies

### READER'S GUIDE

Answers to the **Reading Objectives** questions are on page 105.

**Preteaching Vocabulary**

Have students find the origins of the terms *usury* and *bankruptcy* in an etymological dictionary. Call on volunteers to share their findings with the class.

**Vocabulary PuzzleMaker**

# 2 Teach

## Guided Practice

**L2 Applying Ideas** Have students review the information in **Figure 4.13.** Then ask them to identify the law that protects consumers, and what steps consumers can take, in the following situations:

- A debt collector is calling several times a day.
- A consumer discovers that a mistake on a credit card bill has not been corrected.
- A consumer is refused a loan but is given no reason for the refusal.
- A consumer discovers that the interest rate on a loan is not what was originally agreed upon.

**Daily Lecture Notes 4-4**

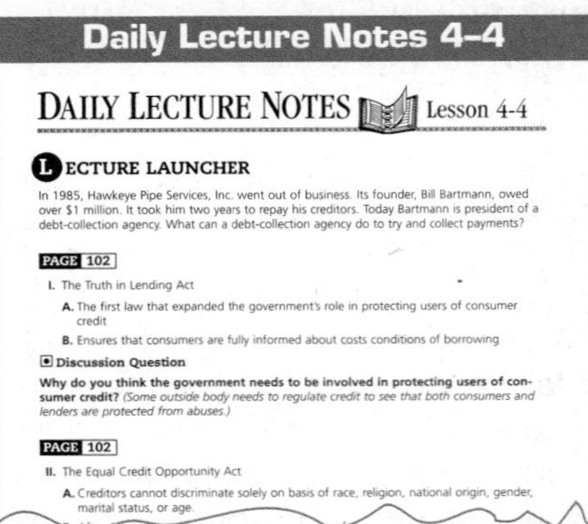
DAILY LECTURE NOTES Lesson 4-4

LECTURE LAUNCHER

In 1985, Hawkeye Pipe Services, Inc. went out of business. Its founder, Bill Bartmann, owed over $1 million. It took him two years to repay his creditors. Today Bartmann is president of a debt-collection agency. What can a debt-collection agency do to try and collect payments?

PAGE 102

I. The Truth in Lending Act
   A. The first law that expanded the government's role in protecting users of consumer credit
   B. Ensures that consumers are fully informed about costs conditions of borrowing

**Discussion Question**

**Why do you think the government needs to be involved in protecting users of consumer credit?** *(Some outside body needs to regulate credit to see that both consumers and lenders are protected from abuses.)*

PAGE 102

II. The Equal Credit Opportunity Act
   A. Creditors cannot discriminate solely on basis of race, religion, national origin, gender, marital status, or age.

See the **Web Activity Lesson Plan** at ett.glencoe.com for an introduction, lesson description, and answers to the **Student Web Activity** for this chapter.

## The Truth in Lending Act

The Truth in Lending Act of 1968 was the first of a series of major federal laws that greatly expanded the government's role in protecting users of consumer credit. An important aspect of the government regulation of credit is to make sure that everyone has equal access. **Figure 4.13** presents the important points about this act and other major federal government laws to regulate credit.

## The Equal Credit Opportunity Act

In 1974 Congress enacted the Equal Credit Opportunity Act (ECOA) as an addition to the Truth in Lending Act of 1968. Among other things, those who provide credit cannot deny you such credit solely on the basis of your race, religion, national origin, gender, marital status, or age. In addition, no one is allowed to discriminate against you in offering credit simply because your income might come from public assistance benefits.

Historically, credit discrimination against married women has been the norm. The 1974 Credit Act made it illegal for a creditor to require an applicant's spouse unless an application for credit was made jointly by husband and wife. If a woman qualifies on her own for the amount and terms of credit requested, she does not have to get her husband to sign the credit application. See **Figure 4.14** on page 104.

## State Usury Laws

**usury law:** *law restricting the amount of interest that can be charged for credit*

A law restricting the amount of interest that can be charged for credit is called a **usury law.** Some states set up different maximum rates for different types of consumer credit. Maximum rates on charge accounts and credit cards, for example, are often about 18 percent a year, or 1½ percent per month. Consumer finance agencies, in contrast, are often allowed to charge higher rates because their loans involve higher risks.

The maximum rates from usury laws were controversial in past years when interest restrictions in many states were as low as 6 or 10 percent. When interest rates in general began to rise in the early 1970s, many lenders complained that they could not keep within such restrictions and still make a profit. In states that were slow to raise interest restrictions, some lenders cut back

ECONOMICS Online

**Student Web Activity** Visit the *Economics Today and Tomorrow* Web site at ett.glencoe.com and click on ***Chapter 4—Student Web Activities*** to learn more about the Fair Debt Collection Practices Act.

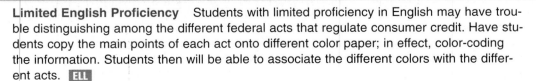

## Meeting Special Needs

**Limited English Proficiency** Students with limited proficiency in English may have trouble distinguishing among the different federal acts that regulate consumer credit. Have students copy the main points of each act onto different color paper; in effect, color-coding the information. Students then will be able to associate the different colors with the different acts. ELL

Refer to *Inclusion for the Social Studies Classroom Strategies and Activities* for students with different learning styles.

## FIGURE 4.13 Major Federal Laws Regulating Consumer Credit

| Name of Law | Main Purpose | Major Provisions |
|---|---|---|
| **Truth in Lending Act (1968)** | Ensures that consumers are fully informed about the costs and conditions of borrowing. | • Creditors must keep borrowers informed of a credit agreement's annual percentage rate, the way charges and fees are calculated, and the payment schedule.<br>• Consumers have a 3-day cooling-off period in which to cancel certain contracts.<br>• Consumers are liable for only the first $50 in unauthorized purchases made on a credit card before it is reported lost or stolen. |
| **Fair Credit Reporting Act (1970)** | Protects the privacy and accuracy of information in a credit check. | • If refused credit, a consumer can request from the lender the name and address of the credit bureau issuing the report.<br>• The credit bureau, if requested, must provide at least a summary of a consumer's credit file.<br>• If the consumer claims part of the file is in error, the bureau must correct the record or explain it. |
| **Equal Credit Opportunity Act (1974)** | Prohibits discrimination in giving credit on the basis of sex, race, religion, marital status, age, or receipt of public assistance. | • Questions about age, sex, and marital status can be asked only if those questions relate directly to a person's ability to repay a loan.<br>• Loan applicants must receive notice of a decision within 30 days. If the loan is denied, the lender must give the reasons. |
| **Fair Credit Billing Act (1974)** | Sets up a procedure for the quick correction of mistakes that appear on consumer credit accounts. | • Consumers have 60 days to notify a creditor of a disputed item on a billing statement. The creditor must correct the mistake or explain the charge.<br>• While the mistake is checked, the consumer can withhold payment of the disputed sum.<br>• Under certain circumstances, a consumer can withhold payment for defective merchandise. |
| **Fair Debt Collection Practices Act (1977)** | Prevents abuse by professional debt collectors; does not apply to banks or other businesses that collect their own accounts. | • Collectors can contact a person other than the debtor only to discover the debtor's location.<br>• The debtor cannot be contacted at an inconvenient time or place.<br>• All harassing behavior is prohibited, including the threat of violence, annoying phone calls, etc. |

103

### Guided Reading Activity 4-4

Name ______ Date ______ Class ______

GUIDED READING Activity 4-4

For use with textbook pages 101–105

GOVERNMENT REGULATION OF CREDIT

OUTLINING

**Directions:** Locate the heading in your textbook. Then use the information under the heading to help you write each answer.

I. The Truth in Lending Act—What is the main purpose of the Truth in Lending Act of 1968?

II. The Equal Credit Opportunity Act
A. What does the Equal Credit Opportunity Act prevent?
B. Historically, who used to be hurt by credit discrimination?

III. State Usury Laws
A. What is a usury law?

## Independent Practice

**L1 Summarizing Ideas** Ask students to find a recent article on either consumer credit laws or bankruptcy. Encourage them to write a summary of the article. Have students share their articles. Then lead the class in a discussion of the latest developments in credit regulation and bankruptcy. BLOCK SCHEDULING

### Economic Connection to... *Literature*

**Punishing Debtors** In the past, failure to pay debts was a punishable offense, often by public humiliation. In England, for example, debtors in the 1600s were put in the stocks. In the 1800s, English debtors had their names published prominently in popular newspapers. People with chronic debt problems usually were thrown in prison until their debts were paid. Imprisonment for debt remained on the statute books until 1869.

## Cooperative Learning

Organize students into an equal number of small groups. Have half the groups research federal consumer credit laws. Direct the other groups to research consumer credit laws enacted by their state and local governments. Then have all groups combine the materials they have gathered to create an illustrated bulletin-board display titled Government Regulation of Consumer Credit. BLOCK SCHEDULING

# 3 Assess

## Meeting Lesson Objectives

Assign Section 4 Assessment as homework or an in-class activity.

Use **Interactive Tutor Self-Assessment Software** to review Section 4.

### Section Quiz 4–4

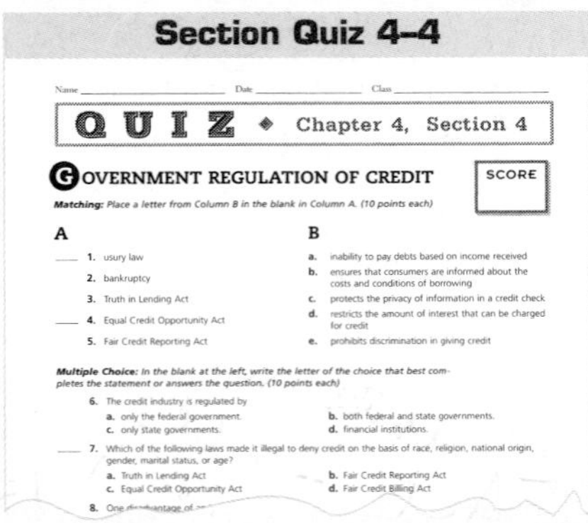

Name ______ Date ______ Class ______

QUIZ ◆ Chapter 4, Section 4

GOVERNMENT REGULATION OF CREDIT

SCORE

***Matching:*** *Place a letter from Column B in the blank in Column A. (10 points each)*

| A | B |
|---|---|
| ____ 1. usury law | a. inability to pay debts based on income received |
| 2. bankruptcy | b. ensures that consumers are informed about the costs and conditions of borrowing |
| 3. Truth in Lending Act | c. protects the privacy of information in a credit check |
| ____ 4. Equal Credit Opportunity Act | d. restricts the amount of interest that can be charged for credit |
| 5. Fair Credit Reporting Act | e. prohibits discrimination in giving credit |

***Multiple Choice:*** *In the blank at the left, write the letter of the choice that best completes the statement or answers the question. (10 points each)*

6. The credit industry is regulated by
   a. only the federal government.
   b. both federal and state governments.
   c. only state governments.
   d. financial institutions.

____ 7. Which of the following laws made it illegal to deny credit on the basis of race, religion, national origin, gender, marital status, or age?
   a. Truth in Lending Act
   b. Fair Credit Reporting Act
   c. Equal Credit Opportunity Act
   d. Fair Credit Billing Act

8. One [illegible]

### Visual Instruction FIGURE 4.14

**Answer:** *Equal Credit Opportunity Act*

on the amount of credit they offered. Others stopped lending completely. Many consumers, particularly those who were poor credit risks, found it hard to obtain credit.

People opposed to raising interest restrictions claimed that people with lower incomes would not be able to afford credit. Supporters of higher rate restrictions claimed that low rates made credit less available because it was less profitable for lenders. Low rates actually hurt those they were supposed to help.

## Personal Bankruptcy

Every day in the United States, thousands of families get into financial trouble because they have ignored the total costs of all their borrowing. They have too many credit cards, too many charge accounts, and own a home that has too large a mortgage. Just because someone offers you credit or allows you to borrow does not mean that you should accept. Buying on credit is a serious consumer activity. See **Figure 4.15.**

If debtors take out too many loans, use too many credit cards, and pile up debts that they cannot pay off, they may have to file personal **bankruptcy.** When a bankruptcy is approved through a bankruptcy court, debtors must give up most of what they own, which is then distributed to their creditors. The Constitution authorizes Congress to establish bankruptcy laws. Certain debts, such as taxes, must continue to be paid, however.

**bankruptcy:** *the inability to pay debts based on income received*

If you declare personal bankruptcy, be aware that the bankruptcy proceedings remain on your credit record for 10 years. During this period, it is very difficult to reestablish credit and borrow funds for items such as a new car or home. That is why

FIGURE 4.14

**Women and Credit** Changes in laws regarding credit have improved a woman's opportunities to borrow money. ***What law made it illegal for creditors to deny credit on the basis of marital status?***



### Relevant Issues in Economics

**Declaring Bankruptcy** Some Americans think that filing for bankruptcy has become too easy. These people want the bankruptcy laws to be revised. They suggest that Chapter 7 bankruptcy—where all debts except taxes, mortgages, student loans, child support, and alimony are wiped out—should be limited to people with low incomes. Anyone earning above the national median income would have to file for bankruptcy under Chapter 13. This entails the setting up of a repayment schedule designed to retire at least a third of the debt.

choosing bankruptcy to get out of your credit "mess" should be a last resort. Also, when you declare bankruptcy, you are making sure that your creditors will never be paid off (at least not in full) for what they loaned out.

**FIGURE 4.15**

**Using Credit** Just because credit card companies make it easy to obtain credit does not mean that you should accept their offers. ***What are some questions you should ask yourself before buying on credit?***

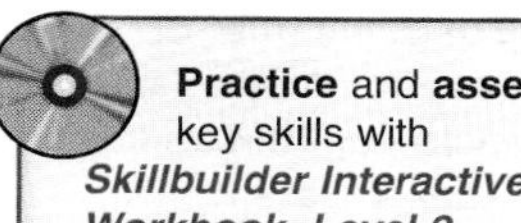

**Practice** and **assess** key skills with *Skillbuilder Interactive Workbook, Level 2.*

## SECTION 4 Assessment

### Understanding Key Terms

1. **Define** usury law, bankruptcy.

### Reviewing Objectives

2. **Graphic Organizer** Create a chart like the one below to describe how the Truth in Lending Act, the Fair Credit Reporting Act, the Equal Credit Opportunity Act, and the Fair Credit Billing Act have affected consumer credit.

| Legislation | Effect on Consumer Credit |
|---|---|
| | |
| | |
| | |

3. What are state usury laws?
4. Why might a person declare personal bankruptcy?

### Applying Economic Concepts

5. **State Usury Laws** The effect of a usury law is often a shortage of available loans. What circumstances might create a *surplus* of available loans?

### Critical Thinking Activity

6. **Making Comparisons** Research the two types of bankruptcy known as Chapter 7 and Chapter 13. Which requires debtors to set up a repayment plan? Which deletes the debt completely? What are the long-term effects of each type on one's future?





## Reteach

Ask students to rewrite the subheadings in Section 4 as questions. Then have them review the section and draft answers to their questions.

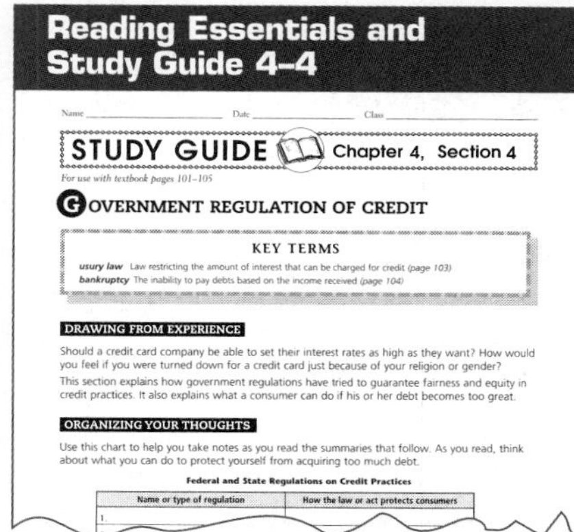
**Reading Essentials and Study Guide 4–4**

Name ______ Date ______ Class ______

STUDY GUIDE Chapter 4, Section 4

*For use with textbook pages 101–105*

GOVERNMENT REGULATION OF CREDIT

KEY TERMS

***usury law*** Law restricting the amount of interest that can be charged for credit *(page 103)*

***bankruptcy*** The inability to pay debts based on the income received *(page 104)*

DRAWING FROM EXPERIENCE

Should a credit card company be able to set their interest rates as high as they want? How would you feel if you were turned down for a credit card just because of your religion or gender?

This section explains how government regulations have tried to guarantee fairness and equity in credit practices. It also explains what a consumer can do if his or her debt becomes too great.

ORGANIZING YOUR THOUGHTS

Use this chart to help you take notes as you read the summaries that follow. As you read, think about what you can do to protect yourself from acquiring too much debt.

**Federal and State Regulations on Credit Practices**

| Name or type of regulation | How the law or act protects consumers |
|---|---|
| 1. | |

### Visual Instruction FIGURE 4.15

**Answer:** *Do I really require this item? Can I postpone purchasing the item? Have I done comparison shopping for credit, finding the lowest interest rate?* See **Figure 4.5** on page 87 for other questions one should ask before buying on credit.

## 4 Close

As a closing activity, have students discuss the importance of credit regulation laws for consumers.

## SECTION 4 Assessment Answers

1. All definitions can be found in the Glossary.
2. Truth in Lending Act: consumers informed about the costs and conditions of borrowing; Fair Credit Reporting Act: privacy and accuracy of credit check are protected; Equal Credit Opportunity Act: cannot be refused credit because of sex, race, religion, marital status, age, or receipt of public assistance; Fair Credit Billing Act: mistakes that appear on consumer credit accounts are now quickly corrected
3. state laws that set limits on the amount of interest lenders may charge
4. too many loans, uses too many credit cards, and piles up unpayable debts
5. Answers may include if interest rates are too high, fewer people will demand loans offered by many creditors.
6. Chapter 13 requires debtors to set up a repayment plan, while Chapter 7 deletes most of the debt completely. Students also will note that both have long-term effects on a person's future, since a bankruptcy filing remains on that person's credit history for 10 years.

## Background

In mid-1999, American Express Co. announced that Chenault would assume the positions of chief executive officer and chairman in the early 2000s.

# Teach

Point out that Chenault feels that business people can gain a great deal from participating in activities outside of work. He believes that "there is a tremendous career benefit that people can gain from work outside their day job. You may be placed in a leadership position at an earlier stage than you might at your job. There is often an opportunity to hone other skills, like public speaking, management, strategic thinking."

Continue by mentioning that Chenault also thinks that people allow company business to dictate too much of their day-to-day schedule. He suggests that there is just as much to be gained from spending some time with friends and family and doing charity work.

Conclude by asking students to offer their opinions on Chenault's views on what can be gained from participating in activities outside the job.

# People & Perspectives

## Kenneth Chenault

*ENTREPRENEUR (1951–)*

- **President and chief operating officer of the American Express Company**
- **Board member of several companies, including IBM and Quaker Oats**
- **Board member of several educational, sports, and charitable organizations**
- **Recipient of many awards recognizing business achievements and charity work**

After working as a lawyer and a business consultant, Kenneth Chenault accepted a position at the American Express Company in 1981. An energetic worker and imaginative problem solver, Chenault rose steadily through company ranks, and in 1997 he was named president and chief operating officer.

Chenault believes that it is not so much *what* or *who* you know, but what you *do:*

*"Having a solid track record, building relationships with the people that you work with, and then impressing them with your abilities will make people in a position to help your career take note. As a result, you will earn the respect of the people who know your work well, rather than simply meeting people who may or may not have occasion to help you."*

As an African American, Chenault has faced obstacles in his career. Taking a practical approach to the situation, he believes, helps people to confront and overcome such obstacles:

*"Everyone, regardless of their ethnic, religious, age, gender, . . . or other differences has to contend with obstacles. So you have to isolate what you can control, from what you can't. You can't control people's biases. You can control your own performance, your own behavior and the values you choose to uphold.*

*I also think it's important to cultivate a measure of resilience. And, perhaps unfortunately, the best teacher of resilience is failure. There is nothing quite like overcoming failure with your character and values intact, to reinforce the fact that learning from your mistakes can be one of life's most important lessons."*

### *Checking for Understanding*

1. **What, according to Kenneth Chenault, is the key to success?**
2. **What advice does Chenault give people for confronting and overcoming obstacles?**



### Answers to *Checking for Understanding*

1. what you *do* in your job, rather than what you know or who you know
2. People should isolate what they cannot control, such as people's biases. Then they should focus on what they can control–their own performance, their own behavior, and the values they choose to uphold. In addition, Chenault thinks it is important for people to cultivate a measure of resilience and to learn from failure.

CHAPTER  Summary

Chapter Overview Visit the *Economics Today and Tomorrow* Web site at ett.glencoe.com and click on ***Chapter 4—Chapter Overviews*** to review chapter information.

## SECTION 1 Americans and Credit

- **Credit** is the receiving of funds either directly or indirectly to buy goods and services today with the promise to pay for them in the future.
- The amount owed—the debt—is equal to the **principal** plus **interest.**
- Many people buy **durable goods** and obtain **mortgages** using **installment debt.**
- People go into debt because they do not want to wait to purchase an item with cash, and they want to spread the debt payments over the life of the item being purchased.

## SECTION 2 Sources of Loans and Credit

- The major financial institutions that lend consumers funds include **commercial banks, savings and loan associations, credit unions,** and **finance companies.**
- A **charge account** allows a customer to buy goods or services from a particular company and pay for them later.
- A **credit card,** often charging high interest, may be used at stores, restaurants, or other businesses.
- **Finance charges** tell you the monthly cost of credit in dollars and cents.
- The **annual percentage rate** tells you the annual cost of credit in percentages.

## SECTION 3 Applying for Credit

- After you have filled out a credit application, a **credit bureau** will perform a **credit check** and determine your **credit rating.**
- Before granting you credit, a creditor looks at your capacity to pay, your character, and any **collateral** you may have.
- Your responsibilities as a borrower include paying on time, keeping records of your debt, and not spending more than you can repay.

## SECTION 4 Government Regulation of Credit

- Legislation states that those who provide credit cannot deny you such credit solely on the basis of your race, religion, national origin, gender, marital status, or age.
- A **usury law** restricts the amount of interest that can be charged for credit, but also leads to a shortage of available credit.
- People who cannot repay their debts may have to file personal **bankruptcy.**



## Economics Journal

**Credit and Debt** Ask students to keep track of the advertisements concerning debt and credit they see on television, in newspapers and magazines, or hear on the radio. Have them list the types of companies that advertise to offer credit. Also, ask them to note which companies offer credit for major purchases and which offer credit for small purchases. Then have them use the information they have gathered to write a paragraph supporting or refuting the following statement: Credit is too easily available to too many people.

ECONOMICS & YOU

Going Into Debt

Chapter 10
Disc 1, Side 1

If you do not have access to a videodisc player, the ***Economics & You*** programs are also available in VHS.

Use the **Chapter 4 Summary** to preview, review, condense, or reteach the chapter.

## Preview/Review

**Vocabulary PuzzleMaker Software** reinforces the key terms used in Chapter 4.

**Interactive Tutor Self-Assessment Software** allows students to review Chapter 4 content.

## Condense

Have students listen to the Chapter 4 **Audio Program** (also available in Spanish) in the TCR. Assign the Chapter 4 Audio Program Activity and give students the Chapter 4 Audio Program Test.

## Reteach

Have students complete **Reteaching Activity** 4 in the TCR (Spanish Reteaching Activities are also available).

# CHAPTER 4 Assessment and Activities

ECONOMICS Online

Have students visit the *Economics Today and Tomorrow* Web site at ett.glencoe.com to review Chapter 4 and take the Self-Check Quiz.

GLENCOE TECHNOLOGY

 MindJogger Videoquiz

Use MindJogger to review Chapter 4 content.

## Identifying Key Terms

1. c
2. a
3. d
4. e
5. b

## Recalling Facts and Ideas

1. principal plus any interest and fees
2. In both cases, interest must be paid for the use of someone else's purchasing power.
3. consumer durables and real property
4. People want or need items immediately and wish to spread the payments over time.
5. commercial bank, savings and loan association, savings bank, credit union, finance company, consumer finance company
6. Visa, MasterCard, and other cards issued through banks
7. finance charges
8. credit history, capacity to pay, character, collateral
9. Secured loans are backed by collateral; unsecured loans are made based on the reputation of the borrower.

CHAPTER 

# Assessment and Activities

ECONOMICS Online

**Self-Check Quiz** Visit the *Economics Today and Tomorrow* Web site at ett.glencoe.com and click on ***Chapter 4—Self-Check Quizzes*** to prepare for the Chapter Test.

## Identifying Key Terms

*Write the letter of the definition in Column B that correctly defines each term in Column A.*

**Column A**

1. principal
2. usury law
3. collateral
4. annual percentage rate
5. unsecured loan

**Column B**

a. restricts the amount of interest that can be charged for credit
b. requires only a promise to repay
c. amount of money borrowed in a loan
d. something of value that a borrower uses as a promise of loan repayment
e. cost of credit expressed as a yearly percentage

## Recalling Facts and Ideas

**Section 1**

1. What do you have to pay when you borrow?
2. How is taking out a loan similar to buying an item on credit?
3. What type of goods do people typically use installment debt to buy?
4. Why do people use credit?

**Section 2**

5. What are the six types of basic lending institutions in our economy?
6. What are some of the most common types of credit cards used today?
7. When you take out a loan, what do you call the total cost of credit expressed in dollars and cents?

**Section 3**

8. When you make an application for a loan, what are four factors that a creditor looks at to determine whether you are creditworthy?
9. What is the difference between a secured and an unsecured loan?
10. What are your responsibilities as a borrower?

**Section 4**

11. What does the Equal Credit Opportunity Act of 1974 prohibit?
12. What are three important federal laws regulating consumer credit?
13. How can usury laws be harmful to the people they are trying to help?

## Thinking Critically

1. **Making Comparisons** In deciding whether to pay cash or use credit for a purchase, what are the costs involved and the benefits of each choice?



10. Borrowers must repay the loan on time, keep records of charges made, and notify card issuers promptly if credit cards are lost or stolen.
11. It prohibits discrimination in lending based on factors–such as race, age, and sex–that have no bearing on an applicant's ability to repay a loan.
12. Any three of the following: Truth in Lending Act, Fair Credit Reporting Act, Equal Credit Opportunity Act, Fair Credit Billing Act, Fair Debt Collection Practices Act
13. When interest rates in general begin to rise, many lenders feel that they could not keep within ceilings set by usury laws and still make a profit. Therefore, they cut back on the amount of credit they offer. As a result, many consumers, particularly those who are poor credit risks, find it hard to obtain credit.

2. **Synthesizing Information** Imagine that you need both a car loan and a home mortgage. Use a chart like the one below to help decide which of the six types of lending institutions discussed in this chapter would be most appropriate for each loan.

| Financial Institution | Services | Car or Home Loan? |
|---|---|---|
| | | |
| | | |
| | | |

3. **Drawing Conclusions** If you declare personal bankruptcy, your creditors clearly lose. What ethical concerns should you have before ever taking this action?

## Applying Economic Concepts

**The Role of Government** Sometimes credit cards are lost or stolen. The owner must take steps to keep his or her card from being used by an unauthorized person. Research the Truth in Lending Act to find out what a credit card holder must do when his or her card is lost or stolen.

## Cooperative Learning Project

Work in small groups to create a loan application that is appropriate for high school students, and circulate it in class. After going over the application, discuss why it is or is not difficult to decide who should receive loans. Is it difficult to decide who should *not* receive loans?

## Reviewing Skills

**Using a Database** Call various retail stores and gas stations and ask them to send you a credit card application. Analyze the applications, then prepare a database that organizes the answers to the following questions.

1. What questions asked on each application are virtually the same?
2. What questions asked on the gas station applications are different than those asked on the retail store applications?
3. Were any questions asked that you think violate the Equal Credit Opportunity Act? Explain.

## Technology Activity

**Using the Internet** If you ever wish to borrow money, your credit rating will be important. You can determine what your credit rating is by going to the Internet.

Enter the words *credit rating* in your search engine. You will find numerous sites that will give you a credit check on yourself. A wealth of online credit reporting services are available, and some of these reporting services are free.

## Analyzing the Global *Economy*

The first banks arose in Europe during the Middle Ages. Indeed, the word *bank* comes from the *banca*, or bench, that moneychangers set up at medieval fairs to exchange currencies, transfer funds, receive deposits, and arrange loans. Research these early financial institutions and the interest rates they charged their customers.



## CHAPTER 4 Assessment and Activities

### Applying Economic Concepts

Card holders must notify issuers of lost or stolen cards immediately. Card holders are responsible for the first $50 of new charges on a lost or stolen card.

### Cooperative Learning Project

Discussions should focus on what lenders might look for in terms of creditworthiness of high school students.

### Reviewing Skills

Encourage students to review the guidelines in the Practicing the Skill section of the Skills feature on page 95.

### Technology Activity

Encourage students to share their findings with the rest of the class.

### Analyzing the Global Economy

Have students present their findings in a brief illustrated report.

### Chapter Bonus Test Question

ASK: How does a credit card differ from a debit card? *A credit card allows consumers to make cashless purchases by giving them access to loans. A debit card does not provide a loan. Instead, it makes cashless purchases possible by enabling customers to transfer funds electronically from their bank accounts directly to the business where they purchased goods.*

## Thinking Critically

1. The benefit of buying on credit is being able to enjoy the good or service now rather than later. The cost is whatever the borrower must pay in interest or lost opportunities to buy other items. The benefit of buying with cash is that the buyer does not incur debt. The costs are the time the buyer may have to wait to buy while saving and the lost opportunities to buy other items.
2. Charts should reflect that banks, savings banks, savings and loan associations, and some larger credit unions are more appropriate for mortgage loans.
3. Answers may vary. Many students will suggest that people should strongly consider their reputations and the promises they have made before deciding not to fully repay their creditors.

# CHAPTER 5 Resource Manager

## Teaching Transparency

### Economic Concepts Transparency 2

ECONOMIC CONCEPTS Transparency 2

OPPORTUNITY COST & TRADE-OFFS

## Application and Enrichment

### Enrichment Activity 5

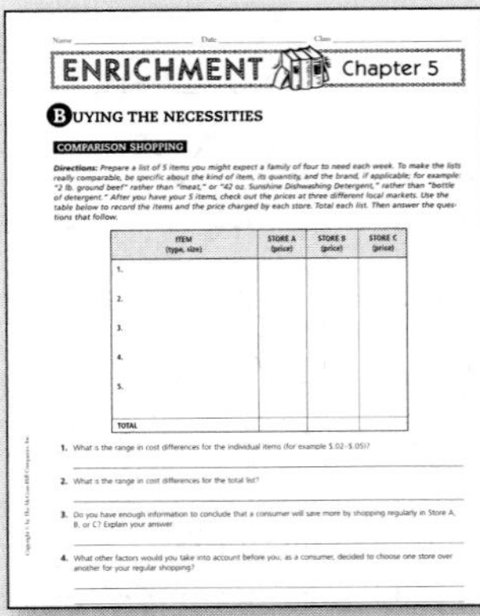
ENRICHMENT Chapter 5

BUYING THE NECESSITIES

COMPARISON SHOPPING

### Consumer Applications Activity 9

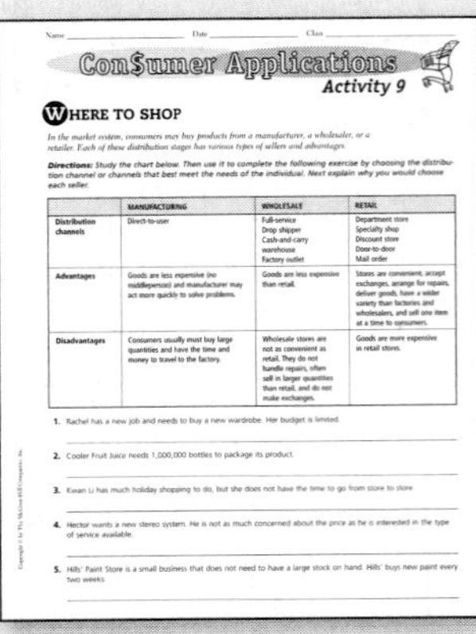
Con$umer Applications Activity 9

WHERE TO SHOP

### Free Enterprise Activity 11

FREE ENTERPRISE ACTIVITY 11

EXPRESSED AND IMPLIED WARRANTIES

## Application and Enrichment

### Cooperative Learning Simulations and Problems 11

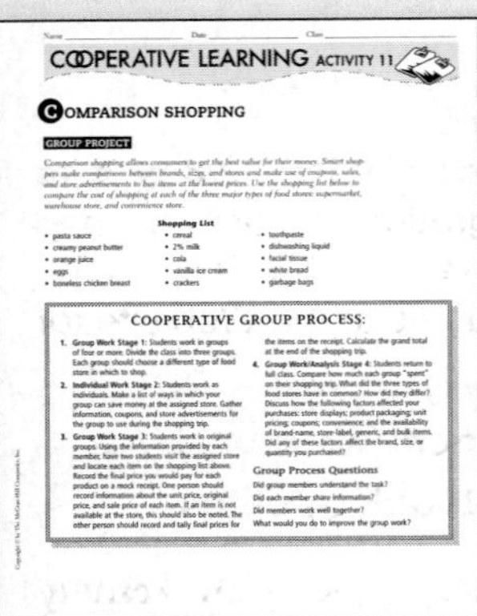
COOPERATIVE LEARNING ACTIVITY 11

COMPARISON SHOPPING

GROUP PROJECT

COOPERATIVE GROUP PROCESS:

### Primary and Secondary Source Readings 6, 12

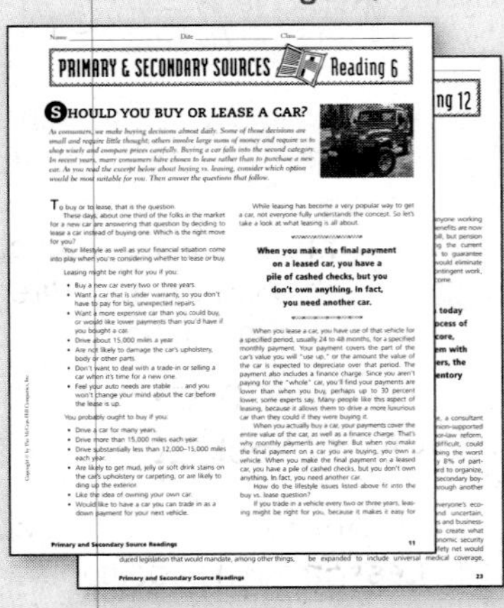
PRIMARY & SECONDARY SOURCES Reading 6

SHOULD YOU BUY OR LEASE A CAR?

### Math Practice for Economics Activity 11

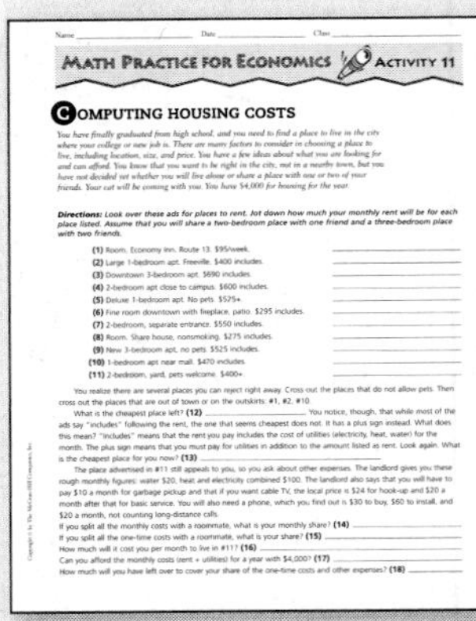
MATH PRACTICE FOR ECONOMICS ACTIVITY 11

COMPUTING HOUSING COSTS

### Economic Cartoons Activity 11

ECONOMIC CARTOON 11

BUYING A HOME



EXAMINING THE CARTOON

## Review and Reinforcement

### Critical Thinking Activity 11

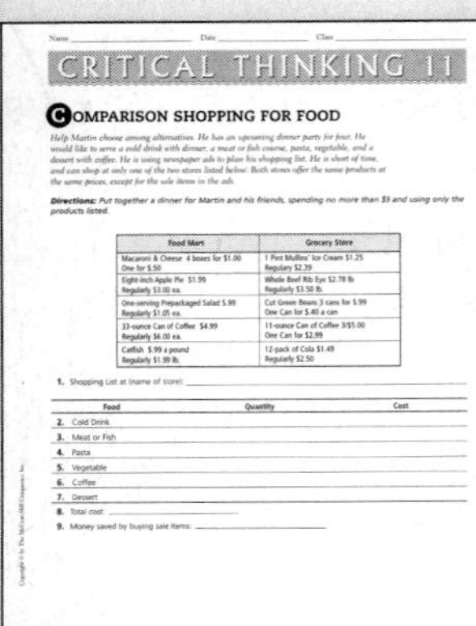
CRITICAL THINKING 11

COMPARISON SHOPPING FOR FOOD

### Reteaching Activity 5

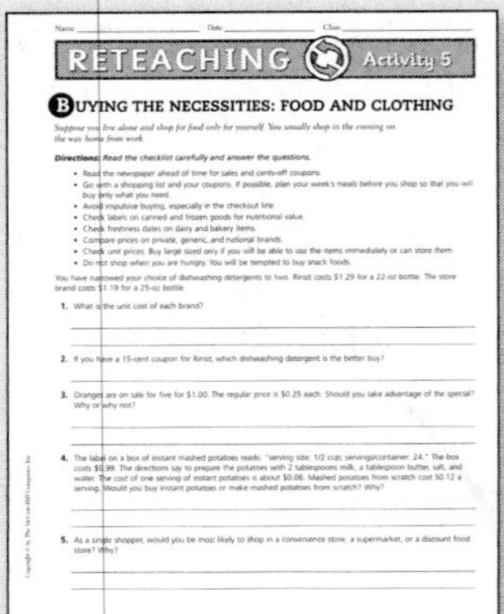
RETEACHING Activity 5

BUYING THE NECESSITIES: FOOD AND CLOTHING

### Economic Vocabulary Activity 5

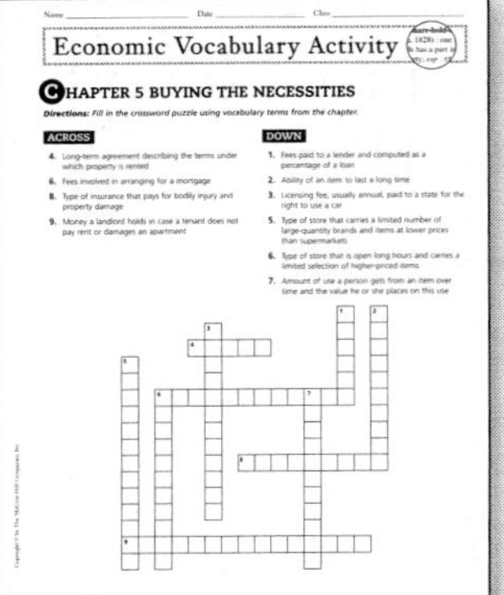
Economic Vocabulary Activity

CHAPTER 5 BUYING THE NECESSITIES

ACROSS

DOWN

### Reinforcing Economic Skills 12

Reinforcing Economic Skills Chapter 12

FINDING THE MAIN IDEA

Letter to Shareholders

# CHAPTER 5 Resource Manager

## Assessment and Evaluation

Chapter 5 Test Form A

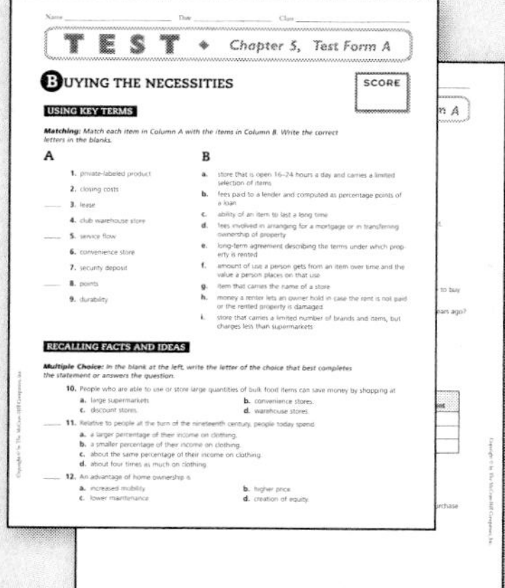

TEST • Chapter 5, Test Form A

BUYING THE NECESSITIES

SCORE

USING KEY TERMS

RECALLING FACTS AND IDEAS

Chapter 5 Test Form B

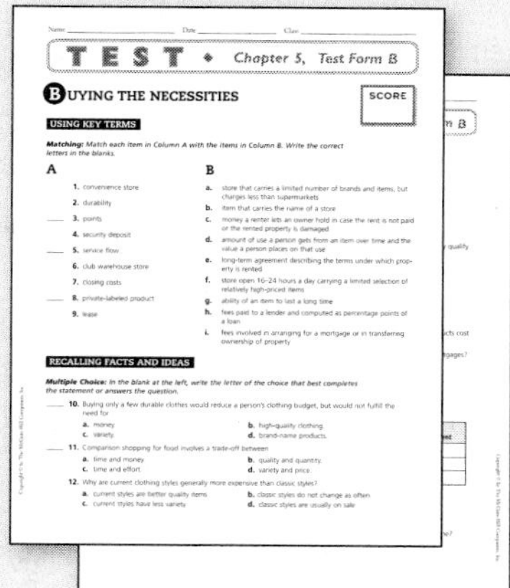

TEST • Chapter 5, Test Form B

BUYING THE NECESSITIES

SCORE

USING KEY TERMS

RECALLING FACTS AND IDEAS

Performance Assessment Activity 11

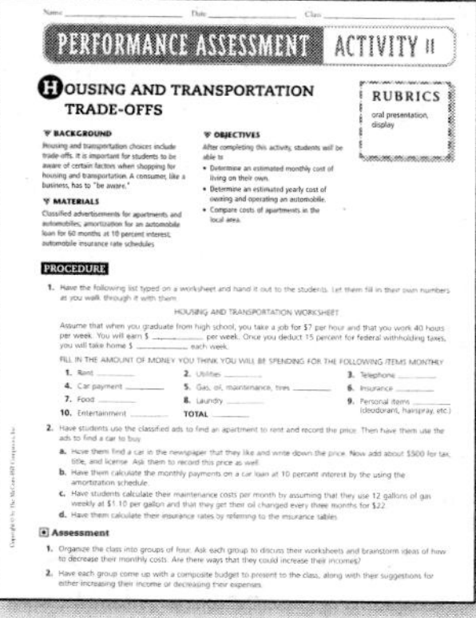

PERFORMANCE ASSESSMENT ACTIVITY 11

HOUSING AND TRANSPORTATION TRADE-OFFS

RUBRICS

PROCEDURE

ExamView® Pro Testmaker

## Technology and Multimedia

 Vocabulary PuzzleMaker Software

 Interactive Tutor Self-Assessment Software

 ExamView® Pro Testmaker

 NBR *Economics & You* Video Program (English/Spanish)

 Presentation Plus!

 Glencoe Skillbuilder Interactive Workbook CD-ROM, Level 2

 Interactive Lesson Planner

 MindJogger Videoquiz

 Interactive Economics! CD-ROM

Audio Program (English or Spanish)

## Spanish Resources

 Spanish Economic Concepts Transparency 2

 Spanish Vocabulary Activity 5

 Spanish Reteaching Activity 5

Spanish Section Quizzes for Chapter 5

 Spanish Chapter 5 Audio Program, Activity, and Test

## ECONOMICS Online

You and your students can visit ett.glencoe.com—the Web site companion to **Economics Today and Tomorrow.** This innovative integration of electronic and print media offers your students a wealth of opportunities. The student text directs students to the Web site for the following options:

- **Chapter Overviews**
- **Self-Check Quizzes**
- **Student Web Activities**
- **Textbook Updates**

Answers are provided for you in the **Web Activity Lesson Plan.** Additional Web resources and Interactive Puzzles are also available.

Use the Glencoe Web site for additional resources. All essential content is covered in the Student Edition.

## Additional Resources

### Reading for the Student

*Consumer Reports Buying Guide.* Boulder, CO: Guide on how to shop, containing product ratings, product recommendations, and buying advice.

### Reading for the Teacher

Underhill, Paco. *Why We Buy: The Science of Shopping.* New York: Simon & Schuster, 1999. Provides a readable explanation of consumer behavior.

# CHAPTER 5 Resource Manager

## Section Resources

| Reading Objectives | Reproducible Resources | Technology/Multimedia Resources |
|---|---|---|
| **Section 1**<br>**Shopping for Food**<br>• What are the advantages of comparison food shopping?<br>• What are the advantages and disadvantages of shopping at club warehouse stores? | Reproducible Lesson Plan 5-1<br>Daily Lecture Notes 5-1<br>Guided Reading Activity 5-1<br>Reading Essentials and Study Guide 5-1<br>Daily Focus Activity 34<br>Section Quiz 5-1* | Daily Focus Transparency 34<br>Economic Concepts Transparency 2<br>Vocabulary PuzzleMaker<br>Interactive Tutor Self-Assessment Software<br>MindJogger Videoquiz<br>NBR's *Economics & You**<br>Presentation Plus!<br>ExamView® Pro Testmaker<br>Economic Survival: A Financial Simulation |
| **Section 2**<br>**Clothing Choices**<br>• What three factors determine clothing value?<br>• When should you take advantage of clothing sales? | Reproducible Lesson Plan 5-2<br>Daily Lecture Notes 5-2<br>Guided Reading Activity 5-2<br>Reading Essentials and Study Guide 5-2<br>Daily Focus Activity 35<br>Section Quiz 5-2* | Daily Focus Transparency 35<br>Vocabulary PuzzleMaker<br>Interactive Tutor Self-Assessment Software<br>MindJogger Videoquiz<br>Presentation Plus!<br>ExamView® Pro Testmaker |
| **Section 3**<br>**To Rent or to Buy**<br>• What three rules should determine how much you spend for a house?<br>• What are the rights and responsibilities of renters? | Reproducible Lesson Plan 5-3<br>Daily Lecture Notes 5-3<br>Guided Reading Activity 5-3<br>Reading Essentials and Study Guide 5-3<br>Daily Focus Activity 36<br>Section Quiz 5-3*<br>Reinforcing Economic Skills 12 | Daily Focus Transparency 36<br>Vocabulary PuzzleMaker<br>Interactive Tutor Self-Assessment Software<br>MindJogger Videoquiz<br>NBR's *Economics & You**<br>Presentation Plus!<br>ExamView® Pro Testmaker<br>Economic Survival: A Financial Simulation |
| **Section 4**<br>**Buying and Operating a Vehicle**<br>• What are the trade-offs when buying a vehicle?<br>• What costs are involved in operating a vehicle? | Reproducible Lesson Plan 5-4<br>Daily Lecture Notes 5-4<br>Guided Reading Activity 5-4<br>Reading Essentials and Study Guide 5-4<br>Daily Focus Activity 37<br>Section Quiz 5-4* | Daily Focus Transparency 37<br>Vocabulary PuzzleMaker<br>Interactive Tutor Self-Assessment Software<br>MindJogger Videoquiz<br>NBR's *Economics & You**<br>Presentation Plus!<br>ExamView® Pro Testmaker |

*Also available in Spanish

# CHAPTER 5 Resource Manager

## ACTIVITY From the Classroom of

**Jeff Harris**
**Dinuba High School**
**Dinuba, California**

### Driving to Work

In this activity, students "find a job and buy a vehicle." First, students describe a job that is of interest to them and explain what actions they need to take to be qualified for this job. Have students write to a potential employer and obtain a job application. Copy the various applications and have students practice filling them out.

Next, students should "buy" a vehicle. Have students summarize in a paragraph the type of car they want. Then have them research the down payment, interest rates, monthly payments, and insurance costs of their chosen vehicle. Encourage them to visit a car lot and speak to a sales representative. If possible, have students obtain quotes on the Internet.

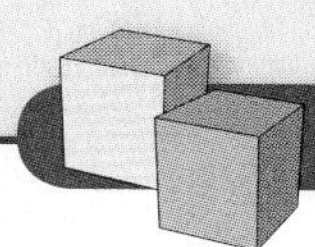

## Block Schedule

Activities that are particularly suited to use within the block scheduling framework are identified throughout this chapter by the following designation: BLOCK SCHEDULING

## Easy Planning and Preparation!

Use Glencoe's **Presentation Plus!**, a Microsoft PowerPoint® application, to teach **Buying the Necessities.** With this multimedia teacher tool, you can customize ready-made presentations. At your fingertips are interactive transparencies, on-screen lecture notes, audiovisual presentations, and links to the Internet and to other Glencoe multimedia.

### Interactive Lesson Planner

Planning has never been easier! Organize your week, month, semester, or year with all the lesson helps you need to make teaching creative, timely, and relevant—the way it is meant to be. The Interactive Lesson Planner opens Glencoe's **Chapter 5** resources, helps you build your schedule, and tracks your progress.

## Key to Ability Levels

**Teaching strategies have been coded for varying learning styles and abilities.**

- L1 BASIC activities for all students
- L2 AVERAGE activities for average to above-average students
- L3 CHALLENGING activities for above-average students
- ELL ENGLISH LANGUAGE LEARNER activities

## National Council on Economic Education

## THE EconomicsAmerica AND EconomicsInternational PROGRAMS

### Voluntary Standards Emphasized in Chapter 5

**Content Standard 1** Students will understand that productive resources are limited. Therefore, people cannot have all the goods and services they want; as a result, they must choose some things and give up others.

**Content Standard 2** Students will understand that effective decision making requires comparing the additional costs of alternatives with the additional benefits. Most choices involve doing a little more or a little less of something; few choices are all-or-nothing decisions.

### Resources Available from NCEE

- *Capstone: The Nation's High School Economics Course*
- *Personal Finance Economics: Wallet Wisdom*
- *Focus: High School Economics*
- *Personal Decision Making: Focus on Economics*

**To order these materials, or to contact your State Council on Economic Education about workshops and programs, call 1-800-338-1192 or visit the NCEE Web site at http://www.nationalcouncil.org**

ECONOMICS & YOU

Buying the Necessities

Chapter 11
Disc 1, Side 1

ASK: What are the trade-offs in buying a new vs. a used car of the same make? *A new car requires fewer immediate repairs but costs more than a used car.*

 Also available in VHS.

## Chapter Overview

Chapter 5 explains or describes the value of comparison shopping for food, how to obtain the best value in clothing for the price, the advantages and disadvantages of buying or renting a home, and the costs of buying a vehicle.

### GLENCOE TECHNOLOGY

Use **MindJogger Videoquiz** VHS to preview Chapter 5 content.

ECONOMICS Online

Introduce students to chapter content and key terms by having them access **Chapter 5—Chapter Overviews** at ett.glencoe.com

# CHAPTER 5

# Buying the Necessities

### Why It's Important

*What are the costs of owning a car? How much should you budget for clothes and food? Should you rent or buy a house? This chapter will help you learn to shop wisely for the necessities.*

*To learn more about buying a home or car, view the* **Economics & You** *Chapter 11 video lesson:* **Buying the Necessities**

ECONOMICS Online

**Chapter Overview** Visit the *Economics Today and Tomorrow* Web site at ett.glencoe.com and click on ***Chapter 5—Chapter Overviews*** to preview chapter information.

## CHAPTER LAUNCH ACTIVITY

Tell students to imagine that a friend has asked for advice on buying a new outfit for school. Mention that the friend has $120 to spend. Then lead a discussion with students on how they would help the friend. Suggest that they draw up a list of questions they might ask the friend about style, quality, durability, and comfort of the clothing desired. Point out that in this chapter they will learn that consumers need to answer such questions when purchasing clothes.

SECTION 1

# Shopping for Food

## Cover Story

*The Columbus Dispatch*, May 26, 1999

Here's a new idea from Yoder's: sour cream in a squeeze-top bottle. It's a good idea if you use sour cream mostly for topping baked potatoes, nachos, and fajitas. It's probably not a good idea if you use it primarily as an ingredient. The 16-ounce plastic bottles sell for $1.99. That compares with $1.39 for Yoder's regular 16-ounce cartons of sour cream.

### Reader's Guide

**Terms to Know**
- club warehouse store
- convenience store
- private-labeled products

**Reading Objectives**
1. What are the advantages of comparison food shopping?
2. What are the advantages and disadvantages of shopping at club warehouse stores?

Americans consume a great variety of foods. They can choose from thousands of different food products and buy them at thousands of stores. Hundreds of brands offer numerous choices: for example, sour cream in a 16-ounce container, sour cream in a squeeze-top bottle, sour cream mixed with chives in an 8-ounce container, and so on. In all, American consumers spend hundreds of billions of dollars a year on food. In this section, you'll learn how to get the most from your food dollars.

## Comparison Shopping

Because American families spend so much for food, comparison shopping is important. It involves making comparisons among brands and sizes before you buy. You need to decide not only what to shop for but where to shop as well.



## SECTION 1 RESOURCE MANAGER

**Reproducible Masters**
- Reproducible Lesson Plan 5–1
- Reading Essentials and Study Guide 5–1
- Guided Reading Activity 5–1
- Section Quiz 5–1
- Daily Focus Activity 34
- Daily Lecture Notes 5–1

**Multimedia**
- Daily Focus Transparency 34
- Vocabulary PuzzleMaker
- Interactive Tutor Self-Assessment Software
- ExamView® Pro Testmaker
- MindJogger Videoquiz
- NBR's *Economics & You*
- Presentation Plus!
- Economic Survival: A Financial Simulation



# 1 Focus

## Overview

Section 1 explains or describes the basic principles of comparison shopping for food; the differences among brand-name, generic, and private-labeled products; and the trade-off among price, quality, and quantity in shopping for food.

### BELLRINGER
**Motivational Activity**

Project **Daily Focus Transparency 34** and have students answer the questions.

This activity is also available as a blackline master.

**Daily Focus Transparency 34**

### Reader's Guide

Answers to the **Reading Objectives** questions are on page 115.

**Preteaching Vocabulary**

Ask students to search through used magazines and newspapers to find advertisements that show club warehouse stores, convenience stores, and private-labeled products. Encourage students to share their advertisements with other members of the class.

**Vocabulary PuzzleMaker**

# 2 Teach

## Guided Practice

**L1** Making Comparisons Draw a two-column chart on the board, with "Advantages" and "Disadvantages" as column headings. Ask students to copy the chart into their notebooks twice. Then have them use one chart to compare club warehouse stores and convenience stores, and the other to compare brand-name products, private-labeled products, and generic products.

**Daily Lecture Notes 5-1**

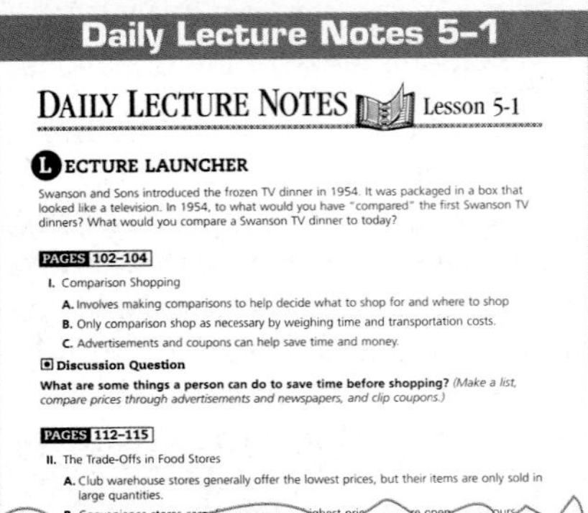

DAILY LECTURE NOTES Lesson 5-1

LECTURE LAUNCHER

Swanson and Sons introduced the frozen TV dinner in 1954. It was packaged in a box that looked like a television. In 1954, to what would you have "compared" the first Swanson TV dinners? What would you compare a Swanson TV dinner to today?

PAGES 102–104

I. Comparison Shopping
   A. Involves making comparisons to help decide what to shop for and where to shop
   B. Only comparison shop as necessary by weighing time and transportation costs.
   C. Advertisements and coupons can help save time and money.

**Discussion Question**

**What are some things a person can do to save time before shopping?** *(Make a list, compare prices through advertisements and newspapers, and clip coupons.)*

PAGES 112–115

II. The Trade-Offs in Food Stores
   A. Club warehouse stores generally offer the lowest prices, but their items are only sold in large quantities.
   B. Convenience stores ca…

## FIGURE 5.1 Checklist for Food Shopping

**The following are helpful tips for getting the most from your money when you shop for food:**

1. Read the newspapers ahead of time for sales and cents-off coupons.
2. Go with a shopping list and coupons. Plan a week's worth of meals so that you will buy only what you need. A list will also help you avoid additional trips to the store.
3. Avoid impulsive buying, or buying without thinking about the purchase beforehand. Be careful in the checkout line because nonessential items are placed by the cash register.
4. Buy nutritional items first. Check labels on canned and frozen goods for nutritional value.
5. Check freshness dates on dairy and bakery items.
6. Compare prices on private, generic, and national brands.
7. Check unit prices. Buy large sizes if you can use the items immediately or can store them.
8. Do not shop when you are hungry or thirsty. You will be tempted to buy more than you need.

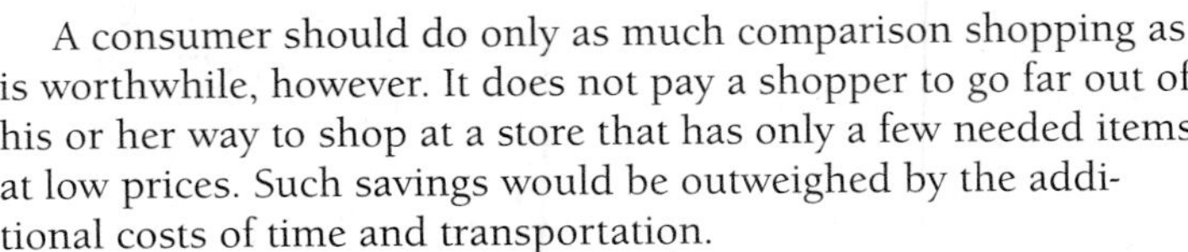

A consumer should do only as much comparison shopping as is worthwhile, however. It does not pay a shopper to go far out of his or her way to shop at a store that has only a few needed items at low prices. Such savings would be outweighed by the additional costs of time and transportation.

Remember, your time has an opportunity cost. The more time you spend comparison shopping for food, the less time you have to do anything else. Reading advertisements is a timesaving, inexpensive way to comparison shop. Food store ads describe sales and often contain cents-off coupons. **Figure 5.1** lists this tip as well as other suggestions to follow in your food shopping.

## Trade-Offs in Food Stores

Americans typically do their food shopping in either supermarkets or **club warehouse stores,** such as Costco. These stores usually sell a limited number of brands and items, but they often sell them by the case. Warehouse stores typically charge the lowest prices for food.

**club warehouse store:** *store that carries a limited number of large-quantity brands and items and is less expensive than supermarkets*



## Meeting Special Needs

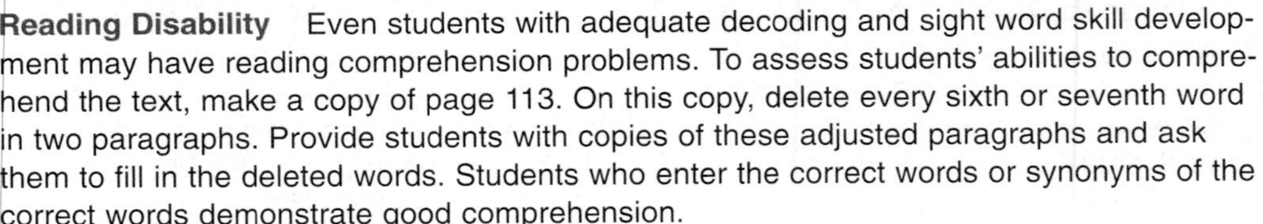

**Reading Disability** Even students with adequate decoding and sight word skill development may have reading comprehension problems. To assess students' abilities to comprehend the text, make a copy of page 113. On this copy, delete every sixth or seventh word in two paragraphs. Provide students with copies of these adjusted paragraphs and ask them to fill in the deleted words. Students who enter the correct words or synonyms of the correct words demonstrate good comprehension.

Refer to *Inclusion for the Social Studies Classroom Strategies and Activities* for students with different learning styles.

Occasionally, you may want to use a **convenience store**, such as 7-Eleven, for just that reason—because it's convenient. They are usually open 16 to 24 hours a day, but carry a limited selection of items. The trade-off here is that you may be saving time to buy a few items you need, but you will pay a relatively higher price than you would elsewhere.

**convenience store:** *store open 16 to 24 hours a day, carrying a limited selection of relatively higher-priced items*

Although club warehouse stores offer the largest potential savings for your food dollars, there is a trade-off. Most food items come only in relatively large-quantity containers. So you may end up buying a "value-pack" of soups that has 24 cans, for example. Unless your family is large and eats canned soup regularly, you will have unused cans of soup in your cupboard. Therein lies an opportunity cost. You have tied up your funds in an inventory of food. Although the lost interest on those funds may not be great in any single week, it can add up to a significant amount over a several-year period.

In contrast, a large inventory can be a benefit. When you have a relatively well-stocked cupboard of food items, you do not have to return to the store to buy food so often. Thus, you save in time and the costs of transportation.

**private-labeled products:** *lower-priced store-brand products carried by some supermarket chains and club wholesale chains*

### Brand-Name Products Versus Private-Labeled Products

When you go shopping in virtually any food store, many of the food items have well-known brand names. Some food stores also carry regional brands that are found only in certain areas of the country.

As an alternative to expensive national brands, some big supermarket chains, as well as club wholesale chains, carry their own store-brand products. These are also called **private-labeled products.** According to some consumer surveys, it is possible to save as much as 40 percent by buying store-brand (private-labeled) products. As shown in **Figure 5.2,** you can save even more when you buy generic or bulk items.

**FIGURE** 

**Generic and Bulk Foods**

Some food products are available in brand-name, store-label, generic, or bulk form. Generally, price decreases in that order. ***What is the difference between private-labeled products and generic products?***

Uncle Ben's converted Rice Original
BRAND NAME
Rice
$2.59
32 OZ.

**Guided Reading Activity 5-1**

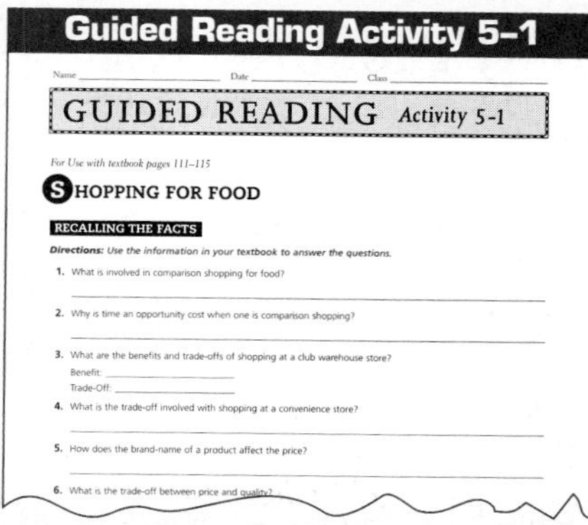

GUIDED READING Activity 5-1

SHOPPING FOR FOOD

RECALLING THE FACTS

1. What is involved in comparison shopping for food?
2. Why is time an opportunity cost when one is comparison shopping?
3. What are the benefits and trade-offs of shopping at a club warehouse store?
4. What is the trade-off involved with shopping at a convenience store?
5. How does the brand-name of a product affect the price?
6. What is the trade-off between price and quality?

## Independent Practice

L2 Applying Ideas Have students work in groups to conduct a price comparison investigation at local supermarkets. Have them find the unit cost of brand-name, private-label, and generic forms of orange juice, spaghetti, canned tomatoes, oatmeal, and several other commonly purchased items. Ask groups to present their findings in a brief report noting which type of product they think is the best value and why.
ELL BLOCK SCHEDULING

**Visual Instruction FIGURE 5.2**

**Answer:** *Private-labeled products are store-brand products carried by some big supermarket chains as well as club wholesale chains. Generic products have no brand or store identification.*

## Cooperative Learning

Organize students into groups, and have groups brainstorm and develop a checklist of shopping reminders aimed at getting the maximum value for every dollar spent on food purchases. Have group representatives present their checklists for review and discussion by the class. Then have the class select the best elements from each to create a class checklist. Finally, select members of each group to work together to create a poster featuring their shopping checklists. Display the poster prominently in the classroom.
BLOCK SCHEDULING

## ECONOMIC SURVIVAL
### A Financial Simulation

To help students learn to manage their own finances, have the class play the game **Economic Survival: A Financial Simulation**, in which each student enters the workforce, rents an apartment, and deals with everyday events. The simulation takes five days to complete and may be extended for an additional two weeks.

**ECONOMICS & YOU**

**Buying the Necessities**

Chapter 11
Disc 1, Side 1

**ASK:** What are some guidelines you should follow when buying food? *comparison shopping, clipping coupons, making a shopping list, checking labels and freshness, not shopping when hungry*

Also available in VHS.

# 3 Assess

## Meeting Lesson Objectives

Assign Section 1 Assessment as homework or an in-class activity.

### The Trade-Off Between Quality, Price, and Quantity

There is often a trade-off between quality and price in the products you buy. A lower-priced generic dishwasher soap might leave a slight film on your drinking glasses, for example, compared to a more expensive national-brand alternative.

Often you will find that the larger the quantity of any item you buy in a supermarket, the lower the per-unit price. Most states require stores to provide unit pricing for food and other products. See **Figure 5.3.** This practice makes it easy to compare prices not only for different brands, but for different sizes of the same brand. For example, the price of milk might be expressed in terms of cents per ounce. You can then tell how much you save per ounce if you buy milk in larger containers.

**Cents-Off Coupons** Many manufacturers give cents-off coupons. To take advantage of them, a consumer has to buy the brand, size, and quantity named on the coupon. The store then reduces the price paid by the amount printed on the coupon. The manufacturer, in turn, pays that amount to the store.

If you make a habit of using coupons, you can reduce your food bill by more than 10 percent over a one-year period. The use of cents-off coupons, however, requires time—the time to collect and match them to items when shopping. Because time is a scarce resource, you have to decide if the money you save using coupons is worth the time you spend. In addition, coupons tempt you to buy brand-name products you might not otherwise buy—thus *not* saving you money at all.

**FIGURE** 

**Unit Pricing** Trying to compare the prices of different amounts of a product—one gallon of Product A versus one half-gallon of Product B—can be confusing. Unit pricing allows you to compare like amounts: ounces to ounces, pounds to pounds, and so on.



## Visual Learning Activity

**Geography and Economics** On the board, draw a map showing a house, then a club warehouse store some distance away, a convenience store close by, and a supermarket about midway between the two. Ask students to write a paragraph explaining which store they might use to buy which items and why. ELL

## Economic Connection to... MATH

# Do Coupons Add Up to Savings?

You have a problem. Spread out on the table in front of you are half a dozen discount coupons for breakfast cereal. The discounts offered range from $.75 to $1.50. Which discount coupon will you choose?

The majority of studies of consumer behavior suggest that the answer is simple. The larger the discount, the more likely consumers are to clip and use the coupon. A recent study, however, suggests that the answer may not be so straightforward.

Most subjects in this study seemed to think that the size of the discount was an indication of price. The products featured on coupons offering greater discounts, study subjects felt, probably were very expensive. Consumers, therefore, may *not* clip and use a coupon offering a large discount because they feel it might not result in real savings. ■

**Practice** and **assess** key skills with *Skillbuilder Interactive Workbook, Level 2.*

## SECTION 1 Assessment

### Understanding Key Terms

1. **Define** club warehouse store, convenience store, private-labeled products.

### Reviewing Objectives

2. What are the advantages of comparison food shopping?
3. **Graphic Organizer** Use a diagram like the one below to describe the advantages and disadvantages of shopping at a club warehouse store.

### Applying Economic Concepts

4. **Trade-Offs** Do you think using cents-off coupons is worth the time spent clipping and matching them to products that you might buy? Why or why not?

### Critical Thinking Activity

5. **Making Comparisons** List your five favorite foods. Then visit five different food stores, or scan food advertisements in newspapers or on television commercials, and compare the prices of your listed items at each store. Explain why you think the stores had similar or different prices for each item.



## SECTION 1 Assessment Answers

1. All definitions can be found in the Glossary.
2. Comparison shopping gives consumers more groceries or better quality for their money.
3. Advantages: large potential for savings, buying in bulk saves time and transportation costs; Disadvantages: ties up funds in food inventories, limited brands
4. Answers will vary. Ensure that students explain the trade-offs involved in coupon clipping.
5. Answers will vary.



Use **Interactive Tutor Self-Assessment Software** to review Section 1.

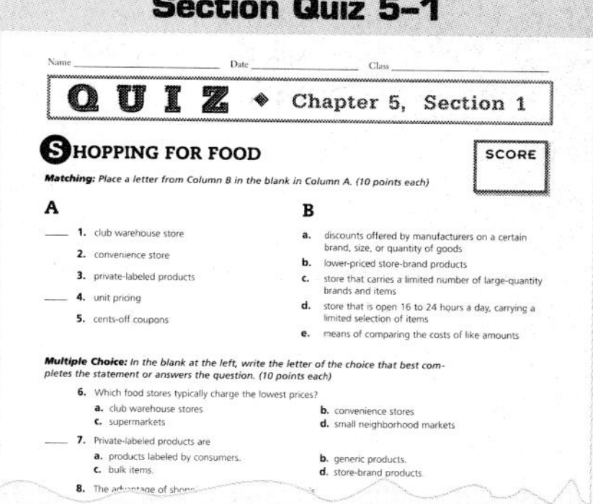

Section Quiz 5-1

Name ______ Date ______ Class ______

QUIZ ◆ Chapter 5, Section 1

SHOPPING FOR FOOD

SCORE

***Matching:*** *Place a letter from Column B in the blank in Column A. (10 points each)*

| A | B |
|---|---|
| ____ 1. club warehouse store | a. discounts offered by manufacturers on a certain brand, size, or quantity of goods |
| ____ 2. convenience store | b. lower-priced store-brand products |
| ____ 3. private-labeled products | c. store that carries a limited number of large-quantity brands and items |
| ____ 4. unit pricing | d. store that is open 16 to 24 hours a day, carrying a limited selection of items |
| ____ 5. cents-off coupons | e. means of comparing the costs of like amounts |

***Multiple Choice:*** *In the blank at the left, write the letter of the choice that best completes the statement or answers the question. (10 points each)*

____ 6. Which food stores typically charge the lowest prices?
a. club warehouse stores
b. convenience stores
c. supermarkets
d. small neighborhood markets

____ 7. Private-labeled products are
a. products labeled by consumers.
b. generic products.
c. bulk items.
d. store-brand products.

8. The advantage of shop...

## Reteach

Have students summarize the section by writing in their own words the main points of the content under each section subheading.

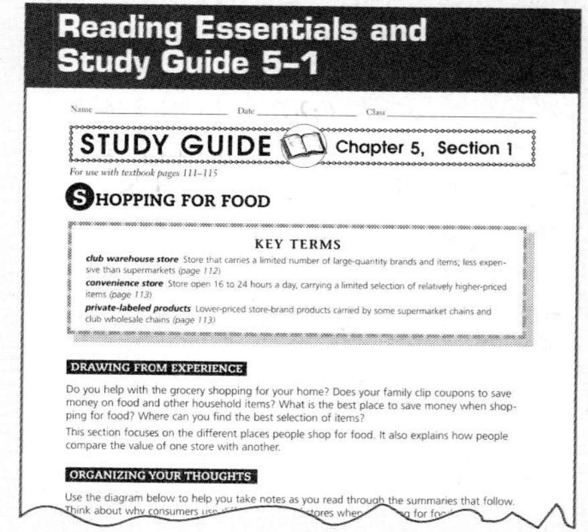

Reading Essentials and Study Guide 5-1

Name ______ Date ______ Class ______

STUDY GUIDE Chapter 5, Section 1

*For use with textbook pages 111–115*

SHOPPING FOR FOOD

KEY TERMS

***club warehouse store*** Store that carries a limited number of large-quantity brands and items; less expensive than supermarkets *(page 112)*

***convenience store*** Store open 16 to 24 hours a day, carrying a limited selection of relatively higher-priced items *(page 113)*

***private-labeled products*** Lower-priced store-brand products carried by some supermarket chains and club wholesale chains *(page 113)*

DRAWING FROM EXPERIENCE

Do you help with the grocery shopping for your home? Does your family clip coupons to save money on food and other household items? What is the best place to save money when shopping for food? Where can you find the best selection of items?

This section focuses on the different places people shop for food. It also explains how people compare the value of one store with another.

ORGANIZING YOUR THOUGHTS

Use the diagram below to help you take notes as you read through the summaries that follow. Think about why consumers use ... stores when ... for food...

## 4 Close

Have students write a brief paragraph explaining the importance of making wise decisions when purchasing food.

## Background

You might mention that Lloyd Ward was recognized by his alma mater in 1998 when the Michigan State University Alumni Association presented him with the Distinguished Alumni Award. This honor is given to Michigan State alumni who have made exceptional contributions to life in the United States.

## Teach

Draw students' attention to Ward's approach to failures. Then point out that Ward feels that not punishing people for failures is not enough. Rather, he feels that redefining failure requires building a "framework for people to feel the room to explore, take risks, and innovate." Conclude by asking students how they think this approach might affect the morale of workers at Maytag.

# People & Perspectives

## Lloyd Ward

*ENTREPRENEUR (1950–)*

- **President and chief executive officer of Maytag Corporation, one of North America's leading producers of premium brand home appliances**
- **Named "Executive of the Year" in 1995 by *Black Enterprise Magazine***
- **Ranked among the top 25 business executives of 1998 by *Business Week***

In the 1969–1970 season, Lloyd Ward captained the Michigan State University men's basketball team. His ability to motivate his teammates quickly became apparent. Ward continued to exhibit leadership qualities as he rose through the ranks of the business world. During his time at Maytag, Ward has become known as a team builder. He believes that motivated workers can help to get customers excited about the company's products:

> *"The focus [at Maytag] before was never disappoint the consumer, satisfy the consumer, be out there with a reliable, dependable product. Now we think of 'wowing' the customer, exceeding their expectations, and providing them with fundamental new benefits they are willing to pay for."*

Such a drastic change in approach involves giving up old and familiar ways of doing business. Persuading workers to adopt new ways, Ward believes, must be undertaken in a positive fashion:

> *"The challenge within our company is not so much people accepting new ideas as having them forget old ideas. A compelling vision provides a context to let go of tradition and the way things were done before so they can look at new things.*
>
> *You need to celebrate your failures as much as your successes. Said another way, you need to redefine failure as a learning experience. Everything you do is an opportunity to deepen focus and get better understanding, so you can do significantly better in your next try."*

### Checking for Understanding

1. **What does Ward mean by "wowing" the customer?**
2. **Why does Ward think that people should celebrate their failures as much as their successes?**

116

### Answers to *Checking for Understanding*

1. By "wowing" the customer, Ward means providing products that exceed customers' expectations and that provide customers with new benefits.
2. Ward thinks that people should celebrate their failures by redefining failure as a learning experience. By doing this, Ward suggests, people deepen their focus and improve their understanding, enabling them to do significantly better the next time.

SECTION 2

# Clothing Choices

## Cover Story

*The Washington Post*, February 1, 1999

The nation's 27 million teenagers, who set many trends in casual clothing, spend about $84 weekly, on average, of which $56 is their own money. They are making more shopping decisions and are picking the brands. A ranking of teens' "one favorite" store placed J.C. Penney first, Old Navy second, and Tommy Hilfiger third.

A lot of 16- and 17-year-olds are working, and they can buy Tommy and Polo clothing and Eddie Bauer jackets.

### Reader's Guide

**Terms to Know**

- durability
- service flow

**Reading Objectives**

1. What three factors determine clothing value?
2. When should you take advantage of clothing sales?

Americans spend about $400 billion annually on clothing and other personal products. Most people could save considerable income by purchasing only a few very durable pieces of clothing. The clothes, however, would not serve another purpose—variety. In this section, you'll learn that variety, for Americans, is typically the motivating factor involved in clothing choice.

## Comparing Clothing Value

Comparison shopping is an important part of buying wisely. Comparing value in clothing means more than simply purchasing an item from the store that offers the best price. Clothing value depends on at least three other factors: style, cost of care, and durability. See **Figure 5.4** on page 118.



## SECTION 2 RESOURCE MANAGER

**Reproducible Masters**

- Reproducible Lesson Plan 5–2
- Reading Essentials and Study Guide 5–2
- Guided Reading Activity 5–2
- Section Quiz 5–2
- Daily Focus Activity 35
- Daily Lecture Notes 5–2

**Multimedia**

- Daily Focus Transparency 35
- Vocabulary PuzzleMaker
- Interactive Tutor Self-Assessment Software
- ExamView® Pro Testmaker
- MindJogger Videoquiz
- Presentation Plus!



# 1 Focus

## Overview

Section 2 describes three factors that determine clothing value, and explains when consumers should take advantage of clothing sales.

### BELLRINGER
**Motivational Activity**

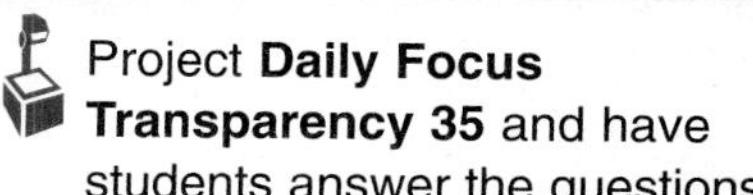

Project **Daily Focus Transparency 35** and have students answer the questions.

This activity is also available as a blackline master.

**Daily Focus Transparency 35**

FOCUS ACTIVITIES
Transparency 35

CLOTHING CHOICES

"The fashion wears out more apparel than the man."
—William Shakespeare

"Don King purchased 110 pairs of shoes from one store, for which he paid $64,100, tax included. . . ." [T]he popular media enjoy touting abnormalities in buying behavior. As a consequence, our youth . . . learn that hyperspending is the main reward for becoming affluent in America. . . . [But the real] rewards are more intangible than product related. . . .
—Thomas J. Stanley and William D. Danko, *The Millionaire Next Door*

"[The ladies of Cranford] dress very independent of fashion; as they observe, 'What does it signify how we dress here at Cranford, where everybody knows us?' And if they go from home, their reason is equally cogent: 'What does it signify how we dress here, where nobody knows us?'"
—Mrs. Gaskell, 19th-century writer

1. What does the quotation from Shakespeare mean?
2. According to Stanley and Danko, what helps drive young people's perceptions that the wealthy spend a lot of money on fashion?

Daily Focus Transparencies

### Reader's Guide

Answers to the **Reading Objectives** questions are on page 120.

**Preteaching Vocabulary**

Call on volunteers to offer definitions of the **Terms to Know**. Then have students locate the terms in the Glossary to check the accuracy of volunteers' definitions.

**Vocabulary PuzzleMaker**

# 2 Teach

## Guided Practice

**L1 Applying Ideas** Have students list 5 to 10 items of their favorite clothing from their wardrobes. Then ask students to evaluate each item of clothing in terms of durability, style, and cost of care. Call on volunteers to present their results and explain why they purchased the various items of clothing. ELL

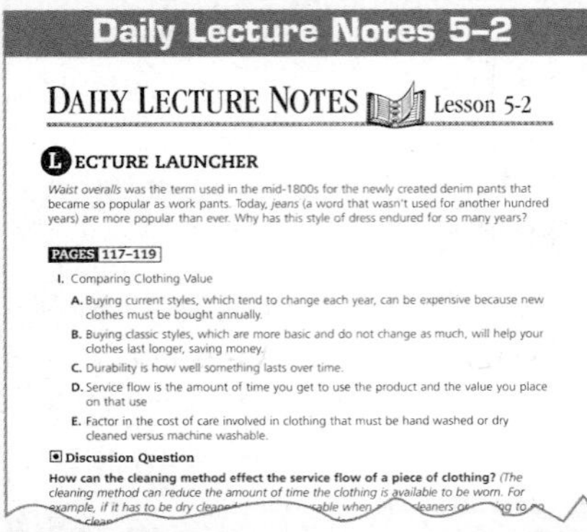

**Daily Lecture Notes 5-2**

DAILY LECTURE NOTES Lesson 5-2

**LECTURE LAUNCHER**

*Waist overalls* was the term used in the mid-1800s for the newly created denim pants that became so popular as work pants. Today, *jeans* (a word that wasn't used for another hundred years) are more popular than ever. Why has this style of dress endured for so many years?

PAGES 117–119

I. Comparing Clothing Value
   - A. Buying current styles, which tend to change each year, can be expensive because new clothes must be bought annually.
   - B. Buying classic styles, which are more basic and do not change as much, will help your clothes last longer, saving money.
   - C. Durability is how well something lasts over time.
   - D. Service flow is the amount of time you get to use the product and the value you place on that use
   - E. Factor in the cost of care involved in clothing that must be hand washed or dry cleaned versus machine washable.

**Discussion Question**

**How can the cleaning method effect the service flow of a piece of clothing?** *(The cleaning method can reduce the amount of time the clothing is available to be worn. For example, if it has to be dry clea*

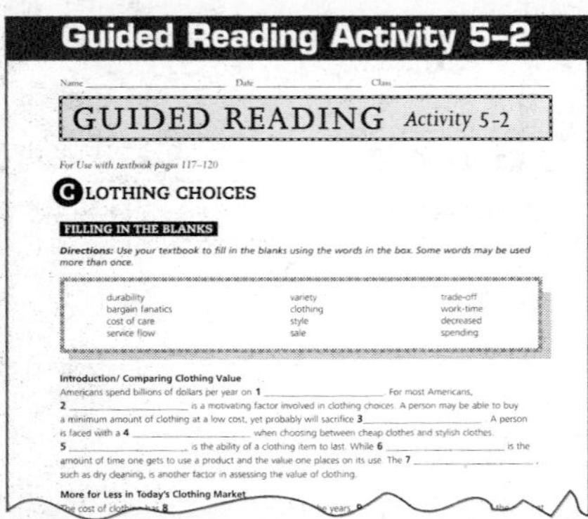

**Guided Reading Activity 5-2**

Name ______ Date ______ Class ______

GUIDED READING *Activity 5-2*

*For Use with textbook pages 117–120*

**CLOTHING CHOICES**

**FILLING IN THE BLANKS**

***Directions:*** *Use your textbook to fill in the blanks using the words in the box. Some words may be used more than once.*

| | | |
|---|---|---|
| durability | variety | trade-off |
| bargain fanatics | clothing | work-time |
| cost of care | style | decreased |
| service flow | sale | spending |

**Introduction/ Comparing Clothing Value**

Americans spend billions of dollars per year on **1** ______. For most Americans, **2** ______ is a motivating factor involved in clothing choices. A person may be able to buy a minimum amount of clothing at a low cost, yet probably will sacrifice **3** ______. A person is faced with a **4** ______ when choosing between cheap clothes and stylish clothes. **5** ______ is the ability of a clothing item to last. While **6** ______ is the amount of time one gets to use a product and the value one places on its use. The **7** ______, such as dry cleaning, is another factor in assessing the value of clothing.

**More for Less in Today's Clothing Market**

**A** Style
*We often buy clothing styles that preserve our self-image. Clothing conveys a message to others about what you do, what you believe, and who you are.*

**FIGURE 5.4**

**Clothing Value** When making clothing purchases, many people want to have different looks for different occasions. Also, people in different climates need different wardrobes for summer and winter.

**B** Cost of Care
*Dry-cleaning costs can vary widely, from $3 per shirt to $10 for a skirt or sweater.*

**C** Durability
*When comparison shopping for clothing, you should try to determine how long an item will last and how long you will need it. Then you should compare prices. Suppose you think Coat A will last twice as long as Coat B, and Coat A costs only 20 percent more. Coat A, then, is a better buy.*

**Style** You may be able to buy the minimum amount of clothing you need at a very low cost. You will, however, generally give up style to do it. You are faced with a trade-off. Should you buy stylish clothes each year to keep up with fashion, but then have less money to spend on other items? Or should you buy less stylish clothes, which results in more money to do other things?

**Durability** The ability of an item to last is known as **durability.** The longer a piece of clothing—or any item—lasts, the more durable it is. When you purchase an item of clothing, you are purchasing it for the service flow that it yields. **Service flow** is the amount of time you get to use a product and the value you place on this use. If you buy a jacket that will last three years and costs $300, the cost per annual service flow is $100.

**durability:** *ability of an item to last a long time*

**service flow:** *amount of use a person gets from an item over time and the value a person places on this use*



## Meeting Special Needs

**Poor Math Skills** Some students may have trouble calculating savings on items offered in clothing sales. Inform them that they can use the following equation to find the dollar savings on a sale item:

R[% rate] × P[original price] = S[savings]

Demonstrate how to use the equation with this example: **If a store advertises 25 percent off a $40 blouse, what is the savings?** *0.25 × $40 = $10*

Refer to *Inclusion for the Social Studies Classroom Strategies and Activities* for students with different learning styles.

**Cost of Care** The cost of care is another factor in assessing value. Two shirts or blouses may cost the same, but one may require dry cleaning, which is more expensive than hand or machine washing. When deciding on the best choice in a clothing purchase, you must consider maintenance costs.

## More for Less

By value shopping, consumers can help themselves in budgeting clothing allowances. It is worth noting, however, that the cost of clothing has decreased significantly over the years. Seventy years ago, a good suit cost about $40. It took an average consumer almost 80 hours to earn enough income to buy that suit. Today a comparable suit sells for just over $500, but costs the average worker the equivalent of 40 hours of work. Over the past 100 years, a pair of name-brand jeans has fallen in *work-time cost* by more than half. This means that clothing basics cost much less than they did in the early 1900s. See **Figure 5.5.**

**Clothing Sales** Although a smaller percentage of one's budget goes to clothing purchases now than in the past, it is still the wise consumer who buys clothing on sale. Because clothing sales are so numerous throughout the year, however, it is easy to become a bargain fanatic—buying sale items just because they are on sale. Before going shopping, make a list of the clothing you require. Having this list along may help you keep your spending within limits. It is wise to determine your wants as well as your realistic needs before shopping at any sale. **Figure 5.6** on page 120 can help you evaluate these wants.

**FIGURE** 

**Work-Time Cost** As a percentage of their budget, Americans spend far less on clothing today than in the past—5.3 percent today as compared to 8.4 percent in 1972–73, and 14.1 percent in 1901. A higher proportion of a family's income can be spent on other things such as education or family vacations.





## Independent Practice

**L2 Creating Wall Charts** Organize students into groups, and have them create wall charts illustrating the changes in young people's clothing styles during the twentieth century. Have groups display their finished wall charts around the room. Then lead students in a discussion of what influence, if any, durability, style, and cost of care considerations had on fashion change.

ELL BLOCK SCHEDULING

# 3 Assess

## Meeting Lesson Objectives

Assign Section 2 Assessment as homework or an in-class activity.

Use **Interactive Tutor Self-Assessment Software** to review Section 2.

### Section Quiz 5-2

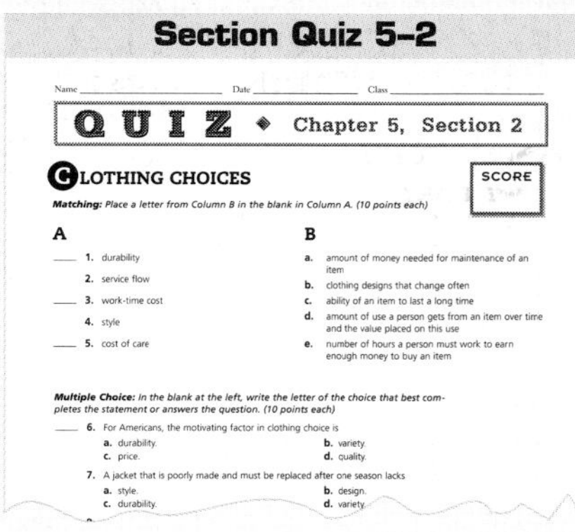

Name ______ Date ______ Class ______

QUIZ ◆ Chapter 5, Section 2

CLOTHING CHOICES

SCORE

***Matching:*** *Place a letter from Column B in the blank in Column A. (10 points each)*

| A | B |
|---|---|
| ____ 1. durability | a. amount of money needed for maintenance of an item |
| 2. service flow | b. clothing designs that change often |
| ____ 3. work-time cost | c. ability of an item to last a long time |
| 4. style | d. amount of use a person gets from an item over time and the value placed on this use |
| ____ 5. cost of care | e. number of hours a person must work to earn enough money to buy an item |

***Multiple Choice:*** *In the blank at the left, write the letter of the choice that best completes the statement or answers the question. (10 points each)*

____ 6. For Americans, the motivating factor in clothing choice is
a. durability. b. variety.
c. price. d. quality.

7. A jacket that is poorly made and must be replaced after one season lacks
a. style. b. design.
c. durability. d. variety.

## Cooperative Learning

Have students work in small groups to research and analyze advertising of clothing sales by various kinds of stores. Tell groups that the object of this activity is to determine whether the advertising gives consumers clear and sufficient information about the merchandise on sale, original and sale prices, savings percentages, and exchange and refund policies. Encourage groups to include broadcast advertising, circulars, catalogs, and newspaper advertisements in their analyses. Have group representatives present their findings to the class for evaluation and discussion.

## Reteach

Have students outline the section. Have them explain in an accompanying paragraph how the content of the section applies to their lives.

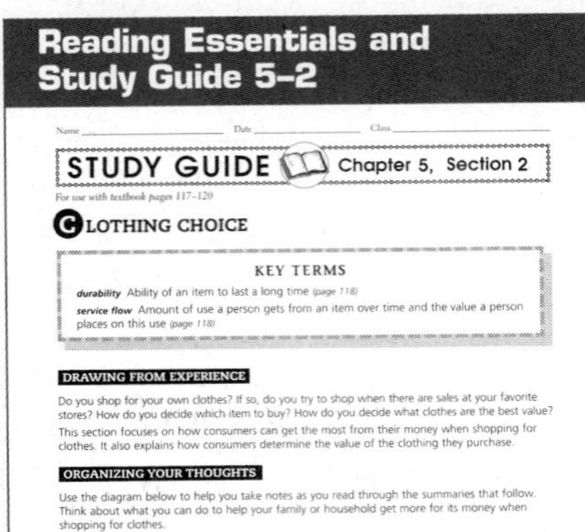

**Reading Essentials and Study Guide 5-2**

Name ______ Date ______ Class ______

STUDY GUIDE Chapter 5, Section 2

*For use with textbook pages 117–120*

CLOTHING CHOICE

KEY TERMS

***durability*** Ability of an item to last a long time *(page 118)*

***service flow*** Amount of use a person gets from an item over time and the value a person places on this use *(page 118)*

DRAWING FROM EXPERIENCE

Do you shop for your own clothes? If so, do you try to shop when there are sales at your favorite stores? How do you decide which item to buy? How do you decide what clothes are the best value?

This section focuses on how consumers can get the most from their money when shopping for clothes. It also explains how consumers determine the value of the clothing they purchase.

ORGANIZING YOUR THOUGHTS

Use the diagram below to help you take notes as you read through the summaries that follow. Think about what you can do to help your family or household get more for its money when shopping for clothes.

## 4 Close

Ask students to discuss how the information in this section might help them make wiser clothing-purchase decisions.

**FIGURE 5.6** **Checklist for Determining Clothing Wants**

**In deciding on clothing purchases, ask yourself the following questions:**

1. What do I already have? Check the condition of the clothes you have, and see what you want to replace.
2. What clothes do I wish to have for school? For my job? For my social life? For recreational activities?
3. How many changes of clothes do I require to meet my minimum standards for cleanliness, variety, and social status?
4. How do my answers to questions 1 through 3 compare with the amount of income I have to spend?
5. Should I pay cash or charge my purchases? Consider the trade-offs involved in paying cash or using credit.

**Practice** and **assess** key skills with ***Skillbuilder Interactive Workbook, Level 2.***

## SECTION 2 Assessment

### Understanding Key Terms

1. **Define** durability, service flow.

### Reviewing Objectives

2. **Graphic Organizer** Create a diagram like the one below to describe three factors that determine clothing value.

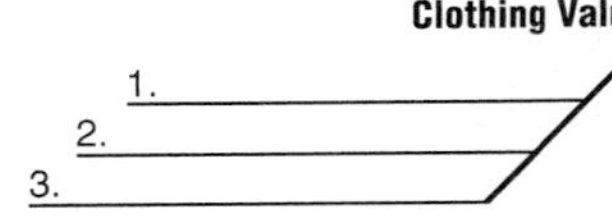


3. When should you take advantage of clothing sales?

### Applying Economic Concepts

4. **Work-Time Cost** Ask your parents and grandparents to remember the cost of a pair of jeans, a jacket, and a pair of tennis shoes when they were teenagers. Then ask them to remember the amount they were paid (by the hour) for any jobs they held as teenagers. Calculate their work-time cost of buying those items.

### Critical Thinking Activity

5. **Synthesizing Information** A store advertises jeans at 33 percent off the original price of $37. What is the sale price? *For help in understanding percentages, see page xix in the Economic Handbook.*



## SECTION 2 Assessment Answers

1. All definitions can be found in the Glossary.
2. Style, Durability, and Cost of Care
3. after you have determined your needs and realistic wants
4. Answers will vary.
5. $24.79

# SECTION 3

# To Rent or to Buy

## Cover Story

*The Columbus Dispatch*, June 3, 1999

Consumers have a case of home-buying fever. New-home sales reached their second-highest level on record in April as buyers, trying to stay ahead of rising mortgage rates, rushed to close deals.

The median price of new homes sold in April climbed to a record $159,500. The median is the midpoint where half cost more and half cost less. The average sales price rose to $193,100, also a record.

### Reader's Guide

**Terms to Know**

- closing costs
- points
- lease
- security deposit

**Reading Objectives**

1. What three rules should determine how much you spend for a house?
2. What are the rights and responsibilities of renters?

Some people will save for years in order to buy a small house. Others take out huge mortgages to purchase large homes. Still others are content to rent a house, condo, or apartment most of their lives. In this section, you'll learn about renting versus buying.

**Figure 5.7** on page 122 compares the advantages and disadvantages of owning and renting. Wise consumers should consider both when deciding whether to buy or to rent housing.

## How Much Should You Spend?

When you decide to buy a house, it is important that you do not take on financial obligations that are beyond your budget. As **Figure 5.8** on page 123 shows, lenders use certain rules to help buyers determine how much housing they can afford.





# 1 Focus

## Overview

Section 3 explains or describes the pros and cons of renting or buying a home and the rights and responsibilities of renters.

### BELLRINGER
**Motivational Activity**

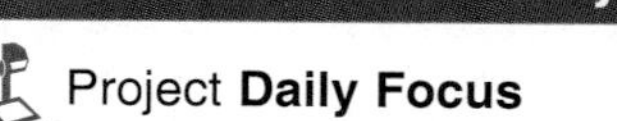

Project **Daily Focus Transparency 36** and have students answer the questions.

This activity is also available as a blackline master.

**Daily Focus Transparency 36**

FOCUS ACTIVITIES
Transparency 36

CONSUMER DECISIONS: HOUSING

Types of Housing

| HOUSING | CHARACTERISTICS |
|---|---|
| Single-Family Houses | Separate from other dwellings; surrounded by land; most expensive. |
| Cooperatives | Own share of building and land; one-term lease on apartment; operating costs of building and land divided among owners; need approval of all owners to make changes. |
| Condominiums | Each apartment individually owned; can sell or make changes; share ownership of common areas; pay fee for upkeep of common areas. |
| Town Houses | A house that shares common sidewalls with other similiar houses; front and back yard; less expensive than single-family houses. |
| Mobile Homes | Less expensive to buy and maintain; lower taxes; need to find land; decline in value; easily damaged during storms. |

1. What are the major types of housing?
2. Which type of housing is most common in your area? Why?

Daily Focus Transparencies

### Reader's Guide

Answers to the **Reading Objectives** questions are on page 127.

**Preteaching Vocabulary**

Have students read the Glossary definitions of the **Terms to Know**. Then ask students to use the terms to write a scenario about choosing a place to live.

**Vocabulary PuzzleMaker**

## SECTION 3 RESOURCE MANAGER

**Reproducible Masters**

- Reproducible Lesson Plan 5–3
- Reading Essentials and Study Guide 5–3
- Guided Reading Activity 5–3
- Section Quiz 5–3
- Daily Focus Activity 36
- Daily Lecture Notes 5–3

**Multimedia**

- Daily Focus Transparency 36
- Vocabulary PuzzleMaker
- Interactive Tutor Self-Assessment Software
- ExamView® Pro Testmaker
- MindJogger Videoquiz
- NBR's *Economics & You*
- Presentation Plus!
- Economic Survival: A Financial Simulation

# 2 Teach

## Guided Practice

**L1** Evaluating Information Organize students into groups and ask each group member to evaluate each of the advantages or disadvantages listed in **Figure 5.7.** Suggest that group members rate each renting advantage and disadvantage with a score of 1 through 3, where 1 is a minor advantage or disadvantage, 2 is average, and 3 is major. Then have them follow the same process for the advantages and disadvantages of buying a home. Have groups tally the scores for each advantage and disadvantage. Then have groups use their results to write several statements on the advantages and disadvantages of renting and buying a home. If students need guidance, suggest the following as a beginning statement: The major advantage in buying a home is . . .

### Daily Lecture Notes 5-3

DAILY LECTURE NOTES Lesson 5-3

LECTURE LAUNCHER

In 1997, Americans spent around $119 billion on home improvements. In the year 2005, it is predicted they will spend $180 billion on home improvements. What kind of improvements might add to the value of your home?

PAGES 121–123

I. How Much Should You Spend?
  A. Avoid spending more than you can afford.
  B. You will need the cash down payment and closing costs.
  C. Be aware of points or fees paid to the lender.

Discussion Question

**Why should people plan ahead and research when spending large sums of money?** *(People should be informed decision makers at all times, but especially when investing or spending large amounts of money to avoid hidden costs and high debt.)*

PAGES 123–124

II. Financing the Purchase of a House
  A. Many different types of mortgages and financing packages are available.
  B. Mortgages involve do... ...rest.

## FIGURE 5.7 Advantages and Disadvantages of Owning and Renting

**Home Ownership Advantages**

- Freedom of use; owners can remodel whenever or however they choose
- Pride of ownership; people tend to take better care of things they own
- Greater privacy
- Usually a good investment that in the past has risen in value as much as, or more than, the general rise in prices
- Significant income tax benefits
- Creation of *equity,* the market value of the property minus the mortgage payments still owed
- Good credit rating if mortgage payments are made on time
- Property to use as collateral for other loans

**Home Ownership Disadvantages**

- Less mobility, especially in years when interest rates on mortgages are high and housing is difficult to sell
- Moving to another property because the present one is too small, too big, and so on is time-consuming
- Necessity of a large outlay of money for a down payment
- Maintenance costs, real estate taxes, and possible depreciation
- Less money for other purchases because of high monthly mortgage payments
- Possibility of overextending a family's debt load to make home improvements or repairs

**Renting Advantages**

- Greater mobility; a renter does not have to worry about trying to sell property
- Feeling of freedom to choose another place to live if dissatisfied with current rental unit
- Paying only a small security deposit rather than a large down payment
- No direct maintenance costs, real estate taxes, or depreciation
- Good credit rating if rent is paid on time
- More money for other purchases because monthly rental payments are often less than monthly mortgage payments
- No temptation to overspend on home improvements

**Renting Disadvantages**

- No freedom of use; renters may not remodel or even paint without the owner's permission
- No return on rental money; a renter will never own the property regardless of how much rent he or she pays, regardless of the length of this period of time
- Few or no tax benefits
- Less privacy
- Little feeling of responsibility for seeing that the property is well taken care of
- No property for use as collateral
- Need to wait for maintenance work at the convenience of the owner

## Meeting Special Needs

**Hearing Disability** Students with hearing difficulties may have problems taking part in group activities. Encourage students to assist their hearing-impaired classmates by allowing them extra time to read information in the textbook and by reviewing group activity directions with them.

Refer to *Inclusion for the Social Studies Classroom Strategies and Activities* for students with different learning styles.

**FIGURE 5.8** **Lender's Rules** It would be unwise for both you and the lender if you spent more than a third of your income on the mortgage. ***Why?***

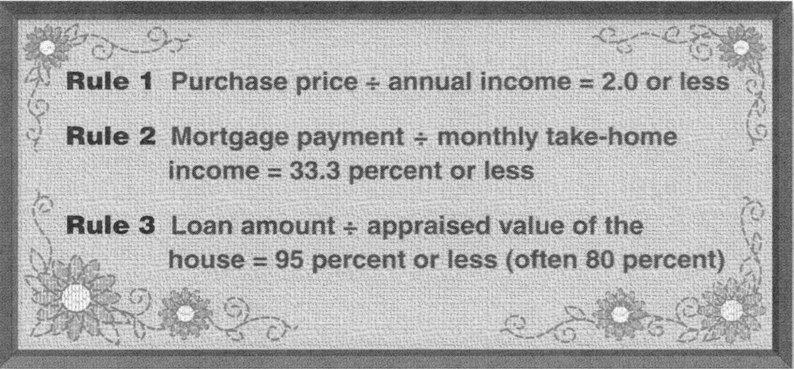

Rule 1 Purchase price ÷ annual income = 2.0 or less
Rule 2 Mortgage payment ÷ monthly take-home income = 33.3 percent or less
Rule 3 Loan amount ÷ appraised value of the house = 95 percent or less (often 80 percent)


In addition to the cash down payment, you will need money for **closing costs.** These are costs involved in arranging for a mortgage or in transferring ownership of the property. Closing costs can include fees for such items as the title search, legal costs, loan application, credit report, house inspections, and taxes. Although the person buying the house usually pays these fees, the seller may agree to pay part or all of them if this will make it easier to sell the house.

<u>**closing costs:**</u> *fees involved in arranging for a mortgage or in transferring ownership of property*

In arranging for a mortgage, it is also important to know about points, which are included in closing costs. **Points** are the fees paid to the lender and computed as a percentage of the loan. Each point the lender charges equals 1 percent of the amount borrowed. Lenders charge points—usually one to four—when they believe that the current interest rate is not high enough to pay the expenses involved in handling the mortgage and still make a profit.

<u>**points:**</u> *fees paid to a lender and computed as a percentage of a loan*

**ECONOMICS Online**

**Student Web Activity** Visit the *Economics Today and Tomorrow* Web site at **ett.glencoe.com** and click on ***Chapter 5—Student Web Activities*** to compare home prices in your area and around the country.

## Purchasing a House

One of the major problems facing today's home buyer is obtaining a mortgage. **Figure 5.9** on page 124 shows several kinds of mortgages that are available.





**Visual Instruction FIGURE 5.8**

**Answer:** *The borrower might not be able to make the mortgage payments, and the lender would have to foreclose on the mortgage.*

**Guided Reading Activity 5-3**

GUIDED READING Activity 5-3

TO RENT OR BUY

See the **Web Activity Lesson Plan** at *ett.glencoe.com* for an introduction, lesson description, and answers to the **Student Web Activity** for this chapter.

### Cooperative Learning

Organize students into an equal number of small groups, and tell groups to imagine that they are real estate specialists at a consumer information service. Have half the groups prepare an illustrated pamphlet titled "Buying a Home—What You Need to Know." Direct the rest of the groups to prepare a similar pamphlet titled "A Renters' Guide—What You Need to Know." Inform groups that the information contained in their pamphlets should be suitable for first-time buyers and renters. Call on groups to present and explain their pamphlets. BLOCK SCHEDULING

**L1 Understanding Ideas** Ask students to calculate the total check a buyer would have to present at closing for the following priced houses if the down payment is $20,000 and closing costs are $2,500 plus two points.

a. $75,000 *($23,600)*
b. $100,000 *($24,100)*
c. $125,000 *($24,600)*
d. $150,000 *($25,100)*
e. $200,000 *($26,100)*

Give students extra practice by adjusting the down payment, closing costs less points, and the number of points.

## Independent Practice

**L2 Applying Ideas** Ask students to find the average starting wage for several occupations. Next, have students carefully review Lender's Rules in **Figure 5.8** on page 123. Then have students calculate the value of houses they could afford if they worked at each selected occupation. Call on volunteers to share their findings with the class.

### Visual Instruction FIGURE 5.9

After students have reviewed the material in **Figure 5.9**, encourage them to search through the housing section of a newspaper to find the latest interest rates for the various kinds of mortgages. Have students compare their findings and decide which mortgage provides the best value.

## FIGURE 5.9 Types of Mortgages

| Type of Mortgage | Interest Rate Changes | Monthly Payment Changes | Description |
|---|---|---|---|
| **Standard Fixed-Rate Mortgage** | No | No | Interest rate and monthly payments remain the same over the term of the mortgage—usually 15 to 30 years. |
| **Flexible Rate Mortgage** | Yes | Yes | Interest rate and monthly payments float up or down along with interest rates in general. Rates can increase by no more than a few percentage points over the life of a mortgage, whereas there is often no limit on the amount of decrease. Three such plans are variable rate mortgage (VRM), adjustable rate mortgage (ARM), and renegotiable rate mortgage (RRM). |
| **Federal Housing Administration (FHA) Mortgage** | No | No | The FHA will insure the entire amount of its mortgages. This added security makes it possible for borrowers to obtain a larger loan than they would with an uninsured mortgage. |
| **Graduated Payment Mortgage (GPM)** | No | Yes | Interest rate is usually fixed for the life of the mortgage. Monthly payments are small at the beginning and increase gradually over the years. GPMs are used by people who expect their incomes to increase steadily from year to year. |
| **Veterans Administration (VA) Mortgage** | No | No | These loans can be obtained only by qualified veterans or their widows. The interest rate is generally lower than for other mortgages. The VA guarantees a large percentage of the loan. Loans with no down payment are possible under the VA program. |

A mortgage usually involves a down payment and interest. If you buy a house for $100,000 and make a $20,000 down payment, you will need to obtain a mortgage for the remaining $80,000. The mortgage will then be repaid in monthly installments that include interest on the loan. Property taxes, homeowners insurance, and mortgage insurance are often included on your mortgage payment as well.

## Renter Rights and Responsibilities

**lease:** *long-term agreement describing the terms under which property is rented*

Most renters sign a **lease**, or contract, that contains several clauses. A prospective tenant should read the lease carefully. Most



### Free Enterprise Activity

Have students consult real estate agents or mortgage company officers to discover how monthly mortgage payments are calculated. Next, ask students to calculate the average monthly payment on a 30-year fixed-rate mortgage at 7.5 percent interest for the following amounts borrowed: (a) $30,000; (b) 50,000; (c) $80,000; (d) $100,000; and (e) $125,000. Then ask students to do the same calculations for a 15-year fixed-rate mortgage.

leases are for one to three years, although sometimes you may pay extra to get a six-month or nine-month lease.

**Tenant Rights** Among the rights of tenants is the use of the property for the purpose stated in the lease. Tenants also have the right to a certain amount of privacy. A landlord usually cannot enter an apartment anytime he or she chooses. A landlord may enter only to make necessary repairs or to show the apartment to a potential renter.

**Tenant Responsibilities** In turn, the tenant's responsibilities include paying the rent on time and taking reasonable care of the property. If major repairs, such as replacing a leaky roof, are needed, the tenant is responsible for notifying the landlord.

Often a lease will limit how an apartment can be used. The lease may forbid pets, for example, or forbid anyone other than the person named on the lease from living there. In signing a lease, the tenant is usually required to give the owner a **security deposit,** or money for the owner to hold in case the rent is not paid or the apartment is damaged. The security deposit, usually equal to one month's rent, is returned after the tenant has moved. The amount returned depends on the condition of the apartment, as determined by the landlord. See **Figure 5.10**.

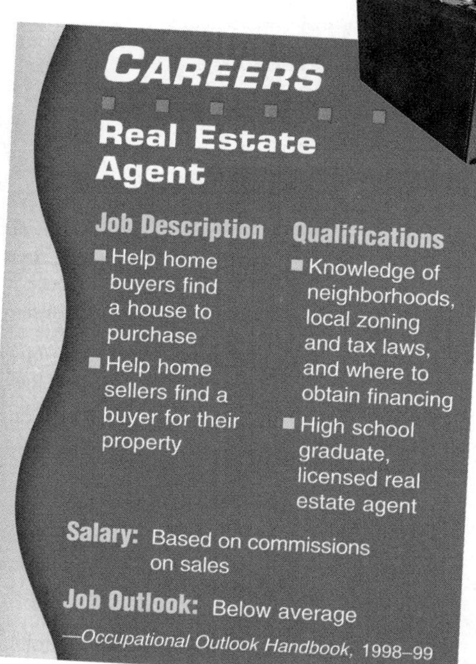

## Careers

### Real Estate Agent

**Job Description**
- Help home buyers find a house to purchase
- Help home sellers find a buyer for their property

**Qualifications**
- Knowledge of neighborhoods, local zoning and tax laws, and where to obtain financing
- High school graduate, licensed real estate agent

**Salary:** Based on commissions on sales

**Job Outlook:** Below average

*—Occupational Outlook Handbook, 1998–99*

**security deposit:** *money a renter lets an owner hold in case the rent is not paid or an apartment is damaged*

**FIGURE 5.10**

**Security Deposit** To make sure you get your apartment security deposit returned, do an initial "walk through" with the landlord to record any damage that already exists. In addition, take dated photos when you move in and when you leave. ***How much are renters usually required to pay as a security deposit?***

**L2 Interviewing** Organize students into small groups to interview either real estate agents or rental agents about their occupations. Suggest that students ask questions about such topics as specialized training, responsibilities, and work schedules. You might also suggest that students ask the agents to describe a "typical" workday. After interviews have been conducted, ask groups to prepare and present a short oral report on their findings.

**ECONOMIC SURVIVAL**
**A Financial Simulation**

To help students learn to manage their own finances, have the class play the game **Economic Survival: A Financial Simulation,** in which each student enters the workforce, rents an apartment, and deals with everyday events. The simulation takes five days to complete and may be extended for an additional two weeks.

**Visual Instruction FIGURE 5.10**

**Answer:** *usually one month's rent*

## Extending the Content

**Other Housing Costs** Owning a home entails many expenses—most notably the cost of improvements, maintenance, and repair. The roof may need to be repaired or replaced, a brick wall may need tuck-pointing, or several rooms may need painting or papering. Further, some home owners might want to make additions to their homes—a family room, a study, or another bedroom, perhaps. According to U.S. Bureau of the Census estimates, property owners spent about $117 billion on housing maintenance and repairs in 1998. The bulk of this amount—$80 billion—went on home improvements, such as room additions. The rest went to maintenance and repair needed to keep homes in ordinary working condition.

# CHAPTER 5

SECTION 3, Pages 121–127

ECONOMICS & YOU

**Buying the Necessities**

Chapter 11
Disc 1, Side 1

**ASK: Why is it necessary for home owners to purchase insurance?** *A home is an investment. Insurance is necessary to protect this investment.*

 Also available in VHS.

**Visual Instruction FIGURE 5.11**

Ask students to review the information in **Figure 5.11.** Have pairs of students role-play the parts of landlord and prospective tenant. Have pairs develop a lease that satisfies the requirements of both landlord and tenant.

# 3 Assess

## Meeting Lesson Objectives

Assign Section 3 Assessment as homework or an in-class activity.

Use **Interactive Tutor Self-Assessment Software** to review Section 3.

**FIGURE 5.11** **Checklist for Clauses in Housing Leases**

**Avoid these types of clauses in leases:**

1. **Confession-of-judgment clause:** The lawyer for the rental owner has the right to plead guilty for you in court if the owner thinks his or her rights have been violated. With a confession-of-judgment clause–illegal in some states–you are admitting guilt before committing any act.
2. **Inability-to-sue clause:** You give up your right to sue the owner if you suffer injury or damage through some fault of the owner, such as neglected repair work.
3. ***Arbitrary clauses,* or those based on one's wishes rather than a rule or law:** The owner has the right to cancel the lease because he or she is dissatisfied with your behavior. An arbitrary clause may
   - forbid hanging pictures.
   - forbid overnight guests (to make sure the apartment is occupied only by the renter).
   - forbid subleasing, or the leasing of the apartment by the tenant to someone else.
   - allow the owner or a representative, such as a plumber, to enter your apartment when you are not home.
   - make you legally responsible for all repairs.
   - make you obey rules that have not yet been written.

**If possible, add these clauses to your lease:**

1. The appliances that come with the apartment–dishwasher, garbage disposal, and air conditioner, for example.
2. The apartment community facilities you have been promised–recreation room, parking space, swimming pool–and whether you must pay extra for their use.
3. Any other promises made by the owner, such as painting the apartment (and what color).
4. The right to cancel your lease if you are transferred to a job in another city. Usually you must agree to pay a certain amount to do this, which should be stated in the lease.
5. The right to put in lighting fixtures, shelves, and so on, and have them remain your property when you move. Otherwise, they become part of the apartment and you may not take them with you.

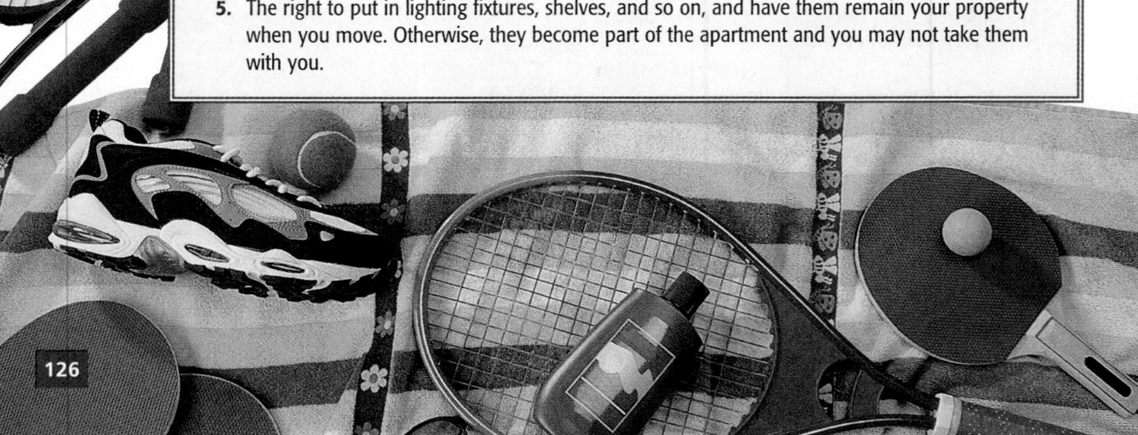

126

**Relevant Issues in Economics**

**Housing Starts** The housing industry accounts for about 5 percent of overall economic activity in the United States. Not surprisingly, economists are very interested in activity in housing construction. In fact, they use housing starts—the beginning of construction of new single-family homes, townhouses, and multifamily apartment buildings—to track economic trends. Sustained declines in housing starts indicate that the economy is slowing down and may be entering a recession. In contrast, increases in housing construction activity signal that an economic expansion is underway.

The tenant is also required to give *notice,* or a formal warning, if he or she plans to move before the term of the lease is up. In this event, the landlord may ask for several months' rent to pay for any time the apartment is empty before a new tenant moves in.

**Landlord Responsibilities** In many states, landlords must make sure that their apartments have certain minimum services, such as heat, and that they are fit to live in. Landlords may also have to obey building safety laws. For example, fire escapes and smoke detectors may be required. Leases usually call for the landlord to make repairs within a reasonable amount of time. In many states, a tenant has the right to pay for the repairs and withhold that amount of rent if the landlord does not make the repairs. **Figure 5.11** details important items that should not be in your lease or that you should have added to your lease.

## Housing in Japan

Land prices in Tokyo and other large cities in Japan are so high that most people feel they cannot buy a home. High land prices also mean that Japanese houses are quite small. On average, a house in Japan has 5 rooms and covers a floor space of about 110 square yards. In comparison, the average American home has 5.5 rooms and some 191 square yards of floor space. Average floor space is even smaller in Japan's cities—only 74 square yards in Tokyo. ■

**Practice** and **assess** key skills with *Skillbuilder Interactive Workbook, Level 2.*

# SECTION 3 Assessment

### Understanding Key Terms

1. **Define** closing costs, points, lease, security deposit.

### Reviewing Objectives

2. What three rules should determine how much you spend on a house?
3. **Graphic Organizer** Use a chart like the one below to summarize the rights and responsibilities of renters.

| Renter Rights | Renter Responsibilities |
|---|---|
| | |
| | |
| | |

### Applying Economic Concepts

4. **Demand** Based on the advantages and disadvantages listed in **Figure 5.7** on page 122, do you think you would like to rent or buy a house when you live independently? Explain your choice.

### Critical Thinking Activity

5. **Synthesizing Information** Imagine you are applying for a mortgage. The monthly mortgage payment will be $800, whereas your monthly take-home income is $1,800. According to **Figure 5.8,** should the lender grant you the mortgage? Why or why not? *For help in understanding percentages, see page xix in the Economic Handbook.*



## SECTION 3 Assessment Answers

1. All definitions can be found in the Glossary.
2. The purchase price should be no more than twice the consumer's annual income; the mortgage payment should be less than one-third of the consumer's monthly take-home pay; the loan amount should be 95 percent or less of the value of the house.
3. Rights: use of property for the purpose stated in the lease, a certain amount of privacy; Responsibilities: paying the rent on time, taking reasonable care of the property, fulfilling the terms of the lease
4. Answers will vary. Ensure that students are fully aware of the advantages and disadvantages of their choice.
5. According to Lender's Rules, mortgage payments should be less than 33.3 percent of monthly take-home pay. Since 33.3 percent of $1,800 is about $599—much less than $800—the lender should not grant the mortgage.



**Section Quiz 5-3**

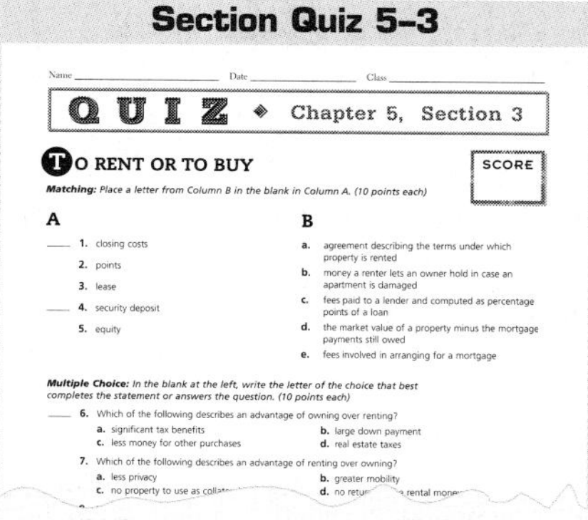
Name ________ Date ________ Class ________

QUIZ ◆ Chapter 5, Section 3

TO RENT OR TO BUY — SCORE

*Matching: Place a letter from Column B in the blank in Column A. (10 points each)*

| A | B |
|---|---|
| ____ 1. closing costs | a. agreement describing the terms under which property is rented |
| ____ 2. points | b. money a renter lets an owner hold in case an apartment is damaged |
| ____ 3. lease | c. fees paid to a lender and computed as percentage points of a loan |
| ____ 4. security deposit | d. the market value of a property minus the mortgage payments still owed |
| ____ 5. equity | e. fees involved in arranging for a mortgage |

*Multiple Choice: In the blank at the left, write the letter of the choice that best completes the statement or answers the question. (10 points each)*

____ 6. Which of the following describes an advantage of owning over renting?
a. significant tax benefits b. large down payment
c. less money for other purchases d. real estate taxes

____ 7. Which of the following describes an advantage of renting over owning?
a. less privacy b. greater mobility
c. no property to use as coll... d. no retur... rental mone...

## Reteach

Randomly assign one of the three main subheadings of the section to each student. Then ask students to create a visual—sketch, cartoon, or web diagram, for example—that illustrates the main ideas of their assigned subheading. Call on volunteers to present and discuss their visuals. **ELL**

**Reading Essentials and Study Guide 5-3**

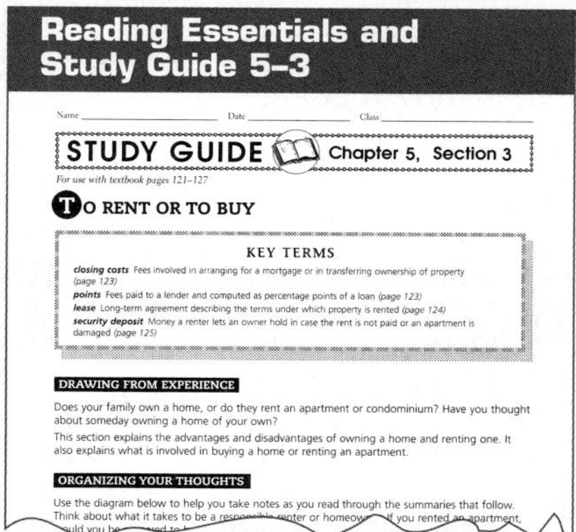
Name ________ Date ________ Class ________

STUDY GUIDE Chapter 5, Section 3

For use with textbook pages 121–127

TO RENT OR TO BUY

KEY TERMS

**closing costs** Fees involved in arranging for a mortgage or in transferring ownership of property (page 123)
**points** Fees paid to a lender and computed as percentage points of a loan (page 123)
**lease** Long-term agreement describing the terms under which property is rented (page 124)
**security deposit** Money a renter lets an owner hold in case the rent is not paid or an apartment is damaged (page 125)

DRAWING FROM EXPERIENCE

Does your family own a home, or do they rent an apartment or condominium? Have you thought about someday owning a home of your own?

This section explains the advantages and disadvantages of owning a home and renting one. It also explains what is involved in buying a home or renting an apartment.

ORGANIZING YOUR THOUGHTS

Use the diagram below to help you take notes as you read through the summaries that follow. Think about what it takes to be a responsible renter or homeowner. If you rented an apartment...

# 4 Close

Discuss with students why it is important to create a mutually acceptable tenant-landlord relationship in advance of signing a lease.

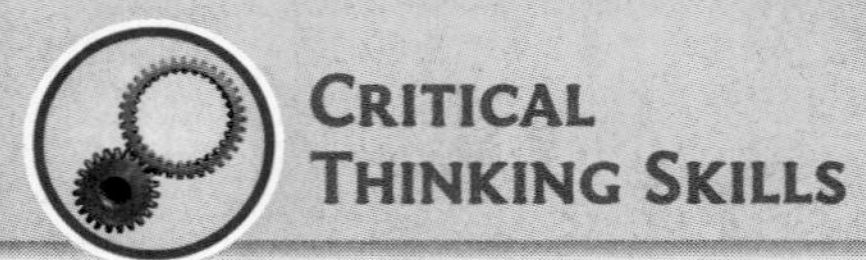


## Finding the Main Idea

Begin by asking students how they studied for their last big test. Did they try to memorize every fact, or did they look for main ideas and try to understand those? Then tell students that this skill lesson provides techniques that will help them identify the main ideas in the material they read.

Review the guidelines in the **Learning the Skill** section, applying them to the excerpt from *Business Week*. Finally, ask students to complete the **Practicing the Skill** questions.

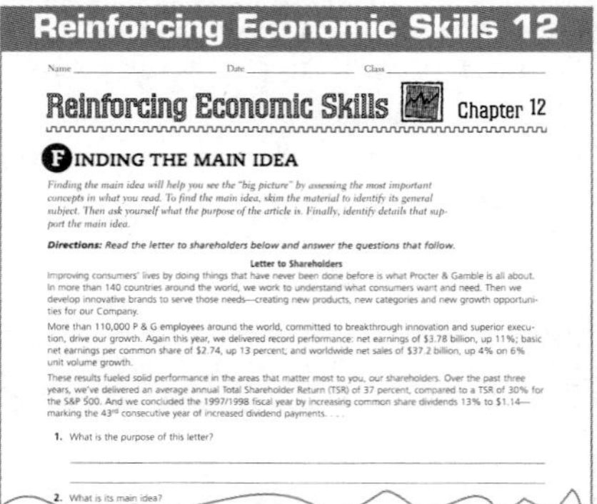

**Reinforcing Economic Skills 12**

Name ______________ Date ______________ Class ______________

**Reinforcing Economic Skills** Chapter 12

**FINDING THE MAIN IDEA**

*Finding the main idea will help you see the "big picture" by assessing the most important concepts in what you read. To find the main idea, skim the material to identify its general subject. Then ask yourself what the purpose of the article is. Finally, identify details that support the main idea.*

***Directions:*** *Read the letter to shareholders below and answer the questions that follow.*

**Letter to Shareholders**

Improving consumers' lives by doing things that have never been done before is what Procter & Gamble is all about. In more than 140 countries around the world, we work to understand what consumers want and need. Then we develop innovative brands to serve those needs—creating new products, new categories and new growth opportunities for our Company.

More than 110,000 P & G employees around the world, committed to breakthrough innovation and superior execution, drive our growth. Again this year, we delivered record performance: net earnings of $3.78 billion, up 11%; basic net earnings per common share of $2.74, up 13 percent; and worldwide net sales of $37.2 billion, up 4% on 6% unit volume growth.

These results fueled solid performance in the areas that matter most to you, our shareholders. Over the past three years, we've delivered an average annual Total Shareholder Return (TSR) of 37 percent, compared to a TSR of 30% for the S&P 500. And we concluded the 1997/1998 fiscal year by increasing common share dividends 13% to $1.14—marking the 43rd consecutive year of increased dividend payments. . . .

1. What is the purpose of this letter?

2. What is its main idea?

### GLENCOE TECHNOLOGY

**Glencoe Skillbuilder Interactive Workbook, Level 2**

This interactive CD-ROM reinforces student mastery of essential social studies skills.

## CRITICAL THINKING SKILLS

# Finding the Main Idea

*Finding the main idea will help you see the "big picture" by organizing information and assessing the most important concepts to remember.*

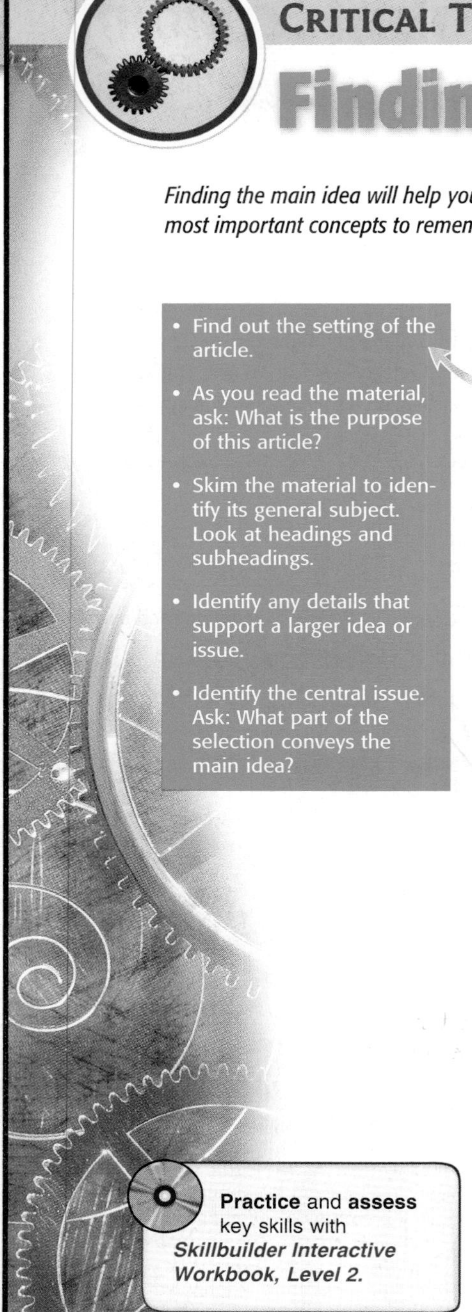

- Find out the setting of the article.
- As you read the material, ask: What is the purpose of this article?
- Skim the material to identify its general subject. Look at headings and subheadings.
- Identify any details that support a larger idea or issue.
- Identify the central issue. Ask: What part of the selection conveys the main idea?

### LEARNING THE SKILL

To learn how to find the main idea, follow the steps listed on the left.

### PRACTICING THE SKILL

Read the excerpt below, then answer the questions that follow.

> *"Car shoppers who rely on the Web have traditionally bought models fresh from the factory. But Internet sales of used cars are on the rise. The Net can help you choose a model, search available inventory, and evaluate specific cars. . . . What's more, you can find low-mileage luxury cars that have just come off lease—with time remaining on their warranties. And once you've settled on your pick, you can apply for financing online."*
>
> —*Business Week*, August 9, 1999

1. Where did this article appear?
2. When was it written?
3. What was the purpose of this article?
4. What is the main idea of this article?
5. What additional details support the main idea?

### APPLICATION ACTIVITY

Bring to class an article that you have found in a newspaper, magazine, or real estate buying guide that deals with home buying or apartment rental hints. Identify the main idea and explain why it is important.

**Practice and assess** key skills with ***Skillbuilder Interactive Workbook, Level 2.***



**Answers to PRACTICING THE SKILL**

1. in the magazine *Business Week*
2. in August 1999
3. to inform readers about used-car sales on the Internet
4. that Internet sales of used cars are on the rise
5. information on the various used-car services available on the Internet

APPLICATION ACTIVITY Articles and responses will vary.

SECTION 

# Buying and Operating a Vehicle

## COVER STORY

*THE COLUMBUS DISPATCH*, MAY 27, 1999

With cars and trucks driving off dealer lots at a fast clip, automakers have decided now is the time to build factories and expand others.

Even with excess capacity at factories that make passenger cars, demand is so great for their highly profitable sport-utility vehicles and pickup trucks that carmakers are willing to risk adding plants to cash in on the good times.

### READER'S GUIDE

**Terms to Know**

- registration fee
- liability insurance

**Reading Objectives**

1. What are the trade-offs when buying a vehicle?
2. What costs are involved in operating a vehicle?

As with every decision in life, when you decide to buy a particular type of car, you are going to make a trade-off that involves an opportunity cost. Three of the major trade-offs include the following:

**(1)** Usually, the smaller the engine, the less gas an automobile burns. This makes a car with a smaller engine less costly to operate, but the car will accelerate less quickly. See **Figure 5.12** on page 130.

**(2)** Newer automobiles cost more, but they require fewer repairs than older ones. See **Figure 5.13** on page 131 for tips on choosing a new or used car.

## 1 Focus

### Overview

Section 4 explores the costs of buying and operating a vehicle and provides a checklist for automobile buyers.

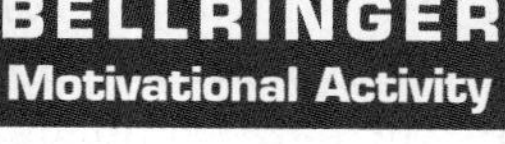

**BELLRINGER**
**Motivational Activity**

Project **Daily Focus Transparency 37** and have students answer the questions.

This activity is also available as a blackline master.

**Daily Focus Transparency 37**

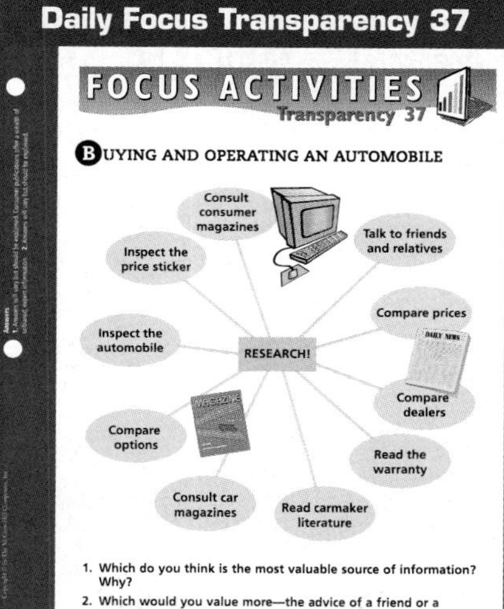


### READER'S GUIDE

Answers to the **Reading Objectives** questions are on page 133.

**Preteaching Vocabulary**

Ask students to use the **Terms to Know** to write a paragraph about buying a vehicle.

**Vocabulary PuzzleMaker**

## SECTION 4 RESOURCE MANAGER

**Reproducible Masters**

- Reproducible Lesson Plan 5–4
- Reading Essentials and Study Guide 5–4
- Guided Reading Activity 5–4
- Section Quiz 5–4
- Daily Focus Activity 37
- Daily Lecture Notes 5–4

**Multimedia**

- Daily Focus Transparency 37
- Vocabulary PuzzleMaker
- Interactive Tutor Self-Assessment Software
- ExamView® Pro Testmaker
- MindJogger Videoquiz
- NBR's *Economics & You*
- Presentation Plus!

# 2 Teach

## Guided Practice

**L2** Evaluating Information On the board, draw a two-column chart with "New Car" and "Used Car" as column headings. Call on students to identify the costs of owning and operating each kind of car. Enter their responses in the appropriate columns. Then have students discuss which–a used car or a new car–would be the more economical purchase.

### Daily Lecture Notes 5–4

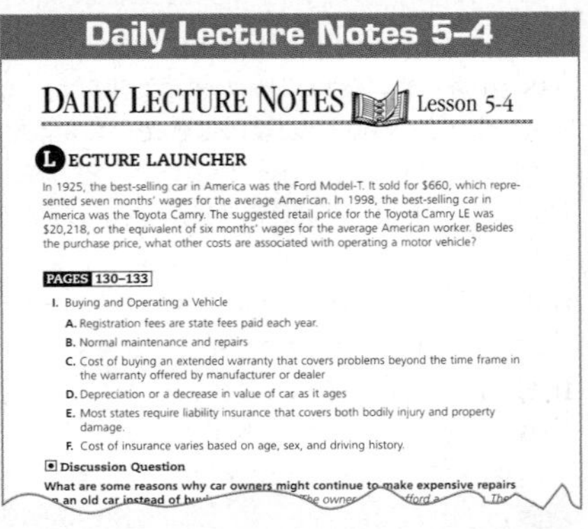

DAILY LECTURE NOTES Lesson 5-4

**LECTURE LAUNCHER**

In 1925, the best-selling car in America was the Ford Model-T. It sold for $660, which represented seven months' wages for the average American. In 1998, the best-selling car in America was the Toyota Camry. The suggested retail price for the Toyota Camry LE was $20,218, or the equivalent of six months' wages for the average American worker. Besides the purchase price, what other costs are associated with operating a motor vehicle?

PAGES 130–133

I. Buying and Operating a Vehicle
   A. Registration fees are state fees paid each year.
   B. Normal maintenance and repairs
   C. Cost of buying an extended warranty that covers problems beyond the time frame in the warranty offered by manufacturer or dealer
   D. Depreciation or a decrease in value of car as it ages
   E. Most states require liability insurance that covers both bodily injury and property damage.
   F. Cost of insurance varies based on age, sex, and driving history.

**Discussion Question**

**What are some reasons why car owners might continue to make expensive repairs an old car instead of bu**

### Visual Instruction FIGURE 5.12

**Answer:** *Smaller cars usually burn less gas. This makes smaller cars less costly to operate.*

FIGURE 5.12

**Trade-Offs** Some of the trade-offs you'll make when purchasing an automobile include small car versus large car, new versus used, and powerful engine versus having to buy less gasoline. ***What is an advantage of owning a small car?***

**(3)** The smaller the automobile, the more energy efficient it is. In an accident, however, larger automobiles usually protect passengers better.

## Buying and Operating a Vehicle

Buying a car involves opportunity costs. One is the amount of money and time spent shopping for the car. Another is the amount of money and time spent in actually purchasing the car. Because of limited resources, most people have to borrow funds to buy a car. The costs of the loan are the down payment, the monthly payments on the principal, and the interest on the loan.

**registration fee:** *licensing fee, usually annual, paid to a state for the right to use a car*

**Registration Fee** The owner of an automobile must pay a state licensing fee, or a **registration fee,** to use the car. Usually the fee must be paid annually. In many states, the amount of the fee varies depending on the car's age, weight, type, and value.

**Normal Maintenance and Major Repairs** The amount of normal maintenance–oil and filter changes and minor tune-ups–depends on the amount the car is driven and how carefully the owner maintains the car. Major repairs are those that are normally unexpected and expensive. They include rebuilding the transmission and replacing the exhaust system. No one can guarantee that an automobile will not require major repairs while you own it, but you can follow certain steps to reduce the probability.

You should check the repair records of different cars before deciding on a particular make and model. If you are considering a used car, you should also take it to a diagnostic center, or have a mechanic check it. Sometimes dealers offer warranties on used cars for a limited time period, such as 30 days, or you can purchase a warranty covering a longer period of time.



## Meeting Special Needs

**Language Disability** Students who have a limited command of language might benefit from the following activity. Have students read sentences or short paragraphs from Section 4. Then have them restate these sentences or paragraphs by giving an example of how they would apply the information to an actual experience—buying gasoline or having a car repaired, for example. Listen carefully to ensure that students are not restating phrases directly from the section.

Refer to *Inclusion for the Social Studies Classroom Strategies and Activities* for students with different learning styles.

## FIGURE 5.13 Checklist for Buying an Automobile

**These tips will help you in making a good choice of a new car or used car:**

1. Ask friends and relatives about their satisfaction or dissatisfaction with their cars.
2. Read articles about different makes and models in car magazines such as *Car and Driver* and *Road & Track*.
3. Read *Consumer Reports* and *Consumers' Research Magazine* for reviews of new automobiles. Carefully read their reports on repair records of different models.
4. Visit dealers and read brochures about their vehicles, keeping in mind that these pamphlets promote the best features.
5. Personally inspect various makes and models in automobile showrooms.
6. Check what is covered by the service warranty. A used car may still be covered under the original manufacturer's warranty. Also, some dealers offer their own limited warranties for used cars.
7. After you decide on a particular make and model, compare the prices offered by several dealers.
8. If you are buying a vehicle off the lot rather than ordering one, check the options–air conditioning, a CD player, special paint, and so on–and their prices. If you do not want any options, the dealer may lower the price.
9. If you are buying a used car, have an automobile diagnostic center or a mechanic not connected with the dealer check it. Add the cost of needed repairs to the dealer's price. This is the real cost of the automobile to you.
10. Make sure the listed price includes federal excise taxes and dealer preparation charges. An *excise tax* is a tax on the manufacture, sale, or use of specific products, such as liquor, gasoline, and automobiles. Dealer preparation charges can include the costs of cleaning, installing certain options, and checking the car's engine before you drive it away. State and local sales taxes will be added to the total cost later.
11. Check various dealers for the reputation of their service departments. Your warranty usually allows you to take your car to any dealer selling that make of car.
12. Do not put a deposit on a car unless you are sure you are going to buy it. You may have a problem getting your deposit back if you change your mind.



**Guided Reading Activity 5-4**

GUIDED READING Activity 5-4

BUYING AND OPERATING A VEHICLE

OUTLINING

*Directions:* Locate the heading in your textbook. Then use the information under the heading to help you write each answer.

I. Introduction
A. What are the benefits of having an automobile with a small engine?
B. What is a disadvantage of owning a smaller automobile?

II. Buying and Operating a Vehicle
A. Introduction —What are the opportunity costs involved in buying a car?
B. Registration Fee—What is a registration fee?
C. Normal Maintenance and Major Repairs
1. What are some examples of normal car maintenance?

## Independent Practice

**L2 Creating a Buyer's Guide** Organize students into groups, and ask groups to use the checklist in **Figure 5.13** to create a buyer's guide to automobiles. Suggest that groups include a list of steps buyers might take in investigating various car models. You might also suggest that they include evaluation measures–fuel efficiency and safety features, for example–against which buyers might rate various models. Encourage groups to present their finished guides for review by the class. BLOCK SCHEDULING

## Cooperative Learning

Organize students into groups to research and develop a fact book on the direct and indirect contribution of the automobile to the American economy. Have groups survey information on automobile manufacturing and sales, gasoline usage, maintenance products and service, automobile insurance, and public works—highways, for example. Direct groups to combine written reports with charts and graphs as needed. Ask groups to display their completed fact books around the classroom. BLOCK SCHEDULING

**ECONOMICS & YOU**

**Buying the Necessities**

Chapter 11
Disc 1, Side 1

**ASK: What are the advantages and disadvantages of both leasing and financing a car?** *The monthly payment for a leased car may be lower than the payment required to finance the same car. However, the consumer must return the car at the end of the lease period, whereas at the end of the financing period, the consumer owns the car.*

 Also available in VHS.

# 3 Assess

## Meeting Lesson Objectives

Assign Section 4 Assessment as homework or an in-class activity.

Use **Interactive Tutor Self-Assessment Software** to review Section 4.

## FIGURE 5.14 Factors Affecting Automobile Insurance Rates

**When you buy automobile insurance, the rate you are charged is determined not only by your age and sex, but also by the following:**

1. **The type of car you drive.** Insurance companies consider the safety record of a car and the costs to repair it if it is involved in an accident.
2. **Where you drive.** If the rate of thefts and accidents is high in an area, the risk to the insurance company is greater. A city, for example, would have more thefts and accidents than would a rural area. Therefore, the rate the insurance company charges in a city will be higher.
3. **What you use the car for.** If you drive your car for business on a daily basis, the rate will be higher than if you use it only for errands and occasional trips.
4. **Marital status.** In general, married men and women have lower accident rates than single men and women and, therefore, pay lower insurance rates.
5. **Safety record.** If you have a history of accidents and traffic tickets, then you will be charged a high rate. Whether a new driver has had driver education is often considered in determining a rate.
6. **Number of drivers.** The number of drivers using a car increases the insurance rate.

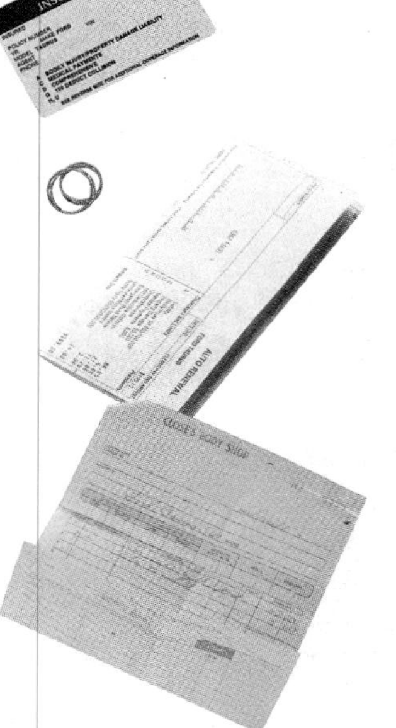

**Extended Warranty** One way to guard against having to pay for major repairs is to buy extended warranty coverage. New-car warranties generally protect owners for all major repairs except tune-ups and damage resulting from improper use of the automobile. New-car warranties usually last only a few years, or up to a certain limit of miles or kilometers. These warranties, however, can often be extended for another one, two, or three years by paying additional money when the car is purchased.

**Depreciation** *Depreciation*—a decline in value over time—takes place as an item wears out or becomes outdated. Age is the major factor. A car loses value every year even if it is not driven because an automobile is a durable good. All durable goods deteriorate, or become worse over time.

Another cause of depreciation is the technology and features of new makes and models. These changes make older models obsolete—out of date and out of style.

The amount of depreciation caused by physical wear and tear varies. It depends on how hard a car is driven, how many miles



## Free Enterprise Activity

**Transportation Business Plan** Have students work in groups to develop a transportation business plan in which students who have cars earn money by providing rides to those who do not. Direct groups to provide written explanations of how their plans are economically beneficial to both drivers and riders.

or kilometers it is driven, and how well it is maintained. Generally, cars depreciate about 20 percent each year.

**Insurance** A major cost of owning an automobile, especially for someone under age 25, is insurance. Many states require that liability insurance be purchased before an automobile can be licensed. **Liability insurance** pays for bodily injury as well as property damage if you are in an accident.

**liability insurance:** *insurance that pays for bodily injury and property damage*

Insurance companies classify drivers in various ways, usually according to age, gender, and marital status. Rates depend on the category into which a person fits. The categories, in turn, are based on statistics showing that different types of drivers have different accident rates.

Young people almost always have to pay higher insurance rates. For example, single males in the 16–25 age group have the highest accident rate of all drivers. Not surprisingly, most insurance companies charge these drivers the highest insurance rates. Married women ages 25–45 have the fewest accidents and the lowest rates.

**Figure 5.14** shows factors in addition to age and sex that affect insurance rates. Rates cannot vary too widely, however, because states set limits on the rates that companies can charge within state borders.

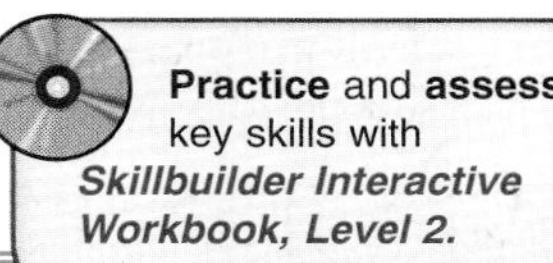

**Practice** and **assess** key skills with *Skillbuilder Interactive Workbook, Level 2.*

## SECTION 4 Assessment

### Understanding Key Terms

1. **Define** registration fee, liability insurance.

### Reviewing Objectives

2. What are the trade-offs when buying a vehicle?
3. **Graphic Organizer** Use a chart like the one below to identify the costs of operating a vehicle.

### Applying Economic Concepts

4. **Insurance Risk** Apply the six factors in **Figure 5.14** to your personal driving situation. Are you a risk for insurance companies? Why or why not?

### Critical Thinking Activity

5. **Making Comparisons** Search the Internet for information on automobile insurance in your community. Write an article detailing what companies sell insurance and how much they charge for basic coverage for drivers in your age group.



## SECTION 4 Assessment Answers

1. All definitions can be found in the Glossary.
2. Trade-offs include: buying a smaller car that burns less gasoline and is less costly to operate, but losing on acceleration and power; buying a newer car that requires fewer repairs than older ones, buts costs more; buying a smaller car that is more energy-efficient and easier to maneuver, but losing the protection provided by a larger car in an accident
3. Costs of operating a vehicle: registration fee, normal maintenance, major repairs, depreciation, insurance
4. Answers will vary. Ensure that student responses are realistic.
5. Articles will vary. Have students compare and discuss their findings.



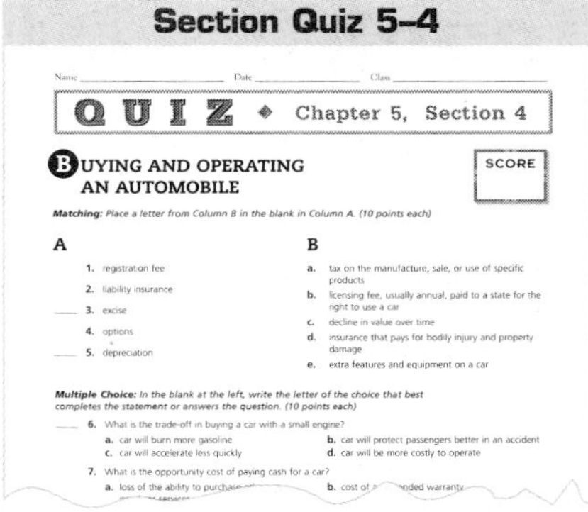

Section Quiz 5-4

QUIZ ◆ Chapter 5, Section 4

BUYING AND OPERATING AN AUTOMOBILE

SCORE

*Matching: Place a letter from Column B in the blank in Column A. (10 points each)*

| A | B |
|---|---|
| 1. registration fee | a. tax on the manufacture, sale, or use of specific products |
| 2. liability insurance | b. licensing fee, usually annual, paid to a state for the right to use a car |
| 3. excise | c. decline in value over time |
| 4. options | d. insurance that pays for bodily injury and property damage |
| 5. depreciation | e. extra features and equipment on a car |

*Multiple Choice: In the blank at the left, write the letter of the choice that best completes the statement or answers the question. (10 points each)*

6. What is the trade-off in buying a car with a small engine?
a. car will burn more gasoline
b. car will protect passengers better in an accident
c. car will accelerate less quickly
d. car will be more costly to operate

7. What is the opportunity cost of paying cash for a car?

## Reteach

Ask students to list the main subheadings of Section 4, leaving space in between each subheading. Then ask students to write a summary sentence for each of the subheadings.

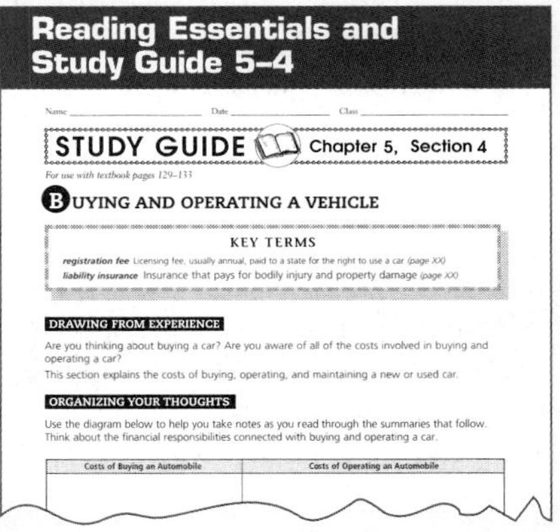

Reading Essentials and Study Guide 5-4

STUDY GUIDE Chapter 5, Section 4

For use with textbook pages 129–133

BUYING AND OPERATING A VEHICLE

KEY TERMS

**registration fee** Licensing fee, usually annual, paid to a state for the right to use a car (page XX)
**liability insurance** Insurance that pays for bodily injury and property damage (page XX)

DRAWING FROM EXPERIENCE

Are you thinking about buying a car? Are you aware of all of the costs involved in buying and operating a car?
This section explains the costs of buying, operating, and maintaining a new or used car.

ORGANIZING YOUR THOUGHTS

Use the diagram below to help you take notes as you read through the summaries that follow. Think about the financial responsibilities connected with buying and operating a car.

| Costs of Buying an Automobile | Costs of Operating an Automobile |
|---|---|

## 4 Close

Have students write a paragraph about the main issues consumers must consider when purchasing a vehicle.

BusinessWeek
**SPOTLIGHT**

# Teach

The Global Positioning System (GPS) consists of 24 satellites circling the Earth. Signals from three of these satellites allow for a high level of navigational accuracy. These satellite signals—along with electronic signals from the speedometer, a gyroscope that measures turns, and software in the car—translate the location information into maps and routes.

## BusinessWeek ONLINE

To find up-to-date news and analysis on the economy, business, technology, markets, entrepreneurs, investments, and finance, have students search feature articles and special reports on the *Business Week* Web site. www.businessweek.com

## Sidelight

The GPS has many uses. In 1999 mountaineers on the summit of Mount Everest used equipment linked to the GPS to measure the elevation of the mountain. They determined that it was 29,035 feet—7 feet higher than officially accepted measurements.

# BusinessWeek

# SPOTLIGHT ON THE ECONOMY

## Backseat Driver on the Dash

**Check It Out! In this chapter you learned about the costs of owning and operating an automobile. In this article, read to learn about a new option available on some current makes and models.**

The most striking thing about Alpine Electronics' computer navigation system for cars is its dead-on accuracy. Using a global-positioning system keyed to satellites and combined with gyroscopic motion sensors, the car knows its position within, at worst, half a city block. This is combined with a map database from Navigation Technologies (NavTech) that knows about details as small as right-turn cutouts at intersections.

When driving, the five-inch LCD display, which is bright enough to be seen even in strong sunlight, offers a choice between a map view, which can zoom from block-level detail to a city overview, and a diagram of driving instructions. A synthesized female voice warns you of turns, usually with ample time to maneuver safely. The display and controls are laid out to be informative without being distracting.

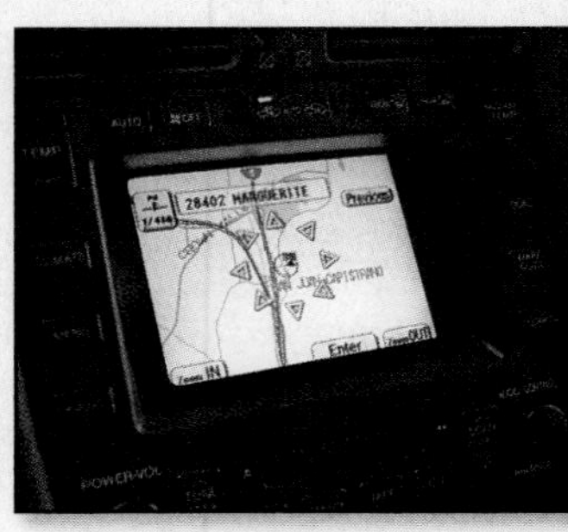

NavTech's database divides the U.S. into nine regions. You get one with the unit, and additional ones cost $150. Major metropolitan areas have block-by-block detail for all streets. Rural areas and smaller cities offer only major roads.

The only really serious flaw . . . is the cost. The price [$2,000], whether as an option in a few luxury models or as an aftermarket add-on, is way too steep for most consumers.

Of course, it wasn't long ago that auto CD players—and even antilock brakes—were luxury options, too. With prices likely to slide down the technology cost curve quickly, it's not hard to imagine the day when in-car navigation systems become standard features.



### Think About It

1. **How does the computer navigation system for automobiles work?**
2. **What is the main flaw of this system, and why may that change in the near future?**



### Answers to *Think About It*

1. It uses a global-positioning system keyed to satellites and gyroscopic motion sensors to pinpoint the automobile's position within half a city block.
2. Its major flaw is its cost. Like other one-time luxuries—CD players, for example—the price of the in-car navigation system is expected to drop considerably in the future.

# CHAPTER  Summary

**Chapter Overview** Visit the *Economics Today and Tomorrow* Web site at ett.glencoe.com and click on ***Chapter 5—Chapter Overviews*** to review chapter information.

## SECTION 1 Shopping for Food

- Comparison shopping for food involves making comparisons among brands, sizes, and stores.
- Reading advertisements and collecting cents-off coupons is a timesaving, inexpensive way to comparison shop.
- Supermarkets or **club warehouse stores** usually charge the lowest prices for food, whereas **convenience stores** may save you time.
- Per-unit pricing of goods makes it easy to compare prices.
- If you make a habit of using coupons, you can reduce your food bill by more than 10 percent over a one-year period.

## SECTION 2 Clothing Choices

- Americans spend about $400 billion annually on clothing and other personal products.
- Clothing value depends on price, style, **durability,** and cost of care.
- When you purchase an item of clothing, you are purchasing it for the **service flow** that it yields.
- The work-time cost of clothing has decreased over the past 100 years, but it is still the wise consumer who buys clothing on sale.

## SECTION 3 To Rent or to Buy

- There are economic and psychological advantages and disadvantages to both owning your own home and renting.
- If you choose to buy a house, you will probably need to obtain a mortgage, which involves a cash down payment, monthly installments, and interest, plus money for **closing costs** and **points.**
- Most renters pay a **security deposit** and sign a **lease** that protects their rights as well as lists their responsibilities.
- Tenant responsibilities include paying the rent on time and taking reasonable care of the property.

## SECTION 4 Buying and Operating a Vehicle

- Some of the trade-offs you'll make when purchasing an automobile include small car versus large car, new versus used, and powerful engine versus having to buy less gasoline.
- The costs of operating an automobile include the **registration fee,** normal maintenance, major repairs, depreciation, and **liability insurance.**
- One way to guard against having to pay for major repairs is to buy extended warranty coverage.



## Economics Journal

**Consumer Decision Making** Have students record the number of times they go from one place to another during a week's period. For each journey, have students list the distance traveled, the mode of transportation, and any alternative modes of transportation that they might have used. After students have completed this "travel log," ask them to record the total number of routes and the total miles they traveled. Then have them develop a transportation map of their most frequently traveled routes. Encourage students to write a paragraph discussing the most efficient way for them to get to the places they need to go.

# CHAPTER 5 Summary

**ECONOMICS & YOU**

**Buying the Necessities**

Chapter 11
Disc 1, Side 1

If you do not have access to a videodisc player, the ***Economics & You*** programs are also available in VHS.

Use the **Chapter 5 Summary** to preview, review, condense, or reteach the chapter.

## Preview/Review

**Vocabulary PuzzleMaker Software** reinforces the key terms used in Chapter 5.

**Interactive Tutor Self-Assessment Software** allows students to review Chapter 5 content.

## Condense

Have students listen to the Chapter 5 **Audio Program** (also available in Spanish) in the TCR. Assign the Chapter 5 Audio Program Activity and give students the Chapter 5 Audio Program Test.

## Reteach

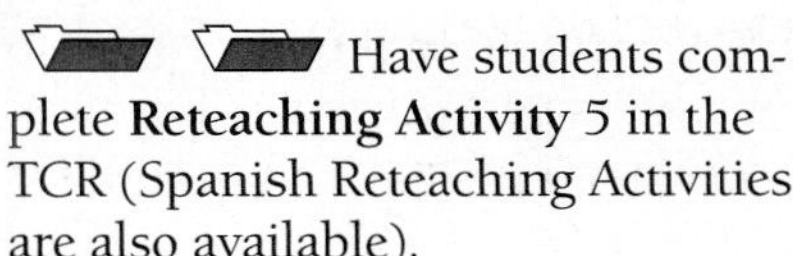

Have students complete **Reteaching Activity** 5 in the TCR (Spanish Reteaching Activities are also available).

Have students visit the *Economics Today and Tomorrow* Web site at ett.glencoe.com to review Chapter 5 and take the Self-Check Quiz.

**GLENCOE TECHNOLOGY**

**MindJogger Videoquiz**

Use MindJogger to review Chapter 5 content.

## Identifying Key Terms

1. b
2. d
3. c
4. h
5. a
6. g
7. f
8. i
9. e
10. j

## Recalling Facts and Ideas

1. Answers may vary but typically will include: doing only the amount of comparison shopping that time and transportation costs justify; reading store and manufacturer advertisements; comparing stores; comparing brands.
2. The trade-off in buying a generic brand is that price may be lower and quantity may be greater, but quality may be less.
3. price, style, cost of care, durability
4. Generally, the more expensive the item, the more durable it is expected to be. Thus, the longer the time of use, the more economical the price.
5. less mobility, less choice, large outlay of money, maintenance costs, real estate taxes, possible depreciation, high mortgage payments, and possibility of overextending debt load
6. no freedom of use, no return on rental money, few tax benefits, little sense of responsibility, no collateral, may have to wait for maintenance
7. providing tenants with minimum services, such as heat and safe living conditions; providing reasonable maintenance; maintaining tenant's right to privacy
8. loan expenses, including down payment, interest, and monthly payments
9. registration fee, normal maintenance and major repairs, depreciation, and insurance

CHAPTER 5

# Assessment and Activities

**Self-Check Quiz** Visit the *Economics Today and Tomorrow* Web site at ett.glencoe.com and click on ***Chapter 5—Self-Check Quizzes*** to prepare for the Chapter Test.

## Identifying Key Terms

*Write the letter of the definition in Column B that correctly defines each term in Column A.*

**Column A**

1. service flow
2. durability
3. security deposit
4. registration fee
5. liability insurance
6. club warehouse store
7. private-labeled products
8. lease
9. closing costs
10. points

**Column B**

a. pays for injury or property damage
b. stream of benefits from using a good
c. usually one month's rent left on deposit
d. how long something lasts
e. fee charged by lender for paperwork, taxes, and other activities
f. goods with the store's label on them
g. large stores requiring a membership
h. money paid to license a vehicle
i. agreement describing rental terms
j. fees paid to a lender, normally when interest rates are low

## Recalling Facts and Ideas

**Section 1**

1. What is one of the best ways to engage in comparison shopping for food products?
2. What is the trade-off involved when you buy a generic brand rather than a brand-name product?

**Section 2**

3. What four factors influence the kind of clothing choices people make?
4. What is the normal relationship between how long an article of clothing will last and its price?

**Section 3**

5. What are some of the disadvantages of owning a house?
6. What are some of the disadvantages of renting a house or an apartment?
7. State three responsibilities of landlords.

**Section 4**

8. If you do not pay cash for a car, what expense must be included in the cost of buying the car?
9. What is included in the cost of operating an automobile?

## Thinking Critically

1. **Understanding Cause and Effect** Why do you think automobile insurance companies charge more for unmarried males between the ages of 16 and 25 than they do for married males between these ages?

2. **Making Comparisons** The two basic types of mortgages used today are flexible rate and fixed rate. Create a chart like the one below to explain the advantages and disadvantages of each.

| Type of mortgage | Advantages | Disadvantages |
|---|---|---|
| | | |
| | | |

## Applying Economic Concepts

**Competition and Market Structure** Examine the food ads in your local newspaper for one week. List those food items that are common to each ad. Compare the prices from the different food stores for the common items. What is the largest percentage difference between the highest and lowest prices?

## Reviewing Skills

**Finding the Main Idea** In *The Theory of the Leisure Class* (1899), economist Thorstein Veblen criticized the leisure class, or the rich, and its spending habits. He talked about "conspicuous consumption," which is buying goods and services to impress others.

List examples of conspicuous consumption that you notice throughout the day—whether on television or in real life. Write a paragraph explaining what kinds of products are typically consumed in this way.

## Technology Activity

**Using the Internet** On the Census Bureau Web site, look up the section of the most recent Census of Housing entitled *Selected Housing Characteristics by States and Counties.* Make a table listing the following statistics for your county: (1) number of total housing units; (2) number of units occupied by owners; and (3) number occupied by renters.

## Cooperative Learning Project

Organize into six groups. Call separate automobile insurance agents and ask for a rate quote by giving the following facts:

- ☐ Age: 21
- ☐ Gender: at least 3 males and 3 females should make the calls
- ☐ Automobile type: 2000 Chevy Malibu
- ☐ Use: Drive to college and part-time job (80 miles a week)
- ☐ Coverage desired: 100/300/50, which means up to $100,000 for one person injured in an accident, up to a total of $300,000 for all personal injuries suffered in the accident, and up to $50,000 for damages to private or public property caused by the accident
- ☐ Collision and comprehensive deductible: $500; no medical or towing

After each group receives its quotes, compare your information:

1. Which agent/insurance company gave the highest quote? The lowest?
2. Was there a substantial difference between the insurance rates for females and males?
3. What was the average percentage difference between the rates quoted for females and males?

## Analyzing the Global Economy

Use the Internet to find automobile dealerships in major cities around the world. Compare the prices of new and used cars in various cities.



## CHAPTER 5 Assessment and Activities

### Applying Economic Concepts

Answers will vary. Encourage students to share and compare their findings.

### Reviewing Skills

Paragraphs will vary.

### Technology Activity

Have students present their findings in a chart or table. Encourage students to display their charts or tables on the bulletin board.

### Cooperative Learning Project

Answers will vary. Groups might present their findings in a chart or table.

### Analyzing the Global Economy

You might have students work in groups to create collages of different makes and models of cars and their prices.

### Chapter Bonus Test Question

ASK: Why do many states require car owners to carry liability insurance? *to ensure that that there will be compensation for other people for injuries or damage to property in case of an accident*

## Thinking Critically

1. Answers may vary. Most students will suggest that unmarried males between the ages of 16 and 25 have more accidents and, therefore, are the greater insurance risk.
2. Fixed rate advantage: offers security of a rate that will not change; Disadvantage: rate remains the same even if interest rates fall. Flexible rate advantage: rates can increase by no more than a few percentage points over the life of a mortgage, whereas there is often no limit on the amount of decrease; Disadvantage: uncertainty if interest rates are volatile

# 1 Focus

Direct students' attention to the prices listed under the various cities. Point out that these are average prices, based on surveys of many stores, restaurants, gasoline stations, and movie theaters.

# 2 Teach

Have students note the varying prices of lunch from city to city. Then point out that there are many reasons for these differences. First, the type of food might be of varying qualities. Second, the costs of production vary greatly from country to country. For instance, labor tends to be cheaper in less developed countries, such as India.

## Global Economy

**A Day on the Town** First, you go downtown to meet a friend for lunch. Later, a friend invites you to a movie. On the way to the theater, you stop and buy gasoline for your car. Check the map below to see what your day might cost in various cities around the world.*

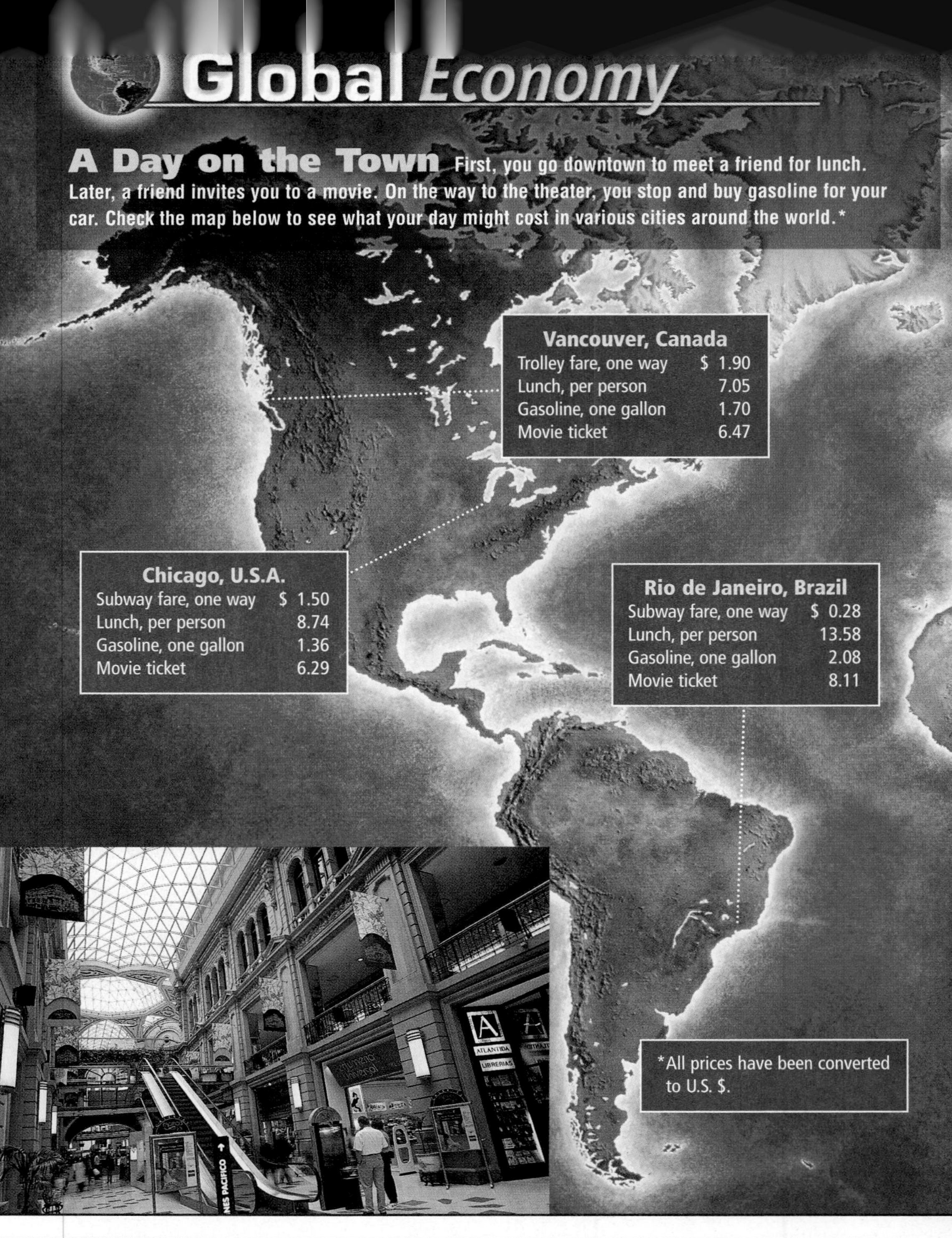

Vancouver, Canada
Trolley fare, one way $ 1.90
Lunch, per person 7.05
Gasoline, one gallon 1.70
Movie ticket 6.47
Chicago, U.S.A.
Subway fare, one way $ 1.50
Lunch, per person 8.74
Gasoline, one gallon 1.36
Movie ticket 6.29
Rio de Janeiro, Brazil
Subway fare, one way $ 0.28
Lunch, per person 13.58
Gasoline, one gallon 2.08
Movie ticket 8.11
*All prices have been converted to U.S. $.


## Teacher's Notes

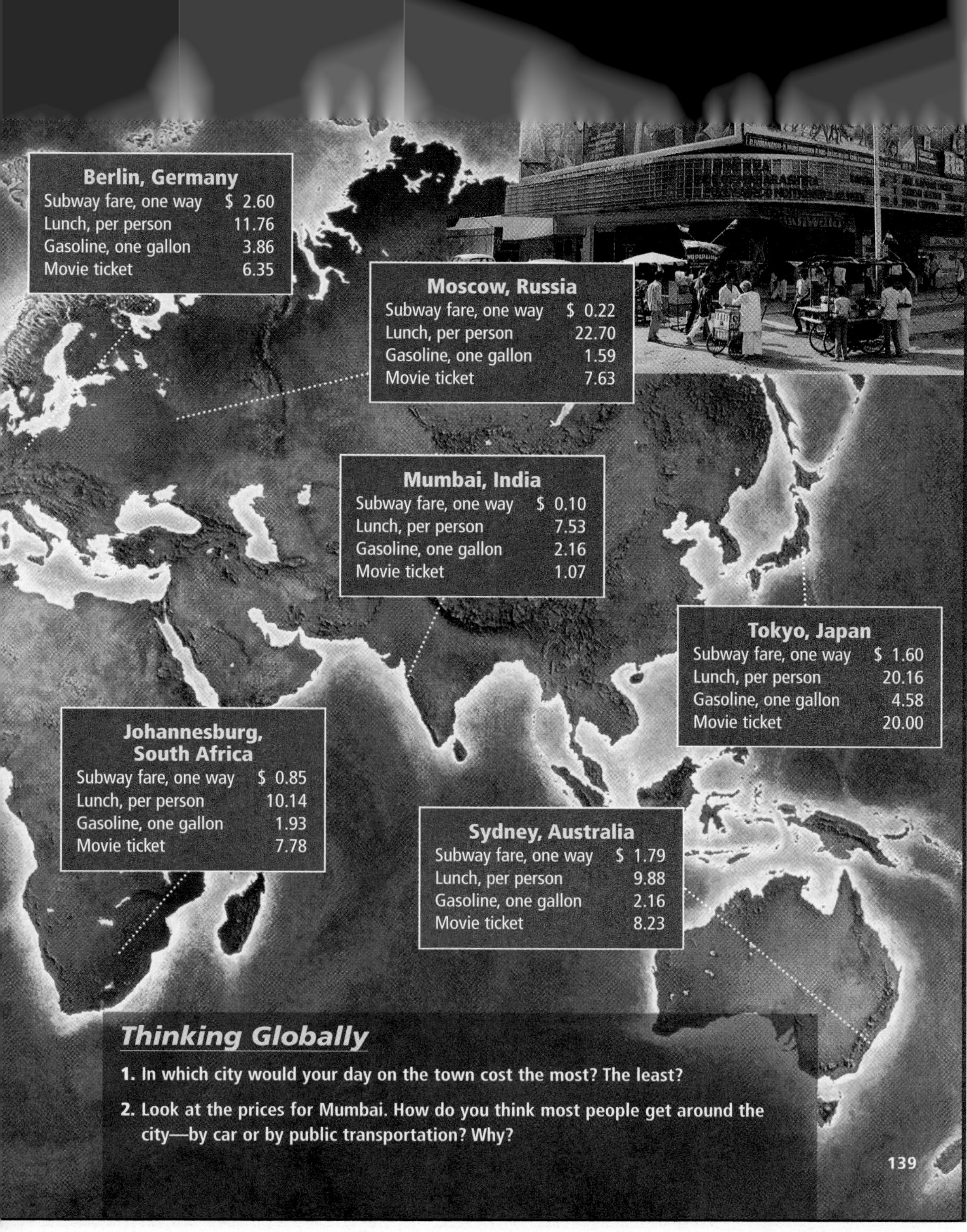

Berlin, Germany
Subway fare, one way $ 2.60
Lunch, per person 11.76
Gasoline, one gallon 3.86
Movie ticket 6.35
Moscow, Russia
Subway fare, one way $ 0.22
Lunch, per person 22.70
Gasoline, one gallon 1.59
Movie ticket 7.63
Mumbai, India
Subway fare, one way $ 0.10
Lunch, per person 7.53
Gasoline, one gallon 2.16
Movie ticket 1.07
Tokyo, Japan
Subway fare, one way $ 1.60
Lunch, per person 20.16
Gasoline, one gallon 4.58
Movie ticket 20.00
Johannesburg, South Africa
Subway fare, one way $ 0.85
Lunch, per person 10.14
Gasoline, one gallon 1.93
Movie ticket 7.78
Sydney, Australia
Subway fare, one way $ 1.79
Lunch, per person 9.88
Gasoline, one gallon 2.16
Movie ticket 8.23


### *Thinking Globally*

1. In which city would your day on the town cost the most? The least?
2. Look at the prices for Mumbai. How do you think most people get around the city—by car or by public transportation? Why?

139

## Answers to *Thinking Globally*

1. The day on the town would cost the most in Tokyo. It would cost the least in Mumbai.
2. by public transportation, because the subway fare is only 10¢, while a gallon of gasoline is over $2

## 3 Assess

Have students answer the **Thinking Globally** questions.

## 4 Close

You might close this feature by asking students the following question: Which of the prices did you find the most surprising? Why?

### ? Did You Know

Which is the most expensive city in the world? According to a study conducted by the European Union (EU), the most expensive city in the world for business travelers is Moscow, closely followed by Tokyo, Buenos Aires, and Hong Kong. Another study by the EU found that the most expensive EU city to live in was Copenhagen, followed by Paris and Berlin.

# CHAPTER 6 Resource Manager

## Teaching Transparency

### Economic Concepts Transparency 10

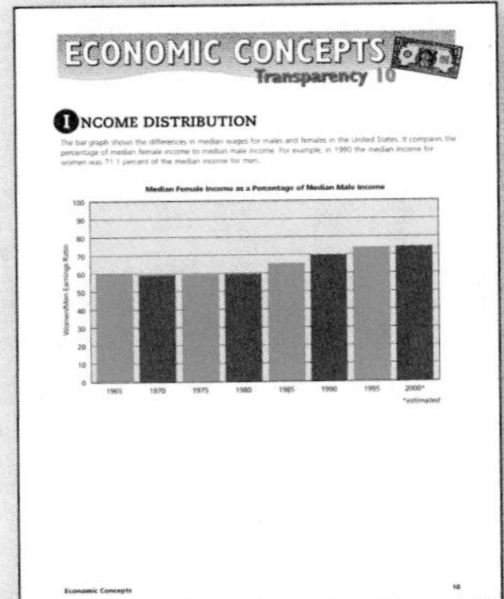
ECONOMIC CONCEPTS Transparency 10

INCOME DISTRIBUTION

Median Female Income as a Percentage of Median Male Income

## Application and Enrichment

### Enrichment Activity 6

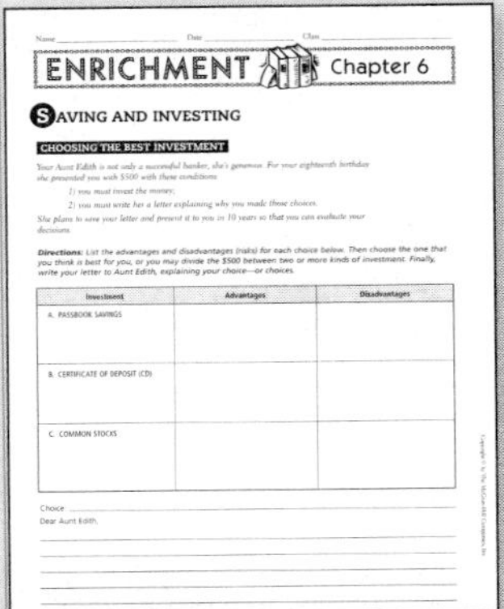
ENRICHMENT Chapter 6

SAVING AND INVESTING

CHOOSING THE BEST INVESTMENT

### Consumer Applications Activity 12

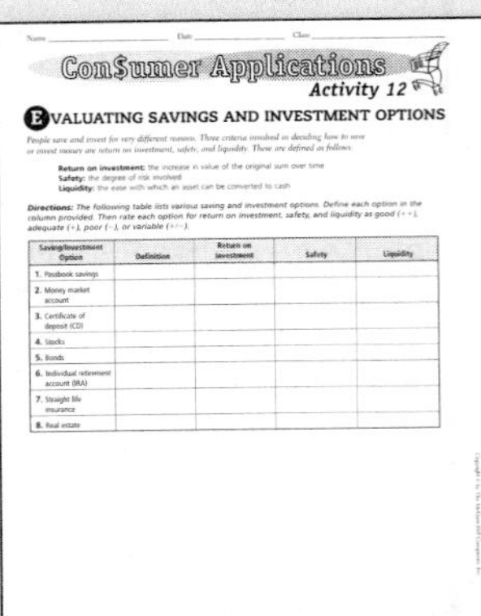
Consumer Applications Activity 12

EVALUATING SAVINGS AND INVESTMENT OPTIONS

### Free Enterprise Activity 12

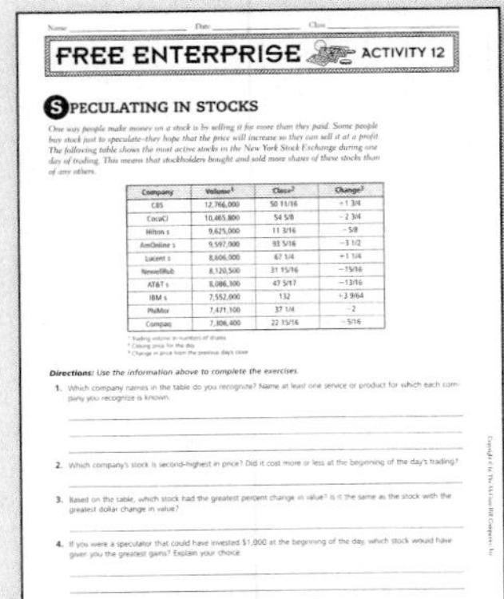
FREE ENTERPRISE ACTIVITY 12

SPECULATING IN STOCKS

## Application and Enrichment

### Cooperative Learning Simulations and Problems 12

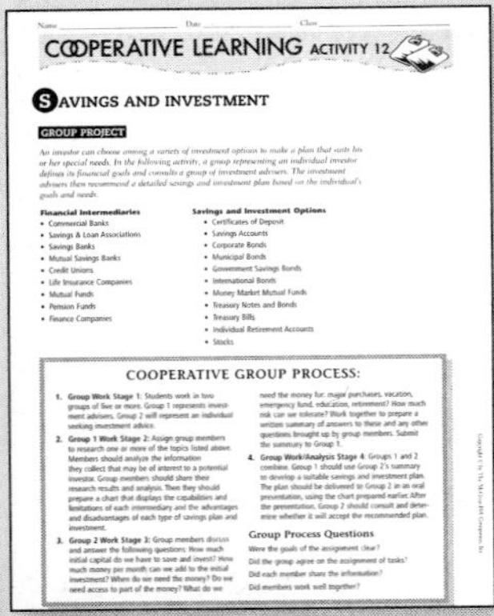
COOPERATIVE LEARNING ACTIVITY 12

SAVINGS AND INVESTMENT

COOPERATIVE GROUP PROCESS:

### Primary and Secondary Source Reading 12

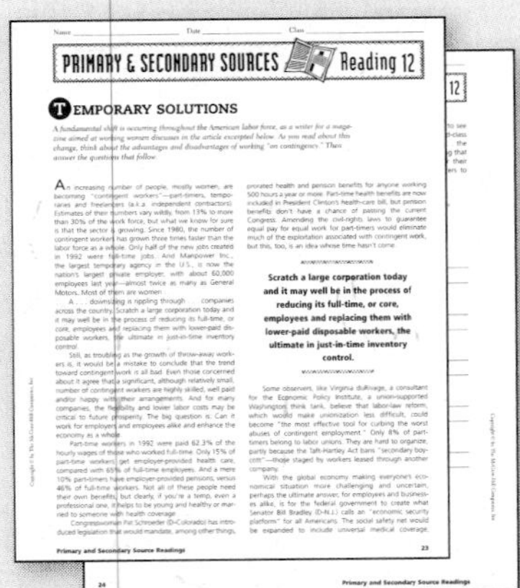
PRIMARY & SECONDARY SOURCES Reading 12

TEMPORARY SOLUTIONS

### Math Practice for Economics Activity 12

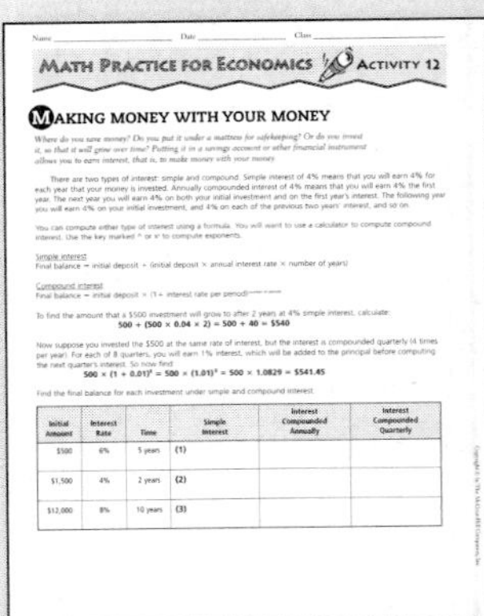
MATH PRACTICE FOR ECONOMICS ACTIVITY 12

MAKING MONEY WITH YOUR MONEY

### Economic Cartoons Activity 12

ECONOMIC CARTOON 12

TWO LITTLE WORDS: DOT COM

EXAMINING THE CARTOON

## Review and Reinforcement

### Critical Thinking Activity 12

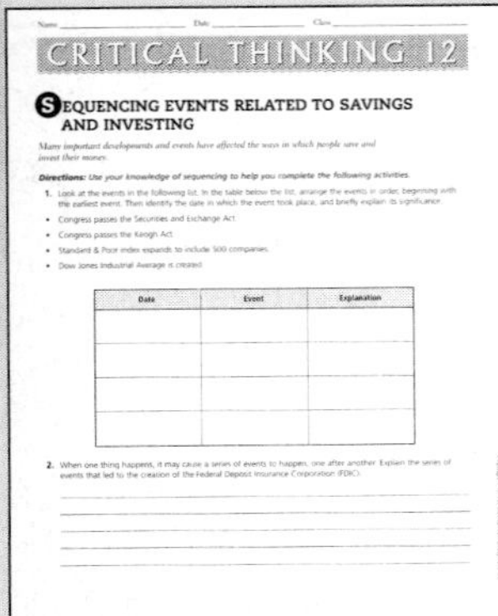
CRITICAL THINKING 12

SEQUENCING EVENTS RELATED TO SAVINGS AND INVESTING

### Reteaching Activity 6

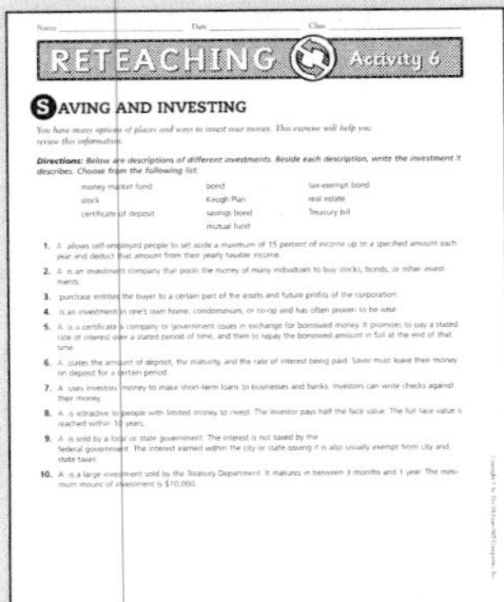
RETEACHING Activity 6

SAVING AND INVESTING

### Economic Vocabulary Activity 6

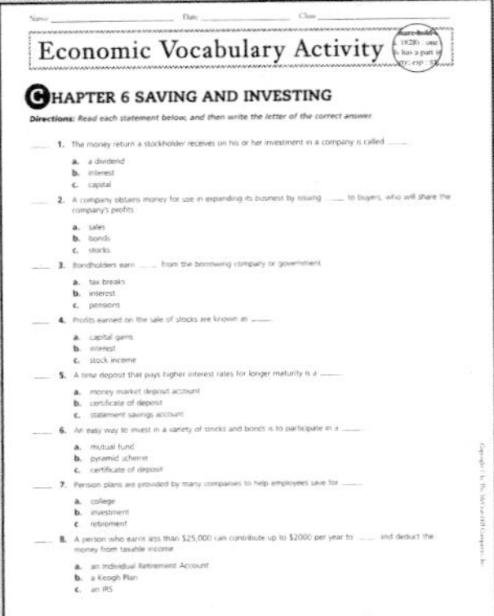
Economic Vocabulary Activity

CHAPTER 6 SAVING AND INVESTING

### Reinforcing Economic Skills 24

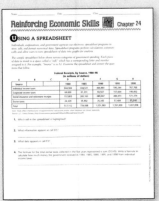

Reinforcing Economic Skills Chapter 24

USING A SPREADSHEET

# CHAPTER 6 Resource Manager

## Assessment and Evaluation

Chapter 6 Test Form A

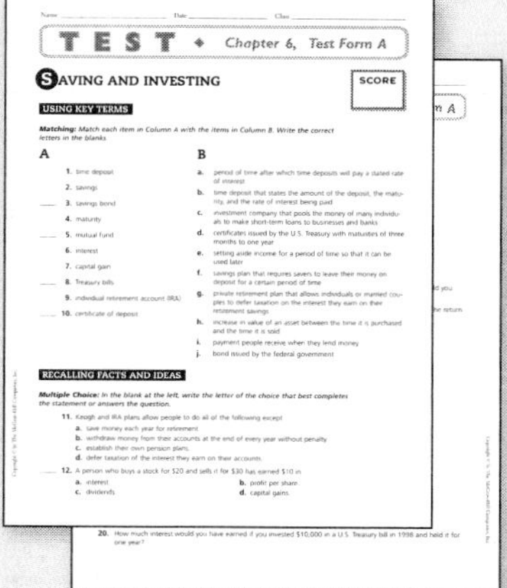

Chapter 6 Test Form B

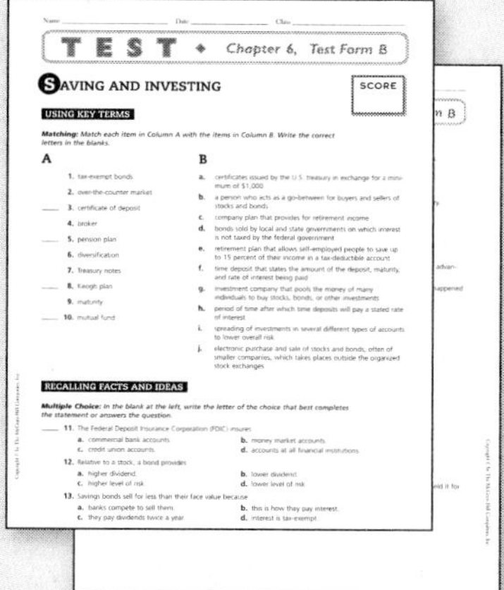

Performance Assessment Activity 12

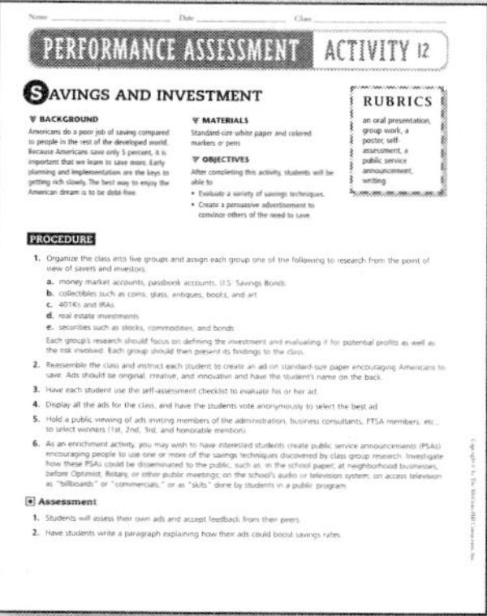

ExamView® Pro Testmaker

## Technology and Multimedia

 Vocabulary PuzzleMaker Software

 Interactive Tutor Self-Assessment Software

 ExamView® Pro Testmaker

 NBR *Economics & You* Video Program (English/Spanish)

 Presentation Plus!

 Glencoe Skillbuilder Interactive Workbook CD-ROM, Level 2

 Interactive Lesson Planner

 MindJogger Videoquiz

 Interactive Economics! CD-ROM

Audio Program (English or Spanish)

## ECONOMICS Online

You and your students can visit *ett.glencoe.com*—the Web site companion to **Economics Today and Tomorrow.** This innovative integration of electronic and print media offers your students a wealth of opportunities. The student text directs students to the Web site for the following options:

- **Chapter Overviews**
- **Student Web Activities**
- **Self-Check Quizzes**
- **Textbook Updates**

Answers are provided for you in the **Web Activity Lesson Plan.** Additional Web resources and Interactive Puzzles are also available.

Use the Glencoe Web site for additional resources. All essential content is covered in the Student Edition.

## Spanish Resources

 Spanish Economic Concepts Transparency 10

 Spanish Vocabulary Activity 6

Spanish Reteaching Activity 6

 Spanish Section Quizzes for Chapter 6

 Spanish Chapter 6 Audio Program, Activity, and Test

## Additional Resources

### Reading for the Student

*Real Life Consumer Economics,* revised ed. New York: Scholastic Books, 1990. Lessons on food, clothing, and shelter; money and credit; and taxes and economics.

### Multimedia Material

*Investments and Risk Capital.* From the Running Your Own Business Series. Videotape, 24 min. Public Television Library, 475 L'Enfant Plaza, SW, Washington, D.C. 20024

# CHAPTER 6 Resource Manager

## Section Resources

| Reading Objectives | Reproducible Resources | Technology/Multimedia Resources |
|---|---|---|
| **Section 1**<br>**Why Save?**<br>• When should you save?<br>• How do passbook, statement, and money market accounts differ?<br>• What are the advantages of time deposits? | Reproducible Lesson Plan 6-1<br>Daily Lecture Notes 6-1<br>Guided Reading Activity 6-1<br>Reading Essentials and Study Guide 6-1<br>Daily Focus Activity 42<br>Section Quiz 6-1*<br>Reinforcing Economic Skills 24 | Daily Focus Transparency 42<br>Vocabulary PuzzleMaker<br>Interactive Tutor Self-Assessment Software<br>MindJogger Videoquiz<br>Presentation Plus!<br>ExamView® Pro Testmaker |
| **Section 2**<br>**Investing: Taking Risks With Your Savings**<br>• How do stocks and bonds differ?<br>• What investment funds are available in stock and bond markets? | Reproducible Lesson Plan 6-2<br>Daily Lecture Notes 6-2<br>Guided Reading Activity 6-2<br>Reading Essentials and Study Guide 6-2<br>Daily Focus Activity 43<br>Section Quiz 6-2* | Daily Focus Transparency 43<br>Economic Concepts Transparency 10<br>Vocabulary PuzzleMaker<br>Interactive Tutor Self-Assessment Software<br>MindJogger Videoquiz<br>NBR's *Economics & You**<br>Interactive Economics!<br>Presentation Plus!<br>ExamView® Pro Testmaker<br>Economic Survival: A Financial Simulation |
| **Section 3**<br>**Special Savings Plans and Goals**<br>• What kinds of retirement investments are available?<br>• How much should you save and invest? | Reproducible Lesson Plan 6-3<br>Daily Lecture Notes 6-3<br>Guided Reading Activity 6-3<br>Reading Essentials and Study Guide 6-3<br>Daily Focus Activity 44<br>Section Quiz 6-3* | Daily Focus Transparency 44<br>Vocabulary PuzzleMaker<br>Interactive Tutor Self-Assessment Software<br>MindJogger Videoquiz<br>NBR's *Economics & You**<br>Presentation Plus!<br>ExamView® Pro Testmaker |

*Also available in Spanish

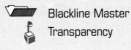

Blackline Master
Transparency

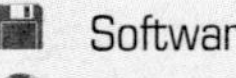
Software

CD-ROM

Videodisc

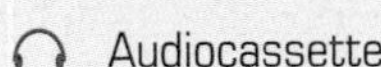
Audiocassette

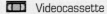

Videocassette

# CHAPTER 6 Resource Manager

## ACTIVITY From the Classroom of

**Roger C. Lyder**
**Pelhan High School**
**Pelhan, New Hampshire**

### Finding a Job

Have students research a particular career and create a presentation for the class. Research the educational entry requirements, salary ranges, growth prospects, prime locations, and offshoots. Students should interview a person in that career in order to get an insider's view.

Then have students practice writing their resumes. These should include their school experience, skills, work experience, and references.

## Easy Planning and Preparation!

Use Glencoe's **Presentation Plus!**, a Microsoft PowerPoint® application, to teach **Saving and Investing.** With this multimedia teacher tool, you can customize ready-made presentations. At your fingertips are interactive transparencies, on-screen lecture notes, audiovisual presentations, and links to the Internet and to other Glencoe multimedia.

### Interactive Lesson Planner

Planning has never been easier! Organize your week, month, semester, or year with all the lesson helps you need to make teaching creative, timely, and relevant—the way it is meant to be. The Interactive Lesson Planner opens Glencoe's **Chapter 6** resources, helps you build your schedule, and tracks your progress.

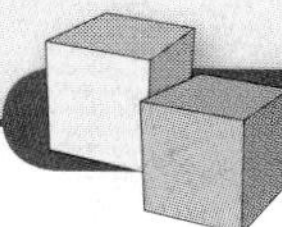

## Block Schedule

Activities that are particularly suited to use within the block scheduling framework are identified throughout this chapter by the following designation: BLOCK SCHEDULING

## Key to Ability Levels

**Teaching strategies have been coded for varying learning styles and abilities.**

L1 BASIC activities for all students
L2 AVERAGE activities for average to above-average students
L3 CHALLENGING activities for above-average students
ELL ENGLISH LANGUAGE LEARNER activities

National Council on Economic Education

## THE EconomicsAmerica AND EconomicsInternational PROGRAMS

### Voluntary Standards Emphasized in Chapter 6

**Content Standard 12** Students will understand that interest rates, adjusted for inflation, rise and fall to balance the amount saved with the amount borrowed, thus affecting the allocation of scarce resources between present and future uses.

**Content Standard 10** Students will understand that institutions evolve in market economics to help individuals and groups accomplish their goals. Banks, labor unions, corporations, legal systems, and not-for-profit organizations are examples of important institutions.

### Resources Available from NCEE

- *Personal Finance Economics: Wallet Wisdom*
- *Learning from the Market: Integrating the Stock Market Game™ Across the Curriculum*
- *Personal Decision Making: Focus on Economics*

To order these materials, or to contact your State Council on Economic Education about workshops and programs, call 1-800-338-1192 or visit the NCEE Web site at http://www.nationalcouncil.org

## Introducing CHAPTER 6

**ECONOMICS & YOU**

Saving and Investing

Chapter 13
Disc 1, Side 1

**ASK:** What is the key principle of investing? *risk versus return*

Also available in VHS.

### Chapter Overview

Most Americans make more income at their jobs than they require for immediate necessities. At the same time, however, many large purchases cost more than a worker earns in a single pay period. Thus, wage earners must decide whether to save their extra earnings for large purchases or invest them for future use. **Chapter 6** describes various types of savings accounts and investment opportunities and explains the advantages and disadvantages of each.

### GLENCOE TECHNOLOGY

Use **MindJogger Videoquiz** VHS to preview Chapter 6 content.

### ECONOMICS Online

Introduce students to chapter content and key terms by having them access **Chapter 6—Chapter Overviews** at *ett.glencoe.com*

# CHAPTER 6

# Saving and Investing

### Why It's Important

*Why should you save? What is the difference between saving and investing? This chapter will explain reasons for saving, as well as the various institutions and investments in which to put your money.*

*To learn more about investment strategies, view the* **Economics & You** *Chapter 13 video lesson:* **Saving and Investing**

### ECONOMICS Online

**Chapter Overview** Visit the *Economics Today and Tomorrow* Web site at ett.glencoe.com and click on ***Chapter 6—Chapter Overviews*** to preview chapter information.

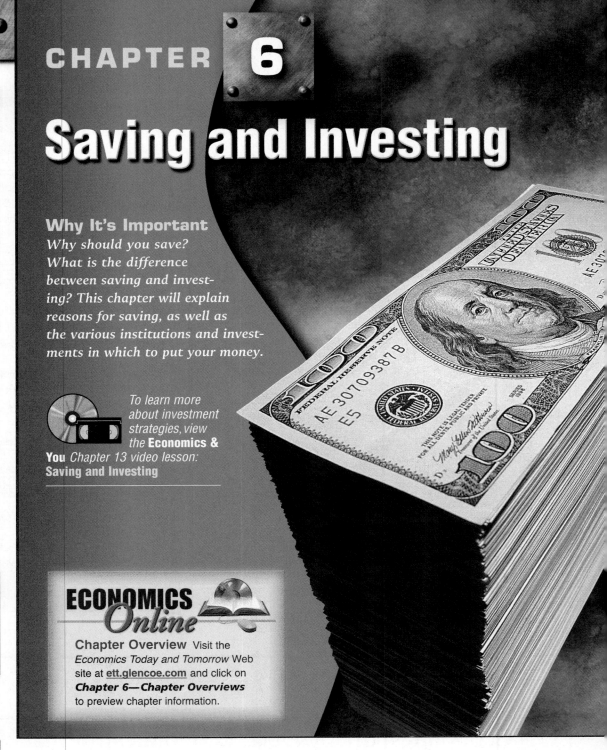

### CHAPTER LAUNCH ACTIVITY

Have students imagine they have $5,000 to save or invest as they please. Offer students the following savings and investment options: a money market account, paying 4 percent interest, on which they can write four checks each month; a three-year certificate of deposit (CD) that pays 6 percent interest; a stock whose value has nearly tripled in the last 18 months. Call on volunteers to identify the option they would choose and why. After students have offered their answers, lead the class in a discussion of two very important factors in savings and investment decisions—risk and return.

# SECTION 1 Why Save?

## Cover Story

*The Columbus Dispatch*, May 29, 1999

Money is burning a hole in consumers' pockets. Again last month, U.S. wage earners spent nearly as much as they made, contributing to record low savings.

But consumers have good reason to be out there spending. They've got jobs, their incomes are rising, confidence is high, and the stock market is booming.

This trend dragged down the savings rate—savings as a percentage of after-tax income—to a record low.

### Reader's Guide

**Terms to Know**

- saving
- interest
- passbook savings account
- statement savings account
- money market deposit account
- time deposits
- maturity
- certificates of deposit

**Reading Objectives**

1. When should you save?
2. How do passbook, statement, and money market accounts differ?
3. What are the advantages of time deposits?

Economists define ***saving*** as the setting aside of income for a period of time so that it can be used later. You may already be saving some of your income for a future use, such as buying a DVD system or continuing your education. See **Figure 6.1** on page 142. As you read this section, you'll learn why saving is important to you and the economy as a whole.

*saving: setting aside income for a period of time so that it can be used later*

## Deciding to Save

Any saving that you do now may be only for purchases that require more funds than you usually have at one time. When you are self-supporting and have more responsibilities, you will probably save for other reasons, such as having funds in case of emergencies and for your retirement.

**Results of Saving** When an individual saves, the economy as a whole benefits. Saving provides money for others to invest or spend. Saving also allows businesses to expand, which provides increased income for consumers and raises the standard of living.



## SECTION 1 RESOURCE MANAGER

**Reproducible Masters**

- Reproducible Lesson Plan 6–1
- Reading Essentials and Study Guide 6–1
- Guided Reading Activity 6–1
- Section Quiz 6–1
- Daily Focus Activity 42
- Daily Lecture Notes 6–1

**Multimedia**

- Daily Focus Transparency 42
- Vocabulary PuzzleMaker
- Interactive Tutor Self-Assessment Software
- ExamView® Pro Testmaker
- MindJogger Videoquiz
- Presentation Plus!



# 1 Focus

## Overview

**Section 1** describes the different kinds of savings accounts available through savings institutions, and explains the advantages and disadvantages of time deposits as compared with other savings accounts.

**BELLRINGER**
**Motivational Activity**

Project **Daily Focus Transparency 42** and have students answer the questions.

This activity is also available as a blackline master.

**Daily Focus Transparency 42**

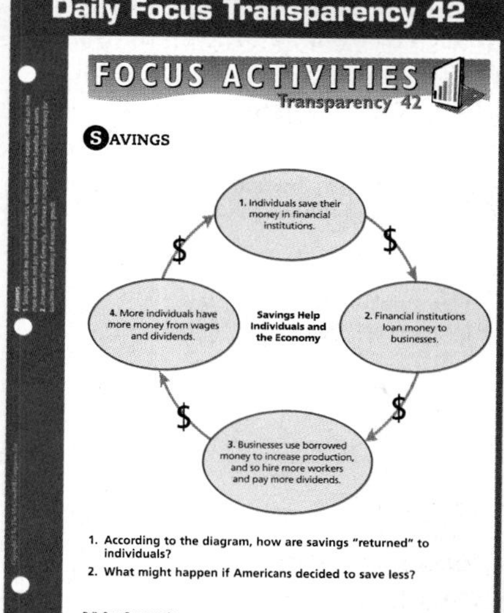


### Reader's Guide

Answers to the **Reading Objectives** questions are on page 144.

**Preteaching Vocabulary**

Provide each student with eight index cards. On one side of each card, have students write one of the **Terms to Know**. Ask students to write each definition on the reverse side of the appropriate index card. Encourage students to use these cards as learning aids as they work through the section.

**Vocabulary PuzzleMaker**

## CHAPTER 6
SECTION 1, Pages 141–144

# 2 Teach

## Guided Practice

**L1 Understanding Ideas** Write the following terms on the board, leaving ample space between each term: passbook savings account, statement savings account, money market deposit account, certificate of deposit. Call on volunteers to identify what they think are the advantages and disadvantages of each. (As guidance, you might suggest that the advantage of a passbook savings account is easy availability of funds, while the disadvantage is a relatively low interest rate.) Note responses on the board. Conclude by asking students which type of account they might use to save for the following: a new coat, a car, a retirement account. In a closing discussion, have students explain their choices.

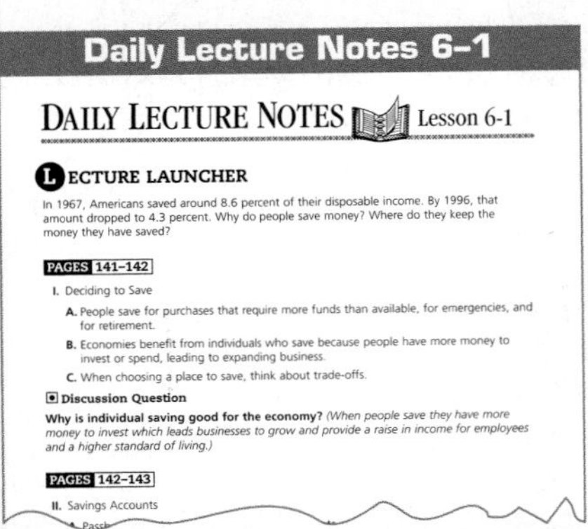

**Daily Lecture Notes 6–1**

DAILY LECTURE NOTES Lesson 6-1

**LECTURE LAUNCHER**

In 1967, Americans saved around 8.6 percent of their disposable income. By 1996, that amount dropped to 4.3 percent. Why do people save money? Where do they keep the money they have saved?

PAGES 141–142

I. Deciding to Save

**A.** People save for purchases that require more funds than available, for emergencies, and for retirement.

**B.** Economies benefit from individuals who save because people have more money to invest or spend, leading to expanding business.

**C.** When choosing a place to save, think about trade-offs.

**Discussion Question**

**Why is individual saving good for the economy?** *(When people save they have more money to invest which leads businesses to grow and provide a raise in income for employees and a higher standard of living.)*

PAGES 142–143

II. Savings Accounts

**Visual Instruction FIGURE 6.1**

**Answer:** *Saving makes more income available for spending in the future.*

**FIGURE 6.1**

**Saving Goals** Your saving goals will change as you move through life. Today you may be saving for a stereo, whereas in the future you may save for a college education. ***How does saving affect your future spending habits?***

**Where to Save** Generally, when people think of saving, they think of putting their funds in a savings bank or a similar financial institution where it will earn interest. **Interest** is the payment people receive when they lend money, or allow someone else to use their money. A person receives interest on his or her savings plan for as long as funds are in the account.

**interest:** *payment people receive when they lend money or allow someone else to use their money*

You actually have many options regarding places in which to put your savings. As you learned in Chapter 4, the most common places are commercial banks, savings and loan associations, savings banks, and credit unions. Investigate the financial institutions in your area and the services they offer.

In comparison shopping for the best savings plan, you need to consider the trade-offs. Some savings plans allow immediate access to your money but pay a low rate of interest. Others pay higher interest and allow immediate use of your money, but require a large minimum balance.

## Savings Accounts

Passbook savings accounts are also called regular savings accounts. With a **passbook savings account**, the depositor receives a booklet in which deposits, withdrawals, and interest are recorded. A customer must present the passbook each time one of these *transactions*, or business operations, takes place.

**passbook savings account:** *account for which a depositor receives a booklet in which deposits, withdrawals, and interest are recorded*

A **statement savings account** is basically the same type of account. Instead of a passbook that must be presented for each transaction, however, the depositor receives a monthly statement showing all transactions. The chief appeal of these accounts is that they offer easy availability of funds. The depositor can usually withdraw funds at any time without paying a *penalty*—forfeiting any money—but there is a trade-off. The interest paid on passbook and statement accounts is low compared to the interest on other savings plans.

**statement savings account:** *account similar to a passbook savings account except that the depositor receives a monthly statement showing all transactions*

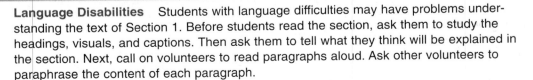

**Meeting Special Needs** 

**Language Disabilities** Students with language difficulties may have problems understanding the text of Section 1. Before students read the section, ask them to study the headings, visuals, and captions. Then ask them to tell what they think will be explained in the section. Next, call on volunteers to read paragraphs aloud. Ask other volunteers to paraphrase the content of each paragraph.

Refer to *Inclusion for the Social Studies Classroom Strategies and Activities* for students with different learning styles.

A **money market deposit account** (MMDA) is another type of account that pays relatively high rates of interest and allows immediate access to money through checks. The trade-off is that these accounts have a $1,000 to $2,500 minimum balance requirement. Customers can usually make withdrawals from a money market account in person at any time, but they are allowed to write only a few checks a month against the account.

### Comparing Saving Rates

The percent of income that Americans save fell steadily in the 1990s. Today, the saving rate—the percentage of disposable personal income saved—stands well below 5 percent. How does this compare to the saving rates of other countries? Below are some recent statistics on saving rates for several industrialized nations. ■

| Country | Saving rate |
|---|---|
| Canada | 4.6% |
| France | 12.5% |
| Germany | 12.4% |
| Great Britain | 11.6% |
| Italy | 13.4% |
| Japan | 13.2% |

## Time Deposits

The term ***time deposits*** refers to a wide variety of savings plans that require a saver to deposit his or her funds for a certain period of time. The period of time is called the **maturity,** and may vary from seven days to eight years or more. Time deposits are often called **certificates of deposit** (CDs), or savings certificates. CDs state the amount of the deposit, the maturity, and the rate of interest being paid.

Time deposits offer higher interest rates than passbook or statement savings accounts. The longer the maturity, the higher the interest rate that is paid. For example, a CD with a short-term maturity of 90 days pays less interest than a CD with a two-year maturity. Savers who cash a time deposit before maturity pay a penalty.

**Insuring Deposits** When the stock market collapsed in 1929, the resulting crisis wiped out people's entire savings. Congress passed, and President Franklin Roosevelt signed, legislation to protect deposits. This legislation created the Federal Deposit Insurance Corporation (FDIC).

Today there are several federal agencies that insure most banks and savings institutions. See **Figure 6.2** on page 144. Each depositor's money in a particular savings institution is insured up to $100,000. If an insured institution fails, each depositor will be paid the full amount of his or her savings up to $100,000 for each legally separate account.

**money market deposit account:** *account that pays relatively high rates of interest, requires a minimum balance, and allows immediate access to money*

**time deposits:** *savings plans that require savers to leave their money on deposit for certain periods of time*

**maturity:** *period of time at the end of which time deposits will pay a stated rate of interest*

**certificates of deposit:** *time deposits that state the amount of the deposit, maturity, and rate of interest being paid*





**Guided Reading Activity 6-1**

GUIDED READING Activity 6-1

WHY SAVE?

FILLING IN THE BLANKS

## Independent Practice

**L2 Gathering Information** Have students work in small groups to investigate the interest rates paid on passbook savings accounts, statement savings accounts, money market deposit accounts, and certificates of deposit at local banks today. Have groups present their findings in a brief report. Encourage students to extend their report by calculating the return after a year for each account on a deposit of $5,000.

BLOCK SCHEDULING

# 3 Assess

## Meeting Lesson Objectives

Assign Section 1 Assessment as homework or an in-class activity.

Use **Interactive Tutor Self-Assessment Software** to review Section 1.

### Cooperative Learning

Have students work in small groups to create an advertisement or brochure for a local savings institution. Suggest that they include in their advertisements or brochures the types of accounts their institutions offer and the benefits and possible uses of such accounts. Encourage groups to display their advertisements and brochures around the class. ELL

CHAPTER 6
SECTION 1, Pages 141–144

Section Quiz 6-1

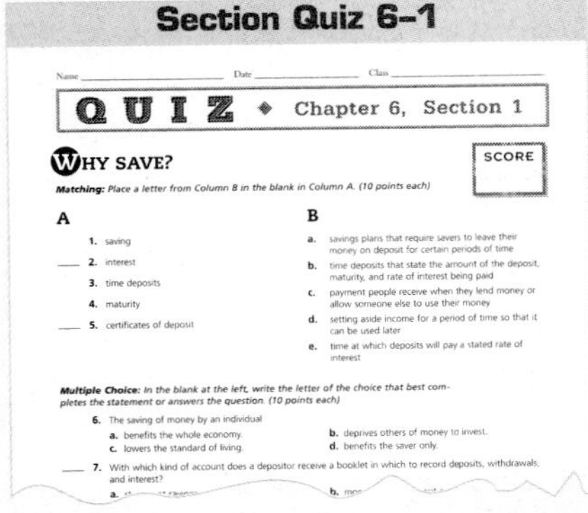

## Reteach

Ask students to summarize the section by writing topic sentences for each of the major subheadings.

Reading Essentials and Study Guide 6-1

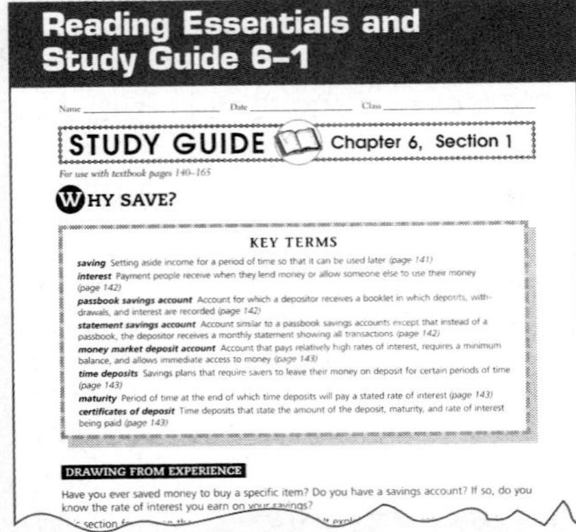

## 4 Close

Ask students to write a slogan or saying that answers the question "Why save?"

FIGURE 6.2 **Savings Institutions' Services and Insurers**

| Institution | Savings Services Offered | Insured by | Number of Institutions* |
|---|---|---|---|
| **Commercial banks** | Passbook and statement savings accounts, certificates of deposit, money market accounts | Federal Deposit Insurance Corporation (FDIC) | 8,774 |
| **Savings and loan associations (S&Ls)/savings banks** | Passbook and statement savings accounts, certificates of deposit, money market accounts | S&Ls: Savings Association Insurance Fund (SAIF)/FDIC | 1,687 |
| **Credit unions** | Share drafts**, share accounts, share certificates | National Credit Union Share Insurance Fund | 10,995 |

*Number of savings institutions changes often
**Interest-earning account similar to checking account

**Practice** and **assess** key skills with ***Skillbuilder Interactive Workbook, Level 2.***

## SECTION 1 Assessment

### Understanding Key Terms

1. **Define** saving, interest, passbook savings account, statement savings account, money market deposit account, time deposits, maturity, certificates of deposit.

### Reviewing Objectives

2. What are three reasons that people save?
3. **Graphic Organizer** Use a chart like the one below to explain the differences among passbook, statement, and money market savings accounts.

| Type of account | Similarities | Differences |
|---|---|---|
| | | |
| | | |

4. What are the advantages of time deposits?

### Applying Economic Concepts

5. **Saving** Why is it more difficult for the beginning saver to open a money market deposit account than a passbook savings account?

### Critical Thinking Activity

6. **Synthesizing Information** If your bank pays 5.5 percent interest on savings deposits, what is the simple interest paid in the third year on an initial $100 deposit? What is the total amount in the account after three years? What is the amount after three years if the interest was compounded annually? *For help in understanding interest rates, see page xxii in the Economic Handbook.*



## SECTION 1 Assessment Answers

1. All definitions can be found in the Glossary.
2. to make large purchases, for emergencies, for retirement
3.

| Type of account | Similarities | Differences |
|---|---|---|
| Passbook savings account | Relatively easy availability of funds | Low minimum deposit, low interest rates |
| Statement savings account | Relatively easy availability of funds | Low minimum deposit, low interest rates |
| Money market deposit account | Relatively easy availability of funds | Relatively high minimum deposit, relatively high interest rates |

4. Time deposits offer higher interest rates than passbook or statement savings accounts.
5. Money market accounts often require initial deposits of $1,000 to $2,500.
6. $5.50; $116.50; $117.42

**Savings Bonds** The United States government issues **savings bonds** as one of its ways of borrowing money. They range in face value from $50 up to $10,000. The purchase of a U.S. savings bond is similar to buying a bank's certificate of deposit. A very safe form of investment, savings bonds are attractive to people with limited money to invest. Another attraction is that the interest earned is not taxed until the bond is turned in for cash.

A person buying a savings bond pays half the bond's face value. You could purchase a $50 bond, then, for only $25. The bond increases in value every 6 months until its full face value is reached. (The *Rule of 72* tells you how long it takes for the bond to mature: Divide the number 72 by the interest rate.) If you choose to redeem a U.S. savings bond before it matures, you are guaranteed a certain rate of interest, which changes depending on rates of interest in the economy.

**savings bonds:** *bonds issued by the federal government as a way of borrowing money; they are purchased at half the face value and increase every 6 months until full face value is reached*

**T-Bills, T-Notes, and T-Bonds** The Treasury Department of the federal government also sells several types of larger investments. **Treasury bills** mature in 3 months to 1 year. The minimum amount of investment for Treasury bills is $10,000. **Treasury notes** have maturity dates of 2 to 10 years, and **Treasury bonds** mature in 10 or more years. Notes and bonds are sold in minimums of $1,000 or $5,000. The interest on all three of these government securities is exempt from state and local income taxes, but not from federal income tax.

**Treasury bills:** *certificates issued by the U.S. Treasury in exchange for a minimum amount of $10,000 and maturing in 3 months to 1 year*

**Treasury notes:** *certificates issued by the U.S. Treasury in exchange for minimum amounts of $1,000 or $5,000 and maturing in 2 to 10 years*

**Treasury bonds:** *certificates issued by the U.S. Treasury in exchange for minimum amounts of $1,000 or $5,000 and maturing in 10 or more years*

## Stock and Bond Markets

Stocks are bought and sold through brokers or on the Internet. A **broker** is a person who acts as a go-between for buyers and sellers. If an investor is interested in buying or trading corporate shares, he or she can contact a brokerage firm, which will perform the service for a fee.

Thousands of full-service brokerage firms throughout the country buy and sell stocks daily for ordinary investors. The fees they charge to perform the trades—up to $500—depend on the dollar amounts invested or traded. Today, however, if an investor has an account with an Internet brokerage firm, the cost for the same trade may be as low as $7.

**broker:** *person who acts as a go-between for buyers and sellers of stocks and bonds*

**Savings Bond**

**L2 Making Comparisons** Write the terms "Stocks" and "Bonds" on the board. Call on volunteers to come to the board and list facts about these two financial assets under the appropriate heading. Then have students use information on the board to discuss the following: You have $5,000 to invest. What would be the advantages and disadvantages of investing your funds in stock? In bonds?

Project **Economic Concepts Transparency 10** and have students discuss the accompanying questions.

### Economic Connection to... History

**Savings Bonds** During World War II special savings bonds—called war bonds—were issued to raise funds for the war effort. These bonds were issued in denominations of $10, $25, $50, $75, $100, $200, $500, $1,000, $10,000, and $100,000, and could be purchased at 75 percent of the face amount.

### Free Enterprise Activity

Tell students to suppose that they have set a goal to save enough money to pay for their college tuition. Ask them to select one of the financial assets—or combination of financial assets—discussed in Section 2 that would best help them attain this goal. Then have students write a brief essay explaining why they chose a particular asset or combination of assets. Encourage students to read their essays to the class.

## Independent Practice

**L3 Writing a Report** Randomly assign the following media to students: radio and television, news magazines, and the Internet. Have students research what kinds of investment information and advice are available on their assigned media. Ask students to write a detailed report and critique of one example they locate. Call on volunteers to present their reports to the class.

### ECONOMIC SURVIVAL A Financial Simulation

To help students learn to manage their own finances, have the class play the game **Economic Survival: A Financial Simulation**, in which each student enters the workforce, rents an apartment, and deals with everyday events. The simulation takes five days to complete and may be extended for an additional two weeks.

### Visual Instruction FIGURE 6.5

After students have viewed **Figure 6.5**, point out that the New York Stock Exchange was founded in May 1792 by a group of 24 brokers. They met under a tree on what today is Wall Street.

There are well over 100 online brokerage firms, with more springing up on the Web every day. It is estimated that 10 million American investors use the Internet to make trades every year.

**Stock Exchanges** Brokerage houses communicate with the busy floors of the stock exchanges. See **Figure 6.5.** The largest stock exchange, or stock market, is the New York Stock Exchange (NYSE) in New York City. There are also supplemental stock exchanges and regional exchanges—such as the Midwest Stock Exchange in Chicago—and exchanges in other countries—such as the London and Tokyo stock exchanges.

To be listed on these exchanges, a corporation offering stock must prove to the exchange that it is in good financial condition. Most of the companies traded on stock exchanges are among the largest, most profitable corporations in the country.

**over-the-counter market:** *electronic purchase and sale of stocks and bonds, often of smaller companies, which takes place outside the organized stock exchanges*

**Over-the-Counter Markets** Stocks can also be sold on the **over-the-counter market,** an electronic marketplace for stocks not listed on the organized exchanges. The largest volume of over-the-counter stocks are quoted on the National Association of Securities Dealers Automated Quotations (NASDAQ) national market system, which merged with the American Stock Exchange in 1998.

FIGURE  6.5

**Buying Stocks or Bonds** If you decide to buy stocks or bonds, you usually have to contact a broker (by phone or through the Internet). You pay the broker a fee to purchase the stock at one of the stock exchanges. The stock exchanges act as a market between buyers and sellers of securities, or stocks.

150

### Relevant Issues in Economics

**Minorities and the Stock Market** Studies have found that the vast majority of American stockholders are white. African Americans and Hispanics each account for only 5 percent of investors, while only 2 percent of investors are Asian. Recently, investment companies have made efforts to tap these underserved minority markets. One company has undertaken regular surveys of African American investors to see how it might better serve them. Other companies advertise prominently in business magazines aimed at Hispanics and Asians. Still others have translated prospectuses for their various financial assets into Spanish and Chinese.

Unlike organized stock exchanges, over-the-counter stocks are not traded in any specific place. Brokerage firms hold shares of stocks that they buy and sell for investors. For example, assume that XYZ Corporation is a company that sells computers. If an investor wanted to buy stock in it, he or she would check the NASDAQ listings in the local newspaper or on the Internet. This table of over-the-counter stocks would list XYZ Corporation, the number of shares of stock sold the day before, and the price at which shares were bought and sold that day. The investor would then call a broker or use the Internet to buy a certain number of shares. Usually stocks are sold in amounts of 100 shares, but some brokers will handle smaller amounts.

**Bond Markets** The New York Exchange Bond Market and the American Exchange Bond Market are the two largest bond exchanges. Bonds, including U.S. government bonds, are sold over-the-counter and on the Internet.

### Careers

#### Stock Broker

**Job Description**
- Relay investors' stock orders to the floor of a securities exchange
- Offer financial counseling and advice on the purchase or sale of particular securities

**Qualifications**
- College degree
- Pass a state licensing exam and the General Securities Registered Representative Exam

**Median Salary:** $38,800

**Job Outlook:** above average

—*Occupational Outlook Handbook*, 1998–99

**Mutual Funds** Many people invest in the stock market by placing some of their savings in a **mutual fund**, an investment company that pools the money of many individuals to buy stocks, bonds, or other investments. See **Figure 6.6.** Most mutual funds hold a variety of stocks or bonds. Losses in one area are likely to be made up by gains in another.

<u>mutual fund:</u> *investment company that pools the money of many individuals to buy stocks, bonds, or other investments*

One popular mutual fund invests in stocks used in an index. An *index* is a measuring system that tracks stock prices over the long run. The Dow-Jones Industrial Average (DJIA) and Standard & Poor's (S&P) are the two most common indexes. The DJIA tracks

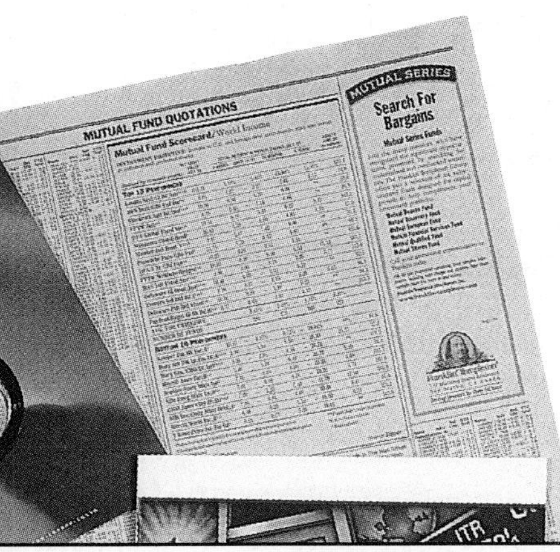


FIGURE  6.6

**Mutual Funds** The small investor should find out how the mutual fund he or she may choose has performed compared to index funds over a period of several years. ***Why are index funds watched so closely?***



## CHAPTER 6
SECTION 2, Pages 146–153

### INTERACTIVE ECONOMICS!

**LESSON 10: PERSONAL FINANCE**

Have students study the section of the Lesson 10 "Tutorial" that deals with stocks, stock markets, and mutual funds. Students will learn how to buy and sell stocks and mutual funds. The "Tutorial" also examines the effects that supply and demand have on the stock market.

Supplied in both CD-ROM and disk formats.

### Visual Instruction FIGURE 6.6

**Answer:** *because most mutual funds use the S&P 500 as the yardstick against which they compare their returns on stocks*

## 3 Assess

### Meeting Lesson Objectives

Assign Section 2 Assessment as homework or an in-class activity.

Use **Interactive Tutor Self-Assessment Software** to review Section 2.

### Extending the Content

**International Bonds** Foreign governments also issue bonds. However, for the most part they are available only in large denominations, usually starting at $1 million. As a result, only institutional investors—pension funds and insurance companies, for example—purchase these international bonds. Another unique aspect of international bonds is that interest and principal payments often are made in the currency of the issuing country rather than in dollars.

## ? Did You Know

The 30 stocks listed on the Dow-Jones include: Allied Signal, Aluminum Co. of America, American Express, AT&T, Boeing, Caterpillar, Citigroup, Coca-Cola, Dupont, Eastman Kodak, Exxon, General Electric, General Motors, Hewlett-Packard, The Home Depot, Intel, International Business Machines, International Paper, J.P. Morgan, Johnson & Johnson, McDonald's Corp., Merck & Co., Microsoft, Minnesota Mining & Manufacturing, Philip Morris, Procter & Gamble, SBC Communications, United Technologies, Wal-Mart Stores, and Walt Disney.

### Section Quiz 6–2

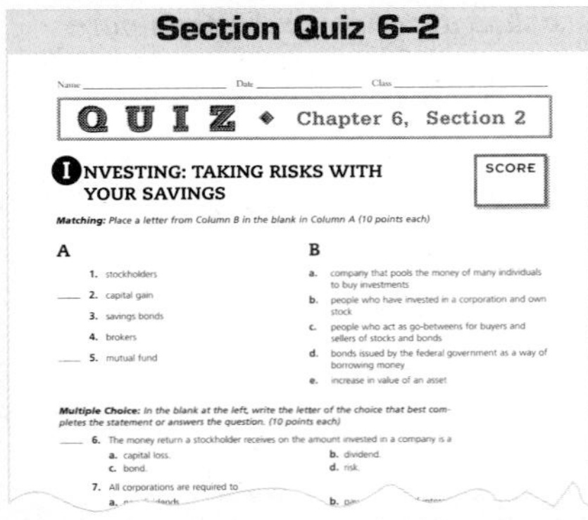

Name ______ Date ______ Class ______

**QUIZ** ◆ Chapter 6, Section 2

**INVESTING: TAKING RISKS WITH YOUR SAVINGS**

SCORE

***Matching:*** *Place a letter from Column B in the blank in Column A (10 points each)*

| A | B |
|---|---|
| ___ 1. stockholders | a. company that pools the money of many individuals to buy investments |
| ___ 2. capital gain | b. people who have invested in a corporation and own stock |
| ___ 3. savings bonds | c. people who act as go-betweens for buyers and sellers of stocks and bonds |
| ___ 4. brokers | d. bonds issued by the federal government as a way of borrowing money |
| ___ 5. mutual fund | e. increase in value of an asset |

***Multiple Choice:*** *In the blank at the left, write the letter of the choice that best completes the statement or answers the question. (10 points each)*

___ 6. The money return a stockholder receives on the amount invested in a company is a
a. capital loss. b. dividend.
c. bond. d. risk.

___ 7. All corporations are required to

## Reteach

Have students construct a chart showing the major characteristics of the financial assets discussed in Section 2.

## Economic Connection to... History

### The Dow-Jones and S&P

The Dow was created in 1896 by Charles Dow, cofounder of Dow Jones & Co. It soon became a permanent feature in the company's newspaper, *The Wall Street Journal,* which is one of the world's most influential business publications. The Dow index grew from its original 12 stocks to 30 by 1928.

It wasn't until 1926 that Standard & Poor's introduced a broader stock index, which tracked the nation's 90 biggest companies. The now-familiar S&P 500 stock index expanded in 1957 to include the 500 biggest companies.

Although it may seem odd that the Dow uses only 30 companies to measure a market with more than 10,000 stocks, those 30 companies have a combined market value of over $2.5 trillion. The S&P's 500 companies have a combined market value of $10.5 trillion—more than three-fourths of the nation's publicly owned stocks. ■

the stocks of 30 of the largest American companies to measure the well-being of the stock market as a whole; the S&P 500 index tracks 500 companies.

Most mutual funds use the S&P 500 as the yardstick against which they compare their returns on stocks. The long-run return from index funds is higher than can be expected from almost any other investment. By investing in a broad-based index fund, investors will almost surely do better over the long run than by investing in individual stocks or in a managed mutual fund. A *managed mutual fund* is one in which the managers adjust the mix of stocks and move often in and out of the market to try to generate the highest yield.

**money market fund:** *type of mutual fund that uses investors' money to make short-term loans to businesses and banks*

**Money Market Funds** One type of mutual fund, called a **money market fund,** normally uses investors' money to buy the short-term debt of businesses and banks. Most money market funds allow investors to write checks against their money in the fund. Any check, however, must be above some minimum amount, usually $500. The investor then earns money only on the amount left in the account.

Banks, savings and loan associations, and savings banks now offer a similar service, called *money market deposit accounts* (MMDA). A major advantage of MMDAs is that the federal government insures them against loss. Mutual funds and money market funds are not insured by the federal government.



## Critical Thinking Activity

**Synthesizing Information** Have students identify which of the following investments will provide the best return at the end of one year.

1. $8,000 invested in a corporate bond paying annual interest of 6 percent
2. $9,000 invested in $25 stock whose value grows by 5 percent over the year
3. $10,000 invested in a government bond paying annual interest of 4 percent

*$8,000 invested in a corporate bond—return will be $480, as compared to $450 for stock and $400 for government bond*

| **Table 1** | |
|---|---|
| **CATEGORIES OF EXPENDITURES** | **MONTHLY COST** |
| Rent | |
| Rental insurance | |
| Telephone | |
| Electricity | |
| Gas heat | |
| Car payment | |
| Car insurance | |
| Car expenses (gas and repairs) | |
| Furniture expenses | |
| Clothing expenses | |
| Food (Eating in) | |
| Eating out | |
| Medical insurance | |
| Medical expenses | |
| Credit card bill | |
| Savings account | |
| Checking account | |
| Stocks and bonds | |
| IRA or Roth IRA | |
| Entertainment | |
| Laundry and Toiletries | |
| Other | |
| TOTAL OF EXPENSES | |

| **Table 2** | |
|---|---|
| **MENUS** | **PRICES OF ITEMS** |
| Monday | |
| | |
| Tuesday | |
| | |
| Wednesday | |
| | |
| Thursday | |
| | |
| Friday | |
| | |
| Saturday | |
| | |
| Sunday | |
| | TOTAL |

## STEP C Creating an Economic Model

Use the results of your cost analyses in Table 1 to draw a bar graph visually showing how your income compares to your expenditures. Draw your graph on poster board to use in a presentation to the rest of the class. In your presentation you should also include visuals of the type of apartment you chose to rent, the furniture you selected, the type of automobile you bought, evidence of car and medical insurance costs, and your calculations for credit card interest fees.

## STEP D Lab Report Analysis

1. What was your largest monthly expense?
2. How much money did you have left over at the end of the month?
3. What expense(s) surprised you the most? Why?
4. What expenditures did you have to reduce in order to meet your other monthly expenses?

# 3 Assess

Have students answer the **Lab Report Analysis** questions.

# 4 Close

Discuss with students the trade-offs they made to minimize costs and meet their wants. Ask them if they would like to change these trade-offs and, if so, why.

## ? Did You Know

Vacations are one expense not included in the Economics Lab budget. In 1999, the average American spent a little under $1,000 on a summer vacation.

## Answers to Lab Report Analysis

The largest monthly expense is rent. The rest of the students' budgets will vary, however. In a review session of this Economics Lab, have students compare and discuss their budgets.

# UNIT 3 Resource Manager

The following transparencies may be used at any time during Unit 3.

## Economic Forms and Financial Pages Transparencies

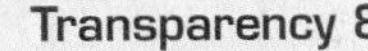

Transparency 8

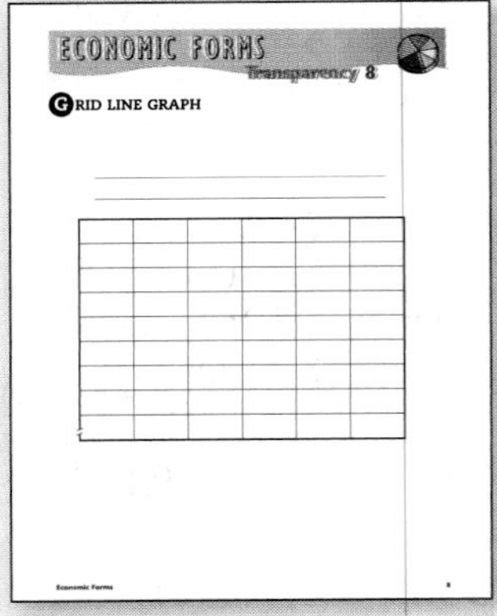

ECONOMIC FORMS
Transparency 8

GRID LINE GRAPH

Transparency 10

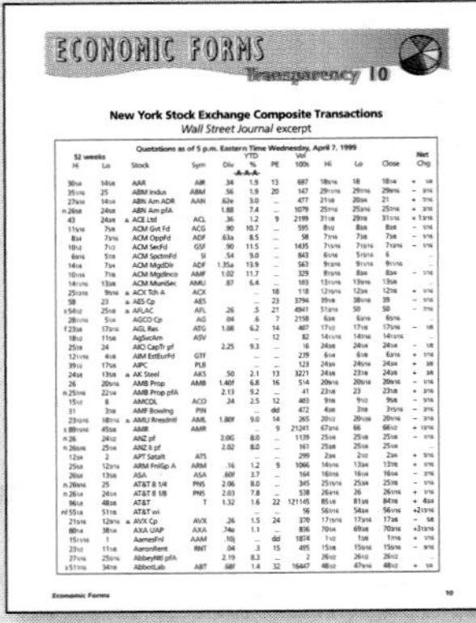

ECONOMIC FORMS
Transparency 10

New York Stock Exchange Composite Transactions
*Wall Street Journal excerpt*

Transparency 14

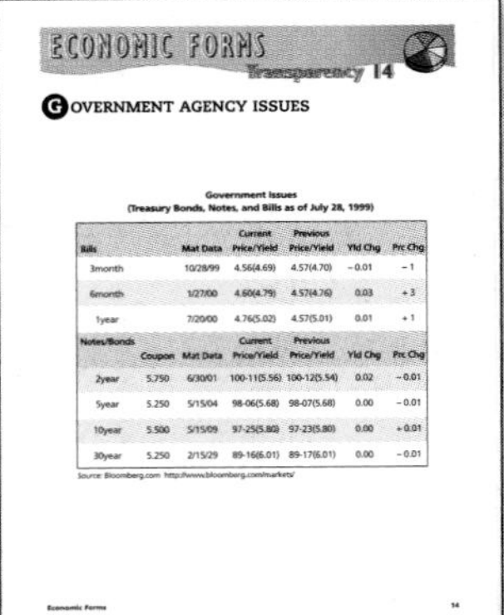

ECONOMIC FORMS
Transparency 14

GOVERNMENT AGENCY ISSUES

Government Issues
(Treasury Bonds, Notes, and Bills as of July 28, 1999)

## Economic Concepts Transparencies

Transparency 7

ECONOMIC CONCEPTS
Transparency 7

MARKETS AND PRICES



Transparency 8

ECONOMIC CONCEPTS
Transparency 8

SUPPLY AND DEMAND

Transparency 9

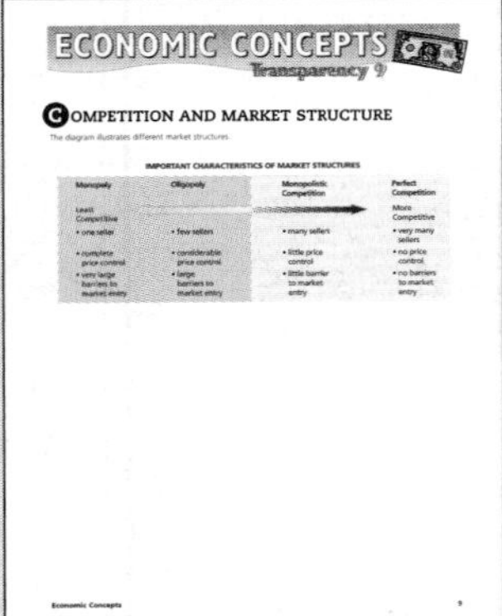

ECONOMIC CONCEPTS
Transparency 9

COMPETITION AND MARKET STRUCTURE

## Real-World Economics

Have your students learn about investing and managing their financial futures by participating in the exciting simulation **The Stock Market Game**.™ See page T24 for more information.

Strengthen students' research, cooperation, presentation, and critical thinking skills by having them compete in the **Fed Challenge**. See page T26 for further information.

## Additional Glencoe Resources for This Unit

- Nightly Business Report *Economics & You* Video Program
- Economic Survival: A Financial Simulation
- Interactive Economics! Software

# UNIT 3 Resource Manager

## Assessment and Evaluation

Unit 3 Test
Form A

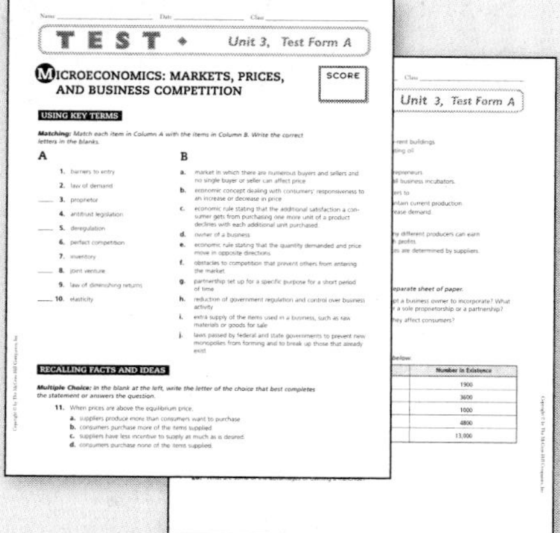

Unit 3 Test
Form B

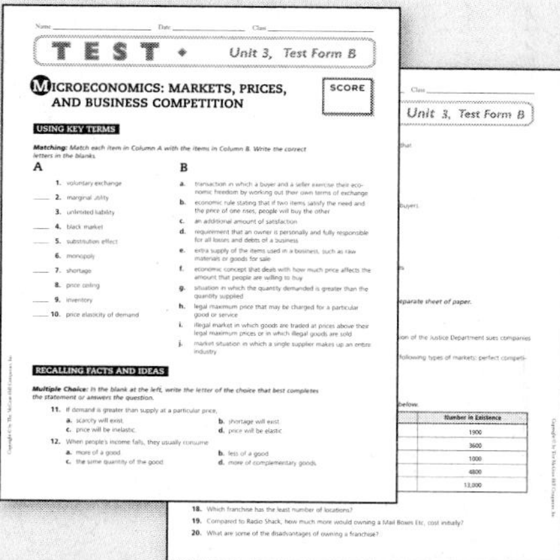

**Use the following tools to easily assess student learning:**

- Performance Assessment Strategies and Activities
- Section Quizzes
- Chapter and Unit Tests
- ExamView® Pro Testmaker
- Interactive Tutor Self-Assessment Software
- SAT I/II Test Practice
- MindJogger Videoquiz
- ett.glencoe.com

## Application and Enrichment

Economics Laboratory 2

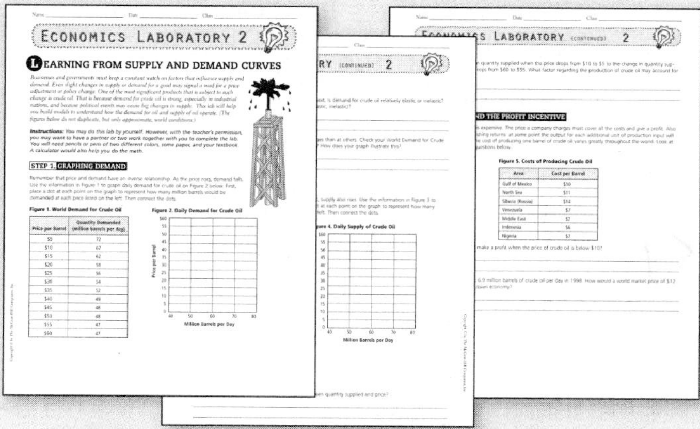

*Business Week* Focus on the New Economy

## ECONOMICS Online

*Glencoe's Web sites provide additional resources. All essential content is covered in the Student Edition.*

**ett.glencoe.com**

Visit the **Economics Today and Tomorrow** Web site for Chapter Overviews, Textbook Updates, Student Web Activities, Web Activity Lesson Plans, and Self-Check Quizzes.

**socialstudies.glencoe.com**

Visit the **Glencoe Social Studies** Web site for additional social studies activities, updates, and links to other sites.

**Glencoe's *Guide to Using the Internet*** provides an introduction to many of the current Internet technologies, social studies and professional resources, and teaching strategies.

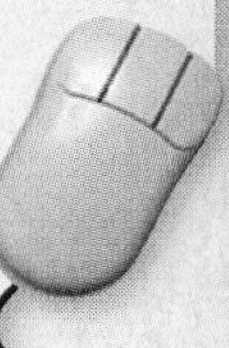

## Unit Objectives

After studying this unit, students will be able to:

- **Explain** the laws of supply and demand as they apply to voluntary markets.
- **Characterize** the types of business organizations.
- **Discuss** how competition and monopolies affect prices.

## Unit Overview

**Unit 3** introduces the laws of supply and demand, business organizations, and the effect of competition and monopolies on prices.

**Chapter 7** explains the demand curve, elasticity of demand, the supply curve, and supply and demand in a voluntary market.

**Chapter 8** describes starting a business, kinds of business organizations, the corporate world, and franchises.

**Chapter 9** explains perfect competition, monopoly, oligopoly, monopolistic competition, and government policies toward competition.

### 00:00 Out of Time?

If time does not permit teaching each chapter in this unit, you may use the **Audio Program** that includes a 1-page activity and a 1-page test for each chapter.

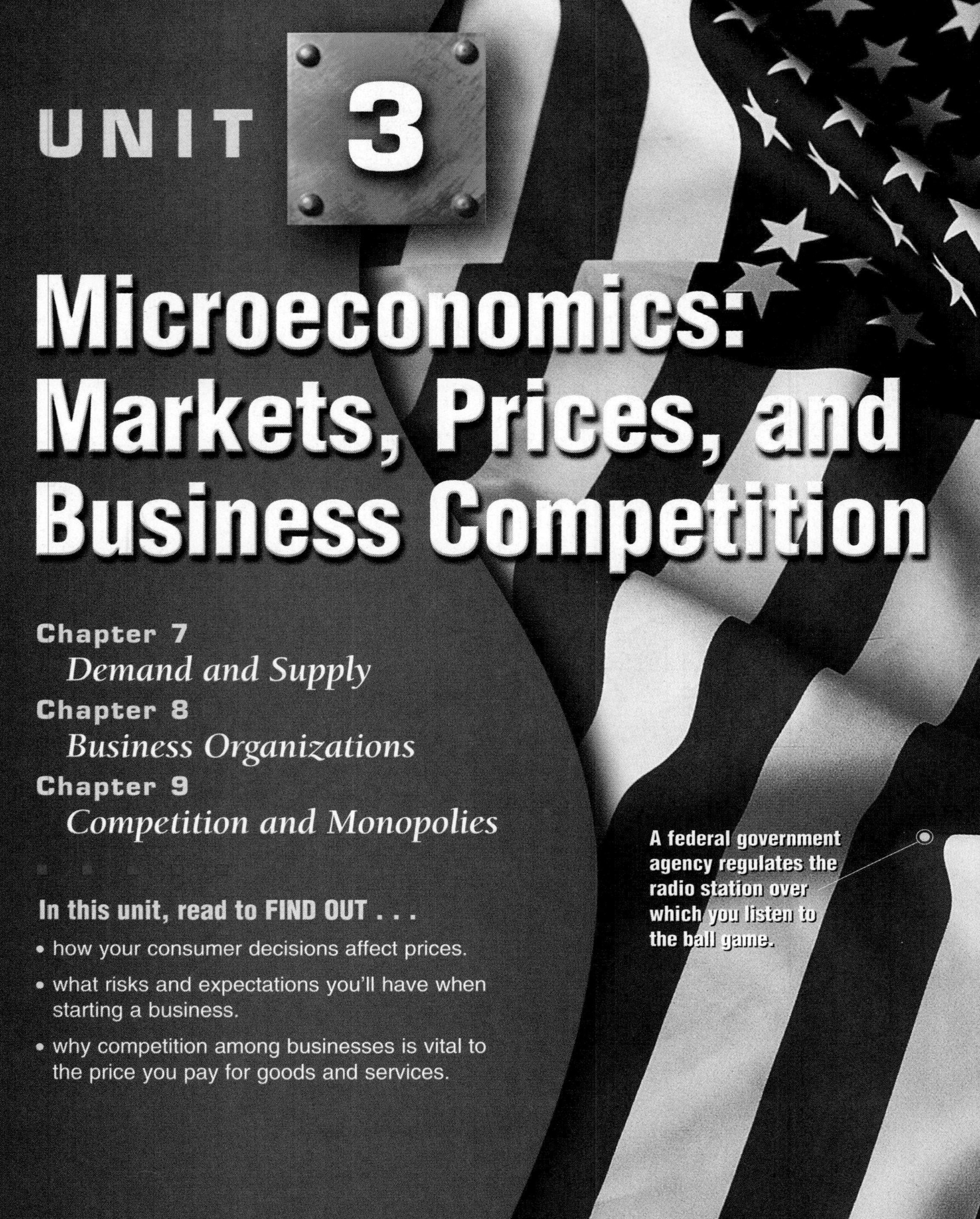

# UNIT 3

# Microeconomics: Markets, Prices, and Business Competition



**In this unit, read to FIND OUT . . .**

- how your consumer decisions affect prices.
- what risks and expectations you'll have when starting a business.
- why competition among businesses is vital to the price you pay for goods and services.

A federal government agency regulates the radio station over which you listen to the ball game.

## ECONOMIC SIMULATION

**Supply Affects Price** List the following crops on the board: corn, wheat, soybeans, oats. Tell students that they are farmers who can grow 10,000 bushels of one crop. Have each student write his or her decision of what to plant. By a show of hands, count the number of students who grew each crop. Next to each crop listed on the board, write the total number of bushels grown. Then post a price for each crop, using the following formulas: Largest crop=$1.00 per bushel; Second largest=$2.00 per bushel; Third largest=$3.00 per bushel; Smallest=$4.00 per bushel. After students calculate how much they earned, ask whether these prices would affect their planting decision for the next year. Discuss why supply affected price.

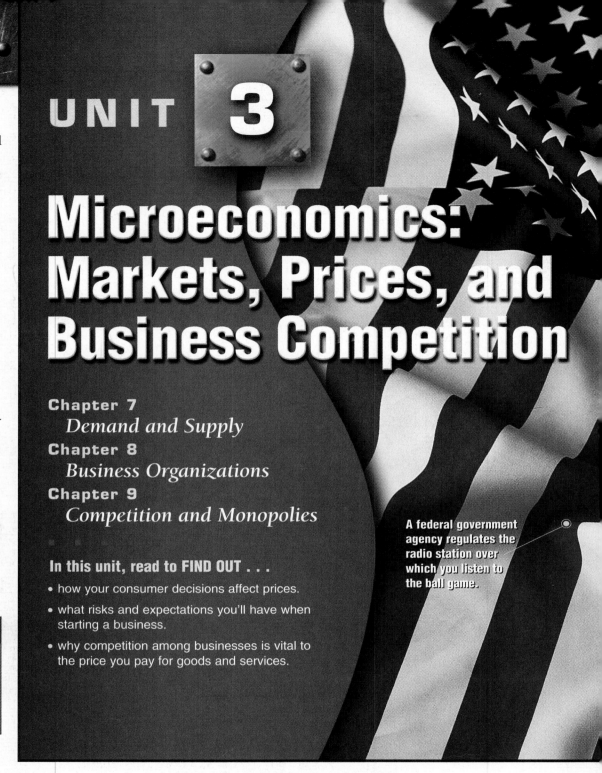

Rawlings® currently holds a monopoly on manufacturing all baseballs for major league and minor league teams.
Some major league owners form partnerships to buy their teams.
The price of these tickets was determined by the interaction of demand and supply.
A winning team often results in a shortage of game tickets.
NEW YORK YANKEES
167

# Introducing UNIT 3

## Making It Relevant

ASK: How much does a baseball glove cost? *Answers should vary, suggesting that prices for baseball gloves differ widely.* Discuss with students the possible reasons for the different prices. *(brand name, type of glove, type of store, quality of leather, and so on)*

Suggest to students that the price of a baseball glove depends on demand for that glove relative to supply. In turn, the other factors can influence demand. For example, advertising may increase demand for a particular brand name, thus affecting the price.

**BusinessWeek ONLINE**

To find up-to-date news and analysis on the economy, business, technology, markets, entrepreneurs, investments, and finance, have students search feature articles and special reports on the *Business Week* Web site.
www.businessweek.com

**EXTRA CREDIT PROJECT**

Choose a business in or near your community. Contact the business by phone or by letter and arrange for a visit and an interview. Explain that you want to find out how the business got started, how it is organized, how it determines consumer wants and needs, and what plans it has for the future. Obtain permission to take photographs of the business. Write a feature about the business and display it with your photographs on a classroom bulletin board.

# CHAPTER 7 Resource Manager

## Teaching Transparency

### Economic Concepts Transparency 8

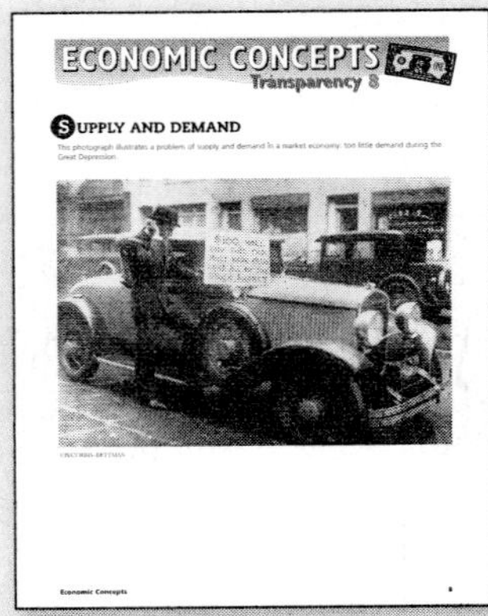
ECONOMIC CONCEPTS Transparency 8

SUPPLY AND DEMAND

## Application and Enrichment

### Enrichment Activity 7

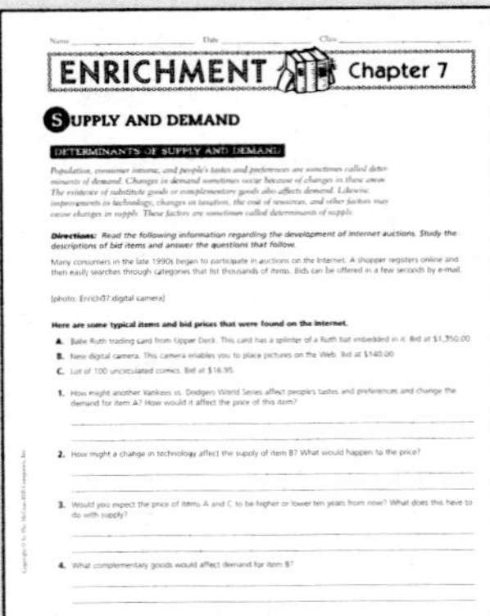
ENRICHMENT Chapter 7

SUPPLY AND DEMAND

### Consumer Applications Activity 5

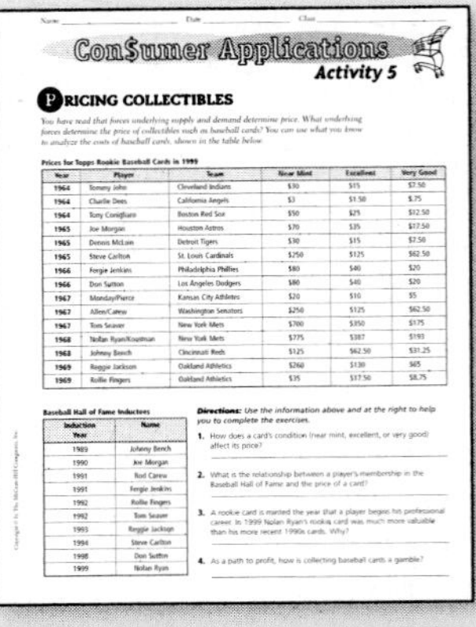
Con$umer Applications Activity 5

PRICING COLLECTIBLES

### Free Enterprise Activity 8

FREE ENTERPRISE ACTIVITY 8

SELLING ASSETS

## Application and Enrichment

### Cooperative Learning Simulations and Problems 4, 5

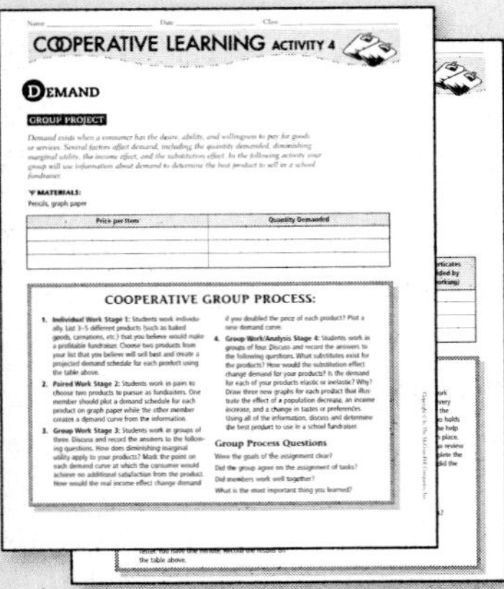
COOPERATIVE LEARNING ACTIVITY 4

DEMAND

COOPERATIVE GROUP PROCESS:

### Primary and Secondary Source Reading 5

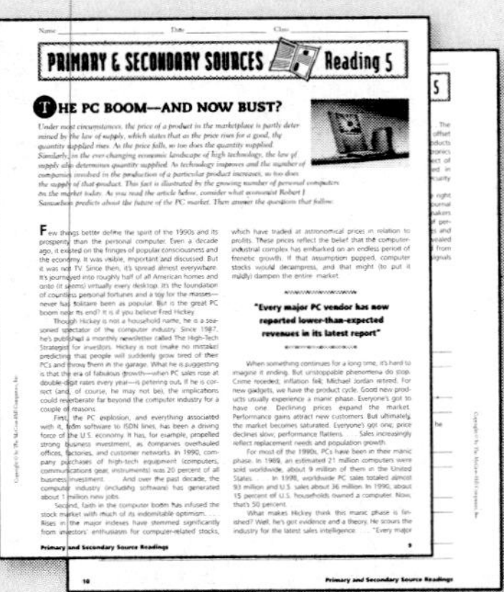
PRIMARY & SECONDARY SOURCES Reading 5

THE PC BOOM—AND NOW BUST?

"Every major PC vendor has now reported lower-than-expected revenues in its latest report"

### Math Practice for Economics Activities 4, 5

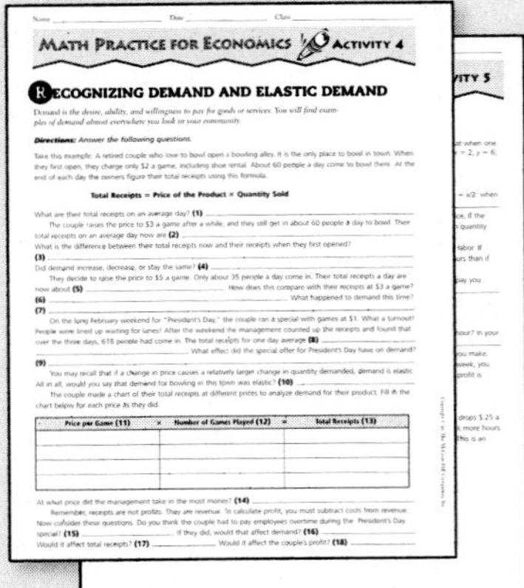
MATH PRACTICE FOR ECONOMICS ACTIVITY 4

RECOGNIZING DEMAND AND ELASTIC DEMAND

### Economic Cartoons Activities 4, 5

ECONOMIC CARTOON 4

DEMAND!

## Review and Reinforcement

### Critical Thinking Activities 4, 5

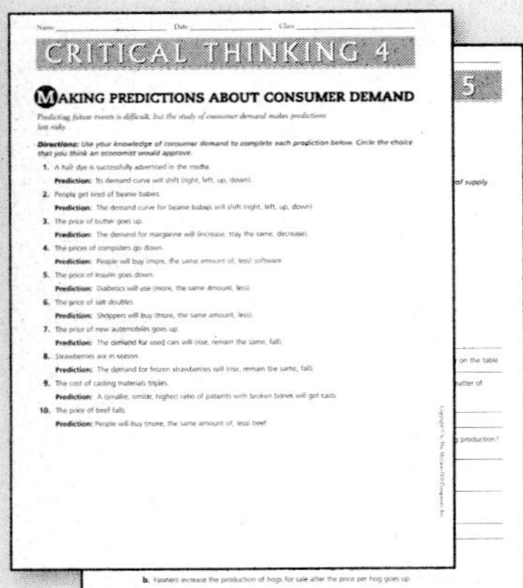
CRITICAL THINKING 4

MAKING PREDICTIONS ABOUT CONSUMER DEMAND

### Reteaching Activity 7

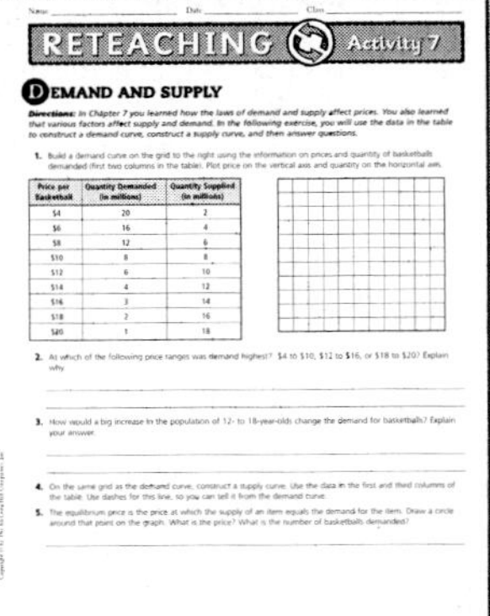
RETEACHING Activity 7

DEMAND AND SUPPLY

### Economic Vocabulary Activity 7

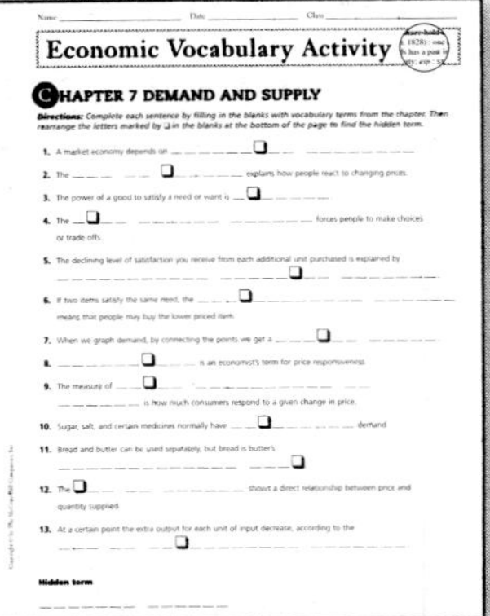
Economic Vocabulary Activity

CHAPTER 7 DEMAND AND SUPPLY

### Reinforcing Economic Skills 10

Reinforcing Economic Skills Chapter 10

UNDERSTANDING CAUSE AND EFFECT

# CHAPTER 7 Resource Manager

## Assessment and Evaluation

Chapter 7 Test Form A

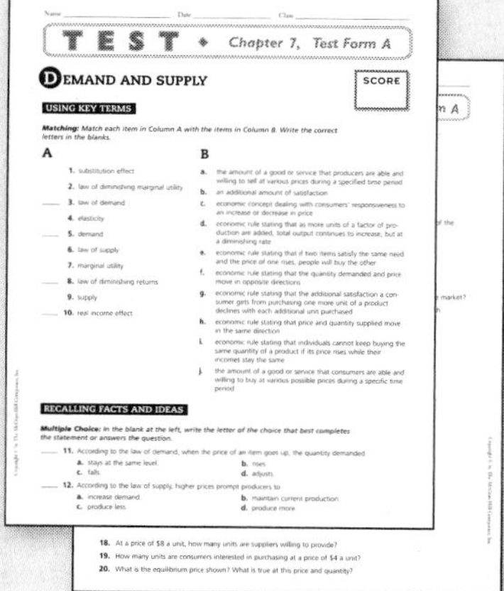

Chapter 7 Test Form B

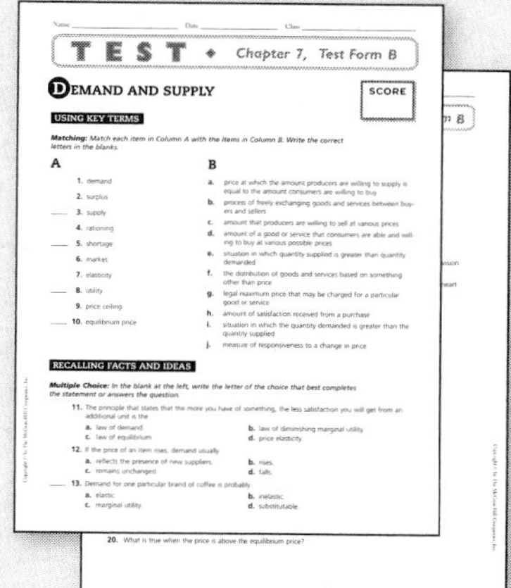

Performance Assessment Activities 4, 5

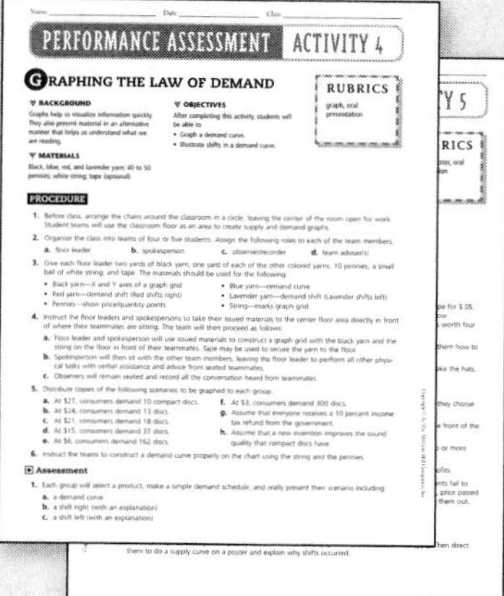

ExamView® Pro Testmaker

## Technology and Multimedia

 Vocabulary PuzzleMaker Software

 Interactive Tutor Self-Assessment Software

 ExamView® Pro Testmaker

 NBR *Economics & You* Video Program (English/Spanish)

 Presentation Plus!

 Glencoe Skillbuilder Interactive Workbook CD-ROM, Level 2

 Interactive Lesson Planner

 MindJogger Videoquiz

 Interactive Economics! CD-ROM

Audio Program (English or Spanish)

## ECONOMICS Online

You and your students can visit ett.glencoe.com—the Web site companion to **Economics Today and Tomorrow.** This innovative integration of electronic and print media offers your students a wealth of opportunities. The student text directs students to the Web site for the following options:

- **Chapter Overviews**
- **Self-Check Quizzes**
- **Student Web Activities**
- **Textbook Updates**

Answers are provided for you in the **Web Activity Lesson Plan.** Additional Web resources and Interactive Puzzles are also available.

Use the Glencoe Web site for additional resources. All essential content is covered in the Student Edition.

## Spanish Resources

 Spanish Economic Concepts Transparency 8

 Spanish Vocabulary Activity 7

 Spanish Reteaching Activity 7

 Spanish Section Quizzes for Chapter 7

 Spanish Chapter 7 Audio Program, Activity, and Test

## Additional Resources

### Reading for the Student

*Economic Activity and Markets.* Federal Reserve Bank of St. Louis. Explains how the economic activity of individuals is coordinated in producing goods and services.

### Reading for the Teacher

*Supply and Demand.* Gainesville, FL: Center for Economic Education, University of Florida, 1996. Provides ideas on how to teach supply and demand.

# CHAPTER 7 Resource Manager

## Section Resources

| Reading Objectives | Reproducible Resources | Technology/Multimedia Resources |
|---|---|---|
| **Section 1**<br>**Demand**<br>• How does the principle of voluntary exchange operate in a market economy?<br>• What does the law of demand state?<br>• How do the real income effect, the substitution effect, and diminishing marginal utility relate to the law of demand? | Reproducible Lesson Plan 7-1<br>Daily Lecture Notes 7-1<br>Guided Reading Activity 7-1<br>Reading Essentials and Study Guide 7-1<br>Daily Focus Activity 9<br>Section Quiz 7-1* | Daily Focus Transparency 9<br>Vocabulary PuzzleMaker<br>Interactive Tutor Self-Assessment Software<br>MindJogger Videoquiz<br>NBR's *Economics & You**<br>Interactive Economics!<br>Presentation Plus!<br>ExamView® Pro Testmaker |
| **Section 2**<br>**The Demand Curve and Elasticity of Demand**<br>• What does a demand curve show?<br>• What are the determinants of demand?<br>• How does the elasticity of demand affect the price of a given product? | Reproducible Lesson Plan 7-2<br>Daily Lecture Notes 7-2<br>Guided Reading Activity 7-2<br>Reading Essentials and Study Guide 7-2<br>Daily Focus Activity 10<br>Section Quiz 7-2* | Daily Focus Transparency 10<br>Vocabulary PuzzleMaker<br>Interactive Tutor Self-Assessment Software<br>MindJogger Videoquiz<br>NBR's *Economics & You**<br>Interactive Economics!<br>Presentation Plus!<br>ExamView® Pro Testmaker |
| **Section 3**<br>**The Law of Supply and the Supply Curve**<br>• What does the law of supply state?<br>• How does the incentive of greater profits affect quantity supplied?<br>• What do a supply schedule and supply curve show?<br>• What are the four determinants of supply? | Reproducible Lesson Plan 7-3<br>Daily Lecture Notes 7-3<br>Guided Reading Activity 7-3<br>Reading Essentials and Study Guide 7-3<br>Daily Focus Activity 13<br>Section Quiz 7-3*<br>Reinforcing Economic Skills 10 | Daily Focus Transparency 13<br>Vocabulary PuzzleMaker<br>Interactive Tutor Self-Assessment Software<br>MindJogger Videoquiz<br>NBR's *Economics & You**<br>Interactive Economics!<br>Presentation Plus!<br>ExamView® Pro Testmaker |
| **Section 4**<br>**Putting Supply and Demand Together**<br>• How is the equilibrium price determined?<br>• How do changes in equilibrium price occur?<br>• How do shortages and surpluses affect price?<br>• How do price ceilings and price floors restrict the free exchange of prices? | Reproducible Lesson Plan 7-4<br>Daily Lecture Notes 7-4<br>Guided Reading Activity 7-4<br>Reading Essentials and Study Guide 7-4<br>Daily Focus Activity 14<br>Section Quiz 7-4* | Daily Focus Transparency 14<br>Economic Concepts Transparency 8<br>Vocabulary PuzzleMaker<br>Interactive Tutor Self-Assessment Software<br>MindJogger Videoquiz<br>NBR's *Economics & You**<br>Interactive Economics!<br>Presentation Plus!<br>ExamView® Pro Testmaker |

*Also available in Spanish

Blackline Master
Transparency

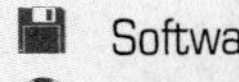
Software
CD-ROM

Videodisc

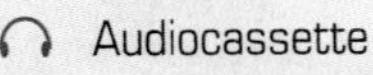
Audiocassette

Videocassette

# CHAPTER 7 Resource Manager

## ACTIVITY From the Classroom of

**Richard Joyce**
**Wilmington High School**
**Wilmington, Illinois**

### Demand, Supply, and the "Blinker" Test

Demand and supply curves shift to the left or right when demand or supply as a whole changes. To help students remember the direction of the change, use the "blinker" test. ASK: When driving a car, if you push the blinker (turn signal) control up, which way are you turning? *(right)* Remember that an increase in demand or supply always moves the curve to the right. ASK: Which way do you push the blinker (turn signal) control when you are turning left? *(down)* So when demand or supply decreases, the curve always shifts to the left. Repeat with the class "up to the right, down to the left."

## Easy Planning and Preparation!

Use Glencoe's **Presentation Plus!**, a Microsoft PowerPoint® application, to teach **Demand and Supply.** With this multimedia teacher tool, you can customize ready-made presentations. At your fingertips are interactive transparencies, on-screen lecture notes, audio-visual presentations, and links to the Internet and to other Glencoe multimedia.

### Interactive Lesson Planner

Planning has never been easier! Organize your week, month, semester, or year with all the lesson helps you need to make teaching creative, timely, and relevant—the way it is meant to be. The Interactive Lesson Planner opens Glencoe's **Chapter 7** resources, helps you build your schedule, and tracks your progress.

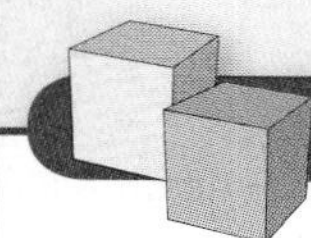

## Block Schedule

Activities that are particularly suited to use within the block scheduling framework are identified throughout this chapter by the following designation: BLOCK SCHEDULING

## Key to Ability Levels

**Teaching strategies have been coded for varying learning styles and abilities.**

L1 BASIC activities for all students
L2 AVERAGE activities for average to above-average students
L3 CHALLENGING activities for above-average students
ELL ENGLISH LANGUAGE LEARNER activities

## National Council on Economic Education

### THE EconomicsAmerica AND EconomicsInternational PROGRAMS

#### Voluntary Standards Emphasized in Chapter 7

**Content Standard 7** Students will understand that markets exist when buyers and sellers interact. This interaction determines market prices and thereby allocates scarce goods and services.

**Content Standard 8** Students will understand that prices send signals and provide incentives to buyers and sellers. When supply or demand changes, market prices adjust, affecting incentives.

#### Resources Available from NCEE

- *Focus: High School Economics*
- *MCG–Economics and Entrepreneurship*
- *Capstone: The Nation's High School Economics Course*

To order these materials, or to contact your State Council on Economic Education about workshops and programs, call 1-800-338-1192 or visit the NCEE Web site at http://www.nationalcouncil.org

*Introducing* CHAPTER 7

ECONOMICS & YOU

What Is Demand?

Chapter 5
Disc 1, Side 1

ASK: What is the law of demand? *When a product's price falls, consumers are more likely to buy it.*

Also available in VHS.

## Chapter Overview

Consumers base their decisions to buy goods and services on anticipated satisfaction, price, and their incomes. Businesses set prices according to the profit desired, the demand anticipated, and the competition expected. **Chapter** 7 discusses the laws of supply and demand and the ways in which a voluntary market affects them.

**GLENCOE TECHNOLOGY**

Use **MindJogger Videoquiz** VHS to preview Chapter 7 content.

Introduce students to chapter content and key terms by having them access **Chapter 7—Chapter Overviews** at *ett.glencoe.com*

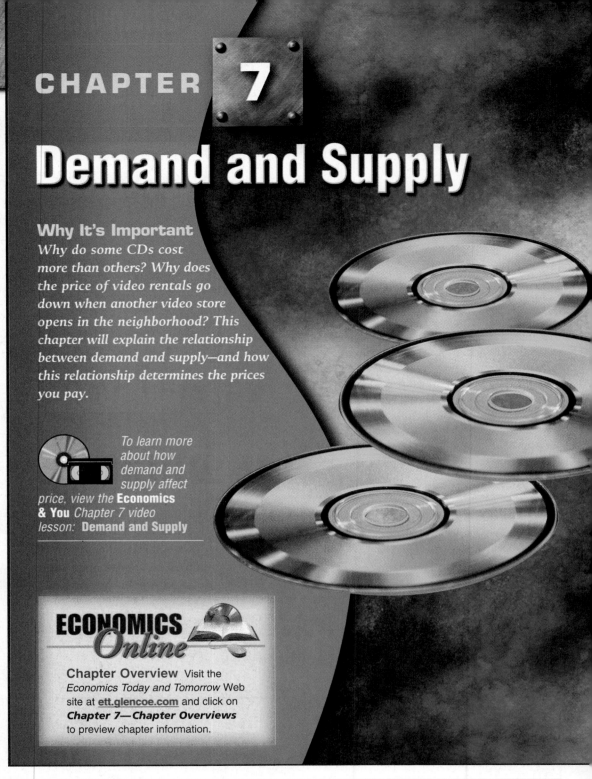

CHAPTER 7

# Demand and Supply

**Why It's Important**

*Why do some CDs cost more than others? Why does the price of video rentals go down when another video store opens in the neighborhood? This chapter will explain the relationship between demand and supply—and how this relationship determines the prices you pay.*

*To learn more about how demand and supply affect price, view the* **Economics & You** *Chapter 7 video lesson:* **Demand and Supply**

ECONOMICS Online

**Chapter Overview** Visit the *Economics Today and Tomorrow* Web site at ett.glencoe.com and click on ***Chapter 7—Chapter Overviews*** to preview chapter information.

## CHAPTER LAUNCH ACTIVITY

In 1998 the President of the United States earned a salary of $200,000 plus a $50,000 expense account. That same year Mike Piazza signed a seven-year contract to play baseball for the New York Mets for $13 million per year—more than 50 times the President's annual salary. **ASK: Why do major league players get paid higher salaries than the President of the United States?** Discuss the effects of demand for and supply of skilled players. Point out nonfinancial incentives for a person to run for the presidency (leadership, political objectives, service to nation). Contrast public and private sector salaries and discuss reasons for the disparity.

SECTION  1 Demand

## Cover Story

*Business Week*, February 15, 1999

The morning after the *Delia's* catalog arrives, the halls of Paxton High School in Jacksonville, Florida, are buzzing. That's when all the girls bring in their copies from home and compare notes.

"Everyone loves *Delia's*," says Emily Garfinkle, 15. "It's the big excitement."

If you've never heard of *Delia's*, chances are you don't know a girl between 12 and 17. The New York cataloger, with a database of 4 million names, has become one of the hottest names in retailing by selling downtown fashion to girls everywhere.

### Reader's Guide

**Terms to Know**

- demand
- supply
- market
- voluntary exchange
- law of demand
- quantity demanded
- real income effect
- substitution effect
- utility
- marginal utility
- law of diminishing marginal utility

**Reading Objectives**

1. How does the principle of voluntary exchange operate in a market economy?
2. What does the law of demand state?
3. How do the real income effect, the substitution effect, and diminishing marginal utility relate to the law of demand?

The word *demand* has a special meaning in economics. *Delia's* catalog may be sent to 4 million people, but that doesn't mean 4 million people demand clothes from the retailer. Many girls may *want* to order items from the catalog. As you read this section, however, you'll learn that demand includes only those people who are willing *and* able to pay for a product or service.

## The "Marketplace"

When you buy something, do you ever wonder why it sells at that particular price? Few individual consumers feel they have any influence over the price of an item. In a market economy,





## 1 Focus

### Overview

Section 1 explains or describes the principle of voluntary exchange as it applies to a market economy, and how the real income effect, the substitution effect, and diminishing marginal utility each alter quantity demanded.

### BELLRINGER
**Motivational Activity**

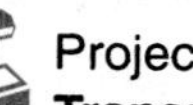

Project **Daily Focus Transparency 9** and have students answer the questions.

This activity is also available as a blackline master.

**Daily Focus Transparency 9**

FOCUS ACTIVITIES Transparency 9

WHAT DETERMINES CHANGES IN DEMAND?

1. How will demand change if you think these products are going out of style?
2. How would the lower prices of substitute goods affect the demand for the products shown here?

Daily Focus Transparencies

### Reader's Guide

Answers to the **Reading Objectives** questions are on page 175.

**Preteaching Vocabulary**

Ask students to work in small groups to create improvisational scenes about buying goods in a store. Each scene should illustrate one of the **Terms to Know**.

Vocabulary PuzzleMaker

### SECTION 1 RESOURCE MANAGER

**Reproducible Masters**

- Reproducible Lesson Plan 7–1
- Reading Essentials and Study Guide 7–1
- Guided Reading Activity 7–1
- Section Quiz 7–1
- Daily Focus Activity 9
- Daily Lecture Notes 7–1

**Multimedia**

- Daily Focus Transparency 9
- Vocabulary PuzzleMaker
- Interactive Tutor Self-Assessment Software
- ExamView® Pro Testmaker
- MindJogger Videoquiz
- NBR's *Economics & You*
- Interactive Economics!
- Presentation Plus!

# 2 Teach

## Guided Practice

**L1** Classifying Encourage students to discuss the reasons for the choices they made during their most recent purchases. Have them tell whether the reasons came under the real income effect, the substitution effect, or the law of diminishing marginal utility.

**Daily Lecture Notes 7-1**

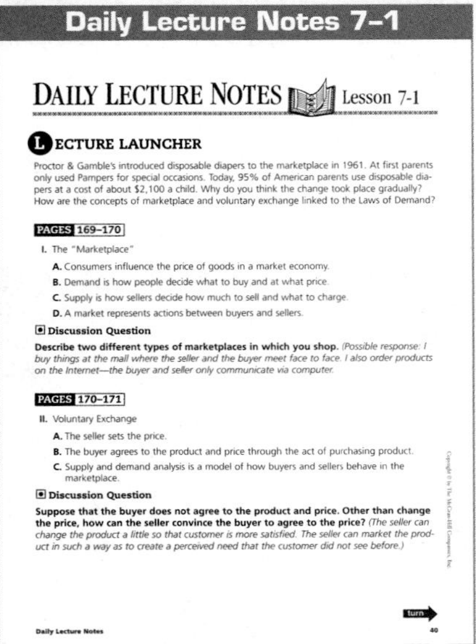

DAILY LECTURE NOTES Lesson 7-1

**LECTURE LAUNCHER**

Proctor & Gamble's introduced disposable diapers to the marketplace in 1961. At first parents only used Pampers for special occasions. Today, 95% of American parents use disposable diapers at a cost of about $2,100 a child. Why do you think the change took place gradually? How are the concepts of marketplace and voluntary exchange linked to the Laws of Demand?

**PAGES 169–170**

I. The "Marketplace"
   - **A.** Consumers influence the price of goods in a market economy.
   - **B.** Demand is how people decide what to buy and at what price.
   - **C.** Supply is how sellers decide how much to sell and what to charge.
   - **D.** A market represents actions between buyers and sellers.

**Discussion Question**

**Describe two different types of marketplaces in which you shop.** *(Possible response: I buy things at the mall where the seller and the buyer meet face to face. I also order products on the Internet—the buyer and seller only communicate via computer.*

**PAGES 170–171**

II. Voluntary Exchange
   - **A.** The seller sets the price.
   - **B.** The buyer agrees to the product and price through the act of purchasing product.
   - **C.** Supply and demand analysis is a model of how buyers and sellers behave in the marketplace.

**Discussion Question**

**Suppose that the buyer does not agree to the product and price. Other than change the price, how can the seller convince the buyer to agree to the price?** *(The seller can change the product a little so that customer is more satisfied. The seller can market the product in such a way as to create a perceived need that the customer did not see before.)*



turn

Daily Lecture Notes 40

**Visual Instruction FIGURE 7.1**

Call on volunteers to identify other examples of local, national, and international markets. **Answer:** *voluntary exchange*

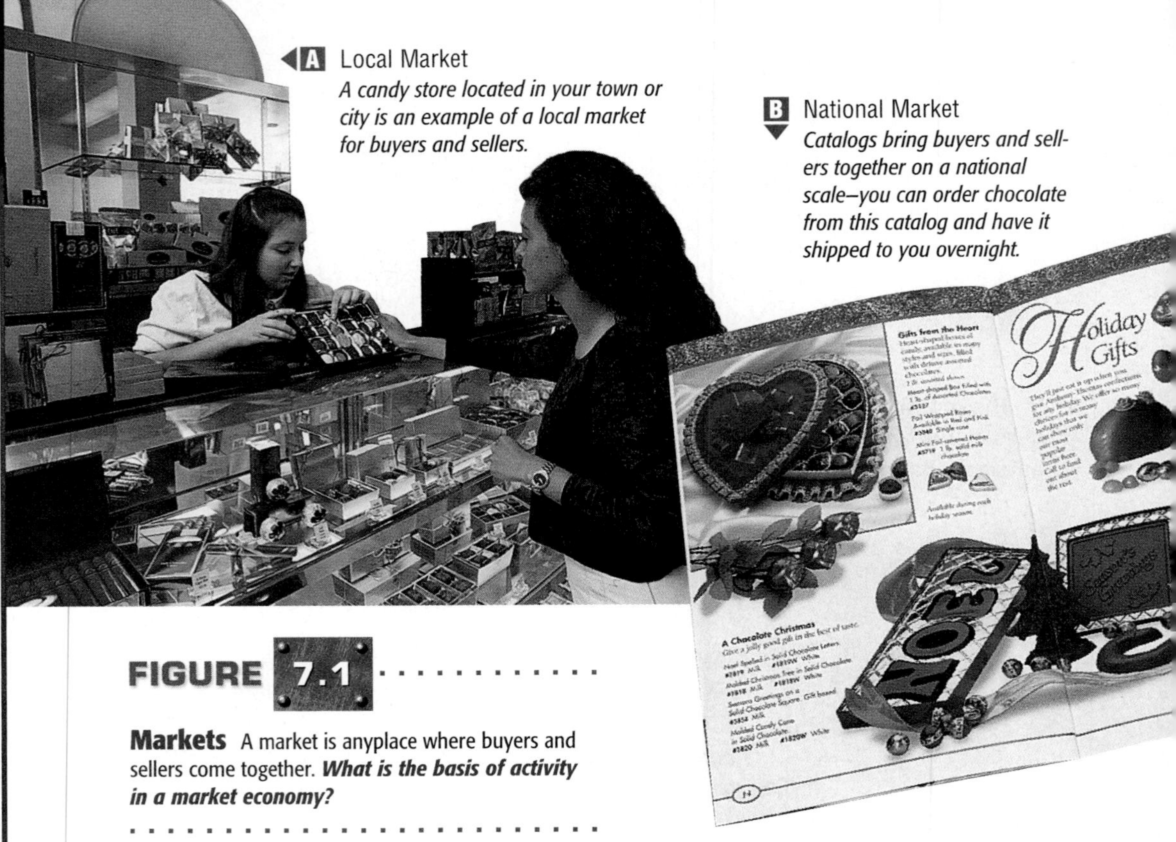


**A** Local Market *A candy store located in your town or city is an example of a local market for buyers and sellers.*

**B** National Market *Catalogs bring buyers and sellers together on a national scale—you can order chocolate from this catalog and have it shipped to you overnight.*

**FIGURE 7.1**

**Markets** A market is anyplace where buyers and sellers come together. ***What is the basis of activity in a market economy?***

**demand:** *the amount of a good or service that consumers are able and willing to buy at various possible prices during a specified time period*

**supply:** *the amount of a good or service that producers are able and willing to sell at various prices during a specified time period*

**market:** *the process of freely exchanging goods and services between buyers and sellers*

**voluntary exchange:** *a transaction in which a buyer and a seller exercise their economic freedom by working out their own terms of exchange*

however, all consumers individually and collectively have a great influence on the price of all goods and services. To understand this, let's look first at how people in the marketplace decide what to buy and at what price. This is **demand.** Then we'll examine how the people who want to sell those things decide how much to sell and at what price. This is **supply.**

What is the marketplace? A **market** represents the freely chosen actions between buyers and sellers of goods and services. As **Figure 7.1** shows, a market for a particular item can be local, national, international, or a combination of these. In a market economy, individuals—whether as buyers or sellers—decide for themselves the answers to the WHAT?, HOW?, and FOR WHOM? economic questions you studied in Chapter 2.

## Voluntary Exchange

The basis of activity in a market economy is the principle of **voluntary exchange.** A buyer and a



### Meeting Special Needs

**English Language Learners** Students with limited English vocabularies may have difficulty understanding phrases such as "real income effect," "substitution effect," and "diminishing marginal utility." Write the phrases on the board, and have student volunteers draw illustrations with stick figures under each phrase that visualize these concepts. **ELL**

Refer to *Inclusion for the Social Studies Classroom Strategies and Activities* for students with different learning styles.

**C** International Market *The World Wide Web has helped create a massive international market. Chocolate lovers anywhere in the world can order chocolate in seconds from this Swiss manufacturer.*

seller exercise their economic freedom by working toward satisfactory terms of an exchange. For example, the seller of an automobile sets a price based on his or her view of market conditions, and the buyer, through the act of buying, agrees to the product and the price. In order to make the exchange, both the buyer and the seller must believe they will be better off–richer or happier–after the exchange than before.

The supplier's problem of what to charge and the buyer's problem of how much to pay is solved voluntarily in the market exchange. Supply and demand analysis is a model of how buyers and sellers operate in the marketplace. Such analysis is a way of explaining cause and effect in relation to price.

## The Law of Demand

*Demand,* in economic terms, represents all of the different quantities of a good or service that consumers will purchase at various prices. It includes both the willingness and the ability to pay. A person may say he or she wants a new CD. Until that person is both willing *and able* to buy it, however, no demand for CDs has been created by that individual.

The law of demand explains how people react to changing prices in terms of the quantities demanded of a good or service. There is an *inverse,* or opposite, relationship between quantity demanded and price. The **law of demand** states:

*As price goes up, quantity demanded goes down.*
*As price goes down, quantity demanded goes up.*

**law of demand:** *economic rule stating that the quantity demanded and price move in opposite directions*



**L2 Analyzing** Ask students how many soft drinks they would buy at 25¢ a can, at 50¢, at $1, at $1.50, and so on. Note prices and quantities on the board. Then ask students to write a generalization about demand based on these figures. *As price rises, quantity demanded decreases.*

### Guided Reading Activity 7-1

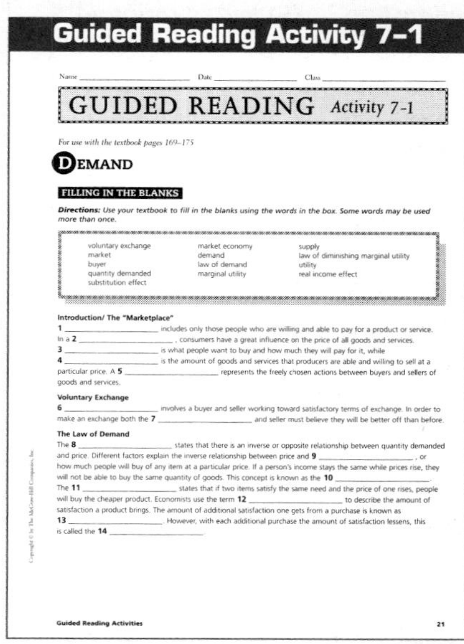

Name ____________ Date ____________ Class ____________

GUIDED READING Activity 7-1

*For use with the textbook pages 169–175*

DEMAND

FILLING IN THE BLANKS

***Directions:*** *Use your textbook to fill in the blanks using the words in the box. Some words may be used more than once.*

| | | |
|---|---|---|
| voluntary exchange | market economy | supply |
| market | demand | law of diminishing marginal utility |
| buyer | law of demand | utility |
| quantity demanded | marginal utility | real income effect |
| substitution effect | | |

**Introduction/ The "Marketplace"**

**1** ____________ includes only those people who are willing and able to pay for a product or service. In a **2** ____________, consumers have a great influence on the price of all goods and services. **3** ____________ is what people want to buy and how much they will pay for it, while **4** ____________ is the amount of goods and services that producers are able and willing to sell at a particular price. A **5** ____________ represents the freely chosen actions between buyers and sellers of goods and services.

**Voluntary Exchange**

**6** ____________ involves a buyer and seller working toward satisfactory terms of exchange. In order to make an exchange both the **7** ____________ and seller must believe they will be better off than before.

**The Law of Demand**

The **8** ____________ states that there is an inverse or opposite relationship between quantity demanded and price. Different factors explain the inverse relationship between price and **9** ____________, or how much people will buy of any item at a particular price. If a person's income stays the same while prices rise, they will not be able to buy the same quantity of goods. This concept is known as the **10** ____________. The **11** ____________ states that if two items satisfy the same need and the price of one rises, people will buy the cheaper product. Economists use the term **12** ____________ to describe the amount of satisfaction a product brings. The amount of additional satisfaction one gets from a purchase is known as **13** ____________. However, with each additional purchase the amount of satisfaction lessens, this is called the **14** ____________

Guided Reading Activities 21

### Cooperative Learning

Organize students in teams of three to play the "Up or Down?" game. Select two teams and give each team member a flash card on which a large arrow is drawn. Present scenarios—for example, the price of CDs goes up, but income remains the same—then ask, "Will quantity demanded go up or go down?" Team members should display their flash cards with the arrow pointing in the correct direction. If any team member displays the flash card incorrectly, that team is disqualified, and a new team joins the game. Continue the game until all teams have competed.

ECONOMICS & YOU

What Is Demand?

Chapter 5
Disc 1, Side 1

ASK: What is the law of demand? *The law of demand states that as prices fall, the quantity of a product demanded increases.*

Also available in VHS.

## Independent Practice

**L2 Cartooning** Have students create cartoons that show how people in different occupations might affect demand for goods and services in different ways. Encourage students to display their cartoons around the classroom. ELL

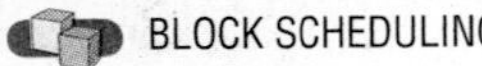
BLOCK SCHEDULING

**quantity demanded:** *the amount of a good or service that a consumer is willing and able to purchase at a specific price*

Several factors explain the inverse relation between price and **quantity demanded,** or how much people will buy of any item at a particular price. These factors include real income, possible substitutes, and diminishing marginal utility.

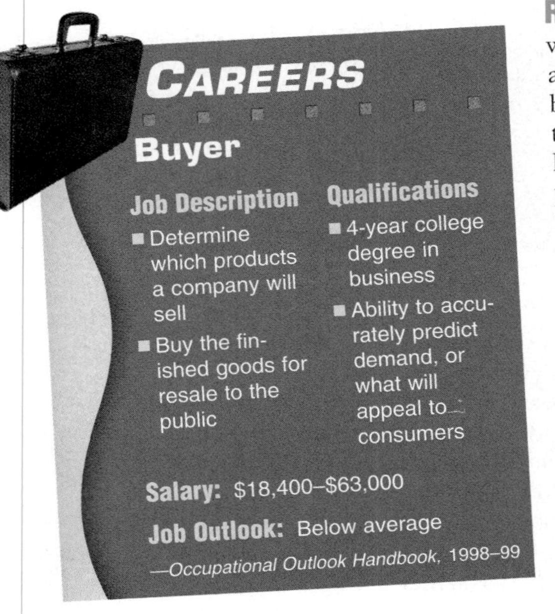

CAREERS
Buyer
Job Description
■ Determine which products a company will sell
■ Buy the finished goods for resale to the public
Qualifications
■ 4-year college degree in business
■ Ability to accurately predict demand, or what will appeal to consumers
Salary: $18,400–$63,000
Job Outlook: Below average
—Occupational Outlook Handbook, 1998–99


**Real Income Effect** No one—not even the wealthiest person in the world—will ever be able to buy everything he or she might possibly want. People's incomes limit the amount they are able to spend. Individuals cannot keep buying the same quantity of a good if its price rises while their income stays the same. This concept is known as the **real income effect** on demand.

**real income effect:** *economic rule stating that individuals cannot keep buying the same quantity of a product if its price rises while their income stays the same*

Suppose that you normally fill your car's gas tank twice a month, spending $15 each time. This means you spend $30 per month on gasoline. If the price of gasoline rises, you may have to spend $40 per month. If the price continues to rise while your income does not, eventually you will not be able to fill the gas tank twice per month because your *real income,* or purchasing power, has been reduced. In order to keep buying the same amount of gasoline, you would need to cut back on buying other things. The real income effect forces you to make a trade-off in your gasoline purchases. The same is true for every item you buy, particularly those you buy on a regular basis. See **Figure 7.2.**

**Substitution Effect** Suppose there are two items that are not exactly the same but which satisfy basically the same need. Their cost is about the same. If the price of one falls, people will most likely buy it instead of the other, now higher-priced, good. If the price of one rises in relation to the price of the other, people will buy the now lower-priced good. This principle is called the **substitution effect.**

**substitution effect:** *economic rule stating that if two items satisfy the same need and the price of one rises, people will buy the other*

Suppose, for example, that you listen to both CDs and audiocassettes. If the price of audiocassettes drops dramatically, you will probably buy more cassettes and fewer CDs. Alternately, if the price of audiocassettes doubles, you will probably increase the number of CDs you buy in relation to cassettes. If the price of both CDs *and* audiocassettes increases, you may decide to purchase other music substitutes such as concert tickets or music videos.



## Extending the Content

**Marginal Utility** In some ways, marginal utility frustrated early economists because they wanted a numerical measure of utility, much like prices or quantity demanded. They tried a hypothetical measure called a *util,* but they soon had to abandon any notions of exact measurement because utility is so subjective. To illustrate, if 20 people were asked how much satisfaction they received from a second glass of lemonade, each one would give a different answer. Economists later developed the concept of indifference curves (a topic usually covered in college classes), which can be used to derive all of the propositions in economics without having to actually measure utility.

## Economic Connection to... *Literature*

# Tom Sawyer Creates Demand

Author Mark Twain introduced a different twist on the meaning of *demand* in his story "The Glorious Whitewasher." Tom Sawyer is forced to whitewash his aunt's fence. To convince other boys to do the work, Tom pretends to find it enjoyable and to consider it a special privilege. The other boys end up paying Tom to let them whitewash the fence:

*Tom said to himself that it was not such a hollow world, after all. He had discovered a great law of human action, without knowing it—namely, that in order to make a man or a boy covet* [demand] *a thing, it is only necessary to make the thing difficult to attain.* ■

—From *The Adventures of Tom Sawyer,* 1876

**Diminishing Marginal Utility** Almost everything that people like, desire, use, or think they would like to use, gives satisfaction. The term that economists use for satisfaction is *utility.* **Utility** is defined as the power that a good or service has to satisfy a want. Based on utility, people decide what to buy and how much they are willing and able to pay. In deciding to make a purchase, they decide the amount of satisfaction, or use, they think they will get from a good or service.

**utility:** *the ability of any good or service to satisfy consumer wants*

Consider the utility that can be derived from buying a cold soft drink at a baseball game on a hot day. At $3 per cup, how many will you buy? Assuming that you have some

**FIGURE 7.2**

**Real Income Effect** If the price of gasoline rises but your income does not, you obviously cannot continue buying the same amount of gas AND everything else you normally purchase. The real income effect can work in the opposite direction, too. If you are already buying two fill-ups a month and the price of gasoline drops in half, your real income then increases. You will have more purchasing power and will probably increase your spending.

**L3 Business Planning** Have students develop plans to increase demand for a given item or service. Have them include in their plans the pitfalls, risks, and trade-offs they foresee and the measures they suggest to deal with them.

**INTERACTIVE ECONOMICS!**

**LESSON 3: DEMAND**

Have students review "A Change in Demand" and "A Change in the Quantity Demanded." Then have them draw two graphs—one showing a change in quantity demanded, the other showing a change in demand.

Supplied in both CD-ROM and disk formats.

**Visual Instruction FIGURE 7.2**

Ask students to consider how their purchasing decisions might be affected if the two fill-ups provided just enough gasoline to drive to and from work during the month. *Students will note that they will need to buy less of other items.*

## Extending the Content

**William Stanley Jevons** The first person to propose the theory of marginal utility was English economist William Stanley Jevons in his book *The Theory of Political Economy* (1871). Jevons illustrated diminishing marginal utility with the example of food. Assume that a person's daily food intake is divided into 10 parts, Jevons said. The first part is very important to the person, for without it he or she would starve. The second provides satisfaction, but not as much as the first, and so on, up to the tenth part. "Each increment of food is less necessary, or possesses less utility, than the previous one," Jevons concluded.

# 3 Assess

## Meeting Lesson Objectives

Assign Section 1 Assessment as homework or an in-class activity.

Use **Interactive Tutor Self-Assessment Software** to review Section 1.

**Section Quiz 7-1**

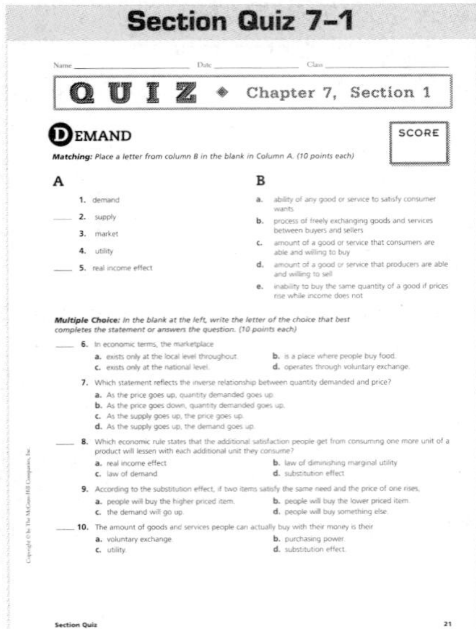

Name ______ Date ______ Class ______

**QUIZ** ◆ Chapter 7, Section 1

**DEMAND** SCORE

***Matching:*** *Place a letter from column B in the blank in Column A. (10 points each)*

**A**

**1.** demand
____ **2.** supply
**3.** market
**4.** utility
____ **5.** real income effect

**B**

**a.** ability of any good or service to satisfy consumer wants
**b.** process of freely exchanging goods and services between buyers and sellers
**c.** amount of a good or service that consumers are able and willing to buy
**d.** amount of a good or service that producers are able and willing to sell
**e.** inability to buy the same quantity of a good if prices rise while income does not

***Multiple Choice:*** *In the blank at the left, write the letter of the choice that best completes the statement or answers the question. (10 points each)*

____ **6.** In economic terms, the marketplace
**a.** exists only at the local level throughout. **b.** is a place where people buy food.
**c.** exists only at the national level. **d.** operates through voluntary exchange.

**7.** Which statement reflects the inverse relationship between quantity demanded and price?
**a.** As the price goes up, quantity demanded goes up.
**b.** As the price goes down, quantity demanded goes up.
**c.** As the supply goes up, the price goes up.
**d.** As the supply goes up, the demand goes up.

____ **8.** Which economic rule states that the additional satisfaction people get from consuming one more unit of a product will lessen with each additional unit they consume?
**a.** real income effect **b.** law of diminishing marginal utility
**c.** law of demand **d.** substitution effect

**9.** According to the substitution effect, if two items satisfy the same need and the price of one rises,
**a.** people will buy the higher priced item. **b.** people will buy the lower priced item.
**c.** the demand will go up. **d.** people will buy something else.

____ **10.** The amount of goods and services people can actually buy with their money is their
**a.** voluntary exchange. **b.** purchasing power.
**c.** utility. **d.** substitution effect.



Section Quiz 21

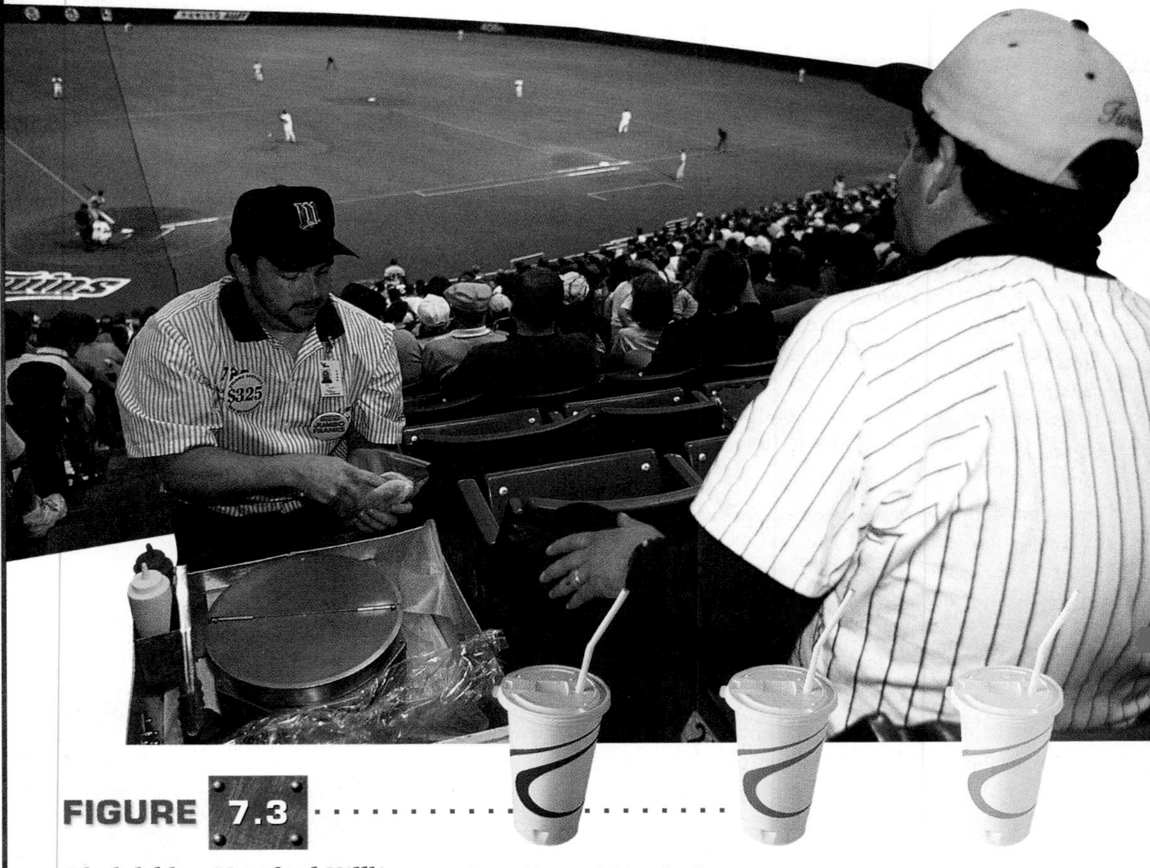

**FIGURE 7.3**

**Diminishing Marginal Utility** Regardless of how satisfying the first taste of an item is, satisfaction declines with additional consumption. Assume, for example, that at a price of $3.25 per hot dog, you have enough after buying three. Thus, the value you place on additional satisfaction from a fourth hot dog would be less than $3.25. According to what will give you the most satisfaction, you will save or spend the $3.25 on something else. Eventually you would receive no additional satisfaction, even if a vendor offered the product at zero price.

**marginal utility:** *an additional amount of satisfaction*

**law of diminishing marginal utility:** *rule stating that the additional satisfaction a consumer gets from purchasing one more unit of a product will lessen with each additional unit purchased*

money, you will buy at least one. Will you buy a second one? A third one? A fifth one? That decision depends on the additional utility, or satisfaction, you expect to receive from each additional soft drink. Your *total* satisfaction will rise with each one bought. The amount of *additional* satisfaction, or **marginal utility,** will diminish, or lessen, with each additional cup, however. This example illustrates the **law of diminishing marginal utility.**



## Cooperative Learning

Point out to students that businesses sometimes engage in price wars to attract consumers. Then organize students into several groups and ask groups to research recent price wars in the gasoline or airline industries to discover the impact on demand. Encourage groups to present their findings in illustrated reports.

At some point, you will stop buying soft drinks. Perhaps you don't want to wait in the concession line anymore. Perhaps your stomach cannot handle another soft drink. Just the thought of another cola makes you nauseated. At that point, the satisfaction that you receive from the soft drink is less than the value you place on the $3 that you must pay. As **Figure 7.3** shows, people stop buying an item when one event occurs—when the satisfaction from the next unit of the same item becomes less than the price they must pay for it.

What if the price drops? Suppose the owner of the ballpark decided to sell soft drinks for $2 each after the fifth inning. You might buy at least one additional soft drink. Why? If you look at the law of diminishing marginal utility again, the reason becomes clear. People will buy an item to the point at which the satisfaction from the last unit bought is equal to the price. At that point, people will stop buying. This concept explains part of the law of demand. As the price of an item decreases, people will generally buy more.

**Practice** and **assess** key skills with *Skillbuilder Interactive Workbook, Level 2.*

## SECTION 1 Assessment

### Understanding Key Terms

1. **Define** demand, supply, market, voluntary exchange, law of demand, quantity demanded, real income effect, substitution effect, utility, marginal utility, law of diminishing marginal utility.

### Reviewing Objectives

2. How does the principle of voluntary exchange operate in a market economy?
3. What is the law of demand?
4. **Graphic Organizer** Create a chart like the one in the next column to show how an increase and decrease in real income, the price of substitutes, and utility influence the quantity demanded for a given product or service.

| Cause | Effect on Quantity Demanded |
|---|---|
| | |
| | |
| | |

### Applying Economic Concepts

5. **Diminishing Marginal Utility** Describe an instance in your own life when diminishing marginal utility caused you to decrease your quantity demanded of a product or service.

### Critical Thinking Activity

6. **Making Predictions** Imagine that you sell popcorn at the local football stadium. Knowing about diminishing marginal utility, how would you price your popcorn after half-time?





## Reteach

Draw a seesaw on the board. Ask students to write a brief explanation of how a seesaw illustrates the relationship between price and quantity demanded.

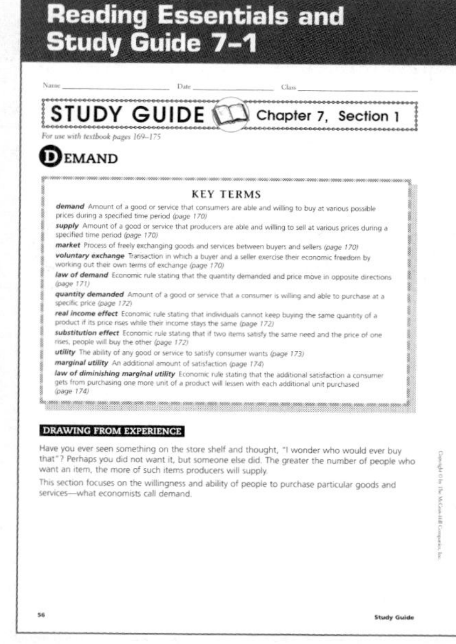

**Reading Essentials and Study Guide 7–1**

Name ______ Date ______ Class ______

STUDY GUIDE Chapter 7, Section 1

*For use with textbook pages 169–175*

DEMAND

KEY TERMS

***demand*** Amount of a good or service that consumers are able and willing to buy at various possible prices during a specified time period *(page 170)*

***supply*** Amount of a good or service that producers are able and willing to sell at various prices during a specified time period *(page 170)*

***market*** Process of freely exchanging goods and services between buyers and sellers *(page 170)*

***voluntary exchange*** Transaction in which a buyer and a seller exercise their economic freedom by working out their own terms of exchange *(page 170)*

***law of demand*** Economic rule stating that the quantity demanded and price move in opposite directions *(page 171)*

***quantity demanded*** Amount of a good or service that a consumer is willing and able to purchase at a specific price *(page 172)*

***real income effect*** Economic rule stating that individuals cannot keep buying the same quantity of a product if its price rises while their income stays the same *(page 172)*

***substitution effect*** Economic rule stating that if two items satisfy the same need and the price of one rises, people will buy the other *(page 172)*

***utility*** The ability of any good or service to satisfy consumer wants *(page 173)*

***marginal utility*** An additional amount of satisfaction *(page 174)*

***law of diminishing marginal utility*** Economic rule stating that the additional satisfaction a consumer gets from purchasing one more unit of a product will lessen with each additional unit purchased *(page 174)*

DRAWING FROM EXPERIENCE

Have you ever seen something on the store shelf and thought, "I wonder who would ever buy that"? Perhaps you did not want it, but someone else did. The greater the number of people who want an item, the more of such items producers will supply.

This section focuses on the willingness and ability of people to purchase particular goods and services—what economists call demand.



56 Study Guide

## 4 Close

Have students write an example from personal experience of how price, real income, or the substitution effect changed their decision to buy a good or service.

## SECTION 1 Assessment Answers

1. All definitions can be found in the Glossary.
2. Buyers and sellers work out their own terms of exchange.
3. The law of demand states that there is an inverse relationship between quantity demanded and price.
4. increase in real income=increase in quantity demanded; decrease in real income=decrease in quantity demanded; price of substitute goes up=quantity demanded of other item goes up; price of substitute goes down=quantity demanded of other item goes down; utility increases=quantity demanded increases; utility decreases=quantity demanded decreases
5. Answers will vary but should indicate that students understand that diminishing marginal utility is the lower level of satisfaction resulting from additional purchases.
6. Students should suggest that the price of popcorn could be reduced after half-time.

BusinessWeek
**Spotlight**

# Teach

As students read the article, have them identify four characteristics of Millard S. Drexler that they believe make him a successful entrepreneur. *(attention to detail, hands-on style, imagination, marketing knowledge, friendly–likes to talk to customers and clerks)*

ASK: What other personal characteristics might help make an entrepreneur successful?

**BusinessWeek ONLINE**

To find up-to-date news and analysis on the economy, business, technology, markets, entrepreneurs, investments, and finance, have students search feature articles and special reports on the *Business Week* Web site. www.businessweek.com

**Sidelight**

Gap began in 1979 as a small retail clothing marketer in Boise, Idaho. The first clothing that Gap sold was made of denim and wool—suitable for the tough Idaho winters.

# BusinessWeek

## Spotlight on the Economy

## Daddy GAP

**Check It Out!** **In this chapter you learned how demand can increase as tastes and preferences change. In the following article, read to learn how one entrepreneur was successful in increasing demand for Gap clothing.**

By the way he talks, you'd think Millard S. Drexler was the chief of some fragile startup instead of the CEO at powerhouse apparel retailer Gap Inc. Virtually no detail—from window displays to fabric blends—is too minute to escape the 54-year-old's attention. Every week, Drexler strolls anonymously into Gap stores from coast to coast to schmooze with consumers and clerks alike in a constant drive to improve the company's products and services.

This hands-on style has been Drexler's trademark since he took the helm at Gap in 1995. Never mind that he runs a company of 81,000 workers in one of the most mature industries around. To Drexler, Gap is still a fledgling. "We are limited only by our imagination," he says.

Old Navy beachwear

Imagination is something that Drexler, known for his marketing and merchandising savvy, has plenty of. In a cluttered marketplace, he has managed to create distinct identities for Gap, Banana Republic, and Old Navy brands. Memorable TV ads over the past years include "jump and jive" dancers for Gap and zany spots for Old Navy.

Banana Republic dress shirts

All that has helped Gap soar, reversing the flat performance of the early '90s even when many other retailers have struggled. Thanks to strong showings at all of its divisions, Gap is expected to earn $775 million, up 45% from last year, on estimated revenues of $8.8 billion in 1998. And then there's Gap's success on the Internet. Experts say Gap has one of the most popular shopping sites around.

### *Think About It*

1. **How did Drexler create distinct identities for his brands?**
2. **What evidence in the article shows Drexler's fear of his customers' tastes and preferences moving away from Gap?**

Millard S. Drexler



### Answers to *Think About It*

1. He used unique television advertising to identify his brands.
2. He likes to walk around his stores and talk with customers and clerks, and he pays attention to details like window displays and fabric blends.

SECTION 2

# The Demand Curve and Elasticity of Demand

## Cover Story

*The Washington Post*, November 30, 1998

America's biggest export is . . . its pop culture—movies, TV programs, music, books and computer software.

. . . The McDonald's restaurants that are opening at a rate of six a day around the world, the baggy jeans and baseball caps that have become a global teenage uniform, the Barbie dolls and Hot Wheels increasingly demanded by children, are all seen as part of the same U.S. invasion.

### Reader's Guide

**Terms to Know**

- demand schedule
- demand curve
- complementary good
- elasticity
- price elasticity of demand
- elastic demand
- inelastic demand

**Reading Objectives**

1. What does a demand curve show?
2. What are the determinants of demand?
3. How does the elasticity of demand affect the price of a given product?

In Section 1 you learned that quantity demanded is based on price. Sometimes, however, more of a particular product is demanded at almost every possible price. Think about it. If Hot Wheels toy cars are placed for sale in the international market, more will be demanded at each and every price offered. We then say that demand for Hot Wheels has increased.

## Graphing the Demand Curve

How can you learn to distinguish between quantity demanded and demand? And how do economists show these relationships



## Section 2 Resource Manager

**Reproducible Masters**

- Reproducible Lesson Plan 7–2
- Reading Essentials and Study Guide 7–2
- Guided Reading Activity 7–2
- Section Quiz 7–2
- Daily Focus Activity 10
- Daily Lecture Notes 7–2

**Multimedia**

- Daily Focus Transparency 10
- Vocabulary PuzzleMaker
- Interactive Tutor Self-Assessment Software
- ExamView® Pro Testmaker
- MindJogger Videoquiz
- NBR's *Economics & You*
- Interactive Economics!
- Presentation Plus!



# 1 Focus

## Overview

Section 2 explains or describes graphing the demand curve, what factors determine demand, and elastic and inelastic demand.

### Bellringer
**Motivational Activity**

Project **Daily Focus Transparency 10** and have students answer the questions.

This activity is also available as a blackline master.

**Daily Focus Transparency 10**

CONSUMER TASTES AFFECT DEMAND

1. What conclusion or conclusions about consumer tastes can you draw from the photographs?
2. How do the photographs indicate a wealthy economy?

### Reader's Guide

Answers to the **Reading Objectives** questions are on page 185.

**Preteaching Vocabulary**

Write the term *elastic demand* on the board. Then place a large rubber band over your hands. Move your hands to stretch and ease the band. As you move your hands, ask students to guess what the term might mean.

Vocabulary PuzzleMaker

# 2 Teach

## Guided Practice

**L1 Understanding Ideas** Reinforce students' understanding of the relationship between movement of the demand curve and changes in demand by underscoring that a shift to the left in the demand curve indicates a decrease in demand, while a shift to the right indicates an increase. Then call on volunteers to suggest a phrase or saying that sums up this relationship.

### Daily Lecture Notes 7–2

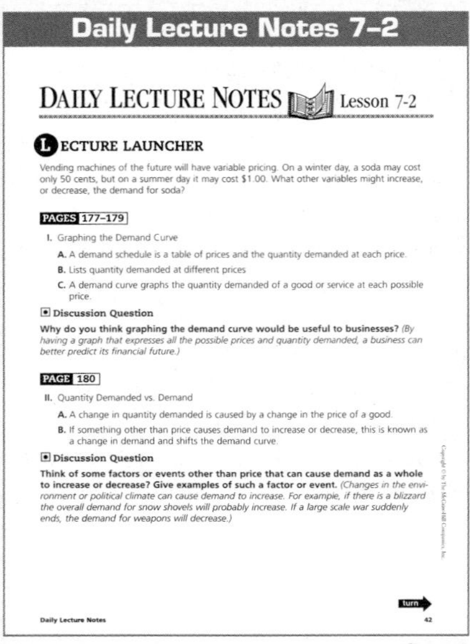

DAILY LECTURE NOTES Lesson 7-2

**LECTURE LAUNCHER**

Vending machines of the future will have variable pricing. On a winter day, a soda may cost only 50 cents, but on a summer day it may cost $1.00. What other variables might increase, or decrease, the demand for soda?

PAGES 177–179

I. Graphing the Demand Curve
   - **A.** A demand schedule is a table of prices and the quantity demanded at each price.
   - **B.** Lists quantity demanded at different prices
   - **C.** A demand curve graphs the quantity demanded of a good or service at each possible price.

**Discussion Question**

**Why do you think graphing the demand curve would be useful to businesses?** *(By having a graph that expresses all the possible prices and quantity demanded, a business can better predict its financial future.)*

PAGE 180

II. Quantity Demanded vs. Demand
   - **A.** A change in quantity demanded is caused by a change in the price of a good.
   - **B.** If something other than price causes demand to increase or decrease, this is known as a change in demand and shifts the demand curve.

**Discussion Question**

**Think of some factors or events other than price that can cause demand as a whole to increase or decrease? Give examples of such a factor or event.** *(Changes in the environment or political climate can cause demand to increase. For example, if there is a blizzard the overall demand for snow shovels will probably increase. If a large scale war suddenly ends, the demand for weapons will decrease.)*



turn

Daily Lecture Notes 42

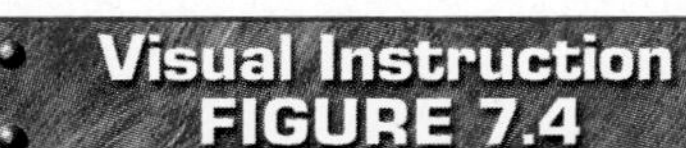


**Answer to Part C:** *900*

in a visual way? It is said that a picture is worth a thousand words. For much of economic analysis, the "picture" is a graph that shows the relationship between two statistics or concepts.

The law of demand can be graphed. As you learned in Section 1, the relationship between the quantity demanded and price is inverse—as the price goes up, the quantity demanded goes down. As the price goes down, the quantity demanded goes up.

Take a look at *Parts A, B,* and *C* of **Figure 7.4.** The series of three parts shows how the price of goods and services affects the quantity demanded at each price. *Part A* is a **demand schedule**—a table of prices and quantity demanded. The numbers show that as the price per CD decreases, the quantity demanded increases. For example, at a cost of $20 each, 100 million CDs will be demanded. When the cost decreases to $12 each, 900 million CDs will be demanded.

**demand schedule:** *table showing quantities demanded at different possible prices*

## FIGURE 7.4 Graphing the Demand Curve

**Demand Can Be Shown Visually** Note how the three parts use a different format to show the same thing. Each shows the law of demand—as price falls, quantity demanded increases.

Also, note that in Parts B and C we refer to the quantity of CDs demanded *per year.* We could have said one day, one week, one month, or two years. The longer the time period, the more likely that factors *other than price* will affect the demand for a given product.

**A Demand Schedule**

| Price per CD | Quantity demanded (in millions) | Points in Part B |
|---|---|---|
| $20 | 100 | A |
| $19 | 200 | B |
| $18 | 300 | C |
| $17 | 400 | D |
| $16 | 500 | E |
| $15 | 600 | F |
| $14 | 700 | G |
| $13 | 800 | H |
| $12 | 900 | I |
| $11 | 1,000 | J |
| $10 | 1,100 | K |

**Part A Demand Schedule** The numbers in the demand schedule above show that as the price per CD decreases, the quantity demanded increases. Note that at $16 each, a quantity of 500 million CDs will be demanded.

### Meeting Special Needs

**Visual Learning Difficulty** Students with visual difficulties may find the graphing techniques presented in this section helpful. Encourage students to use graphing as a way of taking notes and summarizing information throughout the course. You might suggest that students use rulers or index cards to help them keep track of columns and rows when they interpret tables and charts.

Refer to *Inclusion for the Social Studies Classroom Strategies and Activities* for students with different learning styles.

In *Part B,* the numbers from the schedule in *Part A* have been plotted onto a graph. The bottom (or horizontal) axis shows the quantity demanded. The side (or vertical) axis shows the price per CD. Each pair of price and quantity demanded numbers represents a point on the graph. These points are labeled A through K.

Now look at *Part C* of **Figure 7.4.** When the points from *Part B* are connected with a line, we end up with the **demand curve.** A demand curve shows the quantity demanded of a good or service at each possible price. Demand curves slope downward (fall from left to right). In *Part C* you can see the inverse relationship between price and quantity demanded.

**Student Web Activity** Visit the *Economics Today and Tomorrow* Web site at ett.glencoe.com and click on ***Chapter 7—Student Web Activities*** to see how changes in population affect demand.

**demand curve:** *downward-sloping line that shows in graph form the quantities demanded at each possible price*

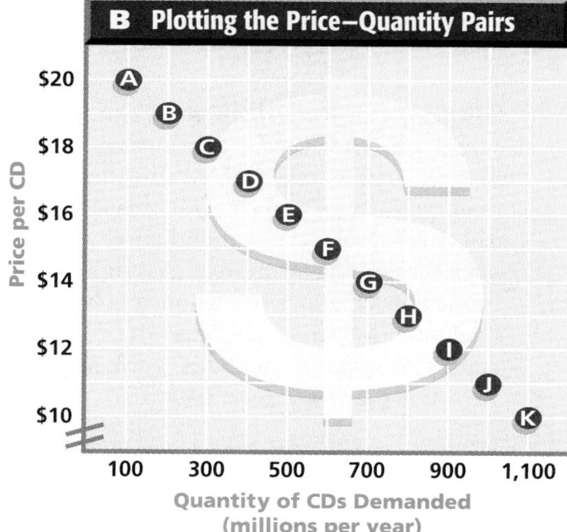


**Part B Plotting Quantity Demanded** Note how the price and quantity demanded numbers in the demand schedule (Part A) have been transferred to a graph in Part B above. Find letter E. It represents a number of CDs demanded (500 million) at a specific price ($16).

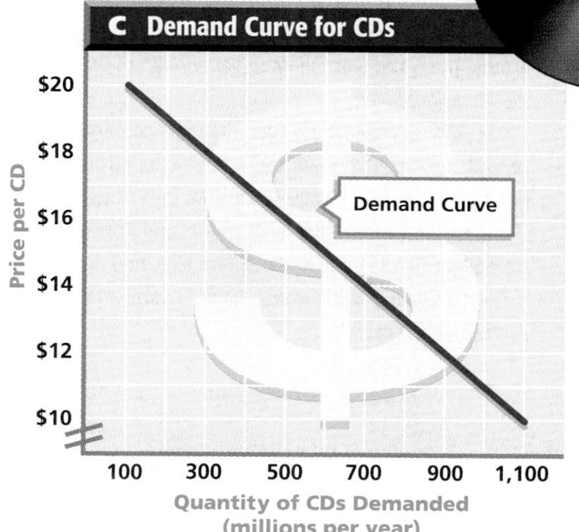


**Part C Demand Curve** The points in Part B have been connected with a line in Part C above. This line is the demand curve, which always falls from left to right. How many CDs will be demanded at a price of $12 each?





ECONOMICS Online

See the **Web Activity Lesson Plan** at *ett.glencoe.com* for an introduction, lesson description, and answers to the **Student Web Activity** for this chapter.

L2 **Explaining Ideas** Ask students to explain what would happen to the demand for CDs in the following situations:

1. There is an overall increase in wages.
2. A chain of appliance stores puts all CD players on sale.
3. The price of audiocassettes increases dramatically.

*Demand would increase in all situations. Wage increases give consumers more income to buy more CDs; demand for CD players and CDs would increase, as they are complementary goods; demand for CDs would increase because CDs and audiocassettes are substitute goods.*

Conclude by asking students to present other situations that might lead to a rise in demand for CDs.

## Free Enterprise Activity

To increase students' understanding of the effects of a change in demand in a free enterprise economy, present the following scenario: A disease destroys much of the coffee crop in South America. How might this affect the price of coffee? *The price increases.* The demand for substitute products? *Demand for substitute drinks, such as soft drinks and juices, might increase.* The demand for complementary products? *Demand for complementary products, such as sugar, might fall.* Have students present these changes in the form of graphs.

**Guided Reading Activity 7-2**

Name ______ Date ______ Class ______

GUIDED READING Activity 7-2

For use with textbook pages 177–185

THE DEMAND CURVE AND THE ELASTICITY OF DEMAND

RECALLING THE FACTS

*Directions: Use the information in your textbook to answer the questions.*

1. What is shown on a demand schedule?
2. What is a demand curve?
3. How is a change in quantity demanded similar to and different from a change in demand?
Similar:
Different:
4. What three changes can affect the demand for a specific product?
Change in
Change in
Change in
5. What is a complementary product?

## Independent Practice

**L2** Graphing Information Have students consult with a local merchant to ascertain the demand for a particular product over a set time period. Suggest that they present their findings in graph form. Encourage students to complement their graphs with a paragraph explaining what factors most affected demand for the product.

## Global Economy

**Hollywood North?**

American movies and television programs are popular in foreign markets. The bustling "American" city scenes and wide open landscapes, however, most likely were filmed in Canada. A favorable exchange rate for the American dollar and government tax breaks make moviemaking much cheaper in Canada than in the United States. Today, three of the top seven movie and television production centers—Vancouver, Toronto, and Montreal—are in Canada.

## Quantity Demanded vs. Demand

Remember that quantity demanded is a specific point along the demand curve. A *change in quantity demanded* is caused by a change in the price of the good, and is shown as a movement along the demand curve. Sometimes, however, something other than price causes demand as a whole to increase or decrease. This is known as a *change in demand* and is shown as a *shift* of the entire demand curve to the left (decrease in demand) or right (increase in demand). If demand increases, people will buy more per year at all prices. If demand decreases, people will buy less per year at all prices. What causes a change in demand as a whole?

## Global Economy

### Demand for American TV Shows

Every year, hundreds of television-program buyers from around the world visit major studios in Los Angeles. What do they buy? *ER, Chicago Hope,* and *NYPD Blue* are hits in western European countries such as England, the Netherlands, and Germany. And people around the world can't seem to get enough of *Buffy the Vampire Slayer.*

Sci-fi is very big. *The X-Files* airs in 60 countries. In central Europe, "they want cars to be exploded 14 stories high," says Klaus Hallig, who buys for Poland, Hungary, the Czech Republic, Bulgaria, and Romania. He bought *Cannon, Bonanza, Miami Vice,* and the *A-Team,* as well as *Little House on the Prairie* and *Highway to Heaven.* ■

## Determinants of Demand

Many factors can affect demand for a specific product. Among these factors are changes in population, changes in income, changes in people's tastes and preferences, the existence of substitutes, and the existence of complementary goods.

**Changes in Population** When population increases, opportunities to buy and sell increase. Naturally, the demand for most products increases. This means that the demand curve for, say, television sets, shifts to the right. At each price, more television sets will be demanded simply because the consumer population increases. Look at *Part A* of **Figure 7.5** on page 182.

**Changes in Income** The demand for most goods and services depends on income. Your demand for CDs would certainly decrease if your income dropped in half and you expected it to stay there. You would buy fewer CDs at all possible prices. The demand curve for CDs would shift to the left as shown in *Part B* of **Figure 7.5** on page 182. If your income went up, however, you might buy more CDs even if the price of CDs doubled. Buying more CDs at all possible prices would shift the demand curve to the right.



## Visual Learning Activity

**Understanding Shifts in the Demand Curve** Draw the following diagram on the board:

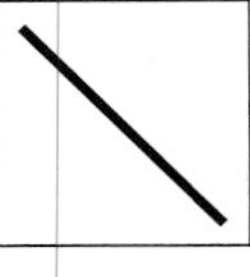

Call on volunteers to come to the board and draw arrows—indicating the direction of movement of the demand curve—and the new demand curve for each of the following:

1. The demand curve for CDs if all wages increased by 20 percent. *Demand curve shifts to the right.*
2. The demand curve for the popular toy "Winnie Widget" after it is replaced by another fad. *Demand curve shifts to the left.*
3. The demand curve for margarine if the price of butter falls. *Demand curve shifts to the left.*

**Changes in Tastes and Preferences** One of the key factors that determine demand is people's tastes and preferences. *Tastes and preferences* refer to what people like and prefer to choose. When an item becomes a fad, more are sold at every possible price. The demand curve shifts to the right as shown in *Part C* of **Figure 7.5** on page 183.

**Substitutes** The existence of substitutes also affects demand. People often think of butter and margarine as substitutes. Suppose that the price of butter remains the same and the price of margarine falls. People will buy more margarine and less butter at all prices of butter. See *Part D* of **Figure 7.5** on page 183.

**Complementary Goods** When two goods are complementary products, the decrease in the price of one will increase the demand for it as well as its complementary good. Cameras and film are complementary goods. Suppose the price of film remains the same. If the price of cameras drops, people will probably buy more of them. They will also probably buy more film to use with the cameras. Therefore, a decrease in the price of cameras leads to an increase in the demand for its **complementary good,** film. As a result, the demand curve for film will shift to the right as shown in *Part E* of **Figure 7.5** on page 183.

**complementary good:** *a product often used with another product*

## The Price Elasticity of Demand

The law of demand is straightforward: The higher the price charged, the lower the quantity demanded–and vice versa. If you sold DVDs, how could you use this information? You know that if you lower prices, consumers will buy more DVDs. By how much should you lower the cost, however? You cannot really answer this question unless you know how responsive consumers will be to a decrease in the price of DVDs. Economists call this price responsiveness **elasticity.** The measure of the **price elasticity of demand** is *how much* consumers respond to a given change in price.

**elasticity:** *economic concept dealing with consumers' responsiveness to an increase or decrease in price of a product*

**price elasticity of demand:** *economic concept that deals with how much demand varies according to changes in price*

**Elastic Demand** For some goods, a rise or fall in price greatly affects the amount people are willing to buy. The demand for these goods is considered elastic–consumers can be flexible when buying or not buying these items. For example, one particular brand of coffee probably has a very

**ECONOMICS & YOU**

**Demand and Supply**

Chapter 7
Disc 1, Side 1

**ASK: How will an increase in the price of an inelastic good, such as prescription medicine, affect the quantity demanded?** *In general, most people will be willing to buy prescription medicine to stay healthy, regardless of the price. Quantity demanded for these medicines, therefore, will not significantly decrease if their prices rise.*

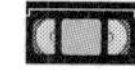 Also available in VHS.

**INTERACTIVE ECONOMICS!**

**LESSON 3: DEMAND**

Have students study the "Advanced Topics Menu," which focuses on determinants of demand elasticity. After clicking on the information provided, students should list the underlying determinants of elasticity on note cards. Have students quiz each other with their cards.

Supplied in both CD-ROM and disk formats.

### Cooperative Learning

Organize the class into small groups. Ask group members to hold discussions on the point at which the real income effect becomes a significant deterrent to buying new items. Have group members then discuss how they use the substitution effect in their own purchases. Finally, have groups use the information developed during discussions to create a short report to business on the buying habits and economic decision making of young consumers. Suggest that groups use graphs, charts, and other appropriate visual materials to illustrate their booklets. BLOCK SCHEDULING

**Visual Instruction FIGURE 7.5**

Direct students' attention to Part A of **Figure 7.5.** ASK: What eventually would happen to the demand curve for toys if there were a decline in the birthrate? Why? *The demand curve would move to the left, because there would be a decline in demand for toys at each and every price.*

**L2 Planning a Trip** Ask students to plan for a trip they would like to take, such as a boating or camping trip. In their preparation for the trip they should list all the goods they will need and the quantities in which they will need them. Have students make notations on their lists to indicate the elasticity of each item.

BLOCK SCHEDULING

## FIGURE 7.5 Determinants of Demand

**Changes in Demand** Many factors can affect demand for a specific product. When demand changes, the entire demand curve shifts to the left or the right.

**Part A Change in Demand if Population Increases** When population increases, opportunities to buy and sell increase. The demand curve labeled D1 represents demand for television sets before the population increased. The demand curve labeled D2 represents demand after the population increased.

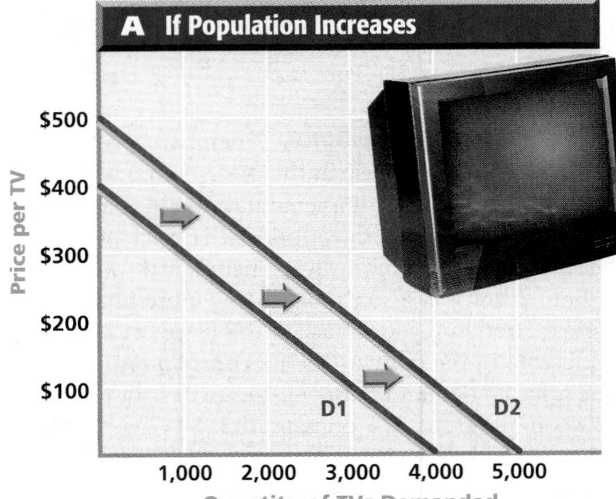


**Part B Change in Demand if Your Income Decreases** The demand curve D1 represents CD demand before income decreased. The demand curve D2 represents CD demand after income decreased. If your income goes up, however, you may buy more CDs at all possible prices, which would shift the demand curve to the right.

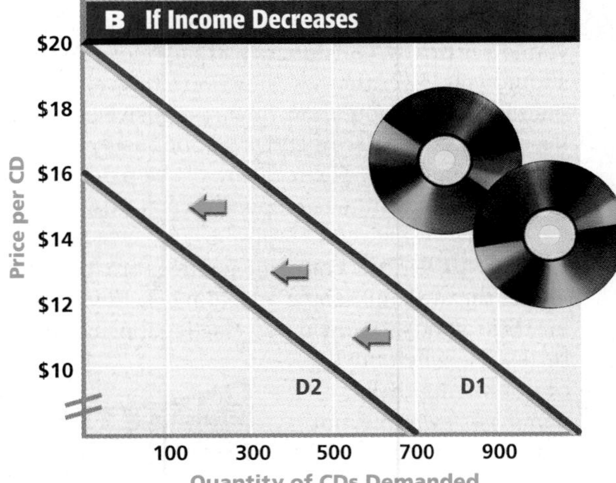




**Relevant Issues in Economics**

**Highways Substitute for Railroads** In the 1950s, the federal government began construction of the interstate highway system. Partly because taxes helped support the development of highways, shipping goods by truck was less costly than shipping by rail. As a result, the trucking industry grew, while railroads declined. Today, many nations have more efficient railroad systems than does the United States. Ask students to discuss the following: Should the federal government also have subsidized railroads in the 1950s? Why or why not?

**Part C Change in Demand if an Item Becomes a Fad** When a product becomes a fad, more of it is demanded at all prices, and the entire demand curve shifts to the right. Notice how D1–representing demand for Beanie Babies™ before they became popular–becomes D2–demand after they became a fad.

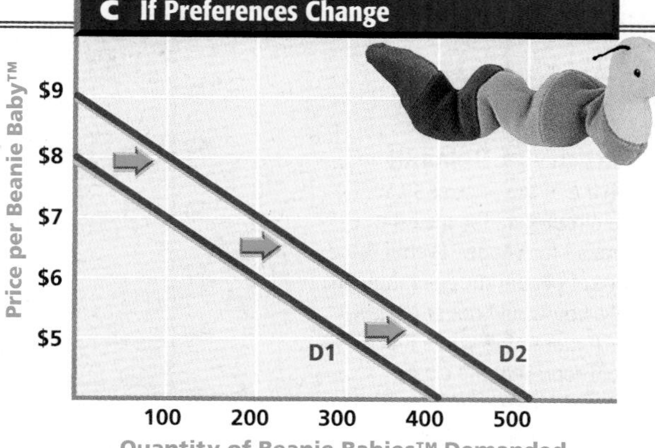


**Part D Change in Demand for Substitutes** As the price of the substitute (margarine) decreases, the demand for the item under study (butter) also decreases. If, in contrast, the price of the substitute (margarine) increases, the demand for the item under study (butter) also increases.

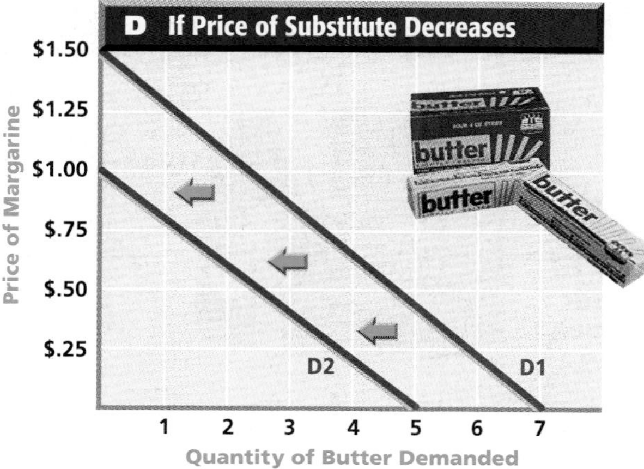


**Part E Change in Demand for Complementary Goods**
A decrease in the price of cameras leads to an increase in the demand for film, its complementary good. As a result, the demand curve for film will shift to the right. The opposite would happen if the price of cameras increased, thereby decreasing the demand for the complementary good, film.

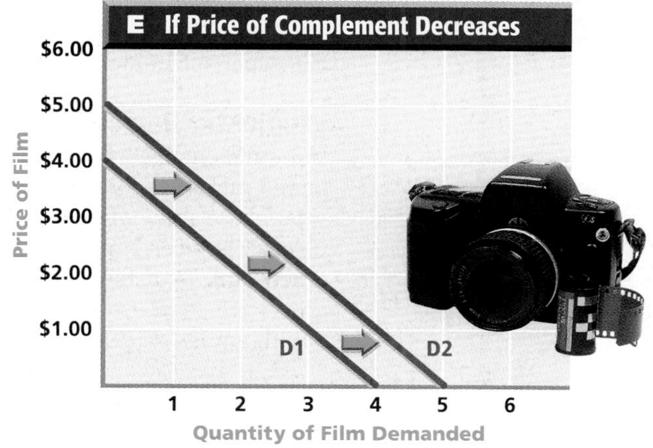




L2 Developing Visual Materials
Ask students to explore the effect of recycling on the demand for raw materials. Have them concentrate on recyclable materials, such as engine oil, metals, and wood pulp. Suggest they present their data in graphs and charts for use as examples in a class discussion.

## Economic Connection to... Technology

Demand for ice-cold soft drinks is greater during hot weather than in the winter months. The management of the Coca-Cola Company thinks this rather obvious fact should be reflected in prices charged at vending machines, and they have developed technology to do just that. A computer chip in the vending machine responds to temperature sensors, and raises the price of soft drinks as the weather gets warmer. The company is looking at other ways to make vending-machine prices more reflective of demand. One idea is to link price to traffic at a machine. If few people buy from the machine, prices might drop automatically.

## Cooperative Learning

Remind students that economists distinguish between needs and wants. Needs are relatively few, while wants are almost limitless. Organize students into small groups. Direct each group to select a good or service and then write a brief research report on how marketing and advertising may create demand for this good or product by clouding the distinction between needs and wants. Call on a volunteer from each group to present the group's findings.

## Visual Instruction FIGURE 7.6

Demand for soft drinks and T-bone steaks is elastic because substitutes for these products exist. Demand for salt and lightbulbs tends to be inelastic because the percentage of a person's total budget devoted to the purchase of these goods is relatively small.

# 3 Assess

## Meeting Lesson Objectives

Assign Section 2 Assessment as homework or an in-class activity.

Use **Interactive Tutor Self-Assessment Software** to review Section 2.

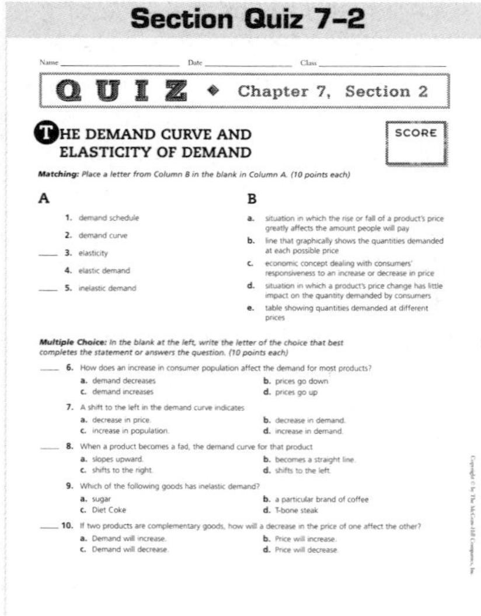

### Section Quiz 7-2

Name ______________ Date ______________ Class ______________

**QUIZ** ◆ Chapter 7, Section 2

**THE DEMAND CURVE AND ELASTICITY OF DEMAND**

SCORE

***Matching:*** *Place a letter from Column B in the blank in Column A. (10 points each)*

| A | B |
|---|---|
| ____ 1. demand schedule | a. situation in which the rise or fall of a product's price greatly affects the amount people will pay |
| ____ 2. demand curve | b. line that graphically shows the quantities demanded at each possible price |
| ____ 3. elasticity | c. economic concept dealing with consumers' responsiveness to an increase or decrease in price |
| ____ 4. elastic demand | d. situation in which a product's price change has little impact on the quantity demanded by consumers |
| ____ 5. inelastic demand | e. table showing quantities demanded at different prices |

***Multiple Choice:*** *In the blank at the left, write the letter of the choice that best completes the statement or answers the question. (10 points each)*

____ 6. How does an increase in consumer population affect the demand for most products?
a. demand decreases   b. prices go down
c. demand increases   d. prices go up

____ 7. A shift to the left in the demand curve indicates
a. decrease in price.   b. decrease in demand.
c. increase in population.   d. increase in demand.

____ 8. When a product becomes a fad, the demand curve for that product
a. slopes upward.   b. becomes a straight line.
c. shifts to the right.   d. shifts to the left.

____ 9. Which of the following goods has inelastic demand?
a. sugar   b. a particular brand of coffee
c. Diet Coke   d. T-bone steak

____ 10. If two products are complementary goods, how will a decrease in the price of one affect the other?
a. Demand will increase.   b. Price will increase.
c. Demand will decrease.   d. Price will decrease.



22 Section Quiz

## FIGURE 7.6

**Elasticity of Demand**
Curve A at the price of \$5.50 could represent the inelastic demand for pepper. Even if the price of pepper dropped dramatically, you would not purchase much more of it. Curve B at \$5.50 could represent the elastic demand for steaks. If the price drops just a little, many people will buy much more steak.

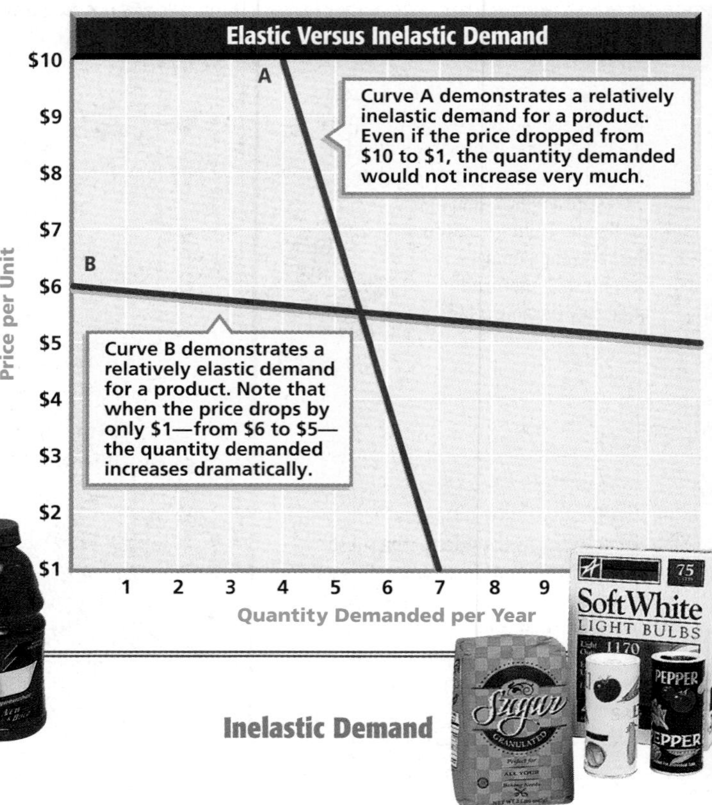


COFFEE

Elastic Demand

**elastic demand:** *situation in which the rise or fall in a product's price greatly affects the amount that people are willing to buy*

**elastic demand.** Consumers consider the many competing brands of coffee to be almost the same. A small rise in the price of one brand will probably cause many consumers to purchase the cheaper substitute brands.

**inelastic demand:** *situation in which a product's price change has little impact on the quantity demanded by consumers*

### Inelastic Demand

If a price change does not result in a substantial change in the quantity demanded, that demand is considered inelastic—consumers are usually not flexible and will purchase some of the item no matter what it costs. Salt, pepper, sugar, and certain types of medicine normally have **inelastic demand.** By using two demand curves in one diagram—as shown in **Figure 7.6**—you can compare a relatively inelastic demand with a relatively elastic demand.

### What Determines Price Elasticity of Demand?

Why do some goods have elastic demand and others have inelastic demand?



## Critical Thinking Activity

**Classifying** Have students work in pairs to compile a list of substitutes for the following items: wallpaper, grapefruit, belt, chess set, carpet. *(Possible answers: paint, orange, suspenders, checkers, tile)* Then have students list complementary goods for each of the following items: Ping-Pong table, aquarium, cup, bed, tennis shoes. *(Possible answers: Ping-Pong balls, tropical fish, saucer, pillows, shoelaces)*

At least three factors determine the price elasticity of demand for a particular item: the existence of substitutes; the percentage of a person's total budget devoted to the purchase of that good; and the time consumers are given to adjust to a change in price.

Clearly, the more substitutes that exist for a product, the more responsive consumers will be to a change in the price of that good. A diabetic needs insulin, which has virtually no substitutes. The price elasticity of demand for insulin, therefore, is very low–it is inelastic. The opposite is true for soft drinks. If the price of one goes up by very much, many consumers may switch to another.

The percentage of your total budget spent on an item will also determine whether its demand is elastic or inelastic. For example, the portion of a family's budget devoted to pepper is very small. Even if the price of pepper doubles, most people will keep buying about the same amount. The demand for pepper, then, is relatively inelastic. Housing demand, in contrast, is relatively elastic because it represents such a large proportion of a household's yearly budget.

Finally, people take time to adjust to price changes. If the price of electricity goes up tomorrow, your demand will be inelastic. The longer the time allowed to reduce the amount of electricity you use, however, the greater the price elasticity of demand.

**Practice** and **assess** key skills with ***Skillbuilder Interactive Workbook, Level 2.***

## SECTION 2 Assessment

### Understanding Key Terms

1. **Define** demand schedule, demand curve, complementary good, elasticity, price elasticity of demand, elastic demand, inelastic demand.

### Reviewing Objectives

2. What does a demand curve show?
3. **Graphic Organizer** Create a diagram like the one below to show the determinants of demand.

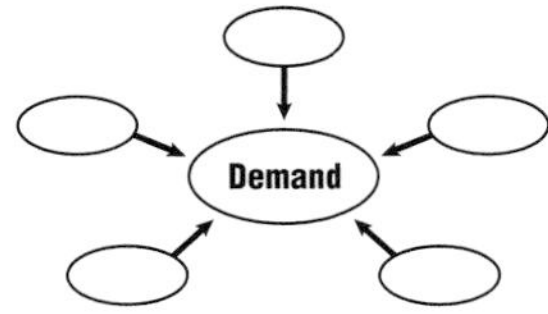


4. How does the elasticity of demand affect the price for a given product?

### Applying Economic Concepts

5. **Demand Elasticity** Provide an example of two products or services for which you have elastic demand and inelastic demand. Explain your choices.

### Critical Thinking Activity

6. **Making Comparisons** Write a paragraph describing how demand and quantity demanded are similar, and how they are different. Use the examples you provided in question 5 to help make the comparison in your paragraph.





## Reteach

Ask students to use the **Terms to Know** to write a paragraph summarizing this section.

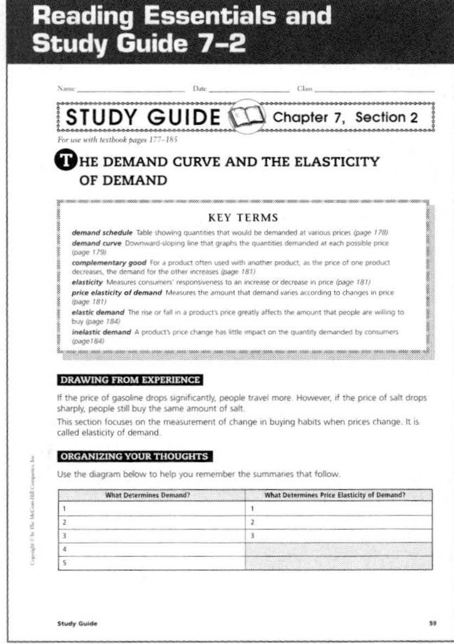

**Reading Essentials and Study Guide 7-2**

Name ______ Date ______ Class ______

STUDY GUIDE Chapter 7, Section 2

*For use with textbook pages 177–185*

THE DEMAND CURVE AND THE ELASTICITY OF DEMAND

KEY TERMS

***demand schedule*** Table showing quantities that would be demanded at various prices *(page 178)*

***demand curve*** Downward-sloping line that graphs the quantities demanded at each possible price *(page 179)*

***complementary good*** For a product often used with another product, as the price of one product decreases, the demand for the other increases *(page 181)*

***elasticity*** Measures consumers' responsiveness to an increase or decrease in price *(page 181)*

***price elasticity of demand*** Measures the amount that demand varies according to changes in price *(page 181)*

***elastic demand*** The rise or fall in a product's price greatly affects the amount that people are willing to buy *(page 184)*

***inelastic demand*** A product's price change has little impact on the quantity demanded by consumers *(page184)*

DRAWING FROM EXPERIENCE

If the price of gasoline drops significantly, people travel more. However, if the price of salt drops sharply, people still buy the same amount of salt.

This section focuses on the measurement of change in buying habits when prices change. It is called elasticity of demand.

ORGANIZING YOUR THOUGHTS

Use the diagram below to help you remember the summaries that follow.

| What Determines Demand? | What Determines Price Elasticity of Demand? |
|---|---|
| 1 | 1 |
| 2 | 2 |
| 3 | 3 |
| 4 | |
| 5 | |

Study Guide 59

## 4 Close

Have students list goods and services that have elastic, moderately elastic, and inelastic demands in their household. Have them create a chart, noting whether the demand for each item responds to changes in price, income, quality, need, available substitutes, time adjustments, or taste.

## SECTION 2 Assessment Answers

1. All definitions can be found in the Glossary.
2. the number of items that will be demanded at every given price
3. Determinants of demand: existence of substitutes, prices of complementary goods, changes in population, income, tastes and preferences
4. A product with elastic demand is likely to be priced lower because consumers can switch among the various substitutes.
5. Examples will vary. Students should consider the factors that cause demand to be elastic or inelastic.
6. Paragraphs will vary but should note that demand and quantity demanded both show the desire, willingness, and ability to buy; and that quantity demanded changes in response to price changes of a product, while demand changes in response to such factors as consumer income, consumer tastes, and prices of related products.

# 1 Focus

## Overview

Section 3 explains or describes how the incentive of greater profit—including the law of diminishing returns—affects supply, and what the supply curve shows.

### BELLRINGER
**Motivational Activity**

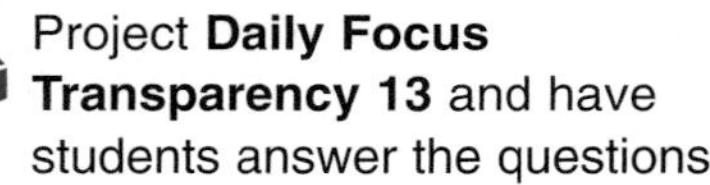

Project **Daily Focus Transparency 13** and have students answer the questions.

This activity is also available as a blackline master.

**Daily Focus Transparency 13**

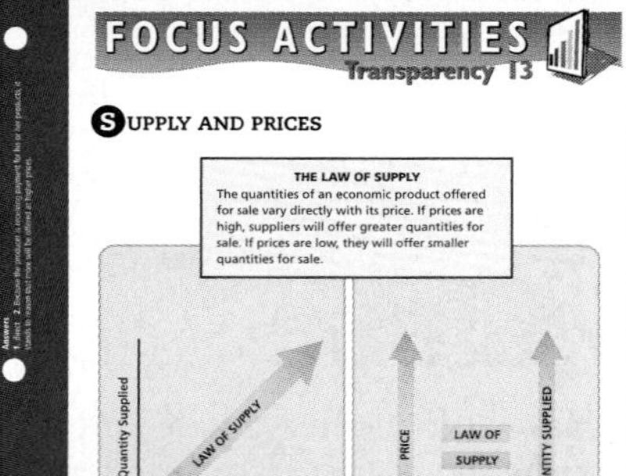

FOCUS ACTIVITIES
Transparency 13

SUPPLY AND PRICES

THE LAW OF SUPPLY
The quantities of an economic product offered for sale vary directly with its price. If prices are high, suppliers will offer greater quantities for sale. If prices are low, they will offer smaller quantities for sale.



1. According to the Law of Supply, is the relationship between price and quantity supplied direct or indirect?
2. Explain why producers supply greater quantities of a good or a service when prices rise.

Daily Focus Transparencies

### Reader's Guide

Answers to the **Reading Objectives** questions are on page 192.

**Preteaching Vocabulary**

Refer students to the **Terms to Know.** Then call on volunteers to skim the section to locate these terms and read them in context.

**Vocabulary PuzzleMaker**

SECTION 3

# The Law of Supply and the Supply Curve

### Reader's Guide

**Terms to Know**
- law of supply
- quantity supplied
- supply schedule
- supply curve
- technology
- law of diminishing returns

**Reading Objectives**
1. What is the law of supply?
2. How does the incentive of greater profits affect quantity supplied?
3. What do a supply schedule and supply curve show?
4. What are the four determinants of supply?

## Cover Story

*The Washington Post*, July 20, 1998

The first billion is always the hardest. It took Jeff Bezos four years. He made his second over the last few weeks. Even by the overheated standards of the late '90s, this is quick.

. . . He owns 19.8 million shares of the online bookseller Amazon.com, which he founded in 1994.

As you've learned, consumers demand products and services at the lowest possible prices. In contrast, suppliers—like Jeff Bezos of the Internet company Amazon.com—exist to make a profit—hopefully, a big profit. As you read this section, you'll learn about the law of supply and how it is geared toward making profits.

## The Law of Supply

To understand how prices are determined, you have to look at both demand and *supply*—the willingness and

## SECTION 3 RESOURCE MANAGER

**Reproducible Masters**
- Reproducible Lesson Plan 7–3
- Reading Essentials and Study Guide 7–3
- Guided Reading Activity 7–3
- Section Quiz 7–3
- Daily Focus Activity 13
- Daily Lecture Notes 7–3

**Multimedia**
- Daily Focus Transparency 13
- Vocabulary PuzzleMaker
- Interactive Tutor Self-Assessment Software
- ExamView® Pro Testmaker
- MindJogger Videoquiz
- NBR's *Economics & You*
- Interactive Economics!
- Presentation Plus!

## FIGURE 7.11

**Equilibrium Price** In a market economy, the forces underlying demand and supply have a push-pull relationship that ultimately leads to an equilibrium price. In our particular example, this is $15 per CD. If the price were to go above $15, the quantity demanded would be less than the quantity supplied. If the price fell below $15 per CD, the quantity demanded would exceed the quantity supplied.

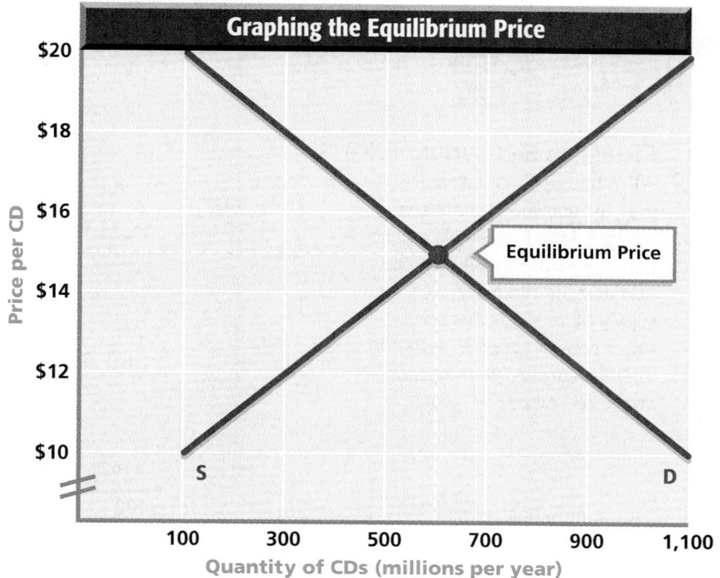


quantity supplied falls. As the price goes up, the quantity demanded falls and the quantity supplied rises.

Is there a price at which the quantity demanded and the quantity supplied meet? Yes. This level is called the **equilibrium price.** At this price, the quantity supplied by sellers is the same as the quantity demanded by buyers. One way to visualize equilibrium price is to put supply and demand curves on one graph, as shown in **Figure 7.11.** Where the two curves intersect is the equilibrium price. At that price, shown in the graph above, the quantity of CDs that consumers are willing and able to purchase is 600 million per year. And suppliers are willing to supply exactly that same amount.

<u>equilibrium price:</u> *the price at which the amount producers are willing to supply is equal to the amount consumers are willing to buy*

## Shifts in Equilibrium Price

What happens when there is an increase in the demand for CDs? Assume that scientists prove that listening to more music increases life span. This discovery will cause the entire demand curve to shift outward to the right, as shown in **Figure 7.12** on page 196.

What about changes in supply? You can show these in a similar fashion. Assume that there is a major breakthrough in the technology of producing CDs. The supply curve shifts outward to the right. The new equilibrium price will fall, and both the *quantity supplied* and the *quantity demanded* will increase.





# 2 Teach

## Guided Practice

**L2 Analyzing Ideas** Write the following list of items on the board: wheat, calculators, gasoline, tickets to concert. Have students work in small groups to brainstorm reasons why one of the items on the list might experience changes in price equilibrium. Ask group representatives to discuss these reasons. Encourage them to illustrate their discussions with drawings of supply and demand curves.

### Daily Lecture Notes 7-4

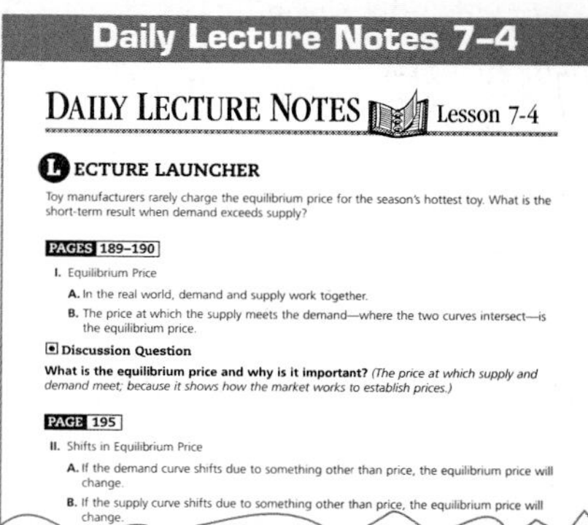

DAILY LECTURE NOTES Lesson 7-4

**LECTURE LAUNCHER**

Toy manufacturers rarely charge the equilibrium price for the season's hottest toy. What is the short-term result when demand exceeds supply?

**PAGES 189–190**

I. Equilibrium Price
   A. In the real world, demand and supply work together.
   B. The price at which the supply meets the demand—where the two curves intersect—is the equilibrium price.

**Discussion Question**

**What is the equilibrium price and why is it important?** *(The price at which supply and demand meet; because it shows how the market works to establish prices.)*

**PAGE 195**

II. Shifts in Equilibrium Price
   A. If the demand curve shifts due to something other than price, the equilibrium price will change.
   B. If the supply curve shifts due to something other than price, the equilibrium price will change.

### Visual Instruction FIGURE 7.11

As students are studying **Figure 7.11**, point out that economists say that the price system acts as a form of communication between consumers and producers. ASK: How does this communication take place? *Most students will suggest that if consumers demand less than is supplied at a particular price, then producers know that they have to adjust prices.*

### Meeting Special Needs

**Speech Disabilities** Have students research to find historic examples of how shortages put pressure on prices to rise. Then have them deliver short speeches about their findings. Students with speech disabilities may want to develop their speeches as a written assignment or have a classmate deliver the speeches they write. Encourage speechwriters to direct their presenters so that their speeches are delivered in the way they wish them to be heard.

Refer to *Inclusion for the Social Studies Classroom Strategies and Activities* for students with different learning styles.

**Guided Reading Activity 7-4**

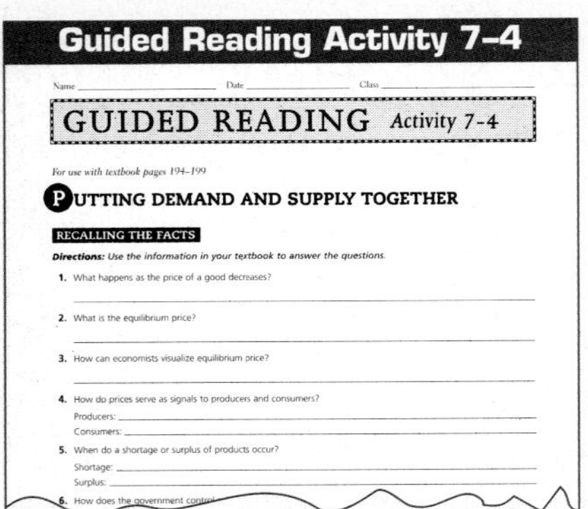
Name ______ Date ______ Class ______

GUIDED READING Activity 7-4

For use with textbook pages 194–199

PUTTING DEMAND AND SUPPLY TOGETHER

RECALLING THE FACTS

*Directions: Use the information in your textbook to answer the questions.*

1. What happens as the price of a good decreases?
2. What is the equilibrium price?
3. How can economists visualize equilibrium price?
4. How do prices serve as signals to producers and consumers?
Producers:
Consumers:
5. When do a shortage or surplus of products occur?
Shortage:
Surplus:
6. How does the government control

**ECONOMICS & YOU**

Demand and Supply

Chapter 7
Disc 1, Side 1

ASK: As the price of vacation homes increases, what will happen to the supply of and demand for such properties? *The supply of homes will rise, and the demand for such properties will fall.*

 Also available in VHS.

**Visual Instruction FIGURE 7.12**

**Answer:** *Quantity demanded and supplied would decrease, and the price would fall.*

**FIGURE 7.12**

**Change in Equilibrium Price**
When the supply or demand curves shift, the equilibrium price also changes. Note that the old equilibrium price was $15. But now the new demand curve intersects the supply curve at a higher price—$17. ***What could happen if, instead, scientists proved that listening to music decreases life span?***

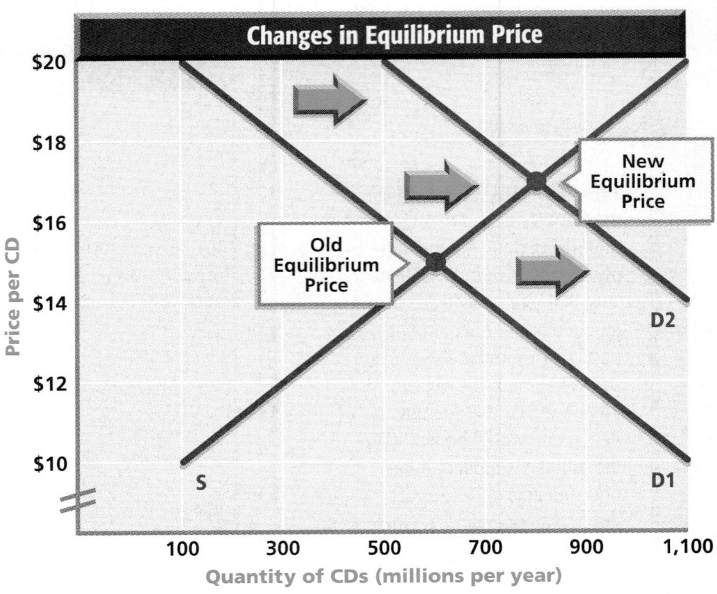


## Prices Serve as Signals

In the United States and other countries with mainly free enterprise systems, prices serve as signals to producers and consumers. Rising prices signal producers to produce more and consumers to purchase less. Falling prices signal producers to produce less and consumers to purchase more.

**shortage:** *situation in which the quantity demanded is greater than the quantity supplied at the current price*

**Shortages** A **shortage** occurs when, at the current price, the quantity demanded is greater than the quantity supplied. If the market is left alone—without government regulations or other restrictions—shortages put pressure on prices to rise. At a higher price, consumers reduce their purchases, whereas suppliers increase the quantity they supply.

**surplus:** *situation in which quantity supplied is greater than quantity demanded at the current price*

**Surpluses** At prices above the equilibrium price, suppliers produce more than consumers want to purchase in the marketplace. Suppliers end up with **surpluses**—large inventories of goods—and this and other forces put pressure on the price to drop to the equilibrium price. If the price falls, suppliers have less incentive to supply as much as before, whereas consumers begin to purchase a greater quantity. The decrease in price toward the equilibrium price, therefore, eliminates the surplus.

**Shortage of Games**



**Cooperative Learning**

Have students work in small groups to create a board game called "Supply and Demand." Give students the following directions: Choose six items you would like to sell in a discount store. Write the name and a different quantity (1–10) of each item on the back of index cards. Label five spaces on the game board to indicate determinants of increasing demand. Label another five spaces to indicate decreasing demand. Stacks of cards can indicate determinants that increase and decrease supply. Create rules to support the object of the game: to achieve the highest sales possible. BLOCK SCHEDULING

**Market Forces** One of the benefits of the market economy is that when it operates without restriction, it eliminates shortages and surpluses. Whenever shortages occur, the market ends up taking care of itself—the price goes up to eliminate the shortage. Whenever surpluses occur, the market again ends up taking care of itself—the price falls to eliminate the surplus. Let's take a look at what happens to the availability of goods and services when the government—not market forces—becomes involved in setting prices.

## Price Controls

Why would the government get involved in setting prices? One reason is that in some instances it believes the market forces of supply and demand are unfair, and it is trying to protect consumers and suppliers. Another reason is that special interest groups use pressure on elected officials to protect certain industries.

**Price Ceilings** A **price ceiling** is a government-set maximum price that can be charged for goods and services. Imagine trying to bring a 12-foot tree into your house that has 8-foot ceilings. The ceiling prevents the top of the tree from going up. Similarly, a *price ceiling* prevents prices from going above a specified amount. For example, city officials might set a price ceiling on what landlords can charge for rent. As *Part A* of **Figure 7.13** on page 198 shows, when a price ceiling is set below the equilibrium price, a shortage occurs.

Effective price ceilings—and resulting shortages—often lead to nonmarket ways of distributing goods and services. The government may resort to **rationing**, or limiting, items that are in short supply. A policy of rationing is expensive, however. Taxpayers must pay the cost of printing ration coupons, setting up offices to distribute the coupons, and maintaining the bureaucracy involved in enforcing who gets how much of the rationed goods.

Shortages also may lead to a **black market**, in which illegally high prices are charged for items that are in short supply. As **Figure 7.14** on page 199 shows, items often sold on the black market include tickets to sporting events.

<u>price ceiling:</u> *a legal maximum price that may be charged for a particular good or service*

<u>rationing:</u> *the distribution of goods and services based on something other than price*

<u>black market:</u> *"underground" or illegal market in which goods are traded at prices above their legal maximum prices or in which illegal goods are sold*

Ration Coupons

Surplus Cheese

Project **Economic Concepts Transparency** 8 and have students discuss the accompanying questions.

## Independent Practice

L2 **Writing Editorials** ASK: Should the prices of any goods and services be fixed in a market economy? Give the students a set period of time to organize their ideas on this subject. Then ask them to write a newspaper editorial supporting or opposing fixed prices. Call on volunteers to read their editorials to the class.

### Economic Connection to... History

**Wage and Price Controls**

In the early 1970s, stagflation wracked the American economy. To combat this economic slowdown accompanied by high inflation, President Richard Nixon imposed a 90-day wage and price freeze. At the end of this period, he set ceilings on annual wage and price increases—5.5 percent for wages and 2.5 percent for prices. These measures helped to stabilize the economy. However, when the ceilings were lifted in 1973, prices rose sharply. As a result, President Nixon imposed new wage and price controls. These controls, in one form or another, remained in place until 1981, when President Ronald Reagan repealed them.

### Critical Thinking Activity

**Cause and Effect** Shortages and surpluses are signals that the market sends to producers of goods and services. A shortage or surplus can be viewed as the initial event in a series of cause-effect relationships that result in a change in supply. Ask students to detail the cause-effect events of a shortage. *Shortage occurs, retailers attempt to obtain more product from wholesalers, wholesalers seek producers to supply additional product, new producers enter the market offering additional product at higher price. Higher price is passed on to consumer.*

# CHAPTER 7
SECTION 4, Pages 194–199

**INTERACTIVE ECONOMICS!**

**LESSON 5: PRICE DETERMINATION**

Have students click on "Prices as Signals." Then have them quiz a partner on the way prices act as signals to consumers and producers.

Supplied in both CD-ROM and disk formats.

**Visual Instruction FIGURE 7.13**

**Answer to Part B:** *2 million workers*

## 3 Assess

### Meeting Lesson Objectives

Assign Section 4 Assessment as homework or an in-class activity.

Use **Interactive Tutor Self-Assessment Software** to review Section 4.

**Section Quiz 7-4**

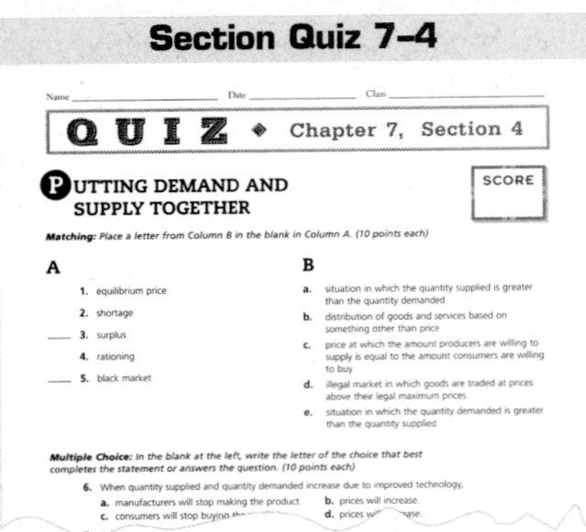
Name ______ Date ______ Class ______

**QUIZ** ◆ Chapter 7, Section 4

**PUTTING DEMAND AND SUPPLY TOGETHER**

SCORE

***Matching:** Place a letter from Column B in the blank in Column A. (10 points each)*

**A**

1. equilibrium price
2. shortage
3. surplus
4. rationing
5. black market

**B**

a. situation in which the quantity supplied is greater than the quantity demanded
b. distribution of goods and services based on something other than price
c. price at which the amount producers are willing to supply is equal to the amount consumers are willing to buy
d. illegal market in which goods are traded at prices above their legal maximum prices
e. situation in which the quantity demanded is greater than the quantity supplied

***Multiple Choice:** In the blank at the left, write the letter of the choice that best completes the statement or answers the question. (10 points each)*

6. When quantity supplied and quantity demanded increase due to improved technology,
a. manufacturers will stop making the product.
b. prices will increase.
c. consumers will stop buying th
d. prices wi ase.

**price floor:** *a legal minimum price below which a good or service may not be sold*

**Price Floors** A **price floor,** in contrast, is a government-set *minimum* price that can be charged for goods and services. Price floors—more common than price ceilings—prevent prices from dropping too low. When are low prices a problem? Assume that about 30 of your classmates all want jobs after school. The local fast-food restaurant can hire 30 students at $4.15 an hour, but the government has set a minimum wage—a price floor—of $5.15 an hour. Some of you will get hired, and you'll happily earn $5.15 an hour. Not all of you will get hired at that wage, however, which leads to a surplus of unemployed workers as shown in *Part B* of **Figure 7.13.** If the market were left on its own, the equilibrium price of $4.15 per hour would have all of you employed.

Besides affecting the minimum wage, price floors have been used to support agricultural prices. If the nation's farmers have a bumper crop of wheat, for example, the country has a huge surplus of wheat. The market, if left alone, would take care of the

## FIGURE 7.13 Price Ceilings and Price Floors

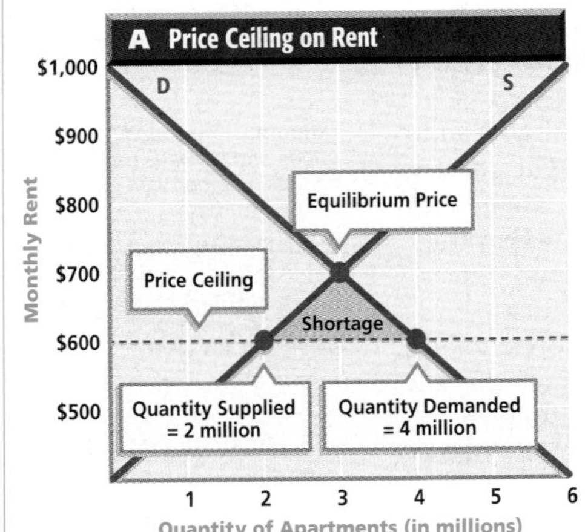


**Part A Price Ceiling** More people would like to rent at the government-controlled price, but apartment owners are unwilling to build more rental units if they cannot charge higher rent. This results in a shortage of apartments to rent.

**B Price Floor on Wages**

$7.15 / $6.15 / $5.15 / $4.15 / $3.15 / $2.15 — Hourly Wage

Quantity Demanded = 2 million; Quantity Supplied = 4 million; Surplus; Price Floor; Equilibrium Price; S; D

1 2 3 4 5 6 — Quantity of Workers (in millions)

**Part B Price Floor** The fast-food restaurant business wants to hire students at $4.15 an hour, but the government has set a minimum wage—a price floor—of $5.15 an hour. ***What is the surplus of workers with a price floor of $5.15 per hourly wage?***



### Free Enterprise Activity

Encourage students to bring to class items—such as books, CDs, and audiocassettes—that they would like to sell. (If students would prefer not to sell items, they might trade them and then return them at the end of the activity.) Have students "set up shop" with one or more partners to offer their goods for sale. Have partners set initial prices on their goods and try to sell them. After a set period of "selling time," have partners review their sales and, if necessary, adjust their prices. Hold a second period of selling time. Once again, have partners review their sales and prices. In a follow-up discussion, have partners talk about how they came to their pricing decisions.

**FIGURE 7.14**

**Black Market** Scalpers selling high-priced, limited tickets—such as these tickets to a World Cup Soccer match—are part of the black market. ***How do price ceilings on tickets to sporting events lead to shortages?***

surplus by having the price drop. As prices decrease, remember, quantity supplied decreases and quantity demanded increases. But the nation's farmers might not earn enough to make a profit or even pay their bills if the price drops too much. So the government sometimes sets a price floor for wheat, which stops the price per bushel from dropping below a certain level. The farmers know this, so instead of reducing their acreage of wheat—which would reduce the surplus—they keep producing more wheat.

**Practice** and **assess** key skills with *Skillbuilder Interactive Workbook, Level 2.*

## SECTION 4 Assessment

### Understanding Key Terms

1. **Define** equilibrium price, shortage, surplus, price ceiling, rationing, black market, price floor.

### Reviewing Objectives

2. How is the equilibrium price determined?
3. How do shifts in equilibrium price occur?
4. **Graphic Organizer** Create a diagram like the one below to show how shortages and surpluses affect prices.

5. How do price ceilings and price floors restrict the free exchange of prices?

### Applying Economic Concepts

6. **Shortages** Explain how a shortage of professional sports tickets determines the general price of those tickets.

### Critical Thinking Activity

7. **Understanding Cause and Effect** Draw a series of three graphs.
   - The first graph should show an equilibrium price for sunglasses.
   - The second graph should show the shift that would occur if research proved wearing sunglasses increased I.Q.
   - The third graph should show the shift that would occur if research proved that wearing sunglasses caused acne. *For help in using graphs, see page xv in the Economic Handbook.*





### Visual Instruction FIGURE 7.14

**Answer:** *Because price ceilings prevent prices from going too high, producers do not want to supply large amounts of goods or services on which they can gain few profits. A reduced supply leads to a shortage.*

## Reteach

Have students use the **Terms to Know** to write a paragraph explaining how equilibrium price is attained.

**Reading Essentials and Study Guide 7–4**

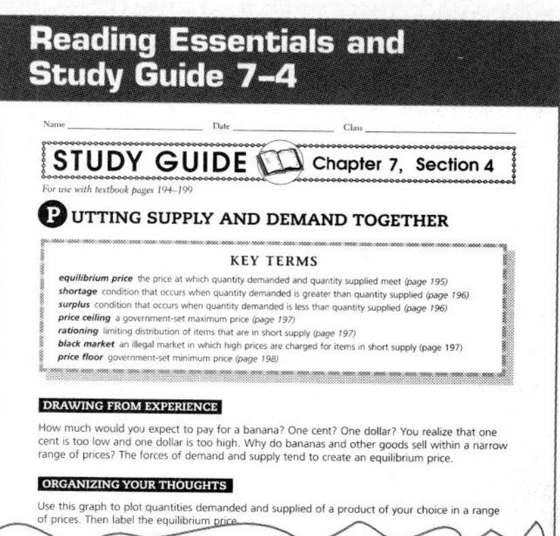

Name ______ Date ______ Class ______

STUDY GUIDE Chapter 7, Section 4

*For use with textbook pages 194–199*

PUTTING SUPPLY AND DEMAND TOGETHER

KEY TERMS

***equilibrium price*** the price at which quantity demanded and quantity supplied meet *(page 195)*
***shortage*** condition that occurs when quantity demanded is greater than quantity supplied *(page 196)*
***surplus*** condition that occurs when quantity demanded is less than quantity supplied *(page 196)*
***price ceiling*** a government-set maximum price *(page 197)*
***rationing*** limiting distribution of items that are in short supply *(page 197)*
***black market*** an illegal market in which high prices are charged for items in short supply (page 197)
***price floor*** government-set minimum price *(page 198)*

DRAWING FROM EXPERIENCE

How much would you expect to pay for a banana? One cent? One dollar? You realize that one cent is too low and one dollar is too high. Why do bananas and other goods sell within a narrow range of prices? The forces of demand and supply tend to create an equilibrium price.

ORGANIZING YOUR THOUGHTS

Use this graph to plot quantities demanded and supplied of a product of your choice in a range of prices. Then label the equilibrium price.

## 4 Close

Have students create a visual representation that illustrates equilibrium. You might suggest a set of scales in balance—with "supply" written in one scale and "demand" written in the other—as an example. **ELL**

## SECTION 4 Assessment Answers

1. All definitions can be found in the Glossary.
2. Equilibrium price is located where demand and supply curves intersect.
3. Equilibrium price changes occur when supply or demand curves shift.
4. Shortages cause prices to rise, surpluses cause prices to fall.
5. They prevent prices from finding an equilibrium between the quantity demanded and supplied.
6. Shortages cause prices to rise; therefore, a shortage of sports tickets will cause their price to rise.
7. First graph should be a standard equilibrium price graph. Second graph should show an increase in equilibrium price; third graph should show a decrease.

## Background

Alfred Marshall was the most influential economist of his time. In developing the theory of supply and demand, he reconciled classical economists, who believed that production controlled price, and contemporary economists, who claimed that demand set prices. Marshall believed that free competition and private enterprise would lead to better social conditions and full employment.

# Teach

Have volunteers read aloud paragraphs of the quoted excerpts from Marshall's *Elements of Economics.* Then have students paraphrase the paragraphs by writing a topic sentence for each. Finally, direct students to answer the questions in **Checking for Understanding.**

You might have students read additional chapters in *Elements of Economics* and report on Marshall's theory of welfare economics.

People & Perspectives

# Alfred Marshall

*ECONOMIST (1842–1924)*

- **Began career as a mathematician**
- **Chaired political economy at Cambridge University, England**
- **Developed supply and demand analysis**
- **Published *Principles of Economics* (1890) and *Elements of Economics* (1892)**

Alfred Marshall is known for introducing the concept of supply and demand analysis to economics. The following excerpt from *Elements of Economics* explains the concept of equilibrium:

"*The simplest case of balance, or equilibrium, between desire and effort is found when a person satisfies one of his wants by his own direct work. When a boy picks blackberries for his own eating, the action of picking may itself be pleasurable for a while. . . .*

*Equilibrium is reached, when at last his eagerness to play and his disinclination for the work of picking counterbalance the desire for eating. The satisfaction which he can get from picking fruit has arrived at its maximum. . . .*"

Marshall also explained how equilibrium is established in a local market. Buyers and sellers, having perfect knowledge of the market, freely compete for their own best interests. In so doing they arrive at a price that exactly equates supply and demand.

"*. . . [A price may be] called the true equilibrium price: because if it were fixed on at the beginning, and adhered to throughout, it would exactly equate demand and supply. (i.e. the amount which buyers were willing to purchase at that price would be just equal to that for which sellers were willing to take that price). . . .*

*In our typical market then we assume that the forces of demand and supply have free play; that there is no combination among dealers on either side; but each acts for himself, and there is much free competition; that is, buyers generally compete freely with buyers, and sellers compete freely with sellers.*"

### *Checking for Understanding*

1. **What does Marshall mean by "equilibrium between desire and effort"?**
2. **What is an equilibrium price?**



### Answers to *Checking for Understanding*

1. Answers will vary but should indicate the point at which satisfaction created by effort has arrived at its maximum. Students should note that at this point, additional effort takes away from the pleasure of attaining the desire.
2. An equilibrium price is a price that is fixed at the beginning and adhered to throughout marketing. It equates supply and demand.

# CHAPTER  Summary

**Chapter Overview** Visit the *Economics Today and Tomorrow* Web site at ett.glencoe.com and click on ***Chapter 7—Chapter Overviews*** to review chapter information.

## SECTION 1 Demand

- **Demand** represents a consumer's willingness and ability to pay.
- The **law of demand** states as price goes up, **quantity demanded** goes down. As price goes down, quantity demanded goes up.
- Factors explaining the inverse relationship between quantity demanded and price include the **real income effect,** the **substitution effect,** and **diminishing marginal utility**—or how one's additional satisfaction for a product lessens with each additional purchase of it.

## SECTION 2 The Demand Curve and Elasticity of Demand

- The downward-sloping **demand curve** signifies that as the price falls, the quantity demanded increases.
- Changes in population, income, tastes and preferences, and the existence of substitutes, or **complementary goods,** affect demand.
- The **price elasticity of demand** is a measure of *how much* consumers respond to a price change.
- If a small change in price causes a large change in quantity demanded, the demand for that good is said to be **elastic.**
- If a price change does not result in much of a change in the quantity demanded, that demand is considered **inelastic.**

## SECTION 3 The Law of Supply and the Supply Curve

- The **law of supply** states as the price rises for a good, the **quantity supplied** also rises. As the price falls, the quantity supplied falls.
- The upward-sloping **supply curve** shows this direct relationship between quantity supplied and price.
- Four factors determine supply in a market economy. These include the price of inputs, the number of firms in the industry, taxes, and **technology.**

## SECTION 4 Putting Supply and Demand Together

- In free enterprise systems, prices serve as signals to producers and consumers.
- The point at which the quantity demanded and the quantity supplied meet is called the **equilibrium price.**
- A **shortage** causes prices to rise, signaling producers to produce more and consumers to purchase less.
- A **surplus** causes prices to drop, signaling producers to produce less and consumers to purchase more.
- A **price ceiling,** which prevents prices from going above a specified amount, often leads to shortages and **black market** activities.
- A **price floor** prevents prices such as a minimum wage from dropping too low.



CHAPTER 7 Summary

**ECONOMICS & YOU**

**Demand and Supply**

Chapter 7
Disc 1, Side 1

If you do not have access to a videodisc player, the ***Economics & You*** programs are also available in VHS.

Use the **Chapter 7 Summary** to preview, review, condense, or reteach the chapter.

## Preview/Review

**Vocabulary PuzzleMaker Software** reinforces the key terms used in Chapter 7.

**Interactive Tutor Self-Assessment Software** allows students to review Chapter 7 content.

## Condense

Have students listen to the Chapter 7 **Audio Program** (also available in Spanish) in the TCR. Assign the Chapter 7 Audio Program Activity and give students the Chapter 7 Audio Program Test.

## Reteach

Have students complete **Reteaching Activity** 7 in the TCR (Spanish Reteaching Activities are also available).

## Economics Journal

**Voluntary Exchange** In American retail stores, consumers may either accept the posted price or decide to shop for a better price elsewhere. However, in certain markets—used cars for example—buyer and seller usually must agree on the price. Have students keep journal entries of the various advertised prices of a few selected makes and model years of used cars over a period of two weeks. Ask students to write a few lines in answer to the following: What risks do buyer and seller each assume when the buyer must "make an offer"?

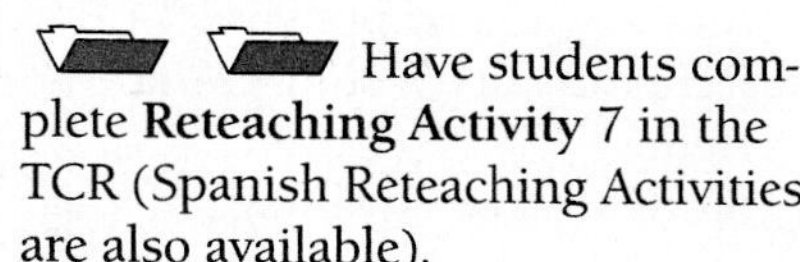

Have students visit the *Economics Today and Tomorrow* Web site at ett.glencoe.com to review Chapter 7 and take the Self-Check Quiz.

MindJogger Videoquiz

Use MindJogger to review Chapter 7 content.

## Identifying Key Terms

1. Paragraphs will vary.
2. Paragraphs will vary.

## Recalling Facts and Ideas

1. voluntary exchange
2. quantity demanded falls
3. real income effect; substitution effect
4. The demand curve moves to the right.
5. Elastic demand means consumers are more responsive to price changes. Inelastic means they are less responsive.
6. Demand curves shift to the right.
7. more, to take advantage of increased profits
8. Supply curve would shift to the left.
9. There is a surplus.
10. There is a shortage.

# CHAPTER 7 Assessment and Activities

**Self-Check Quiz** Visit the *Economics Today and Tomorrow* Web site at ett.glencoe.com and click on ***Chapter 7—Self-Check Quizzes*** to prepare for the Chapter Test.

## Identifying Key Terms

*Write a short paragraph about demand using all of the following terms.*

- law of demand
- quantity demanded
- law of diminishing marginal utility
- real income effect
- substitution effect
- demand curve
- price elasticity of demand

*Write a short paragraph about supply using all of the following terms.*

- law of supply
- law of diminishing returns
- supply curve
- shortage
- equilibrium price
- surplus

## Recalling Facts and Ideas

### Section 1

1. What is the basis of most activity in a market economy?
2. What generally happens to quantity demanded when the price of a good goes up (and other prices stay the same)?
3. When the price of a good changes, what effects tend to create the law of demand?

### Section 2

4. How do we show in a graph an increase in the demand for a good?
5. What is the distinction between elastic and inelastic demand?
6. If income and population increase, what tends to happen to demand curves?

### Section 3

7. Do suppliers tend to produce less or more when the price goes up? Why?
8. What would an increase in taxes do to the position of the supply curve?

### Section 4

9. If the price of a product is above its equilibrium price, what is the result?
10. If the price of a product is below its equilibrium price, what is the result?

## Thinking Critically

1. **Making Generalizations** To what extent do you think the law of demand applies in the world around you? Are there any goods or services that you think do not follow the law of demand? Explain.
2. **Making Comparisons** If you had to guess the relative price elasticities of demand for CDs compared to that of insulin needed by diabetics, what would you state?



## Thinking Critically

1. Answers will vary. Students should offer reasons in support of their answers.
2. Demand for CDs, a luxury, is elastic. Demand for insulin, a necessity for diabetics, is inelastic.
3. Predictions will vary.

3. **Making Predictions** Technology has decreased the cost of producing goods and services. Create a chart like the one below and list four goods or services that you think will be changed by technology in your lifetime. Explain how you think each change will affect your life.

| Technological Change | Effect on My Life |
|---|---|
| 1. | |
| 2. | |
| 3. | |
| 4. | |

## Applying Economic Concepts

**Supply and Demand** Some prices change in our economy very seldom, whereas others change all the time, even daily. Make a list of products whose prices change slowly, if at all. Make another list of products whose prices you think change quickly.

## Cooperative Learning Project

Working in groups of four, each group will interview a local merchant. Ask the following questions and others you think are relevant: What determines the prices you charge? What determines when you change prices? Are there any costs to you of changing prices (such as reprinting price lists)? One person in each group should write a summary of the interview. Then compare these summaries.

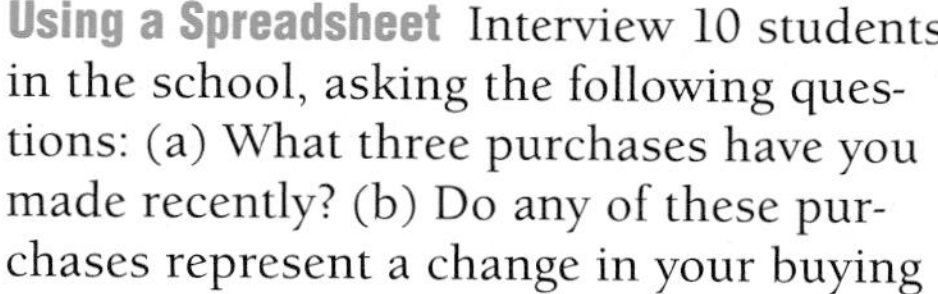

## Technology Activity

**Using a Spreadsheet** Interview 10 students in the school, asking the following questions: (a) What three purchases have you made recently? (b) Do any of these purchases represent a change in your buying habits? (c) Was the change caused by a change in income, a change in tastes and preferences, or a change in the price of substitutes or complements? Summarize the information you obtained by placing it in a spreadsheet.

## Reviewing Skills

**Understanding Cause and Effect** Look at the graph below, then answer the questions that follow.

1. How many pounds of beef are supplied at $1.89 per pound?
2. How many pounds are supplied at $2.69 per pound?
3. What can you infer as the cause-and-effect relationship here?

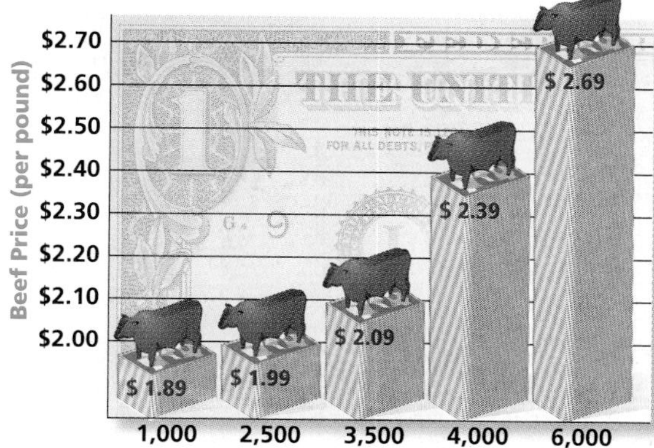


## Analyzing the Global Economy

Clip articles from newspapers or magazines that show the laws of supply and/or demand operating in other parts of the world. Possibilities would be weather damages to crops and economic conditions affecting housing starts, and so on.



# CHAPTER 7 Assessment and Activities

## Applying Economic Concepts

Answers will vary, but students may note that the price of housing usually changes slowly, whereas the prices of other countries' currencies change every day and, in fact, change every second.

## Cooperative Learning Project

Students might present their summaries in the form of a feature article about the merchant and his or her business.

## Technology Activity

Encourage students to compare their spreadsheets.

## Reviewing Skills

1. 1,000,000 pounds
2. 6,000,000 pounds
3. Rising prices cause producers to supply more beef.

## Analyzing the Global Economy

Students might combine their articles in a class scrapbook.

### Chapter Bonus Test Question

ASK: In the American economy, what forces other than supply and demand help to set prices? *government regulations, such as price ceilings and floors*

# 1 Focus

Tell students that the Middle East contains more than half of the world's known oil reserves. (In contrast, the United States has only 2 percent of the world's supplies.) However, the region accounts for only about one-third of the world's oil production. This is because the Organization of Petroleum Exporting Countries (OPEC)—the oil cartel—exercises considerable control over production in the region.

# 2 Teach

Direct students to study the map annotations and to note the sources of the oil consumed in the United States. Then discuss the significance of U.S. dependence on foreign oil. ASK: What events could obstruct the flow of foreign oil to the United States? How would that affect the American economy? *Students may suggest that political unrest, wars, terrorism, and changing trade relations all might interrupt the flow of imported oil. This could disrupt activity in the United States economy, because nearly half of the country's oil consumption is met by foreign sources.*

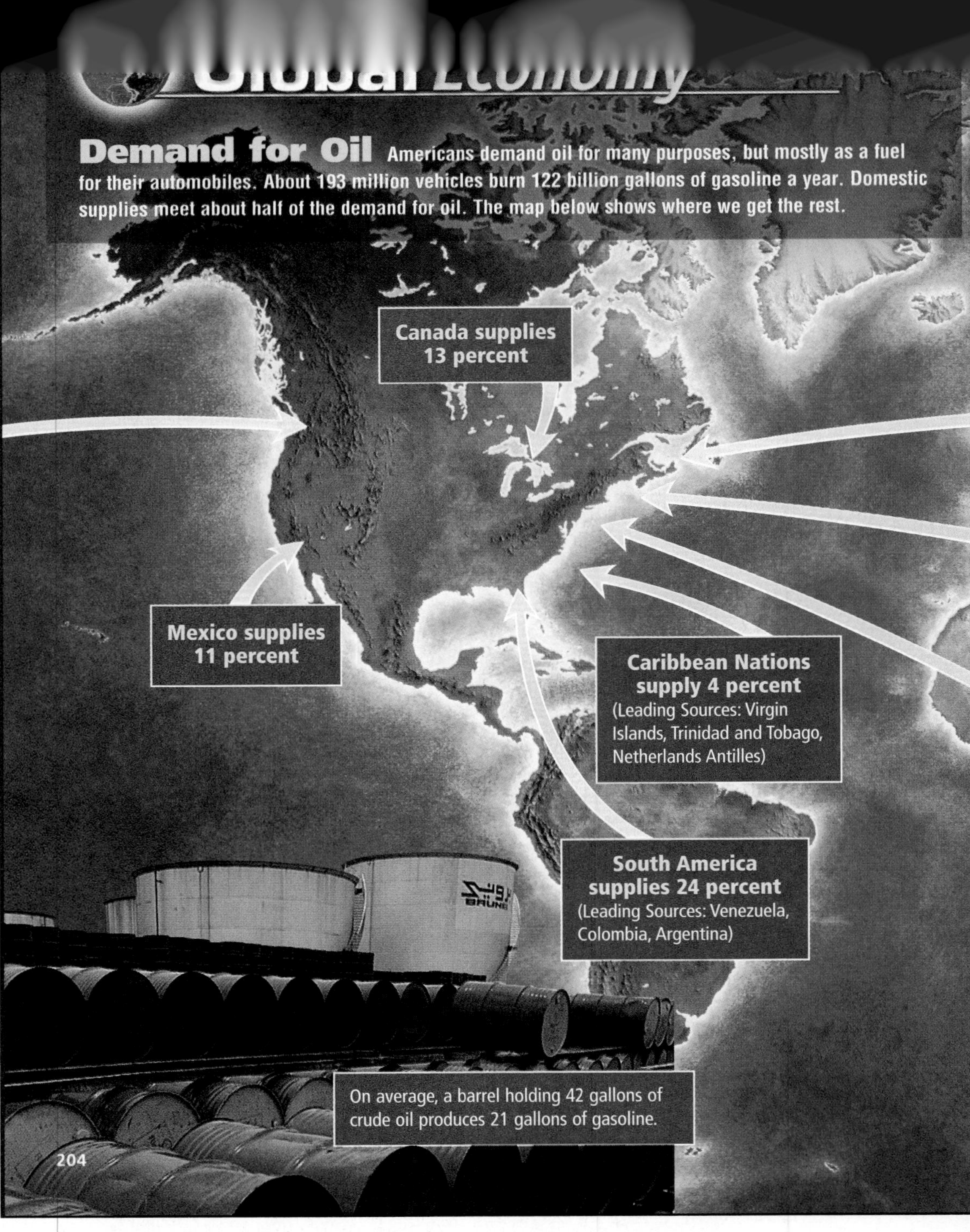

Global Economy
Demand for Oil Americans demand oil for many purposes, but mostly as a fuel for their automobiles. About 193 million vehicles burn 122 billion gallons of gasoline a year. Domestic supplies meet about half of the demand for oil. The map below shows where we get the rest.
Canada supplies 13 percent
Mexico supplies 11 percent
Caribbean Nations supply 4 percent (Leading Sources: Virgin Islands, Trinidad and Tobago, Netherlands Antilles)
South America supplies 24 percent (Leading Sources: Venezuela, Colombia, Argentina)
On average, a barrel holding 42 gallons of crude oil produces 21 gallons of gasoline.
204


## Teacher's Notes

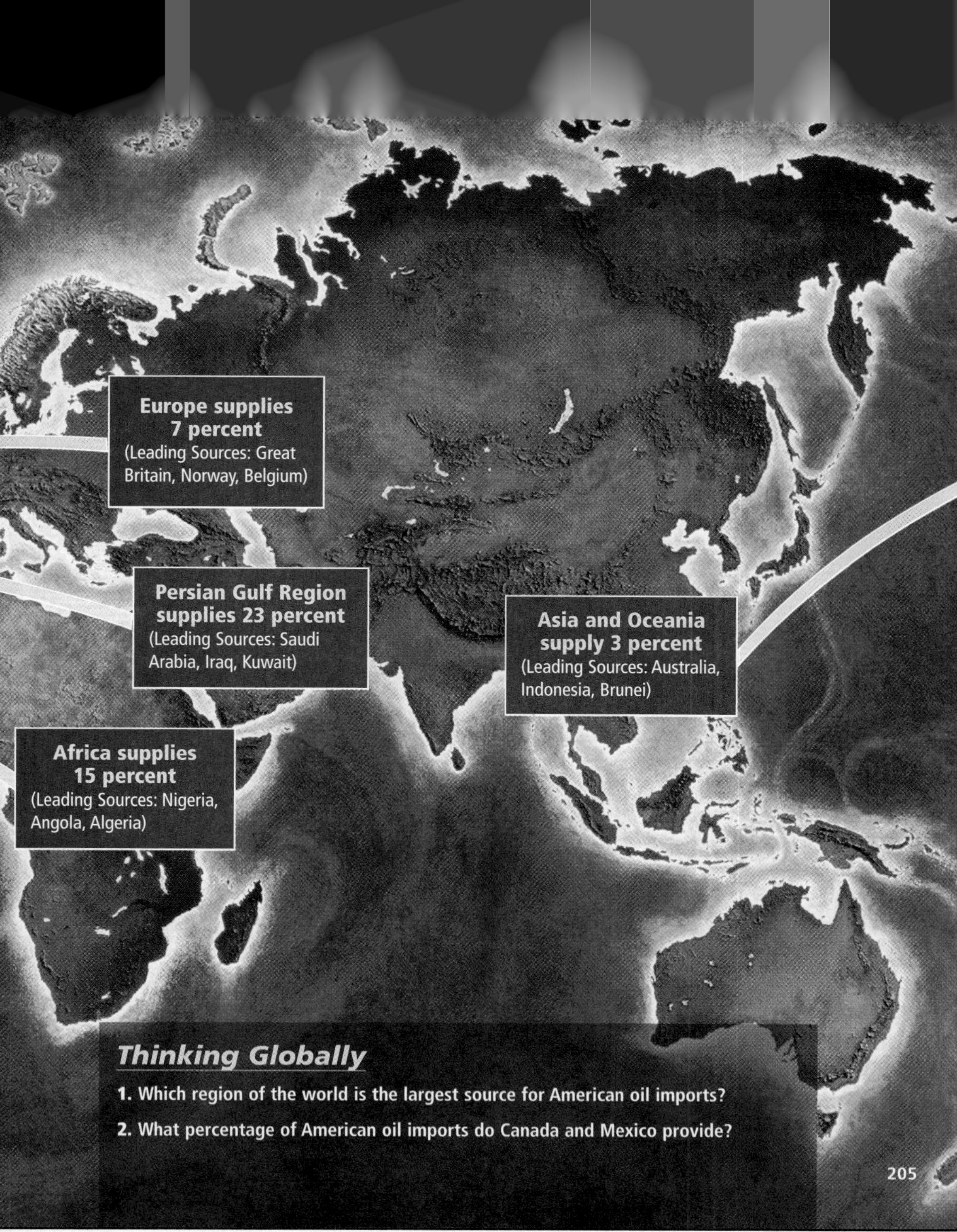
Europe supplies 7 percent
(Leading Sources: Great Britain, Norway, Belgium)
Persian Gulf Region supplies 23 percent
(Leading Sources: Saudi Arabia, Iraq, Kuwait)
Asia and Oceania supply 3 percent
(Leading Sources: Australia, Indonesia, Brunei)
Africa supplies 15 percent
(Leading Sources: Nigeria, Angola, Algeria)
205

### *Thinking Globally*

1. Which region of the world is the largest source for American oil imports?
2. What percentage of American oil imports do Canada and Mexico provide?

## 3 Assess

Have students answer the **Thinking Globally** questions.

## 4 Close

Have students assume that they are experts assigned to study the United States's dependence on foreign oil. Ask them what recommendations they might make to the government to protect the country from oil shortages due to a disruption of the flow of foreign oil.

### Did You Know

The United States accounts for only about 5 percent of the world's population. However, it consumes close to 25 percent of the world's oil.

### Answers to *Thinking Globally*

1. South America
2. 24 percent

# CHAPTER 8 Resource Manager

## Teaching Transparency

### Economic Concepts Transparency 7

ECONOMIC CONCEPTS Transparency 7

MARKETS AND PRICES

## Application and Enrichment

### Enrichment Activity 8

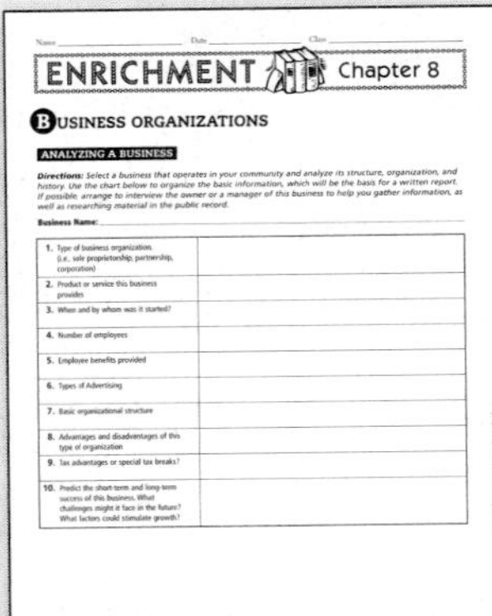

ENRICHMENT Chapter 8

BUSINESS ORGANIZATIONS

### Consumer Applications Activity 4

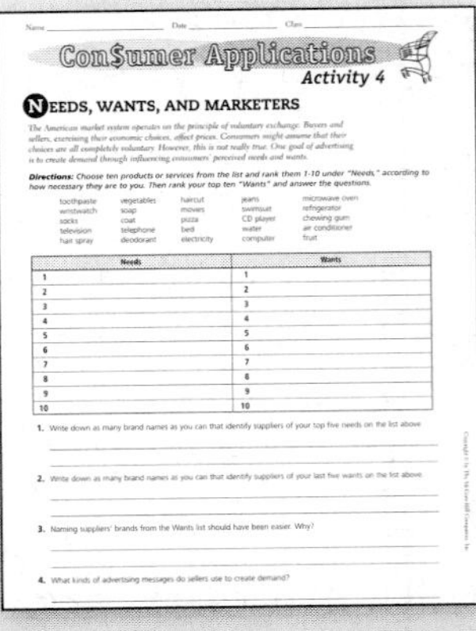

Con$umer Applications Activity 4

NEEDS, WANTS, AND MARKETERS

### Free Enterprise Activity 3

FREE ENTERPRISE ACTIVITY 3

CHOOSING A BUSINESS ORGANIZATION

## Application and Enrichment

### Cooperative Learning Simulations and Problems 3

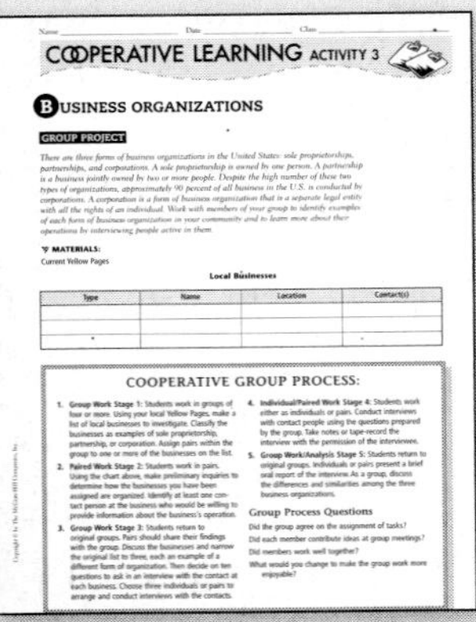

COOPERATIVE LEARNING ACTIVITY 3

BUSINESS ORGANIZATIONS

### Primary and Secondary Source Reading 8

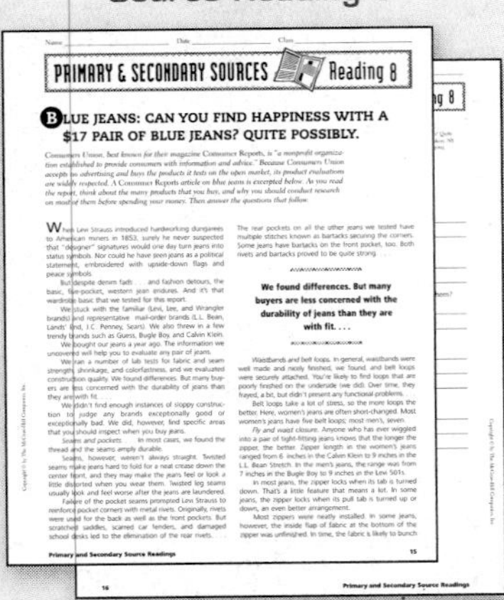

PRIMARY & SECONDARY SOURCES Reading 8

BLUE JEANS: CAN YOU FIND HAPPINESS WITH A $17 PAIR OF BLUE JEANS? QUITE POSSIBLY.

### Math Practice for Economics Activity 3

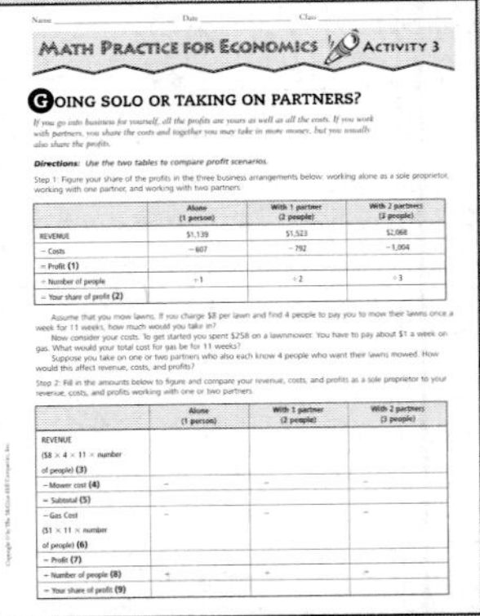

MATH PRACTICE FOR ECONOMICS ACTIVITY 3

GOING SOLO OR TAKING ON PARTNERS?

### Economic Cartoons Activity 3

ECONOMIC CARTOON 3

PRODUCER PAINS

## Review and Reinforcement

### Critical Thinking Activity 3

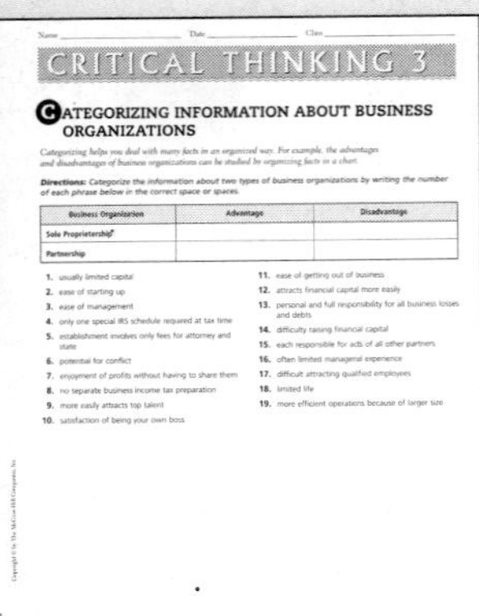

CRITICAL THINKING 3

CATEGORIZING INFORMATION ABOUT BUSINESS ORGANIZATIONS

### Reteaching Activity 8

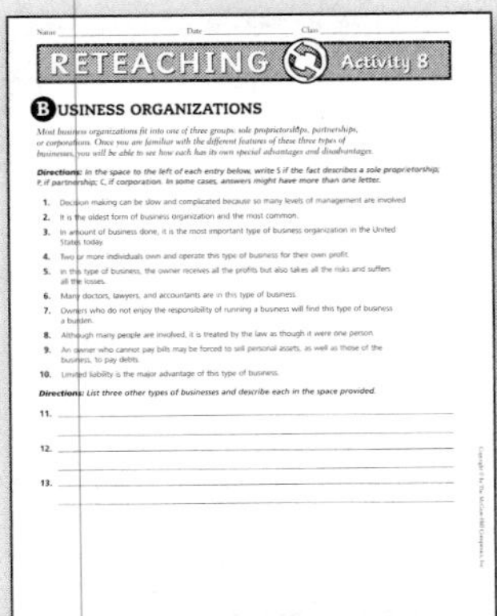

RETEACHING Activity 8

BUSINESS ORGANIZATIONS

### Economic Vocabulary Activity 8

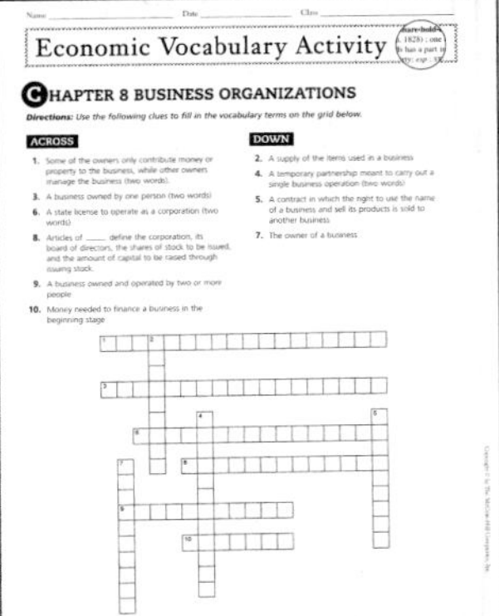

Economic Vocabulary Activity

CHAPTER 8 BUSINESS ORGANIZATIONS

### Reinforcing Economic Skills 21

Reinforcing Economic Skills Chapter 21

USING THE INTERNET

# CHAPTER 8 Resource Manager

## Assessment and Evaluation

Chapter 8 Test Form A

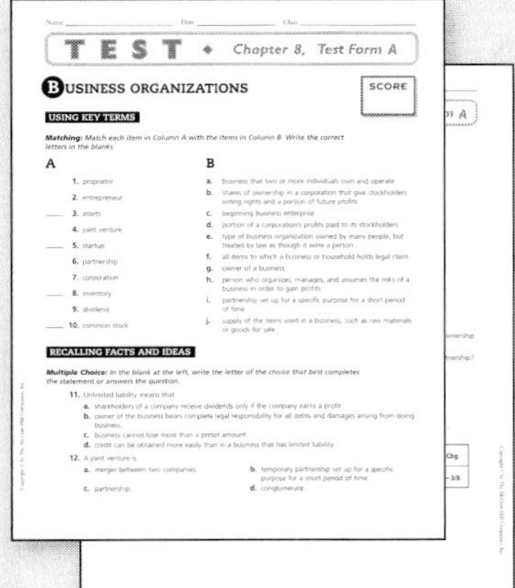

TEST • Chapter 8, Test Form A

BUSINESS ORGANIZATIONS

SCORE

USING KEY TERMS

RECALLING FACTS AND IDEAS

Chapter 8 Test Form B

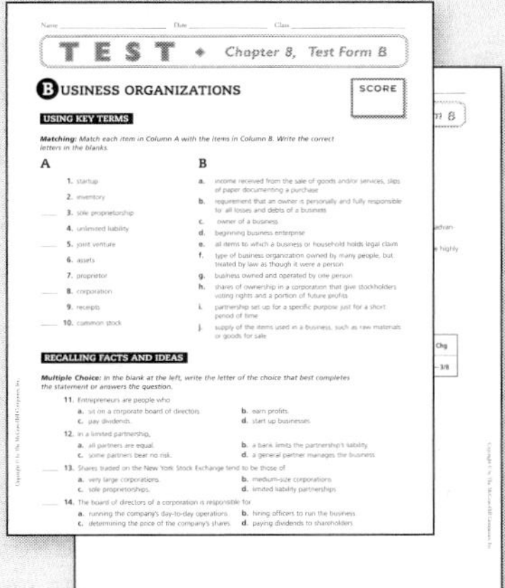

TEST • Chapter 8, Test Form B

BUSINESS ORGANIZATIONS

SCORE

USING KEY TERMS

RECALLING FACTS AND IDEAS

Performance Assessment Activity 3

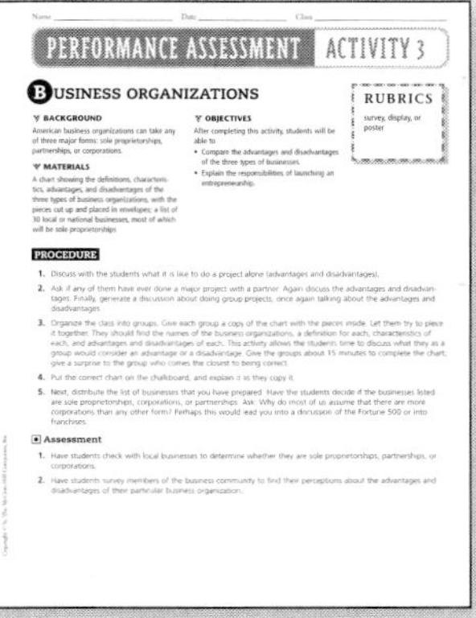

PERFORMANCE ASSESSMENT ACTIVITY 3

BUSINESS ORGANIZATIONS

RUBRICS

PROCEDURE

ExamView® Pro Testmaker

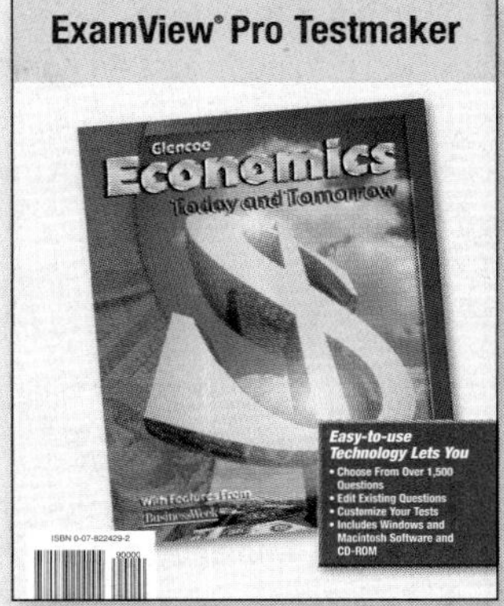


## Technology and Multimedia

 Vocabulary PuzzleMaker Software

 Interactive Tutor Self-Assessment Software

 ExamView® Pro Testmaker

 NBR *Economics & You* Video Program (English/Spanish)

 Presentation Plus!

 Glencoe Skillbuilder Interactive Workbook CD-ROM, Level 2

Interactive Lesson Planner

 MindJogger Videoquiz

 Interactive Economics! CD-ROM

 Audio Program (English or Spanish)

You and your students can visit *ett.glencoe.com*—the Web site companion to **Economics Today and Tomorrow.** This innovative integration of electronic and print media offers your students a wealth of opportunities. The student text directs students to the Web site for the following options:

- **Chapter Overviews**
- **Student Web Activities**
- **Self-Check Quizzes**
- **Textbook Updates**

Answers are provided for you in the **Web Activity Lesson Plan.** Additional Web resources and Interactive Puzzles are also available.

Use the Glencoe Web site for additional resources. All essential content is covered in the Student Edition.

## Spanish Resources

 Spanish Economic Concepts Transparency 7

 Spanish Vocabulary Activity 8

 Spanish Reteaching Activity 8

 Spanish Section Quizzes for Chapter 8

 Spanish Chapter 8 Audio Program, Activity, and Test

## Additional Resources

### Reading for the Student

Drucker, Peter F. *Concept of the Corporation.* New Brunswick, NJ: Transaction Publishers, 1993. The classic study of the American corporation.

### Multimedia Material

*The Business File.* PBS. Video. *Forming a Business: Corporation/Proprietorships and Partnerships* provide detailed information on business organizations.

# CHAPTER 8 Resource Manager

## Section Resources

| Reading Objectives | Reproducible Resources | Technology/Multimedia Resources |
|---|---|---|
| **Section 1**<br>**Starting a Business**<br>• What things must be done before starting a business?<br>• What four elements are involved in every business? | Reproducible Lesson Plan 8-1<br>Daily Lecture Notes 8-1<br>Guided Reading Activity 8-1<br>Reading Essentials and Study Guide 8-1<br>Daily Focus Activity 16<br>Section Quiz 8-1*<br>Reinforcing Economic Skills 21 | Daily Focus Transparency 16<br>Vocabulary PuzzleMaker<br>Interactive Tutor Self-Assessment Software<br>MindJogger Videoquiz<br>Presentation Plus!<br>ExamView® Pro Testmaker |
| **Section 2**<br>**Sole Proprietorships and Partnerships**<br>• What are the advantages and disadvantages of a sole proprietorship?<br>• What are the advantages and disadvantages of a partnership? | Reproducible Lesson Plan 8-2<br>Daily Lecture Notes 8-2<br>Guided Reading Activity 8-2<br>Reading Essentials and Study Guide 8-2<br>Daily Focus Activity 19<br>Section Quiz 8-2* | Daily Focus Transparency 19<br>Economic Concepts Transparency 7<br>Vocabulary PuzzleMaker<br>Interactive Tutor Self-Assessment Software<br>MindJogger Videoquiz<br>NBR's *Economics & You**<br>Presentation Plus!<br>ExamView® Pro Testmaker |
| **Section 3**<br>**The Corporate World and Franchises**<br>• What are the advantages and disadvantages of corporations?<br>• How are corporations typically structured?<br>• What types of businesses are involved in franchises? | Reproducible Lesson Plan 8-3<br>Daily Lecture Notes 8-3<br>Guided Reading Activity 8-3<br>Reading Essentials and Study Guide 8-3<br>Daily Focus Activity 15<br>Section Quiz 8-3* | Daily Focus Transparency 15<br>Vocabulary PuzzleMaker<br>Interactive Tutor Self-Assessment Software<br>MindJogger Videoquiz<br>Presentation Plus!<br>ExamView® Pro Testmaker |

*Also available in Spanish

Blackline Master
Transparency

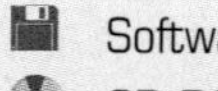
Software
CD-ROM

Videodisc
Audiocassette

Videocassette

# CHAPTER 8 Resource Manager

## ACTIVITY From the Classroom of

**Denny C. Jackson**
**Switzerland County High School**
**Vevay, Indiana**

### Starting a Business

Have students start a mock business—specifically, a hotel business. Working in pairs, they must write a business plan that includes everything from initial financing options to staffing considerations to what "free items" will be provided to hotel guests. See pages 230–231 in the Student Edition for more details.

## Easy Planning and Preparation!

Use Glencoe's **Presentation Plus!**, a Microsoft PowerPoint® application, to teach **Business Organizations.** With this multimedia teacher tool, you can customize ready-made presentations. At your fingertips are interactive transparencies, on-screen lecture notes, audiovisual presentations, and links to the Internet and to other Glencoe multimedia.

**Interactive Lesson Planner**
Planning has never been easier! Organize your week, month, semester, or year with all the lesson helps you need to make teaching creative, timely, and relevant—the way it is meant to be. The Interactive Lesson Planner opens Glencoe's **Chapter 8** resources, helps you build your schedule, and tracks your progress.

## Key to Ability Levels

**Teaching strategies have been coded for varying learning styles and abilities.**

L1 BASIC activities for all students
L2 AVERAGE activities for average to above-average students
L3 CHALLENGING activities for above-average students
ELL ENGLISH LANGUAGE LEARNER activities

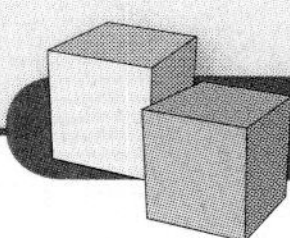

## Block Schedule

Activities that are particularly suited to use within the block scheduling framework are identified throughout this chapter by the following designation: BLOCK SCHEDULING

## National Council on Economic Education

## THE EconomicsAmerica AND EconomicsInternational PROGRAMS

### Voluntary Standards Emphasized in Chapter 8

**Content Standard 10** Students will understand that institutions evolve in market economies to help individuals and groups accomplish their goals. Banks, labor unions, corporations, legal systems, and not-for-profit organizations are examples of important institutions.

**Content Standard 14** Entrepreneurs are people who take the risks of organizing productive resources to make goods and services. Profit is an important incentive that leads entrepreneurs to accept the risks of business failure.

### Resources Available from NCEE

- *MCG–Economics and Entrepreneurship*
- *Entrepreneurship in the U.S. Economy*
- *Learning from the Market: Integrating the Stock Market Game™ Across the Curriculum*

To order these materials, or to contact your State Council on Economic Education about workshops and programs, call 1-800-338-1192 or visit the NCEE Web site at http://www.nationalcouncil.org

*Introducing* CHAPTER 8

ECONOMICS & YOU

Business Organizations

Chapter 4
Disc 1, Side 1

ASK: What are three important planning activities to undertake before starting a business? *Answers may include conducting a feasibility study to see if the business will attract customers, developing a business plan, and arranging for financing.*

Also available in VHS.

## Chapter Overview

Chapter 8 describes or explains how businesses are started and the advantages and disadvantages of sole proprietorships, partnerships, and corporations as business organizations.

### GLENCOE TECHNOLOGY

Use **MindJogger Videoquiz** VHS to preview Chapter 8 content.

### ECONOMICS Online

Introduce students to chapter content and key terms by having them access **Chapter 8—Chapter Overviews** at ett.glencoe.com

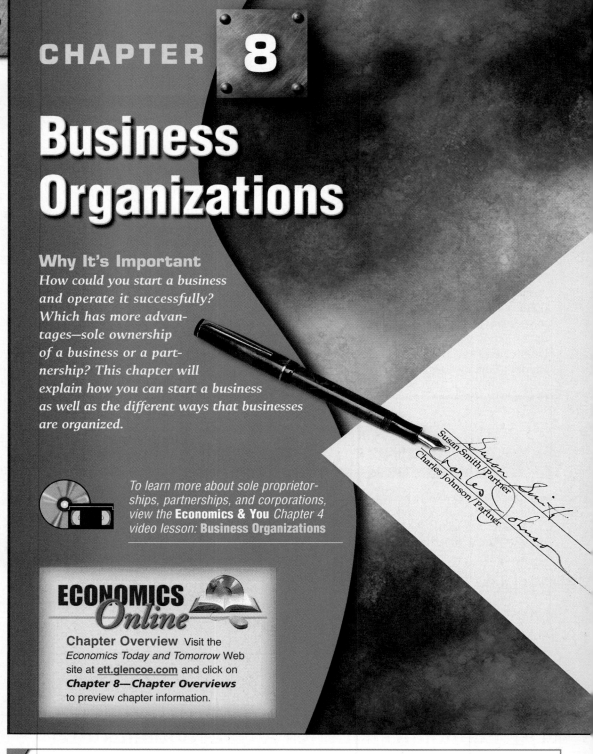

# CHAPTER 8

# Business Organizations

### Why It's Important

*How could you start a business and operate it successfully? Which has more advantages—sole ownership of a business or a partnership? This chapter will explain how you can start a business as well as the different ways that businesses are organized.*



*To learn more about sole proprietorships, partnerships, and corporations, view the* **Economics & You** *Chapter 4 video lesson:* **Business Organizations**

### ECONOMICS Online

**Chapter Overview** Visit the *Economics Today and Tomorrow* Web site at ett.glencoe.com and click on ***Chapter 8—Chapter Overviews*** to preview chapter information.

## CHAPTER LAUNCH ACTIVITY

Ask students to imagine they want to start a business. Have students identify the type of business they would like to start. Also, have them consider the resources they would need, and the decisions they would have to make to run this business. Finally, ask students to consider if they would like to run the business by themselves or if they would like to run it with assistance or financial backing of others. Have students review their responses to these questions as they work through Chapter 8.

# SECTION 1

# Starting a Business

## COVER STORY

*KIPLINGER'S PERSONAL FINANCE MAGAZINE*, DECEMBER 1998

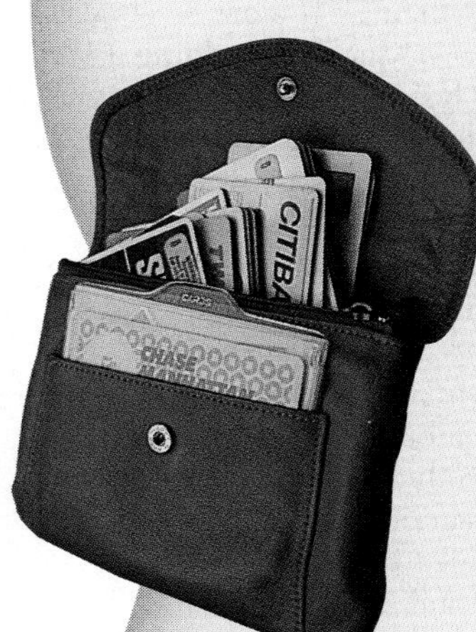

The perfect place for your credit cards is in a Beeping Wallet—a billfold with a microchip that beeps every 20 seconds when a credit card has been removed. It's both a last-gasp warning [to not spend money] and a reminder to replace the card, says David Kopel, the wallet's inventor, who says he came up with the idea after his wife lost a credit card.

### READER'S GUIDE

**Terms to Know**

- entrepreneur
- startup
- small business incubator
- inventory
- receipts

**Reading Objectives**

1. What things must be done before starting a business?
2. What four elements are involved in every business?

How many times have you seen a product for sale and said, "That was *my* idea"? Or you see an item, nod your head, and think, "That's a good idea. I wonder how they thought of that"? Many new products and services arise from personal experience–as in the case of David Kopel's Beeping Wallet. In this section, you'll learn how to take your idea and start a business.

## Getting Started

Suppose that you have been tinkering with electronic equipment since you were a child. By now you can take apart and reassemble cassette and CD players, VCRs, most computers, and



## SECTION 1 RESOURCE MANAGER

**Reproducible Masters**

- Reproducible Lesson Plan 8–1
- Reading Essentials and Study Guide 8–1
- Guided Reading Activity 8–1
- Section Quiz 8–1
- Daily Focus Activity 16
- Daily Lecture Notes 8–1

**Multimedia**

- Daily Focus Transparency 16
- Vocabulary PuzzleMaker
- Interactive Tutor Self-Assessment Software
- ExamView® Pro Testmaker
- MindJogger Videoquiz
- Presentation Plus!



# 1 Focus

## Overview

Section 1 explains the steps involved in starting a business and the four elements of business operation that entrepreneurs need to consider.

**BELLRINGER**
**Motivational Activity**

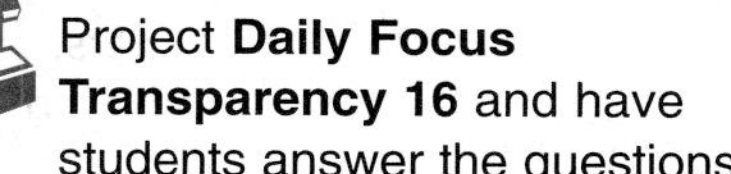

Project **Daily Focus Transparency 16** and have students answer the questions.

This activity is also available as a blackline master.

**Daily Focus Transparency 16**

ENTERING THE WORLD OF BUSINESS

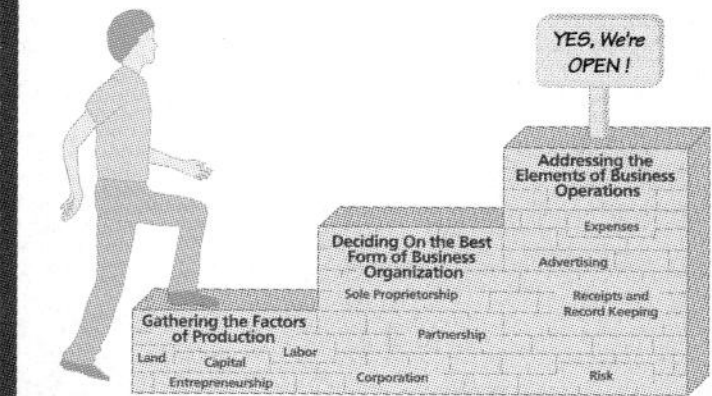


1. What are the four factors of production?
2. How might the second step, deciding on the best form of business organization, affect the third step, addressing the elements of business operation?

### READER'S GUIDE

Answers to the **Reading Objectives** questions are on page 211.

**Preteaching Vocabulary**

Direct students to study the Glossary definitions of the **Terms to Know**. Then have students use these terms to write a paragraph about starting a business.

**Vocabulary PuzzleMaker**

# 2 Teach

## Guided Practice

**L1 Classifying Information** On the board, draw a four-column table with "Expenses," "Advertising," "Record Keeping," and "Risk" as column headings. Call on volunteers to come to the board and enter examples of elements of business operation in the appropriate columns. Then ask students to use the information to write a brief explanation of what entrepreneurs need to consider in operating a business.

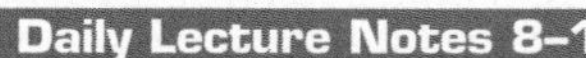

**Daily Lecture Notes 8–1**

DAILY LECTURE NOTES  Lesson 8-1

**LECTURE LAUNCHER**

Sometimes technological advances eliminate entire businesses. For example, before the refrigerator, ice farms were a big business. Workers would cut ice from frozen freshwater lakes, store it in large blocks, and then distribute it to homes to help keep things cool. What do you think were the risks of starting a refrigeration business? Do you think an ice farmer entering the refrigeration business would have an advantage over others who might enter this business?

PAGES 207–209

I. Getting Started

A. People who decide to start a business and are willing to take risks are entrepreneurs.

B. Collect information about the business, the factors of production for the product, and learn about taxes and laws relating to the business.

C. Federal and state government offer help to small businesses.

D. The Internet has a great deal of information to help entrepreneurs.

**Discussion Question**

**Think of a new business you might like to start. What are some of the types of information you would need to gather before you started the company?** *(Answers will vary, but students should be able to relate the ideas of taxes and laws specifically to their product. They should also break down some of the factors of production and list questions relating to*

**Visual Instruction FIGURE 8.1**

**Answer:** *to make profits*

**ECONOMICS Online**

See the **Web Activity Lesson Plan** at ett.glencoe.com for an introduction, lesson description, and answers to the **Student Web Activity** for this chapter.

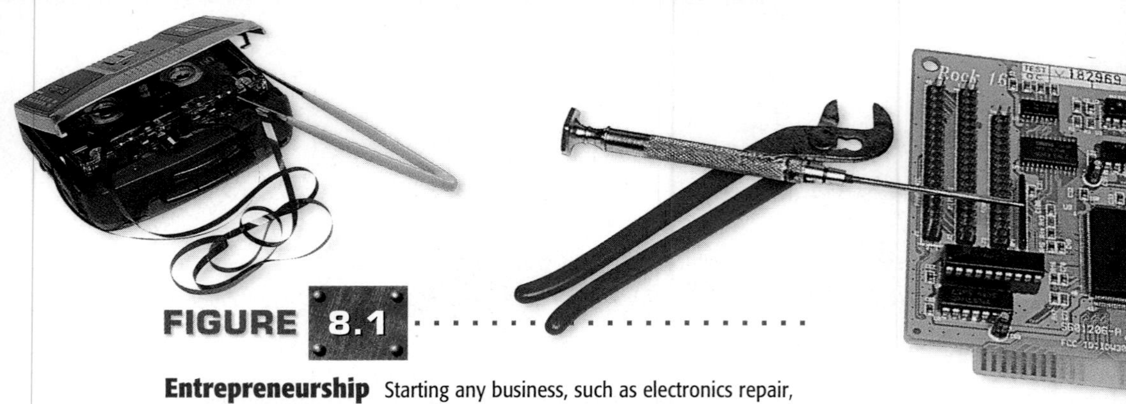

**FIGURE 8.1**

**Entrepreneurship** Starting any business, such as electronics repair, is risky. ***Why do people take the risk of becoming entrepreneurs?***

other electronic equipment without difficulty. You are so good at repairing this kind of equipment that you have been doing it for friends and relatives for some time. Then an idea occurs to you: Why not charge people for your services? Why not go into business for yourself? By starting your own business, you will become an entrepreneur.

A person who makes the decision to start a business is an **entrepreneur** because he or she is willing to take a risk. See **Figure 8.1.** People usually decide to start a business to gain profits, to "do something on their own," or to be their own boss.

*entrepreneur: person who organizes, manages, and assumes the risks of a business in order to gain profits*

After making the decision to start a business, entrepreneurs must gather the relevant factors of production to produce their good or service and decide on the form of business organization that best suits their purposes. (You'll learn about the types of business organizations in Sections 2 and 3.)

Anyone hoping to become an entrepreneur must also learn as much as possible about the business he or she plans to start. This process includes learning about the laws, regulations, and tax codes that will apply to the business.

*startup: a beginning business enterprise*

**Student Web Activity** Visit the *Economics Today and Tomorrow* Web site at ett.glencoe.com and click on ***Chapter 8—Student Web Activities*** to learn more about the Small Business Administration.

**Help From Government** For a person who wants to start a small business, help is available. The federal government's Small Business Administration often helps finance **startups**, or new small businesses. State departments of commerce and community affairs also offer assistance. Many community college and university campuses have small business development centers that are federally funded to help a small business get started.



**Meeting Special Needs**

**Memory Disability** Note taking is an important skill to develop, especially for students with organization or memory problems. Demonstrate the importance of note taking by telling students that good notes will help them to focus on significant information in the text and to organize that information in understandable formats. Add that good notes aid memory by helping students to review for tests. Work with students to review note-taking procedures. Encourage students to adopt those procedures that work best for them.

Refer to *Inclusion for the Social Studies Classroom Strategies and Activities* for students with different learning styles.

A **small business incubator** might also aid businesses in your area. Just as incubators help hatch chicks, there are business incubators that help "hatch" small businesses. They are often operated with state and federal funds. A small business incubator might provide a low-rent building, management advice, and computers. The incubator's goal is to generate job creation and economic growth, particularly in economically depressed areas.

**small business incubator:** *government-funded agency that assists new businesses by providing advice or low-rent buildings and supplies*

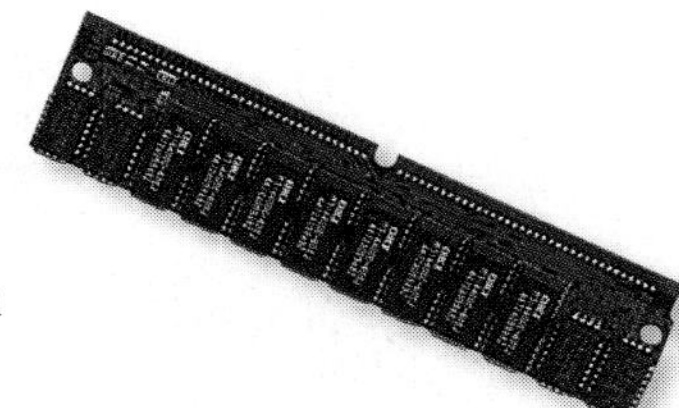

**Help From the Internet** Although new entrepreneurs can get help from government agencies, the Internet also provides a huge amount of information on how to start a business. By using search engines, you can find Web sites that explain everything from putting together a business plan to learning the "secrets to success."

## Elements of Business Operation

Every business must consider four basic elements: expenses, advertising, record keeping, and risk.

**Expenses** You've probably heard the saying, "You have to spend money to make money." This is true when considering business expenses: new equipment, wages, insurance, taxes, electricity, telephone service, and so on. And depending on the kind of job you do, you may need replacement parts. At first, you might buy parts only as you need them for a particular job. In time, you will find it easier to have an **inventory,** or supply of items that are used in your business. See *Part A* of **Figure 8.2** on page 210.

**inventory:** *extra supply of the items used in a business, such as raw materials or goods for sale*

Wages are an expense. Because you could be working for someone else and earning an income, you should pay yourself a wage equal to what you could earn elsewhere. It's important not to forget this *opportunity cost* when you figure out the profits and losses your new business is making.

Will your business make a profit? Add your wages to your other expenses, including taxes. Then subtract your total expenses from your **receipts,** or the money income you've received from customers, and you will have your profit. Keep records of how much you owe and to whom, and of how much your business is taking in. You will need this information to do your taxes.

**receipts:** *income received from the sale of goods and/or services; also, slips of paper documenting a purchase*



### Did You Know

The term *entrepreneur* derives from the French word *entreprendre*, which means "to undertake," "to adventure," or "to try."

### Guided Reading Activity 8–1

Name ______ Date ______ Class ______

GUIDED READING Activity 8-1

*For use with the textbook pages 207–211*

**STARTING A BUSINESS**

**OUTLINING**

***Directions:*** *Locate the heading in your textbook. Then use the information under the heading to help you write each answer.*

I. Getting Started
  A. Introduction
    1. What is an entrepreneur?
    2. After deciding to start a business, what must entrepreneurs do?
  B. Help from Government
    1. Which government agency helps small businesses get started?
    2. What is a small business incubator?
  C. Help From the Internet—How might one use the Internet to help start a business?
II. Elements of Business Operation

### Did You Know

According to the National Business Incubation Association, North American incubators have created nearly 19,000 companies still in business, and more than 245,000 jobs.

## Independent Practice

**L2 Applying Ideas** Have students identify an interest they have that they could channel into a business. Then ask students to create a flyer, a newspaper advertisement, or a Web site advertisement promoting their businesses.

### Free Enterprise Activity

Organize students into several small groups. Direct the groups to locate new businesses in the community. Have these groups interview the owners of the businesses to discover what steps they took to get started. Tell groups specifically to ask the owners what was the most difficult aspect of starting up a new business. Encourage groups to present their findings in oral reports to the class. BLOCK SCHEDULING

## Visual Instruction FIGURE 8.2

Direct students' attention to Part C in **Figure 8.2.** ASK: Why should business owners file the physical evidence of their business purchases? *because business purchases can be deducted from the taxes they owe*

# 3 Assess

## Meeting Lesson Objectives

Assign Section 1 Assessment as homework or an in-class activity.

Use **Interactive Tutor Self-Assessment Software** to review Section 1.

### Section Quiz 8-1

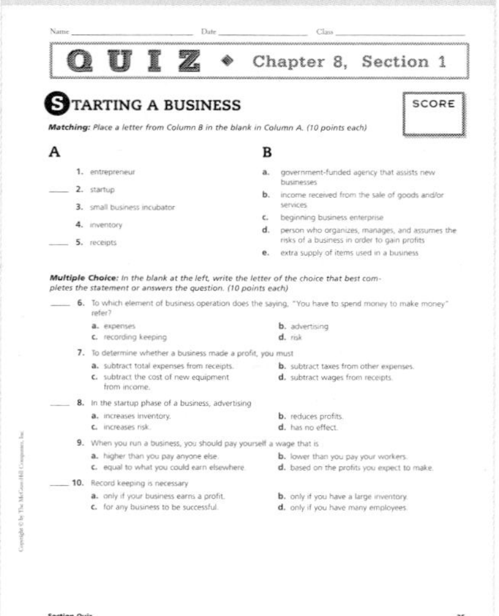

Name ______ Date ______ Class ______

QUIZ ◆ Chapter 8, Section 1

STARTING A BUSINESS

SCORE

***Matching:*** *Place a letter from Column B in the blank in Column A. (10 points each)*

**A**

____ 1. entrepreneur

____ 2. startup

____ 3. small business incubator

____ 4. inventory

____ 5. receipts

**B**

a. government-funded agency that assists new businesses

b. income received from the sale of goods and/or services

c. beginning business enterprise

d. person who organizes, manages, and assumes the risks of a business in order to gain profits

e. extra supply of items used in a business

***Multiple Choice:*** *In the blank at the left, write the letter of the choice that best completes the statement or answers the question. (10 points each)*

____ 6. To which element of business operation does the saying, "You have to spend money to make money" refer?
a. expenses
b. advertising
c. recording keeping
d. risk

____ 7. To determine whether a business made a profit, you must
a. subtract total expenses from receipts.
b. subtract taxes from other expenses.
c. subtract the cost of new equipment from income.
d. subtract wages from receipts.

____ 8. In the startup phase of a business, advertising
a. increases inventory.
b. reduces profits.
c. increases risk.
d. has no effect.

____ 9. When you run a business, you should pay yourself a wage that is
a. higher than you pay anyone else.
b. lower than you pay your workers.
c. equal to what you could earn elsewhere.
d. based on the profits you expect to make.

____ 10. Record keeping is necessary
a. only if your business earns a profit.
b. only if you have a large inventory.
c. for any business to be successful.
d. only if you have many employees.

Copyright © by The McGraw-Hill Companies, Inc.

Section Quiz 25

## FIGURE 8.2

### Elements of Business Operation

**A ▶ Expenses**

*The supplies you need to do your job are included under expenses. Let's imagine that you want to start a painting business. As part of your expenses, you will need to purchase brushes, paint, and ladders. As your business grows, you might invest in paint sprayers or electric sanders so you can complete jobs more quickly. This new equipment will eventually add to your income, but will probably require more money than you have on hand at the startup phase of your business.*

**◀ B Advertising**

*The cost of advertising often reduces profits substantially in the startup phase of a business. After you have several satisfied customers, however, information about your business may spread by word of mouth.*

**C ▶ Record Keeping**

*Maintaining accurate records of your expenses and receipts is vital—especially when you're doing your taxes.*

**D ▶ Risk**

*Many startups fail. If you work for a boss, your overall risks are usually small. As your own boss, your risks are greater, but so are the potential rewards. The profits you expect to make are your incentive for taking those risks.*

210

## Relevant Issues in Economics

**Small Business and the American Economy** How important are small businesses to the American economy? According to the Small Business Administration, there are 23 million small businesses in the United States. These businesses employ more than 50 percent of the private workforce and are the principal source of new jobs. In addition, these businesses generate more than half of the gross domestic product of the United States.

**Advertising** To start a business, you must make potential customers aware that your goods or services are available for a price. You could have flyers printed and distributed to advertise your business, as shown in *Part B* of **Figure 8.2.** You could also buy advertising space in newspapers or on various Web sites.

**Record Keeping** No matter how small your business, having a system to track your expenses and income is key to your success. Probably one of the first things you'll need is a computer. See *Part C* of **Figure 8.2.** You should also purchase or download from the Internet the programs that will allow you to track your expenses and receipts. These programs write checks, calculate your monthly profits and losses, tell you the difference between what you own and what you owe (called *net worth*), and so on.

The slips of paper that document your purchases of supplies—also known as *receipts*—must be filed in a safe place. Business purchases can be deducted from the amount of taxes you owe.

**Risk** Every business involves risks. You must balance the risks against the advantages of being in business for yourself. See *Part D* of **Figure 8.2.** For example, if you spend part of your savings to pay for advertising and equipment, you are taking a risk. You may not get enough business to cover these costs.

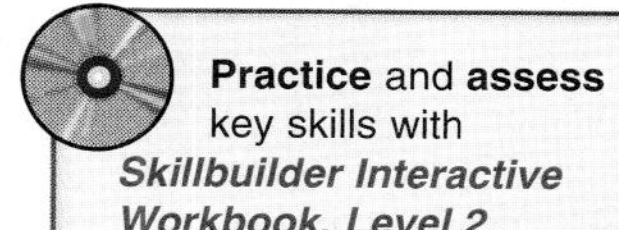

**Practice** and **assess** key skills with ***Skillbuilder Interactive Workbook, Level 2.***

## SECTION 1 Assessment

### Understanding Key Terms

1. **Define** entrepreneur, startup, small business incubator, inventory, receipts.

### Reviewing Objectives

2. What are at least three things you must do before starting a business?
3. **Graphic Organizer** Create a diagram like the one below to explain the four elements common to all businesses.

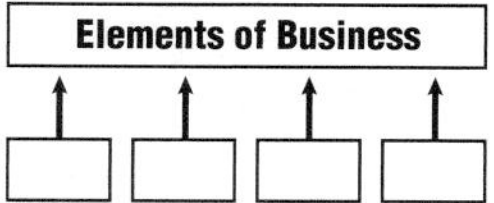


### Applying Economic Concepts

4. **Entrepreneurship** Think of a product or service that you would like to produce. Be sure to consider a business that you know something about or could easily find information about. Also research if there is a demand for that product or service. What initial expenses would you have as a startup?

### Critical Thinking Activity

5. **Synthesizing Information** Using your answer to question 4, compile a table listing all expenses for your startup for one month. *For help in using tables, see page xvii in the Economic Handbook.*



## SECTION 1 Assessment Answers

1. All definitions can be found in the Glossary.
2. Gather the relevant factors of production to produce goods or services, decide on the form of business organization to use, and learn as much as possible about the business.
3. Expenses, Advertising, Record Keeping, Risk
4. Answers will vary.
5. Tables will vary.



## Reteach

Ask students to rewrite the subheads in Section 1 as questions. Then pair students and have partners exchange their questions. Ask students to reread the section to discover the answers to the questions.

**Reading Essentials and Study Guide 8–1**

Name ______ Date ______ Class ______

STUDY GUIDE Chapter 8, Section 1

*For use with textbook pages 207–211*

**STARTING A BUSINESS**

KEY TERMS

***entrepreneur*** Person who hopes to gain profit from the risks of organizing, managing, and starting a business *(page 208)*

***startup*** the process of beginning a business or enterprise *(page 208)*

***small business incubator*** A government-funded agency which provides low-cost buildings and supplies or advice to help new businesses to grow *(page 209)*

***inventory*** Ready supply of extra goods or raw materials necessary for the operation of a business *(page 209)*

***receipts*** Records, such as slips of paper or data stored in computer files, which keep track of sales and purchases; also, income received from the sale of a good or service *(page 209)*

**DRAWING FROM EXPERIENCE**

Have you ever wanted to start your own business? What product or service would you sell? How would you organize your business? Do you need any special equipment or advice to start your business? How would you tell people about your business?

This section focuses on the decisions and the steps a person takes to start a business.

**ORGANIZING YOUR THOUGHTS**

Use the diagram below to help you take notes as you read the summaries that follow. Think about the things that must be done to start a business and the four elements involved in every business.

| Steps to Starting a New Business | Four Elements of Every Business |
| --- | --- |
| 1. | 1. |
| 2. | 2. |
| 3. | 3. |
| 4. | 4. |



Study Guide 69

## 4 Close

Write the words *risk* and *reward* on the board. Then ask students to use the words to write a sentence about starting a new business.

# Technology Skills

## Using the Internet

Begin by stressing that the Internet, when used correctly, can be a powerful research tool. First, it offers access to a world of resources that may not be available at the local public library. Further, the Internet often can provide more recent information than might be available in books or periodicals.

Guide students through the steps listed in **Practicing the Skill.** Point out that students often can identify the type of Web page they have located by domain designations that end a URL. Provide the following examples: *.com* is a commercial organization, *.org* is a nonprofit organization, *.gov* is a government organization, and *.edu* is an educational organization. Conclude by assigning the **Application Activity.**

**Reinforcing Economic Skills 21**

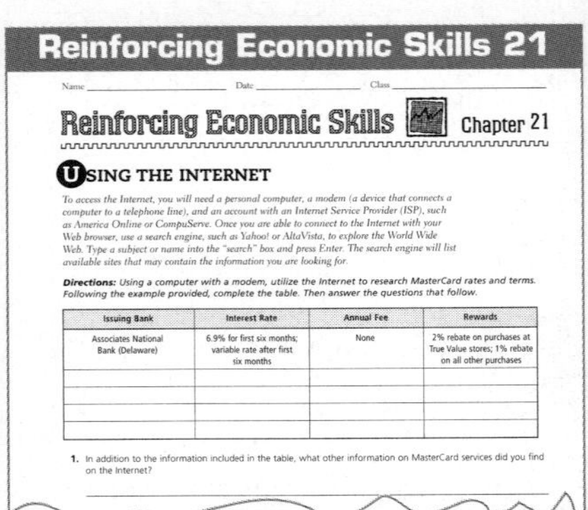

Name ______ Date ______ Class ______

**Reinforcing Economic Skills** Chapter 21

**USING THE INTERNET**

*To access the Internet, you will need a personal computer, a modem (a device that connects a computer to a telephone line), and an account with an Internet Service Provider (ISP), such as America Online or CompuServe. Once you are able to connect to the Internet with your Web browser, use a search engine, such as Yahoo! or AltaVista, to explore the World Wide Web. Type a subject or name into the "search" box and press Enter. The search engine will list available sites that may contain the information you are looking for.*

***Directions:*** *Using a computer with a modem, utilize the Internet to research MasterCard rates and terms. Following the example provided, complete the table. Then answer the questions that follow.*

| Issuing Bank | Interest Rate | Annual Fee | Rewards |
|---|---|---|---|
| Associates National Bank (Delaware) | 6.9% for first six months; variable rate after first six months | None | 2% rebate on purchases at True Value stores; 1% rebate on all other purchases |
| | | | |
| | | | |
| | | | |
| | | | |

1. In addition to the information included in the table, what other information on MasterCard services did you find on the Internet?

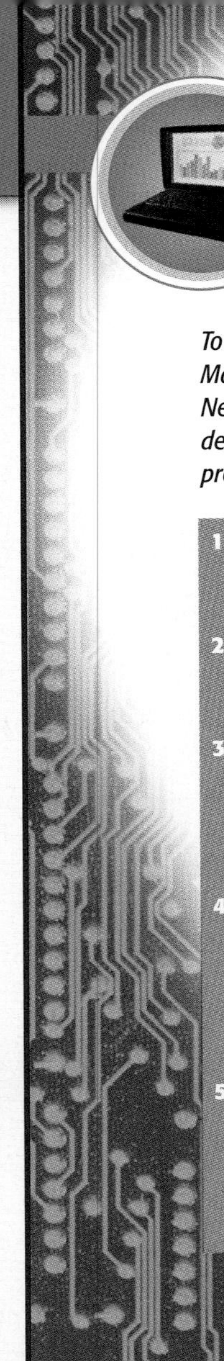

## Technology Skills

# Using the Internet

*To learn more about almost any topic imaginable, use the Internet—a global network of computers. Many features, such as E-mail, interactive educational classes, and shopping services, are offered on the Net. To get on the Internet, you need three things: (a) a personal computer or WebTV, (b) a modem—or device that connects your computer to a telephone line, and (c) an account with an Internet service provider (ISP). An ISP is a company that enables you to log on to the Internet, usually for a fee.*

### Learning the Skill

After you are connected, the easiest way to access Internet sites is to use a "Web browser," a program that lets you view and explore information on the World Wide Web. The Web consists of many documents called "Web sites," each of which has its own address, or Uniform Resource Locator (URL). Many URLs start with the keystrokes *http://*

If you don't know the exact URL of a site, commercial "search engines" such as Yahoo! or AltaVista can help you find information. Type a subject or name into the "search" box, then press Enter. The search engine lists available sites that may have the information you are looking for.

### Practicing the Skill

To learn how the Internet can help business startups, follow the steps listed on the left.

1. Log on to the Internet and access a search engine.
2. Search by typing *small business incubator* in the search engine.
3. Scroll the list of Web pages that appears when the search is complete. Select a page to bring up and read or print.
4. If you get "lost" on the Internet, click on the "back arrow" key at the top of the screen until you find a site that looks familiar.
5. Continue selecting sites until you have enough information to write a short report on the help available to startups from small business incubators.

### Application Activity

Follow the above procedures to locate information about the number of women-owned businesses. Use the information you gather to create a chart or bar graph depicting the number, sales, and workforces of women-owned businesses.



### Answers to Practicing the Skill

Ensure that students accompany their reports with a list of the sources that they used. You might lead a class discussion in which students share their experiences in doing Internet research.

SECTION 2

# Sole Proprietorships and Partnerships

## COVER STORY

*NEWSWEEK*, APRIL 5, 1999

In the movie *The Net,* Sandra Bullock played a victimized computer hacker who, in one scene, orders a pizza on her computer. The moment flashed by most moviegoers . . . , but it gave Tim Glass an idea—not for a better movie but an Internet company. With three longtime friends and colleagues, [Glass] set about recruiting restaurants to post their menus online. The goal: point-and-click ordering. They called the company Cyberslice. . . .

### READER'S GUIDE

**Terms to Know**

- sole proprietorship
- proprietor
- unlimited liability
- assets
- partnership
- limited partnership
- joint venture

**Reading Objectives**

1. What are the advantages and disadvantages of a sole proprietorship?
2. What are the advantages and disadvantages of a partnership?

Businesses can be organized in a number of ways. Some have one owner. Others, like Tim Glass's Cyberslice company, have multiple owners or partners. In this section, you'll learn that the two most common ways of organizing business in the United States are sole proprietorships and partnerships.

## Sole Proprietorships

The most basic type of business organization is the **sole proprietorship**, a business owned by one person. It is the oldest

<u>sole proprietorship:</u> *business owned and operated by one person*



## SECTION 2 RESOURCE MANAGER

**Reproducible Masters**

- Reproducible Lesson Plan 8–2
- Reading Essentials and Study Guide 8–2
- Guided Reading Activity 8–2
- Section Quiz 8–2
- Daily Focus Activity 19
- Daily Lecture Notes 8–2

**Multimedia**

- Daily Focus Transparency 19
- Economic Concepts Transparency 7
- Vocabulary PuzzleMaker
- Interactive Tutor Self-Assessment Software
- ExamView® Pro Testmaker
- MindJogger Videoquiz
- NBR's *Economics & You*
- Presentation Plus!



# 1 Focus

## Overview

**Section 2** describes two types of business organizations—sole proprietorships and partnerships—and explains the advantages and disadvantages of each.

### BELLRINGER
**Motivational Activity**

Project **Daily Focus Transparency 19** and have students answer the questions.

This activity is also available as a blackline master.

**Daily Focus Transparency 19**

FOCUS ACTIVITIES
Transparency 19

SOLE PROPRIETORSHIPS IN THE UNITED STATES

| Nonfarm Sole Proprietorships in the United States (approximate figures) | | |
|---|---|---|
| Total Number of Sole Proprietorships | 16,154,000 | |
| Percent of Sole Proprietorships Engaged in Different Types of Business Activity | Forestry and fishing | 2% |
| | Mining | 1% |
| | Construction | 1% |
| | Manufacturing | 3% |
| | Transportation | 4% |
| | Wholesale and retail | 18% |
| | Finance, insurance, real estate | 9% |
| | Services | 50% |
| | Other | 12% |
| Total receipts (in millions) | $790,630 | |
| Net income (in millions) | $166,799 | |

Source: *Statistical Abstract of the United States*

1. How many nonfarm sole proprietorships are in business in the United States?
2. What is the most common business activity of sole proprietorships?

Daily Focus Transparencies

### READER'S GUIDE

Answers to the **Reading Objectives** questions are on page 217.

**Preteaching Vocabulary**

Have students create word-search puzzles using the **Terms to Know.** Then have students locate the definitions of these terms in the Glossary and rewrite them as clues for their puzzles.

**Vocabulary PuzzleMaker**

# 2 Teach

## Guided Practice

**L1 Understanding Ideas** Organize the class into two groups. Tell members of one group that they have set up a CD store as a sole proprietorship. Inform members of the other group that they also have opened a CD store. However, it is organized as a partnership. Have students write a letter to a friend describing this new business venture by weighing the strengths and weaknesses of their chosen form of business organization. Call on volunteers to read their letters to the class.

### Daily Lecture Notes 8–2

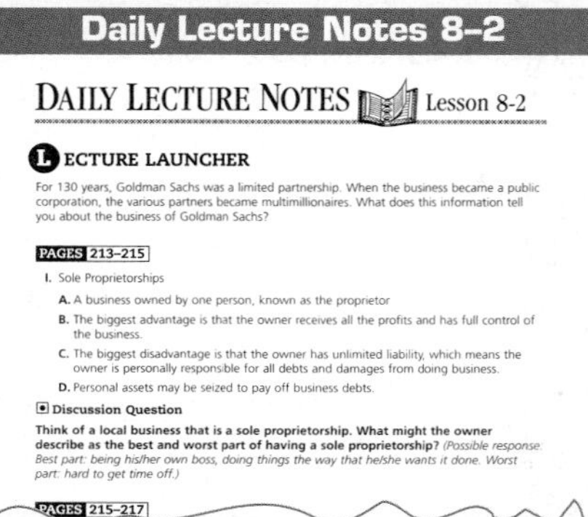

DAILY LECTURE NOTES Lesson 8-2

**LECTURE LAUNCHER**

For 130 years, Goldman Sachs was a limited partnership. When the business became a public corporation, the various partners became multimillionaires. What does this information tell you about the business of Goldman Sachs?

PAGES 213–215

I. Sole Proprietorships
   A. A business owned by one person, known as the proprietor
   B. The biggest advantage is that the owner receives all the profits and has full control of the business.
   C. The biggest disadvantage is that the owner has unlimited liability, which means the owner is personally responsible for all debts and damages from doing business.
   D. Personal assets may be seized to pay off business debts.

**Discussion Question**

**Think of a local business that is a sole proprietorship. What might the owner describe as the best and worst part of having a sole proprietorship?** *(Possible response: Best part: being his/her own boss, doing things the way that he/she wants it done. Worst part: hard to get time off.)*

PAGES 215–217

### Visual Instruction FIGURE 8.3

Review the content of **Figure 8.3** with students. ASK: Which advantage would be most important to you in deciding to start a sole proprietorship? Which disadvantage would be most important in dissuading you from starting a sole proprietorship?

## FIGURE 8.3 Advantages and Disadvantages of Sole Proprietorships

| | Advantages | Disadvantages |
|---|---|---|
| **Profits and Losses** | • Proprietor receives all the profits because he or she takes all the risks. | • Losses are not shared. |
| **Liability** | | • The proprietor has unlimited liability.<br>• If the firm is unable to pay its bills, the proprietor can be forced to sell personal assets as well as the business to pay debts. |
| **Management** | • Decisions on starting and running the business can be made quickly.<br>• Business operations are less complicated than other types of businesses.<br>• There are generally fewer government regulations. | • A proprietor must handle all decision making, even for unfamiliar areas of the business. This is a severe problem for many sole proprietorships. |
| **Taxes** | • Taxes are usually low because a proprietor pays only personal income taxes on profits. | |
| **Personal Satisfaction** | • The proprietor has high satisfaction in being his or her own boss.<br>• The owner can make the business into whatever he or she wants it to be. | • Running a sole proprietorship is demanding and time-consuming.<br>• If the proprietor does not enjoy responsibility, he or she will find ownership a burden. |
| **Financing Growth** | • Proprietors can obtain credit relatively easily. Lenders know they can take over the assets of the business as well as personal assets of the proprietor if the loan is not paid back. | • A sole proprietor must rely on his or her own funds plus funds that can be borrowed.<br>• Borrowing large amounts can be difficult. |
| **Life of the Business** | | • If the proprietor dies, goes bankrupt, or is unwilling or unable to work, the business will probably fail.<br>• Uncertainty about the future increases the risk both to employees and creditors. |

214 CHAPTER 8

## Meeting Special Needs

**Visual Learning Disability** Students with visual-spatial processing problems may have difficulty reading tables. Because information in textbooks often is presented in tabular form, it is important for students to be proficient in reading and interpreting tables. Refer students to **Figure 8.3** on page 214 and **Figure 8.4** on page 216. Point out that they can quickly gain a broad understanding of the content of the table by identifying the column and row headings.

Refer to *Inclusion for the Social Studies Classroom Strategies and Activities* for students with different learning styles.

form of business organization and also the most common. The colonies of Maryland and Pennsylvania were founded as sole proprietorships.

When we speak of a **proprietor**, we are referring to the owner of a business. The word *proprietor* comes from the Latin word *proprietas*, meaning "property." A business is a kind of property.

The United States has more than 16 million such businesses, and many of them are small. For that reason, they usually are easier and less expensive to start and run. You probably have contact with many sole proprietorships every day without realizing it.

The biggest advantages of sole proprietorships are that the proprietor has full pride in owning the business and receives all the profits. The biggest disadvantage is that the proprietor has **unlimited liability**, or complete legal responsibility for all debts and damages arising from doing business. Personal **assets**, or items of value such as houses, cars, jewelry, and so on, may be seized to pay off business debts. **Figure 8.3** lists these and other advantages and disadvantages of operating a sole proprietorship.

**proprietor:** *owner of a business*

**unlimited liability:** *requirement that an owner is personally and fully responsible for all losses and debts of a business*

**assets:** *all items to which a business or household holds legal claim*

**partnership:** *business that two or more individuals own and operate*

## Partnerships

Earlier in this chapter, we imagined that you had started an electronics repair business. Suppose your business is doing so well that your workload leaves you little time to do anything else. You could expand your business by hiring an employee. However, you also need financial capital to buy new equipment, and you would rather not take out a loan. You decide to take on a partner.

The best solution is to look for someone who can keep books, order supplies, handle customers, and invest in the business. You offer to form a **partnership**, a business that two or more individuals own and operate. You sign a partnership agreement that is legally binding. It describes the duties of each partner, the division of profits, and the distribution of assets should the partners end the agreement.

Much like sole proprietorships, an advantage of partnerships is the pride of sharing ownership in a business–and contributing to it in a specialized way that benefits all the partners. A disadvantage is that, like the sole proprietor, the partners have unlimited liability. **Figure 8.4** on page 216 shows other advantages and disadvantages of partnerships.

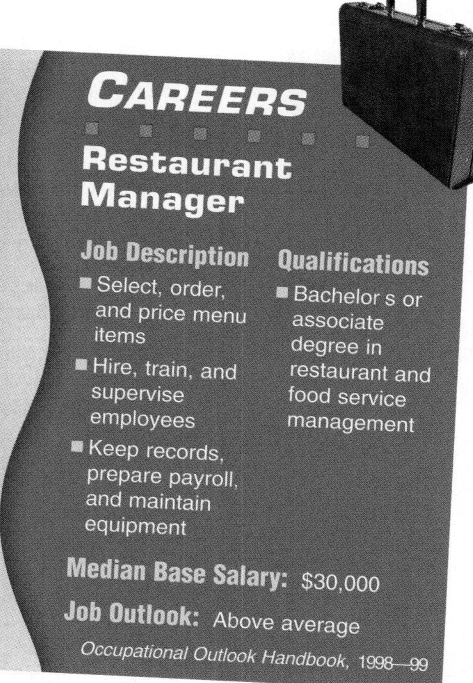

CAREERS
Restaurant Manager
Job Description
Select, order, and price menu items
Hire, train, and supervise employees
Keep records, prepare payroll, and maintain equipment
Qualifications
Bachelor s or associate degree in restaurant and food service management
Median Base Salary: $30,000
Job Outlook: Above average
Occupational Outlook Handbook, 1998–99






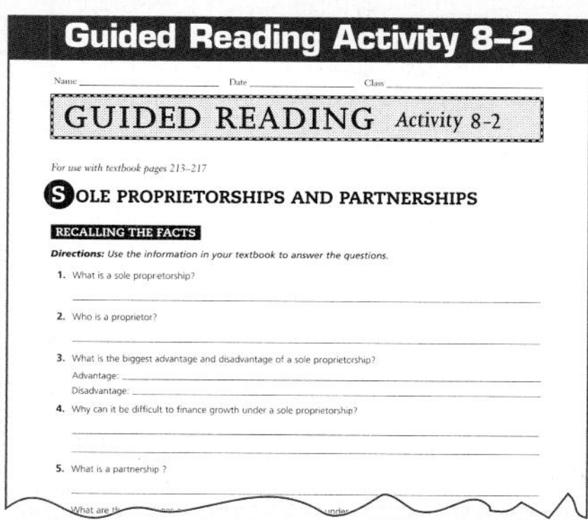

Guided Reading Activity 8-2
GUIDED READING Activity 8-2
SOLE PROPRIETORSHIPS AND PARTNERSHIPS
RECALLING THE FACTS


Project **Economic Concepts Transparency** 7 and have students discuss the accompanying questions.

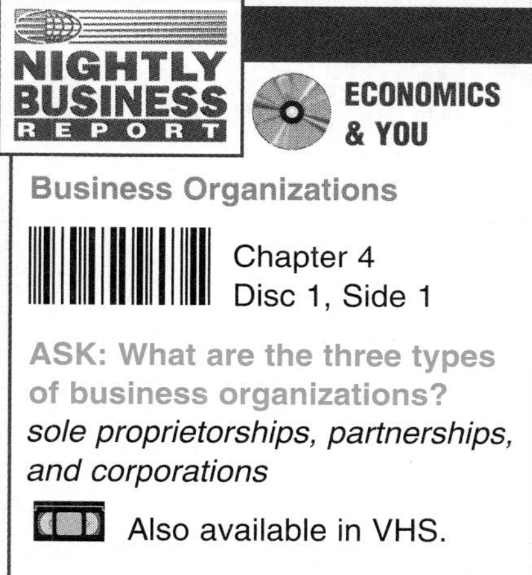

NIGHTLY BUSINESS REPORT
ECONOMICS & YOU
Business Organizations
Chapter 4
Disc 1, Side 1
ASK: What are the three types of business organizations?
sole proprietorships, partnerships, and corporations
Also available in VHS.


## Cooperative Learning

Organize students into groups of three or four. Inform groups that they have decided to set up a painting and decorating company as a partnership. Have each group draw up an agreement among the partners. Point out that the agreement should address such issues as the role each partner plays in providing capital and running the company, how each partner will share in the profits and losses of the company, and what will happen to the partnership and its assets or debts if one or more partners dies or decides to leave. Call on group representatives to share their agreements with the class.

BLOCK SCHEDULING

## Independent Practice

**L2 Writing a Report** Ask students to work in small groups to draw up a report on several businesses in the community. Suggest that they locate three sole proprietorships and three partnerships. Direct groups to include in their reports such information as goods and/or services provided, number of factories, stores, or offices, number of employees, and so on. Encourage students to conclude their reports with observations on whether the businesses chose the most appropriate form of organization for their operations.

# 3 Assess

## Meeting Lesson Objectives

Assign Section 2 Assessment as homework or an in-class activity.

Use **Interactive Tutor Self-Assessment Software** to review Section 2.

**Section Quiz 8–2**

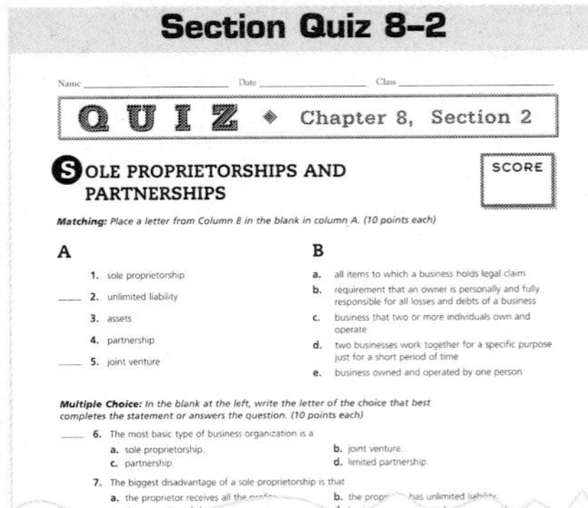
Name ______ Date ______ Class ______

QUIZ ◆ Chapter 8, Section 2

SOLE PROPRIETORSHIPS AND PARTNERSHIPS — SCORE

*Matching:* Place a letter from Column B in the blank in column A. (10 points each)

| A | B |
|---|---|
| ___ 1. sole proprietorship | a. all items to which a business holds legal claim |
| ___ 2. unlimited liability | b. requirement that an owner is personally and fully responsible for all losses and debts of a business |
| ___ 3. assets | c. business that two or more individuals own and operate |
| ___ 4. partnership | d. two businesses work together for a specific purpose just for a short period of time |
| ___ 5. joint venture | e. business owned and operated by one person |

*Multiple Choice:* In the blank at the left, write the letter of the choice that best completes the statement or answers the question. (10 points each)

___ 6. The most basic type of business organization is a
a. sole proprietorship. b. joint venture.
c. partnership. d. limited partnership.

___ 7. The biggest disadvantage of a sole proprietorship is that
a. the proprietor receives all the ... b. the proprietor has unlimited liability
c. ... d. ...

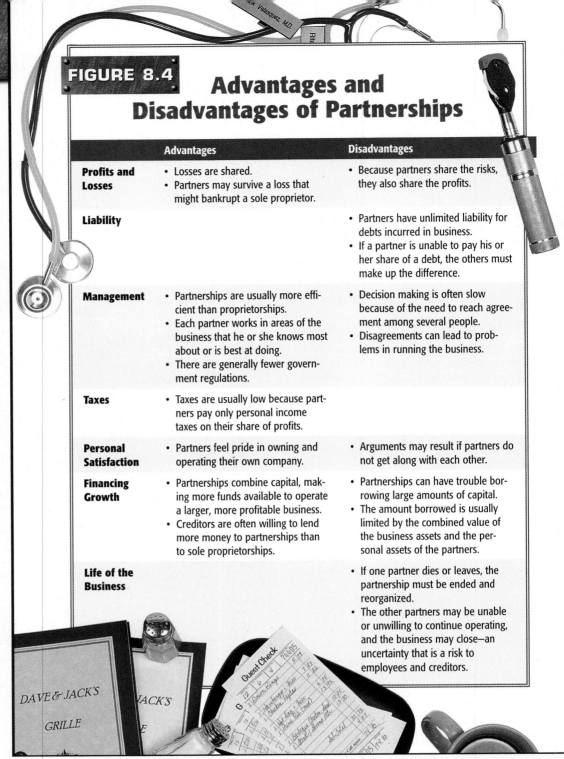

## FIGURE 8.4 Advantages and Disadvantages of Partnerships

| | Advantages | Disadvantages |
|---|---|---|
| **Profits and Losses** | • Losses are shared.<br>• Partners may survive a loss that might bankrupt a sole proprietor. | • Because partners share the risks, they also share the profits. |
| **Liability** | | • Partners have unlimited liability for debts incurred in business.<br>• If a partner is unable to pay his or her share of a debt, the others must make up the difference. |
| **Management** | • Partnerships are usually more efficient than proprietorships.<br>• Each partner works in areas of the business that he or she knows most about or is best at doing.<br>• There are generally fewer government regulations. | • Decision making is often slow because of the need to reach agreement among several people.<br>• Disagreements can lead to problems in running the business. |
| **Taxes** | • Taxes are usually low because partners pay only personal income taxes on their share of profits. | |
| **Personal Satisfaction** | • Partners feel pride in owning and operating their own company. | • Arguments may result if partners do not get along with each other. |
| **Financing Growth** | • Partnerships combine capital, making more funds available to operate a larger, more profitable business.<br>• Creditors are often willing to lend more money to partnerships than to sole proprietorships. | • Partnerships can have trouble borrowing large amounts of capital.<br>• The amount borrowed is usually limited by the combined value of the business assets and the personal assets of the partners. |
| **Life of the Business** | | • If one partner dies or leaves, the partnership must be ended and reorganized.<br>• The other partners may be unable or unwilling to continue operating, and the business may close—an uncertainty that is a risk to employees and creditors. |

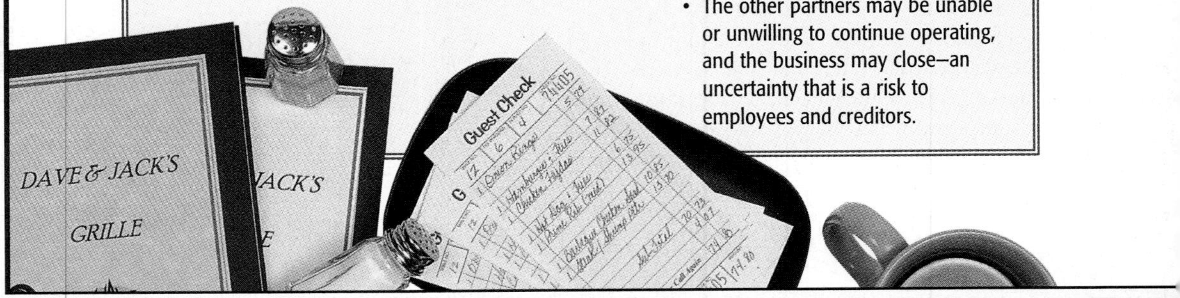

## Free Enterprise Activity

Point out that many school districts throughout the country have encouraged the establishment of student-run businesses—concession stands, bookstores, and so on—in schools. Have students work in small groups to research the topic of student-run businesses. Then ask groups to prepare a report identifying the types of businesses they think students might run in their school. Suggest that they support their recommendations with statistics and other information garnered from their research. BLOCK SCHEDULING

**Limited Partnerships** A **limited partnership** is a special form of partnership in which the partners are not equal. One partner is called the *general partner.* This person (or persons) assumes all of the management duties and has full responsibility for the debts of the limited partnership. The other partners are "limited" because all they do is contribute money or property. They have no voice in the partnership's management.

The advantage to the limited partners is that they have no liability for the losses beyond what they initially invest. The disadvantage, of course, is that they have no say in how the business is run.

limited partnership: *special form of partnership in which one or more partners have limited liability but no voice in management*

**Joint Ventures** Sometimes individuals or companies want to do a special project together. They do not have any desire to work together after the project is done. What they might do is form a **joint venture**—a temporary partnership set up for a specific purpose just for a short period of time.

joint venture: *partnership set up for a specific purpose just for a short period of time*

Suppose investors want to purchase real estate as a short-term investment. They may later plan to resell the property for profit. At that point, the joint venture ends.

**Practice** and **assess** key skills with *Skillbuilder Interactive Workbook, Level 2.*

## SECTION 2 Assessment

### Understanding Key Terms

1. **Define** sole proprietorship, proprietor, unlimited liability, assets, partnership, limited partnership, joint venture.

### Reviewing Objectives

2. What are the advantages and disadvantages of a sole proprietorship?
3. What are the advantages and disadvantages of a partnership?
4. **Graphic Organizer** Create a diagram like the one in the next column, then compare the similarities and differences between partnerships and sole proprietorships. In your diagram, list the characteristics that are unique to partnerships and sole proprietorships in the outer part of each oval. Where the ovals overlap, write the characteristics shared by both.

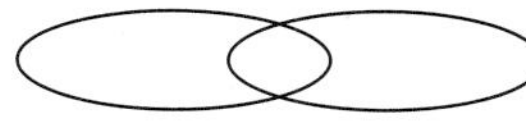

### Applying Economic Concepts

5. **Partnership** Make a list describing at least five character traits that you would want a business partner to possess in order to have a successful partnership with him or her.

### Critical Thinking Activity

6. **Categorizing Information** Imagine you are sole owner of an ice cream parlor. Make a spreadsheet listing all the daily and weekly duties you have to perform *in addition to* making ice cream.



## CHAPTER 8
SECTION 2, Pages 213–217

### Reteach

Pair students, and have partners take turns quizzing each other on the advantages and disadvantages of sole proprietorships and partnerships. For example, one partner states an advantage or disadvantage and the other partner must identify whether it refers to a sole proprietorship or a partnership.

**Reading Essentials and Study Guide 8–2**

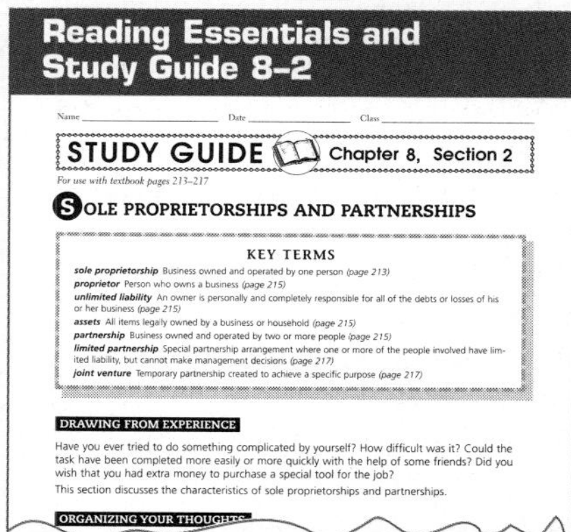

Name ______ Date ______ Class ______

STUDY GUIDE Chapter 8, Section 2

*For use with textbook pages 213–217*

SOLE PROPRIETORSHIPS AND PARTNERSHIPS

KEY TERMS

***sole proprietorship*** Business owned and operated by one person *(page 213)*
***proprietor*** Person who owns a business *(page 215)*
***unlimited liability*** An owner is personally and completely responsible for all of the debts or losses of his or her business *(page 215)*
***assets*** All items legally owned by a business or household *(page 215)*
***partnership*** Business owned and operated by two or more people *(page 215)*
***limited partnership*** Special partnership arrangement where one or more of the people involved have limited liability, but cannot make management decisions *(page 217)*
***joint venture*** Temporary partnership created to achieve a specific purpose *(page 217)*

DRAWING FROM EXPERIENCE

Have you ever tried to do something complicated by yourself? How difficult was it? Could the task have been completed more easily or more quickly with the help of some friends? Did you wish that you had extra money to purchase a special tool for the job?

This section discusses the characteristics of sole proprietorships and partnerships.

ORGANIZING YOUR THOUGHTS

### 4 Close

Write the following on the board: I prefer the sole proprietorship (or partnership) as a business organization because . . .

Ask students to complete the sentence. Then call on volunteers to share and discuss their sentences with the class.

## SECTION 2 Assessment Answers

1. All definitions can be found in the Glossary.
2. Advantages: owner keeps all profits, business decisions can be made quickly, taxes usually low, own boss, relatively easy to get credit. Disadvantages: owner responsible for all losses, unlimited liability, make all business decisions, huge time demands, must depend on own and borrowed funds.
3. Advantages: losses are shared, taxes usually low, partnerships combine the funds of several partners. Disadvantages: profits are shared among partners, decision making sometimes slow, may have trouble borrowing money, partnership must be reorganized if one partner leaves or dies.
4. Similarities: pride in owning and running business, relatively easy to set up, low taxes, unlimited liability for debts, may have trouble borrowing large amounts of money, life of business uncertain. Differences: partners may focus on particular areas of business whereas sole proprietor is alone, decision making quicker in sole proprietorship, sole proprietors must handle all decisions whereas decision making shared among partners.
5. Encourage students to explain why they consider certain character traits important.
6. Have students compare their spreadsheets and note the similarities and differences.

## Background

Mention that even though he is in his eighties, John H. Johnson remains actively involved with the company he founded, serving as publisher and chief executive officer. His daughter, Linda Johnson Rice, who serves as president and chief operating officer, handles the day-to-day business of the company.

## Teach

Point out that Johnson feels that to start a good business "you have to have a good idea. You look for opportunities, and you look for services you can render; either those that aren't being rendered at all, or those that you can provide better." He adds that good luck and hard work play no small part in business success.

Have students discuss how Johnson's ideas on business success are reflected in his experience with Johnson Publishing Company.

# People & Perspectives

## John H. Johnson

*ENTREPRENEUR (1918–)*

- **Began publishing *Negro Digest* in 1942**
- **Published first issue of *Ebony* in 1945**
- **Was one of the first entrepreneurs to recognize and take advantage of the tremendous business opportunities in the African American community**
- **Produces American Black Achievement Awards for television, first aired in 1978**
- **Launched *Ebony South Africa* in 1995**

John Johnson began his career in 1942 at the age of 24. He used a $500 loan on his mother's furniture to start *Negro Digest*, a magazine devoted to the accomplishments of African Americans. Today Johnson Publishing Company, Inc., is the world's largest African American-owned publishing company. This media empire includes *Ebony, Jet, Ebony Man,* and *Ebony South Africa* magazines and Black Entertainment Television (BET). Also part of the company are Fashion Fair Cosmetics and Supreme Beauty Products.

Like many minority-owned companies, Johnson faced many setbacks:

*"The first 25 years were difficult, trying to get circulation and to break through in advertising to get large companies to recognize that black consumers had money and would respond to advertising directed to them. The first 20 years or so in business, we couldn't get a bank loan."*

Although the second 25 years have been easier, Johnson says African American startups will face many of the same hurdles he did:

*"But if you have the staying power and wherewithal, that is assuming you have a good product and market to sell to, you'll be successful. Never say never about new things."*

Johnson has no plans to sell his company or take it public for the following reason:

*"If you go public, the stockholders, the board of directors, the SEC [Securities and Exchange Commission] are all your bosses and you've got to listen to them. We only have three board members: [daughter] Linda, her mother [Eunice Johnson], and I."*

### *Checking for Understanding*

1. **What products does Johnson provide?**
2. **Why does Johnson refuse to turn his business into a corporation?**

218

### Answers to *Checking for Understanding*

1. several magazines, including *Ebony, Jet, Ebony Man,* and *Ebony South Africa;* Black Entertainment Television; and cosmetic products
2. because stockholders, the board of directors, and the SEC would all have a say in how the business is run

SECTION 3

# The Corporate World and Franchises

## COVER STORY

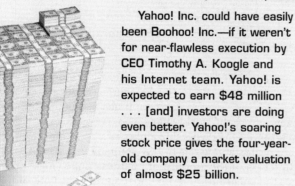

*BUSINESS WEEK*, JANUARY 11, 1999

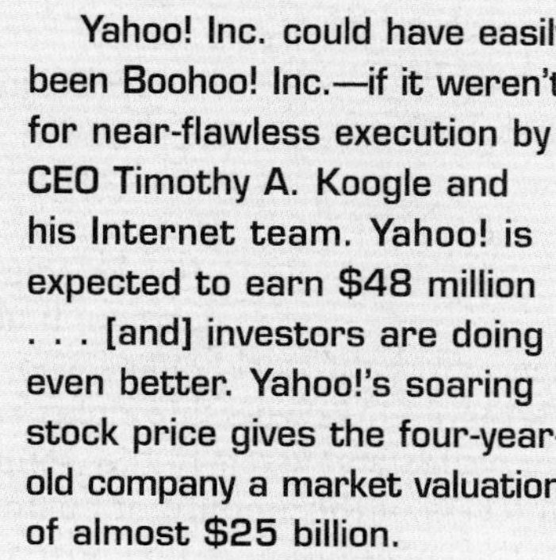

Yahoo! Inc. could have easily been Boohoo! Inc.—if it weren't for near-flawless execution by CEO Timothy A. Koogle and his Internet team. Yahoo! is expected to earn $48 million . . . [and] investors are doing even better. Yahoo!'s soaring stock price gives the four-year-old company a market valuation of almost $25 billion.

### READER'S GUIDE

**Terms to Know**

- corporation
- stock
- limited liability
- articles of incorporation
- corporate charter
- common stock
- dividend
- preferred stock
- franchise

**Reading Objectives**

1. What are the advantages and disadvantages of corporations?
2. How are corporations typically structured?
3. What types of businesses are involved in franchises?

Profits are a good thing. As a sole proprietor, you keep all the profits. In a partnership, you share the profits with one or several partners. In a corporation, like Yahoo! Inc., the profits are dispersed among thousands of shareholders. So why do entrepreneurs incorporate? In this section, read to learn why and how corporations are formed.

## Why Form a Corporation?

Suppose your electronics repair business has grown. You now have several partners and have turned your garage into a



## SECTION 3 RESOURCE MANAGER

**Reproducible Masters**

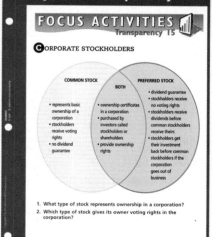

- Reproducible Lesson Plan 8–3
- Reading Essentials and Study Guide 8–3
- Guided Reading Activity 8–3
- Section Quiz 8–3
- Daily Focus Activity 15
- Daily Lecture Notes 8–3

**Multimedia**

- Daily Focus Transparency 15
- Vocabulary PuzzleMaker
- Interactive Tutor Self-Assessment Software
- ExamView® Pro Testmaker
- MindJogger Videoquiz
- Presentation Plus!



# 1 Focus

## Overview

Section 3 explains the advantages and disadvantages of corporations, and describes franchises.

### BELLRINGER
Motivational Activity

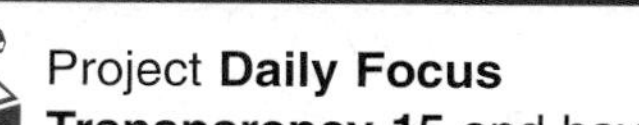

Project **Daily Focus Transparency 15** and have students answer the questions.

This activity is also available as a blackline master.

**Daily Focus Transparency 15**

CORPORATE STOCKHOLDERS

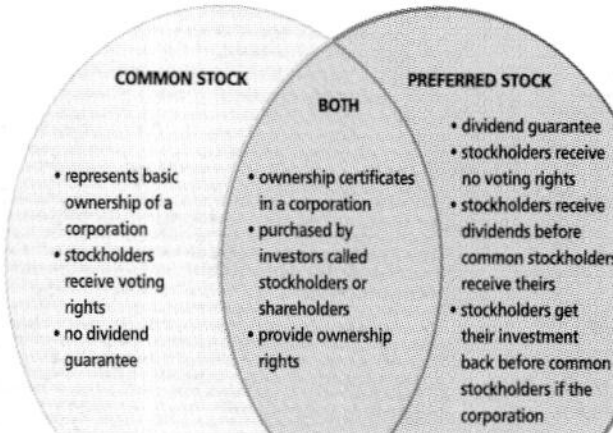


1. What type of stock represents ownership in a corporation?
2. Which type of stock gives its owner voting rights in the corporation?

Daily Focus Transparencies

### READER'S GUIDE

Answers to the **Reading Objectives** questions are on page 225.

**Preteaching Vocabulary**

Have students skim the section to find the definitions of the **Terms to Know.** Then ask students to use each of the terms in a sentence.

**Vocabulary PuzzleMaker**

# 2 Teach

## Guided Practice

**L1 Making Comparisons** Have students study **Figure 8.6** on page 222. Next, refer students to the charts detailing the advantages and disadvantages of sole proprietorships and partnerships (**Figure 8.3** on page 214 and **Figure 8.4** on page 216). Have students create a graphic organizer that compares sole proprietorships, partnerships, and corporations by noting these organizations' similarities and differences.

**Daily Lecture Notes 8–3**

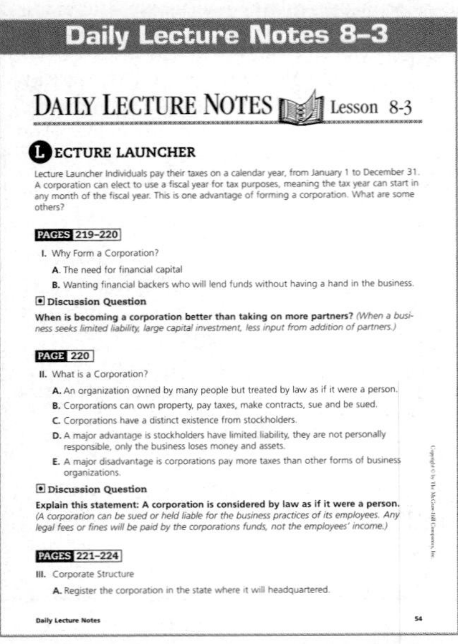

DAILY LECTURE NOTES Lesson 8-3

**LECTURE LAUNCHER**

Lecture Launcher Individuals pay their taxes on a calendar year, from January 1 to December 31. A corporation can elect to use a fiscal year for tax purposes, meaning the tax year can start in any month of the fiscal year. This is one advantage of forming a corporation. What are some others?

PAGES 219–220

I. Why Form a Corporation?
   - A. The need for financial capital
   - B. Wanting financial backers who will lend funds without having a hand in the business.

**Discussion Question**

**When is becoming a corporation better than taking on more partners?** *(When a business seeks limited liability, large capital investment, less input from addition of partners.)*

PAGE 220

II. What is a Corporation?
   - A. An organization owned by many people but treated by law as if it were a person.
   - B. Corporations can own property, pay taxes, make contracts, sue and be sued.
   - C. Corporations have a distinct existence from stockholders.
   - D. A major advantage is stockholders have limited liability, they are not personally responsible, only the business loses money and assets.
   - E. A major disadvantage is corporations pay more taxes than other forms of business organizations.

**Discussion Question**

**Explain this statement: A corporation is considered by law as if it were a person.** *(A corporation can be sued or held liable for the business practices of its employees. Any legal fees or fines will be paid by the corporations funds, not the employees' income.)*

PAGES 221–224

III. Corporate Structure
   - A. Register the corporation in the state where it will headquartered.

Daily Lecture Notes 54



**corporation:** *type of business organization owned by many people but treated by law as though it were a person; it can own property, pay taxes, make contracts, and so on*

shop. You would like to expand and rent a store so that your business is more visible. You would also like to buy the latest equipment, charge a little less than your competitors, and capture a larger share of the market for electronics repair work. You need financial capital, however.

You have decided that you do not want any more partners. You would have to consult with them about every detail of the business as you do now with your present partners. What you want are financial backers who will let you use their funds while letting you run the business. What you are proposing is a corporation.

**Global Economy**

### Big Business!

Many modern corporations are huge. A study conducted in the mid-1990s found that some of these corporations have bigger economies than the countries in which they operate! More than half of the world's 100 largest economies, the study revealed, were corporations, not nations. General Motors, the United States's largest corporation, had the 26th largest economy. This placed it above 167 nations, including Denmark, South Africa, Turkey, and Saudi Arabia. ■

## What Is a Corporation?

A **corporation** is an organization owned by many people but treated by law as though it were a person. A corporation can own property, pay taxes, make contracts, sue and be sued, and so on. It has a separate and distinct existence from the stockholders who own the corporation's stock. **Stock** represents ownership rights to a certain portion of the future profits and assets of the company that issues the stock.

**stock:** *share of ownership in a corporation that entitles the buyer to a certain part of the future profits and assets of the corporation*

In terms of the amount of business done (measured in dollars), the corporation is the most significant type of business organization in the United States today. **Figure 8.5** on page 221 compares corporations to other forms of businesses in terms of numbers and proportion of total business revenue. You can see that although corporations make up only about 20 percent of all businesses, they earn about 90 percent of all business revenues.

Like sole proprietorships and partnerships, corporations have advantages as well as disadvantages. One of the major advantages of a corporation is **limited liability.** If a corporation goes bankrupt or is sued, only the business loses money and assets, not the stockholders. A major disadvantage of corporations is that they are taxed more heavily than other forms of business organizations. Look at **Figure 8.6** on page 222 to read about other advantages and disadvantages of corporations.

**limited liability:** *requirement in which an owner's responsibility for a company's debts is limited to the size of the owner's investment in the firm*



**Meeting Special Needs**

**Fine Motor Skills Problems** Students who have difficulties with fine motor skills are often slow and inefficient writers. This puts such students at a disadvantage, because most assignments require some type of writing. Teach these students to read short segments of text and to use an abridged form of note taking, in which they write only single words and related facts.

Refer to *Inclusion for the Social Studies Classroom Strategies and Activities* for students with different learning styles.

## Corporate Structure

In order to form a corporation, its founders must do three things. First, they must register their company with the government of the state in which it will be headquartered. Second, they must sell stock. Third, along with the other shareholders, they must elect a board of directors.

**Registering the Corporation** Every state has laws governing the formation of corporations, but most state laws are similar. Suppose that you and your partners decide to form a corporation. You will have to file the **articles of incorporation** with the state in which you will run your corporation. In general, these articles include four items:
**(1)** Name, address, and purpose of the corporation;
**(2)** Names and addresses of the initial board of directors (these men and women will serve until the first stockholders' meeting, when a new board may be elected);
**(3)** Number of shares of stock to be issued;
**(4)** Amount of money capital to be raised through issuing stock.
If the articles are in agreement with state law, the state will grant you a **corporate charter**—a license to operate from that state.

**articles of incorporation:** *document listing basic information about a corporation that is filed with the state where the corporation will be headquartered*

**corporate charter:** *license to operate granted to a corporation by the state where it is established*

### FIGURE 8.5

**Business Organizations** Although proprietorships make up about 73 percent of American businesses, they generate only about 5 percent of total business revenues. ***What percentage of American businesses are partnerships?***

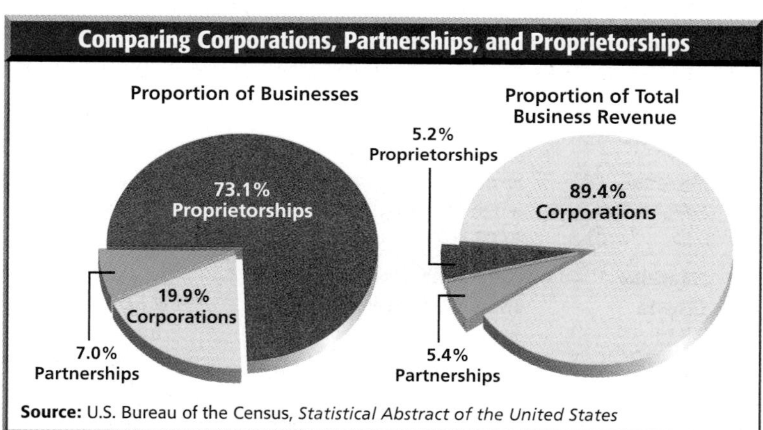


**Source:** U.S. Bureau of the Census, *Statistical Abstract of the United States*

For an online update of this graph, visit ett.glencoe.com and click on ***Textbook Updates—Chapter 8.***



### Relevant Issues in Economics

**Statistics on Business Organizations** Statistics on the number, profits, and sales and operations income of business organizations are collected by the Internal Revenue Service (IRS) from annual tax returns. Published figures are not current, because businesses do not file tax returns until after the tax year is over. Some businesses get extensions from the IRS to file at an even later date. When all the tax returns have been received, the IRS may take several months to analyze and collate the data and prepare it for publication. As a result, the information for a particular year may not be available until three years later.

**L2 Interpreting Ideas** Provide students with recent issues of *Business Week, Forbes, Fortune, The Wall Street Journal,* or the business sections of local newspapers. Ask students to review the periodicals they receive to locate articles on American corporations. Have them note the major issues covered in these articles. Then have students use their findings to write a few paragraphs on corporations in the American economy. Call on volunteers to read their paragraphs to the class.

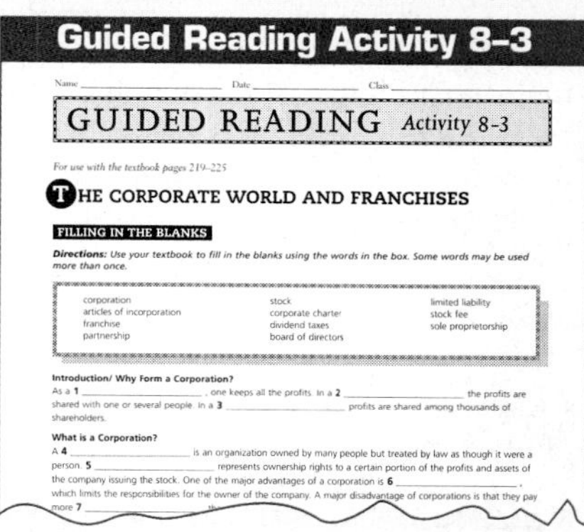

**Guided Reading Activity 8–3**

Name ______ Date ______ Class ______

GUIDED READING Activity 8-3

*For use with the textbook pages 219–225*

THE CORPORATE WORLD AND FRANCHISES

FILLING IN THE BLANKS

***Directions:*** *Use your textbook to fill in the blanks using the words in the box. Some words may be used more than once.*

| | | |
|---|---|---|
| corporation | stock | limited liability |
| articles of incorporation | corporate charter | stock fee |
| franchise | dividend taxes | sole proprietorship |
| partnership | board of directors | |

**Introduction/ Why Form a Corporation?**
As a **1** ______, one keeps all the profits. In a **2** ______ the profits are shared with one or several people. In a **3** ______ profits are shared among thousands of shareholders.

**What is a Corporation?**
A **4** ______ is an organization owned by many people but treated by law as though it were a person. **5** ______ represents ownership rights to a certain portion of the profits and assets of the company issuing the stock. One of the major advantages of a corporation is **6** ______, which limits the responsibilities for the owner of the company. A major disadvantage of corporations is that they pay more **7** ______

### Visual Instruction FIGURE 8.5

Have students study the graphs in **Figure 8.5**. Then ask them to use information in the graphs to make generalizations about the three kinds of business organizations. If students need guidance, offer the following example: Corporations make up a small percentage of businesses but generate the most revenue.
**Answer:** *about 7 percent*

## Independent Practice

**L2 Making Connections** Ask students to research the origins of the word *corporation*. Then have them write a paragraph detailing how the term came to be applied to the modern business organization. Call on volunteers to share their paragraphs with the class.

### Visual Instruction FIGURE 8.6

Have students review the information in **Figure 8.6.** Then ask students to speculate on how working for a corporation might be different from working for a sole proprietorship or partnership.

### Global Economy

**Economic Giant**

Mitsubishi, a Japanese company involved in automobile, electrical, and chemical industries, is the largest corporation in the world. It has the world's $22^{nd}$ largest economy, larger than that of India—a country with a population of more than 1 billion people.

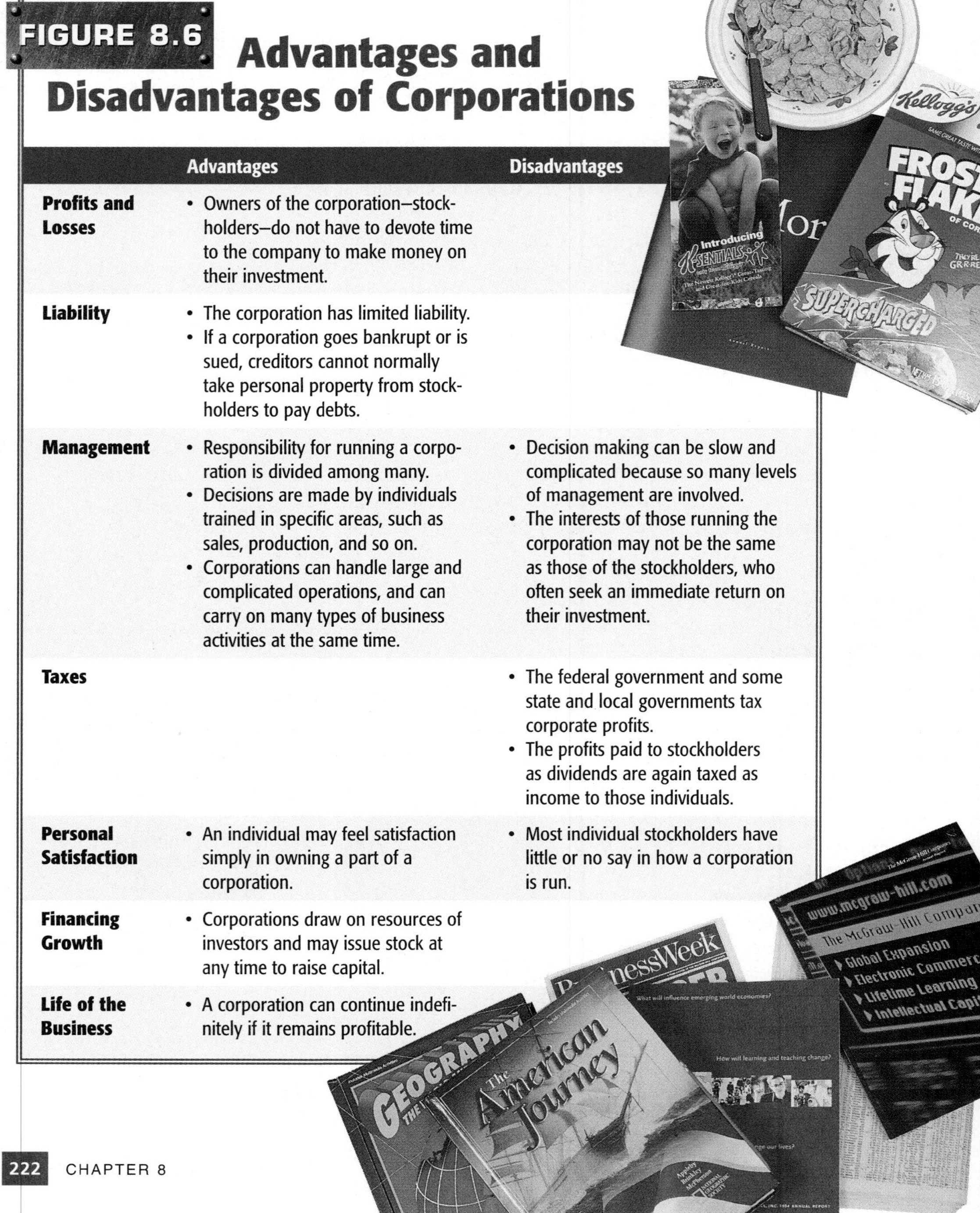


**FIGURE 8.6 Advantages and Disadvantages of Corporations**

| | Advantages | Disadvantages |
|---|---|---|
| **Profits and Losses** | • Owners of the corporation–stockholders–do not have to devote time to the company to make money on their investment. | |
| **Liability** | • The corporation has limited liability.<br>• If a corporation goes bankrupt or is sued, creditors cannot normally take personal property from stockholders to pay debts. | |
| **Management** | • Responsibility for running a corporation is divided among many.<br>• Decisions are made by individuals trained in specific areas, such as sales, production, and so on.<br>• Corporations can handle large and complicated operations, and can carry on many types of business activities at the same time. | • Decision making can be slow and complicated because so many levels of management are involved.<br>• The interests of those running the corporation may not be the same as those of the stockholders, who often seek an immediate return on their investment. |
| **Taxes** | | • The federal government and some state and local governments tax corporate profits.<br>• The profits paid to stockholders as dividends are again taxed as income to those individuals. |
| **Personal Satisfaction** | • An individual may feel satisfaction simply in owning a part of a corporation. | • Most individual stockholders have little or no say in how a corporation is run. |
| **Financing Growth** | • Corporations draw on resources of investors and may issue stock at any time to raise capital. | |
| **Life of the Business** | • A corporation can continue indefinitely if it remains profitable. | |



### Cooperative Learning

Organize students into groups, and tell groups to imagine they are editorial teams working on an economic history textbook. Their task is to develop ideas for a four- to six-page pictorial essay on the history of corporations in the United States. Ask groups to draw up a plan for the essay, including an introduction, illustration ideas, brief captions for illustrations, and ideas for linking paragraphs. Call on groups to present their plans to the class. ELL BLOCK SCHEDULING

**Selling Stock** To raise funds for the expansion of your electronics repair business, you could sell shares of either common or preferred stock in your new corporation. **Common stock** gives the investor part ownership in the corporation, a right to a percentage of the company's future profits, and voting rights at the annual stockholders' meeting. However, it does not *guarantee* a **dividend**—a money return on the money invested in a company's stock. Holders of **preferred stock** do not have voting rights in the corporation, but they are guaranteed a certain amount of dividend each year. Plus, if the corporation goes out of business, holders of preferred stock have first claim on whatever value is left in the company after creditors have been paid.

If your corporation were to become large, you might find its stock traded in the local over-the-counter market. *Over-the-counter* means that individual brokerage firms hold quantities of shares of stock that they buy and sell for investors. Should your corporation continue to grow, its stocks may be traded on a stock exchange.

**common stock:** *shares of ownership in a corporation that give stockholders voting rights and a portion of future profits (after holders of preferred stock are paid)*

**dividend:** *portion of a corporation's profits paid to its stockholders*

**preferred stock:** *shares of ownership in a corporation that give stockholders a portion of future profits (before any profits go to holders of common stock), but no voting rights*

**Naming a Board of Directors** To become incorporated, a company must have a board of directors. You and your partners, as founders of the corporation, would select the first board for your corporation. After that, stockholders at their annual stockholders' meetings would elect the board. The bylaws of the corporation govern this election. Bylaws are a set of rules describing how stock will be sold and dividends paid, with a list of the duties of the company's officers. They are written after the corporate charter has been granted.

## Economic Connection to... History

### Franchises, Franchises, Everywhere!

The inventor and entrepreneur Isaac Singer began the practice of franchising in the United States. In the mid-1800s, Singer signed agreements with several merchants that allowed them to market his sewing machines.

The interstate highway system caused the practice of franchising to explode in the 1950s. Increasing automobile ownership took more Americans on the road, where they looked for familiar motels, restaurants, and gas stations they knew and trusted. Today more than 3,000 American companies franchise. Their 550,000 franchise outlets sell about $800 billion in goods and services each year. ■



**L3 Illustrating Ideas** Ask students to use library resources to locate an annual report of a corporation headquartered in or near their community. Have them use information in the report to construct an organizational chart for the corporation similar to the chart on pages 224–225. Suggest that students include information such as the number of shareholders and the names of the various office holders in their charts. Have students display their organizational charts around the classroom.

### Global Economy

**European Franchises**

There are nearly 145,000 franchise outlets operating in the European countries of Austria, Belgium, Denmark, France, Germany, Great Britain, Hungary, Italy, the Netherlands, Portugal, Spain, and Sweden. These franchises generate about $83 billion in business each year.

### Free Enterprise Activity

Organize students into groups, and tell them to decide on a franchise each would like to operate. Have group members assign the following tasks among themselves:

1. Listing the group's reasons for wanting to obtain the franchise.
2. Finding out the procedure for obtaining the franchise.
3. Interviewing a franchise operator to discover the pros and cons of franchising.
4. Developing a plan for financing the franchise.

Have groups compile the information they obtain into an oral report. Call on group representatives to present their reports to the class. BLOCK SCHEDULING

# CHAPTER 8

SECTION 3, Pages 219–225

## Visual Instruction FIGURE 8.7

After students have reviewed **Figure 8.7**, ask them the following question: What is the role of the board of directors in the running of a corporation? *The board is responsible for supervising and controlling the corporation. It hires various company officers to run day-to-day business operations.* **Answer:** *purchasing manager, research and development director, factory manager*

# 3 Assess

## Meeting Lesson Objectives

Assign Section 3 Assessment as homework or an in-class activity.

Use **Interactive Tutor Self-Assessment Software** to review Section 3.

### Section Quiz 8–3

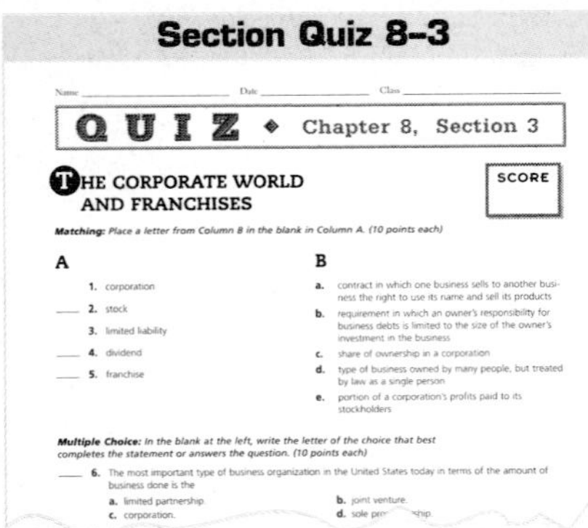

Name ________ Date ________ Class ________

QUIZ ◆ Chapter 8, Section 3

THE CORPORATE WORLD AND FRANCHISES

SCORE

***Matching:** Place a letter from Column B in the blank in Column A. (10 points each)*

**A**

1. corporation
2. stock
3. limited liability
4. dividend
5. franchise

**B**

a. contract in which one business sells to another business the right to use its name and sell its products
b. requirement in which an owner's responsibility for business debts is limited to the size of the owner's investment in the business
c. share of ownership in a corporation
d. type of business owned by many people, but treated by law as a single person
e. portion of a corporation's profits paid to its stockholders

***Multiple Choice:** In the blank at the left, write the letter of the choice that best completes the statement or answers the question. (10 points each)*

6. The most important type of business organization in the United States today in terms of the amount of business done is the
   a. limited partnership.
   b. joint venture.
   c. corporation.
   d. sole pro[illegible]ship.



**FIGURE 8.7** **Corporate Chain of Command** A typical board of directors hires officers to run the company. ***In this organizational chart, who reports to the vice president of manufacturing?***

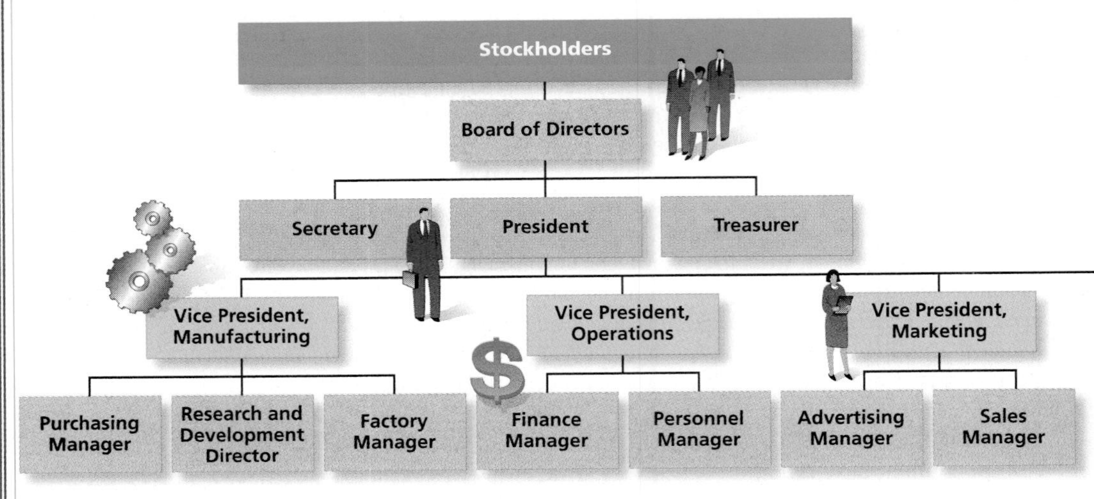


The board is responsible for supervising and controlling the corporation. It does not run business operations on a day-to-day basis. Instead, it hires officers for the company—president, vice president(s), secretary, and treasurer—to run the business and hire other employees. **Figure 8.7** shows the typical structure of a corporation.

## Franchises

*franchise: contract in which one business (the franchiser) sells to another business (the franchisee) the right to use the franchiser's name and sell its products*

Many hotel, motel, gas station, and fast-food chains are franchises. A **franchise** is a contract in which a franchiser sells to another business the right to use its name and sell its products. The person or business buying these rights, called the franchisee, pays a fee that may include a percentage of all money taken in. If a person buys a motel franchise, for example, that person agrees to pay the motel chain a certain fee plus a portion of the profits for as long as his or her motel stays in business. In return, the chain will help the franchisee set up the motel. Often, the chain will have a training program to teach the franchisee about the business and set the standards of business operations.



## Extending the Content

**Raising Capital for Corporations** Selling stock is not the only way a corporation can raise capital to develop and expand. A corporation also can issue bonds. Typically issued in multiples of $1,000 or $5,000, corporate bonds are debt obligations, or IOUs. That is, when investors buy bonds, they are lending money to the issuing corporation. Bonds carry a promise to repay the purchasing price, or principal, on a specified maturity date. Bonds also pay a stated rate of interest, usually in semiannual installments.

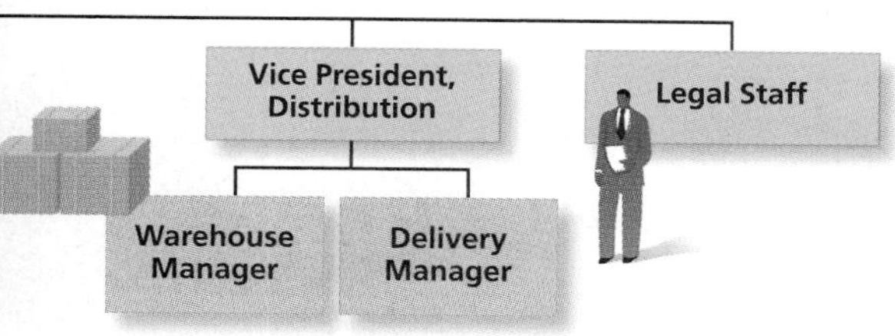


**Practice** and **assess** key skills with *Skillbuilder Interactive Workbook, Level 2.*

# SECTION 3 Assessment

### Understanding Key Terms

1. **Define** corporation, stock, limited liability, articles of incorporation, corporate charter, common stock, dividend, preferred stock, franchise.

### Reviewing Objectives

2. What are the advantages and disadvantages of corporations?
3. **Graphic Organizer** Create a diagram like the one below to show how corporations are typically structured.

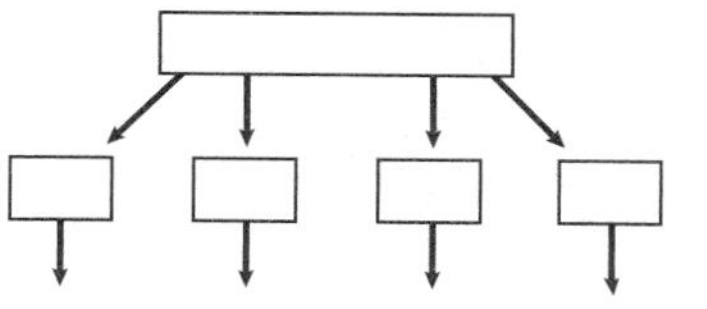

4. What types of businesses are involved in franchises?

### Applying Economic Concepts

5. **Franchises** In what industry would you franchise if offered the opportunity? Explain the possible advantages and help available from other franchises in the same industry. Then describe possible disadvantages of setting up a franchise in your chosen industry.

### Critical Thinking Activity

6. **Making Comparisons** Look in the financial pages of a recent newspaper to analyze how the stocks of three corporations have performed. What was the closing price for each? What were their 52-week highs? *For help in reading the financial page, see page xxiii in the Economic Handbook.*



# SECTION 3 Assessment Answers

1. All definitions can be found in the Glossary.
2. Advantages: owners need not devote time to make money on investment, corporation has limited liability, responsibility for running company shared among many, feeling of satisfaction from owning part of corporation, corporations can draw on resources of many investors and may issue stock to raise funds, corporation can exist indefinitely. Disadvantages: slow decision making, higher taxes, shareholders have little say in running of company.
3. Refer students to **Figure 8.7** on pages 224–225.
4. hotels, motels, gas stations, fast-food chains
5. Answers will vary.
6. Answers will vary. Suggest that students present their findings in chart form.



## Reteach

Ask students to rewrite the major subheadings as newspaper headlines. Then have them write outlines for articles to accompany these headlines.

Reading Essentials and Study Guide 8–3

Name ______ Date ______ Class ______

STUDY GUIDE Chapter 8, Section 3

*For use with textbook pages 218–224*

THE CORPORATE WORLD AND FRANCHISES

KEY TERMS

***corporation*** Business organization owned by many people, but treated as a person by law. For example, it can own property, pay taxes, and make contracts *(page 220)*

***stock*** Allows a person to purchase a specific part of a corporation's future profits or assets *(page 220)*

***limited liability*** An owner's responsibility for the company's debts is limited only to the size of the owner's investment *(page 220)*

***articles of incorporation*** registers basic information about the corporation with the state where the corporation will have its headquarters *(page 221)*

***corporate charter*** A license to operate a corporation within a state's borders *(page 221)*

***common stock*** ownership shares in a corporation, which allow its owners voting rights and a portion of future profits after preferred stockholders are paid *(page 223)*

***dividend*** A portion of the corporation's profit paid to stockholders *(page 223)*

***preferred stock*** An ownership share in a corporation that does not have voting rights, but stockholders receive a portion of future profit before others *(page 223)*

***franchise*** One business, the franchiser, sells the right to use its name and products to another company known as the franchisee *(page 224)*

DRAWING FROM EXPERIENCE

Have you ever been a member of a club or team? How was your organization created? Do you

# 4 Close

Lead students in a discussion of the following question: Which type of business organization—sole proprietorship, partnership, or corporation—is the most important for the American economy?

BusinessWeek
**SPOTLIGHT**

# Teach

Point out that while Burger King is trying to attract customers from the skies, other fast-food franchises are attempting to get their earth-bound customers to "drop in" several times a day. Working on the "day parts" concept–that different times of the day are identified with certain foods–franchisers are opening franchise combinations. For example, food giant Allied Domecq has opened several "trombos." These combine three fast-food franchises–Dunkin' Donuts (breakfast); Togo's, a sub sandwich and salad restaurant (lunch); and Baskin-Robbins (afternoon and evening).

**BusinessWeek ONLINE**

To find up-to-date news and analysis on the economy, business, technology, markets, entrepreneurs, investments, and finance, have students search feature articles and special reports on the *Business Week* Web site. www.businessweek.com

## Sidelight

On March 31, 1998, Burger King announced a new addition to its menu for the following day—the Left-handed Whopper. Left-handers flocked to Burger King outlets to buy the sandwich. They should have taken a closer look at the calendar—it was April 1, April Fool's Day!

# BusinessWeek

# SPOTLIGHT ON THE ECONOMY

## Hate to Eat and Fly, but . . .

**Check It Out!** In this chapter you learned about franchises and corporations. In the following article, read to learn how one franchise has expanded its service in an unusual way.

Now that the drive-through window is a fixture of the fast-food world, Burger King is perfecting the fly-through. A Burger King in suburban London dubs the addition to its regular restaurant the "Whopper Chopper," a landing pad where helicopter pilots can drop in, grab some grub, and fly out without leaving the cockpit.

Pilots call first to alert Burger King that they are landing. An employee dashes out and calls the order in. Then it is delivered to the waiting chopper. "This is more like the old diners where someone comes out to take your order," says Jon Clarke, a Burger King spokesperson in London. "It's a bit more personal."

Pilots agree. "I think this is a great idea," says Mark Barry-Jackson, an Aeromega pilot. "Finding suitable places to stop and refuel passengers has always been difficult." The landing pad, which is under a helicopter traffic lane, was so popular it was closed over the holidays so it could be made big enough to handle military choppers, whose pilots had heard about the place. Burger King, still testing the concept, won't comment on its profitability. But the fly-through is an idea that may just take off.

### Think About It

1. How does this Burger King franchise accommodate customers who are helicopter pilots?
2. What do you think is positive about franchises in general? Negative?

### Answers to *Think About It*

1. It offers a "fly-through" service, delivering meals to waiting helicopters on a landing pad next to the restaurant.
2. Answers will vary. Some students might suggest such positives as set standards for the goods and services offered by franchises. Other students might see this sameness as a negative, since it leads to bland, unimaginative products.

# CHAPTER 8 Summary

**Chapter Overview** Visit the *Economics Today and Tomorrow* Web site at ett.glencoe.com and click on ***Chapter 8—Chapter Overviews*** to review chapter information.

## SECTION 1 Starting a Business

- People usually decide to start a business to gain profits, to "do something on their own," or to be their own boss.
- **Entrepreneurs** must gather the relevant factors of production and decide on the form of business organization that best suits their purposes.
- For those wanting to start a small business, help is available from the government and from the Internet.
- Every business must consider four basic elements: expenses, advertising, **receipts** and record keeping, and risk.

## SECTION 2 Sole Proprietorships and Partnerships

- The most basic type of business organization is the **sole proprietorship,** a business owned by one person.
- The biggest advantages of sole proprietorships are that the proprietor has full pride in owning the business and receives all the profits.
- The biggest disadvantage is that the proprietor has **unlimited liability** and can lose personal **assets** as well as the business.
- A **partnership** is a business organization owned by two or more individuals.
- A legally binding partnership agreement describes the duties of each partner, the division of profits, and the distribution of assets should the partnership end.
- In a **limited partnership,** one general partner assumes the management duties and debt responsibility, while the limited partners contribute money but have no liability.

## SECTION 3 The Corporate World and Franchises

- A **corporation** can own property, pay taxes, make contracts, and sue and be sued.
- One of the major advantages of a corporation is **limited liability.**
- A major disadvantage is that corporations are taxed more heavily than other forms of business organizations.
- To form a corporation, its founders must register with the state government, sell **stock,** and elect a board of directors.
- A **franchise** is a contract in which a franchiser sells to another business the right to use its name and sell its products.



## Economics Journal

**Business Organizations** Have students keep track of all the goods that they and their families purchase during one week. Have them list these items with the name of the businesses where they were purchased. Direct students to indicate the size of each business—small, medium, or large—and whether each business has one or several owners. At the end of the week, ask students to compile the information they have gathered in a chart with the following column headings: "Goods and Services Purchased," "Size of Business," "Ownership." Call on volunteers to display their charts to the class. Have them explain why they buy certain goods from particular businesses.

CHAPTER 8 Summary

**ECONOMICS & YOU**

**Business Organizations**

Chapter 4
Disc 1, Side 1

If you do not have access to a videodisc player, the ***Economics & You*** programs are also available in VHS.

Use the **Chapter 8 Summary** to preview, review, condense, or reteach the chapter.

## Preview/Review

**Vocabulary PuzzleMaker Software** reinforces the key terms used in Chapter 8.

**Interactive Tutor Self-Assessment Software** allows students to review Chapter 8 content.

## Condense

Have students listen to the Chapter 8 **Audio Program** (also available in Spanish) in the TCR. Assign the Chapter 8 Audio Program Activity and give students the Chapter 8 Audio Program Test.

## Reteach

Have students complete **Reteaching Activity** 8 in the TCR (Spanish Reteaching Activities are also available).

**ECONOMICS Online**

Have students visit the *Economics Today and Tomorrow* Web site at ett.glencoe.com to review Chapter 8 and take the Self-Check Quiz.

**GLENCOE TECHNOLOGY**

 **MindJogger Videoquiz**

Use MindJogger to review Chapter 8 content.

## Identifying Key Terms

1. c
2. g
3. a
4. e
5. j
6. f
7. b
8. i
9. h
10. d

## Recalling Facts and Ideas

1. advertising and risk
2. opportunity cost
3. Small Business Administration, state departments of commerce and community affairs, community college and university small business centers, small business incubators, the Internet
4. sole proprietorship
5. Disadvantages: owner responsible for all losses, unlimited liability, make all business decisions, huge time demands, must depend on own funds and what can be borrowed.
6. In a partnership, partners play a role in operating the business and have unlimited liability. In a limited partnership, one general partner runs the business and has unlimited liability, while the limited partners play little part in the business and are liable only for what they have invested.
7. A limited partnership lasts as long as the partners agree to do business together, whereas a joint venture is a temporary partnership set up for a specific purpose and time period.
8. It is registered in the state where it will be headquartered, it sells stock, and it elects a board of directors.
9. the state in which the corporation will be headquartered
10. stockholders
11. The franchiser sells the right to use its name and its product or service to the franchisee. The franchisee pays a fee and a share of the profits. In return, the franchiser helps train the franchisee to run the business efficiently.

# CHAPTER 8 Assessment and Activities

**Self-Check Quiz** Visit the *Economics Today and Tomorrow* Web site at **ett.glencoe.com** and click on ***Chapter 8—Self-Check Quizzes*** to prepare for the Chapter Test.

## Identifying Key Terms

*Identify the letter of the definition in Column B that correctly defines each term in Column A.*

**Column A**

1. inventory
2. corporate charter
3. assets
4. franchise
5. unlimited liability
6. sole proprietorship
7. partnership
8. stock
9. joint venture
10. corporation

**Column B**

a. items of value
b. business owned by two or more people
c. supply of items that are used in business
d. business owned by many people, but treated as a person itself
e. contract in which a business sells the right to use its name to another business
f. business owned by one person
g. right to operate
h. temporary partnership
i. ownership shares in a business
j. legal responsibility for all debts incurred when doing business

## Recalling Facts and Ideas

**Section 1**

1. Every business involves expenses and receipts and record keeping. What are two other elements?
2. When you calculate your profits, it is especially important for you to include the value of your time. What is this called?
3. If you need help in starting a small business, where can you look?

**Section 2**

4. What is the most common form of business organization?
5. What are the disadvantages of a sole proprietorship?
6. What is the difference between a partnership and a limited partnership?
7. What is the difference between a limited partnership and a joint venture?

**Section 3**

8. What are the elements of every corporation?
9. Who grants corporate charters?
10. Which group within a corporation chooses the board of directors?
11. How does a franchise operate?

## Thinking Critically

1. **Drawing Inferences** Why do you have to include the opportunity cost of your time when you calculate your profits in your own business?
2. **Drawing Conclusions** Why would a person decide in favor of a partnership rather than a sole proprietorship?
3. **Understanding Cause and Effect** Create a diagram like the one below and identify three problems in a corporation that might be caused by its complex organizational structure.

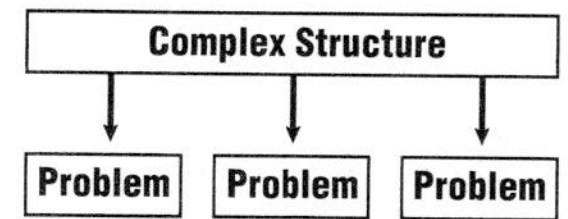


## Applying Economic Concepts

**Economic Institutions and Incentives** In this chapter you have read about numerous advantages and disadvantages of different types of business organizations. Make a list of the following: sole proprietorship, partnership, limited partnership, joint venture, corporation, and franchise. After each type, indicate the single most important advantage that you believe this form of business organization has.

## Technology Activity

**Developing Multimedia Presentations** Think of a product or service you would like to produce. Create a multimedia presentation promoting that product or service. Utilize video, graphics, and music in your presentation. Share your presentation with the rest of the class.

## Reviewing Skills

**Using the Internet** Several business news magazines—*Forbes, Fortune,* and *Business Week*—report the top several hundred corporations in America every year. Find out what the top five corporations are, then use the Internet to locate each company's home page. Once you have located each site, access them and use the information to prepare an oral report on each company's (1) number of employees, (2) total sales in billions of dollars, (3) total market value as given by the stock market, and (4) change in ranking from the previous year.

## Cooperative Learning Project

Working in groups of four, select a corporation listed in the financial pages of a newspaper. Then use business magazines and financial and annual reports, if possible, to determine the annual earnings, dividends, and stock prices of that corporation over the past year. Compare the corporation with those selected by other groups and discuss which stocks would have been the best investments during the past year.

## Analyzing the Global Economy

Notice the labels on your clothes, shoes, and food. Find out in which countries these items were made or produced. Then research one of the top five corporations within one of those countries. Is its corporate structure similar to the structure found in American corporations? Explain.



# CHAPTER 8
## Assessment and Activities

### Applying Economic Concepts

Answers will vary. Ask students to explain why they consider the selected advantages the most important.

### Technology Activity

Presentations will vary.

### Reviewing Skills

After students have presented their reports, ask them to identify the corporations they expected to see on the list and those they were surprised to see.

### Cooperative Learning Project

Prior to students undertaking this project, review with them the meaning of the various symbols used in the financial pages.

### Analyzing the Global Economy

It might be helpful for students to draw diagrams of the structure of their selected corporations.

### Chapter Bonus Test Question

ASK: How might stockholders influence the operations of a corporation? *by exercising their right to vote in elections for the board of directors*

## Thinking Critically

1. because the time used in running the business could have been used to do something else, including working for a wage
2. to expand the business, to share the work, to gain a partner with specific expertise, or to share in business losses
3. decision-making process becomes very complex because of the many layers of management; decision-making process tends to be slow; difficult to identify source of decisions because of many layers of management

Economics Lab

# 1 Focus

Point out to students that in a free market, businesses succeed or fail, in part, because of the preparation and research proprietors undertake before the business is even open. Underscore that well-prepared business owners have a better chance of success than those who rely on instinct and enthusiasm alone. Conclude by informing students that the purpose of this lab is to provide an opportunity to practice the type of preparation and planning that setting up a business requires.

# 2 Teach

Begin by ensuring that all pairs possess, or have access to, all the materials listed in Step A. As pairs work through the procedures in Step B, ensure that they are making reasoned decisions. That is, have them write full explanations of why each decision or determination was made. In Step C, suggest that pairs prepare an oral report to accompany their presentations of drawings and models.

It will take several sessions to satisfactorily complete this Economics Lab. Therefore, establish set times for review of students' progress.

Economics Lab

# *Setting Up a Business*

From the classroom of Denny C. Jackson, Switzerland County High School, Vevay, Indiana

In Chapter 8 you learned about the different types of business organizations and what it takes to start a business. In this lab, you will set up a hotel business.

## STEP A Tools Needed

- ✔ Hotel directories
- ✔ Hotel franchise circulars
- ✔ Vacation/travel guides (for location of the hotel)
- ✔ Drawing paper
- ✔ Colored pencils
- ✔ Clear plastic folder
- ✔ Computer with access to the Internet (optional)
- ✔ Supplies necessary to build a scale model of your hotel

## STEP B Procedures to Follow

1. Work with a partner to research points 2 through 8.
2. Determine the location of your hotel. Use travel guides to identify the "generators" that will draw people to your hotel: national park, theme park, university, airport, isolated interstate, tour groups, and so on.
3. Decide whether your hotel should be an independent or a franchise. Explain your choice.
4. Determine the makeup of the hotel. How many rooms? Restaurant and lounge? Swimming pool? Gift shop? Game room and health spa?

**Teacher's Notes**

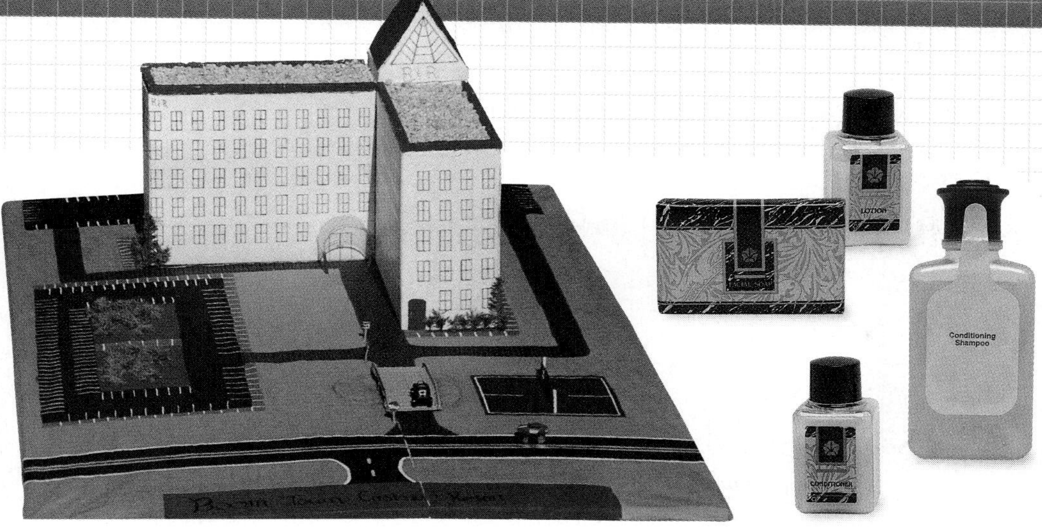


5. Decide on the number and wages of employees you will need for all shifts: a manager, assistant managers, front desk clerks, housekeeping staff, maintenance staff, restaurant staff, and so on.
6. Decide the layout of the rooms as well as their décor. Also design the exterior of the hotel, including parking facilities, subway access, and so on.
7. Determine what you will charge per room. Report on what items are included in the room (shampoo, coffee maker, satellite TV, and so on).
8. Determine how you will obtain the funds needed to begin: banking institution, grant or loan from a small business incubator, etc.

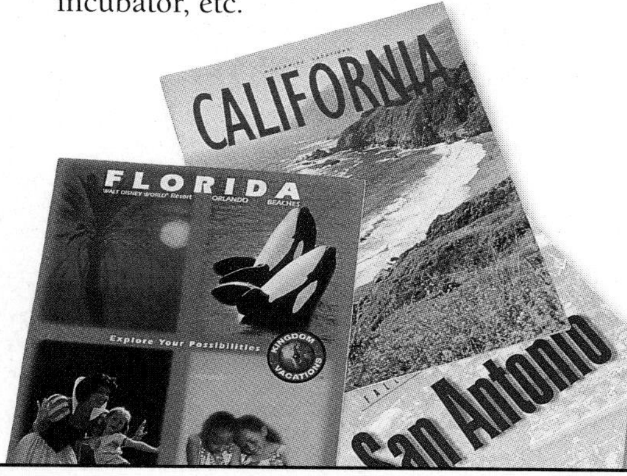


## STEP C Creating an Economic Model

Use the results of your research to create at least two drawings: one showing the layout of the rooms, and one showing the exterior of the hotel. Then create a scale model of your hotel. Present your drawings and model to the rest of the class.

## STEP D Lab Report Analysis

After completing your presentation, answer the following questions:

1. Why did you choose an independent or franchise?
2. Why did you choose the specific location of your hotel?
3. How did you arrive at the room rate?
4. What did you decide to include in the total project?

### Answers to Lab Report Analysis

Have students refer to the reasoned explanations they wrote for Step B before answering the Lab Report Analysis questions. In a concluding session, have students share and discuss their answers.

# 3 Assess

Have students answer the **Lab Report Analysis** questions.

# 4 Close

To conclude the Economics Lab, point out that the hotel and motel industry is a leader in franchising. Ask students why they think this is so.

### Did You Know

An economic impact survey on the travel and tourism industries conducted in 1998 found that Americans who stayed in U.S. hotels and motels in the United States accounted for an estimated $256 billion in spending. This total included such expenditure categories as lodging, transportation, food, shopping, and entertainment.

# CHAPTER 9 Resource Manager

## Teaching Transparency

### Economic Concepts Transparency 9

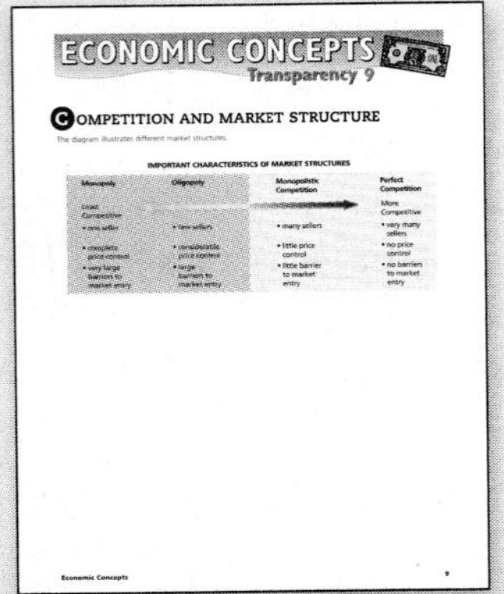

ECONOMIC CONCEPTS Transparency 9

COMPETITION AND MARKET STRUCTURE

## Application and Enrichment

### Enrichment Activity 9

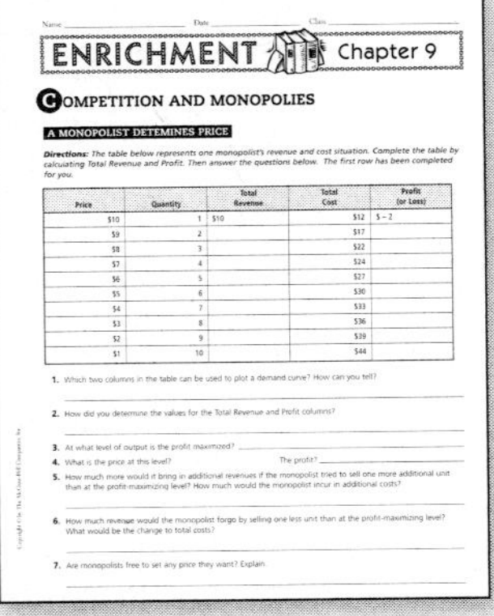

ENRICHMENT Chapter 9

COMPETITION AND MONOPOLIES

A MONOPOLIST DETERMINES PRICE

### Consumer Applications Activity 8

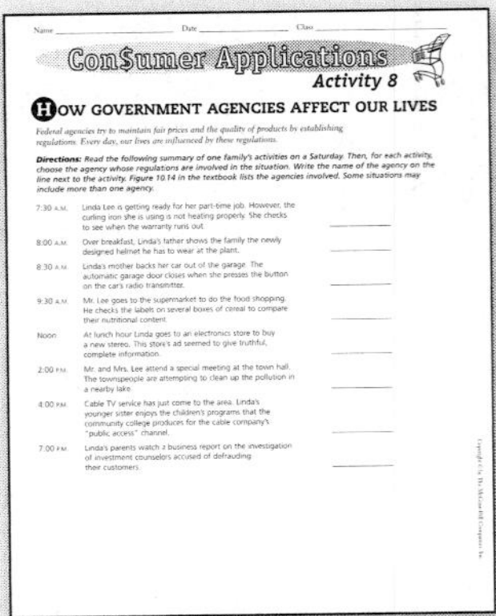

Consumer Applications Activity 8

HOW GOVERNMENT AGENCIES AFFECT OUR LIVES

### Free Enterprise Activity 6

FREE ENTERPRISE ACTIVITY 6

MARKET CONDITIONS

## Application and Enrichment

### Cooperative Learning Simulations and Problems 8

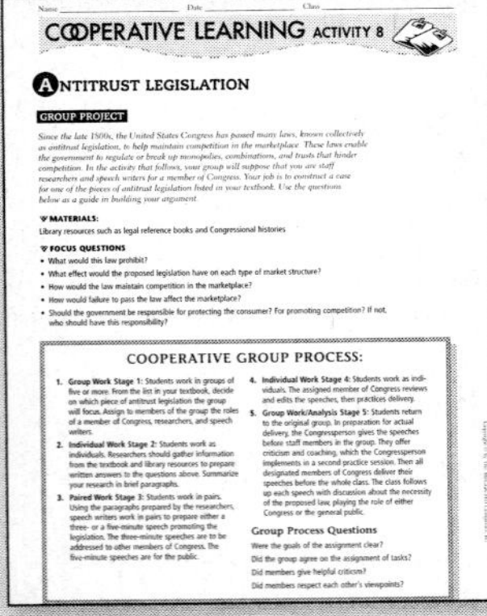

COOPERATIVE LEARNING ACTIVITY 8

ANTITRUST LEGISLATION

COOPERATIVE GROUP PROCESS:

### Primary and Secondary Source Reading 9

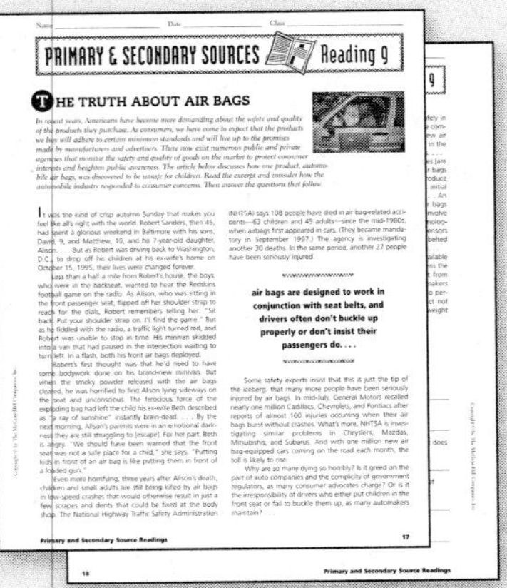

PRIMARY & SECONDARY SOURCES Reading 9

THE TRUTH ABOUT AIR BAGS

air bags are designed to work in conjunction with seat belts, and drivers often don't buckle up properly or don't insist their passengers do. . . .

### Math Practice for Economics Activity 7

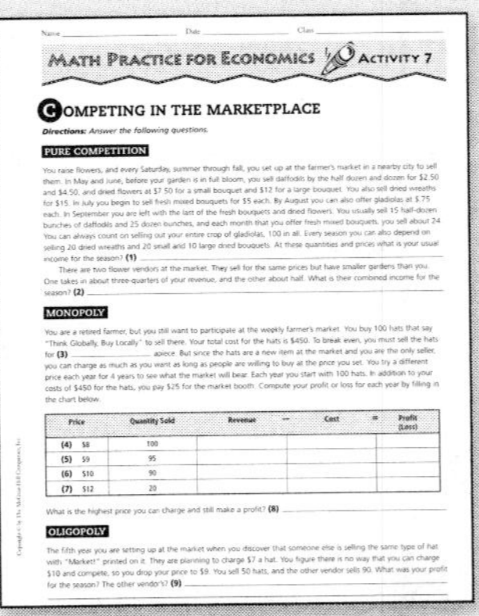

MATH PRACTICE FOR ECONOMICS ACTIVITY 7

COMPETING IN THE MARKETPLACE

PURE COMPETITION

MONOPOLY

OLIGOPOLY

### Economic Cartoons Activity 8

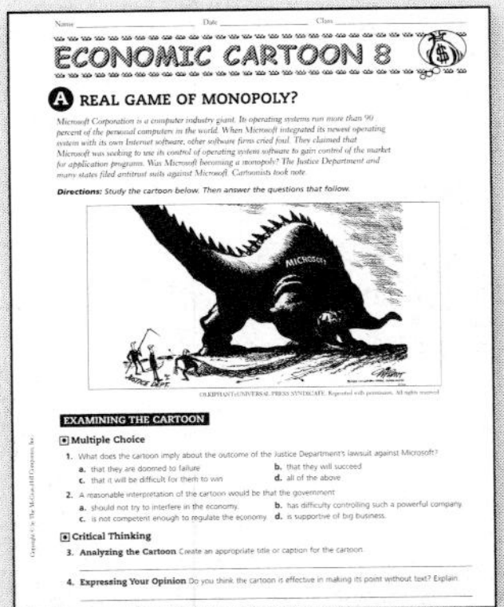

ECONOMIC CARTOON 8

A REAL GAME OF MONOPOLY?

EXAMINING THE CARTOON

## Review and Reinforcement

### Critical Thinking Activity 8

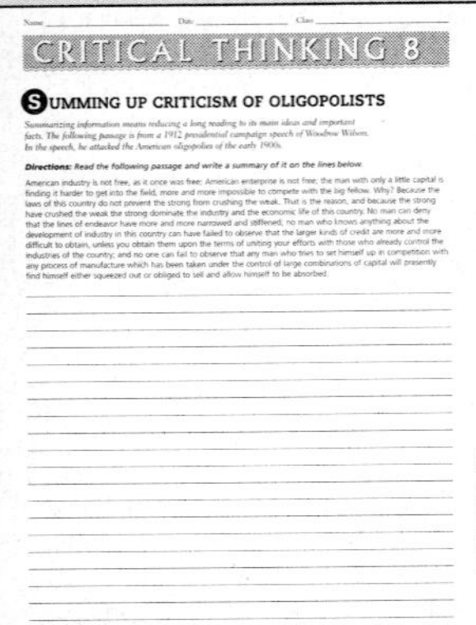

CRITICAL THINKING 8

SUMMING UP CRITICISM OF OLIGOPOLISTS

### Reteaching Activity 9

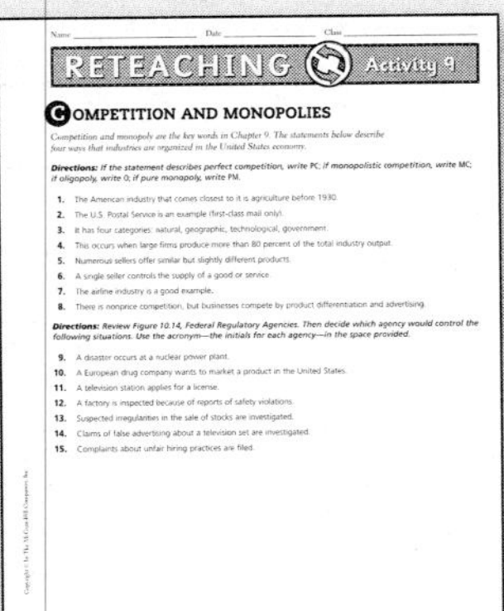

RETEACHING Activity 9

COMPETITION AND MONOPOLIES

### Economic Vocabulary Activity 9

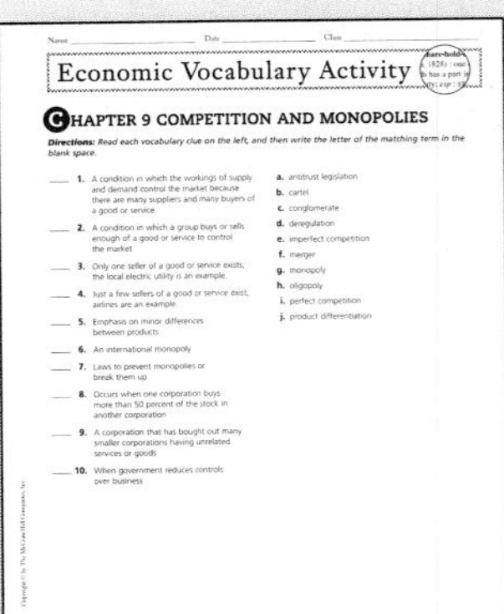

Economic Vocabulary Activity

CHAPTER 9 COMPETITION AND MONOPOLIES

### Reinforcing Economic Skills 16

Reinforcing Economic Skills Chapter 16

DRAWING INFERENCES AND CONCLUSIONS

# CHAPTER 9 Resource Manager

## Assessment and Evaluation

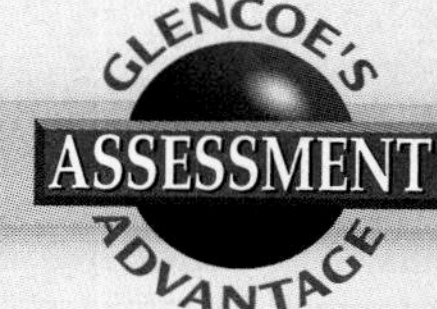


Chapter 9 Test Form A

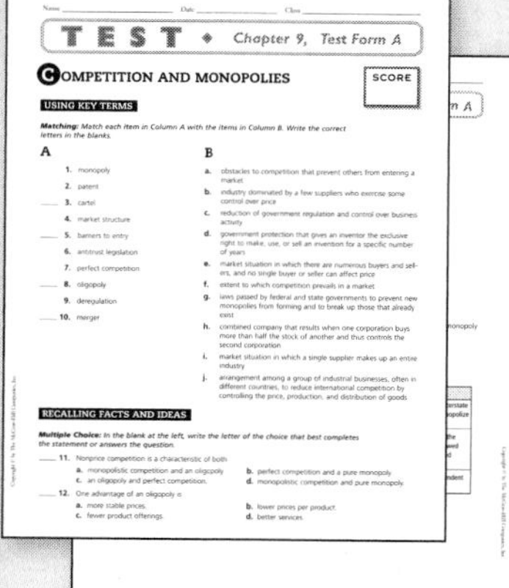

Chapter 9 Test Form B

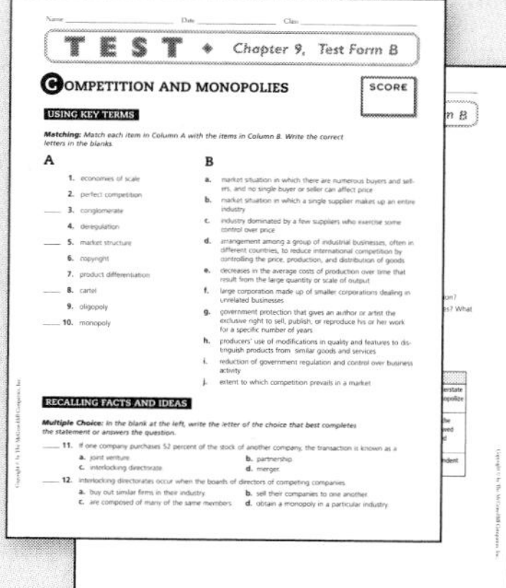

Performance Assessment Activity 8

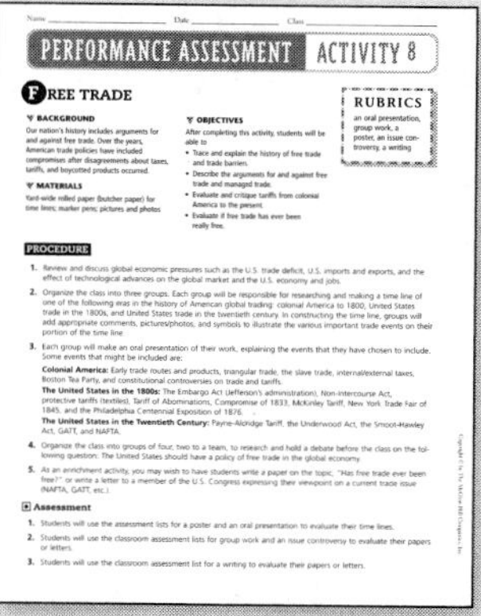

ExamView® Pro Testmaker

## Technology and Multimedia

 Vocabulary PuzzleMaker Software

 Interactive Tutor Self-Assessment Software

 ExamView® Pro Testmaker

 NBR *Economics & You* Video Program (English/Spanish)

 Presentation Plus!

 Glencoe Skillbuilder Interactive Workbook CD-ROM, Level 2

 Interactive Lesson Planner

 MindJogger Videoquiz

 Interactive Economics! CD-ROM

Audio Program (English or Spanish)

You and your students can visit ett.glencoe.com—the Web site companion to **Economics Today and Tomorrow.** This innovative integration of electronic and print media offers your students a wealth of opportunities. The student text directs students to the Web site for the following options:

- **Chapter Overviews**
- **Student Web Activities**
- **Self-Check Quizzes**
- **Textbook Updates**

Answers are provided for you in the **Web Activity Lesson Plan.** Additional Web resources and Interactive Puzzles are also available.

Use the Glencoe Web site for additional resources. All essential content is covered in the Student Edition.

## Spanish Resources

 Spanish Economic Concepts Transparency 9

 Spanish Vocabulary Activity 9

 Spanish Reteaching Activity 9

 Spanish Section Quizzes for Chapter 9

 Spanish Chapter 9 Audio Program, Activity, and Test

## Additional Resources

### Reading for the Student

Keenan, Diane, et al. *Economics U$A: High School Activity Packs.* The Annenberg/CPB Collection. Companion text for the video series mentioned below.

### Multimedia Material

*Economics U$A: Monopoly/Oligopolies.* The Annenberg/CPB Collection. Color video, 60 mins. Discusses the nature of these two theoretical models of competition.

# CHAPTER 9 Resource Manager

## Section Resources

| Reading Objectives | Reproducible Resources | Technology/Multimedia Resources |
|---|---|---|
| **Section 1**<br>**Perfect Competition**<br>• What are the five conditions of perfect competition?<br>• Why is agriculture often considered an example of perfect competition?<br>• How does perfect competition benefit society? | Reproducible Lesson Plan 9-1<br>Daily Lecture Notes 9-1<br>Guided Reading Activity 9-1<br>Reading Essentials and Study Guide 9-1<br>Daily Focus Activity 20<br>Section Quiz 9-1*<br>Reinforcing Economic Skills 16 | Daily Focus Transparency 20<br>Economic Concepts Transparency 9<br>Vocabulary PuzzleMaker<br>Interactive Tutor Self-Assessment Software<br>MindJogger Videoquiz<br>NBR's *Economics & You**<br>Presentation Plus!<br>ExamView® Pro Testmaker |
| **Section 2**<br>**Monopoly, Oligopoly, Monopolistic Competition**<br>• What are four characteristics of a pure monopoly?<br>• What characterizes an oligopoly?<br>• What are five characteristics of monopolistic competition? | Reproducible Lesson Plan 9-2<br>Daily Lecture Notes 9-2<br>Guided Reading Activity 9-2<br>Reading Essentials and Study Guide 9-2<br>Daily Focus Activity 21<br>Section Quiz 9-2* | Daily Focus Transparency 21<br>Vocabulary PuzzleMaker<br>Interactive Tutor Self-Assessment Software<br>MindJogger Videoquiz<br>NBR's *Economics & You**<br>Presentation Plus!<br>ExamView® Pro Testmaker |
| **Section 3**<br>**Government Policies Toward Competition**<br>• What is the difference between interlocking directorates and mergers?<br>• What is the purpose of federal regulatory agencies?<br>• How has some regulation hurt consumers? | Reproducible Lesson Plan 9-3<br>Daily Lecture Notes 9-3<br>Guided Reading Activity 9-3<br>Reading Essentials and Study Guide 9-3<br>Daily Focus Activity 22<br>Section Quiz 9-3* | Daily Focus Transparency 22<br>Vocabulary PuzzleMaker<br>Interactive Tutor Self-Assessment Software<br>MindJogger Videoquiz<br>NBR's *Economics & You**<br>Presentation Plus!<br>ExamView® Pro Testmaker |

*Also available in Spanish

Blackline Master
Transparency

Software

CD-ROM

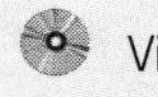
Videodisc

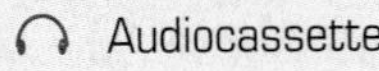
Audiocassette

Videocassette

# CHAPTER 9 Resource Manager

## ACTIVITY From the Classroom of

**Wendy S. Field**
**SCT BOCES Technical-Occupational Center**
**Elmira, New York**

### Medical Center

Have students develop a private medical business. Their outline should include a marketing plan that includes a competitor analysis; a financing plan that explains the costs of running the business; a staffing plan that lists needs versus costs; and a supplier plan that lists the medical supplies needed as well as general items such as business cards and filing cabinets.

Students must then research the aspects of government involvement in their medical business. Zoning regulations and environmental protections must be researched. In addition, students can use the Internet to find what local, state, and federal OSHA regulations must be met. Have students share their plans in an oral report.

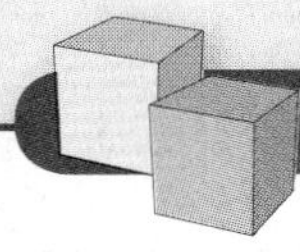

## Block Schedule

Activities that particularly suited to use within the block scheduling framework are identified throughout this chapter by the following designation: BLOCK SCHEDULING

## *Easy Planning and Preparation!*

Use Glencoe's **Presentation Plus!**, a Microsoft PowerPoint® application, to teach **Competition and Monopolies.** With this multimedia teacher tool, you can customize ready-made presentations. At your fingertips are interactive transparencies, on-screen lecture notes, audiovisual presentations, and links to the Internet and to other Glencoe multimedia.

### Interactive Lesson Planner

Planning has never been easier! Organize your week, month, semester, or year with all the lesson helps you need to make teaching creative, timely, and relevant—the way it is meant to be. The Interactive Lesson Planner opens Glencoe's **Chapter 9** resources, helps you build your schedule, and tracks your progress.

## Key to Ability Levels

**Teaching strategies have been coded for varying learning styles and abilities.**

- L1 BASIC activities for all students
- L2 AVERAGE activities for average to above-average students
- L3 CHALLENGING activities for above-average students
- ELL ENGLISH LANGUAGE LEARNER activities

## National Council on Economic Education

## THE EconomicsAmerica AND EconomicsInternational PROGRAMS

### Voluntary Standards Emphasized in Chapter 9

**Content Standard 9** Students will understand that competition among sellers lowers costs and prices, and encourages producers to produce more of what consumers are willing and able to buy.

**Content Standard 16** Students will understand that there is an economic role for government to play in a market economy whenever the benefits of a government policy outweigh its costs.

### Resources Available from NCEE

- *Capstone: The Nation's High School Economics Course*
- *Focus: High School Economics*
- *MCG–Economics and Entrepreneurship*
- *Economics in Transition: Command to Market*
- *From Plan to Market*

To order these materials, or to contact your State Council on Economic Education about workshops and programs, call 1-800-338-1192 or visit the NCEE Web site at http://www.nationalcouncil.org

ECONOMICS & YOU

Competition and Monopolies

Chapter 8
Disc 1, Side 1

ASK: What is likely to happen to the prices of products and services when competition is lacking? *Prices are likely to increase.*

 Also available in VHS.

## Chapter Overview

**Chapter 9** explains or describes the influence of competition on supply and demand and price, perfect competition and pure monopoly, oligopoly and monopolistic competition, and government regulation of business.

### GLENCOE TECHNOLOGY

Use **MindJogger Videoquiz** VHS to preview Chapter 9 content.

### ECONOMICS Online

Introduce students to chapter content and key terms by having them access **Chapter 9—Chapter Overviews** at *ett.glencoe.com*

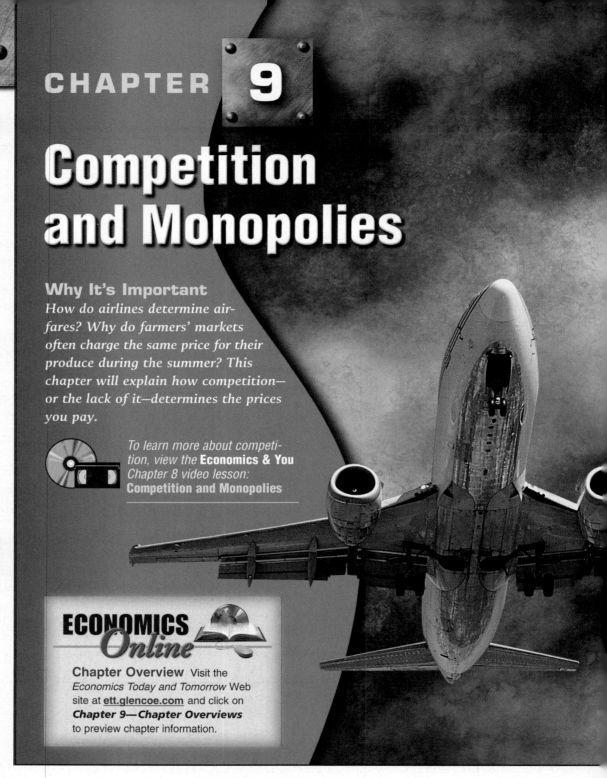

# CHAPTER 9

# Competition and Monopolies

### Why It's Important

*How do airlines determine airfares? Why do farmers' markets often charge the same price for their produce during the summer? This chapter will explain how competition—or the lack of it—determines the prices you pay.*

*To learn more about competition, view the* **Economics & You** *Chapter 8 video lesson:* **Competition and Monopolies**

### ECONOMICS Online

**Chapter Overview** Visit the *Economics Today and Tomorrow* Web site at ett.glencoe.com and click on ***Chapter 9—Chapter Overviews*** to preview chapter information.

## CHAPTER LAUNCH ACTIVITY

Tell students to imagine they want to buy a CD player. Ask them what factors they might consider in making such a purchase. Note their responses on the board. Next, underscore responses such as price, quality, and special features and point out that students assume they will have a choice of these items. Continue by mentioning that there is a choice in the market because companies compete for business. Have students consider what purchasing a CD player would be like if there were no competition. Conclude by informing students that they will learn about competition—and the lack of competition—in the market in this chapter.

SECTION 1

# Perfect Competition

## Cover Story

*Business Week*, March 22, 1999

By December, Boston could get a lot closer to New York and Washington—at least by train. That's when Amtrak's new high-speed rail service, dubbed Acela, will start operating. With Acela, some New York–Boston trips will take just 3 hours, vs. 4½ now. And all new trains will have computer jacks and food service. Amtrak aims to compete head-on with airline shuttles.

### Reader's Guide

**Terms to Know**

- market structure
- perfect competition

**Reading Objectives**

1. What are the five conditions of perfect competition?
2. Why is agriculture often considered an example of perfect competition?
3. How does perfect competition benefit society?

Competition—one of the basic characteristics of our market economic system—is advantageous to consumers for several reasons. First, it provides us with choices. As noted in the *Cover Story* above, people traveling from Boston to New York now have a choice of going by plane or train. Competition is advantageous for another reason as well. Having many competing suppliers of a product leads to a surplus and, thus, lower prices. As you can imagine, for this reason each supplier would like to have as little competition as possible.

## Market Structure

In Chapter 8 you learned that businesses are set up based on the number of owners—sole proprietorship, partnership, corporation. In this chapter you'll learn that businesses are also categorized by **market structure**—or by the amount of competition they face. **Figure 9.1** on page 234 shows the four basic market structures in

**market structure:** *the extent to which competition prevails in particular markets*



## Section 1 Resource Manager

**Reproducible Masters**

- Reproducible Lesson Plan 9–1
- Reading Essentials and Study Guide 9–1
- Guided Reading Activity 9–1
- Section Quiz 9–1
- Daily Focus Activity 20
- Daily Lecture Notes 9–1

**Multimedia**

- Daily Focus Transparency 20
- Economic Concepts Transparency 9
- Vocabulary PuzzleMaker
- Interactive Tutor Self-Assessment Software
- ExamView® Pro Testmaker
- MindJogger Videoquiz
- NBR's *Economics & You*
- Presentation Plus!



# 1 Focus

## Overview

Section 1 explains or describes perfect competition and the conditions that are needed for perfect competition to exist.

**BELLRINGER**
**Motivational Activity**

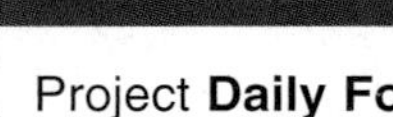

Project **Daily Focus Transparency 20** and have students answer the questions.

This activity is also available as a blackline master.

**Daily Focus Transparency 20**

PERFECT COMPETITION

1. Why do you think all of the apples have similar prices?
2. The land and equipment pictured on the left act as barriers that might make farming less than perfectly competitive. Why?

Daily Focus Transparencies

### Reader's Guide

Answers to the **Reading Objectives** questions are on page 237.

**Preteaching Vocabulary**

Ask students to speculate on the meaning of the terms *market structure* and *perfect competition*. Note students' ideas on the board. Then have students compare their definitions with those in the Glossary.

Vocabulary PuzzleMaker

# 2 Teach

## Guided Practice

**L1 Classifying Information** Review the conditions of perfect competition with students. Then on the board, construct a table with the following column headings: "Market Size," "Product," "Market Entry," "Information," "Control Over Price." Call on volunteers to come to the board and, in the appropriate column, note the way these five conditions are reflected in perfect competition.

### Daily Lecture Notes 9-1

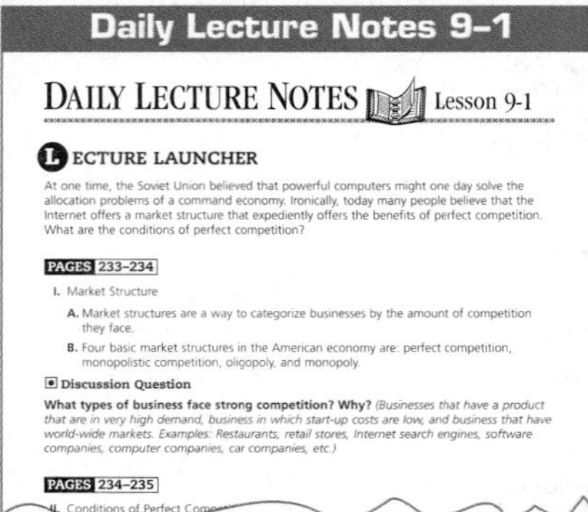

DAILY LECTURE NOTES Lesson 9-1

LECTURE LAUNCHER

At one time, the Soviet Union believed that powerful computers might one day solve the allocation problems of a command economy. Ironically, today many people believe that the Internet offers a market structure that expediently offers the benefits of perfect competition. What are the conditions of perfect competition?

PAGES 233–234

I. Market Structure
   A. Market structures are a way to categorize businesses by the amount of competition they face.
   B. Four basic market structures in the American economy are: perfect competition, monopolistic competition, oligopoly, and monopoly.

**Discussion Question**

**What types of business face strong competition? Why?** *(Businesses that have a product that are in very high demand, business in which start-up costs are low, and business that have world-wide markets. Examples: Restaurants, retail stores, Internet search engines, software companies, computer companies, car companies, etc.)*

PAGES 234–235

II. Conditions of Perfect Comp

### Visual Instruction FIGURE 9.1

Ask students to study **Figure 9.1**. Then ask students what might be the advantages and disadvantages of a perfectly competitive market.

**FIGURE 9.1** **Comparing Market Structures** Markets that are either perfectly competitive or pure monopolies are rare. Most industries in the United States fit one of the other two forms.

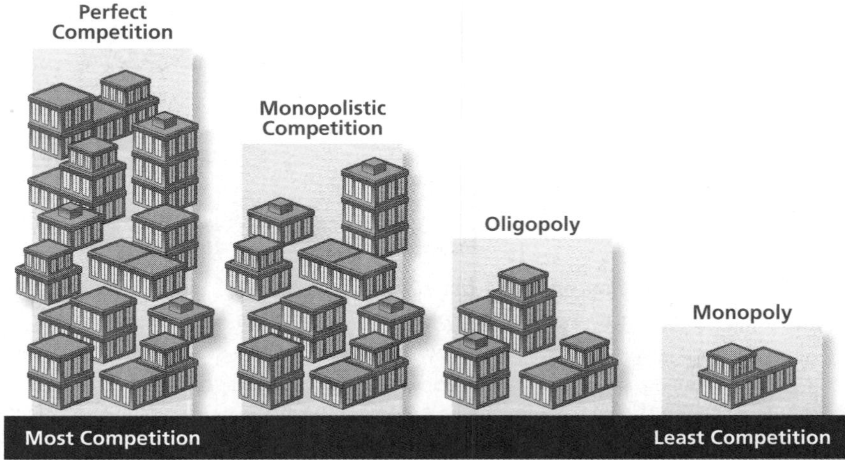


the American economy: perfect competition, monopolistic competition, oligopoly, and monopoly. In this section you'll learn about the ideal market structure of perfect competition.

## Conditions of Perfect Competition

All businesses must engage in some form of competition as long as other businesses produce similar goods or services. When a market includes so many sellers of a particular good or service that each seller accounts for a small part of the total market, a special situation exists. Economists term it **perfect competition.** For perfect competition to take place, five conditions must be met:

**perfect competition:** *market situation in which there are numerous buyers and sellers, and no single buyer or seller can affect price*

**(1) A Large Market** Numerous buyers and sellers must exist for the product.

**(2) A Similar Product** The good or service being sold must be nearly identical. See **Figure 9.2.**

**(3) Easy Entry and Exit** Sellers already in the market cannot prevent competition, or



### Meeting Special Needs

**Learning Strategy** Students with learning challenges often have difficulty applying learning strategies in different situations. To help students use the "Survey, Question, Read, Recite, and Review" strategy, have them construct a chart with the following questions as column headings: "Did I skim for the title, headings, and main ideas?" "Did I ask questions?" "Did I answer my questions?" Work through the section with students. As they move through the procedures, have them place a check mark in the appropriate column on their charts.

Refer to *Inclusion for the Social Studies Classroom Strategies and Activities* for students with different learning styles.

entrance into the market. In addition, the initial costs of investment are small, and the good or service is easy to learn to produce.

**(4) Easily Obtainable Information** Information about prices, quality, and sources of supply is easy for both buyers and sellers to obtain.

**(5) Independence** The possibility of sellers or buyers working together to control the price is almost nonexistent.

**No Control Over Price** When the above five conditions are met, the workings of supply and demand control the price, not a single seller or buyer. On the supply side, perfect competition requires a large number of suppliers of a similar product. On the demand side, perfect competition requires a large number of informed buyers who know exactly what the market price is for the good or service.

In a perfectly competitive market, the market price is the equilibrium price. Total supply and total demand are allowed to interact to reach the equilibrium price—the only price at which quantity demanded equals quantity supplied. In a world of perfect competition, each individual seller would accept that price. Because so many buyers and sellers exist, one person charging a higher or lower price would not affect the market price.

**Information Is Key** True perfect competition is rarely seen in the real world. Nonetheless, fierce competition does exist in many sectors of the economy. While information about prices, quality, and sources of supply might have been hard and costly to obtain in the past, that is not true today. Virtually anyone with access to the Internet can find out the lowest prices of just about anything.

**Perfect Competition**

Having a similar product and easy entry into the market—such as greenhouses do—are two conditions of perfect competition. ***What three other conditions must be met for perfect competition?***

235

## Cooperative Learning

Organize students into several small groups, and tell groups that they have been asked to prepare educational materials to teach the concept of perfect competition. Direct groups to create wall charts, posters, or some other form of pictorial display on perfect competition, using agriculture as an example. Call on groups to use their materials to teach the concept to the rest of the class. ELL BLOCK SCHEDULING

# CHAPTER 9

SECTION 1, Pages 233–237

**Guided Reading Activity 9-1**

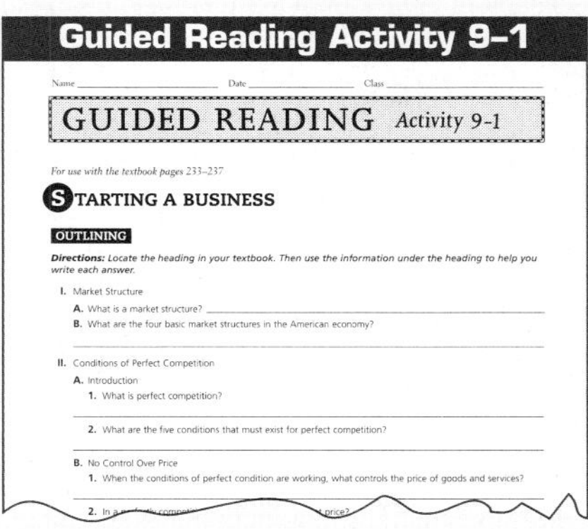
GUIDED READING Activity 9-1

STARTING A BUSINESS

OUTLINING

I. Market Structure
A. What is a market structure?
B. What are the four basic market structures in the American economy?

II. Conditions of Perfect Competition
A. Introduction
1. What is perfect competition?
2. What are the five conditions that must exist for perfect competition?
B. No Control Over Price
1. When the conditions of perfect condition are working, what controls the price of goods and services?

**ECONOMICS & YOU**

**Competition and Monopolies**

Chapter 8
Disc 1, Side 1

**ASK: Why does lack of competition lead to higher prices?** *When competition is lacking, the pressure to compete is reduced. Prices for goods and services, therefore, are likely to go up.*

 Also available in VHS.

Project **Economic Concepts Transparency** 9 and have students discuss the accompanying questions.

**Visual Instruction FIGURE 9.2**

**Answer:** *a large market, easily obtainable information about prices and products, little possibility of sellers and buyers working together to control price*

## Independent Practice

L2 Applying Ideas Organize students into several groups. Tell groups that their task is to write a 45-second to 1-minute radio advertisement that explains the benefits of perfect competition. Suggest that groups listen to examples of radio ads before undertaking the task. Call on groups to "broadcast" their advertisements to the class. BLOCK SCHEDULING

## Did You Know

The demand curve for an individual business in a perfectly competitive market is a horizontal line at the going market price. At that price, the business can sell all the output it wants.

# 3 Assess

## Meeting Lesson Objectives

Assign Section 1 Assessment as homework or an in-class activity.

Use **Interactive Tutor Self-Assessment Software** to review Section 1.

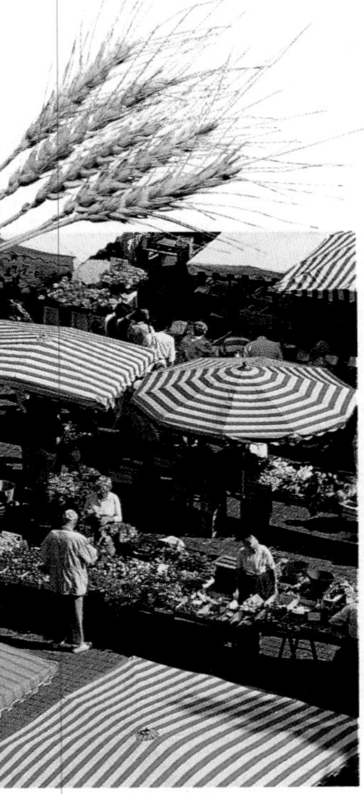

## Agriculture as an Example

Few perfectly competitive industries exist in the United States. The one that perhaps comes closest is the agricultural market. It is often used as an example of perfect competition because individual farmers have almost no control over the market price of their goods. **Figure 9.3** applies the five conditions of perfect competition to the wheat market.

**No Control Over Wheat Prices** No single farmer has any great influence on price. The interaction of supply and demand determines the price of wheat. The supply is the total supply of all the wheat that farmers produce. The demand is the total demand for all uses of wheat. The equilibrium price is the price where supply and demand intersect.

Individual wheat farmers have to accept the market price. If the price is $3 per bushel, that is the price every farmer receives. Farmers who attempt to raise their price above $3 will find that no one will buy their wheat. Neither will a farmer sell his or her crop for less than $3 per bushel.

**Unique Situation** The demand for wheat and other agricultural products is somewhat different from the demand for many other products. People's demand for wheat is, for the most part, inelastic. People can use wheat in only so many ways, and people can eat only so many wheat products. So even if the price of wheat were to increase or drop dramatically, quantity demanded would not change significantly. The supply side of most agricultural markets is also unique. It is highly dependent on conditions over which farmers have little or no control, as shown in **Figure 9.4.**

### FIGURE 9.3

**The Wheat Market as a Perfect Competitor**

1. **A Large Market** Thousands of wheat farmers grow wheat, and thousands of wholesalers buy wheat.
2. **A Similar Product** All wheat is fairly similar.
3. **Easy Entry and Exit** The costs of renting farmland are relatively low, and farming methods can be learned.
4. **Easily Obtainable Information** Information about wheat prices is fairly easy to obtain. Indeed, it can be obtained on the Internet in a few seconds.
5. **Independence** The possibility of thousands of wheat farmers banding together to control the price is very small.



## Visual Learning Activity

**Graphic Organizer** Have students create a graphic organizer titled "The Wheat Market—Perfect Competition." Direct students to draw a web similar to the one here. The web should have "The Wheat Market as Perfect Competitor" written in the central oval. Students should complete the web by entering the conditions of perfect competition in the wheat market in the outer ovals.

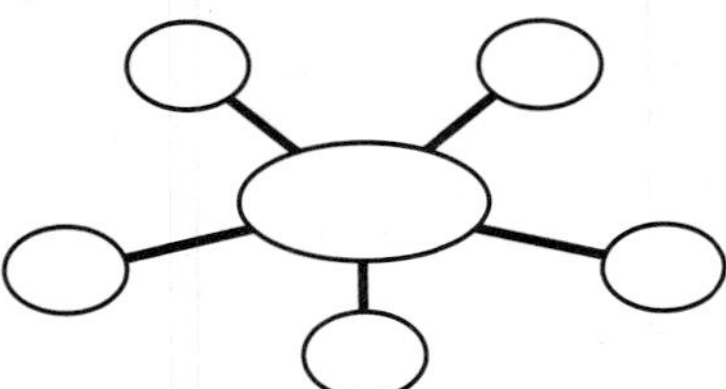

## Benefits to Society

The intense competition in a perfectly competitive industry forces the price down to one that just covers the costs of production plus a small profit. This price is beneficial because it means that consumers are paying only for what has been put in to make those products—the opportunity cost of the use of land, labor, capital, and entrepreneurship. The price that consumers pay for such products is a correct signal about the value of those products in society.

Perfectly competitive industries yield economic efficiency. All inputs are used in the most advantageous way possible, and society therefore enjoys an efficient allocation of productive resources.

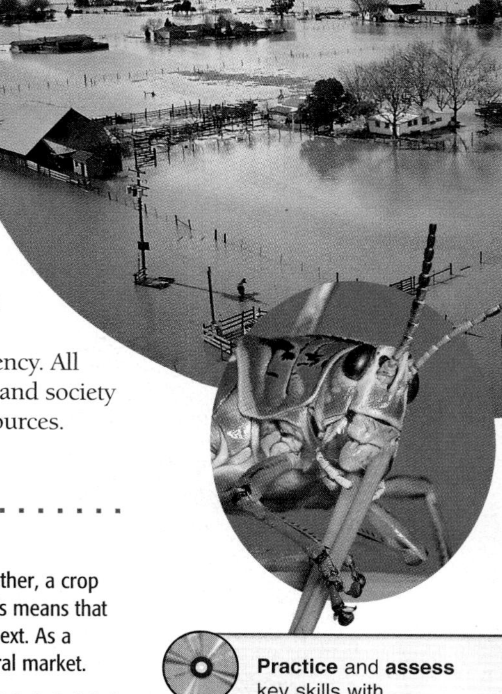

FIGURE 

**Agricultural Disasters Affect Supply** Variations in weather, a crop disease, or a crop-destroying insect can wipe out entire harvests. This means that farmers may have a good harvest one year and a poor harvest the next. As a result, there are widely fluctuating supplies of goods in the agricultural market.

**Practice** and **assess** key skills with *Skillbuilder Interactive Workbook, Level 2.*

## SECTION 1 Assessment

### Understanding Key Terms

1. **Define** market structure, perfect competition.

### Reviewing Objectives

2. **Graphic Organizer** Use a diagram like the one below to explain the five conditions of perfect competition.

Perfect Competition

3. Why is agriculture often considered an example of perfect competition?
4. How does perfect competition benefit society?

### Applying Economic Concepts

5. **Perfect Competition** Explain how a local fast-food restaurant manager faces almost perfect competition in the demand for high school employee labor.

### Critical Thinking Activity

6. **Summarizing Information** In this section, you learned that the Internet has made the United States economy more competitive. Use a search engine to find information about the market price of your favorite automobile.



### Section Quiz 9-1

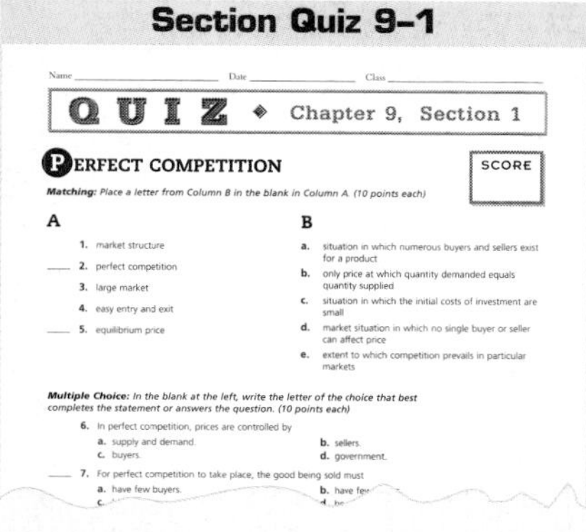
Name ______ Date ______ Class ______

QUIZ ◆ Chapter 9, Section 1

PERFECT COMPETITION SCORE

**Matching:** *Place a letter from Column B in the blank in Column A. (10 points each)*

| A | B |
|---|---|
| ___ 1. market structure | a. situation in which numerous buyers and sellers exist for a product |
| ___ 2. perfect competition | b. only price at which quantity demanded equals quantity supplied |
| ___ 3. large market | c. situation in which the initial costs of investment are small |
| ___ 4. easy entry and exit | d. market situation in which no single buyer or seller can affect price |
| ___ 5. equilibrium price | e. extent to which competition prevails in particular markets |

**Multiple Choice:** *In the blank at the left, write the letter of the choice that best completes the statement or answers the question. (10 points each)*

___ 6. In perfect competition, prices are controlled by
a. supply and demand. b. sellers.
c. buyers. d. government.

___ 7. For perfect competition to take place, the good being sold must
a. have few buyers. b. have few

### Reteach

To reinforce students' understanding of perfect competition, have them develop an annotated outline of this section.

### Reading Essentials and Study Guide 9-1

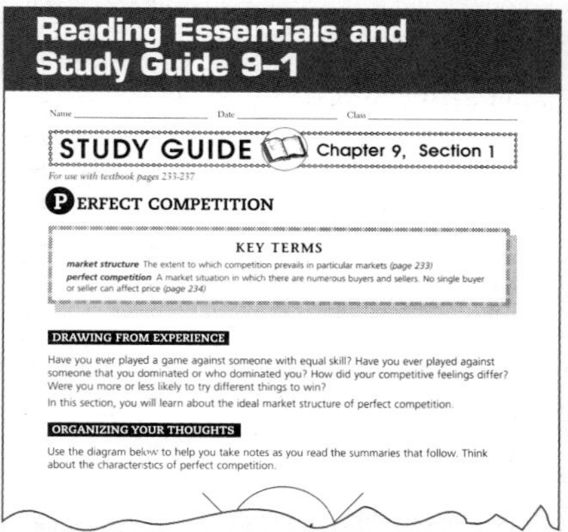
Name ______ Date ______ Class ______

STUDY GUIDE Chapter 9, Section 1

For use with textbook pages 233–237

PERFECT COMPETITION

KEY TERMS

**market structure** The extent to which competition prevails in particular markets (page 233)

**perfect competition** A market situation in which there are numerous buyers and sellers. No single buyer or seller can affect price (page 234)

DRAWING FROM EXPERIENCE

Have you ever played a game against someone with equal skill? Have you ever played against someone that you dominated or who dominated you? How did your competitive feelings differ? Were you more or less likely to try different things to win?

In this section, you will learn about the ideal market structure of perfect competition.

ORGANIZING YOUR THOUGHTS

Use the diagram below to help you take notes as you read the summaries that follow. Think about the characteristics of perfect competition.

## 4 Close

Ask students to write a paragraph using the following as a topic sentence: It is practically impossible to meet all the conditions for perfect competition.

## SECTION 1 Assessment Answers

1. All definitions can be found in the Glossary.
2. Five conditions: a large market, a similar product, easy entry and exit into the market, easily obtainable information, independence
3. Agriculture meets the conditions of perfect competition: many farmers and many buyers of farm products; farm products fairly similar; costs of renting farmland relatively low, and farming methods can be learned; information about farm prices readily available; possibility of thousands of farmers banding together to control price very small.
4. Perfect competition encourages economic efficiency by forcing price down to where it covers costs plus a small profit. This means that consumers are paying only what has been put in to make those products.
5. The high school student labor pool is large; most students have similar qualifications; entry into the high school labor pool is easy; information about students' qualifications and wage requirements is readily available; it is unlikely that students would band together to set wages.
6. Have students discuss the prices they found.

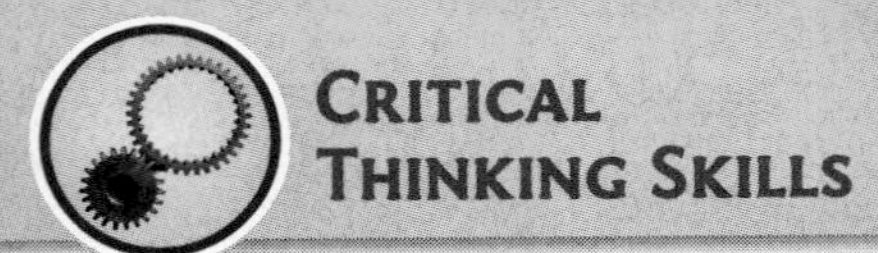

## Critical Thinking Skills

### Drawing Inferences and Conclusions

Write the following sentence on the board, and tell students that it is a headline that might have appeared in the sports pages of a newspaper: "Another Year of Futility–Hawks Fail to Make the Playoffs Again!"

Ask students what information about the team they can draw from the headline. *Most students will infer that it has been some time since the Hawks had a successful season.* Next, ask students to suggest how the writer feels about the situation. *Students may suggest that the writer seems upset or frustrated.* Then point out that in this exercise, students have been drawing inferences and conclusions–a key skill of critical thinkers.

**Reinforcing Economic Skills 16**

Name ________ Date ________ Class ________

**Reinforcing Economic Skills** Chapter 16

**DRAWING INFERENCES AND CONCLUSIONS**

*Drawing inferences involves "reading between the lines," or drawing conclusions that are not stated directly in the text. To draw inferences and make conclusions, read the information carefully and list the important facts. Then apply related information from other sources as well as your own knowledge and insight to develop some conclusions about these facts.*

***Directions:*** *Study the tables below and answer the questions that follow.*

| Country | Infant Deaths per 1,000 Live Births | Number of Television Sets per 1,000 People | Private Consumption per capita (dollars) |
|---|---|---|---|
| Bangladesh | 79 | 7 | 1,049 |
| Finland | 5 | 519 | 11,431 |
| Morocco | 55 | 145 | 2,454 |
| United States | 8 | 776 | 18,507 |

| Country | Health Spending (percent of GNP) | People per Hospital Bed | Gross National Product per capita (millions of dollars) |
|---|---|---|---|
| Bangladesh | 2.4 | 5,479 | 240 |
| Finland | 8.3 | 93 | 20,580 |
| Morocco | 3.4 | 775 | 3,340 |
| United States | 14.3 | 221 | 26,980 |

*Source: World Development Indicators*

**GLENCOE TECHNOLOGY**

**Glencoe Skillbuilder Interactive Workbook, Level 2**

This interactive CD-ROM reinforces student mastery of essential social studies skills.

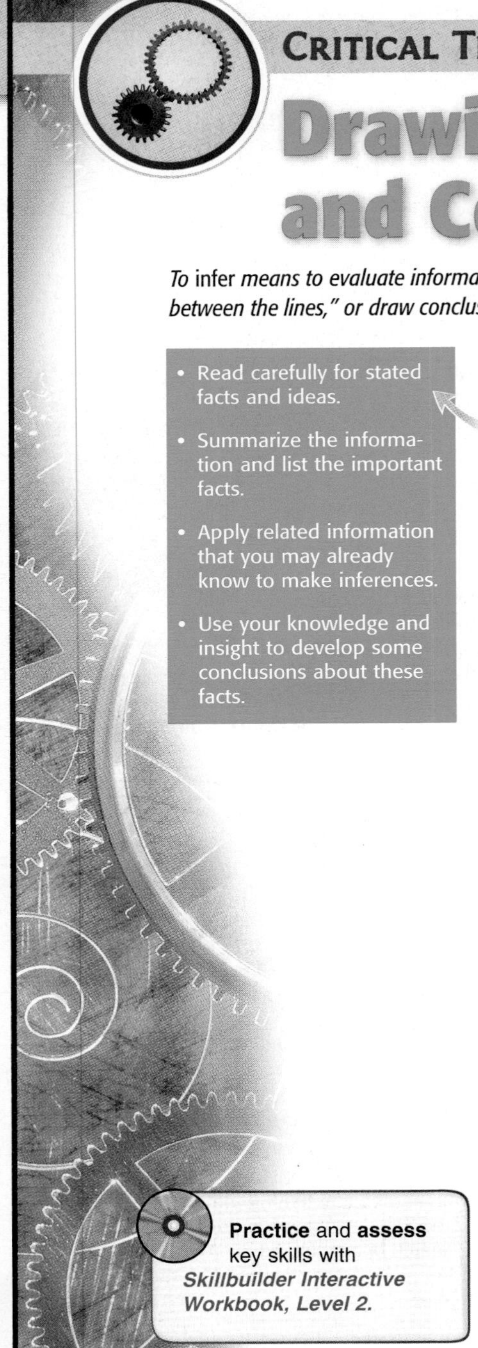

## Critical Thinking Skills

# Drawing Inferences and Conclusions

*To* infer *means to evaluate information and arrive at a conclusion. When you make inferences, you "read between the lines," or draw conclusions that are not stated directly in the text.*

- Read carefully for stated facts and ideas.
- Summarize the information and list the important facts.
- Apply related information that you may already know to make inferences.
- Use your knowledge and insight to develop some conclusions about these facts.

### Learning the Skill

To learn how to make inferences and draw conclusions, follow the steps listed on the left.

### Practicing the Skill

Read the passage below, then answer the questions.

*"[A] landmark 1996 bill gave farmers the freedom to plant what they wanted, when they wanted. But it also swept away much of the financial safety net of price supports for U.S. crops. . . . The next time agriculture hit a downdraft, would Washington really let the market work?*

*Dumb question. In 1999, Uncle Sam will dole out some $14.4 billion to farmers. . . .*

*This is no way to run farm policy. Indeed, it's a simple law of economics that the prospect of bailouts in times of trouble leads farmers to take more risks, such as planting additional, marginal acres. That makes the system less efficient. . . ."*

–*Business Week*, June 28, 1999

1. What facts are presented in the passage?
2. What can you infer about the occupation of the passage's author? Is he or she a farmer? Explain.
3. Can you conclude that the agricultural sector is a perfectly competitive market? Explain.

### Application Activity

Apply the five conditions of perfect competition to the soft drink industry. Would you conclude that it is perfectly competitive? Explain.

**Practice and assess** key skills with ***Skillbuilder Interactive Workbook, Level 2.***



### Answers to Practicing the Skill

1. A landmark bill, passed in 1996, gave farmers the freedom to plant what they want, when they want. In 1999, the federal government will give $14.4 billion to farmers.
2. The author is probably not a farmer. The author does not want to bail out farmers in times of trouble.
3. Most students will conclude that it is not a perfectly competitive market, because government policy interferes with the forces of supply and demand in price setting.

**Application Activity** Students' research should lead them to understand that the soft drink industry in the U.S. is oligopolistic among the several large soft drink manufacturers.

SECTION 2

# Monopoly, Oligopoly, Monopolistic Competition

## Cover Story

*Business Week*, February 1, 1999

When Gillette Co. unveiled Mach3, the world's first triple-blade razor, it took a bold gamble. . . . Mach3 cartridges were to sell for around $1.60 each. Skeptics predicted the personal-care giant would soon be forced to cut that price. But the price is holding and Mach3 has become the No. 1 blade and razor.

What's the secret to pricing power? For starters, a commitment to innovation. Gillette spent nearly $1 billion on the development and initial marketing of Mach3.

### Reader's Guide

**Terms to Know**

- monopoly
- barriers to entry
- economies of scale
- patent
- copyright
- oligopoly
- product differentiation
- cartel
- monopolistic competition

**Reading Objectives**

1. What are four characteristics of a pure monopoly?
2. What characterizes an oligopoly?
3. What are five characteristics of monopolistic competition?

Imagine spending $1 billion on the development and advertising of a razor blade—a common shaving tool. Would that much advertising be worth it? It would if customers paid whatever price you asked for the razors. As you read this section, you'll learn that advertising plays a major role in two types of market structures.

## Imperfect Competition

As mentioned in Section 1, perfect competition is an ideal type of market structure. Most industries in the United States, in



## Section 2 Resource Manager

**Reproducible Masters**

- Reproducible Lesson Plan 9–2
- Reading Essentials and Study Guide 9–2
- Guided Reading Activity 9–2
- Section Quiz 9–2
- Daily Focus Activity 21
- Daily Lecture Notes 9–2

**Multimedia**

- Daily Focus Transparency 21
- Vocabulary PuzzleMaker
- Interactive Tutor Self-Assessment Software
- ExamView® Pro Testmaker
- MindJogger Videoquiz
- NBR's *Economics & You*
- Presentation Plus!



# 1 Focus

## Overview

Section 2 explains and describes the concepts and characteristics of pure monopoly, oligopoly, and monopolistic competition.

### Bellringer

**Motivational Activity**

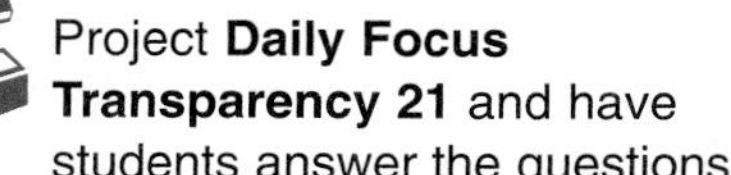

Project **Daily Focus Transparency 21** and have students answer the questions.

This activity is also available as a blackline master.

**Daily Focus Transparency 21**

MONOPOLIES, OLIGOPOLIES, AND MONOPOLISTIC COMPETITION

1. Why does the government pass laws that reduce competition, as in the case of the U.S. Postal Service?
2. Why would the need for high-cost capital keep people from getting into a market such as the aluminum-producing industry?

Daily Focus Transparencies

### Reader's Guide

Answers to the **Reading Objectives** questions are on page 246.

**Preteaching Vocabulary**

List the **Terms to Know** on the board. Have volunteers skim the section to find each term and read and define it in context.

Vocabulary PuzzleMaker

# 2 Teach

## Guided Practice

**L1 Classifying Information** On the board, construct a table with the following vertical column headings: "Number of Sellers," "Product," "Entry Into Market," "Control Over Price." Use "Monopoly," "Oligopoly," and "Monopolistic Competition" as horizontal column headings. Have students compare these three types of imperfect competition by completing the table.

**Daily Lecture Notes 9-2**

DAILY LECTURE NOTES Lesson 9-2

LECTURE LAUNCHER

In the mid-1800s, speculators would cut the telegraph wires connecting Boston to New York. When steamships came into Boston Harbor with information about events in Europe's market, the telegraphs could not be sent. The speculators would arrange to have a horse and rail express deliver the news to them first. What are some other ways that a business might try to control a particular market.

PAGES 239–240

I. Imperfect Competition

A. Most industries are a form of imperfect competition.

B. There are three types of imperfect competition that differ in how much competition and control over price the seller has.

Discussion Question

**Why do you think that U.S. industries mainly have imperfect competition?** *(Answers will vary, but should touch on the difficulty of perfect competition and how capitalistic economies create conditions for imperfect competition.)*

PAGES 240–243

II. Monopoly

**Visual Instruction FIGURE 9.5**

Have students study **Figure 9.5.** Ask them to read the paragraphs under the subheading "Types of Monopolies." ASK: Which type of monopoly is Figure 9.5? *natural monopoly*

**FIGURE 9.5**

**Local Electric Companies**
Because some local electric utilities are the sole providers, and the consumer has no other option, they are monopolies.

**monopoly:** *market situation in which a single supplier makes up an entire industry for a good or service with no close substitutes*

**barriers to entry:** *obstacles to competition that prevent others from entering a market*

contrast, represent some form of *imperfect* competition. Economists classify these three types of imperfect market structures as monopoly, oligopoly, or monopolistic competition. They differ from one another on the basis of how much competition and control over price the seller has.

## Monopoly

The most extreme form of imperfect competition is a pure **monopoly**, in which a single seller controls the supply of the good or service and thus determines the price. A few such markets do exist in the real world. As shown in **Figure 9.5,** some local electric utility companies are the sole providers for a community. The consumers have no other option but to purchase electric power from these monopolies.

**Characteristics of a Monopoly** A monopoly is characterized by four conditions:

**(1) A Single Seller** Only one seller exists for a good or service.
**(2) No Substitutes** There are no close substitutes for the good or service that the monopolist sells.
**(3) No Entry** The monopolist is protected by obstacles to competition that prevent others from entering the market.
**(4) Almost Complete Control of Market Price** By controlling the available supply, the monopolist can control the market price.

In a pure monopoly, the supplier can raise prices without fear of losing business to competitors. Unless buyers choose to pay the new price, they have nowhere else to buy the good or service. A monopolist, however, cannot charge outrageous prices. Even in a monopolistic market, the law of demand is still operating. As the price of a good or service rises, consumers buy less.

**Barriers to Entry** If a monopoly is collecting all the profits in a particular industry, why don't other businesses rush in to get a share of those profits? As mentioned above, a monopoly is protected by **barriers to entry**—obstacles that prevent others from entering the market.

The most obvious barrier into a monopolistic market is a legal one. Some state laws, for example, prevent a competing electric, gas, or water company from operating in an area where a public utility company already provides service. The reasoning against competition in public utility industries is the fear that too much competition may lead to wasteful duplication. Imagine the

**Meeting Special Needs**

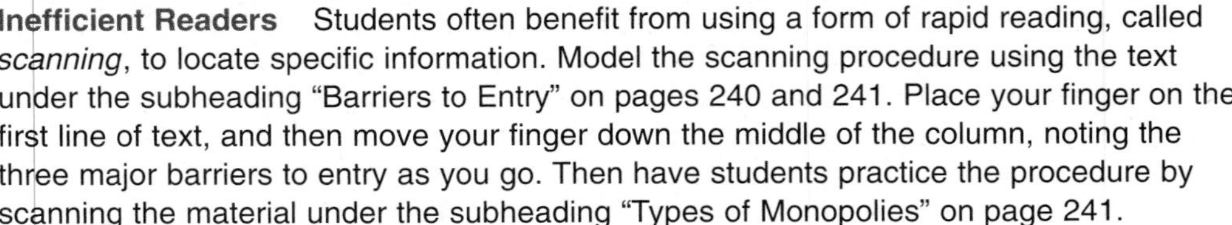

**Inefficient Readers** Students often benefit from using a form of rapid reading, called *scanning*, to locate specific information. Model the scanning procedure using the text under the subheading "Barriers to Entry" on pages 240 and 241. Place your finger on the first line of text, and then move your finger down the middle of the column, noting the three major barriers to entry as you go. Then have students practice the procedure by scanning the material under the subheading "Types of Monopolies" on page 241.

Refer to *Inclusion for the Social Studies Classroom Strategies and Activities* for students with different learning styles.

inefficiency of three or four competing water companies all trying to lay water mains along your street.

Another barrier to entry is the cost of getting started. Called "excessive money capital costs," this barrier is found in industries such as cars and steel, in which initial investment is high because of the amount and cost of the equipment. See **Figure 9.6.**

Ownership of essential raw materials can also provide a barrier to entry. A good example is the diamond industry. The DeBeers Company of South Africa controls the marketing of nearly all the world's diamonds.

**Types of Monopolies** Pure monopolies can be separated into four categories depending on why the monopoly exists. As shown in **Figure 9.7** on page 242, the four types of monopolies are natural, geographic, technological, and government.

In the past it was thought to be more efficient, or natural, to have just one company providing a public good or service. This belief led the government to grant exclusive rights to *natural monopolies*–providers of such things as utilities, bus service, and cable TV. The large size, or scale, of most natural monopolies seemed to give them **economies of scale**–by which they could produce the largest amount for the lowest cost. It is now being realized that advances in technology can make these industries more competitive, however. Government is making moves to deregulate and open them up for competition.

A grocery store in a remote Alaskan village is an example of a monopoly caused by geographic factors. Because the potential for profits is so small, other businesses choose not to enter, thus giving the sole provider a *geographic monopoly.* These types of monopolies are declining, however, as competition arises from mail-order and Internet catalogs and delivery services.

If you invent something, you are capable of having a *technological monopoly* over your invention. A government **patent** gives you the exclusive right to manufacture, rent, or sell your invention for a specified number of years–usually 17. Similarly, a United States **copyright** protects art, literature, song lyrics, and other creative works for the life of the author plus 50 years.

A *government monopoly* is similar to a natural monopoly, except the monopoly is held by the government itself. The construction and maintenance of roads and bridges, for example, are the responsibility of local, state, and national governments.

**economies of scale:** *low production costs resulting from the large size of output*

**patent:** *exclusive right to make, use, or sell an invention for a specified number of years*

**copyright:** *exclusive right to sell, publish, or reproduce creative works for a specified number of years*

**FIGURE** 

**Barriers to Entry** Huge startup costs keep some businesses from entering certain industries.

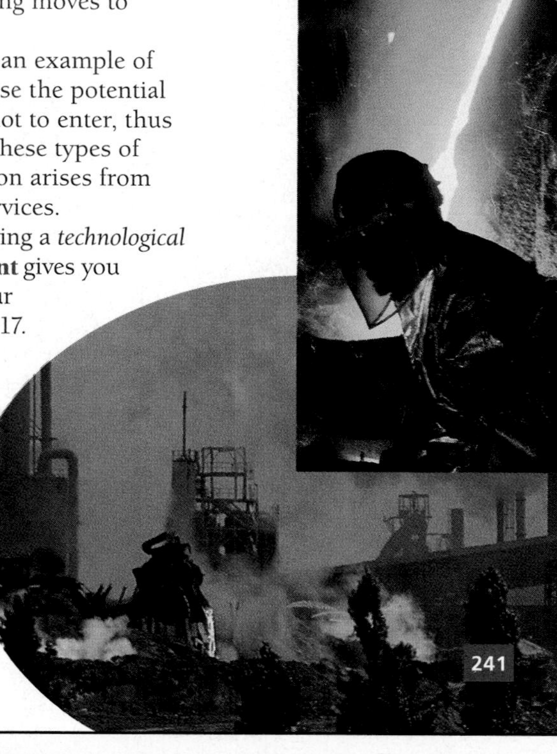


CHAPTER 9
SECTION 2, Pages 239–246

**L2 Demonstrating Ideas** After reviewing the section with the class, organize students into several small groups. Assign each group one of the following market structures: monopoly, oligopoly, monopolistic competition. Ask groups to develop a scenario, skit, or charade that might be used to teach the class the major characteristics of their assigned market structures. After the presentations are completed, lead the class in a discussion of the similarities and differences among the three market structures.

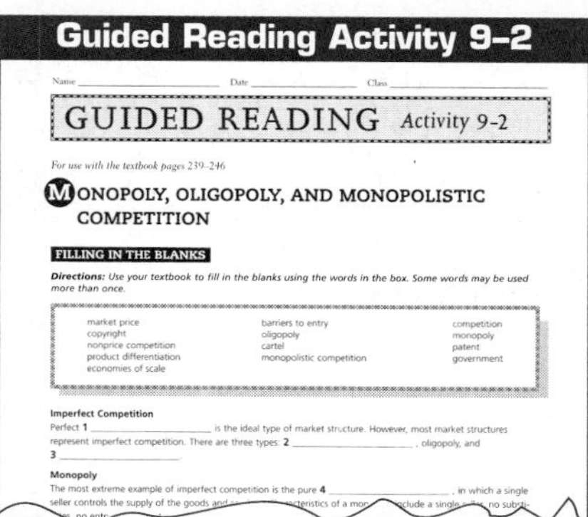

**Guided Reading Activity 9-2**

Name ______ Date ______ Class ______

GUIDED READING Activity 9-2

*For use with the textbook pages 239–246*

**MONOPOLY, OLIGOPOLY, AND MONOPOLISTIC COMPETITION**

**FILLING IN THE BLANKS**

***Directions:*** *Use your textbook to fill in the blanks using the words in the box. Some words may be used more than once.*

| | | |
|---|---|---|
| market price | barriers to entry | competition |
| copyright | oligopoly | monopoly |
| nonprice competition | cartel | patent |
| product differentiation | monopolistic competition | government |
| economies of scale | | |

**Imperfect Competition**

Perfect **1** ______ is the ideal type of market structure. However, most market structures represent imperfect competition. There are three types: **2** ______, oligopoly, and **3** ______.

**Monopoly**

The most extreme example of imperfect competition is the pure **4** ______, in which a single seller controls the supply of the goods and

## Did You Know

The Aluminum Company of America (ALCOA) provides an example of how ownership of essential raw materials can block other companies from entering a market. Around the turn of the twentieth century, ALCOA controlled almost all the sources of bauxite, the ore from which aluminum is made. For many years, ALCOA maintained its near monopoly by refusing to sell bauxite to potential competitors.

## Cooperative Learning

Organize students into several groups, and have groups select an oligopolistic industry. Have groups create a multimedia exhibit that illustrates how firms in their selected industries practice product differentiation. Inform groups that their exhibits might include collages of magazine and newspaper advertisements, videotapes of television advertisements, and audiotapes of radio advertisements. Encourage groups to display their exhibits around the classroom. ELL BLOCK SCHEDULING

## Visual Instruction FIGURE 9.7

Draw students' attention to Part B in **Figure 9.7**. Remind students that technological monopolies are established by government patents. Then inform students that during the 1990s, the U.S. Patent and Trademarks Office issued an average of about 117,000 patents each year.
**Answer:** *Answers may vary. Many students will suggest that because of economies of scale, some natural monopolies and government monopolies may be justified.*

**ECONOMICS & YOU**

**Competition and Monopolies**

Chapter 8
Disc 1, Side 1

**ASK: How is a monopoly different from an oligopoly?** *A monopoly exists when only one producer of a product or service exists. An oligopoly exists when only a few producers compete in a market.*

Also available in VHS.

**FIGURE 9.7**

**Types of Monopolies** Monopolies exist for several reasons. ***Which type of monopoly, if any, do you think is justified? Explain your response.***

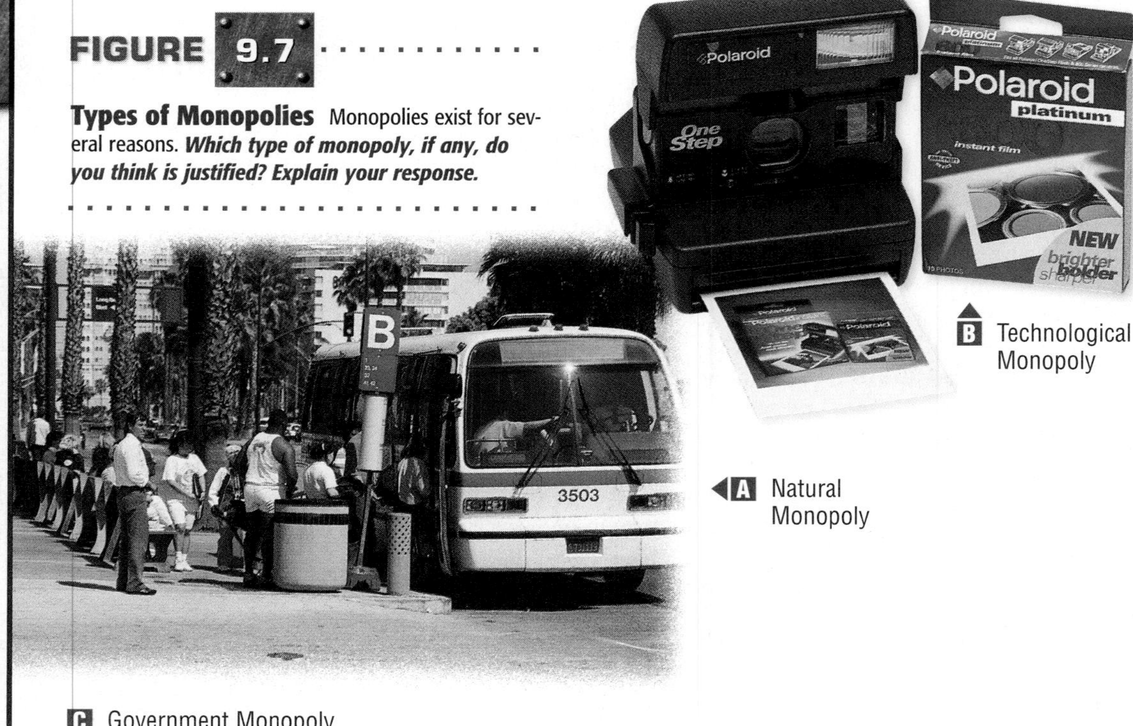


B Technological Monopoly

A Natural Monopoly

C Government Monopoly

D Geographic Monopoly



## Free Enterprise Activity

Ask students to identify several businesses in their community that are monopolistic competitors. Then organize the class into groups, and assign each group one of these businesses. Have groups conduct research and interview company officers to discover the competitive strategies of their assigned companies. Have groups present their findings in the form of brief written reports. Encourage groups to illustrate their reports with appropriate visual materials.

**How Important Are Monopolies Today?** Monopolies are far less important than they once were. As noted earlier, geographic monopolies have little effect because of potential competition from mail-order businesses and electronic commerce on the Internet. Natural monopolies are being broken up by technology and government deregulation.

Technological monopolies rarely last longer than the life of the patent—if even *that* long. Why? Competitors can make and patent slight variations in new products quickly. The microcomputer revolution in the early 1980s followed such a pattern. One company copied another's product, making changes and adding features to obtain a patent of its own.

### Reducing Postal Monopolies

The monopoly that national postal services have enjoyed is now being whittled away by technology. Overnight delivery companies such as Federal Express, Airborne Express, and United Parcel Service (UPS) offer faster delivery but at premium prices. And the widespread use of fax machines and electronic mail (E-mail) has virtually eliminated any remaining monopoly power that national postal services held. ■

## Oligopoly

Unlike a monopoly with just one supplier, an **oligopoly** is an industry dominated by *several* suppliers who exercise some control over price. For a market structure to be labeled an oligopoly, it must meet the following conditions:

**oligopoly:** *industry dominated by a few suppliers who exercise some control over price*

**(1) Domination by a Few Sellers** Several large firms are responsible for 70 to 80 percent of the market.

**(2) Barriers to Entry** Capital costs are high, and it is difficult for new companies to enter major markets.

**(3) Identical or Slightly Different Products** The goods and services provided by oligopolists—such as airline travel, domestic automobiles, and kitchen appliances—are very similar.

**(4) Nonprice Competition** Advertising emphasizes minor differences and attempts to build customer loyalty.

**(5) Interdependence** Any change on the part of one firm will cause a reaction on the part of other firms in the oligopoly.

**Figure 9.8** on page 244 shows a number of industries in which the four largest firms produce more than 80 percent of the total industry output. All of these industries are oligopolies.

Oligopolies are not considered as harmful to consumers as monopolies. Consumers may pay more than if they were buying in a perfectly competitive market. Oligopolistic markets, however, tend to have generally stable prices. They also offer consumers a wider variety of products than would a perfectly competitive industry.





## Independent Practice

**L1 Creating Posters** Have students work in small groups to create posters that illustrate the four types of monopolies. Display finished posters around the classroom. ELL

### Economic Connection to... History

**Early Monopolies** The European shipping companies that operated under royal charters in the 1500s and 1600s were among the earliest monopolies. Rulers gave these companies exclusive rights to trade in Asia and other regions.

**L2 Applying Ideas** Ask students to locate a real example of one of the four types of monopolies. Then have students write a case study comparing their selected example with an "ideal type" of monopoly. Call on volunteers to share their case studies with the class.

### Relevant Issues in Economics

**The HHI** How do economists determine the level of competition in a market? They use a measure called the Herfindahl-Hirschman Index (HHI). The HHI is calculated by totaling data on the market shares of all companies in a market. The higher the HHI score, the less competitive the market. A review of the HHI shows that the least competitive industries in the United States include airlines, automobiles and trucks, tobacco, brewing, snack foods, and soft drinks.

**Visual Instruction FIGURE 9.8**

ASK: How do oligopolists compete? *through nonprice competition, or product differentiation* Offer aspirin as an example of product differentiation. Point out that all aspirin tablets are made from the same ingredients. Often a drug company, through advertising, leads consumers to believe that its aspirin brings greater or faster pain relief than a competitor's brand.

**Global Economy**

**OPEC**

Among the best-known cartels is the Organization of Petroleum Exporting Countries (OPEC). Formed in 1960, OPEC is an association of 11 oil producing and exporting countries—Algeria, Libya, Nigeria, Indonesia, Iran, Iraq, Kuwait, Qatar, Saudi Arabia, the United Arab Emirates, and Venezuela.

**FIGURE 9.8** **Oligopolies** Oligopolies exist in a number of industries throughout the United States. Here several industries are highlighted.

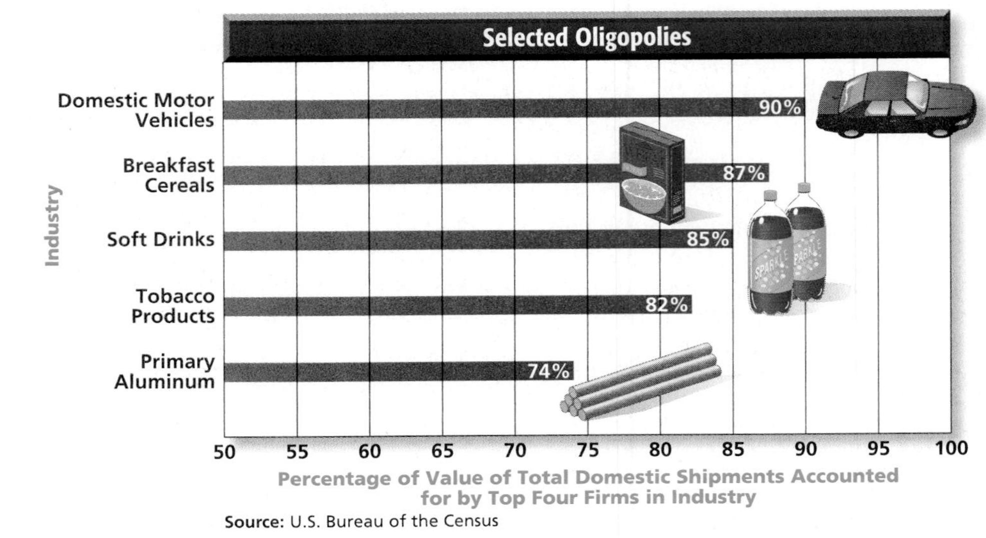


**Source:** U.S. Bureau of the Census

**Product Differentiation** We mentioned earlier that oligopolists engage in *nonprice* competition. What does this mean? Let's use automobiles as an example. Several large auto manufacturers have an oligopoly on the domestic car market. They all make cars, trucks, and sport utility vehicles. However, they spend millions, if not billions, of advertising dollars per year to differentiate their products in your mind–and to win your consumer dollars.

The price you pay for brand names is not just based on supply and demand. Rather, it is based on **product differentiation**–the real or perceived differences in the good or service that make it more valuable in consumers' eyes.

**product differentiation:** *manufacturers' use of minor differences in quality and features to try to differentiate between similar goods and services*

**Interdependent Behavior** With so few firms in an oligopoly, whatever one does, the others are sure to follow. When one airline cuts its airfares to gain market share, for example, the other major airlines lower theirs even more. Although this type of *price war* is initially good for consumers in the form of lower prices, it may force an airline out of business if prices drop too much. Fewer airlines lead to less competition, which raises prices in the long run.



**Extending the Content**

**Cartels** Cartels usually are successful when they sell a product that has inelastic demand—oil, for example. However, the success of a cartel is not guaranteed. It is relatively easy for members to violate any one of the price, production, or distribution conditions agreed to by the cartel. For example, the Organization of Petroleum Exporting Countries (OPEC)—the oil cartel—has found it increasingly difficult to control world oil prices because a number of its members regularly exceed the agreed output levels.

In contrast, if competing firms in an oligopoly secretly agree to raise prices or to divide the market, they are performing an illegal act called *collusion*. Heavy penalties, such as fines and even prison terms, are levied against companies found guilty of collusion in the United States.

**Cartels** An important form of collusion is the cartel. A **cartel** is an arrangement among groups of industrial businesses, often in different countries, to reduce international competition by controlling price, production, and the distribution of goods. Such firms seek monopoly power.

**cartel:** *arrangement among groups of industrial businesses to reduce international competition by controlling the price, production, and distribution of goods*

## Monopolistic Competition

The most common form of market structure in the United States is **monopolistic competition**, in which a large number of sellers offer similar but slightly different products. Obvious examples are brand-name items such as toothpaste, cosmetics, and designer clothes. To be a monopolistic competitor, five conditions must be met:

**monopolistic competition:** *market situation in which a large number of sellers offer similar but slightly different products and in which each has some control over price*

**(1) Numerous Sellers** No single seller or small group dominates the market.

**(2) Relatively Easy Entry** Entry into the market is easier than in a monopoly or oligopoly. One drawback is the high cost of advertising.

**(3) Differentiated Products** Each supplier sells a slightly different product to attract customers.

**(4) Nonprice Competition** Businesses compete by using product differentiation and by advertising.

**(5) Some Control Over Price** By building a loyal customer base through product differentiation, each firm has some control over the price it charges.

Many of the characteristics of monopolistic competition are the same as those of an oligopoly. The major difference is in the number of sellers of a product. As you recall, in an oligopoly a few companies dominate an industry, and control over price is interdependent. Monopolistic competition has many firms, no real interdependence, and some slight difference among products.

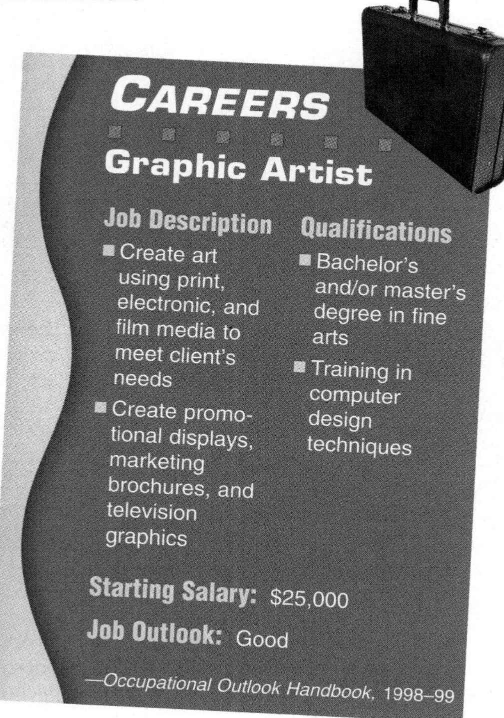

CAREERS
Graphic Artist
Job Description
■ Create art using print, electronic, and film media to meet client's needs
■ Create promotional displays, marketing brochures, and television graphics
Qualifications
■ Bachelor's and/or master's degree in fine arts
■ Training in computer design techniques
Starting Salary: $25,000
Job Outlook: Good
—Occupational Outlook Handbook, 1998–99




## Critical Thinking Activity

**Synthesizing Information** Point out that advertising employs a variety of methods to persuade consumers to buy products. These methods include humor, celebrity endorsements, and appeals to fear. You might provide the following examples: Humor—a child running from room to room while unraveling a toilet roll to advertise a new "extra strength" toilet tissue. Celebrity Endorsement—a baseball star stating that a particular make of car is the "only one" for him. Appeals to Fear—pictures of young children playing while a voice-over says, "Who'll care for them when you're gone?" to sell life insurance. Have students create their own examples of these three kinds of advertising persuasion.



# 3 Assess

## Meeting Lesson Objectives

Assign Section 2 Assessment as homework or an in-class activity.

Use **Interactive Tutor Self-Assessment Software** to review Section 2.

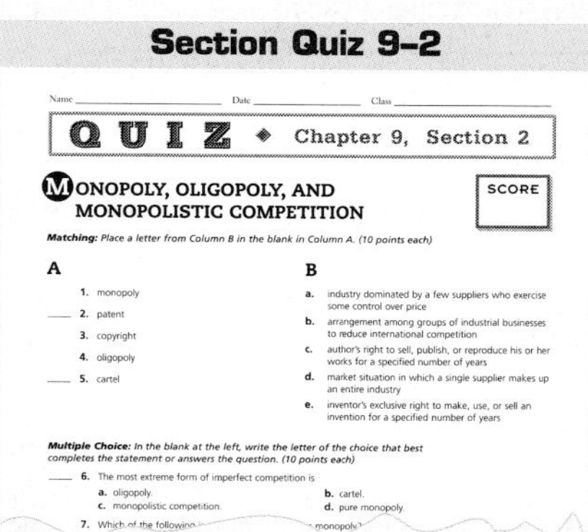
**Section Quiz 9-2**

Name ______ Date ______ Class ______

QUIZ ◆ Chapter 9, Section 2

MONOPOLY, OLIGOPOLY, AND MONOPOLISTIC COMPETITION

SCORE

***Matching:*** *Place a letter from Column B in the blank in Column A. (10 points each)*

| A | B |
|---|---|
| 1. monopoly | a. industry dominated by a few suppliers who exercise some control over price |
| ____ 2. patent | b. arrangement among groups of industrial businesses to reduce international competition |
| 3. copyright | c. author's right to sell, publish, or reproduce his or her works for a specified number of years |
| 4. oligopoly | d. market situation in which a single supplier makes up an entire industry |
| ____ 5. cartel | e. inventor's exclusive right to make, use, or sell an invention for a specified number of years |

***Multiple Choice:*** *In the blank at the left, write the letter of the choice that best completes the statement or answers the question. (10 points each)*

____ 6. The most extreme form of imperfect competition is
a. oligopoly. b. cartel.
c. monopolistic competition. d. pure monopoly.

7. Which of the following ... monopoly?

## Visual Instruction FIGURE 9.9

While students are studying **Figure 9.9**, point out that a cosmetics company may produce several product lines. Each line is aimed at a different market segment. By having several lines, the company competes with other companies in several areas of the cosmetics market.

## Reteach

Have students write five questions about the section. Then ask students to exchange questions and write answers to the questions they received.

### Reading Essentials and Study Guide 9–2

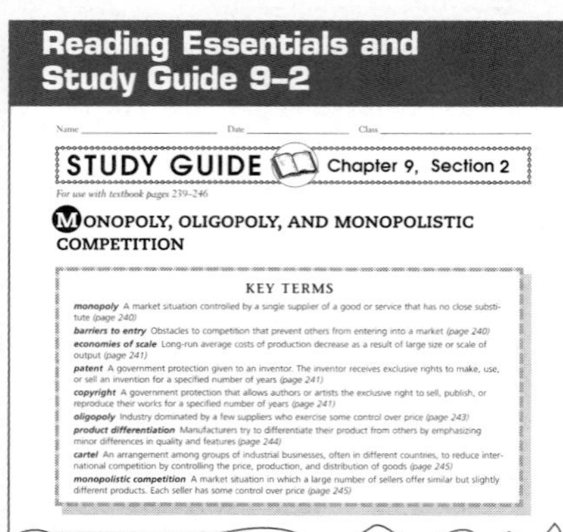

Name ______ Date ______ Class ______

STUDY GUIDE Chapter 9, Section 2

*For use with textbook pages 239–246*

MONOPOLY, OLIGOPOLY, AND MONOPOLISTIC COMPETITION

KEY TERMS

***monopoly*** A market situation controlled by a single supplier of a good or service that has no close substitute *(page 240)*

***barriers to entry*** Obstacles to competition that prevent others from entering into a market *(page 240)*

***economies of scale*** Long-run average costs of production decrease as a result of large size or scale of output *(page 241)*

***patent*** A government protection given to an inventor. The inventor receives exclusive rights to make, use, or sell an invention for a specified number of years *(page 241)*

***copyright*** A government protection that allows authors or artists the exclusive right to sell, publish, or reproduce their works for a specified number of years *(page 241)*

***oligopoly*** Industry dominated by a few suppliers who exercise some control over price *(page 243)*

***product differentiation*** Manufacturers try to differentiate their product from others by emphasizing minor differences in quality and features *(page 244)*

***cartel*** An arrangement among groups of industrial businesses, often in different countries, to reduce international competition by controlling the price, production, and distribution of goods *(page 245)*

***monopolistic competition*** A market situation in which a large number of sellers offer similar but slightly different products. Each seller has some control over price *(page 245)*

## 4 Close

Ask students which of the three market structures discussed in this section they think is the most beneficial for consumers. Have them explain their answers.

**Advertising** Competitive advertising is even more important in monopolistic competition than it is in oligopolies. As shown in **Figure 9.9,** advertising attempts to persuade consumers that the product being advertised is different from, and superior to, any other. When successful, advertising enables companies to charge more for their products. That's why companies like Nike, The Gap, and Procter & Gamble pour millions of dollars into their advertising budgets every year.

**FIGURE 9.9**

**Advertising** Ads lead to product differentiation and competition for consumer dollars. Businesses also compete for shelf space–space on store shelves for displaying their products and attracting buyers.

**Practice** and **assess** key skills with ***Skillbuilder Interactive Workbook, Level 2.***

## SECTION 2 Assessment

### Understanding Key Terms

1. **Define** monopoly, barriers to entry, economies of scale, patent, copyright, oligopoly, product differentiation, cartel, monopolistic competition.

### Reviewing Objectives

2. What are the four characteristics of a pure monopoly?
3. What characteristics of an oligopoly allow it to have a limited control over price?
4. **Graphic Organizer** Use a chart like the one in the next column to compare a monopolistic competitor to an oligopoly in regard to these categories: number of sellers, difficulty of market entry, product differentiation, nonprice competition, and amount of control over price.

| Category | Monopolistic Competition | Oligopoly |
|---|---|---|
| | | |
| | | |
| | | |

### Applying Economic Concepts

5. **Product Differentiation** Give three examples of products you have bought recently based on advertising, not price. How does your consumer behavior justify product differentiation?

### Critical Thinking Activity

6. **Synthesizing Information** Develop a print or video advertisement using yourself as the hardworking product. Use product differentiation to explain why an employee should "purchase" you.



## SECTION 2 Assessment Answers

1. All definitions can be found in the Glossary.
2. single seller, no substitutes, no entry into market, control over price
3. domination by a few sellers, substantial barriers to entry into market, similar products, product differentiation, interdependent behavior
4. See next column.
5. Answers will vary.
6. Advertisements will vary. Encourage students to share their advertisements with the class.

4.

| Category | Monopolistic Competition | Oligopoly |
|---|---|---|
| Number of Sellers | Many | Few |
| Difficulty of Market Entry | Easy | Difficult |
| Product Differentiation | A Fair Amount | A Fair Amount |
| Nonprice Competition | A Fair Amount | A Fair Amount |
| Amount of Control Over Price | Limited | Some |

# BusinessWeek

## Spotlight on the Economy

# Celebrity Can Really Be a Gas

**Check It Out!** **In this chapter, you learned that oligopolists and monopolistic competitors use product differentiation to attract customers. In the following article, read to learn how one celebrity puts nonprice competition to work for him.**

Mario Andretti

Air Jordan shoes. Martha Stewart towels. Now, how's this for the latest in celebrity branding? Mario Andretti unleaded. Yes, the 58-year-old retired racing legend is licensing his name to Texaco gas stations on the West Coast in the hopes of eventually taking the Andretti gas brand nationwide.

The first 37,000-square-foot Andretti mega-station opened in San Francisco in January. It has 10 gas pumps, as well as a Burger King and Starbucks, which lease space from Mario Andretti Petroleum LP. In coming months, Texaco will put the Andretti label on five existing California gas stations, adding "Winning Finish" car washes and "Quick Pit" service bays, branding exclusive to Andretti.

Celebrity evidently sells well. Sales at the San Francisco flagship already total 80% of first-year projected revenues of $5 million, says the partnership. The gas isn't any better than rivals', admits Andretti. But he boasts that the service is. The Indy 500 champ regularly visits his namesake station to make sure. He sometimes even lends a hand to surprised motorists. "I'll pump your gas and clean your windshield, no problem," he says. Now, if he would only drive folks home in the evening rush . . .

–Reprinted from March 8, 1999 issue of *Business Week* by special permission, copyright © 1999 by The McGraw-Hill Companies, Inc.

### *Think About It*

1. **Are goods or services more important at Andretti's mega-station?**
2. **How does Andretti differentiate his products from others?**

Andretti SpeedMart
Burger King Drive-Thru
Starbucks Coffee
Car Wash



### Answers to *Think About It*

1. services; Andretti freely admits that the product he sells–gasoline–is no better than that of his rivals.
2. by using his celebrity as a former racing car champion

BusinessWeek Spotlight

# Teach

Point out that celebrity endorsement is a popular advertising tool for many companies. They willingly pay millions of dollars to celebrities for the right to use their faces or names to sell products. Have students identify several celebrities and the products they endorse. Then ask students if, and why, they might be influenced to buy because of a celebrity endorsement.

### BusinessWeek ONLINE

To find up-to-date news and analysis on the economy, business, technology, markets, entrepreneurs, investments, and finance, have students search feature articles and special reports on the *Business Week* Web site. www.businessweek.com

### Sidelight

Mario Andretti and his son Michael—also a race car driver—are involved in several other auto-related businesses. These include Andretti Enterprises, which provides materials and services to more than 450 car wash operators in the eastern United States, and the Race Rock Cafes, restaurants in Orlando and Las Vegas that have a "racing car" theme.

# 1 Focus

## Overview

Section 3 explains the agencies and laws the federal government established to protect competition in the American economy.

### BELLRINGER
**Motivational Activity**

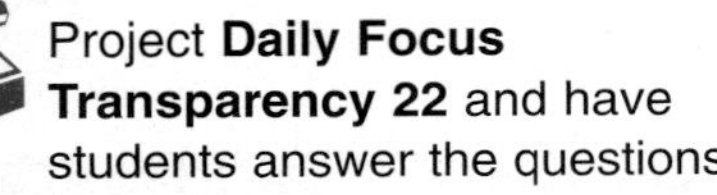

Project **Daily Focus Transparency 22** and have students answer the questions.

This activity is also available as a blackline master.

**Daily Focus Transparency 22**

### Reader's Guide

Answers to the **Reading Objectives** questions are on page 253.

**Preteaching Vocabulary**

Have students find the definitions of the **Terms to Know** in the Glossary. Then ask students to write a brief paragraph explaining how horizontal, vertical, and conglomerate mergers differ.

Vocabulary PuzzleMaker

SECTION 3

# Government Policies Toward Competition

### Reader's Guide

**Terms to Know**

- interlocking directorate
- antitrust legislation
- merger
- conglomerate
- deregulation

**Reading Objectives**

1. What is the difference between interlocking directorates and mergers?
2. What is the purpose of federal regulatory agencies?
3. How has some regulation hurt consumers?

## Cover Story

*Bergen Record*, April 23, 1999

The Federal Trade Commission (FTC) reviews mergers to ensure that they do not substantially lessen competition. The agency certainly was busy in 1998. In that year, the number of announced mergers involving American companies exceeded 7,750. A survey conducted in 1999 suggests that the FTC's workload will not dwindle in the near future. Of the companies polled in the survey, more than one third said that they intended to acquire other companies within the year.

Historically, one of the goals of government in the United States has been to encourage competition in the economy. In this section, you'll learn about the federal laws and regulatory agencies–including the Federal Trade Commission mentioned above–that attempt to force monopolies to act more competitively.

## Antitrust Legislation

The industrial expansion after the Civil War fueled the rise of big businesses. John D. Rockefeller's Standard Oil Company was the most notorious for driving competitors out of business and pressuring customers not to deal with rival oil companies. He also placed members of Standard Oil's board of directors onto

## SECTION 3 RESOURCE MANAGER

**Reproducible Masters**

- Reproducible Lesson Plan 9–3
- Reading Essentials and Study Guide 9–3
- Guided Reading Activity 9–3
- Section Quiz 9–3
- Daily Focus Activity 22
- Daily Lecture Notes 9–3

**Multimedia**

- Daily Focus Transparency 22
- Vocabulary PuzzleMaker
- Interactive Tutor Self-Assessment Software
- ExamView® Pro Testmaker
- MindJogger Videoquiz
- NBR's *Economics & You*
- Presentation Plus!

the board of a competing corporation. Because the same group of people, in effect, controlled both companies, it was less tempting for them to compete with one another. This practice of creating **interlocking directorates** was perfected by Rockefeller.

**interlocking directorate:** *a board of directors, the majority of whose members also serve as the board of directors of a competing corporation*

**Sherman Antitrust Act** Public pressure against Rockefeller's monopoly, or trust, over the oil business led Congress to pass the Sherman Antitrust Act in 1890. The law sought to protect trade and commerce against unlawful restraint and monopoly. The Sherman Act was important **antitrust legislation,** or laws to prevent new monopolies or trusts from forming and to break up those that already exist.

**antitrust legislation:** *federal and state laws passed to prevent new monopolies from forming and to break up those that already exist*

**Clayton Act** Because the language in the Sherman Act was so vague, a new law was passed in 1914 to sharpen its antitrust provisions. The Clayton Act prohibited or limited a number of very specific business practices that lessened competition substantially. The Clayton Act, however, does not state what the term *substantially* means. As a result, it is up to the federal government to make a subjective decision as to whether the merging of two corporations would substantially lessen competition. **Figure 9.10** on page 250 details the Clayton Act and other antitrust legislation.

## Mergers

Most antitrust legislation deals with restricting the harmful effects of mergers. A **merger** occurs when one corporation joins

**merger:** *a combined company that results when one corporation buys more than half the stock of another corporation and, thus, controls the second corporation*

### Economic Connection to...

### Muckrakers

The rise of monopolies in the late 1800s contributed to the development of a new kind of journalism—muckraking. The muckrakers wrote stories exposing corruption in business and politics. One of the most famous muckrakers was Ida Tarbell. She wrote a series of articles that attacked John D. Rockefeller's monopoly, the Standard Oil Company.

In great detail, Tarbell showed how Rockefeller used unfair practices to drive his competitors out of business. She even likened Rockefeller to a crooked gambler: "Mr. Rockefeller has systematically played with loaded dice. . . . Business played in this way . . . is fit only for tricksters." Tarbell's words led to a government investigation of Standard Oil's business practices. ■





# 2 Teach

## Guided Practice

**L1 Identifying Ideas** Ask students to identify the various antitrust laws discussed in this section. Note their responses on the board. Then, for each listed response, call on volunteers to explain the purpose of the law.

**Daily Lecture Notes 9-3**

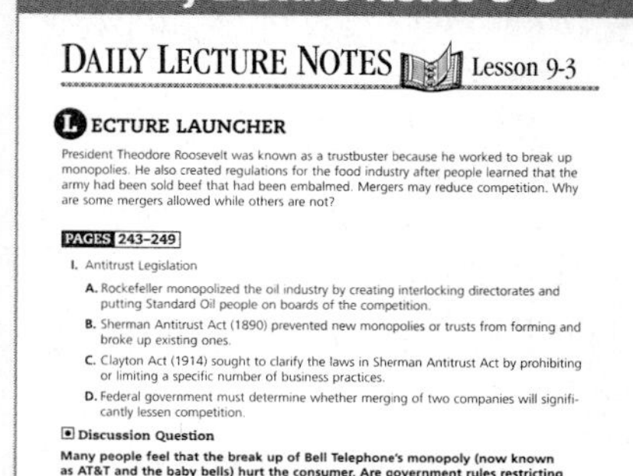
DAILY LECTURE NOTES Lesson 9-3

**LECTURE LAUNCHER**

President Theodore Roosevelt was known as a trustbuster because he worked to break up monopolies. He also created regulations for the food industry after people learned that the army had been sold beef that had been embalmed. Mergers may reduce competition. Why are some mergers allowed while others are not?

PAGES 243–249

I. Antitrust Legislation

A. Rockefeller monopolized the oil industry by creating interlocking directorates and putting Standard Oil people on boards of the competition.

B. Sherman Antitrust Act (1890) prevented new monopolies or trusts from forming and broke up existing ones.

C. Clayton Act (1914) sought to clarify the laws in Sherman Antitrust Act by prohibiting or limiting a specific number of business practices.

D. Federal government must determine whether merging of two companies will significantly lessen competition.

**Discussion Question**

**Many people feel that the break up of Bell Telephone's monopoly (now known as AT&T and the baby bells) hurt the consumer. Are government rules restricting monopolies always good? If not, [illegible] you think the [illegible] should be changed so [illegible]**

### Economic Connection to... History

**The Trustbuster** During the presidency of Theodore Roosevelt, the Department of Justice started more antitrust suits against corporations than it had in all of the three previous administrations. Because of this vigorous enforcement of the Sherman Antitrust Act, Roosevelt earned the nickname "The Trustbuster."

### Meeting Special Needs

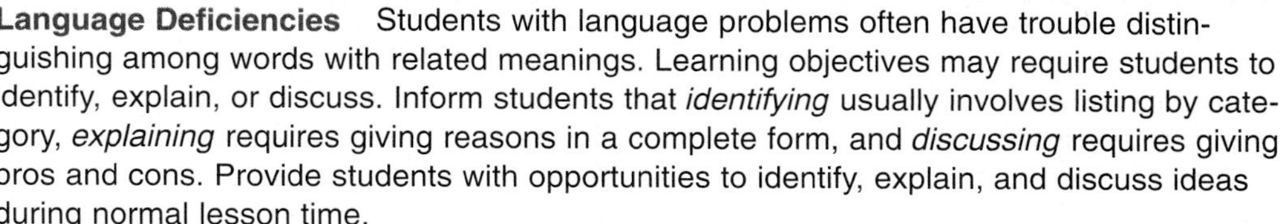

**Language Deficiencies** Students with language problems often have trouble distinguishing among words with related meanings. Learning objectives may require students to identify, explain, or discuss. Inform students that *identifying* usually involves listing by category, *explaining* requires giving reasons in a complete form, and *discussing* requires giving pros and cons. Provide students with opportunities to identify, explain, and discuss ideas during normal lesson time.

Refer to *Inclusion for the Social Studies Classroom Strategies and Activities* for students with different learning styles.

## Guided Reading Activity 9-3

Name ______ Date ______ Class ______

GUIDED READING Activity 9-3

*For use with textbook pages 248–253*

GOVERNMENT POLICIES TOWARD COMPETITION

RECALLING THE FACTS

***Directions:*** *Use the information in your textbook to answer the questions.*

1. What are interlocking directorates?
2. Why is the Sherman Antitrust Act important?
3. What is antitrust legislation?
4. What is the purpose of the Clayton Act?
5. What subjective decision must the federal government make related to the Clayton Act?

**ECONOMICS & YOU**

**Competition and Monopolies**

Chapter 8
Disc 1, Side 1

**ASK:** Why do companies in the same industry sometimes merge? *to cut costs and become more profitable*

 Also available in VHS.

## Visual Instruction FIGURE 9.10

Have students study **Figure 9.10.** ASK: Why was the Clayton Antitrust Act passed? *Because the language in the Sherman Act was so vague, the Clayton Act was passed to sharpen its antitrust provisions.*

## FIGURE 9.10 Antitrust Legislation

| Federal Law | Function |
|---|---|
| **Sherman Antitrust Act (1890)** | Outlawed agreements and conspiracies that restrain interstate trade. Made it illegal to monopolize or even attempt to monopolize any part of interstate commerce. |
| **Clayton Act (1914)** | Restricted *price discrimination*—the practice of selling the same good to different buyers at different prices. Prohibited sellers from requiring that a buyer not deal with a competitor. Outlawed interlocking directorates between competitors. Outlawed mergers that lessen competition substantially. |
| **Federal Trade Commission Act (1914)** | Established the Federal Trade Commission (FTC) as an independent antitrust agency. Gave the FTC power to bring court cases against private businesses engaging in unfair trade practices. |
| **Robinson-Patman Act (1936)** | Strengthened the law against charging different prices for the same product to different buyers. An amendment to the Clayton Act of 1914. |
| **Celler-Kefauver Antimerger Act (1950)** | Strengthened the law against firms joining together to control too large a part of the market. An amendment to the Clayton Act of 1914. |
| **Hart-Scott-Rodino Antitrust Improvements Act (1976)** | Restricted mergers that would lessen competition. Required big corporations planning to merge to notify the Federal Trade Commission (FTC) and the Department of Justice, who would then decide whether to challenge the merger under the terms of the Clayton Act of 1914. |

with another corporation. As shown in **Figure 9.11,** three kinds of mergers exist: horizontal, vertical, and conglomerate.

When the two corporations that merge are in the same business, a *horizontal merger* has occurred. An example of a horizontal merger occurs when Video Store A buys Video Store B. When corporations involved in a "chain" of supply merge, this is called a *vertical merger.* An example would be a paper company buying the lumber mill that supplies it with pulp or buying the office supply business that sells its paper.

Another type of merger is the conglomerate merger. A **conglomerate** is a huge corporation involved in at least four or more unrelated businesses. Procter & Gamble is an example of a multinational conglomerate. With operations in 70 countries,

conglomerate: *large corporation made up of smaller corporations dealing in unrelated businesses*



## Cooperative Learning

Organize the class into an even number of groups. Assign half the groups the topic of the aviation industry; assign the other groups the topic of the telecommunications industry. Have groups investigate the impact of deregulation on their assigned industry. Direct groups to use their findings to develop a brief, illustrated report. Ensure that various tasks are shared among group members so that all members are fully involved in the project. Ask group representatives to present their finished reports to the class.

 BLOCK SCHEDULING

it produces or has acquired such businesses as Cover Girl cosmetics, Pert Plus shampoo, Clearasil skin care, Folgers coffee, Pringles potato chips, Jif peanut butter, Crest toothpaste, NyQuil cough medicine, Dawn dish soap, Cheer and Tide laundry detergent, Pampers diapers, and Charmin toilet paper.

## Regulatory Agencies

Besides using antitrust laws to foster a competitive atmosphere, the government uses direct regulation of business pricing and product quality. **Figure 9.12** on page 252 lists several regulatory agencies that oversee various industries and services. These agencies exist at the federal, state, and even local levels.

**FIGURE 9.11** **Mergers** Horizontal mergers involve businesses that make the same product or provide the same service. Vertical mergers take place when firms taking part in different steps of manufacturing come together. A conglomerate is a firm that has at least four businesses, each making unrelated products.

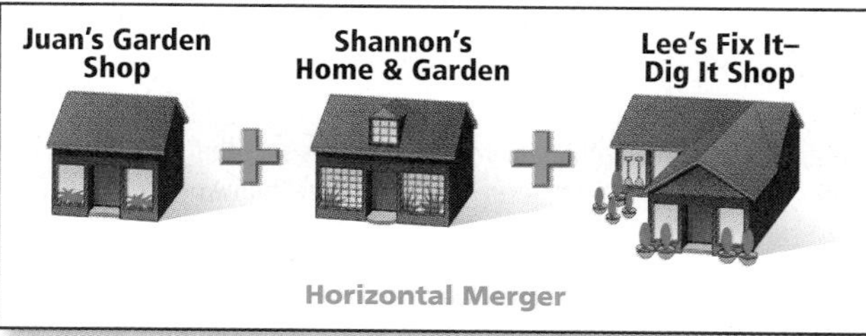


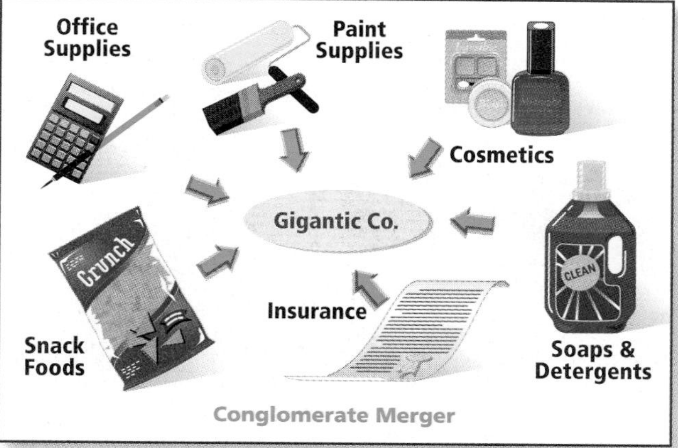


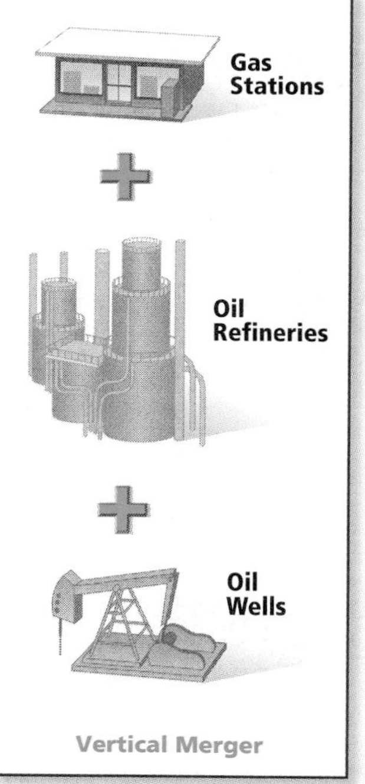


## Free Enterprise Activity

Direct students' attention to the discussion about conglomerate Procter & Gamble on page 251. Then have students work in small groups to conduct research to find a conglomerate that has operations in their state. Direct groups to find advertisements, labels, and other visual materials of the various products produced by the conglomerate's businesses. Have groups use these materials to create a collage titled "Portrait of a Conglomerate." Encourage groups to display their collages around the room. ELL

BLOCK SCHEDULING



## Independent Practice

**L2 Writing Newspaper Articles** Ask students to choose two corporations in the community and imagine they have merged. Have students write a newspaper article about this merger and its impact on the local economy. Encourage students to present their articles in newspaper format—in columns accompanied by appropriate visuals. Call on volunteers to share their articles with the class. BLOCK SCHEDULING

### Did You Know

Some mergers create rather interesting names. In 1908, two Cincinnati banks, the Third National Bank and the Fifth National Bank, merged to become the Fifth Third Bank. In 1975, the bank changed its name again—to Fifth Third Bancorp.

**L3 Writing Editorials** Ask students to write newspaper editorials that support or oppose the following statement: Government antitrust laws and agencies protect competition and benefit consumers. Call on volunteers to share their articles with the class.

# 3 Assess

## Meeting Lesson Objectives

Assign Section 3 Assessment as homework or an in-class activity.

Use **Interactive Tutor Self-Assessment Software** to review Section 3.

### Section Quiz 9-3

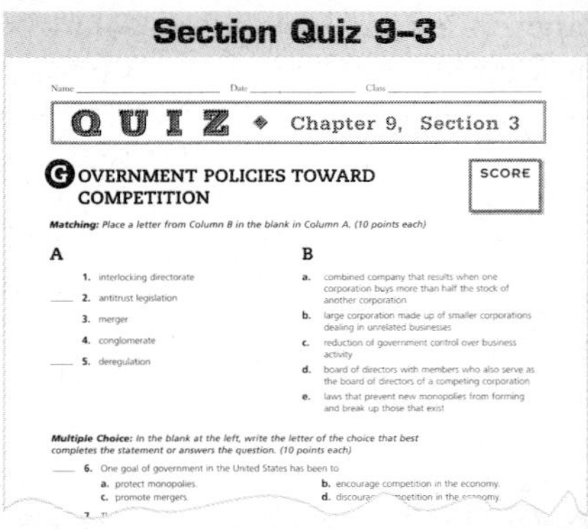

Name ______ Date ______ Class ______

**QUIZ** ◆ Chapter 9, Section 3

**GOVERNMENT POLICIES TOWARD COMPETITION**

SCORE

***Matching:*** *Place a letter from Column B in the blank in Column A. (10 points each)*

| A | B |
|---|---|
| ___ 1. interlocking directorate | a. combined company that results when one corporation buys more than half the stock of another corporation |
| ___ 2. antitrust legislation | b. large corporation made up of smaller corporations dealing in unrelated businesses |
| ___ 3. merger | c. reduction of government control over business activity |
| ___ 4. conglomerate | d. board of directors with members who also serve as the board of directors of a competing corporation |
| ___ 5. deregulation | e. laws that prevent new monopolies from forming and break up those that exist |

***Multiple Choice:*** *In the blank at the left, write the letter of the choice that best completes the statement or answers the question. (10 points each)*

___ 6. One goal of government in the United States has been to

a. protect monopolies.
b. encourage competition in the economy.
c. promote mergers.
d. discoura[illegible]petition in the economy.

### Visual Instruction FIGURE 9.12

Have students review the information in **Figure 9.12**. ASK: Which agency might conduct tests on the safety of a new drug? *Food and Drug Administration* Which agency might you contact if you have questions about the regulation of cable television? *Federal Communications Commission* Which agency might investigate charges of insider trading of stock? *Securities and Exchange Commission*

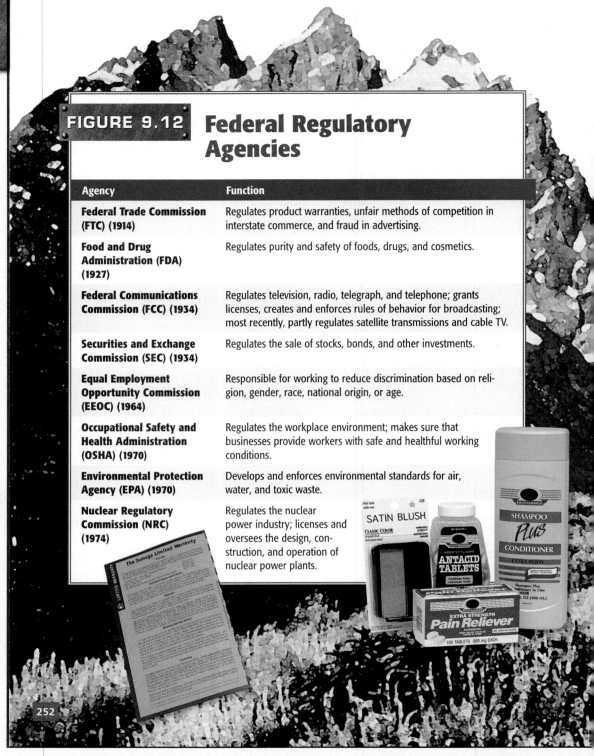

## FIGURE 9.12 Federal Regulatory Agencies

| Agency | Function |
|---|---|
| **Federal Trade Commission (FTC) (1914)** | Regulates product warranties, unfair methods of competition in interstate commerce, and fraud in advertising. |
| **Food and Drug Administration (FDA) (1927)** | Regulates purity and safety of foods, drugs, and cosmetics. |
| **Federal Communications Commission (FCC) (1934)** | Regulates television, radio, telegraph, and telephone; grants licenses, creates and enforces rules of behavior for broadcasting; most recently, partly regulates satellite transmissions and cable TV. |
| **Securities and Exchange Commission (SEC) (1934)** | Regulates the sale of stocks, bonds, and other investments. |
| **Equal Employment Opportunity Commission (EEOC) (1964)** | Responsible for working to reduce discrimination based on religion, gender, race, national origin, or age. |
| **Occupational Safety and Health Administration (OSHA) (1970)** | Regulates the workplace environment; makes sure that businesses provide with safe and healthful working conditions. |
| **Environmental Protection Agency (EPA) (1970)** | Develops and enforces environmental standards for air, water, and toxic waste. |
| **Nuclear Regulatory Commission (NRC) (1974)** | Regulates the nuclear power industry; licenses and oversees the design, construction, and operation of nuclear power plants. |

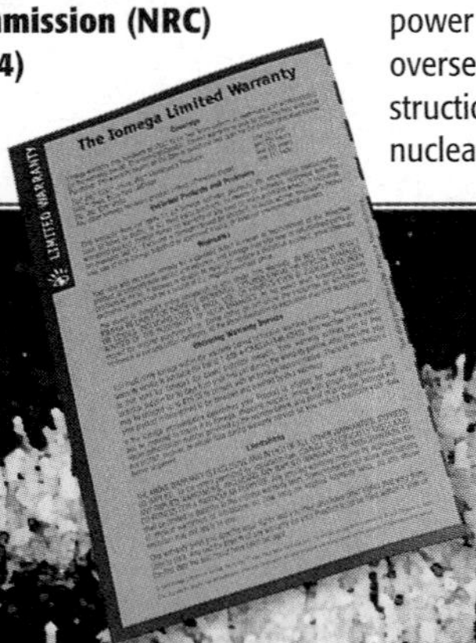

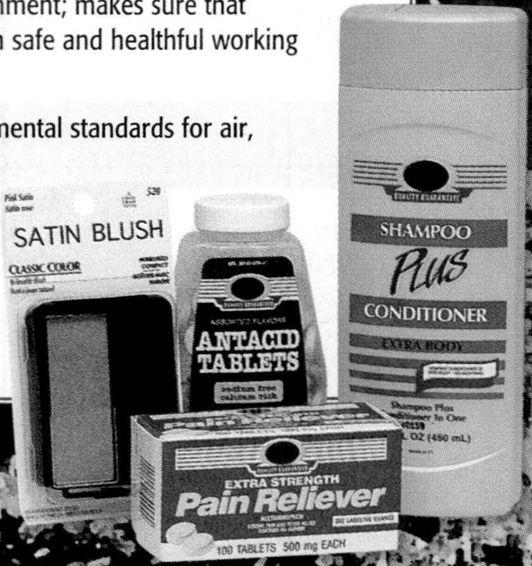

## Extending the Content

**Nutrition Information** Government regulatory agencies can use the weapon of public disclosure—the requirement that businesses reveal information to the public. For example, the Food and Drug Administration (FDA) requires food producers to provide basic information on nutritional content of most food products. Nutrition information labels follow a standard format, listing amounts per serving of calories, protein, carbohydrates, fiber, fat, cholesterol, and other nutrients and vitamins. Since the FDA sets serving sizes, consumers are able to see which products offer the best nutritional value for the price.

**Deregulation** Although the aim of government regulations is to promote efficiency and competition, recent evidence indicates that something quite different has occurred. In the 1980s and 1990s, many industries were **deregulated**—the government reduced regulations and control over business activity. It was found that in trying to protect consumers from unfair practices, government regulations had actually *decreased* the amount of competition in the economy.

As an example, the Federal Communications Commission (FCC) had for years regulated the basic channels in the television market. With deregulation came the entry of competitive pay-TV, cable, and satellite systems.

Many economists speculate about what would happen if the government removed its watchdog responsibility toward mergers in general. Economists assume prices would rise. If, however, the price increases caused profits to be excessive, other sellers would find ways to enter the market. Consumers would benefit eventually from a competitive supply of goods and services.

**Student Web Activity** Visit the *Economics Today and Tomorrow* Web site at ett.glencoe.com and click on ***Chapter 9—Student Web Activities*** to learn more about conglomerates.

**deregulation:** *reduction of government regulation and control over business activity*

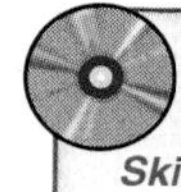

**Practice** and **assess** key skills with *Skillbuilder Interactive Workbook, Level 2.*

## SECTION 3 Assessment

### Understanding Key Terms

1. **Define** interlocking directorate, antitrust legislation, merger, conglomerate, deregulation.

### Reviewing Objectives

2. What is the difference between interlocking directorates and mergers?
3. **Graphic Organizer** Use a chart like the one below to describe the purpose of five federal regulatory agencies.

| Agency | Purpose |
|---|---|
| | |
| | |
| | |

4. How has some regulation hurt consumers?

### Applying Economic Concepts

5. **Regulation** If the shampoo you just bought caused your hair to fall out, which regulatory agency should you contact to complain? Why? What agency should you contact if the new washing machine your parents just bought breaks down, and the manufacturer refuses to honor the warranty?

### Critical Thinking Activity

6. **Categorizing Information** Type *conglomerate* into a search engine. Research one of the conglomerates that you find, and list all the businesses or products owned by that conglomerate.





**ECONOMICS Online**

See the **Web Activity Lesson Plan** at ett.glencoe.com for an introduction, lesson description, and answers to the **Student Web Activity** for this chapter.

### Reteach

Have students reread selected paragraphs. Then have them close their textbooks and write from memory five facts about government policies toward competition.

**Reading Essentials and Study Guide 9-3**

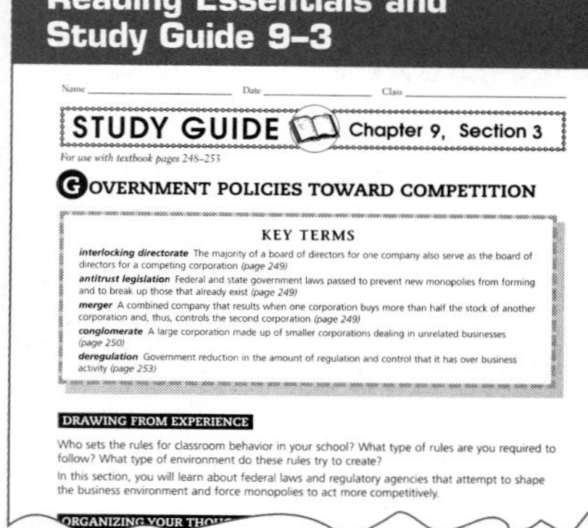

Name ______ Date ______ Class ______

STUDY GUIDE Chapter 9, Section 3

*For use with textbook pages 248–253*

GOVERNMENT POLICIES TOWARD COMPETITION

KEY TERMS

***interlocking directorate*** The majority of a board of directors for one company also serve as the board of directors for a competing corporation *(page 249)*

***antitrust legislation*** Federal and state government laws passed to prevent new monopolies from forming and to break up those that already exist *(page 249)*

***merger*** A combined company that results when one corporation buys more than half the stock of another corporation and, thus, controls the second corporation *(page 249)*

***conglomerate*** A large corporation made up of smaller corporations dealing in unrelated businesses *(page 250)*

***deregulation*** Government reduction in the amount of regulation and control that it has over business activity *(page 253)*

DRAWING FROM EXPERIENCE

Who sets the rules for classroom behavior in your school? What type of rules are you required to follow? What type of environment do these rules try to create?

In this section, you will learn about federal laws and regulatory agencies that attempt to shape the business environment and force monopolies to act more competitively.

## 4 Close

Have students discuss the following questions: What was the initial goal of government antitrust legislation? In your opinion, how successful has it been?

## SECTION 3 Assessment Answers

1. All definitions can be found in the Glossary.
2. With an interlocking directorate, some members of the boards of directors of different corporations are the same. With a merger, two corporations join together.
3. See Figure 9.12 for possible entries for the chart.
4. Some government regulations have decreased the amount of competition in the economy.
5. the Food and Drug Administration, because it regulates the purity and safety of cosmetics, such as shampoo; the Federal Trade Commission, because it regulates product warranties
6. Lists will vary.

## Background

In 1975 William Gates—a 20-year-old Harvard dropout—founded Microsoft with business partner Paul Allen. The company's big break came in 1980, when IBM asked Gates and Allen to provide the operating system for its new personal computer. (The operating system is the software program that manages the inner workings of a computer.) Today Microsoft is the worldwide leader in software for personal computers. In 2000, Bill Gates stepped down as CEO of Microsoft, assuming the position of Chief Software Architect.

# Teach

Have students read Gates's thoughts on how computers have transformed—and will transform—business. Next, ask students to write questions they might like to ask Gates about his vision of business in the future. Call on volunteers to share their questions with the class. ASK: Based on the information in this feature, how do you think Bill Gates might answer these questions?

Assign the **Checking for Understanding** questions. After students have completed this assignment, have them search for more information on Microsoft—location of head offices, company organization, recent sales and income figures, and so on. Encourage students to present their findings in a brief written report.

People & Perspectives

## William Gates

*ENTREPRENEUR (1955–)*

- Cofounder and chief executive officer of Microsoft
- Recipient of the 1993 Price Waterhouse Leadership Award for Lifetime Achievement
- "The richest man in America" according to *Forbes Magazine*'s annual survey

In the book *The Road Ahead* (1996), Bill Gates explains his vision of an interconnected world built around the Internet:

*"Over the next decade, businesses worldwide will be transformed. Intranets will revolutionize the way companies share information internally, and the Internet will revolutionize how they communicate externally. Corporations will redesign their nervous systems to rely on the networks that reach every member of the organization and beyond into the world of suppliers, consultants, and customers. These changes will let companies be more effective and often smaller. In the longer run, as broadband networks make physical proximity to urban services less essential, many businesses will decentralize and disperse their activities, and cities may be downsized too.*

*Even the smallest of all businesses, the individual earning a living in a profession or as an artist, has been empowered by the PC. One person without any staff can produce reports, handle correspondence, bill customers, and maintain a credible business presence—all surprisingly easily. In field after field, the tools of the trade have been transformed by PCs and software.*

*All of these electronic innovations—e-mail, shared screens, videoconferencing, and video phone calls—are ways of overcoming physical separation. As they become commonplace, they'll change not just the way we work together but also the distinction we make between the workplace and everywhere else."*

### Checking for Understanding

1. **In Gates's opinion, what will be the long-term impact of intranets and the Internet?**
2. **How does Gates characterize electronic innovations?**



### Answers to *Checking for Understanding*

1. Intranets and the Internet will revolutionize the way businesses communicate internally and externally over the next decade.
2. They are ways of overcoming physical separation among individuals and businesses.

# CHAPTER 9 Summary

**Chapter Overview** Visit the *Economics Today and Tomorrow* Web site at ett.glencoe.com and click on ***Chapter 9—Chapter Overviews*** to review chapter information.

## SECTION 1 Perfect Competition

- There are four basic **market structures** in the United States: **monopoly, oligopoly, monopolistic competition,** and **perfect competition.**
- Perfect competition is characterized by numerous buyers and sellers, an identical product, easy entry into the market, easy access to information about prices, and no control over price.
- The market for agricultural products is often used as an example of perfect competition because individual farmers have almost no control over the market price of their goods.
- When perfect competition exists, society benefits from its efficient allocation of productive resources.

## SECTION 2 Monopoly, Oligopoly, Monopolistic Competition

- In a monopoly, a single seller controls the supply of the good or service and thus determines the price.
- A monopoly is protected by **barriers to entry,** which could be government regulations, a large initial investment, or ownership of raw materials.
- Four types of monopolies exist: natural monopoly, geographic monopoly, technological monopoly, and government monopoly.
- Natural monopolies are often advantageous in that they give the company an **economy of scale**—which means because of its size, the company can produce the largest amount for the lowest cost.
- An oligopoly is an industry dominated by several suppliers who exercise some control over price.
- Oligopolies and monopolistic competitors use **product differentiation** to make their products more valuable in consumers' eyes.
- Advertising brand names is vital in the market structure known as monopolistic competition, in which a large number of sellers offer similar but slightly different products.

## SECTION 3 Government Policies Toward Competition

- The government has passed **antitrust legislation** to prevent monopolies from forming or to break up those that already exist.
- Two famous pieces of antitrust legislation are the Sherman Antitrust Act and the Clayton Act.
- Three kinds of mergers exist: horizontal, vertical, and conglomerate.
- Federal regulatory agencies oversee various types of industries to ensure fair pricing and product quality.
- **Deregulating** some industries in the 1980s and 1990s resulted in more competition among businesses.



## Economics Journal

**Product Differentiation** Direct students to monitor family purchases of such items as soft drinks, breakfast cereals, toothpaste, and soap over a set period of time. Have them list these items, the brands of these items, and the reasons why the particular brands were chosen—price, quality, brand loyalty, and so on. At the end of the time period, have students present their findings in chart form. Ask students to accompany their charts with a brief analysis of their findings, noting how many of the decisions on brands were influenced by advertisements seen by family members.

# CHAPTER 9 Summary

**ECONOMICS & YOU**

**Competition and Monopolies**

Chapter 8
Disc 1, Side 1

If you do not have access to a videodisc player, the ***Economics & You*** programs are also available in VHS.

Use the **Chapter 9 Summary** to preview, review, condense, or reteach the chapter.

## Preview/Review

**Vocabulary PuzzleMaker Software** reinforces the key terms used in Chapter 9.

**Interactive Tutor Self-Assessment Software** allows students to review Chapter 9 content.

## Condense

Have students listen to the Chapter 9 **Audio Program** (also available in Spanish) in the TCR. Assign the Chapter 9 Audio Program Activity and give students the Chapter 9 Audio Program Test.

## Reteach

Have students complete **Reteaching Activity 9** in the TCR (Spanish Reteaching Activities are also available).

# CHAPTER 9
## Assessment and Activities

ECONOMICS Online

Have students visit the *Economics Today and Tomorrow* Web site at ett.glencoe.com to review Chapter 9 and take the Self-Check Quiz.

**GLENCOE TECHNOLOGY**

**MindJogger Videoquiz**

Use MindJogger to review Chapter 9 content.

### Identifying Key Terms

1. d
2. e
3. a
4. j
5. g
6. b
7. c
8. f
9. i
10. h

### Recalling Facts and Ideas

1. no control
2. The products are nearly identical.
3. agriculture
4. monopoly, oligopoly, monopolistic competition
5. Geographic monopoly: where an individual seller has control over the market because of geographic location. Technological monopoly: where a seller has developed a new manufacturing process or has invented something entirely new and receives a government patent for the development or invention.
6. limited control
7. numerous sellers
8. Horizontal merger: where one company acquires another company in the same business. Vertical merger: where one company acquires another company from which it buys or to which it sells.
9. through antitrust legislation and regulatory agencies

### Thinking Critically

1. Answers may vary, but might include the following: When there are no government controls at work, the agricultural market is almost perfectly competitive. In an agricultural market, there are thousands of farmers (sellers) and thousands of wholesalers (buyers). With so many farmers, no one farmer has influence on price. And it is unlikely that farmers—or farmers and

CHAPTER 

# Assessment and Activities

ECONOMICS Online

**Self-Check Quiz** Visit the *Economics Today and Tomorrow* Web site at ett.glencoe.com and click on ***Chapter 9—Self-Check Quizzes*** to prepare for the Chapter Test.

## Identifying Key Terms

*Write the letter of the definition in Column B that correctly defines each term in Column A.*

**Column A**

1. barriers to entry
2. deregulation
3. conglomerate
4. interlocking directorate
5. geographic monopoly
6. merger
7. monopolistic competition
8. oligopoly
9. government monopoly
10. antitrust legislation

**Column B**

a. large corporation made up of unrelated businesses
b. the joining of two corporations
c. characterized by many firms but differentiated products
d. obstacles that prevent new companies from being formed
e. removing government restrictions from industries
f. characterized by a few firms with differentiated products
g. a store located in an isolated area
h. passed to prevent monopolies
i. building and maintaining local roads and bridges
j. situation in which some of the board of directors for competing companies are the same people

## Recalling Facts and Ideas

**Section 1**

1. In a perfectly competitive market structure, how much control does a single seller have over market price?
2. What is the relationship between the types of products that sellers sell in a perfectly competitive market?
3. What is one example of an almost perfectly competitive market?

**Section 2**

4. What are the three types of market structures with imperfect competition?
5. What is the difference between a geographic monopoly and a technological monopoly?
6. How much control does an oligopoly have over price?
7. In monopolistic competition, how many sellers are there?

**Section 3**

8. What is the difference between a horizontal merger and a vertical merger?
9. What two methods does the federal government use to keep businesses competitive?

## Thinking Critically

1. **Finding the Main Idea** Explain in a paragraph how supply and demand work in the agricultural market when government controls are not operating.
2. **Making Generalizations** Re-create the spider map below, then write two ways that the free enterprise system works to break the three powers of monopolies noted.

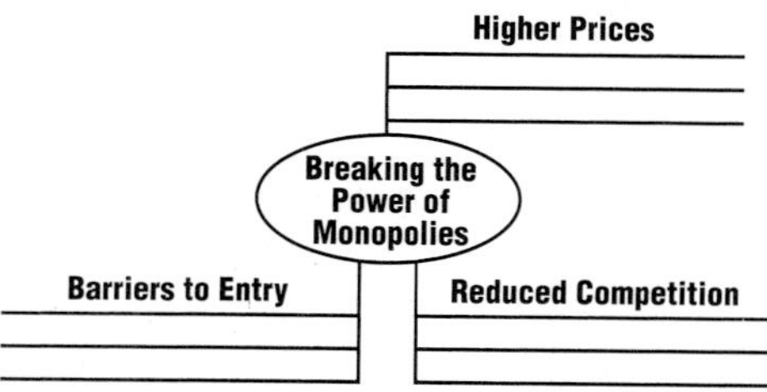


3. **Making Comparisons** What are the fundamental differences between the goals of antitrust legislation and the goals of federal government regulatory agencies?

## Applying Economic Concepts

**Competition and Market Structure** Make a list of the four types of monopolies that exist. Under each type, list three real examples—whether at the federal, state, or local levels.

## Cooperative Learning Project

Organize into groups of three—with one group member representing monopolies; another, oligopolies; and the third, monopolistic competition. Each member of each group should clip business advertisements and articles that characterize his or her market structure. As a group, compare the ads (and businesses) that each person collected. Defend your reasoning behind placing a particular company in its particular grouping.

## Reviewing Skills

**Drawing Inferences and Conclusions** Using **Figure 9.12** on page 252, infer which federal regulatory agency would be responsible for the following "ingredients" of making pizza.

1. Checks the freshness of milk that makes mozzarella cheese.
2. Determines that shipping rates are fair for the pepperoni arriving from out-of-state.
3. Makes sure the pizza advertisement on TV is truthful.
4. Enforces safe working conditions for employees in the pizza parlor.
5. Makes sure that the pizza parlor disposes of waste in a safe manner.

## Technology Activity

**Using the Internet** Choose one of the regulatory agencies mentioned in this chapter and use your Internet search engine to go directly to that agency's home page. Use the information you obtain to write a report summarizing the main functions of that agency.

## Analyzing the Global Economy

Procter & Gamble was mentioned in this chapter as an example of a multinational conglomerate. Use the Internet to find out (a) in how many countries P&G has manufacturing operations; (b) how many countries buy P&G products; (c) how many people are employed by P&G; and (d) what its annual worldwide sales are. Also note the names of products used in Africa, Asia, Europe, and Latin America. Write a report about your findings, and share your report with the rest of the class.



# CHAPTER 9
## Assessment and Activities

### Applying Economic Concepts

Examples will vary. Have students compare their lists to note any similarities.

### Cooperative Learning Project

Encourage groups to post their ads and articles on the bulletin board.

### Reviewing Skills

1. Food and Drug Administration
2. Federal Trade Commission
3. Federal Communications Commission
4. Occupational Safety and Health Administration
5. Environmental Protection Agency

### Technology Activity

Call on volunteers to share their reports with the rest of the class.

### Analyzing the Global Economy

Suggest that students illustrate their reports with appropriate tables, charts, graphs, and maps.

### Chapter Bonus Test Question

ASK: What are the four types of market structures discussed in this chapter? Provide examples of industries that match, or closely match, each of these market structures. *perfect competition, monopoly, oligopoly, monopolistic competition; examples will vary*

wholesalers—will band together to try to control price. Therefore, price is determined by the interaction of supply and demand.

2. Answers may include: Overcoming barriers to entry—technological advances and profit motive; Overcoming higher prices—law of demand prevents monopolists from charging outrageous prices and government regulations set some price ceilings; Overcoming reduced competition—government deregulation and technological advances.
3. The goals of antitrust legislation are to prevent new monopolies from developing and to break up those that already exist. The goal of regulatory agencies is to regulate business pricing and product quality to protect consumers and businesses from unfair practices.

# Focus on Free Enterprise

## 1 Focus

Mention that in the little more than 20 years since its founding, The Home Depot has grown to more than 800 stores. These outlets averaged more than $25 billion in sales each year—nearly 15 percent of the market for home-improvement products.

## 2 Teach

Direct students to read the feature. Then ask them to note the new approach to home-improvement products retailing introduced by Bernie Marcus, Arthur Blank, and Pat Farrar. Also, have them identify other aspects of The Home Depot operation that they find different or interesting. Conclude by asking students to discuss how these approaches contributed to The Home Depot's success.

### ? Did You Know

The Home Depot's stock is publicly traded and is included in the Standard & Poor's 500 Index and the Dow-Jones Industrial Average.

---

CASE STUDY

## Focus on Free Enterprise

# The Home Depot

***When Bernie Marcus and Arthur Blank lost their jobs at Handy Dan, a chain of home improvement stores in California, they knew what they were going to do. They would open their own home improvement store—and it would be the best in the United States. Just exactly how they were going to do this, they were not sure. It became clear to them, however, when they visited a store in Long Beach called Homeco.***

### A Different Approach

Homeco did not look, or work, like any other home improvement store Marcus and Blank had seen. The huge barn-like space was stacked from floor to ceiling with a vast array of home supplies. Every item was offered at a rock-bottom price. And there were tradespeople—painters, carpenters, plumbers, electricians, and so on—throughout the store ready to give shoppers help and advice. Marcus and Blank recognized that this blend of warehouse retailing and superior customer service was the way to go. They quickly asked Homeco's owner, Pat Farrah, to join them in their business venture.

Shortly after, Marcus, Blank, and Farrah moved their operations to Atlanta, Georgia. They opened their first store—called The Home Depot—there in 1978. The store operated on four simple principles. First, stock a

*Bernie Marcus (left) and Arthur Blank*



### Free Enterprise Activity

**More About The Home Depot** The Home Depot has major plans for expansion in the new century. It wants to open more stores in foreign countries. And, in 1999, it opened a convenience-style hardware store in New Brunswick, New Jersey. This is a first of a chain of stores, called Villager's Hardware, designed for smaller locations. The Home Depot fully expects to have 1,900 stores in business by 2003. Have students track the stock prices for The Home Depot for one month.

large assortment of merchandise. Second, charge the lowest prices. Third, provide excellent customer service. Finally, cater to both the do-it-yourself amateur and the construction-industry professional.

The early days were a struggle. Sometimes, the partners did not have the cash to buy supplies. So Farrah stacked the store with empty paint cans and boxes to make it look as though it were well stocked. Over time, however, business began to pick up, and Marcus, Blank, and Farrah opened several more stores.

### Building an Empire

In 1981 the partners took a major step, selling shares in the company. With the $4 million they made from the sale, they began an ambitious expansion program. First, The Home Depot began to establish a foothold in other states. Then the company went international, opening stores elsewhere in the Western Hemisphere. By 1999, it had outlets in 44 states, Puerto Rico, Canada, and Chile.

### Sharing the Wealth

Since its earliest days, The Home Depot has offered employees the chance to share in its success. It gives many workers the choice of taking shares instead of year-end cash bonuses. Workers also have a chance to buy shares at discount rates. This practice, Arthur Blank thinks, simply is good business. When workers own stock, he says, they "feel that they own the stores, that they own the merchandise, that they have total responsibility for the customers in their aisles, and that they create the value." Many workers certainly have benefited from the practice. About 1,000 of them have stock portfolios worth more than $1 million.

The Home Depot also makes an effort to share its good fortune with the communities in which it operates. In 1999 alone, it budgeted $15 million for charity. It also encourages its workers to volunteer for local charitable organizations.

#### *Free Enterprise in Action*

**1. What new approach did The Home Depot bring to the home improvement industry?**

**2. Why does Arthur Blank think that offering stock to employees is good business practice?**

## 3 Assess

Have students answer the **Free Enterprise in Action** questions.

## 4 Close

Close by asking students to discuss the following: Would The Home Depot's approach work in other areas of retailing? Why or why not?

### Did You Know

The Home Depot has been ranked by *Fortune Magazine* as America's Most Admired Specialty Retailer for six consecutive years.

### Answers to *Free Enterprise In Action*

1. The approach followed four basic principles: stock a large assortment of merchandise; charge the lowest prices; provide excellent customer service; and cater to both the do-it-yourself amateur and the construction-industry professional.
2. Blank feels that when workers own stock, they feel that they own the stores and the merchandise and that they have responsibility for their customers. This will tend to encourage them to make a greater effort.

# UNIT 4 Resource Manager

The following transparencies may be used at any time during Unit 4.

## Economic Forms and Financial Pages Transparencies

### Transparency 4

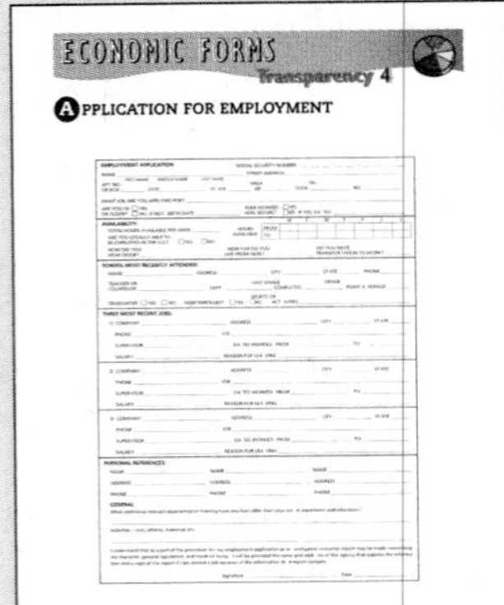
ECONOMIC FORMS
Transparency 4
APPLICATION FOR EMPLOYMENT

### Transparency 10

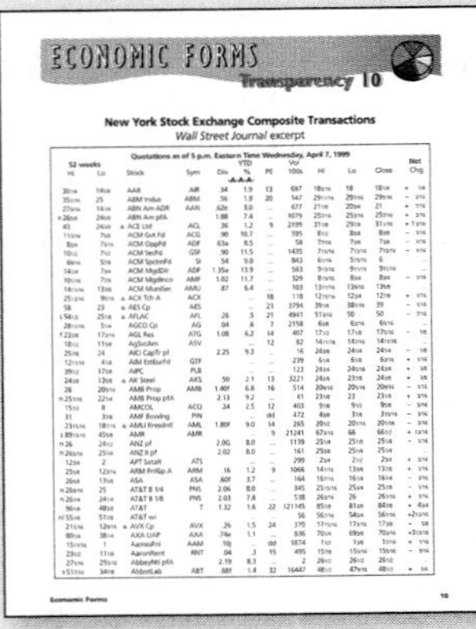
ECONOMIC FORMS
Transparency 10
New York Stock Exchange Composite Transactions
Wall Street Journal excerpt

### Transparency 11

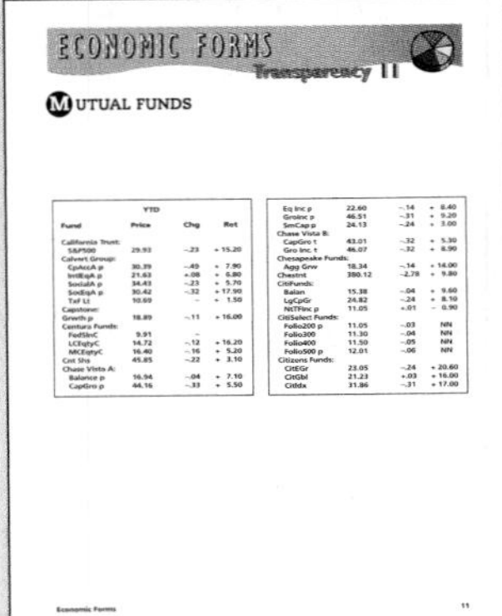
ECONOMIC FORMS
Transparency 11
MUTUAL FUNDS

## Economic Concepts Transparencies

### Transparency 3

ECONOMIC CONCEPTS
Transparency 3
PRODUCTIVITY

### Transparency 5

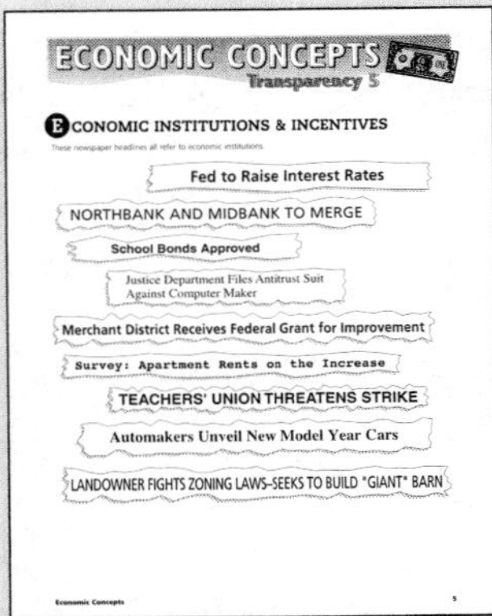
ECONOMIC CONCEPTS
Transparency 5
ECONOMIC INSTITUTIONS & INCENTIVES
Fed to Raise Interest Rates
NORTHBANK AND MIDBANK TO MERGE
School Bonds Approved
Justice Department Files Antitrust Suit Against Computer Maker
Merchant District Receives Federal Grant for Improvement
Survey: Apartment Rents on the Increase
TEACHERS' UNION THREATENS STRIKE
Automakers Unveil New Model Year Cars
LANDOWNER FIGHTS ZONING LAWS–SEEKS TO BUILD "GIANT" BARN

### Transparency 16

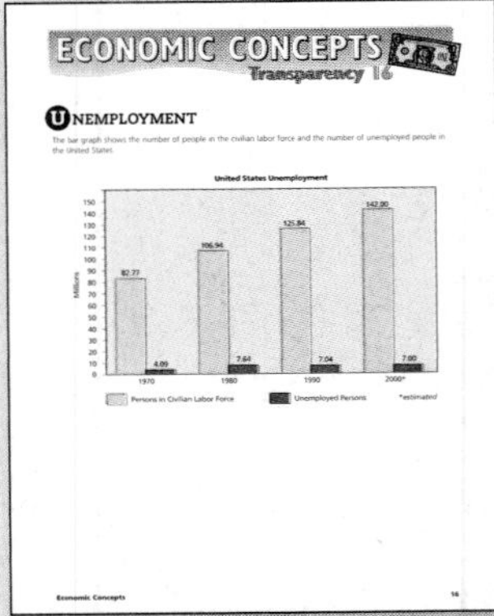
ECONOMIC CONCEPTS
Transparency 16
UNEMPLOYMENT


## Real-World Economics

Have your students learn about investing and managing their financial futures by participating in the exciting simulation **The Stock Market Game™**. See page T24 for more information.

Strengthen students' research, cooperation, presentation, and critical thinking skills by having them compete in the **Fed Challenge**. See page T26 for further information.

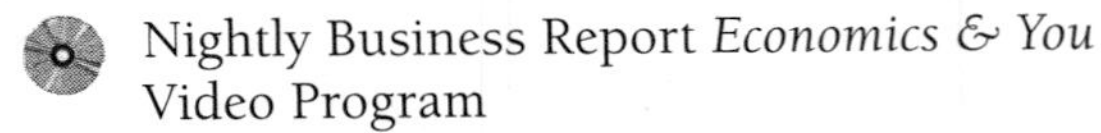

## Additional Glencoe Resources for This Unit

- Nightly Business Report *Economics & You* Video Program
- Economic Survival: A Financial Simulation
- Interactive Economics! Software

# UNIT 4 Resource Manager

## Assessment and Evaluation

GLENCOE'S ASSESSMENT ADVANTAGE

Unit 4 Test
Form A

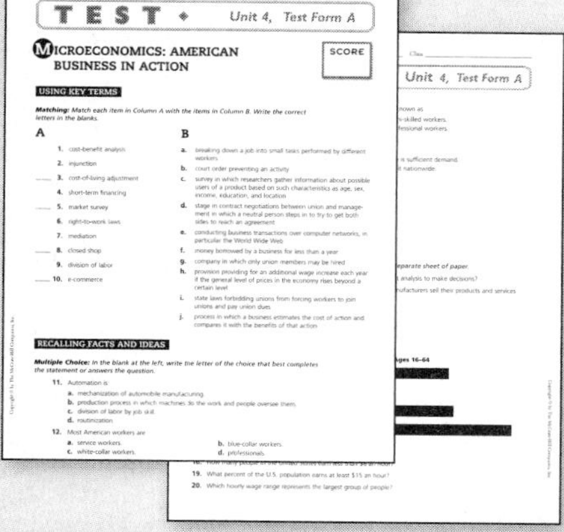
TEST ✦ Unit 4, Test Form A

MICROECONOMICS: AMERICAN BUSINESS IN ACTION

SCORE

USING KEY TERMS

RECALLING FACTS AND IDEAS

Unit 4 Test
Form B

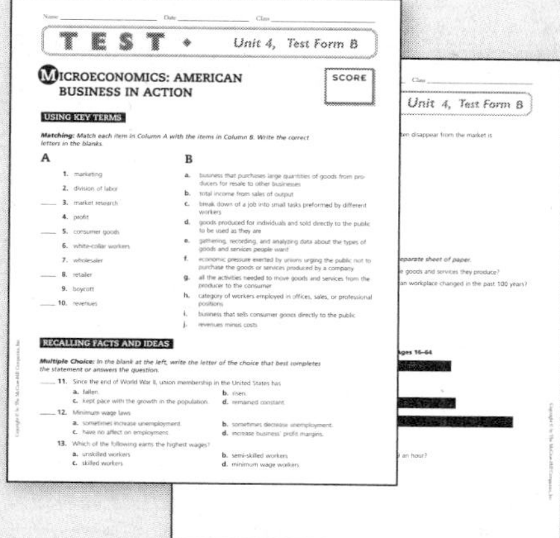
TEST ✦ Unit 4, Test Form B

MICROECONOMICS: AMERICAN BUSINESS IN ACTION

SCORE

USING KEY TERMS

RECALLING FACTS AND IDEAS

**Use the following tools to easily assess student learning:**

- Performance Assessment Strategies and Activities
- Section Quizzes
- Chapter and Unit Tests
- ExamView® Pro Testmaker
- Interactive Tutor Self-Assessment Software
- SAT I/II Test Practice
- MindJogger Videoquiz
- ett.glencoe.com

## Application and Enrichment

Economics Laboratory 4

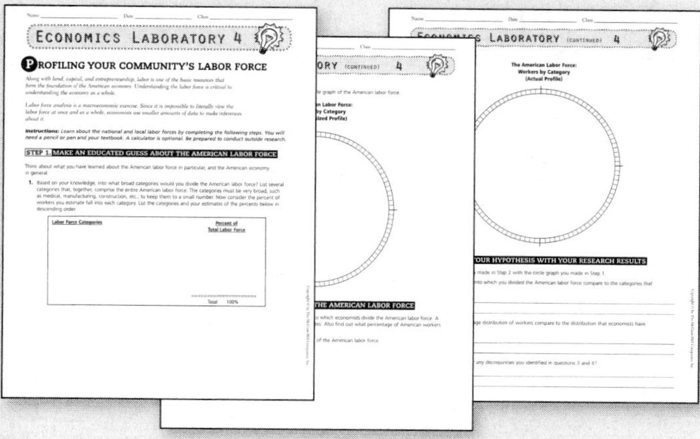
ECONOMICS LABORATORY 4

PROFILING YOUR COMMUNITY'S LABOR FORCE

STEP 1 MAKE AN EDUCATED GUESS ABOUT THE AMERICAN LABOR FORCE

Labor Force Categories

Percent of Total Labor Force

Total 100%

ECONOMICS LABORATORY (CONTINUED) 4

The American Labor Force: Workers by Category (Actual Profile)

*Business Week* Focus on the New Economy

## ECONOMICS Online

*Glencoe's Web sites provide additional resources. All essential content is covered in the Student Edition.*

*ett.glencoe.com*

Visit the **Economics Today and Tomorrow** Web site for Chapter Overviews, Textbook Updates, Student Web Activities, Web Activity Lesson Plans, and Self-Check Quizzes.

*socialstudies.glencoe.com*

Visit the **Glencoe Social Studies** Web site for additional social studies activities, updates, and links to other sites.

**Glencoe's *Guide to Using the Internet*** provides an introduction to many of the current Internet technologies, social studies and professional resources, and teaching strategies.

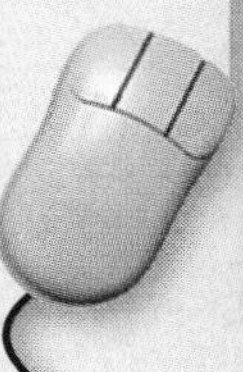

## Unit Objectives

After studying this unit, students will be able to:

- **Specify** sources and types of financing and methods of production available to companies.
- **Explain** basic marketing principles and distribution of goods and services.
- **Describe** the makeup of the American labor force, the labor movement, and collective bargaining procedures.

## Unit Overview

The three chapters in **Unit 4** discuss finance and production, marketing and distribution, and the role of labor in producing goods.

**Chapter 10** explains or describes investment financing, types of financing for business, and the production process.

**Chapter 11** explains how goods are marketed, and describes how goods are distributed from producer to consumer.

**Chapter 12** describes the American labor force and discusses management/labor relations.

### 00:00 Out of Time?

If time does not permit teaching each chapter in this unit, you may use the **Audio Program** that includes a 1-page activity and a 1-page test for each chapter.

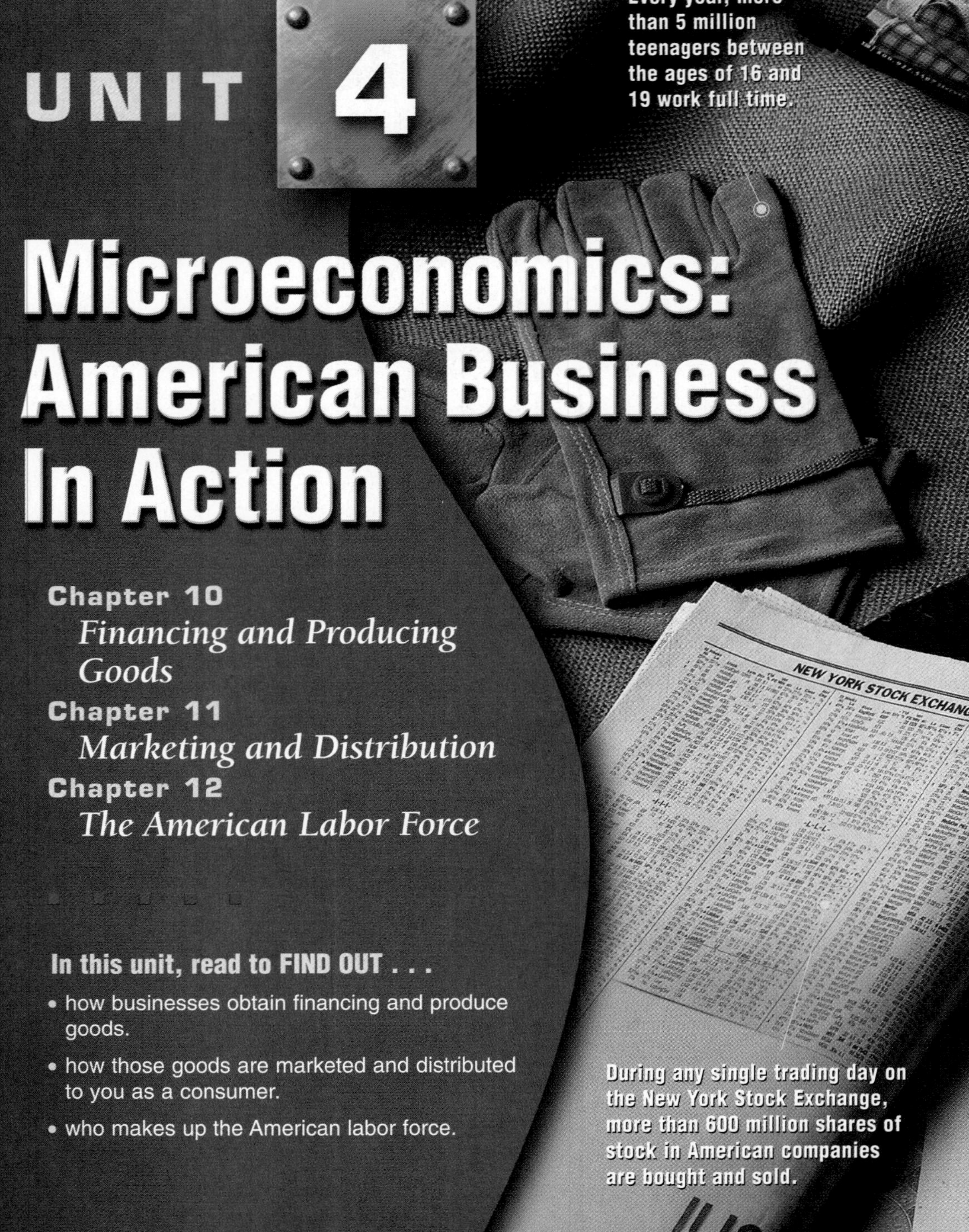


# UNIT 4

# Microeconomics: American Business In Action



**In this unit, read to FIND OUT . . .**

- how businesses obtain financing and produce goods.
- how those goods are marketed and distributed to you as a consumer.
- who makes up the American labor force.

Every year, more than 5 million teenagers between the ages of 16 and 19 work full time.

During any single trading day on the New York Stock Exchange, more than 600 million shares of stock in American companies are bought and sold.

## ECONOMIC SIMULATION

**Business Financing** Organize the class into four groups. Ask three of the groups to assume that they own businesses that plan to expand. Have each group brainstorm to decide what its business is and what assets the business owns. Then each group should draw up plans for business expansion, including reasons for expansion, estimated cost of expansion (up to $100,000), and projected profits after expansion. Ask the fourth group to play the role of a financial institution with $200,000 currently available to lend. Have the first three groups present their expansion plans to the financial institution group. Have members of this group review the plans and decide how much they will lend each of the other groups and the terms and interest rates of the loans.

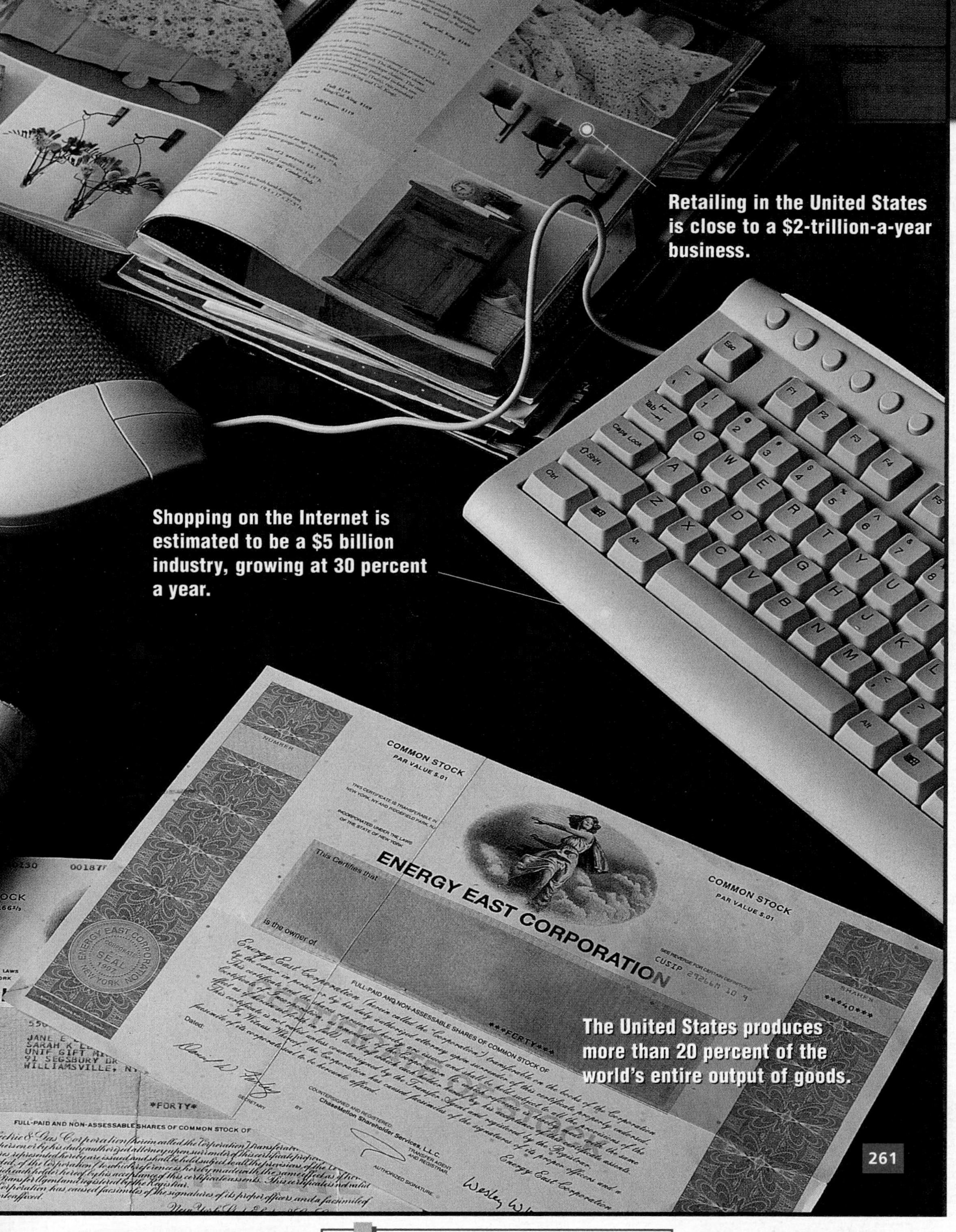

Retailing in the United States is close to a $2-trillion-a-year business.
Shopping on the Internet is estimated to be a $5 billion industry, growing at 30 percent a year.
The United States produces more than 20 percent of the world's entire output of goods.
COMMON STOCK
ENERGY EAST CORPORATION
261


Introducing UNIT 4

## Making It Relevant

Poll students to see if any of them have part-time jobs. Ask those who do have jobs what contribution they think they make to the economy. *Most will respond that they help produce goods and services and, by spending their income, they act as consumers, too.* Point out that in this unit they will learn, among other things, the contribution of the American labor force to the economy.

**BusinessWeek ONLINE**

To find up-to-date news and analysis on the economy, business, technology, markets, entrepreneurs, investments, and finance, have students search feature articles and special reports on the *Business Week* Web site. www.businessweek.com

## EXTRA CREDIT PROJECT

Point out to students that the marketing strategy a company uses depends on the target market. Ask students to research the strategies companies use to market products to one of the American economy's major markets—young people. If students have difficulty finding information, suggest the following books: Gene Del Vecchio, *Creating Ever-Cool: A Marketer's Guide to a Kid's Heart;* James U. McNeal, *The Kids Market: Myths and Realities;* Peter Zollo, *Wise Up to Teens: Insights into Marketing and Advertising to Teens.* Have students present their findings in a brief written report.

# CHAPTER 10 Resource Manager

## Teaching Transparency

### Economic Concepts Transparency 3

## Application and Enrichment

### Enrichment Activity 10

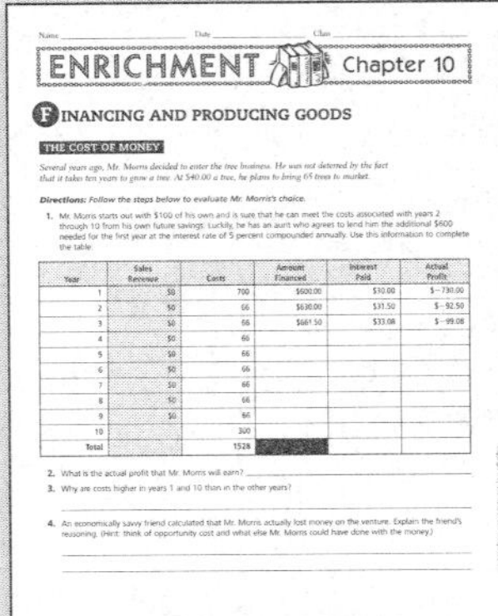

### Consumer Applications Activity 17

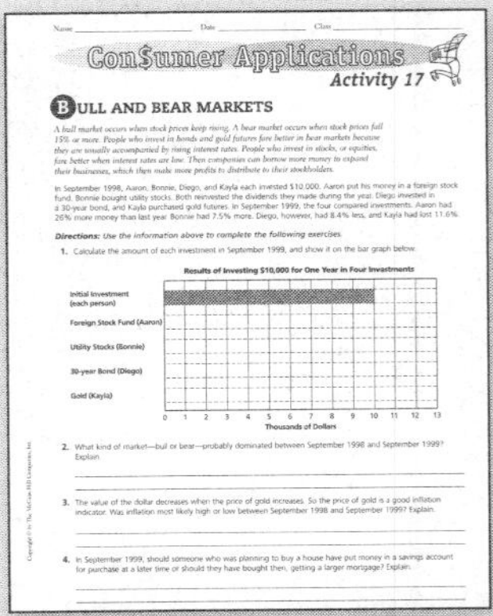

### Free Enterprise Activity 17

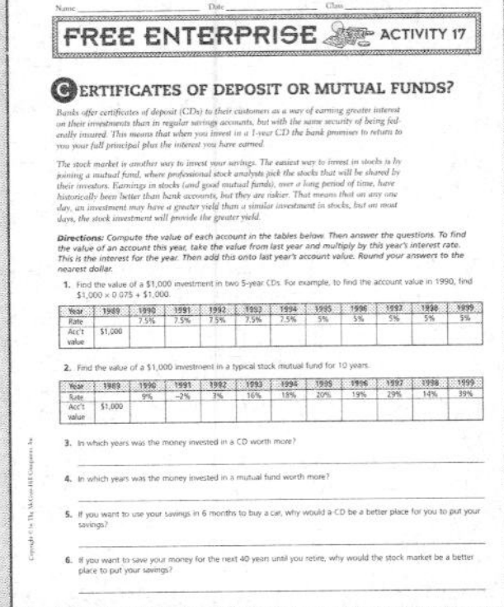

## Application and Enrichment

### Cooperative Learning Simulations and Problems 17

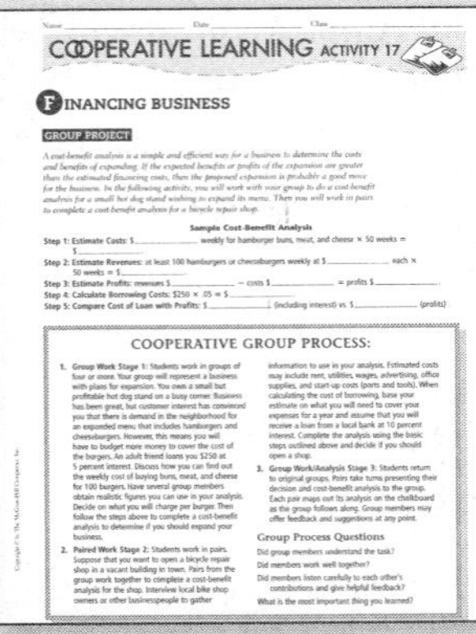

### Primary and Secondary Source Reading 17

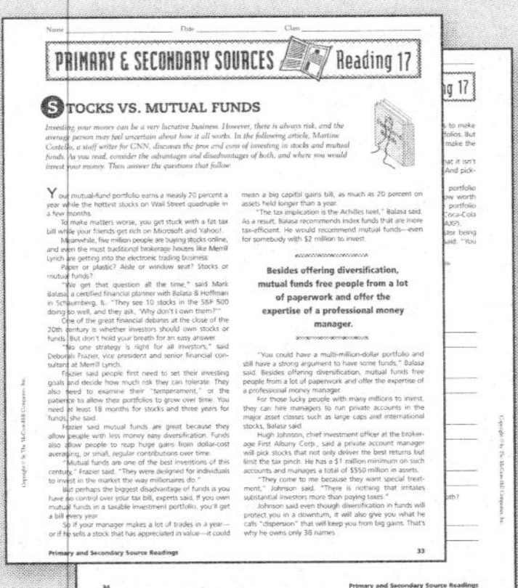

### Math Practice for Economics Activity 17

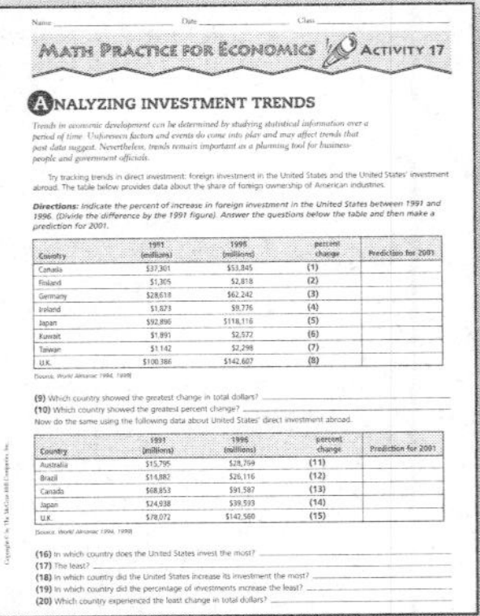

### Economic Cartoons Activity 17

## Review and Reinforcement

### Critical Thinking Activity 17

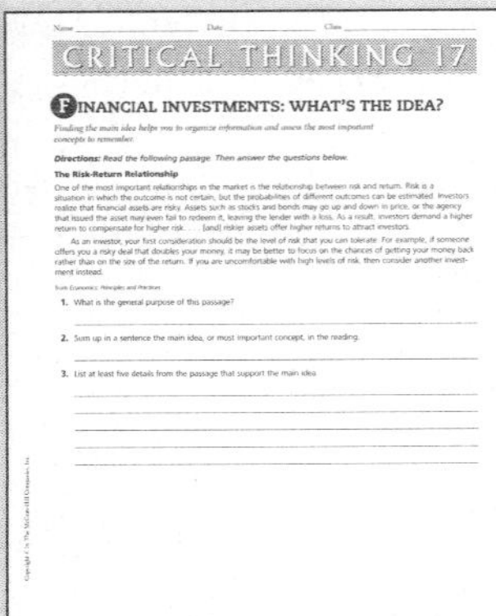

### Reteaching Activity 10

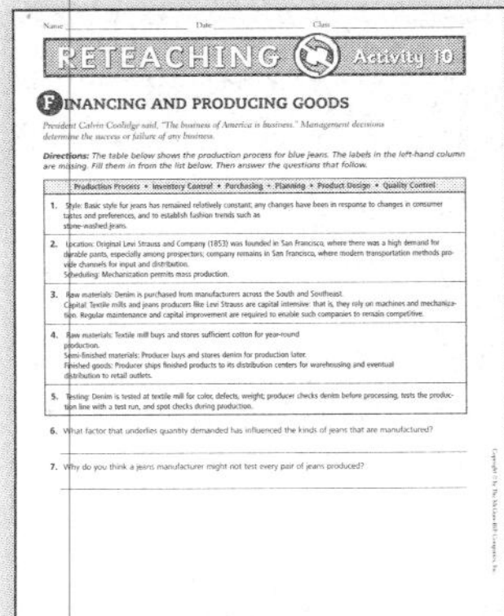

### Economic Vocabulary Activity 10

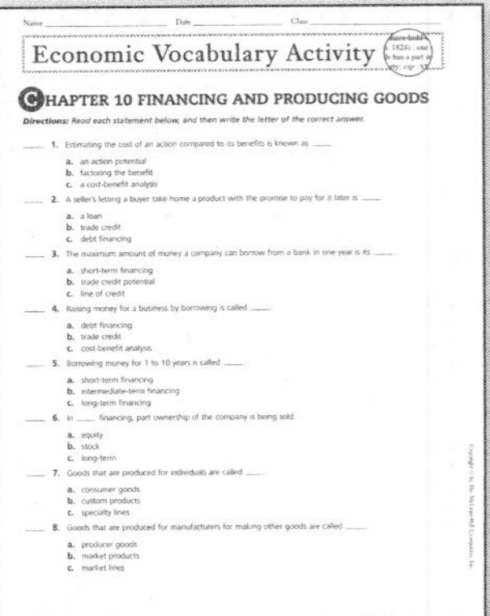

### Reinforcing Economic Skills 14

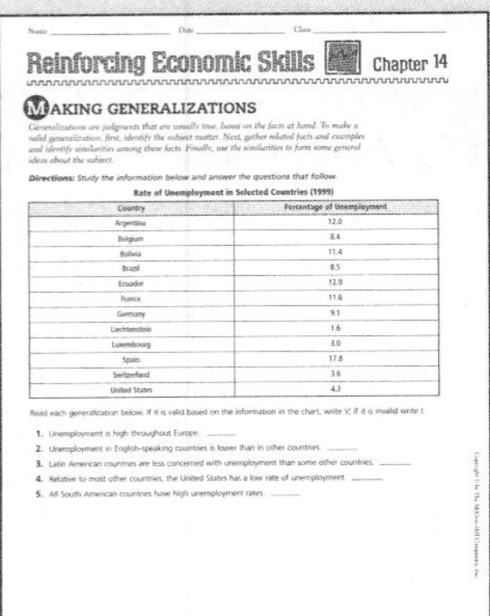

# CHAPTER 10 Resource Manager

## Assessment and Evaluation

Chapter 10 Test Form A

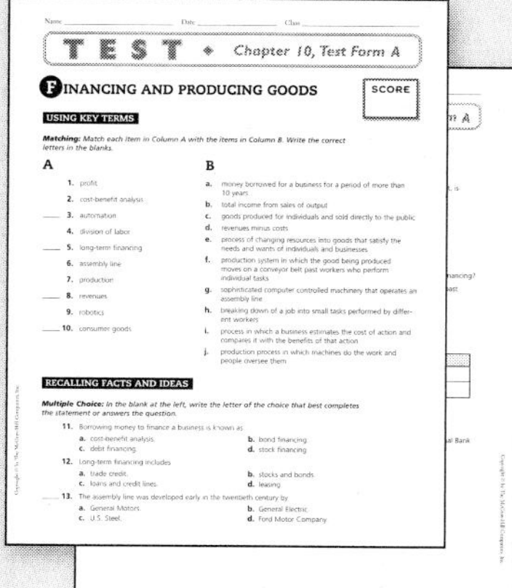
TEST • Chapter 10, Test Form A

FINANCING AND PRODUCING GOODS

USING KEY TERMS

RECALLING FACTS AND IDEAS

Chapter 10 Test Form B

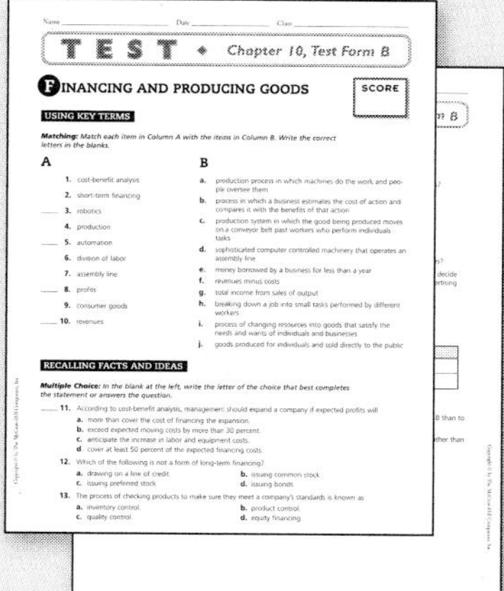
TEST • Chapter 10, Test Form B

FINANCING AND PRODUCING GOODS

USING KEY TERMS

RECALLING FACTS AND IDEAS

Performance Assessment Activity 17

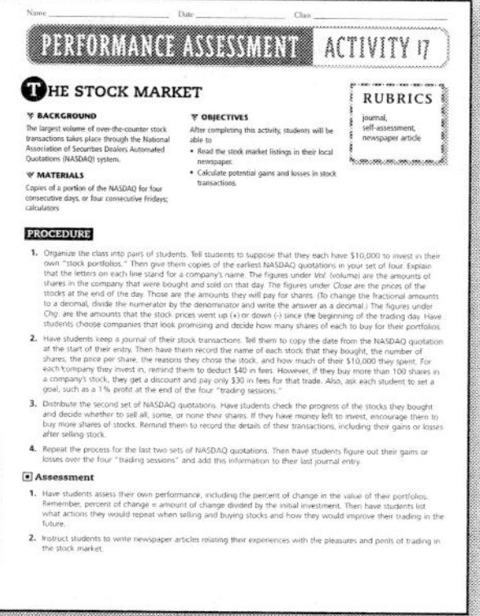
PERFORMANCE ASSESSMENT ACTIVITY 17

THE STOCK MARKET

RUBRICS

PROCEDURE

ExamView® Pro Testmaker

## Technology and Multimedia

-  Vocabulary PuzzleMaker Software
-  Interactive Tutor Self-Assessment Software
-  ExamView® Pro Testmaker
-  NBR *Economics & You* Video Program (English/Spanish)
-  Presentation Plus!
-  Glencoe Skillbuilder Interactive Workbook CD-ROM, Level 2
- Interactive Lesson Planner
-  MindJogger Videoquiz
- Interactive Economics! CD-ROM
- Audio Program (English or Spanish)

## ECONOMICS Online

You and your students can visit ett.glencoe.com—the Web site companion to **Economics Today and Tomorrow.** This innovative integration of electronic and print media offers your students a wealth of opportunities. The student text directs students to the Web site for the following options:

- **Chapter Overviews**
- **Self-Check Quizzes**
- **Student Web Activities**
- **Textbook Updates**

Answers are provided for you in the **Web Activity Lesson Plan.** Additional Web resources and Interactive Puzzles are also available.

Use the Glencoe Web site for additional resources. All essential content is covered in the Student Edition.

## Spanish Resources

-  Spanish Economic Concepts Transparency 3
-  Spanish Vocabulary Activity 10
-  Spanish Reteaching Activity 10
-  Spanish Section Quizzes for Chapter 10
-  Spanish Chapter 10 Audio Program, Activity, and Test

## Additional Resources

### Reading for the Student

Dowd, Merle E. *Money, Banking, and Credit Made Simple.* Garden City, NY: Doubleday and Company, 1994.

### Multimedia Material

*Economics in a Changing World: Production.* Churchill Media. VHS videocassette, 24 min. Uses location footage and interviews to explore the basic concepts of the production process.

# CHAPTER 10 Resource Manager

## Section Resources

| Reading Objectives | Reproducible Resources | Technology/Multimedia Resources |
|---|---|---|
| **Section 1**<br>**Investing in the Free Enterprise System**<br>• How does a business decide whether to expand or not?<br>• Why are people willing to finance business investment?<br>• How does competition for financing determine how resources are allocated in a market economy? | Reproducible Lesson Plan 10-1<br>Daily Lecture Notes 10-1<br>Guided Reading Activity 10-1<br>Reading Essentials and Study Guide 10-1<br>Daily Focus Activity 46<br>Section Quiz 10-1*<br>Reinforcing Economic Skills 14 | Daily Focus Transparency 46<br>Vocabulary PuzzleMaker<br>Interactive Tutor Self-Assessment Software<br>MindJogger Videoquiz<br>NBR's *Economics & You**<br>Presentation Plus!<br>ExamView® Pro Testmaker |
| **Section 2**<br>**Types of Financing for Business Organizations**<br>• What are three general kinds of debt financing?<br>• What four factors should companies consider in choosing the right financing? | Reproducible Lesson Plan 10-2<br>Daily Lecture Notes 10-2<br>Guided Reading Activity 10-2<br>Reading Essentials and Study Guide 10-2<br>Daily Focus Activity 47<br>Section Quiz 10-2* | Daily Focus Transparency 47<br>Vocabulary PuzzleMaker<br>Interactive Tutor Self-Assessment Software<br>MindJogger Videoquiz<br>Interactive Economics!<br>Presentation Plus!<br>ExamView® Pro Testmaker |
| **Section 3**<br>**The Production Process**<br>• What are the four major steps in production operations?<br>• How has technology changed production methods since the early 1800s? | Reproducible Lesson Plan 10-3<br>Daily Lecture Notes 10-3<br>Guided Reading Activity 10-3<br>Reading Essentials and Study Guide 10-3<br>Daily Focus Activity 48<br>Section Quiz 10-3* | Daily Focus Transparency 48<br>Economic Concepts Transparency 3<br>Vocabulary PuzzleMaker<br>Interactive Tutor Self-Assessment Software<br>MindJogger Videoquiz<br>Presentation Plus!<br>ExamView® Pro Testmaker |

*Also available in Spanish

Blackline Master
Transparency

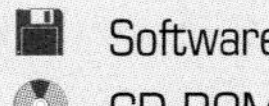
Software
CD-ROM

Videodisc
Audiocassette

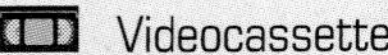
Videocassette

# CHAPTER 10 Resource Manager

## ACTIVITY From the Classroom of

**Charles Cleveland**
**Belen Jesuit Preparatory School**
**Miami, Florida**

### The Stock Market Game™

Have students participate in The Stock Market Game™ (Internet version). Students simulate actual stock transactions for a 12-week period. Working in small groups, students create an investment company name and invest $100,000. Stocks and values are monitored. At the end of the 12-week period, students report the strategies they used and their results.

## Key to Ability Levels

**Teaching strategies have been coded for varying learning styles and abilities.**

L1 BASIC activities for all students
L2 AVERAGE activities for average to above-average students
L3 CHALLENGING activities for above-average students
ELL ENGLISH LANGUAGE LEARNER activities

## Easy Planning and Preparation!

Use Glencoe's **Presentation Plus!**, a Microsoft PowerPoint® application, to teach **Financing and Producing Goods.** With this multimedia teacher tool, you can customize ready-made presentations. At your fingertips are interactive transparencies, on-screen lecture notes, audiovisual presentations, and links to the Internet and to other Glencoe multimedia.

### Interactive Lesson Planner

Planning has never been easier! Organize your week, month, semester, or year with all the lesson helps you need to make teaching creative, timely, and relevant—the way it is meant to be. The Interactive Lesson Planner opens Glencoe's **Chapter 10** resources, helps you build your schedule, and tracks your progress.

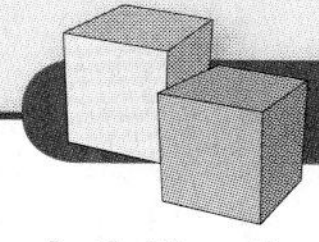

## Block Schedule

Activities that are particularly suited to use within the block scheduling framework are identified throughout this chapter by the following designation: BLOCK SCHEDULING

## National Council on Economic Education

## THE EconomicsAmerica AND EconomicsInternational PROGRAMS

### Voluntary Standards Emphasized in Chapter 10

**Content Standard 10** Students will understand that institutions evolve in market economies to help individuals and groups accomplish their goals. Banks, labor unions, corporations, legal systems, and not-for-profit organizations are examples of important institutions. A different kind of institution, clearly defined and well enforced property rights, is essential to a market economy.

**Content Standard 15** Students will understand that investment in factories, machinery, new technology, and the health, education, and training of people can raise future standards of living.

### Resources Available from NCEE

- *Capstone: The Nation's High School Economics Course*
- *Focus: High School Economics*
- *Learning from the Market: Integrating The Stock Market Game™ Across the Curriculum*
- *MCG–Economics and Entrepreneurship*

To order these materials, or to contact your State Council on Economic Education about workshops and programs, call 1-800-338-1192 or visit the NCEE Web site at http://www.nationalcouncil.org

ECONOMICS & YOU

Financing and Producing Goods

Chapter 19
Disc 1, Side 2

ASK: What should a company look for when borrowing money? *When debt financing, companies need to find the best repayment schedule at the lowest interest rate.*

 Also available in VHS.

## Chapter Overview

Chapter 10 explains or describes the sources and allocation of funds for business investment, how businesses make financing decisions, different production methods, and the impact of technology on these methods.

**GLENCOE TECHNOLOGY**

Use **MindJogger Videoquiz** VHS to preview Chapter 10 content.

Introduce students to chapter content and key terms by having them access **Chapter 10—Chapter Overviews** at *ett.glencoe.com*

# CHAPTER 10

# Financing and Producing Goods

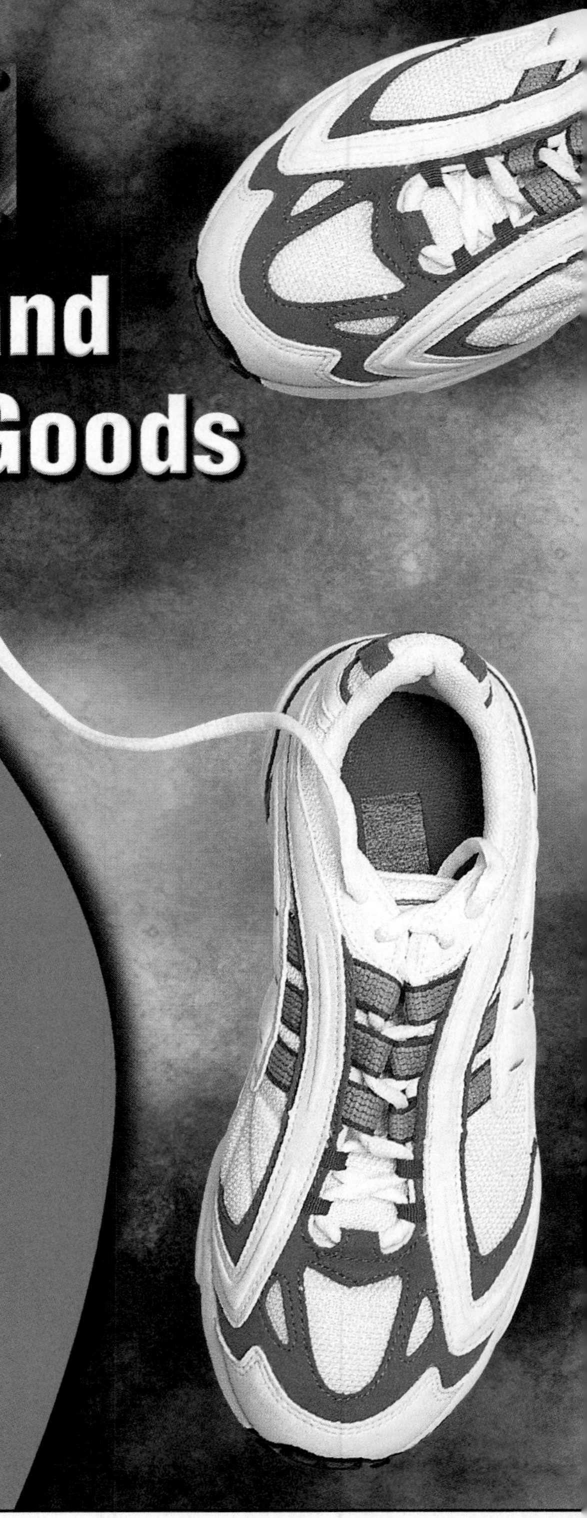

## Why It's Important

*How do shoe manufacturers get started? How could you get started if you wanted to open a business? This chapter will explain how companies obtain the financing needed to open for business, and how they try to work efficiently to make profits.*

*To learn more about factors that affect efficiency and profitability, view the* **Economics & You** *Chapter 19 video lesson:* **Financing and Producing Goods**

**ECONOMICS Online**

**Chapter Overview** Visit the *Economics Today and Tomorrow* Web site at ett.glencoe.com and click on ***Chapter 10—Chapter Overviews*** to preview chapter information.

## CHAPTER LAUNCH ACTIVITY

Organize students into several small groups. Tell groups to imagine that they are the owners of a small business that makes advertising posters. The company has just received a huge order—10,000 posters—that must be delivered in a week. Ask groups to draw up an outline of the production process the company might follow to fill this order. Call on group representatives to share their outlines with the rest of the class. Then tell students that in this chapter they will learn that all companies develop a production process to produce goods and services.

SECTION 

# Investing in the Free Enterprise System

## Cover Story

*The Chicago Tribune*, May 26, 1999

Finding money for your small business is often as deflating as looking for a job. It can be an arduous process of networking, mailing people information about yourself and then calling to see what they think.

A Chicago company is using the Internet to try to streamline the money-hunting process for entrepreneurs by connecting them with venture capitalists. Venture Capital Online has signed up more than 80 venture capital firms nationwide representing $15 billion in capital. It has 200 possible deals in the pipeline. . . .

### Reader's Guide

**Terms to Know**
- financing
- cost-benefit analysis
- revenues
- profits

**Reading Objectives**
1. How does a business decide whether to expand or not?
2. Why are people willing to finance business investment?
3. How does competition for financing determine how resources are allocated in a market economy?

If you were an entrepreneur, you would face many hurdles on your road to success. One hurdle would be finding sufficient financing to pay for your company's current needs—such as parts and tools—and its long-term needs—such as growth. **Financing** is the obtaining of funds, or money capital. As you read this section, you'll learn that both the short-term and long-term needs of businesses can be financed in a variety of ways.

financing: *obtaining funds or money capital for business expansion*



## Section 1 Resource Manager

**Reproducible Masters**
- Reproducible Lesson Plan 10–1
- Reading Essentials and Study Guide 10–1
- Guided Reading Activity 10–1
- Section Quiz 10–1
- Daily Focus Activity 46
- Daily Lecture Notes 10–1

**Multimedia**
- Daily Focus Transparency 46
- Vocabulary PuzzleMaker
- Interactive Tutor Self-Assessment Software
- ExamView® Pro Testmaker
- MindJogger Videoquiz
- NBR's *Economics & You*
- Presentation Plus!



# 1 Focus

## Overview

**Section 1** explains or describes how savings are used as investment funds to finance business startup and growth, how companies use cost-benefit analyses, and how bidding for funds affects the allocation of resources in a free market economy.

### Bellringer
**Motivational Activity**

Project **Daily Focus Transparency 46** and have students answer the questions.

This activity is also available as a blackline master.

**Daily Focus Transparency 46**

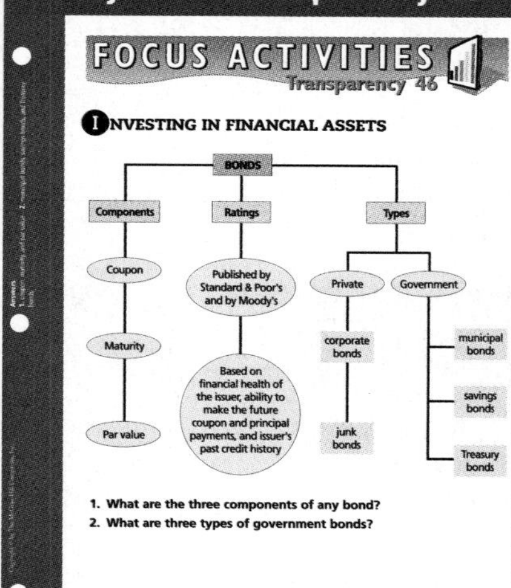


### Reader's Guide

Answers to the **Reading Objectives** questions are on page 268.

**Preteaching Vocabulary**

Have students read the Glossary definition of the term *cost-benefit analysis*. Then have them draw a rough cost-benefit analysis outlining the costs and benefits of buying a car.

**Vocabulary PuzzleMaker**

# 2 Teach

## Guided Practice

**L1 Illustrating Ideas** Review the text under the subheading "Before You Pursue Financing" on pages 265–266. Then have students create a flowchart illustrating the steps businesses must take before obtaining financing for business startup or expansion. Direct students to accompany each step on the flowchart with an appropriate title and illustration. Call on volunteers to present and discuss their flowcharts. ELL

### Daily Lecture Notes 10-1

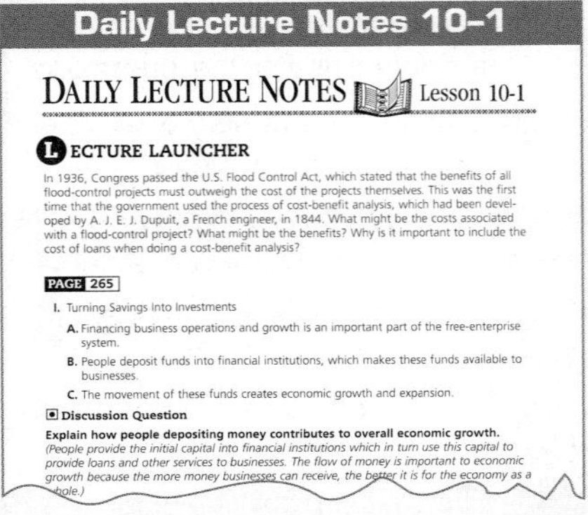
DAILY LECTURE NOTES Lesson 10-1

LECTURE LAUNCHER

In 1936, Congress passed the U.S. Flood Control Act, which stated that the benefits of all flood-control projects must outweigh the cost of the projects themselves. This was the first time that the government used the process of cost-benefit analysis, which had been developed by A. J. E. J. Dupuit, a French engineer, in 1844. What might be the costs associated with a flood-control project? What might be the benefits? Why is it important to include the cost of loans when doing a cost-benefit analysis?

PAGE 265

I. Turning Savings Into Investments
   A. Financing business operations and growth is an important part of the free-enterprise system.
   B. People deposit funds into financial institutions, which makes these funds available to businesses.
   C. The movement of these funds creates economic growth and expansion.

Discussion Question

**Explain how people depositing money contributes to overall economic growth.**
*(People provide the initial capital into financial institutions which in turn use this capital to provide loans and other services to businesses. The flow of money is important to economic growth because the more money businesses can receive, the better it is for the economy as a whole.)*

### Visual Instruction FIGURE 10.1

After students have reviewed Figure 10.1, ask: How might the same individual be both a lender and a borrower in the process of financing business expansion? *The owner of a business might ask a bank for a loan, while personally having funds on deposit at the bank in the form of savings accounts or CDs.*

## FIGURE 10.1

**Financing Business Expansion** Businesses are able to obtain financing because you and other income earners do not spend all that you earn during a year. Through saving, you and others who save make resources available to finance business expansion in the United States.

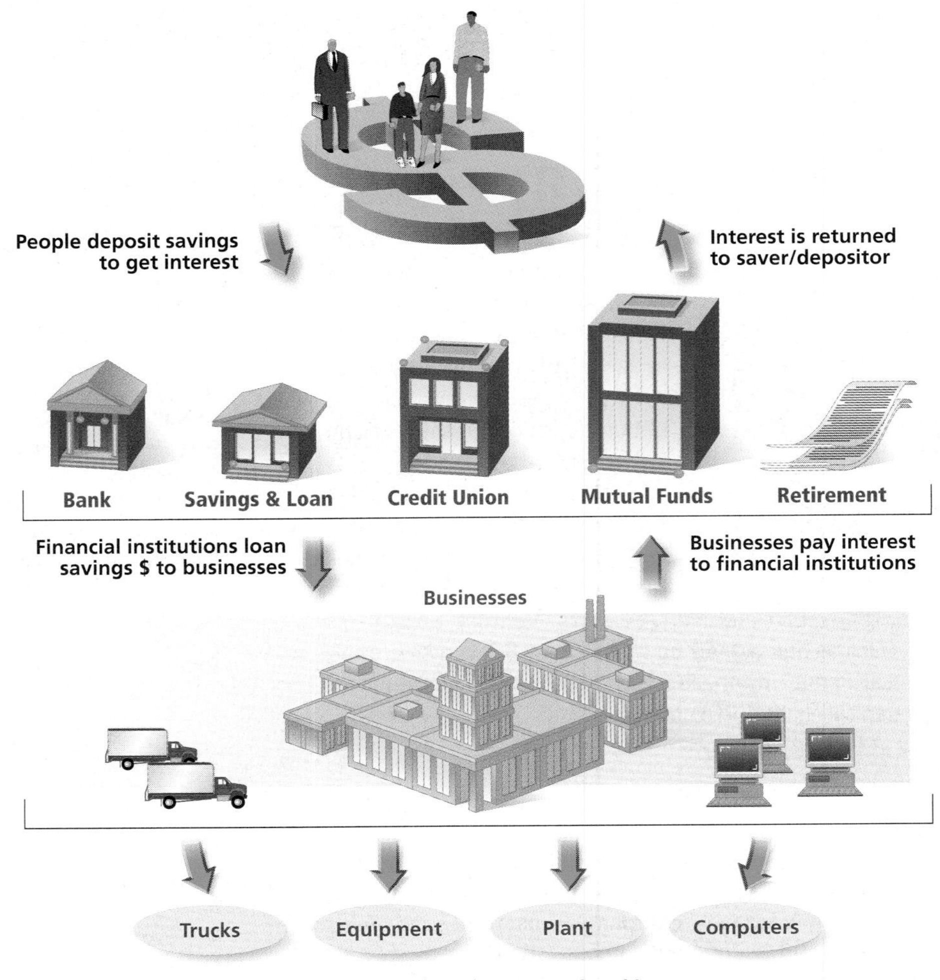
People deposit savings to get interest
Interest is returned to saver/depositor
Bank
Savings & Loan
Credit Union
Mutual Funds
Retirement
Financial institutions loan savings $ to businesses
Businesses pay interest to financial institutions
Businesses
Trucks
Equipment
Plant
Computers
Businesses use savings $ to expand and improve

### Meeting Special Needs

**Limited English Proficiency** Students with limited English proficiency may have difficulty understanding how bidding for funds in a free market affects the allocation of resources. Ask these students to imagine that they have $10,000 to invest and that five business owners have asked to borrow the money to finance expansion. Point out that, as investors, they would probably decide to give funds to the most creditworthy business owner whose company has the best performance record. In conclusion, mention that by making such a decision they have helped to determine the allocation of scarce financial resources.

Refer to *Inclusion for the Social Studies Classroom Strategies and Activities*.

## Critical Thinking Skills

# Making Generalizations

*Generalizations* ***are judgments that are usually true, based on the facts at hand. If you say, "We have a great soccer team," you are making a generalization. If you also say that your team is undefeated, you are providing evidence to support your generalization.***

- Identify the subject matter.
- Collect factual information and examples relevant to the topic.
- Identify similarities among these facts.
- Use these similarities to form some general ideas about the subject.

### Learning the Skill

To learn how to make a valid generalization, follow the steps listed on the left.

### Practicing the Skill

Read the excerpt below, then identify whether each generalization that follows is valid or invalid. Explain your answers.

> "*At the Lintumespsan Middle School, six miles outside of Helsinki, kids as young as 10 are showing up with mobile phones. They're supposed to turn them off during class hours, but some of them always forget. What's worse, the children have their phones rigged to ring with a few bars from songs by Guns N' Roses and the Leningrad Cowboys. . . . Some 58% of all Finns own a mobile phone–the highest penetration in the world. . . . Mobile-phone subscribers can request their bank balances, weather updates, traffic reports, even the latest headlines from Cable News Network, through short-message services.*"
>
> –*Business Week*, May 3, 1999

1. All Finns own mobile phones.
2. Many Finnish school children own mobile phones.
3. In Finland, mobile phones are used for more than just talking to friends.
4. Mobile-phone sales are increasing in Finland.

### Application Activity

Read at least three editorials in your local newspaper. Then make a generalization about each editorial.

**Practice** and **assess** key skills with ***Skillbuilder Interactive Workbook, Level 2.***



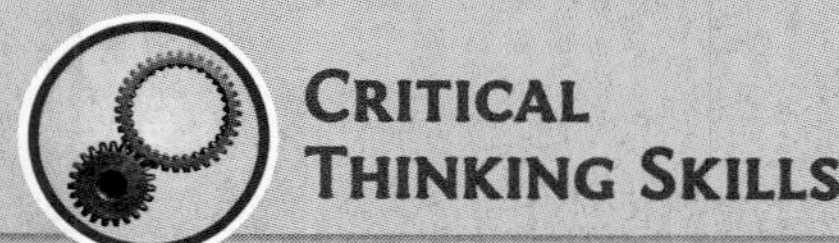

## Critical Thinking Skills

### Making Generalizations

Have students review the Expected Profits bar graph on page 267. Ask them what the graph shows about the relationship between revenues and profits. *As revenues increase, profits increase.* Tell students that they have just made a generalization about this relationship. Then point out that the ability to make generalizations is useful in seeing patterns in large amounts of information.

Next, work through the **Practicing the Skill** questions with students. Conclude by assigning the **Application Activity.**

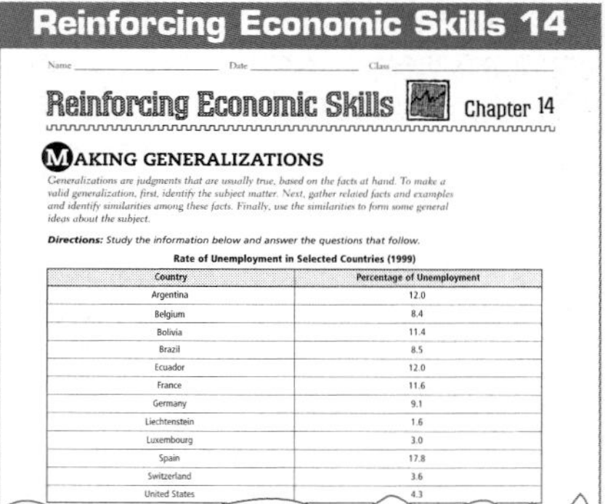

**Reinforcing Economic Skills 14**

Name ______ Date ______ Class ______

**Reinforcing Economic Skills** Chapter 14

**Making Generalizations**

*Generalizations are judgments that are usually true, based on the facts at hand. To make a valid generalization, first, identify the subject matter. Next, gather related facts and examples and identify similarities among these facts. Finally, use the similarities to form some general ideas about the subject.*

***Directions:*** *Study the information below and answer the questions that follow.*

**Rate of Unemployment in Selected Countries (1999)**

| Country | Percentage of Unemployment |
|---|---|
| Argentina | 12.0 |
| Belgium | 8.4 |
| Bolivia | 11.4 |
| Brazil | 8.5 |
| Ecuador | 12.0 |
| France | 11.6 |
| Germany | 9.1 |
| Liechtenstein | 1.6 |
| Luxembourg | 3.0 |
| Spain | 17.8 |
| Switzerland | 3.6 |
| United States | 4.3 |

### Glencoe Technology

**Glencoe Skillbuilder Interactive Workbook, Level 2**

This interactive CD-ROM reinforces student mastery of essential social studies skills.

### Answers to Practicing the Skill

1. Invalid; the excerpt states that 58 percent of Finns own mobile phones.
2. Invalid; the excerpt states that children as young as 10 are turning up at one school *with* mobile phones–it does not mention ownership. Perhaps a better generalization would be: Some Finnish schoolchildren use mobile phones.
3. Valid: the excerpt lists the various services that can be used by owners of mobile phones.
4. Invalid; the excerpt does not address phone sales.

**Application Activity** Have students exchange and discuss their clippings and generalizations.

# 1 Focus

## Overview

Section 2 describes the types of short-term, intermediate-term, and long-term financing available to businesses, and outlines four factors businesses consider before borrowing funds.

### BELLRINGER
**Motivational Activity**

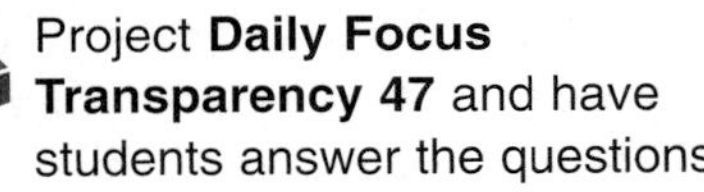

Project **Daily Focus Transparency 47** and have students answer the questions.

This activity is also available as a blackline master.

**Daily Focus Transparency 47**

FOCUS ACTIVITIES
Transparency 47

B USINESS FINANCE OPTIONS

"Getting back to those interest rates, could you be a little more specific than 'it's going to cost a pretty penny?'"

Sources of Business Finance

Short-Term Financing—To Respond to a Cash-Flow Problem
- Family and Friends
- Trade Credit
- Bank Loans
- Line of Credit

Medium-Term Financing—Borrowing Money for 1 to 10 Years
- Bank Loans
- Leasing

Long-Term Financing—Debt to Finance Expansion
- Bonds
- Equity Finance
  - Common Stock
  - Preferred Stock

1. What type of financing would a corporation planning a major expansion use?
2. Why are interest rates on loans so important to business decisions?

Daily Focus Transparencies

### READER'S GUIDE

Answers to the **Reading Objectives** questions are on page 275.

**Preteaching Vocabulary**

Have students study the **Terms to Know**. Then ask students to write questions for which each term is an answer.

**Vocabulary PuzzleMaker**

SECTION 2

# Types of Financing for Business Operations

### READER'S GUIDE

**Terms to Know**
- debt financing
- short-term financing
- intermediate-term financing
- long-term financing

**Reading Objectives**
1. What are three general kinds of debt financing?
2. What four factors should companies consider in choosing the right financing?

## COVER STORY

*FORBES MAGAZINE*, JULY 8, 1998

When a company sells stock to the public for the first time, it is called an initial public offering, or *IPO.* This has proved an especially profitable method of raising capital for Internet companies. In the first six months of 1998, for example, 10 Internet companies floated IPOs, raising $514 million. This was more than twice the amount raised by Internet IPOs in the same period in 1997.

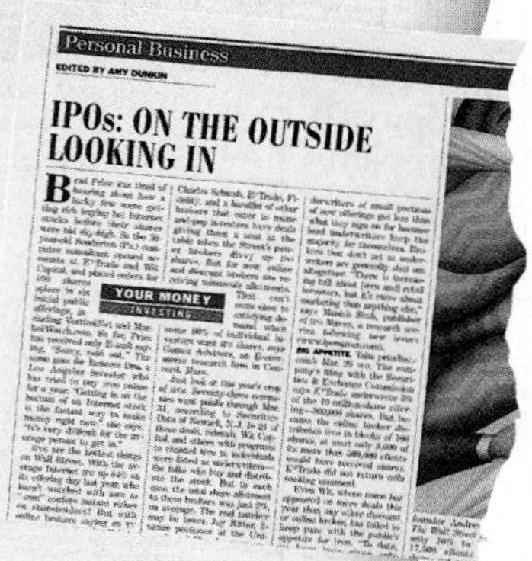

Personal Business

IPOs: ON THE OUTSIDE LOOKING IN

YOUR MONEY

Businesses, like individuals, must undergo a certain process when borrowing funds. A business that wants to borrow must show creditworthiness by undergoing a credit check. A credit rating of good, average, or poor is then assigned to the business. Like an individual who borrows money, a business must pay interest on its loan and repay it within a stated period of time. As you read this section, you'll learn about the financing options from which businesses may choose.

## SECTION 2 RESOURCE MANAGER

**Reproducible Masters**
- Reproducible Lesson Plan 10–2
- Reading Essentials and Study Guide 10–2
- Guided Reading Activity 10–2
- Section Quiz 10–2
- Daily Focus Activity 47
- Daily Lecture Notes 10–2

**Multimedia**
- Daily Focus Transparency 47
- Vocabulary PuzzleMaker
- Interactive Tutor Self-Assessment Software
- ExamView® Pro Testmaker
- MindJogger Videoquiz
- Interactive Economics!
- Presentation Plus!

## Three Kinds of Financing

Raising money for a business through borrowing, or **debt financing,** can be divided into three categories: short-term, intermediate-term, and long-term financing.

**debt financing:** *raising money for a business through borrowing*

**Short-Term Financing** When a business borrows money for any period of time less than a year, it has obtained **short-term financing. Figure 10.3** describes several types of short-term

**short-term financing:** *money borrowed by a business for any period of time less than a year*

### FIGURE 10.3 Short-Term Financing

**Trade Credit**

*Trade credit* is extended by one firm to another business buying the firm's goods. It allows the buyer to take possession of goods immediately and pay for them at some future date—usually 30 to 90 days later.

Businesses often receive a discount—2 percent, for example—if they pay their bill within 10 days. If a business does not repay the bill in that amount of time, it is, in effect, paying 2 percent interest for the use of the trade credit.

**Unsecured Loans**

Most short-term bank credit for businesses is in the form of unsecured bank loans. These are loans not guaranteed by anything other than the promise to repay them.

The borrower must sign a *promissory note* to repay the money in full by a specified time and with a specified rate of interest. The usual repayment period is one year.

**Secured Loans**

Secured loans are backed by *collateral*—something of value that borrowers will lose if they do not repay a loan. Businesses offer as collateral property such as machinery, inventories, or *accounts receivable*—money owed to a business by its customers.

**Line of Credit**

A *line of credit* is a maximum amount of money a company can borrow from a bank during a period of time, usually one year.

Rather than apply each time for a loan, a company may automatically borrow up to the amount of the line of credit—$100,000, for example.

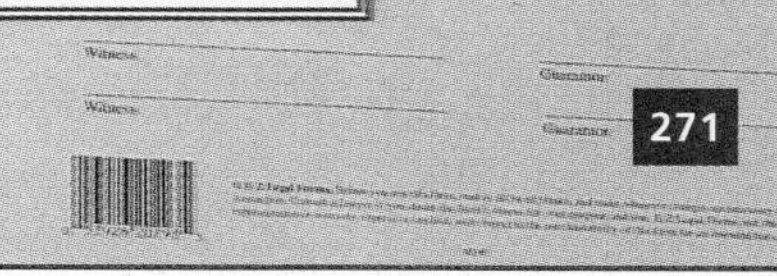



## Meeting Special Needs

**Reading Disability** Students with reading or organizational problems may have trouble classifying the different types of financing. Have students draw cartoons or other visuals to illustrate the different forms of financing. For example, for *line of credit,* students might draw several people waiting in line at a window labeled "Credit." Remind students to give a title to each of their visuals. Also, suggest that they use different colored paper for short-term, intermediate-term, and long-term financing. The combination of symbols, words, and colors will help students distinguish and group the various forms of financing. ELL

 Refer to *Inclusion for the Social Studies Classroom Strategies and Activities*.

# 2 Teach

## Guided Practice

**L1 Categorizing Ideas** On the board, draw a four-column table with "Type of Financing," "Period of Borrowing," "Examples," and "Why Used?" as column headings. Organize students into four groups, and assign one of the columns to each group. Have group members consult and then send a representative to the board to enter information into their assigned column. Have students copy the completed table into their notebooks. Suggest that they retain the chart for review purposes.

### Daily Lecture Notes 10–2

DAILY LECTURE NOTES 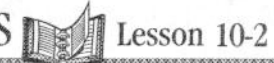 Lesson 10-2

**LECTURE LAUNCHER**

Small businesses provide 67% of workers with their first jobs and initial on the job training in basic skills. Since 1953, the U.S. Small Business Administration (SBA) has provided financial, technical and management assistance to help Americans start and grow their businesses. With a portfolio of business loans, loan guarantees, and disaster loans worth more than $45 billion, the SBA is the nation's largest single financial backer of small business. What kinds of financing are available to businesses?

PAGES 271–274

I. Three Kinds of Financing
   A. Short-Term Financing is when the term of loan is less than one year; used for short-term needs.
   B. Intermediate-Term Financing is when the term of the loan is 1 to 10 years; used when a company wants to expand through land, buildings or equipment.
   C. Long-Term Financing is when the term of loan is longer than 10 years; used for major expansion.

**Discussion Question**

**Suppose you own a printing shop. For what types of expenses would you be likely to take out short-term loans? Explain your reasoning.** *(Answers may vary, but students should suggest items that are paid for and used up quickly. They should also explain how the*

### Visual Instruction FIGURE 10.3

Direct students to the Trade Credit section of **Figure 10.3.** Point out that trade credit accounts for more than half of all business-to-business transactions involving goods. Buyers do not have to tie up money capital in inventory, while sellers increase their sales.

## Visual Instruction FIGURE 10.4

Have students read the information in **Figure 10.4.** Then mention that in recent years many companies have begun to lease, rather than buy, computers and related equipment. Computing technology is developing so rapidly that a machine may be outdated within a year or two. Therefore, a short-term lease, rather than a loan to purchase equipment, may be more cost-effective.

## Guided Reading Activity 10-2

Name ______ Date ______ Class ______

GUIDED READING Activity 10-2

*For use with the textbook pages 270–275*

TYPES OF FINANCING FOR BUSINESS OPERATIONS

OUTLINING

***Directions:** Locate the heading in your textbook. Then use the information under the heading to help you write each answer.*

I. Three Kinds of Financing
  A. Introduction—What are the three categories of debt-financing?
  B. Short-term Financing
    1. What is short-term financing?
    2. Why do companies seek short-term financing?
  C. Intermediate-Term Financing
    1. How long is the borrowing period for intermediate-term financing?
    2. What is a disadvantage of taking a long-term lease instead of a loan?
  D. Long-Term Financing

## Independent Practice

**L3 Writing a Report** Have students research and write a report on the trends in corporate financing from the early 1980s to today. Suggest that, when writing their reports, students take into consideration the impact of the general state of the economy on these trends. Call on volunteers to read their reports and discuss their findings.

## FIGURE 10.4 Intermediate-Term Financing

### Loans

Intermediate-term loans have repayment periods of from 1 to 10 years and generally require collateral such as stocks, bonds, equipment, or machinery. The loan is considered a mortgage if it is secured by property such as the building in which the business is located. Sometimes large, financially sound companies may be able to get unsecured intermediate-term loans.

### Leasing

*Leasing* means renting rather than buying—whether it is a building, machinery, or the like. One advantage of leasing is that the leasing company will often service the machinery at low cost. Another advantage is that the business may deduct a part of the money spent on a lease before figuring income taxes. A disadvantage is that a lease often costs more than borrowing to buy the same equipment.

financing. A business may seek short-term financing for many reasons. A company may have excellent business during the month but not be paid until the beginning of the following month. In the meantime, the company needs funds to pay salaries and its bills. During a growing season, a farmer may have to borrow to buy seed, repair equipment, and pay workers.

**intermediate-term financing:** *money borrowed by a business for 1 to 10 years*

**Intermediate-Term Financing** Borrowing money for 1 to 10 years is considered **intermediate-term financing.** When a company wants to expand its business by buying more land, buildings, or equipment, short-term financing generally is not adequate. For example, if you decided to expand your electronics repair business by opening another shop, you would not apply for a 90-day loan. In 90 days, you would not be able to do enough repair jobs to earn the additional revenue to repay the loan. Instead, you would look for intermediate-term financing such as described in **Figure 10.4.**



## Cooperative Learning

Organize students into several groups, and have groups review recent copies of business periodicals, such as *Business Week, Forbes,* and *Fortune,* and the business sections of newspapers to find articles about companies' plans to expand. Ask groups to write synopses of these articles, paying close attention to how the companies plan to finance expansion. Direct groups to create bulletin-board displays with their articles and synopses.

**Long-Term Financing** Borrowing for longer than 10 years is called **long-term financing.** Long-term financing is used for major expansion, such as building a new plant or buying expensive, long-lasting machines to replace outdated ones. For financing debts lasting 10 to 15 years or more, corporations either issue stock or sell bonds. **Figure 10.5** describes bonds and stocks as

**long-term financing:** *money borrowed by a business for a period of more than 10 years*

## FIGURE 10.5 Long-Term Financing

### Bonds

Bonds promise to pay a stated rate of interest over a stated period of time, and to repay the full amount borrowed at the end of that time.

### Stocks

Selling stock is called *equity financing,* because part of the ownership, or equity, of the company is being sold. Corporations may sell either preferred or common stock. The differences between these types of stock are explained below.

| Common Stock | Preferred Stock |
|---|---|
| **1.** Common stock is issued by all public corporations; it is the stock most often bought and sold. | **1.** Many corporations do not issue preferred stock. |
| **2.** Holders of common stock have voting rights in a corporation. As a group, they elect the board of directors. | **2.** Holders of preferred stock generally have no voting rights. |
| **3.** Common stock may pay dividends based on a corporation's performance. If the company does well, dividends may be high; if it does poorly, the dividends may be low or zero. | **3.** Preferred stock pays a fixed dividend. This amount must be paid before holders of common stock receive any dividends. If a company is unable to pay a fixed dividend on time, it must usually make up the missed payment at a later date. |
| **4.** The value of common stock rises and falls in relation to the corporation's performance and what investors expect it to do in the future. | **4.** The value of preferred stock changes in relation to how well the company is doing. |
| **5.** If a corporation fails, holders of common stock are the last to be paid with whatever money is left after paying all creditors. | **5.** If a corporation fails, holders of preferred stock must be paid before any holders of common stock are paid, but bondholders are paid before any stockholders. |

### Visual Instruction FIGURE 10.5

Have students review the information in **Figure 10.5.** Then point out that long-term financing usually is used when the useful life of the building or equipment being purchased matches or exceeds the length of the debt. For example, a company would purchase a ship with long-term financing because the useful life of the ship will match the length of the long-term debt.

### INTERACTIVE ECONOMICS!

**LESSON 10: PERSONAL FINANCE**

Have students study the Lesson 10 "Tutorial," which focuses on stocks, stock markets, and mutual funds. Students will see how corporations and the stock market work. After students read the "Tutorial," have them complete the "Economics Lab" dealing with terms related to personal finance.

Supplied in both CD-ROM and disk formats.

### Critical Thinking Activity

**Applying Ideas** Ask students to suggest how the following situations might affect a company's debt financing decisions.

1. Interest rates are high. *The company may be reluctant to borrow at high interest rates. It may also be reluctant to issue bonds, since it will have to offer high interest rates to attract investors.*
2. Interest rates start to fall. *The company will be willing to borrow at lower interest rates. Also, it will be willing to issue bonds, since it will not have to offer high interest rates to attract investors.*

# 3 Assess

## Meeting Lesson Objectives

Assign Section 2 Assessment as homework or an in-class activity.

Use **Interactive Tutor Self-Assessment Software** to review Section 2.

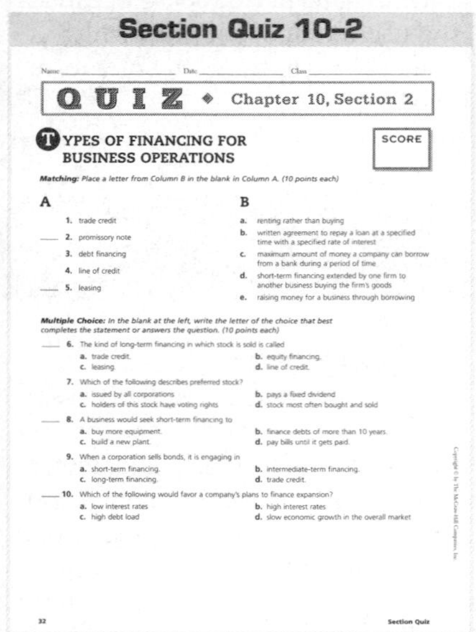

**Section Quiz 10-2**

Name ____________ Date ____________ Class ____________

**QUIZ** ◆ Chapter 10, Section 2

**TYPES OF FINANCING FOR BUSINESS OPERATIONS**

SCORE

***Matching:*** *Place a letter from Column B in the blank in Column A. (10 points each)*

| A | B |
|---|---|
| ____ 1. trade credit | a. renting rather than buying |
| ____ 2. promissory note | b. written agreement to repay a loan at a specified time with a specified rate of interest |
| ____ 3. debt financing | c. maximum amount of money a company can borrow from a bank during a period of time |
| ____ 4. line of credit | d. short-term financing extended by one firm to another business buying the firm's goods |
| ____ 5. leasing | e. raising money for a business through borrowing |

***Multiple Choice:*** *In the blank at the left, write the letter of the choice that best completes the statement or answers the question. (10 points each)*

____ 6. The kind of long-term financing in which stock is sold is called
a. trade credit. b. equity financing.
c. leasing. d. line of credit.

____ 7. Which of the following describes preferred stock?
a. issued by all corporations b. pays a fixed dividend
c. holders of this stock have voting rights d. stock most often bought and sold

____ 8. A business would seek short-term financing to
a. buy more equipment. b. finance debts of more than 10 years.
c. build a new plant. d. pay bills until it gets paid.

____ 9. When a corporation sells bonds, it is engaging in
a. short-term financing. b. intermediate-term financing.
c. long-term financing. d. trade credit.

____ 10. Which of the following would favor a company's plans to finance expansion?
a. low interest rates b. high interest rates
c. high debt load d. slow economic growth in the overall market



32 Section Quiz

methods of long-term financing. Usually only large corporations finance long-term debt by selling bonds. Unlike smaller companies, large corporations with huge assets appear to be better risks to investors who are interested in buying bonds.

## Choosing the Right Financing

Financial managers try to obtain capital at a minimum cost to the company. To do so, they try to choose the best mix of financing. The length of a loan that a company takes out or a corporation's decision regarding whether to sell bonds or issue stock depends on four factors. These factors are the costs of interest, the financial condition of the company, the overall economic climate, and the opinions of the company's owners.

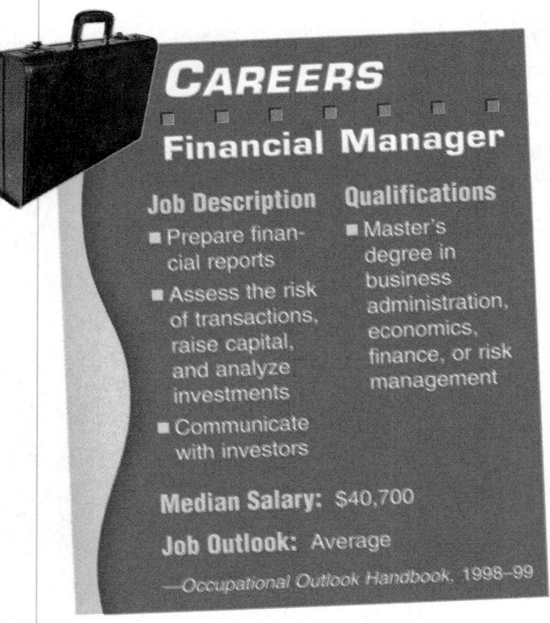


**Interest Costs** When interest rates in general are high, a business may be reluctant to take out a loan. A company may delay its expansion until it can borrow at better interest rates. Or it may take out a series of short-term loans at high rates, hoping that interest rates will drop. When that happens, the company will then take out a long-term loan.

Interest rates also affect the decision to issue bonds. When rates are high, corporations must offer high rates of interest on their bonds to attract investors. When interest rates drop overall, corporations can offer lower rates of return on their bonds.

**Financial Condition of the Company** A company or corporation whose sales and profits are stable or are expected to increase can safely take on more debt—if its current debt is not too large. Financial managers use cost-benefit analysis to determine if the potential profits will cover the cost of financing expansion.

**Market Climate** As shown in **Figure 10.6,** financial managers need to be aware of the market climate when determining whether to sell bonds or issue stock to raise financing. If economic growth in the overall market appears to be slow, investors



### Visual Learning Activity

**Graphic Organizer** Have students use a graphic organizer similar to the one here to describe the three kinds of debt financing available to companies. Direct them to place "Types of Financing" in the central oval, the three types of financing in the intermediate ovals, and examples of these types in the outer ovals.

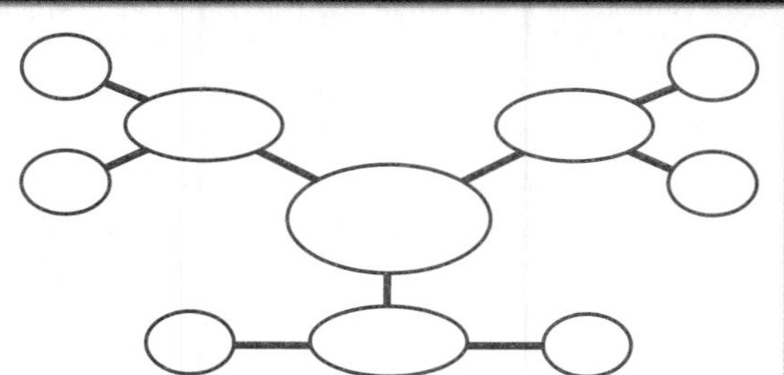

**FIGURE 10.6**

**Market Climate** Business managers must keep an eye on the market climate before obtaining financing. High interest rates combined with a slow economy could spell disaster for a business interested in expanding.

may prefer the fixed rate of return of bonds or preferred stock to the unknown return on common stock.

**Control of the Company** Bonds do not have voting rights attached to them. Most preferred stocks also do not give voting rights to shareholders. The owners of common stocks, however, do have the right to vote in company elections. When debating issues of financing, financial managers may have to gain approval from the owners of common stocks before taking action.

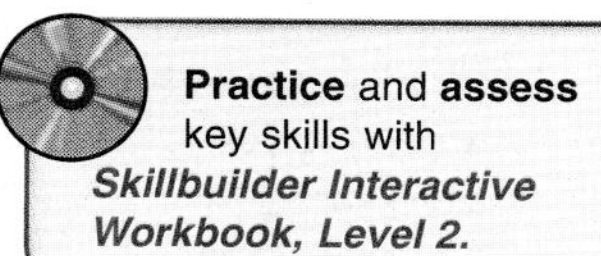

**Practice** and **assess** key skills with *Skillbuilder Interactive Workbook, Level 2.*

## SECTION 2 Assessment

### Understanding Key Terms

1. **Define** debt financing, short-term financing, intermediate-term financing, long-term financing.

### Reviewing Objectives

2. What are three general kinds of debt financing?
3. **Graphic Organizer** Use a diagram like the one in the next column to describe the four factors that affect a company's decision either to obtain financing in the form of loans or to sell bonds or issue stock.

Factors Affecting Loan Choices

### Applying Economic Concepts

4. **Economic Institutions** If you were starting a T-shirt business with limited funds, what type of short-term financing would you pursue first? Why?

### Critical Thinking Activity

5. **Making Comparisons** Write a paragraph describing the difference between secured and unsecured loans.





## Reteach

Have students write a paragraph comparing the three kinds of debt financing available to companies.

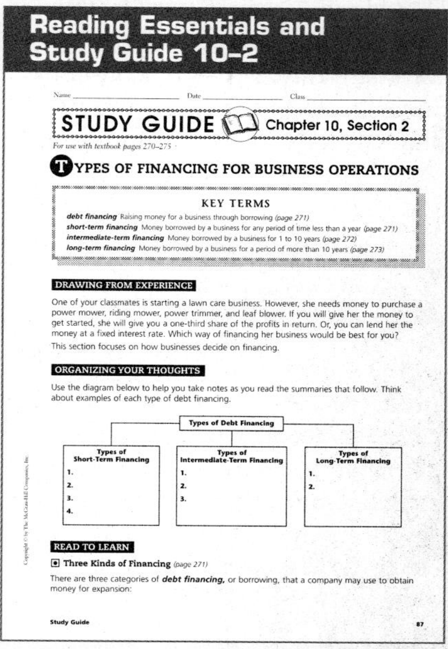

Reading Essentials and Study Guide 10-2

Name ______ Date ______ Class ______

STUDY GUIDE Chapter 10, Section 2

For use with textbook pages 270–275

TYPES OF FINANCING FOR BUSINESS OPERATIONS

KEY TERMS

***debt financing*** Raising money for a business through borrowing *(page 271)*
***short-term financing*** Money borrowed by a business for any period of time less than a year *(page 271)*
***intermediate-term financing*** Money borrowed by a business for 1 to 10 years *(page 272)*
***long-term financing*** Money borrowed by a business for a period of more than 10 years *(page 273)*

DRAWING FROM EXPERIENCE

One of your classmates is starting a lawn care business. However, she needs money to purchase a power mower, riding mower, power trimmer, and leaf blower. If you will give her the money to get started, she will give you a one-third share of the profits in return. Or, you can lend her the money at a fixed interest rate. Which way of financing her business would be best for you?

This section focuses on how businesses decide on financing.

ORGANIZING YOUR THOUGHTS

Use the diagram below to help you take notes as you read the summaries that follow. Think about examples of each type of debt financing.

Types of Debt Financing

| Types of Short-Term Financing | Types of Intermediate-Term Financing | Types of Long-Term Financing |
|---|---|---|
| 1. | 1. | 1. |
| 2. | 2. | 2. |
| 3. | 3. | |
| 4. | | |

READ TO LEARN

**Three Kinds of Financing** *(page 271)*

There are three categories of ***debt financing,*** or borrowing, that a company may use to obtain money for expansion:



Study Guide 87

## 4 Close

Have students create posters illustrating the four factors that influence companies' debt financing decisions.

## SECTION 2 Assessment Answers

1. All definitions can be found in the Glossary.
2. short-term, intermediate-term, and long-term financing
3. Four factors that affect a company's financing plans are interest costs, financial conditions of the company, market climate, and control of the company.
4. Answers may vary. Many students will suggest trade credit, since they have limited funds to spend on inventory.
5. Paragraphs should cover the following points: An unsecured loan is not guaranteed by anything but the promise to repay. The borrower must sign a promissory note to repay the money in full by a specified time and with a specified rate of interest. Secured loans are backed by collateral. Businesses offer property such as machinery, inventories, or accounts receivable as collateral. If a secured loan is not repaid, the lender may claim the collateral.

## Background

Point out that Thomas Sowell began his teaching career in the 1960s. Since that time he has taught at leading universities in the United States, Singapore, Israel, Switzerland, and Germany. Although trained as an economist, Sowell has written extensively on many other subjects, including world history, sociology, politics, and the law.

# Teach

Ask students to read the excerpt and to note how Sowell applies economic concepts to higher education in the United States. Then assign the **Checking for Understanding** questions. After students have completed the assignment, lead them in a class discussion on the following: Should all aspects of life be ruled by economic concepts?

# People & Perspectives

## Thomas Sowell

*ECONOMIST (1930–)*

- **A Rose and Milton Friedman Senior Fellow, The Hoover Institution, Stanford University**
- **Columnist for *Forbes Magazine* and other periodicals; author of a nationally syndicated newspaper column**
- **Published books include *Conquests and Cultures* (1998), *Migrations and Cultures* (1998), and *Race and Culture: A World View* (1994)**

Economics professor and author Thomas Sowell is an outspoken commentator on political, economic, and social issues. Sowell suggests that many of the country's problems can be addressed by applying basic economic concepts to all aspects of life. In this excerpt, Sowell shows how the failure to apply inventory control or the law of supply and demand has created problems in education:

*"When anyone who owns a business discovers that unsold products are piling up on the shelf or in the warehouse, it doesn't take a rocket scientist to figure out that it is time to cut back production until the inventory declines.*

*But no such logic applies in the academic world.*

*Complaints about the excess number of PhDs in the humanities have gone on for years. Every year, for 12 consecutive years, American universities have broken all previous records for the number of PhDs awarded. . . . Forget about supply and demand when it comes to academia.*

*Ironically, doctorates in science, engineering and mathematics have come down somewhat in recent years, even though American companies are recruiting engineers from India, Russia and other places. But in English, history, and other humanities fields, the graduate schools are flooding the market with people for whom there are no jobs."*

—excerpted from the *Jewish World Review*, February 18, 1999

### *Checking for Understanding*

1. **According to Sowell, how has a lack of inventory control created the situation where there are too many PhDs?**
2. **Do you think the subjects university students study should be determined by economic concepts? Why or why not?**
3. **If you were in a position of authority on a college campus, how would you resolve the dilemma?**



### Answers to *Checking for Understanding*

1. There is little call for humanities PhDs in the job market, yet the number of humanities PhDs awarded continues to increase. If inventory control were applied to this situation, no more humanities PhDs would be awarded until those already holding the degree had found jobs.
2. Answers will vary. Ensure that students offer reasons for their answers.
3. Answers will vary. Ensure that students' resolutions are realistic.

SECTION 3

# The Production Process

## Cover Story

*The New York Times*, April 19, 1999

Each month, a purchasing agent for BOC Gases in Murray Hill, New Jersey, logs on to the Internet and looks for a bargain. In this case, the bargain involves not only the price of the product, but an entire cost-saving process set in motion when the on-screen "order" button is clicked.

Nearly 7,000 miles away from New Jersey, in a Japanese gas processing plant, a BOC supplier receives the million-dollar order. . . . And within minutes, a BOC distribution center in San Diego receives electronic notice from Japan that the shipment is on the way.

### Reader's Guide

**Terms to Know**
- production
- consumer goods
- mechanization
- assembly line
- division of labor
- automation
- robotics

**Reading Objectives**
1. What are the four major steps in production operations?
2. How has technology changed production methods since the early 1800s?

After businesses obtain the necessary financing, they can begin production. **Production** is the process of changing resources into goods that satisfy the needs and wants of individuals and other businesses. As noted in the *Cover Story* above, production also involves careful planning in getting raw materials from suppliers on time. As you read this section, you'll learn about all the steps in the production process.

<u>production:</u> *process of changing resources into goods that satisfy the needs and wants of individuals and businesses*

## Steps in Production Operations

Businesses may produce **consumer goods**, or goods sold directly to individuals to be used as they are. As you learned in Chapter 1, businesses may also produce *capital goods*, which are

<u>consumer goods:</u> *goods produced for individuals and sold directly to the public to be used as they are*



## SECTION 3 RESOURCE MANAGER

**Reproducible Masters**
- Reproducible Lesson Plan 10–3
- Reading Essentials and Study Guide 10–3
- Guided Reading Activity 10–3
- Section Quiz 10–3
- Daily Focus Activity 48
- Daily Lecture Notes 10–3

**Multimedia**
- Daily Focus Transparency 48
- Economic Concepts Transparency 3
- Vocabulary PuzzleMaker
- Interactive Tutor Self-Assessment Software
- ExamView® Pro Testmaker
- MindJogger Videoquiz
- Presentation Plus!

# 1 Focus

## Overview

**Section 3** describes the four steps in production operations and discusses the impact of technology on production methods.

### BELLRINGER
**Motivational Activity**

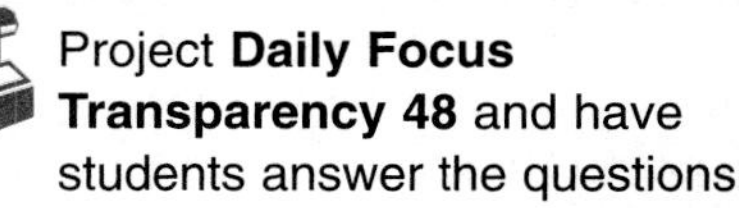

Project **Daily Focus Transparency 48** and have students answer the questions.

This activity is also available as a blackline master.

**Daily Focus Transparency 48**

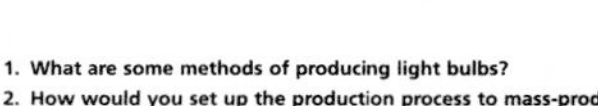

1. What are some methods of producing light bulbs?
2. How would you set up the production process to mass-produce light bulbs?
Daily Focus Transparencies


### Reader's Guide

Answers to the **Reading Objectives** questions are on page 281.

**Preteaching Vocabulary**

Group the **Terms to Know** as follows: 1. production, consumer goods; 2. mechanization, assembly line, division of labor; 3. automation, robotics. Have students show how the terms in each of the groupings are related by using them together in a sentence.

Vocabulary PuzzleMaker

# 2 Teach

## Guided Practice

**L2 Demonstrating Ideas** After reviewing the text under the heading "Steps in Production Operations," organize students into several small groups. Assign each group one of the steps: planning, purchasing, quality control, and inventory control. Ask groups to develop a scenario that illustrates their assigned step in production operations. Call on groups to present their scenarios. After the presentations are completed, lead the class in a discussion of the importance of the steps in creating a successful business.

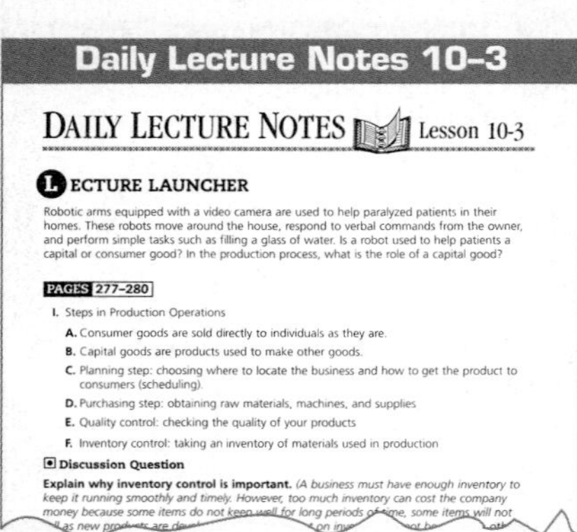

**Daily Lecture Notes 10-3**

DAILY LECTURE NOTES Lesson 10-3

**LECTURE LAUNCHER**

Robotic arms equipped with a video camera are used to help paralyzed patients in their homes. These robots move around the house, respond to verbal commands from the owner, and perform simple tasks such as filling a glass of water. Is a robot used to help patients a capital or consumer good? In the production process, what is the role of a capital good?

PAGES 277–280

I. Steps in Production Operations
   - **A.** Consumer goods are sold directly to individuals as they are.
   - **B.** Capital goods are products used to make other goods.
   - **C.** Planning step: choosing where to locate the business and how to get the product to consumers (scheduling).
   - **D.** Purchasing step: obtaining raw materials, machines, and supplies
   - **E.** Quality control: checking the quality of your products
   - **F.** Inventory control: taking an inventory of materials used in production

**Discussion Question**

**Explain why inventory control is important.** *(A business must have enough inventory to keep it running smoothly and timely. However, too much inventory can cost the company money because some items do not keep well for long periods of time, some items will not*

### Visual Instruction FIGURE 10.7

Have students look carefully at Figure 10.7. ASK: What location factor do you think is involved in placing a sandwich shop next to a movie theater? *Nearness to markets–the audience leaving the theater is a ready market for the sandwich shop.*

**FIGURE 10.7**

**Business Location** Locating a sandwich shop next to a movie theater was a wise business decision. Location is the most important planning decision in starting a retail business.

products used to make other goods. The machines used to assemble automobiles are examples of capital goods.

Besides the actual manufacturing of a good, the production process for both types of goods involves several other operations. These include planning, purchasing, quality control, and inventory control. A fifth operation, product design, will be discussed in Chapter 11.

**Planning** Planning includes choosing a location for the business and scheduling production. *Where* a business is located, or perhaps even more important today–*how* the business will get its products to consumers–is directly related to how successful the business will be. Among the location factors to consider are nearness to markets, raw materials, labor supply, and transportation facilities.

For example, businesses that cater to young people should locate near teen hangouts, universities, and so on. See **Figure 10.7.** Businesses that use coal should locate near their required raw material–coal fields. Businesses that require many unskilled workers should locate near urban areas with a large supply of labor. Finally, a business needs to have access to a means of delivering its products–highways, railroads, airlines, and pipelines.

Scheduling production operations involves setting start and end times for each step in the production process. It includes checking the use of labor, machinery, and materials so that production moves smoothly.

**Purchasing** In order to do business, a company obviously needs the raw materials to produce its goods or offer its services. It also, however, must have machinery, office supplies, telephones, and so on. The people who purchase goods for a business have to decide what to buy, from whom, and at what price. See **Figure 10.8.** To get the best



### Meeting Special Needs

**Writing Disability** A few students who have significant difficulties with written expression may find taking notes virtually impossible. Appoint several "scribes" in the class, and provide them with carbon paper or carbonless copy paper. As the class works through Section 3, have the scribes take complete notes. (They can provide carbons to those who need them at the end of the lesson.) Have poorer note takers write only key words or phrases.

Refer to *Inclusion for the Social Studies Classroom Strategies and Activities* for students with different learning styles.

deal for the company, purchasers must find answers to such questions as:

- Is this the best price?
- Are these goods made well? Will they last?
- Does this supplier offer such services as equipment repair?
- Who pays shipping and insurance costs, and how will goods be shipped?
- How much time is there between ordering goods and receiving them?

**Quality Control** Quality control involves overseeing the grade or freshness of goods, their strength or workability, their construction or design, safety, adherence to federal or industry standards, and many other factors. Quality control systems can be as simple as testing one item per thousand produced or testing each product as it is finished. See **Figure 10.9** on page 280.

**Inventory Control** Almost all manufacturers and many service businesses, such as dry cleaners, need inventories of the materials they use in making their products or offering their services. A production line can come to a complete halt if inventory runs out. Manufacturers and businesses, such as supermarkets, also keep stockpiles of finished goods on hand for sale.

**FIGURE 10.8**

**Purchasing Decisions** Before purchasing goods and services from a supplier, a company must consider the price and quality of those goods as well as services, shipping, and delivery.

**A** Purchasing Inventory

**B** Purchasing Supplier Services

**C** Purchasing Shipping and Delivery Services

### Guided Reading Activity 10-3

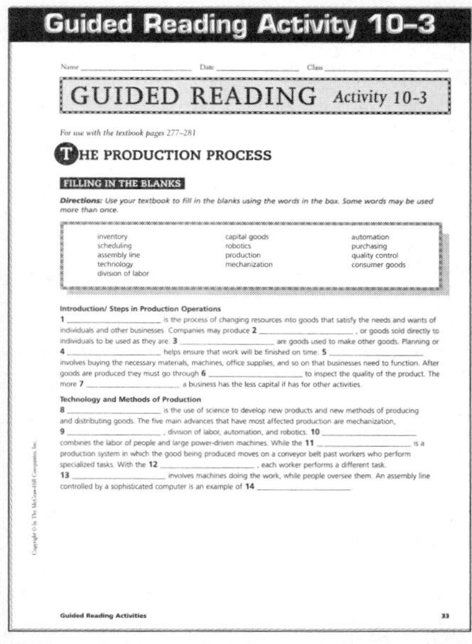

Name ________ Date ________ Class ________

GUIDED READING Activity 10-3

*For use with the textbook pages 277–281*

THE PRODUCTION PROCESS

FILLING IN THE BLANKS

***Directions:*** *Use your textbook to fill in the blanks using the words in the box. Some words may be used more than once.*

| | | |
|---|---|---|
| inventory | capital goods | automation |
| scheduling | robotics | purchasing |
| assembly line | production | quality control |
| technology | mechanization | consumer goods |
| division of labor | | |

**Introduction/ Steps in Production Operations**

**1** ________ is the process of changing resources into goods that satisfy the needs and wants of individuals and other businesses. Companies may produce **2** ________, or goods sold directly to individuals to be used as they are. **3** ________ are goods used to make other goods. Planning or **4** ________ helps ensure that work will be finished on time. **5** ________ involves buying the necessary materials, machines, office supplies, and so on that businesses need to function. After goods are produced they must go through **6** ________ to inspect the quality of the product. The more **7** ________ a business has the less capital it has for other activities.

**Technology and Methods of Production**

**8** ________ is the use of science to develop new products and new methods of producing and distributing goods. The five main advances that have most affected production are mechanization, **9** ________, division of labor, automation, and robotics. **10** ________ combines the labor of people and large power-driven machines. While the **11** ________ is a production system in which the good being produced moves on a conveyor belt past workers who perform specialized tasks. With the **12** ________, each worker performs a different task. **13** ________ involves machines doing the work, while people oversee them. An assembly line controlled by a sophisticated computer is an example of **14** ________.





Project Economic Concepts Transparency 3 and have students discuss the accompanying questions.

### Visual Instruction FIGURE 10.8

After students have studied Figure 10.8, ask: Why might a company purchase goods and services from several different suppliers? *This will encourage competition among the suppliers, resulting in lower prices for the goods and services purchased.*

## Cooperative Learning

Direct students to study the information on purchasing on pages 278–279. Then organize students into several groups, and have groups use this information to develop a format for interviewing purchasing agents about their decision-making procedures. Have each group conduct an interview with a purchasing agent at a company in the community. (Ensure that groups do not duplicate companies or types of businesses.) Have groups present the results of their interviews in brief reports. Encourage them to share and compare these reports.

## Independent Practice

**L2 Creating Time Lines** Have students work in small groups to create a time line showing how new technology has changed production methods in the United States. Suggest that groups make their time lines "oversize"—by taping together sheets of butcher paper. Also, have groups illustrate their time lines with sketches, photographs, charts, graphs, and other suitable visual materials. Direct groups to display their time lines along the classroom walls. ELL BLOCK SCHEDULING

## 3 Assess

### Meeting Lesson Objectives

Assign Section 3 Assessment as homework or an in-class activity.

Use **Interactive Tutor Self-Assessment Software** to review Section 3.

### Visual Instruction FIGURE 10.9

ASK: What might less quality control lead to? *Initially, it will lead to lower production costs and lower prices for consumers. However, it may also lead to a lowering of quality, and consumers may turn to other companies for products of higher quality.*

Inventories are costly, however. There is an opportunity cost involved in maintaining inventory. The more inventory a business has, the less capital it has for other activities. For example, it costs money to warehouse and insure goods against fire and theft. Some goods such as film and medicines spoil if kept beyond a certain period of time. Other goods such as cars and stylish clothes become obsolete, or out of date, in time.

**mechanization:** *combined labor of people and machines*

**assembly line:** *production system in which the good being produced moves on a conveyor belt past workers who perform individual tasks in assembling it*

**division of labor:** *breaking down of a job into small tasks performed by different workers*

**automation:** *production process in which machines do the work and people oversee them*

## Technology and Production

Technology is the use of science to develop new products and new methods for producing and distributing goods and services. From the time of the Industrial Revolution in the late 1700s, technology has changed the methods of production.

**Mechanization** The Industrial Revolution—the beginning of the factory system—came about through **mechanization,** which combines the labor of people and large power-driven machines. With the introduction of spinning and weaving machines in factories, entrepreneurs replaced skilled handiwork with machines run by unskilled workers. The rate of output per labor hour greatly increased as a result.

**FIGURE 10.9**

**Quality Control Trade-Off** The more time spent on quality control—such as this person inspecting vacuum cleaners—the higher the production costs.

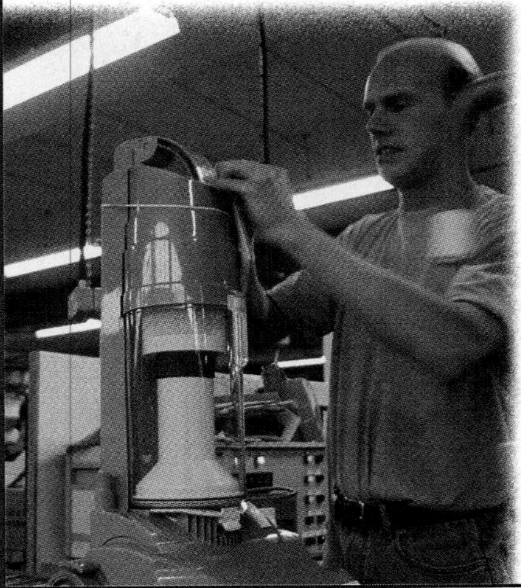

**The Assembly Line** An outgrowth of mechanization was the **assembly line.** An assembly line is a production system in which the good being produced moves on a conveyor belt past workers who perform individual tasks in assembling it. The Ford Motor Company developed the modern assembly-line process early in the twentieth century. Because the assembly line results in more efficient use of machines and labor, the costs of production drop.

**Division of Labor** Assembly-line production is only possible with interchangeable parts made in standard sizes, and with the **division of labor,** or the breaking down of a job into small tasks. A different worker performs each task.

**Automation** Mechanization combines the labor of people and machines. In **automation,** machines do the work and people oversee them. Automation is so common in American society that most of us don't even think about the efficiency of automated traffic signals, doors, or teller machines anymore.

### Extending the Content

**Inventory Control Trade-offs** When making decisions on how much inventory to keep on hand, inventory managers have other costs to consider. If a price of a particular good is expected to rise, the manager may stockpile it to keep down future costs. Often, a supplier will discount large orders, and these discounts may outweigh the other costs of keeping a large inventory.

## Economic Connection to...

# No More Waiting?

In computer science terminology, a "robot" is a software program that can scan E-mail messages to locate key words and phrases and respond appropriately without any human input. Companies that do business on the Internet use robots for all types of customer-service tasks—everything from tracking orders to offering troubleshooting tips. Many computer engineers believe that robots soon will be handling all routine customer questions. Waiting 20 minutes or longer on the telephone for a human customer-service representative may soon be a thing of the past! ■

**Robotics** ***Robotics*** refers to sophisticated, computer-controlled machinery that operates the assembly line. In some industries, robotics regulate every step of the manufacturing process–from the selection of raw materials to processing, packaging, and inventory control.

**robotics:** *sophisticated, computer-controlled machinery that operates an assembly line*

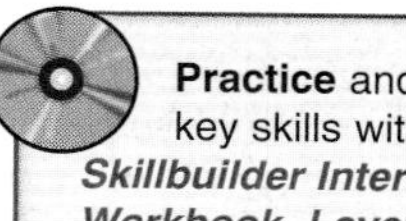

**Practice** and **assess** key skills with ***Skillbuilder Interactive Workbook, Level 2.***

## SECTION 3 Assessment

### Understanding Key Terms

1. **Define** production, consumer goods, mechanization, assembly line, division of labor, automation, robotics.

### Reviewing Objectives

2. What are the most important steps in the production process?
3. **Graphic Organizer** Use a diagram like the one below to explain the factors that have changed production since the early 1800s.

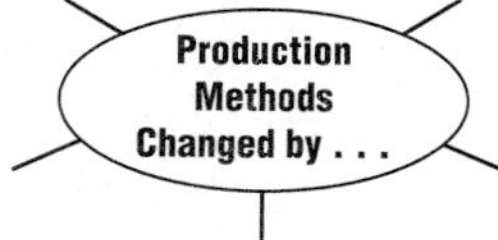


### Applying Economic Concepts

4. **Productivity** Imagine that you are financially prepared to open a small ice-cream cafe. Explain the steps you would follow to begin production. Include information about your planning, purchasing, quality control, and inventory control decisions in your explanation.

### Critical Thinking Activity

5. **Categorizing Information** Make a spreadsheet listing the five advances in technology discussed in this section. For one week, be aware of and count examples of each type of technology. At the end of each day, input your totals in the appropriate column of your spreadsheet. Tabulate your totals at the end of the week. Share your spreadsheet with the rest of the class.



## SECTION 3 Assessment Answers

1. All definitions can be found in the Glossary.
2. planning, purchasing, quality control, and inventory control
3. Factors that have changed production since the early 1800s are mechanization, assembly line, division of labor, automation, and robotics.
4. Most students will suggest that they would begin by planning—choosing a suitable location and developing a production schedule. Next, they would purchase all the materials needed for production—machinery and raw materials. After production was under way, they would check the quality of goods produced. Finally, they would decide what inventory—both materials needed for production and goods produced—to keep on the shelves.
5. Spreadsheets will vary.

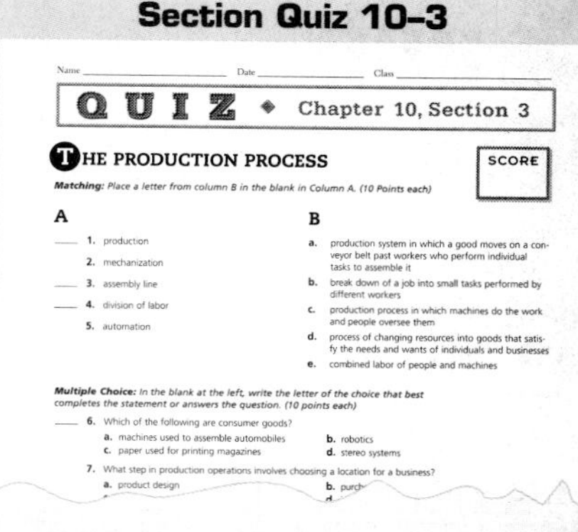

**Section Quiz 10–3**

Name ______ Date ______ Class ______

QUIZ ◆ Chapter 10, Section 3

THE PRODUCTION PROCESS — SCORE

*Matching: Place a letter from column B in the blank in Column A. (10 Points each)*

| A | B |
|---|---|
| ____ 1. production | a. production system in which a good moves on a conveyor belt past workers who perform individual tasks to assemble it |
| 2. mechanization | b. break down of a job into small tasks performed by different workers |
| ____ 3. assembly line | c. production process in which machines do the work and people oversee them |
| ____ 4. division of labor | d. process of changing resources into goods that satisfy the needs and wants of individuals and businesses |
| 5. automation | e. combined labor of people and machines |

*Multiple Choice: In the blank at the left, write the letter of the choice that best completes the statement or answers the question. (10 points each)*

____ 6. Which of the following are consumer goods?
a. machines used to assemble automobiles b. robotics
c. paper used for printing magazines d. stereo systems

7. What step in production operations involves choosing a location for a business?
a. product design b. purch

## Reteach

Ask students to write a summary of the section using the **Terms to Know.**

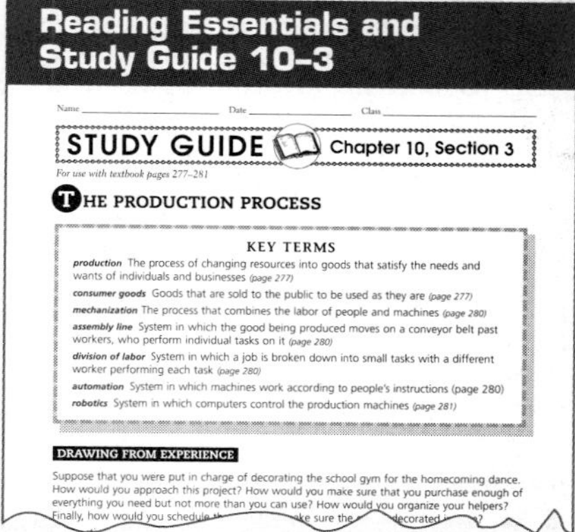

**Reading Essentials and Study Guide 10–3**

Name ______ Date ______ Class ______

STUDY GUIDE Chapter 10, Section 3

*For use with textbook pages 277–281*

THE PRODUCTION PROCESS

KEY TERMS

***production*** The process of changing resources into goods that satisfy the needs and wants of individuals and businesses *(page 277)*

***consumer goods*** Goods that are sold to the public to be used as they are *(page 277)*

***mechanization*** The process that combines the labor of people and machines *(page 280)*

***assembly line*** System in which the good being produced moves on a conveyor belt past workers, who perform individual tasks on it *(page 280)*

***division of labor*** System in which a job is broken down into small tasks with a different worker performing each task *(page 280)*

***automation*** System in which machines work according to people's instructions (page 280)

***robotics*** System in which computers control the production machines *(page 281)*

DRAWING FROM EXPERIENCE

Suppose that you were put in charge of decorating the school gym for the homecoming dance. How would you approach this project? How would you make sure that you purchase enough of everything you need but not more than you can use? How would you organize your helpers? Finally, how would you schedule ...

## 4 Close

Ask students to list the major financing and production decisions that businesses must make.

BusinessWeek
**SPOTLIGHT**

# Teach

In 1998 and 1999, UPS was rated the "World's Most Admired" mail, package, and freight delivery company in a *Fortune* magazine survey. For this survey, the magazine polled senior executives and board members of leading corporations, as well as Wall Street analysts. They were asked to rate companies on such features as quality of management, product or service quality, innovation, financial strength, and commitment to community and the environment.

**BusinessWeek ONLINE**

To find up-to-date news and analysis on the economy, business, technology, markets, entrepreneurs, investments, and finance, have students search feature articles and special reports on the *Business Week* Web site.
www.businessweek.com

**Sidelight**

The Fender stratocaster, with its unique body contour and one pickup out of line, is perhaps the most recognizable guitar in the world. Some of the greatest rock musicians played the "strat," including Buddy Holly, Jimmy Hendrix, Eric Clapton, and Kurt Cobain.

# BusinessWeek

## SPOTLIGHT ON THE ECONOMY

## Going All Out to Pick Up a Gig

**Check It Out! In this chapter you learned that businesses must make wise decisions when selecting a supplier to ship raw materials as well as finished goods. In this article, read to learn how the Fender guitar company made a very wise decision when it selected a shipping agent.**

Who says service is dead? When a big outfit like United Parcel Service is willing to hire a bunch of Dutch rockers to tune a client's guitars, you know that some companies still will do anything to keep a customer happy.

UPS Worldwide Logistics began shipping famed Fender guitars to Europe in April. As happens with stringed instruments, sometimes they arrived out of tune. Previously, the pricey guitars had been sent to 20 European distributors who tuned and tested them. But that was too costly and slow. So, to please Fender, UPS has hired four rock guitarists at its warehouse in [the city of] Roermond, the Netherlands, to do the job. "We've checked disk drives for IBM, but this was a unique challenge," says UPS project manager Ronald Klingeler.

The challenge, however, was met. In May, when the rock group Kiss played a Saturday night concert in Hamburg, it requested a new guitar on Friday—and got one, on time and in tune. Fender says the system will cut costs by 9% and delivery time from months to weeks. But life with a corporate-funded garage band is hard on some UPS guys. Says Klingeler: "When they see a really nice guitar, they always have this urge to try it out and play a song."



### Think About It

1. **What did the supplier (UPS) do to help the client (Fender)?**
2. **By using UPS, how much in production costs is Fender saving?**
3. **How was Fender's delivery time improved?**

### Answers to *Think About It*

1. UPS hired a rock band to tune and test Fender guitars at its warehouse in the Netherlands, rather than sending the guitars out to 30 European distributors for tuning and testing.
2. Fender is saving 9 percent of its production costs by using UPS.
3. Delivery time was cut from months to weeks.

# CHAPTER 10 Summary

Chapter Overview Visit the *Economics Today and Tomorrow* Web site at ett.glencoe.com and click on ***Chapter 10—Chapter Overviews*** to review chapter information.

## SECTION 1 Investing in the Free Enterprise System

- **Financing** business operations and growth is an integral part of our free enterprise system. It all begins with people who save by depositing their funds in a financial institution.
- Financial institutions, in turn, make these deposits available to businesses to finance growth and expansion.
- Businesses usually perform a **cost-benefit analysis** before deciding whether to pursue financing for expansion.
- A cost-benefit analysis involves estimating costs, calculating expected **revenues,** calculating expected **profits,** and calculating the costs of borrowing.

## SECTION 2 Types of Financing for Business Operations

- Raising money for a business through borrowing, or **debt financing,** can be divided into three categories based on length of time of repayment.
- **Short-term financing** is for those businesses that need funds to cover monthly or seasonal budget highs and lows.
- Borrowing money for 1 to 10 years to buy more land, buildings, or equipment is considered **intermediate-term financing.**
- **Long-term financing,** such as issuing stock and selling bonds, is used for major business expansion.
- Financial managers must examine interest costs, the market climate, and the financial condition of the company, as well as inform holders of common stock before obtaining financing.

## SECTION 3 The Production Process

- **Production** is the process of changing resources into goods that satisfy the needs and wants of individuals and other businesses.
- Producing **consumer goods** and capital goods involves planning, purchasing, quality control, and inventory control.
- Planning includes choosing a location for the business and scheduling production.
- The people who purchase goods for a business have to decide what to buy, from whom, and at what price.
- Five major advances in technology—**mechanization,** the **assembly line,** the **division of labor, automation,** and **robotics**—have drastically affected the methods and costs of production.



## Economics Journal

**The Production Process** Ask students to keep track of the consumer products that they use in their homes during a one-week period. At the end of the tracking period, have students select one of the products they listed. Have them investigate how the product is manufactured, how the manufacturer obtains raw materials and other productive resources, and where and how the product is produced. Direct students to present their findings in a brief written report.

# CHAPTER 10 Summary

**ECONOMICS & YOU**

Financing and Producing Goods

Chapter 19
Disc 1, Side 2

If you do not have access to a videodisc player, the ***Economics & You*** programs are also available in VHS.

Use the **Chapter 10 Summary** to preview, review, condense, or reteach the chapter.

## Preview/Review

**Vocabulary PuzzleMaker Software** reinforces the key terms used in Chapter 10.

**Interactive Tutor Self-Assessment Software** allows students to review Chapter 10 content.

## Condense

Have students listen to the Chapter 10 **Audio Program** (also available in Spanish) in the TCR. Assign the Chapter 10 Audio Program Activity and give students the Chapter 10 Audio Program Test.

## Reteach

Have students complete **Reteaching Activity** 10 in the TCR (Spanish Reteaching Activities are also available).

# CHAPTER 10 Assessment and Activities

ECONOMICS Online

Have students visit the *Economics Today and Tomorrow* Web site at ett.glencoe.com to review Chapter 10 and take the Self-Check Quiz.

**GLENCOE TECHNOLOGY**

 **MindJogger Videoquiz**

Use MindJogger to review Chapter 10 content.

## Identifying Key Terms

1. f
2. h
3. e
4. b
5. a
6. c
7. i
8. g
9. d

## Recalling Facts and Ideas

1. by depositing savings in a financial institution (in exchange for interest), which then loans funds to businesses (to finance growth and expansion)
2. Undertake a cost-benefit analysis–estimate all expected operating costs, calculate expected revenues, calculate expected profits, calculate the cost of financing, and determine if expected profits are greater than the cost of financing the operation.
3. to fill in during periods when cash is low and to finance the business while product is being produced–during a farmer's growing season, for example
4. long-term financing
5. Holders of common stock have voting rights in the corporation. As a group, they elect the board of governors.
6. planning, purchasing, and inventory control
7. movement of a product along a conveyor belt past workers who perform individual assembly tasks

## Thinking Critically

1. A saver can be a creditor by depositing funds in a financial institution or by purchasing stocks or bonds. A saver can be a debtor by taking out a loan from a financial institution or by issuing stock or bonds in his or her company.
2. Answers will vary, but most students will suggest that trade credit is the best financing approach in this instance.

# CHAPTER 10 Assessment and Activities

**Self-Check Quiz** Visit the *Economics Today and Tomorrow* Web site at ett.glencoe.com and click on ***Chapter 10—Self-Check Quizzes*** to prepare for the Chapter Test.

## Identifying Key Terms

*Write the letter of the definition in Column B that correctly defines each term in Column A.*

**Column A**

1. revenues
2. consumer goods
3. cost-benefit analysis
4. debt financing
5. profits
6. short-term financing
7. intermediate-term financing
8. assembly line
9. mechanization

**Column B**

a. the money earned after subtracting costs from revenues
b. raising money for a business through borrowing
c. trade credit and promissory notes are involved in this kind of financing
d. combining labor of people and machines
e. process that looks at actions and their benefits
f. total income from sales of output
g. enables workers to perform individual tasks more efficiently
h. sold directly to the public to be used as they are
i. leasing is typical in this kind of financing

## Recalling Facts and Ideas

**Section 1**

1. How do individuals turn savings into investments?
2. Outline the steps you would use in reaching a necessary financial decision.

**Section 2**

3. What are two reasons a business may need short-term financing?
4. Issuing stocks is a form of what type of financing?
5. Do holders of common stock have any rights in a corporation? Explain.

**Section 3**

6. Besides quality control, what other steps are involved in the production process?
7. What does assembly-line production require?

## Thinking Critically

1. **Categorizing Information** Use a diagram like the one below to describe how a saver can be both a creditor and a debtor.

2. **Synthesizing Information** Assume that you have to buy new inventory that you plan to sell off completely by the end of each month. Determine the most appropriate type of financing to use to buy this inventory.

## Applying Economic Concepts

**Making Financing Decisions** Imagine that you own a business. List at least five business expansions you would like to make to your company that would require financing. Explain after each type of business expansion, such as buying 10 desktop computers, what the appropriate type of financing might be. Explain your choices.

## Cooperative Learning Project

Organize into three groups, with each group working on one of the following topics. After the research is complete, each group will report its findings to the class.

A. **Division of Labor** The most famous example of the division of labor focuses on a pin factory, which Adam Smith discussed in his book *The Wealth of Nations*. Group A should do the following: (1) find the passage in the book about the pin factory; (2) develop a chart showing the elements of Adam Smith's arithmetic example; and (3) calculate the percentage increase in productivity due to the division of labor.

B. **Assembly-Line Techniques** This group can divide into two smaller groups. Group B1 will report on how Henry Ford developed the assembly-line process. Group B2 will look at what Eli Whitney developed with the use of interchangeable parts.

C. **Robotics** Group C will research how robotics developed and how much of American manufacturing uses robotics.

## Reviewing Skills

**Making Generalizations** Read the following excerpt, then make a generalization based on the reading.

*"Henry Ford introduced the first moving assembly line in 1913 at his Model T plant in Highland Park, Michigan. Different conveyor systems carried subcomponents to the main assembly line in a finely orchestrated manner. Before the advent of the assembly line, a Model T took more than 12 hours to produce and cost $950. By 1927, after numerous refinements, Model Ts were being turned out in less than half that time, with a price tag of $290 apiece."*

—*Business Week: 100 Years of Innovation*, Summer 1999

## Technology Activity

**Using the Internet** The Small Business Administration (SBA) was designed to help small businesses with short-term financing. Obtain information about the SBA on the Internet. Write an informative brochure for potential small business owners, describing how the SBA can help them get started.

## Analyzing the Global Economy

Engineers at the University of Pennsylvania unveiled the Electronic Numerical Integrator and Computer (ENIAC) for the U.S. government in 1946 to enable artillery men to aim their guns more accurately. ENIAC was made up of 30 separate units, weighed 30 tons, occupied 1,800 square feet, had 17,468 vacuum tubes, and could do nearly 400 multiplications per second. ENIAC, however, was not the first electronic computer. Research the earlier computers built in Britain and Germany.



# CHAPTER 10 Assessment and Activities

## Applying Economic Concepts

Answers will vary. Suggest that students do a quick cost-benefit analysis for each expansion.

## Cooperative Learning Project

Have groups document their research and present their results to the class.

## Reviewing Skills

Generalizations may vary. A possible response is: The assembly line greatly reduced the time and cost of making Model T Fords.

## Technology Activity

Have students share their brochures with the rest of the class.

## Analyzing the Global Economy

Have students present their findings in an illustrated report.

### Chapter Bonus Test Question

ASK: Why might corporations issue bonds and preferred stock rather than common stock when overall economic growth is slow? *Investors would find the fixed rate of return on bonds and preferred stock preferable to the uncertain return on common stock.*

## 1 Focus

Companies around the world spend well over a trillion dollars to market their goods and services. Fewer than 30 countries—most of them in Europe, the Pacific Rim, and North America—account for 90 percent of this spending. About one-third of all advertising dollars are spent by American companies.

## 2 Teach

Point out that each of the countries featured represents a particular level of exposure to advertising spending. Vietnam represents the lowest level, Kenya the next-to-lowest level, Egypt the intermediate level, Russia the next-to-highest level, and Singapore the highest level. (Mention that countries are graded on a per capita spending basis, not total spending.) Then have students compare spending categories among the countries. Ask them to explain why particular categories might be more widely used in some countries than in others.

### ? Did You Know

About one-third of all marketing dollars are spent on promotions—cents-off coupons, sweepstakes, give-aways, and so on—rather than regular advertising.

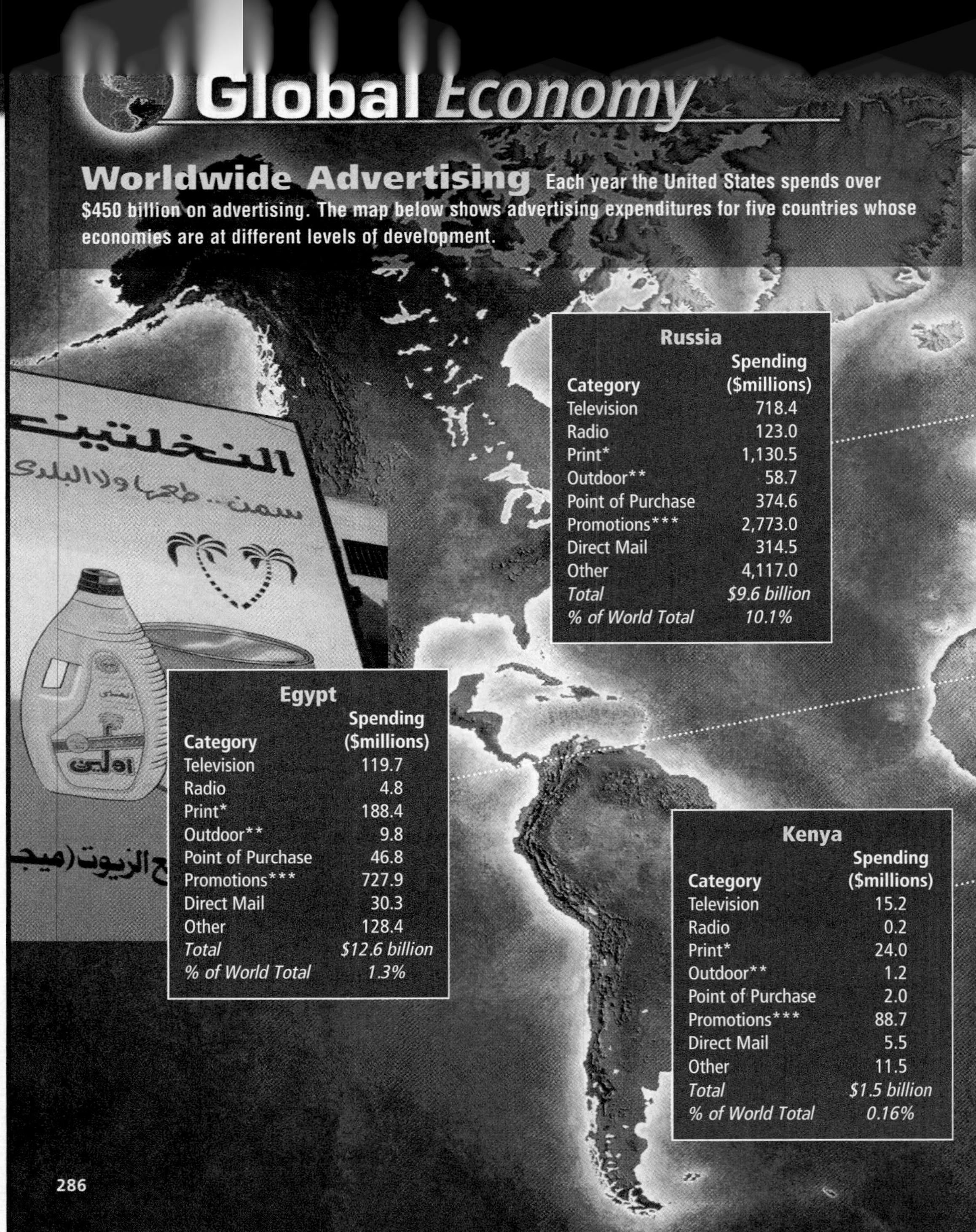

# Global Economy

**Worldwide Advertising** Each year the United States spends over $450 billion on advertising. The map below shows advertising expenditures for five countries whose economies are at different levels of development.

**Russia**

| Category | Spending ($millions) |
|---|---|
| Television | 718.4 |
| Radio | 123.0 |
| Print* | 1,130.5 |
| Outdoor** | 58.7 |
| Point of Purchase | 374.6 |
| Promotions*** | 2,773.0 |
| Direct Mail | 314.5 |
| Other | 4,117.0 |
| *Total* | *$9.6 billion* |
| *% of World Total* | *10.1%* |

**Egypt**

| Category | Spending ($millions) |
|---|---|
| Television | 119.7 |
| Radio | 4.8 |
| Print* | 188.4 |
| Outdoor** | 9.8 |
| Point of Purchase | 46.8 |
| Promotions*** | 727.9 |
| Direct Mail | 30.3 |
| Other | 128.4 |
| *Total* | *$12.6 billion* |
| *% of World Total* | *1.3%* |

**Kenya**

| Category | Spending ($millions) |
|---|---|
| Television | 15.2 |
| Radio | 0.2 |
| Print* | 24.0 |
| Outdoor** | 1.2 |
| Point of Purchase | 2.0 |
| Promotions*** | 88.7 |
| Direct Mail | 5.5 |
| Other | 11.5 |
| *Total* | *$1.5 billion* |
| *% of World Total* | *0.16%* |

286

### Extending the Content

Per capita spending on advertising varies widely between developed and less developed countries. In many of the less developed countries of Africa, Asia, and Latin America, less than $5 per person is spent on advertising. However, in Western Europe, the United States, Canada, Japan, and the stronger economies of the Pacific Rim, per capita spending on advertising stands at nearly $1,400. Japan spends the most per capita—$2,137—on advertising. Another Asian country, Laos, spends the least—just 41 cents.

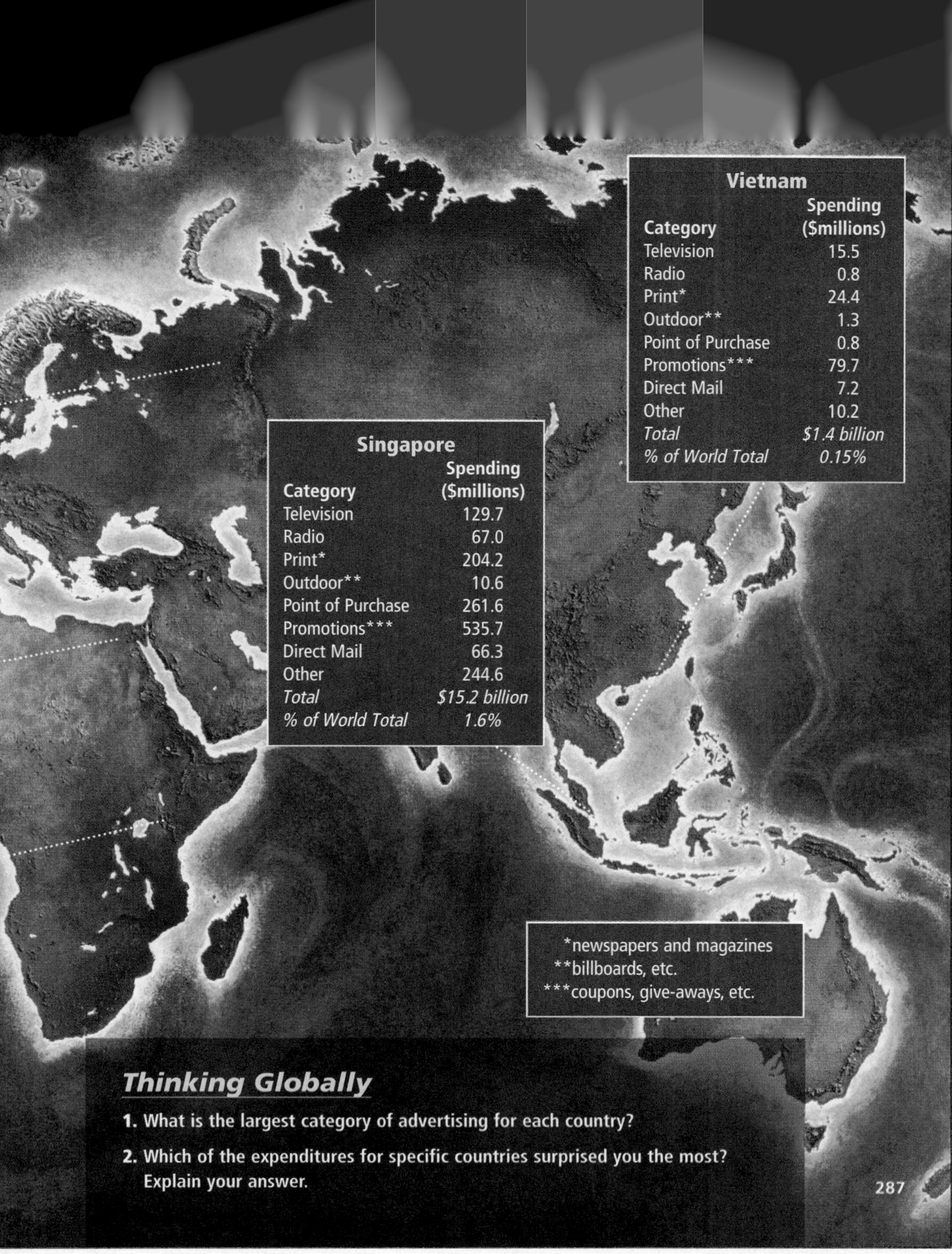

**Vietnam**

| Category | Spending ($millions) |
|---|---|
| Television | 15.5 |
| Radio | 0.8 |
| Print* | 24.4 |
| Outdoor** | 1.3 |
| Point of Purchase | 0.8 |
| Promotions*** | 79.7 |
| Direct Mail | 7.2 |
| Other | 10.2 |
| *Total* | *$1.4 billion* |
| *% of World Total* | *0.15%* |

**Singapore**

| Category | Spending ($millions) |
|---|---|
| Television | 129.7 |
| Radio | 67.0 |
| Print* | 204.2 |
| Outdoor** | 10.6 |
| Point of Purchase | 261.6 |
| Promotions*** | 535.7 |
| Direct Mail | 66.3 |
| Other | 244.6 |
| *Total* | *$15.2 billion* |
| *% of World Total* | *1.6%* |

*newspapers and magazines
**billboards, etc.
***coupons, give-aways, etc.

## *Thinking Globally*

1. What is the largest category of advertising for each country?
2. Which of the expenditures for specific countries surprised you the most? Explain your answer.



## Answers to *Thinking Globally*

1. promotions
2. Answers may vary. Ensure that students offer reasons for their answers.

# 3 Assess

Have students answer the **Thinking Globally** questions.

# 4 Close

Have students use library resources and the Internet to gather similar statistics for the United States. Suggest that they present these statistics in table form.

## ? Did You Know

About two-thirds of the advertising dollars spent around the world are used to market consumer goods and services. The other third is used by businesses to promote their products to other businesses.

# CHAPTER 11 Resource Manager

## Teaching Transparency

### Economic Concepts Transparency 5

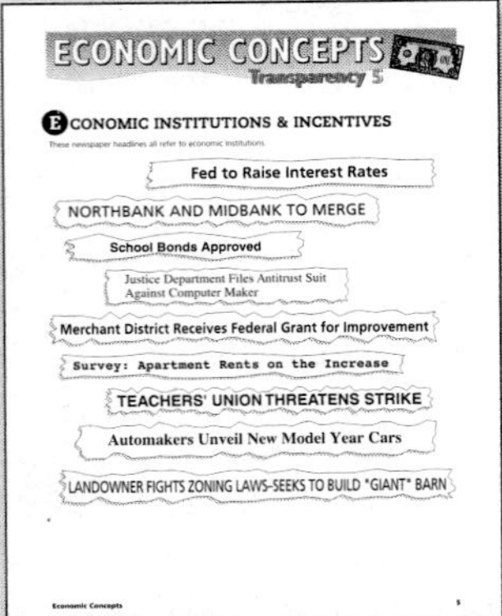

ECONOMIC CONCEPTS Transparency 5

ECONOMIC INSTITUTIONS & INCENTIVES

Fed to Raise Interest Rates

NORTHBANK AND MIDBANK TO MERGE

School Bonds Approved

Justice Department Files Antitrust Suit Against Computer Maker

Merchant District Receives Federal Grant for Improvement

Survey: Apartment Rents on the Increase

TEACHERS' UNION THREATENS STRIKE

Automakers Unveil New Model Year Cars

LANDOWNER FIGHTS ZONING LAWS–SEEKS TO BUILD "GIANT" BARN

## Application and Enrichment

### Enrichment Activity 11

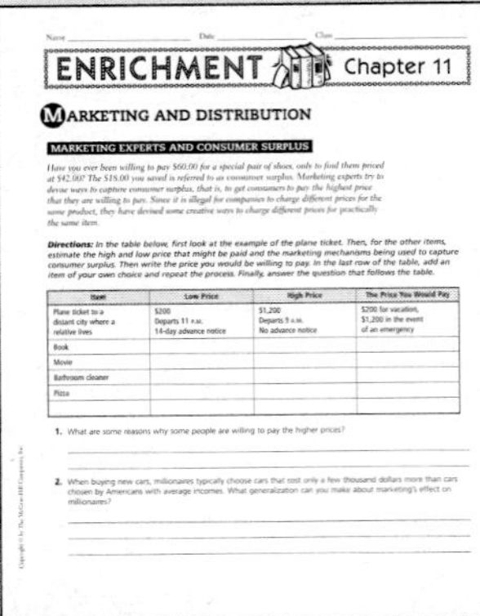

ENRICHMENT Chapter 11

MARKETING AND DISTRIBUTION

MARKETING EXPERTS AND CONSUMER SURPLUS

### Consumer Applications Activity 7

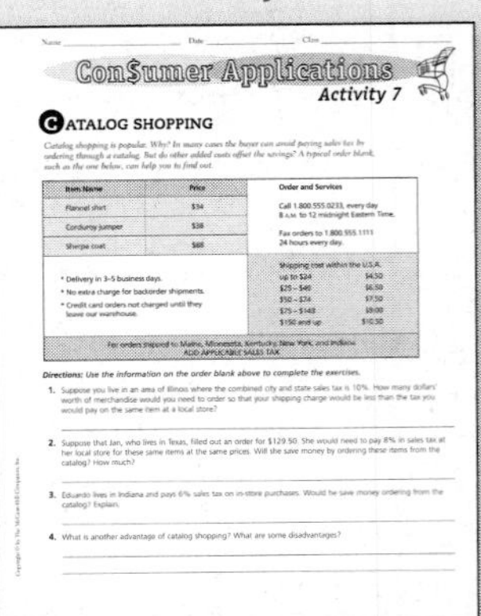

Consumer Applications Activity 7

CATALOG SHOPPING

### Free Enterprise Activity 4

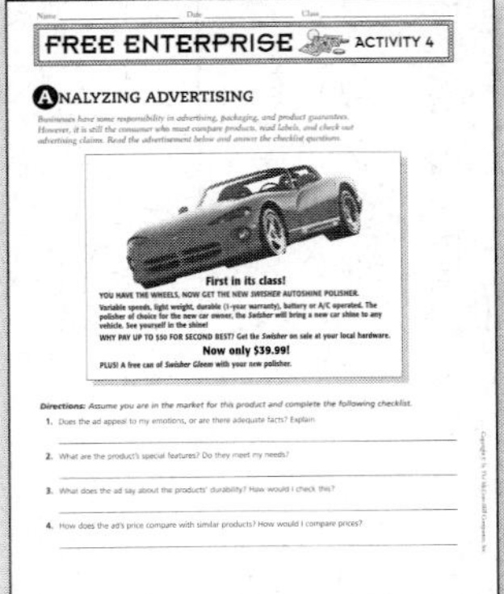

FREE ENTERPRISE ACTIVITY 4

ANALYZING ADVERTISING



## Application and Enrichment

### Cooperative Learning Simulations and Problems 7

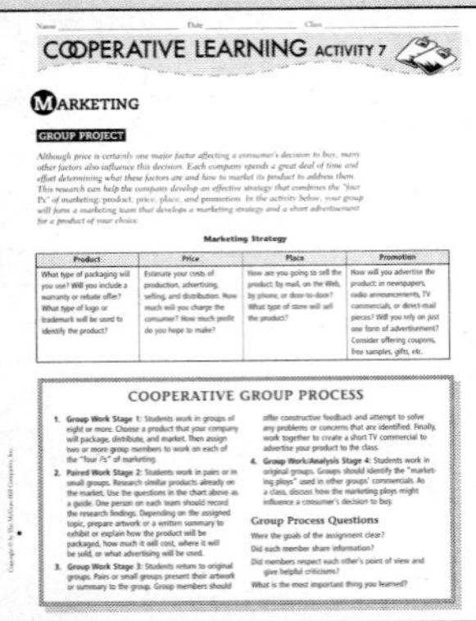

COOPERATIVE LEARNING ACTIVITY 7

MARKETING

GROUP PROJECT

Marketing Strategy

| Product | Price | Place | Promotion |
|---|---|---|---|

COOPERATIVE GROUP PROCESS

Group Process Questions

### Primary and Secondary Source Reading 7

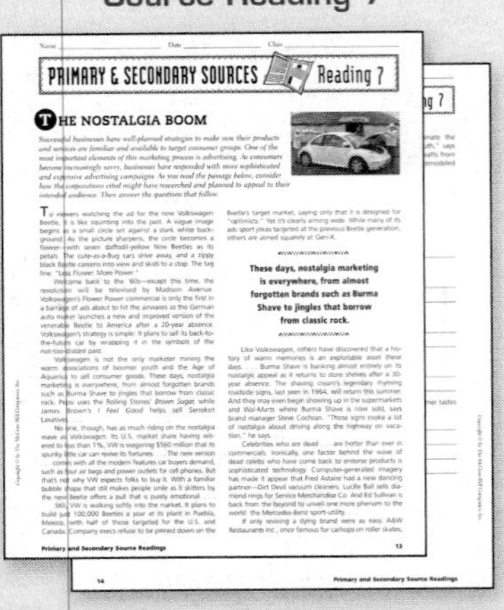

PRIMARY & SECONDARY SOURCES Reading 7

THE NOSTALGIA BOOM

These days, nostalgia marketing is everywhere, from almost forgotten brands such as Burma Shave to jingles that borrow from classic rock.

### Math Practice for Economics Activity 8

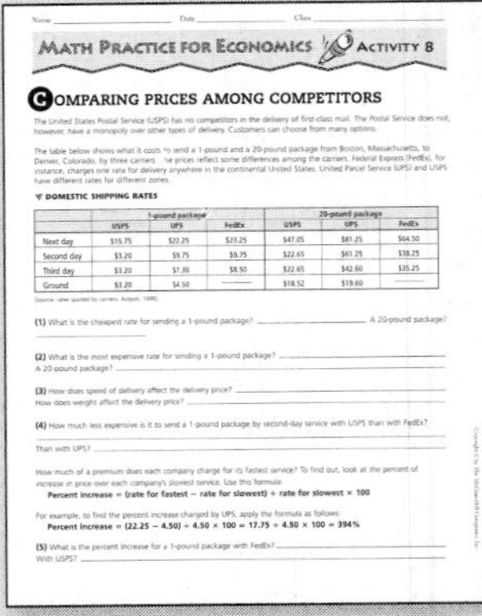

MATH PRACTICE FOR ECONOMICS ACTIVITY 8

COMPARING PRICES AMONG COMPETITORS

### Economic Cartoons Activity 7

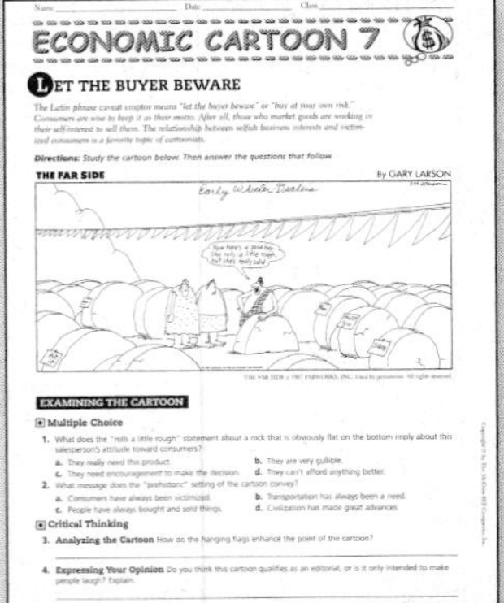

ECONOMIC CARTOON 7

LET THE BUYER BEWARE

THE FAR SIDE By GARY LARSON

EXAMINING THE CARTOON

## Review and Reinforcement

### Critical Thinking Activity 7

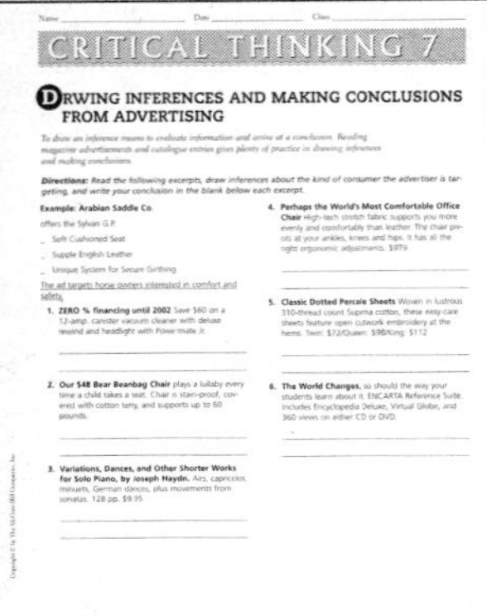

CRITICAL THINKING 7

DRAWING INFERENCES AND MAKING CONCLUSIONS FROM ADVERTISING

### Reteaching Activity 11

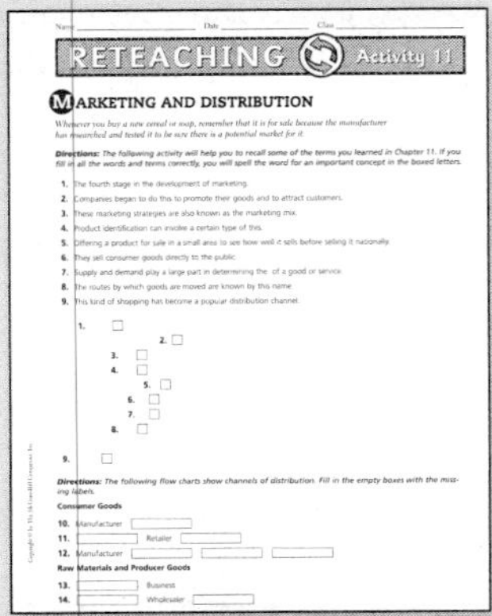

RETEACHING Activity 11

MARKETING AND DISTRIBUTION

### Economic Vocabulary Activity 11

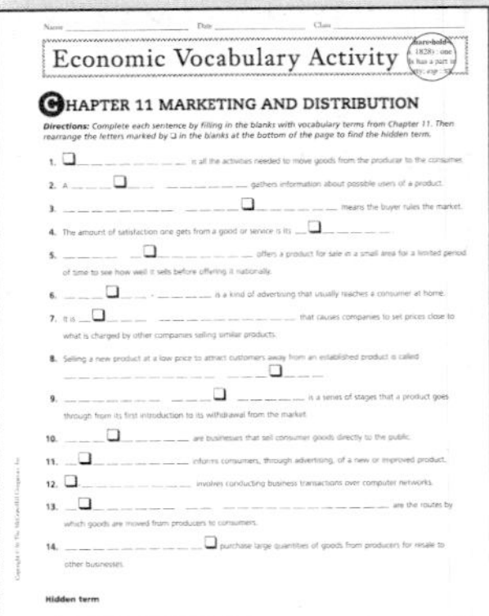

Economic Vocabulary Activity

CHAPTER 11 MARKETING AND DISTRIBUTION

### Reinforcing Economic Skills 25

Reinforcing Economic Skills Chapter 25

DEVELOPING MULTIMEDIA PRESENTATIONS

# CHAPTER 11 Resource Manager

## Assessment and Evaluation

Chapter 11 Test Form A

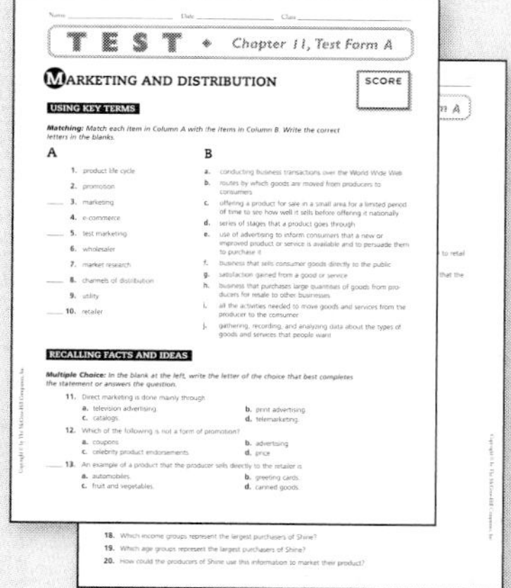


Chapter 11 Test Form B

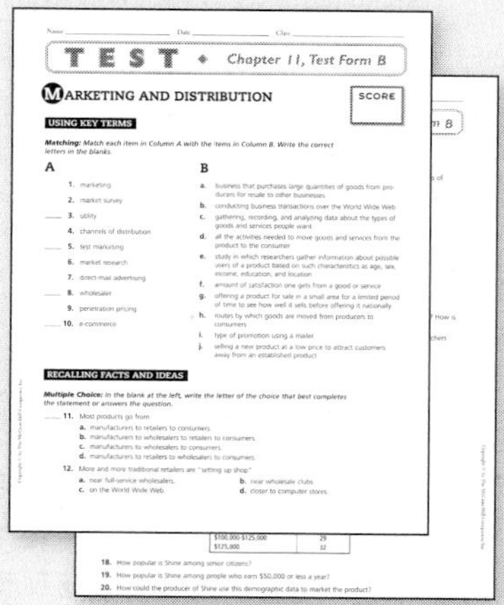


Performance Assessment Activity 7

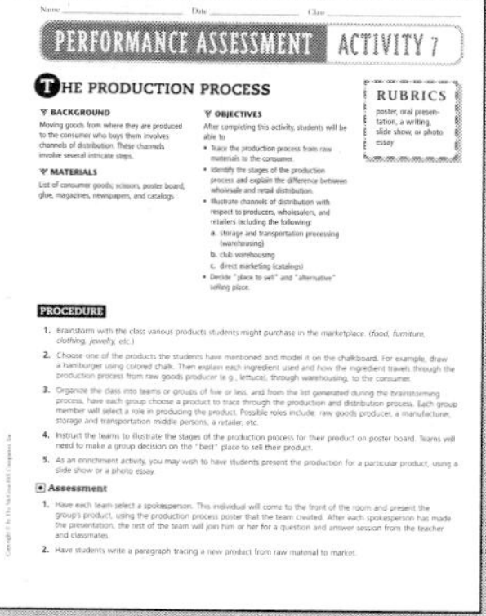


ExamView® Pro Testmaker

## Technology and Multimedia

 Vocabulary PuzzleMaker Software

 Interactive Tutor Self-Assessment Software

 ExamView® Pro Testmaker

 NBR *Economics & You* Video Program (English/Spanish)

 Presentation Plus!

Glencoe Skillbuilder Interactive Workbook CD-ROM, Level 2

 Interactive Lesson Planner

 MindJogger Videoquiz

 Interactive Economics! CD-ROM

 Audio Program (English or Spanish)

## ECONOMICS Online

You and your students can visit ett.glencoe.com—the Web site companion to **Economics Today and Tomorrow.** This innovative integration of electronic and print media offers your students a wealth of opportunities. The student text directs students to the Web site for the following options:

- **Chapter Overviews**
- **Self-Check Quizzes**
- **Student Web Activities**
- **Textbook Updates**

Answers are provided for you in the **Web Activity Lesson Plan.** Additional Web resources and Interactive Puzzles are also available.

Use the Glencoe Web site for additional resources. All essential content is covered in the Student Edition.

## Spanish Resources

 Spanish Economic Concepts Transparency 5

 Spanish Vocabulary Activity 11

 Spanish Reteaching Activity 11

 Spanish Section Quizzes for Chapter 11

 Spanish Chapter 11 Audio Program, Activity, and Test

## Additional Resources

### Reading for the Student

Zollo, Peter. *Wise Up to Teens: Insights Into Marketing and Advertising to Teens.* Ithaca, NY: New Strategist Publications, 1999. Uses real-life examples to show how products are marketed to American teenagers.

### Multimedia Material

*Marketing Perspectives–A Series.* 29 videos. Wisconsin Foundation for Vocational, Technical, and Adult Education.

# CHAPTER 11 Resource Manager

## Section Resources

| Reading Objectives | Reproducible Resources | Technology/Multimedia Resources |
|---|---|---|
| **Section 1**<br>**The Changing Role of Marketing**<br>• How has the role of marketing changed in the United States?<br>• What elements make up market research? | Reproducible Lesson Plan 11-1<br>Daily Lecture Notes 11-1<br>Guided Reading Activity 11-1<br>Reading Essentials and Study Guide 11-1<br>Daily Focus Activity 49<br>Section Quiz 11-1* | Daily Focus Transparency 49<br>Vocabulary PuzzleMaker<br>Interactive Tutor Self-Assessment Software<br>MindJogger Videoquiz<br>NBR's *Economics & You**<br>Presentation Plus!<br>ExamView® Pro Testmaker |
| **Section 2**<br>**The Marketing Mix**<br>• What is the importance of product identification?<br>• Which market strategies depend on price?<br>• How does a firm decide where to sell its products?<br>• What are four types of promotion that a firm may use? | Reproducible Lesson Plan 11-2<br>Daily Lecture Notes 11-2<br>Guided Reading Activity 11-2<br>Reading Essentials and Study Guide 11-2<br>Daily Focus Activity 50<br>Section Quiz 11-2* | Daily Focus Transparency 50<br>Vocabulary PuzzleMaker<br>Interactive Tutor Self-Assessment Software<br>MindJogger Videoquiz<br>Presentation Plus!<br>ExamView® Pro Testmaker |
| **Section 3**<br>**Distribution Channels**<br>• What is the difference between wholesale and retail distribution?<br>• What are two new types of distribution channels? | Reproducible Lesson Plan 11-3<br>Daily Lecture Notes 11-3<br>Guided Reading Activity 11-3<br>Reading Essentials and Study Guide 11-3<br>Daily Focus Activity 51<br>Section Quiz 11-3*<br>Reinforcing Economic Skills 25 | Daily Focus Transparency 51<br>Economic Concepts Transparency 5<br>Vocabulary PuzzleMaker<br>Interactive Tutor Self-Assessment Software<br>MindJogger Videoquiz<br>NBR's *Economics & You**<br>Presentation Plus!<br>ExamView® Pro Testmaker |

*Also available in Spanish

Blackline Master
Transparency

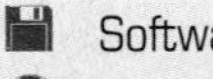
Software

CD-ROM

Videodisc

Audiocassette

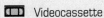

Videocassette

# CHAPTER 11 Resource Manager

## ACTIVITY From the Classroom of

**Bill Nichols**
**The Lovett School**
**Atlanta, Georgia**

### Creating Advertisements

Working with a partner, students will develop a product and create an advertising campaign to sell the product. First, students must decide upon a product to sell. They must outline its features, why a consumer would want to buy it, and what they think they should charge for it. Then students must agree on what two media sources will be used to advertise the product. What is the target group? Students must design both a print advertisement and either a TV or radio ad. Each group should present the advertisements to the rest of the class.

## Easy Planning and Preparation!

Use Glencoe's **Presentation Plus!**, a Microsoft PowerPoint® application, to teach **Marketing and Distribution.** With this multimedia teacher tool, you can customize ready-made presentations. At your fingertips are interactive transparencies, on-screen lecture notes, audiovisual presentations, and links to the Internet and to other Glencoe multimedia.

### Interactive Lesson Planner

Planning has never been easier! Organize your week, month, semester, or year with all the lesson helps you need to make teaching creative, timely, and relevant—the way it is meant to be. The Interactive Lesson Planner opens Glencoe's **Chapter 11** resources, helps you build your schedule, and tracks your progress.

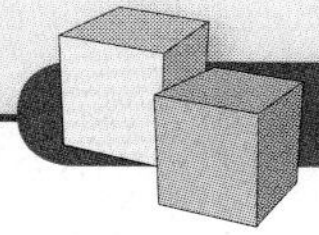

## Block Schedule

Activities that are particularly suited to use within the block scheduling framework are identified throughout this chapter by the following designation: BLOCK SCHEDULING

## Key to Ability Levels

**Teaching strategies have been coded for varying learning styles and abilities.**

L1 **BASIC** activities for all students
L2 **AVERAGE** activities for average to above-average students
L3 **CHALLENGING** activities for above-average students
**ELL** **ENGLISH LANGUAGE LEARNER** activities

## National Council on Economic Education

## THE EconomicsAmerica AND EconomicsInternational PROGRAMS

### Voluntary Standards Emphasized in Chapter 11

**Content Standard 4** Students will understand that people respond predictably to positive and negative incentives.

**Content Standard 8** Students will understand that prices send signals and provide incentives to buyers and sellers. When supply or demand changes, market prices adjust, affecting incentives.

### Resources Available from NCEE

- *Capstone: The Nation's High School Economics Course*
- *Entrepreneurship in the U.S. Economy*
- *Focus: High School Economics*
- *Personal Decision Making: Focus on Economics*

To order these materials, or to contact your State Council on Economic Education about workshops and programs, call 1-800-338-1192 or visit the NCEE Web site at http://www.nationalcouncil.org

ECONOMICS & YOU

Marketing & Distribution

Chapter 17
Disc 1, Side 2

**ASK:** Why has marketing and selling music on the Internet grown so rapidly? *Because of new recording technologies, music can be cheaply and easily distributed over the Internet directly to people's homes.*

 Also available in VHS.

## Chapter Overview

Over the last 100 years, marketing has changed from an aspect of production to a way of creating—and even predicting—demand for a given item. Marketing research, therefore, has become ever more important, and marketers have become more sophisticated in responding to that research.

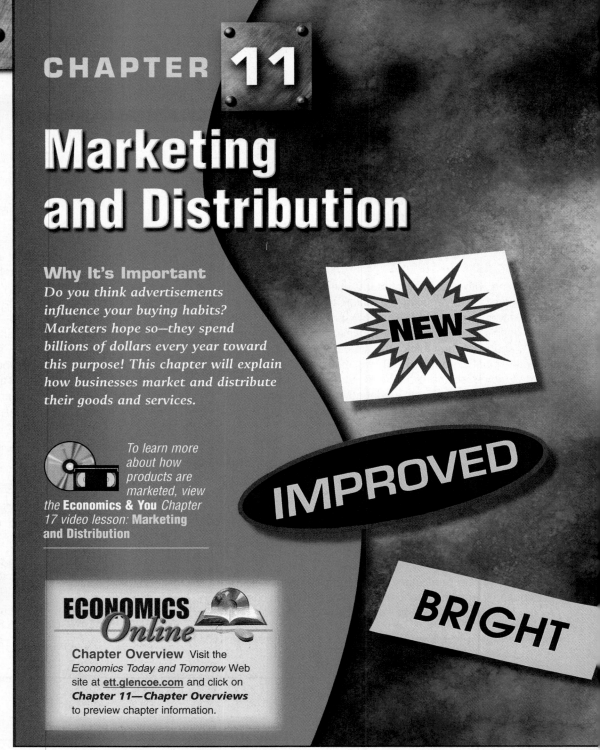

**GLENCOE TECHNOLOGY**

Use **MindJogger Videoquiz** VHS to preview Chapter 11 content.

Introduce students to chapter content and key terms by having them access **Chapter 11—Chapter Overviews** at *ett.glencoe.com*

# CHAPTER 11

# Marketing and Distribution

### Why It's Important

*Do you think advertisements influence your buying habits? Marketers hope so—they spend billions of dollars every year toward this purpose! This chapter will explain how businesses market and distribute their goods and services.*

*To learn more about how products are marketed, view the* **Economics & You** *Chapter 17 video lesson:* **Marketing and Distribution**

NEW

IMPROVED

BRIGHT

**ECONOMICS Online**

**Chapter Overview** Visit the *Economics Today and Tomorrow* Web site at ett.glencoe.com and click on ***Chapter 11—Chapter Overviews*** to preview chapter information.

## CHAPTER LAUNCH ACTIVITY

Have students imagine they have just designed a new fashion belt using discarded industrial strapping. Ask students to describe who they think would be their main customers. If students have difficulty describing potential customers, ask them to suggest ways in which they might find the customer base. Then have them list the ways that they might create demand for the new product. Aid students by mentioning the term *promotion*. Conclude by mentioning to students that the exercise they have just completed closely resembles the tasks undertaken by a company's marketing division.

SECTION 1

# The Changing Role of Marketing

## Cover Story

10 Reasons why you need the fast-acting

*Business Week*, June 7, 1999

Too much marketing today focuses on awareness rather than reasons to buy. In the old days, awareness advertising was more effective. There was less competition. All you had to worry about was whether or not people remembered your product. As technology and more kinds of media have come about, it's no longer enough to be remembered. The consumer has too many choices. Your marketing has to send the message that you are relevant. You need to be sending reasons to buy.

### Reader's Guide

**Terms to Know**

- marketing
- consumer sovereignty
- utility
- market research
- market survey
- test marketing

**Reading Objectives**

1. How has the role of marketing changed in the United States?
2. What elements make up market research?

In addition to financing and producing products, which you learned about in Chapter 10, businesses must promote and eventually sell their products and services. **Marketing** involves all of the activities needed to move goods and services from the producer to the consumer. As you read this section, you'll learn that these activities include market research, advertising and promotion, and distribution.

**marketing:** *all the activities needed to move goods and services from the producer to the consumer*

## The Development of Marketing

Some economists estimate that about 50 percent of the price people pay for an item today is for the cost of marketing. The idea and importance of marketing in the United States have



## Section 1 Resource Manager

**Reproducible Masters**

- Reproducible Lesson Plan 11–1
- Reading Essentials and Study Guide 11–1
- Guided Reading Activity 11–1
- Section Quiz 11–1
- Daily Focus Activity 49
- Daily Lecture Notes 11–1

**Multimedia**

- Daily Focus Transparency 49
- Vocabulary PuzzleMaker
- Interactive Tutor Self-Assessment Software
- ExamView® Pro Testmaker
- MindJogger Videoquiz
- NBR's *Economics & You*
- Presentation Plus!



# 1 Focus

## Overview

**Section 1** describes or explains the development of marketing in the United States and the elements of market research.

### Bellringer

**Motivational Activity**

Project **Daily Focus Transparency 49** and have students answer the questions.

This activity is also available as a blackline master.

**Daily Focus Transparency 49**

FOCUS ACTIVITIES Transparency 49

THE CHANGING ROLE OF MARKETING

| Examples from the Stages of Marketing in America | |
|---|---|
| **Stage** | **Example** |
| I. The Early 1900s | • The National Biscuit Company launches the first million-dollar ad campaign. The product? The Uneeda Biscuit. The slogan? "Lest you forget, we say yet, Uneeda Biscuit." |
| II. The 1920s and 1930s | • Listerine mouthwash says in its ads, "Even your best friend won't tell you." |
| III. The 1950s | • The heaviest-advertised products are automobiles, largely over the new medium of television. |
| IV. The Late 1950s to the 1980s | • Widely-recognized fictional characters are introduced, among them Tony the Tiger, the Pillsbury Doughboy, and the Jolly Green Giant. |
| V. The 1990s | • Direct marketing over the Internet is targeted and personalized—learning what customers like from what they buy and where they browse. |

1. What do you think is the purpose of the characters in the fourth stage of advertising?
2. What is the meaning of the example in the last row of the table?

Daily Focus Transparencies

### Reader's Guide

Answers to the **Reading Objectives** questions are on page 294.

**Preteaching Vocabulary**

Lead the class in a game of "Marketing Lingo." Select two or three students to act as questioners. Have them give short clues to each of the **Terms to Know**, and have the rest of the class try to identify the terms.

**Vocabulary PuzzleMaker**

# 2 Teach

## Guided Practice

**L2 Applying Ideas** Direct students' attention to **Figure 11.1** on pages 290–291. Review the five historical stages of marketing shown. Then organize students into five groups, and assign each group one of the five stages of marketing. Tell groups that they are the marketing department for a company that makes the Wonderful Widget, a multipurpose tool for use around the house. Ask groups to brainstorm ways they might market the Wonderful Widget during their assigned marketing stages. Remind groups to consider the media they might use. Have groups present and discuss their marketing ideas.

### Daily Lecture Notes 11-1

DAILY LECTURE NOTES Lesson 11-1

**LECTURE LAUNCHER**

In 1962, a McDonald's franchise owner introduced the Filet-O-Fish sandwich. He noticed he was losing business on Fridays from Catholic customers and wanted to regain that business. What marketing activities brought the Filet-O-Fish sandwich to the consumer. What are form, place, time, and ownership utility? A typical visit to McDonald's adds to which of these utilities?

PAGES 239–291

I. The Development of Marketing
   - A. The sole purpose of marketing is to convince consumers that a certain product or service will add to their utility.
   - B. Form utility is converting raw materials into desired/needed products.
   - C. Place utility is providing the good/service where the customer wants it to be.
   - D. Time utility is providing the good/service at precisely the time the customer wants it.
   - E. Ownership utility is providing goods/services that people are pleased to own.

**Discussion Question**

**Rank the four types of consumer utility in order of importance. Explain your reasoning.** *(Answers will vary, but students should be able to clearly explain why they ranked the items in the order they did.)*

### Visual Instruction FIGURE 11.1

As students study the information in **Figure 11.1**, ask them which stage they think brought the greatest change in marketing. Encourage them to explain their answers.

changed considerably since 1900. The development of marketing can be traced by analyzing what it has focused on: production, sales, advertising, and **consumer sovereignty**—or consumer as ruler. **Figure 11.1** takes you on a historical "tour" of marketing.

**consumer sovereignty:** *the role of the consumer as ruler of the market when determining the types of goods and services produced*

**utility:** *the amount of satisfaction one gets from a good or service*

**Meeting Consumer Utility** Today, marketing's sole purpose is to convince consumers that a certain product will add to their utility. **Utility** is the ability of any good or service to satisfy consumer wants. Utility can be divided into four major types: form utility, place utility, time utility, and ownership utility.

*Form utility,* created by production, is the conversion of raw materials to finished goods. Examples include transforming cotton cloth into draperies or refining crude oil into gasoline.

*Place utility* is created by having a good or service available where a consumer wants to buy it. Locating a gas station on a busy corner is an example of this type of utility.

## FIGURE 11.1 Stages of Marketing

**A The Early 1900s**

*Producers of consumer goods and services take advantage of new technologies to increase production. Finding that their amount of production exceeds their markets, firms begin using "announcement advertising" to introduce their goods to potential buyers statewide and even nationally. Consumers, no longer having to rely on local producers, become aware of greater choices and respond to the advertising. Less efficient local firms, or those with inferior products, wither and leave the market.*

**B The 1920s and 1930s**

*Rising incomes and the increased wealth of the nation lead consumers to redefine their notions of necessities and luxuries. Greater numbers of consumers can choose among goods and services available. Producers begin to advertise in a manner extolling the virtues of their product compared to the competition. Consumers respond by favoring those companies that present themselves as having the product that best fits their needs. Firms that cannot adequately explain the benefits of their products fail.*



### Meeting Special Needs

**Reading Disability** Students with various reading and information organization problems may have difficulty relating pictures, captions, and the main text. Before students read Section 1, have them study the pictures. Ask them what they think the pictures illustrate. After they have read the section, ask students to again suggest what the pictures illustrate. Then discuss why these particular pictures were included in the section.

Refer to *Inclusion for the Social Studies Classroom Strategies and Activities* for students with different learning styles.

*Time utility* is created by having a good or service available when a consumer wants to buy it. As shown in **Figure 11.2** on page 292, a 24-hour grocery store or all-night restaurant are examples of time utility. Catalog selling is another example of both time and place utility.

*Ownership utility* is the satisfaction one receives from simply owning the good or service. One might purchase a fine art painting for an exorbitant price to have the satisfaction of owning the object. Luxury cars, expensive jewelry, and lawn ornaments also provide ownership utility.

## Market Research

Finding out what consumers want can be difficult. It is crucial that businesses do so, however, because many markets today are national or even global. An increase in sales of a few percentage points can result in millions of dollars in profits. Therefore,

**C ▶ The 1950s**
*During the 1950s, firms began the process of creating demand. They did this by changing their advertising to convince consumers that a specific firm's product, not just a similar product, was a necessity if the consumer was to achieve a desired lifestyle. It was hoped that consumers would view the firm's particular product—whether it was laundry detergent, facial tissue, or breakfast cereal—as an important part of the American way of life.*

**▲ E The 1990s**
*The emergence of the Internet allows even the smallest of firms to advertise inexpensively. Large firms producing for the masses face competition from small businesses that can produce goods and services for small groups or even individuals.*

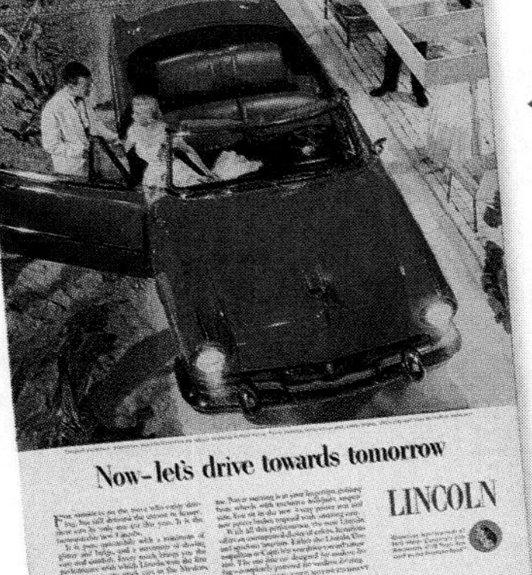


**◀ D The Late 1950s to the 1980s**
*Large national firms find stiff competition from businesses that can imitate their products. Firms begin to research consumer tastes before production in order to be able to specifically satisfy their wants. Advertising focuses on an attempt to have the consumer identify with the person in the advertisement, rather than with the specific product being presented. The recognition that the consumer is ruler of the market—consumer sovereignty—returns. Firms ask consumers what they want and, in effect, fill the specific order much as the local blacksmith had done in the late 1800s.*



## Cooperative Learning

Organize students into several groups, and have groups imagine that they are teams of authors working on a history of marketing in the United States. Tell groups that their task is to create a detailed proposal for the book to send to publishers. Suggest that they include the following in their proposals: book title; a summary of the content; a table of contents with a brief synopsis of each chapter; and a detailed outline of one chapter, including illustration ideas. Call on groups to present and discuss their book proposals.

 BLOCK SCHEDULING



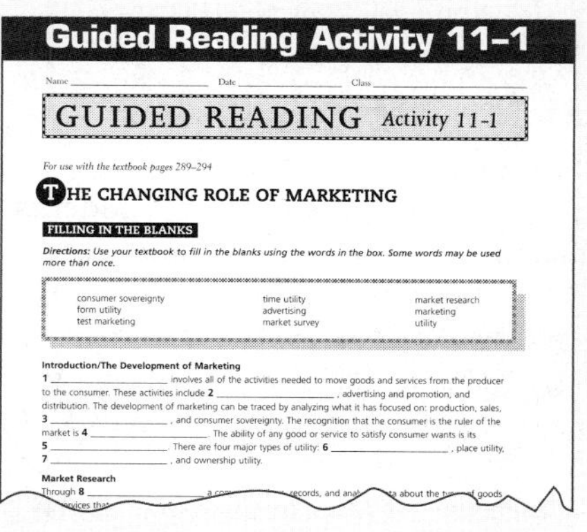

**Guided Reading Activity 11-1**

Name ______ Date ______ Class ______

GUIDED READING Activity 11-1

*For use with the textbook pages 289–294*

THE CHANGING ROLE OF MARKETING

FILLING IN THE BLANKS

***Directions:** Use your textbook to fill in the blanks using the words in the box. Some words may be used more than once.*

| | | |
|---|---|---|
| consumer sovereignty | time utility | market research |
| form utility | advertising | marketing |
| test marketing | market survey | utility |

**Introduction/The Development of Marketing**

**1** ______ involves all of the activities needed to move goods and services from the producer to the consumer. These activities include **2** ______, advertising and promotion, and distribution. The development of marketing can be traced by analyzing what it has focused on: production, sales, **3** ______, and consumer sovereignty. The recognition that the consumer is the ruler of the market is **4** ______. The ability of any good or service to satisfy consumer wants is its **5** ______. There are four major types of utility: **6** ______, place utility, **7** ______, and ownership utility.

**Market Research**

Through **8** ______

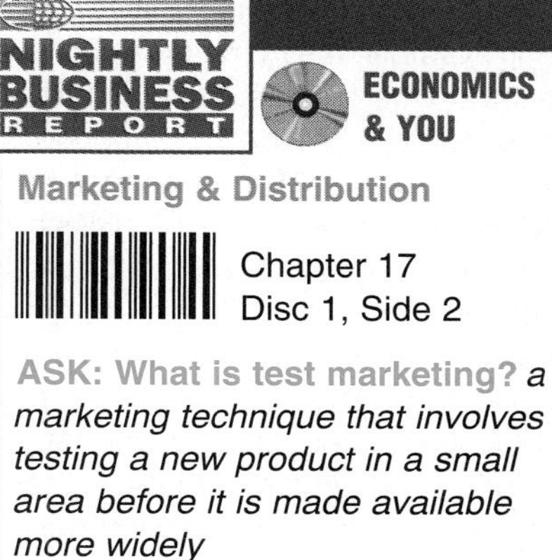

NIGHTLY BUSINESS REPORT

ECONOMICS & YOU

Marketing & Distribution

Chapter 17
Disc 1, Side 2

ASK: What is test marketing? *a marketing technique that involves testing a new product in a small area before it is made available more widely*

Also available in VHS.

## Independent Practice

**L2 Conducting Market Research** Have students work in small groups to develop their own market surveys. Point out that the surveys should be designed to discover what students want from one of the following products: bath soap, movies, news magazines, athletic shoes, computer games, fast food. Then have them survey the school. Ask groups to present their findings in a brief written report.

**Visual Instruction FIGURE 11.2**

**Answer:** *form utility, place utility, and ownership utility*

**Economic Connection to... Technology**

**Virtual Market Research** Some companies now use computer simulations in their market research. For example, they employ a virtual supermarket to gauge consumer preferences. Volunteer shoppers wander through the supermarket on the computer screen, clicking on the items they would like to buy. Using this market research method, one snack-food company discovered that end-of-aisle displays generated more sales than banner advertising above the shelves where the snacks normally were stocked.

**FIGURE 11.2**

**Time Utility** Businesses that are open around the clock satisfy consumers who want to be flexible in their shopping hours—also known as time utility. ***What other types of utility does marketing address?***

before a product is produced or a service is offered, businesses research their market. *Market* in this sense means the people who are potential buyers of the good or service.

Through **market research** a company gathers, records, and analyzes data about the types of goods and services that people want. From automakers to producers of frozen foods, most companies producing consumer goods invest heavily in market research. As shown in **Figure 11.3,** this cost is passed on to consumers.

**market research:** *gathering, recording, and analyzing data about the types of goods and services that people want*

### When Should Market Research Be Done?

Market research may be done at several stages of product development. It can be done at the very beginning when the first ideas about a new product are being developed. It can be conducted again to test sample products and alternative packaging designs.

**FIGURE 11.3**

**Cost of Marketing** As Shoe has found out in the cartoon below, the cost of marketing—or "world tour"—has significantly increased the price of a cup of coffee.

**SHOE**

## Extending the Content

**Development of Market Research** People involved in advertising made major contributions to the development of market research. Advertising executive Claude C. Hopkins invented test marketing and coupon sampling. He explained these practices in his book *Scientific Advertising* (1923)—a classic study of advertising methods that is still in use today. Daniel Starch, a Harvard professor interested in the psychology of advertising, helped to develop advertising research. Among his many contributions was the Starch Test, a tool for evaluating the effectiveness of advertisements by measuring their impact on readers. Ad "starching" remains a key element of advertising research today.

Early market research has several purposes. It helps producers determine whether there is a market for their good or service and what that market is. It can also indicate any changes in quality, features, or design that should be made before a product is offered for sale.

To investigate initial consumer response, market research is often done immediately after a product is released for sale. Some companies even test their advertising to make sure it is attracting the market segment for which the product was designed. Market researchers can also gather information about a product that has been on the market for a while. They then attempt to discover what should be done to maintain or increase sales.

**Market Surveys** The first step in market research is performing a **market survey,** in which researchers gather information about who might be possible users of the product. Such characteristics as age, gender, income, education, and location—urban, suburban, rural—are important to a producer in deciding which market a product should target.

*market survey: information gathered by researchers about possible users of a product based on such characteristics as age, gender, income, education, and location*

A market survey typically involves a series of carefully worded questions. The questions may be administered in the form of a written questionnaire, which is mailed to consumers. Manufacturers of such small appliances as hair dryers and microwave ovens often put a questionnaire on the back of the warranty card that purchasers are to return. Another way to survey the market is by conducting individual interviews or querying focus groups. See **Figure 11.4.**

*test marketing: offering a product for sale in a small area for a limited period of time to see how well it sells before offering it nationally*

**Testing New Products** As a final step before offering a product for national distribution, market researchers will often test-market a product such as a detergent or a toothpaste. **Test marketing** means offering a product for sale in a small area, perhaps several cities, for two months to two years to see how well it sells before offering it nationally.

**FIGURE 11.4**

**Focus Groups** Members of a focus group may test and discuss what they like and dislike about similar, and often competing, products. Generally, the people chosen to be part of the focus group do not know which company has hired them to test the products. The focus group is often observed through a one-way mirror by the marketers of one of the products.



## CHAPTER 11

SECTION 1, Pages 289–294

**L3 Explaining Ideas** Have students imagine they are working on the Frequently Asked Questions (FAQ) page of a market research Web site. The most frequently asked questions are: What do market researchers do? How do market researchers gather information? What is done with this information? Have students conduct research to find answers to these questions. Then have students write the answers as they might appear on a FAQ page. BLOCK SCHEDULING

# 3 Assess

## Meeting Lesson Objectives

Assign Section 1 Assessment as homework or an in-class activity.

Use **Interactive Tutor Self-Assessment Software** to review Section 1.

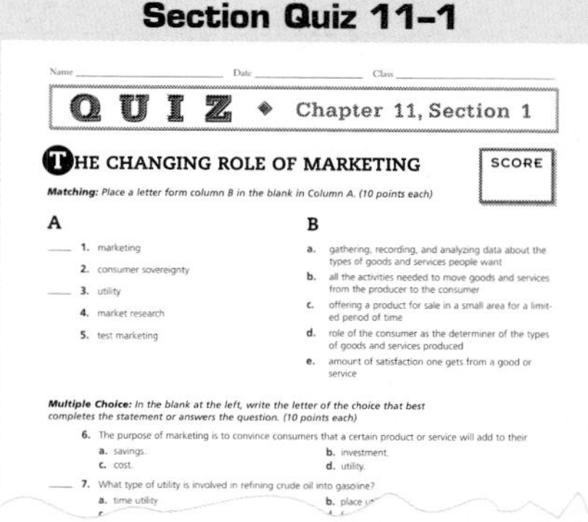

**Section Quiz 11–1**

Name ________ Date ________ Class ________

QUIZ ◆ Chapter 11, Section 1

THE CHANGING ROLE OF MARKETING

SCORE

*Matching: Place a letter form column B in the blank in Column A. (10 points each)*

**A**

___ 1. marketing
___ 2. consumer sovereignty
___ 3. utility
___ 4. market research
___ 5. test marketing

**B**

a. gathering, recording, and analyzing data about the types of goods and services people want
b. all the activities needed to move goods and services from the producer to the consumer
c. offering a product for sale in a small area for a limited period of time
d. role of the consumer as the determiner of the types of goods and services produced
e. amount of satisfaction one gets from a good or service

*Multiple Choice: In the blank at the left, write the letter of the choice that best completes the statement or answers the question. (10 points each)*

___ 6. The purpose of marketing is to convince consumers that a certain product or service will add to their
a. savings. b. investment.
c. cost. d. utility.

___ 7. What type of utility is involved in refining crude oil into gasoline?
a. time utility b. place u...

## Extending the Content

**Market Research Methods** Market researchers use two approaches to gather information—quantitative research and qualitative research. Quantitative research provides numbers. For example, it will show the percentage of the population that prefers product X over product Y. Quantitative information is gathered by interviewing individuals using the same set of questions. Qualitative research tries to discover the reasons behind a particular situation. For example, why do so many people prefer product X over product Y? Market researchers gather qualitative data through open-ended interviews, which focus on broad topics rather than a set series of questions, and through focus groups.

## Reteach

Have students write five questions on the major developments in marketing in the United States. Then pair students and have partners exchange, and then answer, the questions.

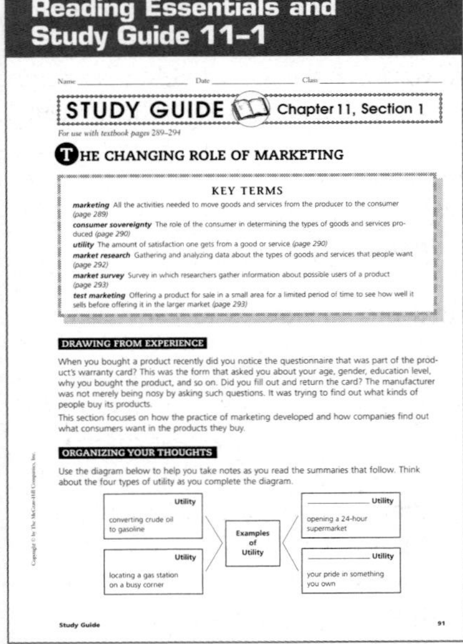

**Reading Essentials and Study Guide 11-1**

Name ______________ Date ______________ Class ______________

STUDY GUIDE Chapter 11, Section 1

*For use with textbook pages 289–294*

THE CHANGING ROLE OF MARKETING

KEY TERMS

***marketing*** All the activities needed to move goods and services from the producer to the consumer *(page 289)*

***consumer sovereignty*** The role of the consumer in determining the types of goods and services produced *(page 290)*

***utility*** The amount of satisfaction one gets from a good or service *(page 290)*

***market research*** Gathering and analyzing data about the types of goods and services that people want *(page 292)*

***market survey*** Survey in which researchers gather information about possible users of a product *(page 293)*

***test marketing*** Offering a product for sale in a small area for a limited period of time to see how well it sells before offering it in the larger market *(page 293)*

DRAWING FROM EXPERIENCE

When you bought a product recently did you notice the questionnaire that was part of the product's warranty card? This was the form that asked you about your age, gender, education level, why you bought the product, and so on. Did you fill out and return the card? The manufacturer was not merely being nosy by asking such questions. It was trying to find out what kinds of people buy its products.

This section focuses on how the practice of marketing developed and how companies find out what consumers want in the products they buy.

ORGANIZING YOUR THOUGHTS

Use the diagram below to help you take notes as you read the summaries that follow. Think about the four types of utility as you complete the diagram.

Examples of Utility

Utility — converting crude oil to gasoline

Utility — locating a gas station on a busy corner

______ Utility — opening a 24-hour supermarket

______ Utility — your pride in something you own

Copyright © by The McGraw-Hill Companies, Inc.

Study Guide 91

## 4 Close

Have students write a paragraph beginning with the following topic sentence: Market research is very helpful at every stage of product development.

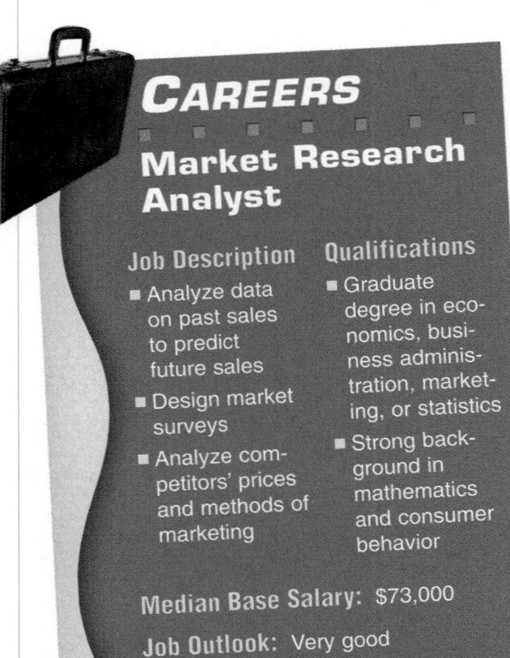

CAREERS
Market Research Analyst
Job Description
■ Analyze data on past sales to predict future sales
■ Design market surveys
■ Analyze competitors' prices and methods of marketing
Qualifications
■ Graduate degree in economics, business administration, marketing, or statistics
■ Strong background in mathematics and consumer behavior
Median Base Salary: $73,000
Job Outlook: Very good
—Occupational Outlook Handbook, 1998–99


For example, before attempting to market a new granola cereal, a company might sell it in several selected areas where the product is most likely to attract the market segment that the company is seeking.

Researchers keep track of the units sold and test different prices and ad campaigns within the test markets. If the product is successful, the company will offer it nationally. If sales are disappointing, the company has two choices. It can make changes based on the data collected in the test market. Or, rather than spend more funds redesigning the product, the company can abandon the idea.

Of all the new products introduced every year in the United States, most are not profitable and do not survive in the marketplace. It is the constant lure of owning a high-profit item, however, that motivates companies to continue developing new products.

**Practice** and **assess** key skills with ***Skillbuilder Interactive Workbook, Level 2.***

## SECTION 1 Assessment

### Understanding Key Terms

1. **Define** marketing, consumer sovereignty, utility, market research, market survey, test marketing.

### Reviewing Objectives

2. **Graphic Organizer** Use a diagram like the one below to make a time line tracing the changing focus of marketing in the United States.

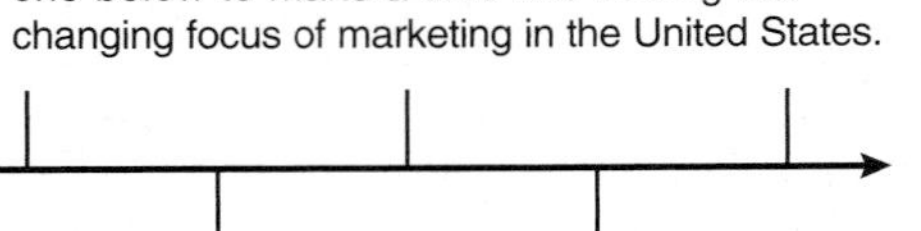

3. What steps are involved in market research?

### Applying Economic Concepts

4. **Market Surveys** Imagine that you have the task of finding the market to buy a new health-food energy bar. What are five questions you would ask consumers in a market survey?

### Critical Thinking Activity

5. **Categorizing Information** Select 10 businesses in your community. Categorize each business according to the type of utility it provides.



## SECTION 1 Assessment Answers

1. All definitions can be found in the Glossary.
2. Time lines will vary but should generally state: Early 1900s focused on production; 1920s and 1930s focused on sales; 1950s promoted a product as a necessity; late 1950s to the 1980s focused on consumer sovereignty; 1990s focused on individual needs.
3. gathering, recording, and analyzing information on a product, then test-marketing the product
4. Answers will vary. Students' questions should focus on such topics as ingredients, product size, price, and so on.
5. Answers will vary. Have students compare their lists to note if there are any variations in categorization.

# BusinessWeek

# SPOTLIGHT ON THE ECONOMY

## Generation Y

**Check It Out!** In this chapter, you learned how important it is for advertisers to know their market. In this article, read to learn how advertisers are marketing their products toward *your* generation.

Today's teens may force marketers to toss their old tricks. Born during a baby bulge that demographers locate between 1979 and 1994, they are as young as 5 and as old as 20. And at 60 million strong, they're the biggest thing to hit the American scene since the 72 million baby boomers. They go by a host of taglines: Generation Y, Echo Boomers, or Millennium Generation.

Indeed, though the echo boom rivals its parents' generation in size, in almost every other way it is very different. This generation is more racially diverse: One in three is not Caucasian. One in four lives in a single-parent household. Three in four have working mothers.

"Most marketers perceive them as kids. When you do that, you fail to take in what they are telling you about the consumers they're becoming," said J. Walker Smith, who specializes in generational marketing. "This is not about teenage marketing. It's about the coming of age of a generation."

Smith and others believe that behind the shift in Gen Y labels lies a shift in values on the part of Gen Y consumers. The marketers that capture Gen Y's attention do so by bringing their messages to the places these kids congregate, whether it's the Internet, a snowboarding tournament, or cable TV. The ads may be funny or disarmingly direct. What they don't do is suggest that the advertiser knows Gen Y better than these savvy consumers know themselves.

Instead, Gen Yers respond to humor, irony, and the (apparently) unvarnished truth. . . .

Marketers who don't bother to learn the interests and obsessions of Gen Y are apt to run up against a brick wall of distrust and cynicism.

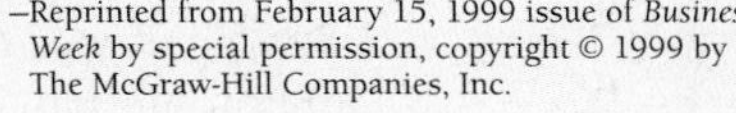



### Think About It

1. **What market does "Generation Y" make up?**
2. **According to the article, how can advertisers reach Gen Yers?**

### Answers to *Think About It*

1. the 60 million young people born between the years 1979 and 1994
2. Advertisers should bring the messages to the places where Generation Yers congregate–such as the Internet, a snowboarding tournament, and cable TV. Also, messages should not suggest that the advertiser knows Generation Yers better than these young people know themselves.

BusinessWeek
**SPOTLIGHT**

## Teach

Point out that some companies use "street teams" to gather marketing information. These teams of young people visit clubs, parks, and malls, talking to their peers about fashion, music, food, and just about everything else. In this way, companies hope to identify trends as they develop. Then ask students to detail what they might say to "street team" members about the ways that companies might market clothes, music, food, and other products. Conclude by asking students how they feel about being targeted as the next big market.

### BusinessWeek ONLINE

To find up-to-date news and analysis on the economy, business, technology, markets, entrepreneurs, investments, and finance, have students search feature articles and special reports on the *Business Week* Web site. www.businessweek.com

### Sidelight

Why are market researchers so interested in Generation Y? Teenagers—a large segment of that group—spend about $141 billion each year. And they are extremely brand loyal.

# 1 Focus

## Overview

Section 2 explains or describes the "four Ps" of marketing–product, price, place, and promotion–and the product life cycle.

**BELLRINGER**
**Motivational Activity**

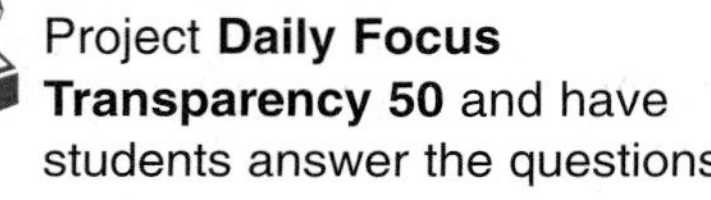

Project **Daily Focus Transparency 50** and have students answer the questions.

This activity is also available as a blackline master.

**Daily Focus Transparency 50**

THE MARKETING MIX

1. Create a new cereal name and package design that will attract consumers.
2. Develop an advertising campaign: write a slogan, choose your preferred type of media, and identify the audience you wish to reach.

Daily Focus Transparencies

### Reader's Guide

Answers to the **Reading Objectives** questions are on page 300.

**Preteaching Vocabulary**

Ask students to write definitions for the **Terms to Know**. Have them check the accuracy of their definitions as they work through Section 2.

Vocabulary PuzzleMaker

SECTION  2

# The Marketing Mix

### Reader's Guide

**Terms to Know**
- price leadership
- penetration pricing
- promotion
- direct-mail advertising
- product life cycle

**Reading Objectives**
1. What is the importance of product identification?
2. Which market strategies depend on price?
3. How does a firm decide where to sell its products?
4. What are four types of promotion that a firm may use?

## Cover Story

*The Washington Post*, February 1, 1999

"Tommy Hilfiger has created a marketing phenomenon by speaking the language of teens," says the company's vice president of worldwide marketing. "Tommy Hilfiger's employees comb the streets, campuses, and nightclubs to see what teenagers are wearing. What teens really dislike is having someone older tell them what to wear. There's nothing worse than a bunch of 35- to 40-year-olds trying to figure out what teenagers want."

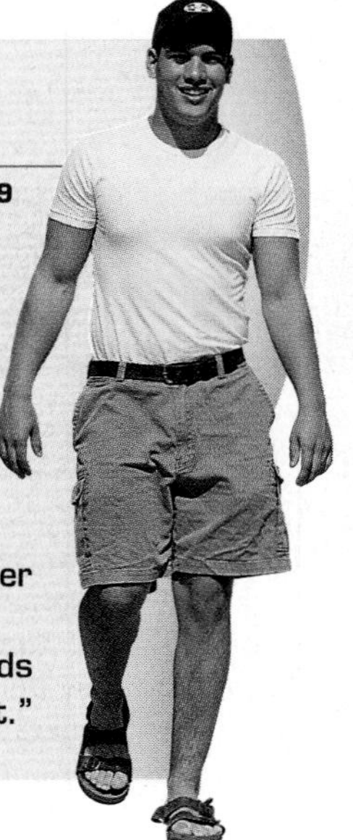

In today's highly competitive world, simply producing a product and offering it for sale is not enough. Through their marketing departments, companies plan a marketing strategy, which details how the company will sell the product effectively. As you read this section, you'll learn that a marketing strategy, or plan, combines the "four Ps" of marketing: product, price, place, and promotion. Decisions about each are based on the data collected through the company's market research. See **Figure 11.5.**

## Product

Market research helps determine *what* good or service to produce. It also helps a company determine what services to offer with the product, how to package it, and what kind of product identification to use.

## SECTION 2 RESOURCE MANAGER

**Reproducible Masters**
- Reproducible Lesson Plan 11–2
- Reading Essentials and Study Guide 11–2
- Guided Reading Activity 11–2
- Section Quiz 11–2
- Daily Focus Activity 50
- Daily Lecture Notes 11–2

**Multimedia**
- Daily Focus Transparency 50
- Vocabulary PuzzleMaker
- Interactive Tutor Self-Assessment Software
- ExamView® Pro Testmaker
- MindJogger Videoquiz
- Presentation Plus!

*Additional services* that accompany a product often help make a sale. Warranties are customary with many manufactured products, but some manufacturers offer special services free or for a small charge. For example, if you buy a camera, you may be able to purchase from the manufacturer a 2-year extended warranty in addition to the 1-year warranty given by the store in which you bought the camera. Automakers used to offer 1-year or 12,000-mile warranties on new cars. Today a 5-year or 50,000-mile warranty is a common offer.

Packaging is also an important factor in selling a product. The "right" packaging combines size, design, and color to attract potential consumers. Compact discs, books, and food are especially dependent on packaging. Such words as *New and Improved* or *Economy Size* are used to attract customers. For economy-minded shoppers, manufacturers add cents-off coupons and rebate offers to their packages.

**FIGURE 11.5**

**The Four Ps of Marketing**

**A** Product
*From the Pillsbury Dough Boy to the familiar Cheerios logo, all of these items are good examples of packaging that achieves product identification.*

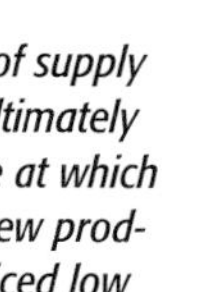

**B** Price
*Although the laws of supply and demand will ultimately determine the price at which a product sells, a new product often will be priced low to attract customers away from better-known products.*

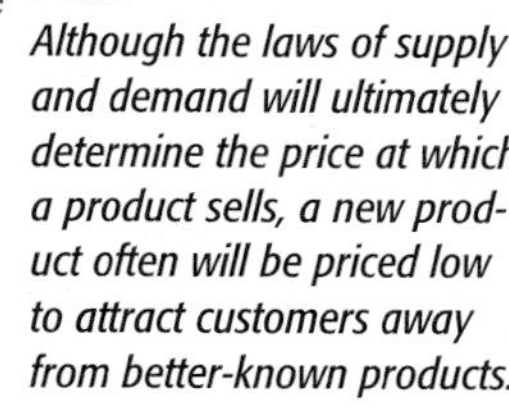

**C** Place
*A marketing department must decide where its company's product should be sold—whether in a specialty store, on the Internet, or through a catalog.*

**D** Promotion
*Product promotion includes the use of advertising to inform customers about a new or improved product. It also dictates where and how a product is physically displayed.*

297

# 2 Teach

## Guided Practice

**L2 Analyzing Ideas** Call on volunteers to identify product slogans and jingles that they know. Note their responses on the board. Ask students what makes these slogans and jingles memorable. Then discuss the importance of memorable slogans and jingles in product identification. Finally, ask students to provide examples of other kinds of product identification—logos, packaging, celebrity endorsements, and so on. **ELL**

### Daily Lecture Notes 11-2

DAILY LECTURE NOTES Lesson 11-2

**LECTURE LAUNCHER**

Sometimes a corporation will start a secondary business under a different name. Both companies might actually sell similar products, but be marketed to different target groups. For example, Gap, Inc. created the company Old Navy, which also sells clothing. The marketing strategy to form two companies can almost always be traced back to the four "Ps" of marketing. What are the four "Ps" of marketing?

**PAGES 296–298**

I. Product
  - **A.** What good or service should be produced?
  - **B.** What services should be offered with the product?
  - **C.** How should product be packaged? Consider size, design, color, catch phrases and coupons or rebates.
  - **D.** How should product be identified? Consider logos, songs, celebrity endorsements, and packaging.
  - **E.** Additional services may be provided to help make a sale.

**Discussion Question**

**Consider a product or service that you bought recently. Describe how the product was marketed.** *(Answers will vary. Students should take into account the packaging, product identification, additional services*

### Visual Instruction FIGURE 11.5

Have students study **Figure 11.5.** Ask them to identify the three major elements in selling a product. *(what services to offer with the product, how to package the product, and what kind of product identification to use)*

### Meeting Special Needs

**Visual Disability** Students with visual difficulties may find it helpful to use charts or graphs whenever they present information. As a practice exercise, have students present the data in the **Economic Connection** feature on page 298 in the form of a bar graph. Assist students by suggesting that they use a scale of one inch: .100.

Refer to *Inclusion for the Social Studies Classroom Strategies and Activities* for students with different learning styles.

**Guided Reading Activity 11-2**

Name ______ Date ______ Class ______

GUIDED READING Activity 11-2

For use with the textbook pages 296–300

THE MARKETING MIX

OUTLINING

*Directions: Locate the heading in your textbook. Then use the information under the heading to help you write each answer.*

I. Product
A. What does market research help determine?
B. Why is packaging important for selling a product?
C. What is the purpose of product identification?

II. Price
A. What is price leadership?
B. What is penetration pricing?

III. Place—Where are various places in which products can be sold?

IV. Promotion

## Independent Practice

**L2 Analyzing Ideas** Have students select a magazine and note the various advertisements. Next, direct students to categorize the advertisements according to the type of product being promoted. Then have students try to identify the type of person at which each of the advertisements is targeted. Ask students to use their ideas to develop a profile of the magazine's readership.
BLOCK SCHEDULING

## Did You Know

Some retailers–especially supermarkets–use a special kind of penetration pricing called the *loss leader.* A loss leader is a product priced at a very low–and sometimes negative–profit margin to attract customers away from competing stores. When in the store, customers will buy other products priced at a normal profit margin. This will make up for the loss on the loss leader.

**Economic Connection to...** 

## Advertising-to-Sales Ratio

Companies measure the effectiveness of their advertising through the advertising-to-sales ratio. This number is calculated by dividing the dollar amount spent on advertising by the dollar amount of sales generated by that advertising. For example, if a $1 million advertising campaign generated $4 million in sales, the advertising-to-sales ratio would be 0.25.

Companies also use the ratio to see which type of advertising—direct mail, television, the Internet, and so on—is most effective. Below are recent advertising-to-sales ratios for the types of advertising most used by businesses. Smaller numbers indicate a greater return on each advertising dollar.

| | |
|---|---|
| Newspapers | .087 |
| Direct Mail | .096 |
| Magazines | .120 |
| Internet | .143 |
| Radio | .172 |
| Television | .204 ■ |

Coupons are used to persuade consumers to make a repeat purchase and develop the habit of buying the product.

Once a product is offered for sale, *product identification* becomes important. Product identification is meant to attract consumers to look at, buy, and remember a particular product. It can involve the use of a logo or certain colors on a package. It can also involve a song or jingle, a certain type of packaging, or anything that can be associated with and identify the product.

### Price

Supply and demand ultimately determine the price of a good or service. Because of the laws of supply and demand, the price at which a product sells may help determine whether it is successful in attracting buyers while still being profitable to its maker. In setting a price, a company has to consider the costs of producing, advertising, selling, and distributing the product, as well as the amount of profit it hopes to make.

Often companies sell similar goods at similar prices. This practice is known as **price leadership.** For example, one major airline may lower its prices, which causes all of the other major airlines to follow by lowering their fares.

Selling a new product at a low price is another marketing strategy called **penetration pricing.** The low price is meant to attract customers away from an established product.

**price leadership:** *practice of setting prices close to those charged by other companies selling similar products*

**penetration pricing:** *selling a new product at a low price to attract customers away from an established product*



## Cooperative Learning

Organize students into several groups, and tell groups they are the marketing division of the Zoom Toy Company. Have group members brainstorm to come up with an idea for a new toy. Then ask groups to develop a marketing program for this new toy. Remind groups that the program should address the "four Ps"—product, price, place, and promotion. Suggest that groups include the following in their campaign materials: a brief report explaining the additional services, packaging, and production identification to be used with the toy; pricing suggestions; ideas on where the toy should be sold; and promotion ideas. Call on groups to present their marketing programs. BLOCK SCHEDULING

## Place

*Where* the product should be sold is another decision of the marketing department. Should it be sold through the mail, by telephone, in department stores, in specialty shops, in supermarkets, in discount stores, door-to-door, or on the Internet? Usually the answer is obvious because of past experience with similar products. A cereal company, for example, would most likely market a new cereal in supermarkets. Another company might decide that its goods would appeal to a limited market. Therefore, it may choose to sell its goods only in specialty shops and on the Internet.

## Promotion

**Promotion** is the use of advertising and other methods to inform consumers that a new or improved product or service is available and to convince them to purchase it. See **Figure 11.6.** Businesses spend billions of dollars each year to advertise through direct-mail pieces and in newspapers, magazines, radio, and television. Increasingly, businesses are also advertising on the World Wide Web.

<u>promotion:</u> *use of advertising to inform consumers that a new or improved product or service is available and to persuade them to purchase it*

<u>direct-mail advertising:</u> *type of promotion using a mailer that usually includes a letter describing the product or service and an order blank or application form*

**Types of Promotion** The particular type of promotion that a producer uses depends on three factors: (1) the product, (2) the type of consumer that the company wants to attract, and (3) the amount of money the company plans to spend. Magazines and catalogs, credit card companies, and insurance companies often use **direct-mail advertising.** The mailer usually includes a letter describing the product or service and an order blank.

Other promotional efforts include free samples, cents-off coupons, gifts, and rebates. Where and how a product is displayed

**FIGURE** 

**Promotion** Product promotion is done in many ways, including having celebrities endorse the product's fine features, as Hawthorne is doing in the cartoon below. ***What are other types of promotion?***

**SHERMAN'S LAGOON**

Reprinted with special permission of King Features Syndicate.



## Extending the Content

**Product Life Cycle** Marketers may use a number of techniques to extend the life of old products. First, they may change the way the product looks. Packaging, labeling, and size can all be redesigned. Second, marketers may find new uses for the product and then change the advertising focus, attempting to persuade consumers that they need the product for its new uses. For example, the makers of Arm & Hammer Baking Soda extended the product's life by persuading consumers that they could use it as a cleaning agent, toothpaste, first aid remedy, antacid, and refrigerator deodorizer.



# 3 Assess

## Meeting Lesson Objectives

Assign Section 2 Assessment as homework or an in-class activity.

Use **Interactive Tutor Self-Assessment Software** to review Section 2.

**Section Quiz 11-2**

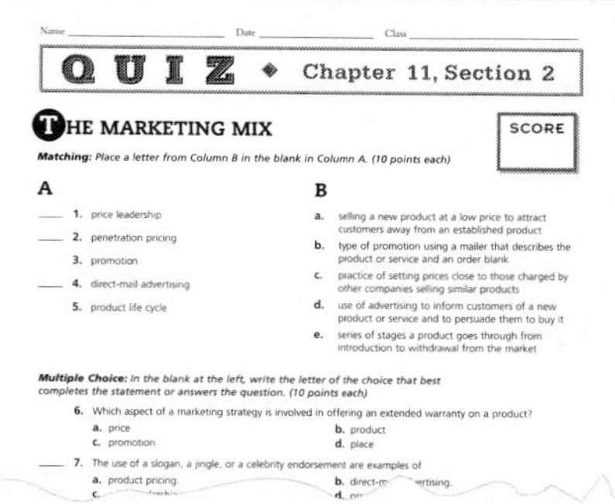

Name ______ Date ______ Class ______

**QUIZ ◆ Chapter 11, Section 2**

**THE MARKETING MIX** SCORE

***Matching:*** *Place a letter from Column B in the blank in Column A. (10 points each)*

**A**

___ 1. price leadership
___ 2. penetration pricing
3. promotion
___ 4. direct-mail advertising
5. product life cycle

**B**

a. selling a new product at a low price to attract customers away from an established product
b. type of promotion using a mailer that describes the product or service and an order blank
c. practice of setting prices close to those charged by other companies selling similar products
d. use of advertising to inform customers of a new product or service and to persuade them to buy it
e. series of stages a product goes through from introduction to withdrawal from the market

***Multiple Choice:*** *In the blank at the left, write the letter of the choice that best completes the statement or answers the question. (10 points each)*

6. Which aspect of a marketing strategy is involved in offering an extended warranty on a product?
a. price b. product
c. promotion d. place

___ 7. The use of a slogan, a jingle, or a celebrity endorsement are examples of
a. product pricing. b. direct-m[illegible]ertising.

## Visual Instruction FIGURE 11.6

After students have studied **Figure 11.6**, ask them to identify the advertising media available to businesses. *(direct mail, newspapers, magazines, radio, television, World Wide Web)* To dramatize the growing use of the Internet as an advertising medium, tell students that in 1999 American businesses spent about $2.8 billion on Web advertising. This figure is expected to grow to $22 billion by 2004.

**Answer:** *direct mail; newspaper, magazine, radio, and television ads; free samples; coupons; free gifts; rebates; product display and placement*

CHAPTER 11
SECTION 2, Pages 296–300

See the **Web Activity Lesson Plan** at *ett.glencoe.com* for an introduction, lesson description, and answers to the **Student Web Activity** for this chapter.

## Reteach

Have students create logos or symbols that represent the "four Ps" of marketing. Ask volunteers to display and explain their logos or symbols.

**Reading Essentials and Study Guide 11-2**

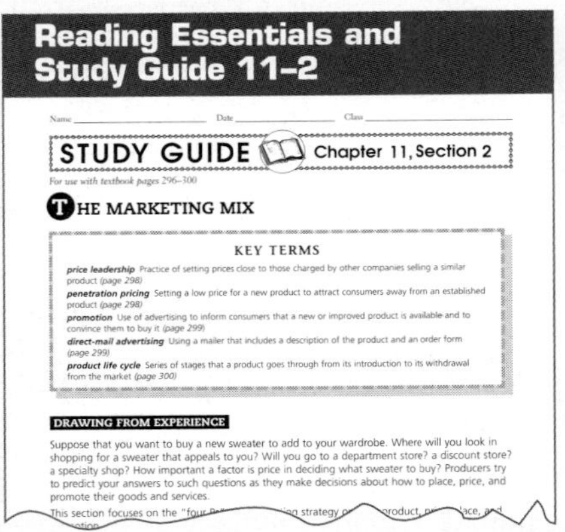
STUDY GUIDE Chapter 11, Section 2

THE MARKETING MIX

KEY TERMS

*price leadership* Practice of setting prices close to those charged by other companies selling a similar product (page 298)

*penetration pricing* Setting a low price for a new product to attract consumers away from an established product (page 298)

*promotion* Use of advertising to inform consumers that a new or improved product is available and to convince them to buy it (page 299)

*direct-mail advertising* Using a mailer that includes a description of the product and an order form (page 299)

*product life cycle* Series of stages that a product goes through from its introduction to its withdrawal from the market (page 300)

DRAWING FROM EXPERIENCE

Suppose that you want to buy a new sweater to add to your wardrobe. Where will you look in shopping for a sweater that appeals to you? Will you go to a department store? a discount store? a specialty shop? How important a factor is price in deciding what sweater to buy? Producers try to predict your answers to such questions as they make decisions about how to place, price, and promote their goods and services.

## 4 Close

Discuss with students how the marketing of a product–the computer, for example–might change over its life cycle.

**Student Web Activity** Visit the *Economics Today and Tomorrow* Web site at ett.glencoe.com and click on ***Chapter 11—Student Web Activities*** to see how Web marketing has become serious business.

are important to promotion as well. For example, magazines are often placed next to checkout lines where people wait.

## Product Life Cycle

Most products go through what is known as a **product life cycle.** This cycle is a series of stages from first introduction to complete withdrawal from the market. The four stages of a typical product life cycle include introduction, growth, maturity, and decline.

**product life cycle:** *series of stages that a product goes through from first introduction to complete withdrawal from the market*

People involved in marketing products need to understand the stages of each product's life cycle because marketing programs are different for each stage. A product in its introductory stage has to be explained and promoted much differently than one in its maturity stage. Also, pricing can vary depending on the stage. Prices of products tend to be relatively high during the growth stage.

Many marketers attempt to extend the life of old products. They may redesign the packaging or find new uses for the product. Advertisements attempt to persuade consumers that they need the product for its new uses.

**Practice** and **assess** key skills with ***Skillbuilder Interactive Workbook, Level 2.***

## SECTION 2 Assessment

### Understanding Key Terms

1. **Define** price leadership, penetration pricing, promotion, direct-mail advertising, product life cycle.

### Reviewing Objectives

2. How does packaging contribute to product identification?
3. What two marketing strategies depend on price?
4. How does a firm decide where to sell its products?
5. **Graphic Organizer** Use a diagram like the one in the next column to explain four ways a firm may promote a product.

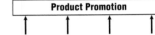

| Product Promotion |
|---|
| ↑ ↑ ↑ ↑ |

### Applying Economic Concepts

6. **Marketing Strategy** Design an advertisement for a new cereal box. Keep in mind that packaging and product identification are two of the most important factors in selling a product.

**Critical Thinking Activity**

7. **Distinguishing Fact From Opinion** Analyze 10 print advertisements in newspapers or magazines. Identify the facts and opinions found in each one.



## SECTION 2 Assessment Answers

1. All definitions can be found in the Glossary.
2. Packaging attracts new customers and creates brand identification.
3. price leadership, price penetration
4. by looking at past experience with similar products
5. Possible ways to promote a product: direct mail; newspaper, magazine, radio, television, or Internet ads; free samples; coupons; gifts; rebates; displays.
6. Advertisements will differ. Encourage students to share and discuss their advertisements.
7. Answers will vary. Have students compare their findings.

# People & Perspectives

## Margaret Whitman

*ENTREPRENEUR (1957–)*

- **President and chief executive officer of eBay Inc., an Internet auction house**
- **Ranked as the richest woman CEO in the world**
- **Voted one of the top 25 "Women on the Web" by a leading women's Internet association**

Margaret "Meg" Whitman has served as the chief executive officer of eBay, the Internet auction house, since March 1998. She is one of the new breed of Internet CEOs whose background is in marketing rather than computer technology. Whitman explains eBay's marketing strategy:

> *"We started with commerce, and what grew out of that was a community. So we think of ourselves as a sort of community-commerce model. And what we've basically done is put in place a venue where people can be successful dealing and communicating with one another. But we also want to expand the kinds of merchandise sold on eBay. . . .*
>
> *[W]e . . . want to get into the kind of merchandise that is not necessarily shippable because it's not economic to ship or you want to see it before you buy it–cars, boats, RVs, things like that. We're also looking at the kind of merchants who sell on eBay. In the beginning, this was strictly about individuals doing business with one another. What happened is that some of those individuals actually became small dealers. . . . Now, we have a lot of merchants who keep their storefronts but in fact their most profitable distribution channel is eBay.*
>
> *We are looking at storefronts as something to think about. Now, all our selling on eBay is in an auction format. And the question is: Are there other formats both our buyers and sellers would want? There are people who don't necessarily like to buy in an auction, and there are sellers who want to sell some of their goods in an auction and some in a storefront . . ."*

### *Checking for Understanding*

1. **Whitman refers to a community-commerce model. Why do you think she uses this characterization?**
2. **What changes in marketing strategy does Whitman foresee for eBay?**





## Background

Inform students that before moving to eBay, Whitman held executive positions at Hasbro Inc., a leading toy company; Florists Transworld Delivery (FTD), the world's largest floral products company; Stride Rite Corporation, a children's shoe company; and the Walt Disney Company. In these positions, she helped to market such well-known brand names as Playskool and Keds.

## Teach

Ask students to identify the "four Ps" of marketing. Then ask them to suggest how the "four Ps" might be applied to a business like eBay–an Internet auction service. Call on volunteers to explain their ideas.

Conclude by asking students to read the excerpt and to answer the **Checking for Understanding** questions.

### Answers to *Checking for Understanding*

1. Answers may vary. Most students will point out that eBay started out as a commercial venture. However, the nature of the venture–an online auction house–helped to create a community where people communicated with one another.
2. Possible changes include getting into merchandise that is not necessarily shippable–large items or items that consumers want to view before buying, reviewing the method of selling, and adding storefronts with fixed prices to the auction approach.

# 1 Focus

## Overview

Section 3 explains the role of producers, wholesalers, and retailers in distribution; the difference between wholesale and retail; and various channels of distribution.

### BELLRINGER
**Motivational Activity**

Project **Daily Focus Transparency 51** and have students answer the questions.

This activity is also available as a blackline master.

**Daily Focus Transparency 51**

FOCUS ACTIVITIES
Transparency 51

DIRECT-MAIL MARKETING

**Totally redesigned: the world's best massage recliner.**

**Twice the rolling action.**

1. What kinds of goods are best suited to direct-mail selling or home-shopping television selling? What are the alternative channels of distribution?
2. Do you think the Get-A-Way Chair from the *Sharper Image Catalog* is particularly well suited to direct selling? Why or why not?

Daily Focus Transparencies

### READER'S GUIDE

Answers to the **Reading Objectives** questions are on page 305.

**Preteaching Vocabulary**

Have students demonstrate their understanding of the **Terms to Know** by using each term correctly in a sentence.

**Vocabulary PuzzleMaker**

SECTION  3

# Distribution Channels

### READER'S GUIDE

**Terms to Know**
- channels of distribution
- wholesalers
- retailers
- e-commerce

**Reading Objectives**
1. What is the difference between wholesale and retail distribution?
2. What are two new types of distribution channels?

## COVER STORY

*BUSINESS WEEK*, FEBRUARY 15, 1999

A rose is a rose is a rose, wrote Gertrude Stein. But don't tell that to flower sellers who are trying to differentiate themselves from their fellow petal-pushers.

To stand out in a crowd, U.S.A. Floral Products, the nation's biggest flower distributor, is test-marketing a plan to sell flowers sporting a tag telling consumers the last date the flowers can be sold for maximum freshness—the equivalent of a "sell by" date on a quart of milk.

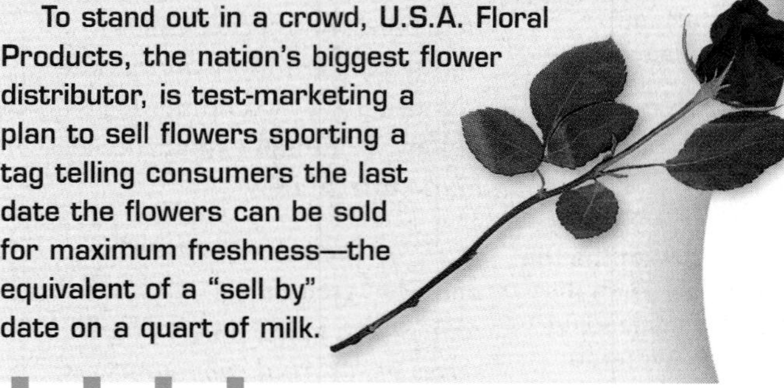

Decisions about distribution, or moving goods from where they are produced to the people who will buy them, is another function of marketing. As you read this section, you'll learn about **channels of distribution**, or the routes by which goods are moved. **Figure 11.7** shows the various distribution channels for different types of goods.

channels of distribution: *routes by which goods are moved from producers to consumers*

## Wholesalers and Retailers

Some consumer goods, such as clothing and farm products, are usually sold by a producer to a wholesaler and then to a retailer, who sells them to consumers. Other consumer goods, such as automobiles, are normally sold by the producer directly to a retailer and then to consumers. With each transaction, or

## SECTION 3 RESOURCE MANAGER

**Reproducible Masters**
- Reproducible Lesson Plan 11–3
- Reading Essentials and Study Guide 11–3
- Guided Reading Activity 11–3
- Section Quiz 11–3
- Daily Focus Activity 51
- Daily Lecture Notes 11–3

**Multimedia**
- Daily Focus Transparency 51
- Economic Concepts Transparency 5
- Vocabulary PuzzleMaker
- Interactive Tutor Self-Assessment Software
- ExamView® Pro Testmaker
- MindJogger Videoquiz
- NBR's *Economics & You*
- Presentation Plus!

## FIGURE 11.7 Channels of Distribution

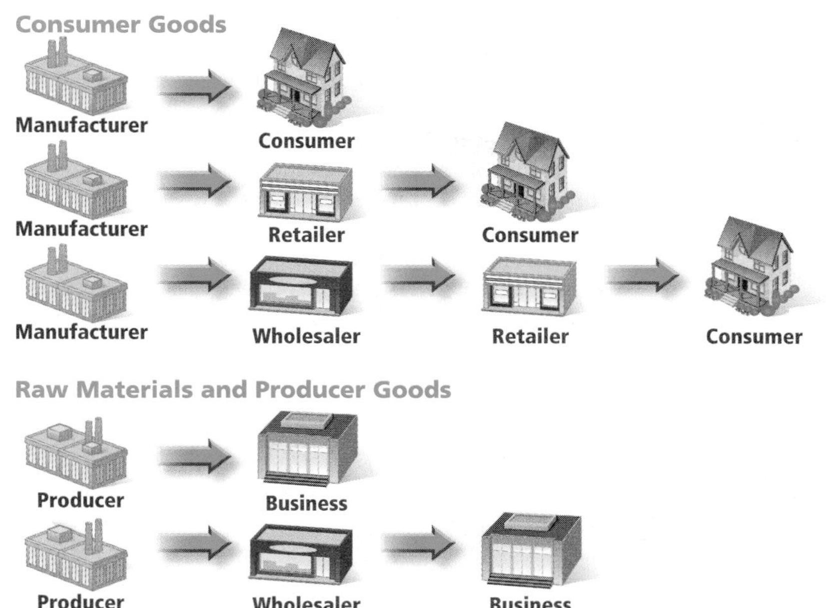


business deal, the price increases. Few goods go directly from producer to consumer; an example of this would be vegetables sold at a farmer's roadside stand. See **Figure 11.8** on page 304.

**Wholesalers** Businesses that purchase large quantities of goods from producers for resale to other businesses (not to consumers) are called **wholesalers.** Various types of wholesalers exist. Some may buy goods from manufacturers and sell them to retail stores that then deal directly with consumers. Others may also buy and sell raw materials or capital goods to manufacturers.

*wholesalers: businesses that purchase large quantities of goods from producers for resale to other businesses*

**Retailers** Businesses that sell consumer goods directly to the public are **retailers.** You are probably familiar with many of them: department stores, discount stores, supermarkets, mail-order houses, specialty stores such as bookshops, and so on.

Traditional retailers have also "set up shop" on the World Wide Web. More and more, there are **e-commerce** retailers that have no physical store anywhere. They are "virtual companies." You'll read more about e-commerce in Chapter 22.

*retailers: businesses that sell consumer goods directly to the public*

*e-commerce: business transactions conducted over computer networks, in particular the World Wide Web*



## CHAPTER 11
SECTION 3, Pages 302–305

# 2 Teach

## Guided Practice

L2 Applying Ideas Direct students to list the various items they and members of their family have purchased over the last week. Next, have students organize listed items into categories–food, clothing, entertainment, and so on. For one item from each category, have students diagram the distribution channel the product followed to get to them, the consumers. Have students compare and discuss their diagrams.

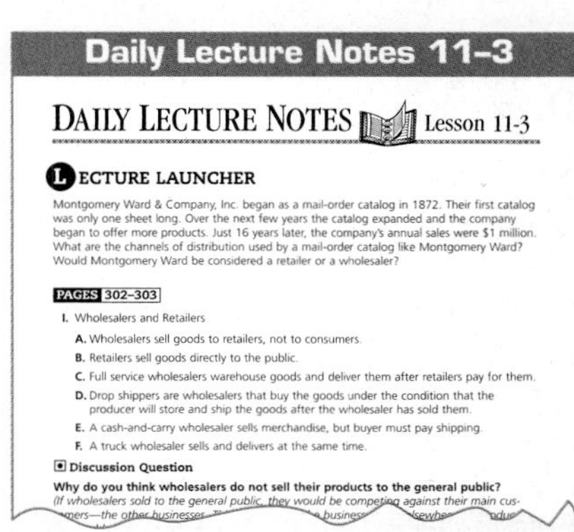
**Daily Lecture Notes 11-3**

DAILY LECTURE NOTES Lesson 11-3

LECTURE LAUNCHER

Montgomery Ward & Company, Inc. began as a mail-order catalog in 1872. Their first catalog was only one sheet long. Over the next few years the catalog expanded and the company began to offer more products. Just 16 years later, the company's annual sales were $1 million. What are the channels of distribution used by a mail-order catalog like Montgomery Ward? Would Montgomery Ward be considered a retailer or a wholesaler?

PAGES 302–303

I. Wholesalers and Retailers
   - A. Wholesalers sell goods to retailers, not to consumers.
   - B. Retailers sell goods directly to the public.
   - C. Full service wholesalers warehouse goods and deliver them after retailers pay for them.
   - D. Drop shippers are wholesalers that buy the goods under the condition that the producer will store and ship the goods after the wholesaler has sold them.
   - E. A cash-and-carry wholesaler sells merchandise, but buyer must pay shipping.
   - F. A truck wholesaler sells and delivers at the same time.

**Discussion Question**

**Why do you think wholesalers do not sell their products to the general public?**
*(If wholesalers sold to the general public, they would be competing against their main cus-*

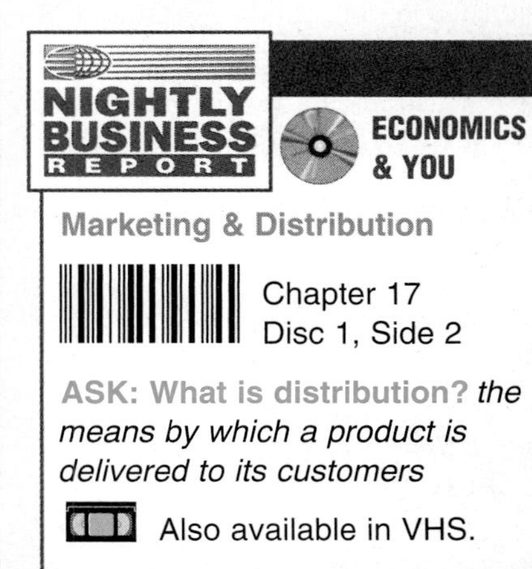

NIGHTLY BUSINESS REPORT
ECONOMICS & YOU
Marketing & Distribution
Chapter 17
Disc 1, Side 2
ASK: What is distribution? the means by which a product is delivered to its customers
Also available in VHS.


## Meeting Special Needs

**Hearing Disability** Students with hearing disabilities may have trouble keeping pace in activities requiring spoken responses to auditory clues. You may want to alter such activities so that clues and responses are written rather than spoken.

Refer to *Inclusion for the Social Studies Classroom Strategies and Activities* for students with different learning styles.

**Guided Reading Activity 11-3**

GUIDED READING Activity 11-3

Project **Economic Concepts Transparency** 5 and have students discuss the accompanying questions.

## Independent Practice

**L3** Research Paper Ask students to research and write a short paper on the development of e-commerce. Suggest that they include such topics as how e-commerce is transacted, any special features of this method of distribution, the changing dollar value of e-commerce, and leading e-businesses. Call on volunteers to read their reports to the class.

# 3 Assess

## Meeting Lesson Objectives

Assign Section 3 Assessment as homework or an in-class activity.

Use **Interactive Tutor Self-Assessment Software** to review Section 3.

## Storage and Transportation

Part of the distribution process includes storing goods for future sales. The producer, wholesaler, or retailer may perform this function. Most retailers keep some inventory on hand for immediate sales. Many have a two- to three-month supply, depending on the type of merchandise.

Transportation involves the physical movement of goods from producers and/or sellers to buyers. In deciding the method of transportation, businesspeople must consider the type of good, such as perishable food. The size and weight of the good are also important. Airfreighting tons of wheat is impractical, but airfreighting small machine parts is not. Speed may be necessary to fulfill a sale or to get fresh fruit to a food plant. The cost of the different types of transportation helps determine how to ship items.

## Distribution Channels

In the last 10 to 15 years, distribution channels have expanded rapidly due to the growth of club warehouse stores and direct marketing.

**Club Warehouse Stores** A typical club warehouse store requires a membership fee—about $35 a year for individuals and more for businesses. Individual club members usually have to be part of a larger group such as a teacher's union or a credit union.

**FIGURE 11.8**

**Wholesalers Versus Retailers** Wholesalers add value to the product by providing time utility and place utility. The consumer benefits from wholesaler networks, but also ends up paying for these services in the final price of the product. In contrast, a local farmer may act as both "manufacturer" and retailer, and prices may be lower. The trade-off is that consumers usually must go out of their way to purchase the product.

### Cooperative Learning

Organize the class into three groups, and assign each group one of the main headings in this section—Wholesalers and Retailers, Storage and Transportation, and Distribution Channels. Have groups create brief pictorial essays, suitable for displaying on the bulletin board, for their assigned topic. Have groups combine their essays to create a bulletin-board display titled "Channels of Distribution." ELL BLOCK SCHEDULING

The club warehouse formula is to buy a limited number of models and brands of each product in such huge quantities that the warehouse gets very favorable prices from the manufacturers. Some of the biggest club warehouses are Costco and Sam's Club (a division of Wal-Mart).

**Direct Marketing** Direct marketing is done mainly through catalogs and over the Internet. Advertising called "space ads" in newspapers and magazines is also direct marketing. Catalog shopping has become a popular distribution channel to avoid state sales taxes. The purchaser normally does not pay sales tax if the catalog company is located in another state. The same holds true for goods purchased through the Internet, although this may change in the future.

Shopping on the Internet has become increasingly popular because of the ease with which it can be done. Anybody with access to the Internet and a valid credit card can order just about anything on the Web.

### Kmart Shoppers

On any given weekend day, 15,000 people come to Guam's hottest spot—Kmart. Reported to be the world's biggest and perhaps busiest Kmart store, its opening drove down prices of everything from shampoo to Cheerios to stereo sets with its famous discounts.

Little shops on this small island always were able to charge high amounts, jacking up prices to cover high shipping costs into the middle of the Pacific Ocean. Shoppers are now grateful for 89-cent cans of Campbell's soup. They must, however, plan their day around getting in and out of the store. It is so big that customers take cell phones so they don't lose their companions in the aisles. ■

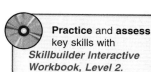

**Practice** and **assess** key skills with *Skillbuilder Interactive Workbook, Level 2.*

## SECTION 3 Assessment

### Understanding Key Terms

1. **Define** channels of distribution, wholesalers, retailers, e-commerce.

### Reviewing Objectives

2. What is the difference between wholesalers and retailers?
3. **Graphic Organizer** Create a diagram like the one below to list and describe four distribution channels for merchandise.

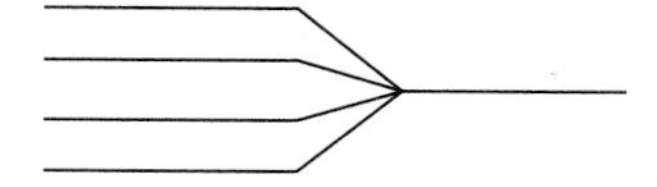

### Applying Economic Concepts

4. **The Role of Government** Research the debate of taxing versus not taxing goods purchased through catalog orders and those purchased on the Internet. What issues are involved, and how many sales tax dollars are estimated to be lost?

### Critical Thinking Activity

5. **Summarizing Information** Type *e-commerce* into your search engine. Research and write a paragraph on the advantages or disadvantages of this type of retailing.



## SECTION 3 Assessment Answers

1. All definitions can be found in the Glossary.
2. Wholesalers buy large quantities of goods to sell to other businesses. Retailers buy goods to sell directly to the public.
3. Answers may include: through wholesalers, through retailers, through club warehouse stores, through the Internet, through catalogs.
4. Answers may vary. Call on volunteers to present their findings to the class. Use these presentations as a starting point for a class discussion on the issue.
5. Answers may vary. Students may wish to use their research findings from this section's Independent Practice activity.

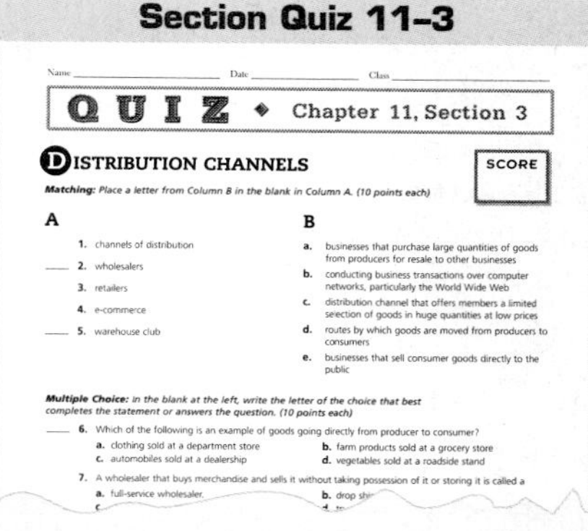

Section Quiz 11-3

Name ______ Date ______ Class ______

QUIZ ◆ Chapter 11, Section 3

DISTRIBUTION CHANNELS

SCORE

***Matching:*** *Place a letter from Column B in the blank in Column A. (10 points each)*

| A | B |
|---|---|
| ____ 1. channels of distribution | a. businesses that purchase large quantities of goods from producers for resale to other businesses |
| ____ 2. wholesalers | b. conducting business transactions over computer networks, particularly the World Wide Web |
| ____ 3. retailers | c. distribution channel that offers members a limited selection of goods in huge quantities at low prices |
| ____ 4. e-commerce | d. routes by which goods are moved from producers to consumers |
| ____ 5. warehouse club | e. businesses that sell consumer goods directly to the public |

***Multiple Choice:*** *In the blank at the left, write the letter of the choice that best completes the statement or answers the question. (10 points each)*

____ 6. Which of the following is an example of goods going directly from producer to consumer?
a. clothing sold at a department store
b. farm products sold at a grocery store
c. automobiles sold at a dealership
d. vegetables sold at a roadside stand

____ 7. A wholesaler that buys merchandise and sells it without taking possession of it or storing it is called a
a. full-service wholesaler.
b. drop sh

## Reteach

To reinforce students' understanding of distribution channels, have them develop an annotated outline of the section.

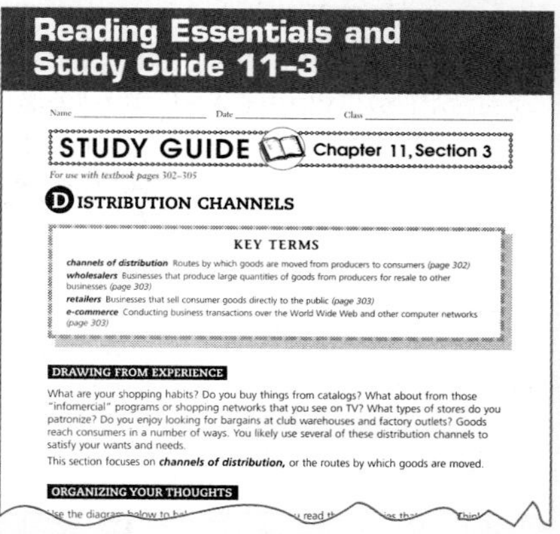

Reading Essentials and Study Guide 11-3

Name ______ Date ______ Class ______

STUDY GUIDE Chapter 11, Section 3

*For use with textbook pages 302–305*

DISTRIBUTION CHANNELS

KEY TERMS

***channels of distribution*** Routes by which goods are moved from producers to consumers *(page 302)*

***wholesalers*** Businesses that produce large quantities of goods from producers for resale to other businesses *(page 303)*

***retailers*** Businesses that sell consumer goods directly to the public *(page 303)*

***e-commerce*** Conducting business transactions over the World Wide Web and other computer networks *(page 303)*

DRAWING FROM EXPERIENCE

What are your shopping habits? Do you buy things from catalogs? What about from those "infomercial" programs or shopping networks that you see on TV? What types of stores do you patronize? Do you enjoy looking for bargains at club warehouses and factory outlets? Goods reach consumers in a number of ways. You likely use several of these distribution channels to satisfy your wants and needs.

This section focuses on ***channels of distribution,*** or the routes by which goods are moved.

ORGANIZING YOUR THOUGHTS

## 4 Close

Have students discuss how technological innovations—the jet airplane or the computer, for example—have affected distribution channels.

## Technology Skills

### Developing Multimedia Presentations

Encourage students to view this skills activity as an adventure rather than homework or a classroom task. A sense of adventure will help create interesting presentations. Next, have students brainstorm a list of possible media that they might use. Do not reject any suggestion—for even those that seen unusual may yield interesting possibilities. You might demonstrate the use of some of these media, showing how they can be integrated into a presentation. You might also invite a guest speaker to discuss or demonstrate the use of computers in developing presentations. Then have students work through the **Practicing the Skill** and **Application Activity** assignments.

**Reinforcing Economic Skills 25**

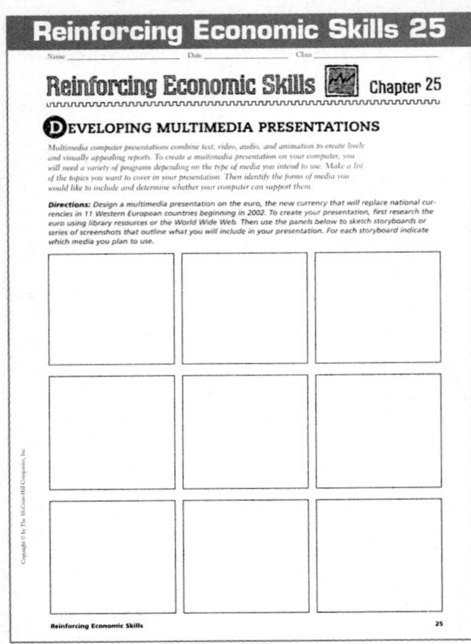

Name ________ Date ________ Class ________

**Reinforcing Economic Skills** Chapter 25

**DEVELOPING MULTIMEDIA PRESENTATIONS**

*Multimedia computer presentations combine text, video, audio, and animation to create lively and visually appealing reports. To create a multimedia presentation on your computer, you will need a variety of programs depending on the type of media you intend to use. Make a list of the topics you want to cover in your presentation. Then identify the forms of media you would like to include and determine whether your computer can support them.*

**Directions:** *Design a multimedia presentation on the euro, the new currency that will replace national currencies in 11 Western European countries beginning in 2002. To create your presentation, first research the euro using library resources or the World Wide Web. Then use the panels below to sketch storyboards or series of screenshots that outline what you will include in your presentation. For each storyboard indicate which media you plan to use.*

Reinforcing Economic Skills 25

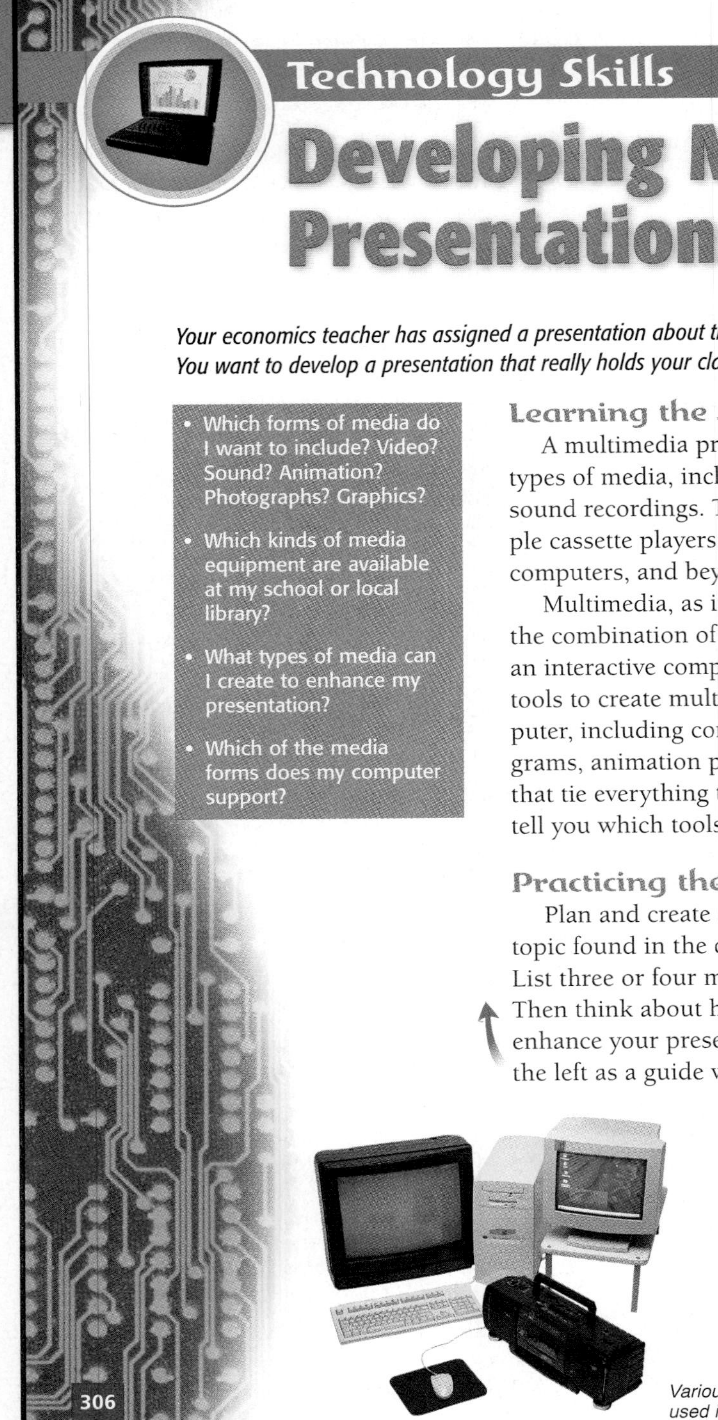

## Technology Skills

# Developing Multimedia Presentations

*Your economics teacher has assigned a presentation about the history of commercials and advertising. You want to develop a presentation that really holds your classmates' attention.*

- Which forms of media do I want to include? Video? Sound? Animation? Photographs? Graphics?
- Which kinds of media equipment are available at my school or local library?
- What types of media can I create to enhance my presentation?
- Which of the media forms does my computer support?

### Learning the Skill

A multimedia presentation involves using several types of media, including photographs, videos, or sound recordings. The equipment can range from simple cassette players, to overhead projectors, to VCRs, to computers, and beyond.

Multimedia, as it relates to computer technology, is the combination of text, video, audio, and animation in an interactive computer program. You need certain tools to create multimedia presentations on a computer, including computer graphics tools and draw programs, animation programs, and authoring systems that tie everything together. Your computer manual will tell you which tools your computer can support.

### Practicing the Skill

Plan and create a multimedia presentation on a topic found in the chapter, such as product promotion. List three or four major ideas you would like to cover. Then think about how multimedia resources could enhance your presentation. Use the questions listed on the left as a guide when planning your presentation.

### Application Activity

Choose an economist from the twentieth century and create a multimedia presentation about his or her theories. Use as many multimedia materials as possible, and share your presentation with the class.

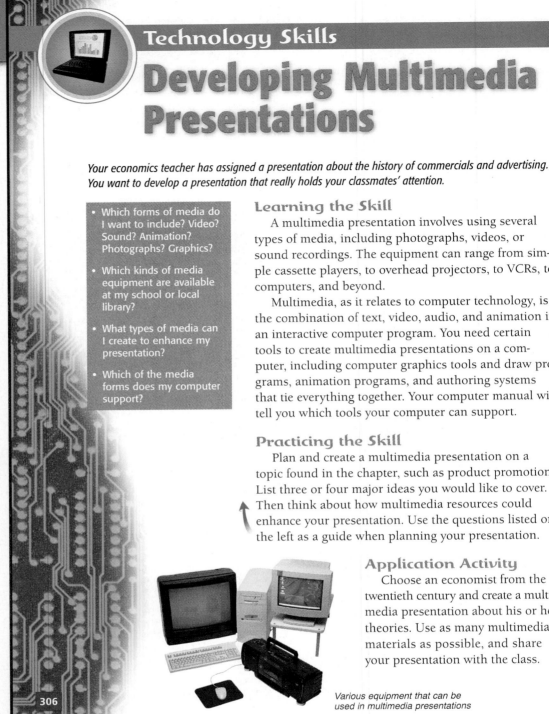

*Various equipment that can be used in multimedia presentations*

306

### Answers to Practicing the Skill

Presentations will vary. Call on volunteers to share and discuss their presentations.

CHAPTER  Summary

**Chapter Overview** Visit the *Economics Today and Tomorrow* Web site at ett.glencoe.com and click on ***Chapter 11—Chapter Overviews*** to review chapter information.

## SECTION 1 The Changing Role of Marketing

- **Marketing** involves all of the activities needed to move goods and services from the producer to the consumer.
- In today's economy, marketing's sole purpose is to convince consumers that a certain product or service will add to their **utility.**
- Utility—the ability of any good or service to satisfy consumer wants—can be divided into four major types: form utility, place utility, time utility, and ownership utility.
- Through **market research** a company gathers, records, and analyzes data about the types of goods and services that people want.
- The first step in market research is performing a **market survey.**
- Before offering a product for national distribution, market researchers will often **test-market** a product.

## SECTION 2 The Marketing Mix

- A marketing plan combines the "four Ps" of marketing: product, price, place, and promotion.
- "Product" means determining what services to offer with the product, how to package it, and what kind of product identification to use.
- In setting a price, a company has to consider the costs of producing, advertising, selling, and distributing, as well as the amount of profit it hopes to make.
- "Place" means determining where a product should be sold.
- **Promotion** is the use of advertising and other methods to inform consumers that a new product is currently available and to convince them to buy it.

## SECTION 3 Distribution Channels

- Deciding what **channels of distribution** to use is another function of marketing.
- Businesses that purchase large quantities of goods from producers for resale to other businesses are called **wholesalers.**
- Businesses that sell consumer goods directly to the public are **retailers.**
- In the last 10 to 15 years, distribution channels have expanded due to the growth of club warehouse stores and direct marketing, including catalog shopping and **e-commerce.**



## Economics Journal

**Marketing** Ask students to select a product they use or are familiar with—a food product, such as breakfast cereal; CD players, training shoes, jeans, pens, computers, computer games, and so on. Ask students to monitor various media for one week and record advertisements for their selected product. Have them note how the product is advertised—what features are stressed, what special services are offered, what logos or other distinguishing marks are used, and so on. Also, have them note how the price of their product varies from advertisement to advertisement. Tell students to use their findings to write a brief essay describing how businesses market their selected product.

ECONOMICS & YOU

Marketing & Distribution

Chapter 17
Disc 1, Side 2

If you do not have access to a videodisc player, the ***Economics & You*** programs are also available in VHS.

Use the **Chapter 11 Summary** to preview, review, condense, or reteach the chapter.

## Preview/Review

**Vocabulary PuzzleMaker Software** reinforces the key terms used in Chapter 11.

**Interactive Tutor Self-Assessment Software** allows students to review Chapter 11 content.

## Condense

Have students listen to the Chapter 11 **Audio Program** (also available in Spanish) in the TCR. Assign the Chapter 11 Audio Program Activity and give students the Chapter 11 Audio Program Test.

## Reteach

Have students complete **Reteaching Activity** 11 in the TCR (Spanish Reteaching Activities are also available).

# CHAPTER 11 Assessment and Activities

Have students visit the *Economics Today and Tomorrow* Web site at ett.glencoe.com to review Chapter 11 and take the Self-Check Quiz.

## GLENCOE TECHNOLOGY

**MindJogger Videoquiz**

Use MindJogger to review Chapter 11 content.

## Identifying Key Terms

1. d
2. c
3. e
4. b
5. a

## Recalling Facts and Ideas

1. Marketing involves activities that add to the utility of a product.
2. announcement advertising; advertising the virtues or benefits of the product; creating demand through advertising; recognition of consumer sovereignty; advertising on the Internet
3. Researchers find out what consumers want through surveys. Researchers conduct surveys at the planning stage, upon customer purchase of goods, and when the product has been on the market for some time.
4. Product–what product to sell, what services to offer with the product, how to package it, and how to develop product identification; Price–what pricing strategy to use; Place–where to sell product; Promotion–using advertising and other methods to inform consumers of product and to persuade them to buy it.
5. through direct mail; advertisements in newspapers, magazines, radio, television, and Internet; free samples; gifts; coupons; rebates; store displays
6. *Place* refers to where a product is sold–mail or telephone order, department stores, specialty shops, supermarkets, discount stores, door-to-door, Internet.
7. maturity, decline
8. routes by which goods are moved to the customer
9. Club warehouses offer less variety, bigger sizes, and greater savings than standard retail stores.
10. producer, wholesaler, or retailer
11. size, weight, and type of good; speed with which delivery must be made; costs of different types of transportation

# CHAPTER 11 Assessment and Activities

**Self-Check Quiz** Visit the *Economics Today and Tomorrow* Web site at ett.glencoe.com and click on ***Chapter 11—Self-Check Quizzes*** to prepare for the Chapter Test.

## Identifying Key Terms

*Write the letter of the definition in Column B that correctly defines each term in Column A.*

**Column A**

1. test marketing
2. penetration pricing
3. price leadership
4. retailer
5. promotion

**Column B**

a. use of advertising to inform consumers about a product and to persuade them to purchase it
b. business that sells goods directly to the consumer
c. selling a new product at a low price to attract new customers away from an established product
d. offering a product in a small area for a limited time to see how well it sells
e. setting prices close to those of competing companies

## Recalling Facts and Ideas

**Section 1**

1. What is the relationship between marketing and utility?
2. What are the historic stages in the development of marketing in the United States?
3. How is market research conducted?

**Section 2**

4. List and describe the "four Ps" of planning a marketing strategy.
5. How are goods and services promoted?
6. What does *place* mean, when referring to marketing?
7. What are the last two stages of a typical product life cycle?

**Section 3**

8. What are distribution channels?
9. How does a club warehouse store differ from a standard retail outlet?
10. Who may perform the storage function of distribution?
11. What are the factors that a business must consider in choosing a method of transporting goods?

## Thinking Critically

1. **Sequencing Information** Suppose you must do a market survey for a new type of running shoe. Use a chart like the one in the next column to list the questions you would ask, and whom and where you would ask the questions.

| Questions | Whom? | Where? |
|---|---|---|
| | | |
| | | |
| | | |

2. **Making Generalizations** What are alternative ways to extend the life of an old product that is in its declining stage?

## Applying Economic Concepts

**The Rising Opportunity Cost of Time** When individuals earn higher incomes, by definition the opportunity cost of their time increases. Economic theory says that they will react in a predictable way–reducing the amount of time they spend shopping. Make a list of the various methods that people can use to reduce the time they spend when they shop for (1) presents for various holidays, Mother's Day, birthdays, etc., (2) food, and (3) photographic and stereo equipment.

## Cooperative Learning Project

Organize into six groups, with each group choosing a particular product from the following categories of consumer goods: home electronics, food, clothing, electric steam generators, automobiles, computers.

After each group has chosen one product or brand within one of the above categories, research the following:

- product packaging
- pricing strategies
- the place where the product is sold
- how the product is promoted
- the product life cycle.

Each group should write a summary of the research results, preferably in graphic form. When the results of each group are completed, compare and contrast the differences in the five categories across the various products.

## Reviewing Skills

**Developing a Multimedia Presentation** Working with a partner, create an advertisement that you think will successfully market a new product. Use multimedia to develop a video commercial, then show the commercial to the rest of the class. Based on your advertising, would they buy the product? Why or why not? (See page 311 for more information on types of advertising appeals.)

## Technology Activity

**Using E-Mail** The club warehouse phenomenon has been around the United States since the 1970s. E-mail 10 friends and relatives to survey their use of club warehouse stores. What percentage patronizes this type of store? What are their reasons for doing so? Did you receive any negative E-mails about warehouse stores (forcing small retailers out of business, for example)? Assemble your responses and summarize them in a paragraph.

## Analyzing the Global Economy

Contact the foreign language teachers in your school to see if they have any advertising materials (print or video) showing commercials from other countries. (Many cable television channels carry foreign stations, too.) Even without translating the language spoken or written, can you understand the purpose of the advertisement? Write several paragraphs describing how marketing in other countries does or does not achieve the same goals as marketing in the United States.



# CHAPTER 11 Assessment and Activities

## Applying Economic Concepts

Answers will vary, but students might identify gifts, groceries, and other items that can be purchased through the mail, by telephone, or on the Internet.

## Cooperative Learning Project

Encourage students to accompany their graphs and charts with written explanations.

## Reviewing Skills

You might use the video presentations as the starting point for a discussion on what makes an effective advertisement.

## Technology Activity

Have students collate their findings to create a class study of the use of club warehouse stores.

## Analyzing the Global Economy

Ask students if they noted any effective approaches in the foreign advertisements that are not used in American ads.

### Chapter Bonus Test Question

ASK: What marketing tool might a hospital use to improve care given to patients? *a market survey of patients*

## Thinking Critically

1. Answers will vary but should include questions about customers' needs and past purchasing practices. People from different age groups and backgrounds might be asked, and interviews might be conducted at malls, sport stores, and so on.
2. Answers will vary but should include finding new uses for the product, changing product packaging and labeling, and changing the focus of advertising.

## Economics Lab

# 1 Focus

Students are bombarded daily with advertisements in newspapers and magazines and on radio, television, and the Internet. To be effective consumers, students must be able to extract valid information from these advertisements. The Economics Lab offers students the opportunity to review the various promotion tactics used by marketers.

# 2 Teach

Begin by ensuring that all groups possess, or have access to, all the materials listed in Step A. As groups work through the procedures in Step B, offer guidance or assistance when needed. In Step C, ask all groups to prepare an oral report to accompany their tally of advertising techniques used.

It will take several sessions to satisfactorily complete this Economics Lab. Therefore, establish set times for review of students' progress.

## Economics Lab

# *Analyzing and Creating Advertisements*

From the classroom of Stephanie Felix, Glendora High School, Glendora, California

In Chapter 11 you learned about marketing and distribution. A function of marketing is product promotion–convincing consumers to buy the product. In this lab, you will examine many advertising techniques used by companies. Then you will develop and market your own product by creating a commercial demonstrating various types of advertising techniques.

### STEP A Tools Needed

- ✔ paper
- ✔ poster board and markers
- ✔ video camera (optional)
- ✔ props for your commercial

### STEP B Procedures to Follow

1. Working in groups of no more than four people, come up with an idea for a product. As a group, submit a one-page typed paper describing your product and answering these questions:
   - What does it do?
   - What is the price?
   - Who is your target market?
   - How are you going to promote your product?
2. On poster board, design the packaging of your product. Include the product's name and any special logos or phrases for product identification.
3. Next, analyze the chart listing **Advertising Techniques** on page 311. Select at least three techniques to incorporate into a commercial about your product.
4. Create a commercial at least 2 minutes long. All members of your group must be included in the commercial.
5. Perform your commercial for the class, or videotape it and bring it to class for viewing.

310

### Teacher's Notes

## Advertising Techniques

| ADVERTISING TECHNIQUE | DESCRIPTION |
|---|---|
| Youthful/Fun | "Use our product and you'll feel like a kid again!" |
| Plain/Humble | "Our product will make you feel natural and simplify your life." |
| Expert Testimony | "I'm a doctor, and I recommend this product." |
| Famous Person | [If Michael Jordan uses the product, it must be cool.] |
| Fear | "If you don't use this, you may regret it." |
| Statistics | "Nine out of ten dentists use this product." |
| Everyone Has One | "Molly the doctor drives this car, and Joe the student does, too." |
| Senses | [Mouth-watering pizza, steaming hot cocoa, sizzling burgers] |
| Snob | "It may be more expensive, but aren't you worth it?" |
| Happy Family | "This diaper makes Susie happy, and if she's happy, I'm happy." |
| Humor | [When you're shopping, you may remember laughing and buy the product.] |
| New and Improved | "Obviously, we made the product better just for you!" |
| Symbol | [Majestic bald eagle, solid Rock of Gibraltar, proud American flag] |
| Overexposure | [News clips, fast speed, quick shots] |
| Healthy | "This product is *good* for you." |
| Attractiveness | "This product will make you attractive." |

## STEP C Creating an Economic Model

Analyze all groups' commercials. Identify and count the types of advertising techniques used in each. As a class, draw a series of bar graphs showing the number of times each technique was used.

## STEP D Lab Report Analysis

After studying each group's commercial, answer the questions below.

1. Which type of advertising technique was used most often?
2. What technique(s) do you think is the most subtle? The most obvious?
3. Which techniques, if any, carry the most validity? Explain your answer.

## Answers to Lab Report Analysis

1. Answers will vary. Ask students why they think this particular technique was the most common.
2. Answers will vary. Ensure that students offer explanations for their answers.
3. Have students explain their reasoning for their choice of the most valid technique.

# 3 Assess

Have students answer the **Lab Report Analysis** questions.

# 4 Close

Share with students the *USA Today* article of the Top Five advertisements. (This article may be found at http://www.usatoday.com/money/index/ad249.htm) Then have students identify the five advertisements they think are the most memorable. Have them explain their choices.

## Did You Know

Advertisers have their own special award—the Clio. First awarded in 1959, the Clio recognizes advertising excellence worldwide in the areas of TV, Print, Outdoor, Radio, Integrated Media, Package Design, Student, and Web Sites.

# CHAPTER 12 Resource Manager

## Teaching Transparency

### Economic Concepts Transparency 16

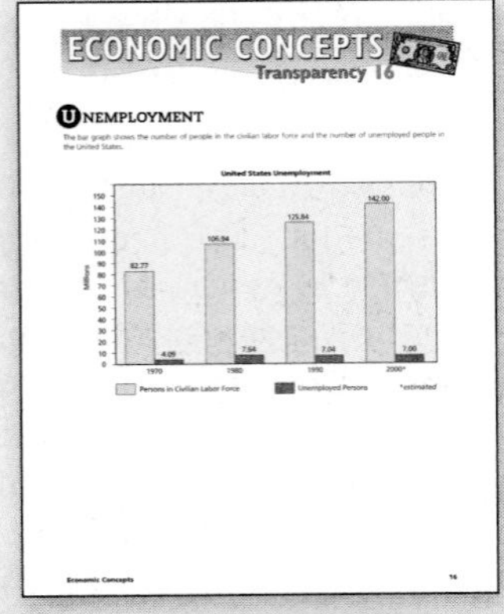

ECONOMIC CONCEPTS Transparency 16

UNEMPLOYMENT

## Application and Enrichment

### Enrichment Activity 12

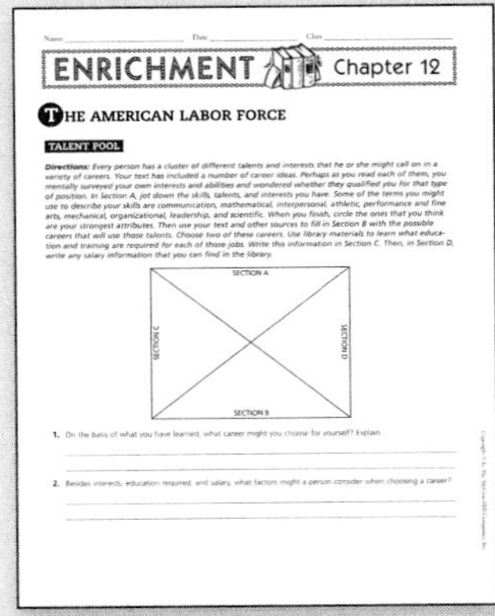

ENRICHMENT Chapter 12

THE AMERICAN LABOR FORCE

TALENT POOL

### Consumer Applications Activity 13

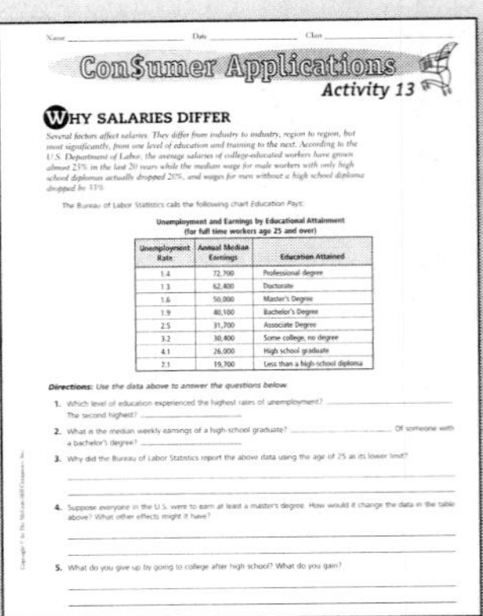

Con$umer Applications Activity 13

WHY SALARIES DIFFER

### Free Enterprise Activity 13

FREE ENTERPRISE ACTIVITY 13

USING ARBITRATION

## Application and Enrichment

### Cooperative Learning Simulations and Problems 13

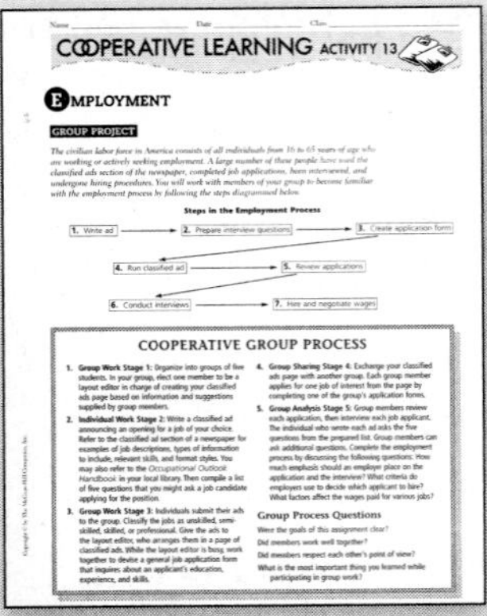

COOPERATIVE LEARNING ACTIVITY 13

EMPLOYMENT

GROUP PROJECT

Steps in the Employment Process

COOPERATIVE GROUP PROCESS

### Primary and Secondary Source Reading 13

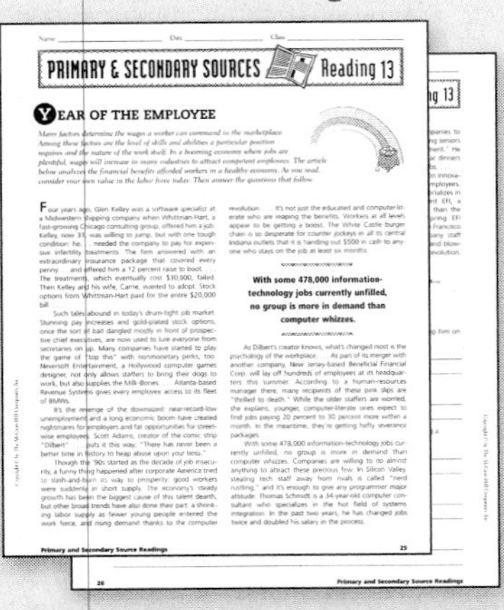

PRIMARY & SECONDARY SOURCES Reading 13

YEAR OF THE EMPLOYEE

### Math Practice for Economics Activity 13

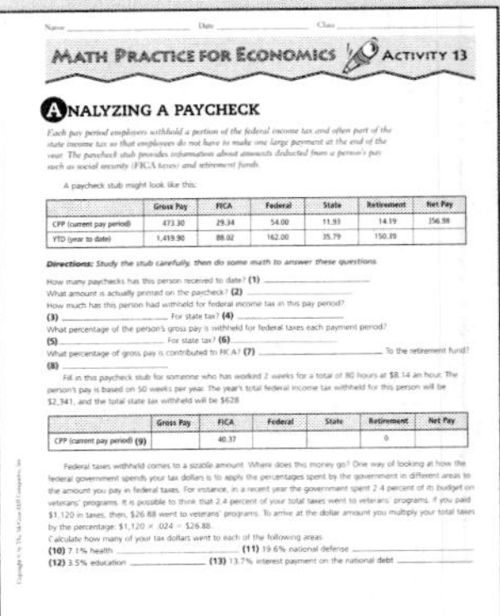

MATH PRACTICE FOR ECONOMICS ACTIVITY 13

ANALYZING A PAYCHECK

### Economic Cartoons Activity 13

ECONOMIC CARTOON 13

QUESTION OF ECONOMIC EQUALITY

EXAMINING THE CARTOON

## Review and Reinforcement

### Critical Thinking Activity 13

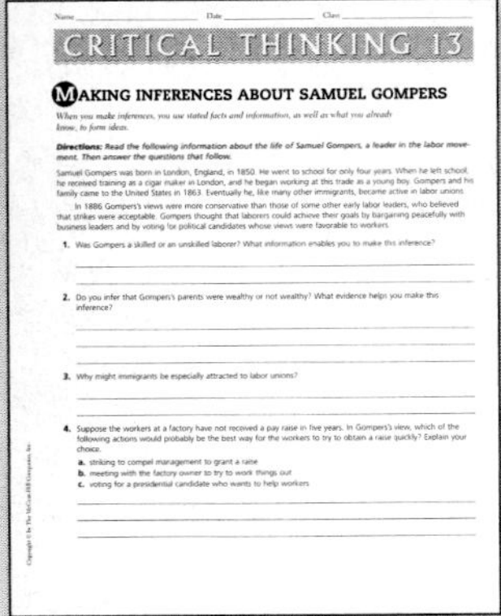

CRITICAL THINKING 13

MAKING INFERENCES ABOUT SAMUEL GOMPERS

### Reteaching Activity 12

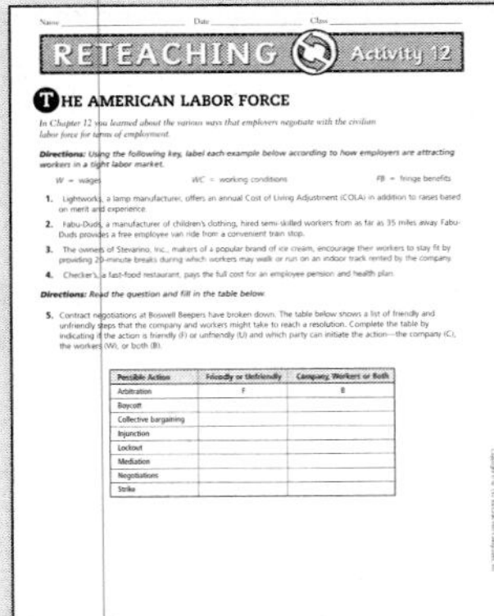

RETEACHING Activity 12

THE AMERICAN LABOR FORCE

### Economic Vocabulary Activity 12

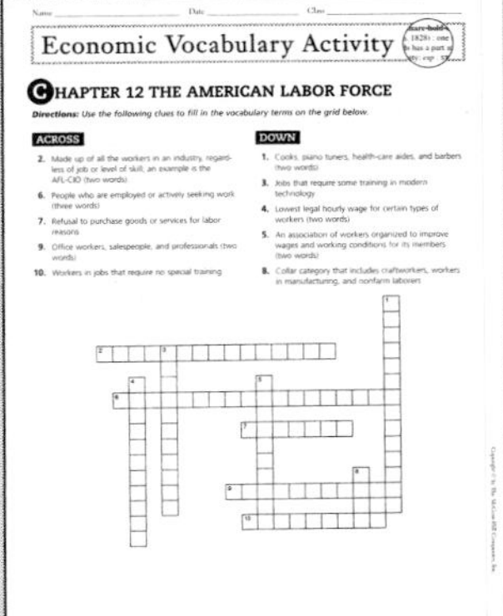

Economic Vocabulary Activity

CHAPTER 12 THE AMERICAN LABOR FORCE

ACROSS

DOWN

### Reinforcing Economic Skills 27

Reinforcing Economic Skills Chapter 27

USING LIBRARY RESOURCES

# CHAPTER 12 Resource Manager

## Assessment and Evaluation

Chapter 12 Test Form A

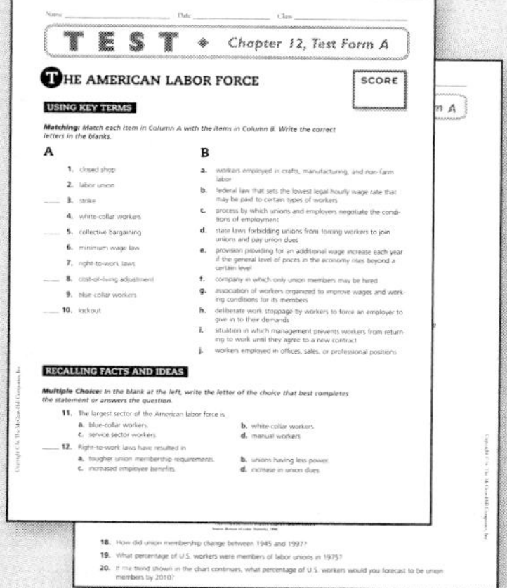


Chapter 12 Test Form B

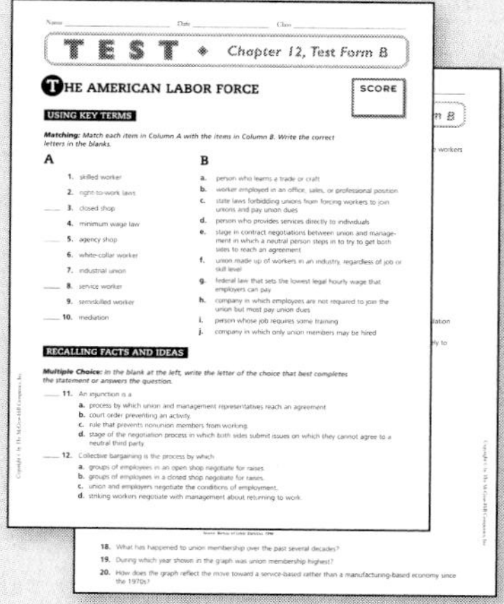


Performance Assessment Activity 13

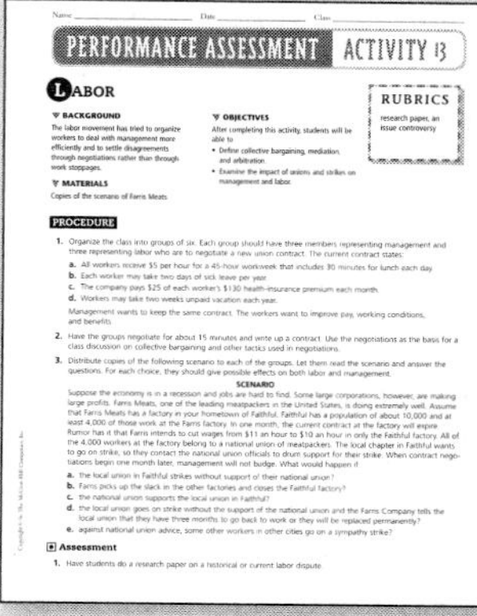


ExamView® Pro Testmaker

## Technology and Multimedia

 Vocabulary PuzzleMaker Software

 Interactive Tutor Self-Assessment Software

 ExamView® Pro Testmaker

 NBR *Economics & You* Video Program (English/Spanish)

 Presentation Plus!

 Glencoe Skillbuilder Interactive Workbook CD-ROM, Level 2

Interactive Lesson Planner

 MindJogger Videoquiz

 Interactive Economics! CD-ROM

 Audio Program (English or Spanish)

## ECONOMICS Online

You and your students can visit ett.glencoe.com—the Web site companion to **Economics Today and Tomorrow.** This innovative integration of electronic and print media offers your students a wealth of opportunities. The student text directs students to the Web site for the following options:

- **Chapter Overviews**
- **Self-Check Quizzes**
- **Student Web Activities**
- **Textbook Updates**

Answers are provided for you in the **Web Activity Lesson Plan.** Additional Web resources and Interactive Puzzles are also available.

Use the Glencoe Web site for additional resources. All essential content is covered in the Student Edition.

## Spanish Resources

 Spanish Economic Concepts Transparency 16

 Spanish Vocabulary Activity 12

 Spanish Reteaching Activity 12

 Spanish Section Quizzes for Chapter 12

 Spanish Chapter 12 Audio Program, Activity, and Test

## Additional Resources

### Reading for the Student

Murray, R. Emmett, and Thomas Geoghegan. *Lexicon of Labor: More Than 500 Key Terms, Biographical Sketches, and Historical Insights Concerning Labor in America.* New York: New Press, 1998. A guide to labor in the United States.

### Reading for the Teacher

Kaufman, Bruce E. *The Economics of Labor Markets.* Hindsdale, IL: Dryden Press, 1997.

# CHAPTER 12 Resource Manager

## Section Resources

| Reading Objectives | Reproducible Resources | Technology/Multimedia Resources |
|---|---|---|
| **Section 1**<br>**Americans at Work**<br>• How are workers categorized according to skill level and training?<br>• How do skill, type of job, and location affect supply and demand in the labor market? | Reproducible Lesson Plan 12-1<br>Daily Lecture Notes 12-1<br>Guided Reading Activity 12-1<br>Reading Essentials and Study Guide 12-1<br>Daily Focus Activity 38<br>Section Quiz 12-1* | Daily Focus Transparency 38<br>Economic Concepts Transparency 16<br>Vocabulary PuzzleMaker<br>Interactive Tutor Self-Assessment Software<br>MindJogger Videoquiz<br>NBR's *Economics & You**<br>Presentation Plus!<br>ExamView® Pro Testmaker |
| **Section 2**<br>**Organized Labor**<br>• What obstacles did labor unions face when they began to organize in the 1800s?<br>• How do closed shops, union shops, and agency shops differ? | Reproducible Lesson Plan 12-2<br>Daily Lecture Notes 12-2<br>Guided Reading Activity 12-2<br>Reading Essentials and Study Guide 12-2<br>Daily Focus Activity 39<br>Section Quiz 12-2* | Daily Focus Transparency 39<br>Vocabulary PuzzleMaker<br>Interactive Tutor Self-Assessment Software<br>MindJogger Videoquiz<br>NBR's *Economics & You**<br>Presentation Plus!<br>ExamView® Pro Testmaker |
| **Section 3**<br>**Collective Bargaining**<br>• What are the major issues over which union contracts are negotiated?<br>• What workers' actions and management responses may accompany a strike?<br>• How has collective bargaining in the United States changed in recent years? | Reproducible Lesson Plan 12-3<br>Daily Lecture Notes 12-3<br>Guided Reading Activity 12-3<br>Reading Essentials and Study Guide 12-3<br>Daily Focus Activity 40<br>Section Quiz 12-3*<br>Reinforcing Economic Skills 27 | Daily Focus Transparency 40<br>Vocabulary PuzzleMaker<br>Interactive Tutor Self-Assessment Software<br>MindJogger Videoquiz<br>NBR's *Economics & You**<br>Presentation Plus!<br>ExamView® Pro Testmaker |

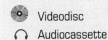

*Also available in Spanish

# CHAPTER 12 Resource Manager

**ACTIVITY**
**From the Classroom of**

**Roger A. Miller**
**New Castle High School**
**New Castle, Indiana**

### Labor and Management

Have students bring in employee manuals from their part-time jobs or from a parent or other relative's workplaces. Study the benefits and procedures listed in the manuals. Have students compare the benefits and discuss why there are differences among them (safety issues, seniority, and so on).

Then have students organize into two groups to take part in a simulated labor dispute. Half the class will be labor; the other half, management. Labor will select an issue or benefit (one missing from the employee manuals) and negotiate for the benefit through collective bargaining with management. Both sides should try to come up with the best solution for the dispute.

### Easy Planning and Preparation!

Use Glencoe's **Presentation Plus!**, a Microsoft PowerPoint® application, to teach **The American Labor Force.** With this multimedia teacher tool, you can customize ready-made presentations. At your fingertips are interactive transparencies, on-screen lecture notes, audiovisual presentations, and links to the Internet and to other Glencoe multimedia.

**Interactive Lesson Planner**

Planning has never been easier! Organize your week, month, semester, or year with all the lesson helps you need to make teaching creative, timely, and relevant—the way it is meant to be. The Interactive Lesson Planner opens Glencoe's **Chapter 12** resources, helps you build your schedule, and tracks your progress.

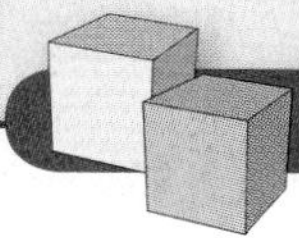

### Block Schedule

Activities that are particularly suited to use within the block scheduling framework are identified throughout this chapter by the following designation: BLOCK SCHEDULING

### Key to Ability Levels

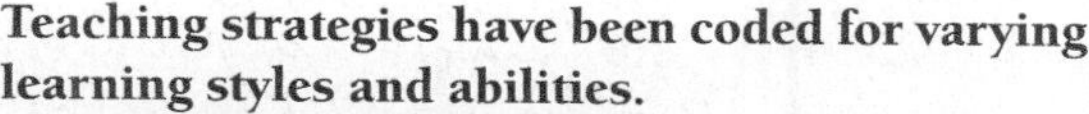

**Teaching strategies have been coded for varying learning styles and abilities.**

L1 BASIC activities for all students
L2 AVERAGE activities for average to above-average students
L3 CHALLENGING activities for above-average students
ELL ENGLISH LANGUAGE LEARNER activities

## National Council on Economic Education

## THE EconomicsAmerica AND EconomicsInternational PROGRAMS

### Voluntary Standards Emphasized in Chapter 12

**Content Standard 10** Students will understand that institutions evolve in market economies to help individuals and groups accomplish their goals.

**Content Standard 13** Students will understand that income for most people is determined by the market value of the productive resources they sell. What workers earn depends, primarily, on the market value of what they produce and how productive they are.

### Resources Available from NCEE

- *Personal Decision Making: Focus on Economics*
- *Personal Finance Economics: Wallet Wisdom*
- *Choices & Changes: Choice Making, Productivity, and Planning*

To order these materials, or to contact your State Council on Economic Education about workshops and programs, call 1-800-338-1192 or visit the NCEE Web site at http://www.nationalcouncil.org

# Introducing CHAPTER 12

ECONOMICS & YOU

The American Labor Force

Chapter 14
Disc 1, Side 1

ASK: Why did unions become popular in the 19th century? *They fought for safer working conditions, shorter working hours, and such benefits as paid health insurance and vacations.*

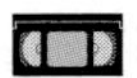 Also available in VHS.

## Chapter Overview

**Chapter 12** explains the composition of the American labor force, how supply and demand affect wages, the development of organized labor, and the procedures and purposes of collective bargaining.

### GLENCOE TECHNOLOGY

Use **MindJogger Videoquiz** VHS to preview Chapter 12 content.

Introduce students to chapter content and key terms by having them access **Chapter 12—Chapter Overviews** at ett.glencoe.com

# CHAPTER 12

# The American Labor Force

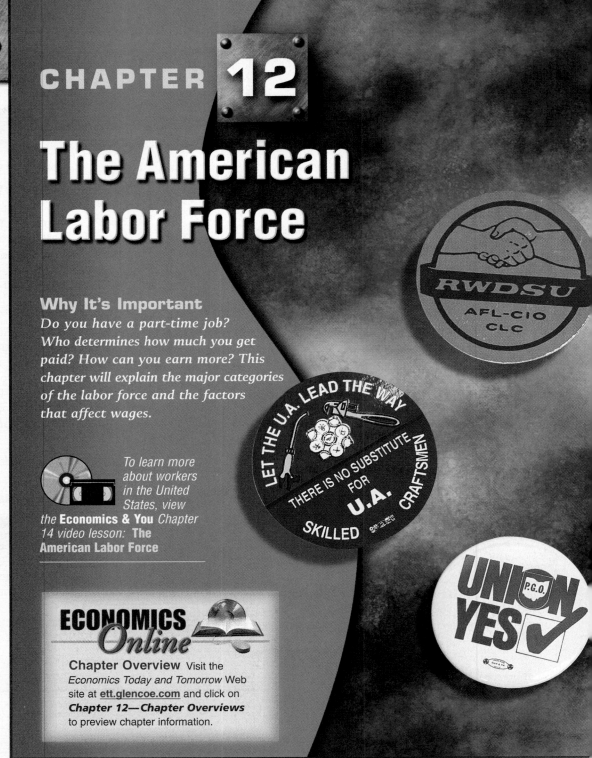

## Why It's Important

*Do you have a part-time job? Who determines how much you get paid? How can you earn more? This chapter will explain the major categories of the labor force and the factors that affect wages.*

*To learn more about workers in the United States, view the* **Economics & You** *Chapter 14 video lesson:* **The American Labor Force**

ECONOMICS Online

**Chapter Overview** Visit the *Economics Today and Tomorrow* Web site at ett.glencoe.com and click on ***Chapter 12—Chapter Overviews*** to preview chapter information.

## CHAPTER LAUNCH ACTIVITY

Encourage students to imagine that they represent workers at a fast-food restaurant or a convenience store and that they are about to negotiate pay and working conditions. Have them consider what they might ask for. Then have them consider what the manager of the restaurant or convenience store might be willing to give. Ask students how they and the manager might be able to bring what is being asked and what is being offered closer together. Guide students toward the idea of compromise. Conclude by pointing out that in this chapter students will learn how compromise plays a major role in the settlement of labor-management disputes.

SECTION 1

# Americans at Work

## COVER STORY

*THE COLUMBUS DISPATCH*, MARCH 17, 1999

Baseball player, president, and cowboy—great jobs, right? Wrong. Try Web site manager, computer systems analyst, and software engineer.

Low stress, short workweeks, and room for advancement put those professions near the top of the list in *Jobs Rated Almanac*, a book ranking 250 of the best and worst jobs in the country.

Nine of the top 10 jobs were in computer or math-related fields. Physical labor fared worst in the rankings, with oil field "roustabouts," lumberjacks, and fishermen taking the final three spots on the list.

### READER'S GUIDE

**Terms to Know**

- civilian labor force
- blue-collar workers
- white-collar workers
- service workers
- unskilled workers
- semiskilled workers
- skilled workers
- professionals
- minimum wage law

**Reading Objectives**

1. How are workers categorized according to skill level and training?
2. How do skill, type of job, and location affect supply and demand in the labor market?

Everyone—from a factory worker to the president of a corporation—belongs to the productive resource known as labor. As you read this section, you'll learn how workers are categorized, how wages are determined, and why employers need to pay more to get (and keep) good workers.

## The Civilian Labor Force

When discussing labor, economists use the term *labor force* in a specific way. The **civilian labor force** is the total number of people 16 years old or older who are either employed or actively

<u>civilian labor force:</u> *total number of people 16 years old or older who are either employed or actively seeking work*



## SECTION 1 RESOURCE MANAGER

**Reproducible Masters**

- Reproducible Lesson Plan 12–1
- Reading Essentials and Study Guide 12–1
- Guided Reading Activity 12–1
- Section Quiz 12–1
- Daily Focus Activity 38
- Daily Lecture Notes 12–1

**Multimedia**

- Daily Focus Transparency 38
- Economic Concepts Transparency 16
- Vocabulary PuzzleMaker
- Interactive Tutor Self-Assessment Software
- ExamView® Pro Testmaker
- MindJogger Videoquiz
- NBR's *Economics & You*
- Presentation Plus!

# 1 Focus

## Overview

**Section 1** describes the different categories of jobs in the American economy and explains how supply and demand determine the wages for various jobs.

**BELLRINGER**
**Motivational Activity**

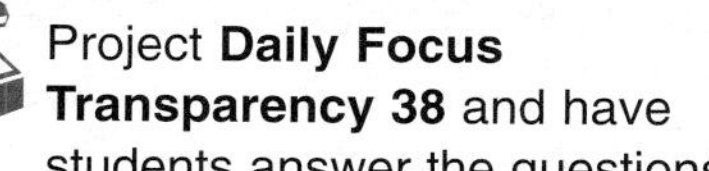

Project **Daily Focus Transparency 38** and have students answer the questions.

This activity is also available as a blackline master.

**Daily Focus Transparency 38**

DETERMINATION OF WAGES

1. Do you agree that economists aren't as important as garbagemen? Why?
2. Why aren't garbagemen paid as much as economists? What factors determine wage rates?

### READER'S GUIDE

Answers to the **Reading Objectives** questions are on page 319.

**Preteaching Vocabulary**

Have students find the definitions of the **Terms to Know** in the Glossary. Then have students use these terms in a paragraph that describes the American labor force.

**Vocabulary PuzzleMaker**

# 2 Teach

## Guided Practice

**L1 Understanding Ideas** Write the four skill categories of labor–unskilled, semiskilled, skilled, and professional–along the top of the board. Call on volunteers to identify jobs that fall in each category. List responses under the appropriate category heading. Then ask students to write a classified advertisement for one job from each category. (To assist students, you might provide them with copies of the classified sections of various newspapers.) Have students compare and discuss their advertisements.

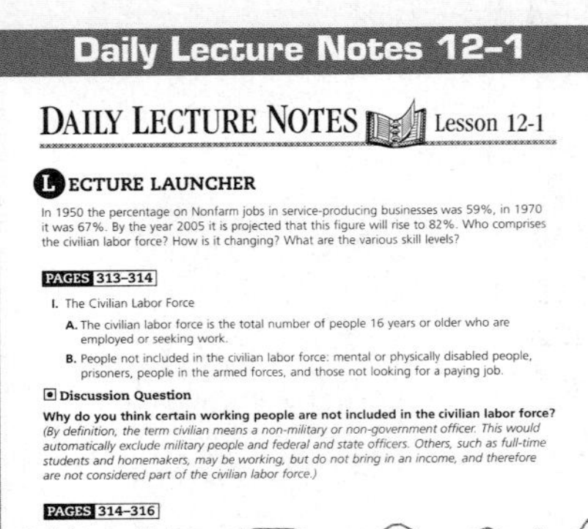
Daily Lecture Notes 12-1

DAILY LECTURE NOTES Lesson 12-1

LECTURE LAUNCHER

In 1950 the percentage on Nonfarm jobs in service-producing businesses was 59%, in 1970 it was 67%. By the year 2005 it is projected that this figure will rise to 82%. Who comprises the civilian labor force? How is it changing? What are the various skill levels?

PAGES 313–314

I. The Civilian Labor Force
   A. The civilian labor force is the total number of people 16 years or older who are employed or seeking work.
   B. People not included in the civilian labor force: mental or physically disabled people, prisoners, people in the armed forces, and those not looking for a paying job.

Discussion Question

**Why do you think certain working people are not included in the civilian labor force?** *(By definition, the term civilian means a non-military or non-government officer. This would automatically exclude military people and federal and state officers. Others, such as full-time students and homemakers, may be working, but do not bring in an income, and therefore are not considered part of the civilian labor force.)*

PAGES 314–316

II. Categories of Workers

### Visual Instruction FIGURE 12.1

**Answer:** *The unemployment rate is based on the civilian labor force. Those not able to work–such as disabled people and those in prison or mental institutions–people in the armed services, and those not looking for a paying job–such as full-time students and homemakers–are not counted as part of the labor force.*

## FIGURE 12.1

**Total Workforce 16 Years and Older**
The number of people age 16 and older who are not in the labor force is not the same number as the nation's unemployment rate. ***Why?***

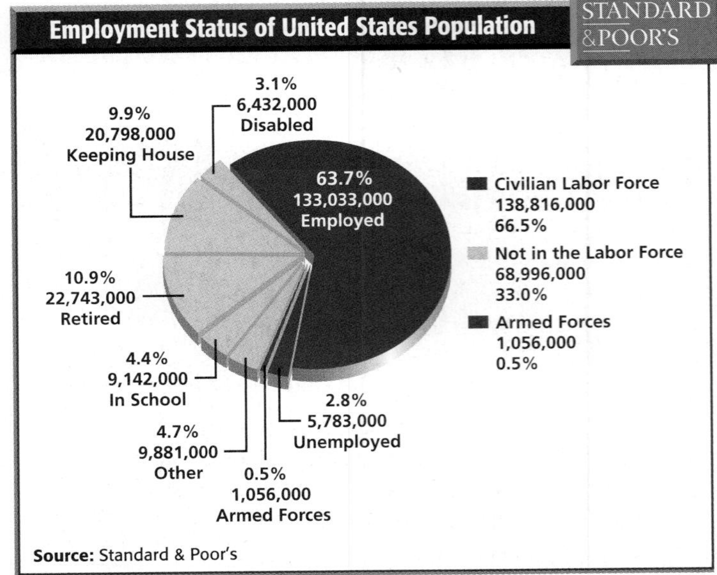

For an online update of this graph, visit ett.glencoe.com and click on ***Textbook Updates—Chapter 12.***

seeking work. Individuals not able to work, such as disabled people or those in prisons or mental institutions, are not included in the civilian labor force. People in the armed forces or those not looking for a paying job, such as full-time students and homemakers, are excluded as well. **Figure 12.1** shows the civilian labor force in comparison to the total working-age population.

## Categories of Workers

Workers in the United States are categorized in several ways. One way is to group them according to the type of work they perform. Another way is by the level of training or education their jobs require.

**Blue-Collar, White-Collar, and Service Workers** During the late 1800s and early 1900s, many farmworkers moved to cities. This migration occurred in part because the increased use of farm machinery required fewer agricultural workers. Higher wages paid to workers in the growing industries of urban areas also lured farmworkers there. Displaced farmers, and others who



### Meeting Special Needs

**Limited Math Skills** When reviewing statistics on wages, students with limited math skills may confuse the terms *mean* and *median*. Help these students by offering the following clues:

1. The median is the middle (both words have a *d* sound, which can be used as a memory aid). Only by ranking the numbers from largest to smallest can you find the middle. If there are two "middle numbers," add them and then divide by two to find the true middle number, or median.
2. The mean is the average—simply add all the numbers and divide by the number of entries.

Refer to *Inclusion for the Social Studies Classroom Strategies and Activities*

entered the workforce because of higher wages, often became **blue-collar workers**—craft workers, workers in manufacturing, and nonfarm laborers.

The largest sector of the labor force is **white-collar workers.** Office workers, salespeople, and highly trained individuals such as physicians and engineers are classified as white-collar workers. This sector experienced steady growth throughout the twentieth century.

In recent years, a shift away from farm work and blue-collar jobs to the service sector of the economy has occurred. **Service workers** are those who provide services directly to individuals. Cooks, piano tuners, health-care aides, and barbers are all service workers. See **Figure 12.2.**

**blue-collar workers:** *category of workers employed in crafts, manufacturing, and nonfarm labor*

**white-collar workers:** *category of workers employed in offices, sales, or professional positions*

**service workers:** *people who provide services directly to individuals*

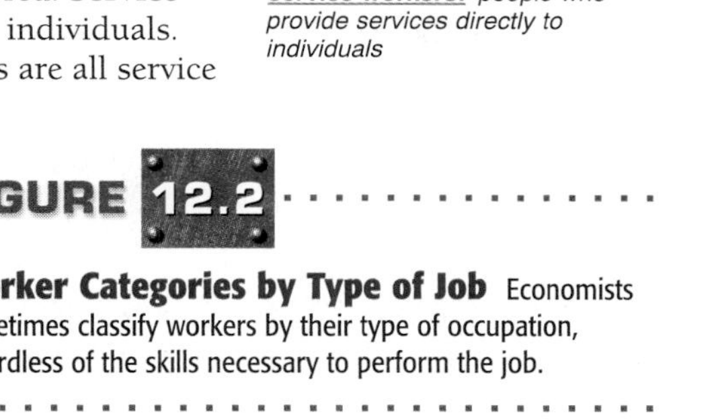

**FIGURE 12.2**

**Worker Categories by Type of Job** Economists sometimes classify workers by their type of occupation, regardless of the skills necessary to perform the job.

**A** *White-collar workers include office workers, salespeople, and highly trained individuals such as engineers.*

**B** *Blue-collar workers include craft workers, workers in manufacturing, and nonfarm laborers.*

**C** *Service workers provide services—haircuts, food service, child care, and so on—directly to individuals.*





**Guided Reading Activity 12-1**

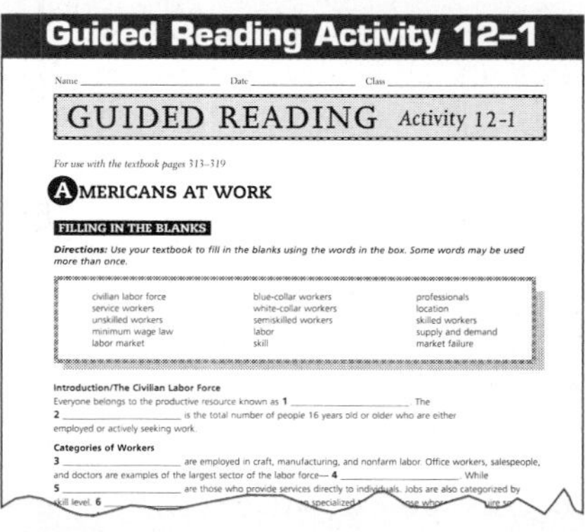

GUIDED READING Activity 12-1

AMERICANS AT WORK

FILLING IN THE BLANKS

Directions: Use your textbook to fill in the blanks using the words in the box. Some words may be used more than once.

| | | |
|---|---|---|
| civilian labor force | blue-collar workers | professionals |
| service workers | white-collar workers | location |
| unskilled workers | semiskilled workers | skilled workers |
| minimum wage law | labor | supply and demand |
| labor market | skill | market failure |

Introduction/The Civilian Labor Force

**ECONOMICS & YOU**

**The American Labor Force**

Chapter 14
Disc 1, Side 1

**ASK: What are the four major categories of workers in the American labor force?** *blue-collar workers, white-collar workers, service workers, and farmworkers*

Also available in VHS.

Project **Economic Concepts Transparency 16** and have students discuss the accompanying questions.

## Cooperative Learning

Organize students into several groups, and have groups create collages that illustrate the United States labor force. Have group members collect magazine, newspaper, and other media pictures of people at work. Inform groups that jobs should range in fields from manual labor to the most recent high-tech developments. Have groups use these pictures to create their collages. Point out that collages should show diversity in terms of range of occupations, types of people working, and types of location. Have groups display their finished collages around the classroom. ELL BLOCK SCHEDULING

**L2 Classifying Information** Call on students to identify the jobs done by people they know or jobs they have read about in newspapers or seen on television. List their responses on the board. Then ask students to construct a three-column chart in their notebooks, using "Jobs," "Labor Category," and "Factors Affecting Supply and Demand" as column headings. Direct students to select 10 jobs from the list on the board and enter them in the first column of the chart. In the second column, have them note whether the jobs are unskilled, semiskilled, skilled, or professional. Ask students to enter in the third column what factors they think might affect how supply and demand determine wages for these jobs. Have students share and compare their finished charts.

**Visual Instruction FIGURE 12.3**

After students have studied **Figure 12.3**, have them suggest how other categories of labor might be illustrated. *Possible answers: unskilled–restaurant worker cleaning a table, landscaping worker raking leaves; professional–doctor examining patient, architect viewing blueprints.*

**unskilled workers:** *people whose jobs require no specialized training*

**semiskilled workers:** *people whose jobs require some training, often using modern technology*

**skilled workers:** *people who have learned a trade or craft either through a vocational school or as an apprentice to an experienced worker*

**professionals:** *highly educated individuals with college degrees and usually additional education or training*

### Jobs Categorized by Skill Level

Another way to categorize workers is by the skills required to perform their occupation. **Unskilled workers** are those whose jobs require no specialized training. Jobs such as waiting on tables and custodial work are considered unskilled, although obviously these types of work require skills such as patience and the ability to pace oneself or to work according to a schedule. Such jobs may also demand the ability to work well with people.

**Semiskilled workers** are those whose jobs require some training, often using modern technology. The job of nurse's aide, for example, is considered a semiskilled occupation.

Someone who has learned a trade or craft, either through a vocational school or as an apprentice to an experienced worker, is considered a **skilled worker.** Police officers and masons hold skilled occupations.

**Professionals** are those with college degrees and usually additional education or training. Also classified as white-collar workers, people who hold professional jobs include teachers, architects, and accountants. As shown in **Figure 12.3,** workers may move from one skill level to another as they gain training and experience.

**FIGURE 12.3**

**Worker Categories by Skill**
This woman moved from a semiskilled position–lumberjack–to a skilled position–manager of the lumberyard.

## Supply and Demand in the Labor Market

The labor market, like other markets, is affected by supply and demand. Suppliers are the workers who offer their services, while the demand comes from employers who require workers.

### Supply and Demand Factors That Affect Wages

Three major factors affect how supply and demand determine prices, or in this case wages, in the labor market. These factors include skill, type of job, and location.

The first factor, *skill,* is the ability a person brings to a job. It may come from talent, initiative, education and/or training, or experience. Because the demand for highly talented individuals is usually high, whereas the supply of such employees is often scarce, a shortage occurs. As you remember from Chapter 7, a shortage usually results in high prices–or high wages. A highly educated brain surgeon and a talented major league home-run hitter, for example, both are paid large sums of money because their skills are in high demand relative to supply.

A worker's initiative also plays a large role in determining wages. Overall, a worker's wages will reflect the value of the

**Free Enterprise Activity**

Point out that wages often include fringe benefits, such as paid vacation time, health insurance, and pension contributions. Organize students into several groups, and have each group select a local company. Have groups visit or write to the personnel departments of these companies to discover what fringe benefits the companies offer. Have groups share their findings with the rest of the class.

## Economic Connection to... Literature

# Shakespeare as Business Guru?

If you want to succeed in business, study the masters: Warren Buffett. Lee Iacocca. Bill Gates. And William Shakespeare.

Shakespeare's plays deal with people in positions of power and responsibility. A workshop at Shakespeare's Globe Theater teaches business leaders to read Shakespeare's works for wisdom that can be applied in the work world.

To weather acts of betrayal, you might turn to *Julius Caesar*. Newly promoted leaders can find parallels with Shakespeare's *Henry V*, who struggles to gain respect in his new role as king. Consider *Hamlet* when you're facing indecision and action. And *Macbeth* teaches how to avoid becoming obsessed with power for its own sake. ■

—*The Columbus Dispatch,* May 27, 1999

product that the worker produces. The worker's productivity will be the major factor in determining his or her success. An employee whose value is easily and generally recognized cannot be underpaid for long by a firm, because another firm will soon entice that worker away with a higher salary.

The *type of job* also affects the amount an employer is willing to pay and a potential employee is willing to accept. Jobs that are unpleasant or dangerous, such as coal mining, often pay higher wages compared to other jobs requiring equal levels of skill. Again, the demand for workers is high, but the supply of laborers willing to do the work may be low.

In contrast, some jobs are enjoyable or prestigious or desirable enough that people are willing to take them even at low wages. Many people take lower-paying jobs in industries such as filmmaking and publishing for these reasons. In these cases, the demand for workers is low, whereas the supply of individuals waiting for prestigious positions is high.

The *location* of both jobs and workers is the third factor in determining wages. If workers are relatively scarce in an area, companies may have to pay high wages to attract workers to move there. Alaska, for example, has the highest wages per person in the country. In contrast, a company in a highly populated area often can hire people

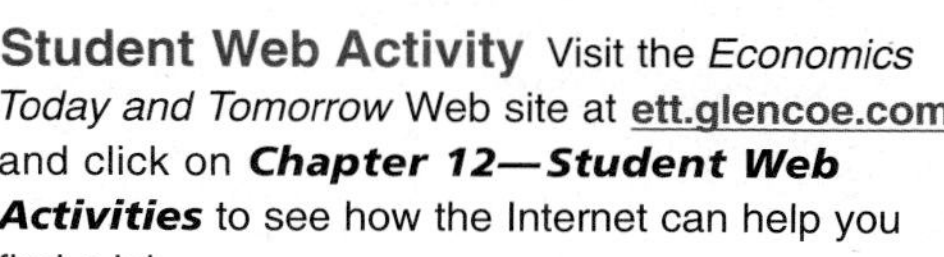

**Student Web Activity** Visit the *Economics Today and Tomorrow* Web site at ett.glencoe.com and click on ***Chapter 12—Student Web Activities*** to see how the Internet can help you find a job.



## Economic Connection to... Literature

**Shakespeare and Business** Why are Shakespeare's plays such a source of ideas for business leaders? According to Richard Olivier, who runs the Globe Theater's workshops, it is because Shakespeare "deals with people in a position of power. There are always kings, dukes, princes, who are put in some kind of dilemma about how to deal with authority, whether it is being threatened by someone or where power has to be negotiated."

## Independent Practice

L3 **Debate** Organize the class into two groups to debate the following: Should professional athletes, rock singers, and movie stars command high salaries for their labors? Suggest that students focus on economic arguments in the debate.

BLOCK SCHEDULING

See the **Web Activity Lesson Plan** at ett.glencoe.com for an introduction, lesson description, and answers to the **Student Web Activity** for this chapter.

## Extending the Content

**Labor Categories** The labels *unskilled, semiskilled, skilled,* and *professional* are helpful in developing a broad picture of the different segments of the labor force. However, some individuals may not fall into a single category. A college student, for example, may work at an unskilled job as server at a fast-food restaurant while he or she attends college. In addition, the definition of the term *technician*—traditionally a skilled position—has begun to change. Some technicians today require considerable training, including a college degree, to prepare them for very difficult and demanding jobs. Moreover, the line between some technicians and scientists—who are considered professionals—is very thin.

**L2 Analyzing Ideas** Point out that the United States labor force has undergone many changes. More often than not, these changes have resulted from the introduction of new technology. Have students research and write an illustrated paper on the impact of the computer and computer-related innovations, such as the Internet, on the labor force. Suggest to students that since these changes are ongoing, they should make the final paragraph of the paper a discussion of possible future changes.

# 3 Assess

## Meeting Lesson Objectives

Assign Section 1 Assessment as homework or an in-class activity.

Use **Interactive Tutor Self-Assessment Software** to review Section 1.

### Visual Instruction FIGURE 12.4

Point out that the cost of living influences regional differences in wages. The cost of living in the North and Midwest, in general, is higher than in the South. Wages, therefore, tend to be higher in the North and Midwest.

at relatively low wages. Even professionals in such a location may not receive high wages. See **Figure 12.4.**

**Restrictions on Wages** If the labor market were perfectly competitive, the changing supply and demand for labor would result in constantly shifting wage rates. The labor market, however, is not perfectly competitive. For one reason, the flow of information about

**FIGURE 12.4**

**Supply and Demand Factors Affecting Wages**

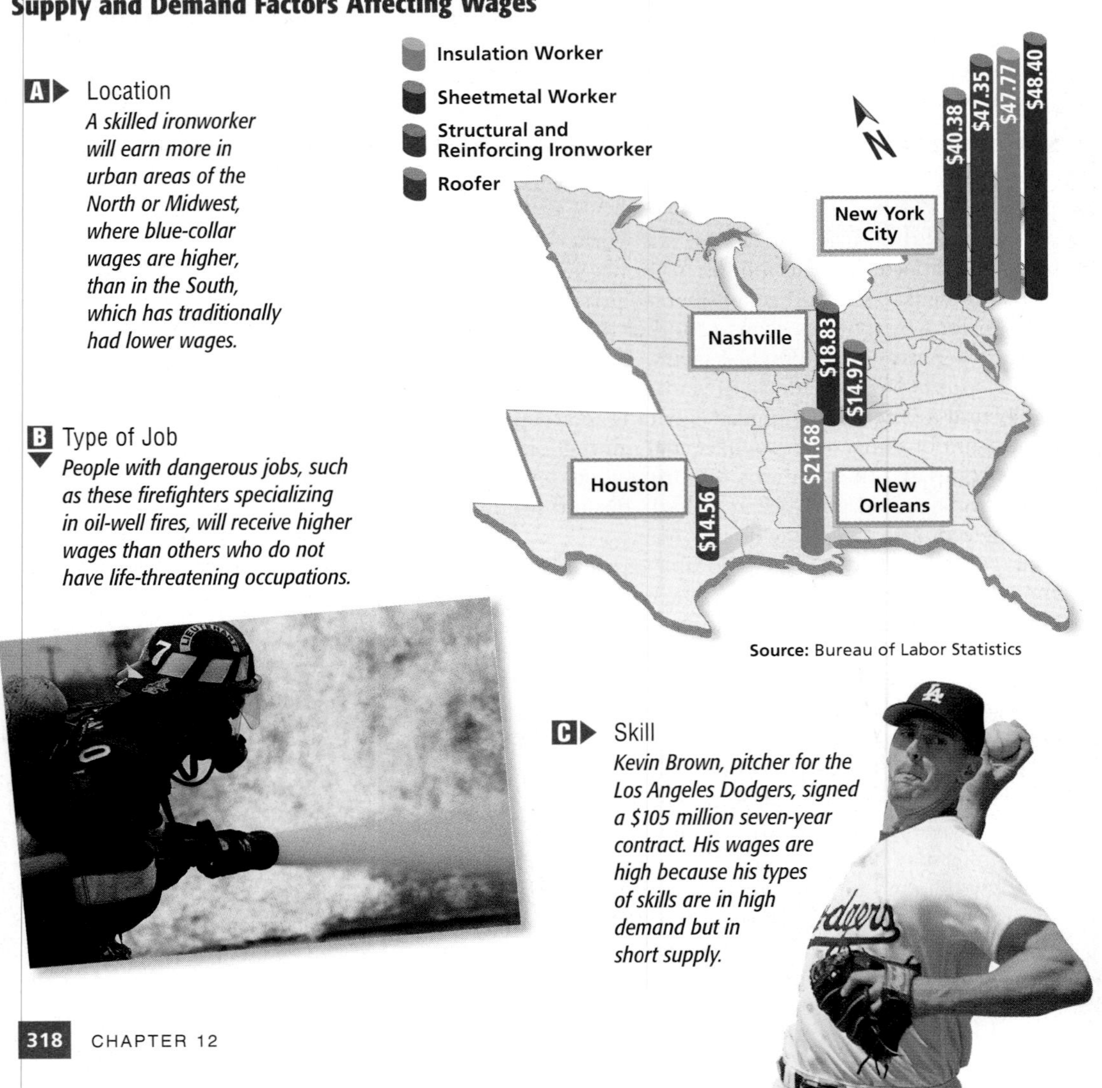


**A ▶ Location** *A skilled ironworker will earn more in urban areas of the North or Midwest, where blue-collar wages are higher, than in the South, which has traditionally had lower wages.*

**B ▼ Type of Job** *People with dangerous jobs, such as these firefighters specializing in oil-well fires, will receive higher wages than others who do not have life-threatening occupations.*

**C ▶ Skill** *Kevin Brown, pitcher for the Los Angeles Dodgers, signed a $105 million seven-year contract. His wages are high because his types of skills are in high demand but in short supply.*



### Relevant Issues in Economics

**Wage Discrimination** Discrimination—unfair treatment based on personal characteristics or beliefs, such as race, gender, or religion—results in differences in wage rates. In the past, women and minorities were excluded from the highest-paying jobs regardless of education or skill. As a result, they were trapped in lower-paying jobs. The Equal Pay Act of 1963—which required businesses to pay men and women the same for equal work—and the 1964 Civil Rights Act—which outlawed discrimination in hiring and firing—helped to end the worst examples of discrimination. Even so, women earn as much as 20 percent less than a man with exactly the same educational achievement and skills.

jobs is imperfect. Workers cannot know exactly what all other employers will pay for their services. Employers, for their part, do not know what all workers are willing to accept. Economists call this lack of information a *market failure.*

Two other factors restrict supply and demand in terms of their influence on wages. One is the federal **minimum wage law,** which sets the lowest legal hourly wage rate that may be paid to certain types of workers. Although the purpose of the minimum wage is to help workers, some studies have shown that the opposite often occurs. An increase in the minimum wage causes some firms to hire fewer low-skilled workers. This can delay the acquisition of job skills by teenagers and minorities and reduce their subsequent attractiveness in the labor force.

**minimum wage law:** *federal law that sets the lowest legal hourly wage rate that may be paid to certain types of workers*

Another factor that restricts the influence of supply and demand on wages is the process of wage negotiations between organized labor (unions) and management. Supply and demand have less influence on wage negotiations than do such things as the company's ability to pay higher wages, the length of the negotiated contract, and seniority–length of time on the job. You'll learn more about organized labor in Sections 2 and 3.

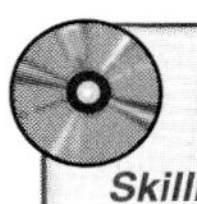

**Practice** and **assess** key skills with ***Skillbuilder Interactive Workbook, Level 2.***

## SECTION 1 Assessment

### Understanding Key Terms

1. **Define** civilian labor force, blue-collar workers, white-collar workers, service workers, unskilled workers, semiskilled workers, skilled workers, professionals, minimum wage law.

### Reviewing Objectives

2. What are four categories of workers as determined by skill level and education?
3. **Graphic Organizer** Create a diagram like the one below to explain how skill, type of job, and location affect supply and demand in the labor market.

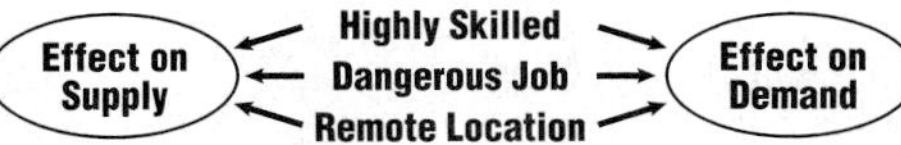


### Applying Economic Concepts

4. **The Civilian Labor Force** Are you technically a member of the civilian labor force? Explain why you are or are not considered part of this group.

### Critical Thinking Activity

5. **Understanding Cause and Effect** Draw two line graphs showing (1) how the labor supply would change in a highly remote location if very high wages were offered to prospective employees, and (2) how the demand for labor would change in a firm that just invested in robotics. *For help in using line graphs, see page xv in the Economic Handbook.*





### Section Quiz 12-1

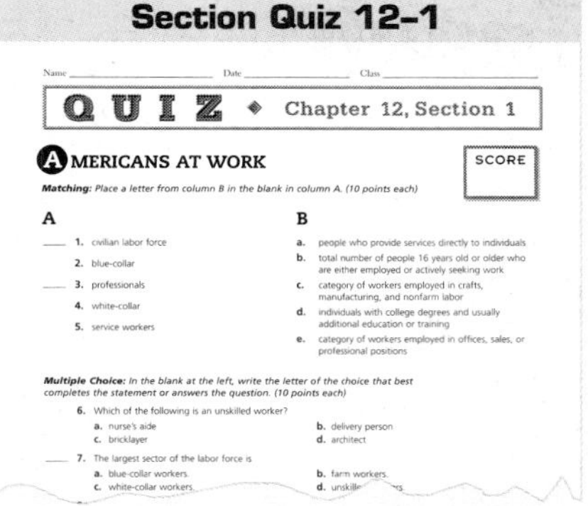

QUIZ ◆ Chapter 12, Section 1

AMERICANS AT WORK

**Matching:** *Place a letter from column B in the blank in column A. (10 points each)*

| A | B |
|---|---|
| ___ 1. civilian labor force | a. people who provide services directly to individuals |
| ___ 2. blue-collar | b. total number of people 16 years old or older who are either employed or actively seeking work |
| ___ 3. professionals | c. category of workers employed in crafts, manufacturing, and nonfarm labor |
| ___ 4. white-collar | d. individuals with college degrees and usually additional education or training |
| ___ 5. service workers | e. category of workers employed in offices, sales, or professional positions |

**Multiple Choice:** *In the blank at the left, write the letter of the choice that best completes the statement or answers the question. (10 points each)*

___ 6. Which of the following is an unskilled worker?
a. nurse's aide b. delivery person
c. bricklayer d. architect

___ 7. The largest sector of the labor force is
a. blue-collar workers. b. farm workers.
c. white-collar workers.

## Reteach

Have students write questions to which the **Terms to Know** are the answers. Call on volunteers to quiz the class with their questions.

### Reading Essentials and Study Guide 12-1

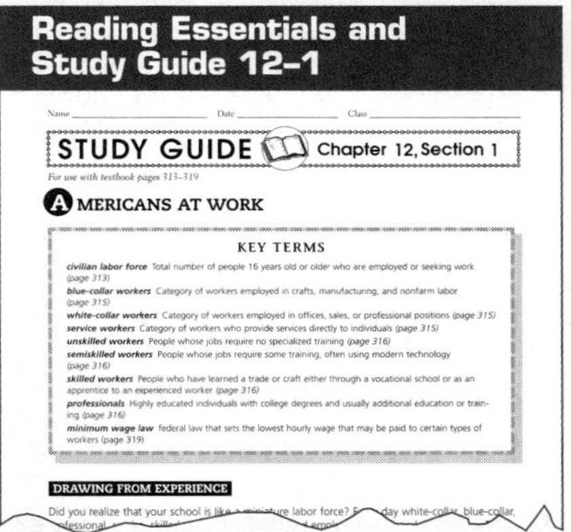

STUDY GUIDE Chapter 12, Section 1

*For use with textbook pages 313–319*

AMERICANS AT WORK

KEY TERMS

***civilian labor force*** Total number of people 16 years old or older who are employed or seeking work (page 313)
***blue-collar workers*** Category of workers employed in crafts, manufacturing, and nonfarm labor (page 315)
***white-collar workers*** Category of workers employed in offices, sales, or professional positions (page 315)
***service workers*** Category of workers who provide services directly to individuals (page 315)
***unskilled workers*** People whose jobs require no specialized training (page 316)
***semiskilled workers*** People whose jobs require some training, often using modern technology (page 316)
***skilled workers*** People who have learned a trade or craft either through a vocational school or as an apprentice to an experienced worker (page 316)
***professionals*** Highly educated individuals with college degrees and usually additional education or training (page 316)
***minimum wage law*** Federal law that sets the lowest hourly wage rate that may be paid to certain types of workers (page 319)

DRAWING FROM EXPERIENCE

Did you realize that your school is like a miniature labor force?

## 4 Close

Have students write a brief paragraph explaining how the forces of supply and demand affect wages.

## SECTION 1 Assessment Answers

1. All definitions can be found in the Glossary.
2. unskilled, semiskilled, skilled, professional
3. The supply of workers in the labor market who fit these categories (Highly Skilled, Dangerous Job, and Remote Location) is low. The demand for labor that fits these categories is high.
4. Answers should indicate that students understand that the civilian labor force consists of people 16 years of age or older who are employed or actively seeking work.
5. Graphs should indicate an increase in supply of labor in the area where high wages are paid and a decrease in the demand for labor in the firm that had invested in robotics.

BusinessWeek
**SPOTLIGHT**

## Teach

To emphasize the problem facing tech companies, mention that a survey conducted in 1999 by the American Management Association found that nearly two-thirds of companies were having trouble filling skilled jobs. Then point out that to tackle this problem, some companies have taken quite extreme measures. Some offer cash "sign-on" bonuses to new employees, while others encourage workers to stay by providing new cars or stock in the company.

### BusinessWeek ONLINE

To find up-to-date news and analysis on the economy, business, technology, markets, entrepreneurs, investments, and finance, have students search feature articles and special reports on the *Business Week* Web site. www.businessweek.com

### Sidelight

Some companies are not taking the enlightened approach recommended by the Hay Group. If they have trouble replacing the workers who have left, they simply load more work on the employees who remain.

# BusinessWeek

## SPOTLIGHT ON THE ECONOMY

# How to Keep the Tech Workers That You've Got

**Check It Out! In Section 1 you learned how supply and demand affect wages. In this article, read to learn what companies should do to keep valued employees.**

With only 7 candidates for every 10 technology jobs, the information technology (IT) staff squeeze is getting worse. Turnover rates are 20% a year and rising. American companies have an estimated 190,000 IT openings. Where to find folks? Here's an idea: Be nicer to the ones you have. That's the key suggestion in a new survey by human-resources consultants at the Hay Group in Philadelphia.

Top reasons tech workers bolt? Poor career development, boring work environment, low pay, not enough chances for promotion, and not enough technology to work on. The answers came from a study of IT professionals who had left their jobs in the prior 12 months. Says Hay Group's Vincent Milich: "It's surprising that even amid this worker shortage, tech companies are still not effectively addressing these key issues."

Milich says companies can combat malaise [onset of illness] by "taking the pulse of the workforce more often and implementing programs that address employees' concerns."

Translated: Pay more, make your company more fun, and help workers develop and advance in their jobs. It's not rocket science, or even as tough as programming C++ yourself, and it's probably less expensive than recruiting and training new workers.



**The Top Five Reasons Tech Workers Quit***

| | Under 30 | Over 30 |
|---|---|---|
| Not enough advancement | 87% | 70% |
| Too boring | 85 | 71 |
| Want more time off | 56 | 43 |
| Want company-paid tuition | 39 | 16 |
| Want more support from boss | 67 | 55 |

*Data: Hay Group

### Think About It

1. **According to the article, in what three ways could companies "address employees' concerns"?**
2. **Why should companies try to hold on to their IT employees?**

### Answers to *Think About It*

1. increase pay, make the company more fun, and help workers develop and advance in their jobs
2. because it is very expensive to recruit and train new workers

SECTION 2

# Organized Labor

## Cover Story

**1884 GOVERNMENT REPORT DESCRIBING WORKING CONDITIONS FOR WOMEN IN A SMALL FACTORY, BOSTON**

The work is dangerous . . . [and they] are liable to get their fingers jammed under the bench, or caught in the die when it comes down to press the parts of the buttons together. A man [although not a surgeon] is provided to dress wounds three times for each individual without charge; afterwards, the person injured must pay all expenses. There are 35 machines in use, and accidents are of very frequent occurrence.

### Reader's Guide

**Terms to Know**

- labor union
- strike
- craft union
- industrial union
- local union
- closed shop
- union shop
- agency shop
- right-to-work laws

**Reading Objectives**

1. What obstacles did labor unions face when they began to organize in the 1800s?
2. How do closed shops, union shops, and agency shops differ?

To have some control over the wages they receive as well as over other working conditions, American workers formed labor unions. A **labor union** is an association of workers organized to improve wages and working conditions for its members. As you read this section, you'll learn that unions are based on the idea that workers as a group will have more influence on management than will individual workers acting alone. (In discussing labor-management relations, the term *management* refers to those in charge of a company—the executives and managers.)

*labor union: association of workers organized to improve wages and working conditions for its members*





# 1 Focus

## Overview

**Section 2** describes the rise of organized labor in the United States and how unions are organized.

### BELLRINGER
**Motivational Activity**

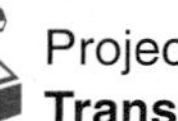

Project **Daily Focus Transparency 39** and have students answer the questions.

This activity is also available as a blackline master.

**Daily Focus Transparency 39**

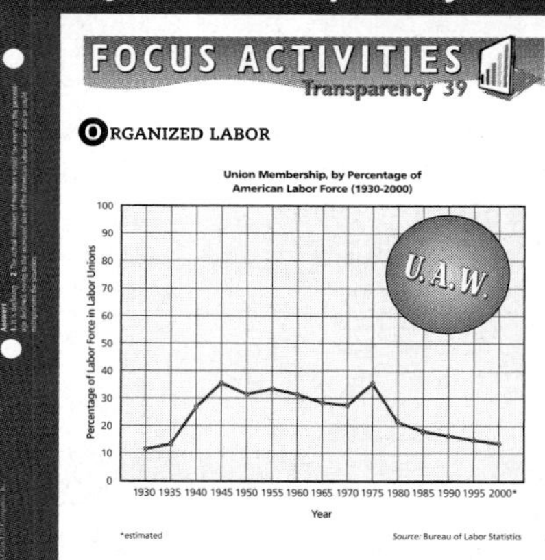



### Reader's Guide

Answers to the **Reading Objectives** questions are on page 326.

**Preteaching Vocabulary**

Have students write two sentences, one explaining the difference between craft unions and industrial unions, the other explaining the differences among a closed shop, a union shop, and an agency shop.

**Vocabulary PuzzleMaker**

## SECTION 2 RESOURCE MANAGER

**Reproducible Masters**

- Reproducible Lesson Plan 12–2
- Reading Essentials and Study Guide 12–2
- Guided Reading Activity 12–2
- Section Quiz 12–2
- Daily Focus Activity 39
- Daily Lecture Notes 12–2

**Multimedia**

- Daily Focus Transparency 39
- Vocabulary PuzzleMaker
- Interactive Tutor Self-Assessment Software
- ExamView® Pro Testmaker
- MindJogger Videoquiz
- NBR's *Economics & You*
- Presentation Plus!

# 2 Teach

## Guided Practice

**L2 Analyzing Ideas** Call on students to identify the reasons why unions were popular and grew in strength during the years from the late 1800s to the mid-1900s. Then point out that since the 1980s, union membership has been declining. Ask students to write a paragraph discussing the possible causes for this change.

**Daily Lecture Notes 12-2**

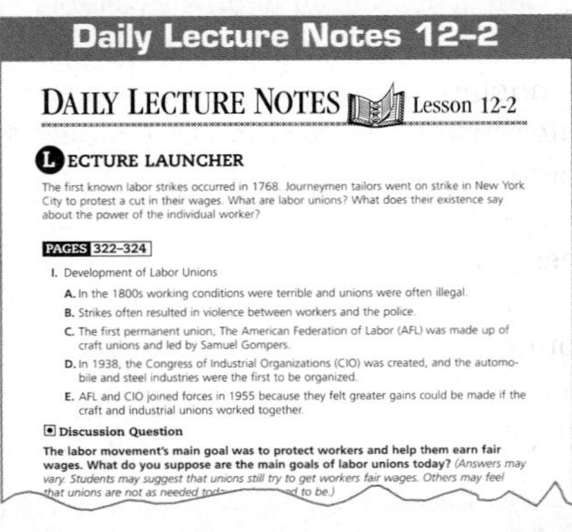

DAILY LECTURE NOTES Lesson 12-2

LECTURE LAUNCHER

The first known labor strikes occurred in 1768. Journeymen tailors went on strike in New York City to protest a cut in their wages. What are labor unions? What does their existence say about the power of the individual worker?

PAGES 322–324

I. Development of Labor Unions
   A. In the 1800s working conditions were terrible and unions were often illegal.
   B. Strikes often resulted in violence between workers and the police.
   C. The first permanent union, The American Federation of Labor (AFL) was made up of craft unions and led by Samuel Gompers.
   D. In 1938, the Congress of Industrial Organizations (CIO) was created, and the automobile and steel industries were the first to be organized.
   E. AFL and CIO joined forces in 1955 because they felt greater gains could be made if the craft and industrial unions worked together.

Discussion Question

**The labor movement's main goal was to protect workers and help them earn fair wages. What do you suppose are the main goals of labor unions today?** *(Answers may vary. Students may suggest that unions still try to get workers fair wages. Others may feel that unions are not as needed tod[illegible] [illegible]ed to be.)*

NIGHTLY BUSINESS REPORT
ECONOMICS & YOU

**The American Labor Force**

Chapter 14
Disc 1, Side 1

**ASK: Why did unions first become popular?** *They fought for safer working conditions, shorter working hours, and such benefits as paid vacations and health insurance.*

Also available in VHS.

**FIGURE 12.5** **Labor's Early Struggle for Recognition** The major weapon for workers to use against management was the strike. More often than not, however, striking unions were viewed as dangerous by the public, who turned against them.

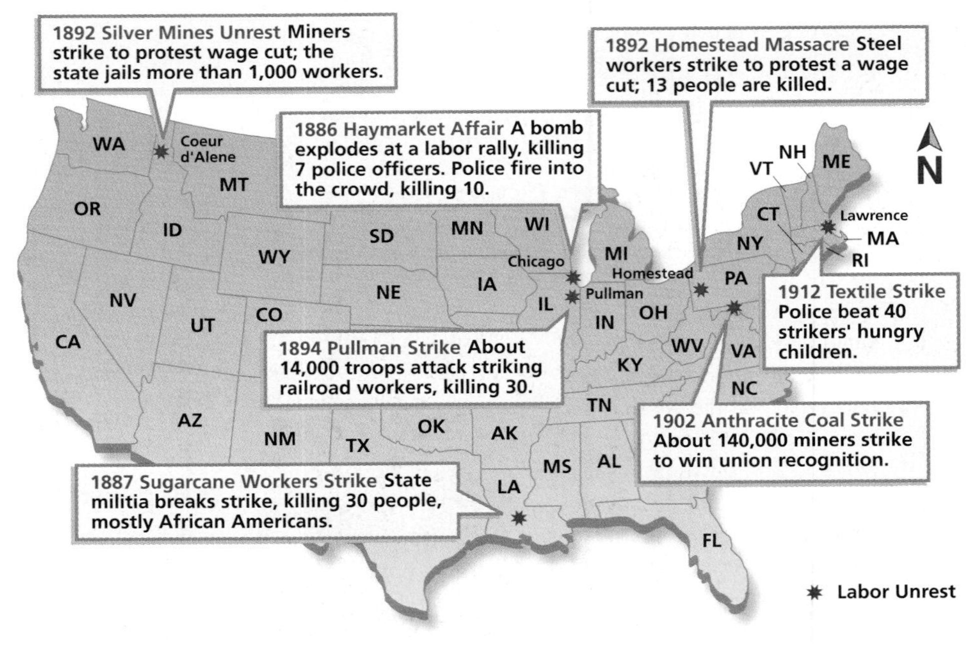
1892 Silver Mines Unrest Miners strike to protest wage cut; the state jails more than 1,000 workers.
1892 Homestead Massacre Steel workers strike to protest a wage cut; 13 people are killed.
1886 Haymarket Affair A bomb explodes at a labor rally, killing 7 police officers. Police fire into the crowd, killing 10.
1912 Textile Strike Police beat 40 strikers' hungry children.
1894 Pullman Strike About 14,000 troops attack striking railroad workers, killing 30.
1902 Anthracite Coal Strike About 140,000 miners strike to win union recognition.
1887 Sugarcane Workers Strike State militia breaks strike, killing 30 people, mostly African Americans.
WA
OR
CA
NV
ID
MT
Coeur d'Alene
WY
UT
AZ
CO
NM
SD
NE
MN
IA
WI
Chicago
IL
Pullman
MI
Homestead
IN
OH
KY
TN
OK
TX
AK
MS
AL
LA
FL
PA
WV
VA
NC
NY
VT
NH
ME
CT
Lawrence
MA
RI
N
Labor Unrest

## Development of Labor Unions

Working conditions in the 1800s were very different from those of today. Buildings were often poorly lighted and ventilated, and the machinery was sometimes dangerous to operate. The workweek was long, and wages were low. No unemployment insurance helped those who were out of work until they found new jobs. Health-care benefits, sick leave, and paid vacations and holidays did not exist.

Workers began to form unions to force employers to improve wages and working conditions, shorten the workday, and end child labor. Unionism, however, met with strong resistance. In the 1800s, state legislatures—influenced by business interests—passed laws against unions, and courts upheld them.

Many businesses refused to hire union members or deal with unions. Workers who were found trying to organize unions were

**Meeting Special Needs**

**Limited English Proficiency** Students with limited English proficiency may have difficulty understanding the types of labor unions that developed and how unions are organized. They may find it easier to comprehend the material if they outline the section. Suggest that they list the different types of unions and levels of union operations and the major characteristics of each in outline form.

Refer to *Inclusion for the Social Studies Classroom Strategies and Activities* for students with different learning styles.

fired and blacklisted—kept from being employed. **Strikes,** or deliberate work stoppages by workers to force an employer to give in to their demands, often resulted in violence between strikers and police, as described in **Figure 12.5.** Not until the mid-1930s did Congress begin to pass laws to regulate labor-management relations. Several of these laws are explained in **Figure 12.6.**

**strike:** *deliberate work stoppage by workers to force an employer to give in to their demands*

**The American Labor Movement** For much of its history, organized labor in the United States has been split into two groups: craft unions and industrial unions. A **craft union** is made up of skilled workers in a specific trade or industry, such as carpentry or printing. The first permanent federation, or organization of national labor unions, was the American Federation of Labor (AFL), composed of craft unions and led by Samuel Gompers. See **Figure 12.7** at right.

**craft union:** *union made up of skilled workers in a specific trade or industry*

**FIGURE 12.7**

**The AFL** Samuel Gompers established the American Federation of Labor and served as its president from 1886 to 1924. Among other causes, he fought for the eight-hour workday.

## FIGURE 12.6 Labor-Management Legislation

| Legislation | Description |
|---|---|
| **Norris-LaGuardia Act, 1932** | Limits the power of the courts to stop picketing and boycotts, and makes yellow-dog contracts illegal. This type of contract is the practice whereby employers require that employees pledge not to join a union. |
| **Wagner Act, 1935** | Guarantees labor's right to organize and bargain collectively. Sets up National Labor Relations Board (NLRB) to oversee the establishment and operation of unions. |
| **Taft-Hartley Act, 1947** | Outlaws certain strike tactics, permits states to pass laws making union shops illegal, and allows the President to delay a strike if it will threaten the nation's health and safety. |
| **Landrum-Griffin Act, 1959** | Increases government control over unions and guarantees union members certain rights, such as freedom of speech in union activities and control over union dues. |





**Guided Reading Activity 12-2**

Name ______ Date ______ Class ______

GUIDED READING Activity 12-2

For use with the textbook pages 321–326

ORGANIZED LABOR

RECALLING THE FACTS

*Directions: Use the information in your textbook to answer the questions.*

1. Why do workers organize into labor unions?
2. What idea are labor unions based on?
3. In the 1800s, how did businesses try to stop labor unions?
4. What is the purpose of a strike?
5. How are craft and industrial unions organized?
Craft unions:
Industrial

## Independent Practice

**L1 Constructing a Time Line** Have students work in small groups to create illustrated time lines of organized labor in the United States from the early 1800s to the present day. Suggest that students include 10 to 15 entries in their time lines. Also, point out that time lines should be constructed with sheets of butcher paper so that they may be displayed on the walls of the classroom. BLOCK SCHEDULING

**Visual Instruction FIGURE 12.6**

Have students review the information in **Figure 12.6.** Then point out that public opinion turned against unions in the mid-1940s. Some people were upset by the labor unrest—in 1946 alone, 116 million workdays were lost to strikes. Other people feared that Communists had infiltrated the unions.

## Cooperative Learning

Organize students into several groups, and have groups investigate the roles that women, African Americans, and other minority groups played in the development of the American labor movement. Have them use their findings to create a brochure that might accompany a museum exhibit on minorities and organized labor in the United States. Suggest that brochures include an overview of the exhibit and several exhibit items—paintings, pictures, charts, graphs, and other visuals—accompanied by explanatory captions. Have groups present and discuss their brochures. BLOCK SCHEDULING

**L2 Writing a Report** Have students select a federal law that regulates organized labor. Have them write a report on this law, discussing the reasons for its enactment; its main points; and any important outcomes for workers, businesses, or the economy as a whole.

## Economic Connection to... History

**May Day** In countries around the world, May 1—May Day—is celebrated as International Workers' Day or Labor Day. One notable exception is the United States, where Labor Day is celebrated on the first Monday in September. May Day actually commemorates an event in American labor history. The American Federation of Labor (AFL) declared a national strike on May 1, 1886, to demand an eight-hour workday. Some 350,000 workers across the United States responded and struck. In the following years, this first major effort to win an eight-hour workday was marked by May Day celebrations in other countries.

**industrial union:** *union made up of all the workers in an industry regardless of job or skill level*

An **industrial union** is made up of all the workers in an industry regardless of job or level of skills. Attempts to organize industrial unions date to the late 1800s and the leadership of Eugene V. Debs, founder of the American Railway Union. The first significant effort to unionize unskilled and semiskilled workers did not begin, however, until the formation of the Congress of Industrial Organizations (CIO) in 1938.

## Global Economy

### Improving Working Conditions Worldwide

Overseas factories drew attention in the 1990s after human-rights groups disclosed that clothing sold in Wal-Mart was produced in a Honduran sweatshop. The Vietnamese factory making Nike products was accused of having dangerous levels of chemicals. The White House convened manufacturers and human-rights groups in 1996 to address such abuses.

Since then, Nike and other companies have taken steps to improve conditions for workers. At Nike's Vietnamese factory, for example, ventilation has been improved and workers are using a less toxic glue. Federal contractors are required to certify that no abusive child labor went into the goods they buy. ■

**The AFL-CIO** During the late 1930s and early 1940s, both the AFL and the CIO launched organizing campaigns that made the lines between industrial and craft unions less clear. AFL unions began recruiting semiskilled and unskilled workers, while the CIO began organizing workers in the skilled trades. The resulting rivalry cost both union federations time and effort.

By the mid-1950s, union leaders realized that the labor movement would make greater gains if craft and industrial unions worked together. As a result, the two federations merged in 1955 to form the present AFL-CIO.

## How Unions Are Organized

Organized labor operates at three levels: the local union, the national or international union, and the federation.

**local union:** *members of a union in a particular factory, company, or geographic area*

**Local Unions** A **local union** consists of the members of a union in a particular factory, company, or geographic area. The local deals with a company by negotiating a contract and making sure the terms of the contract are kept. The influence that a local has often depends on the type of membership policy it has negotiated with management.

**closed shop:** *company in which only union members could be hired*

**union shop:** *company that requires new employees to join a union after a specific period of time*

**agency shop:** *company in which employees are not required to join the union, but must pay union dues*

Not all local unions are alike. Membership requirements and the ways in which management relates to union members vary from one kind of shop to another. In a **closed shop**, companies could hire only union members. The Taft-Hartley Act of 1947 outlawed closed shops, however. In a **union shop**, a new employee must join the union after a specific period of time, usually three months. In an **agency shop**, employees are not required to join the union, but they must pay union dues.



## Extending the Content

**Attitudes Toward Unions** After years of being viewed negatively by many Americans, unions appear to be winning public support once again. A survey conducted in 1999 found that in the six years since 1993, negative attitudes toward unions dropped from 34 percent of the population to 23 percent. In the same period, positive attitudes toward unions showed a moderate rise. Among Americans aged 18–34, positive attitudes exceeded negative attitudes two to one. This approval among younger people, union leaders feel, bodes well for recruitment in the future.

Supporters of union shops and agency shops argue that employees in companies that are unionized should be required to pay union dues because they benefit from contracts the union negotiates. Opponents believe that a person should not be required to join a union.

Since 1947 a number of states, as shown in **Figure 12.8,** have passed **right-to-work laws** that forbid union shops. These laws allow workers to continue working in a particular job without joining a union. The benefits negotiated by the union must be made

**right-to-work laws:** *state laws forbidding unions from forcing workers to join and pay union dues*

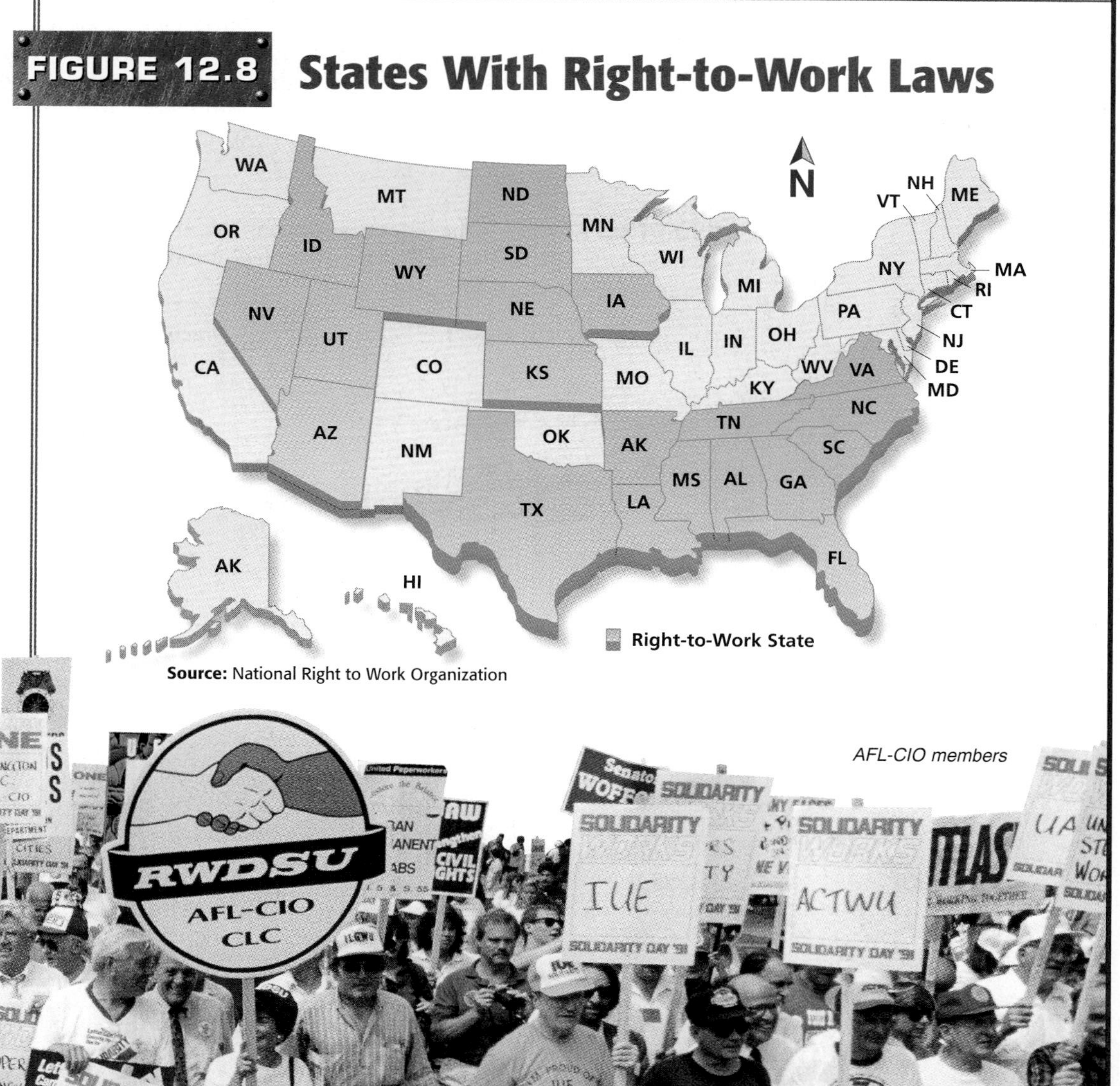


**FIGURE 12.8 States With Right-to-Work Laws**

*AFL-CIO members*

## Relevant Issues in Economics

**Unions and Wages** Economists have tried to evaluate the economic impact of unions by looking at wages in unionized and nonunionized industries. Several studies found that union workers received wages that were 10 to 17 percent higher than those of nonunion workers. However, most economists do not feel that unions have driven up the overall level of wages in the economy. In other words, businesses are not paying wage rates higher than they can bear. Union workers' higher wages, then, come not at the expense of businesses but at the expense of the wages of nonunion workers.



### Visual Instruction FIGURE 12.8

Have students study the map in **Figure 12.8.** **ASK: In which regions of the United States are most right-to-work states found?** *the South and West*

# 3 Assess

## Meeting Lesson Objectives

Assign Section 2 Assessment as homework or an in-class activity.

Use **Interactive Tutor Self-Assessment Software** to review Section 2.

### Section Quiz 12–2

Name ______ Date ______ Class ______

QUIZ ◆ Chapter 12, Section 2

ORGANIZED LABOR

SCORE

***Matching:*** *Place a letter from Column B in the blank in Column A. (10 points each)*

| A | B |
|---|---|
| ___ 1. labor union | a. union made up of all the workers in an industry regardless of job or skill level |
| ___ 2. strike | b. deliberate work stoppage by workers to force an employer to give in to their demands |
| ___ 3. craft union | c. association of workers organized to improve wages and working conditions for its members |
| ___ 4. industrial union | d. company in which only union members may be hired |
| ___ 5. closed shop | e. union made up of skilled workers in a specific trade or industry |

***Multiple Choice:*** *In the blank at the left, write the letter of the choice that best completes the statement or answers the question. (10 points each)*

___ 6. The word *management* refers to
a. those in charge of a company.
b. unskilled workers in a company.
c. union leaders.
d. skilled workers in a company.

7. Which of the following describes reactions to unions in the 1800s?
a. state laws supported unions
b. business ... unions

## Reteach

Have students use the **Terms to Know** to write a summary of Section 2.

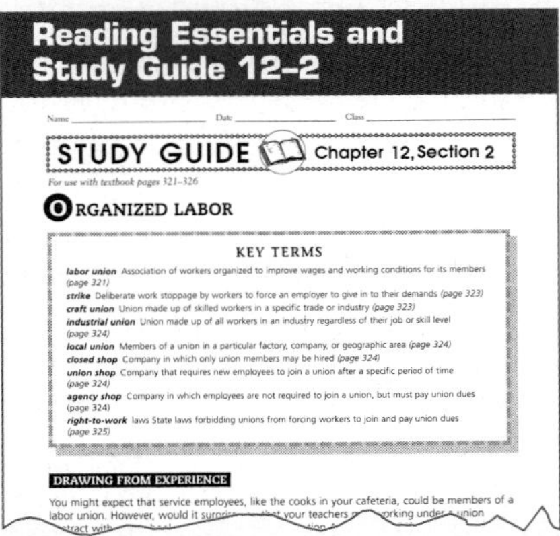

**Reading Essentials and Study Guide 12–2**

Name ______ Date ______ Class ______

STUDY GUIDE Chapter 12, Section 2

*For use with textbook pages 321–326*

ORGANIZED LABOR

KEY TERMS

***labor union*** Association of workers organized to improve wages and working conditions for its members *(page 321)*
***strike*** Deliberate work stoppage by workers to force an employer to give in to their demands *(page 323)*
***craft union*** Union made up of skilled workers in a specific trade or industry *(page 323)*
***industrial union*** Union made up of all workers in an industry regardless of their job or skill level *(page 324)*
***local union*** Members of a union in a particular factory, company, or geographic area *(page 324)*
***closed shop*** Company in which only union members may be hired *(page 324)*
***union shop*** Company that requires new employees to join a union after a specific period of time *(page 324)*
***agency shop*** Company in which employees are not required to join a union, but must pay union dues (page 324)
***right-to-work*** laws State laws forbidding unions from forcing workers to join and pay union dues *(page 325)*

DRAWING FROM EXPERIENCE

You might expect that service employees, like the cooks in your cafeteria, could be members of a labor union. However, would it surpris... your teachers ...orking under a union ...tract with...

# 4 Close

In a class discussion, have students outline the contributions and limitations of labor unions.

available to workers who do not join the union. Unions have less power in states with right-to-work laws than in other states.

**National Unions** Above the locals are the national unions. These organizations are the individual craft or industrial unions that represent locals nationwide. Those unions that also have members in Canada or Mexico are often called international unions.

National unions send in organizers to help employees organize campaigns to set up locals. To help in negotiating a contract between a local and a particular company, the nationals provide lawyers and other staff members. In certain industries such as steel and mining, the national union negotiates the contract for the entire industry. After the majority of union members accept the contract, all the locals within the industry must work under the contract. Some of the largest unions are the International Brotherhood of Teamsters, the United Automobile Workers (UAW), and the United Steelworkers of America (USW).

**Federation Level** At the federation level is the AFL-CIO, which is made up of national and international unions. More than 70 unions with about 13 million members are associated with the AFL-CIO.

**Practice** and **assess** key skills with ***Skillbuilder Interactive Workbook, Level 2.***

## SECTION 2 Assessment

### Understanding Key Terms

1. **Define** labor union, strike, craft union, industrial union, local union, closed shop, union shop, agency shop, right-to-work laws.

### Reviewing Objectives

2. What obstacles did labor unions face when they began to organize in the 1800s?
3. **Graphic Organizer** Create a chart like the one below to summarize the differences among closed shops, union shops, and agency shops.

| Type of Union | Summary |
|---|---|
| | |
| | |

### Applying Economic Concepts

4. **Economic Institutions** List and evaluate the four pieces of legislation highlighted in **Figure 12.6** on page 323. Rate the acts as follows: "+" for acts that benefited unions, "–" for acts that harmed unions, "0" for acts that had a mixed impact on unions.

### Critical Thinking Activity

5. **Synthesizing Information** According to **Figure 12.8** on page 325, is your state a right-to-work state? How do right-to-work laws affect unions? Do you agree or disagree with right-to-work laws? Explain your answer.



## SECTION 2 Assessment Answers

1. All definitions can be found in the Glossary.
2. State laws outlawed unions; businesses refused to hire union members or to deal with union representatives, and often fired and blacklisted union organizers.
3. closed: companies may hire only union workers; union: new employees must join the union after a set period of time, usually three months; agency: employees are not required to join the union, but must pay union dues
4. Norris-LaGuardia Act +; Wagner Act +; Taft-Hartley Act –; Landrum-Griffin Act 0
5. See map on page 325 for right-to-work states. Unions have less power in areas where there are right-to-work laws.

# Walter Reuther

*LABOR LEADER (1907–1970)*

- **President of the United Automobile Workers (UAW), 1946–1970**
- **President of the Congress of Industrial Organizations (CIO), 1952–1955**
- **Helped to bring about the merger of the American Federation of Labor (AFL) and the CIO in 1955**
- **Posthumously awarded the Presidential Medal of Freedom for distinguished civilian service in peacetime in 1995**

Walter Reuther ranks among the greatest American labor leaders of the twentieth century. A driving force in the union-organizing movement of the 1930s and 1940s, he was the first union leader to negotiate for, and win, benefits that workers today take for granted—cost-of-living raises, pension plans, employer-funded health insurance, and profit sharing. Reuther was also deeply involved in the civil rights and environmental movements. As another union leader noted, "Walter Reuther was on the front lines of the battle for a better world." In the excerpt below, Reuther explains his philosophy of unionism:

> *"My main point is that the labor movement is about that problem we face 'tomorrow morning'. . . . The guys have a right to expect the labor movement to deal with that problem. I can't give them some philosophical baloney and say: Well, fellows, you know we're operating way up here in the stratosphere and you shouldn't get excited about these little problems that are bothering you every morning.*
>
> *But to make that the sole purpose of the labor movement is to miss the main target. The labor movement is about changing society. I mean, I don't think I am eloquent when I say to a guy: What good is a dollar an hour more in wages if your neighborhood is burning down? What good is another week's vacation if the lake you used to go to, where you've got a cottage, is polluted and you can't swim in it and the kids can't play in it? What good is another $100 pension if the world goes up in atomic smoke?"*

### *Checking for Understanding*

1. **What do you think Reuther meant by the "little problems that [bother workers] every morning"?**
2. **What did Reuther think was the main "target" of the labor movement?**



## Background

Point out that Walter Reuther was a leader in the Democratic Party, and he served as an adviser to Democratic presidents from Franklin Roosevelt to Lyndon Johnson. Reuther was especially influential during Johnson's administration. He played a major role in the passage of the Civil Rights Act of 1964 and in the development of Johnson's War on Poverty program.

## Teach

After students read the excerpt, underscore that Reuther strongly believed that unions should work to improve society as a whole. ASK: Do you think that unions should be involved in social issues such as civil rights and the environment, or do you think that they should limit their actions to workplace issues such as hours and wages? Encourage students to explain their responses.

### Answers to *Checking for Understanding*

1. Answers may vary. Most students will suggest such problems as paying the bills and making sure families have enough to eat.
2. Reuther thought the main target of unions was to change society.

# 1 Focus

## Overview

Section 3 describes the basic features of collective bargaining and explains how unions have declined in recent years.

### BELLRINGER
**Motivational Activity**

Project **Daily Focus Transparency 40** and have students answer the questions.

This activity is also available as a blackline master.

**Daily Focus Transparency 40**

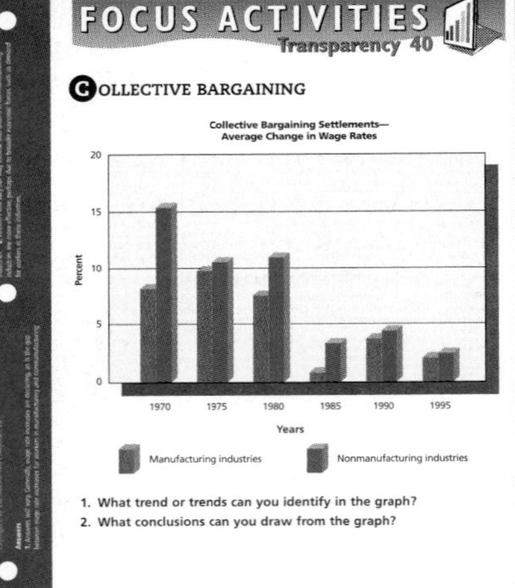


### Reader's Guide

Answers to the **Reading Objectives** questions are on page 333.

**Preteaching Vocabulary**

Have students locate the definitions of the **Terms to Know** in the Glossary. Then have them use each term correctly in sentences.

Vocabulary PuzzleMaker

SECTION 3

# Collective Bargaining

### Reader's Guide

**Terms to Know**

- collective bargaining
- cost-of-living adjustment (COLA)
- mediation
- arbitration
- picketing
- boycott
- lockout
- injunction

**Reading Objectives**

1. What are the major issues over which union contracts are negotiated?
2. What workers' actions and management responses may accompany a strike?
3. How has collective bargaining in the United States changed in recent years?

## Cover Story

*The New York Times*, June 30, 1998

In a move that could lead to the first work stoppage in National Basketball Association history, the 29 league owners Monday agreed to lock out the players and suspend all league business until the two parties sign a new labor agreement.

The lockout will begin at midnight Tuesday night, when the current collective bargaining agreement expires. With no negotiations planned and several major economic issues to be resolved, next season may not start on time.

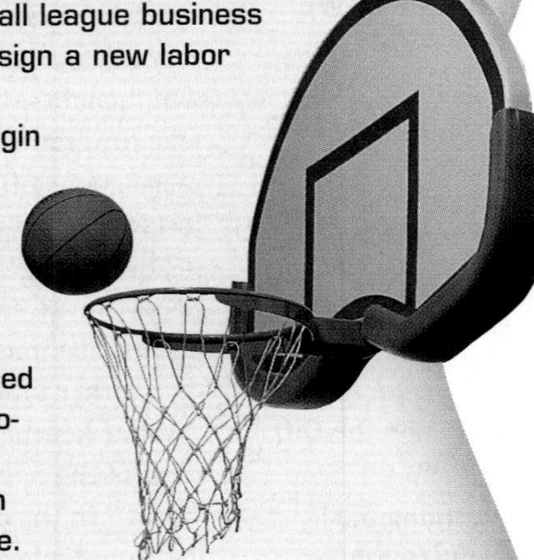

collective bargaining: *process by which unions and employers negotiate the conditions of employment*

**Collective bargaining**, as mentioned above, is the process by which unions and employers negotiate the conditions of employment. At the center of the collective bargaining process is compromise. The company wants to keep wages and benefits low to hold its labor costs down and remain competitive in the market. The union wants to increase wages and benefits for its members as much as possible. As you read this section, you'll learn that both sides must be prepared to give and take a little.

## SECTION 3 RESOURCE MANAGER

**Reproducible Masters**

- Reproducible Lesson Plan 12–3
- Reading Essentials and Study Guide 12–3
- Guided Reading Activity 12–3
- Section Quiz 12–3
- Daily Focus Activity 40
- Daily Lecture Notes 12–3

**Multimedia**

- Daily Focus Transparency 40
- Vocabulary PuzzleMaker
- Interactive Tutor Self-Assessment Software
- ExamView® Pro Testmaker
- MindJogger Videoquiz
- NBR's *Economics & You*
- Presentation Plus!

## Negotiations

Negotiations take place when labor and management meet to discuss in detail a wide range of contract issues. **Figure 12.9** on page 330 lists the most important issues that labor and management may negotiate, including working hours, fringe benefits, and a **cost-of-living adjustment (COLA).** In most cases, negotiations are friendly and result in an agreement that satisfies all parties.

**cost-of-living adjustment (COLA):** *provision calling for an additional wage increase each year if the general level of prices rises*

**Mediation** If negotiations become hostile or compromise breaks down, labor and management may try mediation. **Mediation** occurs when a neutral person steps in and tries to get both sides to reach an agreement. The mediator suggests possible solutions and works to keep the two sides talking with each other.

**mediation:** *a neutral person tries to get both sides to reach an agreement during negotiations*

The federal government, through the Federal Mediation and Conciliation Service (FMCS), provides a mediator free of charge upon request of either union or management. In a typical year, FMCS mediators are involved in thousands of negotiations. A number of state and private mediators also help resolve disputes.

**Arbitration** If mediation fails, the negotiation process may go one step further to arbitration. In **arbitration,** the two sides submit the issues they cannot agree on to a third party for a final decision. Both sides agree in advance to accept the arbitrator's decision, although one or both sides may not be completely happy with the outcome. The FMCS often helps in these cases by providing labor and management with a list of private arbitrators in their area.

**arbitration:** *union and management submit the issues they cannot agree on to a third party for a final decision*

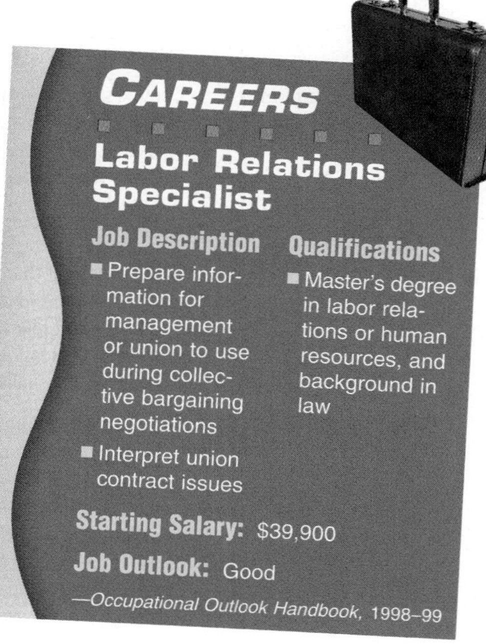

CAREERS
Labor Relations Specialist
Job Description
■ Prepare information for management or union to use during collective bargaining negotiations
■ Interpret union contract issues
Qualifications
■ Master's degree in labor relations or human resources, and background in law
Starting Salary: $39,900
Job Outlook: Good
—Occupational Outlook Handbook, 1998–99


## Strikes and Management

Most contracts are settled at the bargaining table. Sometimes, however, negotiations break down and a strike results. The number of strikes in the United States has declined sharply since 1975, as shown in **Figure 12.10** on page 331.

Strikers usually walk up and down in front of their workplace carrying picket signs that state their disagreement with the company. **Picketing** is meant to discourage workers from crossing the picket line to work for the employer. It is also aimed at embarrassing the company and building public support for the strike.

**picketing:** *action of strikers who walk in front of a workplace carrying signs that state their disagreement with the company*



### Meeting Special Needs

**Learning Disability** To help learning disabled students, illustrate the importance of headings and subheadings for understanding the framework of each section. Model student use by asking questions such as: "What would I do if I wanted to know what each section was about?" For Section 3 read: Negotiations, Mediation, Arbitration; Strikes and Management, Lockouts, Injunctions; and so on. Ask students to rephrase each set of headings using complete sentences.

Refer to *Inclusion for the Social Studies Classroom Strategies and Activities* for students with different learning styles.

# 2 Teach

## Guided Practice

**L1 Illustrating Ideas** Review the text on collective bargaining with students. Ensure that students understand that when conflicts arise between labor and management, mediation and arbitration may be used to find compromises. Then ask students to create a flowchart showing the collective bargaining process. Call on volunteers to display and explain their flowcharts.

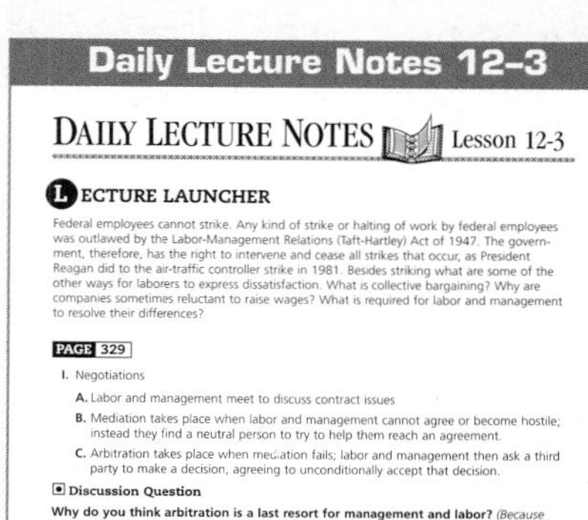
Daily Lecture Notes 12-3

DAILY LECTURE NOTES Lesson 12-3

LECTURE LAUNCHER

Federal employees cannot strike. Any kind of strike or halting of work by federal employees was outlawed by the Labor-Management Relations (Taft-Hartley) Act of 1947. The government, therefore, has the right to intervene and cease all strikes that occur, as President Reagan did to the air-traffic controller strike in 1981. Besides striking what are some of the other ways for laborers to express dissatisfaction. What is collective bargaining? Why are companies sometimes reluctant to raise wages? What is required for labor and management to resolve their differences?

PAGE 329

I. Negotiations

A. Labor and management meet to discuss contract issues

B. Mediation takes place when labor and management cannot agree or become hostile; instead they find a neutral person to try to help them reach an agreement.

C. Arbitration takes place when mediation fails; labor and management then ask a third party to make a decision, agreeing to unconditionally accept that decision.

Discussion Question

**Why do you think arbitration is a last resort for management and labor?** *(Because both sides must agree to do what the arbitrator says before the decisions are even made. Either side might be very disappointed by the contract—in fact, they may find they were*

### Did You Know

When negotiations break down, a process called fact-finding may be used. Under this procedure, labor and management agree to have an independent third party review the issues and recommend possible solutions. Fact-finding is particularly useful when one or both parties have been less than truthful in an attempt to win public support or when one party does not believe the claims of the other.

**L2 Understanding Ideas** On the board, write the title "Unions." Under the title, draw a two-column chart with "Supporters' Views" and "Critics' Views" as column headings. Call on students to come to the board and enter in the chart information on how unions are viewed today. Have students use this information to write a brief essay titled, "Unions Today: Pros and Cons." Have several students read their essays to the class.

## Visual Instruction FIGURE 12.9

Have students review the information in **Figure 12.9**. Then lead them in a discussion of the following questions: How would you rank these issues in order of importance if you represented labor? How would you rank them if you represented management? If you represented labor, which of these issues would you be willing to give the most ground on and why? If you represented management, which of these issues would you be willing to give the most ground on and why? Conclude by pointing out that collective bargaining involves such decisions.

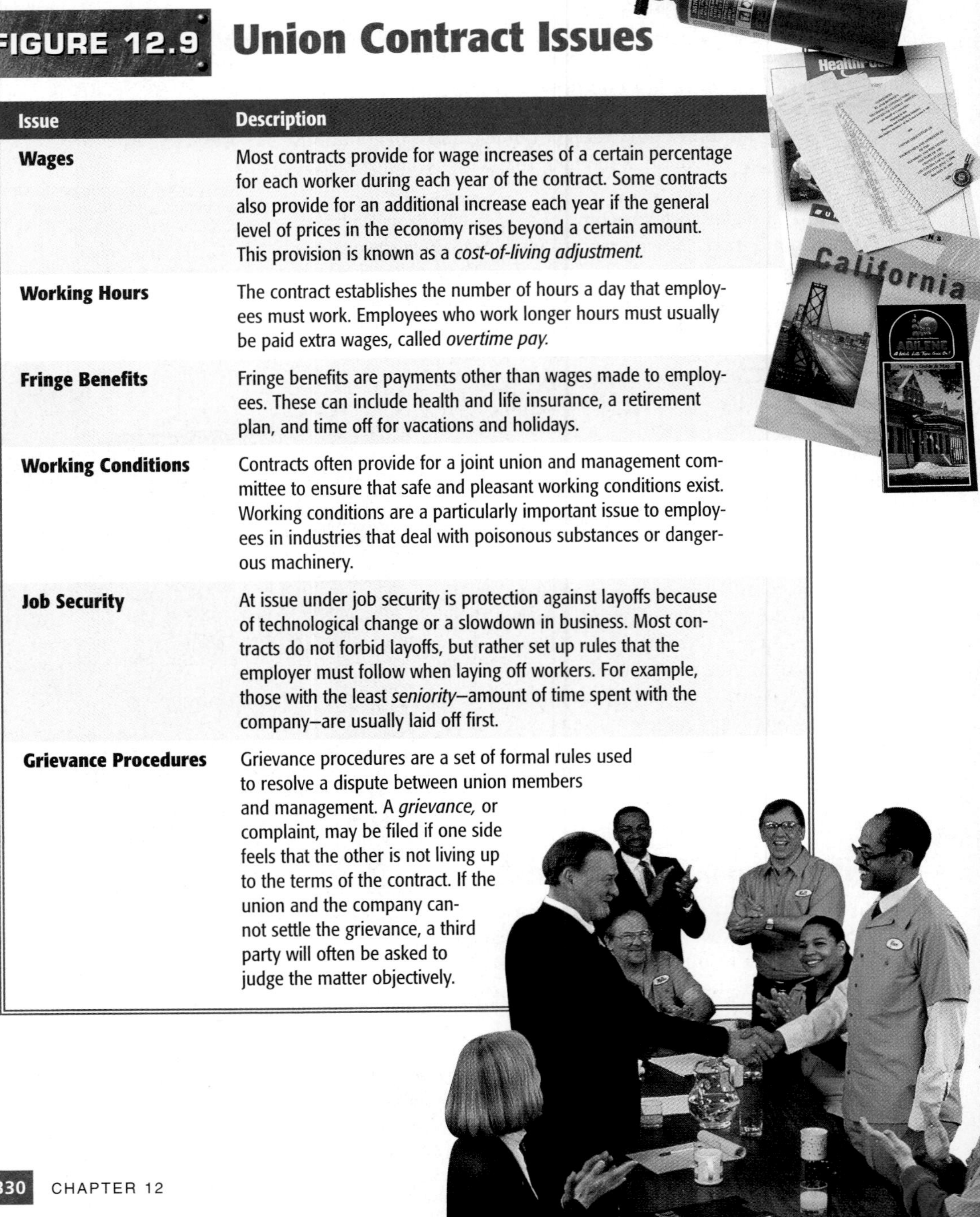

## FIGURE 12.9 Union Contract Issues

| Issue | Description |
|---|---|
| **Wages** | Most contracts provide for wage increases of a certain percentage for each worker during each year of the contract. Some contracts also provide for an additional increase each year if the general level of prices in the economy rises beyond a certain amount. This provision is known as a *cost-of-living adjustment.* |
| **Working Hours** | The contract establishes the number of hours a day that employees must work. Employees who work longer hours must usually be paid extra wages, called *overtime pay.* |
| **Fringe Benefits** | Fringe benefits are payments other than wages made to employees. These can include health and life insurance, a retirement plan, and time off for vacations and holidays. |
| **Working Conditions** | Contracts often provide for a joint union and management committee to ensure that safe and pleasant working conditions exist. Working conditions are a particularly important issue to employees in industries that deal with poisonous substances or dangerous machinery. |
| **Job Security** | At issue under job security is protection against layoffs because of technological change or a slowdown in business. Most contracts do not forbid layoffs, but rather set up rules that the employer must follow when laying off workers. For example, those with the least *seniority*—amount of time spent with the company—are usually laid off first. |
| **Grievance Procedures** | Grievance procedures are a set of formal rules used to resolve a dispute between union members and management. A *grievance,* or complaint, may be filed if one side feels that the other is not living up to the terms of the contract. If the union and the company cannot settle the grievance, a third party will often be asked to judge the matter objectively. |



## Cooperative Learning

Inform students that in recent years, the AFL-CIO and its affiliated unions have made great efforts to recruit new members. Then organize students into several groups, and have groups research how union recruiting methods have changed recently. Suggest that they consider such questions as: Have unions increased spending on recruiting? If so, by how much? Do unions use different recruiting tactics than they did in the past? Are unions aiming recruiting drives at different segments of the working population than they did in the past? Direct groups to use library resources and the Internet in their research. If possible, they might also interview union representatives. Have groups present their findings in oral reports.

Striking unions may also use a boycott to exert more economic pressure against a firm. In a **boycott,** unions urge the public not to purchase goods or services produced by a company. In addition, unions may ask politicians to push management for a settlement or to publicly support the union's demands.

Strikes can drag on for months and even years. After a long period of time, strikers sometimes become discouraged. Some may decide to go back to work without gaining what they wanted. In most cases, however, strikes are settled as management and labor return to the negotiating table and work out an agreement.

**boycott:** *economic pressure exerted by unions urging the public not to purchase the goods or services produced by a company*

**Lockouts** When faced with a strike, management has methods of its own to use against strikers. One is the **lockout,** which occurs when management prevents workers from returning to work until they agree to a new contract. Another tactic is to bring in strikebreakers, called *scabs* by strikers. These are people willing to cross a picket line to work for the terms the company offers.

**lockout:** *situation that occurs when management prevents workers from returning to work until they agree to a new contract*

**FIGURE 12.10**

**Strikes** Compare the trend in strikes with what is happening in union membership. ***How do you think the two are related?***

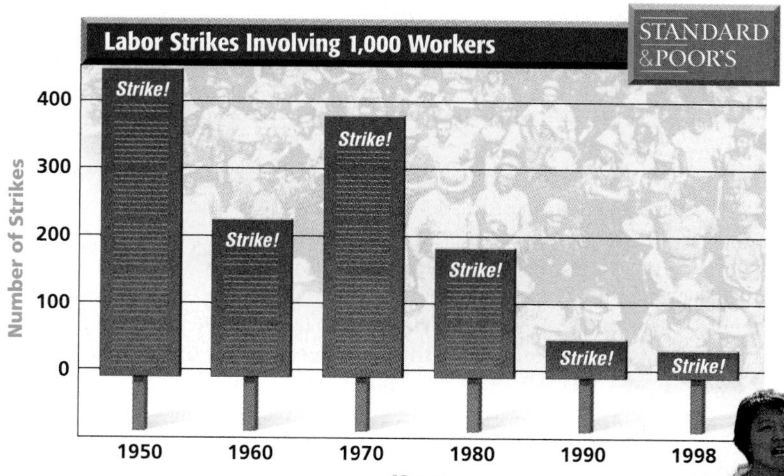

**Labor Strikes Involving 1,000 Workers**

STANDARD & POOR'S

Number of Strikes: 0, 100, 200, 300, 400

Years: 1950, 1960, 1970, 1980, 1990, 1998

Strike! Strike! Strike! Strike! Strike! Strike!

ON STRIKE

**Source:** Standard & Poor's

ECONOMICS Online

For an online update of this graph, visit ett.glencoe.com and click on ***Textbook Updates—Chapter 12.***

## Free Enterprise Activity

Have students role-play a labor-management dispute that must be mediated. Select three students to act as mediators, and have them research conflict resolution methods used in mediation. Then select six students—three to act as union representatives and three to act as management representatives—and have them draw up opposing positions regarding wages, working conditions, and health benefits. Have the mediators negotiate an agreement acceptable to both labor and management. Have the rest of the class critique the mediation, noting what each side lost and gained. BLOCK SCHEDULING



**Guided Reading Activity 12-3**

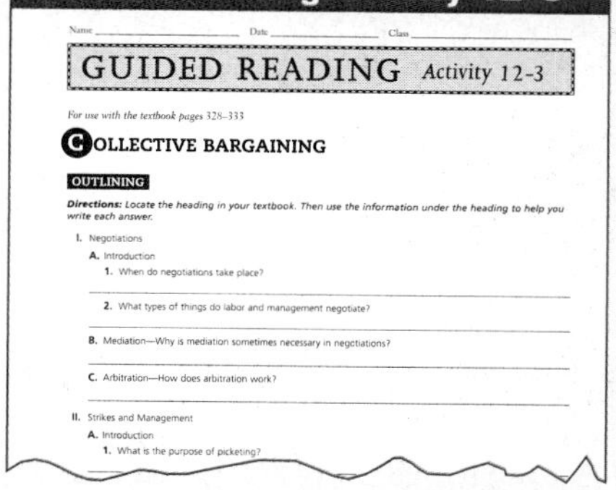

GUIDED READING Activity 12-3

COLLECTIVE BARGAINING

## Independent Practice

**L2 Radio News Reports** Have students research a recent strike in their state. Have them note the reasons for the work stoppage, the procedures used to end the dispute, and the resolution. Have students present their findings in the form of a radio news report lasting two to three minutes. Call on volunteers to "broadcast" their reports to the class. BLOCK SCHEDULING

**Visual Instruction FIGURE 12.10**

**Answer:** *Most students will suggest that as union membership declines, so too will the numbers of strikes, because with fewer unionized workers there are fewer workers to respond to union calls for work stoppages.*

# CHAPTER 12

SECTION 3, Pages 328–333

**Visual Instruction FIGURE 12.11**

ASK: What has happened to union membership since the 1950s? *It has steadily declined.*

**ECONOMICS & YOU**

**The American Labor Force**

Chapter 14
Disc 1, Side 1

**ASK: What positive and negative effects can a strike have on workers?** *It can bring wage increases and greater benefits and security for workers. It also can mean lengthy unemployment and future job insecurity due to the company's loss of revenues and consumer confidence.*

 Also available in VHS.

# 3 Assess

## Meeting Lesson Objectives

Assign Section 3 Assessment as homework or an in-class activity.

Use **Interactive Tutor Self-Assessment Software** to review Section 3.

**FIGURE 12.11**

**Declining Union Membership** The labor movement today faces many problems. The percentage of union members among the labor force reached a high in the mid-1940s and has been declining since 1955.

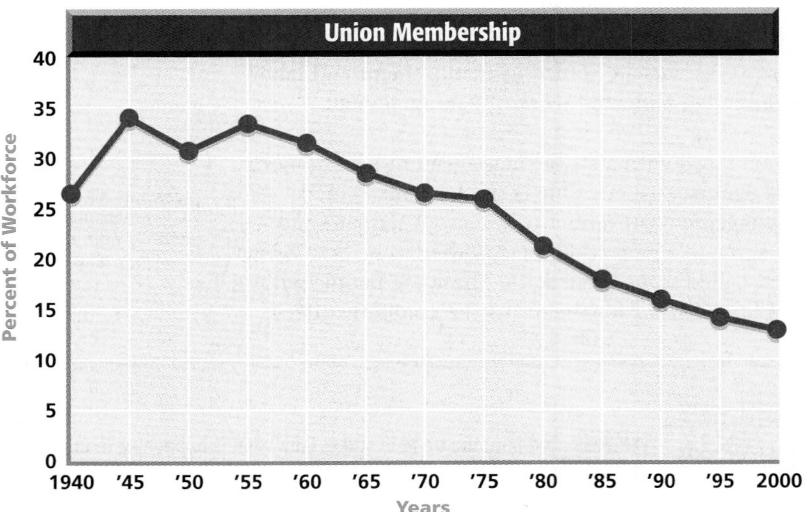


**Source:** U.S. Department of Labor, Bureau of Labor Statistics

For an online update of this graph, visit ett.glencoe.com and click on ***Textbook Updates—Chapter 12.***

**Injunctions** Management sometimes requests a court injunction to limit picketing or to prevent a strike from continuing or even occurring. An **injunction** is a legal order of a court preventing some activity. Under the Taft-Hartley Act of 1947, the President of the United States can obtain an injunction to delay or halt a strike for up to 80 days if the strike will endanger the nation's safety or health. During this cooling-off period, the two sides must try to reach a settlement.

*injunction: court order preventing some activity*

## Decline of Unions

The establishment of the AFL in 1886 is considered the beginning of the modern union era. Since that time, unions have achieved many of their goals. Union supporters list among their accomplishments better wages and working conditions for all employees—union and nonunion. They point out that many workers



## Extending the Content

**Collective Bargaining in Japan** When labor contracts expire in Japan, unions often stage a brief work stoppage to show their power and influence. After workers have returned to work, union and management leaders meet to hammer out a new contract.

now enjoy a sense of security that helps to maintain some control over their jobs and lives.

Union supporters also note that the collective bargaining process has brought more order and fairness to the workplace. It has made clear the rights and responsibilities of both management and labor.

Because working conditions have improved so dramatically over the years, nonunion workers often see little to gain from joining a union. **Figure 12.11** shows how much union membership has declined since the 1940s. In addition, the nature of the economy itself is changing. More jobs are opening in the white-collar and service sectors, whereas blue-collar jobs are decreasing due to automation.

**Critics** The labor movement also has its critics. Some opponents charge that unions have grown so large and bureaucratic that they are out of touch with their members' needs. Others claim that increased wages are passed on to consumers in the form of higher prices.

Employers often argue that union rules decrease productivity. They point to rules that slow the introduction of new technology or require more employees than necessary to do a job. In addition, corruption among some labor leaders has damaged the reputation of organized labor with the public.

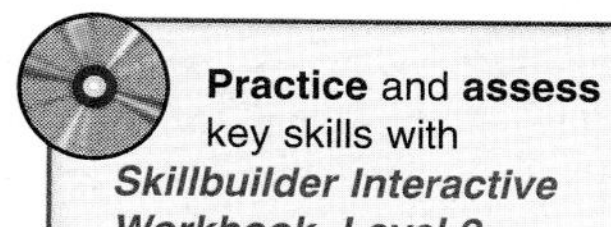

**Practice** and **assess** key skills with *Skillbuilder Interactive Workbook, Level 2.*

## SECTION 3 Assessment

### Understanding Key Terms

1. **Define** collective bargaining, cost-of-living adjustment (COLA), mediation, arbitration, picketing, boycott, lockout, injunction.

### Reviewing Objectives

2. **Graphic Organizer** Create a chart like the one below to list and describe the major issues over which union contracts are negotiated.

| Issue | Description |
|---|---|
| | |
| | |

3. What workers' actions and management responses may accompany a strike?
4. How has collective bargaining in the United States changed in recent years?

### Applying Economic Concepts

5. **Labor Unions** What is your opinion of the influence of unions today? How is your opinion similar to or different from the information given in the text concerning the decline of unionism?

### Critical Thinking Activity

6. **Making Generalizations** Write two newspaper accounts of a fictional local strike. One account should be from the perspective of a union member. The other account should be written from the standpoint of management.



## SECTION 3 Assessment Answers

1. All definitions can be found in the Glossary.
2. Students' answers should include the information found in Figure 12.9 on page 330.
3. workers: picketing, boycotts; management: lockouts, strikebreakers, injunctions
4. It has declined due to the decline in union membership.
5. Answers will vary. Ensure that students support their answers with explanations.
6. Newspaper articles will vary. Have students share and compare their articles.



### Section Quiz 12-3

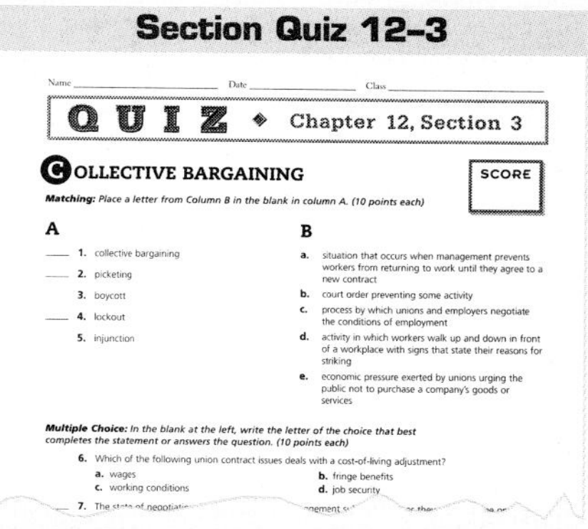

Name ______ Date ______ Class ______

QUIZ ◆ Chapter 12, Section 3

COLLECTIVE BARGAINING

SCORE

*Matching: Place a letter from Column B in the blank in column A. (10 points each)*

| A | B |
|---|---|
| ___ 1. collective bargaining | a. situation that occurs when management prevents workers from returning to work until they agree to a new contract |
| ___ 2. picketing | b. court order preventing some activity |
| 3. boycott | c. process by which unions and employers negotiate the conditions of employment |
| ___ 4. lockout | d. activity in which workers walk up and down in front of a workplace with signs that state their reasons for striking |
| 5. injunction | e. economic pressure exerted by unions urging the public not to purchase a company's goods or services |

*Multiple Choice: In the blank at the left, write the letter of the choice that best completes the statement or answers the question. (10 points each)*

6. Which of the following union contract issues deals with a cost-of-living adjustment?
   a. wages b. fringe benefits
   c. working conditions d. job security

### Reteach

To help students understand collective bargaining procedures and the decline of unions, have them develop an annotated outline of Section 3.

### Reading Essentials and Study Guide 12-3

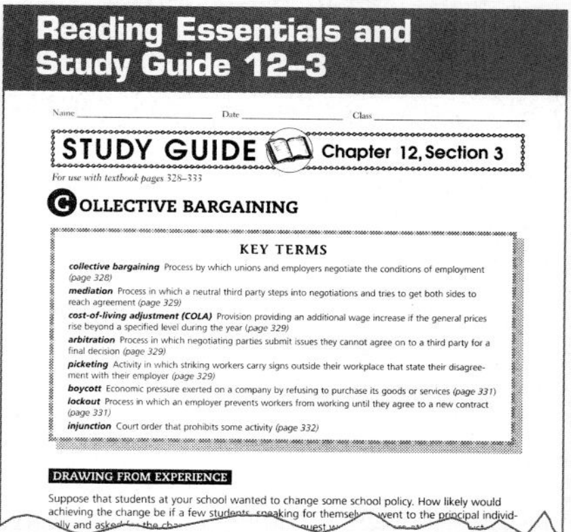

Name ______ Date ______ Class ______

STUDY GUIDE Chapter 12, Section 3

*For use with textbook pages 328–333*

COLLECTIVE BARGAINING

KEY TERMS

***collective bargaining*** Process by which unions and employers negotiate the conditions of employment *(page 328)*

***mediation*** Process in which a neutral third party steps into negotiations and tries to get both sides to reach agreement *(page 329)*

***cost-of-living adjustment (COLA)*** Provision providing an additional wage increase if the general prices rise beyond a specified level during the year *(page 329)*

***arbitration*** Process in which negotiating parties submit issues they cannot agree on to a third party for a final decision *(page 329)*

***picketing*** Activity in which striking workers carry signs outside their workplace that state their disagreement with their employer *(page 329)*

***boycott*** Economic pressure exerted on a company by refusing to purchase its goods or services *(page 331)*

***lockout*** Process in which an employer prevents workers from working until they agree to a new contract *(page 331)*

***injunction*** Court order that prohibits some activity *(page 332)*

DRAWING FROM EXPERIENCE

Suppose that students at your school wanted to change some school policy. How likely would achieving the change be if a few students speaking for themselves went to the principal individ-

## 4 Close

Have students speculate on how issues between unions and management might be handled other than through collective bargaining.

## Using Library Resources

Read through the list of resources—providing actual examples, if possible—and note the types of information that each provides. Inform students that these resources usually can be found in the reference section of the library. Then point out that the reference library has one more very useful resource—the librarian. Asking the librarian for guidance can save a great deal of time if students are researching a topic they know little about.

Work through the questions in the **Practicing the Skill** section, making sure that students understand why certain resources are more appropriate for locating particular kinds of information. Finally, assign the **Application Activity.**

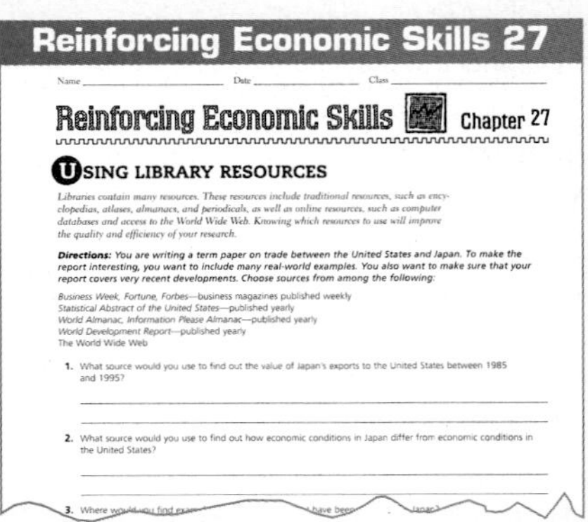

**Reinforcing Economic Skills 27**

Name ______ Date ______ Class ______

Reinforcing Economic Skills Chapter 27

USING LIBRARY RESOURCES

*Libraries contain many resources. These resources include traditional resources, such as encyclopedias, atlases, almanacs, and periodicals, as well as online resources, such as computer databases and access to the World Wide Web. Knowing which resources to use will improve the quality and efficiency of your research.*

***Directions:*** *You are writing a term paper on trade between the United States and Japan. To make the report interesting, you want to include many real-world examples. You also want to make sure that your report covers very recent developments. Choose sources from among the following:*

*Business Week, Fortune, Forbes*—business magazines published weekly
*Statistical Abstract of the United States*—published yearly
*World Almanac, Information Please Almanac*—published yearly
*World Development Report*—published yearly
The World Wide Web

1. What source would you use to find out the value of Japan's exports to the United States between 1985 and 1995?

2. What source would you use to find out how economic conditions in Japan differ from economic conditions in the United States?

### GLENCOE TECHNOLOGY

**Glencoe Skillbuilder Interactive Workbook, Level 2**

This interactive CD-ROM reinforces student mastery of essential social studies skills.

*Study & Writing Skills*

# Using Library Resources

*Your teacher has assigned a major research report, so you go to the library. As you wander the aisles surrounded by books, you wonder: Where do I start my research? Which reference works should I use?*

- **Encyclopedia:** set of books containing short articles on many subjects arranged alphabetically
- **Biographical dictionary:** brief biographies listed alphabetically by last names
- **Atlas:** collection of maps and charts
- **Almanac:** annually updated reference that provides current statistics and historical information on a wide range of subjects
- **Card catalog:** listing of every book in the library, either on cards or computerized; search for books by author, subject, or title
- **Periodical guide:** set of books listing topics covered in magazines and newspaper articles
- **Computer database:** collections of information organized for rapid search and retrieval

**Practice** and **assess** key skills with *Skillbuilder Interactive Workbook, Level 2.*

## *Learning the Skill*

Libraries contain many resources. Listed on the left are brief descriptions of important ones.

## *Practicing the Skill*

Suppose you are assigned a research report dealing with the famous labor leaders Samuel Gompers and Eugene V. Debs. Read the questions below, then decide which of the sources described on the left you would use to answer each question and why.

1. During which years did the men lead their unions?
2. What were the most famous labor actions each dealt with?
3. How did the public react to the labor unions' activities?
4. What benefits do we enjoy today as a result of these two labor leaders?

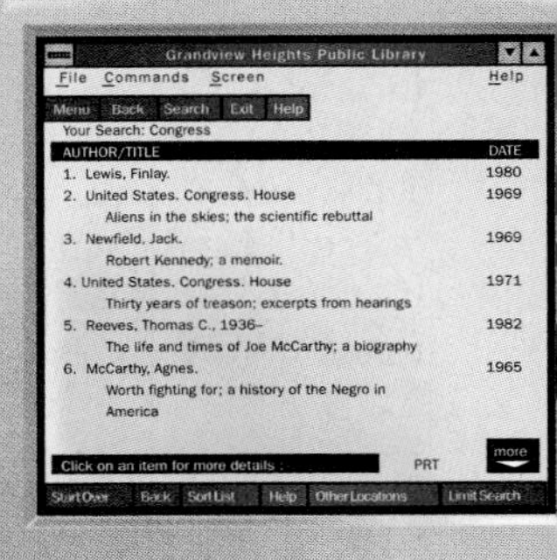


*Computerized card catalog*

## *Application Activity*

Using library resources, research the origins and important leaders of the American Federation of Labor. Present the information you find to the class.

334

### Answers to *Practicing the Skill*

1. Biographical dictionary or encyclopedia—these sources would provide a quick method of finding this specific information. An almanac might also reveal this information.
2. Card catalog or computer database—these sources would provide titles of books in which this broad information might be included.
3. Periodical guides might direct researchers to articles on this subject.
4. Card catalog, computer database, or periodical guides would be best to find information on this specialized information.

*Application Activity* Encourage students to identify the resources they used and why.

CHAPTER  Summary

**Chapter Overview** Visit the *Economics Today and Tomorrow* Web site at ett.glencoe.com and click on ***Chapter 12—Chapter Overviews*** to review chapter information.

## SECTION 1 Americans at Work

- The **civilian labor force** is the total number of people 16 years old or older who are either employed or actively seeking work.
- Workers in the United States are categorized according to the type of work they perform—**blue-collar, white-collar,** or **service worker.**
- Another way to categorize workers is by the skills required to perform their occupation—**unskilled, semiskilled, skilled,** or **professional.**
- Three major factors—skill, type of job, and location—affect how supply and demand determine prices, or in this case wages, in the labor market.
- Factors that restrict supply and demand in terms of their influence on wages include **minimum wage laws** and organized labor.

## SECTION 2 Organized Labor

- A **labor union** is an association of workers organized to improve wages and working conditions for its members.
- Workers began to form unions to force employers to improve working conditions, shorten the workday, and end child labor.
- For much of its history, organized labor in the United States has been split into two groups: **craft unions** and **industrial unions.**
- Organized labor operates at three levels: the **local union,** the national or international union, and the federation.
- Local unions may negotiate a **union shop** or an **agency shop.**

## SECTION 3 Collective Bargaining

- **Collective bargaining** is the process by which unions and employers negotiate the conditions of employment.
- Labor and management may negotiate working hours, wages, fringe benefits, and a **cost-of-living adjustment (COLA).**
- If negotiations become hostile or compromise breaks down, labor and management may try **mediation** or **arbitration.**
- Striking unions may use **picketing** or a **boycott** to exert economic pressure against a firm.
- When faced with a strike, management may use a **lockout** or an **injunction** against strikers.
- The percentage of union members among the labor force reached a high in the mid-1940s and has been declining since 1955.



CHAPTER 12 Summary

ECONOMICS & YOU

The American Labor Force

Chapter 14
Disc 1, Side 1

If you do not have access to a videodisc player, the ***Economics & You*** programs are also available in VHS.

Use the **Chapter 12 Summary** to preview, review, condense, or reteach the chapter.

## Preview/Review

**Vocabulary PuzzleMaker Software** reinforces the key terms used in Chapter 12.

**Interactive Tutor Self-Assessment Software** allows students to review Chapter 12 content.

## Condense

Have students listen to the Chapter 12 **Audio Program** (also available in Spanish) in the TCR. Assign the Chapter 12 Audio Program Activity and give students the Chapter 12 Audio Program Test.

## Reteach

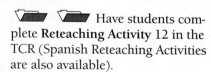

Have students complete **Reteaching Activity** 12 in the TCR (Spanish Reteaching Activities are also available).

## Economics Journal

**Categories of Workers** Over a one-week period, have students keep note of the employed people with whom they come into contact. Students should record the jobs these people do. Next to each job, have students classify it as unskilled, semiskilled, skilled, or professional. At the end of the recording period, have students select one of the jobs they listed. Direct them to interview the people who do these selected jobs. Interview questions should include: How did you get this job? What skills or special knowledge did you need to get hired? What skills or special knowledge did you need to acquire on the job? What do you see in the future for your job? Have students write a brief report summarizing their findings.

# CHAPTER 12 Assessment and Activities

## ECONOMICS Online

Have students visit the *Economics Today and Tomorrow* Web site at ett.glencoe.com to review Chapter 12 and take the Self-Check Quiz.

## GLENCOE TECHNOLOGY

**MindJogger Videoquiz**

Use MindJogger to review Chapter 12 content.

## Identifying Key Terms

1. d
2. a
3. e
4. c
5. g
6. f
7. b

## Recalling Facts and Ideas

1. professional
2. Blue-collar workers are employed in manufacturing and trades, while white-collar workers are employed in office and service jobs.
3. skill level, type of job, and location
4. craft unions and industrial unions
5. American Federation of Labor (AFL) and Congress of Industrial Organizations (CIO)
6. They protect the right of the worker to continue working at a job without joining a union.
7. working hours, fringe benefits, working conditions, job security, and grievance procedures
8. arbitration

# CHAPTER 12 Assessment and Activities

**Self-Check Quiz** Visit the *Economics Today and Tomorrow* Web site at ett.glencoe.com and click on ***Chapter 12—Self-Check Quizzes*** to prepare for the Chapter Test.

## Identifying Key Terms

*Identify the letter of the definition in Column B that correctly defines each term in Column A.*

**Column A**

1. unskilled workers
2. agency shop
3. arbitration
4. injunction
5. right-to-work law
6. closed shop
7. boycott

**Column B**

a. company in which employees are not required to join a union but must pay union dues
b. refusal to purchase the goods and services of a company
c. court order preventing some activity, often a strike
d. those having no special training in job-related skills
e. procedure for settling undecided issues between labor and management by giving them to a third party for a final decision
f. company in which only union members could be hired (now illegal)
g. forbids contracts that require employees to join a union

## Recalling Facts and Ideas

**Section 1**

1. Which category of worker has a higher-education degree as well as additional training?
2. What is the difference between blue-collar and white-collar workers?
3. What factors determine how much a person is paid for his or her work?

**Section 2**

4. What are the major kinds of labor unions?
5. What two union federations merged in 1955?
6. How do right-to-work laws affect workers who do not belong to unions?

**Section 3**

7. Wages are one of the most important major issues in collective bargaining negotiations. What are other important issues?
8. If management and labor have reached a bargaining deadlock, they may try to engage in mediation. If mediation fails, what is the next possible "friendly" step?
9. What do union workers do when they go on strike?
10. What has been the most recent trend in the importance of labor unions in America?



9. They stop all work, and they may also picket and boycott the company.
10. Union membership has been declining and, as a result, union power and influence have declined.

## Thinking Critically

1. Answers may vary, but students should mention that employers compete with one another for better-educated workers by offering higher wages and fringe benefits.

## Thinking Critically

1. **Determining Cause and Effect** Explain why workers with more education and training generally get paid higher wages.
2. **Predicting Consequences** Create a diagram like the one below to explain the factors that may cause a decline in union membership in the future.

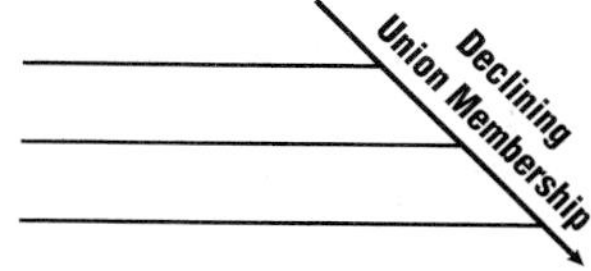


## Applying Economic Concepts

**Economic Costs and Benefits** There are costs and benefits for every activity. Strikes are no exception. Many workers believe that the benefits exceed the costs or they would not strike. List the benefits to workers of going on strike. Then list the costs of going on strike.

## Reviewing Skills

**Using Library Resources** Use library resources to research one of the following labor strikes: Baltimore & Ohio Railroad Workers, 1877; Haymarket Riot, 1886; Homestead Strike, 1892; Pullman Strike, 1894; Anthracite Coal Strike, 1902; Textile Strike in Lawrence, Massachusetts, 1912; Ludlow Massacre in Ludlow, Colorado, 1914. Write a report describing the people or groups involved, the conditions that led to the incident, what happened, and the conclusion.

## Cooperative Learning Project

Analyze the data that follow for the number of unemployed persons over a five-year period. Working in groups, compute the *mean average* number of unemployed.

| | |
|---|---|
| 1994 | 7,996,000 |
| 1995 | 7,404,000 |
| 1996 | 7,236,000 |
| 1997 | 6,739,000 |
| 1998 | 6,210,000 |

Now compute the *median average* unemployment rate for the seven years listed below.

| | |
|---|---|
| 1992 | 7.5 |
| 1993 | 6.9 |
| 1994 | 6.1 |
| 1995 | 5.6 |
| 1996 | 5.4 |
| 1997 | 4.9 |
| 1998 | 4.5 |

*For help in determining averages, see page xx in the Economic Handbook.*

## Technology Activity

**Using a Spreadsheet** Keep track of the employed individuals with whom you come into contact over a one-week period. Write down the types of jobs they do. Then use these jobs as the basis of a spreadsheet showing the training, average salary, and prospects for growth for each job. Use the Internet or sources such as the *Occupational Outlook Handbook* or *O*Net* to find this information.

## Analyzing the Global Economy

France's trucking union struck in 1997, parking their vehicles on roads and highways leading into Paris. Research and report on the reasons for the strike, how long it lasted, the effect on the economy of Paris, and the result of the strike.



2. Answers may include: Workers today receive better wages and have better working conditions than in the past; more jobs are opening in the white-collar and service sectors, which have fewer unions; more people are working at home.

# CHAPTER 12 Assessment and Activities

## Applying Economic Concepts

Benefits: winning strike demands—higher wages, more fringe benefits, better working conditions, more job security, grievance procedures that favor workers, and so on. Costs: loss of wages and other benefits, and possible loss of job if strike is not settled; negative publicity because of the strike; actions of management—lockouts, injunctions, use of strikebreakers.

## Reviewing Skills

Reports will vary. After students have presented their reports, ask them which resources they used in their research and why.

## Cooperative Learning Project

Mean: 7,117,000

Median: 5.6

## Technology Activity

Spreadsheets will vary. Interested students might want to collate job information by industry or skill level to create new spreadsheets.

## Analyzing the Global Economy

Reports will vary. Have students present their findings to the class.

### Chapter Bonus Test Question

**ASK: What is the major difference between mediation and arbitration?** *In mediation, the decision reached is not binding on the two parties. In arbitration, the decision is binding—the parties must accept it.*

CASE STUDY

# Focus on Free Enterprise

## 1 Focus

Inform students that today eBay is the largest online auction house in the world, and Pierre Omidyar and its other principal officers are among the world's richest business executives.

## 2 Teach

Ask students who have taken part in a silent auction to describe how this kind of sale takes place. (The item is shown, and bidders write their bids—there is usually a minimum starting bid and minimum bid raises. After a set period of time, the highest bidder takes the item.) Then point out that this, essentially, is how eBay works—except that the auctions take place online.

### Did You Know

More than 400,000 items are added daily to eBay's auction list. Products available for bid include antiques; books, movies, and music; coins and stamps; computers and computer software; dolls and figures; jewelry and gemstones; photo and electronic equipment; pottery and glass; sports memorabilia; and toys.

CASE STUDY

# Focus on Free Enterprise

# eBay, Inc.

*Star Wars™ toys*

***One night in 1995, while Pierre Omidyar and his fiancée were having dinner, the subject of Pez™ dispensers came up. She was an avid collector of these colorful little candy servers. Where, she wondered, might she meet people with a similar passion to talk and trade? Omidyar, a pioneer of online commerce, knew the place—the Internet.***

Pierre Omidyar and Meg Whitman

### The Online Auctioneer

Omidyar's idea was fairly simple: set up a Web site where people with similar interests could meet to buy and sell unique items—the equivalent of an Internet flea market. Omidyar opened the site—called eBay—in September 1995. A few days later, eBay held its first auction.

An eBay auction follows a set pattern. First, a seller places a description of the item to be sold, often accompanied by photographs, on the Web site. Next, buyers check in and make bids on the item. After a set period of time, usually three to seven days, the auction is closed and the sale item goes to the highest bidder. Six percent of the sale price goes to eBay as a commission.

### Slow Start

At first, business was slow. Just 10 people registered to use eBay's services in 1995. In time, however, more and more people visited the Web site, attracted by the opportunity of finding a bargain. In 1996, eBay made a profit of $150,000. By 1998, profits hit $2.4 million.



### Extending the Content

**The eBay Way of Life** Members of the eBay community can meet in chat rooms provided by the company to discuss common interests and concerns. Sometimes, this has resulted in eBay users from the same geographical area getting together to do charitable work or political organization.

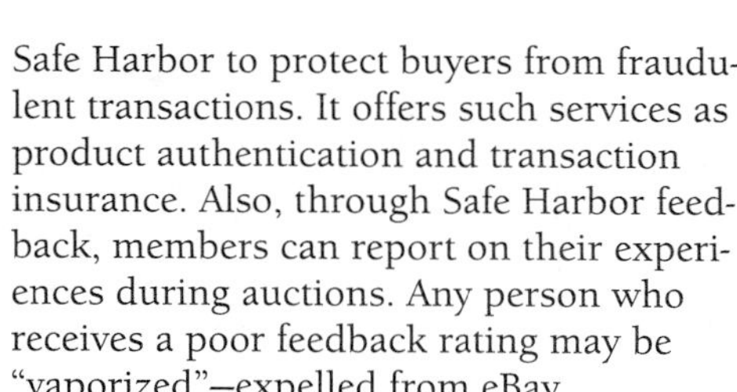
Fiesta®

eBay's success was no accident, mostly due to people Omidyar recruited to run the company. He hired Meg Whitman as chief executive officer of eBay in 1998. Today she is the richest female CEO in the world.

eBay has 7.7 million registered users, with membership growing at an average of 75,000 per week. It has hurtled past being an auction room for Pez™ dispensers and other odd collectibles. It now offers some 3.3 million items in 2,500 categories—everything from Star Wars™ toys to antique pottery.

### The eBay "Community"

Each day, eBay hosts more than 1.8 million auctions, receiving about 3 bids per second. The close interaction that takes place between buyers and sellers during these auctions has helped to create a sense of community among eBay users. In fact, eBay has become a way of life for many. According to surveys, eBay members spend about 130 minutes a month at the Web site.

### Ironing Out Some Wrinkles

With so much activity, it is not surprising that eBay has experienced some instances of fraud. eBay's management, however, has established a system called Safe Harbor to protect buyers from fraudulent transactions. It offers such services as product authentication and transaction insurance. Also, through Safe Harbor feedback, members can report on their experiences during auctions. Any person who receives a poor feedback rating may be "vaporized"—expelled from eBay.

### Future Plans

The rapid rise of eBay has led to the growth of Internet auction companies. In response, Whitman moved to expand the company. In April 1999, eBay acquired a fine-arts auction house through which it plans to host sales of high-priced art items. In addition, eBay has plans to set up local auction sites for large items, such as automobiles and boats. The competition, Whitman states, has been good for eBay. "It has made us more nimble," she says.

Pez™

### *Free Enterprise in Action*

1. **Why might fraud be a problem for a business like eBay? What steps has eBay taken to combat fraud?**
2. **How has eBay responded to the competition provided by other Internet auction sites?**

339

## 3 Assess

Have students answer the **Free Enterprise in Action** questions.

## 4 Close

Have students discuss why they think eBay has been such a great success.

### Did You Know

There are now more than 50 local eBay sites across the United States. In addition, there are special eBay Web pages for users in Australia, Canada, Germany, Great Britain, and Japan.

### Answers to *Free Enterprise In Action*

1. There is a great deal of activity on the Web site, and with users essentially acting on the honor system, some fraud is possible. eBay established a system called Safe Harbor, which offers such services as product authentication and transaction insurance. Also, through Safe Harbor feedback, members can report on their experiences during auctions. Any person who receives a poor feedback rating may be expelled from eBay.
2. It has expanded, acquiring a fine-arts auction house through which to sell high-priced art items and setting up local auction sites for large items, such as automobiles and boats.

# UNIT 5 Resource Manager

The following transparencies may be used at any time during Unit 5.

## Economic Forms and Financial Pages Transparencies

Transparency 1

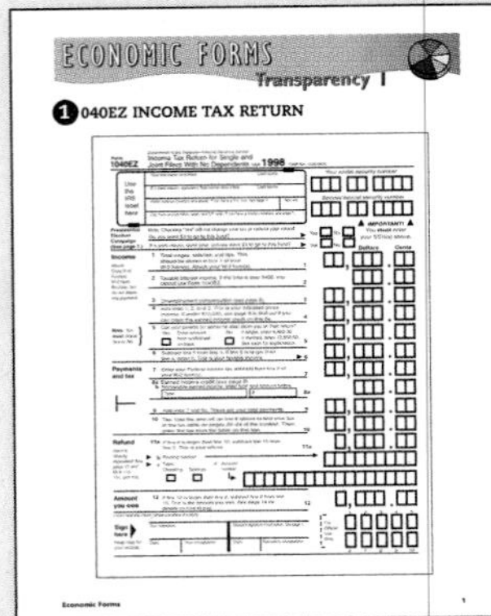


Transparency 2

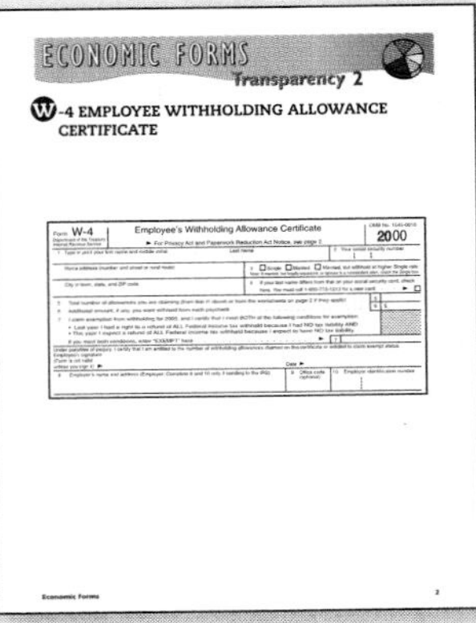


Transparency 3

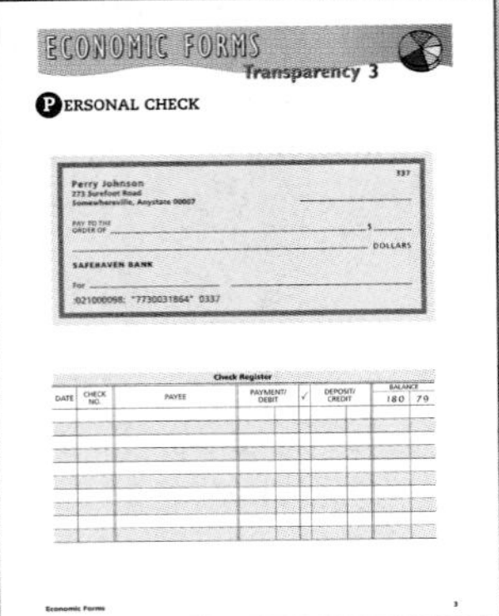


## Economic Concepts Transparencies

Transparency 13

Transparency 14

Transparency 15

Transparency 17

Transparency 18

Transparency 19

## Real-World Economics

Have your students learn about investing and managing their financial futures by participating in the exciting simulation **The Stock Market Game™**. See page T24 for more information.

Strengthen students' research, cooperation, presentation, and critical thinking skills by having them compete in the **Fed Challenge**. See page T26 for further information.

## Additional Glencoe Resources for This Unit

- Nightly Business Report *Economics & You* Video Program
- Economic Survival: A Financial Simulation
- Interactive Economics! Software

# UNIT 5 Resource Manager

## Assessment and Evaluation

Unit 5 Test Form A

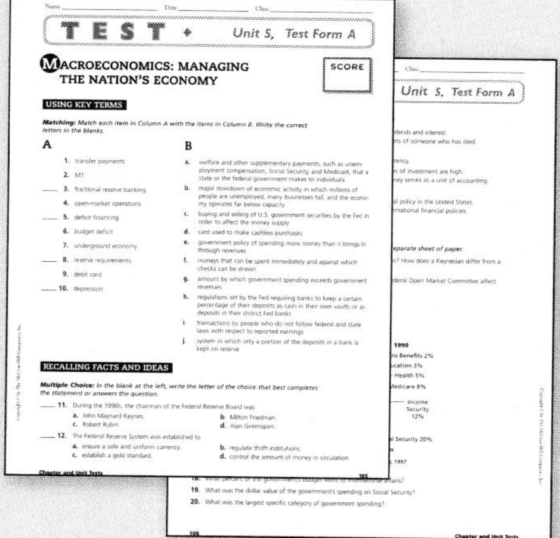

Unit 5 Test Form B

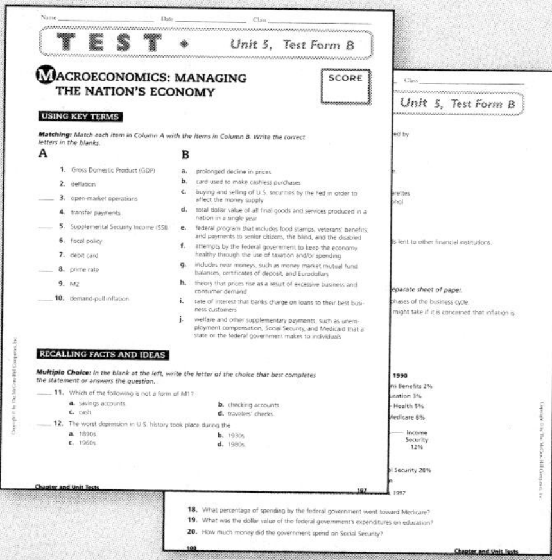

**Use the following tools to easily assess student learning:**

- Performance Assessment Strategies and Activities
- Section Quizzes
- Chapter and Unit Tests
- ExamView® Pro Testmaker
- Interactive Tutor Self-Assessment Software
- SAT I/II Test Practice
- MindJogger Videoquiz
- ett.glencoe.com

## Application and Enrichment

Economics Laboratory 5

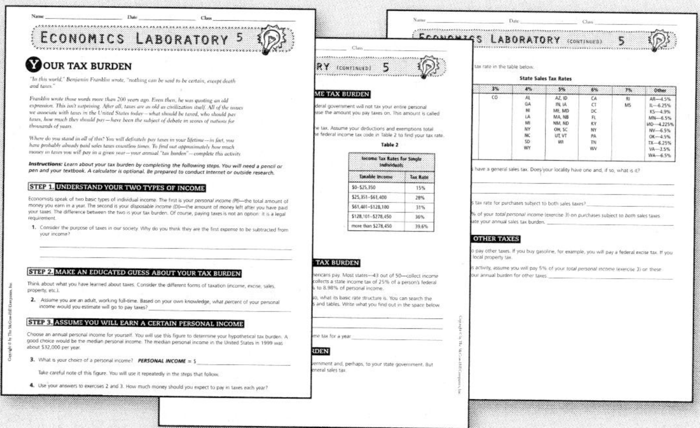

*Business Week* Focus on the New Economy

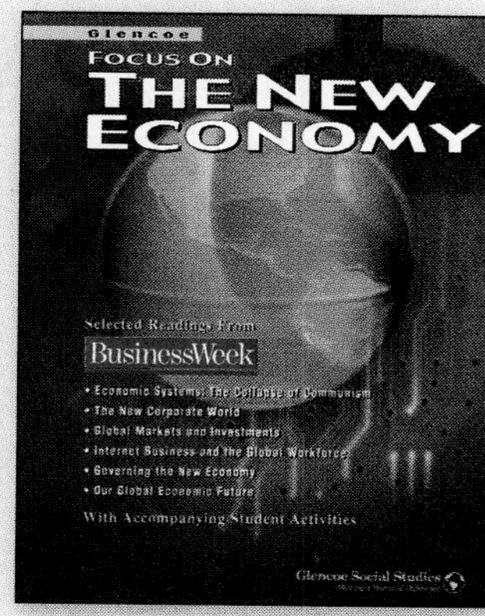


## ECONOMICS Online

*Glencoe's Web sites provide additional resources. All essential content is covered in the Student Edition.*

**ett.glencoe.com**

Visit the **Economics Today and Tomorrow** Web site for **Chapter Overviews, Textbook Updates, Student Web Activities, Web Activity Lesson Plans,** and **Self-Check Quizzes.**

**socialstudies.glencoe.com**

Visit the **Glencoe Social Studies** Web site for additional social studies activities, updates, and links to other sites.

**Glencoe's *Guide to Using the Internet*** provides an introduction to many of the current Internet technologies, social studies and professional resources, and teaching strategies.

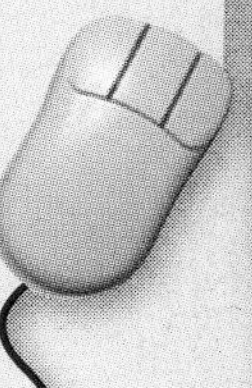

## Unit Objectives

After studying this unit, students will be able to:

- **Explain** how to measure economic performance.
- **Discuss** the Federal Reserve System and United States monetary policy.
- **List** methods used to fight unemployment and inflation.

## Unit Overview

The five chapters of **Unit 5** explain how the nation's economy is managed.

**Chapter 13** describes and explains measures of economic performance.

**Chapter 14** describes the characteristics of money and explains how the banking system works.

**Chapter 15** explains the workings of the Federal Reserve System.

**Chapter 16** describes and explains how the government collects, spends, and owes money.

**Chapter 17** discusses the actions government takes to fight unemployment and inflation.

### 00:00 Out of Time?

If time does not permit teaching each chapter in this unit, you may use the **Audio Program** that includes a 1-page activity and a 1-page test for each chapter.

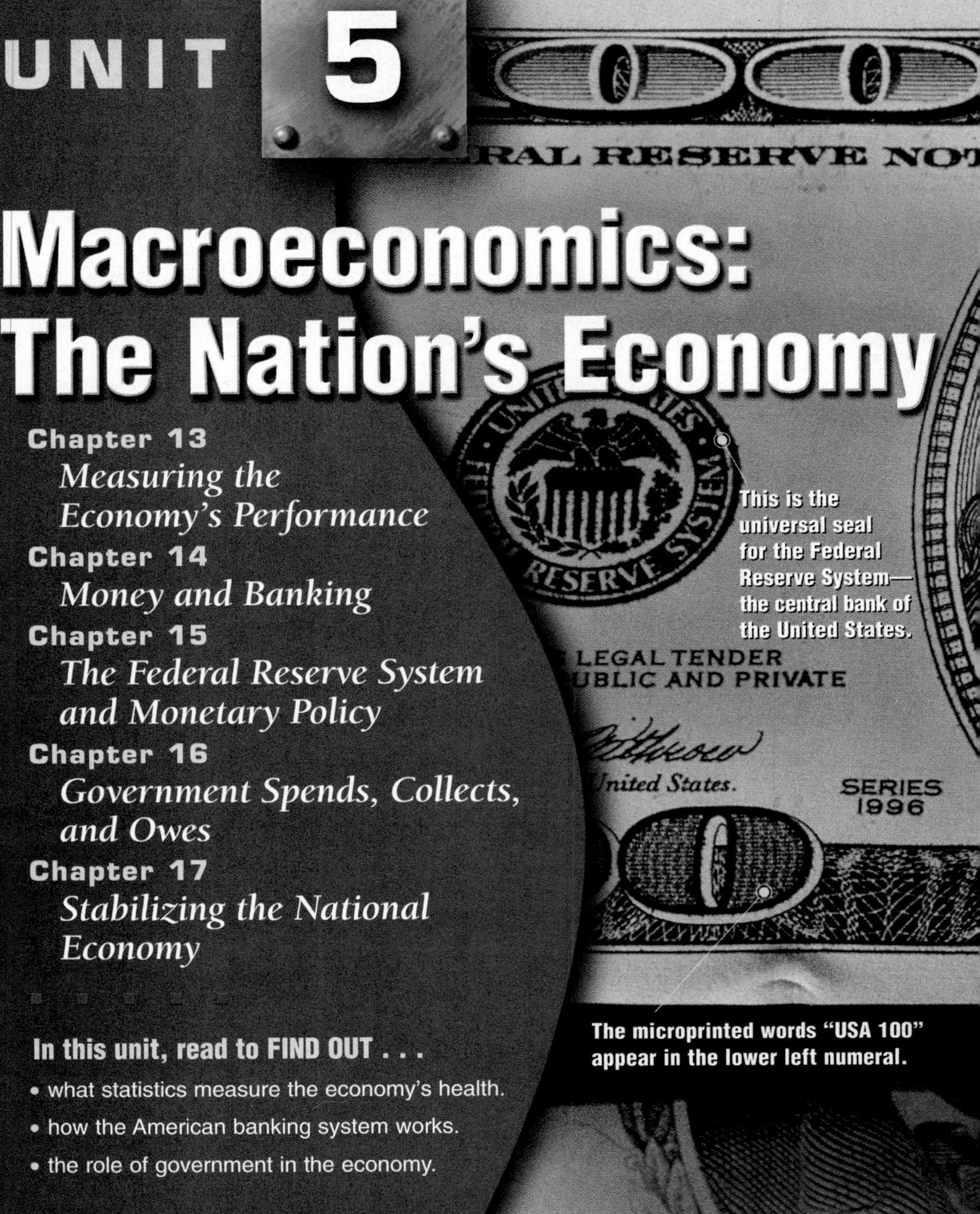


# UNIT 5

# Macroeconomics: The Nation's Economy



**In this unit, read to FIND OUT . . .**

- what statistics measure the economy's health.
- how the American banking system works.
- the role of government in the economy.

This is the universal seal for the Federal Reserve System—the central bank of the United States.

The microprinted words "USA 100" appear in the lower left numeral.

## ECONOMIC SIMULATION

**Stimulating the Economy** Organize students into several groups, and ask groups to imagine they are panels of economic advisers reporting to the President. Then provide the following hypothetical situation: Recently, the national economy has been in a recession, with unemployment at 7 percent and rising, inflation at 4 percent, investment at low levels, and economic growth close to 1.5 percent. The President has asked for recommendations on how to stimulate the economy.

Have groups investigate the different methods that might be used to stimulate the economy. Suggest that they use the information in this unit as a starting point for their investigations. Ask groups to prepare a written report listing their recommendations.

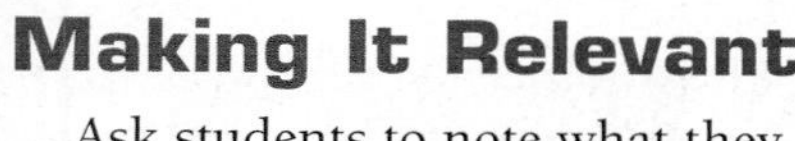

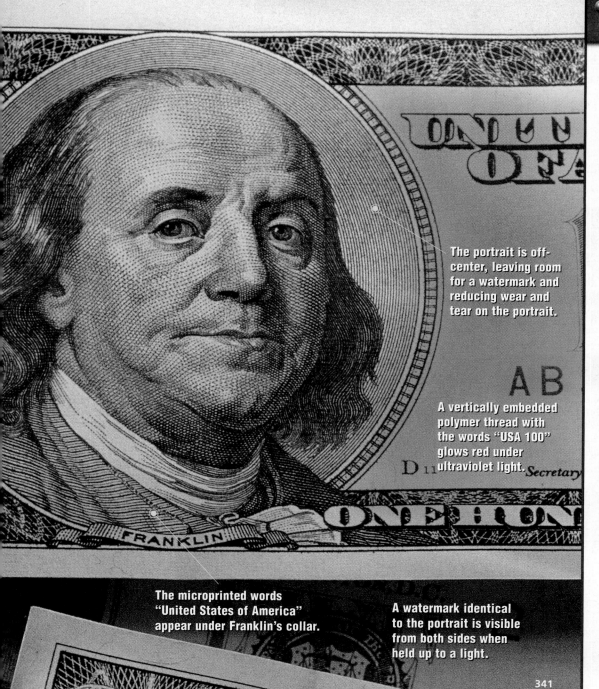


The portrait is off-center, leaving room for a watermark and reducing wear and tear on the portrait.

A vertically embedded polymer thread with the words "USA 100" glows red under ultraviolet light.

The microprinted words "United States of America" appear under Franklin's collar.

A watermark identical to the portrait is visible from both sides when held up to a light.



## Making It Relevant

Ask students to note what they think are the five most important issues in the economy today. Call on volunteers to share their ideas with the rest of the class. On the board, list issues as they are introduced. Circle such issues as taxes, government spending, deficit, national debt, unemployment, inflation, banking, and so on. Ask students to explain why they think these issues are of importance to the American economy. Conclude by mentioning that these issues will be discussed at some length in this unit.

### BusinessWeek ONLINE

To find up-to-date news and analysis on the economy, business, technology, markets, entrepreneurs, investments, and finance, have students search feature articles and special reports on the *Business Week* Web site.
www.businessweek.com

### EXTRA CREDIT PROJECT

Organize the class into several groups. While the class is studying Unit 5, have groups collect newspaper and magazine articles, illustrations, and brochures on economic indicators. At the conclusion of unit study, have groups use the materials they collected to create a collage titled "A Picture of the American Economy." Suggest that groups use annotations or captions to accompany any illustrations they include in their collages. Have groups display their collages around the classroom.

# CHAPTER 13 Resource Manager

## Teaching Transparencies

### Economic Concepts Transparency 13

### Economic Concepts Transparency 14

ECONOMIC CONCEPTS Transparency 13

GROSS DOMESTIC PRODUCT

ECONOMIC CONCEPTS Transparency 14

AGGREGATE SUPPLY



### Economic Concepts Transparency 15

ECONOMIC CONCEPTS Transparency 15

AGGREGATE DEMAND

## Application and Enrichment

### Enrichment Activity 13

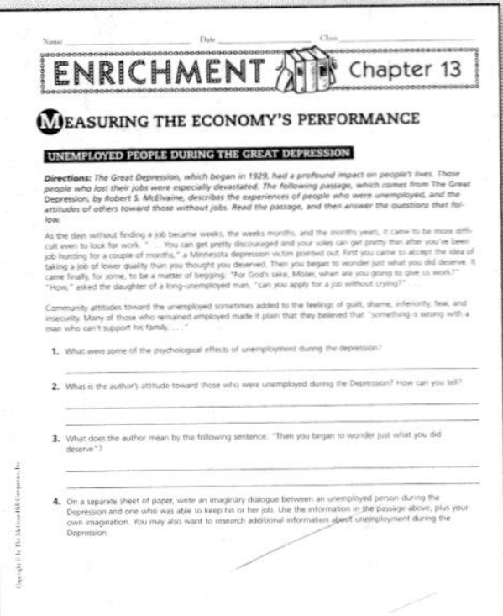

ENRICHMENT Chapter 13

MEASURING THE ECONOMY'S PERFORMANCE

UNEMPLOYED PEOPLE DURING THE GREAT DEPRESSION

### Consumer Applications Activity 18

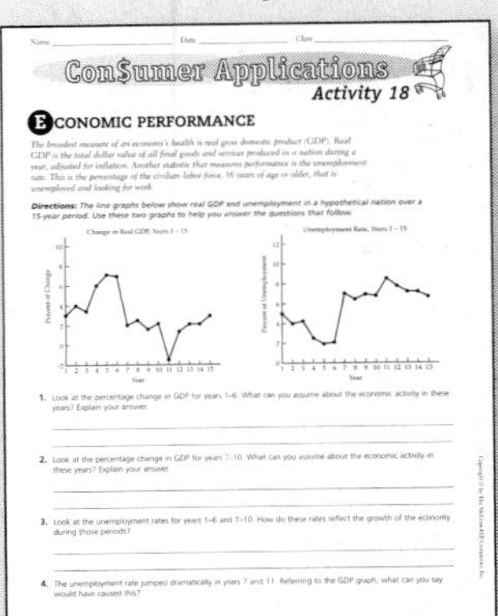

Con$umer Applications Activity 18

ECONOMIC PERFORMANCE

## Application and Enrichment

### Free Enterprise Activity 18

FREE ENTERPRISE ACTIVITY 18

ECONOMIC INDICATORS

### Cooperative Learning Simulations and Problems 18

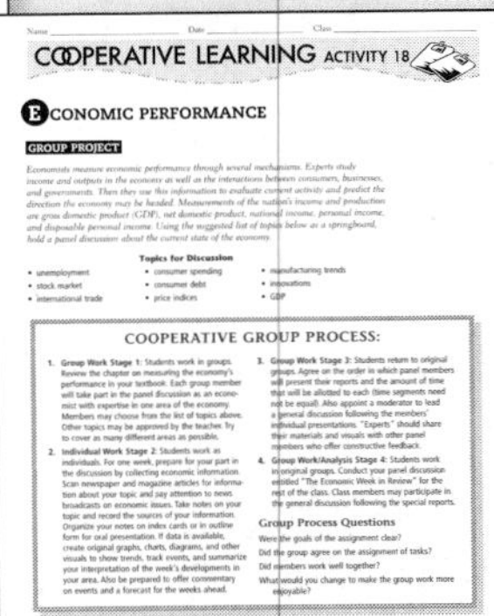

COOPERATIVE LEARNING ACTIVITY 18

ECONOMIC PERFORMANCE

COOPERATIVE GROUP PROCESS:

### Primary and Secondary Source Reading 18

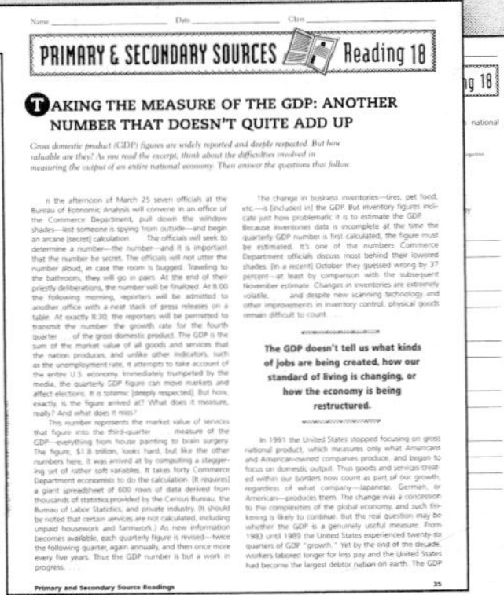

PRIMARY & SECONDARY SOURCES Reading 18

TAKING THE MEASURE OF THE GDP: ANOTHER NUMBER THAT DOESN'T QUITE ADD UP

The GDP doesn't tell us what kinds of jobs are being created, how our standard of living is changing, or how the economy is being restructured.

### Math Practice for Economics Activity 18

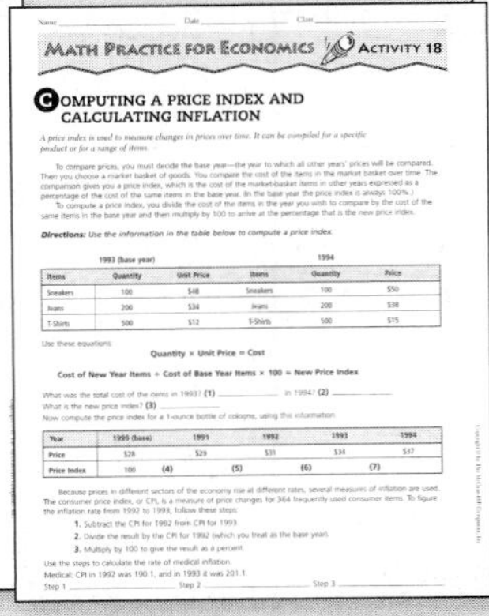

MATH PRACTICE FOR ECONOMICS ACTIVITY 18

COMPUTING A PRICE INDEX AND CALCULATING INFLATION

### Economic Cartoons Activity 18

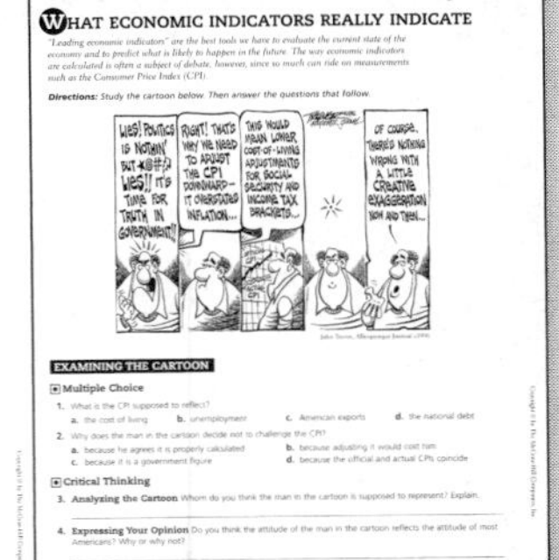

ECONOMIC CARTOON 18

WHAT ECONOMIC INDICATORS REALLY INDICATE

EXAMINING THE CARTOON

## Review and Reinforcement

### Critical Thinking Activity 18

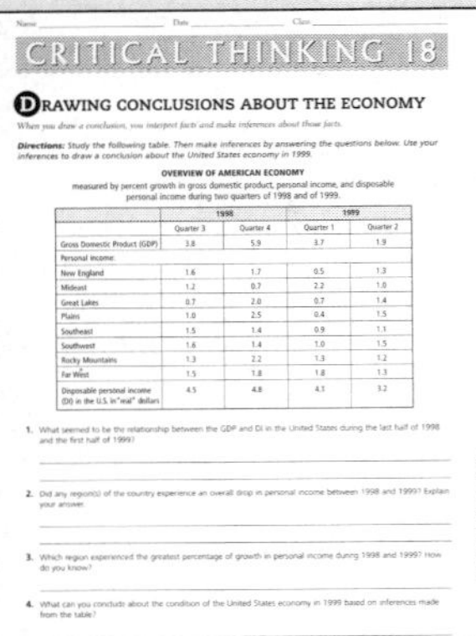

CRITICAL THINKING 18

DRAWING CONCLUSIONS ABOUT THE ECONOMY

OVERVIEW OF AMERICAN ECONOMY

### Reteaching Activity 13

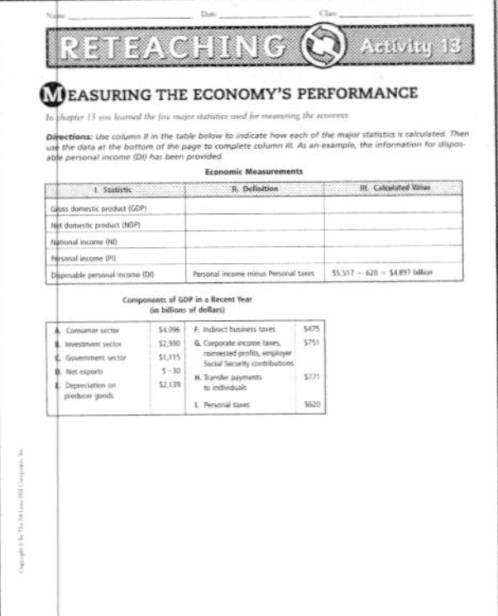

RETEACHING Activity 13

MEASURING THE ECONOMY'S PERFORMANCE

### Economic Vocabulary Activity 13

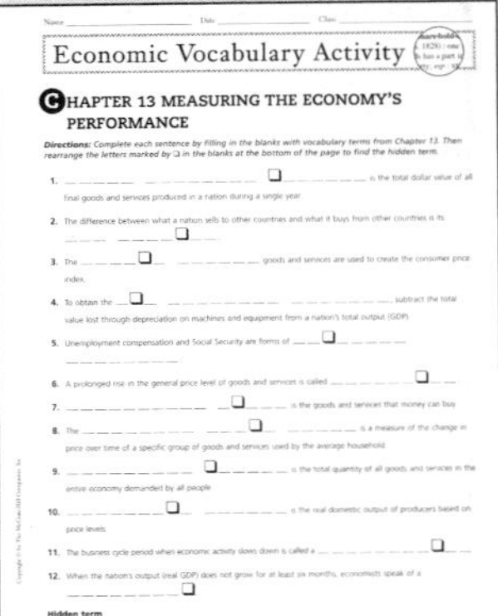

Economic Vocabulary Activity

CHAPTER 13 MEASURING THE ECONOMY'S PERFORMANCE

### Reinforcing Economic Skills 26

Reinforcing Economic Skills Chapter 26

TAKING NOTES

# CHAPTER 13 Resource Manager

## Assessment and Evaluation

Glencoe's Assessment Advantage

Chapter 13 Test Form A

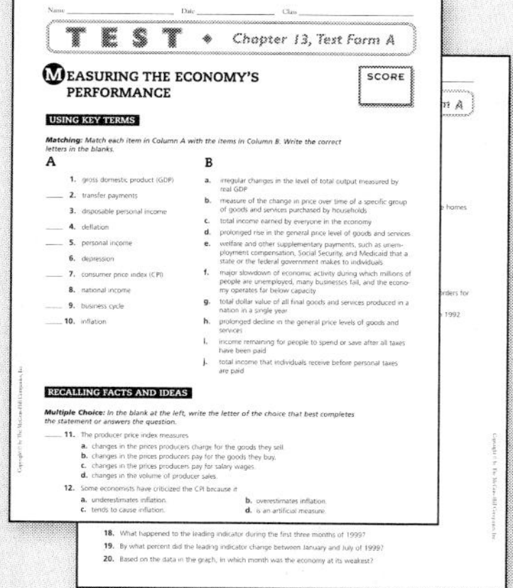


Chapter 13 Test Form B

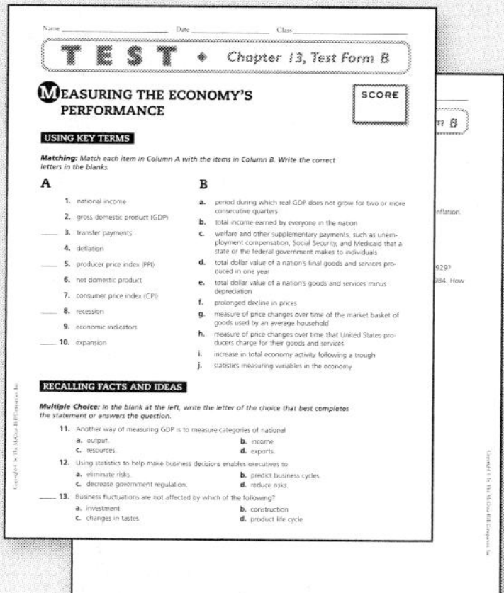


Performance Assessment Activity 18

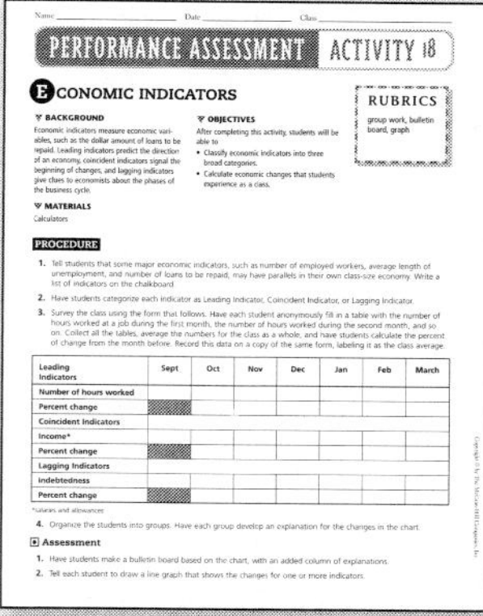


ExamView® Pro Testmaker

## Technology and Multimedia

 Vocabulary PuzzleMaker Software

 Interactive Tutor Self-Assessment Software

 ExamView® Pro Testmaker

 NBR *Economics & You* Video Program (English/Spanish)

 Presentation Plus!

 Glencoe Skillbuilder Interactive Workbook CD-ROM, Level 2

 Interactive Lesson Planner

 MindJogger Videoquiz

 Interactive Economics! CD-ROM

Audio Program (English or Spanish)

## ECONOMICS Online

You and your students can visit ett.glencoe.com—the Web site companion to **Economics Today and Tomorrow.** This innovative integration of electronic and print media offers your students a wealth of opportunities. The student text directs students to the Web site for the following options:

- **Chapter Overviews**
- **Student Web Activities**
- **Self-Check Quizzes**
- **Textbook Updates**

Answers are provided for you in the **Web Activity Lesson Plan.** Additional Web resources and Interactive Puzzles are also available.

Use the Glencoe Web site for additional resources. All essential content is covered in the Student Edition.

## Spanish Resources

 Spanish Economic Concepts Transparencies 13, 14, 15

 Spanish Vocabulary Activity 13

 Spanish Reteaching Activity 13

 Spanish Section Quizzes for Chapter 13

 Spanish Chapter 13 Audio Program, Activity, and Test

## Additional Resources

### Reading for the Student

The Economist *Guide to Economic Indicators: Making Sense of Economics.* New York: John Wiley & Sons, 1998. Written by staff members of *The Economist* magazine.

### Multimedia Material

*Capitalist Dilemmas: Ups and Downs.* Active Learning Consultants. Simulation. Introduces students to business fluctuations.

# CHAPTER 13 Resource Manager

## Section Resources

| Reading Objectives | Reproducible Resources | Technology/Multimedia Resources |
|---|---|---|
| **Section 1**<br>**National Income Accounting**<br>• What four categories of economic activity are used to measure GDP?<br>• How do the three measurements of income—national, personal, and disposable—differ? | Reproducible Lesson Plan 13-1<br>Daily Lecture Notes 13-1<br>Guided Reading Activity 13-1<br>Reading Essentials and Study Guide 13-1<br>Daily Focus Activity 52<br>Section Quiz 13-1*<br>Reinforcing Economic Skills 26 | Daily Focus Transparency 52<br>Economic Concepts Transparency 13<br>Vocabulary PuzzleMaker<br>Interactive Tutor Self-Assessment Software<br>MindJogger Videoquiz<br>NBR's *Economics & You**<br>ExamView® Pro Testmaker |
| **Section 2**<br>**Correcting Statistics for Inflation**<br>• What is the relationship between the purchasing power of money and the rate of inflation?<br>• How do the consumer price index and the producer price index differ in what they measure? | Reproducible Lesson Plan 13-2<br>Daily Lecture Notes 13-2<br>Guided Reading Activity 13-2<br>Reading Essentials and Study Guide 13-2<br>Daily Focus Activity 54<br>Section Quiz 13-2* | Daily Focus Transparency 54<br>Vocabulary PuzzleMaker<br>Interactive Tutor Self-Assessment Software<br>MindJogger Videoquiz<br>Presentation Plus!<br>ExamView® Pro Testmaker |
| **Section 3**<br>**Aggregate Demand and Supply**<br>• Why is there an inverse relationship between aggregate quantity demanded and the price level?<br>• What causes the aggregate supply curve to slope upward?<br>• How do you use aggregate demand and supply analysis to determine the equilibrium price level? | Reproducible Lesson Plan 13-3<br>Daily Lecture Notes 13-3<br>Guided Reading Activity 13-3<br>Reading Essentials and Study Guide 13-3<br>Daily Focus Activity 55<br>Section Quiz 13-3* | Daily Focus Transparency 55<br>Economic Concepts Transparencies 14, 15<br>Vocabulary PuzzleMaker<br>Interactive Tutor Self-Assessment Software<br>MindJogger Videoquiz<br>Interactive Economics!<br>Presentation Plus!<br>ExamView® Pro Testmaker |
| **Section 4**<br>**Business Fluctuations**<br>• What are the phases of a typical business cycle?<br>• What have been the three most severe downturns in the United States economy since the 1920s? | Reproducible Lesson Plan 13-4<br>Daily Lecture Notes 13-4<br>Guided Reading Activity 13-4<br>Reading Essentials and Study Guide 13-4<br>Daily Focus Activity 56<br>Section Quiz 13-4* | Daily Focus Transparency 56<br>Vocabulary PuzzleMaker<br>Interactive Tutor Self-Assessment Software<br>MindJogger Videoquiz<br>Presentation Plus!<br>ExamView® Pro Testmaker |
| **Section 5**<br>**Causes and Indicators of Business Fluctuations**<br>• What are some of the potential causes of business fluctuations?<br>• What are the three broad categories of economic indicators? | Reproducible Lesson Plan 13-5<br>Daily Lecture Notes 13-5<br>Guided Reading Activity 13-5<br>Reading Essentials and Study Guide 13-5<br>Daily Focus Activity 57<br>Section Quiz 13-5* | Daily Focus Transparency 57<br>Vocabulary PuzzleMaker<br>Interactive Tutor Self-Assessment Software<br>MindJogger Videoquiz<br>Presentation Plus!<br>ExamView® Pro Testmaker |

*Also available in Spanish

 Blackline Master  Transparency  Software 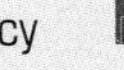 CD-ROM  Videodisc  Audiocassette  Videocassette
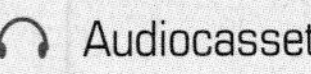

# CHAPTER 13 Resource Manager

## ACTIVITY From the Classroom of

**Eleanor S. Allen**
**Foothill High School**
**Sacramento, California**

### GDP Assessment

Post large letters *C, G, I,* and *X* in four corners of your classroom. As students enter the room, give each person one of the following statements on cards and instruct students to stand by the appropriate sign. If their statement is not counted in GDP, have students sit in their seat. After each group has formed, have them check among themselves to ensure accuracy, and then have each person read his or her card aloud.

**C (Consumer)**
- Teens buy Michael Jordan clothes in record numbers
- New car sales up
- Stores unable to keep up with demand for new calorie-free chocolate ice cream
- Colleges require every student to have a calculator
- New Barbie doll sells quickly
- Haircuts and perms at local beauty salon go on sale
- Tax accountants in greater demand
- Bus rides increase
- Fitness fads increase gym membership
- Diamond sales go up
- Teens rent limousines for Senior Ball

**I (Investment)**
- Intel builds new plant
- GM installs robots for assembly line
- HP expands its Roseville plant
- Wal-Mart opens new stores
- Processing plant for tomatoes built
- Lumber mills renew production
- Microsoft/GE launch new network

**G (Government)**
- Department of Defense orders three new submarines
- Job training program funded by federal government
- New science labs built by Department of Human Services
- New Federal Courthouse under construction
- Third new prison built this year

**X (Foreign)**
- Tractors sold to Poland
- Almonds bought by Germans for marzipan
- Jeeps to Japan
- Airplanes to Saudi Arabia
- Rice to India
- CDs to China

**Not Included in GDP**
- Jim buys a '64 Mustang
- Jill paints her own house
- "Young genius repairs his own computer"
- Electrician takes money "under the table"
- Van Gogh painting sells for record $15 million
- Welfare payments increase

## Easy Planning and Preparation!

Use Glencoe's **Presentation Plus!**, a Microsoft PowerPoint® application, to teach **Measuring the Economy's Performance.** With this multimedia teacher tool, you can customize ready-made presentations. At your fingertips are interactive transparencies, on-screen lecture notes, audiovisual presentations, and links to the Internet and to other Glencoe multimedia.

**Interactive Lesson Planner**

Planning has never been easier! Organize your week, month, semester, or year with all the lesson helps you need to make teaching creative, timely, and relevant—the way it is meant to be. The Interactive Lesson Planner opens Glencoe's **Chapter 13** resources, helps you build your schedule, and tracks your progress.

## National Council on Economic Education

## THE EconomicsAmerica AND EconomicsInternational PROGRAMS

### Voluntary Standards Emphasized in Chapter 13

**Content Standard 18** Students will understand that the nation's overall levels of income, employment, and prices are determined by the interaction of spending and production decisions made by all households, firms, government agencies, and others in the economy.

**Content Standard 19** Students will understand that inflation can reduce the rate of growth of national living standards, because individuals and organizations use resources to protect themselves against the uncertainty of future prices.

### Resources Available from NCEE

- *Capstone: The Nation's High School Economics Course*
- *Focus: High School Economics*
- *Civics and Government: Focus on Economics*

To order these materials, or to contact your State Council on Economic Education about workshops and programs, call 1-800-338-1192 or visit the NCEE Web site at http://www.nationalcouncil.org

ECONOMICS & YOU

Measuring the Economy's Performance

Chapter 20
Disc 1, Side 2

ASK: What is the definition of personal income? *the total income received by individuals before they pay taxes*

 Also available in VHS.

## Chapter Overview

**Chapter 13** describes or explains key statistics used to measure economic performance; consumer and producer price indexes; aggregate supply and demand; business cycles; and the major causes and indicators of these business fluctuations.

### GLENCOE TECHNOLOGY

Use **MindJogger Videoquiz** VHS to preview Chapter 13 content.

Introduce students to chapter content and key terms by having them access **Chapter 13—Chapter Overviews** at *ett.glencoe.com*

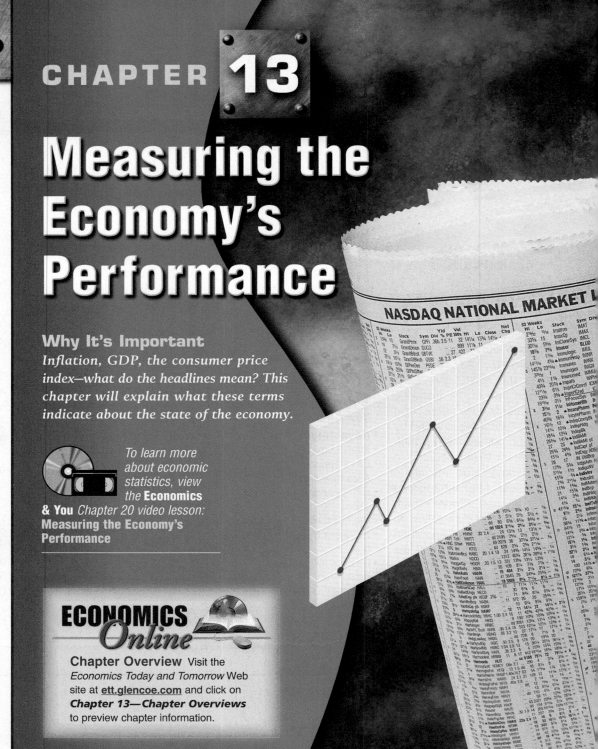

CHAPTER 13

# Measuring the Economy's Performance

### Why It's Important

*Inflation, GDP, the consumer price index—what do the headlines mean? This chapter will explain what these terms indicate about the state of the economy.*

*To learn more about economic statistics, view the* **Economics & You** *Chapter 20 video lesson:* **Measuring the Economy's Performance**

ECONOMICS Online

**Chapter Overview** Visit the *Economics Today and Tomorrow* Web site at ett.glencoe.com and click on ***Chapter 13—Chapter Overviews*** to preview chapter information.

### CHAPTER LAUNCH ACTIVITY

Remind students that in Chapter 7 they studied supply and demand among individual consumers. Then have students imagine they are economic forecasters who must determine the total supply and demand in the economy for a particular month. Ask them to suggest ways they might gather such information and how they might present this information in visual form. Conclude by pointing out that in this chapter students will learn about aggregate supply and demand—supply and demand for the whole economy.

# SECTION 1

# National Income Accounting

## Cover Story

*The Columbus Dispatch*, June 8, 1999

**Oregon and New Hampshire enjoyed the fastest economic growth among the states in 1997, and California's economy remained the biggest, the government said. . . .**

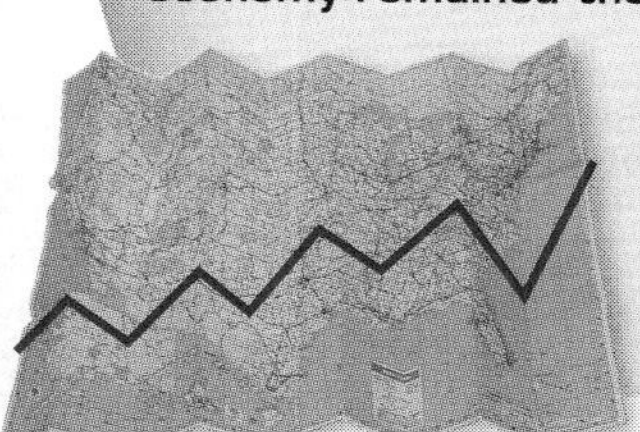

**A Commerce Department report broke down the nation's gross domestic product, the total output of goods and services, to show the amount contributed by each state.**

### Reader's Guide

**Terms to Know**

- national income accounting
- gross domestic product (GDP)
- net exports
- depreciation
- net domestic product (NDP)
- national income (NI)
- personal income (PI)
- transfer payments
- disposable personal income (DI)

**Reading Objectives**

1. What four categories of economic activity are used to measure GDP?
2. How do the three measurements of income—national, personal, and disposable—differ?

People can measure how successful they are economically by the amount of their incomes and by their standard of living, including how much their spendable income will buy. In this section, you'll learn that the success of the overall economy is measured in a similar way.

## National Income Accounting

To determine how healthy the American economy is, economists constantly measure such factors as the amount of goods and services produced yearly by the nation and the amount of income people have to spend. The measurement of the national economy's performance is called **national income accounting.** This area of economics deals with the overall economy's output, or production, and its income.

<u>**national income accounting:**</u> *measurement of the national economy's performance, dealing with the overall economy's output and income*



## SECTION 1 RESOURCE MANAGER

**Reproducible Masters**

- Reproducible Lesson Plan 13–1
- Reading Essentials and Study Guide 13–1
- Guided Reading Activity 13–1
- Section Quiz 13–1
- Daily Focus Activity 52
- Daily Lecture Notes 13–1

**Multimedia**

- Daily Focus Transparency 52
- Economic Concepts Transparency 13
- Vocabulary PuzzleMaker
- Interactive Tutor Self-Assessment Software
- ExamView® Pro Testmaker
- MindJogger Videoquiz
- NBR's *Economics & You*
- Presentation Plus!



# 1 Focus

## Overview

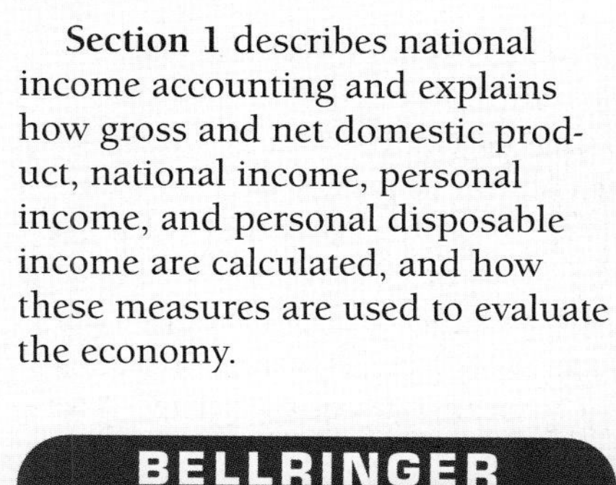

Section 1 describes national income accounting and explains how gross and net domestic product, national income, personal income, and personal disposable income are calculated, and how these measures are used to evaluate the economy.

### BELLRINGER
**Motivational Activity**

Project **Daily Focus Transparency 52** and have students answer the questions.

This activity is also available as a blackline master.

**Daily Focus Transparency 52**

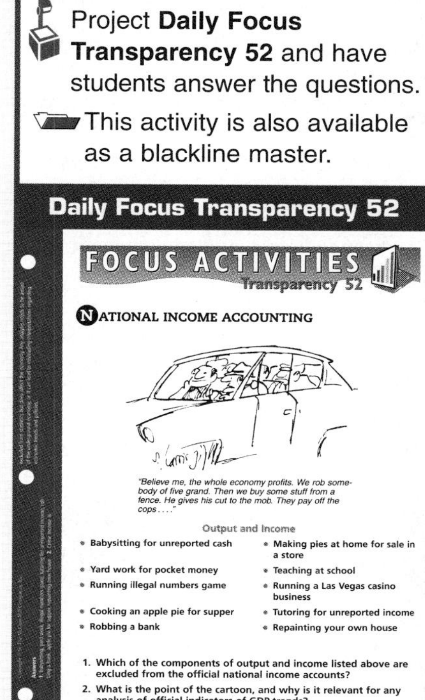


### Reader's Guide

Answers to the **Reading Objectives** questions are on page 348.

**Preteaching Vocabulary**

Have students study the Glossary definitions of the **Terms to Know.** Then have students close their books. State each term in turn, calling on volunteers to define each one.

**Vocabulary PuzzleMaker**

# 2 Teach

## Guided Practice

**L2 Classifying Ideas** On the board, draw a two-column chart using "Strengths" and "Weaknesses" as column headings. Call on volunteers to identify what they think are the strengths and weaknesses of GDP as a measure of economic performance. Note their responses in the appropriate column. Then have students use the information in the chart to write a paragraph explaining why GDP, despite its weaknesses, is a useful measure of the health of the economy.

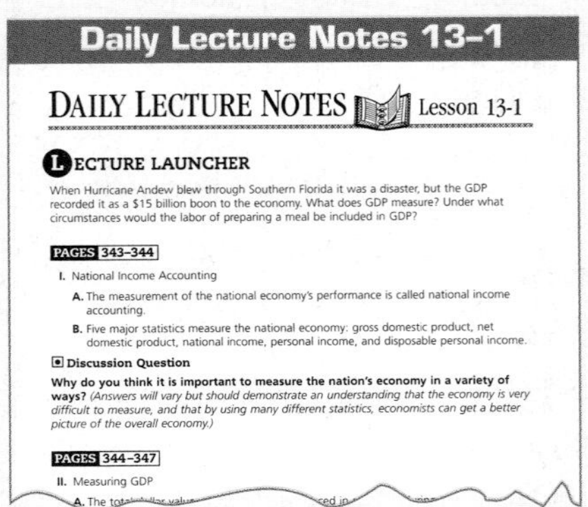

**Daily Lecture Notes 13–1**

DAILY LECTURE NOTES Lesson 13-1

**LECTURE LAUNCHER**

When Hurricane Andew blew through Southern Florida it was a disaster, but the GDP recorded it as a $15 billion boon to the economy. What does GDP measure? Under what circumstances would the labor of preparing a meal be included in GDP?

PAGES 343–344

I. National Income Accounting
  A. The measurement of the national economy's performance is called national income accounting.
  B. Five major statistics measure the national economy: gross domestic product, net domestic product, national income, personal income, and disposable personal income.

**Discussion Question**

**Why do you think it is important to measure the nation's economy in a variety of ways?** *(Answers will vary but should demonstrate an understanding that the economy is very difficult to measure, and that by using many different statistics, economists can get a better picture of the overall economy.)*

PAGES 344–347

II. Measuring GDP

**Visual Instruction FIGURE 13.1**

**Answer:** *$2,238,000,000,000 ($2.2 trillion)*

Five major statistics measure the national economy. These are gross domestic product, net domestic product, national income, personal income, and disposable personal income. Each will be examined separately, starting with the largest overall measurement—gross domestic product. **Figure 13.1** shows gross domestic product and the other four measurements in descending order of value.

## Measuring GDP

<u>gross domestic product (GDP):</u> *total dollar value of all final goods and services produced in a nation in a single year*

The broadest measure of the economy's size is **gross domestic product (GDP).** This is the total dollar value of all *final* goods and services produced in the nation during a single year. This

**FIGURE 13.1**

**GDP and Its Components** Economists start with GDP and subtract various items until they reach the figure measuring disposable personal income—the amount of money people have left to spend after they pay taxes. ***What is the difference in dollars between gross domestic product and disposable personal income?***

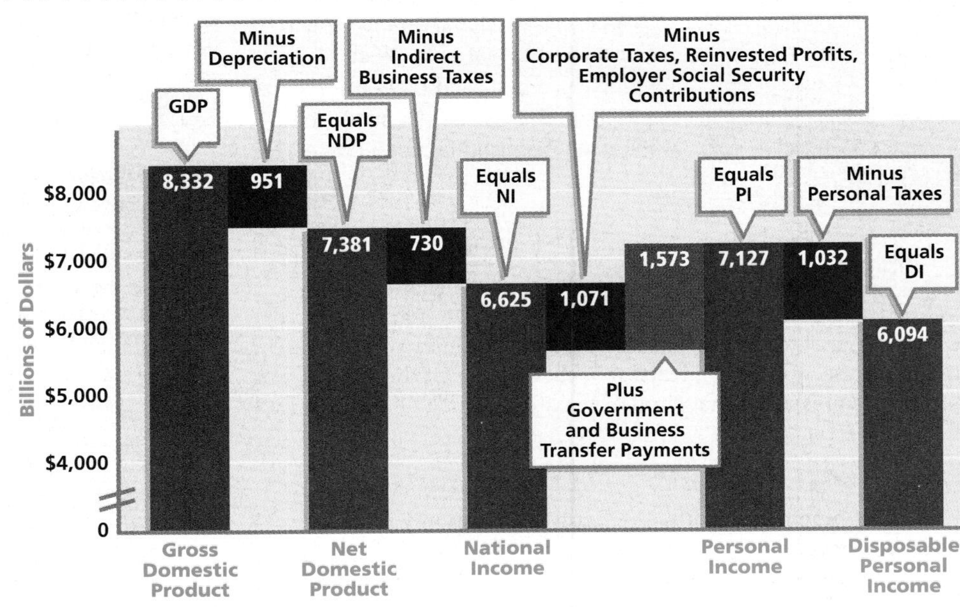


**Source:** Standard & Poor's

For an online update of this graph, visit ett.glencoe.com and click on ***Textbook Updates—Chapter 13.***



## Meeting Special Needs

**Abstract Reasoning Difficulties** Some students have difficulty with abstract information. They may grasp more concrete concepts, such as individual income, but may be confused by the use of income statistics. Work through the calculations of GDP, NDP, NI, PI, and DI. Help students see how the total economic activity of the country affects communities, businesses, and families. Students will be better able to grasp national accounting statistics if they understand that these numbers are relevant to their own lives.

 Refer to *Inclusion for the Social Studies Classroom Strategies and Activities* for students with different learning styles.

figure tells the amount of goods and services produced within the country's borders and made available for purchase in that year.

**Measuring Value** Note the word *value* in the definition. Simply adding up the *quantities* of different items produced would not mean much. Can we really measure the strength of the economy, for example, if we know that 3 billion safety pins and 2 space shuttles were produced?

What we need to know is the total *value* of the items, using some common measure. Economists use the dollar as this common measure of value. As a result, GDP is always expressed in dollar terms. For example, in 1999, GDP for the United States totaled more than $9 trillion.

**Measuring Final Goods and Services** The word *final* in the definition of GDP is also important. Measuring the economy's performance accurately requires that economists add up only the value of final goods and services to avoid *double counting.* For example, GDP does not add the price of computers and memory chips and motherboards if those chips and motherboards are installed in computers for sale. The final price to the buyer already includes the price of the memory chips and motherboards.

Also, only new goods are counted in GDP. The sale price of a used car or a secondhand refrigerator is not counted as part of GDP. Such a sale is not due to the production of the nation, but only transfers a product from one owner to another. If a new battery is put in an old car, however, that new battery is counted as part of GDP. **See Figure 13.2.**

**Computing GDP** To total the amount of GDP, economists add the expenditures made in four categories of the economy. The first category is the *consumer sector (C),* or those goods and services bought by consumers for their direct use. The second category is the *investment sector (I),* or business purchases of tools, machines, buildings, and so on, used to produce other goods. This area also includes money spent on business inventories.

**FIGURE 13.2**

**Avoiding Double Counting**
When calculating GDP, economists count only the value of the final product. The intermediate products that go into making a loaf of wheat bread—wheat that was milled into wheat flour—are not counted in GDP. Only the price of the loaf of bread is counted.

**Student Web Activity** Visit the *Economics Today and Tomorrow* Web site at ett.glencoe.com and click on ***Chapter 13—Student Web Activities*** to learn about your gross state product.



**CHAPTER 13**

**SECTION 1, Pages 343–348**

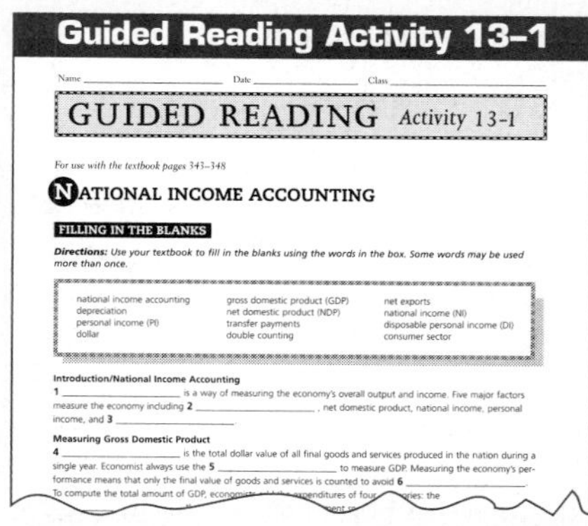

**Guided Reading Activity 13–1**

Name ________ Date ________ Class ________

GUIDED READING Activity 13-1

*For use with the textbook pages 343–348*

NATIONAL INCOME ACCOUNTING

FILLING IN THE BLANKS

***Directions:*** *Use your textbook to fill in the blanks using the words in the box. Some words may be used more than once.*

| | | |
|---|---|---|
| national income accounting | gross domestic product (GDP) | net exports |
| depreciation | net domestic product (NDP) | national income (NI) |
| personal income (PI) | transfer payments | disposable personal income (DI) |
| dollar | double counting | consumer sector |

**Introduction/National Income Accounting**

**1** ________ is a way of measuring the economy's overall output and income. Five major factors measure the economy including **2** ________, net domestic product, national income, personal income, and **3** ________.

**Measuring Gross Domestic Product**

**4** ________ is the total dollar value of all final goods and services produced in the nation during a single year. Economist always use the **5** ________ to measure GDP. Measuring the economy's performance means that only the final value of goods and services is counted to avoid **6** ________.

To compute the total amount of GDP,

**ECONOMICS & YOU**

**Measuring the Economy's Performance**

Chapter 20
Disc 1, Side 2

**ASK: What is gross domestic product?** *the total dollar value of all final goods and services produced in the United States in a single year*

 Also available in VHS.

Project Economic Concepts Transparency 13 and have students discuss the accompanying questions.

See the **Web Activity Lesson Plan** at *ett.glencoe.com* for an introduction, lesson description, and answers to the **Student Web Activity** for this chapter.

## Cooperative Learning

Point out that the Census Bureau collects information on personal income for large metropolitan areas in the United States. Then organize students into several groups, and have groups use the most recent edition of the *Statistical Abstract of the United States* to find the top 10 metropolitan areas in terms of personal income. Have them note how personal income has changed for these metropolitan areas over time. Have groups present their findings in annotated graph form. Encourage groups to display and discuss their graphs.

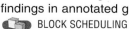

 BLOCK SCHEDULING

## Independent Practice

**L1 Constructing Graphs** Have students locate data and then construct a double line graph showing GDP and NDP for the United States for a recent 10-year period. Direct students to write a caption for the graph that explains which of the two measures more accurately reflects the actual productivity of the economy. ELL

### Visual Instruction FIGURE 13.3

Have students study **Figure 13.3.** ASK: Which sector of the economy receives disposable personal income? *consumer sector*

**L2 Applying Ideas** Point out to students that economists refer to the unpaid work that is not included in GDP as *nonmarket transactions.* Have students record the nonmarket activities they see over a set period of time. Ask students to explain why each of the listed activities is a nonmarket transaction.

**FIGURE 13.3**

**Four Categories of GDP** To compute GDP, economists add the total amount of expenditures from the consumer sector, the investment sector, the government sector, and net exports.

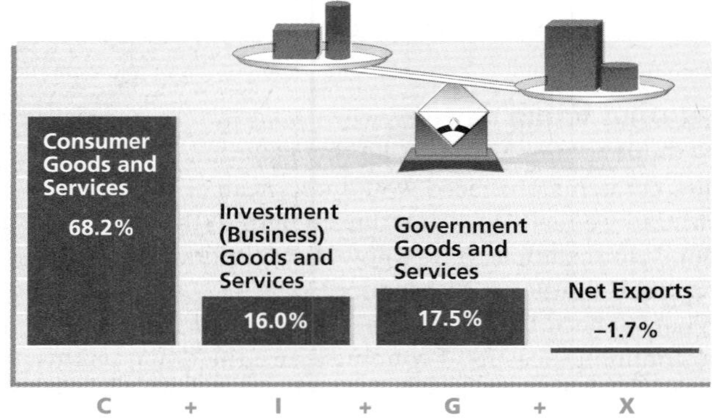


**Source:** *Statistical Abstract of the United States,* 1999

For an online update of this graph, visit ett.glencoe.com and click on ***Textbook Updates—Chapter 13.***

The *government sector (G)* makes up the third category added to GDP. The goods and services bought by federal, state, and local governments range from paper clips to jets. The final category is **net exports** *(X)*, or the difference between what the nation sells to other countries (exports) and what it buys from other countries (imports). This figure may be a plus or minus depending on whether the nation sells more or less to other nations than it buys from them. See **Figure 13.3.**

**net exports:** *difference between what the nation sells to other countries and what it buys from other countries*

**Weaknesses of GDP** The statistics used in computing GDP are accurate only to a point. Statistics about easily measurable things, such as government purchases, are reliable. Some workers, however, are given food, fuel, or housing as part of their

**FIGURE 13.4**

**Non-GDP Work** Unpaid work is not counted as part of GDP, even though it adds to the nation's output. This category includes lawn mowing, maintenance work on a home, baby-sitting, and so on. The government cannot estimate the value of this work accurately.

346

### Extending the Content

**Weaknesses of GDP as a Measurement Tool** Another weakness of GDP is that it measures only the value of quantity, not quality. For example, people buy lightbulbs, but what they really want is light. Lightbulbs can be counted in GDP, but the light they produce is not figured in. Because of technological developments, the quality of light has increased and, therefore, the price of light has fallen. However, GDP measures show a doubling in the price of lightbulbs. As a result, GDP figures may be inaccurate.

wages. GDP can include only an estimate of the value of such goods and services. Moreover, as **Figure 13.4** shows, GDP omits certain areas of economic activity such as unpaid work.

## Net Domestic Product

The loss of value because of wear and tear to durable goods, such as automobiles and refrigerators, is called **depreciation.** The same concept applies to capital goods—machines and equipment. GDP disregards depreciation. It does not take into account that some production merely keeps machines and equipment in working order and replaces them when they wear out.

**Net domestic product (NDP)**—another way of measuring the economy—accounts for the fact that some production is only due to depreciation. NDP takes GDP and subtracts the total loss in value of capital goods caused by depreciation.

**depreciation:** *loss of value because of wear and tear to durable goods and capital goods*

**net domestic product (NDP):** *value of the nation's total output (GDP) minus the total value lost through depreciation on equipment*

### Global Economy

#### Per Capita GDP

One picture of a country's standard of living comes from computing its real GDP per capita—or GDP divided by the total population. This is a measure of the average GDP per resident of a country. Listed below are the 10 nations with the highest per capita GDP.

| | |
|---|---|
| Luxembourg | $33,119 |
| United States | $29,326 |
| Norway | $26,771 |
| Switzerland | $25,902 |
| Denmark | $25,514 |
| Iceland | $24,836 |
| Japan | $24,574 |
| Canada | $23,761 |
| Belgium | $23,242 |
| Austria | $23,077 ■ |

## Measurements of Income

So far, you've learned about GDP and NDP—two major measurements of the nation's output. Three additional measurements look at income—national income, personal income, and disposable personal income.

**National Income** The total amount of income earned by everyone in the economy is called **national income (NI).** NI includes those who use their own labor to earn an income as well as those who make money through the ownership of the other factors of production. NI is equal to the sum of all income resulting from five different areas of the economy. These include wages and salaries, income of self-employed individuals, rental income, corporate profits, and interest on savings and other investments.

If you look again at **Figure 13.1** on page 344, you'll see that national income is equal to NDP minus indirect business taxes, which includes such items as sales taxes and license fees.

**national income (NI):** *total income earned by everyone in the economy*

## CHAPTER 13
SECTION 1, Pages 343–348

# 3 Assess

### Meeting Lesson Objectives

Assign Section 1 Assessment as homework or an in-class activity.

Use **Interactive Tutor Self-Assessment Software** to review Section 1.

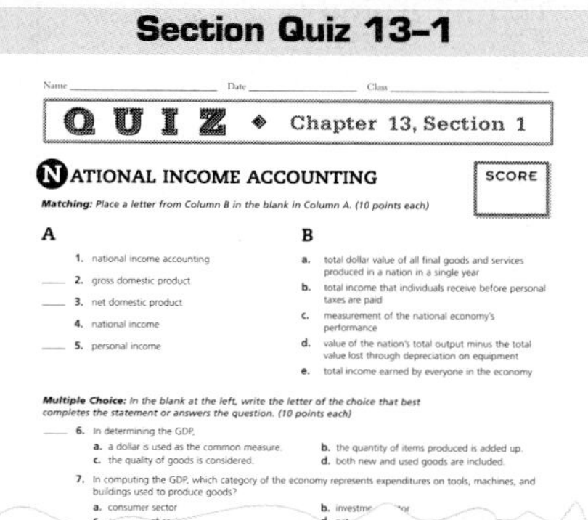

Section Quiz 13-1

Name ________ Date ________ Class ________

QUIZ ◆ Chapter 13, Section 1

NATIONAL INCOME ACCOUNTING

SCORE

***Matching:*** *Place a letter from Column B in the blank in Column A. (10 points each)*

| A | B |
|---|---|
| ___ 1. national income accounting | a. total dollar value of all final goods and services produced in a nation in a single year |
| ___ 2. gross domestic product | b. total income that individuals receive before personal taxes are paid |
| ___ 3. net domestic product | c. measurement of the national economy's performance |
| ___ 4. national income | d. value of the nation's total output minus the total value lost through depreciation on equipment |
| ___ 5. personal income | e. total income earned by everyone in the economy |

***Multiple Choice:*** *In the blank at the left, write the letter of the choice that best completes the statement or answers the question. (10 points each)*

___ 6. In determining the GDP,
a. a dollar is used as the common measure.
b. the quantity of items produced is added up.
c. the quality of goods is considered.
d. both new and used goods are included.

___ 7. In computing the GDP, which category of the economy represents expenditures on tools, machines, and buildings used to produce goods?
a. consumer sector
b. investme[illegible]

### Did You Know

Remind students that the study of the economy as a whole is known as *macroeconomics*. When analyzing macroeconomics, economists essentially are looking at the "big picture" of the economy.

### Relevant Issues in Economics

**GDP and Depreciation** In recent years, the amount used by economists to account for depreciation has been a little more than 10 percent. In 1998, for example, GDP was about $8.3 trillion. Subtracting some $950 billion for depreciation produced an NDP of about $7.4 trillion. Because NDP accounts for depreciation, it is a better measure of the economy's actual productivity than GDP.

## Reteach

Have students write summary paragraphs on each of the following subjects: National Income Accounting, Measuring GDP, Net Domestic Product, Measurements of Income.

**Reading Essentials and Study Guide 13–1**

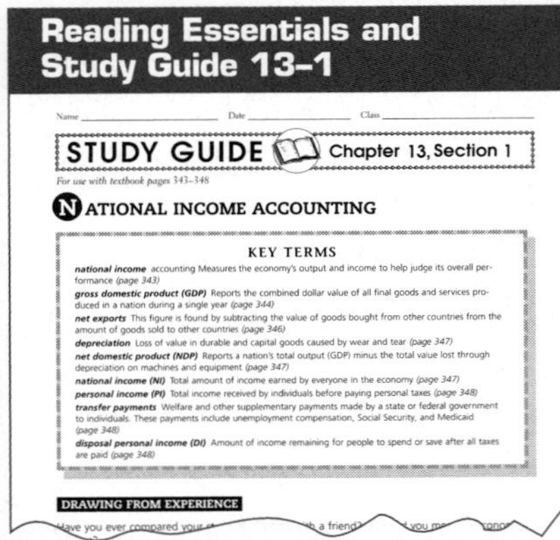

Name ______ Date ______ Class ______

STUDY GUIDE Chapter 13, Section 1

*For use with textbook pages 343–348*

NATIONAL INCOME ACCOUNTING

KEY TERMS

***national income*** accounting Measures the economy's output and income to help judge its overall performance *(page 343)*

***gross domestic product (GDP)*** Reports the combined dollar value of all final goods and services produced in a nation during a single year *(page 344)*

***net exports*** This figure is found by subtracting the value of goods bought from other countries from the amount of goods sold to other countries *(page 346)*

***depreciation*** Loss of value in durable and capital goods caused by wear and tear *(page 347)*

***net domestic product (NDP)*** Reports a nation's total output (GDP) minus the total value lost through depreciation on machines and equipment *(page 347)*

***national income (NI)*** Total amount of income earned by everyone in the economy *(page 347)*

***personal income (PI)*** Total income received by individuals before paying personal taxes *(page 348)*

***transfer payments*** Welfare and other supplementary payments made by a state or federal government to individuals. These payments include unemployment compensation, Social Security, and Medicaid *(page 348)*

***disposal personal income (DI)*** Amount of income remaining for people to spend or save after all taxes are paid *(page 348)*

DRAWING FROM EXPERIENCE

## 4 Close

Have students discuss why economists consider the practice of national income accounting so important.

**personal income (PI):** *total income that individuals receive before personal taxes are paid*

### Personal Income

The total income that individuals receive before personal taxes are paid is called **personal income (PI).** PI can be derived from NI through a two-step process. First, several items are subtracted: corporate income taxes, profits that businesses reinvest in business to expand, and Social Security contributions employers make. These items are subtracted because they represent income that is not available for individuals to spend.

**transfer payments:** *welfare and other supplementary payments that a state or the federal government makes to individuals*

Then transfer payments are added to NI. **Transfer payments** are welfare payments and other assistance payments—unemployment compensation, Social Security, and Medicaid—that a state or the federal government makes to individuals. These transfer payments add to an individual's income even though they are not exchanged for any current productive activity.

**disposable personal income (DI):** *income remaining for people to spend or save after all taxes have been paid*

### Disposable Personal Income

The income that people have left after taxes, including Social Security contributions, is called **disposable personal income (DI).** DI equals PI minus personal taxes. DI is an important indicator of the economy's health because it measures the actual amount of money income people have available to save and spend.

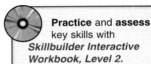

**Practice** and **assess** key skills with ***Skillbuilder Interactive Workbook, Level 2.***

## SECTION 1 Assessment

### Understanding Key Terms

1. **Define** national income accounting, GDP, net exports, depreciation, NDP, NI, PI, transfer payments, DI.

### Reviewing Objectives

2. What four categories of economic activity are used to measure GDP?
3. **Graphic Organizer** Create a diagram like the one below to show what must be subtracted from and added to national income to determine personal income.

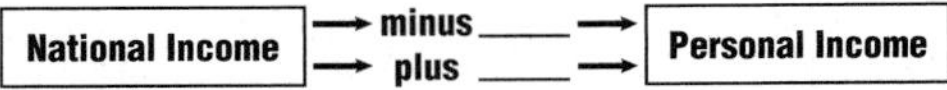


### Applying Economic Concepts

4. **Gross Domestic Product** List five items you have recently purchased. Explain why they should or should not be counted in GDP. Use the terms *value, final,* and *double counting* in your explanations.

### Critical Thinking Activity

5. **Synthesizing Information** Reconstruct **Figure 13.1** on page 344 in the form of a spreadsheet. Start with the dollar figure for GDP, then subtract the dollar figure of depreciation to get NDP. Continue until you have tabulated DI.



## SECTION 1 Assessment Answers

1. All definitions can be found in the Glossary.
2. consumer sector, investment sector, government sector, net exports
3. To derive personal income from national income, corporate income taxes, reinvested business profits, and Social Security contributions made by employers are subtracted; and transfer payments—welfare and other assistance payments—are added.
4. Answers will vary. Call on volunteers to present and discuss their lists.
5. Encourage students to display and compare their spreadsheets.

Study & Writing Skills

# Taking Notes

*Effective note taking involves more than just writing facts in short phrases. It involves breaking up much of the information into meaningful parts so that it can be understood and remembered.*

- When taking notes on material presented in class, write the key points and important facts and figures in a notebook.
- Writing quickly and neatly, use abbreviations and phrases.
- Copy words, statements, or diagrams drawn on the chalkboard.
- Ask the teacher to repeat important points you have missed or do not understand.
- When studying textbook material, organize your notes into an outline (see page 406 for hints on outlining).
- For a research report, take notes on cards. Note cards should include the title, author, and page number of sources.

## Learning the Skill

To learn how to take good notes, follow the steps listed on the left.

## Practicing the Skill

Suppose you are writing a research report on the United States GDP. First, identify main-idea questions about this topic, such as "What does GDP measure?" "What components make up GDP?" and "What are the weaknesses of using GDP to measure the economy?" Then find material about each main-idea question.

Using this textbook as a source, read the material in Section 1 and prepare notes like this:

**Main Idea: What does GDP measure?**
1. GDP is prt of nat'l inc. acct.
2. NIC measrs amt of gds & serv prducd yrly
3. GDP = tot $ vlu of final gds & srvs prdcd in U.S. in 1 yr.

**Main Idea: What components make up GDP?**
1.
2.
3.

## Application Activity

Scan a local newspaper for a short editorial or article about the nation's GDP. Take notes by writing the main idea and supporting facts. Summarize the article using only your notes.

**Practice** and **assess** key skills with ***Skillbuilder Interactive Workbook, Level 2.***

### Taking Notes

Review with students the guidelines to taking notes. As you work through the guidelines, call on volunteers to summarize each point. Then have students study the sample notes included in **Practicing the Skill.** Ask them to translate the abbreviations used in the notes. If students have difficulty, point out that note taking is an individual and personal activity. As long as notes are clear to the writer, any system of shorthand is acceptable.

Assist students with the **Practicing the Skill** activity, reviewing their finished notes. Then assign the **Application Activity.**

**Reinforcing Economic Skills 26**

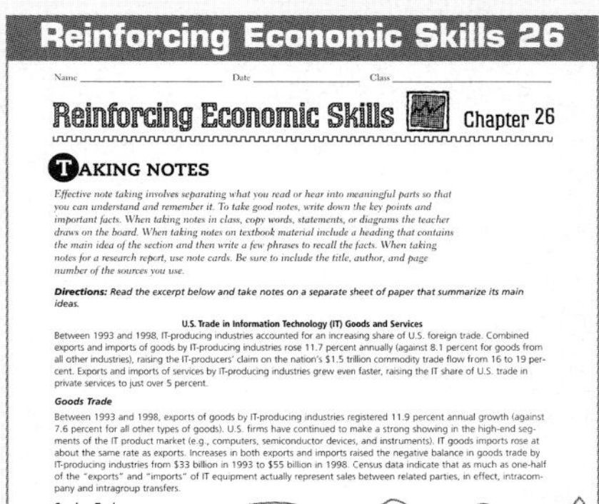

Name ______ Date ______ Class ______

Reinforcing Economic Skills Chapter 26

TAKING NOTES

*Effective note taking involves separating what you read or hear into meaningful parts so that you can understand and remember it. To take good notes, write down the key points and important facts. When taking notes in class, copy words, statements, or diagrams the teacher draws on the board. When taking notes on textbook material include a heading that contains the main idea of the section and then write a few phrases to recall the facts. When taking notes for a research report, use note cards. Be sure to include the title, author, and page number of the sources you use.*

***Directions:*** *Read the excerpt below and take notes on a separate sheet of paper that summarize its main ideas.*

**U.S. Trade in Information Technology (IT) Goods and Services**

Between 1993 and 1998, IT-producing industries accounted for an increasing share of U.S. foreign trade. Combined exports and imports of goods by IT-producing industries rose 11.7 percent annually (against 8.1 percent for goods from all other industries), raising the IT-producers' claim on the nation's $1.5 trillion commodity trade flow from 16 to 19 percent. Exports and imports of services by IT-producing industries grew even faster, raising the IT share of U.S. trade in private services to just over 5 percent.

***Goods Trade***

Between 1993 and 1998, exports of goods by IT-producing industries registered 11.9 percent annual growth (against 7.6 percent for all other types of goods). U.S. firms have continued to make a strong showing in the high-end segments of the IT product market (e.g., computers, semiconductor devices, and instruments). IT goods imports rose at about the same rate as exports. Increases in both exports and imports raised the negative balance in goods trade by IT-producing industries from $33 billion in 1993 to $55 billion in 1998. Census data indicate that as much as one-half of the "exports" and "imports" of IT equipment actually represent sales between related parties, in effect, intracompany and intragroup transfers.

***Services Trade***

**GLENCOE TECHNOLOGY**

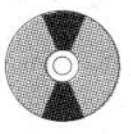

**Glencoe Skillbuilder Interactive Workbook, Level 2**

This interactive CD-ROM reinforces student mastery of essential social studies skills.

### Answers to *Practicing the Skill*

Notes and note-taking styles will vary. Encourage students to use their notes to write a summary of Section 1.

*Application Activity* Summaries will vary. Call on volunteers to share their notes and summaries with the rest of the class.

# 1 Focus

## Overview

**Section 2** describes the effect of inflation on purchasing power and explains how consumer and producer price indexes and real GDP are used to measure changes in average prices.

### BELLRINGER
**Motivational Activity**

Project **Daily Focus Transparency 54** and have students answer the questions.

This activity is also available as a blackline master.

**Daily Focus Transparency 54**

FOCUS ACTIVITIES
Transparency 54

INFLATION

**Records of Inflation**

| The World Record | | |
|---|---|---|
| Time | Place | Description |
| 1922–1923 | Germany | • Between August 1922 and November 1923, inflation ran at an average rate of 3 trillion percent. The economic crisis was a factor in Adolf Hitler's rise to power. |
| **The United States Record** | | |
| Time | Place | Description |
| 1918 | United States | • A 20.4 percent inflation rate this year remains the lowest rate since the CPI was instituted in 1913. |

Sources: *The Guiness Book of World Records, The Word Book Encyclopedia*

1. What type of inflation is each example listed in the table?
2. What is the highest inflation rate ever recorded in the United States?

Daily Focus Transparencies

## READER'S GUIDE

Answers to the **Reading Objectives** questions are on page 354.

**Preteaching Vocabulary**

Have students use the **Terms to Know** to create two word webs, one titled "Inflation and Purchasing Power" and the other titled "Measuring Inflation."

**Vocabulary PuzzleMaker**

SECTION 2

# Correcting Statistics for Inflation

## READER'S GUIDE

**Terms to Know**
- inflation
- purchasing power
- deflation
- consumer price index (CPI)
- market basket
- base year
- producer price index (PPI)
- GDP price deflator
- real GDP

**Reading Objectives**
1. What is the relationship between the purchasing power of money and the rate of inflation?
2. How do the consumer price index and the producer price index differ in what they measure?

## COVER STORY

*BUSINESS WEEK, MAY 31, 1999*

In Wall Street's galaxy, the Phantom Menace is inflation. It's the Dark Side of the economy's Force. The financial markets know that [nonexistent] inflation is the single most important factor supporting the economy's amazing performance of recent years. . . .

That's why the May 14 news of an unexpected 0.7% jump in the April consumer price index, the largest monthly rise in more than nine years, looked as scary as Darth Maul wielding his light saber.

In Section 1, you learned how GDP statistics measure the economy. You also learned that GDP figures can be unreliable because they do not measure unpaid work or depreciation. Another factor that skews GDP figures is **inflation,** or a prolonged rise in the general price level of goods and services. As mentioned in the *Cover Story* above, the presence of inflation can pose a threat to the economy. In this section, you'll learn how inflation affects the current dollar value of GDP as well as your ability to purchase goods and services.

**inflation:** *prolonged rise in the general price level of goods and services*

## SECTION 2 RESOURCE MANAGER

**Reproducible Masters**
- Reproducible Lesson Plan 13–2
- Reading Essentials and Study Guide 13–2
- Guided Reading Activity 13–2
- Section Quiz 13–2
- Daily Focus Activity 54
- Daily Lecture Notes 13–2

**Multimedia**
- Daily Focus Transparency 54
- Vocabulary PuzzleMaker
- Interactive Tutor Self-Assessment Software
- ExamView® Pro Testmaker
- MindJogger Videoquiz
- Presentation Plus!

## The Purchasing Power of Money

When is a dollar not a dollar? When inflation occurs, the prices of goods and services rise. Therefore, the **purchasing power** of the dollar goes down. A dollar's purchasing power is the real goods and services that it can buy. In other words, a dollar cannot buy the same amount as it did before inflation.

How does a drop in the dollar's purchasing power skew GDP? The higher GDP figures that result from inflation do not represent any increase in output. For example, last year an ice-cream cone may have cost $1.00. This year it may cost $1.95. The physical output—in this case, one ice-cream cone—has not changed; only its money value has. To get a true measure of the nation's output in a given year, inflation must be taken into account. **Deflation**, a prolonged *decline* in the general price level, also affects the dollar value of GDP, but deflation rarely happens.

**purchasing power:** *the real goods and services that money can buy; determines the value of money*

**deflation:** *prolonged decline in the general price level of goods and services*

## Measures of Inflation

The government measures inflation in several ways. The three most commonly used measurements are the consumer price index, the producer price index, and the implicit GDP price deflator.

**Consumer Price Index (CPI)** Every month, the government measures the change in price of a specific group of goods and services that the average household uses. This measurement is the **consumer price index (CPI)**. The group of items that are

**consumer price index (CPI):** *measure of the change in price over time of a specific group of goods and services used by the average household*

### Economic Connection to... MATH

## Compiling the CPI

When compiling the CPI, the Bureau of Labor Statistics (BLS) does not record every price of every product bought by everyone in the United States. The BLS instead tries to get a *representative* picture of the prices paid by consumers for all products. A national sample of some 29,000 families provides the BLS with information on their spending habits. This enables the BLS to put together the market basket and to "weight" items according to consumer spending. For example, housing items are given more weight, or importance, than recreation items because most consumers spend more on housing than on recreation. ■

### Meeting Special Needs

**Study Strategy** Students with learning problems often have difficulty generalizing the use of strategies from one situation to another. They need to have periodic review of both the steps of the strategy they are using and the procedures that are used in each of the steps. Tell students that in this section they will use the study strategy independently. Have each student draw a chart with grids to self-evaluate each one of the following: Did I skim for titles, headings, and main ideas? Did I ask questions? Did I answer my questions?

Refer to *Inclusion for the Social Studies Classroom Strategies and Activities* for students with different learning styles.

# 2 Teach

## Guided Practice

**L1 Illustrating Ideas** Review the information on inflation and purchasing power. Then ask students to present the relationship between the rate of inflation and the purchasing power of money in a diagram. If students have difficulty, you might suggest that they draw a "shrinking" dollar that gets smaller as prices rise. Or you might suggest that they draw two arrows, one pointing upward, the other pointing downward. Direct students to title, illustrate, and annotate their diagrams. Call on volunteers to present and explain their diagrams to the class. ELL

### Daily Lecture Notes 13–2

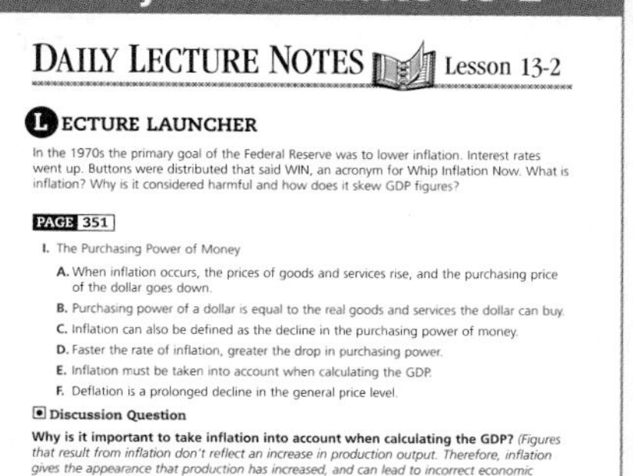

DAILY LECTURE NOTES Lesson 13-2

LECTURE LAUNCHER

In the 1970s the primary goal of the Federal Reserve was to lower inflation. Interest rates went up. Buttons were distributed that said WIN, an acronym for Whip Inflation Now. What is inflation? Why is it considered harmful and how does it skew GDP figures?

PAGE 351

I. The Purchasing Power of Money

A. When inflation occurs, the prices of goods and services rise, and the purchasing price of the dollar goes down.

B. Purchasing power of a dollar is equal to the real goods and services the dollar can buy.

C. Inflation can also be defined as the decline in the purchasing power of money.

D. Faster the rate of inflation, greater the drop in purchasing power.

E. Inflation must be taken into account when calculating the GDP.

F. Deflation is a prolonged decline in the general price level.

**Discussion Question**

**Why is it important to take inflation into account when calculating the GDP?** *(Figures that result from inflation don't reflect an increase in production output. Therefore, inflation gives the appearance that production has increased, and can lead to incorrect economic policies.)*

### Economic Connection to... MATH

In compiling the CPI, the BLS also uses a national sample of about 24,000 families to find out the kinds of stores where people shop.

## Visual Instruction FIGURE 13.5

Discuss with students how increases in the CPI often mean that people have more money, because prices and wages often rise at the same time. However, this extra money has less purchasing power.

## Guided Reading Activity 13-2

GUIDED READING Activity 13-2

CORRECTING STATISTICS FOR INFLATION

RECALLING THE FACTS

Directions: Use the information in your textbook to answer the questions.

1. What is inflation?
2. What is a dollar's purchasing power?
3. How does a drop in the dollar's purchasing power affect GDP?
4. How are deflation and inflation similar and different?
Similarities:
Differences:
5. What does the consumer price index (CPI) measure?

## Independent Practice

**L2 Analyzing Trends** Have students consult the most recent editions of the *Statistical Abstract of the United States* and the *Economic Report of the President* to find CPI and PPI statistics for the 1990s. Have them use their findings to write a paragraph on inflation trends during the decade. Suggest that students illustrate their paragraphs with charts and graphs.

BLOCK SCHEDULING

**FIGURE 13.5**

**Selected Consumer Prices** Price indexes allow you to compare price levels from year to year. When the CPI rises, there is inflation.

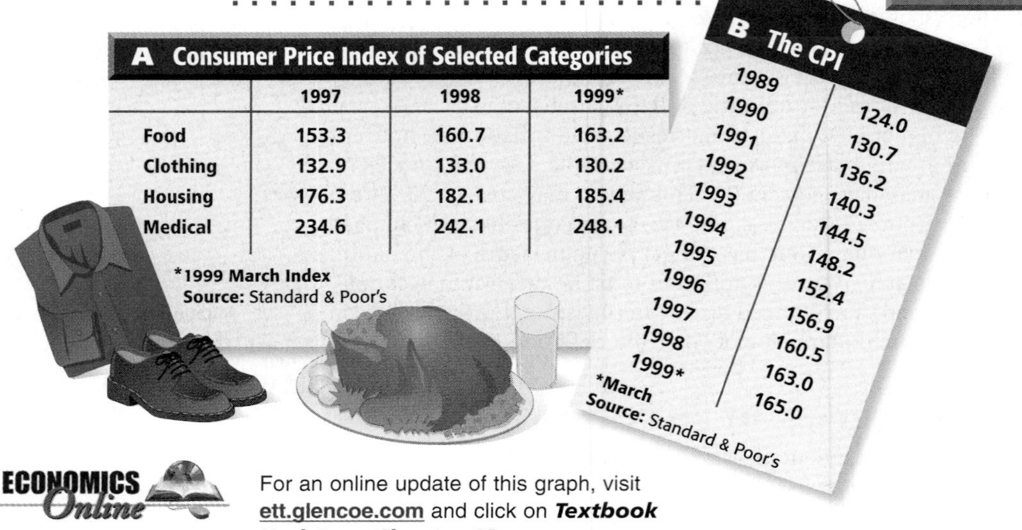

**A Consumer Price Index of Selected Categories**

| | 1997 | 1998 | 1999* |
|---|---|---|---|
| Food | 153.3 | 160.7 | 163.2 |
| Clothing | 132.9 | 133.0 | 130.2 |
| Housing | 176.3 | 182.1 | 185.4 |
| Medical | 234.6 | 242.1 | 248.1 |

*1999 March Index
**Source:** Standard & Poor's

**B The CPI**

| | |
|---|---|
| 1989 | 124.0 |
| 1990 | 130.7 |
| 1991 | 136.2 |
| 1992 | 140.3 |
| 1993 | 144.5 |
| 1994 | 148.2 |
| 1995 | 152.4 |
| 1996 | 156.9 |
| 1997 | 160.5 |
| 1998 | 163.0 |
| 1999* | 165.0 |

*March
**Source:** Standard & Poor's



ECONOMICS Online For an online update of this graph, visit ett.glencoe.com and click on ***Textbook Updates—Chapter 13.***

*market basket: representative group of goods and services used to compile the consumer price index*

priced, called a **market basket,** includes about 90,000 specific goods and services under general categories such as food, housing, transportation, apparel, education, recreation, medical care, and personal care. About every 10 years, the market basket is updated to include new products and services and to reflect more current spending patterns. *Part A* of **Figure 13.5** has broken down the CPI into several major categories, whereas *Part B* shows the overall CPI for several years.

*base year: year used as a point of comparison for other years in a series of statistics*

Employees at the federal Bureau of Labor Statistics (BLS) compile the CPI monthly. They start with prices from a **base year** so that they have a point of comparison for current-day prices. For example, if you paid $1.00 for an ice-cream cone in 1998, and the price of the cone increased to $1.95 in 2001, the cost of an ice-cream cone has risen 95 cents (and in this case, 95 percent) since 1998 ($1.95 − 1.00 = .95).

In compiling the CPI, the BLS's base year is really the average of prices that existed for the three years 1982 to 1984. This base is given a value of 100. CPI numbers for later years indicate the percentage that the market basket price has risen since the base year.



## Cooperative Learning

Inform students that economists use the term *hyperinflation* to describe a situation where the rate of inflation is so high that prices change weekly or daily. Organize students into several groups, and have groups research an example of hyperinflation. If students have difficulty finding an example, you might suggest Germany after World War I or Latin America in the 1980s. Have groups use their findings to create an illustrated report. Direct groups to cover such topics as what caused hyperinflation, what was the impact of hyperinflation on the economy, and how hyperinflation was brought under control.

For example, the 1999 March CPI of 165.0 means that the average price of goods and services in the market basket has risen 65.0 percent since the period 1982–1984 (165.0 − 100 = 65.0). The price level, therefore, rose 65 percent since 1982–1984. The CPI can also be used to calculate inflation for any period, as shown in **Figure 13.6.**

**Producer Price Index** Another important measure of inflation is the **producer price index (PPI).** The PPI is actually a group of indexes that measures the average change in prices that United States producers charge their customers—whether these customers are other producers buying crude materials for further processing or wholesalers who will sell the products to retailers or directly to consumers. Most of the producer prices included in the PPIs are in mining, manufacturing, and agriculture.

The PPIs usually increase before the CPI. Apple producers, for example, may experience a weak harvest. Because of the shortage of apples, the price of apples rises. A bakery that buys apples will eventually increase the price of its apple pies to cover the higher price of apples. Eventually the CPI will increase because consumers will have to pay more for the final products—in this case, apple pies. Therefore, changes in the PPIs often are watched as a hint that inflation and the CPI are going to increase.

**GDP Price Deflator** Government economists account for inflation by issuing another measure of price changes in GDP, called the **GDP price deflator.** This index removes the effects of inflation from GDP so that the overall economy in one year can be compared to another year. When the price deflator is applied to GDP in any year, the new figure is called **real GDP.**

The federal government uses 1992 as its base year to measure real GDP. Each year the price deflator is used to change current, or inflated, GDP to real GDP. For example, GDP in current dollars for 1998 was $8,511.0 billion. To find real GDP for 1998, the government divides 1998 GDP by the 1998 price deflator (112.7) and multiplies the result by 100:

$$\$8{,}511.0 \div 112.7 \times 100 = \$7{,}551.9$$

Real GDP for 1998 was $7,551.9 billion. This figure may now be compared to 1992 GDP of $6,244.4 billion. This is a more meaningful comparison than comparing 1998 GDP in inflated dollars to 1992 GDP. **Figure 13.7** on page 354 shows both current GDP and real GDP (in chained [1992] dollars).

<u>**producer price index (PPI):**</u> *measure of the change in price over time that United States producers charge for their goods and services*

<u>**GDP price deflator:**</u> *price index that removes the effect of inflation from GDP so that the overall economy in one year can be compared to another year*

<u>**real GDP:**</u> *GDP that has been adjusted for inflation by applying the price deflator*

**FIGURE 13.6**

**Calculating Inflation** At the end of 1991, the CPI was 136.2. In March 1999 it was 165.0, which is a difference of 28.8 (165.0 − 136.2 = 28.8). If we now use 1991 as the base year, we can find out by what percentage consumer prices on average rose from 1991 to 1999. We do this by dividing 28.8 by 136.2, which gives us 0.2114 (28.8 ÷ 136.2). When we multiply by 100 to give the result as a percent, we get 21.14 percent.

# 3 Assess

## Meeting Lesson Objectives

Assign Section 2 Assessment as homework or an in-class activity.

Use **Interactive Tutor Self-Assessment Software** to review Section 2.

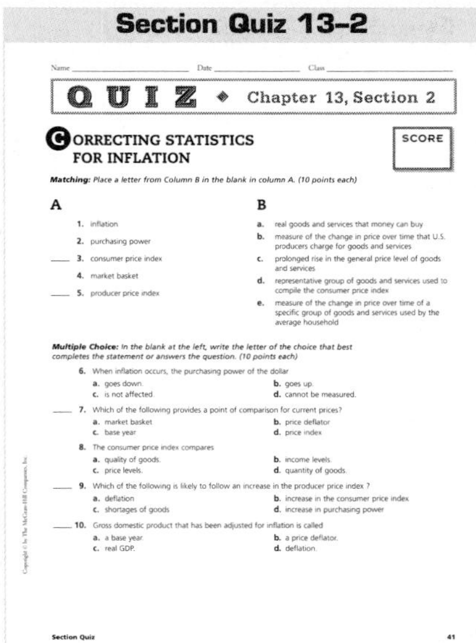

**Section Quiz 13-2**

Name ______ Date ______ Class ______

**QUIZ ◆ Chapter 13, Section 2**

**CORRECTING STATISTICS FOR INFLATION** SCORE

***Matching:*** *Place a letter from Column B in the blank in column A. (10 points each)*

**A**

1. inflation
2. purchasing power
3. consumer price index
4. market basket
5. producer price index

**B**

a. real goods and services that money can buy
b. measure of the change in price over time that U.S. producers charge for goods and services
c. prolonged rise in the general price level of goods and services
d. representative group of goods and services used to compile the consumer price index
e. measure of the change in price over time of a specific group of goods and services used by the average household

***Multiple Choice:*** *In the blank at the left, write the letter of the choice that best completes the statement or answers the question. (10 points each)*

6. When inflation occurs, the purchasing power of the dollar
   a. goes down. b. goes up. c. is not affected. d. cannot be measured.
7. Which of the following provides a point of comparison for current prices?
   a. market basket b. price deflator c. base year d. price index
8. The consumer price index compares
   a. quality of goods. b. income levels. c. price levels. d. quantity of goods.
9. Which of the following is likely to follow an increase in the producer price index ?
   a. deflation b. increase in the consumer price index c. shortages of goods d. increase in purchasing power
10. Gross domestic product that has been adjusted for inflation is called
   a. a base year. b. a price deflator. c. real GDP. d. deflation.

Section Quiz 41

## Relevant Issues in Economics

**The CPI and Product Quality** Economists and policy makers who analyze price indexes to forecast inflation and determine the cost of living know that these indexes are not perfect. Price indexes do not always measure real change because they cannot fully account for changes in quality. For example, prices of color printers may rise 5 percent from one year to the next. However, the level of improvement in the quality of the printers may be much greater than 5 percent. Thus, the cost of living may not have risen much at all.

## Reteach

Have students write summary paragraphs explaining the consumer price index, the producer price index, and the GDP price deflator.

### Reading Essentials and Study Guide 13–2

Name ______ Date ______ Class ______

**STUDY GUIDE** Chapter 13, Section 2

*For use with textbook pages 350–354*

**CORRECTING STATISTICS FOR INFLATION**

**KEY TERMS**

***inflation*** A prolonged rise in the general prices of goods and services *(page 350)*

***purchasing power*** The value of money as determined by measuring the amount of real goods and services that money can purchase *(page 351)*

***deflation*** A lengthy decline in the general price of goods and services *(page 351)*

***consumer price index (CPI)*** Measures the change in price over time for a specific group of goods and services used by the average household *(page 351)*

***market basket*** A group of goods and services used to compile the consumer price index *(page 352)*

***base year*** In a series of statistics, this is the year used as a point of comparison *(page 352)*

***producer price index (PPI)*** Measures the change in price over time that producers charge for their goods and services *(page 353)*

***GDP price deflator*** A price index that permits the comparison of one year's economic performance to another by removing the impact of inflation *(page 353)*

***real GDP*** GDP that has been adjusted for inflation by applying the price deflator *(page 353)*

**DRAWING FROM EXPERIENCE**

How much did you pay for your favorite good, such as a video game or music CD, last year? Did you pay the same price for similar goods this year? If your income stayed the same as last year, could you buy more or less of your favorite good? Economists ask similar questions when they try to judge the impact of ***inflation*** on your ***purchasing power.***

In this section, you will learn about how economists measure inflation.

**ORGANIZING YOUR THOUGHTS**

Use the diagram below to help you take notes as you read the summaries that follow. Think about how inflation affects the current dollar value of GDP as well as your ability to purchase goods and services.

| TERMS | DESCRIPTION |
|---|---|
| Inflation | |
| CPI | |
| PPI | |
| GDP Price Deflator | |



112 Study Guide

## 4 Close

Discuss with students why indicators such as CPI, PPI, and the GDP price deflator are useful to businesses, government, and consumers.

**FIGURE 13.7** **GDP in Current and Chained (1992) Dollars** Real GDP has been adjusted for inflation using 1992 as a base year.

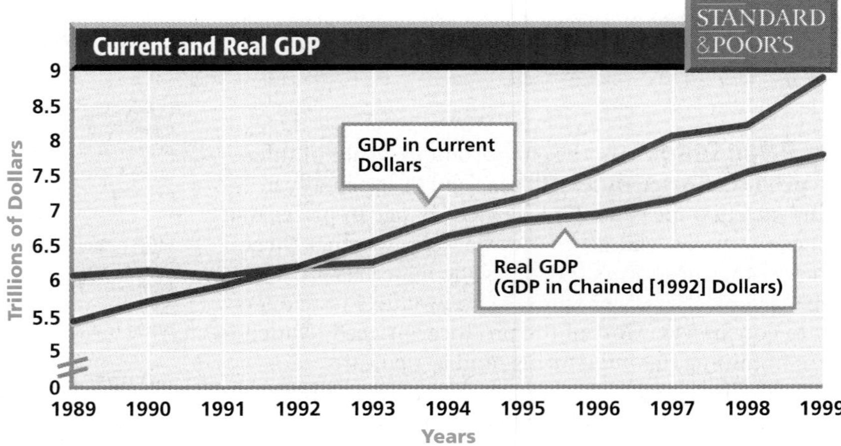


**Source:** Standard & Poor's

For an online update of this graph, visit ett.glencoe.com and click on ***Textbook Updates—Chapter 13.***

**Practice** and **assess** key skills with *Skillbuilder Interactive Workbook, Level 2.*

## SECTION 2 Assessment

### Understanding Key Terms

1. **Define** inflation, purchasing power, deflation, consumer price index, market basket, base year, producer price index, GDP price deflator, real GDP.

### Reviewing Objectives

2. What is the relationship between the purchasing power of money and the rate of inflation?
3. **Graphic Organizer** Use a chart like the one in the next column to show the difference between what the CPI and the PPI measure.

| Index | What It Measures |
|---|---|
| | |

### Applying Economic Concepts

4. **Market Basket** If you were to construct a market basket of goods and services that students typically consume, what would you select?

### Critical Thinking Activity

5. **Making Predictions** If the PPIs measuring crude oil, agricultural products, and lumber decrease for three months in a row, what prediction could you make about the CPI?



## SECTION 2 Assessment Answers

1. All definitions can be found in the Glossary.
2. The purchasing power of money declines as inflation increases.
3. CPI measures change in price over a specified period of time of a group of specific goods and services that the average household uses; PPI measures the average change in prices that United States producers charge their customers.
4. Answers will vary. Have students share and compare their market baskets.
5. Since the PPIs tend to lead the CPI, there will be a decrease in the CPI.

**SPOTLIGHT**

# BusinessWeek

## SPOTLIGHT ON THE ECONOMY

# Unveiling the Secrets of the CPI

**Check It Out!** In this chapter you learned about the consumer price index (CPI). In this article, read to learn about several weaknesses of the CPI and how the Bureau of Labor Statistics (BLS) tries to overcome these weaknesses.

The government tracks inflation in various forms. For instance, the producer price index (PPI) captures changes in prices charged by U.S. goods producers. . . . For the best inflation reading, however, markets look to the CPI. It is the most comprehensive indicator because it covers all goods and services purchased by households. It's the timeliest because the report is released . . . about two weeks after the end of each month. The CPI does include sales and excise taxes.

The CPI is not perfect. The elderly complain that the CPI, although used for adjusting Social Security checks, misses price hikes on drugs. Increases in property taxes show up only indirectly when the BLS calculates rents. And if your employer increases your health-insurance premium, the CPI won't reflect it.

The BLS counters that the consumer price index's aim is to measure prices for a specific basket of goods and services that the average household buys, according to surveys done from 1993 to 1995. This set basket leads to the biggest rap on the CPI: It does not allow for substitution. Say, a drought in Washington means a price jump for Red Delicious apples. Consumers might buy cheaper Granny Smiths. But the CPI would still give more weight to the price of Red Delicious apples.

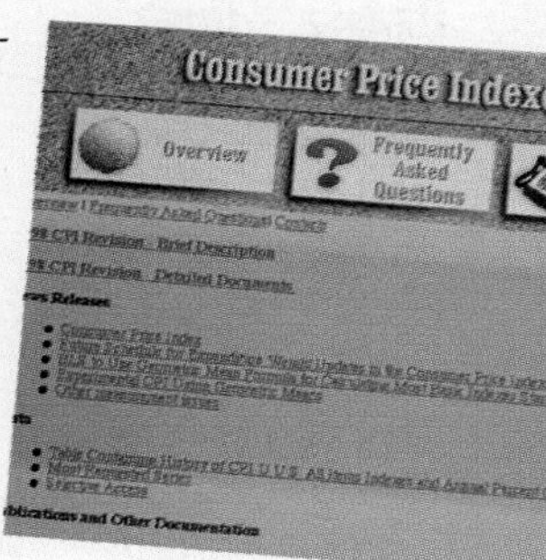


In the mid-1990s, economists criticized the CPI for overestimating inflation. . . . For one thing, said economists, the BLS took too long to include new products, and thus the CPI failed to capture the price reductions that take place in the first years of a product's lifetime. Cell phones, for instance, were costly to use when they were introduced in the 1980s. But competition brought the connection fees down rapidly. However, the BLS did not include cellular phones in the CPI until 1998.

Quality adjustment is another problem. How does the BLS account for air bags in cars, which add costs but save lives?



### Think About It

1. **What does the CPI measure?**
2. **What are three criticisms of the CPI?**



## Teach

Work through the criticisms of the CPI with students. When discussing substitution, point out that the CPI may be thrown off by consumers switching stores. The CPI compares prices in the same stores over time. If, when prices rise, consumers switch to discount stores that charge lower prices, the CPI will exaggerate what shoppers are actually paying. ASK: Why are people concerned that the CPI might be overestimating inflation? *Most students will point out that Social Security payments and some pay raises are tied to inflation.*

### BusinessWeek ONLINE

To find up-to-date news and analysis on the economy, business, technology, markets, entrepreneurs, investments, and finance, have students search feature articles and special reports on the *Business Week* Web site. www.businessweek.com

### Sidelight

The Boskin Commission, set up by the United States Senate Finance Committee in 1996 to examine the CPI, found that the index overestimated inflation by about 1.1 percentage points.

### Answers to *Think About It*

1. changes in prices for a specific basket of goods and services that the average household buys
2. Criticisms include: Certain price increases–on drugs, property taxes, and health insurance premiums, for example–are not reflected in the CPI. The CPI does not allow for substitutions–consumers often substitute when prices of certain goods rise. It overestimates inflation by taking too long to include new products in the market basket. CPI does not account for quality adjustment.

# 1 Focus

## Overview

Section 3 provides an analysis of aggregate demand and aggregate supply in the economy.

### BELLRINGER
**Motivational Activity**

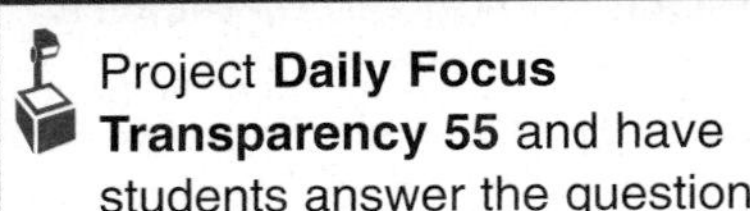

Project **Daily Focus Transparency 55** and have students answer the questions.

This activity is also available as a blackline master.

**Daily Focus Transparency 55**

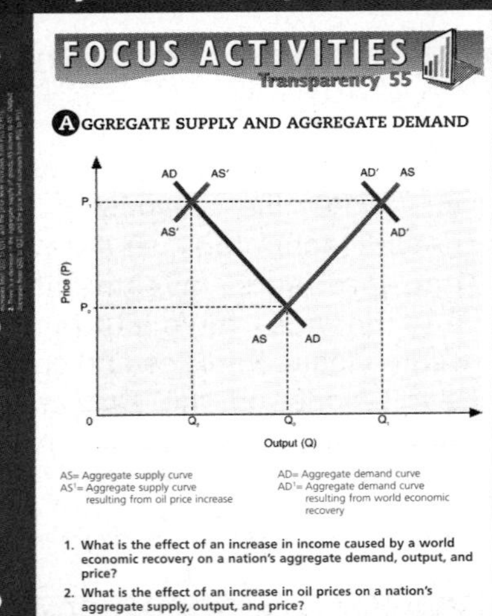

FOCUS ACTIVITIES
Transparency 55
A AGGREGATE SUPPLY AND AGGREGATE DEMAND
AD AS' AD' AS
P₁ P₂
AS' AD' AS AD
Price (P)
Output (Q)
0 Q₁ Q₂ Q₃
AS= Aggregate supply curve
AS'= Aggregate supply curve resulting from oil price increase
AD= Aggregate demand curve
AD'= Aggregate demand curve resulting from world economic recovery
1. What is the effect of an increase in income caused by a world economic recovery on a nation's aggregate demand, output, and price?
2. What is the effect of an increase in oil prices on a nation's aggregate supply, output, and price?
Daily Focus Transparencies


### Reader's Guide

Answers to the **Reading Objectives** questions are on page 359.

**Preteaching Vocabulary**

On the board, draw a simplified sketch of **Figure 13.10**. Have students copy the sketch into their notebooks and label the aggregate demand curve and aggregate supply curve.

**Vocabulary PuzzleMaker**

SECTION 3

# Aggregate Demand and Supply

### Reader's Guide

**Terms to Know**
- aggregates
- aggregate demand
- aggregate demand curve
- aggregate supply
- aggregate supply curve

**Reading Objectives**
1. Why is there an inverse relationship between aggregate quantity demanded and the price level?
2. What causes the aggregate supply curve to slope upward?
3. How do you use aggregate demand and supply analysis to determine the equilibrium price level?

## Cover Story

*Kiplinger's Personal Finance Magazine*, November 1998

It will take a few years for the global economy to achieve a new equilibrium between manufacturing production and consumer demand. Many goods are now in oversupply, and consumer demand is impaired by falling currencies and growth-inhibiting governmental policies. . . . But these are cyclical imbalances of the sort that have occurred for decades and will keep recurring from time to time.

As mentioned in the *Cover Story* above, the laws of supply and demand can be applied to the economy as a whole, as well as to individual consumer decisions. Economists are interested in the demand by all consumers for all goods and services, and the supply by all producers of all goods and services. When we look at the economy as a whole in this way, we are looking at **aggregates**—the summing up of all the individual parts in the economy. As you'll learn in this section, we call these sums aggregate demand and aggregate supply.

**aggregates:** *summation of all the individual parts in the economy*

## Aggregate Demand

**Aggregate demand** is the total quantity of all goods and services in the entire economy demanded by all people. How can we find out the aggregate quantity of goods and services that all citizens will demand at any single point in time? To answer this

**aggregate demand:** *total quantity of goods and services in the entire economy that all citizens will demand at any single time*



### SECTION 3 RESOURCE MANAGER

**Reproducible Masters**
- Reproducible Lesson Plan 13–3
- Reading Essentials and Study Guide 13–3
- Guided Reading Activity 13–3
- Section Quiz 13–3
- Daily Focus Activity 55
- Daily Lecture Notes 13–3

**Multimedia**
- Daily Focus Transparency 55
- Economic Concepts Transparencies 14, 15
- Vocabulary PuzzleMaker
- Interactive Tutor Self-Assessment Software
- ExamView® Pro Testmaker
- MindJogger Videoquiz
- Interactive Economics!
- Presentation Plus!

## FIGURE 13.8

**Aggregate Demand Curve** Although the curve for aggregate demand resembles that for simple demand, it is for the entire economy, not just one good or service. Aggregate demand may increase (curve shifts to the right) if consumers collectively spend more and save less or if better economic conditions are forecast. Aggregate demand may decrease (curve shifts to the left) if higher taxes are imposed on the overall economy or if bleak economic conditions are forecast.

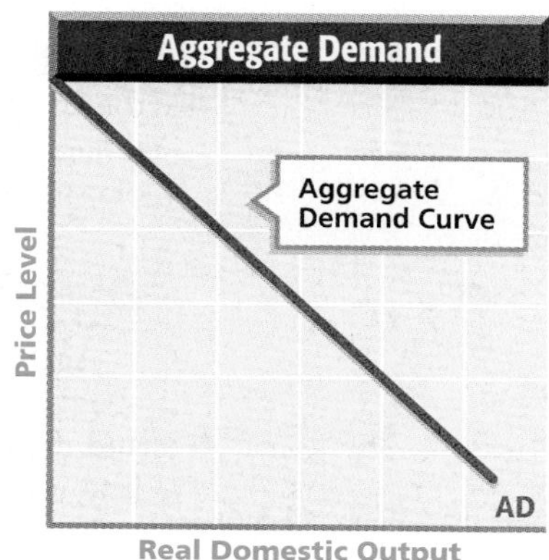


question, we have to relate aggregate demand to something else. As you remember from Chapter 7, the basic law of demand relates the quantity demanded of a specific product to its price. When discussing aggregates, however, we are talking about *all* products. Because there are millions of different prices for all products, aggregate demand cannot be related to prices.

Instead, aggregate demand is related to the *price level*—the average of all prices as measured by a price index. If we use the implicit GDP price deflator as our index, our measure of aggregate demand will be based on real (adjusted for inflation) domestic output. You can see this relationship in **Figure 13.8.** It is called the **aggregate demand curve.**

**aggregate demand curve:** *a graphed line showing the relationship between the aggregate quantity demanded and the average of all prices as measured by the implicit GDP price deflator*

Notice the similarity between the aggregate demand curve labeled AD in **Figure 13.8** and the individual demand curve you studied in Chapter 7 (page 179). Both of these curves slope downward, showing an inverse relationship. As the price level in the nation's economy goes down, a larger quantity of real domestic output is demanded per year. This change in quantity demanded is shown as a movement *along* the AD curve.

There are two main reasons for this inverse relationship. One involves the real purchasing power of your cash, and the other concerns the relative price of goods and services sold to other countries.

Consider the first reason. Inflation causes the purchasing power of your cash to go down. Deflation causes your purchasing power to go up. Therefore, when the price level goes down, the purchasing power of any cash that you hold will go up. You and everyone else will feel slightly richer because you are able to buy more goods and services.



## Meeting Special Needs

**Language Disability** Restating is difficult for students with language problems. They often have trouble finding synonyms for words in the text. Explain that the point of restating is for them to use common language and not to make it sound like the textbook. Have students read through the section for words that might be somewhat complex and restate them in their own words.

Refer to *Inclusion for the Social Studies Classroom Strategies and Activities* for students with different learning styles.



# 2 Teach

## Guided Practice

**L2 Understanding Ideas** Have students review **Figure 13.8** on page 357 and **Figure 13.9** on page 358. ASK: What might happen to the aggregate demand curve if consumers collectively save less and spend more? *The curve would shift to the right, indicating an increase in aggregate demand.* What would happen to the aggregate supply curve if there were a substantial increase in the cost of foreign oil? *The curve would shift to the left, indicating a decrease in aggregate supply.*

**Daily Lecture Notes 13-3**

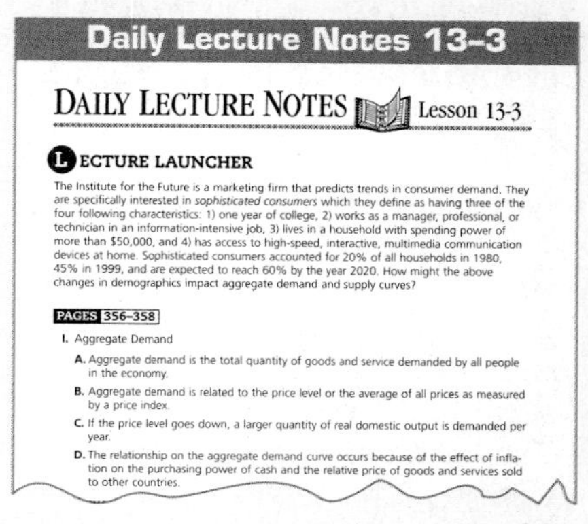

DAILY LECTURE NOTES Lesson 13-3

LECTURE LAUNCHER

The Institute for the Future is a marketing firm that predicts trends in consumer demand. They are specifically interested in *sophisticated consumers* which they define as having three of the four following characteristics: 1) one year of college, 2) works as a manager, professional, or technician in an information-intensive job, 3) lives in a household with spending power of more than $50,000, and 4) has access to high-speed, interactive, multimedia communication devices at home. Sophisticated consumers accounted for 20% of all households in 1980, 45% in 1999, and are expected to reach 60% by the year 2020. How might the above changes in demographics impact aggregate demand and supply curves?

PAGES 356–358

I. Aggregate Demand

A. Aggregate demand is the total quantity of goods and service demanded by all people in the economy.

B. Aggregate demand is related to the price level or the average of all prices as measured by a price index.

C. If the price level goes down, a larger quantity of real domestic output is demanded per year.

D. The relationship on the aggregate demand curve occurs because of the effect of inflation on the purchasing power of cash and the relative price of goods and services sold to other countries.

**Guided Reading Activity 13-3**

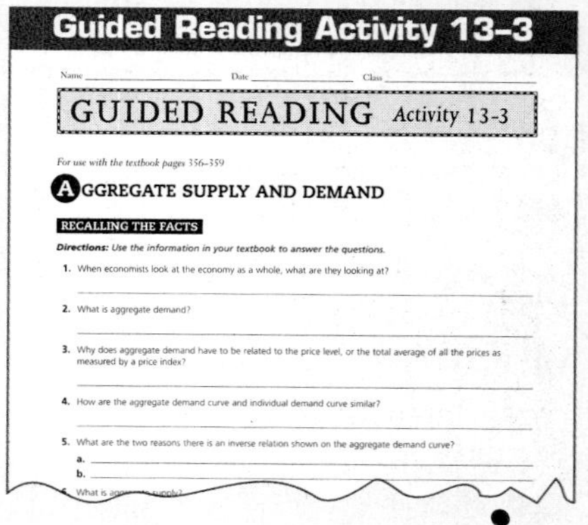

Name Date Class

GUIDED READING Activity 13-3

For use with the textbook pages 356–359

AGGREGATE SUPPLY AND DEMAND

RECALLING THE FACTS

Directions: Use the information in your textbook to answer the questions.

1. When economists look at the economy as a whole, what are they looking at?
2. What is aggregate demand?
3. Why does aggregate demand have to be related to the price level, or the total average of all the prices as measured by a price index?
4. How are the aggregate demand curve and individual demand curve similar?
5. What are the two reasons there is an inverse relation shown on the aggregate demand curve?
a.
b.

Project **Economic Concepts Transparencies 14** and **15** and have students discuss the accompanying questions.

## Independent Practice

**L2** Analyzing Ideas Have students write a short essay that discusses the value to businesses and government of knowing the nation's aggregate demand, aggregate supply, and equilibrium price level. Call on volunteers to read their essays to the class.

**LESSON 6: MACROECONOMIC EQUILIBRIUM**

Have students click on "The Aggregate Supply Curve." **ASK: What do the vertical and horizontal axes show on the aggregate supply curve?** *The vertical axis shows an overall price level such as the consumer price level. The horizontal axis shows real GDP.*

Supplied in both CD-ROM and disk formats.

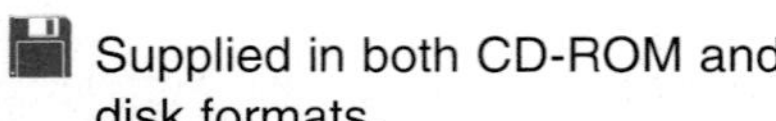

## 3 Assess

Assign Section 3 Assessment as homework or an in-class activity.

Use **Interactive Tutor Self-Assessment Software** to review Section 3.

As for the second reason, when the price level goes down in the United States, our goods become relatively better deals for foreigners who want to buy them. Foreigners then demand more of our goods as exports.

## Aggregate Supply

Aggregate demand is only one side of the picture. Let us look at aggregate supply. As the price of a specific product goes up, and if all other prices stay the same, producers of that product find it profitable to produce more. The same is true for all producers in the economy over a short period of time. If the price level goes up and wages do not, overall profits will rise. Producers will want to supply more to the marketplace—they offer more real domestic output as the price level increases. The reverse is true as the price level falls. This is called **aggregate supply.** You can see this positive relationship in **Figure 13.9**—the **aggregate supply curve.**

aggregate supply: *real domestic output of producers based on the rise and fall of the price level*

aggregate supply curve: *a graphed line showing the relationship between the aggregate quantity supplied and the average of all prices as measured by the implicit GDP price deflator*

## Putting Aggregate Demand and Aggregate Supply Together

Just as we are able to compare demand and supply for a given product to find an equilibrium price and quantity, we can

**FIGURE 13.9**

**Aggregate Supply Curve** Similar to the individual supply curve, the aggregate supply curve shows the amount of real GDP that could be produced at various price levels. Aggregate supply increases (curve shifts to the right) when all firms experience lower costs of production due to lower taxes or interest rates or lower prices for foreign oil, for example. Aggregate supply decreases (curve shifts to the left) for the opposite reasons: higher taxes, higher interest rates, higher prices for foreign oil.

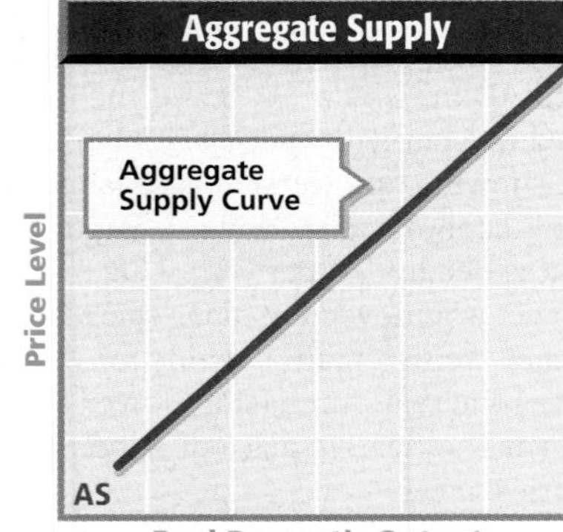


▼ Producers

358

### Cooperative Learning

Organize students into several groups. Have groups use library resources to locate discussions of the factors that might cause changes in aggregate supply and aggregate demand. Then have groups find and clip photographs from current newspapers and magazines that illustrate these factors. Direct groups to use these clippings to create an annotated collage on aggregate supply and demand. Have groups display their collages around the classroom. ELL BLOCK SCHEDULING

## FIGURE 13.10

**National Output and the Price Level** The intersection of aggregate demand and aggregate supply gives the equilibrium price level and national output (real domestic output).

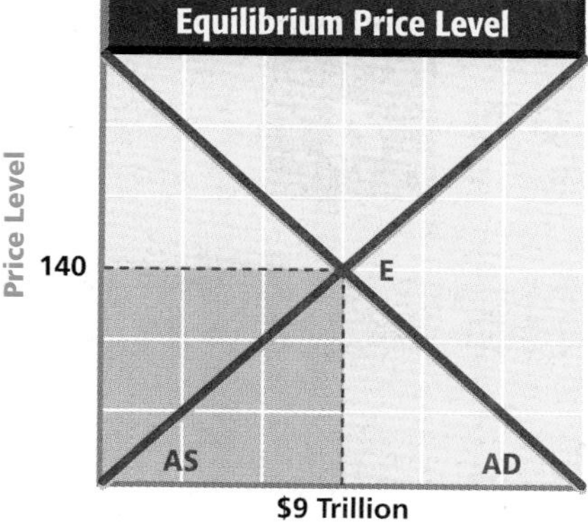


compare aggregate demand and aggregate supply. We do this in **Figure 13.10.**

The equilibrium price level in our example is determined where the aggregate demand curve crosses the aggregate supply curve, or at a GDP price deflator of 140. The equilibrium quantity of real GDP demanded and supplied is $9 trillion. As long as nothing changes in this situation, the economy will produce $9 trillion of real domestic output, and the price level will remain at 140—there will be neither inflation nor deflation.

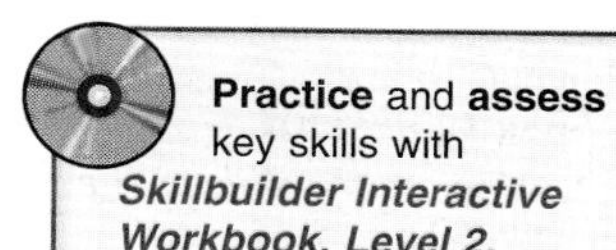

**Practice** and **assess** key skills with ***Skillbuilder Interactive Workbook, Level 2.***

## SECTION 3 Assessment

### Understanding Key Terms

1. **Define** aggregates, aggregate demand, aggregate demand curve, aggregate supply, aggregate supply curve.

### Reviewing Objectives

2. **Graphic Organizer** Create a diagram like the one below to show why there is an inverse relationship between aggregate quantity demanded and the price level.

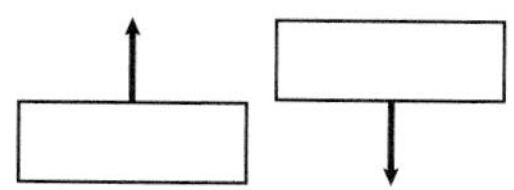

3. What causes the aggregate supply curve to slope upward?
4. How do you use aggregate demand and supply analysis to determine the equilibrium price level?

### Applying Economic Concepts

5. **Aggregate Demand** What would happen to the aggregate demand curve if there was a massive tax cut?

### Critical Thinking Activity

6. **Synthesizing Information** Draw a graph showing both an aggregate demand curve and an aggregate supply curve. Now assume that the price level increases. What happens to aggregate demand and aggregate supply?



## SECTION 3 Assessment Answers

1. All definitions can be found in the Glossary.
2. Relationship is inverse because as price level falls, aggregate quantity demanded rises.
3. As prices rise, suppliers will produce more because they will enjoy greater profits.
4. Overlay aggregate demand and aggregate supply curves—where they intersect represents the equilibrium price level.
5. The curve would move to the right, indicating an increase in aggregate demand.
6. Aggregate demand would decrease while aggregate supply would increase.



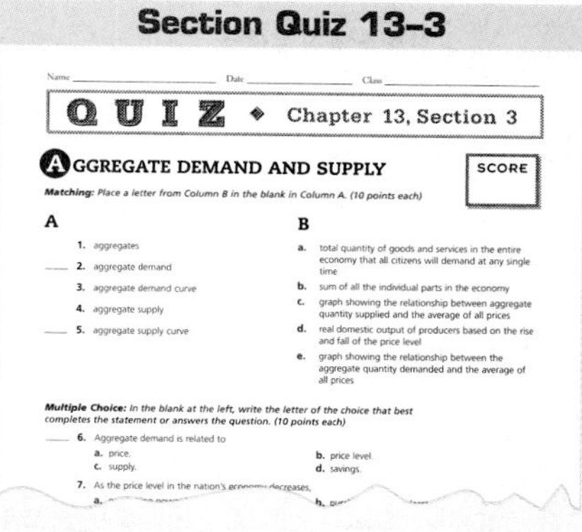

Section Quiz 13-3

Name ______ Date ______ Class ______

QUIZ ◆ Chapter 13, Section 3

AGGREGATE DEMAND AND SUPPLY — SCORE

*Matching: Place a letter from Column B in the blank in Column A. (10 points each)*

| A | B |
|---|---|
| ___ 1. aggregates | a. total quantity of goods and services in the entire economy that all citizens will demand at any single time |
| ___ 2. aggregate demand | b. sum of all the individual parts in the economy |
| ___ 3. aggregate demand curve | c. graph showing the relationship between aggregate quantity supplied and the average of all prices |
| ___ 4. aggregate supply | d. real domestic output of producers based on the rise and fall of the price level |
| ___ 5. aggregate supply curve | e. graph showing the relationship between the aggregate quantity demanded and the average of all prices |

*Multiple Choice: In the blank at the left, write the letter of the choice that best completes the statement or answers the question. (10 points each)*

___ 6. Aggregate demand is related to
a. price. b. price level.
c. supply. d. savings.

7. As the price level in the nation's economy decreases,

## Reteach

Have students summarize the meaning of each of the graphs in this section.

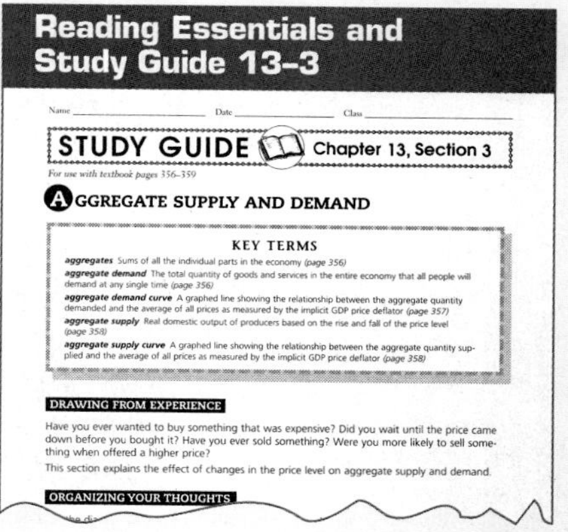

Reading Essentials and Study Guide 13-3

Name ______ Date ______ Class ______

STUDY GUIDE Chapter 13, Section 3

*For use with textbook pages 356–359*

AGGREGATE SUPPLY AND DEMAND

KEY TERMS

***aggregates*** Sums of all the individual parts in the economy *(page 356)*

***aggregate demand*** The total quantity of goods and services in the entire economy that all people will demand at any single time *(page 356)*

***aggregate demand curve*** A graphed line showing the relationship between the aggregate quantity demanded and the average of all prices as measured by the implicit GDP price deflator *(page 357)*

***aggregate supply*** Real domestic output of producers based on the rise and fall of the price level *(page 358)*

***aggregate supply curve*** A graphed line showing the relationship between the aggregate quantity supplied and the average of all prices as measured by the implicit GDP price deflator *(page 358)*

DRAWING FROM EXPERIENCE

Have you ever wanted to buy something that was expensive? Did you wait until the price came down before you bought it? Have you ever sold something? Were you more likely to sell something when offered a higher price?

This section explains the effect of changes in the price level on aggregate supply and demand.

ORGANIZING YOUR THOUGHTS

## 4 Close

Encourage students to write riddles, proverbs, or one-verse poems that explain the relationship between aggregate demand and price level and aggregate supply and price level.

# 1 Focus

## Overview

**Section 4** describes the business cycle from peak through contraction or recession, and trough to recovery; and reviews business fluctuations in the United States.

**BELLRINGER**
**Motivational Activity**

Project **Daily Focus Transparency 56** and have students answer the questions.

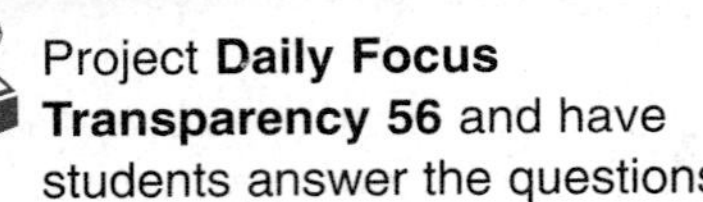

This activity is also available as a blackline master.

**Daily Focus Transparency 56**

FOCUS ACTIVITIES Transparency 56

BUSINESS FLUCTUATIONS

1. What does the photograph illustrate about aggregate demand during the Great Depression of the 1930s?
2. Why was the Great Depression so destructive to workers?

### READER'S GUIDE

Answers to the **Reading Objectives** questions are on page 363.

**Preteaching Vocabulary**

Have students draw a wavy line, similar to the one in **Figure 13.11**, across a sheet of notepaper. Direct them to enter the terms *peak, boom, contraction, recession, depression, trough, expansion,* and *recovery* in appropriate places on the line. Then have students write the definition of each term below the diagram.

**Vocabulary PuzzleMaker**

SECTION  4

# Business Fluctuations

### READER'S GUIDE

**Terms to Know**
- business fluctuations
- business cycle
- peak
- boom
- contraction
- recession
- depression
- trough
- expansion
- recovery

**Reading Objectives**
1. What are the phases of a typical business cycle?
2. What have been the three most severe downturns in the United States economy since the 1920s?

## COVER STORY

*BUSINESS WEEK*, JULY 19, 1999

Happy Birthday. The economic expansion is now 100 months old; six more months, and it will become the longest in U.S. history. But while its longevity gets all the attention, the expansion's most important characteristic may turn out to be its unusual quality. Driven by the kind of technological change that comes along once or twice in a century, this expansion is rewriting a lot of conventional economic wisdom.

Some years inflation is high; other years it is not. The same holds true for unemployment, world trade, and taxes. We have fluctuations in virtually all aspects of our economy. The ups and downs in an economy are called **business fluctuations.** Some people associate these ups and downs in business activity with what has been called the **business cycle**—changes in the level of total output measured by real GDP.

<u>business fluctuations:</u> *ups and downs in an economy*

<u>business cycle:</u> *irregular changes in the level of total output measured by real GDP*

## Model of the Business Cycle

**Figure 13.11** shows an idealized business cycle. According to this model, the phases of a business cycle begin with growth leading to an economic **peak** or **boom**—a period of prosperity. New businesses open, factories are producing at full capacity, and everyone who wants work can find a job.

Eventually, however, real GDP levels off and begins to decline. During this part of the cycle, a **contraction** of the economy

<u>peak/boom:</u> *period of prosperity in a business cycle in which economic activity is at its highest point*

<u>contraction:</u> *part of the business cycle during which economic activity is slowing down*



**SECTION 4 RESOURCE MANAGER**

**Reproducible Masters**
- Reproducible Lesson Plan 13–4
- Reading Essentials and Study Guide 13–4
- Guided Reading Activity 13–4
- Section Quiz 13–4
- Daily Focus Activity 56
- Daily Lecture Notes 13–4

**Multimedia**
- Daily Focus Transparency 56
- Vocabulary PuzzleMaker
- Interactive Tutor Self-Assessment Software
- ExamView® Pro Testmaker
- MindJogger Videoquiz
- Presentation Plus!

occurs. Business activity begins to slow down. If the contraction lasts long enough and is deep enough, the economy can continue downward until it slips into a recession.

A **recession** is any period of at least two quarters—six months—during which real GDP does not grow. In a recession, business activity starts to fall at a rapid rate economy-wide. Factories cut back on production and lay off workers. Consumers, with less income, cut back on purchases. Faced with a worsening economy, fewer new businesses open and some existing ones fail. If a recession becomes extremely bad, it deepens into a **depression.** Then millions of people are out of work, many businesses fail, and the economy operates far below capacity.

At some point, the downward direction of the economy levels off in a **trough.** A trough is the lowest point in the business cycle. It occurs when real GDP stops going down, levels off, and slowly begins to increase. The increase in total economic activity that follows is called an **expansion** or **recovery.** Consumer spending picks up, signaling factories to hire workers and increase production to meet demand. New businesses begin to open. The recovery continues until the economy hits another peak, and a new cycle begins.

recession: *part of the business cycle in which the nation's output (real GDP) does not grow for at least six months*

depression: *major slowdown of economic activity*

trough: *lowest part of the business cycle in which the downward spiral of the economy levels off*

expansion/recovery: *part of the business cycle in which economic activity slowly increases*

## Ups and Downs of Business

In the real world, as you can see from **Figure 13.12** on page 362, the business cycles are not as regular as the model shows. The peaks and troughs are clear, however.

### FIGURE 13.11

**A Model of the Business Cycle**
Business cycles fluctuate between peaks and troughs. ***What does the word model indicate about the business cycle shown?***

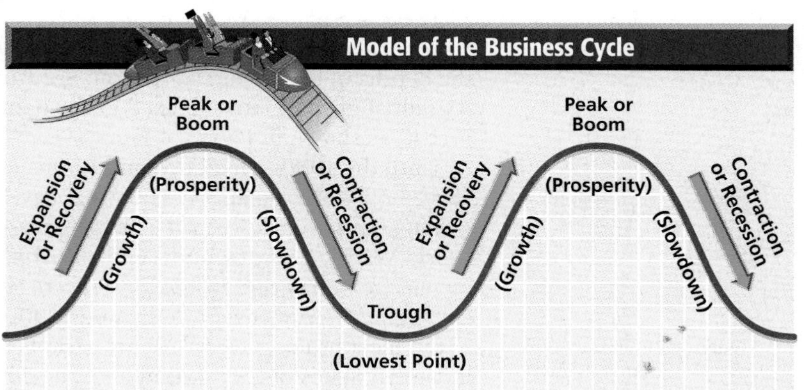




# 2 Teach

## Guided Practice

**L2 Applying Ideas** List the following on the board: employment, income, spending, GDP. Call on volunteers to identify what happens to each of these during recession, trough, and peak phases of the business cycle.

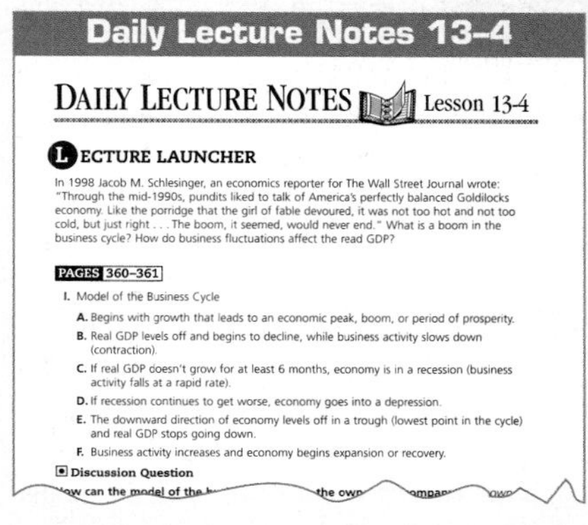
Daily Lecture Notes 13–4

DAILY LECTURE NOTES Lesson 13-4

LECTURE LAUNCHER

In 1998 Jacob M. Schlesinger, an economics reporter for The Wall Street Journal wrote: "Through the mid-1990s, pundits liked to talk of America's perfectly balanced Goldilocks economy. Like the porridge that the girl of fable devoured, it was not too hot and not too cold, but just right . . . The boom, it seemed, would never end." What is a boom in the business cycle? How do business fluctuations affect the read GDP?

PAGES 360–361

I. Model of the Business Cycle
- A. Begins with growth that leads to an economic peak, boom, or period of prosperity.
- B. Real GDP levels off and begins to decline, while business activity slows down (contraction).
- C. If real GDP doesn't grow for at least 6 months, economy is in a recession (business activity falls at a rapid rate).
- D. If recession continues to get worse, economy goes into a depression.
- E. The downward direction of economy levels off in a trough (lowest point in the cycle) and real GDP stops going down.
- F. Business activity increases and economy begins expansion or recovery.

Discussion Question

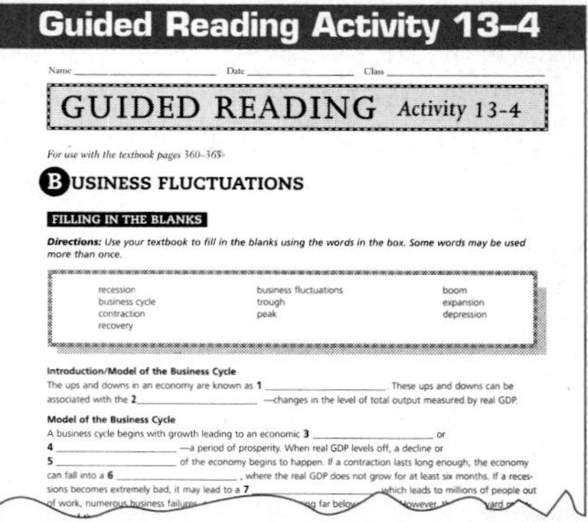
Guided Reading Activity 13–4

Name ______ Date ______ Class ______

GUIDED READING Activity 13-4

*For use with the textbook pages 360–363*

BUSINESS FLUCTUATIONS

FILLING IN THE BLANKS

***Directions:*** *Use your textbook to fill in the blanks using the words in the box. Some words may be used more than once.*

| | | |
|---|---|---|
| recession | business fluctuations | boom |
| business cycle | trough | expansion |
| contraction | peak | depression |
| recovery | | |

**Introduction/Model of the Business Cycle**

The ups and downs in an economy are known as **1** ______. These ups and downs can be associated with the **2** ______ —changes in the level of total output measured by real GDP.

**Model of the Business Cycle**

A business cycle begins with growth leading to an economic **3** ______ or **4** ______ —a period of prosperity. When real GDP levels off, a decline or **5** ______ of the economy begins to happen. If a contraction lasts long enough, the economy can fall into a **6** ______, where the real GDP does not grow for at least six months. If a recessions becomes extremely bad, it may lead to a **7** ______ which leads to millions of people out

Visual Instruction FIGURE 13.11

**Answer:** *It is idealized or theoretical.*

## Meeting Special Needs

**Limited English Proficiency** Students who speak English as a second language may have trouble grasping the terminology and concepts of business fluctuations. Help them find resources, such as photo essays and illustrated histories, that show scenes of each stage of the business cycle. Such images can help students to understand what happens to the economy—and businesses and individuals—in a typical business cycle. ELL

Refer to *Inclusion for the Social Studies Classroom Strategies and Activities* for students with different learning styles.

## Independent Practice

L2 Research Reports Encourage students to conduct research into a major economic depression in the United States. Have them note what caused the depression, how the economy recovered, and what economic changes—if any—came about because of the depression.

## Global Economy

### International Trade and the Great Depression

In the years after World War I, the United States followed a protectionist trade policy. Because foreign countries found it difficult to sell their products in the U.S., they could not make enough money to buy American exports. The effect on the American economy was made worse by the fact that many foreign countries had borrowed heavily from American banks after World War I. Falling export earnings led many of these countries to default on their loans, and this caused havoc in the American banking system.

# 3 Assess

## Meeting Lesson Objectives

Assign Section 4 Assessment as homework or an in-class activity.

Use **Interactive Tutor Self-Assessment Software** to review Section 4.

**FIGURE 13.12** **Business Activity** American business activity declined about 50 percent during the Great Depression, yet bounced back to new highs after World War II.

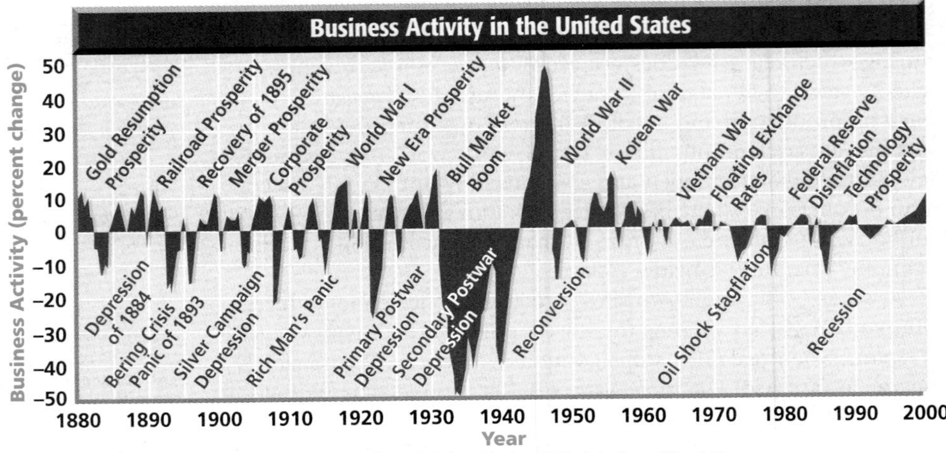


**Sources:** *American Business Activity from 1790 to Today*, 67th ed., AmeriTrust Co., January 1996; plus author's projections

The largest drop that eventually resulted in a depression followed the stock market crash in October 1929. The preceding years had been a time of widespread prosperity, as shown in *Part A* of **Figure 13.13.** By September 1929, heavy speculation had driven stock prices to an all-time peak. Then stock prices started to fall in early October and continued to fall. Suddenly, on October 29, there was a stampede to unload stocks. In one day the total value of all stocks fell by $14 billion.

Not long after the stock market crash, the United States fell into a serious recession. Factories shut down, laying off millions of workers. Businesses and banks failed by the thousands. Real GDP fell sharply over the next few years, pushing the nation into the depths of the Great Depression. See *Part B* of **Figure 13.13.** A gradual upward rise climaxed in the boom period after World War II, as shown in *Part C* of **Figure 13.13.**

Until the 1980s, small ups and downs occurred. The 1980s started off with a small recession that developed into the most serious economic downturn by some measurements since World War II. This downturn ended in 1982 and was followed by relative prosperity, except for a severe stock market crash in October 1987. A recovery in the mid-1990s developed into one of the most prolonged and robust periods of economic growth in United States history, lasting into the 2000s.



## Critical Thinking Activity

**Making Predictions** Remind students that during a recession people may lose their jobs. Newly unemployed people must conserve their resources—this means that they spend much less than when they were employed. When spending does not take place, a chain reaction is set off that affects the whole economy. Ask students to write a short paragraph describing the chain reaction that is set off when a large factory is closed, throwing hundreds of people out of work.

## FIGURE 13.13 Prosperity, Depression, and Boom

Prosperity Before the Crash **A**

*The 1920s had been a decade in which Americans began buying increasing numbers of radios, stoves, and automobiles. During these years, prices remained stable, and the standard of living rose about 3 percent per year.*

**B** Depression Conditions

*The Great Depression of the 1930s forced millions of Americans out of work. Used to the prosperity of the 1920s, Americans during the bust era of the Depression often relied on handouts.*

War Boom **C**

*The United States economy grew rapidly during World War II. There were 17 million new jobs created, and farmers shared in the prosperity as crop prices doubled between 1940 and 1945.*

**Practice** and **assess** key skills with *Skillbuilder Interactive Workbook, Level 2.*

## SECTION 4 Assessment

### Understanding Key Terms

1. **Define** business fluctuations, business cycle, peak or boom, contraction, recession, depression, trough, expansion or recovery.

### Reviewing Objectives

2. What are the phases of a typical business cycle?
3. **Graphic Organizer** Create a time line like the one below to describe the three most severe downturns in the United States economy since the 1920s.

### Applying Economic Concepts

4. **Business Fluctuations** Write three headlines that might have appeared in a newspaper during the years of the Great Depression. Then write three headlines that might have appeared during the expansion of the 1990s. Explain why you chose to write those particular headlines for those time periods.

### Critical Thinking Activity

5. **Understanding Cause and Effect** What actions and reactions throughout the economy may cause a recession to deepen into a depression?



## SECTION 4 Assessment Answers

1. All definitions can be found in the Glossary.
2. peak or boom, a period of prosperity; contraction or recession, a period of slowdown or stagnation; trough, the lowest point in the business cycle; expansion or recovery, a period of steady growth toward another peak
3. Time lines should include the Great Depression, the serious economic downturn in the early 1980s, and the stock market crash in 1987.
4. Headlines will vary. Call on volunteers to read their headlines to the class. After each headline is read, ask students to suggest ideas for an accompanying news story.
5. Students may suggest such actions and reactions as consumers cutting their spending, businesses cutting back on production, and businesses laying off large numbers of workers.



### Section Quiz 13–4

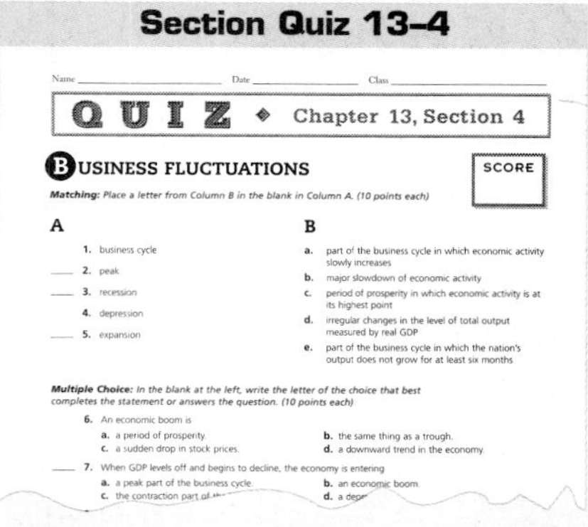

Name ______ Date ______ Class ______

QUIZ ◆ Chapter 13, Section 4

**BUSINESS FLUCTUATIONS** SCORE

***Matching:*** *Place a letter from Column B in the blank in Column A. (10 points each)*

| A | B |
|---|---|
| 1. business cycle | a. part of the business cycle in which economic activity slowly increases |
| ___ 2. peak | b. major slowdown of economic activity |
| ___ 3. recession | c. period of prosperity in which economic activity is at its highest point |
| 4. depression | d. irregular changes in the level of total output measured by real GDP |
| ___ 5. expansion | e. part of the business cycle in which the nation's output does not grow for at least six months |

***Multiple Choice:*** *In the blank at the left, write the letter of the choice that best completes the statement or answers the question. (10 points each)*

6. An economic boom is
   a. a period of prosperity. b. the same thing as a trough.
   c. a sudden drop in stock prices. d. a downward trend in the economy.

___ 7. When GDP levels off and begins to decline, the economy is entering
   a. a peak part of the business cycle. b. an economic boom.
   c. the contraction part of... d. a depr...

## Reteach

Have students write a paragraph describing each of the stages of the business cycle.

### Reading Essentials and Study Guide 13–4

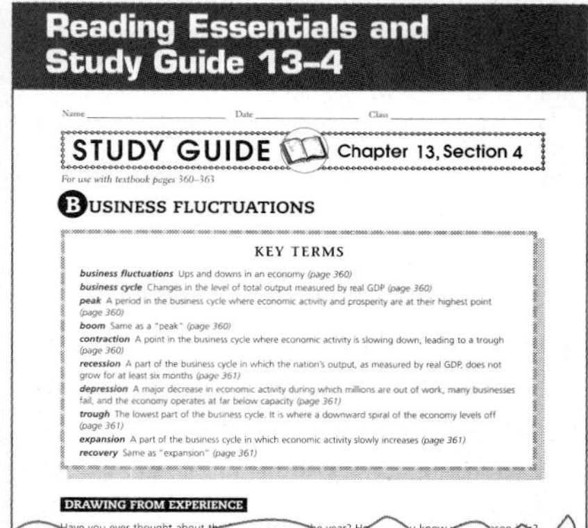

Name ______ Date ______ Class ______

STUDY GUIDE Chapter 13, Section 4

*For use with textbook pages 360–363*

**BUSINESS FLUCTUATIONS**

KEY TERMS

***business fluctuations*** Ups and downs in an economy *(page 360)*
***business cycle*** Changes in the level of total output measured by real GDP *(page 360)*
***peak*** A period in the business cycle where economic activity and prosperity are at their highest point *(page 360)*
***boom*** Same as a "peak" *(page 360)*
***contraction*** A point in the business cycle where economic activity is slowing down, leading to a trough *(page 360)*
***recession*** A part of the business cycle in which the nation's output, as measured by real GDP, does not grow for at least six months *(page 361)*
***depression*** A major decrease in economic activity during which millions are out of work, many businesses fail, and the economy operates at far below capacity *(page 361)*
***trough*** The lowest part of the business cycle. It is where a downward spiral of the economy levels off *(page 361)*
***expansion*** A part of the business cycle in which economic activity slowly increases *(page 361)*
***recovery*** Same as "expansion" *(page 361)*

DRAWING FROM EXPERIENCE

Have you ever thought about ...

## 4 Close

Lead students in a discussion of what might happen to a small business during a typical business cycle.

# 1 Focus

## Overview

**Section 5** discusses the possible causes of business fluctuations and describes the economic indicators used to predict business fluctuations.

### BELLRINGER
**Motivational Activity**

Project **Daily Focus Transparency 57** and have students answer the questions.

This activity is also available as a blackline master.

**Daily Focus Transparency 57**

FOCUS ACTIVITIES
Transparency 57

CAUSES AND INDICATORS OF BUSINESS FLUCTUATIONS

| Economic Indicators | |
|---|---|
| Gross Domestic Product (GDP) | The dollar value of all final goods, services, and structures produced within the nation's borders in a year |
| Housing Starts | The level of activity in the construction sector |
| Retail Sales | The value of goods bought in all possible retail outlets |
| Unemployment Rate | The percentage of workers without jobs who are actively seeking work |
| Consumer Price Index (CPI) | The current cost of a market basket of goods relative to the cost in a base year |
| Interest Rate | The cost of borrowing money for investment |
| Trade Balance | The dollar value of exports minus the dollar value of imports |
| Exchange Rate | The value of the American dollar against other currencies |

1. Which three of the economic indicators listed probably provide the most information about the growth rate of the economy?
2. Which two of the indicators probably provide the most information about price instability and unemployment?

Daily Focus Transparencies

### READER'S GUIDE

Answers to the **Reading Objectives** questions are on page 367.

**Preteaching Vocabulary**

Have students write a few sentences explaining the differences among leading, coincidental, and lagging indicators.

**Vocabulary PuzzleMaker**

SECTION 5

# Causes and Indicators of Business Fluctuations

### READER'S GUIDE

**Terms to Know**
- innovations
- economic indicators
- leading indicators
- coincident indicators
- lagging indicators

**Reading Objectives**
1. What are some of the potential causes of business fluctuations?
2. What are the three broad categories of economic indicators?

## COVER STORY

*COMPTON'S ONLINE ENCYCLOPEDIA*, "BUSINESS CYCLE"

Economists, politicians, and others have been puzzled by business cycles since at least the early 19th century. One of the more unusual explanations was proposed by English economist William Stanley Jevons in the 19th century. He believed the ups and downs of an economy were caused by sunspot cycles, which affected agriculture and caused cycles of bad and good harvests. This hypothesis is not taken seriously today.

For as long as booms and recessions have existed, economists have tried to explain why business fluctuations occur. If they could understand the causes, they reason, then the government could take actions to smooth out business fluctuations. No single theory, however, seems to explain past cycles or to serve as an adequate measure to predict future ones. The difficulty arises because at any given time, several factors are working together to create business fluctuations.

## Causes of Business Fluctuations

For many years economists believed that business fluctuations occurred in regular cycles. Later, economists believed that business



## SECTION 5 RESOURCE MANAGER

**Reproducible Masters**
- Reproducible Lesson Plan 13–5
- Reading Essentials and Study Guide 13–5
- Guided Reading Activity 13–5
- Section Quiz 13–5
- Daily Focus Activity 57
- Daily Lecture Notes 13–5

**Multimedia**
- Daily Focus Transparency 57
- Vocabulary PuzzleMaker
- Interactive Tutor Self-Assessment Software
- ExamView® Pro Testmaker
- MindJogger Videoquiz
- Presentation Plus!

fluctuations were related to changes in the rate of saving and investing. Today economists tend to link business fluctuations to four main forces: business investment, government activity, external factors, and psychological factors.

**Business Investment** Some economists believe that business decisions are the key to business fluctuations. Suppose a firm believes that prospects for future sales are good. Probably it will increase its capital investment: buy new machines, build new factories, expand old ones, and so on. This expansion will create new jobs and more income for consumer spending.

**Innovations**—inventions and new production techniques—can have a similar effect on the economy. When one firm begins to use an innovation, others must imitate the product or production method in order to become competitive again.

When businesses anticipate a downturn in the economy, they cut back on their capital investment and inventories. Producers, in turn, cut back on production to prevent a surplus. Enough inventory cutbacks could lead to a recession.

**Government Activity** A number of economists believe that the changing policies of the federal government are a major reason for business cycles. The government affects business activity in two ways: through its policies on taxing and spending, and through its control over the supply of money available in the economy. You'll learn more about these government actions in Chapters 15 and 16.

**External Factors** Factors outside a nation's economy also influence the business cycle. As you can see from **Figure 13.14**,

### CAREERS

**Statistician**

**Job Description**
- Design surveys and experiments, collect data, and interpret the results
- Use mathematical models to develop economic forecasts

**Qualifications**
- College degree in statistics
- Strong background in computer science recommended

**Average Salary:** $61,030

**Job Outlook:** Favorable

*—Occupational Outlook Handbook, 1998–99*

<u>innovations:</u> *inventions and new production techniques*

**FIGURE 13.14**

**External Factors** War, immigration, crop failures, and the changing availability of raw resources are some external factors that affect business cycles.

# 2 Teach

## Guided Practice

**L1 Analyzing Ideas** Refer students to **Figure 13.15** on page 366. Discuss the different categories of economic indicators to ensure that students understand them. Then ask students to pick an item from each category and, in a brief paragraph, explain how changes in each might indicate a rise or fall in business activity.

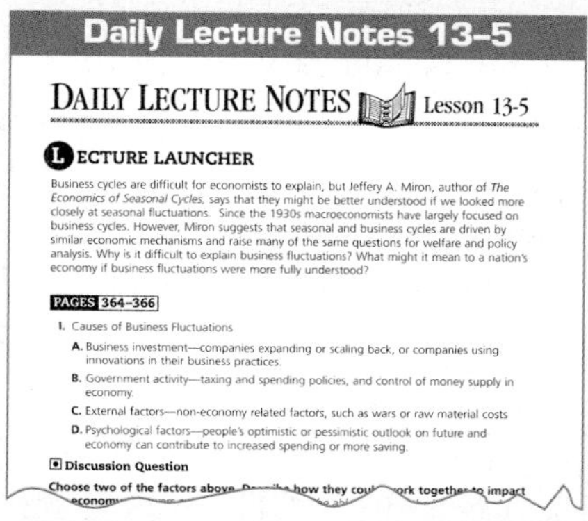

**Daily Lecture Notes 13–5**

DAILY LECTURE NOTES Lesson 13-5

**LECTURE LAUNCHER**

Business cycles are difficult for economists to explain, but Jeffery A. Miron, author of *The Economics of Seasonal Cycles*, says that they might be better understood if we looked more closely at seasonal fluctuations. Since the 1930s macroeconomists have largely focused on business cycles. However, Miron suggests that seasonal and business cycles are driven by similar economic mechanisms and raise many of the same questions for welfare and policy analysis. Why is it difficult to explain business fluctuations? What might it mean to a nation's economy if business fluctuations were more fully understood?

PAGES 364–366

I. Causes of Business Fluctuations
   A. Business investment—companies expanding or scaling back, or companies using innovations in their business practices.
   B. Government activity—taxing and spending policies, and control of money supply in economy.
   C. External factors—non-economy related factors, such as wars or raw material costs
   D. Psychological factors—people's optimistic or pessimistic outlook on future and economy can contribute to increased spending or more saving.

**Discussion Question**

**Choose two of the factors above. [illegible] how they cou[illegible] work together to impact [illegible]**

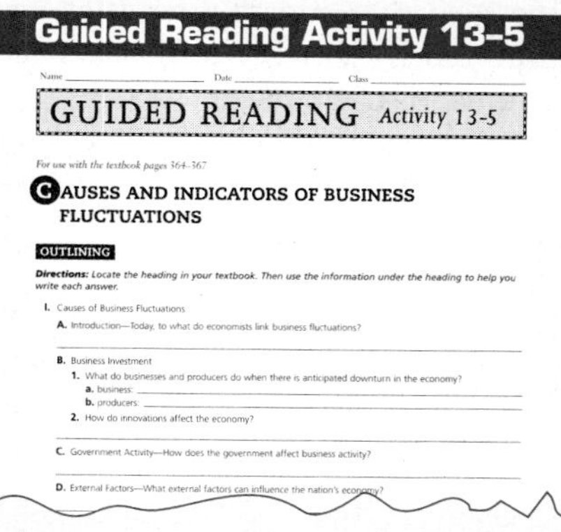

**Guided Reading Activity 13–5**

Name ______ Date ______ Class ______

GUIDED READING Activity 13-5

*For use with the textbook pages 364–367*

**CAUSES AND INDICATORS OF BUSINESS FLUCTUATIONS**

OUTLINING

***Directions:*** *Locate the heading in your textbook. Then use the information under the heading to help you write each answer.*

I. Causes of Business Fluctuations
   A. Introduction—Today, to what do economists link business fluctuations?
   B. Business Investment
      1. What do businesses and producers do when there is anticipated downturn in the economy?
         a. business: ______
         b. producers: ______
      2. How do innovations affect the economy?
   C. Government Activity—How does the government affect business activity?
   D. External Factors—What external factors can influence the nation's economy?

### Meeting Special Needs

**Reading Comprehension Problems** Students with reading comprehension problems may have difficulty understanding how certain statistical measures may lag behind others. Give students the example of the Acme Widget Company, producing 20,000 widgets a week. Sales of the widgets begin to slow but production continues at normal levels. After several weeks of declining sales, production is cut because Acme has a large inventory of widgets. Thus, sales figures are a more sensitive indicator of a coming downturn (or upturn) in the economy than production figures.

Refer to *Inclusion for the Social Studies Classroom Strategies and Activities*.

## Independent Practice

L2 Oral Report Refer students to the discussion of external factors as a cause of business fluctuations. Then have them use library resources and the Internet to investigate the impact of the OPEC oil embargo of 1973 on the American economy. Suggest that they present their findings in a brief oral report.

### Visual Instruction FIGURE 13.15

Inform students that they can track the latest data on leading indicators by visiting The Dismal Scientist Web site at *www.dismal.com/economy/releases/dyn_release.asp?r=usa_leading*

Point out that they can use the menu on the left of the page to link to information on coincident and lagging indicators. (Students might be intrigued by the name of the Web site. Inform them that nineteenth-century Scottish writer Thomas Carlyle referred to economics as the "dismal science.")

# 3 Assess

## Meeting Lesson Objectives

Assign Section 5 Assessment as homework or an in-class activity.

Use **Interactive Tutor Self-Assessment Software** to review Section 5.

**FIGURE 13.15 Major Economic Indicators**

**Leading Indicators**

1. Average weekly hours for production workers in manufacturing
2. Weekly initial claims for unemployment insurance
3. New orders for consumer goods
4. Speed with which companies make deliveries (the busier a company, the longer it will take to fill orders)
5. Number of contracts and orders for plants and equipment
6. Number of building permits issued for private housing units
7. Stock prices
8. Changes in money supply in circulation
9. Changes in interest rates
10. Changes in consumer expectations

**Coincident Indicators**

1. Number of nonagricultural workers who are employed
2. Personal income minus transfer payments
3. Rate of industrial production
4. Sales of manufacturers, wholesalers, and retailers

**Lagging Indicators**

1. Average length of unemployment
2. Size of manufacturing and trade inventories
3. Labor cost per unit of output in manufacturing
4. Average interest rate charged by banks to their best business customers
5. Number of commercial and industrial loans to be repaid
6. Ratio of consumer installment debt to personal income
7. Change in consumer price index for services

wars in particular have an important impact. This impact results from the increase in government spending during wartime.

Another external factor—the availability of raw materials such as oil—may also have an effect on the economy. New sources of raw materials may lower operating costs for certain industries. The sudden loss of raw materials and the resulting higher prices, however, can have the opposite effect.

### Psychological Factors

Finally, it is possible that people's psychological reactions to events also cause business fluctuations. The prospects of peace in a troubled area or the discovery of a new oil field can lead to feelings of confidence and optimism. War or the overthrow of the government of an important trading partner can cause pessimism about the future. These psychological factors sometimes contribute to consumer confidence and increased spending or the lack of confidence and more saving.

## Economic Indicators

Every day, business leaders are faced with the dilemma of trying to predict what will happen to the economy in the coming months and years. To aid decision makers, government and private economists study a number of economic indicators—listed in **Figure 13.15**—to learn about the current and possible future state



### Cooperative Learning

Inform students that the National Bureau of Economic Research (NBER) in Cambridge, Massachusetts, officially tracks the dates of peaks and troughs in the business cycle. Then organize students into groups, and have groups investigate the work of the NBER. Inform groups that a great deal of information may be found on the NBER's Web site at www.nber.org Suggest that they pay special attention to the NBER's listing of peaks and troughs in the American economy. Have groups present their findings in a large illustrated and annotated time line. BLOCK SCHEDULING of the economy. **Economic indicators** are statistics that measure variables in the economy, such as stock prices or the dollar amount of loans to be repaid. Each month, the U.S. Department of Commerce compiles statistics for 78 economic indicators covering all aspects of the state of the U.S. economy.

**economic indicators:** *statistics that measure variables in the economy*

**Leading Indicators** Statistics that point to what will happen in the economy are called **leading indicators.** They seem to lead to a change in overall business activity—whether it is an upward or a downward trend. The Commerce Department keeps track of numerous leading indicators, but the ten listed in **Figure 13.15** are the ones that most concern American economists.

**leading indicators:** *statistics that point to what will happen in the economy*

**Coincident Indicators** Other economic indicators, which usually change at the same time as changes in overall business activity, also help economists. When these **coincident indicators** begin a downswing, they indicate that a contraction in the business cycle has begun. If they begin an upswing, they indicate that the economy is picking up and a recovery is underway.

**coincident indicators:** *economic indicators that usually change at the same time as changes in overall business activity*

**Lagging Indicators** A third set of indicators seems to lag behind changes in overall business activity. For example, it may be six months after the start of a downturn before businesses reduce their borrowing. The amount of change in these **lagging indicators,** whether up or down, gives economists clues as to the duration of the phases of the business cycle.

**lagging indicators:** *indicators that seem to lag behind changes in overall business activity*

**Practice** and **assess** key skills with ***Skillbuilder Interactive Workbook, Level 2.***

## SECTION 5 Assessment

### Understanding Key Terms

1. **Define** innovations, economic indicators, leading indicators, coincident indicators, lagging indicators.

### Reviewing Objectives

2. **Graphic Organizer** Create a diagram similar to the one here to explain four of the potential causes of business fluctuations.

3. What are the three broad categories of economic indicators?

### Applying Economic Concepts

4. **Business Fluctuations** What innovation do you think has had the most influence on expanding the American economy? Why?

### Critical Thinking Activity

5. **Making Predictions** Identify two events that would cause you to predict a contraction of the economy.



## SECTION 5 Assessment Answers

1. All definitions can be found in the Glossary.
2. The four potential causes of business fluctuations are business investment, government activity, external factors, and psychological factors.
3. leading indicators, coincident indicators, lagging indicators
4. Many students will suggest the computer or the Internet, because of the impact e-commerce has had on the American economy.
5. Answers will vary but may include: a fall in the average weekly hours for production workers, a rise in the weekly initial claims for unemployment insurance, a fall in new orders for consumer goods, a fall in the number of building permits issued for private housing units, a fall in stock prices, a rise in interest rates.



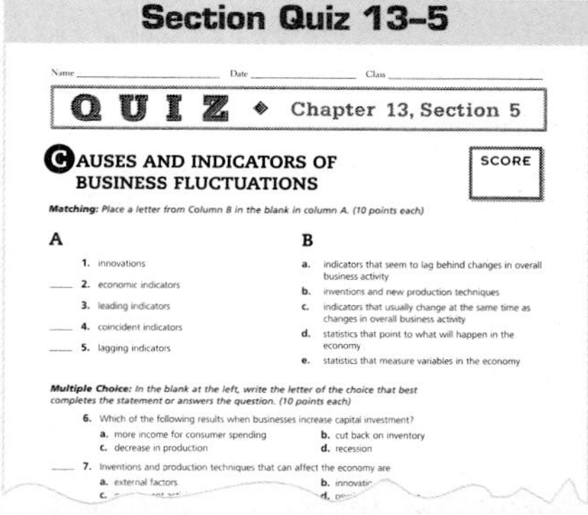

Section Quiz 13–5

Name ______ Date ______ Class ______

QUIZ ◆ Chapter 13, Section 5

CAUSES AND INDICATORS OF BUSINESS FLUCTUATIONS

SCORE

*Matching: Place a letter from Column B in the blank in column A. (10 points each)*

| A | B |
|---|---|
| ____ 1. innovations | a. indicators that seem to lag behind changes in overall business activity |
| ____ 2. economic indicators | b. inventions and new production techniques |
| ____ 3. leading indicators | c. indicators that usually change at the same time as changes in overall business activity |
| ____ 4. coincident indicators | d. statistics that point to what will happen in the economy |
| ____ 5. lagging indicators | e. statistics that measure variables in the economy |

*Multiple Choice: In the blank at the left, write the letter of the choice that best completes the statement or answers the question. (10 points each)*

____ 6. Which of the following results when businesses increase capital investment?
a. more income for consumer spending
b. cut back on inventory
c. decrease in production
d. recession

____ 7. Inventions and production techniques that can affect the economy are
a. external factors
b. innovatic

## Reteach

Organize students into groups, and have groups develop visuals that illustrate the four causes of business fluctuations and the three categories of economic indicators. Have groups present and discuss their illustrations.

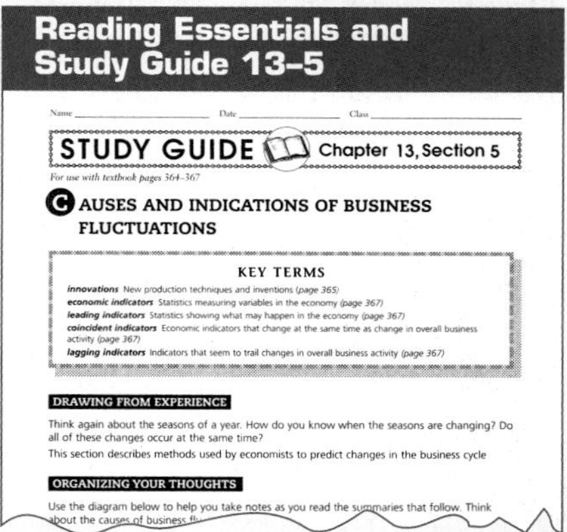

Reading Essentials and Study Guide 13–5

Name ______ Date ______ Class ______

STUDY GUIDE Chapter 13, Section 5

*For use with textbook pages 364–367*

CAUSES AND INDICATIONS OF BUSINESS FLUCTUATIONS

KEY TERMS

***innovations*** New production techniques and inventions *(page 365)*
***economic indicators*** Statistics measuring variables in the economy *(page 367)*
***leading indicators*** Statistics showing what may happen in the economy *(page 367)*
***coincident indicators*** Economic indicators that change at the same time as change in overall business activity *(page 367)*
***lagging indicators*** Indicators that seem to trail changes in overall business activity *(page 367)*

DRAWING FROM EXPERIENCE

Think again about the seasons of a year. How do you know when the seasons are changing? Do all of these changes occur at the same time?

This section describes methods used by economists to predict changes in the business cycle

ORGANIZING YOUR THOUGHTS

Use the diagram below to help you take notes as you read the summaries that follow. Think about the causes of business

## 4 Close

To close this section, lead students in a discussion of why economic forecasting is so difficult.

## Background

Inform students that prior to taking positions at the Federal Reserve Board and the President's Council of Economic Advisers, Janet Yellen was an economics professor at the University of California, Berkeley's Haas School of Business. Interestingly, her predecessor as Chair of the Council of Economic Advisers, Laura D'Andrea Tyson, also was a professor at the Haas School of Business.

# Teach

Ask for volunteers to read aloud from the excerpt. Have students note Yellen's ideas on controlling unemployment and inflation. ASK: What does Yellen think is the purpose of economic policy? (*to promote the well-being of American households*) Have students discuss whether or not they agree with this view.

# People & Perspectives

## Janet Yellen

ECONOMIST (1946–)

- **Chair of President Clinton's Council of Economic Advisers, 1997–99**
- **Member of Federal Reserve Board of Governors, 1994–96**
- **Member of Congressional Budget Office's Panel of Economic Advisers**
- **Professor at the University of California at Berkeley; also held teaching positions at Harvard University and the London School of Economics**

During her career, Janet Yellen has investigated a wide variety of economic issues. She has paid special attention to wages, prices, and unemployment—issues that directly affect ordinary Americans. In her Senate confirmation hearings for the position of governor of the Federal Reserve Board, Yellen stated that she hoped to keep her eye on the people behind the numbers.

*"I think stabilization policy is important—to avoid huge swings in unemployment. When you have the kind of recession we had in 1982 and 1983, for example, you can see the visible toll it takes on households. Perhaps because the causes and consequences of unemployment have been a focus of my research, I consider it easy to remain mindful of the people behind the numbers. In order to avoid high unemployment we must be careful not to push the economy below the NAIRU [Non-Accelerating Inflation Rate of Unemployment—the minimum rate of unemployment consistent with stable inflation], allowing inflation to rise and to become embedded in expectations. Because when that happens, it takes a period of above normal unemployment to lower inflation. That's the painful lesson of the '70s. Even when it comes to inflation we have to remember that prices [in themselves] do not affect social welfare. Inflation matters because of its repercussions on a country's economic performance, which in turn affects the welfare of individuals. Why are we in this business? It seems to me that it's to promote the well-being of American households. That's what it's all about."*

### Checking for Understanding

1. **According to Yellen, why is stabilization policy important?**
2. **Why is it dangerous to let inflation get out of hand?**



### Answers to *Checking for Understanding*

1. to avoid huge swings in unemployment
2. Because when inflation gets out of hand, it takes a period of above-normal unemployment to bring it under control, and this adversely affects the welfare of American households.

# CHAPTER 13 Summary

**Chapter Overview** Visit the *Economics Today and Tomorrow* Web site at ett.glencoe.com and click on ***Chapter 13—Chapter Overviews*** to review chapter information.

## SECTION 1 National Income Accounting

- The measurement of the national economy's performance is called **national income accounting**—and includes five statistical measures.
- **Gross domestic product (GDP)** is the total dollar value of all final goods and services produced in the nation during a single year.
- When **depreciation** is subtracted from GDP, you get a statistic called **net domestic product.**
- Three additional measurements—**national income, personal income,** and **disposable personal income**—look at how much money is available to be spent by businesses and individuals.

## SECTION 2 Correcting Statistics for Inflation

- When **inflation** occurs, the **purchasing power** of the dollar declines.
- Inflation skews GDP by making it appear that more output was produced, when in reality only the prices of goods and services have increased.
- To find **real GDP,** the government measures inflation's effect on current GDP.
- Three common measurements of inflation are the **consumer price index,** the **producer price index,** and the **GDP price deflator.**

## SECTION 3 Aggregate Demand and Supply

- **Aggregate demand** and **aggregate supply** relate the total quantity of all goods and services in the entire economy to the price level.
- Equilibrium exists where the **aggregate demand curve** intersects the **aggregate supply curve,** thus resulting in neither inflation nor deflation.

## SECTION 4 Business Fluctuations

- The economy experiences **business fluctuations.**
- A **business cycle** begins with a **peak** or **boom,** then **contracts** toward a **recession** (and perhaps even a **depression**). The downward spiral hits a **trough,** then increases again in an **expansion** or **recovery.**
- The Great Depression was the worst economic crisis in United States history.

## SECTION 5 Causes and Indicators of Business Fluctuations

- Economists link business fluctuations to four main forces: business investment, government activity, external factors, and psychological factors.
- To help business and government leaders in making economic decisions for the future, economists create and update **economic indicators.**



## Economics Journal

**Economic Forecasting** Ask students to record for one week references in the media to unemployment, consumer spending, manufacturing trends, prices, economic recession, and economic expansion. With each entry, have students indicate whether the issue covered is positive or negative for the overall economy. At the end of the recording period, have students write a report summarizing the overall view of the health of the economy presented in the media. Have students conclude their reports by stating whether they are optimistic or pessimistic about the economy and why.

# CHAPTER 13 Summary

**ECONOMICS & YOU**

**Measuring the Economy's Performance**

Chapter 20
Disc 1, Side 2

If you do not have access to a videodisc player, the ***Economics & You*** programs are also available in VHS.

Use the **Chapter 13 Summary** to preview, review, condense, or reteach the chapter.

## Preview/Review

**Vocabulary PuzzleMaker Software** reinforces the key terms used in Chapter 13.

**Interactive Tutor Self-Assessment Software** allows students to review Chapter 13 content.

## Condense

Have students listen to the Chapter 13 **Audio Program** (also available in Spanish) in the TCR. Assign the Chapter 13 Audio Program Activity and give students the Chapter 13 Audio Program Test.

## Reteach

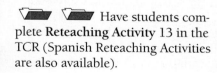

Have students complete **Reteaching Activity** 13 in the TCR (Spanish Reteaching Activities are also available).

## CHAPTER 13 Assessment and Activities

ECONOMICS Online

Have students visit the *Economics Today and Tomorrow* Web site at ett.glencoe.com to review Chapter 13 and take the Self-Check Quiz.

**GLENCOE TECHNOLOGY**

 **MindJogger Videoquiz**

Use MindJogger to review Chapter 13 content.

### Identifying Key Terms

1. d
2. a
3. c
4. f
5. b
6. e

### Recalling Facts and Ideas

1. consumer goods, producer goods
2. wages and salaries, income of self-employed individuals, rental income, corporate profits, interest on savings and other investments
3. personal tax payments, including Social Security contributions
4. consumer price index, producer price index
5. Inflation is a prolonged rise in prices, while deflation is a prolonged fall in prices.
6. by applying the GDP price deflator to remove the effects of inflation
7. The aggregate demand curve slopes downward because as prices fall, a larger quantity of real domestic output is demanded. The aggregate supply curve slopes upward because as prices rise, producers supply more, causing domestic output to rise.
8. equilibrium price level and the equilibrium quantity of real GDP demanded and supplied
9. if consumers save less and spend more, or if better economic conditions are forecast
10. peak, contraction or recession, trough, recovery or expansion
11. Business activity decreases, industry cuts back on production, consumers spend less, workers are laid off, fewer new businesses open, and some existing businesses fail.
12. Great Depression of the 1930s
13. Optimism can lead to increased consumer spending and greater business productivity. Pessimism can make people more cautious, reducing consumer spending.
14. taxing and spending policies and control of the money supply

# CHAPTER 13 Assessment and Activities

ECONOMICS Online

**Self-Check Quiz** Visit the *Economics Today and Tomorrow* Web site at ett.glencoe.com and click on ***Chapter 13—Self-Check Quizzes*** to prepare for the Chapter Test.

## Identifying Key Terms

*Write the letter of the definition in Column B below that correctly defines each term in Column A.*

**Column A**

1. base year
2. trough
3. economic indicators
4. expansion
5. real GDP
6. business cycle

**Column B**

a. point when economic activity is at its lowest
b. figures for the nation's total production that have been corrected for inflation
c. measurement of specific aspects of the economy such as stock prices
d. used as a point of comparison for other years in a series of statistics
e. periodic ups and downs in the nation's economic activity
f. business recovery period, when economic activity increases

## Recalling Facts and Ideas

**Section 1**

1. Net exports and government goods are two components of GDP. What are the other two components?
2. What five categories of income make up national income?
3. If you were given the statistic on disposable personal income, what other information would you need to derive personal income?

**Section 2**

4. What are the most commonly used price indexes?
5. What is the difference between inflation and deflation?
6. How would you determine real GDP if you knew only GDP?

**Section 3**

7. Why does the aggregate demand curve slope downward and the aggregate supply curve slope upward?
8. What is determined at the intersection of the aggregate supply and aggregate demand curves?
9. What would cause the AD curve to shift to the right?

**Section 4**

10. What are the four main phases of a business cycle?
11. When the economy enters a recession, what normally happens?
12. When was the most serious downturn in economic activity in the United States?

**Section 5**

13. How might psychological factors affect the business cycle?
14. What two aspects of government activity affect business cycles?

## Thinking Critically

1. **Making Generalizations** How might knowledge of nationwide economic statistics help you?
2. **Summarizing Information** Create a diagram like the one below to summarize national income accounting. Start with the lowest statistic, disposable personal income, and work your way up to GDP—adding and subtracting the appropriate items.

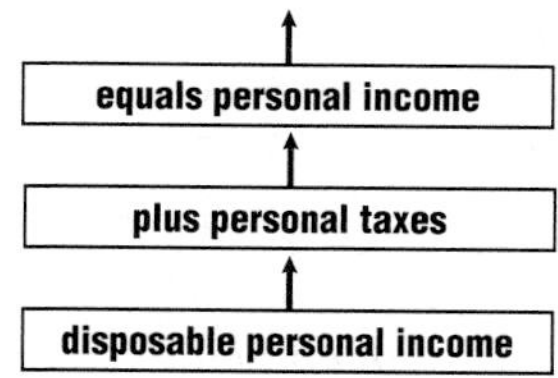


## Applying Economic Concepts

**Business Cycles** Try to analyze what you think occurs throughout the economy during a recession. Make a list of some of the things that business owners may do to react to a recession, such as reduce employees' overtime hours.

## Cooperative Learning Project

To make comparisons between the prices of things in the past and those of today, you have to make the distinction between current prices (often called *nominal values*), and prices adjusted for inflation *(real values)*. Working with a partner, use the following statistics and equation to find real 1998 GDP.

*1998 nominal GDP = $8,511.0 billion*
*1998 price deflator = 112.70*
*nominal GDP ÷ implicit price deflator × 100 = real GDP*

## Reviewing Skills

**Taking Notes** Research lagging indicators, coincident indicators, and leading indicators. Take notes on your research using the following guidelines:

- For each type of indicator, what are the various subgroups?
- How long has the indicator been reported in the United States?
- Can you find instances when the indicator was wildly inaccurate?

From your notes, write a paragraph describing how useful any of these indicators might be in accurately predicting changes in the nation's overall economic activity.

## Technology Activity

**Using the Internet** Use the Internet to find the latest edition of the *Statistical Abstract of the United States*. Locate the tables in the "Prices" section that give price indexes for consumer goods for selected cities and metropolitan areas. Construct a line graph showing the rise in the index for "all items" over the last six years.

## Analyzing the Global Economy

Use the Internet or a source in the library to find out the 10 countries with the highest real GDP. Then compare this list with the 10 countries with the highest real GDP per capita, found in the Global Economy feature on page 347.



# CHAPTER 13 Assessment and Activities

## Applying Economic Concepts

Answers may vary. Students' responses might include the following actions: freeze hiring, raises, and benefits; reduce inventory; cut prices; and, in extreme cases, close plants and sell off assets.

## Cooperative Learning Project

$7,551.9 billion

## Reviewing Skills

Notes and note-taking styles will vary. Call on volunteers to share their notes and paragraphs with the rest of the class.

## Technology Activity

Encourage students to display and discuss their line graphs.

## Analyzing the Global Economy

Have students share their findings. Then discuss why the two lists are different.

### Chapter Bonus Test Question

ASK: What point in the business cycle do the following statements describe?

1. Unemployment is on the rise. *recession*
2. Industrial output reaches new highs. *peak*
3. Consumer spending begins to increase and factories start to hire workers. *recovery*
4. After dipping markedly, real GDP levels off. *trough*

## Thinking Critically

1. Answers may vary. Possible student response: Such knowledge can be useful in determining if it is a good time to change jobs, to make a major investment, or to take on extra debt.
2. disposable personal income + personal taxes = personal income; personal income + corporate taxes, reinvested profits, employer Social Security contributions − government and business transfer payments = national income; national income + indirect business taxes = net domestic product; net domestic product + depreciation = gross domestic product

# Economics Lab

# 1 Focus

Indexes are an invaluable tool for comparing monthly and yearly statistics. The consumer price index, for example, allows economists to track how prices change over time. In this lab, students are given the opportunity to construct their own price index.

# 2 Teach

This lab may be stretched over six weeks—one week for preparation, four weeks for pricing items, and one week for constructing the price index. Because such a long time period is involved, establish set times to review students' progress.

As students start the procedures in Step B, ensure that they have a large enough sample survey to get a realistic spread of food types. When students begin to categorize the foods, you might offer some examples of categories used by the Bureau of Labor Statistics (BLS), the agency that develops the CPI—breakfast cereal, coffee, milk, snack foods, chicken, frozen peas, and so on. In Step C, have students present their index in table form.

Economics Lab

# *Constructing a Market Basket*

From the classroom of Rochelle Tuchman, Shulamith High School, Brooklyn, New York

In Chapter 13 you learned how the consumer price index compares prices for a market basket of about 90,000 goods and services in order to adjust GDP for inflation. In this lab, you'll construct your own market basket and price index.

## STEP A Tools Needed

- ✔ notebook
- ✔ pencil
- ✔ calculator
- ✔ transportation to local supermarket

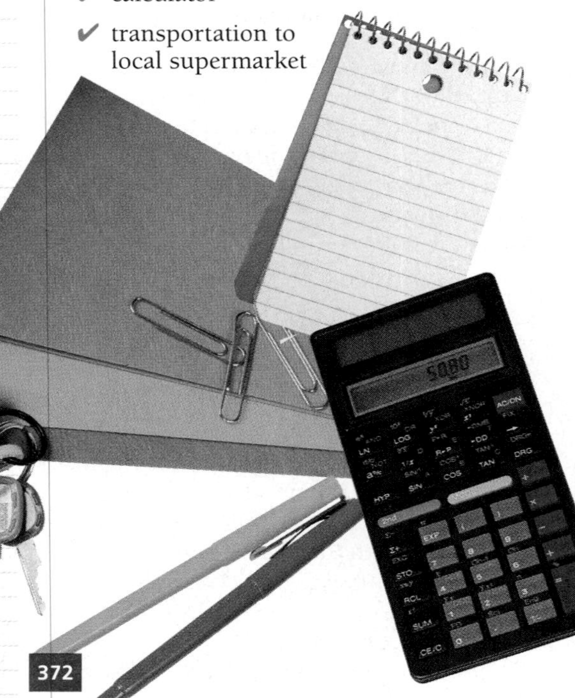



## STEP B Procedures to Follow

1. Survey students in your school to see what kinds of food their families eat the most.
2. Identify five categories of food that are purchased most often (and that are available in a supermarket): frozen pizza, pasta, soda, and so on.
3. Then identify three specific items in each category, including brand name and size (16 ounces, for example).
4. Also identify the locations of supermarkets in your community where the items can be purchased.
5. Now price your specific items on a per-week basis for one month. You must price the same product(s) in the same supermarket on the same day each week.
6. After the first visit to the supermarket, add up the total amount of the 15 items in your market basket. This number will signify your base year.
7. After each of the remaining three visits to the supermarket, add up the total amount of your market basket again, and compare the new totals to your base year.

### Teacher's Notes

## STEP C Creating an Economic Model

Use your totals to construct a price index. It should begin with a listing of your market basket contents and quantities. Week 1, your base year, will have a value of 100. Index numbers for Weeks 2, 3, and 4 will show the percentage that the market basket price has risen since the "base year." Remember, to calculate the percentage of change, subtract 100 (base year value) from the new figure: [Week 2 figure] − 100 = percent change of market basket.

## STEP D Lab Report Analysis

Study the price index you created in Step C, then answer the questions below.

1. What was the total amount of your market basket in your base year?
2. By how much did your price index change from your base year (Week 1) to Week 4?
3. Were you surprised by the results of your price index? Explain.

## 3 Assess

Have students answer the **Lab Report Analysis** questions.

## 4 Close

To conclude, you might have students discuss what trends in prices are shown in their indexes.

### ? Did You Know

The thousands of items used for the consumer price index are organized into about 200 categories. These categories, in turn, are arranged in 8 major groups. The major groups are: food and beverages; housing; apparel; transportation; medical care; recreation; education and communication; and other goods and services.

### Answers to Lab Report Analysis

1. Answers will vary.
2. Answers will vary. Students should express their answers as a percentage.
3. Answers will vary. Ensure that students fully explain their answers.

# CHAPTER 14 Resource Manager

## Teaching Transparency

### Economic Concepts Transparency 6

ECONOMIC CONCEPTS Transparency 6

EXCHANGE, MONEY, AND INTERDEPENDENCE

## Application and Enrichment

### Enrichment Activity 14

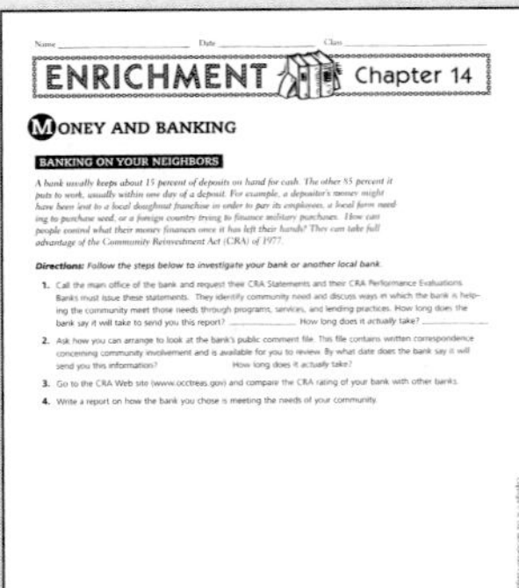

ENRICHMENT Chapter 14

MONEY AND BANKING

BANKING ON YOUR NEIGHBORS

### Consumer Applications Activity 16

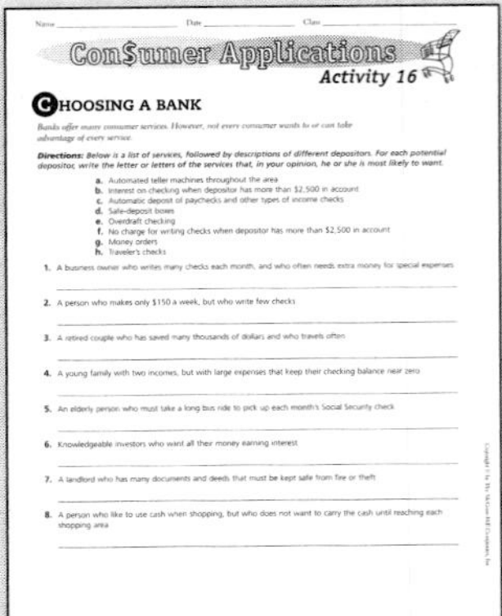

Consumer Applications Activity 16

CHOOSING A BANK

### Free Enterprise Activity 16

FREE ENTERPRISE ACTIVITY 16

TYPES, FUNCTIONS, AND CHARACTERISTICS OF MONEY

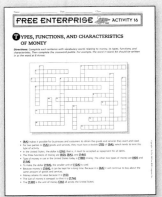

## Application and Enrichment

### Cooperative Learning Simulations and Problems 16

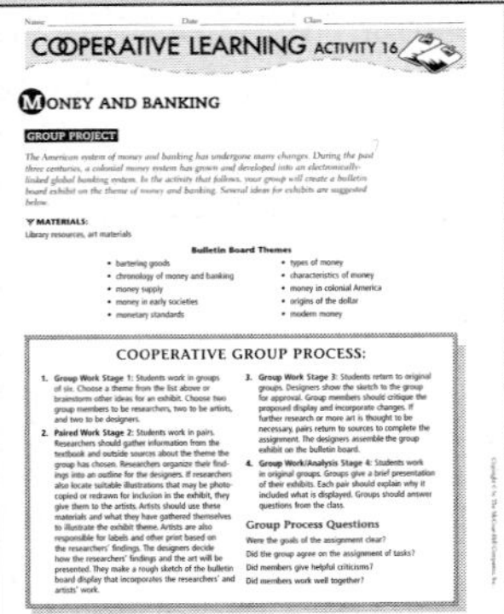

COOPERATIVE LEARNING ACTIVITY 16

MONEY AND BANKING

COOPERATIVE GROUP PROCESS:

### Primary and Secondary Source Reading 16

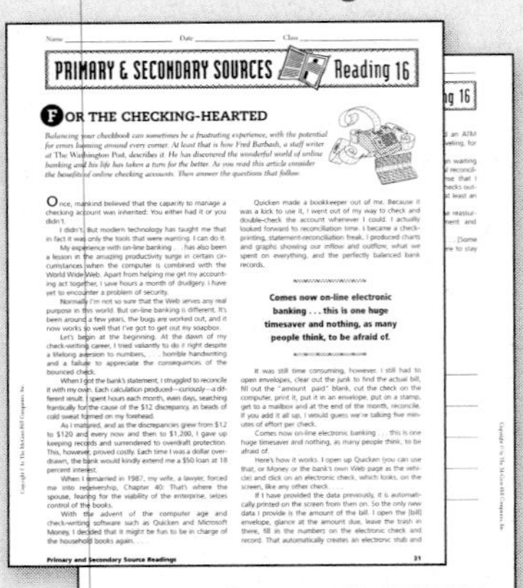

PRIMARY & SECONDARY SOURCES Reading 16

FOR THE CHECKING-HEARTED

### Math Practice for Economics Activity 16

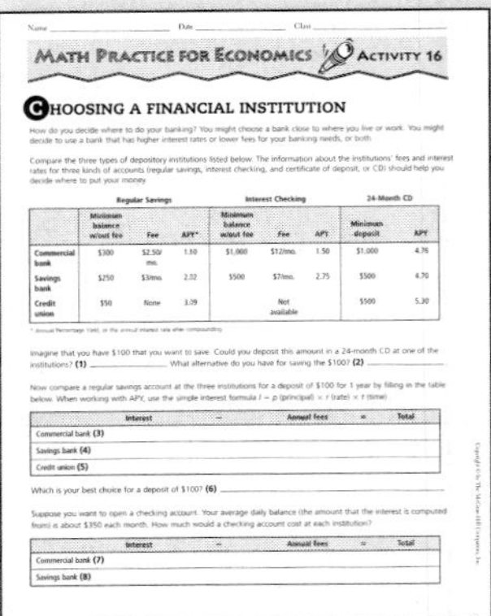

MATH PRACTICE FOR ECONOMICS ACTIVITY 16

CHOOSING A FINANCIAL INSTITUTION

### Economic Cartoons Activity 17

ECONOMIC CARTOON 17

DAY TRADING—BIG WINNINGS, BIG LOSSES

## Review and Reinforcement

### Critical Thinking Activity 16

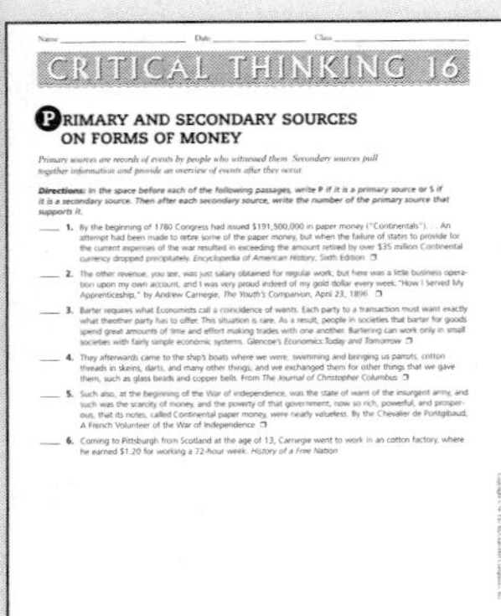

CRITICAL THINKING 16

PRIMARY AND SECONDARY SOURCES ON FORMS OF MONEY

### Reteaching Activity 14

RETEACHING Activity 14

MONEY AND BANKING

### Economic Vocabulary Activity 14

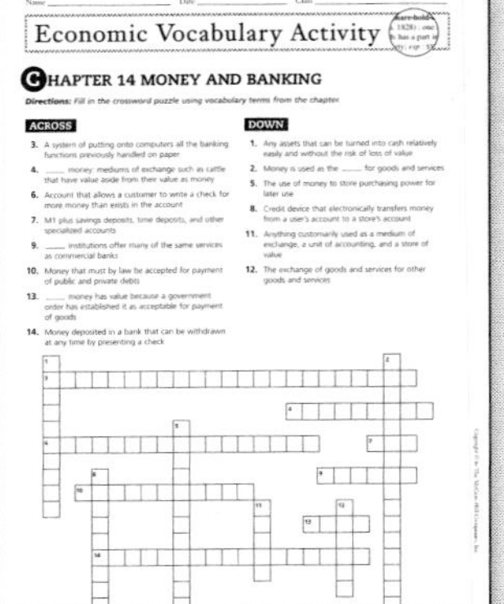

Economic Vocabulary Activity

CHAPTER 14 MONEY AND BANKING

### Reinforcing Economic Skills 20

Reinforcing Economic Skills Chapter 20

SYNTHESIZING INFORMATION

# CHAPTER 14 Resource Manager

## Assessment and Evaluation

GLENCOE'S ASSESSMENT ADVANTAGE

Chapter 14 Test Form A

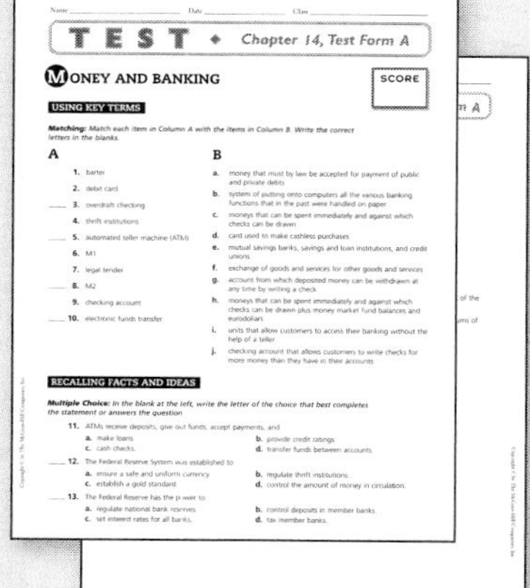
TEST • Chapter 14, Test Form A

MONEY AND BANKING

Chapter 14 Test Form B

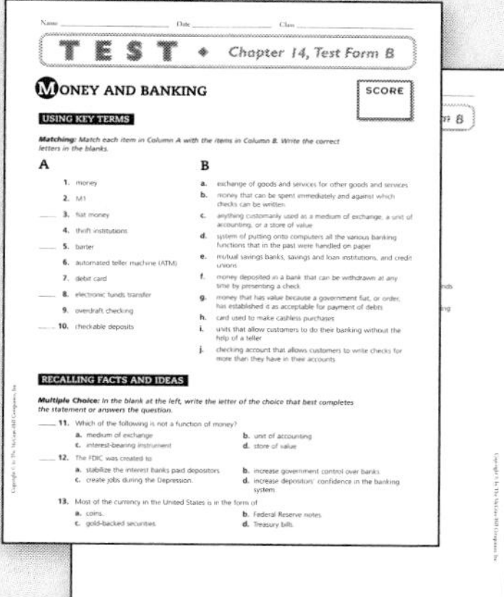
TEST • Chapter 14, Test Form B

MONEY AND BANKING

Performance Assessment Activity 16

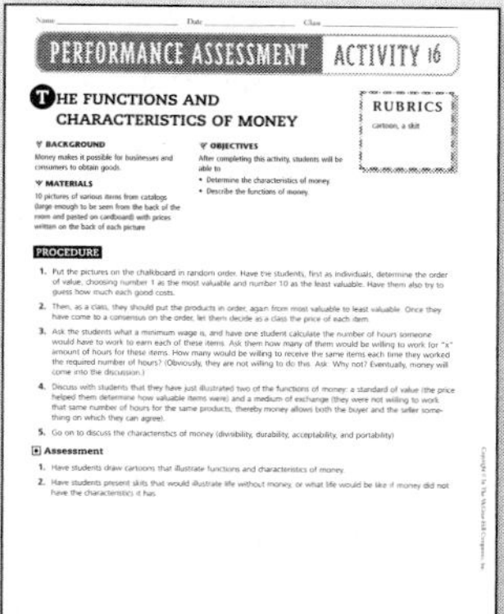
PERFORMANCE ASSESSMENT ACTIVITY 16

THE FUNCTIONS AND CHARACTERISTICS OF MONEY

ExamView® Pro Testmaker

## Technology and Multimedia

- Vocabulary PuzzleMaker Software
- Interactive Tutor Self-Assessment Software
- ExamView® Pro Testmaker
- NBR *Economics & You* Video Program (English/Spanish)
- Presentation Plus!
- Glencoe Skillbuilder Interactive Workbook CD-ROM, Level 2
- Interactive Lesson Planner
- MindJogger Videoquiz
- Interactive Economics! CD-ROM
- Audio Program (English or Spanish)

## ECONOMICS Online

You and your students can visit ett.glencoe.com—the Web site companion to **Economics Today and Tomorrow.** This innovative integration of electronic and print media offers your students a wealth of opportunities. The student text directs students to the Web site for the following options:

- **Chapter Overviews**
- **Student Web Activities**
- **Self-Check Quizzes**
- **Textbook Updates**

Answers are provided for you in the **Web Activity Lesson Plan.** Additional Web resources and Interactive Puzzles are also available.

Use the Glencoe Web site for additional resources. All essential content is covered in the Student Edition.

## Spanish Resources

 Spanish Economic Concepts Transparency 6

 Spanish Vocabulary Activity 14

 Spanish Reteaching Activity 14

 Spanish Section Quizzes for Chapter 14

 Spanish Chapter 14 Audio Program, Activity, and Test

## Additional Resources

### Reading for the Teacher

Carr, Glenna D., et al. *Finance: Money, Banks, and Credit,* revised ed. Gainesville, FL: Center for Economic Education. Ideas on how to teach the functions and uses of money.

### Multimedia Material

*"The Banking System"–Economics USA.* The Annenberg/CPB Collection, 19 Gregory Drive, South Burlington, VT 05403. Color videos, 60 min. each.

# CHAPTER 14 Resource Manager

## Section Resources

| Reading Objectives | Reproducible Resources | Technology/Multimedia Resources |
|---|---|---|
| **Section 1**<br>**The Functions and Characteristics of Money**<br>• What are the three functions of money?<br>• What are the six major characteristics of money? | Reproducible Lesson Plan 14-1<br>Daily Lecture Notes 14-1<br>Guided Reading Activity 14-1<br>Reading Essentials and Study Guide 14-1<br>Daily Focus Activity 58<br>Section Quiz 14-1*<br>Reinforcing Economic Skills 20 | Daily Focus Transparency 58<br>Economic Concepts Transparency 6<br>Vocabulary PuzzleMaker<br>Interactive Tutor Self-Assessment Software<br>MindJogger Videoquiz<br>NBR's *Economics & You**<br>Presentation Plus!<br>ExamView® Pro Testmaker |
| **Section 2**<br>**History of American Money and Banking**<br>• What are some of the most important events in the history of money and banking?<br>• What are six services provided by banks and savings institutions?<br>• How has electronic banking changed banking services? | Reproducible Lesson Plan 14-2<br>Daily Lecture Notes 14-2<br>Guided Reading Activity 14-2<br>Reading Essentials and Study Guide 14-2<br>Daily Focus Activity 59<br>Section Quiz 14-2* | Daily Focus Transparency 59<br>Vocabulary PuzzleMaker<br>Interactive Tutor Self-Assessment Software<br>MindJogger Videoquiz<br>NBR's *Economics & You**<br>Presentation Plus!<br>ExamView® Pro Testmaker |
| **Section 3**<br>**Types of Money in the United States**<br>• What is the difference between money and near moneys?<br>• What does the M2 definition of money include? | Reproducible Lesson Plan 14-3<br>Daily Lecture Notes 14-3<br>Guided Reading Activity 14-3<br>Reading Essentials and Study Guide 14-3<br>Daily Focus Activity 60<br>Section Quiz 14-3* | Daily Focus Transparency 60<br>Vocabulary PuzzleMaker<br>Interactive Tutor Self-Assessment Software<br>MindJogger Videoquiz<br>Presentation Plus!<br>ExamView® Pro Testmaker |

*Also available in Spanish

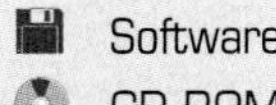

# CHAPTER 14 Resource Manager

## ACTIVITY From the Classroom of

**Doug Woods**
**Washington High School**
**Cherokee, Illinois**

### Mobile Money

Organize the class into four groups. Have each group construct a four-sided placard (or use a medium-sized box) that represents the following concepts about money:

Side 1—History of money
Side 2—Functions of money
Side 3—Kinds of money
Side 4—Foreign currency

Have students use photographs, time lines, quotes, and so on to enhance their display. Students should construct the placards so that they can be hung in the classroom like mobiles.

## Easy Planning and Preparation!

Use Glencoe's **Presentation Plus!**, a Microsoft PowerPoint® application, to teach **Money and Banking.** With this multimedia teacher tool, you can customize ready-made presentations. At your fingertips are interactive transparencies, on-screen lecture notes, audio-visual presentations, and links to the Internet and to other Glencoe multimedia.

### Interactive Lesson Planner

Planning has never been easier! Organize your week, month, semester, or year with all the lesson helps you need to make teaching creative, timely, and relevant—the way it is meant to be. The Interactive Lesson Planner opens Glencoe's **Chapter 14** resources, helps you build your schedule, and tracks your progress.

## Block Schedule

Activities that are particularly suited to use within the block scheduling framework are identified throughout this chapter by the following designation: BLOCK SCHEDULING

## Key to Ability Levels

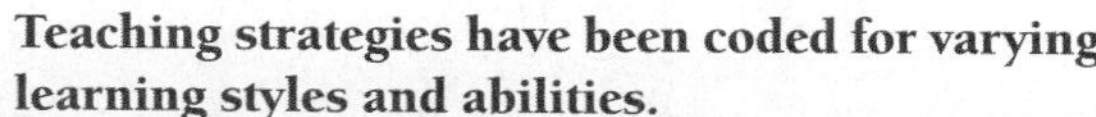

**Teaching strategies have been coded for varying learning styles and abilities.**

L1 BASIC activities for all students
L2 AVERAGE activities for average to above-average students
L3 CHALLENGING activities for above-average students
ELL ENGLISH LANGUAGE LEARNER activities

## National Council on Economic Education

## THE EconomicsAmerica AND EconomicsInternational PROGRAMS

### Voluntary Standards Emphasized in Chapter 14

**Content Standard 10** Students will understand that institutions evolve in market economies to help individuals and groups accomplish their goals. Banks, labor unions, corporations, legal systems, and not-for-profit organizations are examples of important institutions.

**Content Standard 11** Students will understand that money makes it easier to trade, borrow, save, invest, and compare the values of goods and services.

### Resources Available from NCEE

- *Capstone: The Nation's High School Economics Course*
- *Focus: International Trade*
- *United States History: Eyes on the Economy, Vol. 1 and Vol. 2*
- *Personal Decision Making: Focus on Economics*

To order these materials, or to contact your State Council on Economic Education about workshops and programs, call 1-800-338-1192 or visit the NCEE Web site at http://www.nationalcouncil.org

ECONOMICS & YOU

Money and Banking

Chapter 18
Disc 1, Side 2

ASK: What new nontraditional functions have banks taken on? *selling stocks, insurance, mutual funds*

Also available in VHS.

## Chapter Overview

Chapter 14 describes or explains the functions and characteristics of money, modern banking services, the role of money and banking in the development of the United States, and the types of money in use in the United States today.

### *GLENCOE* TECHNOLOGY

Use **MindJogger Videoquiz** VHS to preview Chapter 14 content.

Introduce students to chapter content and key terms by having them access **Chapter 14—Chapter Overviews** at *ett.glencoe.com*

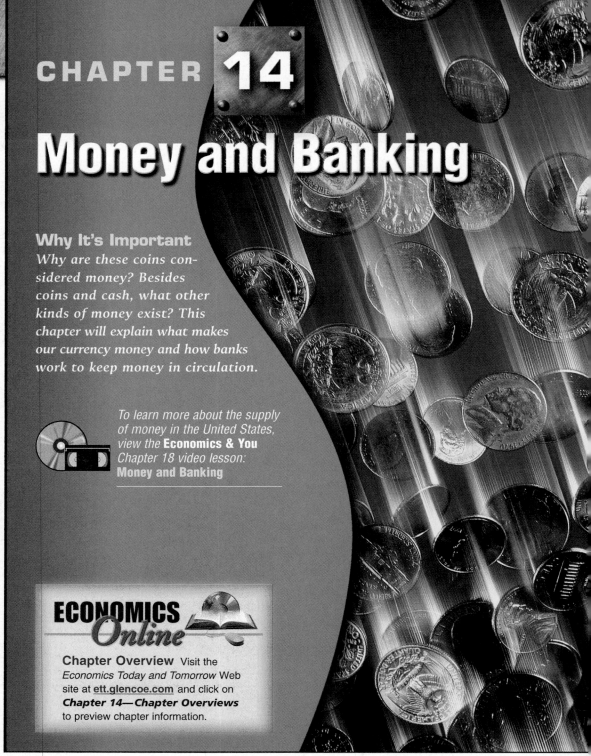

# CHAPTER 14 Money and Banking

### Why It's Important

*Why are these coins considered money? Besides coins and cash, what other kinds of money exist? This chapter will explain what makes our currency money and how banks work to keep money in circulation.*

*To learn more about the supply of money in the United States, view the* ***Economics & You*** *Chapter 18 video lesson:* **Money and Banking**

ECONOMICS *Online*

**Chapter Overview** Visit the *Economics Today and Tomorrow* Web site at ett.glencoe.com and click on ***Chapter 14—Chapter Overviews*** to preview chapter information.

## CHAPTER LAUNCH ACTIVITY

Have students write a short story about a typical day in a country where there is no money. Have them describe how they might do everyday activities—buying lunch at the school cafeteria or getting gasoline for the car, for example. Call on volunteers to read their stories to the class. Conclude by informing students that in Chapter 14 they will learn about the role of money in the American economy.

SECTION 1

# The Functions and Characteristics of Money

## COVER STORY

*DISCOVER*, OCTOBER 1998

[W]ealthy citizens [in Mesopotamia] were flaunting money at least as early as 2500 B.C. and perhaps a few hundred years before that. "There's just no way to get around it," says Marvin Powell, a historian at Northern Illinois University in De Kalb. "Silver in Mesopotamia functions like our money today. It's a means of exchange. People use it for a storage of wealth, and they use it for defining value."

### READER'S GUIDE

**Terms to Know**

- money
- medium of exchange
- barter
- unit of accounting
- store of value
- commodity money
- representative money
- fiat money
- legal tender

**Reading Objectives**

1. What are the three functions of money?
2. What are the six major characteristics of money?

For thousands of years, money has made it possible for businesses to obtain easily what they need from suppliers and for consumers to obtain goods and services. What, however, is money? As you read this section, you'll learn the answer to this question.

## The Functions of Money

The basis of the market economy is voluntary exchange. In the American economy, the exchange usually involves money in return for a good or service. Most Americans think of money as bills, coins, and checks. Historically, though, and in other economies, money might be shells, gold, or even goods such as sheep.



## SECTION 1 RESOURCE MANAGER

**Reproducible Masters**

- Reproducible Lesson Plan 14–1
- Reading Essentials and Study Guide 14–1
- Guided Reading Activity 14–1
- Section Quiz 14–1
- Daily Focus Activity 58
- Daily Lecture Notes 14–1

**Multimedia**

- Daily Focus Transparency 58
- Economic Concepts Transparency 6
- Vocabulary PuzzleMaker
- Interactive Tutor Self-Assessment Software
- ExamView® Pro Testmaker
- MindJogger Videoquiz
- NBR's *Economics & You*
- Presentation Plus!

# 1 Focus

## Overview

Section 1 describes or explains the three functions of money, the three types of money, and money's six major characteristics.

**BELLRINGER**
**Motivational Activity**

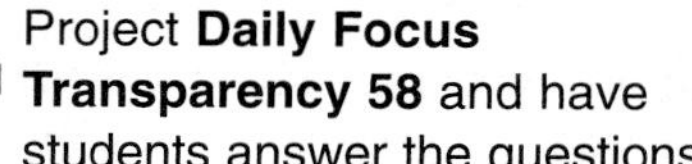

Project **Daily Focus Transparency 58** and have students answer the questions.

This activity is also available as a blackline master.

**Daily Focus Transparency 58**

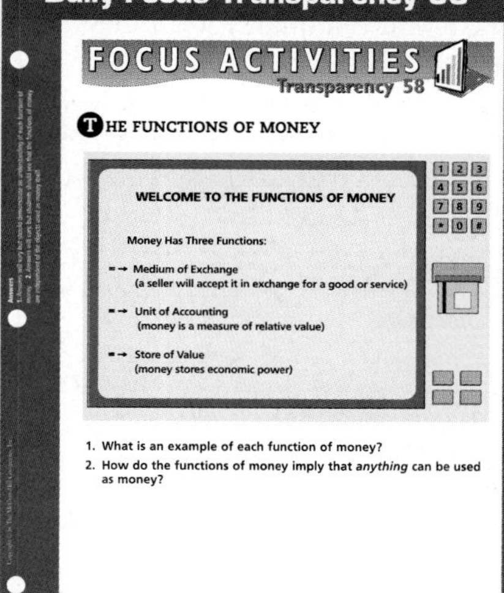

FOCUS ACTIVITIES
Transparency 58

THE FUNCTIONS OF MONEY

WELCOME TO THE FUNCTIONS OF MONEY
Money Has Three Functions:
Medium of Exchange
(a seller will accept it in exchange for a good or service)
Unit of Accounting
(money is a measure of relative value)
Store of Value
(money stores economic power)



1. What is an example of each function of money?
2. How do the functions of money imply that *anything* can be used as money?

Daily Focus Transparencies

### READER'S GUIDE

Answers to the **Reading Objectives** questions are on page 379.

**Preteaching Vocabulary**

Have students locate the definitions of the **Terms to Know** in the Glossary. Then ask them to identify the terms that relate to the functions of money and the terms that describe the types of money.

**Vocabulary PuzzleMaker**

# 2 Teach

## Guided Practice

**L1 Understanding Ideas** On the board, draw a two-column chart with "Function or Characteristic" and "The Dollar" as column headings. In the first column, list the three functions and six characteristics of money. Then have students view a dollar bill. Ask them to identify how the dollar fulfills each function and demonstrates each characteristic. Note their responses in the appropriate row in the chart. Have students use the information in the chart to write a paragraph answering the following question: How and why does the dollar bill qualify as money?

### Daily Lecture Notes 14-1

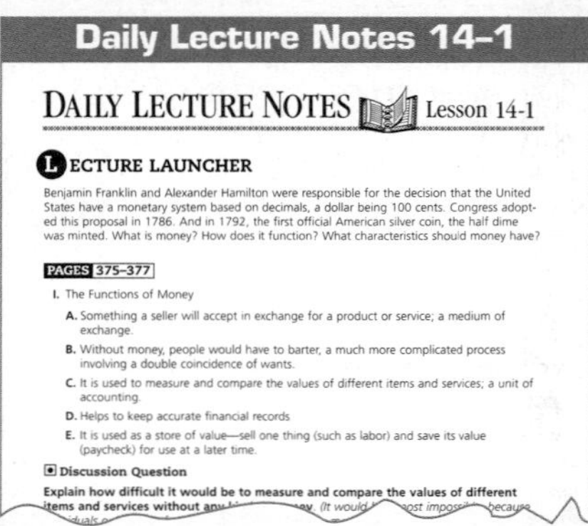
DAILY LECTURE NOTES Lesson 14-1

LECTURE LAUNCHER

Benjamin Franklin and Alexander Hamilton were responsible for the decision that the United States have a monetary system based on decimals, a dollar being 100 cents. Congress adopted this proposal in 1786. And in 1792, the first official American silver coin, the half dime was minted. What is money? How does it function? What characteristics should money have?

PAGES 375–377

I. The Functions of Money
   A. Something a seller will accept in exchange for a product or service; a medium of exchange.
   B. Without money, people would have to barter, a much more complicated process involving a double coincidence of wants.
   C. It is used to measure and compare the values of different items and services; a unit of accounting.
   D. Helps to keep accurate financial records
   E. It is used as a store of value—sell one thing (such as labor) and save its value (paycheck) for use at a later time.

**Discussion Question**

**Explain how difficult it would be to measure and compare the values of different items and services without any**



**money:** *anything customarily used as a medium of exchange, a unit of accounting, and a store of value*

**medium of exchange:** *use of money in exchange for goods or services*

**barter:** *exchange of goods and services for other goods and services*

**unit of accounting:** *use of money as a yardstick for comparing the values of goods and services in relation to one another*

**Figure 14.1** shows several items that have been used as money. For example, Native Americans used wampum—beads made from shells. People in the Fiji Islands have used whales' teeth.

Economists identify money by certain functions. Anything that is used as a medium of exchange, a unit of accounting, and a store of value is considered **money.** See **Figure 14.2.**

**Medium of Exchange** To say that money is a **medium of exchange** simply means that a seller will accept it in exchange for a good or service. Most people are paid for their work in money, which they then can use to buy whatever they need or want. Without money, people would have to **barter**—exchange goods and services for other goods and services.

Barter requires what economists call a double coincidence of wants. Each party to a transaction must want exactly what the other person has to offer. This situation is rare. As a result, people in societies that barter for goods spend great amounts of time and effort making trades with one another. Bartering works only in small societies with fairly simple economic systems.

**Unit of Accounting** Money is the yardstick that allows people to compare the values of goods and services in relation to one another. In this way, money functions as a **unit of accounting.** Each nation uses a basic unit to measure the value of goods, as it uses the foot or meter to measure distance. In the United States, this base unit of value is the dollar. In Japan, it is the yen; in much of Europe, the euro. An item for sale is marked with a price that indicates its value in terms of that unit.

By using money prices as a factor in comparing goods, people can determine whether one item is a better bargain than another. A single unit of accounting also allows people to keep accurate financial records—records of debts owed, income saved, and so on.

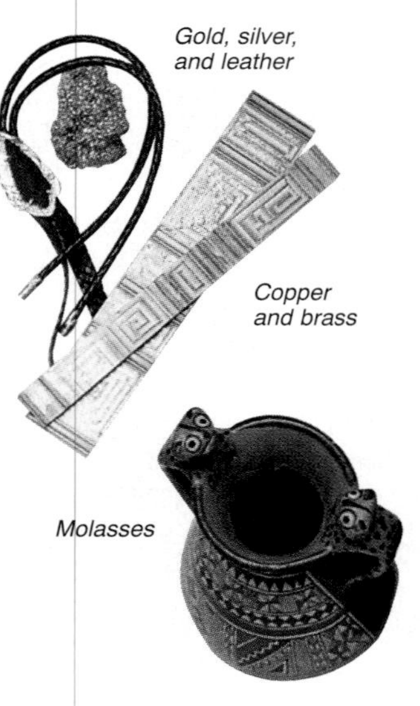


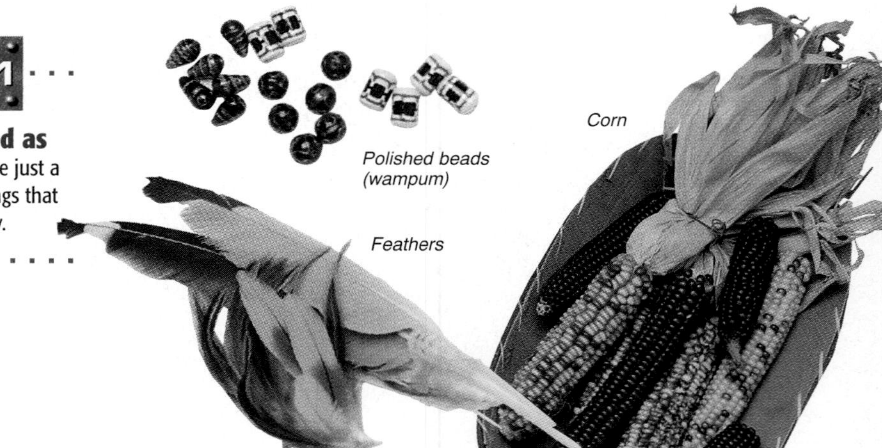


**FIGURE 14.1**

**Selected Items Used as Money** These items are just a sample of the various things that have been used as money.



### Meeting Special Needs

**Learning Disorder** Show students with learning disorders the importance of headings and subheadings for understanding the framework of each section. Illustrate the method to students by asking them what they would do if they wanted to discover what Section 1 was about. Read aloud the section's headings and subheadings. As you read each one, ask students to rephrase it in a complete sentence.

Refer to *Inclusion for the Social Studies Classroom Strategies and Activities* for students with different learning styles.

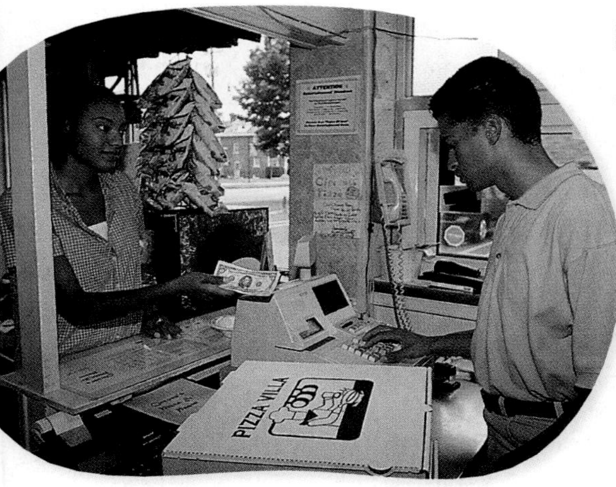


**FIGURE 14.2**

**Three Functions of Money** All money serves three functions. The money this woman holds is serving as a medium of exchange; the vendor will accept it in exchange for a pizza. The money is also a unit of accounting–the products in the market are all priced in dollars, so the woman can compare values of different items. Finally, the money serves as a store of value–the woman has stored her purchasing power in the form of dollars.

**Store of Value** Money also serves as a **store of value.** You can sell something, such as your labor, and store the purchasing power that results from the sale in the form of money for later use. People usually receive their money income once a week, once every two weeks, or once a month. In contrast, they usually spend their income at different times during a pay period. To be able to buy things between paydays, a person can store some of his or her income in cash and some in a checking account. It is important to note that in periods of rapid and unpredictable inflation, money is less able to act as a store of value.

**store of value:** *use of money to store purchasing power for later use*

## Characteristics of Money

Anything that people are willing to accept in exchange for goods can serve as money. At various times in history, cattle, salt, animal hides, gems, and tobacco have been used as mediums of exchange. Each of these items has certain characteristics that make it better or worse than others for use as money. Cattle, for example, are difficult to transport, but they are durable. Gems are easy to carry, but they are not easy to split into small pieces to use.

**Figure 14.3** on page 378 lists the characteristics that to some degree all items used as money must have. Almost

**Global Economy**

### Russia's Barter Economy

Because Russian currency is not trusted, real money plays a fairly small part in Russia's economy today. Most business is conducted by barter or with IOUs. For example, workers rarely receive wages in the form of cash. A bicycle factory outside the city of Perm pays its workers in bicycles! To get cash, the workers have to sell their "paychecks." More often than not, they simply trade the bicycles for the products they want. ■



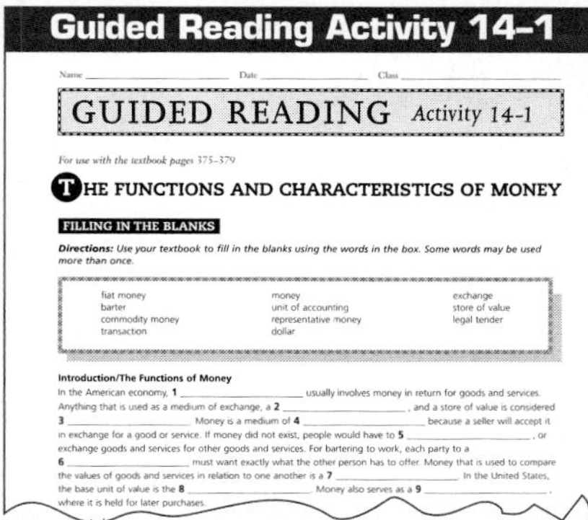
**Guided Reading Activity 14-1**

Name ______ Date ______ Class ______

GUIDED READING *Activity 14-1*

*For use with the textbook pages 375–379*

**THE FUNCTIONS AND CHARACTERISTICS OF MONEY**

**FILLING IN THE BLANKS**

***Directions:*** *Use your textbook to fill in the blanks using the words in the box. Some words may be used more than once.*

| | | |
|---|---|---|
| fiat money | money | exchange |
| barter | unit of accounting | store of value |
| commodity money | representative money | legal tender |
| transaction | dollar | |

**Introduction/The Functions of Money**

In the American economy, **1** ______ usually involves money in return for goods and services. Anything that is used as a medium of exchange, a **2** ______, and a store of value is considered **3** ______. Money is a medium of **4** ______ because a seller will accept it in exchange for a good or service. If money did not exist, people would have to **5** ______, or exchange goods and services for other goods and services. For bartering to work, each party to a **6** ______ must want exactly what the other person has to offer. Money that is used to compare the values of goods and services in relation to one another is a **7** ______. In the United States, the base unit of value is the **8** ______. Money also serves as a **9** ______, where it is held for later purchases.

Project **Economic Concepts Transparency 6** and have students discuss the accompanying questions.

**Money and Banking**

Chapter 18
Disc 1, Side 2

**ASK:** What function does money serve when you save it for a future purchase? *store of value*

Also available in VHS.

## Cooperative Learning

Organize the class into small groups, and have groups review **Figure 14.1** on page 376. Direct groups to use library resources and the Internet to discover the various items that have been used for money through the ages. Have groups use their findings to create an illustrated chart titled "Money—Not Just Bills and Coins." Suggest that they include such information as where and when each item has been used as money. Encourage groups to display their completed charts around the classroom. ELL BLOCK SCHEDULING

## Independent Practice

L2 Illustrating Ideas Tell students they have been asked to teach a lesson on the functions and characteristics of money. Have them work in small groups to develop two teaching visual aids—one to teach the functions of money, the other to teach the characteristics of money. Call on groups to display and explain their teaching aids.

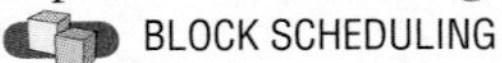 BLOCK SCHEDULING

# 3 Assess

## Meeting Lesson Objectives

Assign Section 1 Assessment as homework or an in-class activity.

Use **Interactive Tutor Self-Assessment Software** to review Section 1.

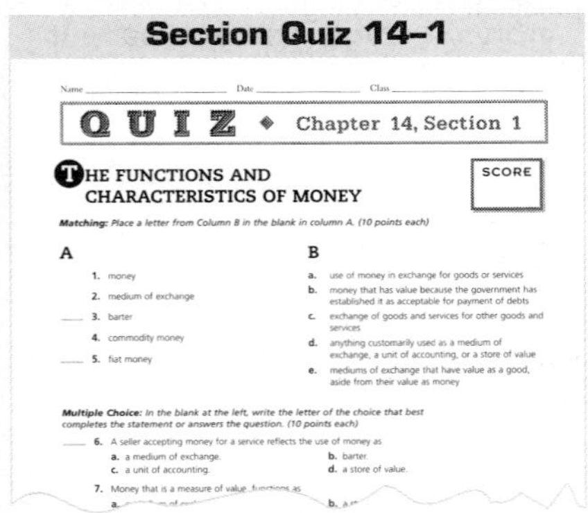

**Section Quiz 14–1**

Name ______ Date ______ Class ______

QUIZ ◆ Chapter 14, Section 1

THE FUNCTIONS AND CHARACTERISTICS OF MONEY

SCORE

***Matching:*** *Place a letter from Column B in the blank in column A. (10 points each)*

| A | B |
|---|---|
| ___ 1. money | a. use of money in exchange for goods or services |
| ___ 2. medium of exchange | b. money that has value because the government has established it as acceptable for payment of debts |
| ___ 3. barter | c. exchange of goods and services for other goods and services |
| ___ 4. commodity money | d. anything customarily used as a medium of exchange, a unit of accounting, or a store of value |
| ___ 5. fiat money | e. mediums of exchange that have value as a good, aside from their value as money |

***Multiple Choice:*** *In the blank at the left, write the letter of the choice that best completes the statement or answers the question. (10 points each)*

___ 6. A seller accepting money for a service reflects the use of money as
a. a medium of exchange. b. barter.
c. a unit of accounting. d. a store of value.

___ 7. Money that is a measure of value functions as

## FIGURE 14.3 Characteristics of Money

| Characteristic | Description |
|---|---|
| **Durable** | Money must be able to withstand the wear and tear of being passed from person to person. Paper money lasts one year on average, but old bills can be easily replaced. Coins, in contrast, last for years. |
| **Portable** | Money must be easy to carry. Though paper money is not very durable, people can easily carry large sums of paper money. |
| **Divisible** | Money must be easily divided into small parts so that purchases of any price can be made. Carrying coins and small bills makes it possible to make purchases of any amount. |
| **Stable in Value** | Money must be stable in value. Its value cannot change rapidly or its usefulness as a store of value will decrease. |
| **Scarce** | Whatever is used as money must be scarce. That is what gives it value. |
| **Accepted** | Whatever is used as money must be accepted as a medium of exchange in payment for debts. In the United States, acceptance is based on the knowledge that others will continue to accept paper money, coins, and checks in exchange for desired goods and services. |

any item that meets most of these criteria can be and probably has been used as money. Precious metals—particularly gold and silver—are especially well suited as mediums of exchange, and have often been used as such throughout history. It is only in more recent times that paper money has been widely used as a medium of exchange.

## Types of Money

**commodity money:** *a medium of exchange such as cattle or gems that has value as a commodity or good aside from its value as money*

**representative money:** *money that is backed by an item of value, such as gold or silver*

Mediums of exchange such as cattle and gems are considered **commodity money.** They have a value as a commodity, or good, aside from their value as money. Cattle are used for food. Gems are used for jewelry.

**Representative money** is money backed by—or exchangeable for—a valuable item such as gold or silver. Typically, the amount of representative money in circulation, or in use by people, was limited because it was linked to some scarce good, such as gold.

At one time, the United States government issued representative money in the form of silver and gold certificates. In addition, private banks accepted deposits of gold bars or silver ingots



## Extending the Content

**A Resurgence of Barter** In recent years, barter has become a favored method of doing business for many American companies. There are about 400 trade exchanges—agencies that organize and assist barter transactions—in the United States and Canada. These exchanges represent nearly 400,000 businesses and oversee more than $4 billion in barter business each year. Companies pay between $200 and $500 to join a trade exchange and then pay a monthly fee of about $30. Usually, a trade broker arranges a company's trades and tracks what the company owes and is owed in barter "dollars."

## Economic Connection to... History

# A Chocolate Lover's Dream

The Aztec in Central America used cacao beans, from which chocolate is made, as money. Prices varied from a few beans for a piece of fruit to several thousand for an enslaved person.

Aztec merchants had to take care when selling expensive items. Payment usually came stored in sacks, and the sacks might contain counterfeit money—bean husks filled with mud. ■

(called bullion) in exchange for paper money called banknotes. The notes were a promise to convert the paper money back into coin or bullion on demand. These banks were supposed to keep enough gold or silver in reserve–on hand–to redeem their banknotes. That did not always happen, however.

Today all United States money is **fiat money**, meaning that its face value occurs through government fiat, or order. It is in this way declared **legal tender.**

**fiat money:** *money that has value because a government fiat, or order, has established it as acceptable for payment of debts*

**legal tender:** *money that by law must be accepted for payment of public and private debts*

**Practice** and **assess** key skills with ***Skillbuilder Interactive Workbook, Level 2.***

## SECTION 1 Assessment

### Understanding Key Terms

1. **Define** money, medium of exchange, barter, unit of accounting, store of value, commodity money, representative money, fiat money, legal tender.

### Reviewing Objectives

2. What are the three functions of money?
3. **Graphic Organizer** Create a diagram like the one below to describe the six major characteristics of money.

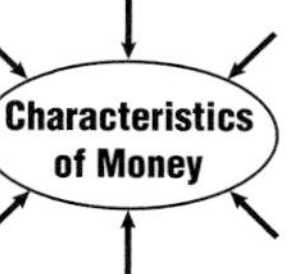


### Applying Economic Concepts

4. **Money** Imagine that you live in a bartering society. List 10 items that you use frequently, and then identify alternative goods that you would be willing to trade for them.

### Critical Thinking Activity

5. **Making Comparisons** Make a chart with five columns. In the first column, list Commodity Money, Representative Money, and Fiat Money. In the other four columns, write Description, Example, Advantage, and Disadvantage. Fill in the chart, comparing the three types of money. *(For help in using charts, see page xvii in the Economic Handbook.)*



## ? Did You Know ?

As well as cacao beans, the Aztecs also used cotton cloaks, beads, shells, and copper bells as money.

## Reteach

Have students use the main headings and subheadings to write an outline of Section 1.

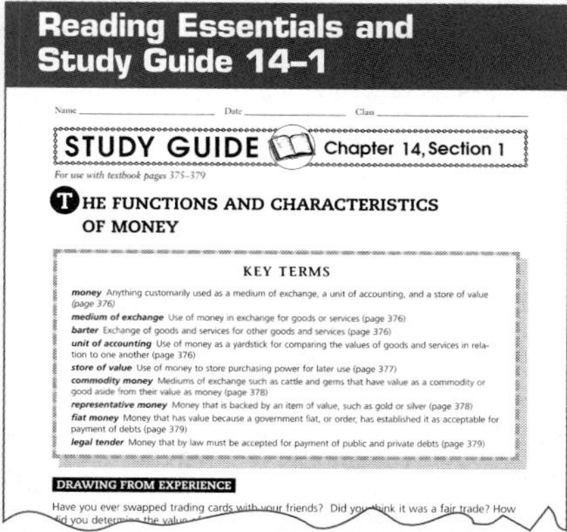

**Reading Essentials and Study Guide 14-1**

Name ________ Date ________ Class ________

STUDY GUIDE Chapter 14, Section 1

*For use with textbook pages 375–379*

THE FUNCTIONS AND CHARACTERISTICS OF MONEY

KEY TERMS

***money*** Anything customarily used as a medium of exchange, a unit of accounting, and a store of value (page 376)

***medium of exchange*** Use of money in exchange for goods or services (page 376)

***barter*** Exchange of goods and services for other goods and services (page 376)

***unit of accounting*** Use of money as a yardstick for comparing the values of goods and services in relation to one another (page 376)

***store of value*** Use of money to store purchasing power for later use (page 377)

***commodity money*** Mediums of exchange such as cattle and gems that have value as a commodity or good aside from their value as money (page 378)

***representative money*** Money that is backed by an item of value, such as gold or silver (page 378)

***fiat money*** Money that has value because a government fiat, or order, has established it as acceptable for payment of debts (page 379)

***legal tender*** Money that by law must be accepted for payment of public and private debts (page 379)

DRAWING FROM EXPERIENCE

Have you ever swapped trading cards with your friends? Did you think it was a fair trade? How

## 4 Close

Have students write a short paragraph that answers the following question: What is money? Call on volunteers to read and discuss their paragraphs.

## SECTION 1 Assessment Answers

1. All definitions can be found in the Glossary.
2. medium of exchange, store of value, unit of accounting
3. Six major characteristics are durability, portability, divisibility, stability in value, scarcity, and acceptability.
4. Lists will vary. Have students share and compare their lists to see if any trades are possible.
5. Commodity—Examples: cattle, gems, and salt. Adv: It can be used for purposes other than money. Dis: Some commodities might not be portable, and they may not be easy to divide. Representative—Examples: silver and gold certificates, banknotes. Adv: It maintains its value. Dis: Banks may not keep enough of the valuable backing item on deposit to redeem all representative money. Fiat—Example: dollar bill. Adv: acceptable everywhere for business transactions.

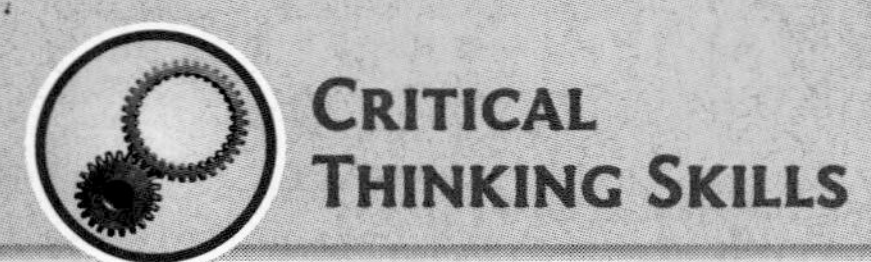

## CRITICAL THINKING SKILLS

### Synthesizing Information

Point out that synthesizing might involve integrating information from many different kinds of sources. For example, researching the various items used for money might involve the study and integration of information from time lines, charts, tables, graphs, periodical articles, and books.

**Reinforcing Economic Skills 20**

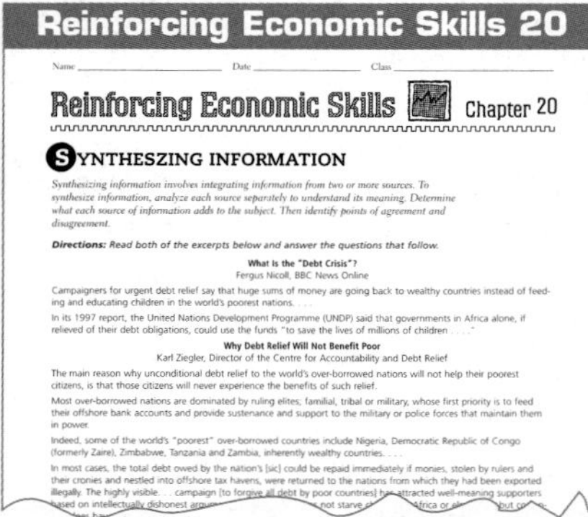

Name ______ Date ______ Class ______

**Reinforcing Economic Skills** Chapter 20

**SYNTHESZING INFORMATION**

*Synthesizing information involves integrating information from two or more sources. To synthesize information, analyze each source separately to understand its meaning. Determine what each source of information adds to the subject. Then identify points of agreement and disagreement.*

***Directions:** Read both of the excerpts below and answer the questions that follow.*

**What Is the "Debt Crisis"?**
Fergus Nicoll, BBC News Online

Campaigners for urgent debt relief say that huge sums of money are going back to wealthy countries instead of feeding and educating children in the world's poorest nations. . . .

In its 1997 report, the United Nations Development Programme (UNDP) said that governments in Africa alone, if relieved of their debt obligations, could use the funds "to save the lives of millions of children . . . ."

**Why Debt Relief Will Not Benefit Poor**
Karl Ziegler, Director of the Centre for Accountability and Debt Relief

The main reason why unconditional debt relief to the world's over-borrowed nations will not help their poorest citizens, is that those citizens will never experience the benefits of such relief.

Most over-borrowed nations are dominated by ruling elites; familial, tribal or military, whose first priority is to feed their offshore bank accounts and provide sustenance and support to the military or police forces that maintain them in power.

Indeed, some of the world's "poorest" over-borrowed countries include Nigeria, Democratic Republic of Congo (formerly Zaire), Zimbabwe, Tanzania and Zambia, inherently wealthy countries. . . .

In most cases, the total debt owed by the nation's [sic] could be repaid immediately if monies, stolen by rulers and their cronies and nestled into offshore tax havens, were returned to the nations from which they had been exported illegally. The highly visible. . . campaign [to forgive all debt by poor countries] has attracted well-meaning supporters based on intellectually dishonest

**GLENCOE TECHNOLOGY**

**Glencoe Skillbuilder Interactive Workbook, Level 2**

This interactive CD-ROM reinforces student mastery of essential social studies skills.

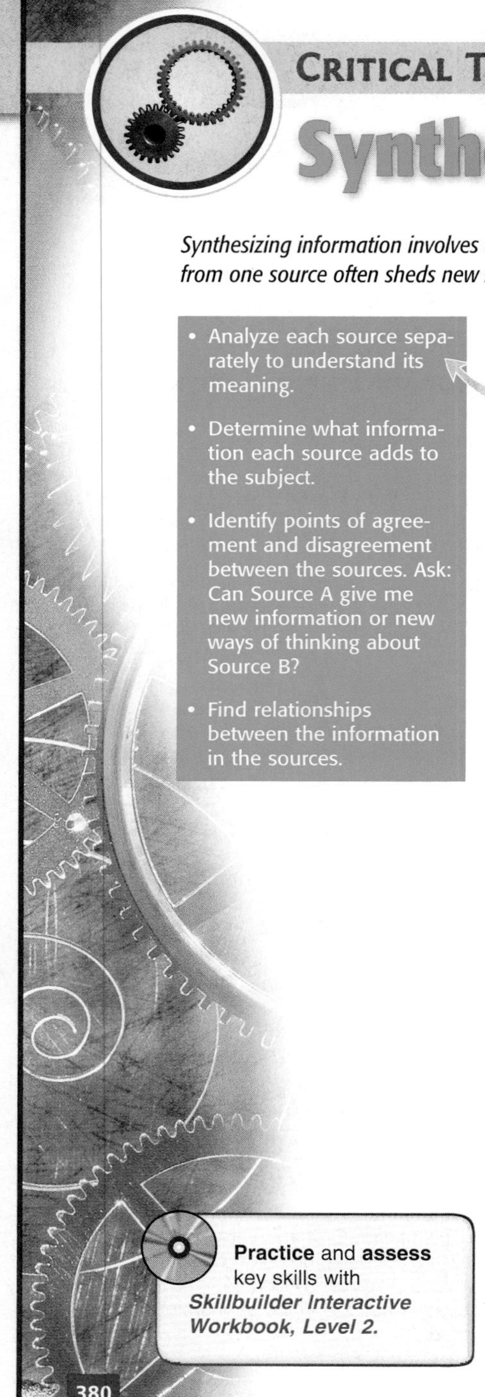

## CRITICAL THINKING SKILLS

# Synthesizing Information

*Synthesizing information involves combining information from two or more sources. Information gained from one source often sheds new light upon other information.*

- Analyze each source separately to understand its meaning.
- Determine what information each source adds to the subject.
- Identify points of agreement and disagreement between the sources. Ask: Can Source A give me new information or new ways of thinking about Source B?
- Find relationships between the information in the sources.

### LEARNING THE SKILL

To learn how to synthesize information, follow the steps listed on the left.

### PRACTICING THE SKILL

Study the sources below, then answer the questions.

**Source A** *"At present 60% to 70% of all dollars in circulation are used abroad. Today Panama is the best-known country that is 'dollarized,' but 11 others use the U.S. dollar. The best route for the emerging market countries is to unilaterally dollarize. . . . [T]he dollar could serve as the linchpin of a new global financial architecture, one that would eliminate currency crises, lower interest rates, and stimulate growth."*
–*Forbes,* May 3, 1999

**Source B** *"When a country abandons its currency, it surrenders a central symbol of national identity. . . . We are courting trouble if many countries dollarize. They would blame us for their problems; and they would try to influence U.S. policies, pushing for either lower or higher interest rates."*
–*Newsweek,* May 17, 1999

1. What is the main subject of each source?
2. Does Source B support or contradict Source A? Explain.
3. Summarize what you learned from both sources.

### APPLICATION ACTIVITY

Find two sources of information on banking practices. What are the main ideas in the sources? How does each source add to your understanding of the topic?

**Practice** and **assess** key skills with *Skillbuilder Interactive Workbook, Level 2.*



### Answers to PRACTICING THE SKILL

1. The main idea is about other countries adopting the dollar as their currency.
2. Source B contradicts Source A. Source A states that dollarizing would be the linchpin of a new global financial system, which would eliminate currency crises, lower interest rates, and stimulate economic growth. Source B states that dollarizing could create trouble for the United States and bring about fluctuating interest rates.
3. Some sources suggest that dollarizing could be the beginning of global financial security, while others suggest that it could create economic problems for the U.S.

APPLICATION ACTIVITY Answers will vary. Have students share and compare their reports.

SECTION 2

# History of American Money and Banking

## COVER STORY

*BUSINESS WEEK*, APRIL 27, 1998

The $1,000,000,000,000 bank. Once, it was unimaginable. But in eight days in April [1998], three eye-popping megamergers have brought the prospect of the first trillion-dollar bank within sight. Suddenly, it seems to be the all-but-certain climax of the cycle of ever-larger combinations that have already reshaped the [banking] industry.

### READER'S GUIDE

**Terms to Know**

- overdraft checking
- electronic funds transfer (EFT)
- automated teller machine (ATM)

**Reading Objectives**

1. What are some of the most important events in the history of American money and banking?
2. What are six services provided by banks and savings institutions?
3. How has electronic banking changed banking services?

American banking has included everything from wampum to "virtual" money—banking in cyberspace on the Internet. In this section, you'll learn about the development of and changes in the United States banking industry.

## History of American Banking

Because the history of money in the United States is so closely tied to the development of the banking system, the time line in **Figure 14.4** on pages 382–383 describes both. During the colonial period, England did not permit the American colonies to print money or mint coins. Bartering for goods was common.



## SECTION 2 RESOURCE MANAGER

**Reproducible Masters**

- Reproducible Lesson Plan 14–2
- Reading Essentials and Study Guide 14–2
- Guided Reading Activity 14–2
- Section Quiz 14–2
- Daily Focus Activity 59
- Daily Lecture Notes 14–2

**Multimedia**

- Daily Focus Transparency 59
- Vocabulary PuzzleMaker
- Interactive Tutor Self-Assessment Software
- ExamView® Pro Testmaker
- MindJogger Videoquiz
- NBR's *Economics & You*
- Presentation Plus!



# 1 Focus

## Overview

Section 2 describes important events in the history of American money and banking, the services provided by banks and savings institutions, and the impact of electronic banking on banking services.

### BELLRINGER

**Motivational Activity**

Project **Daily Focus Transparency 59** and have students answer the questions.

This activity is also available as a blackline master.

**Daily Focus Transparency 59**

FOCUS ACTIVITIES Transparency 59

THE BANK PANIC OF 1907

1. Describe what is taking place in this photo. Is there anything unusual about this banking scene?
2. When a bank like the one in the photograph failed, runs on the bank followed. How would you explain a run on the bank?

Daily Focus Transparencies

### READER'S GUIDE

Answers to the **Reading Objectives** questions are on page 385.

**Preteaching Vocabulary**

Provide each student with three index cards. Direct students to write definitions for the **Terms to Know.** Collect the cards and randomly read aloud two definitions for each term. Have students vote on which they think is the correct definition. Then have them locate the definitions in the Glossary.

Vocabulary PuzzleMaker

# 2 Teach

## Guided Practice

**L1 Constructing a Time Line** Review with students the information in **Figure 14.4.** Organize students into groups, and direct groups to create a time line on the history of money and banking in the United States. Assign each group a time period from the 1780s to the present. Then have groups assemble pictures or create drawings that illustrate important events in American money and banking during their assigned time period. Display the time lines around the classroom. **ELL**

### Daily Lecture Notes 14-2

DAILY LECTURE NOTES Lesson 14-2

**LECTURE LAUNCHER**

In its early years, the United States had an unusually large number of banks compared to other countries. This was in large part due to the demands of an expanding frontier. People needed capital to purchase land and materials for building, and there was little communication between the eat coast and the frontier. In the course of American history, how has banking changed? What services do banks offer today?

**PAGES 381–384**

I. History of American Banking
   - **A.** England farebode Colonial America from using printed money or minted coins.
   - **B.** Bartering of various goods was used in place of money.
   - **C.** When the war came, the Continental Congress issued bills of credit (Continentals) to pay war debts.
   - **D.** Too many Continentals were issued and they became worthless.
   - **E.** After the war, the United States began to mint its own coins backed by gold and silver.

**Discussion Question**

**Why were Continentals worthless?** *(Because the Congress issued too many of them. Their fortunes rose and fell with the tides of the Revolutionary War.)*

**PAGE 384**

### Visual Instruction FIGURE 14.4

Refer students to **Figure 14.4** and draw their attention to the entry for 1811. Point out that banks that issued more currency than they could back with gold and silver were called *wildcat banks.* Many of these banks were located in areas so remote that people said only a wildcat could find them.

## FIGURE 14.4 Time Line of American Money and Banking

| Years | Events |
|---|---|
| **1780s** | The new nation has no reliable medium of exchange. National leaders disagree on a type of banking system. One group, led by Alexander Hamilton, believes a national banking system is necessary for development. The opposition, led by Thomas Jefferson, argues that only states should have the right to charter banks. |
| **1791** | Congress establishes the First Bank of the United States and gives it a 20-year charter. The bank is a private business, although the government supplies one-fifth of its starting capital. It serves as a depository for government funds, makes loans to the government and private individuals and businesses, and regulates the activities of banks with state charters. It also issues banknotes backed by gold. |
| **1792** | Congress passes the Coinage Act, which organizes a mint and establishes the dollar as the basic unit of currency for the nation. The Act also places the nation on a bimetallic monetary standard—the value of the dollar is fixed according to specific quantities of both silver and gold. |
| **1811** | Congress refuses to renew the charter of the First Bank because of questions about its legality and fears that it is gaining too much power. Without federal controls, dozens of state-chartered banks lend money and issue banknotes freely, many of which are not backed by enough gold or silver reserves. |
| **1816** | Congress establishes the Second Bank of the United States after the financial confusion caused by the War of 1812. Like the First Bank, it brings some order to the banking system. It pressures state-chartered banks to limit lending and to keep enough gold and silver in reserve to redeem their banknotes. Opposition to a strong national bank remains, however. In 1832 President Andrew Jackson vetoes legislation to extend the Second Bank's charter. |
| **1830s–1860s** | The end of the Second Bank brings another rapid rise in state-chartered banks. The amount of money in circulation varies widely. Such shifts in the amount of money available result in major fluctuations in business activity and prices. |
| **Civil War** | To help pay for the war, the United States issues fiat money—the first time since the Revolutionary War. These United States notes, called *greenbacks,* change in value as confidence in the Union army rises or falls. Difficulties in raising money for the war make clear the need for a better monetary and banking system. In 1863 and 1864, Congress passes the National Bank acts. These acts establish a system of federally chartered private banks, called *national banks.* The government also sets up a safe, uniform currency by requiring that all national banknotes be fully backed by government bonds. The *Comptroller of the Currency* is created to grant charters for national banks and to oversee their activities. |



382

### Meeting Special Needs

**Comprehension and Organization Problems** Taking notes requires the ability to consolidate and summarize information so that it is sufficiently clear and complete. To help students take good notes, ask them to read the subsection titled "Electronic Banking" on pages 384 and 385. Direct them to take notes as they read. Then pair students, and have partners teach each other the subsection information using only their notes. Have students discuss the effectiveness of their notes in providing essential information. Direct them to identify unclear or missing information. Finally, have them repeat the reading and note-taking process to improve their notes.

| Years | Events |
|---|---|
| Late 1860s–Early 1900s | The nation shifts to a gold monetary standard in 1869. The federal government begins redeeming early 1860s greenbacks for gold coins. Despite the new banking system, problems remain. There is no simple way to regulate the amount of national banknotes in circulation, so periodic shortages of money occur. Financial panics occur in 1873, 1884, 1893, and 1907. Many banks with low reserves are forced to close. |
| 1913 | To control the amount of money in circulation, Congress establishes the Federal Reserve System. It serves as the nation's central bank with power to regulate reserves in national banks, make loans to member banks, and control the growth of the money supply. In 1914 the system begins issuing paper money called *Federal Reserve notes*. These notes soon become the major form of currency in circulation. |
| 1929 | The Great Depression begins. Stocks and other investments lose much of their value. Bankrupt businesses and individuals are unable to repay their loans. |
| 1929–1934 | A financial panic causes thousands of banks to collapse. When President Franklin Roosevelt takes office in March 1933, he declares a "bank holiday," closing all banks. Each bank is allowed to reopen only after it proves it is financially sound. Congress passes the Glass-Steagall Banking Act in June, establishing the Federal Deposit Insurance Corporation (FDIC). This new agency helps restore public confidence in banks by insuring funds of individual depositors in case of a bank failure.<br><br>The nation switches from a gold standard to a fiat monetary standard. The government stops converting greenbacks into gold, calls in all gold coins and certificates, and prohibits private ownership of gold. |
| 1930s–1960s | Banking reforms of the 1930s allow banks to enter a period of long-term stability, in which few banks fail. |
| Late 1960s–1970s | Congress passes a series of laws to protect consumers in dealing with financial institutions. The Truth in Lending Act of 1968, the Equal Credit Opportunity Act of 1974, and the Community Reinvestment Act of 1977 make clear the rights and responsibilities of banks and consumers.<br><br>Banks begin using computers to transfer money electronically and to handle many banking activities. Congress passes the Electronic Funds Transfer Act of 1978 to protect consumers using these new services. |
| 1980s–present | As part of the general move toward deregulation of business, Congress passes the Depository Institutions Deregulation and Monetary Control Act in 1980.<br><br>Deregulation allows the savings and loan industry to make risky loans. Many S&Ls face bankruptcy. Congress passes the Financial Institutions Reform, Recovery, and Enforcement Act of 1989. The full cost of bailing out the S&Ls is $300 billion, or about $4,000 per United States family in future taxes. The FDIC takes over regulation of the thrift institutions industry. Banking continues to evolve, incorporating technology such as e-cash on the Internet. |



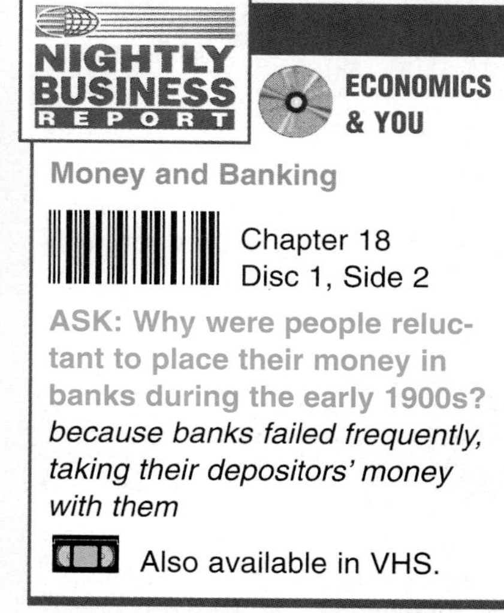

NIGHTLY BUSINESS REPORT
ECONOMICS & YOU
Money and Banking
Chapter 18
Disc 1, Side 2
ASK: Why were people reluctant to place their money in banks during the early 1900s?
because banks failed frequently, taking their depositors' money with them
Also available in VHS.


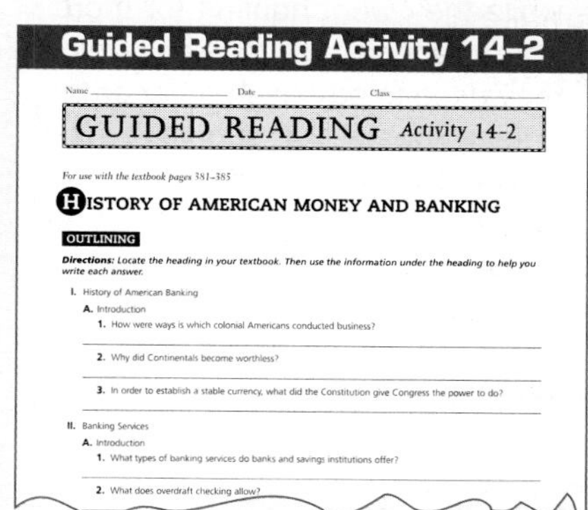
**Guided Reading Activity 14-2**

Name ______ Date ______ Class ______

GUIDED READING Activity 14-2

For use with the textbook pages 381–385

HISTORY OF AMERICAN MONEY AND BANKING

OUTLINING

*Directions:* Locate the heading in your textbook. Then use the information under the heading to help you write each answer.

I. History of American Banking
A. Introduction
1. How were ways in which colonial Americans conducted business?
2. Why did Continentals become worthless?
3. In order to establish a stable currency, what did the Constitution give Congress the power to do?

II. Banking Services
A. Introduction
1. What types of banking services do banks and savings institutions offer?
2. What does overdraft checking allow?

## Independent Practice

**L1 Making Comparisons** Have students review the text on electronic banking transfers on pages 384 and 385. Then have them write a few paragraphs discussing the advantages and disadvantages of EFT as compared to using checks or making payments in cash. Call on volunteers to read their paragraphs to the class.

## Cooperative Learning

Organize students into several groups, and have groups investigate the services offered by local banks and savings institutions. Each group should focus on a different bank or savings institution and present their findings in the form of an illustrated chart. Have groups display and discuss their finished charts. Then lead all students in a discussion of which bank or savings institution is best suited to their banking needs. ELL

BLOCK SCHEDULING

See the **Web Activity Lesson Plan** at ett.glencoe.com for an introduction, lesson description, and answers to the **Student Web Activity** for this chapter.

**Economic Connection to... History**

In colonial times, frontier hunters often left their deerskins, or buckskins, at trading posts while they went hunting for more. They received a receipt, which they used to pay each other or the trading posts for supplies. The value of the buckskins that hunters left—and the receipt—usually was about a dollar. The common name for a dollar—*buck*—derives from this practice.

# 3 Assess

## Meeting Lesson Objectives

Assign Section 2 Assessment as homework or an in-class activity.

Use **Interactive Tutor Self-Assessment Software** to review Section 2.

**Student Web Activity** Visit the *Economics Today and Tomorrow* Web site at **ett.glencoe.com** and click on ***Chapter 14—Student Web Activities*** to see how online banking works.

Though scarce, some European gold and silver coins also circulated in the colonies. The Spanish *dolár,* later called the "dollar" by colonists, was one of the more common coins.

The Revolutionary War brought even more confusion to the already haphazard colonial money system. To help pay for the war, the Continental Congress issued bills of credit, called Continentals, that could be used to pay debts. So many of these notes were issued that they became worthless, and people often refused to accept them. The phrase "not worth a Continental" became a way of describing something of little value.

After the war, establishing a reliable medium of exchange became a major concern of the new nation. The Constitution, ratified in 1788, gave Congress the power to mint coins, although private banks were still allowed to print banknotes representing gold and silver on deposit.

## Banking Services

Banks and savings institutions today offer a wide variety of services, including checking accounts, interest on certain types of checking accounts, automatic deposit and payment, storage of valuables, transfer of money from one person to another, and overdraft checking. **Overdraft checking** allows a customer to write a check for more money than exists in his or her account. The bank lends the needed amount and the customer pays the money back, usually at a relatively high rate of interest.

**overdraft checking:** *checking account that allows a customer to write a check for more money than exists in his or her account*

In general, the types of banking services are the same across the country. The exact terms and conditions of the services, however, vary from state to state according to each state's banking laws. When choosing a bank or savings institution, you should investigate the bank's service charges.

## Electronic Banking

One of the most important changes in banking began in the late 1970s with the introduction of the computer. With it came **electronic funds transfer (EFT),** a system of putting onto computers all the various banking functions that in the past had to be handled on paper. One of the most common features

**electronic funds transfer (EFT):** *system of putting onto computers all the banking functions that in the past were handled on paper*



**Extending the Content**

**ATM Transaction Charges** Using an ATM is a relatively easy task. The customer inserts his or her card, enters an identification code, and then makes a transaction. If the customer is making a withdrawal at an ATM not owned by his or her bank, a fee—usually between $1 and $2.50—is charged. Since each transaction costs only about 25 cents, some consumers have accused banks of profiting unfairly. Banks have responded by arguing that charging a fee for convenience services is standard business practice. Recently, some local governments have passed laws that prevent banks from charging ATM fees. In response, a few banks have programmed their ATMs to reject cards of customers who do not bank with them.

of EFT is **automated teller machines (ATMs).** These units let consumers do their banking without the help of a teller.

Today you can even do your banking from home. You can see your account balances, transfer funds from a savings account to a checking account, and often even apply for a loan—all on the Internet.

*__automated teller machines (ATMs):__ units that allow consumers to do their banking without the help of a teller*

**EFT Concerns** Although EFT can save time, trouble, and costs in making transactions, it does have some drawbacks. The possibility of tampering and lack of privacy are increased because all records are stored in a computer. A person on a computer terminal could call up and read or even alter the account files of a bank customer in any city, if he or she knew how to get around the safeguards built into the system. In response to these and other concerns, the Electronic Fund Transfer Act of 1978 describes the rights and responsibilities of participants in EFT systems. For example, EFT customers are responsible for only $50 in losses when someone steals or illegally uses their ATM card, if they report the card missing within two days. If they wait more than two days, they could be responsible for as much as $500. Users are also protected against computer mistakes.

**Practice** and **assess** key skills with ***Skillbuilder Interactive Workbook, Level 2.***

## SECTION 2 Assessment

### Understanding Key Terms

1. **Define** overdraft checking, electronic funds transfer (EFT), automated teller machine (ATM).

### Reviewing Objectives

2. **Graphic Organizer** Create a time line like the one below to list and describe at least five of the most important events in the history of American money and banking. See **Figure 14.4** on pages 382–383 for information.

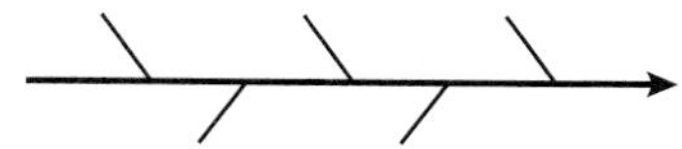

3. What are six services offered by banks and savings institutions?
4. How has electronic banking changed banking services?

### Applying Economic Concepts

5. **Money** In 1934 the government stopped backing paper money with gold. Some experts have proposed a return to the gold standard. Do you think this would be a good idea? Why or why not?

### Critical Thinking Activity

6. **Drawing Inferences** Why do you think coins have been a more desirable form of money than paper currency throughout American history?



## SECTION 2 Assessment Answers

1. All definitions can be found in the Glossary.
2. Time lines will vary.
3. Students' answers may include interest on certain kinds of checking accounts, automatic deposit and payment, storage of values, transfer of money, and overdraft checking.
4. Electronic banking has made banking transactions simpler, quicker, and less expensive. Tampering and lack of privacy are increased because all records are stored in computers.
5. Some students may agree, because dollars would be backed by something of value. Others might disagree because the amount of money in circulation would be controlled by the amount of U.S. gold.
6. Some students will suggest that people believed that coins made of gold and silver maintained their value better than paper money. Others might suggest that coins are more durable than paper currency.



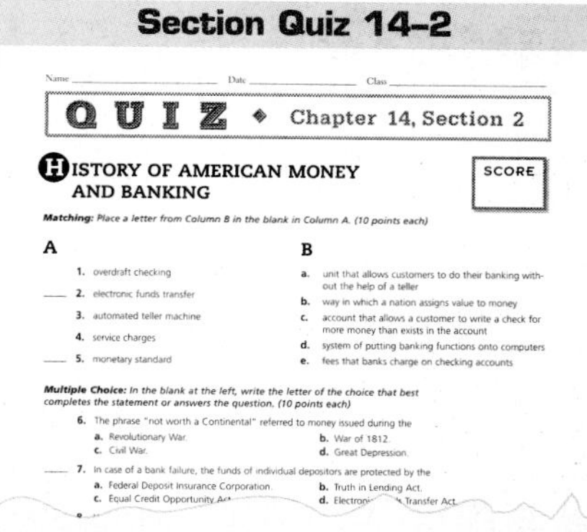

**Section Quiz 14-2**

Name ______ Date ______ Class ______

QUIZ ◆ Chapter 14, Section 2

HISTORY OF AMERICAN MONEY AND BANKING

SCORE

***Matching:*** *Place a letter from Column B in the blank in Column A. (10 points each)*

| A | B |
|---|---|
| ___ 1. overdraft checking | a. unit that allows customers to do their banking without the help of a teller |
| ___ 2. electronic funds transfer | b. way in which a nation assigns value to money |
| ___ 3. automated teller machine | c. account that allows a customer to write a check for more money than exists in the account |
| ___ 4. service charges | d. system of putting banking functions onto computers |
| ___ 5. monetary standard | e. fees that banks charge on checking accounts |

***Multiple Choice:*** *In the blank at the left, write the letter of the choice that best completes the statement or answers the question. (10 points each)*

___ 6. The phrase "not worth a Continental" referred to money issued during the
a. Revolutionary War. b. War of 1812.
c. Civil War. d. Great Depression.

___ 7. In case of a bank failure, the funds of individual depositors are protected by the
a. Federal Deposit Insurance Corporation. b. Truth in Lending Act.
c. Equal Credit Opportunity Act d. Electroni[illegible] Transfer Act.

## Reteach

Have students write review questions based on the section headings. Then pair students, and have partners quiz each other on section content using their questions.

**Reading Essentials and Study Guide 14-2**

Name ______ Date ______ Class ______

STUDY GUIDE Chapter 14, Section 2

*For use with textbook pages 381–385*

HISTORY OF AMERICAN MONEY AND BANKING

KEY TERMS

***overdraft checking*** Checking account that allows a customer to write a check for more money than exists in his or her account (page 384)

***electronic funds transfer (EFT)*** System of putting onto computers all the various banking functions that in the past were handled on paper (page 384)

***automated teller machines (ATMs)*** Units that allow consumers to do their banking without the help of a teller (page 385)

**DRAWING FROM EXPERIENCE**

In the United States, the FDIC (Federal Deposit Insurance Corporation) insures bank deposits. Would you feel confident about putting your money in a bank if your deposit was not insured?

This section focuses on the history of banking and currency in the U.S. It also explains current banking practices and services.

**ORGANIZING YOUR THOUGHTS**

Use the time line below to help [illegible]

## 4 Close

Ask students to write a paragraph in support of or opposed to the following statement: Technological developments have greatly improved banking services for consumers.

BusinessWeek
**SPOTLIGHT**

# Teach

You might point out that bank service fees—especially those charged for the use of ATMs—have become a major issue. Some state and local governments, citing the Electronic Funds Transfer Act of 1978, have sought to control the types and levels of fees that banks can charge.

**BusinessWeek ONLINE**

To find up-to-date news and analysis on the economy, business, technology, markets, entrepreneurs, investments, and finance, have students search feature articles and special reports on the *Business Week* Web site.
www.businessweek.com

**Sidelight**

Throughout much of the 1990s, banks earned record yearly profits. Income from fees grew at more than three times the rate of the increase in profits.

BusinessWeek

# SPOTLIGHT ON THE ECONOMY

## How Higher Fees Hurt Banks

**Check It Out! In this chapter you learned about banking services. In this article, read to learn how consumers are reacting to higher bank fees for those services.**

Anyone who has maintained a checking account over the past decade knows that the rules of the game have been dramatically changing. Specifically, your once friendly bank or thrift institution has probably been imposing a lot more fees and restrictions on your account—in an understandable effort to save money and wring even more profits from your need for its services.

Among other things, many banks now try to save money on handling canceled checks—either by not returning them at all or, more likely, charging either a set monthly amount for all returned checks or a per-check fee. Some also charge customers for using live tellers instead of ATMs. And many have been raising their fees considerably for handling bounced checks and for using other banks' ATMs.

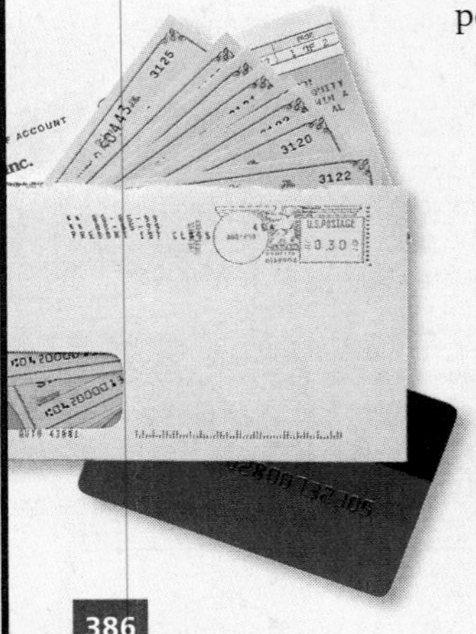

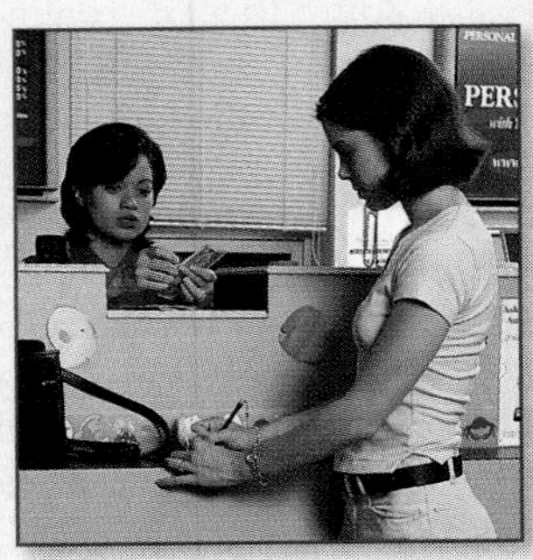

Ironically, reports economist Joanna Stavins in a recent issue of the Federal Reserve Bank of Boston's *New England Economic Review*, most of the gambits don't seem to be paying off. In a study of checking accounts at some 250 banks around the nation in 1997, she found that only two of the features described above appeared to be producing higher revenues: increased charges for bounced checks and higher fixed monthly fees for returning canceled checks.

In all other cases, raising fees or tightening restrictions tended to induce depositors to switch to other institutions—thus lowering the banks' take. Consumers, it seems, are a lot more sensitive to such practices than banks realize.



### Think About It

1. **What actions are banks taking to earn more profits?**
2. **According to Stavins, how are customers reacting to banks' actions?**



### Answers to *Think About It*

1. Actions include not returning canceled checks or charging some kind of fee for their return, charging customers for using live tellers, raising fees for handling bounced checks and for using other banks' ATMs.
2. Many customers have switched to other banking institutions to avoid these various fees and charges.

SECTION 3

# Types of Money in the United States

## COVER STORY

*KIPLINGER'S PERSONAL FINANCE MAGAZINE*, DECEMBER 1998

Lincoln, Jefferson, Roosevelt and Washington. Soon to join those icons of American history on our nation's coinage is Sacajawea, the teenage Shoshone girl who helped guide Lewis and Clark on their historic expedition. According to the explorers' journals, the girl, with her infant son strapped to her back, helped the party navigate through mountain passes, communicate with native tribes, and find edible plants and roots when other food was scarce.

Sacajawea will represent Lady Liberty on the new dollar coin, expected to make its debut in 2000.

### READER'S GUIDE

**Terms to Know**

- checking account
- checkable deposits
- thrift institutions
- debit card
- near moneys
- M1
- M2

**Reading Objectives**

1. What is the difference between money and near moneys?
2. What does the M2 definition of money include?

When you think of money, you may think only of coins and paper bills. As you read this section, you'll learn that money is more than just cash.

*Randy L'Teton, model for the Sacajawea coin*

## Money and Near Moneys

Money in use today consists of more than just currency. It also includes deposits in checking and savings accounts, plus certain other investments.



## SECTION 3 RESOURCE MANAGER

**Reproducible Masters**

- Reproducible Lesson Plan 14–3
- Reading Essentials and Study Guide 14–3
- Guided Reading Activity 14–3
- Section Quiz 14–3
- Daily Focus Activity 60
- Daily Lecture Notes 14–3

**Multimedia**

- Daily Focus Transparency 60
- Vocabulary PuzzleMaker
- Interactive Tutor Self-Assessment Software
- ExamView® Pro Testmaker
- MindJogger Videoquiz
- Presentation Plus!



# 1 Focus

## Overview

Section 3 explains the difference between money and near moneys and describes the components of the M1 and M2 measures of the money supply.

**BELLRINGER**
**Motivational Activity**

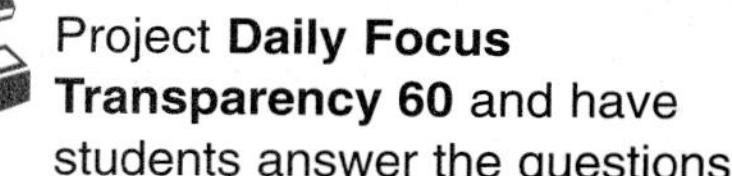

Project **Daily Focus Transparency 60** and have students answer the questions.

This activity is also available as a blackline master.

**Daily Focus Transparency 60**

FOCUS ACTIVITIES
Transparency 60

TYPES OF MONEY

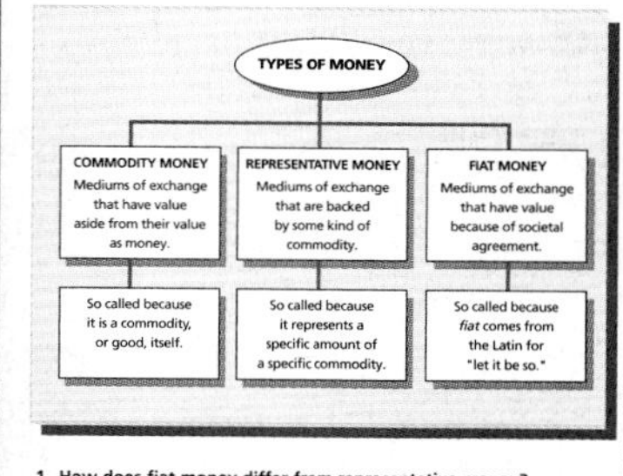



1. How does fiat money differ from representative money?
2. What type of money is used in the United States today?

Daily Focus Transparencies

### READER'S GUIDE

Answers to the **Reading Objectives** questions are on page 391.

**Preteaching Vocabulary**

Call on volunteers to state what they think each of the **Terms to Know** means. As each definition is offered, have students check its accuracy by locating the term in the Glossary.

**Vocabulary PuzzleMaker**

# 2 Teach

## Guided Practice

**L1** Categorizing Information Review with students the information on the money supply on page 391. On the board, draw a two-column chart with "M1" and "M2" as column headings. Call on volunteers to enter the items listed below in the correct columns. (Remind students that some items are part of both measures.)

Travelers' checks *(M1 and M2)*
Money market deposit accounts *(M2)*
Currency *(M1 and M2)*
Checkable deposits *(M1 and M2)*
Savings deposits *(M2)*

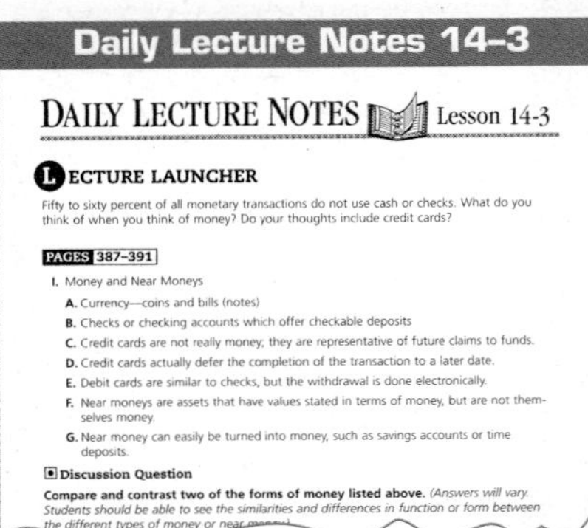

**Daily Lecture Notes 14-3**

DAILY LECTURE NOTES Lesson 14-3

**LECTURE LAUNCHER**

Fifty to sixty percent of all monetary transactions do not use cash or checks. What do you think of when you think of money? Do your thoughts include credit cards?

PAGES 387–391

I. Money and Near Moneys
- **A.** Currency—coins and bills (notes)
- **B.** Checks or checking accounts which offer checkable deposits
- **C.** Credit cards are not really money; they are representative of future claims to funds.
- **D.** Credit cards actually defer the completion of the transaction to a later date.
- **E.** Debit cards are similar to checks, but the withdrawal is done electronically.
- **F.** Near moneys are assets that have values stated in terms of money, but are not themselves money.
- **G.** Near money can easily be turned into money, such as savings accounts or time deposits.

**Discussion Question**

**Compare and contrast two of the forms of money listed above.** *(Answers will vary. Students should be able to see the similarities and differences in function or form between the different types of money or near money.)*

### Visual Instruction FIGURE 14.5

After students have reviewed **Figure 14.5**, point out that checks provide an important record of personal expenditures. Canceled checks are needed in preparing income tax returns or resolving disputes over the payment of bills or credit card accounts.

**Currency** All United States coins in circulation today are token coins. The value of the metal in each coin is less than its exchange value. A quarter, for example, consists of a mixture of copper and nickel. The value of the metal in a quarter, however, is much less than 25 cents. The Bureau of the Mint, which is part of the Treasury Department, makes all coins. About 7 percent of the currency in circulation in the United States today is in the form of coins.

Most of the nation's currency is in the form of Federal Reserve notes issued by Federal Reserve banks. The Bureau of Engraving and Printing, also part of the Treasury Department, prints all Federal Reserve notes. They are issued in denominations of $1,

## FIGURE 14.5

**Writing a Check and Balancing Your Checkbook** Always fill out your checks completely and clearly in ink. See the sample check in Part A. After you write a check to someone or make a deposit into your checking account, write the number, date, and amount in your check register. See the sample register in Part B.

Then, when you receive your monthly bank statement, balance your checkbook by following these steps:

1. Sort your checks by number. Check off each one in your checkbook.
2. Check off your deposit slips.
3. Deduct service charges and bank fees from your checkbook balance.
4. Add to the bank statement balance any deposits that have not cleared.
5. Total the amount of checks that have not cleared. Subtract this total from the amount on your bank statement.

The sample checkbook register in Part B shows that you have a running total of $191.36 in your account. Balance this total against the bank statement in Part C.

**A**

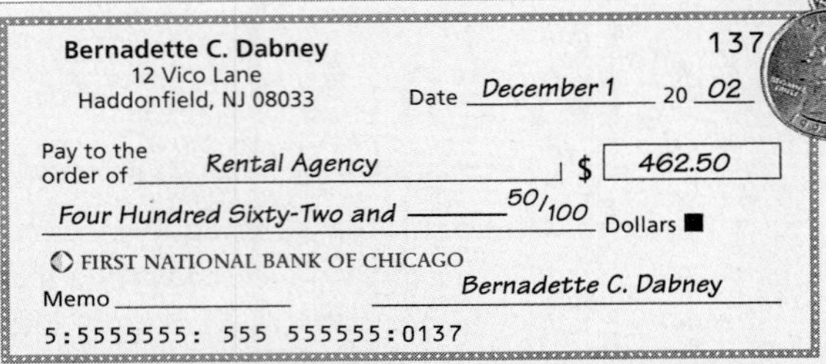

Bernadette C. Dabney
12 Vico Lane
Haddonfield, NJ 08033

137

Date *December 1* 20 *02*

Pay to the order of *Rental Agency* $ *462.50*

*Four Hundred Sixty-Two and 50/100* Dollars

FIRST NATIONAL BANK OF CHICAGO

Memo

*Bernadette C. Dabney*

5:5555555: 555 555555:0137

**B**

| Number | Date | Description | Payment of Debt | Fee | Deposit of Credit | Balance |
|---|---|---|---|---|---|---|
| | | | | | | $ 827.91 |
| 132 | 10/25 | Fashion Shop | $ 73.16 | | $ | $ 754.75 |
| 133 | 11/1 | Rent | 462.50 | | | 292.25 |
| 134 | 11/7 | Phone | 83.00 | | | 209.25 |
| 135 | 11/14 | Cash | 50.00 | | | 159.25 |
| 136 | 11/15 | J.W. Little | 10.00 | | | 149.25 |
| — | 11/22 | John's check | | | 4.00 | 153.25 |
| — | 11/23 | Paycheck | | | 500.61 | 653.86 |
| 137 | 12/1 | Rent | 462.50 | | | 191.36 |

**C**

FIRST NATIONAL BANK OF CHICAGO

Bernadette C. Dabney
12 Vico Lane
Haddonfield, NJ 08033

123-456-7
Account Number
1 Dec. 2002
Statement Date

Summary of Accounts

| Account Number | Previous Balance | Total Credits | Total Debits | Total Charges | Current Balance |
|---|---|---|---|---|---|
| 123-456-7 | 827.91 | 504.61 | 674.66 | 3.00 | 660.86 |

Previous Balance 827.91 Current Balance 660.86

| Debits | Credits | Balance |
|---|---|---|
| Nov. 4 132 73.16 | | 754.75 |
| 8 133 462.50 | | 292.25 |
| 15 134 83.00 | | 209.25 |
| 135 50.00 | | 159.25 |
| | Nov. 22 4.00 | 163.25 |
| | 23 500.61 | 663.86 |
| SC 3.00 | | 660.86 |



### Meeting Special Needs

**Auditory Disability** One type of learning disorder results from inefficient auditory processing. Students with this disability may look as if they are not paying attention when, in reality, they are "lost" in the confusion of language. To help students with this type of disability listen effectively, cue them with a subtle but consistent gesture—a raised hand, for example—when you are coming to an important point.

Refer to *Inclusion for the Social Studies Classroom Strategies and Activities* for students with different learning styles.

$2, $5, $10, $20, $50, and $100. (Larger notes used to be printed, but the practice was stopped to make it harder for criminals to hide large amounts of cash.)

The Treasury Department has also issued United States notes in $100 denominations only. These bills have the words *United States Note* printed across the top and can be distinguished from Federal Reserve notes by a red Treasury seal. United States notes make up less than 1 percent of the paper money in circulation. Both Federal Reserve notes and United States notes are fiat money, or legal tender.

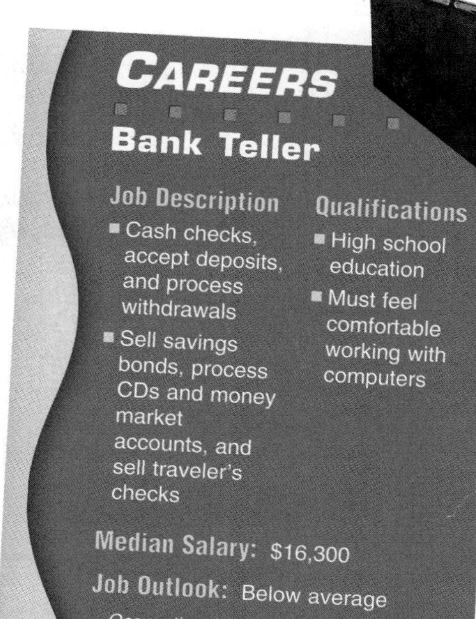


**Checks** A **checking account** is money deposited in a bank that a person can withdraw at any time by writing a check. The bank must pay the amount of the check on demand, or when it is presented for payment. Such accounts used to be called *demand deposits.* Today we call these **checkable deposits,** and a variety of financial institutions offer them.

Commercial banks used to be the only financial institutions that could offer checkable deposits. Today all **thrift institutions**—mutual savings banks, savings and loan associations (S&Ls), and credit unions—offer checkable deposits. In addition, certain brokerage houses offer the equivalent of checking accounts. Merrill Lynch and Fidelity Investments are two examples.

The largest part of the money supply in the United States consists of checkable accounts. **Figure 14.5** shows how to write a check and balance a checkbook.

**Credit Cards and Debit Cards** Even though many people use their credit cards to purchase goods and services, the credit card itself is not money. It acts neither as a unit of accounting nor as a store of value. The use of your credit card is really a loan to you by the issuer of the card, whether it is a bank, retail store, gas company, or American Express. Basically, then, credit card "money" represents a future claim on funds that you will have later. Credit cards defer rather than complete transactions that ultimately involve the use of money.

A **debit card** automatically withdraws money from a checkable account. When you use your debit card to purchase something, you are in effect giving an instruction to your bank to

**checking account:** *account in which deposited money can be withdrawn at any time by writing a check*

**checkable deposits:** *money deposited in a bank that can be withdrawn at any time by presenting a check*

**thrift institutions:** *mutual savings banks, S&Ls, and credit unions that offer many of the same services as commercial banks*

**debit card:** *device used to make cashless purchases; money is electronically withdrawn from the consumer's checkable account and transferred directly to the store's bank account*

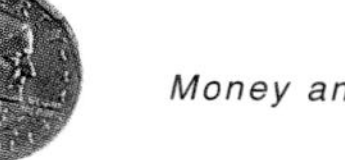



## Cooperative Learning

Organize students into small groups, and have groups investigate how United States money—both coin and paper—is made. Direct groups to discover such information as where money is made, what materials are used, what measures are taken to prevent counterfeiting, and what happens to worn-out currency. Have groups present their findings in illustrated reports. ELL BLOCK SCHEDULING



## Global Economy

**"Dollarizing" South America**

Many South American countries have proposed adopting the dollar as their basic currency. A good deal of business is conducted with dollars. And in some of the larger South American cities, dollars are available at ATMs.

**Guided Reading Activity 14-3**

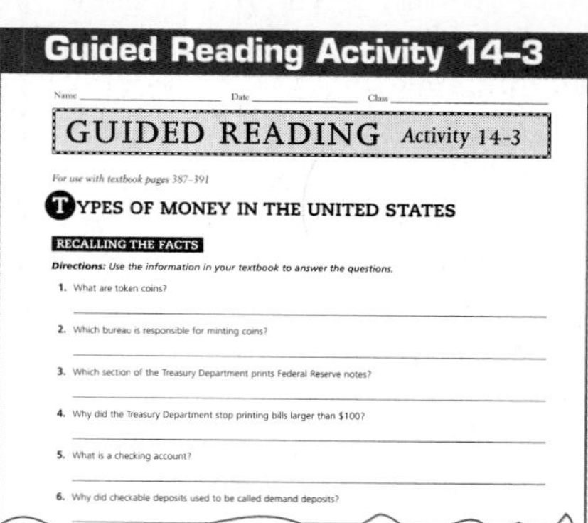
GUIDED READING Activity 14-3

For use with textbook pages 387–391

TYPES OF MONEY IN THE UNITED STATES

RECALLING THE FACTS

*Directions: Use the information in your textbook to answer the questions.*

1. What are token coins?
2. Which bureau is responsible for minting coins?
3. Which section of the Treasury Department prints Federal Reserve notes?
4. Why did the Treasury Department stop printing bills larger than $100?
5. What is a checking account?
6. Why did checkable deposits used to be called demand deposits?

## Independent Practice

**L2 Constructing Graphs** Have students construct a circle graph using the following information:

M1 in 1996
Total = $1,081 billion
Currency = $395 billion
Travelers' checks = $9 billion
Demand deposits = $403 billion
Other checkable deposits = $275 billion.

Then have students use library resources to find the most recent figures on M1. Call on volunteers to discuss how the size and composition of M1 have changed since 1996. BLOCK SCHEDULING

### Visual Instruction FIGURE 14.6

Refer students to **Figure 14.6.** ASK: How have M1 and M2 changed over the 10 years shown in the graph? *Both have increased steadily, with M2 increasing at a slightly faster rate.*

**L3 Writing Newspaper Articles** Have students use library resources and the Internet to find economists' views on whether credit cards should be considered money. Then have them present their findings on this debate in the form of an article for the business section of a newspaper.

# 3 Assess

## Meeting Lesson Objectives

Assign Section 3 Assessment as homework or an in-class activity.

Use **Interactive Tutor Self-Assessment Software** to review Section 3.

**FIGURE 14.6** **M1 and M2** With the deregulation of banking services in the early 1980s, the definition of the money supply was enlarged to include the new types of accounts.

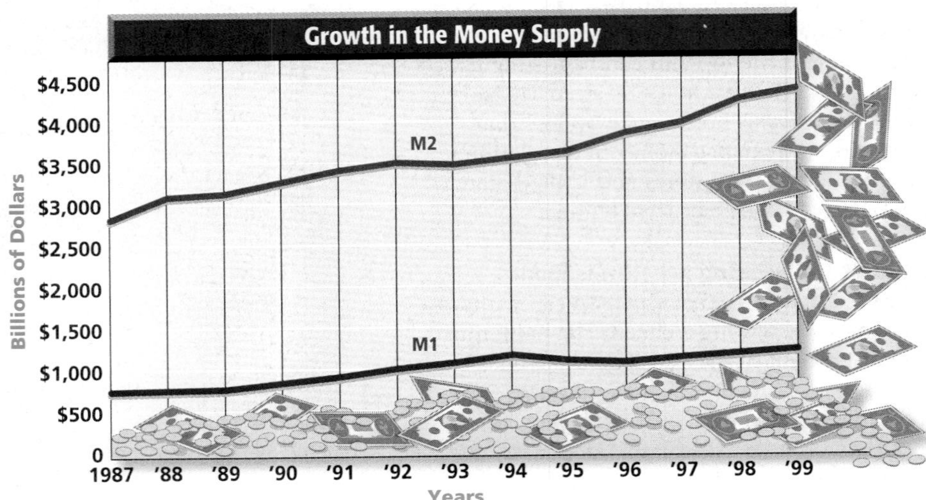


**Source:** Board of Governors of the Federal Reserve System

For an online update of this graph, visit ett.glencoe.com and click on ***Textbook Updates—Chapter 14.***

transfer money directly from your bank account to the store's bank account. The use of a debit card does not create a loan. Debit card "money" is similar to checkable account money.

**near moneys:** *assets, such as savings accounts, that can be turned into money relatively easily and without the risk of loss of value*

**Near Moneys** Numerous other assets are almost, but not exactly, like money. These assets are called **near moneys.** Their values are stated in terms of money, and they have high liquidity in comparison to other investments, such as stocks. Near moneys can be turned into currency or into a means of payment, such as a check, relatively easily and without the risk of loss of value. For example, if you have a bank savings account, you cannot write a check on it. You can, however, go to the bank and withdraw some or all of your funds. You can then redeposit these funds in your checking account or spend it all as cash.



### Visual Learning Activity

**Graphic Organizer** Have students draw two web diagrams similar to the one here. The first web should have three outer ovals, while the second should have two outer ovals. Ask students to write "Money" in the central oval of the first web. They should enter examples of money in the outer ovals. For the second web, have students enter "Near Moneys" in the central oval and examples of near moneys in the outer ovals.

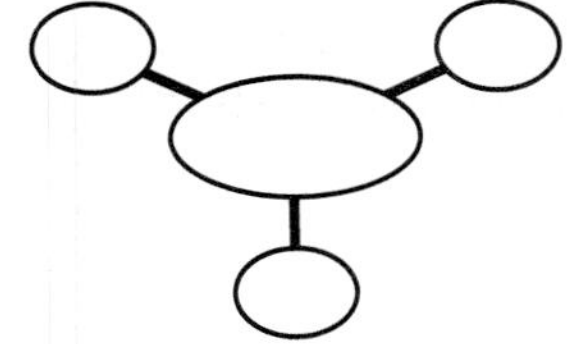

Time deposits and savings account balances are near moneys. Both pay interest, and neither can be withdrawn by check. Time deposits require that a depositor notify the financial institution within a certain period of time, often 10 days, before withdrawing money. Savings accounts do not usually require such notification.

## The Money Supply

How much money is there in the United States today? That question is not so easy to answer. First, the definition of *money supply* must be agreed upon. Currently, two basic definitions are used, although others exist. The first is called M1, and the second M2.

**M1** includes all currency (bills and coins), all checkable deposits, and traveler's checks. **M2** includes everything in M1 plus savings deposits, time deposits, small-denomination certificates of deposit, money market deposit accounts, money market mutual fund balances, and other more specialized account balances. **Figure 14.6** shows the growth of M1 and M2 from 1987 to 1999.

**M1:** *narrowest definition of the money supply; consists of moneys that can be spent immediately and against which checks can be written*

**M2:** *broader definition of the money supply; includes all of M1, plus such near moneys as money market mutual fund balances, certificates of deposit, and Eurodollars*

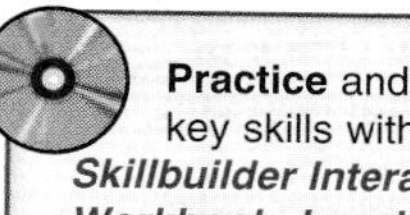

**Practice** and **assess** key skills with ***Skillbuilder Interactive Workbook, Level 2.***

## SECTION 3 Assessment

### Understanding Key Terms

1. **Define** checking account, checkable deposits, thrift institutions, debit card, near moneys, M1, M2.

### Reviewing Objectives

2. **Graphic Organizer** Create a chart like the one below to explain the difference between money and near moneys.

| Money | Near Moneys | Differences |
|---|---|---|
| | | |

3. What does the M2 definition of money include?

### Applying Economic Concepts

4. **Exchange, Money, and Interdependence** What various forms or types of money and near moneys do you use?

### Critical Thinking Activity

5. **Summarizing Information** Use a search engine to find the Bureau of Engraving and Printing Web site. Find out how currency is printed and what security measures are taken to avoid counterfeiting. What steps would you suggest to minimize counterfeiting?



## SECTION 3 Assessment Answers

1. All definitions can be found in the Glossary.
2. Money: currency, checkable deposits at banks and savings institutions, debit cards; Near Moneys: time deposits, savings account balances; Differences: Money is legal tender or checks or debit card transactions that must be paid by banks on demand. Near moneys can be turned into currency or a means of payment—such as a check—relatively easily.
3. M2 includes all of M1 (currency, travelers' checks, and checkable deposits) plus savings deposits, time deposits, small-denomination certificates of deposit, money market deposit accounts, money market mutual fund balances, and other more specialized accounts.
4. Answers will vary.
5. Encourage students to present their findings in an illustrated report.



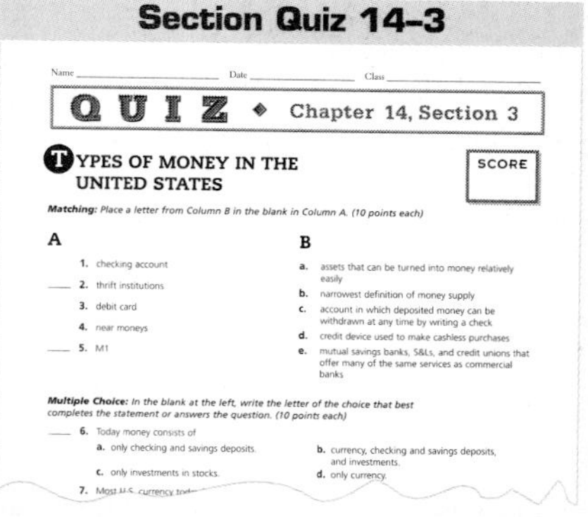
**Section Quiz 14-3**

Name ______ Date ______ Class ______

QUIZ ◆ Chapter 14, Section 3

TYPES OF MONEY IN THE UNITED STATES

SCORE

*Matching: Place a letter from Column B in the blank in Column A. (10 points each)*

| A | B |
|---|---|
| ___ 1. checking account | a. assets that can be turned into money relatively easily |
| ___ 2. thrift institutions | b. narrowest definition of money supply |
| ___ 3. debit card | c. account in which deposited money can be withdrawn at any time by writing a check |
| ___ 4. near moneys | d. credit device used to make cashless purchases |
| ___ 5. M1 | e. mutual savings banks, S&Ls, and credit unions that offer many of the same services as commercial banks |

*Multiple Choice: In the blank at the left, write the letter of the choice that best completes the statement or answers the question. (10 points each)*

___ 6. Today money consists of
a. only checking and savings deposits.
b. currency, checking and savings deposits, and investments.
c. only investments in stocks.
d. only currency.

7. Most U.S. currency tod

## Reteach

Have students use the **Terms to Know** to write two paragraphs—one explaining the difference between money and near moneys, the other describing two measures of money.

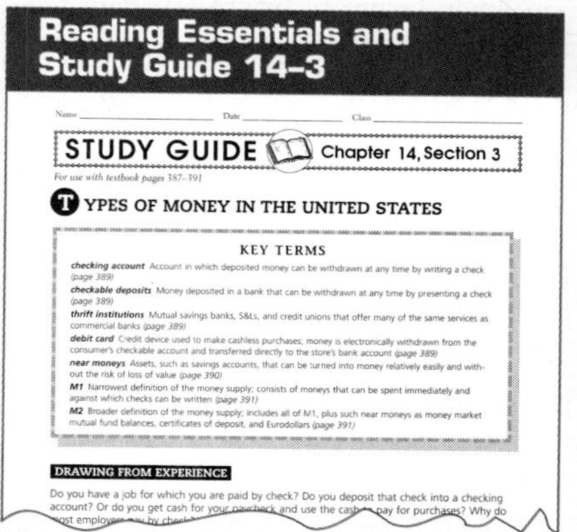
**Reading Essentials and Study Guide 14-3**

Name ______ Date ______ Class ______

STUDY GUIDE Chapter 14, Section 3

*For use with textbook pages 387–391*

TYPES OF MONEY IN THE UNITED STATES

KEY TERMS

***checking account*** Account in which deposited money can be withdrawn at any time by writing a check *(page 389)*

***checkable deposits*** Money deposited in a bank that can be withdrawn at any time by presenting a check *(page 389)*

***thrift institutions*** Mutual savings banks, S&Ls, and credit unions that offer many of the same services as commercial banks *(page 389)*

***debit card*** Credit device used to make cashless purchases; money is electronically withdrawn from the consumer's checkable account and transferred directly to the store's bank account *(page 389)*

***near moneys*** Assets, such as savings accounts, that can be turned into money relatively easily and without the risk of loss of value *(page 390)*

***M1*** Narrowest definition of the money supply; consists of moneys that can be spent immediately and against which checks can be written *(page 391)*

***M2*** Broader definition of the money supply; includes all of M1, plus such near moneys as money market mutual fund balances, certificates of deposit, and Eurodollars *(page 391)*

DRAWING FROM EXPERIENCE

Do you have a job for which you are paid by check? Do you deposit that check into a checking account? Or do you get cash for your paycheck and use the cash to pay for purchases? Why do most employers pay by check

## 4 Close

Have students work in small groups to create posters illustrating the components of American money.

## Background

When introducing this feature, you might mention that Aida Alvarez is the first Hispanic woman, and the first person of Puerto Rican heritage, to hold a cabinet position.

# Teach

Call on volunteers to read Aida Alvarez's three statements. After the first statement, ask students to restate Alvarez's definition in their own words. After the second statement, point out that one area that Alvarez feels the SBA should be fully involved in is microlending–making loans of $1,000 or less. Have students discuss how this might help small businesses. Finally, after the third statement, underscore the importance of small businesses by pointing out that they employ the majority of American workers.

# People & Perspectives

## Aida Alvarez

*GOVERNMENT OFFICIAL (1950–)*

- **Administrator of the United States Small Business Administration (SBA)**
- **Served as director of the Office of Federal Housing Enterprise Oversight (OFHEO), which regulates the operations of the nation's two largest housing finance companies (1993–97)**
- **Worked as an investment banker and a journalist**

In 1997 President Bill Clinton appointed Aida Alvarez to the office of Administrator of the Small Business Administration (SBA). The SBA oversees the development and delivery of a series of financial and business programs designed to aid small businesses. Alvarez has a very broad view of what constitutes a "small business":

*"[The] SBA deals with a whole range of business. There are a number of different size standards to determine whether a business is small or not.*

*One way to look at it is that if a business has 500 or fewer employees it is a small business. We add onto this [number] businesses that can't tap into the lines of credit that they need to grow, even if they are dominant in their field. Those businesses are candidates for the SBA."*

Alvarez feels that the SBA can play a much greater role in the economy:

*". . . I think there is opportunity to turn the SBA into a leading-edge financial agency. As women's businesses continue to grow, I would like to do whatever I can to support them. There also are other communities not being serviced. Minority communities, rural communities, Alaskan native communities."*

Alvarez considers the work of the SBA essential because of the contribution of small businesses to American life:

*". . . [S]mall businesses are the building blocks of sustainable communities. Small businesses create good jobs. Jobs bring security and hope. Hope enables people to invest for the future–to buy homes, establish neighborhoods, educate children, settle down, and rise up."*

### *Checking for Understanding*

1. **According to Alvarez, what is a small business?**
2. **Why does Alvarez consider the work of the SBA essential?**

392

### Answers to *Checking for Understanding*

1. not only businesses with 500 employees or less, but also those businesses that cannot tap into the lines of credit that they need to grow
2. Because of the contribution small businesses make to American life–according to Alvarez–they are the building blocks of sustainable communities, and they create good jobs.

# CHAPTER 14 Summary

**Chapter Overview** Visit the *Economics Today and Tomorrow* Web site at ett.glencoe.com and click on ***Chapter 14—Chapter Overviews*** to review chapter information.

## SECTION 1 The Functions and Characteristics of Money

- **Money** has three functions. It can be used as a **medium of exchange,** a **unit of accounting,** and a **store of value.**
- Anything serving as money must be durable, portable, divisible, stable in value, scarce, and accepted as a medium of exchange in payment for debts.
- Money that has an alternative use as a commodity—cattle, gems, and tobacco, for example—is considered **commodity money.**
- Money that is backed by—or can be exchanged for—gold or silver is known as **representative money.**
- Today all United States money is **fiat money,** or **legal tender.**

## SECTION 2 History of American Money and Banking

- Throughout American history, people have used commodity money, European coins, privately printed banknotes, and many other forms of notes.
- To control the amount of money in circulation, Congress established the Federal Reserve System in 1913. It serves as the nation's central bank. In 1914 the system began issuing paper money called Federal Reserve notes, which soon became the major form of currency.
- The Constitution of the United States gave Congress the power to mint coins. It was not until the Civil War that the government set up a safe, uniform currency.
- In 1934 the nation switched from a gold standard to a fiat money standard.
- **Electronic funds transfer** has revolutionized the banking industry, with customers using **automated teller machines** and even the Internet to do their banking.

## SECTION 3 Types of Money in the United States

- Money today consists of more than just currency. It also includes deposits in **checking accounts** as well as **debit cards** and **near moneys.**
- Economists measure the amount of money in the economy by adding up **M1**—currency, all **checkable deposits,** and traveler's checks. Then they calculate **M2**—all the items in M1 plus savings deposits, time deposits, small-denomination certificates of deposit, and other account balances.



## Economics Journal

**Money and Banking** Have students monitor the currency that comes into their possession during a one-week period. Ask them to keep track of the features that appear on the front and back of each bill or coin, noting the differences among the various denominations of bills and coins. Suggest that students collate their information in a chart with the following column headings: "Unit of Currency," "Front Characteristics," "Back Characteristics." Encourage students to share and compare their charts.

CHAPTER 14 Summary

ECONOMICS & YOU

Money and Banking

Chapter 18
Disc 1, Side 2

If you do not have access to a videodisc player, the ***Economics & You*** programs are also available in VHS.

Use the **Chapter 14 Summary** to preview, review, condense, or reteach the chapter.

## Preview/Review

**Vocabulary PuzzleMaker Software** reinforces the key terms used in Chapter 14.

**Interactive Tutor Self-Assessment Software** allows students to review Chapter 14 content.

## Condense

Have students listen to the Chapter 14 **Audio Program** (also available in Spanish) in the TCR. Assign the Chapter 14 Audio Program Activity and give students the Chapter 14 Audio Program Test.

## Reteach

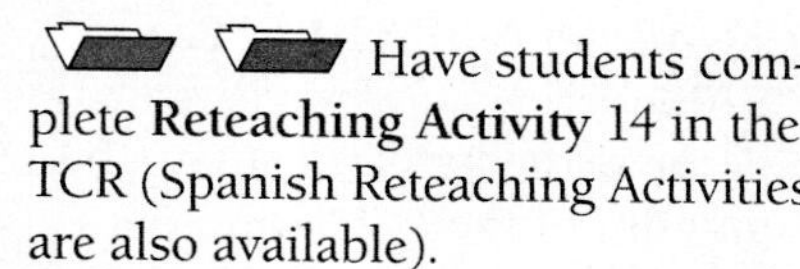

Have students complete **Reteaching Activity** 14 in the TCR (Spanish Reteaching Activities are also available).

## CHAPTER 14
### Assessment and Activities

Have students visit the *Economics Today and Tomorrow* Web site at ett.glencoe.com to review Chapter 14 and take the Self-Check Quiz.

**GLENCOE TECHNOLOGY**

**MindJogger Videoquiz**

Use MindJogger to review Chapter 14 content.

### Identifying Key Terms

1. d
2. c
3. b
4. g
5. f
6. a
7. e

### Recalling Facts and Ideas

1. barter
2. Money also should be portable, stable in value, scarce, and acceptable.
3. fiat
4. bartering
5. in the 1930s at the beginning of the Great Depression
6. automated teller machines (ATMs)
7. \$1, \$2, \$5, \$10, \$20, \$50, and \$100
8. because the bank must pay the amount of the check on demand, or when it is presented for payment
9. Near moneys are almost, but not exactly, like money. Their values are stated in money terms, and they can be turned into currency or a means of payment, such as a check, fairly easily and without loss of value.
10. because, unlike M2, it does not include near moneys

# CHAPTER 14
# Assessment and Activities

**Self-Check Quiz** Visit the *Economics Today and Tomorrow* Web site at ett.glencoe.com and click on ***Chapter 14—Self-Check Quizzes*** to prepare for the Chapter Test.

## Identifying Key Terms

*Write the letter of the definition in Column B that correctly defines each term in Column A.*

**Column A**

1. fiat money
2. checkable deposits
3. M1
4. commodity money
5. near moneys
6. legal tender
7. electronic funds transfer

**Column B**

a. money that by law must be accepted for payment of debts
b. currency in circulation, traveler's checks, plus checking-type deposits
c. money in a bank that can be withdrawn at any time
d. money that has value because the government has established it as acceptable payment for debts
e. computerized banking functions that previously were handled on paper
f. assets that can be turned into money fairly easily
g. money that has value aside from its value as money

## Recalling Facts and Ideas

**Section 1**

1. What is the alternative to using money?
2. Money should be durable and divisible. What other characteristics should money have?
3. Is the type of money used in the United States commodity money, representative money, or fiat money?

**Section 2**

4. What type of system did the early colonists use when they bought and sold goods and services?
5. When was the most serious banking panic of the twentieth century?
6. Electronic banking is increasingly common today. What form of this system do most consumers use?

**Section 3**

7. What are the only denominations of paper currency being issued today by the federal government?
8. Why were checking accounts formerly called demand deposits?
9. What is the distinction between money and near moneys?
10. Why is M1 considered a narrower definition of the money supply than M2?



### Thinking Critically

1. Barter: Costs—requires a double coincidence of wants; that is, each party to the transaction must want exactly what the other person is offering. This takes a great deal of time and effort. Barter goods may not maintain their value. Barter goods may not be portable. Benefits—if trade takes place, it saves the effort of exchanging one item for money and using the money to buy the other. Money: Costs—on occasions, may be a slower process of making transactions than barter. Benefits—money is a medium of exchange that is readily acceptable as payment for goods and services. Money provides a simple and convenient way to compare values of various items. Money retains its value. Money is portable.

## Thinking Critically

1. **Making Comparisons** Create a diagram like the one below to compare the costs and benefits of engaging in barter to the costs and benefits of using money.

| | Costs | Benefits |
|---|---|---|
| Barter | | |
| Money | | |

2. **Making Generalizations** Why are debit cards similar to money, whereas credit cards are not?

## Applying Economic Concepts

**The Functions of Money** The three functions of money are as a medium of exchange, a unit of accounting, and a store of value. Keep track of any time you use money, see money used, or see dollar values written out somewhere. Try to determine in each instance what function the money is serving. For example, if you see a headline that says "Microsoft Corporation Sales Increased to $10 Billion," you know that money is being used as a unit of accounting.

## Cooperative Learning Project

During the 1930s, the United States underwent a tragic economic depression. Work in groups to research the following aspects of daily life.

- What happened to incomes and prices?
- What happened to savings accounts?
- What happened to the availability of jobs?

Each member of each group should research one question. Summarize the group's notes to develop a lecture that describes what actually happened during the Great Depression.

## Reviewing Skills

**Synthesizing Information** Imagine that the country is returning to privately issued banknotes. Design the currency you would like to see in circulation.

Use information from the Bureau of Engraving and Printing's Web site to gather data about the exact measurements of existing currency. Then make a list of items, ideas, people, and so on that are important to you. Utilize your list to help create your currency. Share your design with the rest of the class.

## Technology Activity

**Using a Database** Analyze the currency in your possession. List the features that appear on the front and back of each bill or coin, noting the similarities and differences between the various currencies.

Create a database that could be accessed by foreign visitors to describe the specific features and purposes of each bill and coin. Create fields such as portrait, paper/coin, value, Federal Reserve Bank, watermarks, colors, etc.

## Analyzing the Global Economy

Analyze several foreign coins and paper currencies. Use a magnifying glass if necessary. Make a chart listing the following items noted on each currency: Country of Origin, Monetary Unit, Year of Origin, Watermarks, Identity of People Pictured, Symbols, Natural Features, Buildings or Animals Shown, Other. Compare the foreign currency to United States currency, and share your chart with the rest of the class.



2. Debit cards are considered money because they are similar to checkable account money. Credit cards, on the other hand, create a loan that must be paid at a later date.

# CHAPTER 14 Assessment and Activities

### Applying Economic Concepts

Answers will vary. Suggest that students present their answers in chart form.

### Cooperative Learning Project

Encourage students to find first-person accounts of the Great Depression. Quotations, or sound recordings of eyewitness accounts, will add authenticity to their lectures.

### Reviewing Skills

As students share their designs, ask them to explain why they selected certain design features–people or landmarks shown, size and placement of numbers, colors, and so on.

### Technology Activity

Point out to students that the Economics Journal activity for this chapter is a useful source of information for this activity.

### Analyzing the Global Economy

As students share their charts, have them discuss the major similarities and differences between the foreign currencies and United States currency.

### Chapter Bonus Test Question

ASK: When might barter work as well as or better than an exchange involving money? *Students might suggest the trading of items of similar value—such as compact discs—or when there is a double coincidence of wants—when both parties in the transaction want what the other is offering.*

# 1 Focus

Ask students if they would be willing to sell an item–a baseball cap or a CD, for example–for a few dollars. Although they might argue about the number of dollars, most students would be willing to make the sale. Then ask them if they would be willing to part with that item for shells, or a block of salt, or a string of beads. When students respond in the negative, point out that in the past, these three commodities–and many others–were readily accepted as money. Conclude by informing students that this feature provides a brief review of the major developments in the history of money.

# 2 Teach

Have students read through the information in the boxes. Then have them arrange the information in a chart, categorizing by continent or time period. Suggest that they refer to their charts as they answer the **Thinking Globally** questions.

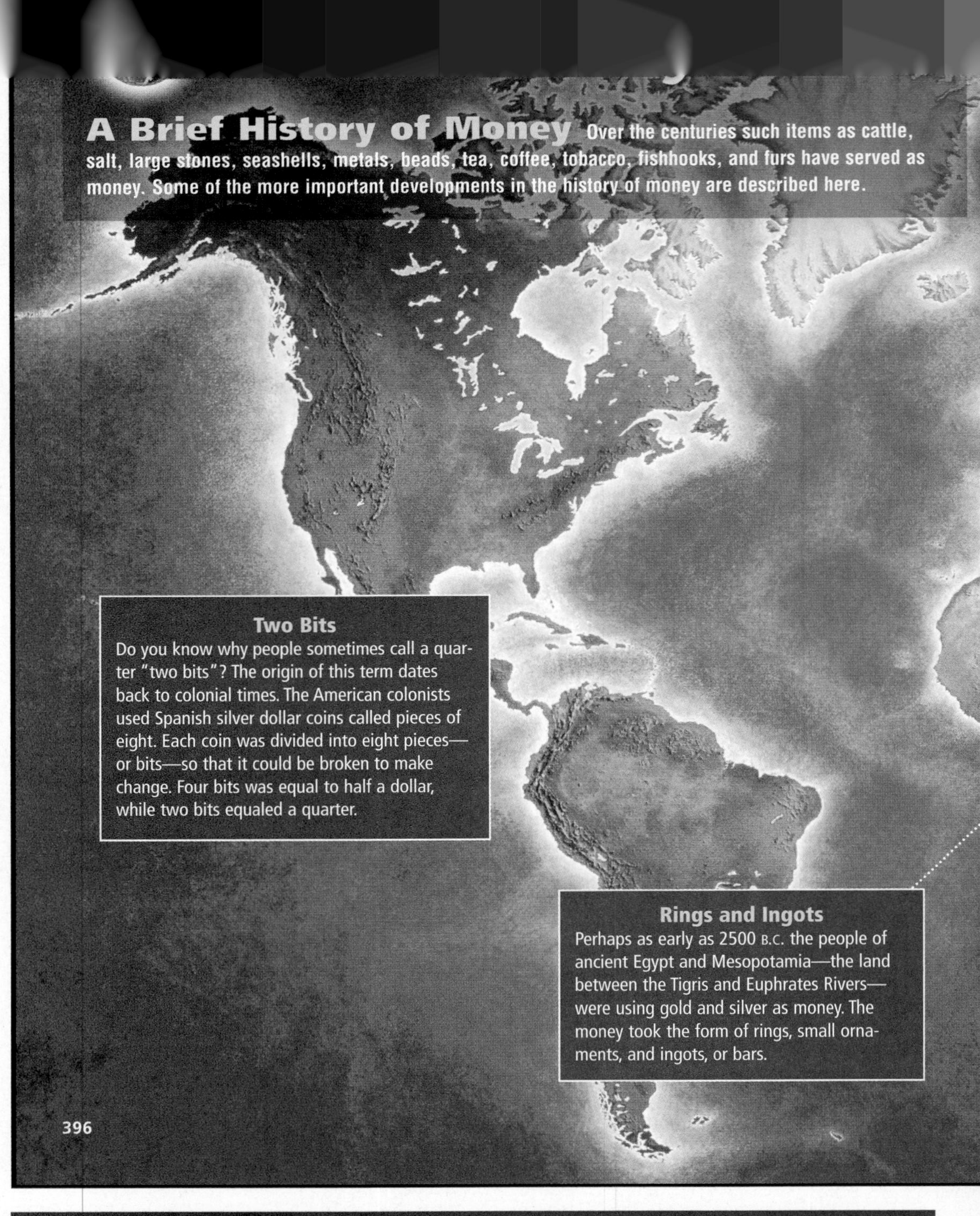

A Brief History of Money Over the centuries such items as cattle, salt, large stones, seashells, metals, beads, tea, coffee, tobacco, fishhooks, and furs have served as money. Some of the more important developments in the history of money are described here.
Two Bits
Do you know why people sometimes call a quarter "two bits"? The origin of this term dates back to colonial times. The American colonists used Spanish silver dollar coins called pieces of eight. Each coin was divided into eight pieces—or bits—so that it could be broken to make change. Four bits was equal to half a dollar, while two bits equaled a quarter.
Rings and Ingots
Perhaps as early as 2500 B.C. the people of ancient Egypt and Mesopotamia—the land between the Tigris and Euphrates Rivers—were using gold and silver as money. The money took the form of rings, small ornaments, and ingots, or bars.
396

## Extending the Content

**Commodity Money** Throughout history people have used commodities—everything from salt to dried fish to coconuts to cattle—as money. Several words with connections to money derive from the commodities once used as a medium of exchange. The English word *salary,* or a fixed income that is paid at regular intervals, comes from the Latin word *salarius,* which means "of salt." Another Latin word, *pecuniarius*—meaning "wealth in cattle"—is the basis for the English word *pecuniary,* which means "related to money."

The First Coins
The Lydians, who lived in what is now western Turkey, probably made the first coins during the 600s B.C. These coins were made of electrum, a mix of gold and silver, and were stamped with pictures of gods or emperors. The Greeks, Persians, and Romans adopted Lydian coining techniques and, in time, the use of coins spread throughout much of Western Europe.
The First Paper Banknotes
The Chinese may have begun to make coins around the same time as the Lydians. These coins were made of bronze and often had holes in them so that they could be carried on a string. The Chinese also began using paper banknotes—printed on paper made from mulberry bark—in the A.D. 800s.
FREEDOM AND JUSTICE · GHANA ·
Cowrie Shells
Cowrie shells have been used as money throughout Asia, Africa, and Oceania. The cowrie was still in use in some African countries as recently as the mid-1900s. The name for Ghana's monetary unit, the cedi, comes from the Ghanaian word meaning "cowrie shell."
Thinking Globally
1. Where did the use of coins develop?
2. What developments in the history of money took place in China?
3. How is the history of money in Africa reflected in the currency of Ghana?
397


# 3 Assess

Have students answer the **Thinking Globally** questions.

# 4 Close

To conclude, ask students to discuss why they think the various items once used as money fell out of favor and were replaced by coins and paper currency.

## ? Did You Know

Native Americans probably used wampum–strings of beads made from clamshells–as money long before the arrival of the Europeans. It was among the most popular mediums of exchange when early European settlers and Native Americans traded. ?

## Answers to *Thinking Globally*

1. The use of coins probably developed during the 600s B.C. in what is now western Turkey. Coins may have developed around the same time in China.
2. The Chinese may have begun to make coins around the same time as the Lydians. The Chinese began using paper banknotes in the A.D. 800s.
3. Cowrie shells have been used as money throughout Africa, and the name for Ghana's monetary unit, the cedi, means "cowrie."

# CHAPTER 15 Resource Manager

## Teaching Transparency

### Economic Concepts Transparency 18

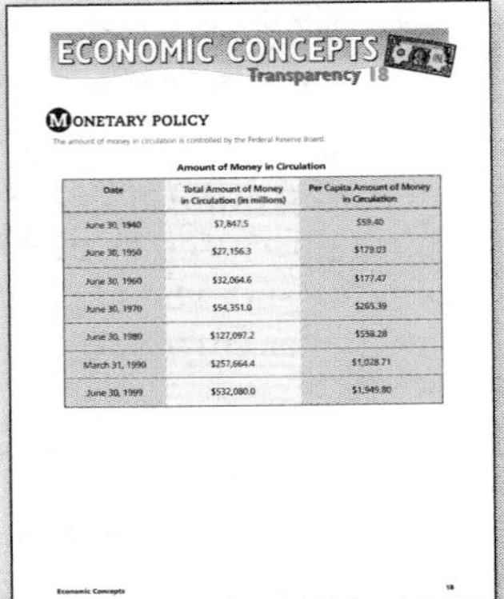

ECONOMIC CONCEPTS Transparency 18

MONETARY POLICY

Amount of Money in Circulation

| Date | Total Amount of Money in Circulation (in millions) | Per Capita Amount of Money in Circulation |
|---|---|---|
| June 30, 1940 | $7,847.5 | $59.40 |
| June 30, 1950 | $27,156.3 | $179.03 |
| June 30, 1960 | $32,064.6 | $177.47 |
| June 30, 1970 | $54,351.0 | $265.39 |
| June 30, 1980 | $127,097.2 | $556.28 |
| March 31, 1990 | $257,664.4 | $1,028.71 |
| June 30, 1999 | $532,080.0 | $1,949.80 |

## Application and Enrichment

### Enrichment Activity 15

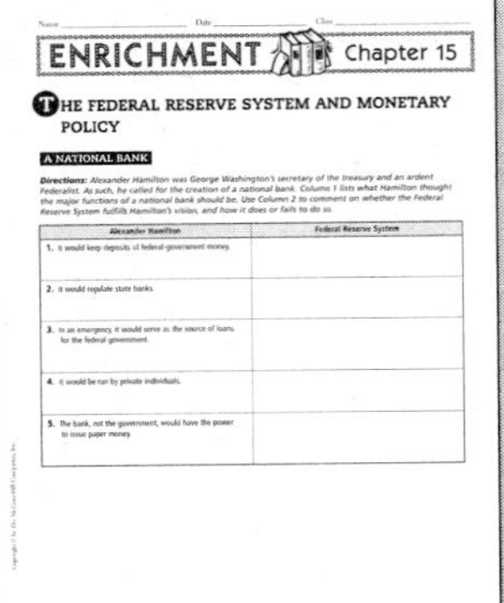

ENRICHMENT Chapter 15

THE FEDERAL RESERVE SYSTEM AND MONETARY POLICY

A NATIONAL BANK

### Consumer Applications Activity 20

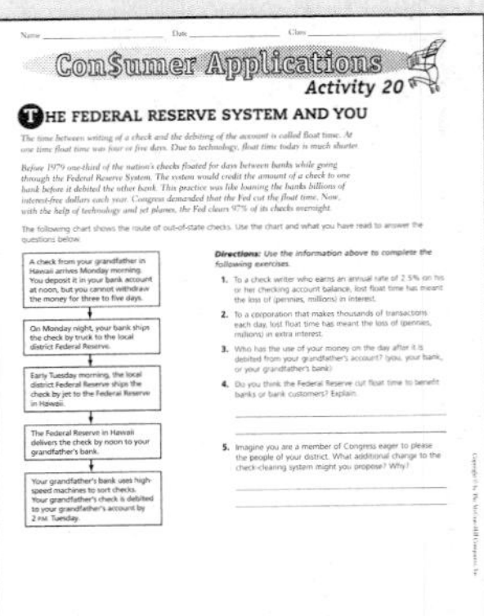

Con$umer Applications Activity 20

THE FEDERAL RESERVE SYSTEM AND YOU

### Free Enterprise Activity 20

FREE ENTERPRISE ACTIVITY 20

DECISION MAKING AT THE FEDERAL RESERVE BOARD

## Application and Enrichment

### Cooperative Learning Simulations and Problems 20

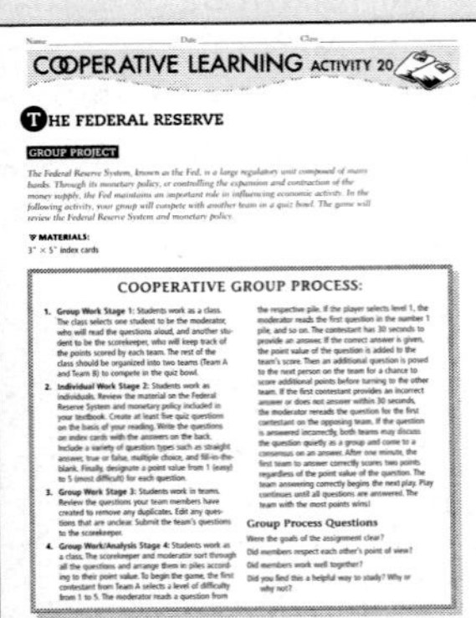

COOPERATIVE LEARNING ACTIVITY 20

THE FEDERAL RESERVE

COOPERATIVE GROUP PROCESS:

### Primary and Secondary Source Reading 20

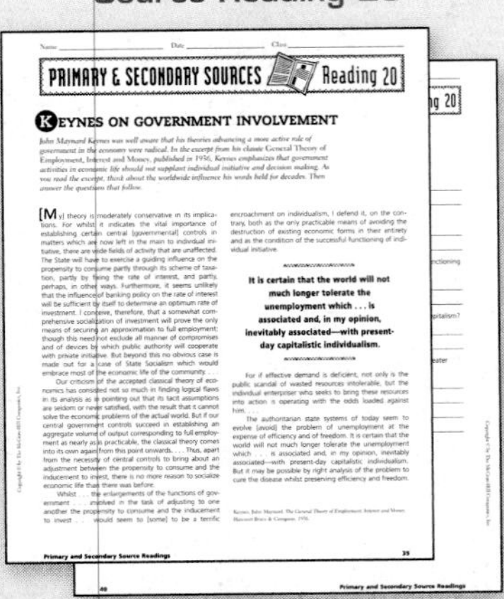

PRIMARY & SECONDARY SOURCES Reading 20

KEYNES ON GOVERNMENT INVOLVEMENT

### Math Practice for Economics Activity 20

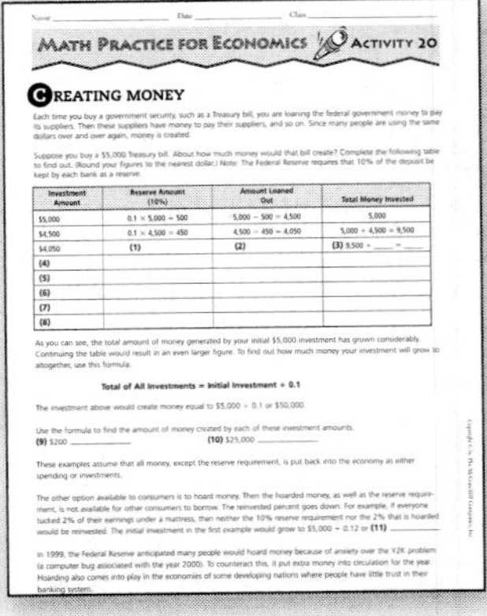

MATH PRACTICE FOR ECONOMICS ACTIVITY 20

CREATING MONEY

### Economic Cartoons Activity 20

ECONOMIC CARTOON 20

WHEN GREENSPAN SPEAKS...



## Review and Reinforcement

### Critical Thinking Activity 20

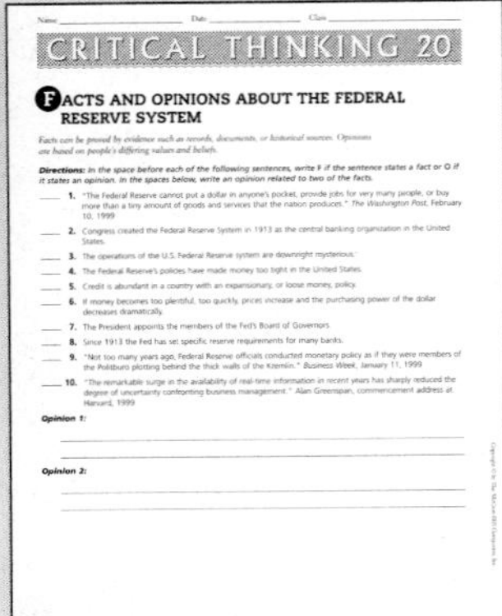

CRITICAL THINKING 20

FACTS AND OPINIONS ABOUT THE FEDERAL RESERVE SYSTEM

### Reteaching Activity 15

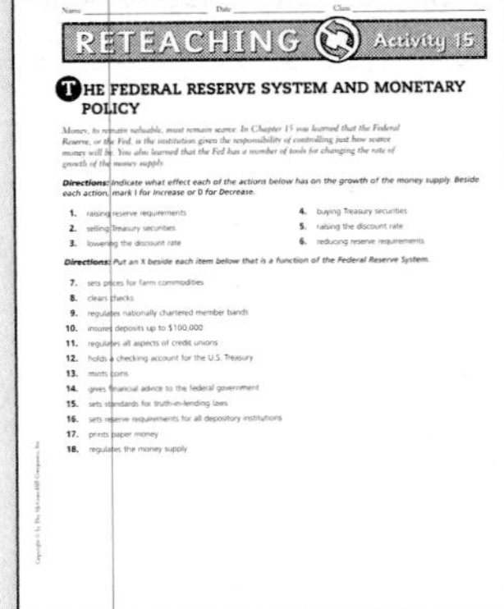

RETEACHING Activity 15

THE FEDERAL RESERVE SYSTEM AND MONETARY POLICY

### Economic Vocabulary Activity 15

Economic Vocabulary Activity

CHAPTER 15 THE FEDERAL RESERVE SYSTEM AND MONETARY POLICY

### Reinforcing Economic Skills 28

Reinforcing Economic Skills Chapter 28

OUTLINING

# CHAPTER 15 Resource Manager

## Assessment and Evaluation

Chapter 15 Test Form A

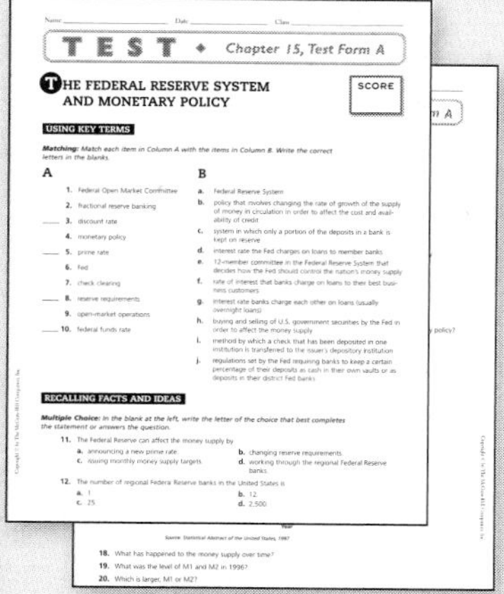
TEST ♦ Chapter 15, Test Form A

THE FEDERAL RESERVE SYSTEM AND MONETARY POLICY

SCORE

USING KEY TERMS

RECALLING FACTS AND IDEAS

Chapter 15 Test Form B

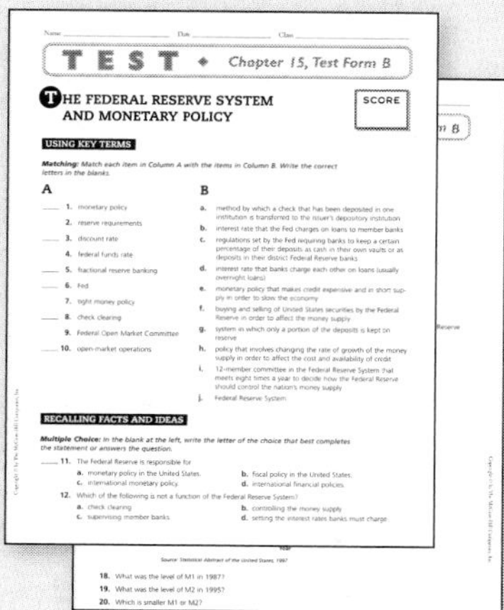
TEST ♦ Chapter 15, Test Form B

THE FEDERAL RESERVE SYSTEM AND MONETARY POLICY

SCORE

USING KEY TERMS

RECALLING FACTS AND IDEAS

Performance Assessment Activity 20

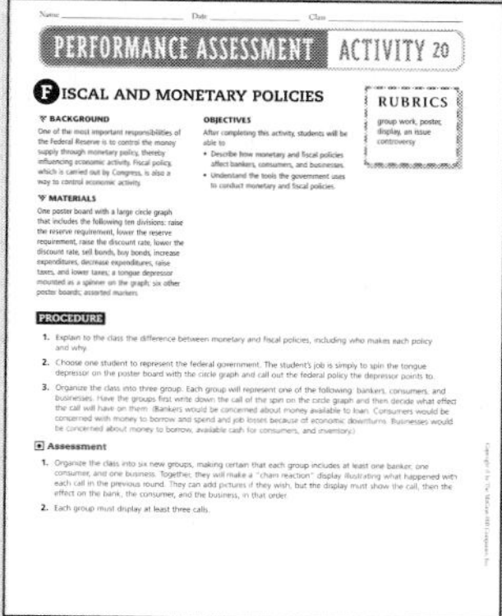
PERFORMANCE ASSESSMENT ACTIVITY 20

FISCAL AND MONETARY POLICIES

RUBRICS

PROCEDURE

ExamView® Pro Testmaker

## Technology and Multimedia

 Vocabulary PuzzleMaker Software

Interactive Tutor Self-Assessment Software

  ExamView® Pro Testmaker

 NBR *Economics & You* Video Program (English/Spanish)

 Presentation Plus!

 Glencoe Skillbuilder Interactive Workbook CD-ROM, Level 2

 Interactive Lesson Planner

 MindJogger Videoquiz

 Interactive Economics! CD-ROM

Audio Program (English or Spanish)

## ECONOMICS Online

You and your students can visit ett.glencoe.com—the Web site companion to **Economics Today and Tomorrow.** This innovative integration of electronic and print media offers your students a wealth of opportunities. The student text directs students to the Web site for the following options:

- **Chapter Overviews**
- **Student Web Activities**
- **Self-Check Quizzes**
- **Textbook Updates**

Answers are provided for you in the **Web Activity Lesson Plan.** Additional Web resources and Interactive Puzzles are also available.

Use the Glencoe Web site for additional resources. All essential content is covered in the Student Edition.

## Spanish Resources

 Spanish Economic Concepts Transparency 18

 Spanish Vocabulary Activity 15

 Spanish Reteaching Activity 15

 Spanish Section Quizzes for Chapter 15

 Spanish Chapter 15 Audio Program, Activity, and Test

## Additional Resources

### Reading for the Student

*A Day at the Fed*, rev. ed. Federal Reserve Bank of New York, 1998. Takes the reader through a typical day at the New York Fed.

### Reading for the Teacher

*Mercantilists and Classicals: Insights from Doctrinal History.* Federal Reserve Bank of Richmond, 1998. Traces the evolution of rival monetary doctrines.

# CHAPTER 15 Resource Manager

## Section Resources

| Reading Objectives | Reproducible Resources | Technology/Multimedia Resources |
|---|---|---|
| **Section 1**<br>**Organization and Functions of the Federal Reserve System**<br>• How is the Federal Reserve System in the United States organized?<br>• What are the functions of the Fed? | Reproducible Lesson Plan 15-1<br>Daily Lecture Notes 15-1<br>Guided Reading Activity 15-1<br>Reading Essentials and Study Guide 15-1<br>Daily Focus Activity 63<br>Section Quiz 15-1*<br>Reinforcing Economic Skills 28 | Daily Focus Transparency 63<br>Vocabulary PuzzleMaker<br>Interactive Tutor Self-Assessment Software<br>MindJogger Videoquiz<br>Interactive Economics!<br>Presentation Plus!<br>ExamView® Pro Testmaker |
| **Section 2**<br>**Money Supply and the Economy**<br>• What are the differences between loose money and tight money policies?<br>• What is the purpose of fractional reserve banking?<br>• How does the money supply expand? | Reproducible Lesson Plan 15-2<br>Daily Lecture Notes 15-2<br>Guided Reading Activity 15-2<br>Reading Essentials and Study Guide 15-2<br>Daily Focus Activity 64<br>Section Quiz 15-2* | Daily Focus Transparency 64<br>Vocabulary PuzzleMaker<br>Interactive Tutor Self-Assessment Software<br>MindJogger Videoquiz<br>NBR's *Economics & You**<br>Interactive Economics!<br>Presentation Plus!<br>ExamView® Pro Testmaker |
| **Section 3**<br>**Regulating the Money Supply**<br>• How can the Fed use reserve requirements to alter the money supply?<br>• How does the discount rate affect the money supply?<br>• How does the Fed use open-market operations?<br>• What are some of the difficulties of carrying out monetary policy? | Reproducible Lesson Plan 15-3<br>Daily Lecture Notes 15-3<br>Guided Reading Activity 15-3<br>Reading Essentials and Study Guide 15-3<br>Daily Focus Activity 62<br>Section Quiz 15-3* | Daily Focus Transparency 62<br>Economic Concepts Transparency 18<br>Vocabulary PuzzleMaker<br>Interactive Tutor Self-Assessment Software<br>MindJogger Videoquiz<br>NBR's *Economics & You**<br>Interactive Economics!<br>Presentation Plus!<br>ExamView® Pro Testmaker |

*Also available in Spanish

Blackline Master
Transparency

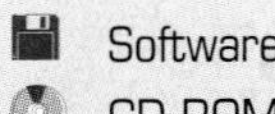
Software
CD-ROM

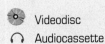

Videodisc
Audiocassette

Videocassette

# CHAPTER 15 Resource Manager

## ACTIVITY From the Classroom of

**Howard D. Merrick, Jr.**
**Pottsville Area High School**
**Pottsville, Pennsylvania**

### Smart Borrowing and Investing

As our society gets ever more complex, students need to better understand the importance of smart borrowing and smart investing. Organize students into groups and have groups visit, phone, or e-mail various banks in the school district. Students should collect information on the types of loans available and their rates. They should also ask about the types of savings or investment plans and their rates. After students have evaluated the differences between various borrowing and savings plans, have them calculate the changes that would occur if the Fed raised or lowered interest rates.

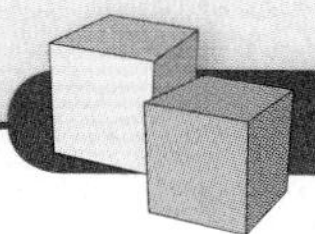

## Block Schedule

Activities that are particularly suited to use within the block scheduling framework are identified throughout this chapter by the following designation: BLOCK SCHEDULING

## Easy Planning and Preparation!

Use Glencoe's **Presentation Plus!**, a Microsoft PowerPoint® application, to teach **The Federal Reserve System and Monetary Policy.** With this multimedia teacher tool, you can customize ready-made presentations. At your fingertips are interactive transparencies, on-screen lecture notes, audiovisual presentations, and links to the Internet and to other Glencoe multimedia.

**Interactive Lesson Planner**

Planning has never been easier! Organize your week, month, semester, or year with all the lesson helps you need to make teaching creative, timely, and relevant—the way it is meant to be. The Interactive Lesson Planner opens Glencoe's **Chapter 15** resources, helps you build your schedule, and tracks your progress.

## Key to Ability Levels

**Teaching strategies have been coded for varying learning styles and abilities.**

L1 **BASIC** activities for all students

L2 **AVERAGE** activities for average to above-average students

L3 **CHALLENGING** activities for above-average students

ELL **ENGLISH LANGUAGE LEARNER** activities

## National Council on Economic Education

## THE EconomicsAmerica AND EconomicsInternational PROGRAMS

### Voluntary Standards Emphasized in Chapter 15

**Content Standard 11** Students will understand that money makes it easier to trade, borrow, save, invest, and compare the values of goods and services.

**Content Standard 20** Students will understand that federal government budgetary policy and the Federal Reserve System's monetary policy influence the overall levels of employment, output, and prices.

### Resources Available from NCEE

- *Capstone: The Nation's High School Economics Course*
- *Civics and Government: Focus on Economics*
- *United States History: Eyes on the Economy, Vol. 2*
- *Personal Finance Economics: Wallet Wisdom*
- *Focus: High School Economics*

To order these materials, or to contact your State Council on Economic Education about workshops and programs, call 1-800-338-1192 or visit the NCEE Web site at http://www.nationalcouncil.org

ECONOMICS & YOU

The Federal Reserve System and Monetary Policy

Chapter 22
Disc 1, Side 2

ASK: What analogy is made about the American economy and the Fed? *The American economy is likened to a car—and the Fed is the driver.*

Also available in VHS.

## Chapter Overview

Chapter 15 describes or explains the organization and functions of the Fed, how and why the supply of money in the United States is regulated, and the differences between tight money policies and loose money policies.

### GLENCOE TECHNOLOGY

Use **MindJogger Videoquiz** VHS to preview Chapter 15 content.

Introduce students to chapter content and key terms by having them access **Chapter 15—Chapter Overviews** at ett.glencoe.com

# CHAPTER 15

# The Federal Reserve System and Monetary Policy

### Why It's Important

*Who determines how much money exists in the United States? This chapter will explain who's in charge of the money supply and how they decide what amount to put into circulation.*

*To learn more about the money supply, view the* **Economics & You** *Chapter 22 video lesson:* **The Federal Reserve System and Monetary Policy**

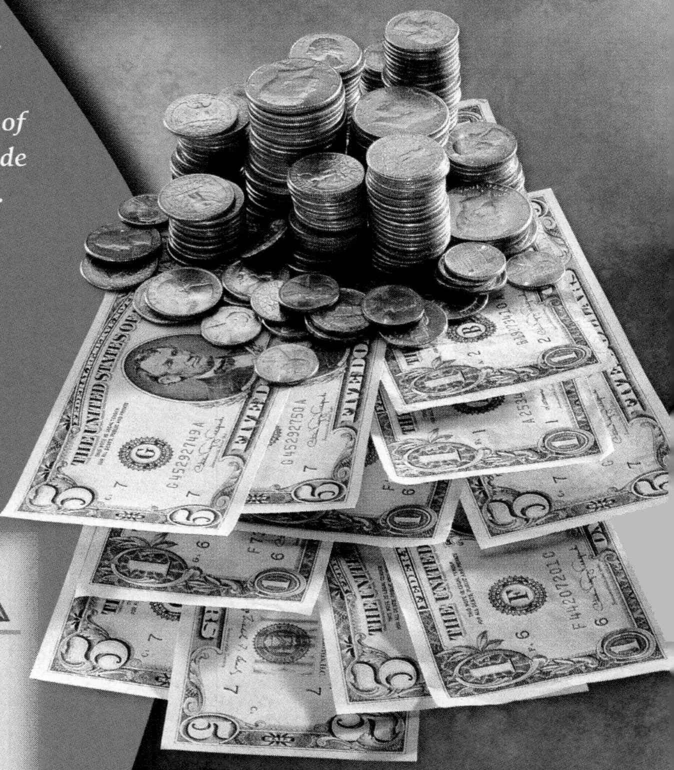

**ECONOMICS Online**

**Chapter Overview** Visit the *Economics Today and Tomorrow* Web site at ett.glencoe.com and click on ***Chapter 15—Chapter Overviews*** to preview chapter information.

## CHAPTER LAUNCH ACTIVITY

Organize the class into small groups, and have groups research local banks' current mortgage rates and mortgage rates five years ago. Have groups note by how much the rates have changed and speculate on why this change occurred. Encourage groups to share their findings with the class. Conclude by informing students that in this chapter they will learn about the institution that influences all interest rates in the economy—the Federal Reserve System.

SECTION 2

# Money Supply and the Economy

## Cover Story

*Business Credit*, July–August 1995

To many people, the operations of the U.S. Federal Reserve System are more than confusing, they can be downright mysterious. Sure, our politicians and newscasters can often be heard referring to "the Fed," but how many of us really understand this complex part of the American government and economy?

### Reader's Guide

**Terms to Know**

- loose money policy
- tight money policy
- fractional reserve banking
- reserve requirements

**Reading Objectives**

1. What are the differences between loose money and tight money policies?
2. What is the purpose of fractional reserve banking?
3. How does the money supply expand?

As you learned in Section 1, the jobs of the Fed today range from processing checks to serving as the government's banker. As you read this section, you'll learn that the Fed's most important function, however, involves control over the rate of growth of the money supply.

## Loose and Tight Money Policies

You may have read a news report in which a business executive complained that money is "too tight." You may have run across a story about an economist warning that money is "too



## Section 2 Resource Manager

**Reproducible Masters**

- Reproducible Lesson Plan 15–2
- Reading Essentials and Study Guide 15–2
- Guided Reading Activity 15–2
- Section Quiz 15–2
- Daily Focus Activity 64
- Daily Lecture Notes 15–2

**Multimedia**

- Daily Focus Transparency 64
- Vocabulary PuzzleMaker
- Interactive Tutor Self-Assessment Software
- ExamView® Pro Testmaker
- MindJogger Videoquiz
- NBR's *Economics & You*
- Interactive Economics!
- Presentation Plus!



# 1 Focus

## Overview

**Section 2** explains the difference between loose money policies and tight money policies, and how fractional reserve banking is used to increase the money supply.

### Bellringer

**Motivational Activity**

Project **Daily Focus Transparency 64** and have students answer the questions.

This activity is also available as a blackline master.

**Daily Focus Transparency 64**

FOCUS ACTIVITIES
Transparency 64

MONETARY POLICY

| Monetary Policy | |
|---|---|
| *WHAT* It Is | The expansion and/or contraction of the money supply in order to influence the cost and availability of credit. This is accomplished by: • The Reserve Requirement • Open Market Operations • Changing the Discount Rate • Margin Requirements • Moral Suasion • Selective Credit Controls |
| *WHY* It Exists | • to keep the economy functioning as efficiently as possible; to help acheive national economic goals |
| *WHO* Makes It | • the Federal Reserve |
| *HOW* It Affects the Economy | • *tight money policy*: interest rates increase; consumers and businesses borrow and spend less, which slows economic growth • *loose money policy*: interest rates decrease; consumers and businesses borrow and spend more, which accelerates economic growth |
| *WHEN* It Is Changed | • when the Fed determines that slowing or accelerating the economy is necessary for overall economic health, or to avoid specific economic problems such as recessions and excess inflation |

1. What is monetary policy?
2. Who determines monetary policy?

Daily Focus Transparencies

### Reader's Guide

Answers to the **Reading Objectives** questions are on page 410.

**Preteaching Vocabulary**

Have students locate and read the definitions of the **Terms to Know** in the Glossary. Then have students use each term correctly in a sentence.

Vocabulary PuzzleMaker

# 2 Teach

## Guided Practice

**L1 Understanding Ideas** Draw a three-column chart with "Deposit," "Required Reserves," and "Excess Reserves" as column headings. Enter $100 in the Deposit column, and tell students that the reserve requirement is 20 percent. Have students enter the loans that can be made until the initial $100 deposit is depleted.

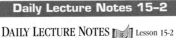

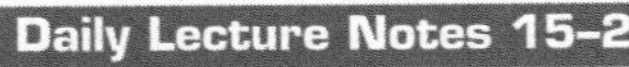

**Daily Lecture Notes 15-2**

DAILY LECTURE NOTES Lesson 15-2

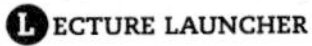

**LECTURE LAUNCHER**

In 1979 inflation had risen to almost 13%. Under the leadership of Paul A. Volcker, the Fed implemented tight monetary policies. This led to the most severe recession the U.S. had experienced since the Great Depression, but Volcker had brought inflation under control. What are tight monetary policies and how do they work to control inflation? How does the Fed go about expanding the money supply?

PAGES 407–408

I. Loose and Tight Money Policies
   A. Monetary policy involves changing the growth rate of the money supply in order to change the cost and availability of credit.
   B. Loose money means credit is plentiful and inexpensive; used to encourage economic growth.
   C. Tight money means credit is in short supply and expensive; used to control inflation.
   D. The goal of monetary policy is to strike a balance between tight and loose money.

**Discussion Question**

**Why is striking a balance between loose and tight money important?** *(It is important to have a balance because too much money (loose) causes inflation and not enough (tight) leads to a shrinking economy. The right balance of the two leads to a prosperous economy with low inflation.)*

**Visual Instruction FIGURE 15.5**

**Answer:** *tight money policy; because this policy causes business activity to slow*

**ECONOMICS & YOU**

**The Federal Reserve and Monetary Policy**

Chapter 22
Disc 1, Side 2

**ASK: Why would the Fed impose a tight money policy?** *to control inflation*

loose." In these cases, the terms *tight* and *loose* are referring to the monetary policy of the Fed. *Monetary policy,* as you recall, involves changing the rate of growth of the money supply in order to affect the cost and availability of credit.

Credit, like any good or service, has a cost. The cost of credit is the interest that must be paid to obtain it. As the cost of credit increases, the quantity demanded decreases. In contrast, if the cost of borrowing drops, the quantity of credit demanded rises.

**Figure 15.5** shows the results of monetary policy decisions. If the Fed implements a **loose money policy** (often called "expansionary"), credit is abundant and inexpensive to borrow. If the Fed follows a **tight money policy** (often called "contractionary"), credit is in short supply and is expensive to borrow.

A loose money policy is implemented to encourage economic growth. You may be wondering why any nation would want a tight money policy, however. The answer is to control inflation. If money becomes too plentiful too quickly, prices increase and the purchasing power of the dollar decreases.

**loose money policy:** *monetary policy that makes credit inexpensive and abundant, possibly leading to inflation*

**tight money policy:** *monetary policy that makes credit expensive and in short supply in an effort to slow the economy*

## Fractional Reserve Banking

Before you can understand how the Fed regulates the nation's money supply, you need to understand the basis of the United States banking system and the way money is created. The banking system is based on what is called **fractional reserve banking.**

Since 1913 the Fed has set specific **reserve requirements** for many banks. This means that they must hold a certain percentage of their total deposits either as cash in their own vaults or as deposits in their Federal Reserve district bank. Banks must hold

**fractional reserve banking:** *system in which only a fraction of the deposits in a bank is kept on hand, or in reserve; the remainder is available to lend*

**reserve requirements:** *regulations set by the Fed requiring banks to keep a certain percentage of their deposits as cash in their own vaults or as deposits in their Federal Reserve district bank*

**FIGURE 15.5**

**Loose Money Versus Tight Money** Look at the chart and determine the differences between loose money policy and tight money policy. ***Which of these policies can lead to a recession? Why is this possible?***

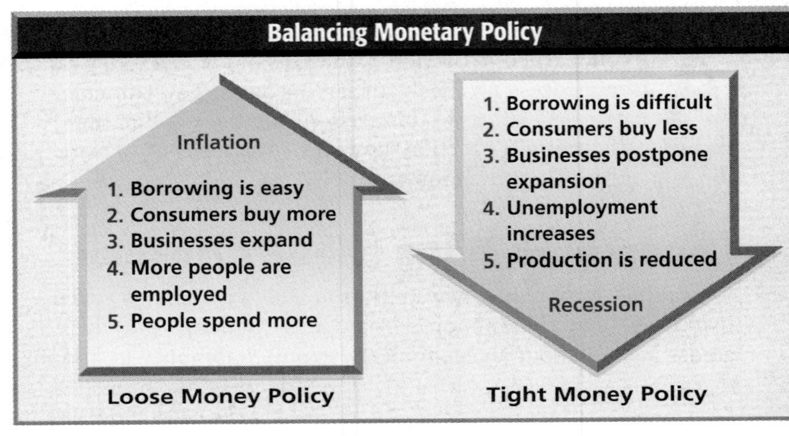

Balancing Monetary Policy
Inflation
1. Borrowing is easy
2. Consumers buy more
3. Businesses expand
4. More people are employed
5. People spend more
Loose Money Policy
1. Borrowing is difficult
2. Consumers buy less
3. Businesses postpone expansion
4. Unemployment increases
5. Production is reduced
Recession
Tight Money Policy




## Meeting Special Needs

**Inefficient Readers** Students with decoding problems may skip unfamiliar words. Often, however, they can comprehend words based on the context. Ask students to scan Section 2 for words that are unfamiliar. Have students write these words in their notebooks. Then encourage students to guess at the meaning of the words based on the context.

Refer to *Inclusion for the Social Studies Classroom Strategies and Activities* for students with different learning styles.

these reserves in case one or more banking customers decide to withdraw large amounts of cash from their checking accounts. Currently, most financial institutions must keep 10 percent of their checkable deposits as reserves with the Fed.

## Money Expansion

Currency is a small part of the money supply. A larger portion consists of funds that the Fed and customers have deposited in banks. Because banks are not required to keep 100 percent of their deposits in reserve, they can use these new reserves to create what is, in effect, new money. See **Figure 15.6.**

### FIGURE 15.6 Expanding the Money Supply

- The chart shows how $1,000 in new reserves expands to $5,000 by simple loans. In Round 1, the Fed deposits $1,000 in Bank A. With a 20 percent reserve requirement, Bank A must hold $200 of the new deposit on reserve. This leaves the bank with $800 of excess reserves.
- In Round 2, Mr. Jones applies to Bank A for an $800 loan to buy a computer. Bank A finds him creditworthy and credits his account with $800. Mr. Jones writes a check to Computer World, which deposits the money at Bank B. Bank B's reserves increase by $800. Of this amount, $160 (20 percent of $800) are required reserves, and the remaining $640 are excess reserves.
- In Round 3, Bank B—to earn profits—loans its excess reserves to Ms. Wang, who wants to borrow $640. She, in turn, buys something from Mr. Diaz, who does his banking at Bank C. He deposits the money from Ms. Wang. Bank C now has $640 in new deposits, of which $128 are required reserves. Bank C now loans $512 of excess reserves to Mrs. Fontana, who buys something from Mrs. Powers, and so on.

| Round | Deposited by | Amount of Deposit | Required Reserves (20%) | Excess Reserves (80%) | Loaned to | Paid to |
|---|---|---|---|---|---|---|
| 1 | the Fed (Bank A) | $1,000 | $200 | $800 | Mr. Jones | Computer World |
| 2 | Computer World (Bank B) | $800 | $160 | $640 | Ms. Wang | Mr. Diaz |
| 3 | Mr. Diaz (Bank C) | $640 | $128 | $512 | Mrs. Fontana | Mrs. Powers |
| 4 | Mrs. Powers (Bank D) | $512 | $102.40 | $409.60 | Mr. Gibbs | Mr. Santana |
| 5 | Mr. Santana (Bank E) | $409.60 | $81.92 | $327.68 | | |
| 6 | All Others | | | | | |
| Eventual Totals | | $5,000 | $1,000 | | | |

409

## Cooperative Learning

Organize students into small groups, and have groups review newspapers and magazines for stories about monetary policy. Have groups make copies of the articles they find and use them to create a collage. For each article, have groups note if it describes a loose monetary policy or a tight monetary policy. Encourage groups to display their collages around the classroom. BLOCK SCHEDULING



**Guided Reading Activity 15-2**

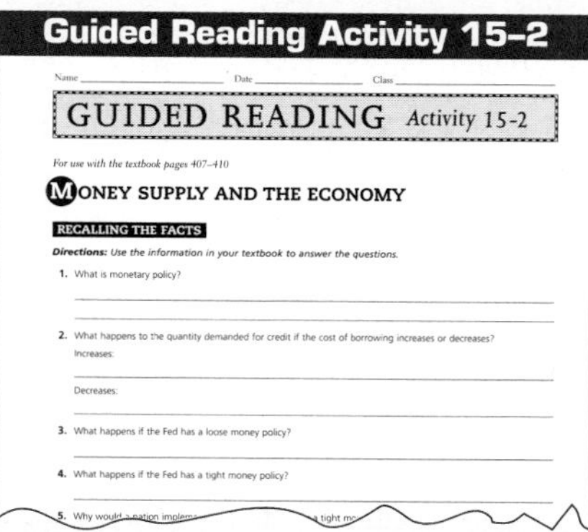
GUIDED READING Activity 15-2
For use with the textbook pages 407–410
MONEY SUPPLY AND THE ECONOMY
RECALLING THE FACTS
Directions: Use the information in your textbook to answer the questions.
1. What is monetary policy?
2. What happens to the quantity demanded for credit if the cost of borrowing increases or decreases?
Increases:
Decreases:
3. What happens if the Fed has a loose money policy?
4. What happens if the Fed has a tight money policy?

## Independent Practice

**L2 Illustrating Ideas** Have students illustrate tight money policy and loose money policy. As an example, suggest drawings of Uncle Sam tightening and loosening a vice on a bag of money. Call on volunteers to display and explain their images.

**INTERACTIVE ECONOMICS!**

**LESSON 8: MONETARY POLICY**

Have students complete the "Economics Lab," which discusses the fractional reserve system.

Supplied in both CD-ROM and disk formats.

## 3 Assess

Assign Section 2 Assessment as homework or an in-class activity.

Use **Interactive Tutor Self-Assessment Software** to review Section 2.

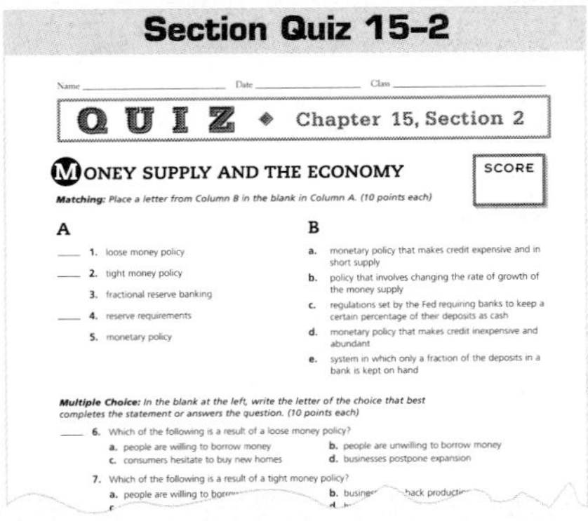

### Section Quiz 15-2

Name ______ Date ______ Class ______

**QUIZ** ◆ Chapter 15, Section 2

**MONEY SUPPLY AND THE ECONOMY** SCORE

***Matching:*** *Place a letter from Column B in the blank in Column A. (10 points each)*

| A | B |
|---|---|
| ____ 1. loose money policy | a. monetary policy that makes credit expensive and in short supply |
| ____ 2. tight money policy | b. policy that involves changing the rate of growth of the money supply |
| 3. fractional reserve banking | c. regulations set by the Fed requiring banks to keep a certain percentage of their deposits as cash |
| ____ 4. reserve requirements | d. monetary policy that makes credit inexpensive and abundant |
| 5. monetary policy | e. system in which only a fraction of the deposits in a bank is kept on hand |

***Multiple Choice:*** *In the blank at the left, write the letter of the choice that best completes the statement or answers the question. (10 points each)*

____ 6. Which of the following is a result of a loose money policy?
a. people are willing to borrow money b. people are unwilling to borrow money
c. consumers hesitate to buy new homes d. businesses postpone expansion

7. Which of the following is a result of a tight money policy?
a. people are willing to borr... b. busine... back productio...

## Reteach

Have students write two paragraphs, one explaining the difference between tight money policy and loose money policy, the other explaining how fractional reserve banking helps to expand the money supply.

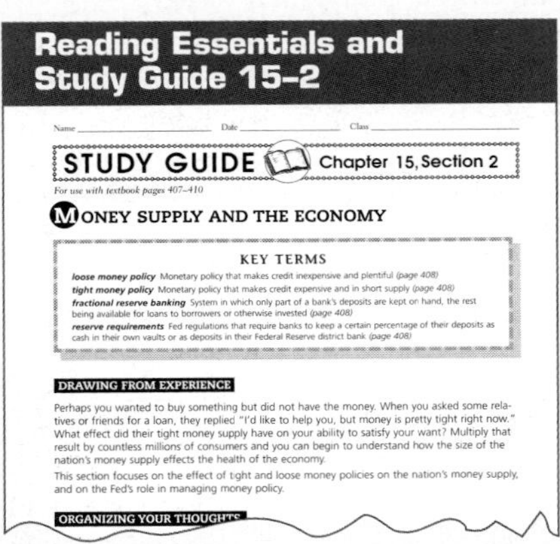

### Reading Essentials and Study Guide 15-2

Name ______ Date ______ Class ______

**STUDY GUIDE** Chapter 15, Section 2

*For use with textbook pages 407–410*

**MONEY SUPPLY AND THE ECONOMY**

**KEY TERMS**

***loose money policy*** Monetary policy that makes credit inexpensive and plentiful *(page 408)*
***tight money policy*** Monetary policy that makes credit expensive and in short supply *(page 408)*
***fractional reserve banking*** System in which only part of a bank's deposits are kept on hand, the rest being available for loans to borrowers or otherwise invested *(page 408)*
***reserve requirements*** Fed regulations that require banks to keep a certain percentage of their deposits as cash in their own vaults or as deposits in their Federal Reserve district bank *(page 408)*

**DRAWING FROM EXPERIENCE**

Perhaps you wanted to buy something but did not have the money. When you asked some relatives or friends for a loan, they replied "I'd like to help you, but money is pretty tight right now." What effect did their tight money supply have on your ability to satisfy your want? Multiply that result by countless millions of consumers and you can begin to understand how the size of the nation's money supply effects the health of the economy.

This section focuses on the effect of tight and loose money policies on the nation's money supply, and on the Fed's role in managing money policy.

**ORGANIZING YOUR THOUGHTS**

## 4 Close

Have students determine whether a high reserve requirement or low reserve requirement is desirable for economic growth.

Suppose Bank A sells a government bond to the Fed and receives $1,000. This is $1,000 in "new" money because the Fed simply creates it by writing a check. With a 20 percent reserve requirement, the bank must hold $200 of that money in reserve. The bank is free to lend the remaining $800.

Suppose a customer asks the same bank for an $800 loan. The bank creates $800 simply by transferring $800 to the customer's checking account. The bank must keep in reserve 20 percent of this new deposit—$160—but now it can lend the remaining $640. This $640 is, in turn, treated as a new deposit. Eighty percent of it—$512—can again be lent. The process continues, with each new deposit giving the bank new funds to continue lending. The original $1,000 becomes $5,000.

Of course, a bank usually does not lend and receive back the same money. Its customers will probably withdraw money and spend it or deposit it in another bank. As the money finds its way into a second and third bank, and so on, each bank can use the non-required reserve portion of the money to make more loans. This process is known as the *multiple expansion of the money supply.*

**Practice** and **assess** key skills with ***Skillbuilder Interactive Workbook, Level 2.***

## SECTION 2 Assessment

### Understanding Key Terms

1. **Define** loose money policy, tight money policy, fractional reserve banking, reserve requirements.

### Reviewing Objectives

2. **Graphic Organizer** Create a chart to describe the effect of loose money and tight money policies on the actions listed below.

| Effect on . . . | Loose Money Policy | Tight Money Policy |
|---|---|---|
| Borrowing | | |
| Consumer buying | | |
| Businesses | | |
| Employment | | |
| Production | | |

3. What is the purpose of fractional reserve banking?
4. How does the money supply expand?

### Applying Economic Concepts

5. **Monetary Policy** If there is a 10 percent reserve requirement, by how much does the money supply expand if the Fed injects $100 of new money? By how much does it expand if the reserve requirement is raised to 20 percent?

### Critical Thinking Activity

6. **Synthesizing Information** Analyze **Figure 15.6** on page 409. Create a similar scenario showing the expansion of the money supply. Begin the expansion by depositing $200 into Bank A. Assume that the reserve requirement is 20 percent.



## SECTION 2 Assessment Answers

1. All definitions can be found in the Glossary.
2.

| Effect on . . . | Loose Money Policy | Tight Money Policy |
|---|---|---|
| Borrowing | Increases | Decreases |
| Consumer buying | Increases | Decreases |
| Businesses | Expand | Contract |
| Employment | Rises | Falls |
| Production | Increases | Decreases |

3. Banks hold a certain percentage of total deposits in reserve to meet Fed requirements, and this helps regulate the money supply.
4. Since banks have to keep only a fraction of deposits in reserve, they are able to lend the excess reserves, thus expanding the money supply.
5. $1,000; $500
6. The money supply will expand by $1,000.

# BusinessWeek

# Spotlight on the Economy

## Why the Fed's Open-Mouth Policy Works

**Check It Out! In this chapter you learned that the Federal Open Market Committee decides whether to raise or lower interest rates to control inflation. In this article, read to learn how the FOMC announces its decisions.**

Not too many years ago, Federal Reserve officials conducted monetary policy as if they were members of the Politburo plotting behind the thick walls of the Kremlin. The Fed's reasoning: Secrecy was essential if central bankers were to avoid political pressure from those who would like to influence Fed policy on interest rates.

But for the past five years, Fed Chairman Alan Greenspan has been dismantling those Kremlin walls, brick by brick. On May 18, we saw the results of his efforts. Instead of waiting six weeks or more to let the markets know what it thought, the policy-setting Federal Open Market Committee broadcast the outcome of its meeting immediately: Yes, the Fed will adopt a tightening bias in light of rising inflation risks. The markets, which had reeled on news of a surprisingly high consumer price index for April, took the news in stride—relieved to see that the Fed was not yet ready to raise rates.

It all worked beautifully. Alan Greenspan, who is a great believer in free markets, loves it when traders do the Fed's work—raising and lowering bond yields to keep the domestic economy on course. As the reaction to the Fed's May 18 announcement shows, the markets are fully capable of taking direction from the Fed.

. . . Now, everyone from home buyers in North Dakota to executives in Florida . . . gets the same information—and the right information—at exactly the same time.



### Think About It

1. **How did Alan Greenspan change the way the FOMC announces its decisions?**
2. **What are the benefits of a transparent monetary policy?**

### Answers to *Think About It*

1. Greenspan ended the secrecy surrounding FOMC decision making and has cut the waiting time between making a decision and announcing it.
2. Everyone—from home buyers to business executives—gets the right information at the same time.

BusinessWeek Spotlight

## Teach

Direct students to read the excerpt and note how Fed Chairman Alan Greenspan changed the way that the Fed announces its decisions. Then have students discuss why they think Greenspan made these changes. *Most students will suggest that by being more open and prompt in announcing the Fed's decisions, Greenspan hopes to stop businesses and investors from speculating on what the decisions might be and taking actions that might be harmful to the economy.*

### BusinessWeek ONLINE

To find up-to-date news and analysis on the economy, business, technology, markets, entrepreneurs, investments, and finance, have students search feature articles and special reports on the *Business Week* Web site. www.businessweek.com

### Sidelight

The Internet has helped speed up the release of information on the Fed's actions. Shortly after decisions have been made, they are placed on the Press Releases page of the Federal Reserve Board of Governors Web site: www.bog.frb.fed.us

# 1 Focus

## Overview

Section 3 discusses the methods the Fed uses to regulate the money supply—the reserve requirement, the discount rate, and open-market operations—and explains the difficulties associated with instituting monetary policy.

**BELLRINGER**
**Motivational Activity**

Project **Daily Focus Transparency 62** and have students answer the questions.

This activity is also available as a blackline master.

**Daily Focus Transparency 62**

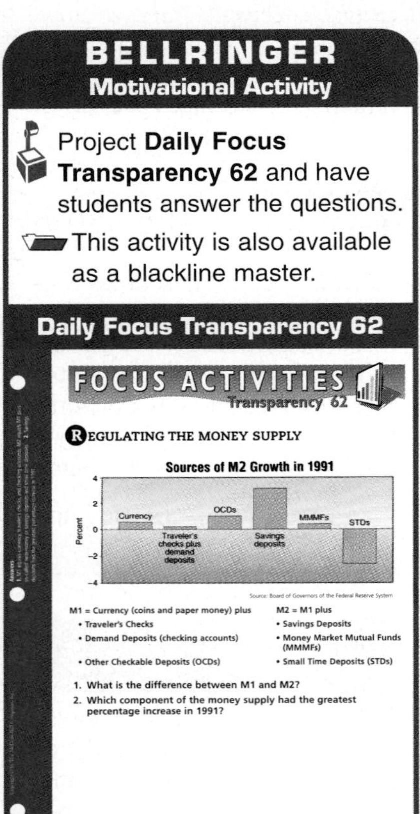


**READER'S GUIDE**

Answers to the **Reading Objectives** questions are on page 417.

**Preteaching Vocabulary**

Have students skim the section to locate the in-text definitions of the **Terms to Know.** Then have them write a brief explanation of the differences among the terms *discount rate, prime rate,* and *federal funds rate.*

Vocabulary PuzzleMaker

SECTION 3

# Regulating the Money Supply

**READER'S GUIDE**

**Terms to Know**
- discount rate
- prime rate
- federal funds rate
- open-market operations

**Reading Objectives**
1. How can the Fed use reserve requirements to alter the money supply?
2. How does the discount rate affect the money supply?
3. How does the Fed use open-market operations?
4. What are some of the difficulties of carrying out monetary policy?

**COVER STORY**

*THE COLUMBUS DISPATCH*, JULY 1, 1999

Like a driver applying a quick tap of the brakes, the Federal Reserve yesterday raised the cost of borrowing to keep the U.S. economy from running ahead too fast.

As a result, consumers can expect to pay a little more when buying homes, cars, and other big-ticket items, as well as when carrying credit-card balances.

The main goal of the Federal Reserve is to keep the money supply growing steadily and the economy running smoothly without inflation. As you'll learn in this section, the Fed uses several tools to achieve a smoothly running economy.

## Changing Reserve Requirements

The Federal Reserve can choose to control the money supply by changing the reserve requirements of financial institutions. The lower the percentage of deposits that must be kept in reserve, the more dollars are available to loan. The reverse is also true.

**SECTION 3 RESOURCE MANAGER**

**Reproducible Masters**
- Reproducible Lesson Plan 15–3
- Reading Essentials and Study Guide 15–3
- Guided Reading Activity 15–3
- Section Quiz 15–3
- Daily Focus Activity 62
- Daily Lecture Notes 15–3

**Multimedia**
- Daily Focus Transparency 62
- Economic Concepts Transparency 18
- Vocabulary PuzzleMaker
- Interactive Tutor Self-Assessment Software
- ExamView® Pro Testmaker
- MindJogger Videoquiz
- NBR's *Economics & You*
- Interactive Economics!

**Figure 15.7** explains how changes in the reserve requirement affect the nation's money supply.

As *Part C* of **Figure 15.7** shows, the Fed may raise reserve requirements. To build up its reserves to meet the new requirement, a bank has several possibilities. It can call in some loans, sell off securities or other investments, or borrow from another bank or from the Federal Reserve. Obviously, because all banks would have to increase their reserves, this action would decrease the amount of money in the economy. Raising reserve requirements, then, could be used to help slow down the economy if it were expanding too rapidly.

Even small changes in the reserve requirement can have major effects on the money supply. As a result, some believe that this tool is not precise enough to make frequent small adjustments to the money supply. In recent years, changing the reserve requirement has not been used to regulate the money supply.

## FIGURE 15.7 Raising and Lowering Reserve Requirements

| Bank Deposits | Reserve Requirement | $ Amount Bank May Loan | Fed Action |
|---|---|---|---|
| **Part A** **$1,000,000** | 10% (10% × $1,000,000 = $100,000) | $900,000 | Suppose a bank has $1 million in deposits, and the reserve requirement is 10 percent. The bank must keep at least $100,000 in reserves. |
| **Part B** **$1,000,000** | 5% (5% × $1,000,000 = $50,000 | $950,000 | If the Fed wanted to increase the money supply, it could lower the reserve requirement to 5 percent, for example. The bank would then need to keep only $50,000 in reserves. It could lend out the other $950,000. This additional $50,000 would expand the money supply many times over as it was lent and redeposited. This could help pull the economy out of a recession. |
| **Part C** **$1,000,000** | 15% (15% × $1,000,000 = $150,000) | $850,000 | Suppose instead that the Fed wanted to decrease the money supply, or at least slow down its rate of growth. It could do this by increasing the reserve requirement from 10 to 15 percent. The bank in this example would then need to keep $150,000 on reserve–$50,000 more than with a 10% reserve requirement. |





# 2 Teach

## Guided Practice

**L1 Organizing Ideas** Write *How the Fed Regulates the Money Supply* on the board. Beneath this title, draw a two-column chart with "Action" and "Impact on Money Supply" as column headings. Call on volunteers to add actions and outcomes to the appropriate columns. Have students copy the completed chart into their notebooks for review purposes.

### Daily Lecture Notes 15-3

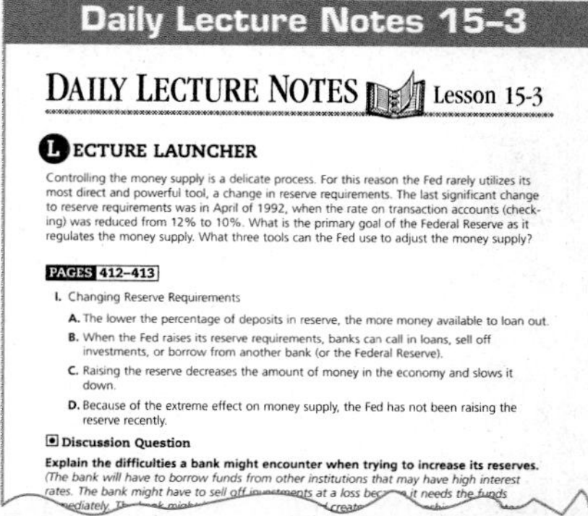

DAILY LECTURE NOTES Lesson 15-3
LECTURE LAUNCHER
Controlling the money supply is a delicate process. For this reason the Fed rarely utilizes its most direct and powerful tool, a change in reserve requirements. The last significant change to reserve requirements was in April of 1992, when the rate on transaction accounts (checking) was reduced from 12% to 10%. What is the primary goal of the Federal Reserve as it regulates the money supply. What three tools can the Fed use to adjust the money supply?
PAGES 412–413
I. Changing Reserve Requirements
A. The lower the percentage of deposits in reserve, the more money available to loan out.
B. When the Fed raises its reserve requirements, banks can call in loans, sell off investments, or borrow from another bank (or the Federal Reserve).
C. Raising the reserve decreases the amount of money in the economy and slows it down.
D. Because of the extreme effect on money supply, the Fed has not been raising the reserve recently.
Discussion Question
Explain the difficulties a bank might encounter when trying to increase its reserves.


### Visual Instruction FIGURE 15.7

Have students review the information in **Figure 15.7**. Then ask the following questions: Which action—the one in Part B or the one in Part C—might the Fed take to halt a downturn in business activity? *(the one in Part B)* Which action—the one in Part B or the one in Part C—might the Fed take to bring inflation under control? *(the one in Part C)*

### Meeting Special Needs

**Mixed Learners** Some students learn best visually, while others are auditory learners. Many are "mixed" learners, who use a combination of visual and auditory cues to learn. Ask students to look at and then think about the information in **Figure 15.7.** Have them read the paragraphs on pages 412 and 413 under the heading "Changing Reserve Requirements." Point out that references in the text to **Figure 15.7** act as a method of combining different cues to facilitate learning.

Refer to *Inclusion for the Social Studies Classroom Strategies and Activities* for students with different learning styles.

**L2 Understanding Ideas** On the board, write several actions that the Fed might take—the Fed lowers the discount rate; the Fed raises the reserve requirement; and the Fed sells Treasury bills, for example. Have students transform each action into a newspaper headline. In brief articles to accompany the headlines, have students outline the impact of each action on the economy.

**ECONOMICS & YOU**

**The Federal Reserve System and Monetary Policy**

Chapter 22
Disc 1, Side 2

**ASK:** What technique does the Fed use to slow down the economy, and how does it work? *The Fed attempts to slow down the economy by raising interest rates. This makes money more expensive to borrow and encourages consumers and businesses to postpone purchases.*

Also available in VHS.

**Guided Reading Activity 15-3**

GUIDED READING Activity 15-3

REGULATING THE MONEY SUPPLY

FILLING IN THE BLANKS

## Changing the Discount Rate

Sometimes a bank will find itself without enough reserves to meet its reserve requirement. This situation may occur if customers unexpectedly borrow a great deal of money or if depositors suddenly withdraw large amounts. The bank must then borrow funds to meet its reserve requirement. One of the ways it can do this is to ask its Federal Reserve district bank for a loan. The district bank, like any other bank, charges interest. The rate of interest the Fed charges its member banks is called the **discount rate.**

**discount rate:** *interest rate that the Fed charges on loans to member banks*

If the bank does borrow from the Fed, this newly created money would then be available for lending to individuals or businesses, thus increasing the money supply. If the discount rate is high, the bank passes its increased costs on to customers in the form of higher interest rates on loans. For example, it might raise its **prime rate**—the interest rate it charges its best business customers. High discount rates, by discouraging borrowing, might keep down the growth of the money supply.

**prime rate:** *rate of interest that banks charge on loans to their best business customers*

In contrast, if the discount rate is low, even a bank with sufficient reserves might borrow money. The loan will raise the bank's reserves and increase its ability to make loans. Thus, a reduction in the discount rate may increase the total money supply.

Changing the discount rate, like changing the reserve requirement, is rarely used by the Fed as a tool of monetary policy. Rather, either through its chairman or its Federal Open Market Committee, the Fed periodically states that it is going to change "the" interest rate. Because there are many interest rates in the economy, which one does the Fed mean?

### Global Economy

### Worldwide Influence

Decisions made by the Federal Open Market Committee (FOMC) may have an impact far beyond the American economy. Immediately after the FOMC announces its actions, American financial markets respond. Traders consider how these actions will affect the economy, and they buy or sell stocks and bonds accordingly. As a result, stock and bond prices rise or fall, sometimes sharply.

By the end of the business day in the United States, financial markets in Asia are opening. Traders and investors there read the Fed's actions and note the response of the American markets, often following the example of their American counterparts. A comparable situation develops a few hours later in Europe, when financial markets open there. As one American financial expert has noted, "The Fed has become the dominant central bank in the world." ■



## Cooperative Learning

Organize students into groups of four. Have groups investigate and write illustrated reports explaining how the Fed's actions affected the overall economy during and immediately after World War I, during the 1920s, during the Great Depression, and during and immediately after World War II. Have group members assign time periods among themselves. Direct each group to combine its reports into a booklet titled "A History of Federal Reserve Policies." BLOCK SCHEDULING

## FIGURE 15.8

**Federal Funds Rate** When the media discusses a rate hike or reduction by the Fed, they are referring to the federal funds rate, or the interest rate that banks charge each other for overnight loans. ***How does an increase in the federal funds rate affect you as a banking customer?***

**FOX TROT**

### Federal Funds Rate

The interest rate the Fed is referring to is the **federal funds rate.** This is the interest rate that banks charge each other for short-term loans (usually overnight). Why would one bank need to borrow from another? Suppose a customer walks into Bank A late in the day and withdraws a large amount. In order to provide funds to the customer, the bank must dip into its required reserves. Before the banking day ends, Bank A must raise its reserves to the required amount or pay a penalty to the Fed.

**federal funds rate:** *interest rate that banks charge each other on loans (usually overnight)*

Bank A could borrow money from the Fed as discussed earlier, but the discount rate may be too high. Instead, Bank A approaches Bank B for a loan. Bank B happens to have excess reserves that day, so it loans Bank A the money it needs at the federal funds rate. This federal funds market is active—billions of dollars of reserves are borrowed and loaned each business day.

If the Fed causes the federal funds rate to drop from 5.25 percent to 5 percent, banks will borrow more and, thus, lend more. This increases business activity in the economy. In contrast, the chairman of the Fed may publicly state the opposite—that the Fed is causing the federal funds rate to rise from, say, 5.5 percent to 5.75 percent. At this higher rate, banks will reduce their borrowing from other banks as well as raise the interest rates they charge their own customers. Economic activity will contract. See **Figure 15.8.**

415

### Visual Instruction FIGURE 15.8

**Answer:** *Banks raise the interest rates they charge their own customers.*

Project **Economic Concepts Transparency 18** and have students discuss the accompanying questions.

### Did You Know

The Fed also makes short-term hard currency loans to regulate the money supply. In the last week of 1999, for example, the Fed made about $20 billion in short-term loans to member banks. Fed officials wanted to make sure that banks had enough reserves in case customers, uncertain of the impact of the computer "millennium bug," withdrew large amounts of cash.

### Independent Practice

**L2 Constructing Graphs** Have students research the average prime interest rates for the last 25 years. Direct students to present their findings in graph form. Ask students to indicate on their graphs the periods when the Fed might have been following a loose money policy and when the Fed might have been following a tight money policy.

### Free Enterprise Activity

Remind students that one method used by the Fed to regulate the nation's money supply is the purchase and sale of government securities. Ask students to conduct research on one kind of government security, the Treasury bill (T-bill). Direct them to find out values, maturities, and interest rates of these securities. Finally, have students examine the advantages and disadvantages of buying T-bills. Ask students to present their findings in brief illustrated reports.

# CHAPTER 15
SECTION 3, Pages 412–417

INTERACTIVE ECONOMICS!

**LESSON 8: MONETARY POLICY**

Have students click on the Advanced Topic "The Reserve Requirement." Then have them click on "Math Practice" and complete the problems.

Supplied in both CD-ROM and disk formats.

## Global Economy

**Varying Discount Rates**

Discount rates vary from nation to nation. At the end of 1999, when the discount rate in the United States stood at 4.75 percent, the discount rate in Canada was 5.0 percent, Great Britain's was 6.0 percent, and Japan's was 0.5 percent.

# 3 Assess

## Meeting Lesson Objectives

Assign Section 3 Assessment as homework or an in-class activity.

Use **Interactive Tutor Self-Assessment Software** to review Section 3.

**open-market operations:** *buying and selling of United States securities by the Fed to affect the money supply*

## Open-Market Operations

Buying and selling government securities, called **open-market operations,** is the major tool the Fed uses to control the money supply. As you may remember from Chapter 10, securities are government IOUs such as Treasury bills, notes, and bonds. The term *open market* is used because these securities are bought and sold in the open market through dealers who specialize in buying and selling government securities. An open market is one that is open to private businesses and not controlled or owned by the government.

When the Fed buys securities—such as Treasury bills—it pays for them by making a deposit in the account of the security dealer's bank. This deposit increases the bank's reserves and therefore the amount of money it can lend, thus increasing the money supply. Remember the *multiple expansion of money* that you learned about in Section 2? When the Fed adds even a relatively small amount of new reserves into the banking system, banks can create money by holding on to required reserves and loaning out the rest.

In contrast, when the Fed sells Treasury bills to a dealer, the dealer's bank must use its deposits to purchase the securities. This action means that banks have fewer reserves to support loans and must reduce their lending. The multiple expansion of money works in reverse by taking more money out of circulation than just the initial withdrawal.

## Difficulties of Monetary Policy

Economists sometimes describe the Fed's control over the money supply as similar to a driver's control over a car. Like a driver, the Fed can accelerate or brake, depending on what phase of the business cycle the economy is in. In reality, the Fed cannot control the money supply as quickly and as surely as a driver can control a car.

One problem is the difficulty in gathering and evaluating information about M1 and M2. As you know, the money supply is measured in terms of M1—currency, traveler's checks, and checkable accounts—and M2—which is M1 plus certain near moneys. In recent years, new savings and investment opportunities have appeared. Keeping track of the growth of M1 and M2 becomes more difficult as money is shifted from savings accounts into interest-paying checkable accounts or from checkable accounts into money market deposit accounts. The increased use of credit cards and electronic transfer funds has also changed the way money circulates through the economy.



## Extending the Content

**Buying Treasury Securities** Many investors buy Treasury securities directly from commercial banks. To avoid the fee that commercial banks charge on such transactions, however, some investors buy directly from a Federal Reserve district bank or one of its branches. Interested buyers must submit an offer for the securities they want to buy. The submission must be made on the appropriate forms and accompanied by payment—either cash or certified check.

Throughout its history, the Fed's monetary policies have been criticized. In some instances of rising inflation, the Fed increased the amount of money in circulation, thereby worsening inflation. During other periods when the economy was slowing down and going into recession, the Fed decreased the money supply. This action made the recession worse.

To prevent such misjudgments, some critics of the Fed have requested that the money supply simply be increased at the same rate every year. They recommend that the Fed *not* engage in monetary policy.

Although the Fed is protected from direct political pressure, it nonetheless still receives conflicting advice from many directions. In addition, the Fed is not the only force working to affect the economy. The spending and taxing policies of the federal government are also at work. The Fed's task is to consider all of these factors as it plots a course for the growth of the economy as well as one that ensures price stability.

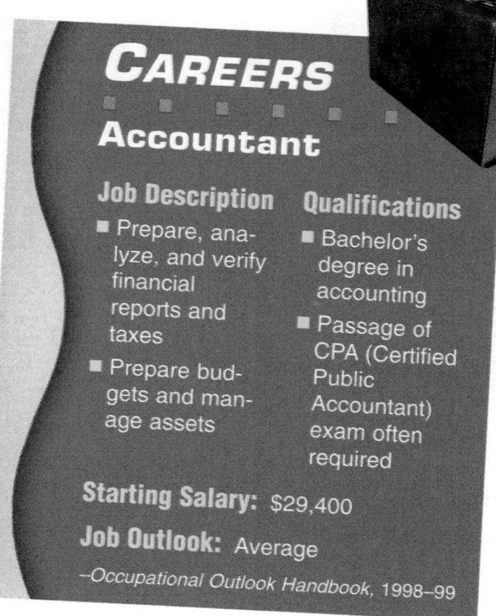

CAREERS
Accountant
Job Description
Prepare, analyze, and verify financial reports and taxes
Prepare budgets and manage assets
Qualifications
Bachelor's degree in accounting
Passage of CPA (Certified Public Accountant) exam often required
Starting Salary: $29,400
Job Outlook: Average
–Occupational Outlook Handbook, 1998–99


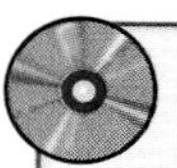

**Practice** and **assess** key skills with *Skillbuilder Interactive Workbook, Level 2.*

# SECTION 3 Assessment

### Understanding Key Terms

1. **Define** discount rate, prime rate, federal funds rate, open-market operations.

### Reviewing Objectives

2. How can the Fed use reserve requirements to alter the money supply?
3. How does the discount rate affect the money supply?
4. What are some of the difficulties of carrying out monetary policy?
5. **Graphic Organizer** Create a diagram like the one in the next column to show how the Fed uses open-market operations to change the money supply.

Fed Buys Securities → ☐ → ☐ → ☐

Fed Sells Securities → ☐ → ☐ → ☐

### Applying Economic Concepts

6. **Monetary Policy** If you were responsible for controlling the nation's money supply, which tool would you use? Why?

### Critical Thinking Activity

7. **Synthesizing Information** Imagine that you are the chairman of the Fed. Write a paragraph to the general public explaining why you are raising the federal funds rate. Include the words "inflation" and "recession" in your explanation.





**Section Quiz 15-3**

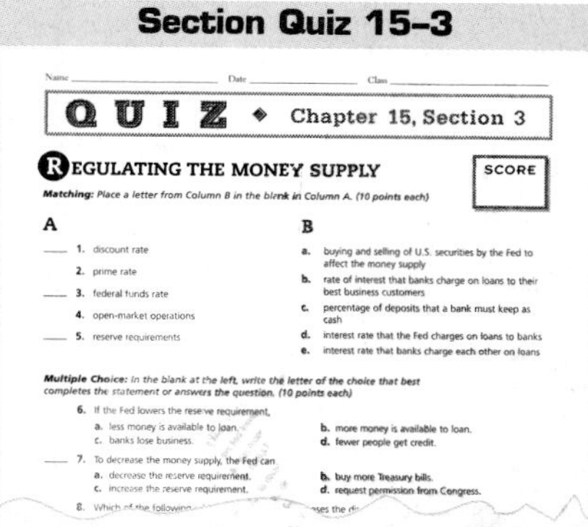

QUIZ ◆ Chapter 15, Section 3

REGULATING THE MONEY SUPPLY

*Matching:* Place a letter from Column B in the blank in Column A. (10 points each)

| A | B |
| --- | --- |
| 1. discount rate | a. buying and selling of U.S. securities by the Fed to affect the money supply |
| 2. prime rate | b. rate of interest that banks charge on loans to their best business customers |
| 3. federal funds rate | c. percentage of deposits that a bank must keep as cash |
| 4. open-market operations | d. interest rate that the Fed charges on loans to banks |
| 5. reserve requirements | e. interest rate that banks charge each other on loans |

*Multiple Choice:* In the blank at the left, write the letter of the choice that best completes the statement or answers the question. (10 points each)

6. If the Fed lowers the reserve requirement,
a. less money is available to loan. b. more money is available to loan.
c. banks lose business. d. fewer people get credit.

7. To decrease the money supply, the Fed can
a. decrease the reserve requirement. b. buy more Treasury bills.
c. increase the reserve requirement. d. request permission from Congress.

## Reteach

Refer students to the Section Objectives on page 412. Have them use information in the section to answer these questions.

**Reading Essentials and Study Guide 15-3**

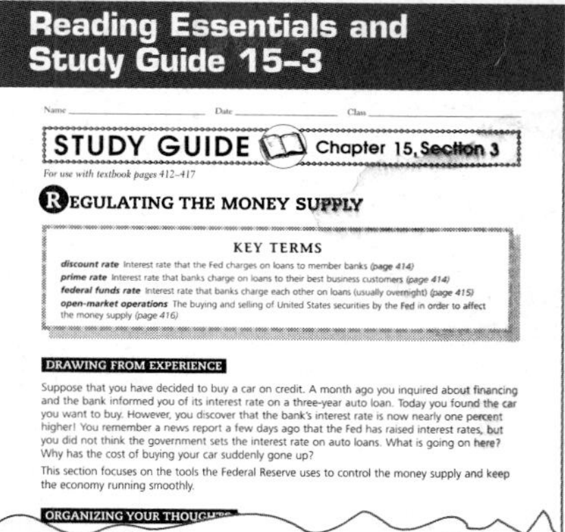

STUDY GUIDE Chapter 15, Section 3

For use with textbook pages 412–417

REGULATING THE MONEY SUPPLY

KEY TERMS

**discount rate** Interest rate that the Fed charges on loans to member banks (page 414)
**prime rate** Interest rate that banks charge on loans to their best business customers (page 414)
**federal funds rate** Interest rate that banks charge each other on loans (usually overnight) (page 415)
**open-market operations** The buying and selling of United States securities by the Fed in order to affect the money supply (page 416)

DRAWING FROM EXPERIENCE

Suppose that you have decided to buy a car on credit. A month ago you inquired about financing and the bank informed you of its interest rate on a three-year auto loan. Today you found the car you want to buy. However, you discover that the bank's interest rate is now nearly one percent higher! You remember a news report a few days ago that the Fed has raised interest rates, but you did not think the government sets the interest rate on auto loans. What is going on here? Why has the cost of buying your car suddenly gone up?

This section focuses on the tools the Federal Reserve uses to control the money supply and keep the economy running smoothly.

ORGANIZING YOUR THOUGHTS

## 4 Close

Call on students to identify and explain the various methods the Fed uses to regulate the money supply.

# SECTION 3 Assessment Answers

1. All definitions can be found in the Glossary.
2. When the Fed raises the reserve requirement, banks must hold more of their deposits in reserve, and this decreases the money supply. When the Fed lowers the reserve requirement, banks must hold less of their deposits in reserve, and this increases the money supply.
3. A reduction in the discount rate increases the money supply, while an increase in the discount rate decreases the money supply.
4. It is difficult to gather and evaluate information on M1 and M2. The Fed often receives conflicting advice on actions to take. The Fed is not the only force working to affect the economy.
5. Diagram should show that when the Fed buys government securities on the open market, it increases the money supply by putting more money into circulation, and when the Fed sells government securities, it decreases the money supply by taking money out of circulation.
6. Some students will suggest the federal funds rate, since it is the tool that has an immediate impact on the economy. Others may suggest open-market operations, since it is the major tool that the Fed uses to control the money supply.
7. Have students share their paragraphs.

## Background

Point out that Greenspan assumed control of the Fed shortly before the stock market crash of 1987. Greenspan has often taken aggressive action to curb the threat of inflation. This earned him harsh criticism from many quarters. However, the United States has experienced a period of sustained growth and low inflation throughout Greenspan's tenure at the Fed.

# Teach

Have students search the Internet for articles on Alan Greenspan and his policies. Tell students that a good starting point for their search might be the Federal Reserve Board of Governors Web site at www.bog.frb.fed.us. By using the menu on the left of the page, they can access speeches made by Greenspan. Have students write brief synopses of the articles they find. Call on volunteers to share their synopses with the rest of the class.

# People & Perspectives

## Alan Greenspan

*ECONOMIST (1926–)*

- **Chairman of the Federal Reserve Board since 1987**
- **Chairman of the Council of Economic Advisers under President Gerald Ford**
- **Member of the Economic Policy Advisory Board under President Ronald Reagan**

As Chairman of the Federal Reserve Board, Alan Greenspan monitors developments in the United States economy—the impact of new technologies, for example. In this excerpt, Greenspan discusses the economic impact of information technology.

*"The American economy, clearly more than most, is in the grip of what the eminent Harvard professor, Joseph Schumpeter, many years ago called 'creative destruction,' the continuous process by which emerging technologies push out the old. Standards of living rise when incomes created by the productive facilities employing older, increasingly [outdated], technologies are marshaled to finance the newly produced capital assets that embody cutting-edge technologies.*

*. . . Of course, large remnants of imprecision still persist, but the remarkable surge in the availability of real-time information in recent years has sharply reduced the degree of uncertainty confronting business management. This has enabled businesses to remove large swaths of now unnecessary inventory, and dispense with [redundant use of] worker[s] and capital. . . . As a consequence, growth in output per work hour has accelerated, elevating the standard of living of the average American worker.*

*. . . Moreover, technological innovations have spread far beyond the factory floor and retail and wholesale distribution channels. Biotech, for example, is revolutionizing medicine and agriculture, with far-reaching consequences for the quality of life not only in the United States but around the world."*

### Checking for Understanding

1. **What does Greenspan mean by the term "creative destruction"?**
2. **How, according to Greenspan, have technological innovations fundamentally changed the economy?**

418

### Answers to *Checking for Understanding*

1. the continuous process by which new technologies push out old technologies
2. Technological innovations have enabled businesses to use workers and capital more efficiently, accelerating growth in output per work hour and elevating the standard of living of the average American worker.

# CHAPTER  15 Summary

**Chapter Overview** Visit the *Economics Today and Tomorrow* Web site at ett.glencoe.com and click on ***Chapter 15—Chapter Overviews*** to review chapter information.

## SECTION 1 Organization and Functions of the Federal Reserve System

- Congress created the Federal Reserve System, or **Fed,** in 1913 as the central banking organization in the United States.
- The Fed is made up of a Board of Governors assisted by the Federal Advisory Council, the **Federal Open Market Committee,** 12 district banks, 25 branch banks, and thousands of member banks.
- Among the Fed's functions are **check clearing,** acting as the federal government's fiscal agent, supervising member state banks, holding reserves, supplying paper currency, and carrying out **monetary policy.**

## SECTION 2 Money Supply and the Economy

- The most important function of the Fed is monetary policy, or controlling the rate of growth of the money supply.
- With a **loose money policy,** credit is abundant and inexpensive to borrow. With a **tight money policy,** credit is in short supply and is expensive to borrow.
- The banking system is based on **fractional reserve banking,** in which banks hold a certain percentage of their total deposits either as cash in their vaults or in Fed banks.
- After banks meet the **reserve requirement,** they can loan out the rest to create what is, in effect, new money.

## SECTION 3 Regulating the Money Supply

- The Fed can control the money supply by changing the reserve requirements of financial institutions. Lowering the requirement allows banks to loan more, thus increasing the money supply.
- Other tools the Fed can use are changing the **discount rate** and **federal funds rate,** which also affect the **prime rate.** By making borrowing more expensive, banks and consumers are discouraged from spending, which halts the growth of the money supply.
- The main tool the Fed uses to control the money supply is **open-market operations**—buying and selling government securities. By depositing money in the banking system (buying securities), the money supply grows. By withdrawing money from the banking system (selling securities), the money supply decreases.



## Economics Journal

**Federal Reserve System** Have students track the paper currency that they handle in one week. Ask them to record the value and issuing Federal Reserve Bank of each note. At the end of the week, have students collate their data in one table to see from which Federal Reserve Banks the various denominations originated. Then direct each student to present the class findings in the form of a bar graph or map of the Federal Reserve System.

# CHAPTER 15 Summary

**ECONOMICS & YOU**

**The Federal Reserve System and Monetary Policy**

Chapter 22
Disc 1, Side 2

If you do not have access to a videodisc player, the ***Economics & You*** programs are also available in VHS.

Use the **Chapter 15 Summary** to preview, review, condense, or reteach the chapter.

## Preview/Review

**Vocabulary PuzzleMaker Software** reinforces the key terms used in Chapter 15.

**Interactive Tutor Self-Assessment Software** allows students to review Chapter 15 content.

## Condense

Have students listen to the Chapter 15 **Audio Program** (also available in Spanish) in the TCR. Assign the Chapter 15 Audio Program Activity and give students the Chapter 15 Audio Program Test.

## Reteach

Have students complete **Reteaching Activity** 15 in the TCR (Spanish Reteaching Activities are also available).

# CHAPTER 15
## Assessment and Activities

Have students visit the *Economics Today and Tomorrow* Web site at ett.glencoe.com to review Chapter 15 and take the Self-Check Quiz.

**GLENCOE TECHNOLOGY**

**MindJogger Videoquiz**

Use MindJogger to review Chapter 15 content.

### Identifying Key Terms

1. b
2. i
3. f
4. j
5. a
6. c
7. g
8. h
9. e
10. d

### Recalling Facts and Ideas

1. It directs the operations of the Federal Reserve System.
2. 12 Federal Reserve Banks and 25 branch banks
3. Department of the Treasury
4. loose money policy and tight money policy
5. A fraction of the money is kept on reserve and the rest is available for loans.
6. because the Fed sets specific reserve requirements for banks
7. changing the discount rate and using open-market operations
8. raise reserve requirements, increase the discount rate, and sell securities on the open market
9. because money is shifted among savings accounts, interest-bearing checkable accounts, and money market deposit accounts, and because of the increased use of credit cards and electronic transfers
10. because sometimes its actions have worsened the situation—either inflation or recession—they were designed to combat

### Thinking Critically

1. The format of flowcharts may vary, but should resemble the illustration in **Figure 15.6.**
2. Member banks, as stockholders in their district bank, may vote for bank's board members and receive dividends on stock.
3. Answers may vary but should suggest that the Fed's actions would be more influenced by shifting political trends.

# CHAPTER 15
# Assessment and Activities

**Self-Check Quiz** Visit the *Economics Today and Tomorrow* Web site at ett.glencoe.com and click on ***Chapter 15—Self-Check Quizzes*** to prepare for the Chapter Test.

## Identifying Key Terms

*Write the letter of the definition in Column B that correctly defines each term in Column A.*

**Column A**

1. Fed
2. prime rate
3. tight money policy
4. reserve requirements
5. monetary policy
6. open-market operations
7. discount rate
8. loose money policy
9. federal funds rate
10. check clearing

**Column B**

a. means of changing the growth rate of the money supply
b. central banking system in the United States
c. purchases and sales of United States securities by the Fed
d. method by which a check deposited in one bank is transferred to another bank
e. the interest paid by banks when they borrow reserves among themselves
f. situation in which credit is expensive to borrow
g. the interest paid by banks when they borrow from a Fed district bank
h. situation in which credit is inexpensive to borrow
i. the interest rate that banks charge their best customers for loans
j. rule that banks keep a certain percentage of their deposits as cash

## Recalling Facts and Ideas

**Section 1**

1. What does the Board of Governors do within the Fed?
2. How many Fed banks and branches are there?
3. Which agency of the federal government supplies paper currency to the economy?

**Section 2**

4. What are the two basic types of monetary policies?
5. In a 10 percent fractional reserve banking system, what happens to the money supply when the Fed injects $100 of new money into the American economy?
6. Why do banks have to keep money in reserve accounts?

**Section 3**

7. The Fed can change the money supply in circulation by changing reserve requirements. What are two other methods that it can use to do this?
8. If the Fed wants to decrease the money supply, what can it do?

9. Why is it difficult for the Fed to gather and evaluate information about M1 and M2?
10. Why do some of the Fed's critics think the Fed should not engage in monetary policy?

## Thinking Critically

1. **Understanding Cause and Effect** Create a flowchart like the one below to show how the banking system creates money.

2. **Making Comparisons** What is the advantage for banks to be members of the Federal Reserve today? How does this differ from the past?
3. **Identifying Alternatives** How do you think the Fed would operate differently if it were under the control of the executive branch?

## Applying Economic Concepts

**Monetary Policy** Look at **Figure 15.2** on page 402. Use the map to answer the following questions.

1. In what federal district do you live?
2. What is the Federal Reserve Bank city of district 9?
3. What is the Federal Reserve Bank city of district 4? What are district 4's branch cities?
4. What are the branch cities of district 11?
5. To what district bank would checks written in Hawaii go first?

## Cooperative Learning Project

Working in groups, imagine that you are members of the Federal Open Market Committee. Eight times a year, you meet to discuss whether changes in the supply of money are necessary. The research staff presents information about the state of the economy. Write a list of the different types of information you think the members of the FOMC should have during their meetings.

## Reviewing Skills

**Outlining** Reread and outline Section 3 of this chapter, using the following as your skeleton:

I. Regulating the Money Supply
   A. Changing reserve requirements
   B. Changing the discount rate
   C. Open-market operations
   D. The difficulties of monetary policy

After outlining the information, develop a convincing argument in favor of one monetary tool over the use of the other two monetary tools. Summarize your argument and present that summary in a short speech to the class using your outline.

## Technology Activity

**Using the Internet** On the Internet, check the most recent issue of the *Federal Reserve Bulletin* for the current reserve requirements and discount rate. Check the same month's issue for the last four years to see how often they have changed and by how much. Track these data on a chart.

## Analyzing the Global Economy

Select a nation and research its central banking organization. Does the country have a "central bank"? If so, how does it regulate the money supply? If not, what controls does the country have in place to avoid inflation or recessions? Present your findings to the class.



# CHAPTER 15
## Assessment and Activities

## Reviewing Skills

I. Regulating the Money Supply
   A. Changing reserve requirements
   B. Changing the discount rate
      1. Prime rate
      2. Federal funds rate
   C. Open-market operations
      1. Buying government securities
      2. Selling government securities
   D. Difficulties of Monetary Policy
      1. Gathering and evaluating information on M1 and M2
      2. Criticism of Fed policies
      3. Conflicting advice on policies
      4. Fed not only force working to affect economy

Arguments and monetary policy tools will vary.

## Technology Activity

Have students share and compare their charts.

## Analyzing the Global Economy

Encourage students to present their findings in an illustrated report.

## Chapter Bonus Test Question

ASK: When the reserve requirement is 5 percent, how much of a $1,000 deposit will be available for loans? *$950* If the reserve requirement is 7 percent, how much of this deposit may be used for loans? *$930*

## Applying Economic Concepts

1. Your Fed district
2. Minneapolis
3. Cleveland; Cincinnati, Pittsburgh
4. El Paso, Houston, San Antonio
5. San Francisco

## Cooperative Learning Project

Answers will vary but might include such items as changes in money supply, discount rate, reserve requirement, and Treasury securities issues and trading.

# CHAPTER 16 Resource Manager

## Teaching Transparency

### Economic Concepts Transparency 19

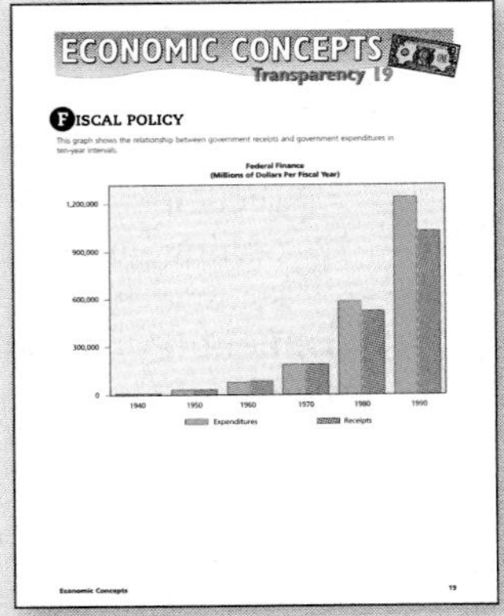

ECONOMIC CONCEPTS Transparency 19

FISCAL POLICY

## Application and Enrichment

### Enrichment Activity 16

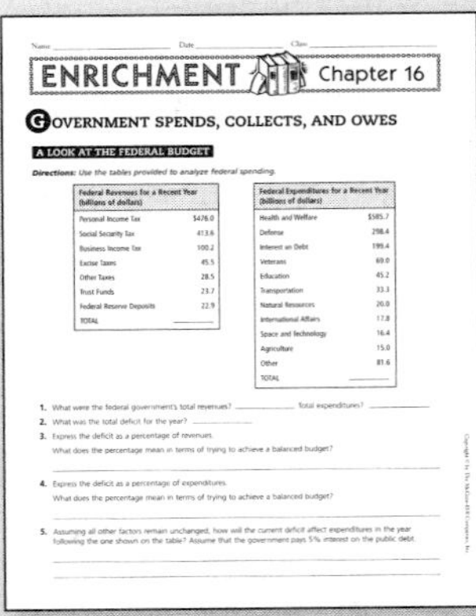

ENRICHMENT Chapter 16

GOVERNMENT SPENDS, COLLECTS, AND OWES

A LOOK AT THE FEDERAL BUDGET

### Consumer Applications Activities 14, 15

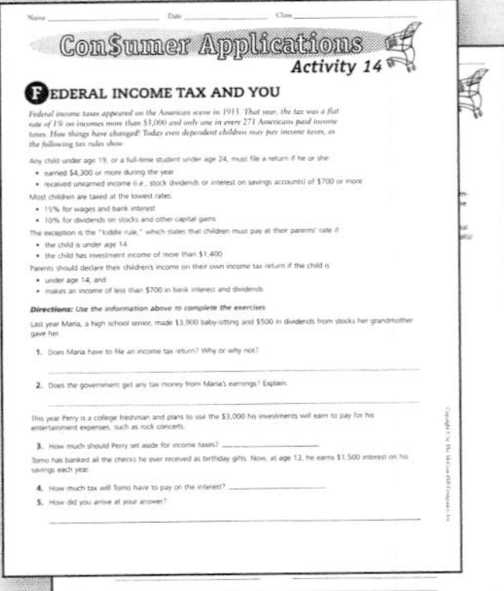

Consumer Applications Activity 14

FEDERAL INCOME TAX AND YOU

### Free Enterprise Activities 14, 15

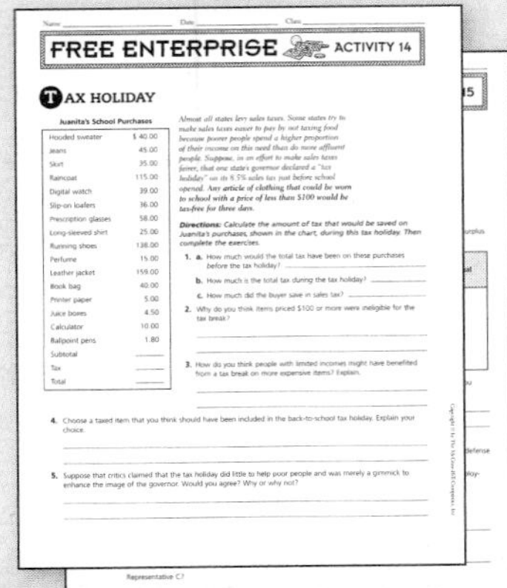

FREE ENTERPRISE ACTIVITY 14

TAX HOLIDAY

## Application and Enrichment

### Cooperative Learning Simulations and Problems 14, 15

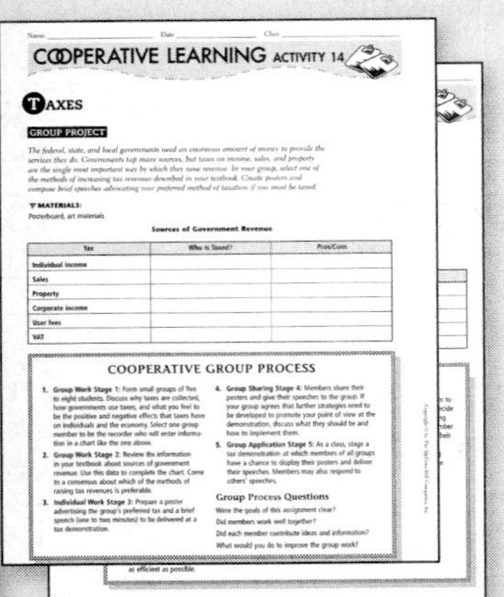

COOPERATIVE LEARNING ACTIVITY 14

TAXES

COOPERATIVE GROUP PROCESS

### Primary and Secondary Source Readings 14, 15

PRIMARY & SECONDARY SOURCES Reading 14

BREAK THE TAX BREAK HABIT

### Math Practice for Economics Activities 14, 15

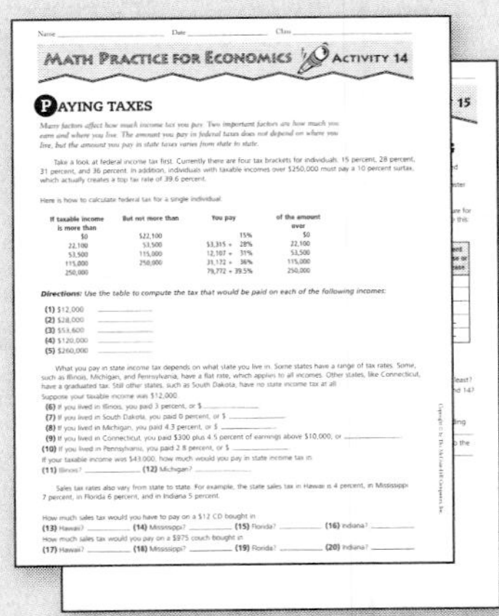

MATH PRACTICE FOR ECONOMICS ACTIVITY 14

PAYING TAXES

### Economic Cartoons Activity 14

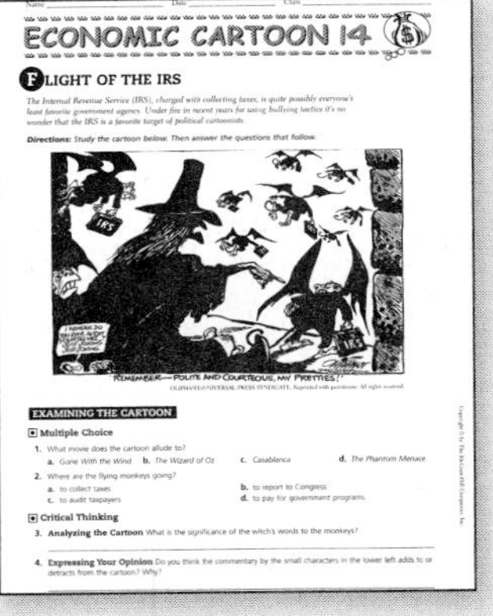

ECONOMIC CARTOON 14

FLIGHT OF THE IRS

## Review and Reinforcement

### Critical Thinking Activities 14, 15

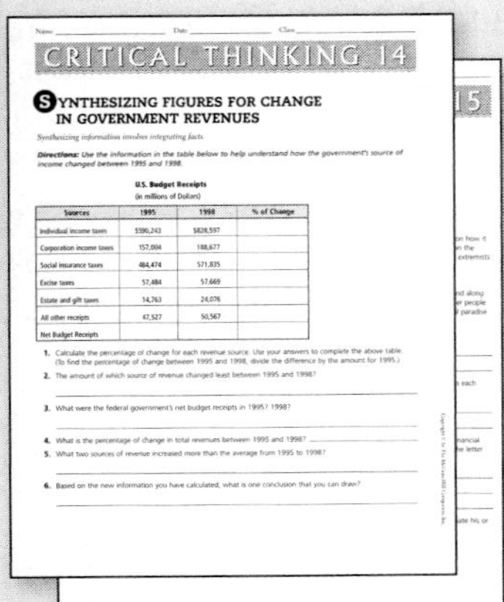

CRITICAL THINKING 14

SYNTHESIZING FIGURES FOR CHANGE IN GOVERNMENT REVENUES

### Reteaching Activity 16

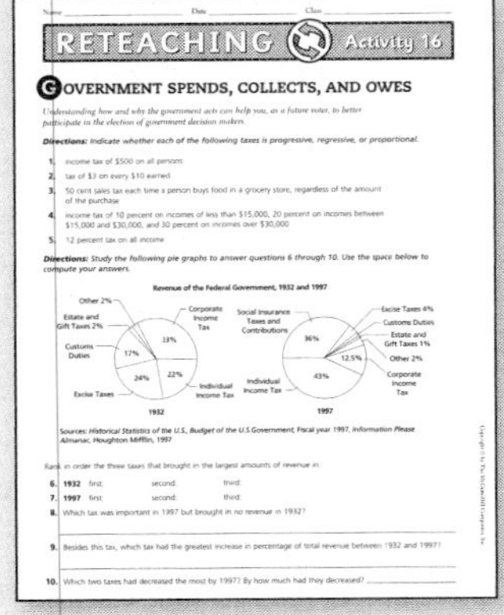

RETEACHING Activity 16

GOVERNMENT SPENDS, COLLECTS, AND OWES

### Economic Vocabulary Activity 16

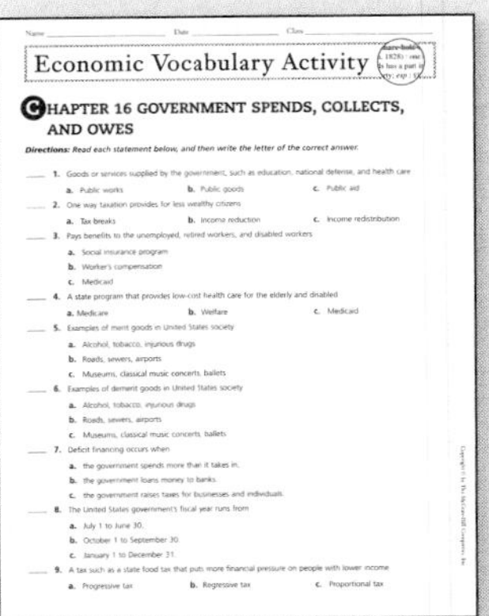

Economic Vocabulary Activity

CHAPTER 16 GOVERNMENT SPENDS, COLLECTS, AND OWES

### Reinforcing Economic Skills 22

Reinforcing Economic Skills Chapter 22

USING E-MAIL

# CHAPTER 16 Resource Manager

## Assessment and Evaluation

Chapter 16 Test Form A

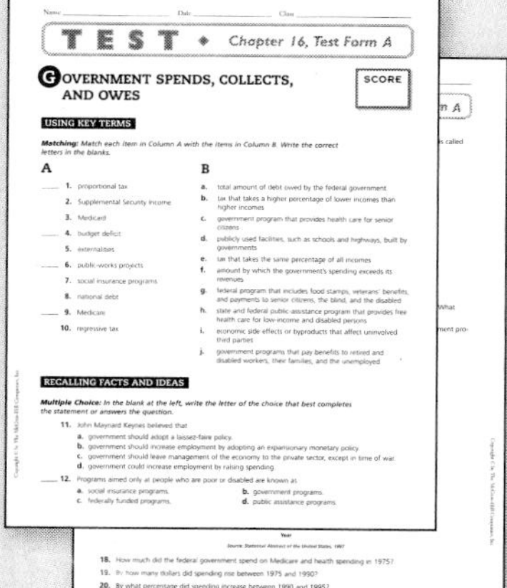

Chapter 16 Test Form B

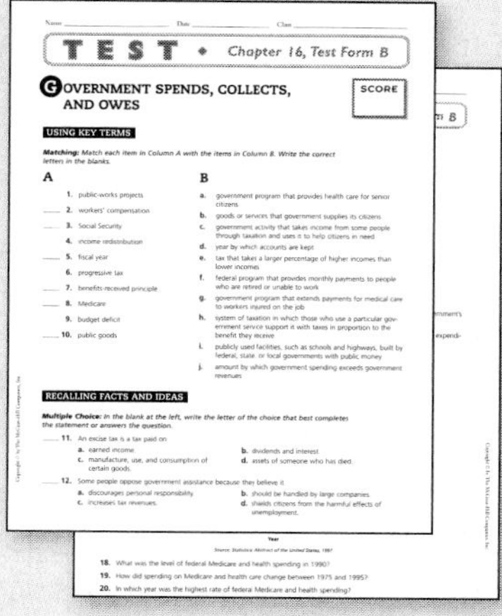

Performance Assessment Activities 14, 15

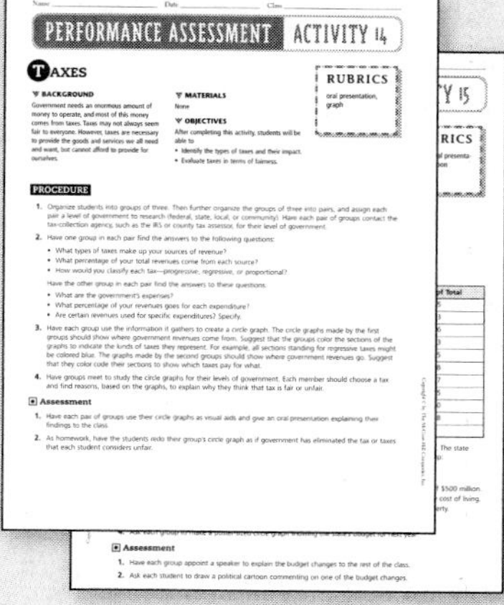

ExamView® Pro Testmaker

## Technology and Multimedia

 Vocabulary PuzzleMaker Software

 Interactive Tutor Self-Assessment Software

 ExamView® Pro Testmaker

 NBR *Economics & You* Video Program (English/Spanish)

 Presentation Plus!

 Glencoe Skillbuilder Interactive Workbook CD-ROM, Level 2

 Interactive Lesson Planner

 MindJogger Videoquiz

 Interactive Economics! CD-ROM

Audio Program (English or Spanish)

## Spanish Resources

 Spanish Economic Concepts Transparency 19

 Spanish Vocabulary Activity 16

 Spanish Reteaching Activity 16

 Spanish Section Quizzes for Chapter 16

 Spanish Chapter 16 Audio Program, Activity, and Test

You and your students can visit ett.glencoe.com—the Web site companion to **Economics Today and Tomorrow.** This innovative integration of electronic and print media offers your students a wealth of opportunities. The student text directs students to the Web site for the following options:

- **Chapter Overviews**
- **Self-Check Quizzes**
- **Student Web Activities**
- **Textbook Updates**

Answers are provided for you in the **Web Activity Lesson Plan.** Additional Web resources and Interactive Puzzles are also available.

Use the Glencoe Web site for additional resources. All essential content is covered in the Student Edition.

## Additional Resources

### Reading for the Student

Clayton, Gary E., et al. *A Guide to Everyday Economic Statistics.* Columbus, OH: McGraw-Hill, 1997. Explains the statistics used to measure the economy.

### Reading for the Teacher

Morgan, Iwan W. *Deficit Government: Taxing and Spending in Modern America.* Chicago: Ivan R. Dee, 1998. Analysis of budget policy trends since the 1930s.

# CHAPTER 16 Resource Manager

## Section Resources

| Reading Objectives | Reproducible Resources | Technology/Multimedia Resources |
|---|---|---|
| **Section 1**<br>**Growth in the Size of Government**<br>• What are two measurements of government growth?<br>• What do some economists believe caused the growth of government? | Reproducible Lesson Plan 16-1<br>Daily Lecture Notes 16-1<br>Guided Reading Activity 16-1<br>Reading Essentials and Study Guide 16-1<br>Daily Focus Activity 65<br>Section Quiz 16-1* | Daily Focus Transparency 65<br>Vocabulary PuzzleMaker<br>Interactive Tutor Self-Assessment Software<br>MindJogger Videoquiz<br>Presentation Plus!<br>ExamView® Pro Testmaker |
| **Section 2**<br>**The Functions of Government**<br>• What are public goods?<br>• Through what two general categories does government redistribute income?<br>• What are some criticisms of government involvement in the economy? | Reproducible Lesson Plan 16-2<br>Daily Lecture Notes 16-2<br>Guided Reading Activity 16-2<br>Reading Essentials and Study Guide 16-2<br>Daily Focus Activity 67<br>Section Quiz 16-2* | Daily Focus Transparency 67<br>Economic Concepts Transparency 19<br>Vocabulary PuzzleMaker<br>Interactive Tutor Self-Assessment Software<br>MindJogger Videoquiz<br>NBR's *Economics & You**<br>Presentation Plus!<br>ExamView® Pro Testmaker |
| **Section 3**<br>**The Federal Budget and the National Debt**<br>• What are the steps in the federal budget-making process?<br>• What are the five largest federal expenditures?<br>• What are the five largest state and local government expenditures?<br>• How does deficit spending increase the national debt? | Reproducible Lesson Plan 16-3<br>Daily Lecture Notes 16-3<br>Guided Reading Activity 16-3<br>Reading Essentials and Study Guide 16-3<br>Daily Focus Activity 68<br>Section Quiz 16-3* | Daily Focus Transparency 68<br>Vocabulary PuzzleMaker<br>Interactive Tutor Self-Assessment Software<br>MindJogger Videoquiz<br>NBR's *Economics & You**<br>Presentation Plus!<br>ExamView® Pro Testmaker |
| **Section 4**<br>**Taxation**<br>• What are the two principles of taxation?<br>• What effect do the three forms of taxation have on taxpayers? | Reproducible Lesson Plan 16-4<br>Daily Lecture Notes 16-4<br>Guided Reading Activity 16-4<br>Reading Essentials and Study Guide 16-4<br>Daily Focus Activity 66<br>Section Quiz 16-4*<br>Reinforcing Economic Skills 22 | Daily Focus Transparency 66<br>Vocabulary PuzzleMaker<br>Interactive Tutor Self-Assessment Software<br>MindJogger Videoquiz<br>Presentation Plus!<br>ExamView® Pro Testmaker |

*Also available in Spanish

Blackline Master

Transparency

Software
CD-ROM

Videodisc
Audiocassette
Videocassette

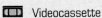

# CHAPTER 16 Resource Manager

## ACTIVITY From the Classroom of

**Christopher S. Ziller**
**Tecumseh High School**
**Lynnville, Indiana**

### YOU Make the Cut!

Students are to take part in the federal budget-making process. Each student or pairs of students should be given one of the following agencies or departments and the amount requested (in billions of dollars) for the fiscal year. Then tell students that the total amount in the federal budget for discretionary spending is $500 billion. Students must research their agency in order to convince the Office of Management and Budget (OMB) to allocate funds to them. Have students present their arguments before the class, and then work together to balance the budget.

- Legislative branch—$3
- Judicial branch—$4
- Agriculture—$15
- Commerce—$5
- Defense-Military—$301
- Education—$35
- Energy—$18
- Health and Human Services—$43
- Housing and Urban Development—$30
- Interior—$9
- Justice—$19
- Labor—$12
- State—$7
- Transportation—$51
- Treasury—$13
- Veterans Affairs—$19
- Corps of Engineers—$4
- Environmental Protection Agency—$7
- Federal Emergency Management Agency—$2
- International Assistance Programs—$12
- National Aeronautics and Space Administration—$14
- National Science Foundation—$4
- Social Security Administration—$6

## Easy Planning and Preparation!

Use Glencoe's **Presentation Plus!**, a Microsoft PowerPoint® application, to teach **Government Spends, Collects, and Owes.** With this multimedia teacher tool, you can customize ready-made presentations. At your fingertips are interactive transparencies, on-screen lecture notes, audiovisual presentations, and links to the Internet and to other Glencoe multimedia.

### Interactive Lesson Planner

Planning has never been easier! Organize your week, month, semester, or year with all the lesson helps you need to make teaching creative, timely, and relevant—the way it is meant to be. The Interactive Lesson Planner opens Glencoe's **Chapter 16** resources, helps you build your schedule, and tracks your progress.

## Key to Ability Levels

**Teaching strategies have been coded for varying learning styles and abilities.**

L1 BASIC activities for all students
L2 AVERAGE activities for average to above-average students
L3 CHALLENGING activities for above-average students
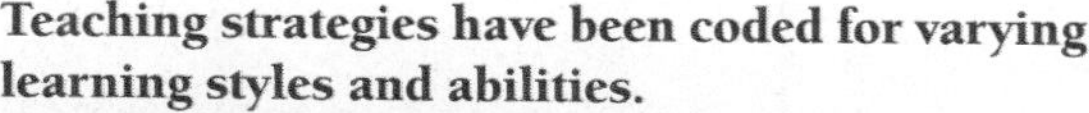
ELL ENGLISH LANGUAGE LEARNER activities

## National Council on Economic Education

## THE EconomicsAmerica AND EconomicsInternational PROGRAMS

### Voluntary Standards Emphasized in Chapter 16

**Content Standard 16** Students will understand that there is an economic role for government to play in a market economy whenever the benefits of a government policy outweigh its costs.

**Content Standard 20** Students will understand that federal government budgetary policy and the Federal Reserve System's monetary policy influence the overall levels of employment, output, and prices.

### Resources Available from NCEE

- *Capstone: The Nation's High School Economics Course*
- *Focus: High School Economics*
- *Civics and Government: Focus on Economics*

To order these materials, or to contact your State Council on Economic Education about workshops and programs, call 1-800-338-1192 or visit the NCEE Web site at http://www.nationalcouncil.org

ECONOMICS & YOU

How Government Spends, Collects, and Owes

Chapter 15
Disc 1, Side 2

ASK: What is the difference between a budget deficit and a budget surplus? *In a budget deficit, the federal government spends more in a year than it receives in revenue from taxes. In a budget surplus, the government takes in more money than it spends.*

Also available in VHS.

## Chapter Overview

Chapter 16 describes or explains the growth of government, the ways in which government contributes to the public good, the budget-making process, the national debt, and the principles of taxation.

### GLENCOE TECHNOLOGY

Use **MindJogger Videoquiz** VHS to preview Chapter 16 content.

Introduce students to chapter content and key terms by having them access **Chapter 16—Chapter Overviews** at *ett.glencoe.com*

# CHAPTER 16

# Government Spends, Collects, and Owes

### Why It's Important

*Who owns national parks and museums? How are tax dollars and your high school related? This chapter will explain why the government collects tax dollars from you, and what it spends those funds on.*

*To learn more about the federal government's debt, view the* **Economics & You** *Chapter 15 video lesson:* **How Government Spends, Collects, and Owes**

**ECONOMICS Online**

**Chapter Overview** Visit the *Economics Today and Tomorrow* Web site at ett.glencoe.com and click on ***Chapter 16—Chapter Overviews*** to preview chapter information.

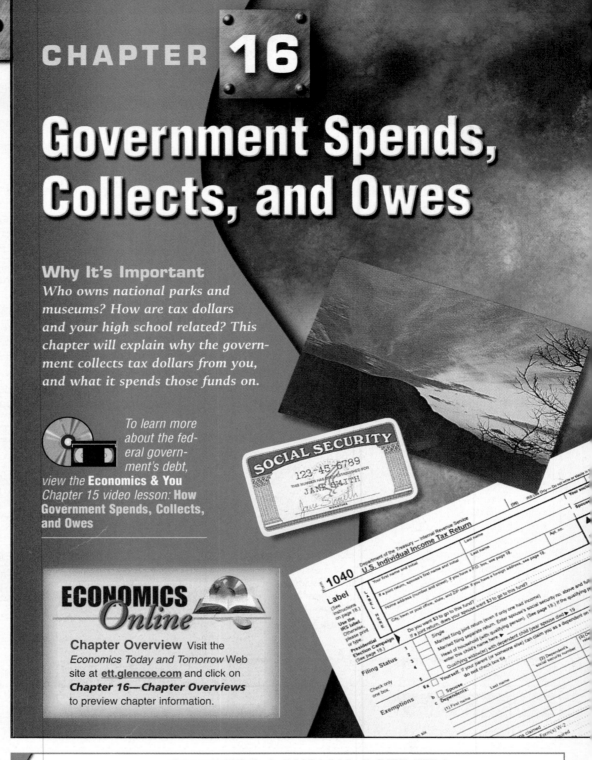

### CHAPTER LAUNCH ACTIVITY

Ask students to identify the ways in which government spending affects their lives. Have students pay special attention to the public goods they use—roads, parks, public transportation, education, and so on. Note their responses on the board. Then have students use the information on the board to write a short paragraph titled "How Government Spending Affects Everyday Life." Call on volunteers to read and discuss their paragraphs.

# SECTION 1

# Growth in the Size of Government

## READER'S GUIDE

**Terms to Know**

- public-works projects
- Medicare

**Reading Objectives**

1. What are two measurements of government growth?
2. What do some economists believe caused the growth of government?

## COVER STORY

*THE NEW YORK TIMES*, APRIL 14, 1999

The [White House] is expected to announce as early as next week requirements for cleaner gasoline and tougher pollution standards for the nation's automobiles. The expected regulations would also force sport utility vehicles and pickup trucks to meet the stricter standards for passenger cars for the first time.

Environmentalists are pleased, but the oil and auto industries say gasoline prices for all drivers and the costs of sport utility vehicles and pickup trucks would be increased.

As you learned in Chapter 2, the United States is not a pure market economy. In addition to the market forces of supply and demand, other forces affect the distribution of resources throughout the economy. As revealed in the *Cover Story* above, the government is one of the most important of these forces. As you read this section, you'll learn that government at every level—local, state, and federal—is involved in almost every aspect of the United States economy.

## Government Growth

Government has grown considerably in the last 70 years or so. In 1929, just before the Great Depression began, government at



## SECTION 1 RESOURCE MANAGER

**Reproducible Masters**

- Reproducible Lesson Plan 16–1
- Reading Essentials and Study Guide 16–1
- Guided Reading Activity 16–1
- Section Quiz 16–1
- Daily Focus Activity 65
- Daily Lecture Notes 16–1

**Multimedia**

- Daily Focus Transparency 65
- Vocabulary PuzzleMaker
- Interactive Tutor Self-Assessment Software
- ExamView® Pro Testmaker
- MindJogger Videoquiz
- Presentation Plus!



# 1 Focus

## Overview

**Section 1** describes the measurements of government growth and explains why government has grown considerably since the Great Depression.

### BELLRINGER
**Motivational Activity**

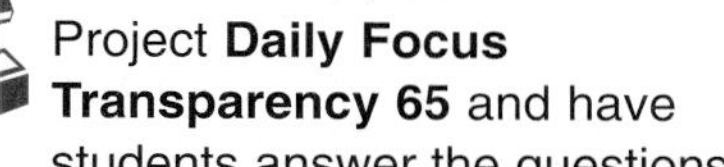

Project **Daily Focus Transparency 65** and have students answer the questions.

This activity is also available as a blackline master.

**Daily Focus Transparency 65**

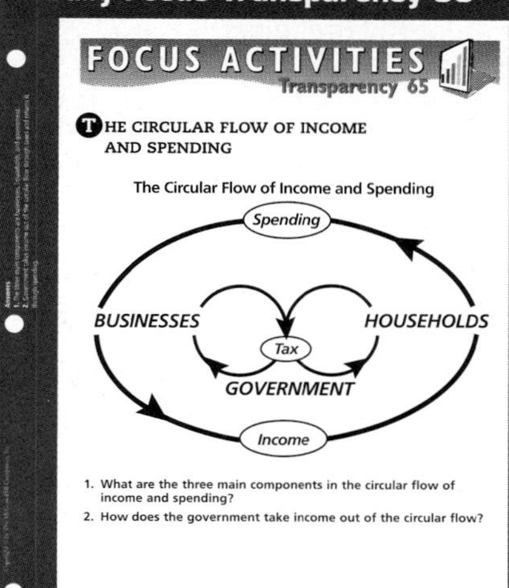

FOCUS ACTIVITIES
Transparency 65
THE CIRCULAR FLOW OF INCOME AND SPENDING
The Circular Flow of Income and Spending
Spending
BUSINESSES
HOUSEHOLDS
Tax
GOVERNMENT
Income
1. What are the three main components in the circular flow of income and spending?
2. How does the government take income out of the circular flow?
Daily Focus Transparencies


## READER'S GUIDE

Answers to the **Reading Objectives** questions are on page 427.

**Preteaching Vocabulary**

Call on volunteers to identify public-works projects that have recently been completed in their community. Ask them to explain what makes these programs public-works projects.

**Vocabulary PuzzleMaker**

# 2 Teach

## Guided Practice

**L1 Understanding Ideas** After reviewing the section with students, draw on the board a graphic organizer similar to the one below.

| *How Government Has Grown* |
|---|
| *Why Government Has Grown* |

Call on volunteers to suggest information that might be added to the graphic organizer. Enter their responses in the appropriate section of the organizer.

### Daily Lecture Notes 16-1

DAILY LECTURE NOTES  Lesson 16-1

**LECTURE LAUNCHER**

In 1956, the Federal Aid Highway Act and the Highway Revenue Act gave the government authority to raise funds for the development of the U.S. Interstate Highway System. To raise this revenue, the government instituted a federal gasoline tax and road tolls. How predominant is the government in the United States economic system? What are the three levels of government and how can they impact the economic choices in a market economy?

PAGES 423–425

I. Government Growth

A. The number of government workers and functions has increased dramatically.

B. Public-works projects are public facilities that are built and paid for with tax dollars.

**Discussion Question**

**Name some public-works projects that you use and consider important.** *(Answers may vary. Students may mention their school, a community center, a town pool, the highways, bus system, etc.)*

PAGES 425–427

I. Why Has Government Grown?

A. During the depression, more government services were needed.

all levels employed slightly more than 3 million civilian workers. During the Depression, however, there was a demand for more government services.

Today, about 2.7 million people work for the federal government alone. If you add local and state employees, the government employs about 20 million civilian workers. This figure represents more than a sixfold increase during a period in which the population only doubled.

The number of government workers has increased because the number of government functions has risen. **Figure 16.1** shows one way of looking at the government activities that affect our lives.

**Figure 16.2** on page 426 shows another way of looking at the economy. As you can see from the graph, the different levels of government have grown at different rates. During the late 1960s, state and local governments spent less than the federal government. The federal government paid for national defense; the salaries of

## FIGURE  16.1

**Government Involvement in the Economy** Government plays a major role in most aspects of our lives. Some individuals believe that government has grown too large and that the private sector should provide goods and services without government intervention. Others argue that government should be even larger.

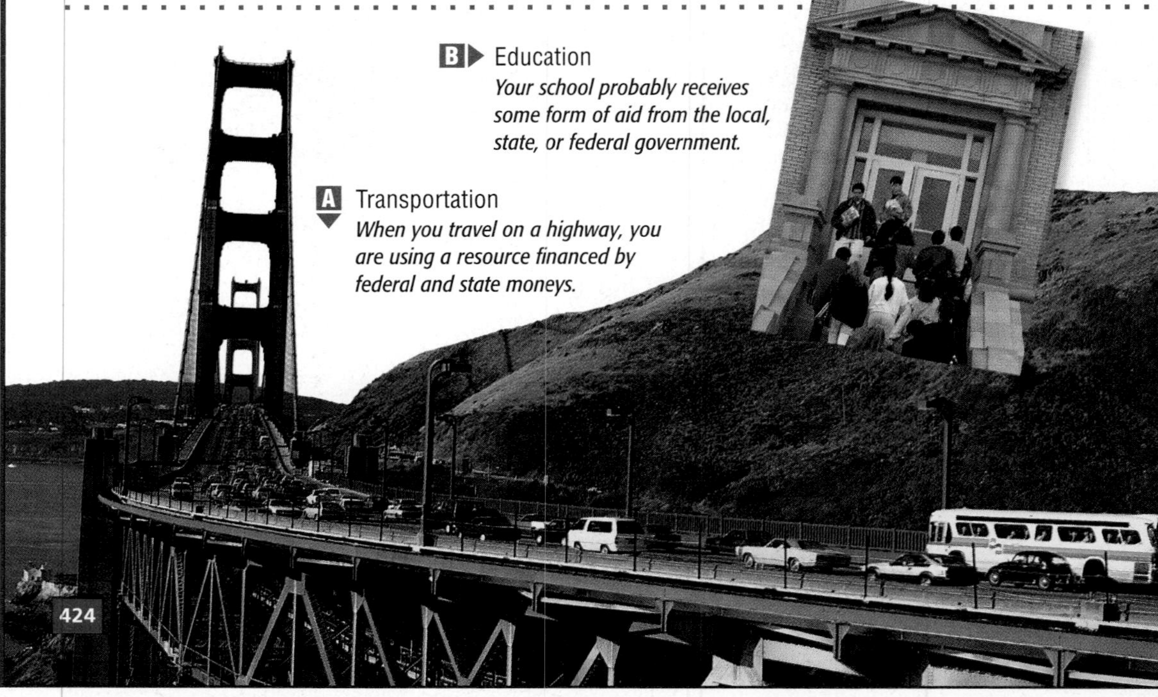

B Education
Your school probably receives some form of aid from the local, state, or federal government.
A Transportation
When you travel on a highway, you are using a resource financed by federal and state moneys.
424

## Meeting Special Needs

**Reading Disability** Students with various reading and organizational problems may have trouble understanding graphs that contain multiple lines of information. They may also have trouble connecting information from two or more graphs. Before students read Section 1, ask them to study **Figures 16.2** and **16.3** on page 426. Have them note what information each line on the graph in **Figure 16.2** provides. Then have them consider how the information provided in **Figure 16.3** adds to what they learned from **Figure 16.2.** Finally, ask students to read the section and discuss how the graphs illustrate the information in the text.

Refer to *Inclusion for the Social Studies Classroom Strategies and Activities*.

members of Congress, federal judges, and the employees of executive departments such as the State Department; and public-works projects. **Public-works projects** are publicly used facilities such as schools and highways that are built and paid for with tax dollars.

This situation continued until about 1970. At that time, federal funds diminished, while state and local government spending for such items as sewers, roads, and schools increased rapidly.

**public-works projects:** *publicly used facilities, such as schools and highways, built by federal, state, or local governments with public money*

## Why Has Government Grown?

Economists have often tried to explain the huge growth in government spending. During the Great Depression, there appeared to be a need for more government services. In the 1940s, the government spent billions of dollars to pay for World War II. Why has the government continued to grow since then?

One theory is that as the nation became richer, especially in the late 1960s and early 1970s, people demanded more government services to even out certain income inequities. Today, total government *purchases* represent over 20 percent of GDP. This figure does not include such items as interest payments on the national debt and transfer payments such as welfare programs. If you add these items, total government *outlays* easily exceed one-third of GDP. See **Figure 16.3** on page 426.

**C** Product Safety *Many goods that you buy are produced in accordance with local, state, and federal regulations.*

**D** Worker Safety *If you have a job, government safety and other regulations often determine your working conditions.*

**E** Taxation *If you own property, buy goods, or earn money income, you probably pay taxes that help pay for many government activities.*

### Cooperative Learning

Organize students into groups to research and develop a plan for a public-works project that would bring a new facility or a needed benefit to the community. Possible projects include a new freeway to ease traffic congestion, a social center for seniors, an ice rink to meet growing interest in hockey and figure skating, or a beautification program for local parks. Have each group write a justification for its selected program—why the facility is needed, how it will benefit the community, and so on. Then direct groups to draw up their plans, considering such factors as cost, funding, availability of labor, and so forth. Call on group representatives to present and discuss their plans. BLOCK SCHEDULING



### Guided Reading Activity 16-1

GUIDED READING Activity 16-1

GROWTH IN THE SIZE OF GOVERNMENT

RECALLING THE FACTS

*Directions: Use the information in your textbook to answer the questions.*

1. At what levels is the government involved in the economy?
2. Why has the number of government workers grown so much over the years?
3. What are some areas of the economy on which the government has an affect?
4. What are public-works projects?
5. Why has the government continued to grow since World War II?
6. How can one figure total government outlays?

## Independent Practice

**L3 Research Reports** Have students work individually or in small groups to research the changing role of government in the economy since the Great Depression. Suggest that they use library resources to find economic history texts covering this time period. Have them present their findings in an illustrated report suitable for displaying on the bulletin board. ELL BLOCK SCHEDULING

## Global Economy

### Governmental Systems

The United States and several other nations—Australia, Austria, India, and Mexico, for example—have a federal system of government, in which power is shared between states or provinces and the central government. However, some nations—France and Italy, for example—have a unitary system, where power and responsibility rest mainly with the central government.

# CHAPTER 16
SECTION 1, Pages 423–427

# 3 Assess

## Meeting Lesson Objectives

Assign Section 1 Assessment as homework or an in-class activity.

Use **Interactive Tutor Self-Assessment Software** to review Section 1.

**Section Quiz 16-1**

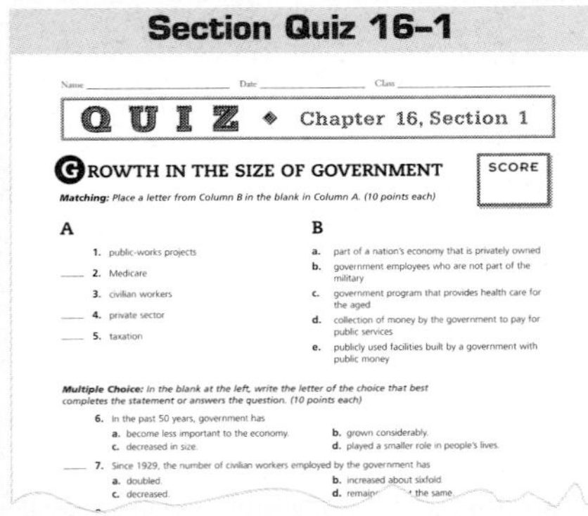

**Visual Instruction FIGURES 16.2 & 16.3**

Have students study Figures 16.2 and 16.3. Then direct them to make freehand copies of the two graphs in their notebooks. Have them extend the lines on the graphs to show at what level they think government spending will be in the years 2005, 2010, and 2015. Call on volunteers to display and explain their predictions.

**The True Size of Government** The size of government cannot be measured merely by the cost of government spending. Any discussion of the government's size must include *where* government spends this money.

When the government taxes you to provide you with a particular service, such as **Medicare** (health care for the aged), this cost of government is included in government spending. What if the

**Medicare:** *government program that provides health care for the aged*

**FIGURE 16.2**

**Government Consumption Expenditures and Gross Investment** Government purchases of goods and services (excluding Social Security and other welfare payments and interest) corrected for inflation show an increase in all levels of government spending.

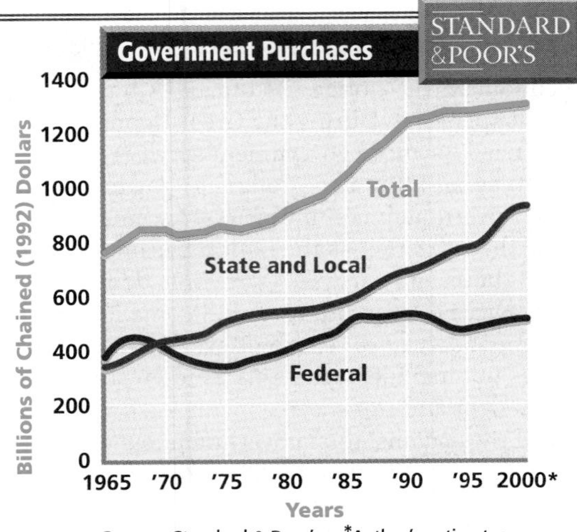


**Source:** Standard & Poor's *Author's estimates

**ECONOMICS Online** For an online update of this graph, visit ett.glencoe.com and click on ***Textbook Updates—Chapter 16.***

**FIGURE 16.3**

**Government Spending as a Percentage of GDP** Total government expenditures–including Social Security and other welfare payments, as well as interest payments–expressed as a percentage of GDP have grown from 1965 to the present.

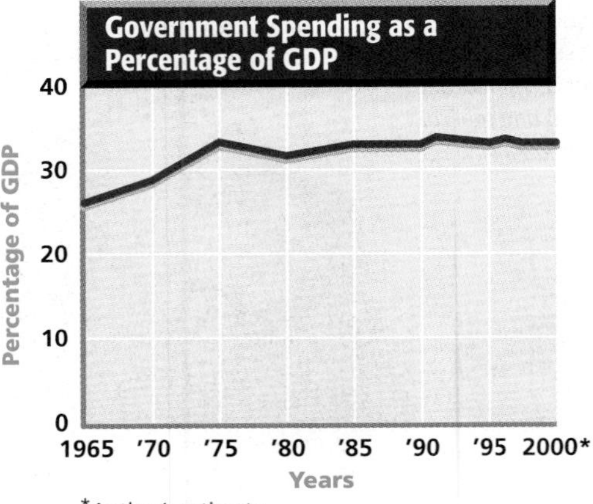


*Author's estimate
**Source:** *Economic Report of the President*, 1999



**Visual Learning Activity**

**Graphs** Draw on the board two diagrams similar to the one below.

Label one diagram "Government Workers" and the other "Government Spending." Then ask students to copy the diagrams into their notebooks and to add information from Section 1 that shows how government has grown over the years. For example, on the "Government Workers" diagram, students might place on the horizontal axis the label "1929" to the left and the label "Today" to the right. On the vertical axis, they might place the label "3 Million Workers" at the bottom and the label "20 Million Workers" at the top. Call on volunteers to display and discuss their diagrams.

government also requires that your employer provide that same service? State governments are doing just that. In Massachusetts, for example, employers with five or more employees must provide medical insurance for each employee. So, the federal government taxes employees to pay for government-provided health insurance, and a state government requires that employers provide health insurance directly. The true size of government, then, may be even greater than government estimates show because some "private sector" spending is required by law.

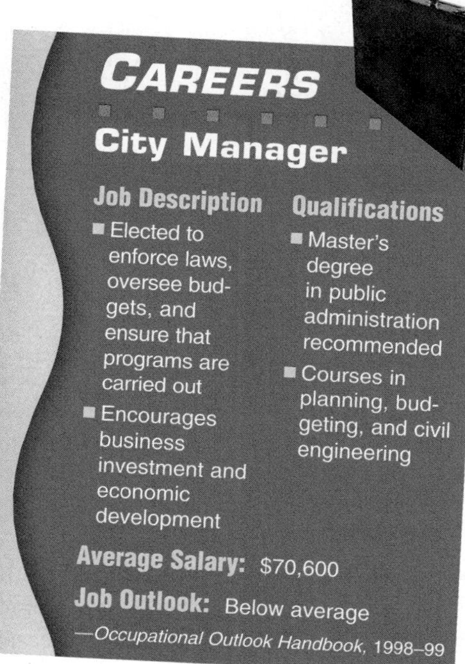

CAREERS
City Manager
Job Description
Elected to enforce laws, oversee budgets, and ensure that programs are carried out
Encourages business investment and economic development
Qualifications
Master's degree in public administration recommended
Courses in planning, budgeting, and civil engineering
Average Salary: $70,600
Job Outlook: Below average
—Occupational Outlook Handbook, 1998–99


**The Growth of Government—Good or Bad?** We know that government in the United States grew throughout the 1900s. Can we say whether this is good or bad for society? Although no one can know how much government is good for society, a general rule to remember is that government taxing and spending has opportunity costs. Government activity displaces private economic decision making along the production possibilities curve, which you learned about in Chapter 1. This private decision making involved in buying and selling is at the core of wealth creation and a rising standard of living for all citizens.

**Practice** and **assess** key skills with *Skillbuilder Interactive Workbook, Level 2.*

## SECTION 1 Assessment

### Understanding Key Terms

1. **Define** public-works projects, Medicare.

### Reviewing Objectives

2. What are two measurements of government growth?
3. **Graphic Organizer** Create a diagram like the one shown in the next column to explain what has caused the growth of government since the 1930s.

(1960s) ____
(1940s) ____
(1930s) ____
Government Grows

### Applying Economic Concepts

4. **The Role of Government** Do you think it is easier to increase or decrease government spending? Why?

### Critical Thinking Activity

5. **Synthesizing Information** According to **Figure 16.2,** by how much did government spending at all levels increase since 1970?





## Reteach

Provide each student with 10 index cards. Have students write questions—one question per card—from information found in Section 1. Pair students, and have partners quiz each other on section content using their question cards.

**Reading Essentials and Study Guide 16-1**

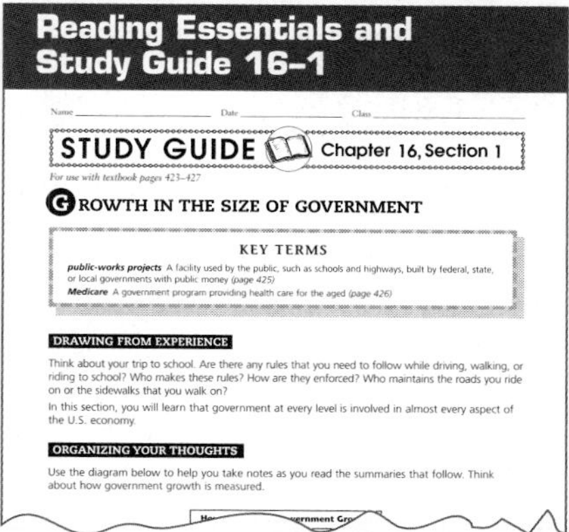


## 4 Close

Have students use information in the section to write a brief essay arguing whether government services should be expanded or reduced. Call on volunteers to read their essays, and use the readings as the starting point for a debate on this issue.

## SECTION 1 Assessment Answers

1. All definitions can be found in the Glossary.
2. the size of the government workforce and government spending
3. 1930s—social needs during the Great Depression; 1940s—expenditures for World War II; 1960s—welfare payments to even out certain income inequities
4. Students should point out that people generally oppose cuts in programs that affect them directly. Cutting programs that are considered wasteful is popular, however.
5. increased by about $500 billion

## Background

Point out that Keynes had many talents. In addition to his work as an economist, he was a journalist of some skill and an influential government official. He also made a small fortune investing in stocks and foreign currencies, and he was a renowned art collector.

# Teach

Mention that these excerpts are taken from Keynes's book *The General Theory of Employment, Interest, and Money.* In this study, Keynes hypothesized that increased government spending could have offset the collapse of business spending that brought on the economic instability of the Great Depression. Then point out that any government taxing or spending policies designed to stimulate the private sector of the economy are usually referred to as *Keynesian economics.*

People & Perspectives

## John Maynard Keynes

*ECONOMIST (1883–1946)*

- **Educated and later taught at Cambridge University**
- **Served as adviser to the British government in the 1930s and 1940s**
- **Keynesian economics named after him**
- **Most influential publication was *The General Theory of Employment, Interest, and Money* (1936)**

John Maynard Keynes originated the school of economic thought referred to as Keynesian economics, which supports the use of government spending and taxing to help the economy. Keynes believed that there was a need for government intervention, in part because an economy may reach an equilibrium level of employment that is below full employment.

Keynes added that the equilibrium level of employment depends on the level of investment. If the level of investment is low, full employment cannot be achieved:

> *"Thus, to justify any given amount of employment there must be an amount of current investment sufficient to absorb the excess of output over what the community chooses to consume when employment is at a given level. . . . It follows, that . . . the equilibrium level of employment, [that is] the level at which there is no inducement to employers as a whole either to expand or contract employment, will depend on the amount of current investment."*

Keynes believed that his theory explained why large pockets of poverty exist in otherwise rich communities or nations:

> *". . . This analysis supplies us with an explanation of the paradox of poverty in the midst of plenty. . . . Moreover the richer the community, the wider will tend to be the gap between its actual and its potential production; and therefore the more obvious and outrageous the defects of the economic system."*

### *Checking for Understanding*

1. **According to Keynes, what is the relationship between employment and current investment?**
2. **According to Keynes, what is the equilibrium level of employment?**



### Answers to *Checking for Understanding*

1. The rate of current investment determines the rate of employment.
2. It is the level at which there is no inducement to employers as a whole either to expand or contract employment.

# SECTION 2

# The Functions of Government

## COVER STORY

*BUSINESS WEEK*, NOVEMBER 30, 1998

Dorsey Ruley is that rare Chicago Bulls fan who has never leaped from his seat at a Michael Jordan moment. Emotional control has nothing to do with it. Ruley is a quadriplegic, bound to a wheelchair. During every game, all he saw was a sea of standing, clapping, stomping fans at Chicago's United Center.

Help may be on the way. A series of court judgments and settlements around the nation in recent months could force arena owners to improve seating for the disabled.

### READER'S GUIDE

**Terms to Know**

- public goods
- income redistribution
- social insurance programs
- Social Security
- workers' compensation
- public-assistance programs
- welfare
- Supplemental Security Income
- Temporary Assistance to Needy Families
- Medicaid
- externalities

**Reading Objectives**

1. What are public goods?
2. Through what two general categories does government redistribute income?
3. What are some criticisms of government involvement in the economy?

The general purpose of government in the United States is to protect individual rights, to promote a stable legal environment for economic activity, and to promote policies that support the general well-being of all citizens. In this section, you'll learn that government tries to accomplish this purpose in four ways: (1) providing public goods, (2) redistributing income, (3) regulating economic activity, and (4) ensuring economic stability.



## SECTION 2 RESOURCE MANAGER

**Reproducible Masters**

- Reproducible Lesson Plan 16–2
- Reading Essentials and Study Guide 16–2
- Guided Reading Activity 16–2
- Section Quiz 16–2
- Daily Focus Activity 67
- Daily Lecture Notes 16–2

**Multimedia**

- Daily Focus Transparency 67
- Economic Concepts Transparency 19
- Vocabulary PuzzleMaker
- Interactive Tutor Self-Assessment Software
- ExamView® Pro Testmaker
- MindJogger Videoquiz
- NBR's *Economics & You*
- Presentation Plus!



# 1 Focus

## Overview

**Section 2** describes or explains public goods, the redistribution of income, and the ways in which government regulates economic activity and promotes economic stability.

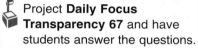

### BELLRINGER
**Motivational Activity**

Project **Daily Focus Transparency 67** and have students answer the questions.

This activity is also available as a blackline master.

**Daily Focus Transparency 67**

FINANCING STATE AND LOCAL PUBLIC WORKS

1. In this photograph, what public works have been damaged by natural disaster?
2. What effect might this damage have on a community and its finances?

Daily Focus Transparencies

### READER'S GUIDE

Answers to the **Reading Objectives** questions are on page 433.

**Preteaching Vocabulary**

Select 11 students and assign each student one of the **Terms to Know**. Have these students create a scenario illustrating their assigned term. The rest of the class should identify the terms being illustrated.

**Vocabulary PuzzleMaker**

# 2 Teach

## Guided Practice

**L1 Identify Understanding** Write at least 25 questions about section content. (Examples: What is the definition of *public goods?* Define and give an example of a demerit good.) Then organize the class into teams, and ask each team a question in turn, allowing teams about 10 seconds to answer. Give a point for each correct answer. Tally scores and award extra credit to the winning team.

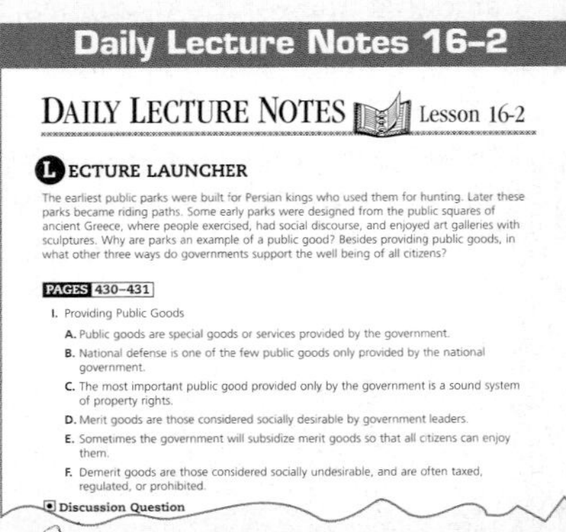

**Daily Lecture Notes 16-2**

DAILY LECTURE NOTES Lesson 16-2

LECTURE LAUNCHER

The earliest public parks were built for Persian kings who used them for hunting. Later these parks became riding paths. Some early parks were designed from the public squares of ancient Greece, where people exercised, had social discourse, and enjoyed art galleries with sculptures. Why are parks an example of a public good? Besides providing public goods, in what other three ways do governments support the well being of all citizens?

PAGES 430–431

I. Providing Public Goods
   - A. Public goods are special goods or services provided by the government.
   - B. National defense is one of the few public goods only provided by the national government.
   - C. The most important public good provided only by the government is a sound system of property rights.
   - D. Merit goods are those considered socially desirable by government leaders.
   - E. Sometimes the government will subsidize merit goods so that all citizens can enjoy them.
   - F. Demerit goods are those considered socially undesirable, and are often taxed, regulated, or prohibited.

Discussion Question

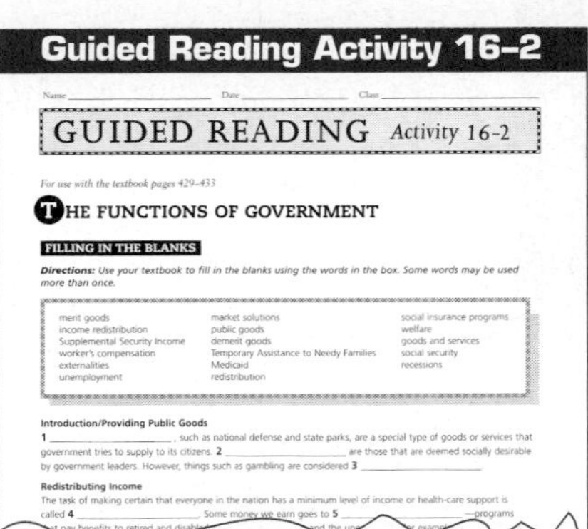

**Guided Reading Activity 16-2**

Name ______ Date ______ Class ______

GUIDED READING Activity 16-2

*For use with the textbook pages 429–433*

THE FUNCTIONS OF GOVERNMENT

FILLING IN THE BLANKS

***Directions:*** *Use your textbook to fill in the blanks using the words in the box. Some words may be used more than once.*

| | | |
|---|---|---|
| merit goods | market solutions | social insurance programs |
| income redistribution | public goods | welfare |
| Supplemental Security Income | demerit goods | goods and services |
| worker's compensation | Temporary Assistance to Needy Families | social security |
| externalities | Medicaid | recessions |
| unemployment | redistribution | |

**Introduction/Providing Public Goods**

**1** ______, such as national defense and state parks, are a special type of goods or services that government tries to supply to its citizens. **2** ______ are those that are deemed socially desirable by government leaders. However, things such as gambling are considered **3** ______.

**Redistributing Income**

The task of making certain that everyone in the nation has a minimum level of income or health-care support is called **4** ______. Some money we earn goes to **5** ______—programs

public goods: *goods or services that government supplies to its citizens; can be used by many individuals at the same time without reducing the benefit each person receives*

## Providing Public Goods

**Public goods** are a special type of goods or services that government tries to supply to its citizens. Many people can use public goods—such as streetlights—at the same time, without reducing the benefit each person receives.

National defense is one of the few public goods only the federal government provides. Usually, the different levels of government share responsibility for other types of public goods—the legal system, for example. Federal, state, and some local governments maintain separate systems of courts, correctional institutions, and law-enforcement agencies.

The most important public good that only government can provide is a sound system of property rights. In such a system, individuals have the right to own factors of production, to risk investment, and to discover new ways of production.

**Merit Goods** In any society, certain goods and services are considered to have special merit. A *merit good* is one that is deemed socially desirable by government leaders—museums, ballets, and classical music concerts, for example. The government may subsidize such goods by requiring all taxpayers to support them. This allows everyone to enjoy such goods for less than the full market price. See **Figure 16.4.**

**Demerit Goods** The opposite of merit goods are *demerit goods*. These are goods that elected government officials have deemed socially undesirable, such as gambling and injurious drugs. The government exercises its role in the area of demerit goods by taxing, regulating, or prohibiting the manufacture, sale, and use of such

THE CITIZENS
OF GEORGIA
WELCOME YOU
TO THEIR PARK

FIGURE 

**Merit Goods** The establishment and maintenance of museums and parks fall under the government function of providing merit goods.

### Meeting Special Needs

**Hearing Disability** Students whose hearing is impaired may have difficulty contributing in role-playing and discussion activities. When assigning such activities, direct students to include letters or memos that can be shared with the class as part of spoken presentations.

Refer to *Inclusion for the Social Studies Classroom Strategies and Activities* for students with different learning styles.

goods. For example, governments justify very high taxes on alcohol and tobacco products because they are demerit goods.

## Redistributing Income

Another function of government is to provide for the public well-being by assisting specific groups such as the aged, the ill, and the poor. Through their elected representatives, Americans have chosen to see that almost everyone in the nation is provided with a certain minimum level of income and health-care support. This task is accomplished primarily through **income redistribution,** or using tax receipts to assist citizens in need. Tax dollars are used to subsidize two general categories of assistance: social insurance programs and public-assistance programs.

**income redistribution:** *government activity that takes income from some people through taxation and uses it to help citizens in need*

**Social Insurance Programs** When you receive a paycheck, you will notice that a portion of your pay has been withheld by various levels of government. Some of this money is earmarked for **social insurance programs**—programs that pay benefits to retired and disabled workers, their families, and the unemployed. These benefits are financed by taxes that you, other workers, and employers pay into the programs. Examples of social insurance programs include **Social Security,** a federal program that provides monthly payments to people who are retired or unable to work. Upon retirement, you are also eligible for Medicare, a federal program that provides low-cost health care for the aged.

Another social insurance program is **workers' compensation,** a state program that provides payments for medical care to workers injured on the job. People who have lost jobs altogether can receive payments through *unemployment insurance.*

**social insurance programs:** *government programs that pay benefits to retired and disabled workers, their families, and the unemployed*

**Social Security:** *federal program that provides monthly payments to people who are retired or unable to work*

**workers' compensation:** *government program that extends payments for medical care to workers injured on the job*

**Public-Assistance Programs** **Public-assistance programs,** often called **welfare,** are different from social insurance programs. Public-assistance programs make payments to individuals based on need, regardless of whether a person has paid taxes into the program.

Included in this category are **Supplemental Security Income,** a federally financed and administered program that makes payments to the aged, blind, and disabled; and **Temporary Assistance to Needy Families,** a state-run program that provides money to needy single parents raising young children. **Medicaid,** a state and federal program that provides free health care for low-income and disabled persons, is another public-assistance program.

**public-assistance programs/welfare:** *government programs that make payments to citizens based on need*

**Supplemental Security Income:** *federal programs that include food stamps, veterans' benefits, and payments to the disabled*

**Temporary Assistance to Needy Families:** *state-run program that provides money to needy single parents*

**Medicaid:** *state and federal public-assistance program that provides free health care for low-income and disabled persons*

**ECONOMICS & YOU**

**Government Spending**

Chapter 16
Disc 1, Side 2

**ASK: What are transfer payments?** *Transfer payments are payments, such as Social Security and welfare, that go from taxpayers to people who are not producing goods and services.*

 Also available in VHS.

Project **Economic Concepts Transparency 19** and have students discuss the accompanying questions.

## Independent Practice

**L3** **Applying Ideas** Have students study the major functions of government regulation listed in **Figure 16.5.** Tell students that different interest groups—business associations, labor unions, environmental groups, and consumer groups, for example—strive to influence government regulation of the economy. Have students identify a good or service and then discover how different interest groups might press for government regulation of the production, distribution, or consumption of that good or service. Encourage students to present their findings to the class in oral reports.

### Cooperative Learning

Organize students into several groups, and tell groups that they are design teams hired to create a brochure for the government. The brochure should inform the general public in a lively and entertaining way of the economic functions of government. Suggest that students make their brochures from one sheet of letter-size paper—folded in half to make a four-page brochure, one page for each of the four functions. Call on groups to display and discuss their brochures. BLOCK SCHEDULING

## Visual Instruction FIGURE 16.5

Have students review the information in **Figure 16.5.** Then call on volunteers to suggest an example for each of the four functions. *Examples may vary but might include: Protecting Consumers–setting safety standards for products; Promoting Competition–reviewing mergers of companies; Supervising Labor and Management–arbitration of labor-management disagreements; Regulating Negative By-Products of Production Process–setting pollution-control standards.*

# 3 Assess

## Meeting Lesson Objectives

Assign Section 2 Assessment as homework or an in-class activity.

Use **Interactive Tutor Self-Assessment Software** to review Section 2.

### Section Quiz 16-2

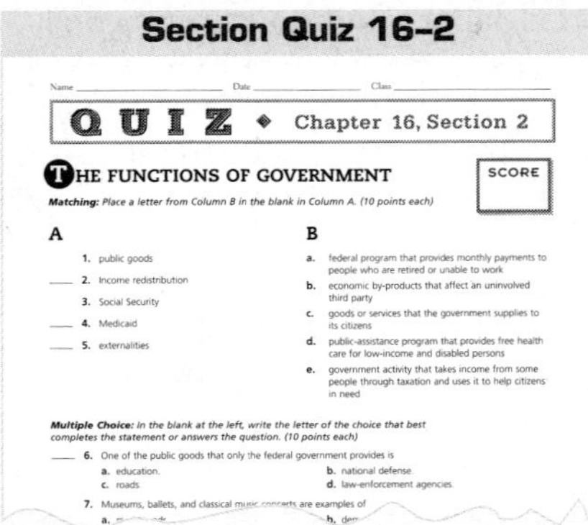

Name ______ Date ______ Class ______

QUIZ ◆ Chapter 16, Section 2

THE FUNCTIONS OF GOVERNMENT

SCORE

**Matching:** *Place a letter from Column B in the blank in Column A. (10 points each)*

**A**

____ 1. public goods
____ 2. Income redistribution
____ 3. Social Security
____ 4. Medicaid
____ 5. externalities

**B**

a. federal program that provides monthly payments to people who are retired or unable to work
b. economic by-products that affect an uninvolved third party
c. goods or services that the government supplies to its citizens
d. public-assistance program that provides free health care for low-income and disabled persons
e. government activity that takes income from some people through taxation and uses it to help citizens in need

**Multiple Choice:** *In the blank at the left, write the letter of the choice that best completes the statement or answers the question. (10 points each)*

____ 6. One of the public goods that only the federal government provides is
a. education.
b. national defense.
c. roads.
d. law-enforcement agencies.

7. Museums, ballets, and classical music concerts are examples of

FIGURE 16.5 **Government Regulations** Government under the American free enterprise system regulates certain aspects of the economy.

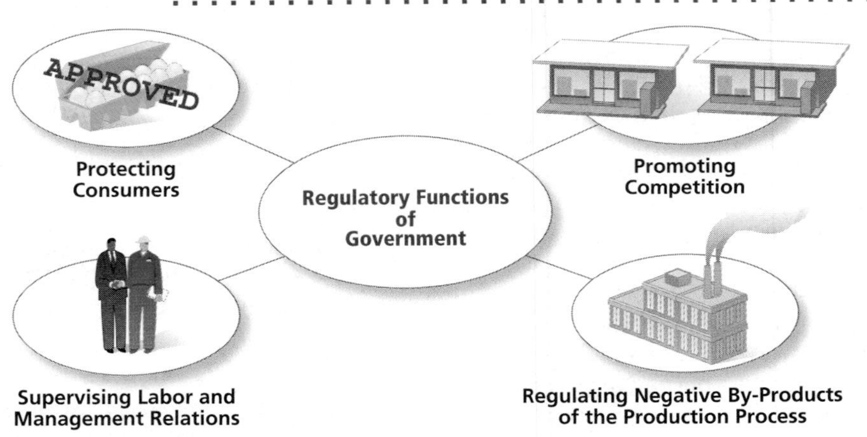


## Regulating Economic Activity

**Figure 16.5** illustrates four ways in which the government intervenes in economic activity. One of the most important regulatory functions concerns the side effects of the production process–also called **externalities.** When a steel mill produces steel, for example, the resulting pollution from the smokestacks may cause health problems in the surrounding area. In the absence of legal rules that limit such pollution, the steel mill does not have to correct these negative externalities. Government has often stepped in to require plants to install equipment that will reduce pollution.

**externalities:** *economic side effects or by-products that affect an uninvolved third party; can be negative or positive*

## Ensuring Economic Stability

Ensuring economic stability has meant smoothing the ups and downs in the nation's overall business activity. Such intervention has been sought to shield citizens from the harmful effects of business fluctuations, including unemployment, high inflation, recessions, and even depressions. In Chapter 17, you'll learn more about the government's attempt to stabilize the economy.



## Extending the Content

**Pollution Permits** The United States Environmental Protection Agency (EPA) and state environment departments have developed an interesting way of dealing with the negative externality of pollution. The EPA and the states sell permits to industries that allow the release of set amounts of pollutants. The money made from these sales is used for environmental cleanup and protection programs. Over time, the number of permits issued will be reduced, and industries will have to install antipollution devices or face stiff fines for violating pollution standards.

## Critics of Government Involvement

There are many critics of government involvement in the economy. They point out that merit goods, for example, should be provided by private organizations. If people pay fewer taxes, they have more disposable income and can choose to fund symphonies or other merit goods if they really want such services.

Opponents of redistribution programs think that most government assistance discourages personal initiative, affects incentives, and harms self-development. Critics of government regulations argue that most regulations raise the prices of goods and services. A better approach, these critics say, would be to encourage market solutions to such problems as pollution.

### Working in Britain

In the mid-1940s, the British government established a welfare system designed to provide its citizens with economic security "from cradle to grave." Over the years, the system grew and now accounts for more than 30 percent of the government's annual budget. Almost half of all Britons receive some form of assistance—from retirement pensions to housing benefits.

In 1999 Prime Minister Tony Blair called for an overhaul of the system. "If you can work," he stated, "you should work." He suggested that people who receive welfare assistance would have to actively seek employment or risk losing their benefits: "The days of an automatic right to benefit will go." ■

**Practice** and **assess** key skills with *Skillbuilder Interactive Workbook, Level 2.*

## SECTION 2 Assessment

### Understanding Key Terms

1. **Define** public goods, income redistribution, social insurance programs, Social Security, workers' compensation, public-assistance programs, welfare, Supplemental Security Income, Temporary Assistance to Needy Families, Medicaid, externalities.

### Reviewing Objectives

2. What are public goods?
3. **Graphic Organizer** Create a chart like the one below to list the programs through which government redistributes income.

| Social Insurance Programs | Public-Assistance Programs |
|---|---|
| | |

4. What are some criticisms of government involvement in the economy?

### Applying Economic Concepts

5. **The Role of Government** List five ways that local, state, and federal government are involved in your daily life. Provide specific examples in your list.

### Critical Thinking Activity

6. **Summarizing Information** In a paragraph, list at least three activities or "goods" that you think should be considered merit goods, or goods that are deemed socially desirable by government leaders. Then describe why you think the government should or should not be involved in providing merit goods to society.





### Global Economy

**Welfare System Changes**

One change to the system that Prime Minister Blair proposed was that unemployment benefits for young people should be limited to six months. After that, they would have to find work or enter a job-training program.

## Reteach

Have students use headings, **Terms to Know**, and caption information to create an outline for a brief essay on the economic functions of government.

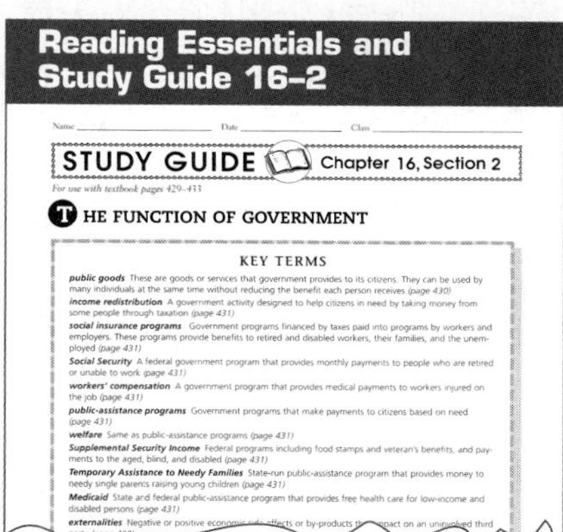

**Reading Essentials and Study Guide 16–2**

Name ______ Date ______ Class ______

STUDY GUIDE Chapter 16, Section 2

*For use with textbook pages 429–433*

THE FUNCTION OF GOVERNMENT

KEY TERMS

***public goods*** These are goods or services that government provides to its citizens. They can be used by many individuals at the same time without reducing the benefit each person receives *(page 430)*

***income redistribution*** A government activity designed to help citizens in need by taking money from some people through taxation *(page 431)*

***social insurance programs*** Government programs financed by taxes paid into programs by workers and employers. These programs provide benefits to retired and disabled workers, their families, and the unemployed *(page 431)*

***Social Security*** A federal government program that provides monthly payments to people who are retired or unable to work *(page 431)*

***workers' compensation*** A government program that provides medical payments to workers injured on the job *(page 431)*

***public-assistance programs*** Government programs that make payments to citizens based on need *(page 431)*

***welfare*** Same as public-assistance programs *(page 431)*

***Supplemental Security Income*** Federal programs including food stamps and veteran's benefits, and payments to the aged, blind, and disabled *(page 431)*

***Temporary Assistance to Needy Families*** State-run public-assistance program that provides money to needy single parents raising young children *(page 431)*

***Medicaid*** State and federal public-assistance program that provides free health care for low-income and disabled persons *(page 431)*

***externalities*** Negative or positive economic side effects or by-products th[illegible]pact on an uninvolved third party *(page 4[illegible]*

## 4 Close

Discuss with students how people at different ages benefit from the four functions of government.

## SECTION 2 Assessment Answers

1. All definitions can be found in the Glossary.
2. Public goods are goods and services government supplies to its citizens.
3. Social Insurance Programs: Social Security, Medicare, workers' compensation; Public-Assistance Programs: Supplemental Security Income, Temporary Assistance to Needy Families, Medicaid
4. Critics feel that public goods should be provided by private organizations and that government assistance discourages personal initiative and reduces incentives as well as raises the prices of goods and services.
5. Answers may include providing schools, roads, water, sanitation; regulating food products, medicines, working conditions; taxing; consumer protection.
6. Answers will vary. Ensure that students explain why their selected goods and services should be considered socially desirable.

BusinessWeek
**Spotlight**

# Teach

Point out that many Americans are concerned over the future of the Social Security system. They fear that as the American population ages, more money will be withdrawn from the system than will be paid into it by workers. Encourage students to research the ideas put forward to secure the future of Social Security. Suggest that a good starting point for research is the Social Security Administration's Web site at www.ssa.gov. Call on volunteers to share their findings with the class.

**BusinessWeek ONLINE**

To find up-to-date news and analysis on the economy, business, technology, markets, entrepreneurs, investments, and finance, have students search feature articles and special reports on the *Business Week* Web site.
www.businessweek.com

**Sidelight**

You do not have to be a senior citizen to receive Social Security. You may be eligible for Social Security if you have a parent who is retired, disabled, or who has died. In 1999, about 3 million children under age 18 received monthly Social Security checks.

# BusinessWeek

## Spotlight on the Economy

## Social Security Is Aptly Named

**Check It Out!** In this chapter you learned that one function of government is to provide for the public well-being. In this article, read to learn how distributing income through Social Security can increase the well-being of the elderly.

One result of the current Social Security debate has been to concentrate the public's mind on the true economic condition of the elderly—and to give the lie to those who describe them as "greedy geezers." While the top 20% of seniors are relatively affluent, reports the Center on Budget & Policy Priorities, almost all of the rest are highly dependent on Social Security.

In 1997, the average Social Security retirement benefit was just $765 a month, and the average check to 65-year-olds was $819 a month—a tidy sum, but hardly a bonanza. Yet, according to the center's analysis, the program provided at least half of the total income of more than 55% of senior citizens and at least 75% of the total income of more than a third.

Social Security's impact on poverty among older Americans is equally revealing. Based on 1997 Census Bureau data, the center finds that the retirement program lifted 11.4 million seniors—or nearly half of the 65-and-older population—out of poverty, cutting the elderly's poverty rate from 47.6% to 11.9%. Means-tested programs, such as Supplemental Security Income, lowered the rate still further to 10.5%—bringing it close to that of other adult Americans.



### Think About It

1. What percentage of senior citizens rely on Social Security to provide half of their income?
2. How many seniors were lifted out of poverty by Social Security payments?

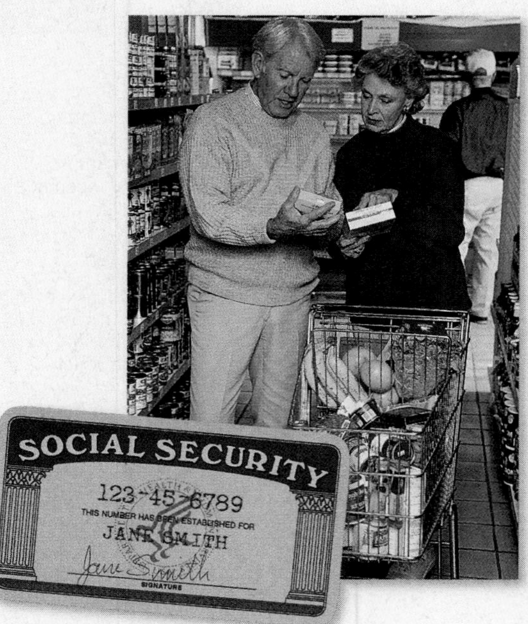




### Answers to *Think About It*

1. more than 55 percent
2. 11.4 million senior citizens

SECTION 3

# The Federal Budget and the National Debt

## Cover Story

*The New York Times*, January 31, 1999

The federal budget deficit is gone, transformed by a strong economy into a string of projected surpluses that should grow larger for years to come. . . .

Eliminating the deficit is hardly the end of the government's financial troubles, however. . . . [T]he national debt was built up over decades of deficit spending—the federal government has not run steady surpluses since the 1920s—and it remains an economic millstone of considerable proportions.

### Reader's Guide

**Terms to Know**

- fiscal year
- budget deficit
- deficit financing
- national debt
- budget surplus

**Reading Objectives**

1. What are the steps in the federal budget-making process?
2. What are the five largest federal expenditures?
3. What are the five largest state and local government expenditures?
4. How does deficit spending increase the national debt?

To carry out all of its functions, government must spend huge sums of money. As a result, the federal budget is huge and has numerous categories. Because all resources are scarce, an increase in spending in one area will cause a decrease in spending in some other area. *Parts A* and *B* of **Figure 16.6** on page 436 show the major areas in which the federal and state and local governments spend their money. As you read this section, you'll learn how the government prepares its budget and decides where to spend its funds.





# 1 Focus

## Overview

Section 3 explains the steps in the federal budget-making process and how deficit spending increases the nation's public debt.

### BELLRINGER
**Motivational Activity**

Project **Daily Focus Transparency 68** and have students answer the questions.

This activity is also available as a blackline master.

**Daily Focus Transparency 68**

FOCUS ACTIVITIES Transparency 68

THE NATIONAL DEBT

Interest Paid on the National Debt 1940–2000

| Year | Interest Paid on National Debt (billions) | Percent of Federal Expenditures |
|---|---|---|
| 1940 | $1 | 11.0 |
| 1950 | $5.7 | 13.4 |
| 1960 | $9.2 | 10.0 |
| 1970 | $19.3 | 9.9 |
| 1980 | $74.9 | 12.7 |
| 1990 | $264.8 | 21.8 |
| 2000* | $370 | 22.5 |

*estimated

Source: *Statistical Abstract of the United States*

1. Write a one-sentence summary of the table.
2. Which decade had the greatest increase in interest paid on the national debt in both dollar terms and as a percentage of federal expenditures?

Daily Focus Transparencies

### Reader's Guide

Answers to the **Reading Objectives** questions are on page 439.

**Preteaching Vocabulary**

Ask students to use the **Terms to Know** to write a description of the federal budget-making process.

Vocabulary PuzzleMaker

## SECTION 3 RESOURCE MANAGER

**Reproducible Masters**

- Reproducible Lesson Plan 16–3
- Reading Essentials and Study Guide 16–3
- Guided Reading Activity 16–3
- Section Quiz 16–3
- Daily Focus Activity 68
- Daily Lecture Notes 16–3

**Multimedia**

- Daily Focus Transparency 68
- Vocabulary PuzzleMaker
- Interactive Tutor Self-Assessment Software
- ExamView® Pro Testmaker
- MindJogger Videoquiz
- NBR's *Economics & You*
- Presentation Plus!

# 2 Teach

## Guided Practice

**L2 Analyzing Ideas** Review the constitutional principle of checks and balances with students. Then work through the flowchart of the federal budget-making process in **Figure 16.7** on page 437. Ask students to write a few sentences explaining how the making of the federal budget demonstrates the principle of checks and balances.

**Daily Lecture Notes 16–3**

DAILY LECTURE NOTES Lesson 16-3

LECTURE LAUNCHER

Social Security first began in 1935 during the Great Depression. By about 2012 more money will go out in benefits than will come in as revenue. This deficit will be covered by the surplus in Social Security, but only until about 2032, when the trust will be bankrupt. How might an increase in spending on Social Security affect the federal budget? What kinds of budgetary decisions will the government have to make between now and 2032?

PAGES 437–438

I. The Budget Making Process
   - A. The Federal Budget is prepared about 18 months before the fiscal year.
   - B. The President, the Office of Management and Budget (OMB) work together to outline a budget plan.
   - C. The President approves budget and then submits it to Congress.
   - D. Congress then examines and discusses the budget, and should pass it before the coming fiscal year.
   - E. Often the budget is not passed until after the fiscal year has already begun.
   - F. The largest category in state and local budgets is education.
   - G. Other large categories include public assistance, hospitals, health maintenance, and highways.

Discussion Question

## Visual Instruction FIGURE 16.6

Have students study the information in **Figure 16.6.** ASK: What categories of spending do you find surprising? Why? Then have students compare the information in Part A with that in Part B. Ask students to combine the data and draw bar graphs showing the total spending for federal, state, and local governments.

## FIGURE 16.6

**Part A Federal Spending** The federal budget is based on a fiscal year, rather than the calendar year. Spending is calculated from the beginning of the budget year on October 1 of one year to September 30 of the next year.

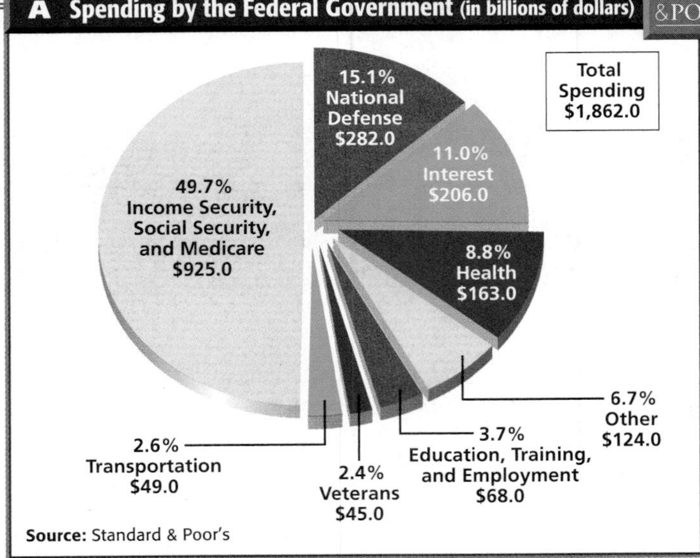


**Part B State and Local Government Spending** State and local government expenditures have increased in recent years, as these governments cover the rising costs of social welfare programs.

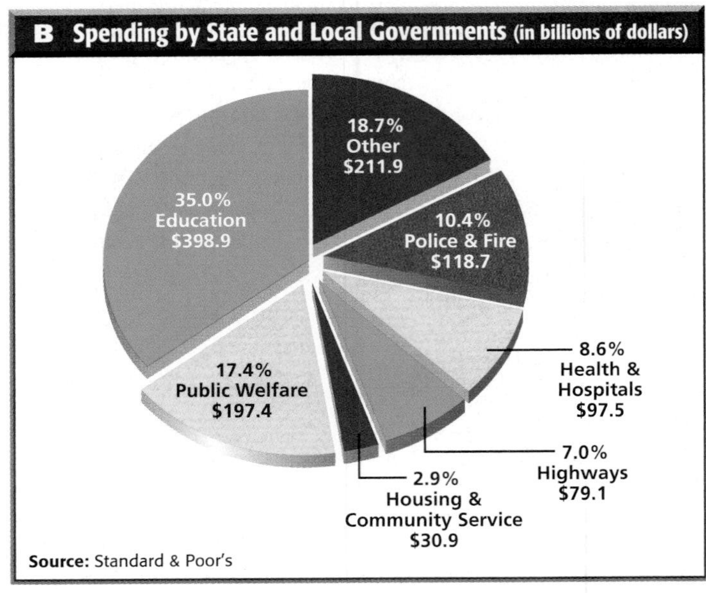

For online updates of these graphs, visit ett.glencoe.com and click on ***Textbook Updates—Chapter 16.***

436 CHAPTER 16

## Meeting Special Needs

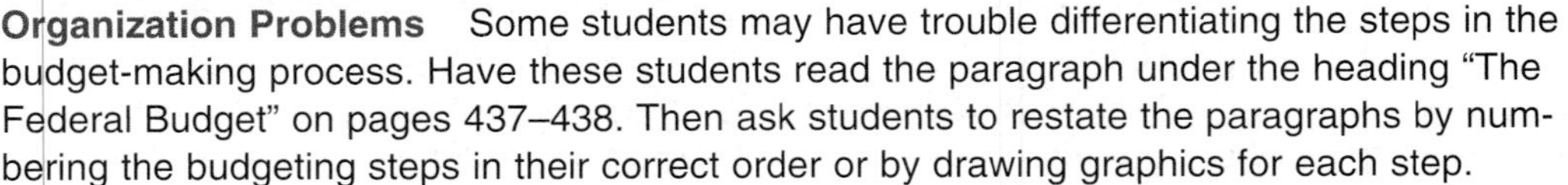

**Organization Problems** Some students may have trouble differentiating the steps in the budget-making process. Have these students read the paragraph under the heading "The Federal Budget" on pages 437–438. Then ask students to restate the paragraphs by numbering the budgeting steps in their correct order or by drawing graphics for each step.

Refer to *Inclusion for the Social Studies Classroom Strategies and Activities* for students with different learning styles.

## FIGURE 16.7

**The Federal Budget-Making Process** The Office of Management and Budget (OMB) starts the budget process, with the advice of the Council of Economic Advisers and the Treasury Department.

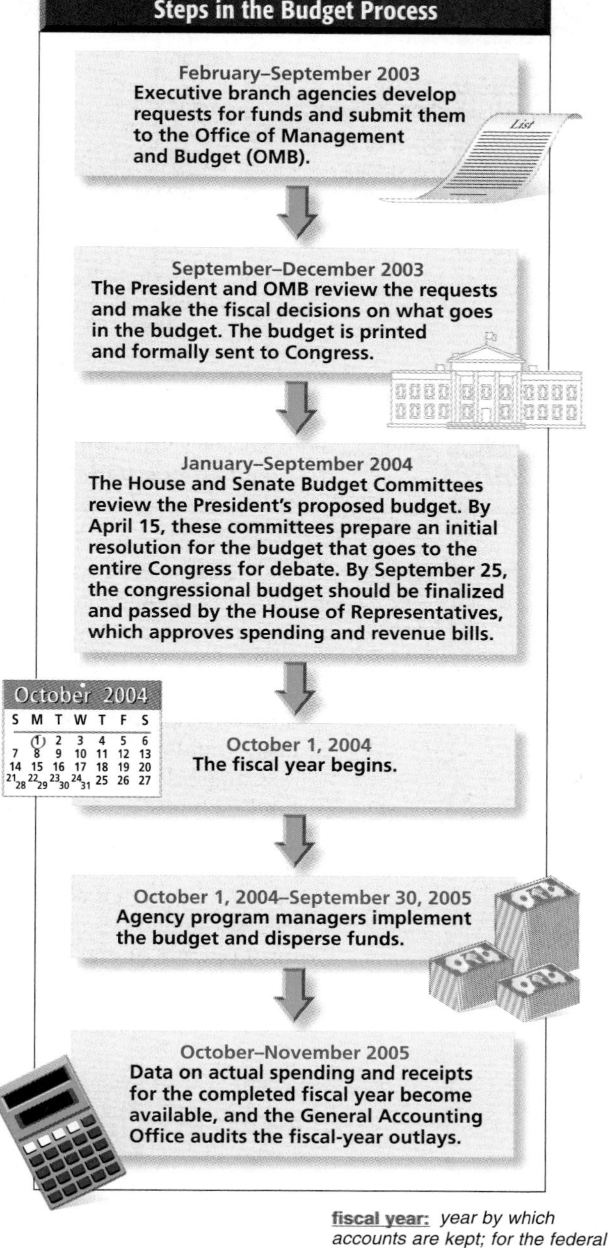

Steps in the Budget Process
February–September 2003
Executive branch agencies develop requests for funds and submit them to the Office of Management and Budget (OMB).
List
September–December 2003
The President and OMB review the requests and make the fiscal decisions on what goes in the budget. The budget is printed and formally sent to Congress.
January–September 2004
The House and Senate Budget Committees review the President's proposed budget. By April 15, these committees prepare an initial resolution for the budget that goes to the entire Congress for debate. By September 25, the congressional budget should be finalized and passed by the House of Representatives, which approves spending and revenue bills.
October 2004
S M T W T F S
1 2 3 4 5 6
7 8 9 10 11 12 13
14 15 16 17 18 19 20
21 22 23 24 25 26 27
28 29 30 31
October 1, 2004
The fiscal year begins.
October 1, 2004–September 30, 2005
Agency program managers implement the budget and disperse funds.
October–November 2005
Data on actual spending and receipts for the completed fiscal year become available, and the General Accounting Office audits the fiscal-year outlays.


*Part B* of **Figure 16.6** shows how state and local governments spend the tax revenues they collect. The largest single category by far in state and local expenditures is education. The "other" expenditure includes expenditures for such things as state parks and state courts.

## The Budget-Making Process

Considerable debate and compromise are necessary in preparing an annual budget. A complicated budget-making process goes on every year, not just in Washington, D.C., but in every state and local government unit as well.

**The Federal Budget** About 18 months before the **fiscal year** begins on October 1, the executive branch of the government begins to prepare a budget, as **Figure 16.7** shows. Working with the President, the Office of Management and Budget (OMB) makes an outline of a tentative budget for the next fiscal year. The various departments and agencies receive this outline and usually start bargaining with the OMB for a larger allocation of federal funds.

**fiscal year:** *year by which accounts are kept; for the federal government, October 1 to September 30 of the next year*



## Cooperative Learning

Point out to students that in recent years there has been considerable debate on a balanced budget amendment to the Constitution. Organize students into groups, and have groups use library and Internet resources to research the major arguments for and against this amendment. Encourage groups to use their findings to create a Web site designed to inform people about the balanced budget amendment debate. Call on groups to display and discuss their Web site designs. BLOCK SCHEDULING



**Guided Reading Activity 16-3**

GUIDED READING Activity 16-3

THE FEDERAL BUDGET AND THE NATIONAL DEBT

OUTLINING

I. The Budget Making Process
A. Introduction—Where does the budget-making process happen?
B. The Federal Budget
1. Who prepares the tentative budget for each fiscal year?
2. How does the budget flow through Congress?
3. How does the government operate if the budget is not passed on time?
II. Deficit Spending and the National Debt

Government Spending

Chapter 16
Disc 1, Side 2

ASK: What circumstances have led to the United States having a national debt? *In certain years, the government has spent more than it received in taxes. It therefore had to borrow money from individuals and other countries. Until the government is able to pay all this money back with interest, we will have a national debt.*

Also available in VHS.

## Independent Practice

**L3 Research** Direct students to conduct research on the federal budget and their state's budget for the present year. Ask them to present their findings in an illustrated report.

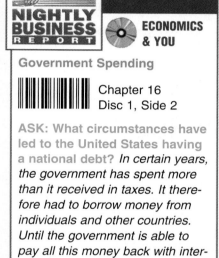

### Visual Instruction FIGURE 16.8

As students review **Figure 16.8**, mention that the national debt grew steadily in the second half of the twentieth century because the federal government ran a deficit in all but 6 of the 59 years between 1940 and 1998.

### Did You Know

On average, the federal government spends about $3.4 million every minute.

## 3 Assess

### Meeting Lesson Objectives

Assign Section 3 Assessment as homework or an in-class activity.

Use **Interactive Tutor Self-Assessment Software** to review Section 3.

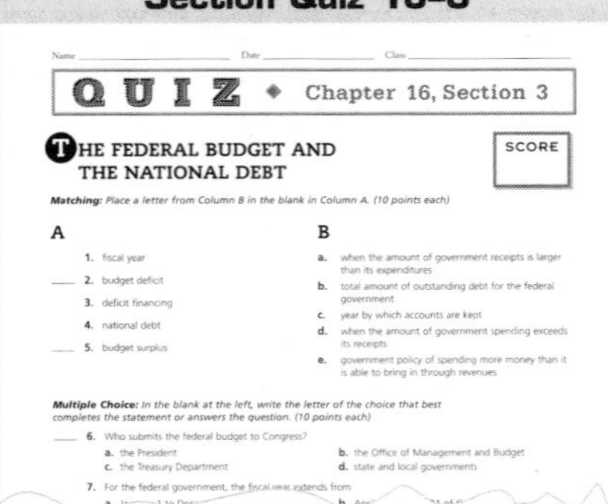

**Section Quiz 16–3**

Name ________ Date ________ Class ________

QUIZ ◆ Chapter 16, Section 3

THE FEDERAL BUDGET AND THE NATIONAL DEBT

SCORE

***Matching:*** *Place a letter from Column B in the blank in Column A. (10 points each)*

| A | B |
|---|---|
| ___ 1. fiscal year | a. when the amount of government receipts is larger than its expenditures |
| ___ 2. budget deficit | b. total amount of outstanding debt for the federal government |
| ___ 3. deficit financing | c. year by which accounts are kept |
| ___ 4. national debt | d. when the amount of government spending exceeds its receipts |
| ___ 5. budget surplus | e. government policy of spending more money than it is able to bring in through revenues |

***Multiple Choice:*** *In the blank at the left, write the letter of the choice that best completes the statement or answers the question. (10 points each)*

___ 6. Who submits the federal budget to Congress?
a. the President
b. the Office of Management and Budget
c. the Treasury Department
d. state and local governments

7. For the federal government, the fiscal year extends from

## FIGURE 16.8

**Net National Debt** The net national debt of the United States increased almost 26 percent between 1992 and 1997. The net national debt started to decline slightly from 1998 on.

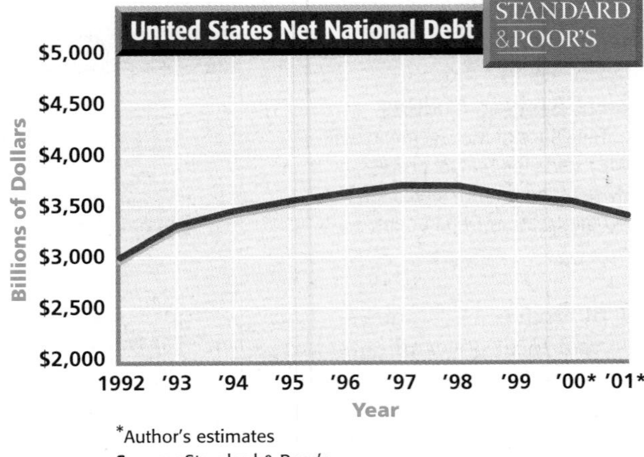


ECONOMICS Online For an online update of this graph, visit ett.glencoe.com and click on ***Textbook Updates—Chapter 16.***

The President reviews and approves the budget plan. The budget is printed, and the President submits the budget to Congress by January. Then various committees and subcommittees of Congress examine the budget's proposals, while the Congressional Budget Office (CBO) advises the committees about different aspects of the budget. Throughout the year, each committee holds a series of discussions.

Congress is supposed to pass two budget resolutions that set binding limits on spending and taxes for the upcoming fiscal year. In practice, however, the required budget resolutions often do not get passed on time. Moreover, when they are passed, the resolutions are not always treated as binding. As a result, the fiscal year sometimes starts without a budget, and the government must operate on the basis of a continuing congressional resolution. Agencies that allocate funds can continue spending as they spent the year before until the new budget resolution is passed.

## Deficit Spending and the National Debt

In spite of the budget process outlined above, federal government revenues have not always been equal to government expenditures. Most years, the federal government spent more than it collected in taxes, causing a **budget deficit.** When a budget deficit occurs, the government must raise the extra funds through

**budget deficit:** *situation when the amount of government spending exceeds its receipts during the fiscal year*



### Relevant Issues in Economics

**Future Government Spending** Some economists feel that the government practice of spending more than it receives will create serious problems in the future, even if there are no budget deficits today. Most of these problems are related to the so-called baby boom generation—Americans born between 1946 and 1964. In the years from 2011 to 2029, some 78 million baby boomers will turn 65. They will collect Social Security benefits and will need medical care, the cost of which—for the most part—will be covered by the federal Medicare program. Currently, Medicare expenses equal about 2.5 percent of GDP. Some economists estimate that by 2030 this figure will rise to about 14 percent.

borrowing. This borrowing is similar to an individual overspending his or her income and using credit. The government's overspending is called **deficit financing.**

**Government Borrowing** Government borrows money to cover the deficit by selling securities to individuals and businesses. Federal securities include Treasury bonds, notes, and bills. When you buy United States savings bonds, you are also lending funds to the federal government. In addition, individual agencies of the federal government, such as the Tennessee Valley Authority, are authorized to sell bonds. State and local governments can borrow by selling bonds to finance some of their activities.

Each year the federal government creates new debt by issuing new securities. At the same time, it retires old debt by paying off bonds, notes, and bills as they come due. The total amount of outstanding debt for the federal government is called the **national debt,** or public debt.

As you can see from **Figure 16.8,** from the beginning of the 1990s until 1997, the dollar amount of the net national debt grew. The government ran a **budget surplus**—government revenues exceeded government expenditures during the fiscal year—in 1998, 1999, and 2000. A budget surplus does not mean that the national debt is reduced, however. It only means that the debt does not grow.

**deficit financing:** *government policy of spending more money than it is able to bring in through revenues*

**national debt:** *total amount of outstanding debt for the federal government*

**budget surplus:** *situation when the amount of government receipts is larger than its expenditures during the fiscal year*

**Practice** and **assess** key skills with *Skillbuilder Interactive Workbook, Level 2.*

## SECTION 3 Assessment

### Understanding Key Terms

1. **Define** fiscal year, budget deficit, deficit financing, national debt, budget surplus.

### Reviewing Objectives

2. **Graphic Organizer** Create a diagram like the one below to describe the steps in the federal budget-making process.

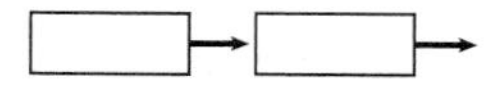

3. What are the five largest federal expenses?
4. What are the five largest state and local expenses?
5. How does deficit spending increase the size of the national debt?

### Applying Economic Concepts

6. **Trade-Offs** If you had to reduce spending at the state and local levels, which categories shown in *Part B* of **Figure 16.6** would you reduce? Why?

### Critical Thinking Activity

7. **Categorizing Information** What is your share of the national debt today? Search the Internet under *national debt* for the debt total, then divide that number by an estimate of the current population.



## SECTION 3 Assessment Answers

1. All definitions can be found in the Glossary.
2. Graphic organizers should resemble **Figure 16.7** on page 437.
3. income security, Social Security, and Medicare; national defense; interest on the debt; health; and other
4. education; other; public welfare; police and fire; health and hospitals
5. When the government uses deficit spending, it must borrow to make up the shortfall. The money that the government has yet to pay back is the national debt. Continued deficit spending will add to the debt.
6. Ensure that students fully explain their choices.
7. Answers will vary but will be in the range of $20,000. Suggest that students visit the Bureau of Public Debt's Web site at *www.publicdebt.treas.gov*. Population estimates may be found on the Bureau of the Census Web site at *www.census.gov*.

## Reteach

Direct each student to write three questions about the federal budget-making process on index cards. Collect and shuffle the cards. Then work through the cards, selecting students at random to answer questions.

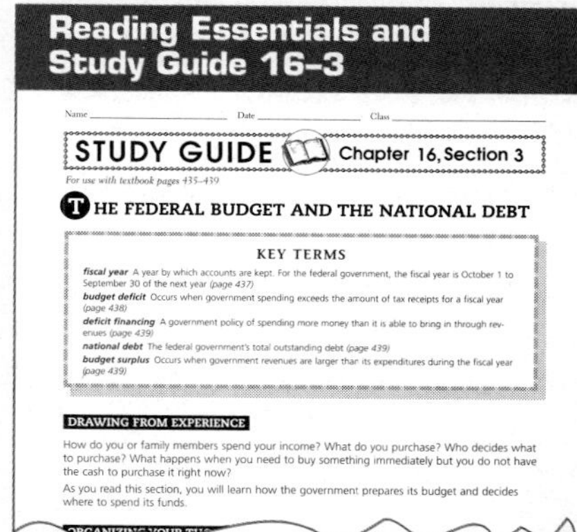

**Reading Essentials and Study Guide 16–3**

Name ______ Date ______ Class ______

STUDY GUIDE Chapter 16, Section 3

*For use with textbook pages 435–439*

THE FEDERAL BUDGET AND THE NATIONAL DEBT

KEY TERMS

***fiscal year*** A year by which accounts are kept. For the federal government, the fiscal year is October 1 to September 30 of the next year *(page 437)*

***budget deficit*** Occurs when government spending exceeds the amount of tax receipts for a fiscal year *(page 438)*

***deficit financing*** A government policy of spending more money than it is able to bring in through revenues *(page 439)*

***national debt*** The federal government's total outstanding debt *(page 439)*

***budget surplus*** Occurs when government revenues are larger than its expenditures during the fiscal year *(page 439)*

DRAWING FROM EXPERIENCE

How do you or family members spend your income? What do you purchase? Who decides what to purchase? What happens when you need to buy something immediately but you do not have the cash to purchase it right now?

As you read this section, you will learn how the government prepares its budget and decides where to spend its funds.

## 4 Close

Lead students in a discussion of the following: Should the federal government be limited to spending only what it collects in taxes? Why or why not?

# 1 Focus

## Overview

Section 4 describes or explains the principles of taxation and the types of taxes collected in the United States.

### BELLRINGER
Motivational Activity

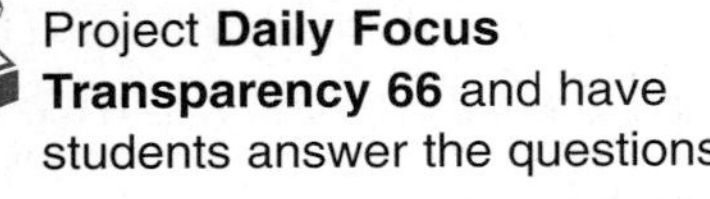

Project **Daily Focus Transparency 66** and have students answer the questions.

This activity is also available as a blackline master.

**Daily Focus Transparency 66**

TAXES—A CONTINUING CONTROVERSY

1. In the cartoon above, what are the people doing outside the door of the Internal Revenue Service?
2. What is the cartoonist saying about how much money the Internal Revenue Service takes away from people in taxes?

Daily Focus Transparencies

### Reader's Guide

Answers to the **Reading Objectives** questions are on page 443.

**Preteaching Vocabulary**

Have students demonstrate their understanding of the **Terms to Know** by writing a sentence showing the difference between the benefits-received principle and the ability-to-pay principle.

**Vocabulary PuzzleMaker**

# SECTION 4 Taxation

### Reader's Guide

**Terms to Know**
- benefits-received principle
- ability-to-pay principle
- proportional tax
- progressive tax
- regressive tax

**Reading Objectives**
1. What are the two principles of taxation?
2. What effect do the three forms of taxation have on taxpayers?

## Cover Story

*The Washington Post*, April 12, 1999

"We'll cut your taxes" is the most repeated campaign promise in the history of American politics. Yet somehow it is still considered visionary, worth a fight. Worth, indeed, a crusade.

Why? It's in our blood. Historically, Americans have hated taxes, and not merely because we had to pay them. We've hated taxes because we've perceived them to be an infringement on our liberty—and the source of big, powerful, and mischievous government. This was true from the beginning. It wasn't just "taxation without representation" that bothered us so much. It was taxation. Period.

You, the American taxpayer, are the source of most of the money the government spends. Almost all federal, state, and local government revenue comes from taxes. In this section, you'll learn about the major kinds of taxes paid in this country.

## Principles of Taxation

**Figure 16.9** lists the major taxes that the various levels of government use to raise revenue. Taxes are usually justified according to one of two major principles. Under the **benefits-received principle,** those who use a particular government service should support it with taxes in proportion to the benefit they receive. Those who do not use a service do not pay taxes for it. A gasoline

**benefits-received principle:** *system of taxation in which those who use a particular government service support it with taxes in proportion to the benefit they receive; those who do not use a service do not pay taxes for it*

## SECTION 4 RESOURCE MANAGER

**Reproducible Masters**
- Reproducible Lesson Plan 16–4
- Reading Essentials and Study Guide 16–4
- Guided Reading Activity 16–4
- Section Quiz 16–4
- Daily Focus Activity 66
- Daily Lecture Notes 16–4

**Multimedia**
- Daily Focus Transparency 66
- Vocabulary PuzzleMaker
- Interactive Tutor Self-Assessment Software
- ExamView® Pro Testmaker
- MindJogger Videoquiz
- Presentation Plus!

## FIGURE 16.9 Major Taxes

| Tax | Description | Type |
|---|---|---|
| **Personal income** | Tax is a percentage of income and a major source of federal revenue; many state governments also levy | Progressive at the federal level, but is sometimes proportional at the state level |
| **Social insurance** | Taxes covered by the Federal Insurance Contributions Act (FICA); second-largest source of federal revenue | Proportional up to $72,600 in 1999, regressive above that (as estimated by the Social Security Administration) |
| **Corporate income** | Federal tax as a percentage of corporate profits; some states also levy | At the federal level, progressive up to $10 million, proportional above that |
| **Excise** | Tax paid by the consumer on the manufacture, use, and consumption of certain goods; major federal taxes are on alcohol, tobacco, and gasoline; some states also levy | Regressive if people with higher incomes spend a lower proportion of income on taxed items |
| **Estate** | Federal tax on the property of someone who has died; some states also levy | Progressive; rate increases with the value of the estate |
| **Inheritance** | State tax paid by those who inherit property | Varies by state |
| **Gift** | Federal tax paid by the person who gives a large gift | Progressive; rate increases with the value of the gift |
| **Sales** | Tax paid on purchases; almost all states as well as many local governments levy; rate varies from state to state and within states; items taxed also vary | Regressive if people with higher incomes spend a lower proportion of income on taxed items |
| **Property** | State and local taxation of the value of property; both real property (such as buildings and land) and personal property (such as stocks, bonds, and home furnishings) may be taxed | Proportional; rate is set by state and local governments |
| **Customs duties** | Tax on imports; paid by the importer | Proportional |





# 2 Teach

## Guided Practice

L2 **Applying Ideas** Direct students to review the discussion of the principles of taxation on pages 440 and 442. Then randomly assign either the benefits-received principle or the ability-to-pay principle to each student. Have students study the types of taxes listed in **Figure 16.9** on page 441, and have them identify which tax fits their assigned principle. Call on volunteers to share their findings with the class.

### Daily Lecture Notes 16-4

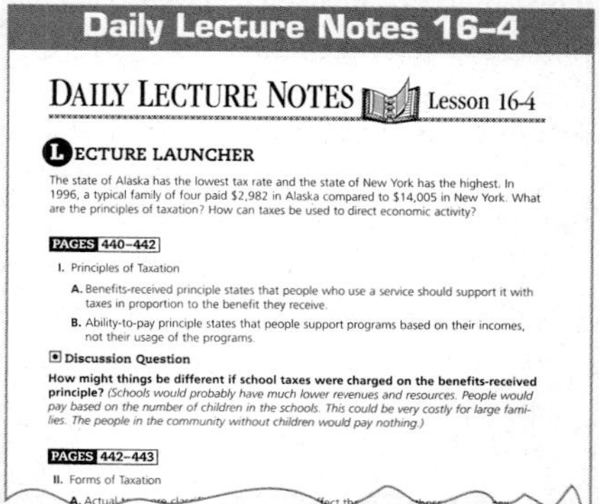

DAILY LECTURE NOTES Lesson 16-4

LECTURE LAUNCHER

The state of Alaska has the lowest tax rate and the state of New York has the highest. In 1996, a typical family of four paid $2,982 in Alaska compared to $14,005 in New York. What are the principles of taxation? How can taxes be used to direct economic activity?

PAGES 440–442

I. Principles of Taxation

A. Benefits-received principle states that people who use a service should support it with taxes in proportion to the benefit they receive.

B. Ability-to-pay principle states that people support programs based on their incomes, not their usage of the programs.

**Discussion Question**

**How might things be different if school taxes were charged on the benefits-received principle?** *(Schools would probably have much lower revenues and resources. People would pay based on the number of children in the schools. This could be very costly for large families. The people in the community without children would pay nothing.)*

PAGES 442–443

II. Forms of Taxation

### Visual Instruction FIGURE 16.9

ASK: What are the three general classifications of taxes? *progressive, proportional, regressive*

### Meeting Special Needs

**Language Comprehension Disability** Students who have difficulty with comprehension or who have limited English proficiency may benefit by reading information and then restating it. Direct students to read sentences from Section 4 and then restate each one in their own words. Listen carefully to students to ensure that they are not simply repeating phrases directly from the book.

Refer to *Inclusion for the Social Studies Classroom Strategies and Activities* for students with different learning styles.

**Guided Reading Activity 16-4**

## Independent Practice

L2 Creating Posters Have students work in small groups to create posters that depict the information in Section 4. Direct groups to make two posters—one illustrating the principles of taxation, the other illustrating the three forms of taxation. Call on groups to display and explain their posters. ELL BLOCK SCHEDULING

**ECONOMICS Online**

See the **Web Activity Lesson Plan** at ett.glencoe.com for an introduction, lesson description, and answers to the **Student Web Activity** for this chapter.

## 3 Assess

Assign Section 4 Assessment as homework or an in-class activity.

Use **Interactive Tutor Self-Assessment Software** to review Section 4.

## Economic Connection to... MATH

### Tax Freedom Day

Every year, the Tax Foundation announces the arrival of "Tax Freedom Day." On this date, the average American has earned enough to pay all of his or her federal, state, and local taxes for the year.

To arrive at this date, Tax Foundation economists use a fairly simple formula. First, they divide per capita taxes (amount paid for all taxes divided by the population) by per capita income (total income earned divided by the population). This shows the percentage of the average American's income that goes for taxes. They then apply this percentage to 365 to find the number of days it would take to "work off" this amount.

In 1999, for example, some 36 percent of income went for taxes ($10,298 divided by $28,878). Applying this percentage to 365 produces 131 days. The average American worked to May 11 to pay all taxes. ■

tax to pay for highway construction and repair is based on the benefits-received principle. Frequent users of the highways often buy more gasoline and, therefore, pay more in gasoline taxes.

A tax based on the benefits-received principle is useful in raising funds to pay for a service only certain individuals use. Many government services—national defense, for example—benefit everyone equally, however. Also, those who most require services, such as the aged and poor, are the individuals least able to pay taxes.

**ability-to-pay principle:** *principle of taxation in which those with higher incomes pay more taxes than those with lower incomes, regardless of the number of government services they use*

Under the **ability-to-pay principle,** those with higher incomes pay more taxes than those with lower incomes, regardless of the number of government services they use. For example, in most cities all property owners, even those without school-aged children, must pay property taxes to support the local school system. Property taxes are calculated as a percentage of the value of a person's home. Thus, wealthier people with more expensive homes pay more property taxes.

**ECONOMICS Online**

**Student Web Activity** Visit the *Economics Today and Tomorrow* Web site at ett.glencoe.com and click on ***Chapter 16—Student Web Activities*** to learn how the federal government spends your tax dollars.

### Forms of Taxation

Actual taxes are classified according to the effect they have on those who are taxed. In the United States today, these classifications include proportional, progressive, and regressive taxes.



### Extending the Content

**Using Taxation To Influence Economic Decisions** Government uses taxation not only to raise revenue, but also to influence the economic decisions of businesses and individuals. Government can adjust taxes to encourage business. State and local governments, for example, may reduce or eliminate taxes for a company to persuade it to locate in a particular area. Taxes also can be used to discourage activities. High taxes on cigarettes and alcohol are designed, in part, to discourage smoking and drinking. Similarly, customs duties make imports more expensive and discourage American consumers from buying foreign goods.

**Proportional Tax** A **proportional tax** is the easiest type of tax to understand. The taxes you owe are simply a proportion of the money income you have earned. If there is a tax of 10 percent on all income and you earn $1,000, then you pay $100 in taxes. If you earn $10,000, you pay $1,000 in taxes, and so on.

<u>proportional tax:</u> *tax that takes the same percentage of all incomes; as income rises, the amount of tax paid also rises*

**Progressive Tax** With a **progressive tax,** when an individual earns a higher income, his or her taxes increase more than in proportion to the increase in money income. A good example of a progressive tax is our federal individual income tax system. As you make more reported income, you pay an increasingly higher percentage of that additional income in taxes to the federal government. A progressive income tax has often been justified on the basis of the ability-to-pay principle.

<u>progressive tax:</u> *tax that takes a larger percentage of higher incomes than lower incomes; justified on the basis of the ability-to-pay principle*

**Regressive Tax** As you might expect, a **regressive tax** is the opposite of a progressive tax. The percentage that you pay in taxes actually goes down as you make more money income. Some economists believe that a good example of a regressive tax is the sales tax on food. They point out that poorer families spend a larger proportion of their income on food. Therefore, the sales tax they pay on food takes up a larger proportion of their total income than a wealthier family pays.

<u>regressive tax:</u> *tax that takes a larger percentage of lower incomes than of higher incomes*

**Practice** and **assess** key skills with *Skillbuilder Interactive Workbook, Level 2.*

## SECTION 4 Assessment

### Understanding Key Terms

1. **Define** benefits-received principle, ability-to-pay principle, proportional tax, progressive tax, regressive tax.

### Reviewing Objectives

2. What are the two principles of taxation?
3. **Graphic Organizer** Create a chart like the one in the next column to explain the three forms of taxation and their effect on taxpayers.

| Type of Tax | Effect on Taxpayer | Example |
|---|---|---|
| | | |

### Applying Economic Concepts

4. **Taxation** List and describe the kinds of taxes you personally pay.

### Critical Thinking Activity

5. **Making Comparisons** Which of the two principles of taxation do you think is the more equitable? Explain your answer.



## SECTION 4 Assessment Answers

1. All definitions can be found in the Glossary.
2. benefits-received principle and ability-to-pay principle
3. Proportional: Taxpayers pay the same proportion of income, some state income taxes; Progressive: Taxpayers with higher incomes pay more than those with lower incomes, federal income tax; Regressive: Percentage taxpayers pay in tax falls as income rises, sales tax on food
4. Answers may include income tax, sales tax, Social Security tax, excise tax, customs duty.
5. Ensure that students give valid reasons for their choice of taxation principle.

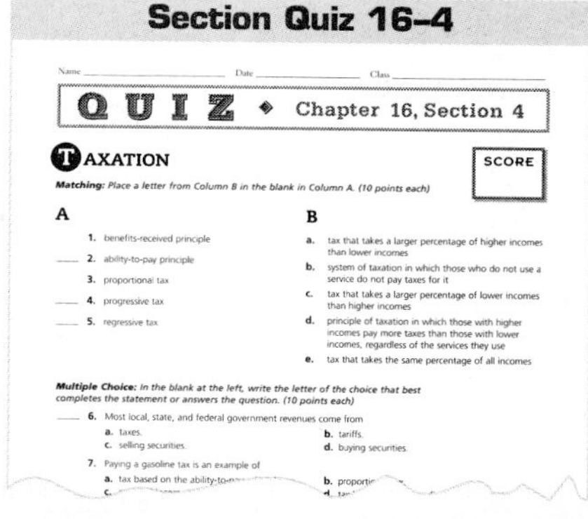

**Section Quiz 16–4**

Name ________ Date ________ Class ________

QUIZ ◆ Chapter 16, Section 4

TAXATION

SCORE

**Matching:** *Place a letter from Column B in the blank in Column A. (10 points each)*

**A**

1. benefits-received principle
2. ability-to-pay principle
3. proportional tax
4. progressive tax
5. regressive tax

**B**

a. tax that takes a larger percentage of higher incomes than lower incomes
b. system of taxation in which those who do not use a service do not pay taxes for it
c. tax that takes a larger percentage of lower incomes than higher incomes
d. principle of taxation in which those with higher incomes pay more taxes than those with lower incomes, regardless of the services they use
e. tax that takes the same percentage of all incomes

**Multiple Choice:** *In the blank at the left, write the letter of the choice that best completes the statement or answers the question. (10 points each)*

6. Most local, state, and federal government revenues come from
   a. taxes. b. tariffs.
   c. selling securities. d. buying securities.
7. Paying a gasoline tax is an example of
   a. tax based on the ability-to- b. proporti

## Reteach

Write the following titles on the board: Principles of Taxation, Forms of Taxation. Ask students to write a brief paragraph on each of these topics.

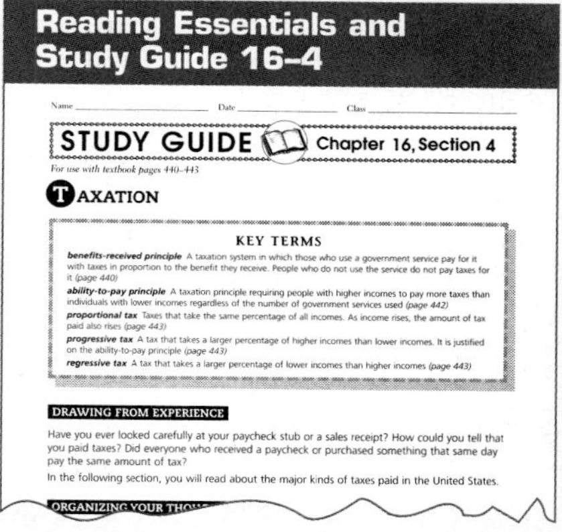

**Reading Essentials and Study Guide 16–4**

Name ________ Date ________ Class ________

STUDY GUIDE Chapter 16, Section 4

*For use with textbook pages 440–443*

TAXATION

KEY TERMS

***benefits-received principle*** A taxation system in which those who use a government service pay for it with taxes in proportion to the benefit they receive. People who do not use the service do not pay taxes for it *(page 440)*

***ability-to-pay principle*** A taxation principle requiring people with higher incomes to pay more taxes than individuals with lower incomes regardless of the number of government services used *(page 442)*

***proportional tax*** Taxes that take the same percentage of all incomes. As income rises, the amount of tax paid also rises *(page 443)*

***progressive tax*** A tax that takes a larger percentage of higher incomes than lower incomes. It is justified on the ability-to-pay principle *(page 443)*

***regressive tax*** A tax that takes a larger percentage of lower incomes than higher incomes *(page 443)*

DRAWING FROM EXPERIENCE

Have you ever looked carefully at your paycheck stub or a sales receipt? How could you tell that you paid taxes? Did everyone who received a paycheck or purchased something that same day pay the same amount of tax?

In the following section, you will read about the major kinds of taxes paid in the United States.

ORGANIZING YOUR THO

## 4 Close

Remind students that one of the goals of the American economy is economic equity. Then have them discuss if—and how—the principles of taxation and the different forms of taxation meet this economic goal.

## Technology Skills

### Using E-Mail

You might begin this skill by taking a class survey to find out which students correspond regularly using E-mail. Encourage students who have the most experience with this form of communication to demonstrate creating and sending a message and opening and printing a received message. At this point, you might mention that it is possible to attach documents or other files to E-mail messages. As an example, suggest that a student might send an essay to a classmate without typing it again as part of the message.

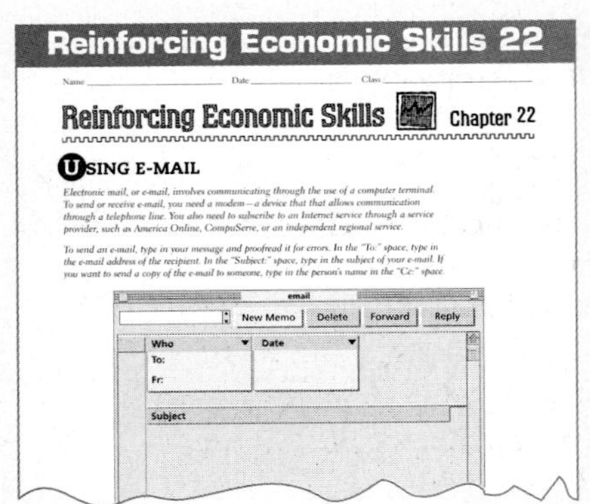

**Reinforcing Economic Skills 22**

Name ______ Date ______ Class ______

**Reinforcing Economic Skills** Chapter 22

**USING E-MAIL**

*Electronic mail, or e-mail, involves communicating through the use of a computer terminal. To send or receive e-mail, you need a modem—a device that that allows communication through a telephone line. You also need to subscribe to an Internet service through a service provider, such as America Online, CompuServe, or an independent regional service.*

*To send an e-mail, type in your message and proofread it for errors. In the "To:" space, type in the e-mail address of the recipient. In the "Subject:" space, type in the subject of your e-mail. If you want to send a copy of the e-mail to someone, type in the person's name in the "Cc:" space.*

# Technology Skills

# Using E-Mail

*Electronic mail, or E-mail, refers to communicating at a distance through the use of a computer. A computer is ready to "talk" to other computers after two things are added to it: (a) a modem—a device that allows communication through a telephone line, and (b) communications software, which lets your computer prepare and send information to the modem.*

1. Select the "Message" function from your communications software.
2. Type in your message, and proofread it for errors.
3. Type in the E-mail address of the recipient. and select the "Send" button.
4. The E-mail system places the message in the receiver's electronic mailbox. He or she may read the message at any time, and send you a return message.
5. When you receive E-mail, the sender's address is on the message—add it to your electronic address book at that time.

## Learning the Skill

To send an E-mail message, follow the steps listed on the left.

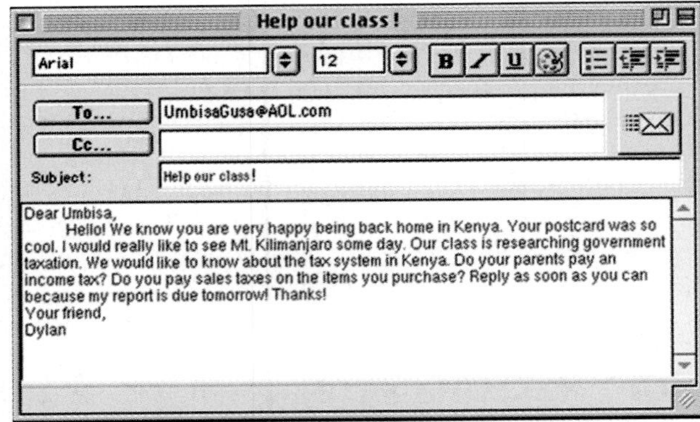



*After you type in your message, you may send it, forward it, and even save it to a file.*

## Practicing the Skill

Select a current issue concerning government taxation to research. Then browse the Internet to obtain the E-mail address of a federal official concerned with the issue. E-mail the official, sharing opinions about the issue, asking questions about the issue, and requesting information.

## Application Activity

E-mail a classmate. Forward the information you received from the government official concerning the issue above. Working together, write a summary of the E-mail correspondence with the official.

444

### Answers to Practicing the Skill

Results will vary. Review students' E-mail messages before they send them to federal officials.

**Application Activity** Answers may vary. Have partners share their summaries with the rest of the class.

# CHAPTER  Summary

## ECONOMICS Online

**Chapter Overview** Visit the *Economics Today and Tomorrow* Web site at ett.glencoe.com and click on ***Chapter 16—Chapter Overviews*** to review chapter information.

### SECTION 1 Growth in the Size of Government

- Government at every level—local, state, and federal—is involved in almost every aspect of the United States economy.
- All levels of government employ about 20 million civilian workers.
- Government finances highways, education, and other **public-works projects.** It also regulates product and worker safety.
- Total government outlays, including actual purchases as well as transfer payments, exceed one-third of GDP.

### SECTION 2 The Functions of Government

- One function of government is to provide **public goods,** such as national parks and national defense.
- Another function of government is to provide for the public well-being through **social insurance programs**—such as **Social Security, Medicare,** and **workers' compensation**—and **public-assistance programs**—such as **Supplemental Security Income** and **Medicaid.**
- A third function of government is to regulate the negative **externalities** of the production process.
- A fourth function—ensuring economic stability—has meant smoothing the ups and downs in the nation's overall business activity.

### SECTION 3 The Federal Budget and the National Debt

- The federal government's largest expenditures include Social Security/Medicare/income security, national defense, interest on the national debt, and health.
- The executive and legislative branches prepare a federal budget for each **fiscal year.**
- Spending more in a fiscal year than it collects in taxes results in the government running a **budget deficit.**
- The total amount accumulated by annual budget deficits is the **national debt.**

### SECTION 4 Taxation

- Under the **benefits-received principle,** people who use a particular government service support it with taxes in proportion to the benefit they receive.
- Under the **ability-to-pay principle,** those with higher incomes pay more taxes than those with lower incomes, regardless of the number of government services they use.
- Major types of taxes include personal income, social insurance, corporate income, sales, and property taxes.
- Taxes are classified according to the effect they have on those who are taxed: **proportional, progressive,** or **regressive.**



## Economics Journal

**Government Involvement in the Economy** Have students list all the activities they do during a three-day period. Next to each item on the list, have students indicate what role the government might have in that activity. As an example, remind students that when they drive, it is usually on a government-provided public road. Have students use this information to write a brief discussion of how government supports, regulates, or taxes them. Suggest that they conclude the discussion with a paragraph on the pros and cons of government involvement in their lives.

CHAPTER 16 Summary

**ECONOMICS & YOU**

**How Government Spends, Collects, and Owes**

Chapter 15
Disc 1, Side 2

If you do not have access to a videodisc player, the ***Economics & You*** programs are available in VHS.

Use the **Chapter 16 Summary** to preview, review, condense, or reteach the chapter.

## Preview/Review

**Vocabulary PuzzleMaker Software** reinforces the key terms used in Chapter 16.

**Interactive Tutor Self-Assessment Software** allows students to review Chapter 16 content.

## Condense

Have students listen to the Chapter 16 **Audio Program** (also available in Spanish) in the TCR. Assign the Chapter 16 Audio Program Activity and give students the Chapter 16 Audio Program Test.

## Reteach

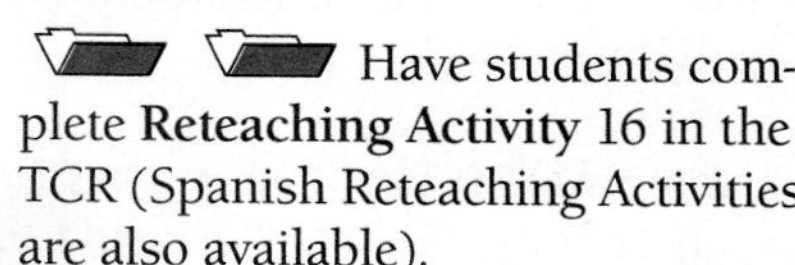

Have students complete **Reteaching Activity** 16 in the TCR (Spanish Reteaching Activities are also available).

## CHAPTER 16 Assessment and Activities

ECONOMICS Online

Have students visit the *Economics Today and Tomorrow* Web site at ett.glencoe.com to review Chapter 16 and take the Self-Check Quiz.

**MindJogger Videoquiz**

Use MindJogger to review Chapter 16 content.

### Identifying Key Terms

1. e
2. f
3. c
4. b
5. h
6. g
7. d
8. a

### Recalling Facts and Ideas

1. Government has grown in terms of workers employed and in terms of spending.
2. over 20 percent
3. provide public goods, redistribute income, regulate economic activity, ensure economic stability
4. Examples may vary but might include national defense, roads, schools, museums, parks, and the legal system.
5. Answers may vary. Students might suggest noise pollution and increased traffic as negative externalities, and new airport businesses–restaurants, stores, and so on–in the neighborhood as positive externalities.
6. about 18 months
7. deficit spending–spending more than is taken in and borrowing to make up the shortfall
8. personal income, social insurance, corporate income, excise, estate, inheritance, gift, sales, property, customs duties
9. proportional

### Thinking Critically

1. around 1970; state and local governments began paying for such things as schools, sewers, and roads
2. Answers will vary but may include: State and local governments may reduce or eliminate taxes for a company to persuade it to locate in a particular area. Taxes also can be used to discourage activities–high taxes on cigarettes and alcohol are

# CHAPTER 16 Assessment and Activities

ECONOMICS Online

**Self-Check Quiz** Visit the *Economics Today and Tomorrow* Web site at ett.glencoe.com and click on ***Chapter 16—Self-Check Quizzes*** to prepare for the Chapter Test.

## Identifying Key Terms

*Write the letter of the definition in Column B that correctly defines each term in Column A.*

**Column A**

1. benefits-received principle
2. public goods
3. ability-to-pay principle
4. income redistribution
5. national debt
6. Medicare
7. Social Security
8. Medicaid

**Column B**

a. public-assistance program that provides free health care to low-income persons
b. taking tax dollars from some to give to others in the form of aid
c. system by which those with higher incomes pay higher taxes
d. provides monthly payments to the retired
e. payment for a particular government service by those who use the service
f. goods and services whose use by one person does not reduce use by another
g. provides health care for the aged
h. amount of money the government owes

## Recalling Facts and Ideas

**Section 1**

1. In what ways has the government grown since the Great Depression?
2. What percent of GDP is accounted for by total government purchases?

**Section 2**

3. What are government's main functions?
4. Give five examples of public goods.
5. What would be a negative externality of having an airport built near your home? What would be a positive externality?

**Section 3**

6. About how long does it take the federal government to prepare a budget?
7. What causes the nation's public debt?

**Section 4**

8. What are the principal taxes that exist in the United States today?
9. If all income were taxed at exactly the same rate, what type of tax would be in existence?

## Thinking Critically

1. **Analyzing Information** Look at **Figure 16.2** on page 426. When did federal government purchases drop below state and local purchases? Why do you think this situation occurred?

2. **Drawing Conclusions** Create a diagram like the one below to explain how you think taxes can encourage or discourage consumer and business behaviors.

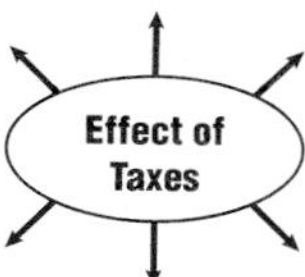


## Applying Economic Concepts

**Principles of Taxation** You learned about two principles of taxation, one of which was the benefits-received principle. Assume that you want to use this principle to justify a progressive income tax system. Write a list of the reasons explaining why, as a person's income goes up, that person receives more benefits from the government and therefore should be taxed progressively.

## Cooperative Learning Project

Work in groups representing at least three regions of the United States. Each member should choose one or more states in the group's region to research. Determine which states in the region have the highest tax rate. The information needed will be:

- Highest tax rate applied to personal income
- Highest tax rate applied to corporate income
- Sales tax rate

Share your information with the rest of your group, and then have the groups present the information to the rest of the class. Which state in which region has the highest tax rate? Which region in general has the highest tax rate?

## Reviewing Skills

**Using E-Mail** Using your communications software, type a message asking 10 registered voters for their opinions on the national debt. In your E-mail, ask the recipients questions such as the following:

1. How serious do you think the national debt is for the future of the United States?
2. What measures, if any, should the federal government take to reduce the national debt?
3. If we do not reduce the national debt, what consequences do you foresee, particularly for the generation currently attending high school?
4. What sacrifices do you think you would be willing to make to help reduce the debt?

## Technology Activity

**Developing Multimedia Presentations** Develop a video tracing your daily routine and examining each part of your life in which the government is involved. For example, if you take a bus to school, videotape the bus and explain that this is an example of property taxes being used to fund school transportation. Continue filming throughout the day as you come in contact with other government services. Show your completed video to the class.

## Analyzing the Global Economy

Compare the federal income tax rate of the United States to other industrialized nations, including the Netherlands, Germany, Sweden, Japan, and France. Which nation has the highest tax rate?



designed, in part, to discourage smoking and drinking. Similarly, customs duties make imports more expensive and discourage American consumers from buying foreign goods.

# CHAPTER 16 Assessment and Activities

## Applying Economic Concepts

Answers will vary, but reasons should reflect an understanding of progressive taxation and the benefits-received principle.

## Cooperative Learning Project

Students might present their information in a chart or a table.

## Reviewing Skills

E-mail responses will vary. Encourage students to share and comment on their responses.

## Technology Activity

Students may wish to work in teams to complete their videos.

## Analyzing the Global Economy

Have students list the nations they research according to tax rates from highest to lowest.

### Chapter Bonus Test Question

ASK: Which principle of taxation is represented by a gasoline tax to pay for highway construction? Why? *benefits-received principle, because drivers who use the highways are the ones who pay the tax*

## Focus on Free Enterprise

# 1 Focus

Have students identify hobbies that they enjoy. Ask them if they think they might be able to develop these hobbies into businesses. Then inform them that this is exactly what the founders of the Trek Bicycle Corporation did.

# 2 Teach

Mention that Trek was a sponsor of Lance Armstrong and the United States Tour de France team of which he was a member. Ask students why they think Trek would be willing to sponsor professional cyclists and cycle teams. *Most students will note that it is good publicity for their product. Others might also suggest that Trek might get useful feedback from professional cyclists, which will help in improving their product.*

CASE STUDY

## Focus on Free Enterprise

# The Trek Bicycle Corporation

***On July 25, 1999, American Lance Armstrong rode through the streets of Paris, France, greeted by thousands of wildly cheering spectators. He was on his way to victory in the Tour de France—the world's greatest bicycle race. Armstrong was just the second American to win this grueling competition, which lasts about three weeks and covers more than 2,000 miles. It was an "all-American" victory, for Armstrong was riding an American-made bike—the Trek 5500 OCLV.***

Lance Armstrong

### The Bike Barn

Trek bikes got their start in Waterloo, Wisconsin, more than 20 years ago. Richard Burke and his friends loved tinkering with bicycles, even making their own bike frames. When other people started admiring their handiwork, they realized they had a real business opportunity.

In 1976 Burke and his friends set up Trek Bicycle Corporation in a rented barn in Waterloo. The company had just five workers and made one product—hand-built steel bike frames. Over time, Trek Bicycle expanded its business, making its own road bicycles using quality parts from American manufacturers. In the early 1980s, Trek introduced a line of mountain bikes. By the end of the decade, Trek was producing bicycle clothing, safety equipment, and children's bikes.

As a result, Trek expanded its production facilities, building three factories in Wisconsin—one right next door to the barn in Waterloo. It also opened facilities in Europe and Japan. Today Trek employs about 2,000 people worldwide

448

## Extending the Content

**Trek Bikes** In 1996, in the first-ever automobile/bicycle company partnership, Trek Bicycle joined with Volkswagen to market an interesting combination—an automobile with a bike attached! The special edition Jetta Trek featured a Volkswagen Jetta combined with a Trek mountain bike. The Volkswagen/Trek partnership continues today—as cosponsors of a mountain bike race team.

Police patrol on Y bikes

and has yearly sales in excess of $550 million. It ranks as one of the world's leading quality bicycle manufacturers.

### Building a Better Bike

Trek Bicycle's success is due to its commitment to product improvement. Trek has continually made research and development one of its top priorities. This focus has resulted in many innovations in bicycle construction. Their carbon fiber frame is one example. Weighing less than 2.5 pounds, it was designed using the same technology that developed the Stealth fighter.

Another example is the aluminum-frame Y bike. The technology used in its construction combined the comfort of mountain bikes with the quickness of road bikes. The Y bike is popular in an unusual market—law enforcement. Many police forces use the Y bike for their bicycle units. Even the President's Secret Service squad patrols the White House grounds on specially designed Y bikes!

Trek's innovations also are popular with people in the industry. In 1995 the Trek engineers who designed the Y bike won *Popular Mechanics* magazine's Design Engineer of the Year Award. In 1996 the Industrial Designers Society of America gave Trek's Y bike its Gold Industrial Excellence Award.

### Future Plans

Trek Bicycle plans to continue developing new and exciting products for cycling enthusiasts. The most recent is a line of bikes built especially for riding in the city—the Urban Assault Vehicle. Trek also wants to solidify itself as an American operation. At present, some 70 percent of Trek bikes are made at the company's Wisconsin facilities. In the next few years, Trek hopes to push this figure higher. For Richard Burke and other Trek executives, "Made in America" is an important and proud boast.

#### *Free Enterprise in Action*

1. **What is the key to Trek Bicycle Corporation's success?**
2. **How do Trek Bicycle's future plans show that the company takes the statement "Made in America" seriously?**



## 3 Assess

Have students answer the **Free Enterprise in Action** questions.

## 4 Close

Ask students to discuss if they would be more willing to buy a product labeled as "Made in America." Have students explain their responses.

### ? Did You Know

To celebrate Armstrong's Tour de France victory, Trek released a "Lance Armstrong Signature" limited edition—just 1,999 models—of the Trek 5500 OCLV.

### Answers to *Free Enterprise In Action*

1. Trek's key to success is its commitment to product improvement.
2. At present, 70 percent of Trek bikes are made at the company's facilities in Wisconsin, and Trek wants to increase this number over the next few years.

# CHAPTER 17 Resource Manager

## Teaching Transparency

### Economic Concepts Transparency 17

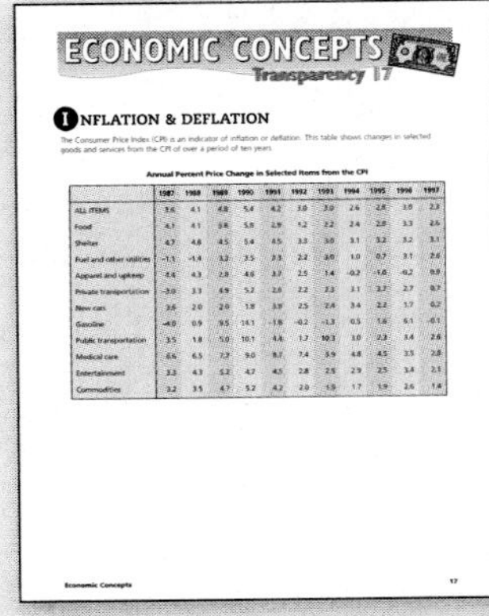
ECONOMIC CONCEPTS Transparency 17

INFLATION & DEFLATION

## Application and Enrichment

### Enrichment Activity 17

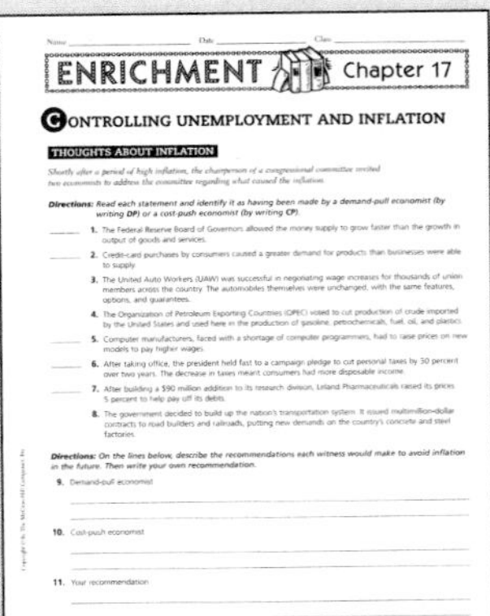
ENRICHMENT Chapter 17

CONTROLLING UNEMPLOYMENT AND INFLATION

### Consumer Applications Activity 21

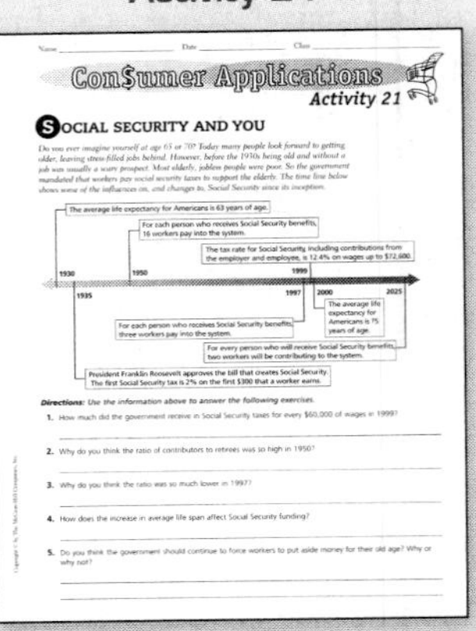
Consumer Applications Activity 21

SOCIAL SECURITY AND YOU

### Free Enterprise Activity 21

FREE ENTERPRISE ACTIVITY 21

POLICIES FOR GROWTH

## Application and Enrichment

### Cooperative Learning Simulations and Problems 21

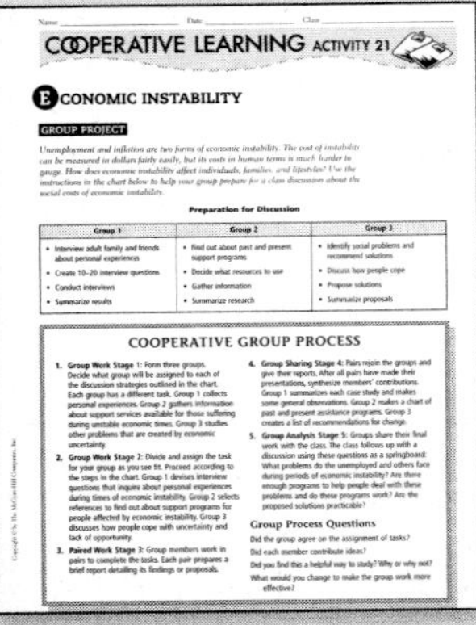
COOPERATIVE LEARNING ACTIVITY 21

ECONOMIC INSTABILITY

COOPERATIVE GROUP PROCESS

### Primary and Secondary Source Reading 21

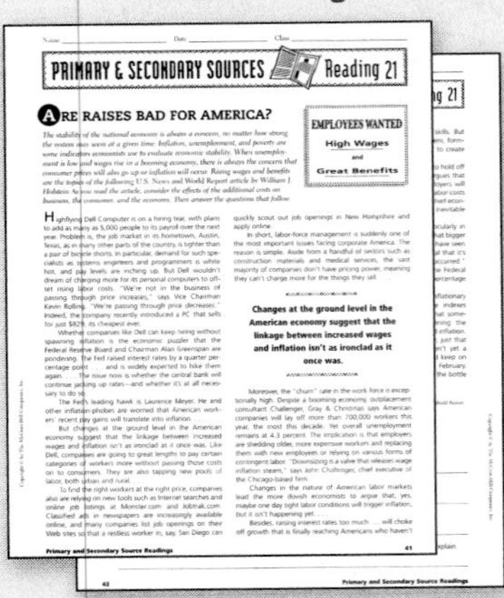
PRIMARY & SECONDARY SOURCES Reading 21

ARE RAISES BAD FOR AMERICA?

### Math Practice for Economics Activity 21

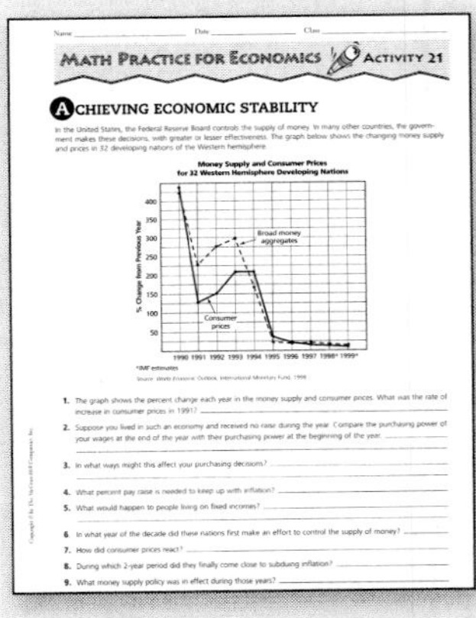
MATH PRACTICE FOR ECONOMICS ACTIVITY 21

ACHIEVING ECONOMIC STABILITY

### Economic Cartoons Activity 21

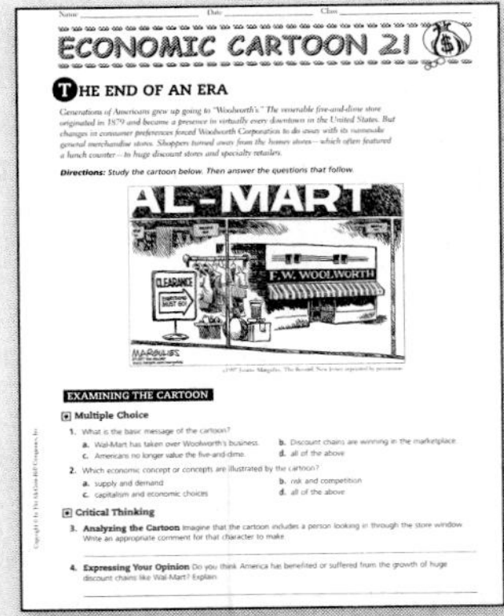
ECONOMIC CARTOON 21

THE END OF AN ERA

## Review and Reinforcement

### Critical Thinking Activity 21

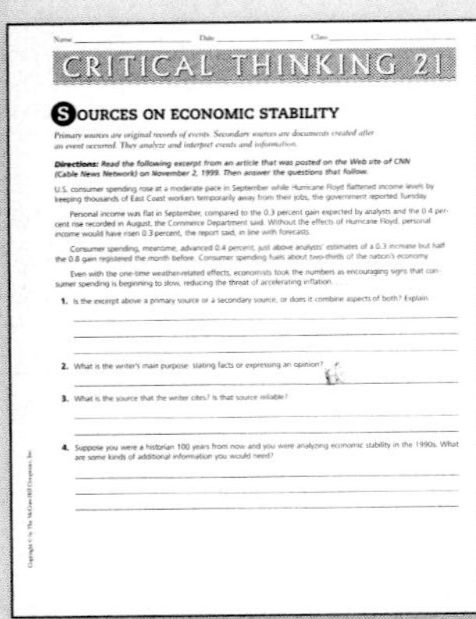
CRITICAL THINKING 21

SOURCES ON ECONOMIC STABILITY

### Reteaching Activity 17

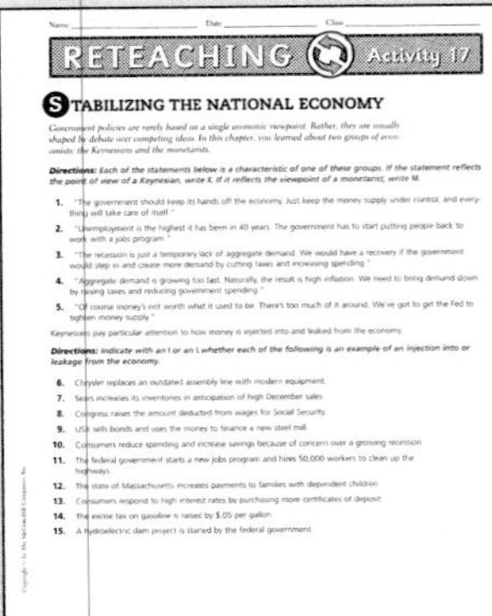
RETEACHING Activity 17

STABILIZING THE NATIONAL ECONOMY

### Economic Vocabulary Activity 17

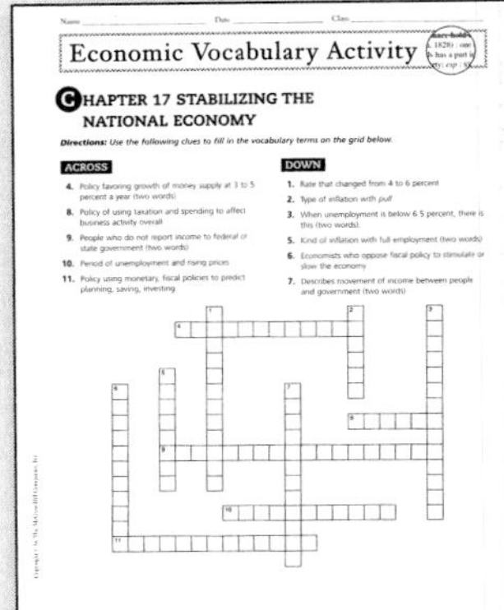
Economic Vocabulary Activity

CHAPTER 17 STABILIZING THE NATIONAL ECONOMY

### Reinforcing Economic Skills 13

Reinforcing Economic Skills Chapter 13

SUMMARIZING INFORMATION

# CHAPTER 17 Resource Manager

## Assessment and Evaluation

Chapter 17 Test Form A

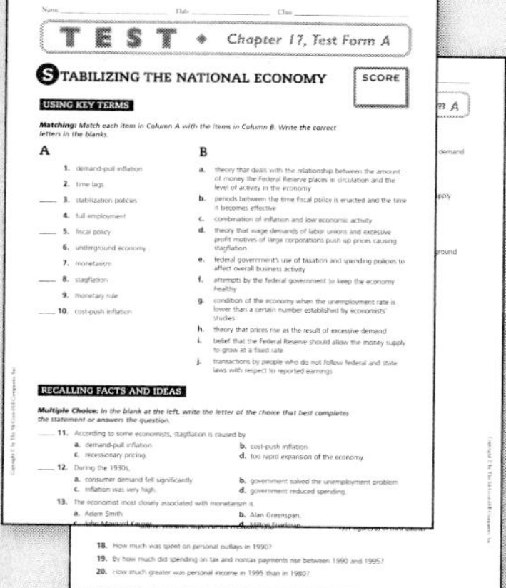

Chapter 17 Test Form B

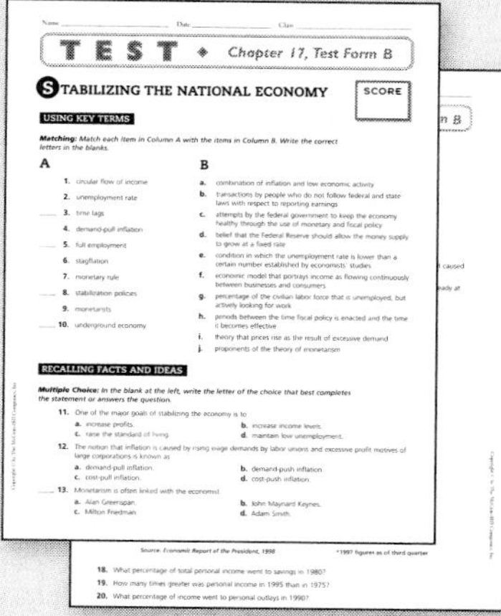

Performance Assessment Activity 21

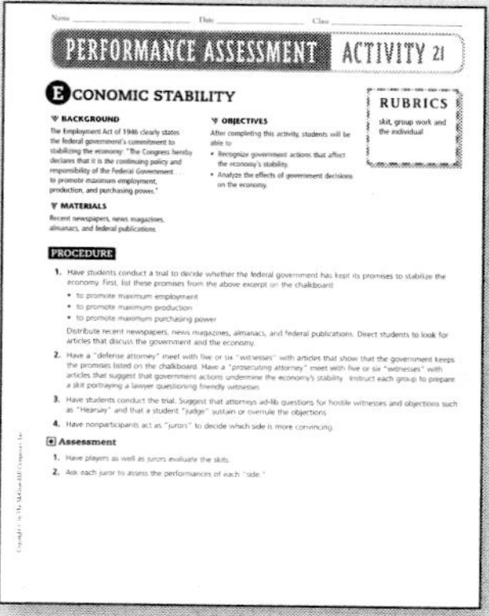

ExamView® Pro Testmaker

## Technology and Multimedia

 Vocabulary PuzzleMaker Software

 Interactive Tutor Self-Assessment Software

 ExamView® Pro Testmaker

 NBR *Economics & You* Video Program (English/Spanish)

 Presentation Plus!

 Glencoe Skillbuilder Interactive Workbook CD-ROM, Level 2

 Interactive Lesson Planner

 MindJogger Videoquiz

 Interactive Economics! CD-ROM

Audio Program (English or Spanish)

## Spanish Resources

 Spanish Economic Concepts Transparency 17

 Spanish Vocabulary Activity 17

 Spanish Reteaching Activity 17

Spanish Section Quizzes for Chapter 17

  Spanish Chapter 17 Audio Program, Activity, and Test

## ECONOMICS Online

You and your students can visit *ett.glencoe.com*—the Web site companion to **Economics Today and Tomorrow.** This innovative integration of electronic and print media offers your students a wealth of opportunities. The student text directs students to the Web site for the following options:

- **Chapter Overviews**
- **Student Web Activities**
- **Self-Check Quizzes**
- **Textbook Updates**

Answers are provided for you in the **Web Activity Lesson Plan.** Additional Web resources and Interactive Puzzles are also available.

Use the Glencoe Web site for additional resources. All essential content is covered in the Student Edition.

## Additional Resources

### Reading for the Student

*The American Economy: Government's Role, Citizen's Choice*, 3rd ed. Washington, D.C.: Close Up Foundation, 1999. Explores government's role in economic policies.

### Multimedia Material

*John Maynard Keynes/Fiscal Policy* and *Monetary Policy/Stabilization Policy* videos in *Economics U$A*. The Annenberg/CPB Collection, South Burlington, VT.

# CHAPTER 17 Resource Manager

| Section Resources | | |
|---|---|---|
| **Reading Objectives** | **Reproducible Resources** | **Technology/Multimedia Resources** |
| **Section 1**<br>**Unemployment and Inflation**<br>• What are two problems the government faces in measuring unemployment?<br>• What are the four kinds of unemployment?<br>• How does demand-pull inflation differ from cost-push inflation? | Reproducible Lesson Plan 17-1<br>Daily Lecture Notes 17-1<br>Guided Reading Activity 17-1<br>Reading Essentials and Study Guide 17-1<br>Daily Focus Activity 70<br>Section Quiz 17-1* | Daily Focus Transparency 70<br>Economic Concepts Transparency 17<br>Vocabulary PuzzleMaker<br>Interactive Tutor Self-Assessment Software<br>MindJogger Videoquiz<br>Presentation Plus!<br>ExamView® Pro Testmaker |
| **Section 2**<br>**The Fiscal Policy Approach to Stabilization**<br>• How does income flow between businesses and consumers?<br>• How can the federal government use fiscal policy to combat unemployment? | Reproducible Lesson Plan 17-2<br>Daily Lecture Notes 17-2<br>Guided Reading Activity 17-2<br>Reading Essentials and Study Guide 17-2<br>Daily Focus Activity 77<br>Section Quiz 17-2*<br>Reinforcing Economic Skills 13 | Daily Focus Transparency 77<br>Vocabulary PuzzleMaker<br>Interactive Tutor Self-Assessment Software<br>MindJogger Videoquiz<br>NBR's *Economics & You**<br>Presentation Plus!<br>ExamView® Pro Testmaker |
| **Section 3**<br>**Monetarism and the Economy**<br>• What do monetarists think the government and the Fed should do to stabilize the economy?<br>• Why do monetarists criticize fiscal policy? | Reproducible Lesson Plan 17-3<br>Daily Lecture Notes 17-3<br>Guided Reading Activity 17-3<br>Reading Essentials and Study Guide 17-3<br>Daily Focus Activity 78<br>Section Quiz 17-3* | Daily Focus Transparency 78<br>Vocabulary PuzzleMaker<br>Interactive Tutor Self-Assessment Software<br>MindJogger Videoquiz<br>Interactive Economics!<br>Presentation Plus!<br>ExamView® Pro Testmaker |

*Also available in Spanish

Blackline Master
Transparency

Software

CD-ROM

Videodisc
Audiocassette

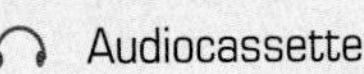
Videocassette

## ACTIVITY From the Classroom of

**Brian Sage**
**Niagara Falls High School**
**Niagara Falls, New York**

### Measuring Local Inflation

The consumer price index (CPI) is the most widely used measure of inflation and is sometimes viewed as an indicator of the effectiveness of government economic policy. Have students research inflation in their local area by constructing a price index similar to the CPI used by the federal government's Bureau of Labor Statistics (BLS).

The BLS measures price changes in the following eight major groups. Examples of categories in each group are listed as well. For each grouping, have several students list at least 10 specific items and price them once a month, then construct a price index to measure local inflation.

- Food and beverages (cookies, cereals, cheese, coffee, chicken, restaurant meals)
- Housing (residential rent, home owners' costs, fuel oil, soaps and detergents)
- Apparel and its upkeep (men's shirts, women's dresses, jewelry)
- Transportation (airline fares, new and used cars, gasoline, car insurance)
- Recreation (newspapers, toys, musical instruments, admission fees)
- Education and communication (tuition, postage, telephone services, computers)
- Other goods and services (haircuts, cosmetics, bank fees)

## Easy Planning and Preparation!

Use Glencoe's **Presentation Plus!**, a Microsoft PowerPoint® application, to teach **Stabilizing the National Economy.** With this multimedia teacher tool, you can customize ready-made presentations. At your fingertips are interactive transparencies, on-screen lecture notes, audiovisual presentations, and links to the Internet and to other Glencoe multimedia.

### Interactive Lesson Planner

Planning has never been easier! Organize your week, month, semester, or year with all the lesson helps you need to make teaching creative, timely, and relevant—the way it is meant to be. The Interactive Lesson Planner opens Glencoe's **Chapter 17** resources, helps you build your schedule, and tracks your progress.

## Key to Ability Levels

**Teaching strategies have been coded for varying learning styles and abilities.**

L1 BASIC activities for all students
L2 AVERAGE activities for average to above-average students
L3 CHALLENGING activities for above-average students
ELL ENGLISH LANGUAGE LEARNER activities

## National Council on Economic Education

## THE EconomicsAmerica AND EconomicsInternational PROGRAMS

### Voluntary Standards Emphasized in Chapter 17

**Content Standard 19** Students will understand that unemployment imposes costs on individuals and nations. Unexpected inflation imposes costs on many people and benefits some others because it arbitrarily redistributes purchasing power. Inflation can reduce the rate of growth of national living standards, because individuals and organizations use resources to protect themselves against the uncertainty of future prices.

### Resources Available from NCEE

- *Capstone: The Nation's High School Economics Course*
- *Civics and Government: Focus on Economics*
- *Focus: High School Economics*

**To order these materials, or to contact your State Council on Economic Education about workshops and programs, call 1-800-338-1192 or visit the NCEE Web site at http://www.nationalcouncil.org**

Introducing CHAPTER 17

ECONOMICS & YOU

Economic Growth and Stability

Chapter 23
Disc 1, Side 2

ASK: Why is unemployment considered a barometer of the economy? *because unemployment tends to rise during recessions and drop during periods of expansion*

 Also available in VHS.

## Chapter Overview

Chapter 17 discusses the causes and effects of unemployment and inflation, and explores the fiscal and monetary policies used by the government to stabilize the economy.

### GLENCOE TECHNOLOGY

Use **MindJogger Videoquiz** VHS to preview Chapter 17 content.

ECONOMICS Online

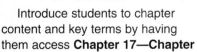

Introduce students to chapter content and key terms by having them access **Chapter 17—Chapter Overviews** at *ett.glencoe.com*

# CHAPTER 17

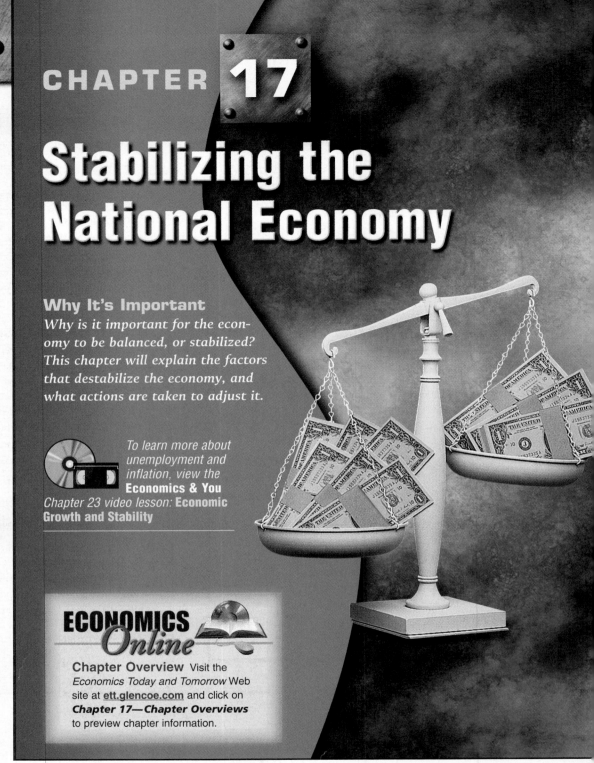

# Stabilizing the National Economy

### Why It's Important

*Why is it important for the economy to be balanced, or stabilized? This chapter will explain the factors that destabilize the economy, and what actions are taken to adjust it.*

*To learn more about unemployment and inflation, view the* **Economics & You** *Chapter 23 video lesson:* **Economic Growth and Stability**

ECONOMICS Online

**Chapter Overview** Visit the *Economics Today and Tomorrow* Web site at ett.glencoe.com and click on ***Chapter 17—Chapter Overviews*** to preview chapter information.

## CHAPTER LAUNCH ACTIVITY

Place a set of scales in front of the class, and inform students that the scales represent the economy. Move the scales by adding weights to either side. At the same time, mention that a condition called inflation can upset economic stability. Balance the scales, then set them in motion again, pointing out that unemployment too can cause the economy to become unstable. Tell students that in this chapter they will learn about different approaches to maintain economic stability.

# SECTION 1

# Unemployment and Inflation

## COVER STORY

*KIPLINGER'S PERSONAL FINANCE MAGAZINE*, SEPTEMBER 1998

A booming economy. Record-low unemployment. A blizzard of pink slips [a note stating that a person has been fired].

What's wrong with this picture? The fact is, even in the best of times hundreds of thousands of people lose their jobs through no fault of their own. . . . You might not get any advance warning, so don't be caught off guard. Have an up-to-date resume and networking system. . . . You want to be able to launch your job search soon after you get the bad news.

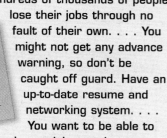

NOTICE OF EMPLOYMENT TERMINATION

NAME:

JOB TITLE:

EFFECTIVE DATE:

Signed,

### READER'S GUIDE

**Terms to Know**

- stabilization policies
- unemployment rate
- full employment
- underground economy
- demand-pull inflation
- stagflation
- cost-push inflation

**Reading Objectives**

1. What are two problems the government faces in measuring unemployment?
2. What are the four kinds of unemployment?
3. How does demand-pull inflation differ from cost-push inflation?

When people are unemployed, they experience uncertainty. In the same way, unemployment in general causes uncertainty in the American economy. To keep the economy healthy and to make the future more predictable for planning, saving, and investing, the federal government uses monetary and fiscal policies. Together these are called **stabilization policies.** Unfortunately, neither policy is always successful in

**stabilization policies:** *attempts by the federal government to keep the economy healthy; includes monetary and fiscal policies*



## SECTION 1 RESOURCE MANAGER

**Reproducible Masters**

- Reproducible Lesson Plan 17–1
- Reading Essentials and Study Guide 17–1
- Guided Reading Activity 17–1
- Section Quiz 17–1
- Daily Focus Activity 70
- Daily Lecture Notes 17–1

**Multimedia**

- Daily Focus Transparency 70
- Economic Concepts Transparency 17
- Vocabulary PuzzleMaker
- Interactive Tutor Self-Assessment Software
- ExamView® Pro Testmaker
- MindJogger Videoquiz
- Presentation Plus!



# 1 Focus

## Overview

**Section 1** describes or explains measures of unemployment, types of unemployment, and the demand-pull and cost-push theories of inflation.

### BELLRINGER

**Motivational Activity**

Project **Daily Focus Transparency 70** and have students answer the questions.

This activity is also available as a blackline master.

**Daily Focus Transparency 70**

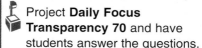

FOCUS ACTIVITIES Transparency 70

UNEMPLOYMENT

Unemployment—Rates and Measures
Unemployment and Unemployment Rates by Occupation and by Sex, 1997
For civilian noninstitutional population 16 years old and over. Rate represents unemployment as a percent of the labor force for each specified group. Based on Current Population Survey.

| OCCUPATION | UNEMPLOYMENT RATE 1997 | | |
|---|---|---|---|
| | Total | Male | Female |
| Total[1] | 4.9 | 4.9 | 5.0 |
| Managerial and professional specialty | 2.0 | 1.9 | 2.1 |
| Executive, administrative, and managerial | 1.9 | 1.8 | 2.0 |
| Professional specialty | 2.0 | 2.0 | 2.1 |
| Technical sales, and administrative support | 4.1 | 3.6 | 4.4 |
| Technicians and related support | 2.4 | 2.2 | 2.6 |
| Sales occupations | 4.9 | 3.6 | 6.2 |
| Administrative support, including clerical | 3.8 | 4.2 | 3.7 |
| Service occupations | 6.7 | 6.5 | 6.8 |
| Private household | 8.4 | 12.6 | 8.2 |
| Protective service | 3.7 | 3.4 | 5.2 |
| Service except private household and protective | 7.0 | 7.6 | 6.7 |
| Precision production, craft, and repair | 4.8 | 4.8 | 5.1 |
| Mechanics and repairers | 3.5 | 3.4 | 4.5 |
| Construction trades | 7.0 | 7.0 | 7.2 |
| Other precision production, craft, and repair | 3.4 | 3.0 | 5.0 |
| Operators, fabricators, and laborers | 7.5 | 7.1 | 8.8 |
| Machine operators, assemblers, inspectors | 6.5 | 5.1 | 8.6 |
| Transportation and material moving occupations | 5.4 | 5.3 | 6.0 |
| Handlers, equipment cleaners, helpers, laborers | 11.1 | 11.3 | 10.5 |
| Construction laborers | 17.1 | 16.9 | 20.8 |
| Farming, forestry, and fishing | 7.1 | 6.9 | 7.8 |

B Base is less than 35,000.
1 Includes people with no previous work experience and those whose last jobs were in the Armed Forces.
Adapted from U.S. Bureau of Labor Statistics, Employment and Earnings, monthly, January issue.

1. Which occupation had the highest unemployment rate?
2. Which occupation had the lowest unemployment rate for men? For women?

Daily Focus Transparencies

### READER'S GUIDE

Answers to the **Reading Objectives** questions are on page 455.

**Preteaching Vocabulary**

Ask students to write questions for which the **Terms to Know** are the answers. Have students use their questions to test each other's comprehension of the terms.

**Vocabulary PuzzleMaker**

# 2 Teach

## Guided Practice

**L2** Making Connections Have students identify the four types of unemployment, and note their responses on the board. Next, have students note any particular jobs that are prone to one or more of the four types of unemployment. Write their ideas under the appropriate unemployment type. Then have students work in small groups to brainstorm ways to eliminate or soften the conditions that cause the four kinds of unemployment. Call on group representatives to share and discuss their ideas.

See the **Web Activity Lesson Plan** at *ett.glencoe.com* for an introduction, lesson description, and answers to the **Student Web Activity** for this chapter.

**Visual Instruction FIGURE 17.1**

**Answer:** *1935*

**Student Web Activity** Visit the *Economics Today and Tomorrow* Web site at ett.glencoe.com and click on ***Chapter 17—Student Web Activities*** to learn how to write an online resume.

solving the complex problems of the economy. As you read this section, you'll learn that two of the biggest threats to a nation's economic stability are high unemployment and inflation.

## Measuring Unemployment

Expert economists advise the President and Congress, but they often disagree about the causes and cures of the economic problems that periodically face the nation. One statistic they all look at, however, is the **unemployment rate**–the percentage of the civilian labor force that is without jobs but that is actively looking for work. See **Figure 17.1.**

**unemployment rate:** *percentage of the civilian labor force that is unemployed but is actively looking for work*

High unemployment is usually a sign that all is not well with the economy. Moreover, the waste of human resources that unemployment causes is an extremely serious problem. As a result, maintaining a low unemployment rate is one of the major goals in stabilizing the economy.

**FIGURE 17.1**

**Unemployment**
Unemployment can reduce living standards, disrupt families, and reduce a person's feeling of self-respect. ***During which year shown did unemployment peak?***

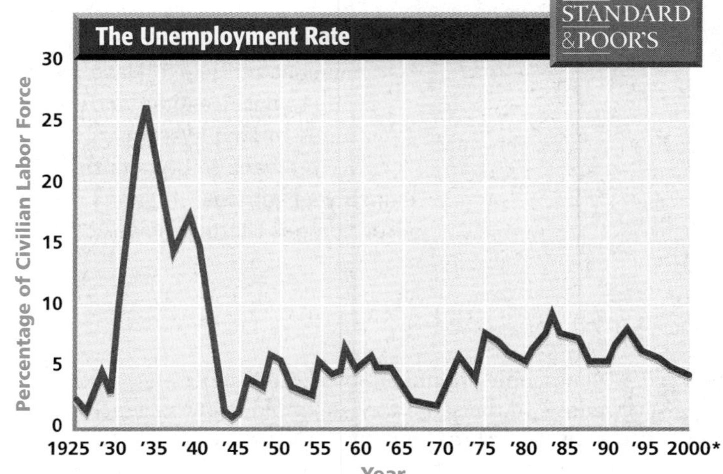


**Source:** Standard & Poor's *Author's estimate

For an online update of this graph, visit ett.glencoe.com and click on ***Textbook Updates—Chapter 17.***



**Meeting Special Needs**

**Reading and Organization Problems** Students who have difficulty categorizing information may find it useful to use a framework for comparing the different types of unemployment discussed in this section. Have students look for the answers to the following questions: What is the nature of this type of unemployment? What are the causes of this type of unemployment? How does this type of unemployment differ from other types? How is it similar? Who does this unemployment affect? If necessary, direct students' search for the information to answer these questions.

 Refer to *Inclusion for the Social Studies Classroom Strategies and Activities*.

## FIGURE 17.2 Types of Unemployment

| Type | Definition | Characteristics |
|---|---|---|
| **Cyclical** | Unemployment associated with up or down fluctuations in the business cycle | Rises during recessions and depressions; falls during recoveries and booms |
| **Structural** | Unemployment caused by changes in the economy, such as technological advances or discoveries of natural resources | Can result when workers are replaced by computers or other machines or when cheaper natural resources are found elsewhere; often affects less skilled workers |
| **Seasonal** | Unemployment caused by changes in the seasons or weather | Affects construction workers, particularly in the Northeast and Midwest; also affects farmworkers needed only during certain months of the growing season |
| **Frictional** | Temporary unemployment between jobs because of firings, layoffs, voluntary searches for new jobs, or retraining | Always exists to some degree because of the time needed between jobs to find new work and the imperfect match between openings and applicants |

**Types of Unemployment** Many types of unemployment exist. **Figure 17.2** describes these kinds of unemployment. Some people work in seasonal jobs or jobs that are sensitive to technological advances or to changes in the marketplace. As a result, not all unemployment can or should be eliminated. Moreover, economists disagree over what the level of full employment should be. Economists today generally have come to consider the economy at **full employment** when the unemployment rate is less than 5 percent.

**full employment:** *condition of the economy when the unemployment rate is lower than a certain percentage established by economists' studies*

It is important to remember that the unemployment rate is only an estimate. The unemployment rate does not include people who are unemployed and have stopped looking for work. Nor does it include people who work in family businesses without receiving pay.

Unemployment is difficult to measure accurately because government statisticians cannot possibly interview every person in and out of the labor force. Survey results are also imperfect because of the existence of the **underground economy.** The underground economy consists of people who do not follow federal and state laws with respect to reporting earnings. Examples might include tax avoiders, gamblers, and drug traffickers.

**underground economy:** *transactions by people who do not follow federal and state laws with respect to reporting earnings*



## Cooperative Learning

Have students work in small groups to track unemployment and inflation in the United States over the last 25 years. Suggest that they use the *Statistical Abstract of the United States*, the *Economic Report of the President,* and similar reference books for their research. Have groups present their findings in a series of illustrated and annotated graphs. Encourage groups to display and discuss their finished graphs.

  BLOCK SCHEDULING



### Daily Lecture Notes 17-1

DAILY LECTURE NOTES Lesson 17-1

LECTURE LAUNCHER

Brazil has had high inflationary periods throughout its history. In mid-1994, its monthly inflation reached 50 percent. In 1997, inflation was at 10%. In the United States what is considered an acceptable level of inflation? Why are inflation and unemployment important to a nation's stability?

PAGES 452–453

I. Measuring Unemployment

A. The unemployment rate is the percentage of the civilian labor force that is without jobs but is actively seeking work.

B. High unemployment is a sign that the economy is not doing well.

C. Types of unemployment: cyclical, structural, seasonal, and frictional

D. Full employment is when the unemployment rate is below 5 percent.

E. The underground economy, consisting of people who do not follow federal and state laws with respect to reporting earnings, makes it difficult to measure true unemployment rates.

**Discussion Question**

**Why can't all unemployment be eliminated?** *(Structural, seasonal, and frictional unemployment will always exist.)*

### Guided Reading Activity 17-1

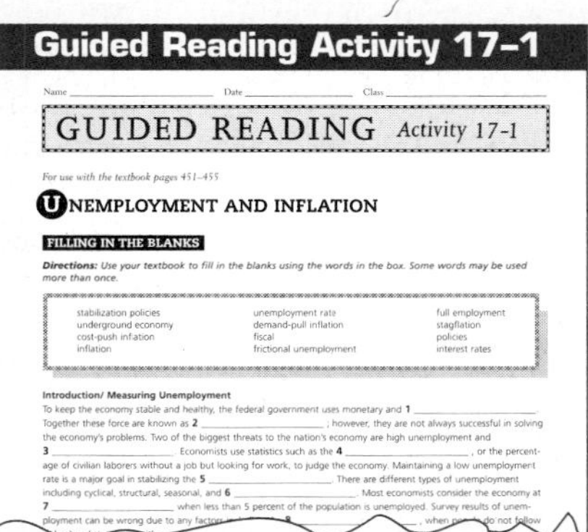

Name ______ Date ______ Class ______

GUIDED READING Activity 17-1

*For use with the textbook pages 451–455*

UNEMPLOYMENT AND INFLATION

FILLING IN THE BLANKS

***Directions:*** *Use your textbook to fill in the blanks using the words in the box. Some words may be used more than once.*

| | | |
|---|---|---|
| stabilization policies | unemployment rate | full employment |
| underground economy | demand-pull inflation | stagflation |
| cost-push inflation | fiscal | policies |
| inflation | frictional unemployment | interest rates |

**Introduction/ Measuring Unemployment**

To keep the economy stable and healthy, the federal government uses monetary and **1** ______. Together these force are known as **2** ______; however, they are not always successful in solving the economy's problems. Two of the biggest threats to the nation's economy are high unemployment and **3** ______. Economists use statistics such as the **4** ______, or the percentage of civilian laborers without a job but looking for work, to judge the economy. Maintaining a low unemployment rate is a major goal in stabilizing the **5** ______. There are different types of unemployment including cyclical, structural, seasonal, and **6** ______. Most economists consider the economy at **7** ______ when less than 5 percent of the population is unemployed. Survey results of unemployment can be wrong due to any factor ... **8** ______, when people do not follow ...

Project **Economic Concepts Transparency 17** and have students discuss the accompanying questions.

## Independent Practice

**L2 Illustrating Ideas** Organize students into groups, and assign each group either cost-push inflation or demand-pull inflation. Have groups develop and perform a scenario that illustrates their assigned cause of inflation. Then have students discuss which cause they think best explains the occurrence of inflation.

 BLOCK SCHEDULING

# 3 Assess

## Meeting Lesson Objectives

Assign Section 1 Assessment as homework or an in-class activity.

Use **Interactive Tutor Self-Assessment Software** to review Section 1.

### Section Quiz 17-1

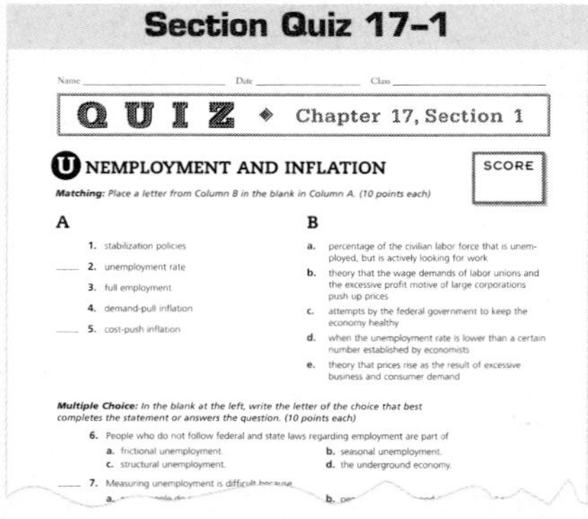

Name ______ Date ______ Class ______

QUIZ ◆ Chapter 17, Section 1

UNEMPLOYMENT AND INFLATION

SCORE

***Matching:*** *Place a letter from Column B in the blank in Column A. (10 points each)*

| A | B |
|---|---|
| ___ 1. stabilization policies | a. percentage of the civilian labor force that is unemployed, but is actively looking for work |
| ___ 2. unemployment rate | b. theory that the wage demands of labor unions and the excessive profit motive of large corporations push up prices |
| ___ 3. full employment | c. attempts by the federal government to keep the economy healthy |
| ___ 4. demand-pull inflation | d. when the unemployment rate is lower than a certain number established by economists |
| ___ 5. cost-push inflation | e. theory that prices rise as the result of excessive business and consumer demand |

***Multiple Choice:*** *In the blank at the left, write the letter of the choice that best completes the statement or answers the question. (10 points each)*

___ 6. People who do not follow federal and state laws regarding employment are part of
a. frictional unemployment.
b. seasonal unemployment.
c. structural unemployment.
d. the underground economy.

___ 7. Measuring unemployment is difficult because

### Economic Connection to... History

**Ancient Job Concerns** Worries about employment are not limited to modern economies. For example, archaeologists have found symbols connected with job placement in the ruins of ancient Babylon.

## Global Economy

### Unemployment

How do United States unemployment statistics compare to those of other industrialized nations?

| U.S. | Japan | France | Germany |
|---|---|---|---|
| **Unemployment Rate** | | | |
| 4.3% | 4.8% | 11.5% | 10.5% |
| **% of Average Wage Received in Benefits** | | | |
| 48% | 51% | 58% | 36% |
| **Length of Time Benefits Are Paid** | | | |
| 6 mo. | 1 yr. | 2 yrs. | 5 yrs. |

**Source:** *The New York Times*, May 9, 1999

## Inflation

A second major problem that may face any nation is inflation. The economy can usually adapt to gradually rising prices. If prices rise about 3 percent every year, for example, everyone comes to expect and understand that. Unpredictable inflation, however, has a destabilizing effect on the economy.

During periods of unpredictable high inflation, creditors raise interest rates to maintain the level of profits they had before inflation began to rise rapidly. This, in turn, may have a slowing effect on the economy's growth.

Inflation may also affect consumers' standard of living. Suppose you receive a 5 percent pay raise in a year in which inflation has risen 8 percent. Your real (adjusted for inflation) income has decreased. Inflation is a particularly serious problem for people who live on *fixed incomes,* such as those who are retired.

Not all economists agree on a single explanation of why inflation occurs. Two competing ideas have developed: the demand-pull theory (prices are *pulled* up by high demand) and the cost-push theory (prices are *pushed* up by high production costs and wages).

**demand-pull inflation:** *theory that prices rise as the result of excessive business and consumer demand; demand increases faster than total supply, resulting in shortages that lead to higher prices*

**Demand-Pull** According to the theory of **demand-pull inflation,** prices rise as the result of excessive business and consumer demand. If economy-wide, or aggregate, demand increases faster than total supply, the resulting shortage will lead to the bidding up of prices.

Demand-pull inflation can occur for several reasons. If the Federal Reserve causes the money supply to grow too rapidly, individuals will spend the additional dollars on a limited supply of goods and services. This increased demand will cause prices to rise. Increases in government spending and in business investment can also increase overall demand. Aggregate demand can also increase if taxes are reduced or consumers begin saving less.

**Cost-Push** The demand-pull theory assumes that increased demand will increase output and reduce unemployment. Experience, however, has shown that rising prices and unemployment



### Visual Learning Activity

**Chart** Point out that some economists illustrate the cost-push theory of inflation with a circle. Draw a circle, and provide students with the following phrases out of order. Have students use arrows and the phrases to illustrate the process of cost-push inflation around the circle.

1. Workers demand higher wages to balance the decline in their purchasing power.
2. Large unions receive wage increases.
3. Businesses pay higher wages, causing their costs to increase.
4. Businesses raise prices to maintain profits.
5. Consumers pay higher prices for goods. (which points back to number 1)

**FIGURE 17.3**

**Effects of Inflation** As Ziggy notes, inflation lowers the purchasing power of people, especially those on fixed incomes.

ZIGGY

..WITH THE HIGH COST OF THINGS NOWADAYS,
..I'M FINDING IT MORE AND MORE DIFFICULT TO GRASP THE CONCEPT OF "PETTY" CASH!



can occur at the same time. This combination of inflation and low economic activity is sometimes called **stagflation.**

According to some economists, stagflation is a result of cost-push inflation at work in the economy. The theory of **cost-push inflation** states that the wage demands of labor unions and the excessive profit motive of large corporations push up prices. When businesses have to pay higher wages, their costs increase. To maintain their profit level, businesses must raise the prices of the goods and services they produce.

During periods of cost-push inflation, unemployment can remain high. Prices are being adjusted for higher wages and profits—not because of increased aggregate demand. Without additional aggregate demand, producers have no reason to increase output by hiring new workers.

**stagflation:** *combination of inflation and low economic activity*

**cost-push inflation:** *theory that higher wages and profits push up prices*

**Practice** and **assess** key skills with ***Skillbuilder Interactive Workbook, Level 2.***

# SECTION 1 Assessment

### Understanding Key Terms

1. **Define** stabilization policies, unemployment rate, full employment, underground economy, demand-pull inflation, stagflation, cost-push inflation.

### Reviewing Objectives

2. What are two problems the government faces in measuring unemployment?
3. **Graphic Organizer** Create a diagram like the one below to describe the four kinds of unemployment.

4. How does demand-pull inflation differ from cost-push inflation?

### Applying Economic Concepts

5. **Inflation and Deflation** Name some factors that could cause the price of each of the following to go up or down: oil, medical care, orange juice, automobiles.

### Critical Thinking Activity

6. **Understanding Cause and Effect** Construct a table that identifies the causes of inflation. List four causes under demand-pull inflation in column 1 and three causes under cost-push inflation in column 2. *For help in constructing tables, see page xx in the Economic Handbook.*





## Reteach

Have students demonstrate their understanding of section content by answering the following questions: How is unemployment measured? What are the four basic types of unemployment? How is demand-pull inflation different from cost-push inflation?

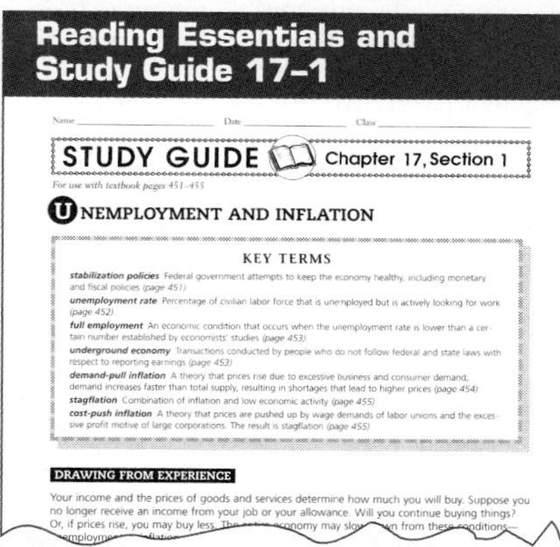

**Reading Essentials and Study Guide 17–1**

Name ______ Date ______ Class ______

STUDY GUIDE Chapter 17, Section 1

*For use with textbook pages 451–455*

UNEMPLOYMENT AND INFLATION

KEY TERMS

***stabilization policies*** Federal government attempts to keep the economy healthy, including monetary and fiscal policies *(page 451)*

***unemployment rate*** Percentage of civilian labor force that is unemployed but is actively looking for work *(page 452)*

***full employment*** An economic condition that occurs when the unemployment rate is lower than a certain number established by economists' studies *(page 453)*

***underground economy*** Transactions conducted by people who do not follow federal and state laws with respect to reporting earnings *(page 453)*

***demand-pull inflation*** A theory that prices rise due to excessive business and consumer demand; demand increases faster than total supply, resulting in shortages that lead to higher prices *(page 454)*

***stagflation*** Combination of inflation and low economic activity *(page 455)*

***cost-push inflation*** A theory that prices are pushed up by wage demands of labor unions and the excessive profit motive of large corporations. The result is stagflation *(page 455)*

DRAWING FROM EXPERIENCE

Your income and the prices of goods and services determine how much you will buy. Suppose you no longer receive an income from your job or your allowance. Will you continue buying things? Or, if prices rise, you may buy less.

## 4 Close

Have students identify some of the ways in which high unemployment and high inflation affect the economy.

## SECTION 1 Assessment Answers

1. All definitions can be found in the Glossary.
2. Statisticians can't interview every person in and out of the labor force; existence of an underground economy.
3. Diagrams should resemble **Figure 17.2** on page 453.
4. Demand-pull inflation results when demand increases faster than total supply. Cost-push inflation results when excessive wage demands of large unions and excessive profit motive of large corporations push up prices.
5. Increase in prices: shortage of oil imports, demand for more medical service, bad weather conditions in orange groves, higher auto production costs or large raises for autoworkers; Decrease in prices: new crude oil discoveries, better health habits, bumper crop, better technology for efficient production
6. Tables should include the following: Demand-pull causes: rapid increase in the money supply; increased government spending and business investment for expansion; reductions in taxes; reductions in consumer saving. Cost-push causes: high production costs; wage demands of large unions; excessive profit motive of large corporations.

BusinessWeek **Spotlight**

# Teach

Encourage students to discuss the kinds of jobs they think will be available for them when they graduate from high school or college. Ask them if they think they will work for one company for several years, or if they think they will move from company to company. Also, ask them what kinds of special skills they think they will need for employment in the twenty-first century. Conclude by informing students that this feature reviews the ways that the job market changed in the 1990s.

**BusinessWeek ONLINE**

To find up-to-date news and analysis on the economy, business, technology, markets, entrepreneurs, investments, and finance, have students search feature articles and special reports on the *Business Week* Web site. www.businessweek.com

**Sidelight**

Technological developments have changed not only how people work, but also *where* they work. A survey carried out in 1999 found that 19.6 million Americans regularly worked at home at least one day per month. In 1990, only 4 million Americans regularly worked at home.

# BusinessWeek

## Spotlight on the Economy

## Your Next Job

**Check It Out!** In this chapter you learned about the four kinds of unemployment. In this article, read to learn how the United States job market looked at the end of the twentieth century.

Employers across the country are facing a newly emboldened American work force. We're living through the tightest U.S. labor market in three decades—a hiring bonanza that is transforming the nature of work. The current hypergrowth in jobs can't last forever; fast-food restaurants won't be paying signing bonuses during the next recession. But the most remarkable changes in the workplace—and our attitudes toward it—will redefine careers well into the 21st century. Just as the Great Depression produced a generation of frugal worry-warts, those of us benefiting from the long jobs boom of the 1990s sport an often brazen self-confidence about how we connect to our jobs. . . .

What is worth knowing? That more Americans are creating entirely new styles of employment. They're found in the expanding ranks of self-employed Free Agents who find financial and professional independence in everything from personal training to urban planning. Or they are the new Nomads, workers who never seem to stop job hunting. There's an emerging class of Globalists, too—those have-laptop-will-travel workers who straddle time zones in today's borderless economy. . . .

The most striking—and frightening—feature of this new landscape is how much it demands of us. Once expertise in a single discipline, like marketing, was enough to ensure a secure corporate future. But today's free agent needs skills in selling himself (how else to drum up business?), finance (to win that bank loan) and technology (is this computer upgrade a wise investment?).



### Think About It

1. According to the article, why are workers so confident about their jobs?
2. How have the new styles of employment changed what is demanded of workers?

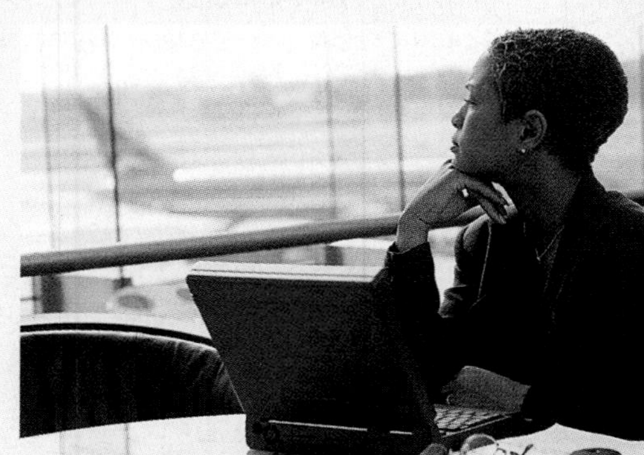



### Answers to *Think About It*

1. because there was a jobs boom throughout the 1990s
2. In the past, expertise in a single discipline was enough to guarantee a successful future. Now, workers must have skills in several areas.

SECTION 2

# The Fiscal Policy Approach to Stabilization

## Cover Story

*The New York Times*, July 14, 1999

For all the recent talk of cutting taxes, Congress rarely cuts them when the economy is growing robustly, as it is now, and unemployment is low. The worry among economists is that the extra money in people's pockets may make an already strong economy too strong, finally stoking inflation after a long period of relatively stable prices.

### Reader's Guide

**Terms to Know**
- fiscal policy
- circular flow of income

**Reading Objectives**
1. How does income flow between businesses and consumers?
2. How can the federal government use fiscal policy to combat unemployment?

Most economists belong to one of two groups on the question of stabilization. One group emphasizes the role of the Federal Reserve in stabilizing the economy, which you learned about in Chapter 15. In this section, you'll learn that the other group concentrates more on the use of **fiscal policy**, the federal government's deliberate use of its taxation rates and expenditures to affect overall business activity.

**fiscal policy:** *federal government's use of taxation and spending policies to affect overall business activity*

## John Maynard Keynes

John Maynard Keynes developed fiscal policy theories during the Great Depression. Keynes believed that the forces of aggregate supply and demand operated too slowly in a serious recession, and that government should step in to stimulate aggregate demand.



## Section 2 Resource Manager

**Reproducible Masters**
- Reproducible Lesson Plan 17–2
- Reading Essentials and Study Guide 17–2
- Guided Reading Activity 17–2
- Section Quiz 17–2
- Daily Focus Activity 77
- Daily Lecture Notes 17–2

**Multimedia**
- Daily Focus Transparency 77
- Vocabulary PuzzleMaker
- Interactive Tutor Self-Assessment Software
- ExamView® Pro Testmaker
- MindJogger Videoquiz
- NBR's *Economics & You*
- Presentation Plus!



# 1 Focus

## Overview

**Section 2** outlines a simple model of how income flows between businesses and consumers, and discusses how Keynesian fiscal policy might be used to control unemployment and inflation.

### Bellringer

**Motivational Activity**

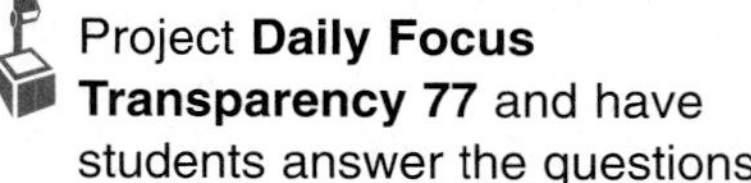

Project **Daily Focus Transparency 77** and have students answer the questions.

This activity is also available as a blackline master.

**Daily Focus Transparency 77**

**STABILIZATION POLICIES**

In the Words of John Maynard Keynes

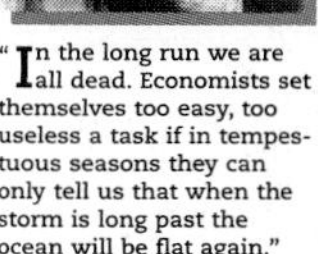

"The important thing for government is to not do things which individuals are doing already, and to do them a little better or a little worse: but to do those things which are at present not done at all."

"I think that Capitalism, wisely managed, can probably be made more efficient for attaining economic ends than any alternative system yet in sight, but that in itself is in many ways extremely objectionable."

"In the long run we are all dead. Economists set themselves too easy, too useless a task if in tempestuous seasons they can only tell us that when the storm is long past the ocean will be flat again."

1. According to Keynes, what things should government do?
2. Reread the second quotation. What might Keynes have felt was "extremely objectionable" about capitalism?

Daily Focus Transparencies

### Reader's Guide

Answers to the **Reading Objectives** questions are on page 460.

**Preteaching Vocabulary**

Have students work in small groups to develop stories or skits that illustrate the term *circular flow of income*. Call on groups to perform their stories or skits.

**Vocabulary PuzzleMaker**

# 2 Teach

## Guided Practice

**L2 Understanding Ideas** Write the terms *unemployment* and *inflation* on the board. Call on students to identify the fiscal policy actions the government can take to fight these two conditions. Enter their responses under the appropriate term. Then have students use the information on the board to write a brief essay titled "Stabilizing the Economy—The Fiscal Policy Approach."

### Daily Lecture Notes 17-2

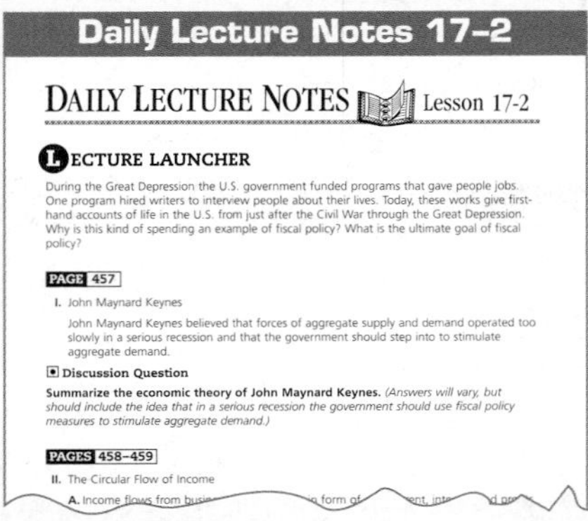
DAILY LECTURE NOTES Lesson 17-2

LECTURE LAUNCHER

During the Great Depression the U.S. government funded programs that gave people jobs. One program hired writers to interview people about their lives. Today, these works give first-hand accounts of life in the U.S. from just after the Civil War through the Great Depression. Why is this kind of spending an example of fiscal policy? What is the ultimate goal of fiscal policy?

PAGE 457

I. John Maynard Keynes

John Maynard Keynes believed that forces of aggregate supply and demand operated too slowly in a serious recession and that the government should step into to stimulate aggregate demand.

Discussion Question

**Summarize the economic theory of John Maynard Keynes.** *(Answers will vary, but should include the idea that in a serious recession the government should use fiscal policy measures to stimulate aggregate demand.)*

PAGES 458–459

II. The Circular Flow of Income

A. Income flows from busi...

### Guided Reading Activity 17-2

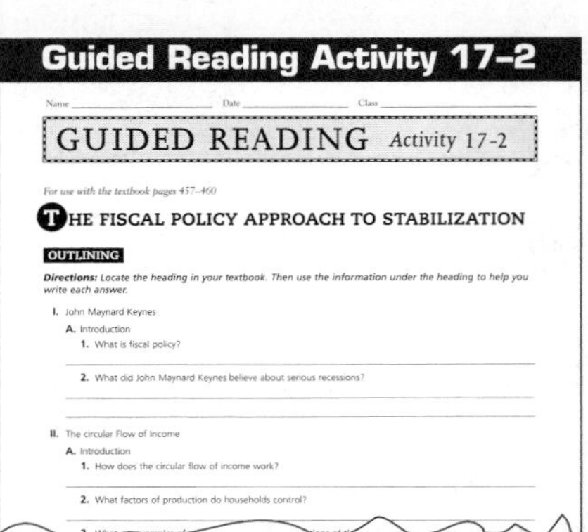
Name ______ Date ______ Class ______

GUIDED READING Activity 17-2

*For use with the textbook pages 457–460*

THE FISCAL POLICY APPROACH TO STABILIZATION

OUTLINING

***Directions:** Locate the heading in your textbook. Then use the information under the heading to help you write each answer.*

I. John Maynard Keynes
   A. Introduction
      1. What is fiscal policy?
      2. What did John Maynard Keynes believe about serious recessions?
II. The circular Flow of Income
   A. Introduction
      1. How does the circular flow of income work?
      2. What factors of production do households control?
      3. Wha...

## The Circular Flow of Income

**circular flow of income:** *economic model that pictures income as flowing continuously between businesses and consumers*

To understand Keynesian theory, you must first understand what is known as the **circular flow of income**. You learned about this model in Chapter 2. The model pictures income as flowing from businesses to households as wages, rents, interest, and profits. Income flows from households to businesses as payments for consumer goods and services.

Not all income, however, follows this circular flow. Some of it is removed from the economy through consumer saving and government taxation. Economists use the term *leakage* to refer to this removal of money income. **Figure 17.4** shows these leakages. Offsetting leakages of income are injections of income into the economy. Injections occur through business investment and government spending.

**FIGURE 17.4** **Circular Flow** Government occupies a central position in the circular flow of income. By using fiscal policy, the federal government partially controls the levels of leakages and injections. This, in turn, may control the overall level of economic activity.

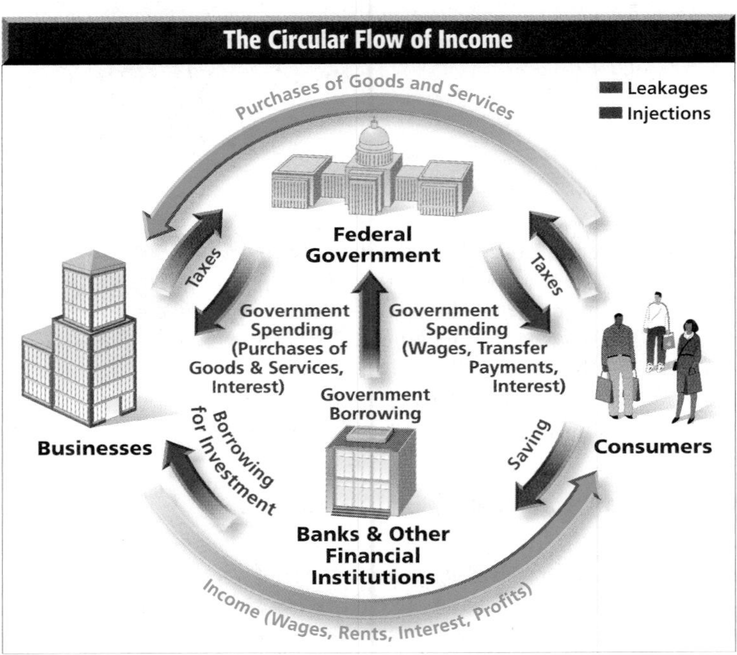




## Meeting Special Needs

**Hearing and Speech Disabilities** Students with hearing or speech problems may be concerned about making oral presentations to the class. Encourage these students to use posters, charts, graphs, and other visuals to supplement their presentations and create confidence in their ability to explain what they know.

Refer to *Inclusion for the Social Studies Classroom Strategies and Activities* for students with different learning styles.

FRANK & ERNEST

FRANK & ERNEST reprinted by permission of Newspaper Enterprise Association, Inc.

**FIGURE 17.5** **Equilibrium** The customer above is unhappy that his income and outgo are in equilibrium. Keynesian economists, however, want injections and leakages (income and outgo) to balance in the circular flow of economic activity.

Ideally, leakages and injections balance each other. See **Figure 17.5.** In this state of equilibrium, the income that households save is reinjected through business investment. Income taken out through taxes is returned through government spending.

## Fiscal Policy and Unemployment

Many public officials and labor leaders have suggested starting jobs programs to reduce unemployment and stimulate the economy. Several suggestions for forming new government-sponsored jobs programs to bring down unemployment rates were made in the early 1980s and again in 1992 and 1993.

Cuts in federal taxes are another way in which fiscal policy has been used in an attempt to speed up economic activity and fight unemployment. Giving businesses tax credits on investments allows them to deduct from their taxes some of the costs of new capital equipment. The goal is to encourage businesses to expand production and hire more workers.

## Fiscal Policy and Inflation

Fiscal policy supporters also believe that inflation can be reduced by such government actions as increasing taxes and/or reducing government spending. They argue that such actions will reduce the aggregate demand for goods and services. Because people are paying higher taxes, they are taking home less spendable income and so must cut back on their purchases. As purchases



## Extending the Content

**Fiscal Policy and the Great Depression** Keynesian economists believe that the Great Depression resulted from a serious imbalance of leakages and injections. In the months following the stock market crash of 1929, the desire and ability of businesses to invest collapsed, reducing output and causing a high rate of unemployment. According to Keynesian theory, government should have filled the gap created when businesses began limiting their investments. The government could have increased injections of government spending or cut taxes. Either action would have given businesses and consumers more disposable income.



## Independent Practice

**L2 Illustrating Ideas** Organize students into groups, and tell them to prepare an information brochure—suitable for ninth grade students—titled "Fiscal Policy: What It Is, What It Does." Call on group representatives to present and discuss their brochures.

**ECONOMICS & YOU**

**Economic Growth and Stability**

Chapter 23
Disc 1, Side 2

**ASK: What is the goal of Keynesian economics?** *It argues for more government involvement in the economy during recessions. The hope is that with more people working due to government projects, demand for products will increase and stimulate the economy.*

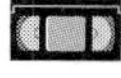 Also available in VHS.

# 3 Assess

## Meeting Lesson Objectives

Assign Section 2 Assessment as homework or an in-class activity.

Use **Interactive Tutor Self-Assessment Software** to review Section 2.

### Section Quiz 17-2

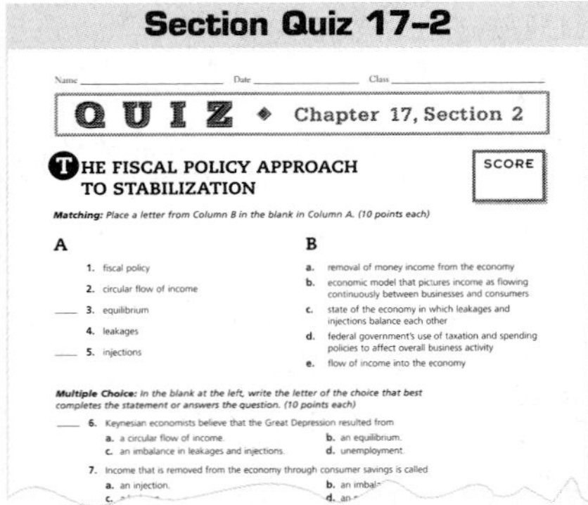

Name ______ Date ______ Class ______

**QUIZ** ◆ Chapter 17, Section 2

**THE FISCAL POLICY APPROACH TO STABILIZATION**

SCORE

***Matching:*** *Place a letter from Column B in the blank in Column A. (10 points each)*

| A | B |
|---|---|
| ___ 1. fiscal policy | a. removal of money income from the economy |
| ___ 2. circular flow of income | b. economic model that pictures income as flowing continuously between businesses and consumers |
| ___ 3. equilibrium | c. state of the economy in which leakages and injections balance each other |
| ___ 4. leakages | d. federal government's use of taxation and spending policies to affect overall business activity |
| ___ 5. injections | e. flow of income into the economy |

***Multiple Choice:*** *In the blank at the left, write the letter of the choice that best completes the statement or answers the question. (10 points each)*

___ 6. Keynesian economists believe that the Great Depression resulted from
a. a circular flow of income. b. an equilibrium.
c. an imbalance in leakages and injections. d. unemployment.

___ 7. Income that is removed from the economy through consumer savings is called
a. an injection. b. an imbal-
c. … d. an …

## Reteach

Have students outline the major aspects of the circular flow of income, fiscal policy and unemployment, and fiscal policy and inflation.

### Reading Essentials and Study Guide 17-2

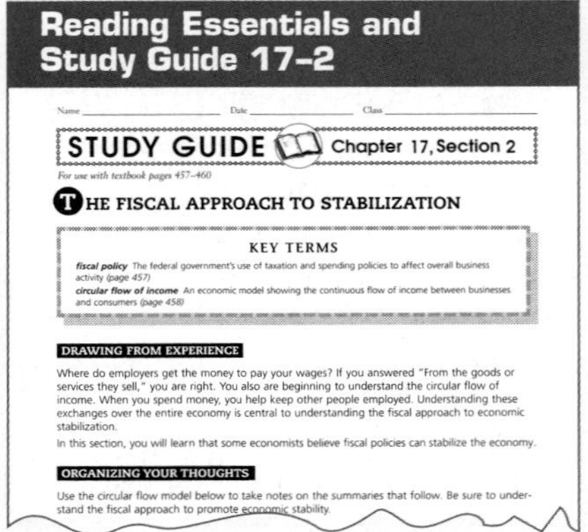

Name ______ Date ______ Class ______

**STUDY GUIDE** Chapter 17, Section 2

*For use with textbook pages 457–460*

**THE FISCAL APPROACH TO STABILIZATION**

**KEY TERMS**

***fiscal policy*** The federal government's use of taxation and spending policies to affect overall business activity *(page 457)*

***circular flow of income*** An economic model showing the continuous flow of income between businesses and consumers *(page 458)*

**DRAWING FROM EXPERIENCE**

Where do employers get the money to pay your wages? If you answered "From the goods or services they sell," you are right. You also are beginning to understand the circular flow of income. When you spend money, you help keep other people employed. Understanding these exchanges over the entire economy is central to understanding the fiscal approach to economic stabilization.

In this section, you will learn that some economists believe fiscal policies can stabilize the economy.

**ORGANIZING YOUR THOUGHTS**

Use the circular flow model below to take notes on the summaries that follow. Be sure to understand the fiscal approach to promote economic stability.

## 4 Close

Have students discuss the kinds of policies Keynesian economists might suggest for the present economic situation in the United States.

## Economic Connection to... History

# Jobs Programs

Jobs programs were created by the federal government during the 1930s. The Federal Art Project employed artists to depict American history and everyday life in public buildings. These artists created more than 2,500 murals and 17,700 sculptures.

The Federal Writers Project employed writers who worked on many different publications. The best known was the *American Guide* series—tour guides that included information on the history, geography, industry, and culture for each of the 48 states. ■

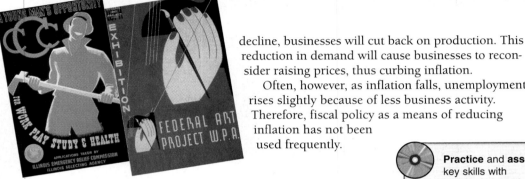

*CCC and WPA posters*

decline, businesses will cut back on production. This reduction in demand will cause businesses to reconsider raising prices, thus curbing inflation.

Often, however, as inflation falls, unemployment rises slightly because of less business activity. Therefore, fiscal policy as a means of reducing inflation has not been used frequently.

**Practice** and **assess** key skills with ***Skillbuilder Interactive Workbook, Level 2.***

## SECTION 2 Assessment

### Understanding Key Terms

1. Define fiscal policy, circular flow of income.

### Reviewing Objectives

2. **Graphic Organizer** Create a diagram like the one below to show what types of income flow from businesses to consumers in the circular flow.

**Businesses** ⇄ **Consumers**

3. How can the federal government use fiscal policy to combat unemployment?

### Applying Economic Concepts

4. **Fiscal Policy** Explain how the government policy of increasing federal, state, or local taxes could eventually lower inflation.

### Critical Thinking Activity

5. **Evaluating Primary and Secondary Sources** Research the Depression-era writings of Studs Terkel and photographs of Dorothea Lange. Write a report describing the economic conditions of the early 1930s and what actions you think the government should have taken to ease the crisis.



## SECTION 2 Assessment Answers

1. All definitions can be found in the Glossary.
2. See **Figure 17.4** on page 458 for diagram ideas and content.
3. The government might combat unemployment by creating new jobs programs or by cutting taxes. Both approaches are designed to stimulate the economy and, by doing so, reduce unemployment.
4. If people are paying higher taxes, they have less income available to make purchases. As purchases decline, businesses will cut back on production and reduce prices.
5. Encourage students to share and discuss their reports with the rest of the class.

## Critical Thinking Skills

# Summarizing Information

*Have you ever read something and just a short time later forgotten what it was all about? Summarizing information—reducing many sentences to just a few well-chosen phrases—helps you remember the main ideas and important facts contained in a longer reading selection.*

- Your summary should be much shorter than the reading selection.
- Your summary should contain the main ideas of the reading selection.
- Your summary should not contain your opinion. It should contain only the opinion of the person who wrote the selection.
- Your summary sentences and phrases should not be copied word for word from the selection. Write a summary in your own words to be sure that you understand the main ideas of the selection.

### Learning the Skill

To learn how to summarize information, follow the guidelines listed on the left.

### Practicing the Skill

Read the excerpt below, then answer the questions.

*"Tomorrow's school, it turns out, may remind parents more of a sleek shopping mall than of the long, chalk-choked corridors of their youth. Retailers and health clubs of today 'have got it figured out,' says Paul Hansen, the principal architect in charge of a $118 million retrofit of Sandburg High School [Chicago]. The new Sandburg will incorporate some of the hottest ideas in school design: a central library that resembles a Barnes & Noble superstore, a gym with updated amenities like a rock-climbing wall, and a food court to replace the cafeteria. . . . Schools of the future will be wired to the hilt. Fiber optics, internal computer networks, videoconferencing, and the like are musts."*

—*Newsweek*, December 14, 1998

1. What is the main idea of this paragraph?
2. What are the supporting details of the main idea?
3. Write a short summary that will help you remember what the paragraph is about.

### Application Activity

Spend 15 minutes reading and summarizing two articles on the front page of today's newspaper. Circle the articles and have a classmate ask you questions about them. How much were you able to remember after summarizing the information?

**Practice** and **assess** key skills with ***Skillbuilder Interactive Workbook, Level 2.***



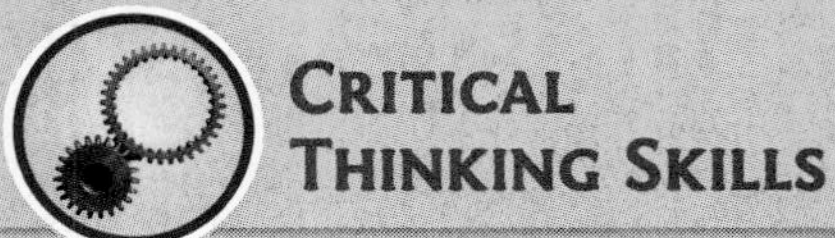

## Critical Thinking Skills

### Summarizing Information

Review the guidelines provided in the **Learning the Skill** section. Working with students, apply these guidelines to the paragraphs under the title "The Circular Flow of Income" on pages 458 and 459. Remind students that they should include information from visuals in their summaries. Then assist students as they work through the **Practicing the Skill** activity.

**Reinforcing Economic Skills 13**

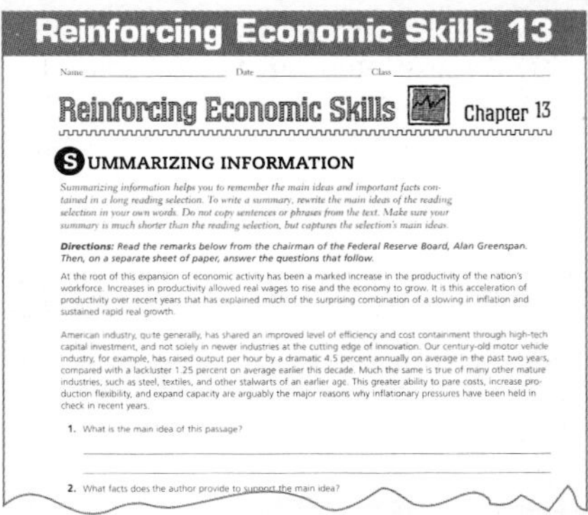

Name ______ Date ______ Class ______

Reinforcing Economic Skills Chapter 13

SUMMARIZING INFORMATION

*Summarizing information helps you to remember the main ideas and important facts contained in a long reading selection. To write a summary, rewrite the main ideas of the reading selection in your own words. Do not copy sentences or phrases from the text. Make sure your summary is much shorter than the reading selection, but captures the selection's main ideas.*

***Directions:** Read the remarks below from the chairman of the Federal Reserve Board, Alan Greenspan. Then, on a separate sheet of paper, answer the questions that follow.*

At the root of this expansion of economic activity has been a marked increase in the productivity of the nation's workforce. Increases in productivity allowed real wages to rise and the economy to grow. It is this acceleration of productivity over recent years that has explained much of the surprising combination of a slowing in inflation and sustained rapid real growth.

American industry, quite generally, has shared an improved level of efficiency and cost containment through high-tech capital investment, and not solely in newer industries at the cutting edge of innovation. Our century-old motor vehicle industry, for example, has raised output per hour by a dramatic 4.5 percent annually on average in the past two years, compared with a lackluster 1.25 percent on average earlier this decade. Much the same is true of many other mature industries, such as steel, textiles, and other stalwarts of an earlier age. This greater ability to pare costs, increase production flexibility, and expand capacity are arguably the major reasons why inflationary pressures have been held in check in recent years.

1. What is the main idea of this passage?
2. What facts does the author provide to support the main idea?

## GLENCOE TECHNOLOGY

**Glencoe Skillbuilder Interactive Workbook, Level 2**

This interactive CD-ROM reinforces student mastery of essential social studies skills.

## Answers to Practicing the Skill

1. Schools of tomorrow will be more like shopping malls than traditional schools.
2. Sandburg school will have a library that looks like a Barnes & Noble superstore, a gym with updated amenities like a rock-climbing wall, and a food court instead of a cafeteria.
3. Summaries will vary. Ensure that students follow the guidelines when writing their summaries.

**Application Activity** You may want to hand out copies of a current newspaper article and have students practice summarizing the information in class.

# 1 Focus

## Overview

Section 3 explains the theory of monetarism, discusses the monetarist approach to government policy, and reviews monetarist criticisms of fiscal policy.

**BELLRINGER**
**Motivational Activity**

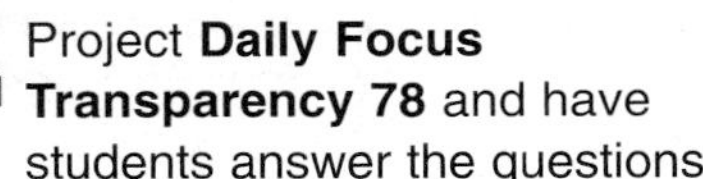

Project **Daily Focus Transparency 78** and have students answer the questions.

This activity is also available as a blackline master.

**Daily Focus Transparency 78**

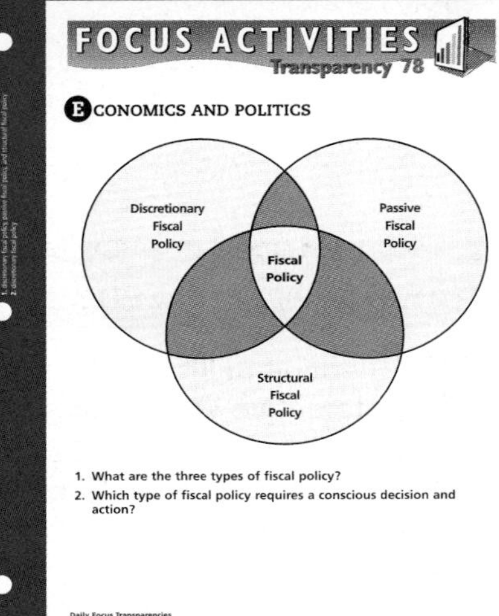


### READER'S GUIDE

Answers to the **Reading Objectives** questions are on page 465.

**Preteaching Vocabulary**

Ask students to use the four **Terms to Know** in an imaginary news story about the economy.

Vocabulary PuzzleMaker

SECTION 3

# Monetarism and the Economy

### READER'S GUIDE

**Terms to Know**
- monetarism
- monetarists
- monetary rule
- time lags

**Reading Objectives**
1. What do monetarists think the government and the Fed should do to stabilize the economy?
2. Why do monetarists criticize fiscal policy?

## COVER STORY

*THE ECONOMIST*, AUGUST 10, 1996

Have monetary policymakers got [inflation] licked? Central bankers will tell you that they have not, and not just out of modesty. Although plenty of them have targets for inflation, none is sure precisely how, or how rapidly, changes in monetary policy affect the economy. So they cannot be certain that a sensible-looking interest-rate cut will not revive inflation—or that a cautious-looking rise will not tip the economy into recession.

Hence the search for . . . a simple rule for choosing [a] monetary policy that keeps inflation down without hitting the economy too hard.

**monetarism:** *theory that deals with the relationship between the amount of money the Fed places in circulation and the level of activity in the economy*

**monetarists:** *supporters of the theory of monetarism, often linked with Milton Friedman*

In this section, you'll learn about **monetarism,** the theory that deals with the relationship between the amount of money the Federal Reserve places in circulation and the level of activity in the economy. The supporters of this theory are called **monetarists.**

## The Theory of Monetarism

Monetarism is often linked with economist Milton Friedman (see page 466). As you remember from Chapter 15, the Federal Reserve can change the growth rate of the money supply. Friedman and many other economists believe that the Fed

## SECTION 3 RESOURCE MANAGER

**Reproducible Masters**
- Reproducible Lesson Plan 17–3
- Reading Essentials and Study Guide 17–3
- Guided Reading Activity 17–3
- Section Quiz 17–3
- Daily Focus Activity 78
- Daily Lecture Notes 17–3

**Multimedia**
- Daily Focus Transparency 78
- Vocabulary PuzzleMaker
- Interactive Tutor Self-Assessment Software
- ExamView® Pro Testmaker
- MindJogger Videoquiz
- Interactive Economics!
- Presentation Plus!

should increase the money supply at a smooth, given percent each year. They argue that when the amount of money in circulation expands too rapidly, people spend more. If the economy is operating below capacity, this extra demand will lead to a rise in output. To produce more, businesses will have to hire more workers, and unemployment will decrease. If there is already full employment, however, the increased aggregate demand will lead to a rise in prices—inflation.

## Government Policy According to Monetarists

Friedman and his monetarist followers believe the economy is so complex and so little understood that government does more harm than good in trying to second-guess businesspeople and consumers. As a result, monetarists generally oppose using fiscal policy to stimulate or slow the economy.

For example, they do not believe the government should operate with budget deficits each year in an attempt to stimulate the economy. Instead, monetarists believe that the government should balance the federal budget. This action would keep government from competing with private business to borrow money in the credit market. It would also reduce the amount of interest that the government must pay each year.

The Fed, according to monetarists, should also stop trying to smooth the ups and downs in the economy. Rather, the Fed should follow a **monetary rule,** or allow the money supply to grow smoothly and consistently at a rate of perhaps 3 to 5 percent per year. Monetarists believe that a steady growth in the money supply within strict guidelines (or targets, as they are called) is the best way to provide businesses and consumers with more certainty about the future. According to monetarism, this policy would result in a controlled expansion of the economy without rapid inflation or high unemployment.

### Careers

**Social Worker**

**Job Description**
- Assist families dealing with unemployment, illness, or serious conflicts
- Refer clients to specialists

**Qualifications**
- Bachelor's degree in social work
- State licensing certification

**Median Salary:** $25,000

**Job Outlook:** Above average

*—Occupational Outlook Handbook, 1998–99*

<u>monetary rule:</u> *monetarists' belief that the Fed should allow the money supply to grow at a smooth, consistent rate per year and not use monetary policy to stimulate or slow the economy*

**Monetarist Theory and the Federal Reserve** Monetarist theory had a major influence on Federal Reserve policies in the 1980s. You can trace the changing monetary policies of the Fed in **Figure 17.6** on page 464.





# 2 Teach

## Guided Practice

**L1 Illustrating Ideas** Draw a large circle on the board. To the side, write the following labels: *Fed increases the money supply. Consumers have more cash. Demand for goods and services increases. Businesses increase output by hiring workers. At full employment, prices rise (inflation).* Call on volunteers to write these labels and arrows on the circle to show the impact of increased money supply on aggregate demand and inflation.

### Daily Lecture Notes 17-3

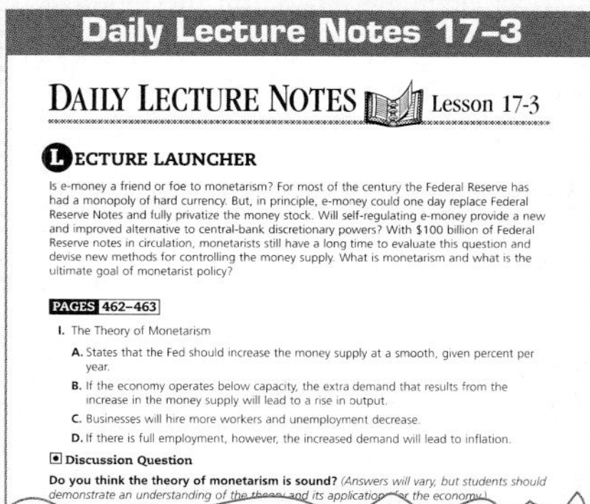

DAILY LECTURE NOTES Lesson 17-3

**LECTURE LAUNCHER**

Is e-money a friend or foe to monetarism? For most of the century the Federal Reserve has had a monopoly of hard currency. But, in principle, e-money could one day replace Federal Reserve Notes and fully privatize the money stock. Will self-regulating e-money provide a new and improved alternative to central-bank discretionary powers? With $100 billion of Federal Reserve notes in circulation, monetarists still have a long time to evaluate this question and devise new methods for controlling the money supply. What is monetarism and what is the ultimate goal of monetarist policy?

**PAGES 462–463**

I. The Theory of Monetarism
   - **A.** States that the Fed should increase the money supply at a smooth, given percent per year.
   - **B.** If the economy operates below capacity, the extra demand that results from the increase in the money supply will lead to a rise in output.
   - **C.** Businesses will hire more workers and unemployment decrease.
   - **D.** If there is full employment, however, the increased demand will lead to inflation.

**Discussion Question**

**Do you think the theory of monetarism is sound?** *(Answers will vary, but students should demonstrate an understanding of the theory and its applications for the economy.)*

### Guided Reading Activity 17-3

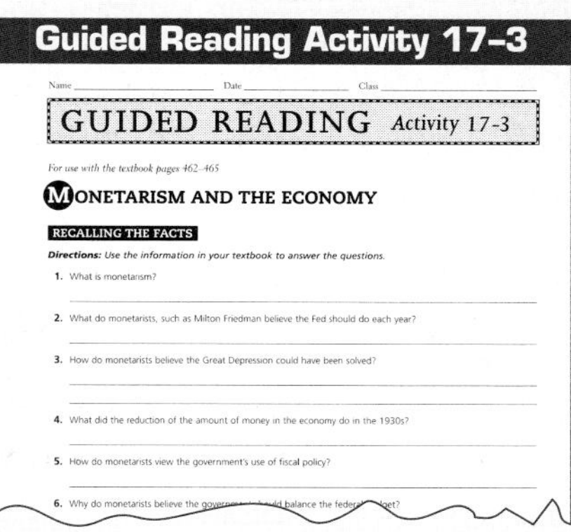

Name ______ Date ______ Class ______

GUIDED READING Activity 17-3

*For use with the textbook pages 462–465*

**MONETARISM AND THE ECONOMY**

**RECALLING THE FACTS**

***Directions:*** *Use the information in your textbook to answer the questions.*

1. What is monetarism?
2. What do monetarists, such as Milton Friedman believe the Fed should do each year?
3. How do monetarists believe the Great Depression could have been solved?
4. What did the reduction of the amount of money in the economy do in the 1930s?
5. How do monetarists view the government's use of fiscal policy?
6. Why do monetarists believe the government should balance the federal budget?

## Meeting Special Needs

**Study Strategy** To help build discussion skills for gifted students, appoint two or three students to plan and lead a class or panel discussion on the different approaches of fiscal policy and monetary policy. Be sure that students limit the focus of the discussion and take into account the class time available.

Refer to *Inclusion for the Social Studies Classroom Strategies and Activities* for students with different learning styles.

## Independent Practice

**L2 Drawing Cartoons** Direct students to create cartoons supporting or opposing monetary policies designed to stabilize the economy. Call on volunteers to display and explain their cartoons.

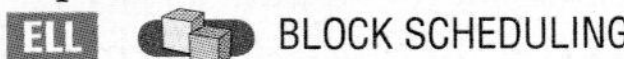

ELL BLOCK SCHEDULING

**LESSON 7: FISCAL POLICY**

Have students study the "Tutorial." Students will learn how the federal government plays both an indirect and a direct role in the economy.

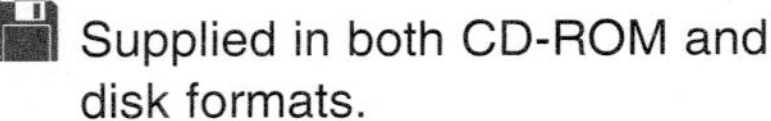

Supplied in both CD-ROM and disk formats.

# 3 Assess

## Meeting Lesson Objectives

Assign Section 3 Assessment as homework or an in-class activity.

Use **Interactive Tutor Self-Assessment Software** to review Section 3.

**Visual Instruction FIGURE 17.6**

**Answer:** *unemployment rose*

## Monetarists' Criticism of Fiscal Policy

Monetarists believe that the theory of fiscal policy never matches the reality of fiscal policy. Two reasons account for this discrepancy. The first reason concerns the political process of fiscal policy. Monetarists point out that no single government body

**FIGURE 17.6**

**Changing Fed Policies** To monetarists, the reduction in the amount of money in circulation can mean only one thing–a reduction in aggregate demand. With less aggregate demand, fewer workers are needed and unemployment increases. ***What happened to the unemployment rate when Fed policies began to lower inflation from 1980–1982?***

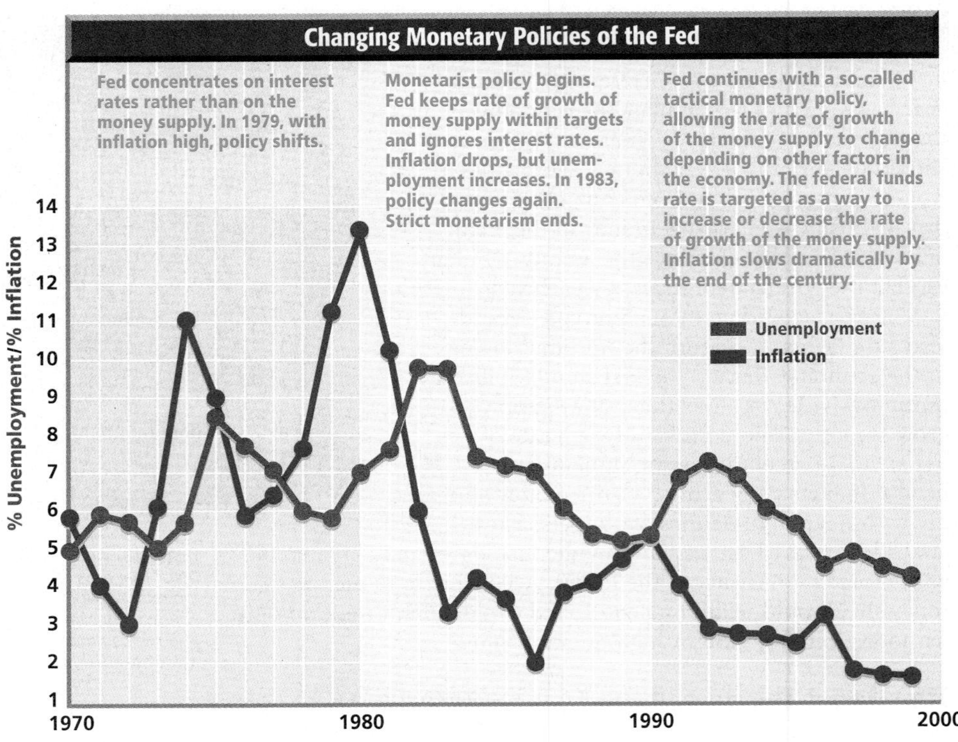

Changing Monetary Policies of the Fed
Fed concentrates on interest rates rather than on the money supply. In 1979, with inflation high, policy shifts.
Monetarist policy begins. Fed keeps rate of growth of money supply within targets and ignores interest rates. Inflation drops, but unemployment increases. In 1983, policy changes again. Strict monetarism ends.
Fed continues with a so-called tactical monetary policy, allowing the rate of growth of the money supply to change depending on other factors in the economy. The federal funds rate is targeted as a way to increase or decrease the rate of growth of the money supply. Inflation slows dramatically by the end of the century.
Unemployment
Inflation
% Unemployment/% Inflation
14
13
12
11
10
9
8
7
6
5
4
3
2
1
1970
1980
1990
2000

Sources: *Economic Report of the President,* 1999; Bureau of Economic Analysis



## Extending the Content

**Monetary Policy and the Great Depression** Monetarists view the Great Depression differently from Keynesian economists. Monetarists do not deny that a lack of business investment in the early 1930s reduced aggregate demand. However, they feel that the fall in aggregate demand resulted from the reduced amount of money in circulation. According to monetarists, the Fed should have greatly increased the amount of money in the economy. Instead, the steps taken by the Fed cut the money supply by one-third between 1929 and 1933. By its actions, the monetarists claim, the Fed turned what would have been just another recession into an economic disaster.

designs and implements fiscal policy. The President, with the aid of the director of the Office of Management and Budget (OMB), the secretary of the Treasury, and the Council of Economic Advisers, designs yet only *recommends* the desired mix of taxes and government expenditures.

Congress, with the aid of many committees (the House Ways and Means Committee, the Senate Finance Committee, and the Senate Budget Committee, to name a few), actually enacts fiscal policy. One built-in organizational problem is that the power to enact fiscal policy does not rest with a single government institution. Disagreement as to the proper fiscal policy emerges among members of Congress and between Congress and the President. Furthermore, being politicians, they have incentives to take actions that will look good today and help them get reelected, but which may hurt the economy in the long run.

Monetarists also point out that even if fiscal policy could be enacted when the President wanted, there are various **time lags** between when it is enacted and when it becomes effective. It takes many months, if not years, for fiscal policy stimuli to cause employment to rise in the economy. Consequently, a fiscal policy designed to combat a recession might not produce results until the economy is already experiencing inflation. In this event, the fiscal policy could worsen the situation.

**time lags:** *periods between the time fiscal policy is enacted and the time it becomes effective*

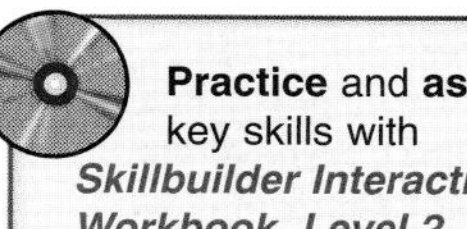

**Practice** and **assess** key skills with *Skillbuilder Interactive Workbook, Level 2.*

# SECTION 3 Assessment

### Understanding Key Terms

1. **Define** monetarism, monetarists, monetary rule, time lags.

### Reviewing Objectives

2. **Graphic Organizer** Create a diagram like the one below to describe what monetarists think the government and the Fed should do to stabilize the economy.

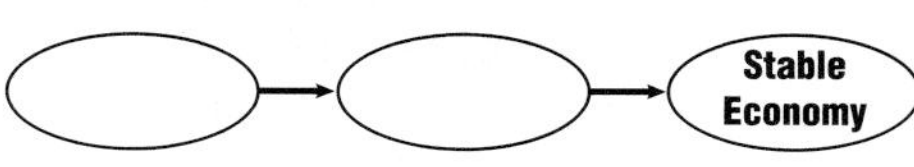


3. Why do monetarists criticize fiscal policy?

### Applying Economic Concepts

4. **Monetarism** Do you agree or disagree with the theory of monetarism? Explain your response.

### Critical Thinking Activity

5. **Making Comparisons** Describe in your own words the difference between monetarism and monetary policy. Share your description with a classmate, making sure he or she understands the difference.





## Section Quiz 17-3

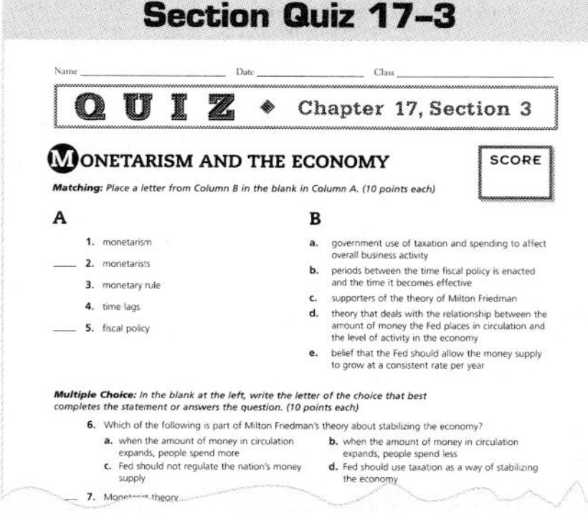

Name _____ Date _____ Class _____

QUIZ ◆ Chapter 17, Section 3

MONETARISM AND THE ECONOMY

SCORE

**Matching:** *Place a letter from Column B in the blank in Column A. (10 points each)*

A

1. monetarism
2. monetarists
3. monetary rule
4. time lags
5. fiscal policy

B

a. government use of taxation and spending to affect overall business activity
b. periods between the time fiscal policy is enacted and the time it becomes effective
c. supporters of the theory of Milton Friedman
d. theory that deals with the relationship between the amount of money the Fed places in circulation and the level of activity in the economy
e. belief that the Fed should allow the money supply to grow at a consistent rate per year

**Multiple Choice:** *In the blank at the left, write the letter of the choice that best completes the statement or answers the question. (10 points each)*

6. Which of the following is part of Milton Friedman's theory about stabilizing the economy?
   a. when the amount of money in circulation expands, people spend more
   b. when the amount of money in circulation expands, people spend less
   c. Fed should not regulate the nation's money supply
   d. Fed should use taxation as a way of stabilizing the economy

## Reteach

Have students review the section content by outlining the chief aspects of monetarism and monetary policy.

## Reading Essentials and Study Guide 17-3

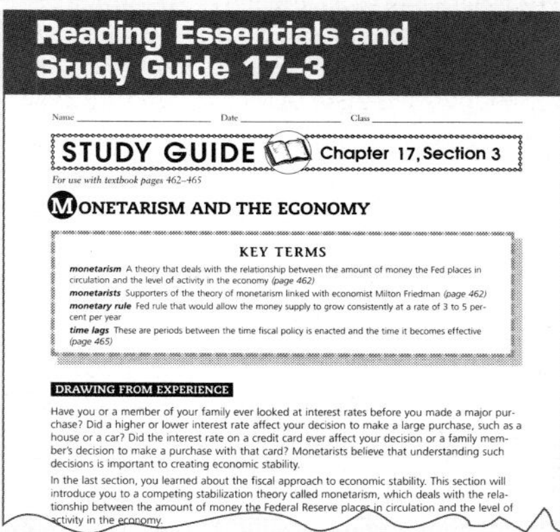

Name _____ Date _____ Class _____

STUDY GUIDE Chapter 17, Section 3

*For use with textbook pages 462–465*

MONETARISM AND THE ECONOMY

KEY TERMS

***monetarism*** A theory that deals with the relationship between the amount of money the Fed places in circulation and the level of activity in the economy *(page 462)*

***monetarists*** Supporters of the theory of monetarism linked with economist Milton Friedman *(page 462)*

***monetary rule*** Fed rule that would allow the money supply to grow consistently at a rate of 3 to 5 percent per year

***time lags*** These are periods between the time fiscal policy is enacted and the time it becomes effective *(page 465)*

DRAWING FROM EXPERIENCE

Have you or a member of your family ever looked at interest rates before you made a major purchase? Did a higher or lower interest rate affect your decision to make a large purchase, such as a house or a car? Did the interest rate on a credit card ever affect your decision or a family member's decision to make a purchase with that card? Monetarists believe that understanding such decisions is important to creating economic stability.

In the last section, you learned about the fiscal approach to economic stability. This section will introduce you to a competing stabilization theory called monetarism, which deals with the relationship between the amount of money the Federal Reserve places in circulation and the level of activity in the economy.

## 4 Close

Have students debate which they think is more effective in stabilizing the economy—fiscal policy or monetary policy.

## SECTION 3 Assessment Answers

1. All definitions can be found in the Glossary.
2. Government should balance the federal budget; the Fed should follow a monetary rule.
3. because, according to monetarists, the economy is too complex for fiscal measures to successfully adjust investment or spending
4. Ensure that students offer valid reasons for their answers.
5. Monetarism is the theory that deals with the relationship between the amount of money in circulation and economic activity, whereas monetary policy is the action taken by the Fed to increase or decrease the money supply.

## Background

Milton Friedman has been called a modern Adam Smith because of his support for free market competition and his opposition to government intervention in the economy. He has been particularly critical of the Federal Reserve System.

## Teach

Call on volunteers to read aloud the excerpts from *Capitalism and Freedom*. Encourage students to write a summary of the points made by Friedman in the excerpts. Then have students answer the **Checking for Understanding** questions.

# People & Perspectives

## Milton Friedman

ECONOMIST (1912–)

- **Won Nobel Prize for Economics in 1976**
- **Leading supporter of monetarism**
- **Publications include *The Monetary History of the U.S. 1867–1960* with Anna J. Schwartz (1963), *Capitalism and Freedom* (1962), and *Free to Choose* with Rose Friedman (1980)**

Milton Friedman has written extensively on the monetary history of the United States. Here, Friedman explains why he does not approve of the Fed and gives a possible alternative solution to regulating the money supply:

*"The establishment of the Federal Reserve System . . . established a separate official body charged with explicit responsibility for monetary conditions, and supposedly clothed with adequate power to achieve monetary stability or, at least, to prevent pronounced instability. It is therefore instructive to compare experience as a whole before and after its establishment–say, from just after the Civil War to 1914 and from 1914 to date.*

*. . . The stock of money, prices, and output was decidedly more unstable after the establishment of the Reserve System than before. . . .*

*. . . Any system which gives so much power and so much discretion to a few men that mistakes–excusable or not–can have such far-reaching effects is a bad system. It is a bad system to believers in freedom just because it gives a few men such power without any effective check by the body politic–this is the key political argument against an 'independent' central bank.*

*. . . My choice at the moment would be . . . instructing the monetary authority to achieve a specified rate of growth in the stock of money. . . . I would specify that the Reserve System shall see to it that the total stock of money so defined rises . . . at an annual rate of X percent, where X is a number between 3 and 5."*

### Checking for Understanding

1. **What is Friedman's argument against an "independent" central bank?**
2. **What rule does Friedman propose to govern decisions of the Federal Reserve System?**



### Answers to *Checking for Understanding*

1. It gives a few people too much power without any checks.
2. Friedman proposes a legislated rule instructing the monetary authority to achieve a specified rate of growth in the stock of money.

# CHAPTER  Summary

Chapter Overview Visit the *Economics Today and Tomorrow* Web site at ett.glencoe.com and click on ***Chapter 17—Chapter Overviews*** to review chapter information.

## SECTION 1 Unemployment and Inflation

- Two of the biggest threats to the nation's economic stability are high unemployment and inflation.
- Maintaining a low **unemployment rate** is a goal of **stabilization policies.**
- The four types of unemployment are cyclical, structural, seasonal, and frictional.
- According to the theory of **demand-pull inflation,** prices rise because excessive business and consumer demand increases faster than total supply.
- The theory of **cost-push inflation** states that the wage demands of labor unions and the excessive profit motive of large corporations push up prices.

## SECTION 2 The Fiscal Policy Approach to Stabilization

- Some economists believe economic stabilization can be met with **fiscal policy**—the federal government's deliberate use of taxation and spending to affect overall business activity.
- John Maynard Keynes developed fiscal policy theories during the Great Depression.
- Keynesian theory states that leakages out of and injections into the **circular flow of income** affect aggregate demand, and should be counteracted by government taxing and spending policies.
- To bring down unemployment, Keynesian economists believe in forming government-sponsored jobs programs and cutting federal taxes.

## SECTION 3 Monetarism and the Economy

- **Monetarists** believe in using the growth rate of the money supply to stabilize the economy.
- The theory of **monetarism** is often linked with economist Milton Friedman.
- Friedman and his supporters believe that the Fed should follow a **monetary rule** by increasing the money supply at a smooth, given percent per year.
- Monetarists criticize fiscal policy because of the political arena in which it is developed, and because **time lags** between enactment and implementation of fiscal policies may worsen the situation.



## Economics Journal

**Economic Stability** Direct students to keep track of the references to U.S. unemployment and inflation that they see in newspapers and magazines or on television for at least a week. For each entry, have students note whether the economic news is positive or negative. Have students use their recorded information to write a brief status report on the economy. Suggest that they answer the following questions in their reports: What is the trend of inflation—up or down? What is the trend for unemployment?

CHAPTER 17 Summary

ECONOMICS & YOU

Economic Growth and Stability

Chapter 23
Disc 1, Side 2

If you do not have access to a videodisc player, the ***Economics & You*** programs are also available in VHS.

Use the **Chapter 17 Summary** to preview, review, condense, or reteach the chapter.

## Preview/Review

**Vocabulary PuzzleMaker Software** reinforces the key terms used in Chapter 17.

**Interactive Tutor Self-Assessment Software** allows students to review Chapter 17 content.

## Condense

Have students listen to the Chapter 17 **Audio Program** (also available in Spanish) in the TCR. Assign the Chapter 17 Audio Program Activity and give students the Chapter 17 Audio Program Test.

## Reteach

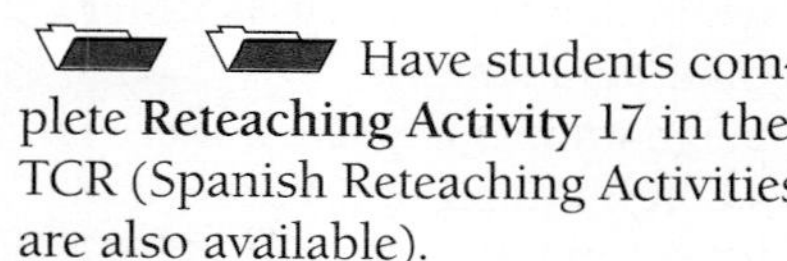

Have students complete **Reteaching Activity** 17 in the TCR (Spanish Reteaching Activities are also available).

# CHAPTER 17
## Assessment and Activities

Have students visit the *Economics Today and Tomorrow* Web site at ett.glencoe.com to review Chapter 17 and take the Self-Check Quiz.

**GLENCOE TECHNOLOGY**

 **MindJogger Videoquiz**

Use MindJogger to review Chapter 17 content.

## Identifying Key Terms

Sample sentences:

1. The unemployment rate is the percentage of the civilian labor force that is unemployed but actively looking for work.
2. Full employment is a condition in which the unemployment rate is lower than a certain percentage–usually 5 percent–established by economists.
3. The underground economy involves transactions by people who do not follow federal or state laws with respect to declaring earnings.
4. Demand-pull inflation results when demand increases faster than total supply.
5. Stagflation exists when there is a combination of inflation and low economic activity.
6. Cost-push inflation results when workers' wage demands and the excessive profit motive of large corporations push up prices.
7. Fiscal policy is the government's use of taxation and spending programs to affect overall business activity.
8. Monetarism is a theory dealing with the relationship between the amount of money in circulation and the level of economic activity.
9. Monetarists feel that the Fed should follow a monetary rule, allowing the money supply to increase by a set amount each year.
10. The period between when fiscal policy is enacted and when it takes effect is called a time lag.

## Recalling Facts and Ideas

1. cyclical, structural, seasonal, frictional
2. excessive business and consumer demand
3. workers' excessive wage demands and excessive profit motive of large corporations
4. consumer saving, government taxation
5. business investment, government spending
6. increase government spending and cut taxes
7. Milton Friedman

---

# CHAPTER 17
# Assessment and Activities

**Self-Check Quiz** Visit the *Economics Today and Tomorrow* Web site at ett.glencoe.com and click on ***Chapter 17—Self-Check Quizzes*** to prepare for the Chapter Test.

## Identifying Key Terms

*Write a one-sentence explanation of each of the following terms.*

1. unemployment rate
2. full employment
3. underground economy
4. demand-pull inflation
5. stagflation
6. cost-push inflation
7. fiscal policy
8. monetarism
9. monetary rule
10. time lags

## Recalling Facts and Ideas

**Section 1**

1. What are the four types of unemployment?
2. What causes demand-pull inflation?
3. What causes cost-push inflation?

**Section 2**

4. What are the leakages out of the circular flow of income?
5. What are the injections of income into the circular flow of income?
6. What do Keynesian economists think the federal government should do to reduce unemployment?

**Section 3**

7. Who is the economist most often linked to monetarism?
8. What do monetarists believe the Fed should do in terms of monetary policy?

## Thinking Critically

1. **Making Generalizations** Why can full employment never be defined as zero unemployment?
2. **Understanding Cause and Effect** Create a diagram like the one below to explain why the unemployment rate might rise if fiscal policy were used to combat inflation.

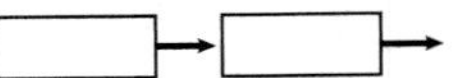

## Technology Activity

**Using the Internet** Choose either unemployment or inflation to investigate further. Using a search engine, type in *unemployment* or *inflation* to locate current statistics on your chosen topic. Visit a government Web site to learn about the most up-to-date statistics. Write a one-page summary of your findings.

## Applying Economic Concepts

**Unanticipated Versus Anticipated Inflation** Unanticipated inflation may affect you in many ways. For example, when inflation is high, banks charge higher interest rates to compensate for inflation. If you borrowed money at the high interest rates and then the rate of inflation fell, you would be worse off. You would be paying too much interest on that borrowed money. Make a list of other problems that you might encounter if there were a change in the rate of inflation that you did not anticipate.

## Reviewing Skills

**Summarizing Information** Read the excerpt below, then answer the questions that follow.

*"In recent years–as the second-longest economic expansion on record has spread its impact–most of the country has experienced a shortage of workers.*

*What's most perplexing is this: Tight labor markets are not affecting the economy the way textbooks say they should.*

*Normally, in the organic life of an economy, tight labor leads to higher wages, which triggers inflation, which leads to higher interest rates, which cause the economy to slow, which then eases the demand for labor.*

*For years now, economists have expected this chain of events to play out. But the scenario has been nipped from the start. Tight labor has not led to spiraling wages."*

–*The Columbus Dispatch*, August 23, 1999

1. According to the article, what should happen when there is a shortage of workers?
2. Summarize what the article states about the economy.

## Cooperative Learning Project

Organize into four groups. The first three groups will each track one of the following: government fiscal policies, monetary policies, and major economic indicators. The last group will create visuals from the information that is collected.

Using the front page of 10 consecutive issues of the *Wall Street Journal*, three groups will record a summary of news in each of their categories. Fiscal policy includes taxes and government spending. Monetary policy includes central bank interest rates, money supply, open-market operations, and reserve requirements. Economic indicators include such measurements as the consumer price index, industrial production, producer prices, retail sales, stocks and bonds, and unemployment. Each item should include the category, the date of the news, and a brief summary of the news.

As the information is being gathered by the first three groups, the last group should begin creating headlines that place the events in chronological order on a bulletin board. To conclude this project, the class should discuss the state of the economy as reflected in the headlines.

## Analyzing the Global Economy

Scan the international section of a newspaper or business magazine. Keep track of the number of times that you read about the topics of unemployment and inflation in other countries. Create a table listing the specific countries, and the specific topics. After each entry, indicate whether the economic news was positive or negative.



# CHAPTER 17 Assessment and Activities

## Technology Activity

Summaries will vary. Encourage students to share and compare their summaries.

## Applying Economic Concepts

Answers will vary but should demonstrate an understanding of the way different rates of inflation affect the value of money.

## Reviewing Skills

1. A shortage of workers leads to higher wages. This, in turn, triggers inflation, which leads to higher interest rates. As a result, the economy slows and the demand for labor eases.
2. Summaries will vary but should note that the usual economic result of labor shortages has not developed.

## Cooperative Learning Project

After discussing the state of the economy, students might extrapolate any implications the news items have for the future of the economy.

## Analyzing the Global Economy

Call on volunteers to share and discuss their findings.

8. Follow the monetary rule and allow the money supply to grow at a constant rate of between 3 and 5 percent each year.

## Thinking Critically

1. Unemployment will always occur because people lose their jobs, leave jobs to further their education, or change jobs. Also, some people work at jobs that are seasonal in nature. Further, technological developments may make certain jobs redundant, leaving some workers unemployed.
2. Diagrams may include: Government would raise taxes and/or reduce spending. This would reduce the aggregate demand for goods and services. Consumers would take home less spendable income. Therefore, they would cut back on spending, causing businesses to cut back on production. The slowdown in production would probably cause unemployment.

### Chapter Bonus Test Question

**ASK: What fiscal policies might be enacted to deal with unemployment?** *Fiscal policies would include increased government spending and tax cuts to stimulate the economy.*

# UNIT 6 Resource Manager

The following transparencies may be used at any time during Unit 6.

## Economic Forms and Financial Pages Transparencies

Transparency 7

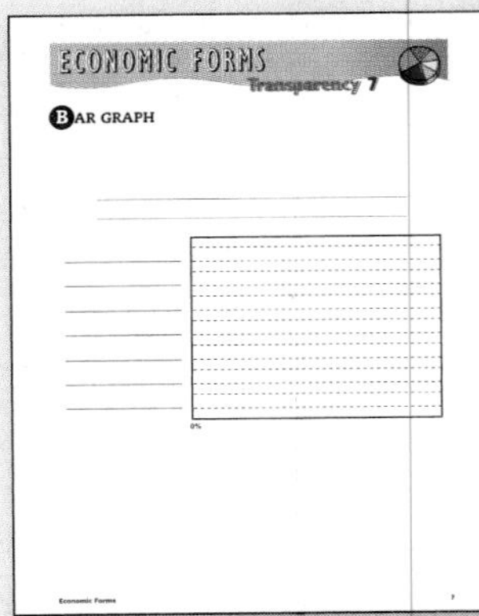


Transparency 13

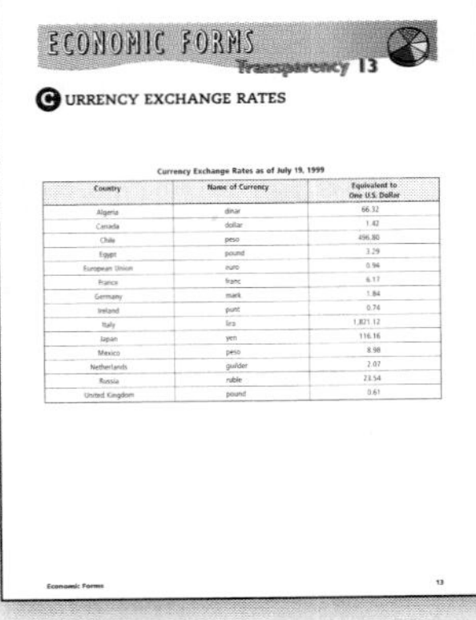


Transparency 14

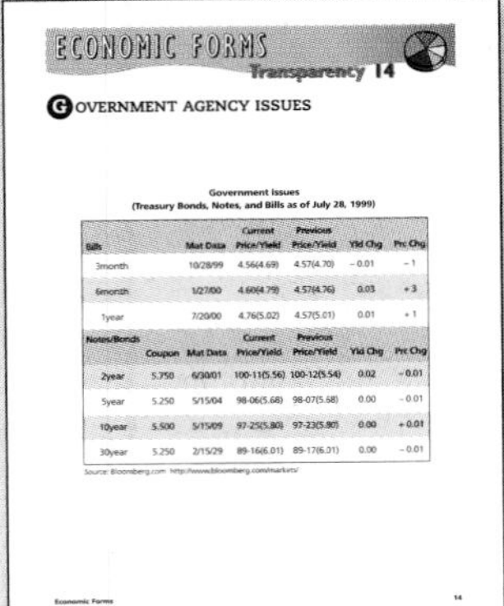


## Economic Concepts Transparencies

Transparency 3

ECONOMIC CONCEPTS Transparency 3 — PRODUCTIVITY

Transparency 4

ECONOMIC CONCEPTS Transparency 4 — ECONOMIC SYSTEMS

Transparency 11

ECONOMIC CONCEPTS Transparency 11 — MARKET FAILURES

Transparency 20

ECONOMIC CONCEPTS Transparency 20 — ABSOLUTE AND COMPARATIVE ADVANTAGE AND BARRIERS TO TRADE

Transparency 21

ECONOMIC CONCEPTS Transparency 21 — EXCHANGE RATES AND BALANCE OF PAYMENTS

Transparency 22

ECONOMIC CONCEPTS Transparency 22 — INTERNATIONAL ASPECTS OF GROWTH AND STABILITY

## Real-World Economics

Have your students learn about investing and managing their financial futures by participating in the exciting simulation **The Stock Market Game™**. See page T24 for more information.

Strengthen students' research, cooperation, presentation, and critical thinking skills by having them compete in the **Fed Challenge**. See page T26 for further information.

## Additional Glencoe Resources for This Unit

- Nightly Business Report *Economics & You* Video Program
- Economic Survival: A Financial Simulation
- Interactive Economics! Software

# UNIT 6 Resource Manager

## Assessment and Evaluation

Unit 6 Test Form A

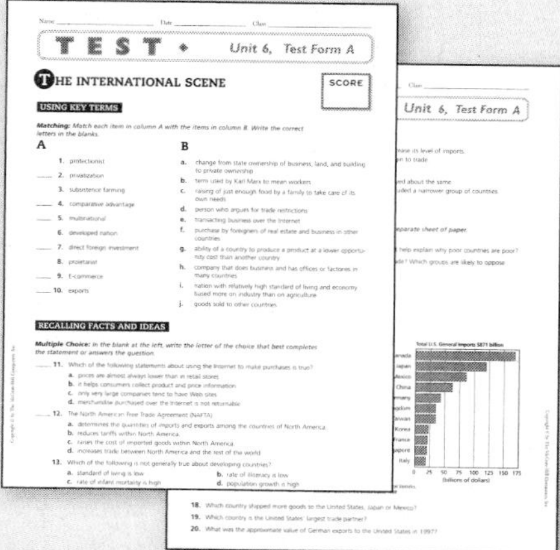

Unit 6 Test Form B

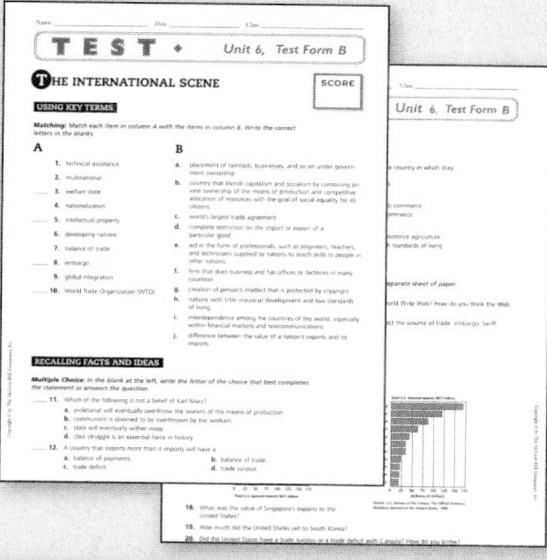

**Use the following tools to easily assess student learning:**

- Performance Assessment Strategies and Activities
- Section Quizzes
- Chapter and Unit Tests
- ExamView® Pro Testmaker
- Interactive Tutor Self-Assessment Software
- SAT I/II Test Practice
- MindJogger Videoquiz
- ett.glencoe.com

## Application and Enrichment

Economics Laboratory 6

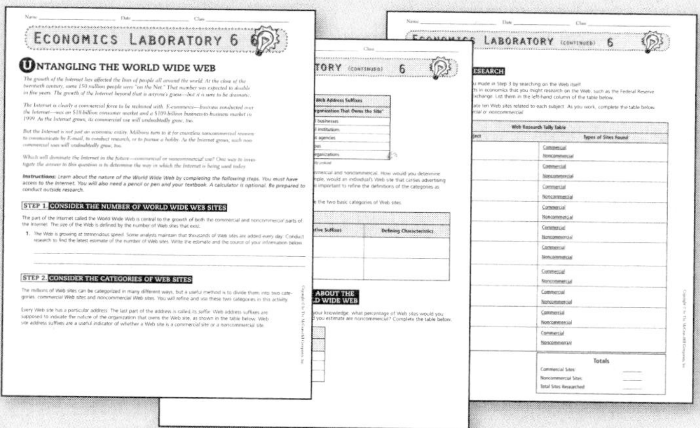

*Business Week* Focus on the New Economy

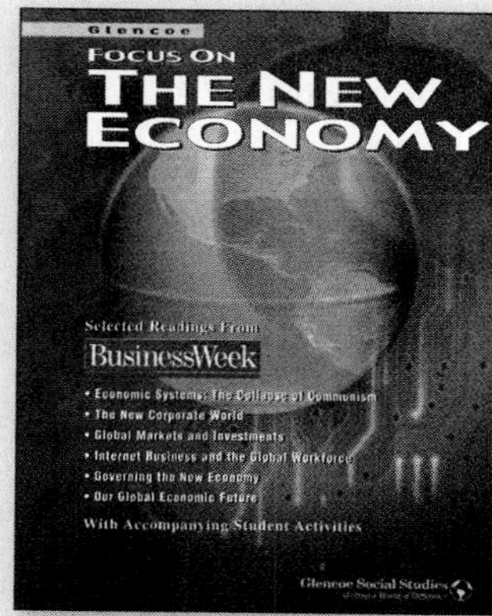


## ECONOMICS Online

*Glencoe's Web sites provide additional resources. All essential content is covered in the Student Edition.*

ett.glencoe.com

Visit the **Economics Today and Tomorrow** Web site for Chapter Overviews, Textbook Updates, Student Web Activities, Web Activity Lesson Plans, and Self-Check Quizzes.

socialstudies.glencoe.com

Visit the **Glencoe Social Studies** Web site for additional social studies activities, updates, and links to other sites.

**Glencoe's *Guide to Using the Internet*** provides an introduction to many of the current Internet technologies, social studies and professional resources, and teaching strategies.

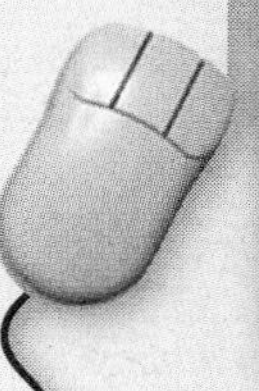

## Unit Objectives

After studying this unit, students will be able to:

- **Explain** imports and exports.
- **Describe** how other nations' economies are becoming more like the American economy.
- **Describe** economic growth in developing nations.
- **Explain** the trend toward a global economy.
- **Discuss** the impact of computer technology on the economy.

## Unit Overview

Unit 6 introduces the global economy. **Chapter 18** explains the benefits of international trade, describes how international trade is financed, and explores the limits placed on it.

**Chapter 19** compares capitalism and socialism and explores economic changes in China, Russia, Sweden, and Latin America.

**Chapter 20** describes the characteristics of developing nations, outlines the obstacles to economic growth, and discusses industrialization and the future.

**Chapter 21** discusses direct foreign investment in the United States and investigates multinational businesses.

**Chapter 22** reviews the impact that the Internet is having on the economy and explores some of the problems related to cybernomics.

### 00:00 Out of Time?

If time does not permit teaching each chapter in this unit, you may use the **Audio Program** that includes a 1-page activity and a 1-page test for each chapter.

# UNIT 6

# The International Scene

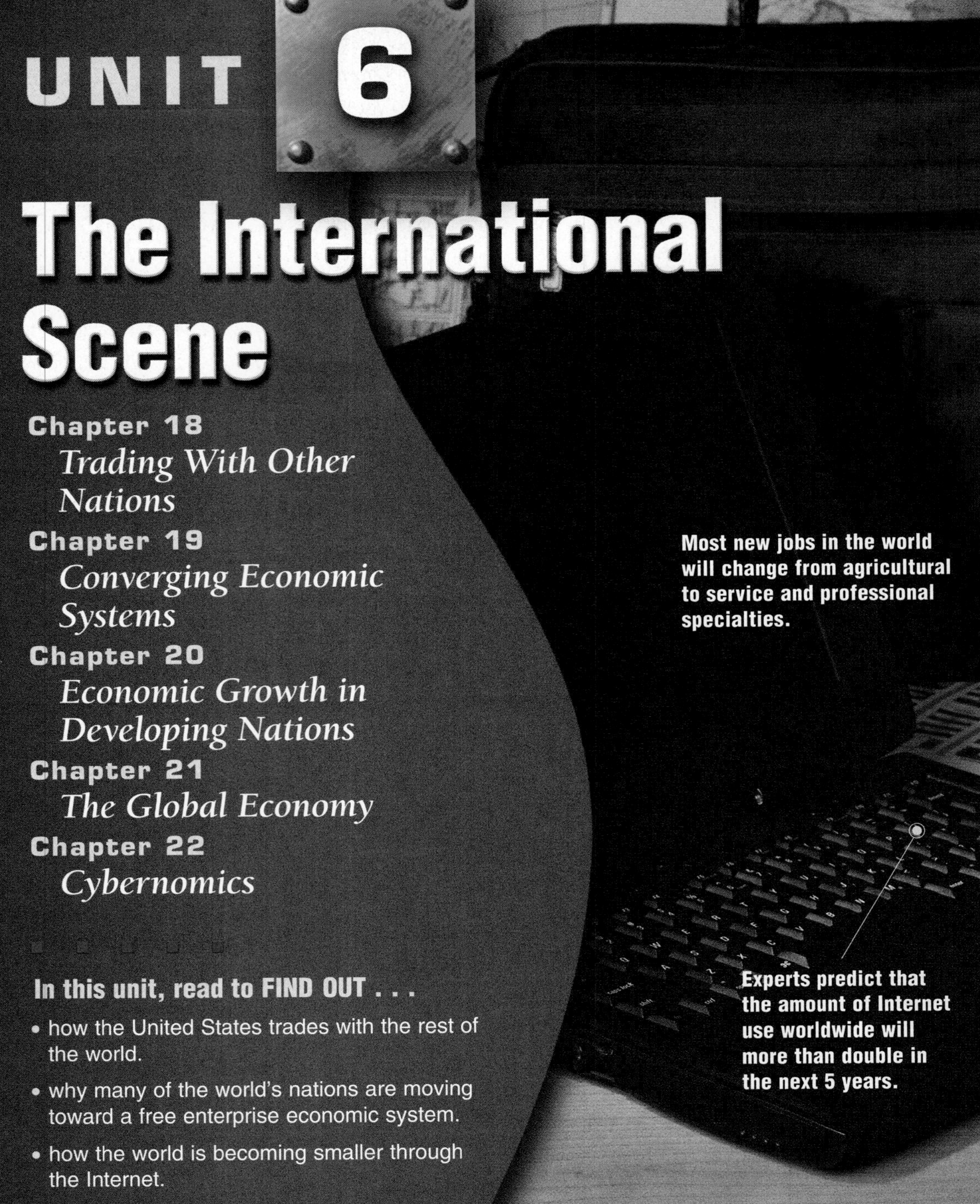



**Most new jobs in the world will change from agricultural to service and professional specialties.**

**Experts predict that the amount of Internet use worldwide will more than double in the next 5 years.**

**In this unit, read to FIND OUT . . .**

- how the United States trades with the rest of the world.
- why many of the world's nations are moving toward a free enterprise economic system.
- how the world is becoming smaller through the Internet.

### ECONOMIC SIMULATION

**International Trade** Have the class role-play a congressional subcommittee meeting on a plan to raise tariffs on imported products—athletic shoes, for example. Select several students to act as subcommittee members and four or five others to act as witnesses—consumer advocates, workers in the shoe-making industry, executives from American shoe manufacturers, and executives from foreign shoe manufacturers. Encourage expert witnesses to make presentations to the subcommittee for or against the raise in tariffs, and have subcommittee members ask them questions. Have the rest of the class act as reporters and write summaries of the procedures.

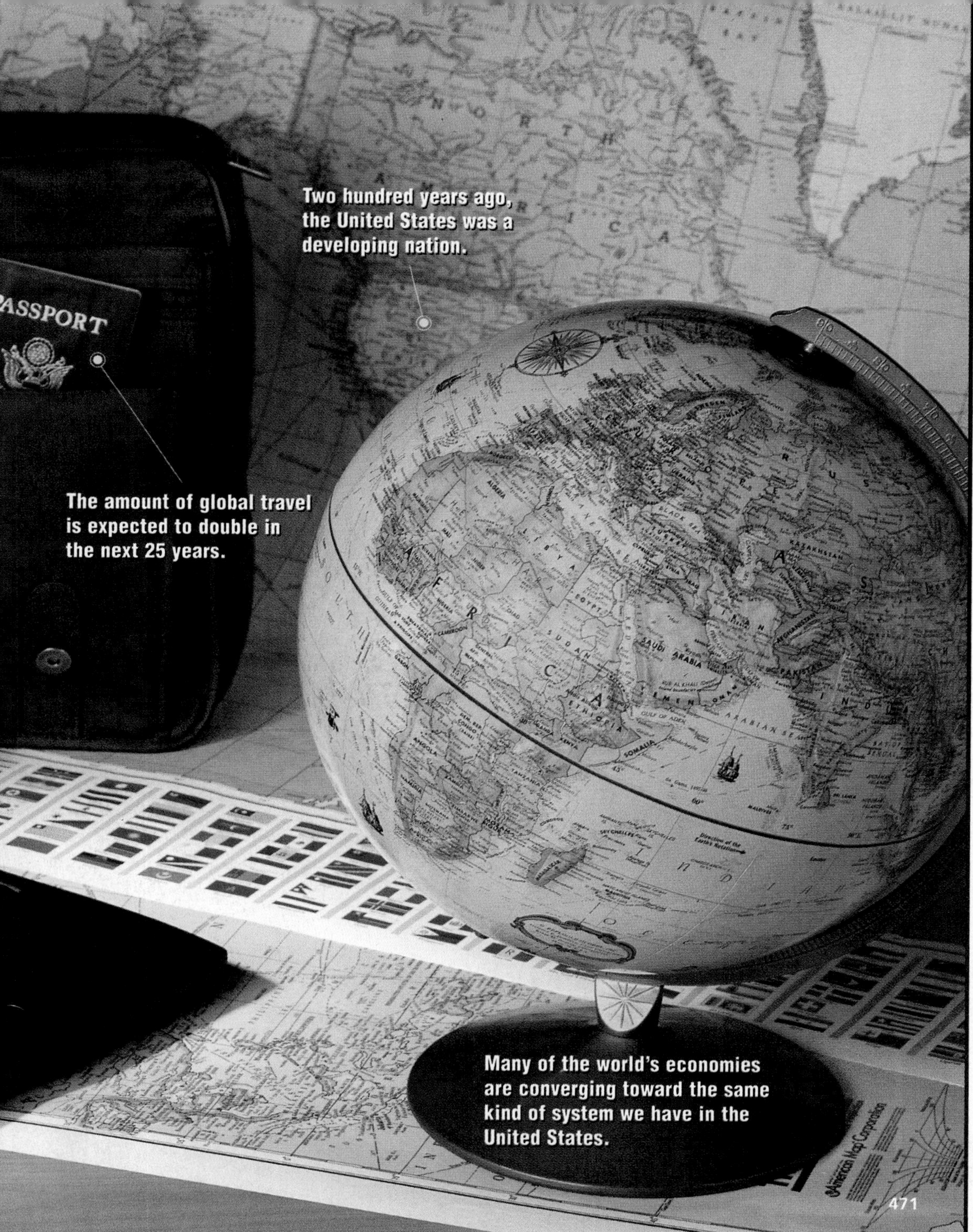

Two hundred years ago, the United States was a developing nation.
The amount of global travel is expected to double in the next 25 years.
Many of the world's economies are converging toward the same kind of system we have in the United States.
PASSPORT
471


*Introducing* UNIT 6

## Making It Relevant

Provide students with copies of newspapers and current affairs magazines. Direct students to skim through these periodicals to locate advertisements for foreign goods. Encourage students to ask themselves the following questions about the advertisements: What good is advertised? Where is it made? How was it transported to the United States? Do American companies make this good? If so, why do you think we buy it from other countries? Have students discuss their answers. Conclude by pointing out that the chapters in this unit deal with such topics as international trade and the growing interconnectedness of the world's economies.

### BusinessWeek ONLINE

To find up-to-date news and analysis on the economy, business, technology, markets, entrepreneurs, investments, and finance, have students search feature articles and special reports on the *Business Week* Web site. www.businessweek.com

### EXTRA CREDIT PROJECT

Have students research organizations such as the Ford Foundation, the International Finance Corporation (IFC), and agencies of the United Nations (UN) that offer loans or grants to economically developing nations. Have students write short reports with graphs showing trends in assistance offered. Suggest that students combine their reports into a pamphlet titled *International Organizations and Economic Development.*

# CHAPTER 18 Resource Manager

## Teaching Transparencies

### Economic Concepts Transparency 20

### Economic Concepts Transparency 21

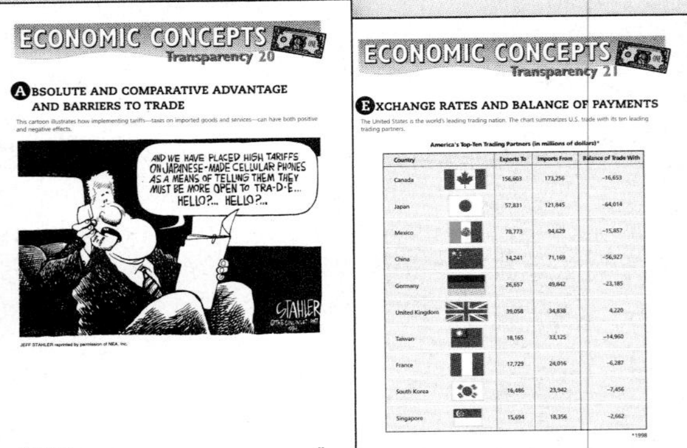

ECONOMIC CONCEPTS Transparency 20

ABSOLUTE AND COMPARATIVE ADVANTAGE AND BARRIERS TO TRADE



ECONOMIC CONCEPTS Transparency 21

EXCHANGE RATES AND BALANCE OF PAYMENTS

## Application and Enrichment

### Enrichment Activity 18

ENRICHMENT Chapter 18

TRADING WITH OTHER NATIONS

### Consumer Applications Activity 22

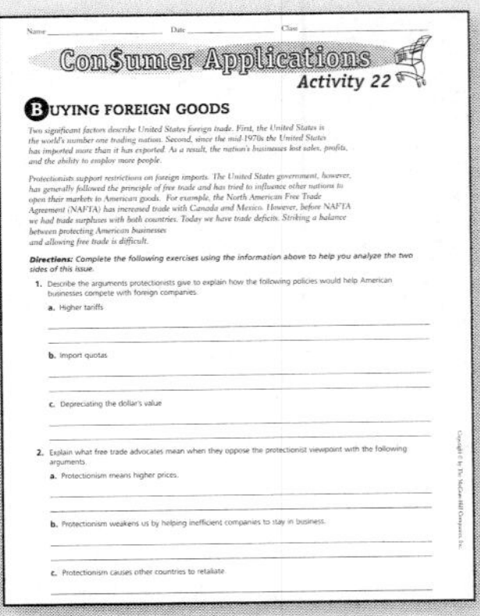

Consumer Applications Activity 22

BUYING FOREIGN GOODS

### Free Enterprise Activity 22

FREE ENTERPRISE ACTIVITY 22

FREE TRADE AND JOBS

## Application and Enrichment

### Cooperative Learning Simulations and Problems 22

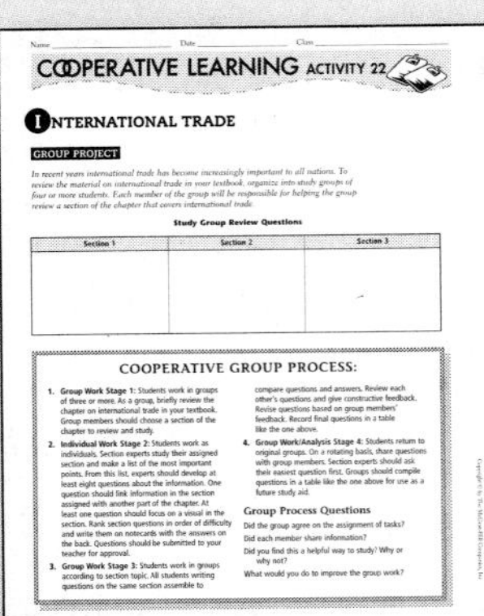

COOPERATIVE LEARNING ACTIVITY 22

INTERNATIONAL TRADE

COOPERATIVE GROUP PROCESS:

### Primary and Secondary Source Reading 22

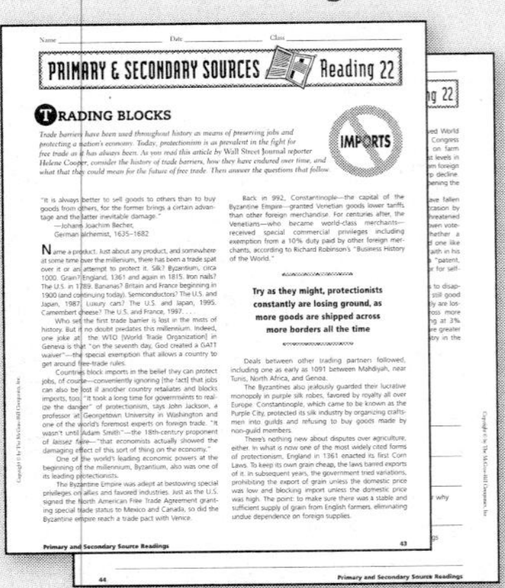

PRIMARY & SECONDARY SOURCES Reading 22

TRADING BLOCKS

### Math Practice for Economics Activity 22

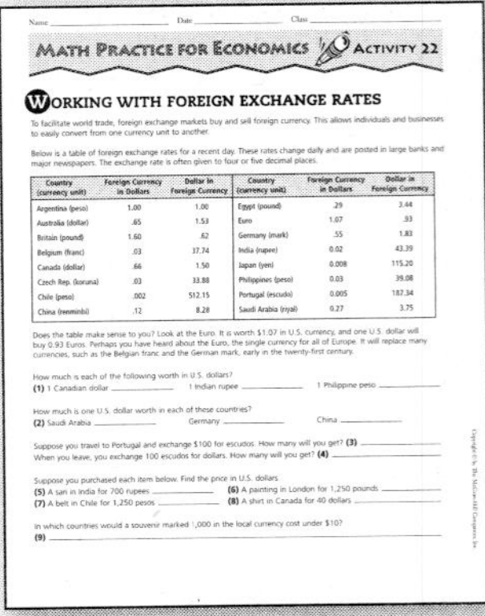

MATH PRACTICE FOR ECONOMICS ACTIVITY 22

WORKING WITH FOREIGN EXCHANGE RATES

### Economic Cartoons Activity 22

ECONOMIC CARTOON 22

GUESS WHO'S COMING TO DINNER

## Review and Reinforcement

### Critical Thinking Activity 22

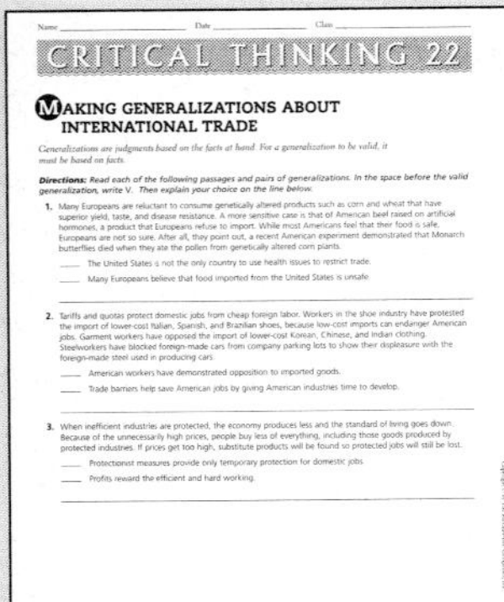

CRITICAL THINKING 22

MAKING GENERALIZATIONS ABOUT INTERNATIONAL TRADE

### Reteaching Activity 18

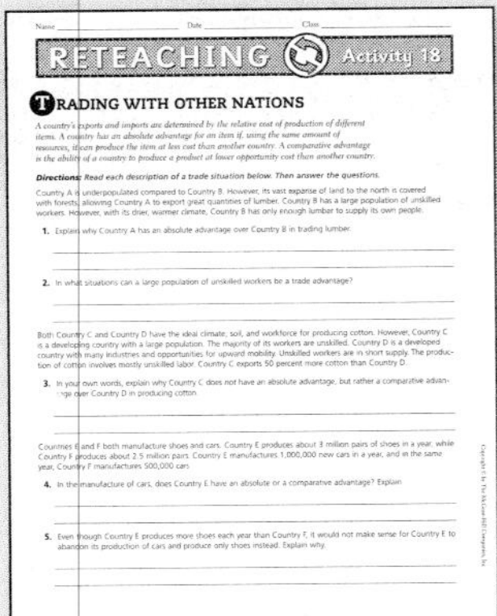

RETEACHING Activity 18

TRADING WITH OTHER NATIONS

### Economic Vocabulary Activity 18

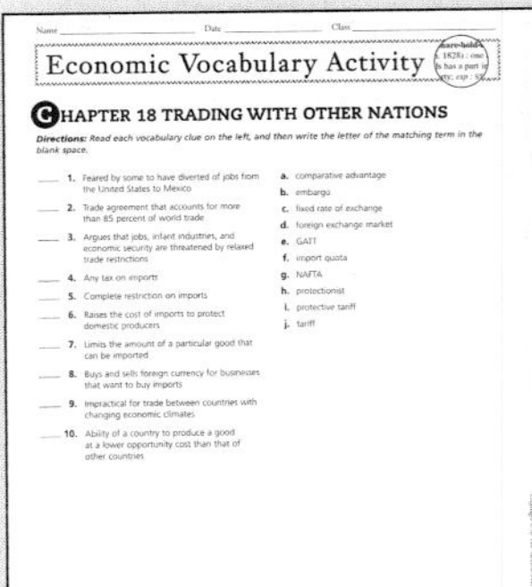

Economic Vocabulary Activity

CHAPTER 18 TRADING WITH OTHER NATIONS

### Reinforcing Economic Skills 29

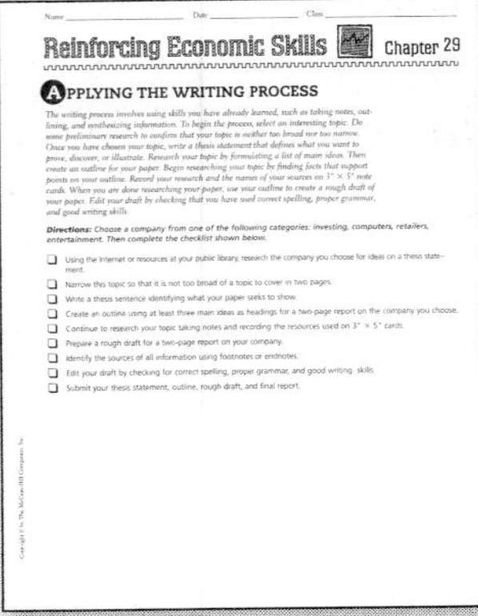

Reinforcing Economic Skills Chapter 29

APPLYING THE WRITING PROCESS

# CHAPTER 18 Resource Manager

## Assessment and Evaluation



Chapter 18 Test Form A

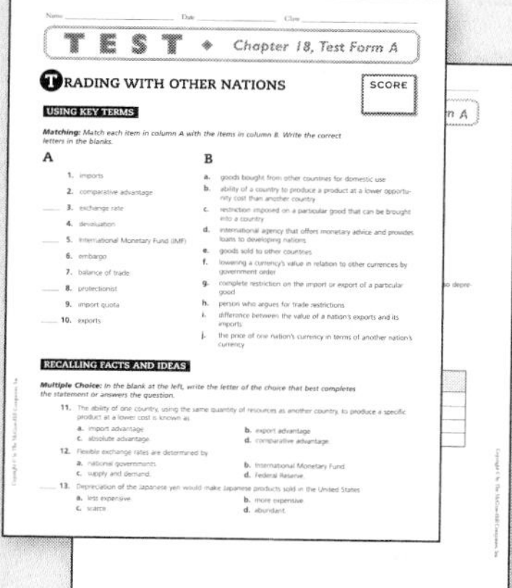
TEST ◆ Chapter 18, Test Form A

TRADING WITH OTHER NATIONS

SCORE

USING KEY TERMS

RECALLING FACTS AND IDEAS

Chapter 18 Test Form B

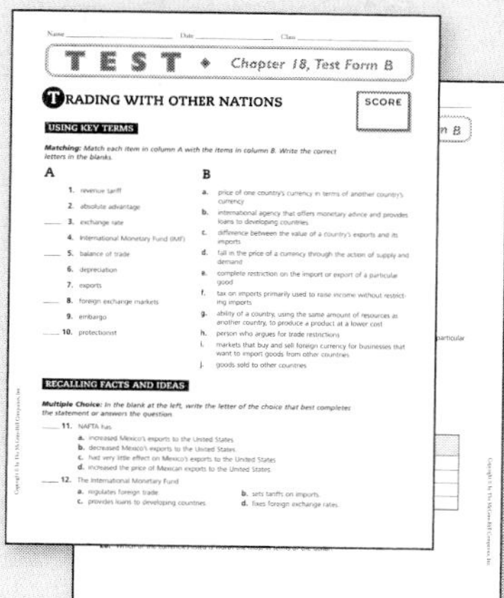
TEST ◆ Chapter 18, Test Form B

TRADING WITH OTHER NATIONS

SCORE

USING KEY TERMS

RECALLING FACTS AND IDEAS

Performance Assessment Activity 22

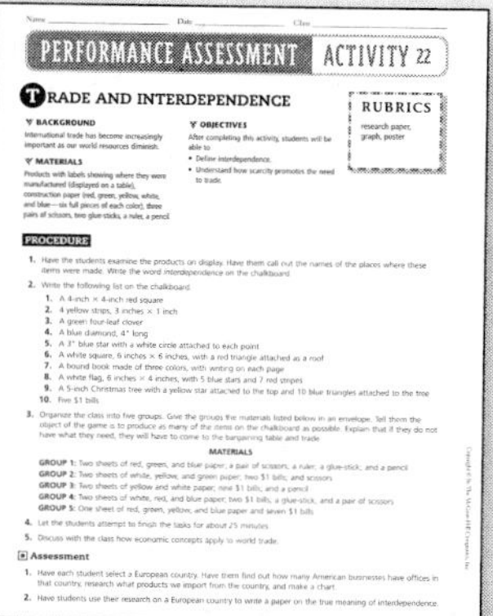
PERFORMANCE ASSESSMENT ACTIVITY 22

TRADE AND INTERDEPENDENCE

RUBRICS

PROCEDURE

ExamView® Pro Testmaker

## Technology and Multimedia

Vocabulary PuzzleMaker Software

Interactive Tutor Self-Assessment Software

ExamView® Pro Testmaker

NBR *Economics & You* Video Program (English/Spanish)

Presentation Plus!

Glencoe Skillbuilder Interactive Workbook CD-ROM, Level 2

Interactive Lesson Planner

MindJogger Videoquiz

Interactive Economics! CD-ROM

Audio Program (English or Spanish)

## ECONOMICS Online

You and your students can visit ett.glencoe.com—the Web site companion to **Economics Today and Tomorrow.** This innovative integration of electronic and print media offers your students a wealth of opportunities. The student text directs students to the Web site for the following options:

- **Chapter Overviews**
- **Student Web Activities**
- **Self-Check Quizzes**
- **Textbook Updates**

Answers are provided for you in the **Web Activity Lesson Plan.** Additional Web resources and Interactive Puzzles are also available.

Use the Glencoe Web site for additional resources. All essential content is covered in the Student Edition.

## Spanish Resources

Spanish Economic Concepts Transparencies 20, 21

Spanish Vocabulary Activity 18

Spanish Reteaching Activity 18

Spanish Section Quizzes for Chapter 18

Spanish Chapter 18 Audio Program, Activity, and Test

## Additional Resources

### Reading for the Student

Miller, R. Willard, and Ruby M. Miller. *America's International Trade: A Reference Handbook.* Santa Barbara, CA: ABC-CLIO, 1995. Principles of international trade.

### Multimedia Material

*Economics U$A: International Trade/Exchange Rates.* The Annenberg/CPB Collection, South Burlington, VT. Video, 60 min. Explores two features of the global economy.

# CHAPTER 18 Resource Manager

## Section Resources

| Reading Objectives | Reproducible Resources | Technology/Multimedia Resources |
|---|---|---|
| **Section 1**<br>**The Benefits of World Trade**<br>• What are the benefits of international trade?<br>• What is the difference between absolute advantage and comparative advantage? | Reproducible Lesson Plan 18-1<br>Daily Lecture Notes 18-1<br>Guided Reading Activity 18-1<br>Reading Essentials and Study Guide 18-1<br>Daily Focus Activity 79<br>Section Quiz 18-1*<br>Reinforcing Economic Skills 29 | Daily Focus Transparency 79<br>Economic Concepts Transparency 20<br>Vocabulary PuzzleMaker<br>Interactive Tutor Self-Assessment Software<br>MindJogger Videoquiz<br>NBR's *Economics & You**<br>Interactive Economics!<br>Presentation Plus!<br>ExamView® Pro Testmaker |
| **Section 2**<br>**Financing World Trade**<br>• Why do nations need a system of currency exchange rates?<br>• How do the forces of supply and demand determine flexible exchange rates?<br>• How do exchange rates affect the balance of trade? | Reproducible Lesson Plan 18-2<br>Daily Lecture Notes 18-2<br>Guided Reading Activity 18-2<br>Reading Essentials and Study Guide 18-2<br>Daily Focus Activity 80<br>Section Quiz 18-2* | Daily Focus Transparency 80<br>Economic Concepts Transparency 21<br>Vocabulary PuzzleMaker<br>Interactive Tutor Self-Assessment Software<br>MindJogger Videoquiz<br>NBR's *Economics & You**<br>Interactive Economics!<br>Presentation Plus!<br>ExamView® Pro Testmaker |
| **Section 3**<br>**Restrictions on World Trade**<br>• How can a nation restrict imports?<br>• What are three arguments for and against free trade?<br>• What are some current international and regional trade agreements? | Reproducible Lesson Plan 18-3<br>Daily Lecture Notes 18-3<br>Guided Reading Activity 18-3<br>Reading Essentials and Study Guide 18-3<br>Daily Focus Activity 81<br>Section Quiz 18-3* | Daily Focus Transparency 81<br>Vocabulary PuzzleMaker<br>Interactive Tutor Self-Assessment Software<br>MindJogger Videoquiz<br>Presentation Plus!<br>ExamView® Pro Testmaker |

*Also available in Spanish

Blackline Master
Transparency

Software
CD-ROM

Videodisc
Audiocassette

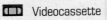

Videocassette

# CHAPTER 18 Resource Manager

## ACTIVITY From the Classroom of

**Marlene Scott**
**Central Decatur High School**
**Leon, Iowa**

### Where in the World?

Have students research the manufacturing origins of bicycle parts. They can use the Internet to locate companies that make various parts to bicycles. In addition, ask students to search their own homes to find and list the various appliances, accessories, and furniture that were made in other countries. Have students compare their lists in class, then discuss the meaning of a "global economy."

## Easy Planning and Preparation!

Use Glencoe's **Presentation Plus!**, a Microsoft PowerPoint® application, to teach **Trading With Other Nations.** With this multimedia teacher tool, you can customize ready-made presentations. At your fingertips are interactive transparencies, on-screen lecture notes, audiovisual presentations, and links to the Internet and to other Glencoe multimedia.

### Interactive Lesson Planner

Planning has never been easier! Organize your week, month, semester, or year with all the lesson helps you need to make teaching creative, timely, and relevant—the way it is meant to be. The Interactive Lesson Planner opens Glencoe's **Chapter 18** resources, helps you build your schedule, and tracks your progress.

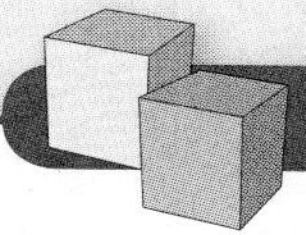

## Block Schedule

Activities that are particularly suited to use within the block scheduling framework are identified throughout this chapter by the following designation: BLOCK SCHEDULING

## Key to Ability Levels

**Teaching strategies have been coded for varying learning styles and abilities.**

L1 BASIC activities for all students
L2 AVERAGE activities for average to above-average students
L3 CHALLENGING activities for above-average students
ELL ENGLISH LANGUAGE LEARNER activities

## National Council on Economic Education

## THE EconomicsAmerica AND EconomicsInternational PROGRAMS

### Voluntary Standards Emphasized in Chapter 18

**Content Standard 5** Students will understand that voluntary exchange occurs only when all participating parties expect to gain. This is true for trade among individuals or organizations within a nation, and among individuals or organizations in different nations.

**Content Standard 6** Students will understand that when individuals, regions, and nations specialize in what they can produce at the lowest cost and then trade with others, both production and consumption increase.

### Resources Available from NCEE

- *Capstone: The Nation's High School Economics Course*
- *MCG–International Trade*
- *Geography: Focus on Economics*
- *Civics and Government: Focus on Economics*

To order these materials, or to contact your State Council on Economic Education about workshops and programs, call 1-800-338-1192 or visit the NCEE Web site at http://www.nationalcouncil.org

ECONOMICS & YOU

International Trade

Chapter 24
Disc 1, Side 2

ASK: What causes a surplus in a nation's balance of trade? *A trade surplus occurs when the value of goods a nation exports is higher than the value of goods imported.*

Also available in VHS.

## Chapter Overview

Chapter 18 explains the benefits of international trade, absolute and comparative advantage, exchange rates, barriers to free trade, and major trade agreements.

### GLENCOE TECHNOLOGY

Use **MindJogger Videoquiz** VHS to preview Chapter 18 content.

### ECONOMICS Online

Introduce students to chapter content and key terms by having them access **Chapter 18—Chapter Overviews** at *ett.glencoe.com*

# CHAPTER 18

# Trading With Other Nations

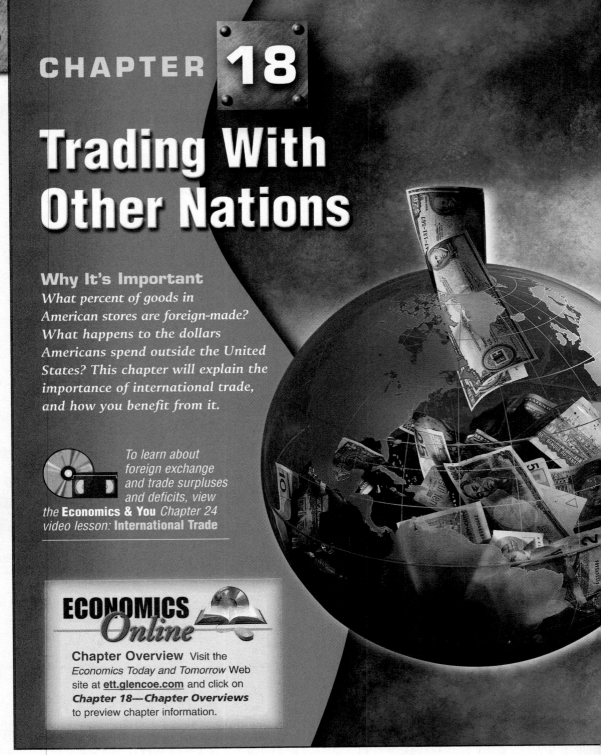

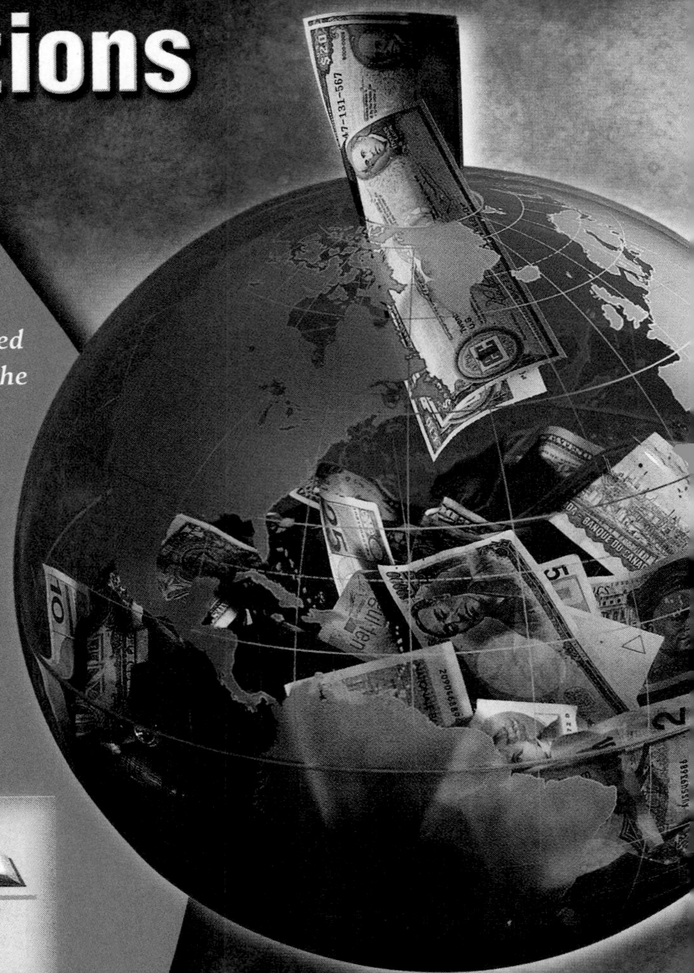

### Why It's Important

*What percent of goods in American stores are foreign-made? What happens to the dollars Americans spend outside the United States? This chapter will explain the importance of international trade, and how you benefit from it.*

*To learn about foreign exchange and trade surpluses and deficits, view the* **Economics & You** *Chapter 24 video lesson:* **International Trade**

### ECONOMICS Online

**Chapter Overview** Visit the *Economics Today and Tomorrow* Web site at **ett.glencoe.com** and click on ***Chapter 18—Chapter Overviews*** to preview chapter information.

## CHAPTER LAUNCH ACTIVITY

Have students imagine that they are owners of a small manufacturing company. Tell them that they have an opportunity to increase sales of the product by exporting it. Ask them to identify the laws, customs, consumer preferences, and other types of information they would need to know about the countries they intend to export to. Discuss their responses, and then inform students that this chapter deals with trade among nations.

SECTION 1

# The Benefits of World Trade

## COVER STORY

*THE WASHINGTON POST*, FEBRUARY 15, 1999

Mickey makes it to Beijing. Getting [the Disney movie] 'Mulan' into Chinese theaters was seen as an essential part of Disney's business plan for this nation of 1.3 billion, with a growing middle class and eager young customers. The film, about a courageous heroine who disguises herself as a man and secretly takes her ailing father's place in battle against the invading Huns, is based on a 1,500-year-old Chinese legend, and the story is as familiar here as Cinderella or Snow White in the United States. 'Mulan' has earned $299 million worldwide.

### READER'S GUIDE

**Terms to Know**

- imports
- exports
- absolute advantage
- specialization
- comparative advantage

**Reading Objectives**

1. What are the benefits of international trade?
2. What is the difference between absolute advantage and comparative advantage?

As you read this section, ask yourself what would happen if the United States could no longer sell goods to other countries or buy goods in return. Before you answer, you should be aware that the value of **imports**—goods bought from other countries for domestic use—is about 13 percent of GDP in the United States. That figure may not seem large, but many inconveniences would result without imports.

**imports:** *goods bought from other countries for domestic use*



## SECTION 1 RESOURCE MANAGER

**Reproducible Masters**

- Reproducible Lesson Plan 18–1
- Reading Essentials and Study Guide 18–1
- Guided Reading Activity 18–1
- Section Quiz 18–1
- Daily Focus Activity 79
- Daily Lecture Notes 18–1

**Multimedia**

- Daily Focus Transparency 79
- Economic Concepts Transparency 20
- Vocabulary PuzzleMaker
- Interactive Tutor Self-Assessment Software
- ExamView® Pro Testmaker
- Interactive Economics!
- NBR's *Economics & You*
- Presentation Plus!



# 1 Focus

## Overview

Section 1 discusses the benefits of international trade and explains the difference between absolute advantage and comparative advantage.

### BELLRINGER

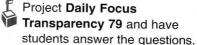

**Motivational Activity**

Project **Daily Focus Transparency 79** and have students answer the questions.

This activity is also available as a blackline master.

**Daily Focus Transparency 79**

ABSOLUTE AND COMPARATIVE ADVANTAGE

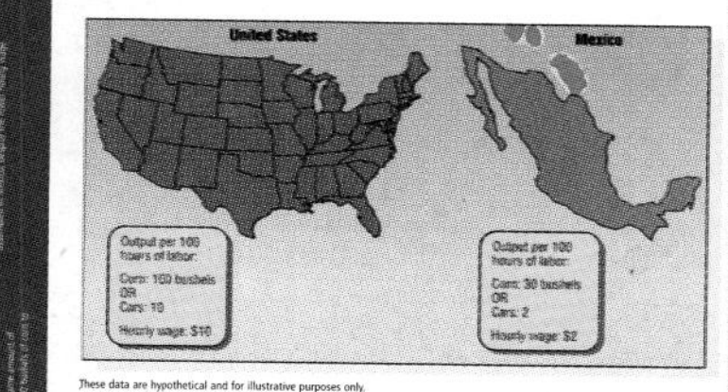


These data are hypothetical and for illustrative purposes only.

1. For each good, identify the country that has an absolute advantage in production. Explain your answer.
2. If it takes 10 hours to assemble a car in the United States and 50 hours in Mexico, what is the cost of assembling a car in each country? Given this information, would U.S. auto makers save money by taking advantage of cheaper labor costs in Mexico? Explain.

Daily Focus Transparencies

### READER'S GUIDE

Answers to the **Reading Objectives** questions are on page 477.

**Preteaching Vocabulary**

Have students explain in their own words the difference between absolute advantage and comparative advantage.

**Vocabulary PuzzleMaker**

# 2 Teach

## Guided Practice

**L2 Analyzing Ideas** Review with students the benefits of trade discussed in this section. Focus on the raw materials and goods the United States would not have without international trade. Have students discuss what would happen if the United States could no longer import such things. Then ask students to use points raised in the discussion to write a paragraph about the importance of international trade to daily life in the United States.

### Daily Lecture Notes 18–1

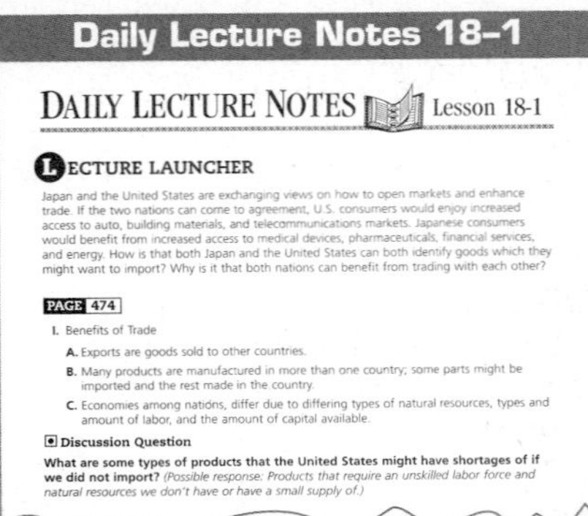
DAILY LECTURE NOTES Lesson 18-1

LECTURE LAUNCHER

Japan and the United States are exchanging views on how to open markets and enhance trade. If the two nations can come to agreement, U.S. consumers would enjoy increased access to auto, building materials, and telecommunications markets. Japanese consumers would benefit from increased access to medical devices, pharmaceuticals, financial services, and energy. How is that both Japan and the United States can both identify goods which they might want to import? Why is it that both nations can benefit from trading with each other?

PAGE 474

I. Benefits of Trade
   A. Exports are goods sold to other countries.
   B. Many products are manufactured in more than one country; some parts might be imported and the rest made in the country.
   C. Economies among nations, differ due to differing types of natural resources, types and amount of labor, and the amount of capital available.

Discussion Question

**What are some types of products that the United States might have shortages of if we did not import?** *(Possible response: Products that require an unskilled labor force and natural resources we don't have or have a small supply of.)*

### Visual Instruction FIGURE 18.1

Offer other examples of American goods that are not completely made in America. Point out that the memory chips used in an American-made IBM computer are made in Taiwan. Also, orange juices are made from concentrate that comes not only from the United States, but also from Mexico and Brazil.

We would have no coffee, chocolate, or pepper. Consider also that more than 60 percent of the radios, television sets, and motorcycles sold in the United States are imported. Many raw materials also come from foreign sources. More than 90 percent of the nation's bauxite, from which aluminum is made, is imported.

## Benefits of Trade

Imports tell only half the story. Many American workers are employed in industries that export their products overseas. **Exports** are goods sold to other countries. For example, more than 40 percent of the nation's engineering and scientific instruments are sold to consumers overseas. In addition, almost two-thirds of the wheat produced in the United States is shipped abroad.

**exports:** *goods sold to other countries*

**Made in the U.S.A.?** Sometimes it is hard to distinguish between goods made in America and those purchased abroad, as shown in **Figure 18.1.** In short, international trade affects you whether you know it or not. We have truly entered the age of a global economy, so learning about international trade is simply learning about everyday life.

**Differences Among Nations** Nations benefit through world trade because each differs in the type and amount of the factors of production it has available for use. The availability of natural resources is one of the most important of these differences.

The type and amount of labor and capital available to a nation are equally important. For example, much of the economy of the United States is based on high-technology production. A highly skilled labor force and large amounts of capital—in the form of advanced equipment and machinery—make this possible. Another nation—with the same natural resources but without the same labor and capital resources—could have a very different economy.

**FIGURE 18.1**

**Who Made the Parts?**
Consider the Boeing 777. This plane is hardly "made in America." International suppliers provide rudders, elevators, outboard flaps, wingtip assemblies, engines, nose-landing gears, nose-landing gear doors, and main-landing gears. Japanese suppliers, in particular, provide cargo doors, fuselage panels, and passenger doors. The complicated Boeing 777 jet aircraft is a jigsaw puzzle in which the pieces come from all over the world.

### Meeting Special Needs

**Organizational Difficulties** Students who have organizational problems may have difficulty translating information from graphic form to written form. Have students work in small groups to study **Figure 18.2** on page 476. Ask them to identify what information the graphic conveys. Encourage students to write their answers in sentence form.

Refer to *Inclusion for the Social Studies Classroom Strategies and Activities* for students with different learning styles.

# Economic Connection to... MATH

## Comparative Advantage

British economist David Ricardo first advanced the theory of comparative advantage in 1817. He used a mathematical example involving the production of wine and cloth in Portugal and England.

In England, it might take 100 workers to make a set amount of cloth and 120 workers to make a set amount of wine. In Portugal, it might take 90 workers to make the same amount of cloth, while the same amount of wine might take 80 workers. Ricardo observed that it would be in the interest of England to focus on making cloth, using the finished product to buy wine. By employing its capital in wine production, Portugal could obtain more cloth from England than it could produce by diverting some capital to cloth manufacturing. ■

## Absolute vs. Comparative

If the United States could produce everything *more cheaply* than every other nation, it might not want to import anything. We know this situation does not exist for any nation, however, because of opportunity cost. All nations must make choices in how they use their scarce resources.

**Absolute Advantage** The particular distribution of resources in a nation often gives it an advantage over another nation in the production of one or more products. Brazil's tropical climate and inexpensive labor make it ideally suited for growing bananas. A country with a moderate climate, such as France, would produce far fewer bananas. Brazil, therefore, has an absolute advantage in banana production over France. **Absolute advantage** is the ability of one country, using the same amount of resources as another country, to produce a particular product at a lower absolute cost.

A nation often finds it profitable to produce and export a limited assortment of goods for which it is particularly suited. This concept is known as **specialization.** See **Figure 18.2** on page 476. For example, Japan's specialization in consumer electronics has led many nations to import these types of products from Japan.

**Comparative Advantage** A nation doesn't need to have an absolute advantage in the production of a certain good to find it profitable to specialize and then to trade with other countries. For example, consider two imaginary nations, Alpha and Beta. Assume that each country produces only soybeans and corn.

<u>absolute advantage:</u> *ability of one country, using the same quantity of resources as another, to produce a particular product at a lower absolute cost*

<u>specialization:</u> *concept that a nation should produce and export a limited assortment of goods for which it is particularly suited in order to remain profitable*



**CHAPTER 18**
SECTION 1, Pages 473–477

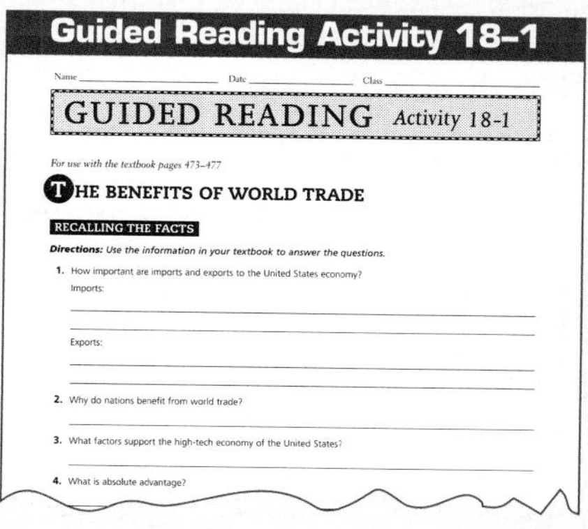
Guided Reading Activity 18-1

Name ______ Date ______ Class ______

GUIDED READING Activity 18-1

For use with the textbook pages 473–477

THE BENEFITS OF WORLD TRADE

RECALLING THE FACTS

*Directions: Use the information in your textbook to answer the questions.*

1. How important are imports and exports to the United States economy?
Imports:
Exports:
2. Why do nations benefit from world trade?
3. What factors support the high-tech economy of the United States?
4. What is absolute advantage?

NIGHTLY BUSINESS REPORT — ECONOMICS & YOU

International Trade

Chapter 24
Disc 1, Side 2

ASK: What factors can lead to a trade war? *A trade imbalance may lead a country to impose tariffs on imported goods. Other nations may respond with trade barriers of their own.*

Also available in VHS.

Project **Economic Concepts Transparency 20** and have students discuss the accompanying questions.

### Cooperative Learning

Direct students' attention to the **Global Economy** feature on pages 494–495. Then organize students into groups, and have groups research and construct a similar map showing the United States's major trading partners. Ensure that all students are involved in the activity by encouraging groups to assign particular tasks to individual members—research, collating statistics, drawing the map, creating map labels, and so on. Call on groups to display and discuss their maps. BLOCK SCHEDULING

## Independent Practice

**L2 Creating a Collage** Have students work in small groups to create a collage of American imports and exports. Suggest that they annotate illustrations in their collages with such information as dollar value of particular imports and exports, chief sources of particular imports, chief destinations of particular exports, and so on. Call on groups to display and discuss their collages. ELL

**LESSON 9: INTERNATIONAL TRADE**

Have students go to the Introduction menu and click on "Finding Comparative Advantage." Ask students to read through the "Tutorial" and find the comparative advantage for both Alpha and Beta.

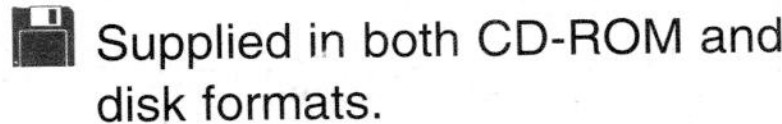
Supplied in both CD-ROM and disk formats.

# 3 Assess

## Meeting Lesson Objectives

Assign Section 1 Assessment as homework or an in-class activity.

Use **Interactive Tutor Self-Assessment Software** to review Section 1.

**FIGURE 18.2**

**Exports and Imports of the United States**

Look at the graph to see what products the United States imports and exports. Name the products that the United States exports more than it imports.

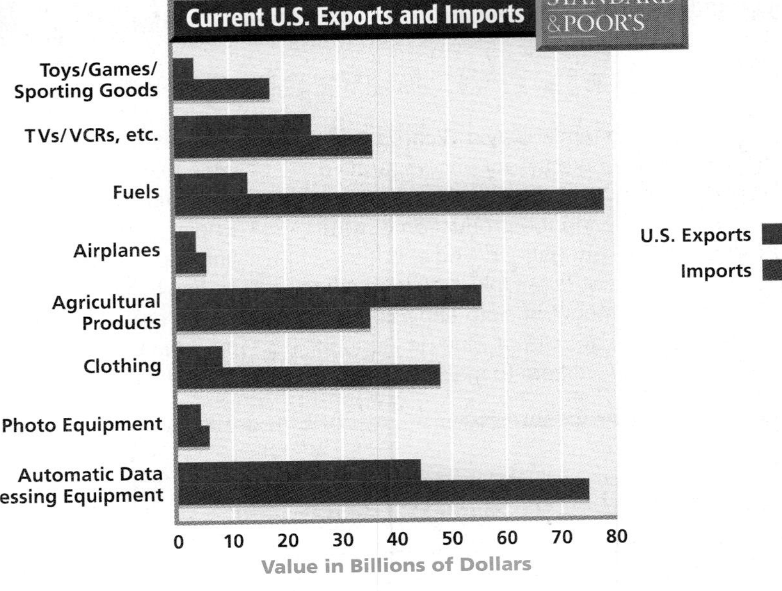


Source: Standard & Poor's

For an online update of this graph, visit ett.glencoe.com and click on ***Textbook Updates—Chapter 18.***

When producing only soybeans, Alpha produces 10 million bushels, while Beta produces only 8 million. The next year, suppose the two countries decide to grow only corn. Alpha produces 50 million bushels, while Beta produces 25 million. According to this example, Alpha has an absolute advantage in the production of both soybeans and corn.

Does this mean that Alpha will produce both crops and, therefore, have no reason to trade with Beta? No. Alpha can produce slightly more soybeans than Beta. In contrast, it can produce a great deal more corn. It would make little sense for Alpha to take land, labor, and capital resources away from the efficient production of corn and use them for the less efficient production of soybeans. Alpha's opportunity cost—what it gives up to get something else—would be less if it invested all its resources in the production of corn. It could export its surplus corn and use the revenues it receives to import soybeans from Beta.

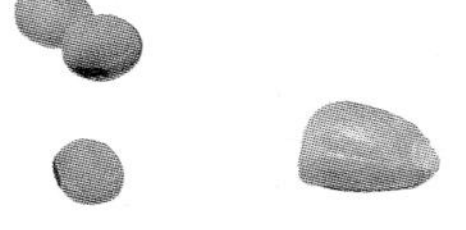

Alpha has a comparative advantage in corn production. **Comparative advantage** is the ability of a country to produce a

**comparative advantage:** *ability of a country to produce a product at a lower opportunity cost than another country*

## Extending the Content

**The Relationship Between Imports and Exports** International trade is an economic activity like any other, and it is subject to the same economic principles. In economic terms, international trade might be viewed as a production process that transforms exports into imports. Nations trade to get imports, and they export other things in order to pay for those imports. A fundamental proposition in international trade is: *In the long run, exports pay for imports.*

product at a *lower opportunity cost* than another country. Beta has a comparative advantage in soybean production. It can produce about the same amount of soybeans as Alpha, but only half as much corn. By using its resources to grow only soybeans, Beta is just giving up the relatively inefficient production of corn. Beta, then, has a lower opportunity cost for soybean production than does Alpha. Beta should produce the maximum amount of soybeans, export soybeans to Alpha, and import corn. Both countries benefit when each country concentrates on that production for which it is relatively most efficient.

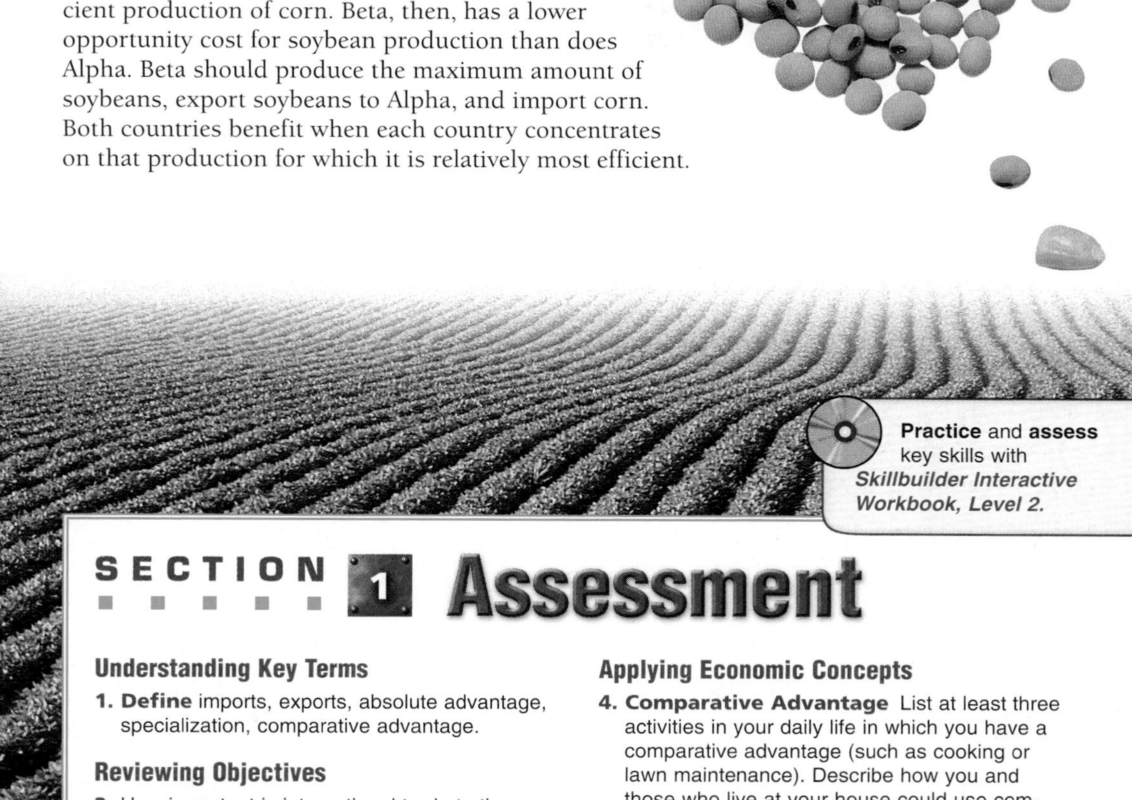

**Practice** and **assess** key skills with *Skillbuilder Interactive Workbook, Level 2.*

## SECTION 1 Assessment

### Understanding Key Terms

1. **Define** imports, exports, absolute advantage, specialization, comparative advantage.

### Reviewing Objectives

2. How important is international trade to the United States economy?
3. **Graphic Organizer** Create a diagram like the one below to explain the difference between absolute advantage and comparative advantage.

Trade
Absolute Advantage | Comparative Advantage

### Applying Economic Concepts

4. **Comparative Advantage** List at least three activities in your daily life in which you have a comparative advantage (such as cooking or lawn maintenance). Describe how you and those who live at your house could use comparative advantage in order to "trade" to get more accomplished.

### Critical Thinking Activity

5. **Synthesizing Information** Use **Figure 18.2** to answer the following question: In what two products do trading partners seem to have the greatest absolute advantage or comparative advantage over the United States? Explain.





### Section Quiz 18-1

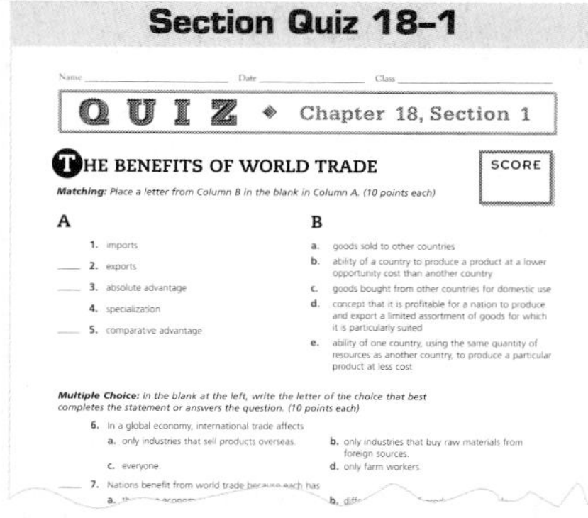

Name ______ Date ______ Class ______

QUIZ ◆ Chapter 18, Section 1

THE BENEFITS OF WORLD TRADE

SCORE

*Matching:* Place a letter from Column B in the blank in Column A. (10 points each)

| A | B |
|---|---|
| ___ 1. imports | a. goods sold to other countries |
| ___ 2. exports | b. ability of a country to produce a product at a lower opportunity cost than another country |
| ___ 3. absolute advantage | c. goods bought from other countries for domestic use |
| ___ 4. specialization | d. concept that it is profitable for a nation to produce and export a limited assortment of goods for which it is particularly suited |
| ___ 5. comparative advantage | e. ability of one country, using the same quantity of resources as another country, to produce a particular product at less cost |

*Multiple Choice:* In the blank at the left, write the letter of the choice that best completes the statement or answers the question. (10 points each)

___ 6. In a global economy, international trade affects
a. only industries that sell products overseas.
b. only industries that buy raw materials from foreign sources.
c. everyone.
d. only farm workers.

___ 7. Nations benefit from world trade because each has

## Reteach

Have each student write three questions for each of the two major headings in Section 1. Collect the questions and use them to test students' understanding of section content.

### Reading Essentials and Study Guide 18-1

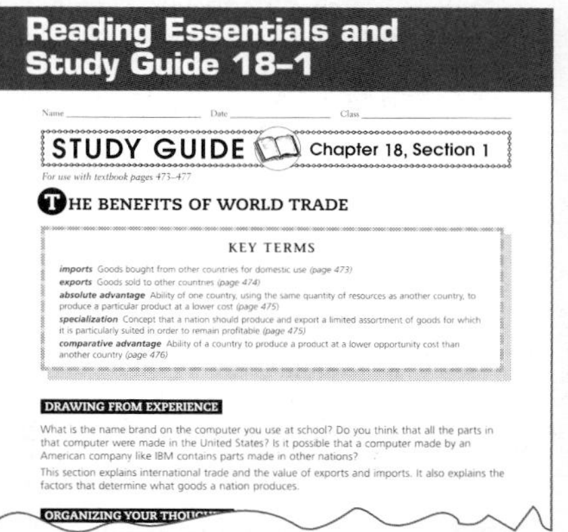

Name ______ Date ______ Class ______

STUDY GUIDE Chapter 18, Section 1

*For use with textbook pages 473–477*

THE BENEFITS OF WORLD TRADE

KEY TERMS

**imports** Goods bought from other countries for domestic use (page 473)
**exports** Goods sold to other countries (page 474)
**absolute advantage** Ability of one country, using the same quantity of resources as another country, to produce a particular product at a lower cost (page 475)
**specialization** Concept that a nation should produce and export a limited assortment of goods for which it is particularly suited in order to remain profitable (page 475)
**comparative advantage** Ability of a country to produce a product at a lower opportunity cost than another country (page 476)

DRAWING FROM EXPERIENCE

What is the name brand on the computer you use at school? Do you think that all the parts in that computer were made in the United States? Is it possible that a computer made by an American company like IBM contains parts made in other nations?

This section explains international trade and the value of exports and imports. It also explains the factors that determine what goods a nation produces.

ORGANIZING YOUR THOUGHTS

## 4 Close

Engage students in a discussion of the ways in which the United States would be poorer without the benefit of international trade.

## SECTION 1 Assessment Answers

1. All definitions can be found in the Glossary.
2. Imports account for about 13 percent of GDP. Also, more than 40 percent of the nation's engineering and scientific instruments are exported. In addition, about two-thirds of the wheat produced in the United States is sold abroad.
3. Absolute advantage—when one country, using the same amount of resources as another country, is able to produce a particular product at a lower absolute cost. Comparative advantage—when a country can produce a particular product at a lower opportunity cost than another country.
4. Answers will vary, but should demonstrate an understanding of the concept of comparative advantage.
5. fuels and clothing

Study & Writing Skills

## Applying the Writing Process

Review the guidelines with students, pointing out the value of developing an outline prior to writing a report. Remind students that an outline may be adjusted at the writing stage if a different order seems more appropriate.

Work through the **Practicing the Skill** activity with students. You might begin this process by asking students why it is useful to narrow the topic. *Narrowing the topic helps to focus research efforts.* Conclude by assigning the **Application Activity.**

**Reinforcing Economic Skills 29**

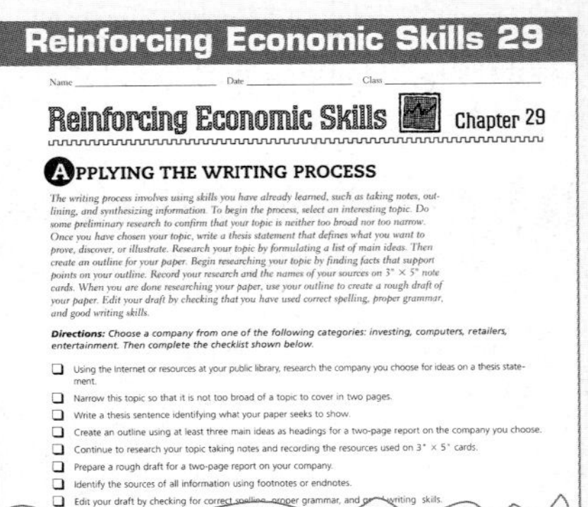

Name ______ Date ______ Class ______

**Reinforcing Economic Skills** Chapter 29

**APPLYING THE WRITING PROCESS**

*The writing process involves using skills you have already learned, such as taking notes, outlining, and synthesizing information. To begin the process, select an interesting topic. Do some preliminary research to confirm that your topic is neither too broad nor too narrow. Once you have chosen your topic, write a thesis statement that defines what you want to prove, discover, or illustrate. Research your topic by formulating a list of main ideas. Then create an outline for your paper. Begin researching your topic by finding facts that support points on your outline. Record your research and the names of your sources on 3" × 5" note cards. When you are done researching your paper, use your outline to create a rough draft of your paper. Edit your draft by checking that you have used correct spelling, proper grammar, and good writing skills.*

***Directions:*** *Choose a company from one of the following categories: investing, computers, retailers, entertainment. Then complete the checklist shown below.*

- ☐ Using the Internet or resources at your public library, research the company you choose for ideas on a thesis statement.
- ☐ Narrow this topic so that it is not too broad of a topic to cover in two pages.
- ☐ Write a thesis sentence identifying what your paper seeks to show.
- ☐ Create an outline using at least three main ideas as headings for a two-page report on the company you choose.
- ☐ Continue to research your topic taking notes and recording the resources used on 3" × 5" cards.
- ☐ Prepare a rough draft for a two-page report on your company.
- ☐ Identify the sources of all information using footnotes or endnotes.
- ☐ Edit your draft by checking for correct spelling, proper grammar, and good writing skills.
- ☐ Submit

**GLENCOE TECHNOLOGY**

**Glencoe Skillbuilder Interactive Workbook, Level 2**

This interactive CD-ROM reinforces student mastery of essential social studies skills.

Study & Writing Skills

# Applying the Writing Process

*Researching and writing allow you to organize your ideas in a logical manner. The writing process involves using skills you have already learned, such as taking notes, outlining, and synthesizing information.*

- Select an interesting topic. Do preliminary research to determine whether your topic is too broad or too narrow.
- Write a thesis statement that defines what you want to prove, discover, or illustrate in your writing. This will be the focus of your entire paper.
- Research your topic by formulating a list of main ideas and preparing note cards listing facts and source information for each main idea.
- Your report should have an introduction, a body, and a conclusion summarizing and restating your findings.
- Each paragraph should express one main idea in a topic sentence. Additional sentences support or explain the main idea by using details and facts.

### Learning the Skill

Use the guidelines listed on the left to help you apply the writing process.

### Practicing the Skill

Suppose you are writing a report on international trade. Answer the following questions about the writing process.

1. How could you narrow this topic?
2. What are three main ideas that should be included in this report?
3. Name three possible sources of information about international trade.
4. What maps, charts, and graphs might you include with your report?

**Practice** and **assess** key skills with ***Skillbuilder Interactive Workbook, Level 2.***

### Application Activity

Research and write a short report on the manufacturing of your favorite automobile. What parts, if any, were imported?



## Answers to *Practicing the Skill*

1. Answers will vary. Students might suggest focusing on regional trade, the United States's major trading partners, or international trade agreements.
2. Answers will vary according to the focus chosen in question 1.
3. Students may suggest the Web sites of trade organizations, almanacs, the *Statistical Abstract,* and so on.
4. Students' reports could include world maps, international trade cartograms, bar graphs comparing imports and exports, and so on.

***Application Activity*** Answers will vary. Ensure that students follow the guidelines in preparing and writing their reports.

SECTION 2

# Financing World Trade

## COVER STORY

*THE COLUMBUS DISPATCH*, SEPTEMBER 7, 1999

If the price of buying a car starts rising in the United States, consumers may need to look no further than the dollar's recent slide against major foreign currencies.

On the other hand, economically depressed Midwestern farmers may find it easier to sell surplus grain overseas if a weak dollar makes it cheaper for foreigners to buy U.S. goods.

The dollar spent much of last week on the skids, flirting with its lowest level of the year against the Japanese yen. . . . It also has lost ground to the euro.

### READER'S GUIDE

**Terms to Know**

- exchange rate
- foreign exchange markets
- fixed rate of exchange
- International Monetary Fund (IMF)
- devaluation
- flexible exchange rates
- depreciation
- balance of trade

**Reading Objectives**

1. Why do nations need a system of currency exchange rates?
2. How do the forces of supply and demand determine flexible exchange rates?
3. How do exchange rates affect the balance of trade?

The United States uses the dollar as its medium of exchange; Mexico, the peso; India, the rupee; and Japan, the yen. As you read this section, you'll learn that to engage in world trade, people must have a way of knowing the **exchange rate**—what the price of their currency is in terms of another nation's currency. They must also be able to exchange one type of currency for another. Why is this so?

**exchange rate:** *the price of one nation's currency in terms of another nation's currency*

A Japanese digital video disk (DVD) manufacturer who exports DVD systems to the United States probably does not want American dollars in payment. The firm needs Japanese currency to pay its workers and suppliers. Fortunately, international



## SECTION 2 RESOURCE MANAGER

**Reproducible Masters**

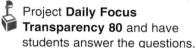

- Reproducible Lesson Plan 18–2
- Reading Essentials and Study Guide 18–2
- Guided Reading Activity 18–2
- Section Quiz 18–2
- Daily Focus Activity 80
- Daily Lecture Notes 18–2

**Multimedia**

- Daily Focus Transparency 80
- Economic Concepts Transparency 21
- Vocabulary PuzzleMaker
- Interactive Tutor Self-Assessment Software
- ExamView® Pro Testmaker
- MindJogger Videoquiz
- NBR's *Economics & You*
- Interactive Economics!

# 1 Focus

## Overview

Section 2 outlines the transition from a fixed rate of exchange to the current flexible rate of exchange among international currencies. It also discusses changes in the United States's balance of trade over the years.

### BELLRINGER
**Motivational Activity**

Project **Daily Focus Transparency 80** and have students answer the questions.

This activity is also available as a blackline master.

**Daily Focus Transparency 80**

WHO BENEFITS FROM A CHEAP DOLLAR?

1. If the exchange rate causes the U.S. dollar to drop in value, will the American tourists in the first photograph be able to buy more goods and services or fewer goods and services in the country they are visiting?
2. How will American workers, such as factory workers producing goods for export, benefit from a weak dollar?

Daily Focus Transparencies

### READER'S GUIDE

Answers to the **Reading Objectives** questions are on page 484.

**Preteaching Vocabulary**

Provide each student with eight index cards. On each card, direct students to write a **Term to Know** on the front and the term's definition on the back. Encourage students to refer to their cards as they work through the section.

**Vocabulary PuzzleMaker**

# 2 Teach

## Guided Practice

L2 **Applying Ideas** Tell students they are going to take a week's vacation in the country of their choice. Lead students in a discussion of what they might spend on their vacation—hotel costs, meals, sightseeing, travel, gifts for family and friends, and so on. Have each student develop a simple budget for the week. Then have them use a newspaper business section to find the cost in the currency of their chosen vacation spot. Encourage students to share their findings. Discuss with students why exchange rates might be a factor in making vacation plans.

### Daily Lecture Notes 18-2

DAILY LECTURE NOTES Lesson 18-2

**LECTURE LAUNCHER**

In 1994, following a crash in the Mexican stock market, the value of the peso fell 42% in just eleven days. Why does world trade depend on the conversion of one currency into another? What is the name for the market in which these conversions take place?

PAGES 480–481

I. Fixed Exchange Rates

A. Under a system of fixed exchange rates, national governments valued their currency in relation to a single standard.

B. Fixed exchange rates made it easy to compare different currencies.

C. Devaluation is to lower a currency's value in relation to other currencies by government order.

D. It is difficult to hold exchange rates constant in an international economy.

**Discussion Question**

**Why do you think it is so difficult to keep the exchange rates constant in an international economy?** *(Different countries have different national economic situations. Some might be flourishing while others are experiencing recession, decline, or slowing of growth. In addition, situations in these countries are changing daily. The more countries you consider, the more difficult it is to keep the comparison between them constant.)*

### Visual Instruction FIGURE 18.3

After students have studied Figure 18.3, have them use the business section of a newspaper to find current exchange rates for the listed currencies.

trade is organized so that individuals and businesses can easily and quickly convert one currency to another. **Foreign exchange markets** allow for these conversions. People in these markets deal in buying and selling foreign currency for businesses that want to import goods from other countries. Some of the currency trading also takes place through banks. **Figure 18.3** shows you what information a typical exchange rate lists on a given day.

foreign exchange markets: *markets dealing in buying and selling foreign currency for businesses that want to import goods from other countries*

## Fixed Exchange Rates

From 1944 to the early 1970s, the foreign exchange market operated with a **fixed rate of exchange.** Under this system, national governments set the value of their currency in relation to a single standard—usually the amount of gold held in reserve. With a fixed rate of exchange, a government could compare its

fixed rate of exchange: *system under which a national government sets the value of its currency in relation to a single standard*

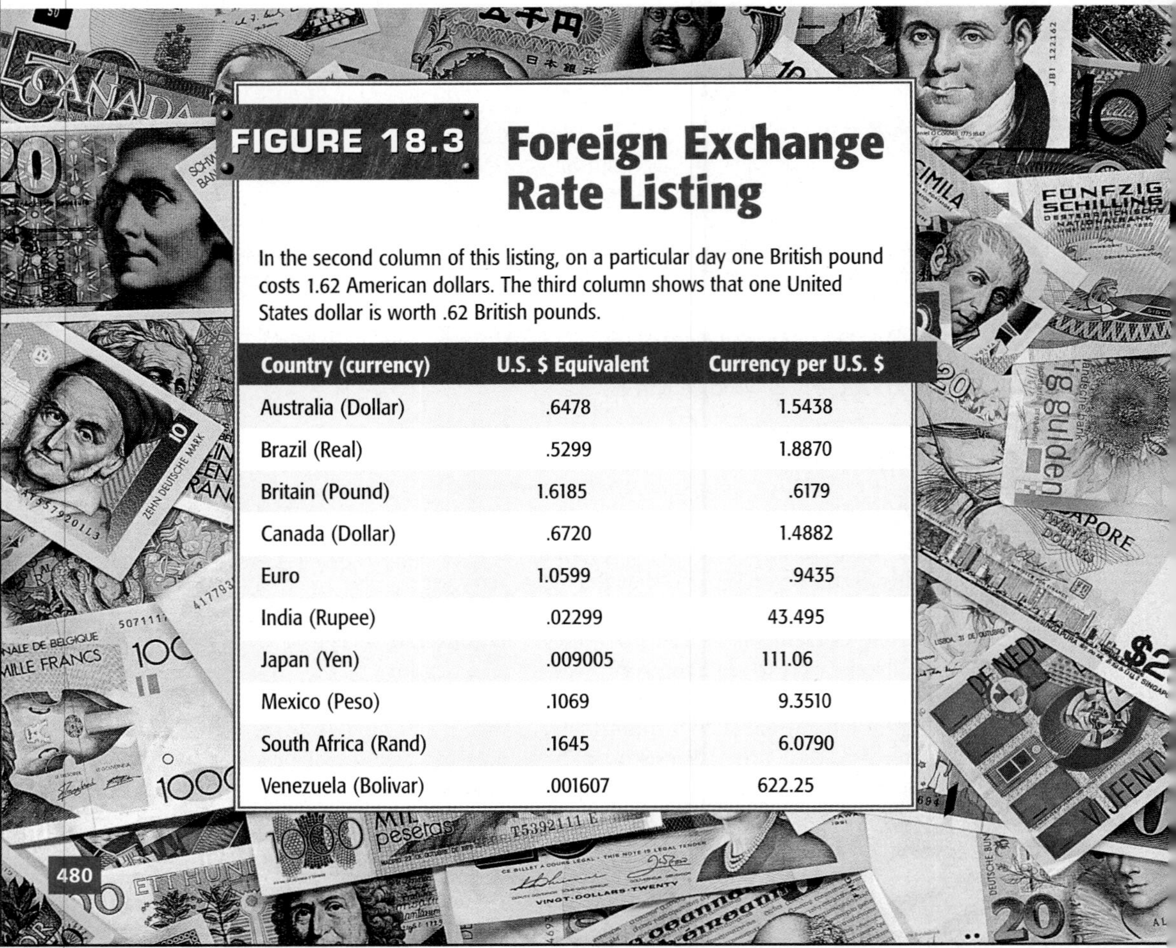

**FIGURE 18.3 Foreign Exchange Rate Listing**

In the second column of this listing, on a particular day one British pound costs 1.62 American dollars. The third column shows that one United States dollar is worth .62 British pounds.

| Country (currency) | U.S. $ Equivalent | Currency per U.S. $ |
|---|---|---|
| Australia (Dollar) | .6478 | 1.5438 |
| Brazil (Real) | .5299 | 1.8870 |
| Britain (Pound) | 1.6185 | .6179 |
| Canada (Dollar) | .6720 | 1.4882 |
| Euro | 1.0599 | .9435 |
| India (Rupee) | .02299 | 43.495 |
| Japan (Yen) | .009005 | 111.06 |
| Mexico (Peso) | .1069 | 9.3510 |
| South Africa (Rand) | .1645 | 6.0790 |
| Venezuela (Bolivar) | .001607 | 622.25 |

### Meeting Special Needs

**Physical Disability** Students who have difficulty with fine motor skills often are slow and inefficient writers. Because most assignments require some measure of writing, these students are at a tremendous disadvantage. Teach these students to read short pieces of text and to use an abbreviated note-taking system of writing only single words and associated facts.

Refer to *Inclusion for the Social Studies Classroom Strategies and Activities* for students with different learning styles.

## FIGURE 18.4

**Effects of Devaluation** These charts show how devaluation of the Japanese yen affects consumers in the United States. ***Do you think an American consumer would prefer to buy a DVD system before or after devaluation? Why?***

**Effects of Official Devaluation of Japanese Yen**

| Before Devaluation | After Devaluation |
|---|---|
| Japanese DVD costs 20,000 yen | Japanese DVD costs 20,000 yen |
| Exchange Rate: 100 yen = $1 U.S. | Exchange Rate: 200 yen = $1 U.S. |
| DVD = $\frac{20{,}000 \text{ yen}}{100 \text{ yen per } \$}$ = $200.00 | DVD = $\frac{20{,}000 \text{ yen}}{200 \text{ yen per } \$}$ = $100.00 |
| An American would have to pay $200 for the Japanese DVD | An American would have to pay $100 for the Japanese DVD |

currency to that of other countries. The **International Monetary Fund (IMF)** supported a fixed exchange rate system. Member governments of the IMF (including the United States) were obligated to keep their foreign exchange rates more or less fixed.

A fixed rate of exchange had some advantages for world trade. Importers and exporters knew exactly how much of a foreign currency they could purchase with their own nation's money. Also, the system allowed central banks to affect the level of exports and imports in their country by devaluing the currency. **Devaluation** means lowering a currency's value in relation to other currencies by government order. **Figure 18.4** shows how the cost of a Japanese DVD system would decrease if Japan devalues its yen by one-half.

This system of fixed exchange rates eventually proved impractical. The basic problem was the difficulty of holding exchange rates fixed in an international economic climate that was constantly changing. Suppose one nation such as the United States suffered from high inflation, and a trading partner such as Japan did not. Then American goods would become very costly for the Japanese to buy. Because the price of Japanese goods would not be rising, Americans could use their inflated, or "cheaper," dollars to buy more Japanese products. The United States would be importing huge quantities of Japanese goods but exporting little to Japan.

<u>International Monetary Fund (IMF):</u> *agency whose member governments once were obligated to keep their foreign exchange rates more or less fixed; today it offers monetary advice and provides loans to developing nations*

<u>devaluation:</u> *lowering a currency's value in relation to other currencies by government order*

**Student Web Activity** Visit the *Economics Today and Tomorrow* Web site at <u>ett.glencoe.com</u> and click on ***Chapter 18—Student Web Activities*** to learn about increased efficiency in international trade.





### Visual Instruction FIGURE 18.4

**Answer:** *after devaluation, because the DVD would cost less in American dollars*

### Guided Reading Activity 18-2

GUIDED READING Activity 18-2

FINANCING WORLD TRADE

OUTLINING

*Directions: Locate the heading in your textbook. Then use the information under the heading to help you write each answer.*

I. Introduction
A. What is the exchange rate?
B. What is the purpose of foreign exchange markets?
II. Fixed Exchange Rates
A. What is a fixed rate of exchange?
B. What were the advantages of a fixed rate of exchange?
C. What is devaluation?
D. Why did fixed exchange rates ...

See the **Web Activity Lesson Plan** at <u>ett.glencoe.com</u> for an introduction, lesson description, and answers to the **Student Web Activity** for this chapter.

Project **Economic Concepts Transparency 21** and have students discuss the accompanying questions.

## Cooperative Learning

Have students work in small groups to interview local bank officers who deal with foreign exchange matters. Encourage students to ask the officers questions on the history of exchange rates, the change from fixed to flexible rates, and problems involving exchange rates—the impact of fluctuating rates on trade, for example. Suggest that students also ask how varying exchange rates might affect local businesses. Direct groups to present the results of their interviews in a brief written report.

ECONOMICS & YOU

International Trade

Chapter 24
Disc 1, Side 2

ASK: What is a floating exchange rate? *The value of each nation's currency changes constantly. Under this mechanism, the market determines the value of goods and services in other nations' currencies.*

 Also available in VHS.

**Global Economy**

**The Big Mac Index**

Inform students that *The Economist* publishes its Big Mac Index in one of its April editions. Encourage students to learn more about the Big Mac Index by visiting *The Economist* Web site at ***www.economist.com/editorial/freeforall/focus/bigmac.html***

**INTERACTIVE ECONOMICS!**

**LESSON 9: INTERNATIONAL TRADE**

Have students click on "Economics Lab." To complete the lab, students should click and drag the terms of trade into the appropriate spaces on the chart.

 Supplied in both CD-ROM and disk formats.

## Flexible Exchange Rates

**flexible exchange rate:** *arrangement in which the forces of supply and demand are allowed to set the price of various currencies*

**depreciation:** *fall in the price of a currency through the action of supply and demand*

On August 15, 1971, President Richard Nixon officially announced what would become the end of fixed American exchange rates. Most of the world's nations turned to a **flexible exchange rate** system. Under this arrangement, the forces of supply and demand are allowed to set the price of various currencies. With flexible exchange rates, a currency's price may change, or float, up or down a little each day. For example, Japanese currency might be trading at 115.6 yen to the dollar on one day and 118.2 yen to the dollar on the next.

The forces actually determining exchange rates are the supply and demand of goods and services that can be bought with a particular currency. For example, suppose the amount of dollars wanted by Japanese exporters is greater than the quantity of dollars supplied by Americans who want to buy Japanese goods. Because the quantity demanded exceeds that supplied, the American dollar will become more expensive in relation to the yen. It will take more yen to equal one dollar. In contrast, if the quantity of dollars American importers supplied is more than the quantity demanded by Japanese exporters, the price of a dollar will become cheaper in relation to the yen. Fewer yen will equal one dollar.

When the price of a currency falls through the action of supply and demand, it is termed **depreciation.** As with devaluation, depreciation of a country's currency improves its competitive edge in foreign trade.

Besides import-export transactions, political or economic instability within a country may encourage people to exchange their currency for a more stable currency, often the United States dollar. In that case, the value of the dollar would rise in relation to the other nation's currency. A country that is experiencing rapid inflation will find its currency falling in value in relation to other currencies.

### The Big Mac Index

One way to see whether a currency is devalued or overvalued against the U.S. dollar is to use the "Big Mac Index" developed by *The Economist.* Economists compare the price of a Big Mac hamburger in the United States to what it costs in another country's local currency. Converting the foreign price to U.S. dollars shows whether the price of a Big Mac is undervalued or overvalued against the U.S. dollar. For example, a Big Mac may cost $2.56 in the United States and 280 yen in Japan (which converts to $2.08 in U.S. currency). The Japanese yen, therefore, is undervalued against the U.S. dollar. ■

| | Big Mac Prices | | |
|---|---|---|---|
| Country | in local currency | in U.S. dollars | Percent under (–) or over (+) valued against dollar |
| U.S. (Dollar) | 2.56 | $2.56 | --- |
| Brazil (Real) | 3.10 | 2.72 | +6 |
| China (Yuan) | 9.90 | 1.20 | –53 |
| Israel (Shekel) | 12.50 | 3.38 | +32 |
| Mexico (Peso) | 17.9 | 2.10 | –18 |
| Russia (Ruble) | 12,000 | 2.00 | –22 |



**Critical Thinking Activity**

**Applying Ideas** Have students solve the following exchange rate problems:

1. A meal at the Carvery restaurant in London costs £25. How much would the meal cost in American dollars if the exchange rate were £1 = $1.65? *(25 × 1.65 = $41.25)*
2. A professional baseball player's salary works out to approximately $33,000. What would the player receive in Canadian dollars if the exchange rate were U.S. $1 = Canadian $0.69? *(33,000 × .69 = Canadian $22,770)*
3. A television set sells for ¥54,300 in Tokyo. How much would it cost in U.S. dollars if the exchange rate were ¥105.40 = $1? *(54,300 ÷ 105.40 = $515.18)*

**FIGURE 18.5** **Balance of Trade** This graph shows how the United States has had a negative balance of trade for the most part since the 1970s.

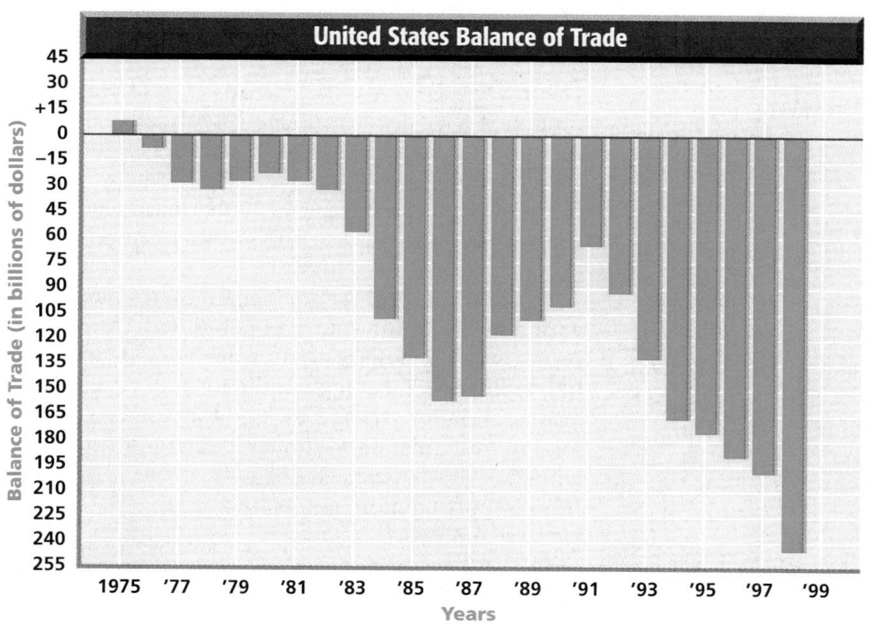


**Source:** Department of Commerce

ECONOMICS Online — For an online update of this graph, visit ett.glencoe.com and click on ***Textbook Updates—Chapter 18.***

## Balance of Trade

A currency's exchange rate can have an important effect on a nation's **balance of trade.** See **Figure 18.5.** The balance of trade is the difference between the value of a nation's exports and its imports. If a nation's currency depreciates, or becomes "weak," the nation will likely export more goods because its products will become cheaper for other nations to buy. If a nation's currency increases in value, or becomes "strong," the amount of its exports will decline.

When the value of goods leaving a nation exceeds the value of those coming in, a positive balance of trade is said to exist. In this case, the nation is bringing in more money as payments for goods

balance of trade: *difference between the value of a nation's exports and its imports*



# CHAPTER 18

SECTION 2, Pages 479–484

## Independent Practice

**L1 Illustrating Ideas** Ask students to research and graph exchange rates over the last five years for a nation of their choice. Have students display their graphs and discuss how varying exchange rates may have affected their selected nation's trade with the United States. BLOCK SCHEDULING

**L2 Summarizing Ideas** Encourage students to review newspapers and magazines for articles on the balance of trade. Have students select two or three articles to summarize. Call on volunteers to present their summaries to the class.

# 3 Assess

## Meeting Lesson Objectives

Assign Section 2 Assessment as homework or an in-class activity.

Use **Interactive Tutor Self-Assessment Software** to review Section 2.

**Section Quiz 18-2**

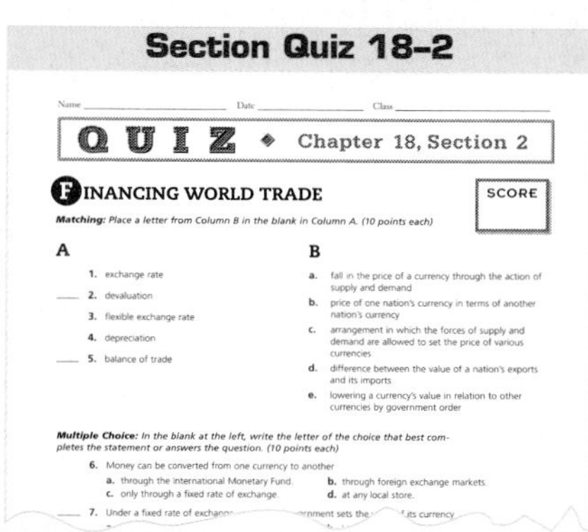
Name Date Class

QUIZ ◆ Chapter 18, Section 2

FINANCING WORLD TRADE SCORE

*Matching: Place a letter from Column B in the blank in Column A. (10 points each)*

| A | B |
|---|---|
| 1. exchange rate | a. fall in the price of a currency through the action of supply and demand |
| 2. devaluation | b. price of one nation's currency in terms of another nation's currency |
| 3. flexible exchange rate | c. arrangement in which the forces of supply and demand are allowed to set the price of various currencies |
| 4. depreciation | d. difference between the value of a nation's exports and its imports |
| 5. balance of trade | e. lowering a currency's value in relation to other currencies by government order |

*Multiple Choice: In the blank at the left, write the letter of the choice that best completes the statement or answers the question. (10 points each)*

6. Money can be converted from one currency to another
a. through the International Monetary Fund. b. through foreign exchange markets.
c. only through a fixed rate of exchange. d. at any local store.

7. Under a fixed rate of exchange

## Free Enterprise Activity

Organize students into groups, and tell groups to imagine they run "international" stores that take many different currencies. Assign each group a different retailing area—clothing and shoes, groceries, electrical appliances, and so on. Have groups investigate the prices charged at local stores for five items in their assigned retailing area. Then have groups use the exchange rate table in a newspaper business section to find equivalent prices in the currencies of Canada, Mexico, two South American countries, two African countries, two European countries, and two Asian countries. Direct groups to use their findings to create price billboards, showing items, countries, and prices. BLOCK SCHEDULING

## Reteach

Have students write a summary of the section using the **Terms to Know** listed on page 479.

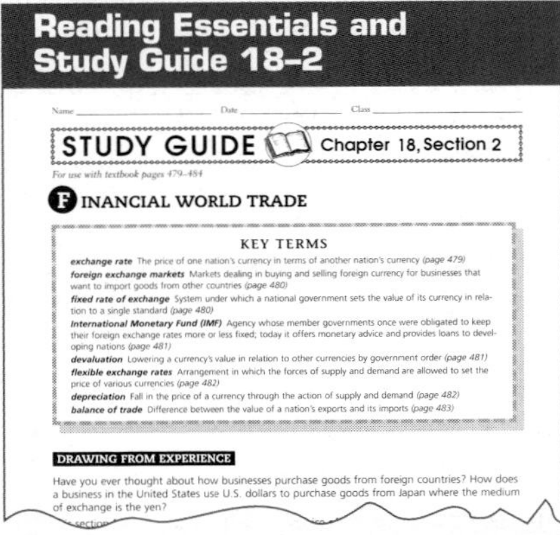
**Reading Essentials and Study Guide 18–2**

Name ______ Date ______ Class ______

STUDY GUIDE Chapter 18, Section 2

*For use with textbook pages 479–484*

FINANCIAL WORLD TRADE

KEY TERMS

***exchange rate*** The price of one nation's currency in terms of another nation's currency *(page 479)*

***foreign exchange markets*** Markets dealing in buying and selling foreign currency for businesses that want to import goods from other countries *(page 480)*

***fixed rate of exchange*** System under which a national government sets the value of its currency in relation to a single standard *(page 480)*

***International Monetary Fund (IMF)*** Agency whose member governments once were obligated to keep their foreign exchange rates more or less fixed; today it offers monetary advice and provides loans to developing nations *(page 481)*

***devaluation*** Lowering a currency's value in relation to other currencies by government order *(page 481)*

***flexible exchange rates*** Arrangement in which the forces of supply and demand are allowed to set the price of various currencies *(page 482)*

***depreciation*** Fall in the price of a currency through the action of supply and demand *(page 482)*

***balance of trade*** Difference between the value of a nation's exports and its imports *(page 483)*

DRAWING FROM EXPERIENCE

Have you ever thought about how businesses purchase goods from foreign countries? How does a business in the United States use U.S. dollars to purchase goods from Japan where the medium of exchange is the yen?

## 4 Close

Ask students to explain why a "strong" dollar would cause a trade deficit.

than it is paying out. A negative balance of trade exists when the value of goods coming into a country is greater than the value of those going out. This situation is called a *trade deficit*. The United States has had a negative balance of trade, or trade deficit, for many years beginning in the 1970s.

**Trade Deficit—Good or Bad?** It is important to realize that a continued trade deficit is not necessarily a bad thing. A trade deficit continues because there are opportunities for foreigners to invest in the United States economy. For example, many Japanese automobile companies have built factories in the United States to satisfy the U.S. demand for Japanese cars. This creates jobs and supporting industries that benefit U.S. citizens.

In addition, because the United States has a stable currency with a low inflation rate, compared with other industrialized countries, U.S. dollars are in worldwide demand. Foreigners like to hold their savings in the form of dollars to protect against inflation in their own countries. As a result of both foreign investment and foreign demand for holding dollars, United States citizens can benefit from importing more goods than we have to export.

**Practice** and **assess** key skills with ***Skillbuilder Interactive Workbook, Level 2.***

## SECTION 2 Assessment

### Understanding Key Terms

1. **Define** exchange rate, foreign exchange markets, fixed rate of exchange, International Monetary Fund (IMF), devaluation, flexible exchange rates, depreciation, balance of trade.

### Reviewing Objectives

2. Why do nations need a system of currency exchange rates?
3. How do the forces of supply and demand determine flexible exchange rates?
4. **Graphic Organizer** Create a diagram like the one in the next column to explain how exchange rates affect the balance of trade.

### Applying Economic Concepts

5. **Flexible Exchange Rates** In what ways does depreciation of a country's currency improve that country's competitiveness in foreign trade?

### Critical Thinking Activity

6. **Synthesizing Information** How does a weak American dollar affect you as a consumer? How does a strong American dollar affect you?



## SECTION 2 Assessment Answers

1. All definitions can be found in the Glossary.
2. to engage in international trade
3. If the amount of dollars wanted by Japanese exporters is greater than the quantity supplied by Americans who buy Japanese goods, the dollar becomes more expensive in relation to the yen; it will take more yen to equal one dollar. Conversely, if the amount of dollars demanded by Japanese exporters is less than the quantity supplied by American buyers, the dollar will be less expensive in relation to the yen.
4. Weak currency→more exports→favorable balance of trade; strong currency→fewer exports→negative balance of trade
5. Depreciation of a country's currency makes that country's exports cheaper, therefore making the country more competitive in foreign trade.
6. Most students will note that a weak dollar will mean they pay more for foreign goods, while a strong dollar will mean that they pay less.

# People & Perspectives

## James Tobin

*ECONOMIST (1918–)*

- Member of John F. Kennedy's Council of Economic Advisers, 1961–1962
- Awarded the Nobel Prize in Economics in 1981
- Author/editor of 16 books and more than 400 articles on economics
- Holds the position of Sterling Professor of Economics Emeritus at Yale University

Nearly 30 years ago, economist James Tobin suggested that a tax should be imposed on foreign exchange transactions to discourage speculation in the foreign exchange markets. With the rise of the global economy and the Internet, economists are reviewing the issue of foreign exchange speculation—and the "Tobin tax"—once again. In the following paragraphs, Tobin explains what the Tobin tax is and how it would work.

*"There are 1.3 trillion dollars a day in foreign exchange transactions. Those transactions would be taxed, at a very low rate, something like one tenth of one percent per dollar per transaction. The taxes would be levied by each country on transactions that originate in the country, and collected by the usual tax authority of that country.*

*If people are involved in making a lot of transactions every day, every week, they would have to pay the tax a lot of times. So they are discouraged from doing that just by the existence of the tax."*

Even though there is discussion among economists about the Tobin tax, Tobin himself is doubtful that it will ever be implemented:

*"I am not optimistic about that. I don't think the financial community, including ministers of finance in major countries and the central banks of those countries, have any use for those taxes. They don't want it. . . . The International Monetary Fund is not going to go for it.*

*People do not like to be taxed. They think it is an interference with the free market."*

### Checking for Understanding

1. **What is the Tobin tax? What is its purpose?**
2. **Why, according to Tobin, will the Tobin tax not be implemented?**





## Background

Some of Tobin's students went on to hold influential government positions. Janet Yellen studied with Tobin at Yale University in the late 1960s and early 1970s. She later served on the Federal Reserve Board of Governors from 1994 to 1996. She also was the chair of President Clinton's Council of Economic Advisers from 1997 to 1999. (Inform students that they may read more about Janet Yellen on page 368.)

## Teach

Ask for volunteers to read aloud from the excerpts. Then point out that some economists have expressed opposition to the Tobin tax because they believe it would harm growth in developing nations by deterring foreign investment. Have students discuss how foreign investment might be discouraged by Tobin's tax.

### Did You Know

Tobin served as an officer in the U.S. Navy during World War II. The author Herman Wouk was a friend and fellow officer of Tobin's in the war years. Wouk modeled one of the characters in his novel *The Caine Mutiny* (1951) on Tobin.

### Answers to *Checking for Understanding*

1. a tax of about one-tenth of 1 percent per dollar on foreign exchange transactions; to discourage speculation in foreign exchange markets
2. because finance ministers of major countries, the central banks of these countries, and the IMF are not supportive of such a tax

# 1 Focus

## Overview

**Section 3** explains how tariffs, quotas, and embargoes can restrict imports; outlines the main arguments for and against free trade; and discusses the major world and regional trade agreements.

**BELLRINGER**
**Motivational Activity**

Project **Daily Focus Transparency 81** and have students answer the questions.

This activity is also available as a blackline master.

**Daily Focus Transparency 81**

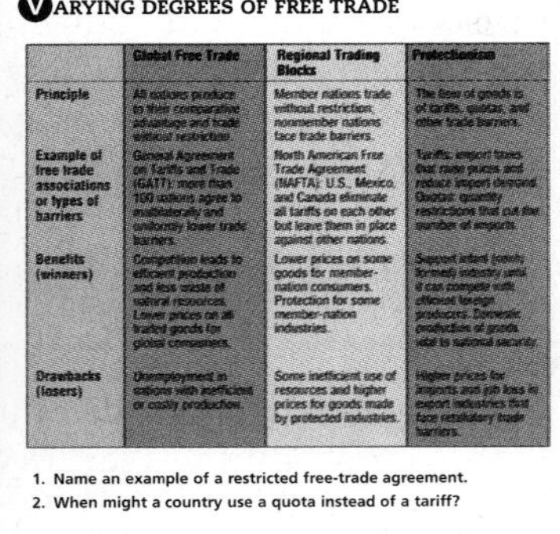

FOCUS ACTIVITIES
Transparency 81

VARYING DEGREES OF FREE TRADE

| | Global Free Trade | Regional Trading Blocks | Protectionism |
|---|---|---|---|
| Principle | All nations produce to their comparative advantage and trade without restriction. | Member nations trade without restriction; nonmember nations face trade barriers. | The flow of goods is of tariffs, quotas, and other trade barriers. |
| Example of free trade associations or types of barriers | General Agreement on Tariffs and Trade (GATT): more than 100 nations agree to multilaterally and uniformly lower trade barriers. | North American Free Trade Agreement (NAFTA): U.S., Mexico, and Canada eliminate all tariffs on each other but leave them in place against other nations. | Tariffs: import taxes that raise prices and reduce import demand. Quotas: quantity restrictions that cut the number of imports. |
| Benefits (winners) | Competition leads to efficient production and less waste of natural resources. Lower prices on all traded goods for global consumers. | Lower prices on some goods for member-nation consumers. Protection for some member-nation industries. | Support infant (newly formed) industry until it can compete with efficient foreign producers. Domestic production of goods vital to national security. |
| Drawbacks (losers) | Unemployment in nations with inefficient or costly production. | Some inefficient use of resources and higher prices for goods made by protected industries. | Higher prices for imports and job loss in export industries that face retaliatory trade barriers. |

1. Name an example of a restricted free-trade agreement.
2. When might a country use a quota instead of a tariff?

Daily Focus Transparencies

## Reader's Guide

Answers to the **Reading Objectives** questions are on page 489.

**Preteaching Vocabulary**

Call on students to explain how each of the **Terms to Know** is related to international trade.

**Vocabulary PuzzleMaker**

SECTION 

# Restrictions on World Trade

## Reader's Guide

**Terms to Know**

- tariff
- revenue tariff
- protective tariff
- import quota
- embargo
- protectionists
- General Agreement on Tariffs and Trade (GATT)
- World Trade Organization (WTO)
- North American Free Trade Agreement (NAFTA)
- European Union (EU)

**Reading Objectives**

1. How can a nation restrict imports?
2. What are three arguments for and against free trade?
3. What are some current international and regional trade agreements?

## Cover Story

*Business Week*, January 18, 1999

The mood was giddy just about everywhere on the Continent as Europe's new currency, the euro, made its grand debut. . . . After years of skepticism from critics on the Continent and abroad, Europe has its common currency.

The long-term effects of melding an 11-nation, $6.5 trillion, 290 million-person region into one economic and financial bloc are giving Continental Europe new [power]. Companies around the world are eager to exploit what they hope will become a true single market.

To trade or not to trade? The difficulties that different currencies cause are only one problem of world trade. There are also natural barriers, which include the differences in languages and cultures between various trading partners. As you read this section, you'll learn that some nations may set restrictions to discourage or limit trade.

## Three Ways to Restrict Imports

Three major barriers to world trade are tariffs, quotas, and embargoes. The most commonly used barrier to free trade is the **tariff**, a tax on imports.

<u>tariff:</u> *tax placed on an imported product*



## SECTION 3 RESOURCE MANAGER

**Reproducible Masters**

- Reproducible Lesson Plan 18–3
- Reading Essentials and Study Guide 18–3
- Guided Reading Activity 18–3
- Section Quiz 18–3
- Daily Focus Activity 81
- Daily Lecture Notes 18–3

**Multimedia**

- Daily Focus Transparency 81
- Vocabulary PuzzleMaker
- Interactive Tutor Self-Assessment Software
- ExamView® Pro Testmaker
- MindJogger Videoquiz
- Presentation Plus!

In many parts of the world,
:en reached in order to increase
theast Asia as well as in Central
ional trade agreements. The
nada and Mexico called the
**eement (NAFTA).** The U.S.
)3. Since then, trade has
the general benefit of all.
gional trade agreement in the
**on (EU).** Currently, the EU con-
itain, Denmark, Italy, Spain,
lgium, the Netherlands, Finland,
er countries have applied to
nuary 1, 1993, the EU began
on trade among its member
of the 15 member nations
as a common currency. Those
n their own national currencies
e EU will have a common cur-
an consumers. It will rival the
ages 494–495.

**North American Free Trade Agreement:** *trade agreement designed to reduce tariff barriers between Mexico, Canada, and the United States*

**European Union:** *organization of European nations whose goal is to encourage economic integration as a single market*

**Practice** and **assess** key skills with ***Skillbuilder Interactive Workbook, Level 2.***

# Assessment

ective tariff,
nists, General
World Trade
e Trade

?

d against free

hart like the
least three

| urpose |
|---|
| |

## Applying Economic Concepts

5. **Free Trade** Assume you are (a) a startup computer software producer, (b) the owner of a retail dress shop, (c) a steelworker whose company just closed, (d) a student working in fast-food service. Write a short argument for or against free trade from the standpoint of each individual.

## Critical Thinking Activity

6. **Summarizing Information** Research opinions about the North American Free Trade Agreement (NAFTA) on the Internet. Scan several articles to identify which groups support NAFTA and which groups oppose the trade agreement. Provide the reasons each group gives for supporting or opposing NAFTA.



# sment Answers

e Glossary.
argoes
through com-
y, comparative
n; arguments
d to protect
national eco-

f the following:

GATT—to establish tariff reductions that are mutually advantageous to all members; WTO—replaced GATT, to reduce tariffs; NAFTA—to increase free trade among United States, Canada, and Mexico; EU—to eliminate trade restrictions among member nations

5. Answers should demonstrate an understanding of the arguments for and against free trade.
6. Encourage students to share their findings.



**Section Quiz 18-3**

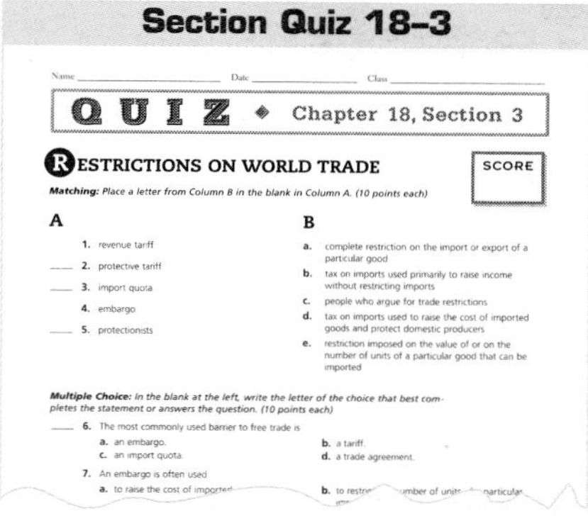
Name ________ Date ________ Class ________

QUIZ ◆ Chapter 18, Section 3

RESTRICTIONS ON WORLD TRADE — SCORE

*Matching: Place a letter from Column B in the blank in Column A. (10 points each)*

| A | B |
|---|---|
| ___ 1. revenue tariff | a. complete restriction on the import or export of a particular good |
| ___ 2. protective tariff | b. tax on imports used primarily to raise income without restricting imports |
| ___ 3. import quota | c. people who argue for trade restrictions |
| ___ 4. embargo | d. tax on imports used to raise the cost of imported goods and protect domestic producers |
| ___ 5. protectionists | e. restriction imposed on the value of or on the number of units of a particular good that can be imported |

*Multiple Choice: In the blank at the left, write the letter of the choice that best completes the statement or answers the question. (10 points each)*

___ 6. The most commonly used barrier to free trade is
a. an embargo. b. a tariff.
c. an import quota. d. a trade agreement.

7. An embargo is often used
a. to raise the cost of imports

## Reteach

Call on students to write two summary paragraphs, one on methods of restricting imports and one on the arguments for and against free trade.

**Reading Essentials and Study Guide 18-3**

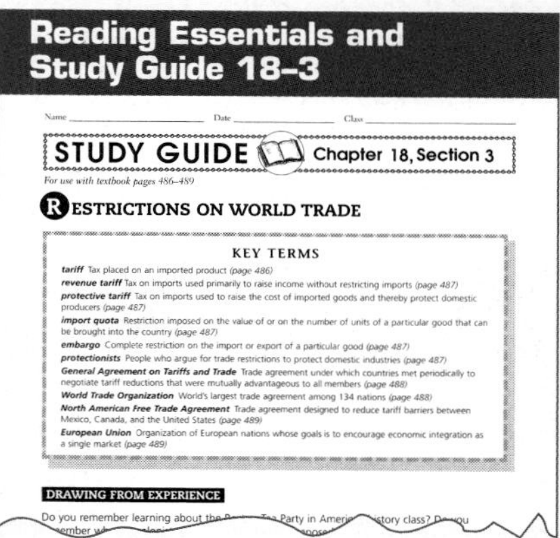
Name ________ Date ________ Class ________

STUDY GUIDE Chapter 18, Section 3

*For use with textbook pages 486–489*

RESTRICTIONS ON WORLD TRADE

KEY TERMS

**tariff** Tax placed on an imported product (page 486)
**revenue tariff** Tax on imports used primarily to raise income without restricting imports (page 487)
**protective tariff** Tax on imports used to raise the cost of imported goods and thereby protect domestic producers (page 487)
**import quota** Restriction imposed on the value of or on the number of units of a particular good that can be brought into the country (page 487)
**embargo** Complete restriction on the import or export of a particular good (page 487)
**protectionists** People who argue for trade restrictions to protect domestic industries (page 487)
**General Agreement on Tariffs and Trade** Trade agreement under which countries met periodically to negotiate tariff reductions that were mutually advantageous to all members (page 488)
**World Trade Organization** World's largest trade agreement among 134 nations (page 488)
**North American Free Trade Agreement** Trade agreement designed to reduce tariff barriers between Mexico, Canada, and the United States (page 489)
**European Union** Organization of European nations whose goals is to encourage economic integration as a single market (page 489)

DRAWING FROM EXPERIENCE

# 4 Close

Ask students if they think the development of large regional trade agreements such as NAFTA and the European Union will encourage protectionism or free trade. Have them explain their answers.

BusinessWeek
**SPOTLIGHT**

# Teach

Point out that NAFTA met with considerable opposition in the United States. Encourage students to research the arguments presented by people against NAFTA. Call on volunteers to present their findings to the class. Then ask students to discuss whether they think opposition to NAFTA is justified.

**BusinessWeek ONLINE**

To find up-to-date news and analysis on the economy, business, technology, markets, entrepreneurs, investments, and finance, have students search feature articles and special reports on the *Business Week* Web site. www.businessweek.com

**Sidelight**

One problem resulting from NAFTA is traffic congestion at border crossings between Mexico and the United States. The crossing point at Laredo, for example, sees about 5,000 cargo trucks each day. The line of traffic waiting to enter the United States often stretches five miles (8 km), and Mexican drivers face a wait of three hours or more just to get to the border checkpoint.

BusinessWeek

# SPOTLIGHT ON THE ECONOMY

## Mexican Makeover

**Check It Out! In this chapter you learned about regional trade agreements. In this article, read to learn how NAFTA has helped to create the world's newest industrial power.**

Mexico's economy is undergoing a stunning transformation. Five years after the launch of the North American Free Trade Agreement (NAFTA), it is fast becoming an industrial power. Free trade with the U.S. and Canada is turning the country from a mere assembler of cheap, low-quality goods into a reliable exporter of sophisticated products, from auto brake systems to laptop computers. Since 1993, exports have more than doubled, to $115 billion. Manufactured goods now make up close to 90% of Mexico's sales abroad, up from 77% five years ago. . . .

Mexico's industrial surge also means that North America is winning back thousands of jobs that had been lost to Asia as U.S. and Canadian companies shifted production to lower-cost production sites in the last decade. Now, for example, IBM is making computer components in Guadalajara that were formerly made in Singapore. And clothing retailers such as Gap Inc. and Liz Claiborne are increasingly buying garments from Mexican contractors, who can offer faster delivery than Asians. . . .

But the makeover of Mexican industry goes far beyond export and investment numbers. From small entrepreneurs to executives of the country's new multinationals, Mexican managers are becoming more confident as they respond to heightened competition at home and to the tough demands of foreign customers.



### Think About It

1. **How has NAFTA affected Mexico's exports?**
2. **How has NAFTA affected Mexico's entrepreneurs?**

### Answers to *Think About It*

1. Since 1993, Mexican exports have more than doubled to $115 billion.
2. They are becoming more confident in their ability to compete.

# 18 Summary

ɪnomics
glencoe.com
*Overviews*

World

supply us with
ınd many
ıdustries that

ɪne country,
as another
ıct at a lower

/ of a country
ɪrtunity cost

l Trade

sinesses
urrency for

ɔn's currency
lly the amount

- Under a **flexible exchange rate** system, the forces of supply and demand are allowed to set the price of various currencies.
- The rate at which a currency is being exchanged can have an important effect on a nation's **balance of trade.**
- If a nation's currency **depreciates,** the nation will likely export more goods and services. If a nation's currency increases in value, the amount of its exports will decline.

## SECTION 3 Restrictions on World Trade

- Three major barriers to world trade are **tariffs, quotas,** and **embargoes.**
- **Protectionists** are in favor of trade restrictions to protect American jobs, to protect national security, and to protect infant industries.
- Those who argue for free trade believe that competition results in better products at lower prices and that restricting imports hurts export industries.
- Recent trade agreements such as the **World Trade Organization,** the **North American Free Trade Agreement,** and the **European Union** have worked to lower trade restrictions.



## Economics Journal

ɪtudents track what they wear for one week. Ask them to
see where each item of clothing was produced. Have them
ɔurnal. At the end of the recording period, have students tally
l a class record. Then ask them to present this information in
for example. Call on students to display their visuals and
d countries.

# CHAPTER 18 Summary

**ECONOMICS & YOU**

International Trade

Chapter 24
Disc 1, Side 2

If you do not have access to a videodisc player, the ***Economics & You*** programs are also available in VHS.

Use the **Chapter 18 Summary** to preview, review, condense, or reteach the chapter.

## Preview/Review

**Vocabulary PuzzleMaker Software** reinforces the key terms used in Chapter 18.

**Interactive Tutor Self-Assessment Software** allows students to review Chapter 18 content.

## Condense

Have students listen to the Chapter 18 **Audio Program** (also available in Spanish) in the TCR. Assign the Chapter 18 Audio Program Activity and give students the Chapter 18 Audio Program Test.

## Reteach

Have students complete **Reteaching Activity** 18 in the TCR (Spanish Reteaching Activities are also available).

# CHAPTER 18
## Assessment and Activities

ECONOMICS Online

Have students visit the *Economics Today and Tomorrow* Web site at ett.glencoe.com to review Chapter 18 and take the Self-Check Quiz.

**GLENCOE TECHNOLOGY**

**MindJogger Videoquiz**

Use MindJogger to review Chapter 18 content.

### Identifying Key Terms

1. e
2. g
3. c
4. h
5. d
6. b
7. f
8. i
9. a

### Recalling Facts and Ideas

1. by determining its own opportunity costs and those of other countries producing the same goods
2. products it cannot produce and raw materials it does not have; many industries then export much of what they produce
3. absolute advantage
4. so that individuals and businesses can easily and quickly convert one currency to another
5. because the international economic climate was constantly changing
6. A revenue tariff raises income. A protective tariff limits imports to protect domestic industries.
7. loss of job security, need to protect infant industries, need to protect national economic security
8. exports

### Thinking Critically

1. Most students will note that American exports should increase, because American products would be cheaper in foreign markets.
2. Tariff placed on imports raises their prices→prices of domestic products remain low→protected industries recoup costs before they must compete with those of other nations.

# CHAPTER 18 Assessment and Activities

**Self-Check Quiz** Visit the *Economics Today and Tomorrow* Web site at ett.glencoe.com and click on ***Chapter 18—Self-Check Quizzes*** to prepare for the Chapter Test.

## Identifying Key Terms

*Write the letter of the definition in Column B that correctly defines each term in Column A.*

**Column A**

1. absolute advantage
2. comparative advantage
3. embargo
4. protectionists
5. balance of trade
6. devaluation
7. depreciation
8. revenue tariff
9. exchange rate

**Column B**

a. price of one country's currency in relation to another country's currency
b. lowering of a currency's value in relation to other currencies
c. complete restriction on the import or export of a particular good
d. difference between the value of a nation's exports and its imports
e. ability of a nation to produce a product at a lower opportunity cost
f. drop in the price of a currency in response to supply and demand
g. ability of a country to use the same amount of resources as another to produce a product at less cost
h. those who oppose the relaxation of trade restrictions
i. tax on imports to raise money

## Recalling Facts and Ideas

**Section 1**

1. How does a country determine whether it has a comparative advantage in the production of certain goods?
2. What does the United States gain from international trade?
3. "America can produce more DVDs per labor hour than can any other country in the world." Is this an example of an absolute advantage or a comparative advantage?

**Section 2**

4. Why are foreign exchange markets necessary?
5. Why was it difficult to maintain a system of fixed rates of exchange?

**Section 3**

6. What is the difference between a revenue tariff and a protective tariff?
7. What are three arguments against free trade?
8. What is also affected when restrictions are put on imports?

of the dol-
ncies,
en to

Create a
how how
allow

national
percent
ts all
nterna-
scribe
interna-
an do
oducts
e or
ically

centrate
e following

earch one

or within
of GDP
orts)
nation

- The top three items that are exported
- The top three items that are imported

Each group will decide what the relationship is between the natural resource base and what is exported and imported. Finally, each group will write a summary of how life in each country would be different if international trade were prohibited.

## Reviewing Skills

**Applying the Writing Process** There are virtually no restrictions on trade within the 50 states, mainly because the Constitution of the United States forbids it. Write a one-page description of problems that might have arisen if the Constitution had been silent on trade among the states. Include in your paper the section or sections in the Constitution that prohibit at least one restriction on international trade.

## Technology Activity

**Developing Multimedia Presentations** Study the list of topics below. Choose one of the topics and explain how you would use at least three types of media in a presentation to best teach the topic to your class.

1. U.S. Exports and Imports
2. Foreign Exchange Markets
3. U.S. Balance of Trade
4. North American Free Trade Agreement

## Analyzing the Global Economy

Use the Internet to find out more about international trade. Type *international trade* into your search engine. From the list of Web sites that appears on the monitor, select at least three. Read and summarize your findings.



# CHAPTER 18 Assessment and Activities

## Applying Economic Concepts

Have students share and compare their lists.

## Cooperative Learning Project

Suggest that students combine their summaries in a booklet titled "International Trade."

## Reviewing Skills

Call on students to read and discuss their descriptions.

## Technology Activity

Ensure that students choose a variety of media for their selected topic.

## Analyzing the Global Economy

Have students share the results of their Internet search with the rest of the class.

### Chapter Bonus Test Question

**ASK: The value of the currency of the nation you plan to vacation in falls against the dollar. How might this affect your vacation?** *A dollar will buy more of the foreign currency, essentially making the vacation cheaper.*

# 1 Focus

Have students locate the original six members of the European Union—France, West Germany, Italy, Belgium, the Netherlands, and Luxembourg—on a world map. Point out that this initial union of several war-torn countries has grown into one of the most powerful trading groups in the world.

# 2 Teach

Have students read the information in the boxes. Then point out that one area of the world is not addressed in the map—the non-EU countries of Western Europe. Inform students that EU exports to this area total $131.6 million, while imports from this area run about $113.3 million. Have students use these figures to calculate the value of the EU's total international trade. *(about $1.6 trillion)*

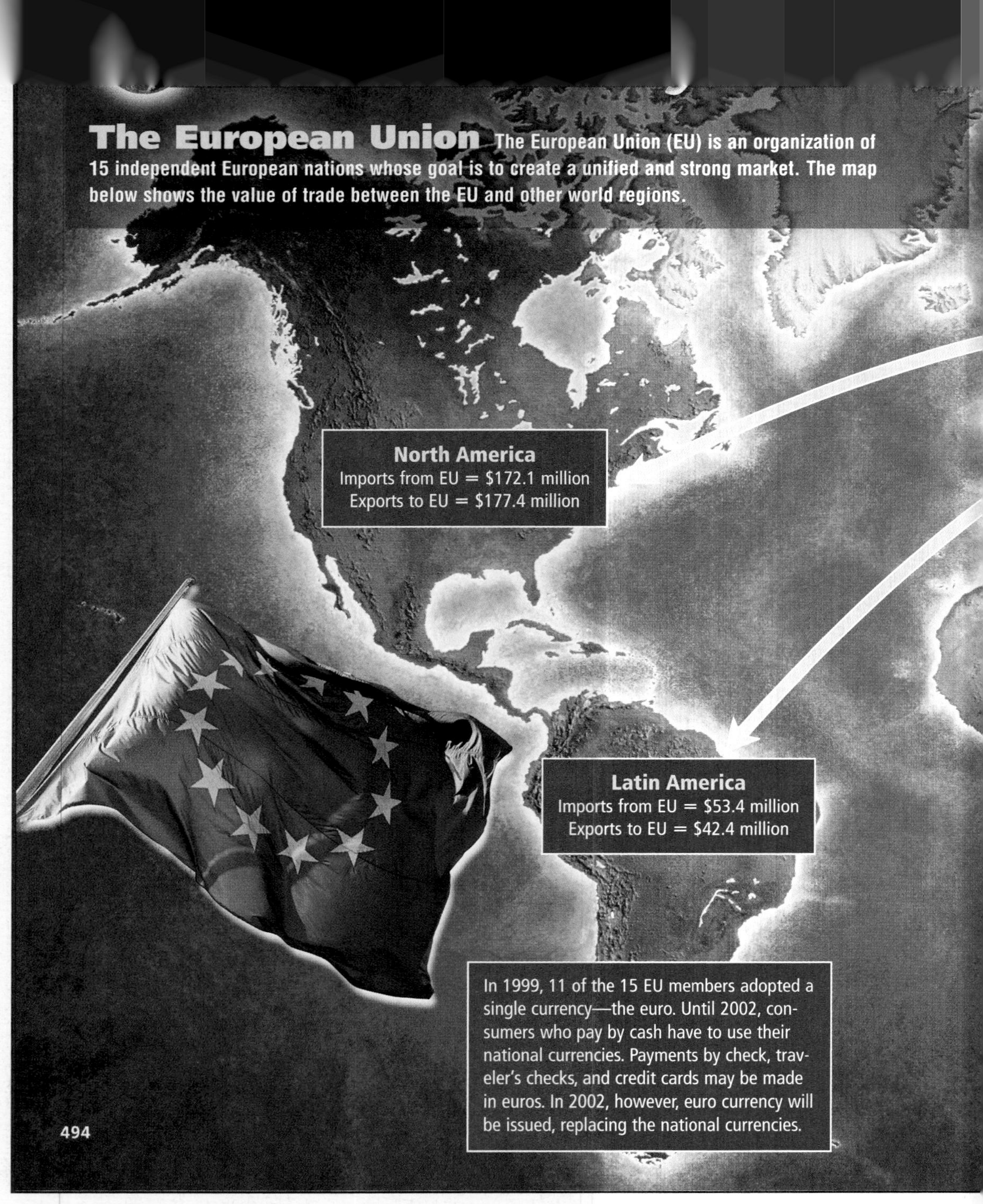

The European Union The European Union (EU) is an organization of 15 independent European nations whose goal is to create a unified and strong market. The map below shows the value of trade between the EU and other world regions.
North America
Imports from EU = $172.1 million
Exports to EU = $177.4 million
Latin America
Imports from EU = $53.4 million
Exports to EU = $42.4 million
In 1999, 11 of the 15 EU members adopted a single currency—the euro. Until 2002, consumers who pay by cash have to use their national currencies. Payments by check, traveler's checks, and credit cards may be made in euros. In 2002, however, euro currency will be issued, replacing the national currencies.
494


## Extending the Content

**The European Union** The EU was first established as the European Economic Community (EEC) in 1957 with just six members—France, West Germany, Italy, Belgium, the Netherlands, and Luxembourg. Its purpose was to speed the economic recovery of war-torn Europe. Since that time, it has added nine new members—Denmark, Great Britain, and Ireland in 1973; Greece in 1981; Portugal and Spain in 1986; and Austria, Finland, and Sweden in 1995.

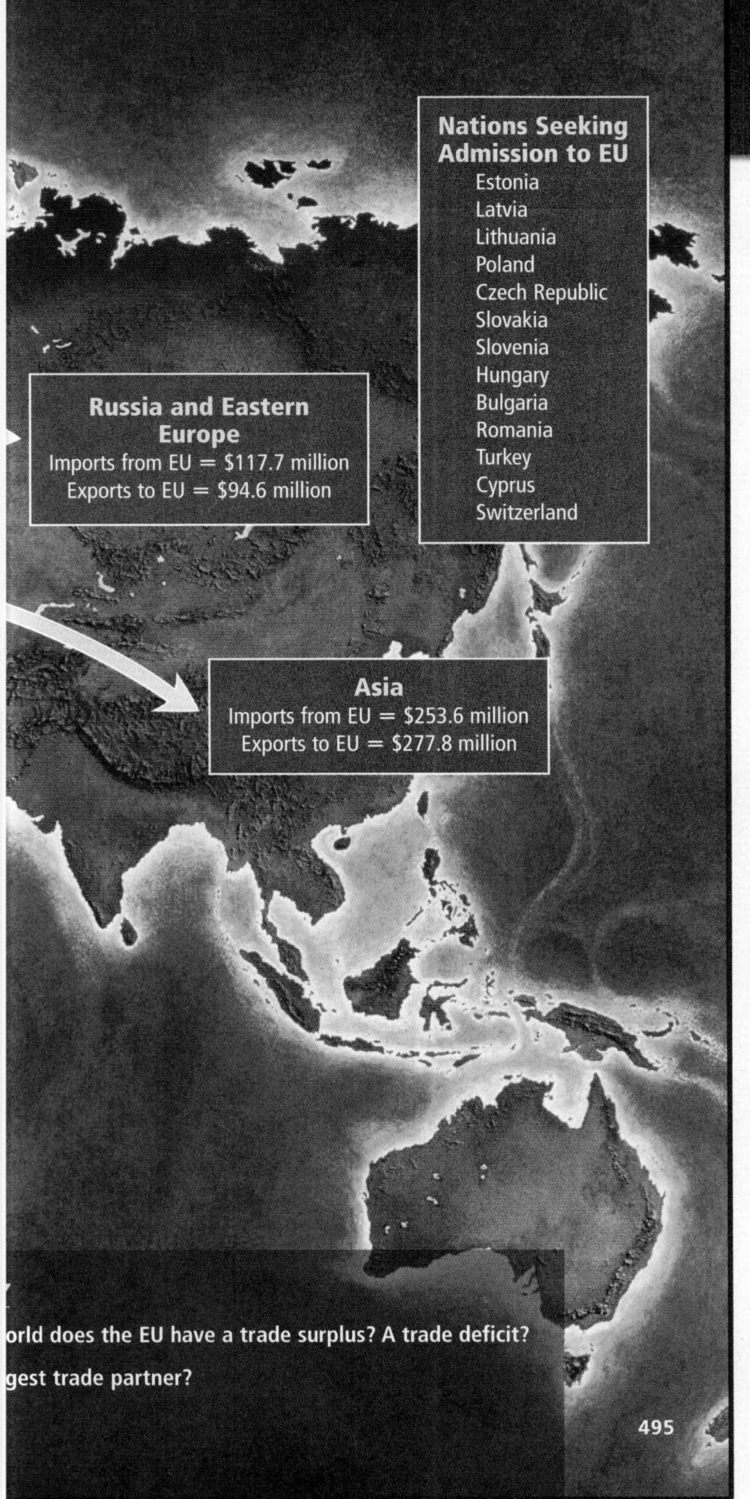

Nations Seeking Admission to EU
Estonia
Latvia
Lithuania
Poland
Czech Republic
Slovakia
Slovenia
Hungary
Bulgaria
Romania
Turkey
Cyprus
Switzerland
Russia and Eastern Europe
Imports from EU = $117.7 million
Exports to EU = $94.6 million
Asia
Imports from EU = $253.6 million
Exports to EU = $277.8 million
orld does the EU have a trade surplus? A trade deficit?
gest trade partner?
495


## 3 Assess

Have students answer the **Thinking Globally** questions.

## 4 Close

Inform students that some people fear the growth of the EU, believing it will harm the United States economy. Others suggest that there is nothing to fear from the growth of the EU, because it will be a free market like the United States. Have students agree or disagree with these views.

### ? Did You Know

One of the attractions of foreign travel for some people is the chance to buy goods, such as liquor, perfume, and jewelry, free of various import duties. EU citizens do not have this opportunity when traveling to other EU countries. The EU banned all duty-free sales on intra-EU trips in July 1999.

### ɡ Globally

ussia and Eastern Europe; Deficit: North America, Africa,

# CHAPTER 19 Resource Manager

## Teaching Transparency

### Economic Concepts Transparency 4

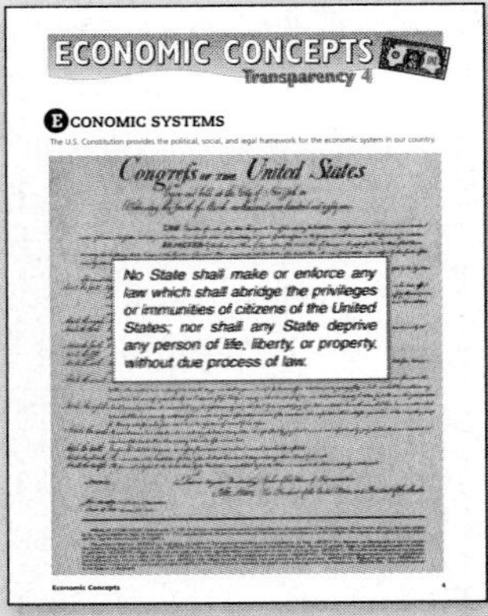

ECONOMIC CONCEPTS Transparency 4

ECONOMIC SYSTEMS

No State shall make or enforce any law which shall abridge the privileges or immunities of citizens of the United States; nor shall any State deprive any person of life, liberty, or property, without due process of law.

## Application and Enrichment

### Enrichment Activity 19

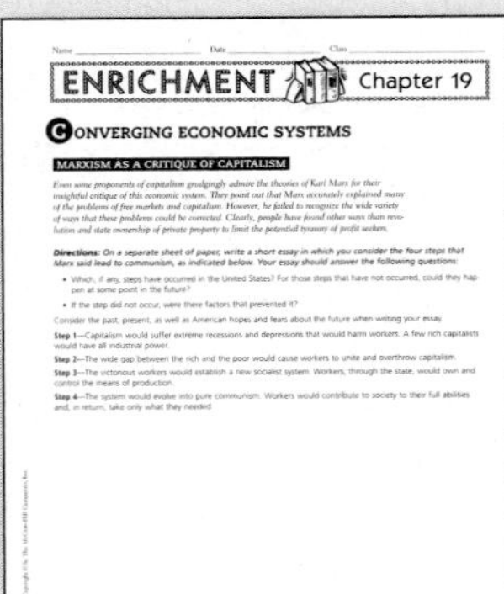

ENRICHMENT Chapter 19

CONVERGING ECONOMIC SYSTEMS

MARXISM AS A CRITIQUE OF CAPITALISM

### Consumer Applications Activity 23

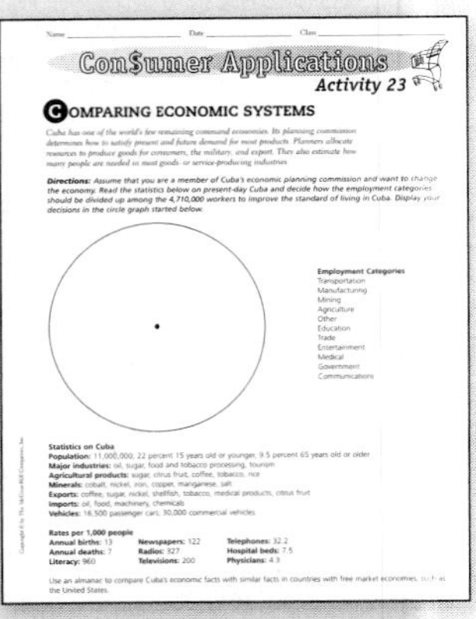

Con$umer Applications Activity 23

COMPARING ECONOMIC SYSTEMS

### Free Enterprise Activity 23

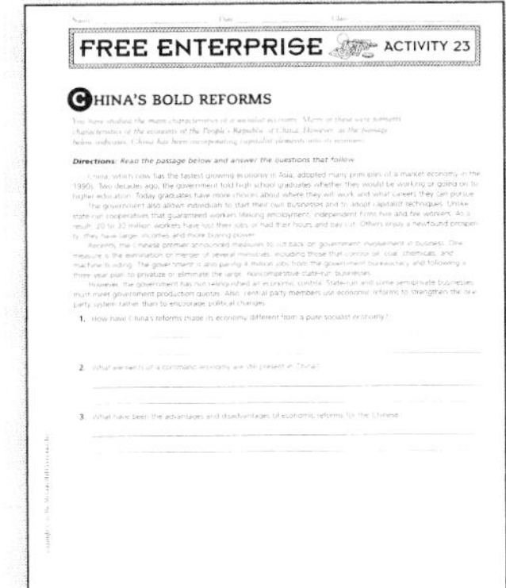

FREE ENTERPRISE ACTIVITY 23

CHINA'S BOLD REFORMS

## Application and Enrichment

### Cooperative Learning Simulations and Problems 23

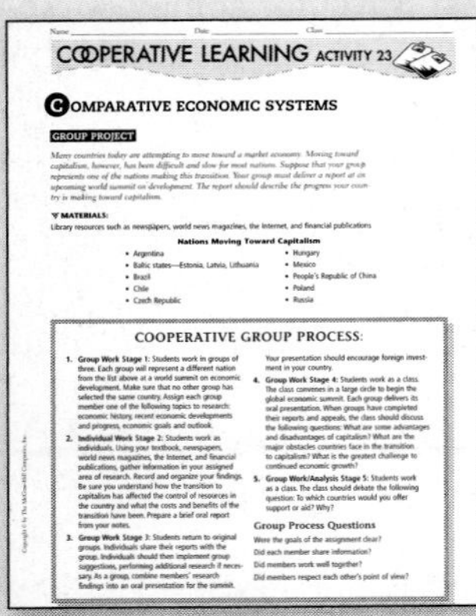

COOPERATIVE LEARNING ACTIVITY 23

COMPARATIVE ECONOMIC SYSTEMS

GROUP PROJECT

COOPERATIVE GROUP PROCESS:

### Primary and Secondary Source Reading 23

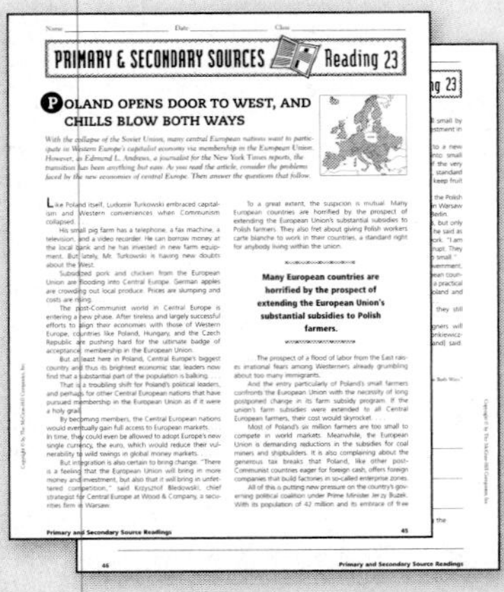

PRIMARY & SECONDARY SOURCES Reading 23

POLAND OPENS DOOR TO WEST, AND CHILLS BLOW BOTH WAYS

Many European countries are horrified by the prospect of extending the European Union's substantial subsidies to Polish farmers.

### Math Practice for Economics Activity 23

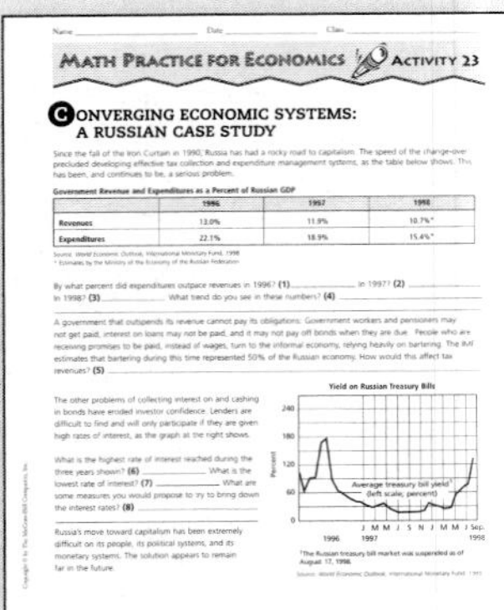

MATH PRACTICE FOR ECONOMICS ACTIVITY 23

CONVERGING ECONOMIC SYSTEMS: A RUSSIAN CASE STUDY

### Economic Cartoons Activity 23

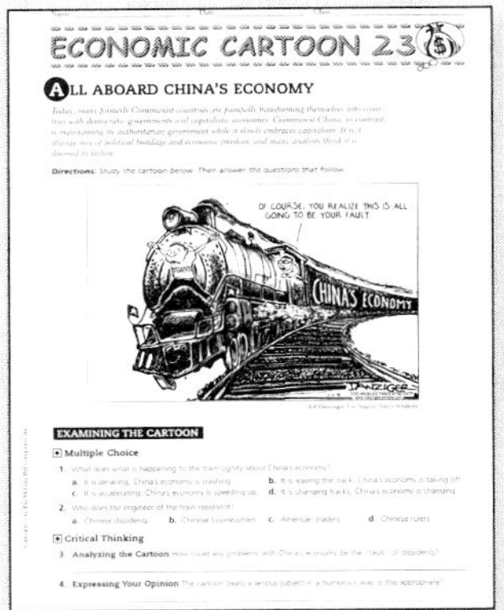

ECONOMIC CARTOON 23

ALL ABOARD CHINA'S ECONOMY



EXAMINING THE CARTOON

## Review and Reinforcement

### Critical Thinking Activity 23

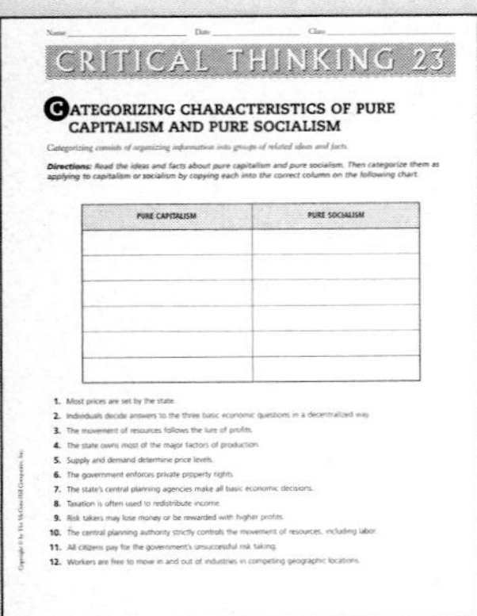

CRITICAL THINKING 23

CATEGORIZING CHARACTERISTICS OF PURE CAPITALISM AND PURE SOCIALISM

| PURE CAPITALISM | PURE SOCIALISM |
|---|---|

### Reteaching Activity 19

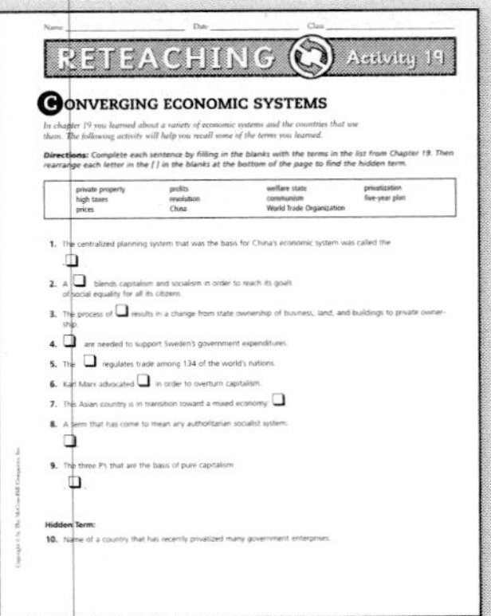

RETEACHING Activity 19

CONVERGING ECONOMIC SYSTEMS

### Economic Vocabulary Activity 19

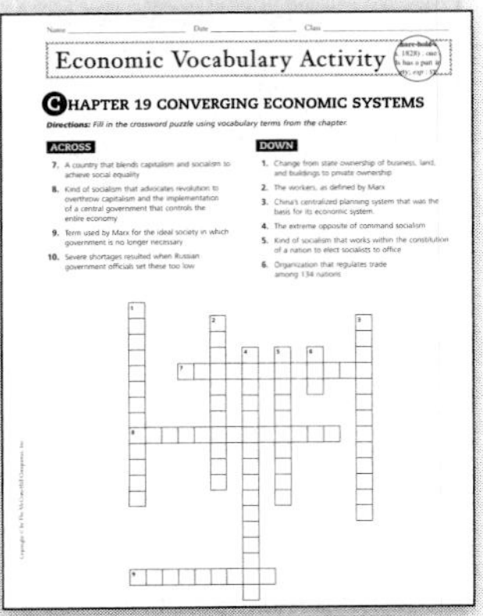

Economic Vocabulary Activity

CHAPTER 19 CONVERGING ECONOMIC SYSTEMS

ACROSS

DOWN

### Reinforcing Economic Skills 15

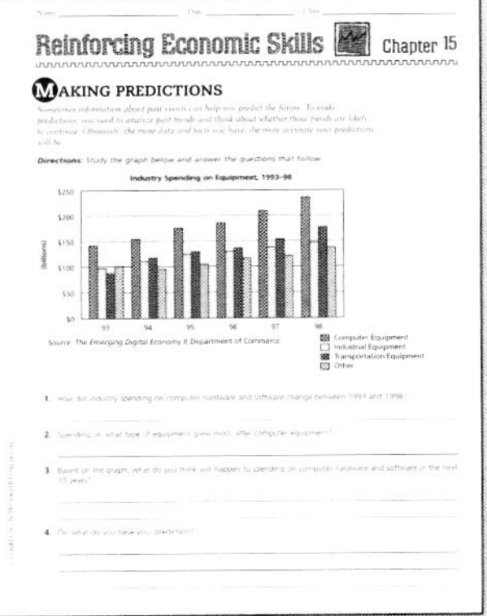

Reinforcing Economic Skills Chapter 15

MAKING PREDICTIONS

## ...PTER 19 Resource Manager

### Assessment and Evaluation

Chapter 19 Test Form B

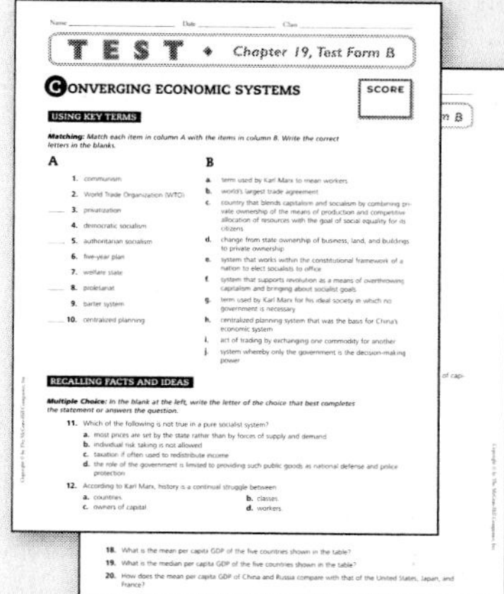

Performance Assessment Activity 23

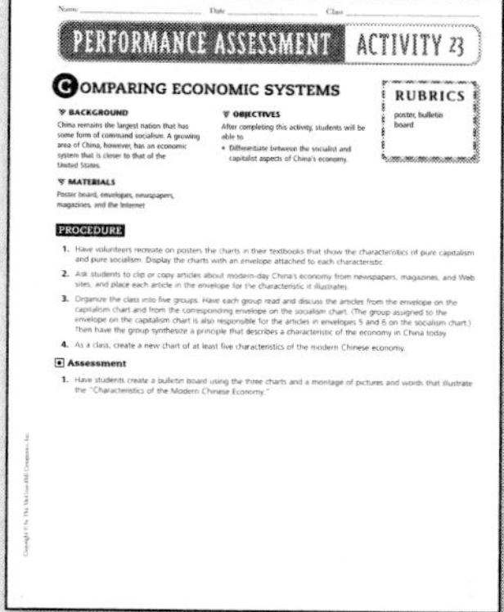

ExamView® Pro Testmaker

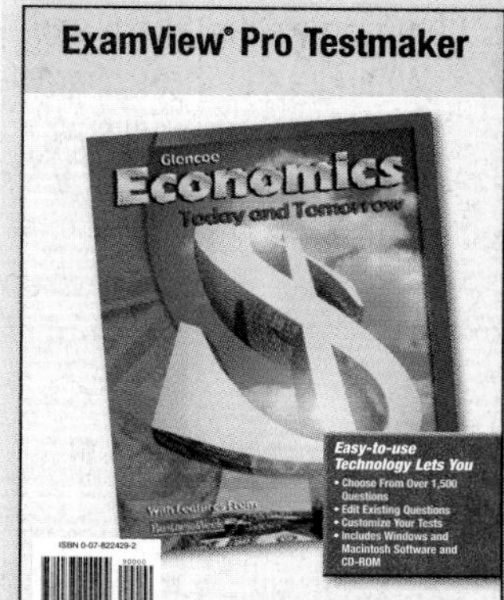

### ...l Multimedia

...ter Software

...Assessment Software

...aker

...Video Program (English/Spanish)

...nteractive Workbook CD-ROM,

...nner

...

...! CD-ROM

...sh or Spanish)

### ...esources

...ncepts Transparency 4

...ctivity 19

...ctivity 19

...es for Chapter 19

...udio Program, Activity, and Test

### ECONOMICS Online

You and your students can visit ett.glencoe.com—the Web site companion to **Economics Today and Tomorrow.** This innovative integration of electronic and print media offers your students a wealth of opportunities. The student text directs students to the Web site for the following options:

- **Chapter Overviews**
- **Self-Check Quizzes**
- **Student Web Activities**
- **Textbook Updates**

Answers are provided for you in the **Web Activity Lesson Plan.** Additional Web resources and Interactive Puzzles are also available.

Use the Glencoe Web site for additional resources. All essential content is covered in the Student Edition.

### Additional Resources

**Reading for the Student**

Schnitzer, Martin, *Comparative Economic Systems,* 8th ed. Cincinnati, OH: Southwestern, 1999. Compares the U.S., Japanese, and German economies.

**Multimedia Material**

*Capitalism, Communism, Socialism: An Introduction.* BFA Educational Media. Video. Details political, economic, and social features of these systems.

# CHAPTER 19 Resource Manager

## Section Resources

| Reading Objectives | Reproducible Resources | Technology/Multimedia Resources |
|---|---|---|
| **Section 1**<br>**Comparing Capitalism and Socialism**<br>• What are the three characteristics of pure market capitalism?<br>• What are the key characteristics of pure socialism?<br>• How did socialism develop?<br>• What are the benefits of capitalism? | Reproducible Lesson Plan 19-1<br>Daily Lecture Notes 19-1<br>Guided Reading Activity 19-1<br>Reading Essentials and Study Guide 19-1<br>Daily Focus Activity 82<br>Section Quiz 19-1* | Daily Focus Transparency 82<br>Economic Concepts Transparency 4<br>Vocabulary PuzzleMaker<br>Interactive Tutor Self-Assessment Software<br>MindJogger Videoquiz<br>NBR's *Economics & You**<br>Presentation Plus!<br>ExamView® Pro Testmaker |
| **Section 2**<br>**Changing Authoritarian Socialism—The Case of China**<br>• How did the Chinese economic system develop following World War II?<br>• What have been two major problems in China's attempt to move to capitalism? | Reproducible Lesson Plan 19-2<br>Daily Lecture Notes 19-2<br>Guided Reading Activity 19-2<br>Reading Essentials and Study Guide 19-2<br>Daily Focus Activity 83<br>Section Quiz 19-2* | Daily Focus Transparency 83<br>Vocabulary PuzzleMaker<br>Interactive Tutor Self-Assessment Software<br>MindJogger Videoquiz<br>NBR's *Economics & You**<br>Presentation Plus!<br>ExamView® Pro Testmaker |
| **Section 3**<br>**Nations Move Toward the Market System**<br>• How has Russia changed since privatization?<br>• How has the Swedish economy been changing?<br>• What changes have recently occurred in Latin American economies? | Reproducible Lesson Plan 19-3<br>Daily Lecture Notes 19-3<br>Guided Reading Activity 19-3<br>Reading Essentials and Study Guide 19-3<br>Daily Focus Activity 84<br>Section Quiz 19-3*<br>Reinforcing Economic Skills 15 | Daily Focus Transparency 84<br>Vocabulary PuzzleMaker<br>Interactive Tutor Self-Assessment Software<br>MindJogger Videoquiz<br>Presentation Plus!<br>ExamView® Pro Testmaker |

*Also available in Spanish

Blackline Master
Transparency

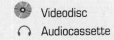

Software
CD-ROM

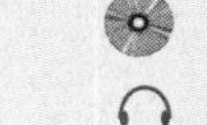
Videodisc
Audiocassette

Videocassette

# CHAPTER 19 Resource Manager

## ACTIVITY From the Classroom of

**Sharon Owens**
**Westerville City Schools**
**Westerville, Ohio**

### Shake Hands or Bow?

As nations around the world move toward a market economy, many American businesses are interacting more and more with different cultures in other countries. Have students write or e-mail an American company that conducts business in foreign countries to discover any cultural or business practices the company has incorporated into its operations. For example, businesspeople in Japan greet each other by bowing. Failure to honor such traditional courtesies may have a negative impact on a company's efforts to do business.

In addition, students can select a specific country and research its culture in relation to business protocol. Then have students work in groups to make a videotape demonstrating the various procedures and key words one should know in order to properly conduct business in their chosen country. Students can show their completed video to the class.

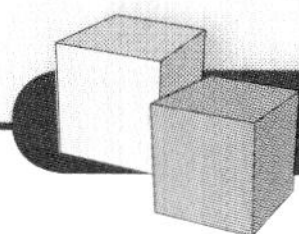

## Block Schedule

Activities that are particularly suited to use within the block scheduling framework are identified throughout this chapter by the following designation: BLOCK SCHEDULING

## Easy Planning and Preparation!

Use Glencoe's **Presentation Plus!**, a Microsoft PowerPoint® application, to teach **Converging Economic Systems.** With this multimedia teacher tool, you can customize ready-made presentations. At your fingertips are interactive transparencies, on-screen lecture notes, audiovisual presentations, and links to the Internet and to other Glencoe multimedia.

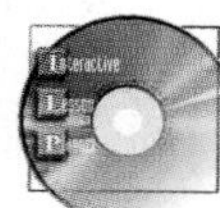

**Interactive Lesson Planner**

Planning has never been easier! Organize your week, month, semester, or year with all the lesson helps you need to make teaching creative, timely, and relevant—the way it is meant to be. The Interactive Lesson Planner opens Glencoe's **Chapter 19** resources, helps you build your schedule, and tracks your progress.

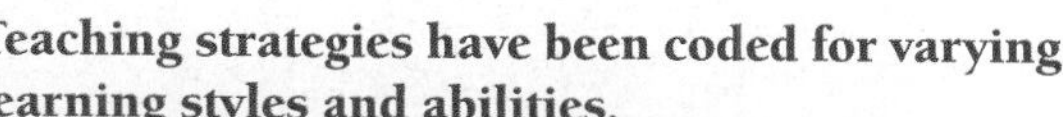

## Key to Ability Levels

**Teaching strategies have been coded for varying learning styles and abilities.**

L1 BASIC activities for all students

L2 AVERAGE activities for average to above-average students

L3 CHALLENGING activities for above-average students

ELL ENGLISH LANGUAGE LEARNER activities

## National Council on Economic Education

## THE EconomicsAmerica AND EconomicsInternational PROGRAMS

### Voluntary Standards Emphasized in Chapter 19

**Content Standard 3** Students will understand that different methods can be used to allocate goods and services. People, acting individually or collectively through government, must choose which methods to use to allocate different kinds of goods and services.

### Resources Available from NCEE

- *Capstone: The Nation's High School Economics Course*
- *Civics and Government: Focus on Economics*
- *Economics in Transition: Command to Market*
- *From Plan to Market*

**To order these materials, or to contact your State Council on Economic Education about workshops and programs, call 1-800-338-1192 or visit the NCEE Web site at http://www.nationalcouncil.org**

ECONOMICS & YOU

Comparative Economic Systems

Chapter 25
Disc 1, Side 2

ASK: What is the main difference between capitalism and socialism? *In capitalism, the factors of production are privately owned and controlled. In socialism, some of the factors of production are owned and controlled by the government.*

 Also available in VHS.

## Chapter Overview

Chapter 19 compares capitalism and socialism, discusses China's progress from a communist economy to a mixed economy, and outlines economic changes in several other countries.

**GLENCOE TECHNOLOGY**

Use **MindJogger Videoquiz** VHS to preview Chapter 19 content.

ECONOMICS Online

Introduce students to chapter content and key terms by having them access **Chapter 19—Chapter Overviews** at *ett.glencoe.com*

# CHAPTER 19

# Converging Economic Systems

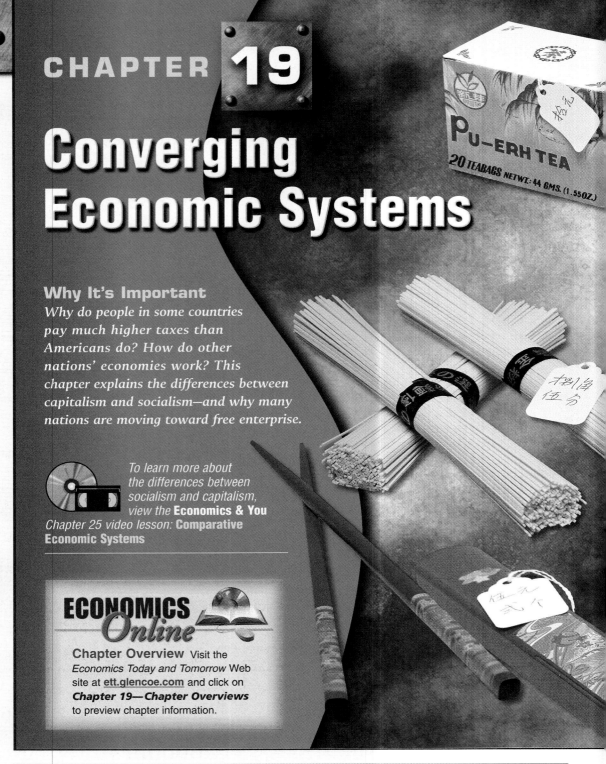

## Why It's Important

*Why do people in some countries pay much higher taxes than Americans do? How do other nations' economies work? This chapter explains the differences between capitalism and socialism—and why many nations are moving toward free enterprise.*

*To learn more about the differences between socialism and capitalism, view the* **Economics & You** *Chapter 25 video lesson:* **Comparative Economic Systems**

ECONOMICS Online

**Chapter Overview** Visit the *Economics Today and Tomorrow* Web site at ett.glencoe.com and click on ***Chapter 19—Chapter Overviews*** to preview chapter information.

## CHAPTER LAUNCH ACTIVITY

Call on students to share with the class the economic choices they have made recently in response to their needs and goals. Have the class discuss how their lives would be different if they were not allowed to make economic choices freely. Encourage students to take notes during the discussion. Then ask them to use their notes to write a paragraph beginning: "Limited economic freedom would . . ." Conclude by pointing out that in this chapter they will learn how socialist economic systems require extensive planning that necessarily limits citizens' economic, political, and social freedoms.

# SECTION 1

# Comparing Capitalism and Socialism

## COVER STORY

*BUSINESS WEEK*, JULY 19, 1999

For more than 15 years, the handful of foreign automakers allowed into China have dutifully assembled the cars and trucks prescribed by Beijing [China's capital]—even if those vehicles didn't make the most economic sense.

. . . For years, China has tightly restricted market access, especially for passenger cars. The government limited the number of players, set production volumes and prices, and dictated what types of vehicles could be made and where. Foreign carmakers have ended up making outmoded vehicles that are too expensive for most Chinese.

### READER'S GUIDE

**Terms to Know**

- proletariat
- communism
- democratic socialism
- authoritarian socialism

**Reading Objectives**

1. What are the three characteristics of pure market capitalism?
2. What are the key characteristics of pure socialism?
3. How did socialism develop?
4. What are the benefits of capitalism?

Some government intervention occurs in the American economy, but generally the marketplace answers the three basic economic questions of WHAT, HOW, and FOR WHOM goods and services should be produced. In command economies, however, the government (not the market) answers these three basic questions.

In this chapter you will study different economic systems. The system that we know best in the United States is market capitalism. The opposite of this system is pure command socialism.



## SECTION 1 RESOURCE MANAGER

**Reproducible Masters**

- Reproducible Lesson Plan 19–1
- Reading Essentials and Study Guide 19–1
- Guided Reading Activity 19–1
- Section Quiz 19–1
- Daily Focus Activity 82
- Daily Lecture Notes 19–1

**Multimedia**

- Daily Focus Transparency 82
- Economic Concepts Transparency 4
- Vocabulary PuzzleMaker
- Interactive Tutor Self-Assessment Software
- ExamView® Pro Testmaker
- MindJogger Videoquiz
- NBR's *Economics & You*
- Presentation Plus!



# 1 Focus

## Overview

**Section 1** outlines the major characteristics of pure market capitalism and pure socialism and explores the benefits of capitalism.

### BELLRINGER

**Motivational Activity**

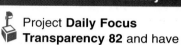

Project **Daily Focus Transparency 82** and have students answer the questions.

This activity is also available as a blackline master.

**Daily Focus Transparency 82**

FOCUS ACTIVITIES
Transparency 82

COMPARISON OF ECONOMIC SYSTEMS

| | Capitalism | Socialism | Authoritarian Socialism/ Communism |
|---|---|---|---|
| Ownership of Resources | Privately owned | Many basic resources and industries owned by government; others privately owned | Most government-owned |
| Source of Economic Decisions | Individuals and businesses | Government makes most industrial decisions; advises private industry | Government devises economic plans for the nation and its industries |
| Role of Workers | Free to choose jobs | Free to choose jobs | Restricted in freedom to choose jobs |
| Social Programs and Their Financing | Government provides social security and unemployment benefits; financed by taxes | Government provides free medical care, education, pensions, and unemployment benefits; financed by taxes | Government provides low-cost housing, free health care, education, and pensions; financed by taxes |
| Examples | United States, Japan, Singapore | Sweden, Great Britain, France | People's Republic of China, North Korea |

1. What are the three major types of economic systems?
2. Which systems provide free medical care? How is it financed?

Daily Focus Transparencies

### READER'S GUIDE

Answers to the **Reading Objectives** questions are on page 501.

**Preteaching Vocabulary**

Have students write sentences using each of the **Terms to Know**. Call on volunteers to read aloud their sentences, omitting the term in each. Ask the rest of the class to identify the missing term.

**Vocabulary PuzzleMaker**

# 2 Teach

## Guided Practice

**L2** Applying Ideas Review the information in **Figure 19.1** with students. Then have students work in small groups to develop scenarios illustrating each of the characteristics of pure market capitalism and pure socialism. Have the rest of the class identify the characteristics that are being illustrated.

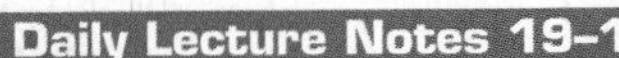

**Daily Lecture Notes 19-1**

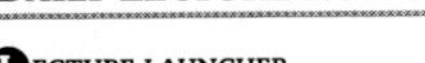

DAILY LECTURE NOTES Lesson 19-1

**LECTURE LAUNCHER**

During the 1800s, Great Britain gained control of Hong Kong, a small territory once belonging to China. As part of the British Empire, Hong Kong flourished economically. In 1997, Hong Kong was returned to China. How this will effect Hong Kong's long-term economy remains to be seen. What are the three basic economic questions that the economic systems of China, Great Britain, and all nations must answer? How are these questions typically answered in a capitalist economy like Great Britain? How are they typically answered in a socialist economy like China?

PAGE 498

I. Pure Market Capitalism
 - **A.** Operates on the basis of the three P's: prices, profits, and private property
 - **B.** A government in a pure capitalist system provides only public goods such as national defense and police protection.

**Discussion Question**

**Is the United States economy functioning under pure capitalism? Explain.** *(Possible response: The U.S. economy is very far from pure capitalism because the government provides much more than just national defense and police protection. In fact, government provides an enormous number (in both percentage and total) of jobs.)*

PAGES 498–500

**ECONOMICS & YOU**

**Comparative Economic Systems**

Chapter 25
Disc 1, Side 2

ASK: How did Marx view history? *He viewed it as a struggle between workers and bosses.*

 Also available in VHS.

## FIGURE 19.1

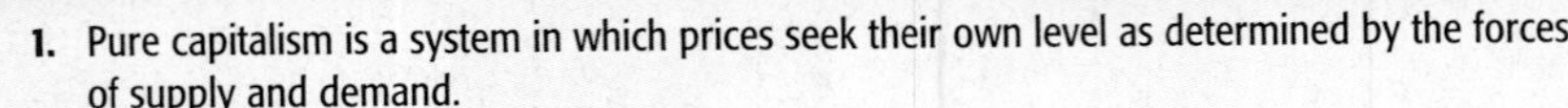

### A Characteristics of Pure Capitalism

1. Pure capitalism is a system in which prices seek their own level as determined by the forces of supply and demand.
2. Resources, including labor, are free to move in and out of industries in competing geographic locations. The movement of resources follows the lure of profits—higher expected profits create an incentive for more resources to go where those profits are expected to occur.
3. Private property rights exist, are legal, and are enforced by the government, or the rule of law.
4. Those who take risks may be rewarded by higher profits. When those risks turn out to be bad business decisions, the risk takers lose money.
5. The three basic economic questions are all decided in a decentralized way by individuals.

### B Characteristics of Pure Socialism

1. Most prices are set by the state, rather than by forces of supply and demand.
2. The movement of resources, particularly labor, is strictly controlled. The central planning authority makes all the decisions.
3. Most of the major factors of production are owned by the state. Private property rights are strictly limited to small tools that an individual needs for an occupation.
4. Individual risk taking is not allowed. The state takes all of the risk when it decides which new companies shall be formed. All citizens pay for unsuccessful risk taking.
5. Economic decisions about what, how, and for whom to produce are all made by state officials through central planning agencies and other administrative units.
6. Taxation is often used to redistribute income.

## Pure Market Capitalism

In its purest theoretical form, market or pure capitalism operates on the basis of the *three Ps:* Prices, Profits, and Private Property. See *Part A* of **Figure 19.1.** Government in a pure capitalist system is limited to providing such public goods as national defense and police protection.

## Pure Socialism

Pure socialism is an economic system in which there is little private property and the state owns virtually all the factors of production. Few examples of pure command socialism exist. Perhaps the



## Meeting Special Needs

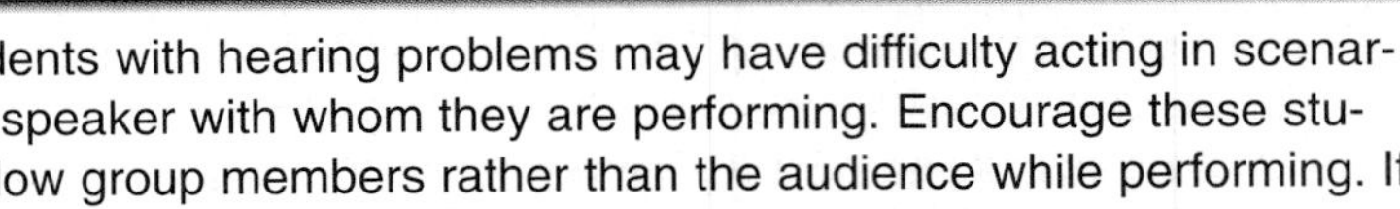

**Hearing Disability** Students with hearing problems may have difficulty acting in scenarios if they cannot see the speaker with whom they are performing. Encourage these students to focus on their fellow group members rather than the audience while performing. If necessary, have groups perform their scenarios facing each other across a table.

Refer to *Inclusion for the Social Studies Classroom Strategies and Activities* for students with different learning styles.

most extensively controlled economies are in North Korea and Cuba. *Part B* of **Figure 19.1** lists the characteristics of pure socialism.

**The Marxian View of Socialism** Socialism as a modern economic system grew out of protests against the problems caused by the Industrial Revolution of the 1800s. Karl Marx viewed history as a continual struggle between various groups, or classes, in society. In his own day, he saw this struggle as going on between capitalists—owners of the land, machines, and factories—and the **proletariat,** or workers. Marx believed capitalists exploited the proletariat, or used them unfairly. According to Marx, the value of goods depends only on how much labor is used in producing them. When capitalists sold a good and kept the profit, they were taking income that rightly belonged to the proletariat.

Despite capitalism's dominance in the nineteenth century, Marx believed it was doomed to fail. He outlined the collapse of capitalism, as shown in **Figure 19.2,** and predicted the

**proletariat:** *term used by Karl Marx referring to workers*

## FIGURE 19.2 The Change From Capitalism to Socialism According to Marx

**The End of Capitalism** Clearly Marx did not accurately predict what would happen in capitalist nations. Indeed, the opposite has proven to be true.

**The Change From Capitalism to Socialism According to Marx**

**Step 1**
Capitalism would suffer extreme recessions and depressions that would harm workers. A few rich capitalists would have all industrial power.

**Step 2**
The wide gap between the rich and the poor would cause workers to unite and overthrow capitalism.

**Step 3**
The victorious workers would establish a new socialist system. Workers, through the state, would own and control the means of production.

**Step 4**
The system would evolve into pure communism. Workers would contribute to society to their full abilities and, in return, take only what they needed.

*Leaders of the 1917 Russian Revolution*



## Cooperative Learning

Organize students into groups, and assign each group either *capitalism, democratic socialism,* or *authoritarian socialism.* Direct groups to describe the organization of a poster-making business under their assigned economic system. Suggest that groups consider the following questions in completing this task: From where will startup funds come? From where will the factors of production come? How will workers be paid? How much will be produced? How will the production process be organized? How will the finished posters be distributed? Have group representatives share their organization plans with the rest of the class. BLOCK SCHEDULING



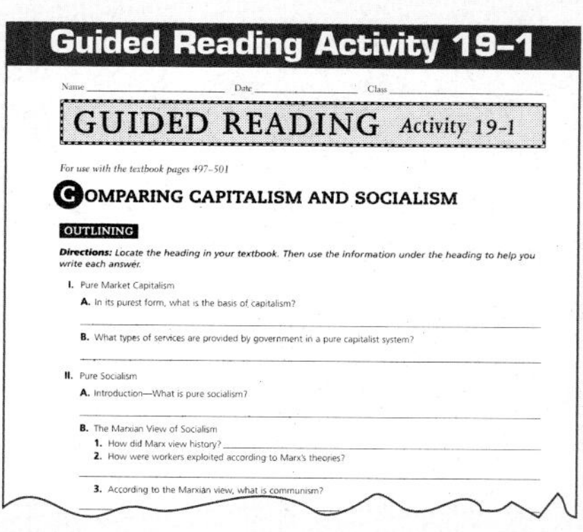

**Guided Reading Activity 19-1**

Name ______ Date ______ Class ______

GUIDED READING Activity 19-1

*For use with the textbook pages 497–501*

**COMPARING CAPITALISM AND SOCIALISM**

OUTLINING

***Directions:*** *Locate the heading in your textbook. Then use the information under the heading to help you write each answer.*

**I.** Pure Market Capitalism
  **A.** In its purest form, what is the basis of capitalism?
  **B.** What types of services are provided by government in a pure capitalist system?
**II.** Pure Socialism
  **A.** Introduction—What is pure socialism?
  **B.** The Marxian View of Socialism
    **1.** How did Marx view history?
    **2.** How were workers exploited according to Marx's theories?
    **3.** According to the Marxian view, what is communism?

Project **Economic Concepts Transparency 4** and have students discuss the accompanying questions.

## Independent Practice

**L2 Making Comparisons** Have students write a brief essay comparing the advantages and disadvantages of capitalism and socialism. Call on volunteers to read and discuss their essays. BLOCK SCHEDULING

**Economic Connection to... History**

**American Socialism** Debs's success in the 1912 election proved to be the high point for the Socialist Party of America. Soon after, the party's popularity began to fade. Many explanations have been given as to why socialism failed to gain lasting support in the United States. One of the most colorful came from the German historian Werner Sombart. In *Why Is There No Socialism in the United States?* (1906), Sombart noted that Americans enjoyed the highest standard of living in the world. "All socialist utopias come to nothing on roast beef and apple pie!" he observed.

## 3 Assess

### Meeting Lesson Objectives

Assign Section 1 Assessment as homework or an in-class activity.

Use **Interactive Tutor Self-Assessment Software** to review Section 1.

**Economic Connection to... History**

## Socialist Party of America

Several political parties that promoted socialism developed in the United States during the late 1800s and early 1900s. The most successful of these, the Socialist Party of America, was founded in 1901. By 1912 party membership had grown to about 118,000. And in the presidential election of that year, the Socialist candidate, Eugene V. Debs, received more than 900,000 votes. ■

communism: *term used by Karl Marx for his ideal society in which no government is necessary*

evolution of socialism into **communism**—an ideal system with no need for a government. Today *communism* has come to mean any authoritarian socialist system that supports revolution as a means to overthrow capitalism and bring about socialist goals. Instead of "no government," communist systems historically have demonstrated that a central government controls the entire economy.

democratic socialism: *system that works within the constitutional framework of a nation to elect socialists to office; the government usually controls only some areas of the economy*

authoritarian socialism: *system that supports revolution as a means to overthrow capitalism and bring about socialist goals; the entire economy is controlled by a central government; also called* communism

**Socialism Since Marx** In the twentieth century, socialism split into two major trends: democratic socialism and authoritarian socialism. **Democratic socialism** is a type of socialist system that works within the constitutional framework of a nation to elect socialists to office. In democratic socialist nations, government usually controls only some areas of the economy.

**Authoritarian socialism**, in contrast, more closely follows Marx's beliefs. Its supporters advocate revolution as the means to overthrow capitalism and bring about socialist goals. In authoritarian socialist nations, a central government controls the entire economy. *Communism*, the term Marx applied to his ideal society, came to mean any authoritarian socialist system.

### The Benefits of Capitalism

Many economists like to compare the advantages and disadvantages of capitalism and socialism. Often such comparisons are based on individual values. Those who place a high value on personal freedom, initiative, and individuality prefer capitalism. Critics of socialism point out that it brings extensive government intervention in all parts of the economy and, by necessity, in people's personal lives.



### Extending the Content

**Socialist Literature** Robert Tressell's novel *The Ragged Trousered Philanthropists* (1914) provides one of the most vivid pictures of working-class life at the beginning of the 1900s. The novel describes a year in the lives of a group of construction workers in a town on England's south coast. The novel also serves as a political tract. In a series of lunch-break discussions among the workers, Tressell explained the basic ideas of socialism. One reader likened these discussions to the works of Karl Marx "simplified into the working men's understanding." *The Ragged Trousered Philanthropists* had an enormous impact on the socialist and labor movements in Great Britain.

Supporters of capitalism point out that capitalism allows for more efficiency in the marketplace and for greater rates of economic growth. Indeed, considerable evidence shows that unregulated economic systems—those that are closer to pure capitalism—have *much higher* rates of economic growth.

**All Economies Are Planned** It is often said that pure socialism requires centralized planning, and pure capitalism does not. In reality, all economies are planned in one way or another. The United States has a highly planned economy. The difference between economic planning here versus in socialist countries is *who* does the planning. Private firms, individuals, and elected government officials do the planning in the American economy. In pure socialist systems, central planners make decisions on behalf of everyone.

Real-world capitalism has some problems. Critics note that income is unequally distributed throughout the economy. They also say that although capitalist nations have enough government-provided goods such as highways, they do not have enough schools and museums for the general public. Such critics clearly value the political goals of socialism.

**Practice** and **assess** key skills with *Skillbuilder Interactive Workbook, Level 2.*

## SECTION 1 Assessment

### Understanding Key Terms

1. **Define** proletariat, communism, democratic socialism, authoritarian socialism.

### Reviewing Objectives

2. What are the three characteristics of pure market capitalism?
3. What are the key characteristics of pure socialism?
4. **Graphic Organizer** Create a diagram like the one below to show the major steps in the development of socialism.

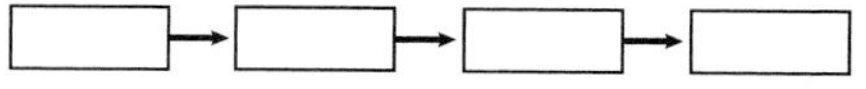

5. What are the benefits of capitalism?

### Applying Economic Concepts

6. **Authoritarian Socialism** Imagine that you live in an authoritarian socialist nation. What arguments might you make to change the economic and political systems?

### Critical Thinking Activity

7. **Making Comparisons** Create a table that compares how each of the following functions is handled under capitalism and democratic socialism: setting price of goods; ownership of production; economic planning; business failures. *For help in creating tables, see page xvii in the Economic Handbook.*





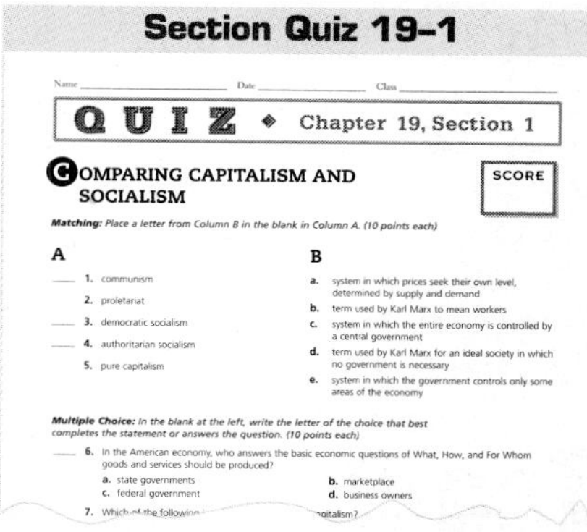

### Section Quiz 19-1

Name ______ Date ______ Class ______

**QUIZ** ◆ Chapter 19, Section 1

**COMPARING CAPITALISM AND SOCIALISM** SCORE

***Matching:*** *Place a letter from Column B in the blank in Column A. (10 points each)*

**A**

____ 1. communism
2. proletariat
____ 3. democratic socialism
____ 4. authoritarian socialism
5. pure capitalism

**B**

**a.** system in which prices seek their own level, determined by supply and demand
**b.** term used by Karl Marx to mean workers
**c.** system in which the entire economy is controlled by a central government
**d.** term used by Karl Marx for an ideal society in which no government is necessary
**e.** system in which the government controls only some areas of the economy

***Multiple Choice:*** *In the blank at the left, write the letter of the choice that best completes the statement or answers the question. (10 points each)*

____ 6. In the American economy, who answers the basic economic questions of What, How, and For Whom goods and services should be produced?
**a.** state governments **b.** marketplace
**c.** federal government **d.** business owners

7. Which of the following ... capitalism?

## Reteach

Ask students to explain how the basic questions of economics—What? How? and For Whom?—are answered in a pure market capitalist economy and a pure socialist economy.

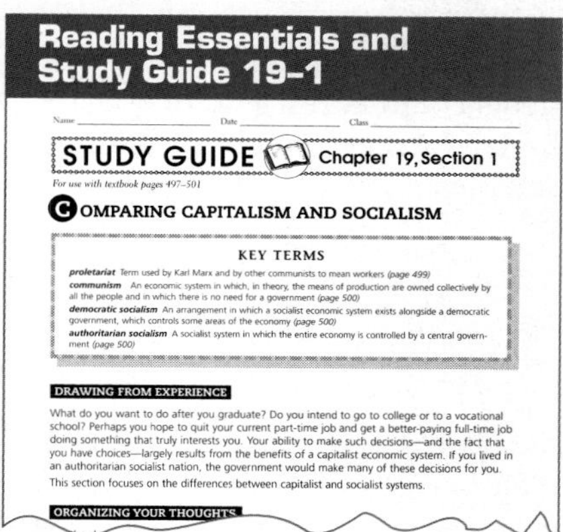

### Reading Essentials and Study Guide 19-1

Name ______ Date ______ Class ______

**STUDY GUIDE** Chapter 19, Section 1

*For use with textbook pages 497–501*

**COMPARING CAPITALISM AND SOCIALISM**

**KEY TERMS**

***proletariat*** Term used by Karl Marx and by other communists to mean workers *(page 499)*
***communism*** An economic system in which, in theory, the means of production are owned collectively by all the people and in which there is no need for a government *(page 500)*
***democratic socialism*** An arrangement in which a socialist economic system exists alongside a democratic government, which controls some areas of the economy *(page 500)*
***authoritarian socialism*** A socialist system in which the entire economy is controlled by a central government *(page 500)*

**DRAWING FROM EXPERIENCE**

What do you want to do after you graduate? Do you intend to go to college or to a vocational school? Perhaps you hope to quit your current part-time job and get a better-paying full-time job doing something that truly interests you. Your ability to make such decisions—and the fact that you have choices—largely results from the benefits of a capitalist economic system. If you lived in an authoritarian socialist nation, the government would make many of these decisions for you.

This section focuses on the differences between capitalist and socialist systems.

**ORGANIZING YOUR THOUGHTS**

## 4 Close

Direct students to work in small groups to design symbols or logos for capitalism and socialism. Call on groups to display and explain their symbols or logos.

## SECTION 1 Assessment Answers

1. All definitions can be found in the Glossary.
2. Prices, Profits, and Private Property: prices set by forces of supply and demand; free movement of resources go to where profits are highest, and risk takers may be rewarded; private property rights exist due to decentralized decision making
3. prices set by government, most resources owned and controlled by government, private property rights strictly limited, no individual risk taking, decision making centralized in the hands of government
4. grew out of problems caused by Industrial Revolution; split into two trends in the 1900s; democratic socialism works within constitutional framework; authoritarian socialism supports revolution to bring about socialist goals
5. Answers should include personal freedom, initiative, individuality, efficiency, economic growth.
6. Answers may include economic comparisons of your nation with living standards in free market systems, emigration of people from your nation, lack of political freedoms.
7. Students' tables should be based on information in **Figure 19.1** on page 498.

## Background

Point out that Marx's theories assumed that communism would develop in the industrialized world. The two great communist revolutions took place in Russia and China, however, both of which had agricultural economies.

# Teach

Have students read aloud the quoted excerpts from *The Communist Manifesto*. Call on volunteers to paraphrase each paragraph in order to gain a better understanding of Marx's ideas. Then have students answer the **Checking for Understanding** questions.

You might have interested students conduct research on Marx to delve deeper into his economic theories.

# People & Perspectives

## Karl Marx

*ECONOMIST (1818–1883)*

- **Born and educated in Germany, but spent much of his adult life in exile in Great Britain**
- **Deeply influenced by the German philosopher Georg Hegel**
- **Publications include *The Communist Manifesto* (1848), *Critique of Political Economy* (1859), and *Das Kapital* (1867)**

Karl Marx outlined his view of socialism in *The Communist Manifesto*, a pamphlet that he wrote with colleague Friedrich Engels in 1848. In the following excerpt, Marx answers two questions: Who are the Communists? What is their basic theory?

*"The Communists do not form a separate party opposed to other working-class parties. They have no interests separate and apart from the proletariat as a whole.*

*. . . The immediate aim of the Communists is the same as that of all other proletarian parties: Formation of the proletariat into a class, overthrow of the bourgeois supremacy, conquest of political power by the proletariat.*

*. . . The distinguishing feature of communism is not the abolition of property generally, but the abolition of bourgeois property. But modern bourgeois private property is the final and most complete expression of the system of producing and appropriating products that is based on class antagonisms, on the exploitation of the many by the few.*

*In this sense, the theory of the Communists may be summed up in the single sentence: Abolition of private property.*

*. . . It has been objected that upon the abolition of private property, all work will cease, and universal laziness will overtake us. According to this, bourgeois society ought long ago to have gone to the dogs through sheer idleness; for those of its members who work, acquire nothing, and those who acquire anything, do not work. The whole of this objection is but another expression of the tautology [needless repetition of an idea]: There can no longer be any wage labor when there is no longer any capital."*

### *Checking for Understanding*

1. **According to Marx, what phrase sums up communist theory?**
2. **Why was the incentive to work an issue Marx had to address?**

502

### Answers to *Checking for Understanding*

1. abolition of private property
2. Marx had to address this issue because some people believed that when private property was abolished, all work would stop and the workers would be overtaken by "universal laziness."

# SECTION 2 Changing Authoritarian Socialism—The Case of China

## COVER STORY

*MANCHESTER GUARDIAN WEEKLY, MARCH 21, 1999*

China took another big step towards opening itself up to private enterprise last week when it changed its constitution to raise the status of the burgeoning business sector.

The landmark decision by the National People's Congress, the country's parliament, allows the private sector to become an important component of what is still referred to as the socialist economy.

### READER'S GUIDE

**Terms to Know**

- five-year plans
- World Trade Organization (WTO)

**Reading Objectives**

1. How did the Chinese economic system develop following World War II?
2. What have been two major problems in China's attempt to move to capitalism?

The People's Republic of China remains the largest nation that has some form of command socialism. As you read this section, however, you'll learn that a growing area of China has an economic system that is much closer to that of the United States.

## Development of China's Economic System

The Communists won China's civil war following World War II. The new government started an economic system based on





# 1 Focus

## Overview

**Section 2** outlines how the Chinese economy developed after World War II, reviews China's transition to a mixed economy, and explores China's future economic prospects.

**BELLRINGER**
**Motivational Activity**

Project **Daily Focus Transparency 83** and have students answer the questions.

This activity is also available as a blackline master.

**Daily Focus Transparency 83**

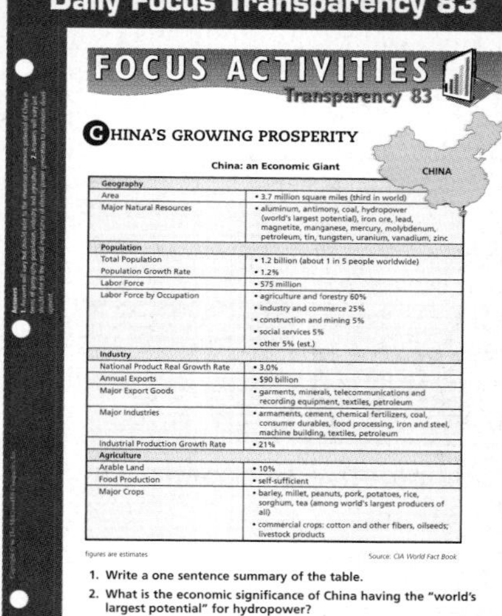
FOCUS ACTIVITIES
Transparency 83

CHINA'S GROWING PROSPERITY

China: an Economic Giant

| Geography | |
|---|---|
| Area | • 3.7 million square miles (third in world) |
| Major Natural Resources | • aluminum, antimony, coal, hydropower (world's largest potential), iron ore, lead, magnetite, manganese, mercury, molybdenum, petroleum, tin, tungsten, uranium, vanadium, zinc |
| **Population** | |
| Total Population | • 1.2 billion (about 1 in 5 people worldwide) |
| Population Growth Rate | • 1.2% |
| Labor Force | • 575 million |
| Labor Force by Occupation | • agriculture and forestry 60% • industry and commerce 25% • construction and mining 5% • social services 5% • other 5% (est.) |
| **Industry** | |
| National Product Real Growth Rate | • 3.0% |
| Annual Exports | • $90 billion |
| Major Export Goods | • garments, minerals, telecommunications and recording equipment, textiles, petroleum |
| Major Industries | • armaments, cement, chemical fertilizers, coal, consumer durables, food processing, iron and steel, machine building, textiles, petroleum |
| Industrial Production Growth Rate | • 21% |
| **Agriculture** | |
| Arable Land | • 10% |
| Food Production | • self-sufficient |
| Major Crops | • barley, millet, peanuts, pork, potatoes, rice, sorghum, tea (among world's largest producers of all) • commercial crops: cotton and other fibers, oilseeds; livestock products |

figures are estimates

Source: *CIA World Fact Book*

1. Write a one sentence summary of the table.
2. What is the economic significance of China having the "world's largest potential" for hydropower?

Daily Focus Transparencies

### READER'S GUIDE

Answers to the **Reading Objectives** questions are on page 506.

**Preteaching Vocabulary**

Have students indicate how the **Terms to Know** are related to China's economic development.

Vocabulary PuzzleMaker

## SECTION 2 RESOURCE MANAGER

**Reproducible Masters**

- Reproducible Lesson Plan 19–2
- Reading Essentials and Study Guide 19–2
- Guided Reading Activity 19–2
- Section Quiz 19–2
- Daily Focus Activity 83
- Daily Lecture Notes 19–2

**Multimedia**

- Daily Focus Transparency 83
- Vocabulary PuzzleMaker
- Interactive Tutor Self-Assessment Software
- ExamView® Pro Testmaker
- NBR's *Economics & You*
- MindJogger Videoquiz
- Presentation Plus!

# 2 Teach

## Guided Practice

**L2 Organizing Ideas** Ask students to write an essay titled "China's March From Communism to Market Economy." Call on volunteers to identify themes, ideas, and facts they think should be included in the essay. Note their responses on the board. Then ask students to use the information on the board to draw up an outline for the essay.

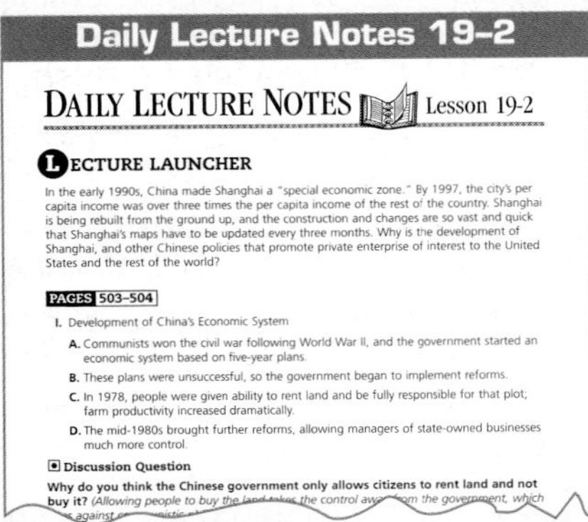
**Daily Lecture Notes 19-2**

DAILY LECTURE NOTES Lesson 19-2

**LECTURE LAUNCHER**

In the early 1990s, China made Shanghai a "special economic zone." By 1997, the city's per capita income was over three times the per capita income of the rest of the country. Shanghai is being rebuilt from the ground up, and the construction and changes are so vast and quick that Shanghai's maps have to be updated every three months. Why is the development of Shanghai, and other Chinese policies that promote private enterprise of interest to the United States and the rest of the world?

PAGES 503–504

I. Development of China's Economic System
  A. Communists won the civil war following World War II, and the government started an economic system based on five-year plans.
  B. These plans were unsuccessful, so the government began to implement reforms.
  C. In 1978, people were given ability to rent land and be fully responsible for that plot; farm productivity increased dramatically.
  D. The mid-1980s brought further reforms, allowing managers of state-owned businesses much more control.

**Discussion Question**

**Why do you think the Chinese government only allows citizens to rent land and not buy it?** *(Allowing people to buy the land takes the control away from the government, which*

**ECONOMICS & YOU**

**Comparative Economic Systems**

Chapter 25
Disc 1, Side 2

**ASK: What are some economic reforms taking place in China?** *privatization of state-run companies, the establishment of special economic zones*

Also available in VHS.

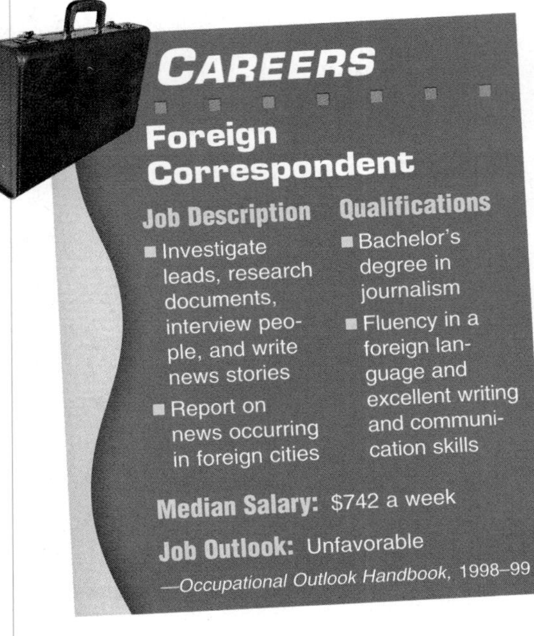


so-called **five-year plans.** The first such five-year plan, implemented in 1953, failed to fully meet expectations. Starting in the mid-1950s, the Chinese began to alter their strict centralized planning.

CAREERS
Foreign Correspondent
Job Description
Investigate leads, research documents, interview people, and write news stories
Report on news occurring in foreign cities
Qualifications
Bachelor's degree in journalism
Fluency in a foreign language and excellent writing and communication skills
Median Salary: $742 a week
Job Outlook: Unfavorable
—Occupational Outlook Handbook, 1998–99

In 1958 they reformed their system to give some decision-making powers to local government rather than restricting them to the central government. The national planning system was transformed into a regional planning system. These reforms did not transform the Chinese economy, however, because it was still not governed by capitalism's *three Ps*—Prices, Profits, and Private Property. Economic conditions worsened after 1958.

In 1978 Chinese leaders designed a reform to motivate people to work harder. Private individuals were permitted to rent land for up to 15 years. Each peasant household became responsible for its own plot of land. Whatever it produced in excess of a minimum amount required by the state remained the property of the household. The results were impressive. Between 1979 and 1984, overall farm productivity increased dramatically.

Another set of reforms and a restructuring of the economy occurred in the mid-1980s. These reforms are continuing today. Managers in state-owned businesses are allowed much more decision-making power than before. After they fulfill state production requirements, they can set production according to market demand. They also are allowed to sell part of their output to whomever they choose at market prices. See **Figure 19.3.**

*five-year plans: centralized planning system that was the basis for China's economic system; eventually was transformed to a regional planning system leading to limited free enterprise*

**FIGURE 19.3**

**The Shift to a Free Market**
China—after the failure of command economies throughout the world—has begun to allow free enterprise.

## Meeting Special Needs

**Reading Disability** Many students who are not good readers are able to locate information in the text when their attention is directed to it. Without direction, however, they often are unable to distinguish between important facts and elaboration. The notes they take, therefore, may contain a great deal of inessential information. In this section, main ideas are obvious but not necessarily stated in the first sentence of the paragraph. Tell students to select a subsection of Section 2. Then have them locate a sentence in each paragraph of the subsection that best states that paragraph's main idea. Have them defend their choices.

 Refer to *Inclusion for the Social Studies Classroom Strategies and Activities*.

# SECTION 1

# Characteristics of Developing Nations

## Cover Story

*The Columbus Dispatch*, June 30, 1999

For coffee drinkers with a social conscience, a share of each coffee dollar now goes to fill the pockets of poor farmers instead of corporations. An importer called Equal Exchange pays coffee growers [in developing countries] a guaranteed minimum price for their beans, while cutting out middlemen to deliver the coffee from tree to table.

Before they began selling to Equal Exchange, some farmers earned as little as 20 cents a pound for their coffee. . . . Now they receive a minimum price of $1.26 a pound, plus a 15-cent premium for coffee grown without the use of chemicals.

### Reader's Guide

**Terms to Know**
- developed nations
- developing nations
- subsistence agriculture
- infant mortality rate

**Reading Objectives**
1. About how many nations in the world are considered developed?
2. What are five economic characteristics of developing nations?
3. Why have poorly defined property rights been a problem in developing countries?

Many Americans may not realize it, but even the poorest families in the United States usually have an income far above the average income in much of the rest of the world. About one-half of the world's population lives at or close to subsistence, with just enough to survive. As you read this section, you'll learn about the characteristics of these *developing countries*.

## SECTION 1 RESOURCE MANAGER

**Reproducible Masters**
- Reproducible Lesson Plan 20–1
- Reading Essentials and Study Guide 20–1
- Guided Reading Activity 20–1
- Section Quiz 20–1
- Daily Focus Activity 86
- Daily Lecture Notes 20–1

**Multimedia**
- Daily Focus Transparency 86
- Vocabulary PuzzleMaker
- Interactive Tutor Self-Assessment Software
- ExamView® Pro Testmaker
- MindJogger Videoquiz
- NBR's *Economics & You*
- Presentation Plus!



# 1 Focus

## Overview

**Section 1** compares developed nations and developing nations and discusses the factors that economists use to measure economic development.

### BELLRINGER
**Motivational Activity**

Project **Daily Focus Transparency 86** and have students answer the questions.

This activity is also available as a blackline master.

**Daily Focus Transparency 86**

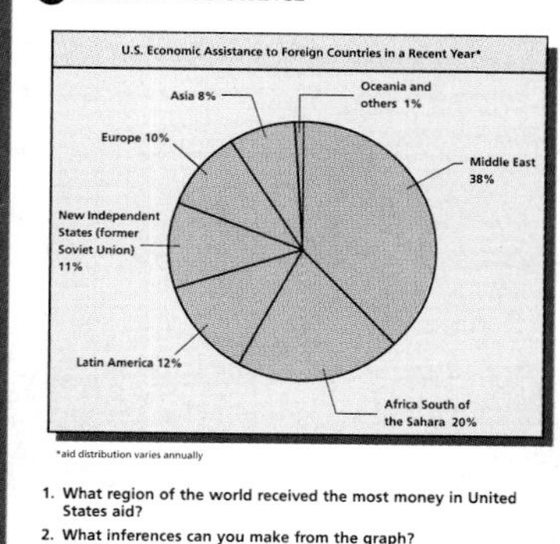


### Reader's Guide

Answers to the **Reading Objectives** questions are on page 521.

**Preteaching Vocabulary**

Have students locate the definitions of the **Terms to Know** in the Glossary. Then have them use all four terms in a brief paragraph that describes what a developing nation is.

**Vocabulary PuzzleMaker**

# 2 Teach

## Guided Practice

**L2 Illustrating Ideas** Call on volunteers to identify the characteristics of developing nations. Note their responses on the board. Then have students work in small groups to produce some form of teaching aid—poster, graphic organizer, illustrated flash cards, and so on—that will help students learn the major features of developing nations. Have groups present and explain their teaching aids. ELL BLOCK SCHEDULING

### Daily Lecture Notes 20-1

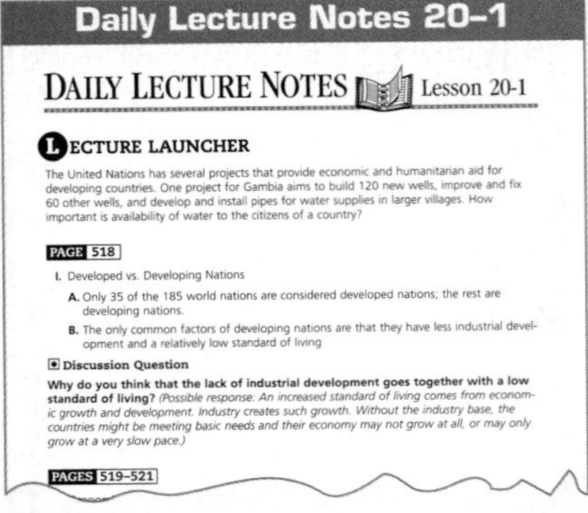

DAILY LECTURE NOTES Lesson 20-1

**LECTURE LAUNCHER**

The United Nations has several projects that provide economic and humanitarian aid for developing countries. One project for Gambia aims to build 120 new wells, improve and fix 60 other wells, and develop and install pipes for water supplies in larger villages. How important is availability of water to the citizens of a country?

PAGE 518

I. Developed vs. Developing Nations
   A. Only 35 of the 185 world nations are considered developed nations; the rest are developing nations.
   B. The only common factors of developing nations are that they have less industrial development and a relatively low standard of living

**Discussion Question**

**Why do you think that the lack of industrial development goes together with a low standard of living?** *(Possible response: An increased standard of living comes from economic growth and development. Industry creates such growth. Without the industry base, the countries might be meeting basic needs and their economy may not grow at all, or may only grow at a very slow pace.)*

PAGES 519–521

### Visual Instruction FIGURE 20.1

**Answer:** *Mexico's average per capita GDP is much larger—about 9 times greater—than that of Madagascar.*

## Developed vs. Developing Nations

**developed nations:** *nations with relatively high standards of living and economies based more on industry than on agriculture*

**developing nations:** *nations with little industrial development and relatively low standards of living*

Of the more than 185 nations in the world, only about 35 are considered **developed nations.** These nations include the United States, Canada, most European countries, Japan, Australia, and New Zealand.

The remaining parts of the world's population live in **developing nations.** These are nations with less industrial development and a relatively low standard of living. Within this general definition, however, nations differ in many ways. **Figure 20.1** compares two developing nations, Madagascar and Mexico. The average income per person in Mexico is only 30 percent that of the United States. Yet Mexico is much more developed and prosperous than almost all other developing nations.

Besides differences in the standard of living among developing nations, great differences often exist within a nation. For example, about 26 percent of India's population lives and works in urban areas, many of which are like those in developed nations. In rural India, however, many families live three to a room, often in mud houses. Only a fraction of these homes have running water and electricity.

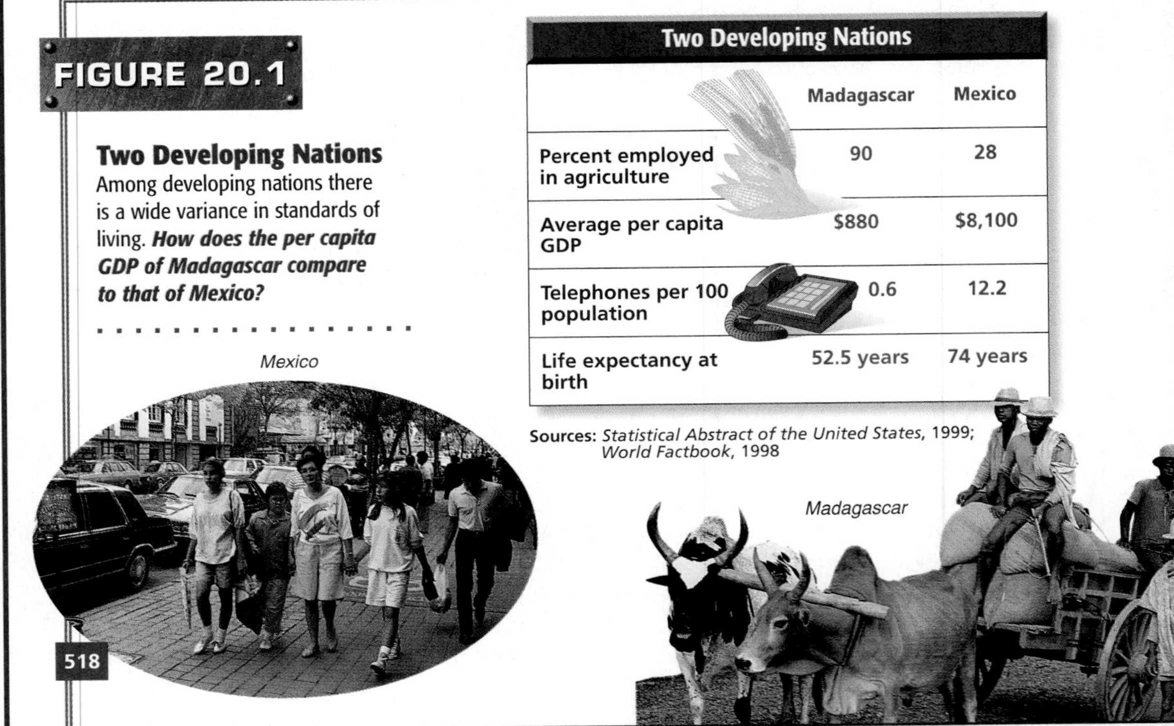


**FIGURE 20.1**

**Two Developing Nations**
Among developing nations there is a wide variance in standards of living. ***How does the per capita GDP of Madagascar compare to that of Mexico?***

**Two Developing Nations**

| | Madagascar | Mexico |
|---|---|---|
| Percent employed in agriculture | 90 | 28 |
| Average per capita GDP | $880 | $8,100 |
| Telephones per 100 population | 0.6 | 12.2 |
| Life expectancy at birth | 52.5 years | 74 years |

**Sources:** *Statistical Abstract of the United States*, 1999; *World Factbook*, 1998

518

### Meeting Special Needs

**Reading Disability** Students with various reading and organizational difficulties may have problems relating graphics and the main text. Before students read Section 1, ask them to review the graphics. Have students identify what the graphics illustrate. Then direct students to read the section, restate what the graphics illustrate, and suggest why the graphics were included in the section.

Refer to *Inclusion for the Social Studies Classroom Strategies and Activities* for students with different learning styles.

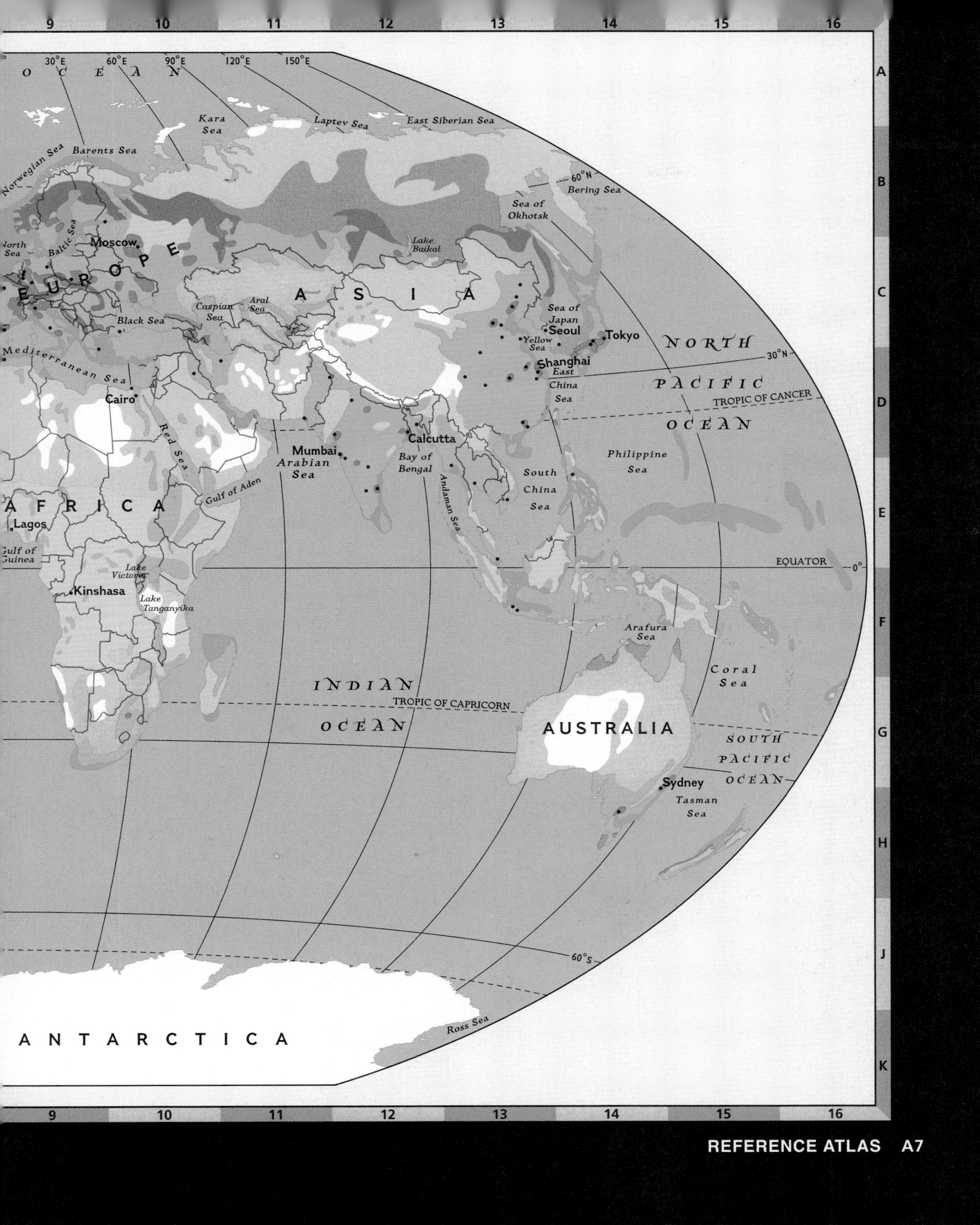

ASIA
EUROPE
AFRICA
AUSTRALIA
ANTARCTICA
Moscow
Cairo
Mumbai
Calcutta
Seoul
Tokyo
Shanghai
Lagos
Kinshasa
Sydney
Kara Sea
Laptev Sea
East Siberian Sea
Barents Sea
Norwegian Sea
Bering Sea
Sea of Okhotsk
Lake Baikal
Caspian Sea
Aral Sea
Black Sea
Mediterranean Sea
Red Sea
Gulf of Aden
Arabian Sea
Bay of Bengal
Andaman Sea
Sea of Japan
Yellow Sea
East China Sea
South China Sea
Philippine Sea
Arafura Sea
Coral Sea
Tasman Sea
Ross Sea
Lake Victoria
Lake Tanganyika
Gulf of Guinea
North Sea
Baltic Sea
NORTH PACIFIC OCEAN
SOUTH PACIFIC OCEAN
INDIAN OCEAN
TROPIC OF CANCER
TROPIC OF CAPRICORN
EQUATOR
30°E
60°E
90°E
120°E
150°E
60°N
30°N
0°
60°S

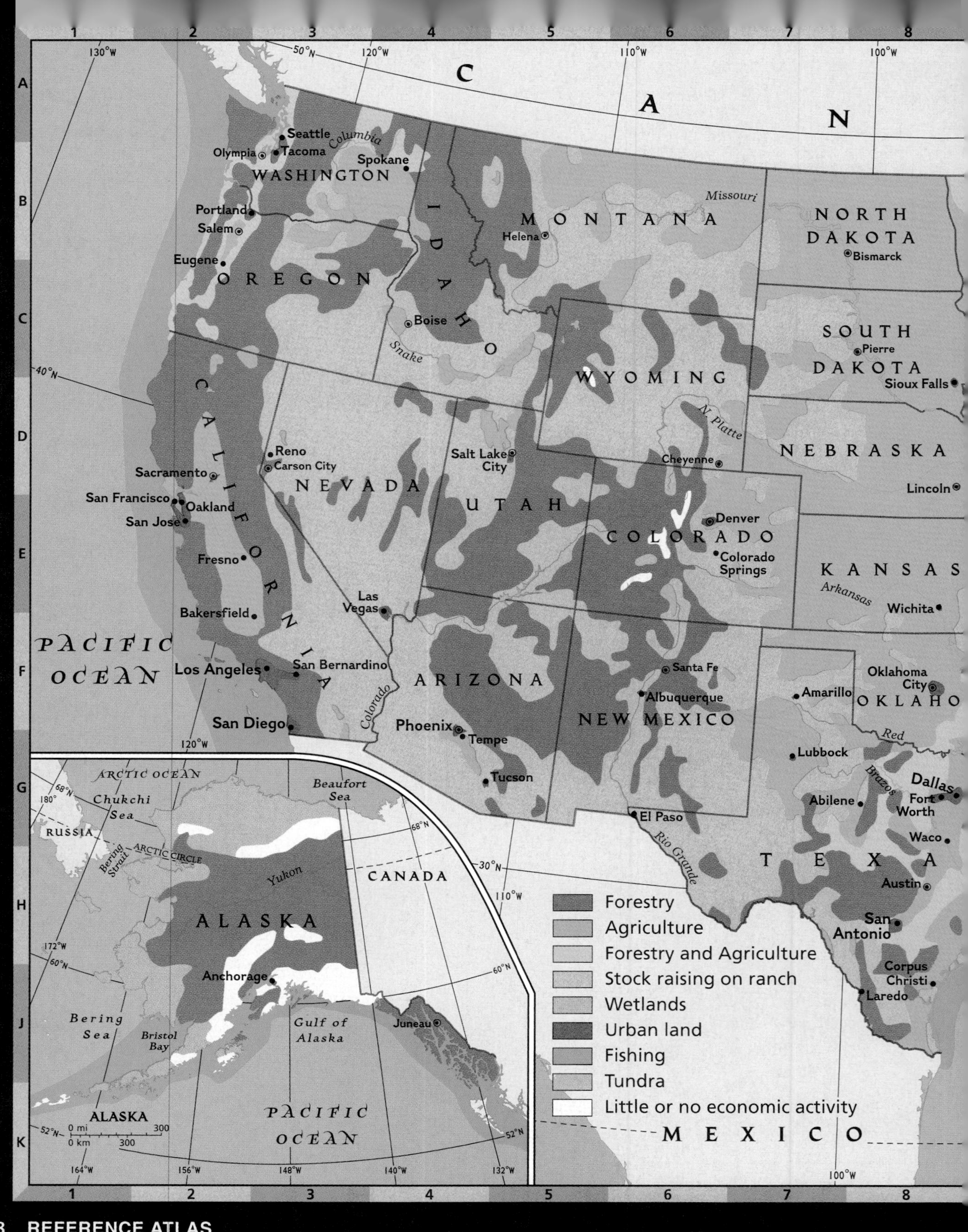

CANADA
PACIFIC OCEAN
WASHINGTON
OREGON
IDAHO
MONTANA
NORTH DAKOTA
SOUTH DAKOTA
WYOMING
NEBRASKA
NEVADA
UTAH
COLORADO
KANSAS
CALIFORNIA
ARIZONA
NEW MEXICO
OKLAHOMA
TEXAS
MEXICO
Seattle
Olympia
Tacoma
Spokane
Portland
Salem
Eugene
Helena
Bismarck
Boise
Pierre
Sioux Falls
Reno
Carson City
Salt Lake City
Cheyenne
Lincoln
Sacramento
San Francisco
Oakland
San Jose
Fresno
Denver
Colorado Springs
Las Vegas
Wichita
Bakersfield
Los Angeles
San Bernardino
Santa Fe
Albuquerque
Amarillo
Oklahoma City
San Diego
Phoenix
Tempe
Tucson
Lubbock
Dallas
Fort Worth
Abilene
El Paso
Waco
Austin
San Antonio
Corpus Christi
Laredo
Columbia
Missouri
Snake
N. Platte
Arkansas
Colorado
Red
Brazos
Rio Grande
ARCTIC OCEAN
Chukchi Sea
Beaufort Sea
RUSSIA
Bering Strait
ARCTIC CIRCLE
Yukon
CANADA
ALASKA
Anchorage
Juneau
Bering Sea
Bristol Bay
Gulf of Alaska
PACIFIC OCEAN
ALASKA
0 mi 300
0 km 300
Forestry
Agriculture
Forestry and Agriculture
Stock raising on ranch
Wetlands
Urban land
Fishing
Tundra
Little or no economic activity

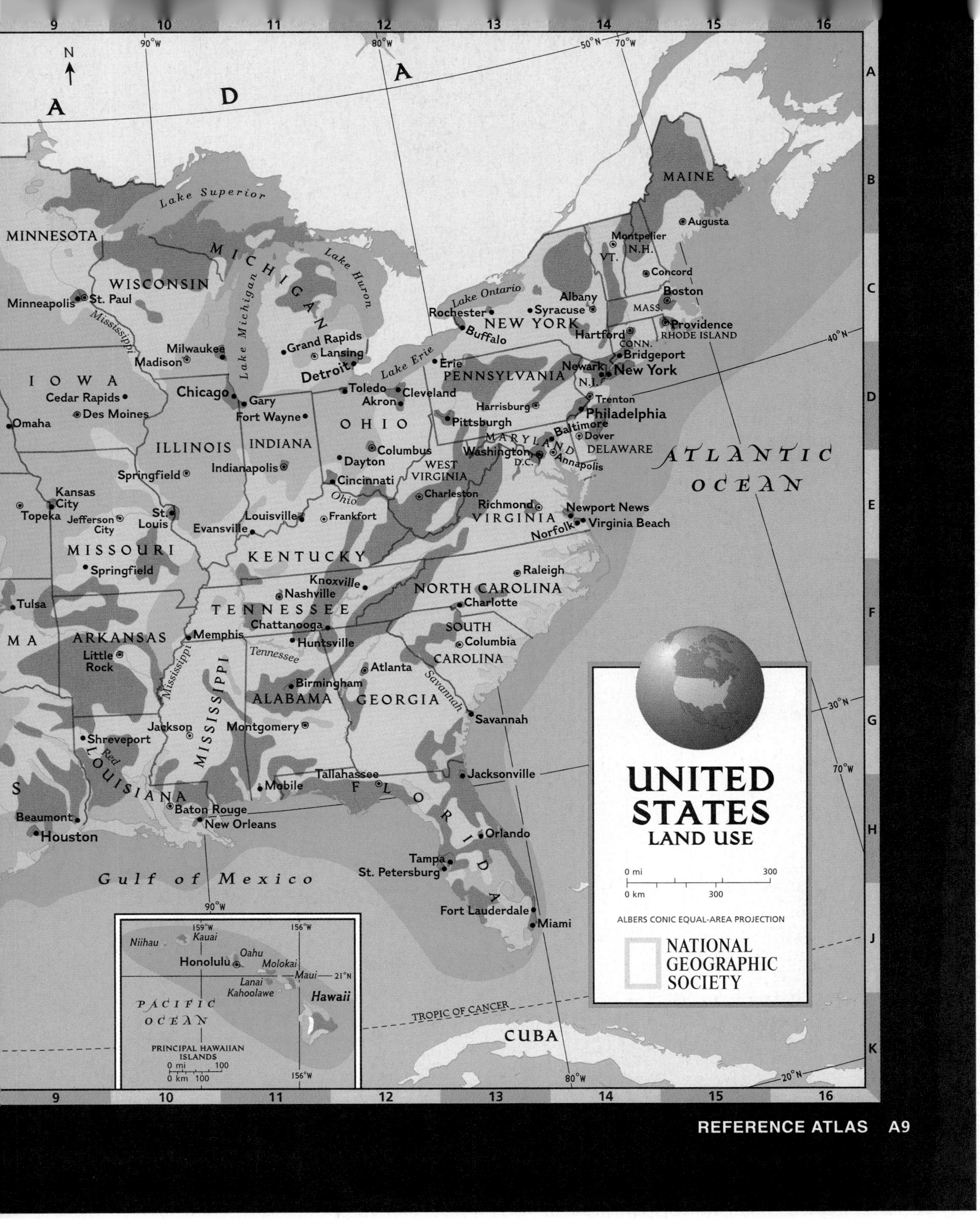
UNITED STATES
LAND USE
ALBERS CONIC EQUAL-AREA PROJECTION
NATIONAL GEOGRAPHIC SOCIETY
ATLANTIC OCEAN
Gulf of Mexico
CUBA
PACIFIC OCEAN
PRINCIPAL HAWAIIAN ISLANDS
MAINE
NEW YORK
PENNSYLVANIA
OHIO
MICHIGAN
WISCONSIN
MINNESOTA
IOWA
ILLINOIS
INDIANA
KENTUCKY
TENNESSEE
NORTH CAROLINA
SOUTH CAROLINA
GEORGIA
FLORIDA
ALABAMA
MISSISSIPPI
LOUISIANA
ARKANSAS
MISSOURI
VIRGINIA
WEST VIRGINIA
MARYLAND
DELAWARE
RHODE ISLAND
TROPIC OF CANCER

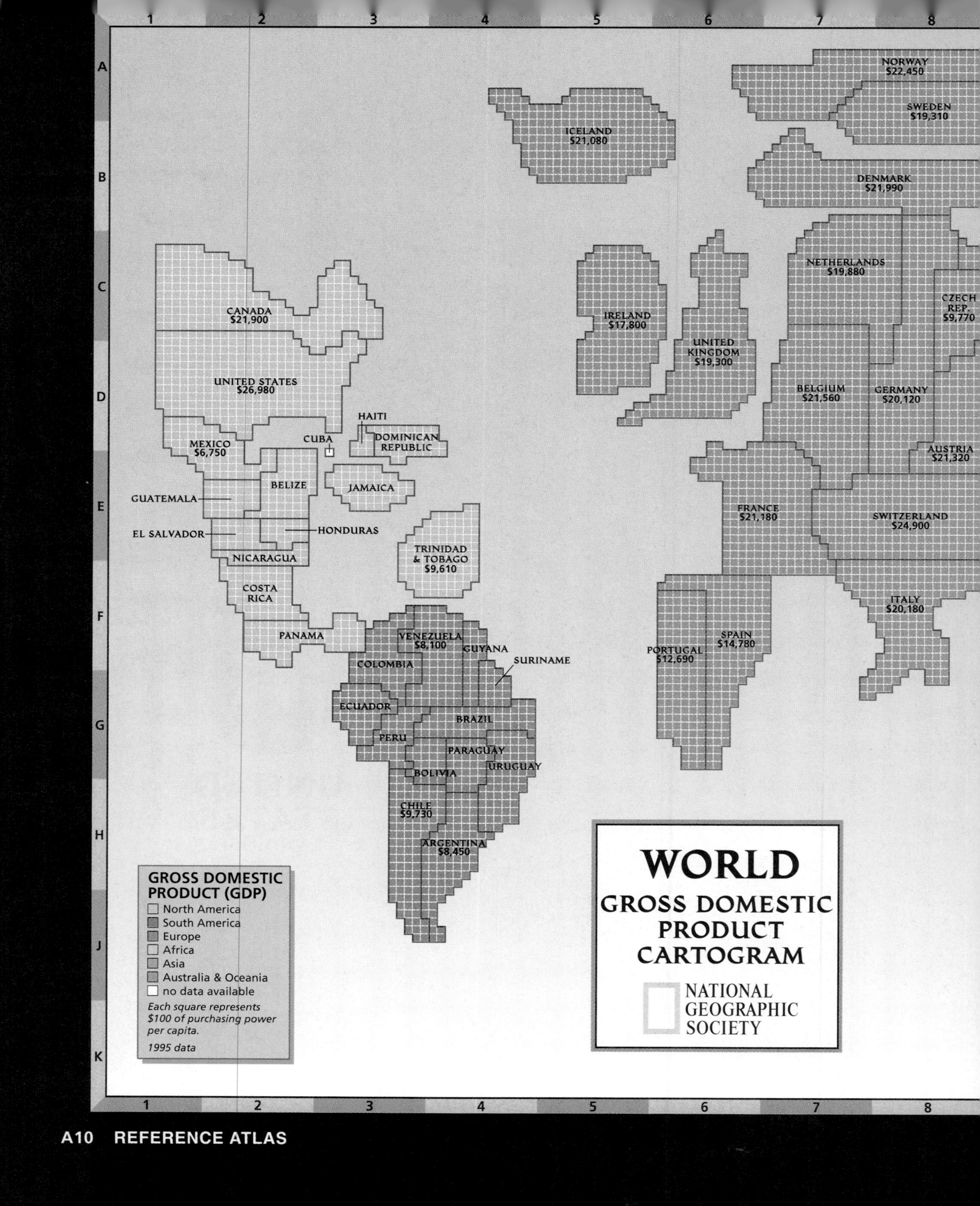
WORLD
GROSS DOMESTIC PRODUCT CARTOGRAM
NATIONAL GEOGRAPHIC SOCIETY
GROSS DOMESTIC PRODUCT (GDP)
North America
South America
Europe
Africa
Asia
Australia & Oceania
no data available
Each square represents $100 of purchasing power per capita.
1995 data
CANADA $21,900
UNITED STATES $26,980
MEXICO $6,750
CUBA
HAITI
DOMINICAN REPUBLIC
JAMAICA
BELIZE
GUATEMALA
EL SALVADOR
HONDURAS
NICARAGUA
COSTA RICA
PANAMA
TRINIDAD & TOBAGO $9,610
VENEZUELA $8,100
GUYANA
SURINAME
COLOMBIA
ECUADOR
PERU
BRAZIL
PARAGUAY
URUGUAY
BOLIVIA
CHILE $9,730
ARGENTINA $8,450
ICELAND $21,080
NORWAY $22,450
SWEDEN $19,310
DENMARK $21,990
IRELAND $17,800
UNITED KINGDOM $19,300
NETHERLANDS $19,880
CZECH REP. $9,770
BELGIUM $21,560
GERMANY $20,120
AUSTRIA $21,320
FRANCE $21,180
SWITZERLAND $24,900
ITALY $20,180
SPAIN $14,780
PORTUGAL $12,690

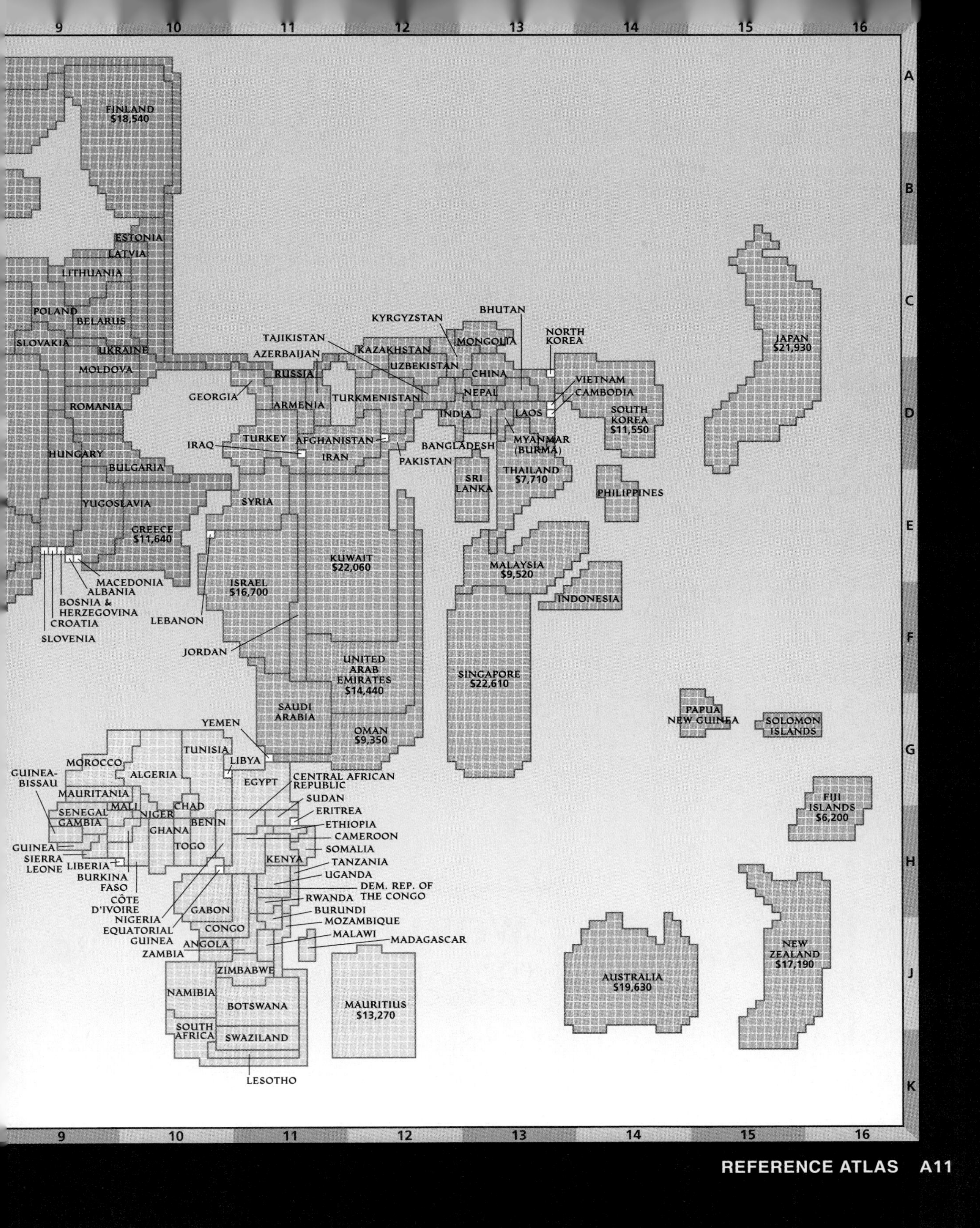
9
10
11
12
13
14
15
16
A
B
C
D
E
F
G
H
J
K
FINLAND
$18,540
ESTONIA
LATVIA
LITHUANIA
POLAND
BELARUS
SLOVAKIA
UKRAINE
MOLDOVA
ROMANIA
HUNGARY
BULGARIA
YUGOSLAVIA
GREECE
$11,640
MACEDONIA
ALBANIA
BOSNIA &
HERZEGOVINA
CROATIA
SLOVENIA
LEBANON
ISRAEL
$16,700
JORDAN
SYRIA
TURKEY
IRAQ
GEORGIA
ARMENIA
RUSSIA
AZERBAIJAN
TAJIKISTAN
KYRGYZSTAN
KAZAKHSTAN
UZBEKISTAN
TURKMENISTAN
AFGHANISTAN
IRAN
PAKISTAN
KUWAIT
$22,060
UNITED
ARAB
EMIRATES
$14,440
SAUDI
ARABIA
OMAN
$9,350
YEMEN
BHUTAN
MONGOLIA
CHINA
NEPAL
INDIA
BANGLADESH
SRI
LANKA
LAOS
MYANMAR
(BURMA)
THAILAND
$7,710
NORTH
KOREA
VIETNAM
CAMBODIA
SOUTH
KOREA
$11,550
JAPAN
$21,930
PHILIPPINES
MALAYSIA
$9,520
INDONESIA
SINGAPORE
$22,610
PAPUA
NEW GUINEA
SOLOMON
ISLANDS
FIJI
ISLANDS
$6,200
NEW
ZEALAND
$17,190
AUSTRALIA
$19,630
MOROCCO
TUNISIA
LIBYA
ALGERIA
EGYPT
GUINEA-
BISSAU
MAURITANIA
MALI
SENEGAL
GAMBIA
NIGER
CHAD
BENIN
GHANA
TOGO
GUINEA
SIERRA
LEONE
LIBERIA
BURKINA
FASO
CÔTE
D'IVOIRE
NIGERIA
EQUATORIAL
GUINEA
CENTRAL AFRICAN
REPUBLIC
SUDAN
ERITREA
ETHIOPIA
CAMEROON
SOMALIA
KENYA
TANZANIA
UGANDA
DEM. REP. OF
THE CONGO
RWANDA
BURUNDI
MOZAMBIQUE
MALAWI
MADAGASCAR
GABON
CONGO
ANGOLA
ZAMBIA
ZIMBABWE
NAMIBIA
BOTSWANA
SOUTH
AFRICA
SWAZILAND
LESOTHO
MAURITIUS
$13,270

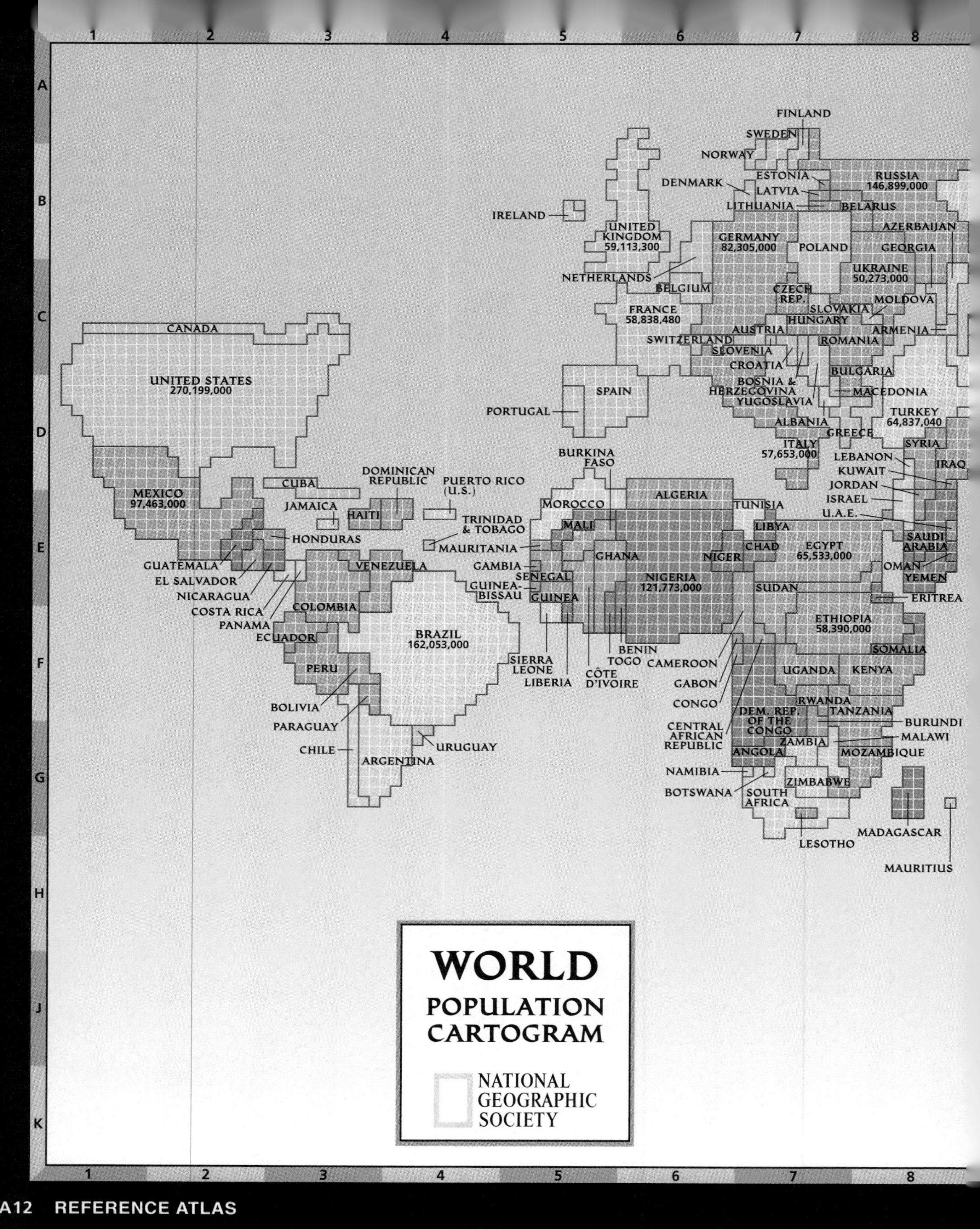
WORLD
POPULATION
CARTOGRAM
NATIONAL
GEOGRAPHIC
SOCIETY
FINLAND
SWEDEN
NORWAY
ESTONIA
RUSSIA
146,899,000
DENMARK
LATVIA
LITHUANIA
BELARUS
IRELAND
UNITED KINGDOM
59,113,300
GERMANY
82,305,000
POLAND
AZERBAIJAN
GEORGIA
UKRAINE
50,273,000
NETHERLANDS
BELGIUM
CZECH REP.
MOLDOVA
FRANCE
58,838,480
SLOVAKIA
HUNGARY
ARMENIA
AUSTRIA
SWITZERLAND
ROMANIA
SLOVENIA
CROATIA
BULGARIA
BOSNIA &
HERZEGOVINA
YUGOSLAVIA
MACEDONIA
TURKEY
64,837,040
SPAIN
PORTUGAL
ALBANIA
GREECE
ITALY
57,653,000
SYRIA
LEBANON
IRAQ
KUWAIT
JORDAN
ISRAEL
U.A.E.
CANADA
UNITED STATES
270,199,000
MEXICO
97,463,000
CUBA
JAMAICA
HAITI
DOMINICAN REPUBLIC
PUERTO RICO (U.S.)
TRINIDAD & TOBAGO
HONDURAS
GUATEMALA
EL SALVADOR
NICARAGUA
COSTA RICA
PANAMA
VENEZUELA
COLOMBIA
ECUADOR
PERU
BRAZIL
162,053,000
BOLIVIA
PARAGUAY
CHILE
ARGENTINA
URUGUAY
BURKINA FASO
MOROCCO
ALGERIA
TUNISIA
LIBYA
MALI
MAURITANIA
GAMBIA
SENEGAL
GUINEA-BISSAU
GUINEA
GHANA
NIGER
CHAD
EGYPT
65,533,000
SAUDI ARABIA
OMAN
YEMEN
NIGERIA
121,773,000
SUDAN
ERITREA
ETHIOPIA
58,390,000
SOMALIA
SIERRA LEONE
LIBERIA
CÔTE D'IVOIRE
BENIN
TOGO
CAMEROON
GABON
CONGO
CENTRAL AFRICAN REPUBLIC
UGANDA
KENYA
RWANDA
DEM. REP. OF THE CONGO
TANZANIA
BURUNDI
ZAMBIA
MALAWI
ANGOLA
MOZAMBIQUE
NAMIBIA
BOTSWANA
ZIMBABWE
SOUTH AFRICA
LESOTHO
MADAGASCAR
MAURITIUS

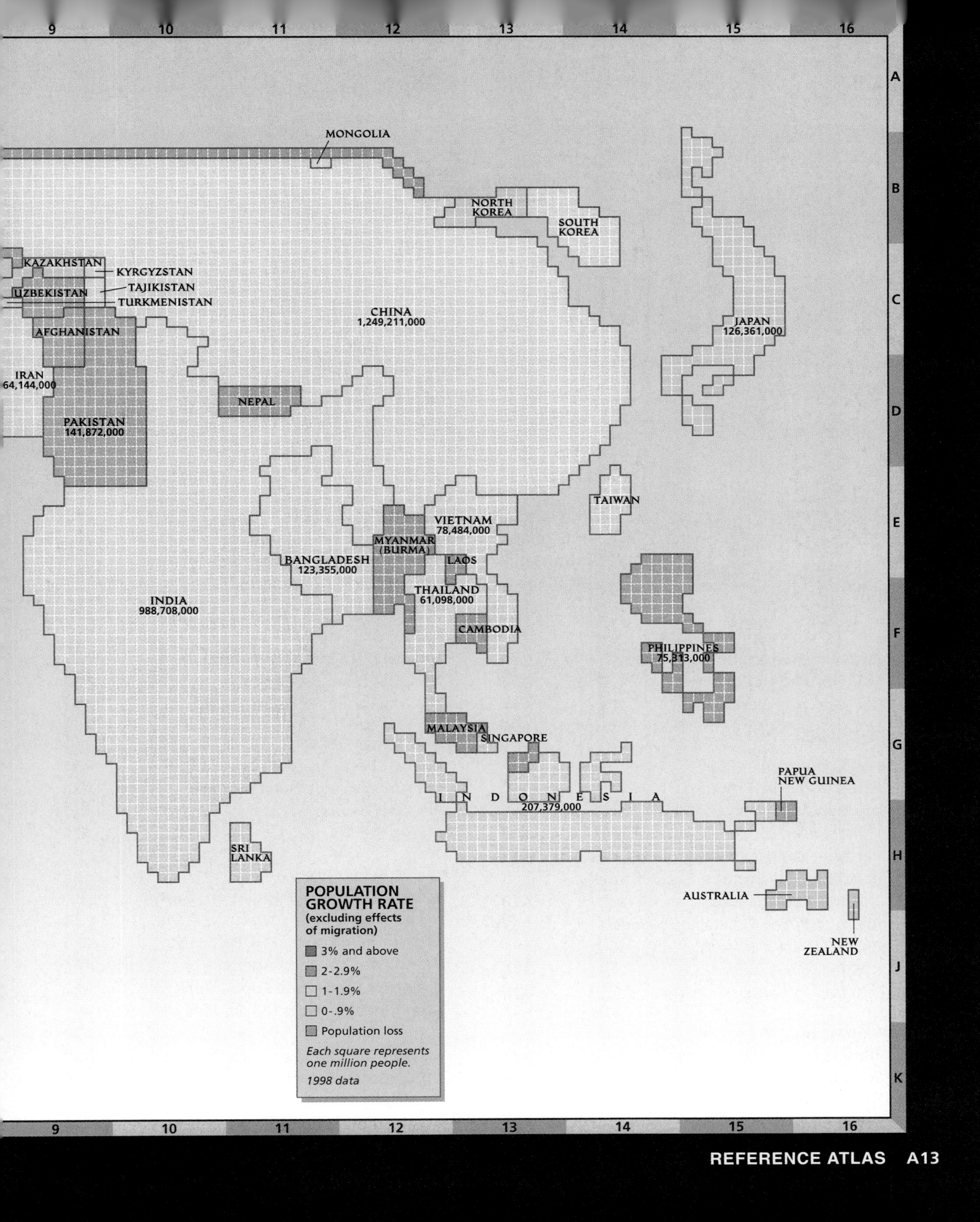

MONGOLIA
NORTH KOREA
SOUTH KOREA
KAZAKHSTAN
KYRGYZSTAN
UZBEKISTAN
TAJIKISTAN
TURKMENISTAN
CHINA
1,249,211,000
JAPAN
126,361,000
AFGHANISTAN
IRAN
64,144,000
NEPAL
PAKISTAN
141,872,000
TAIWAN
VIETNAM
78,484,000
MYANMAR (BURMA)
BANGLADESH
123,355,000
LAOS
THAILAND
61,098,000
INDIA
988,708,000
CAMBODIA
PHILIPPINES
75,313,000
MALAYSIA
SINGAPORE
PAPUA NEW GUINEA
I N D O N E S I A
207,379,000
SRI LANKA
AUSTRALIA
NEW ZEALAND
POPULATION GROWTH RATE
(excluding effects of migration)
3% and above
2-2.9%
1-1.9%
0-.9%
Population loss
Each square represents one million people.
1998 data
9 10 11 12 13 14 15 16
A B C D E F G H J K

## Contents

The data and forecasts for the graphs, tables, and charts in the Databank are based on information from Standard & Poor's. View the ett.glencoe.com Web site for data updates.

## The American People

### U.S. Population Projections, 2000–2050

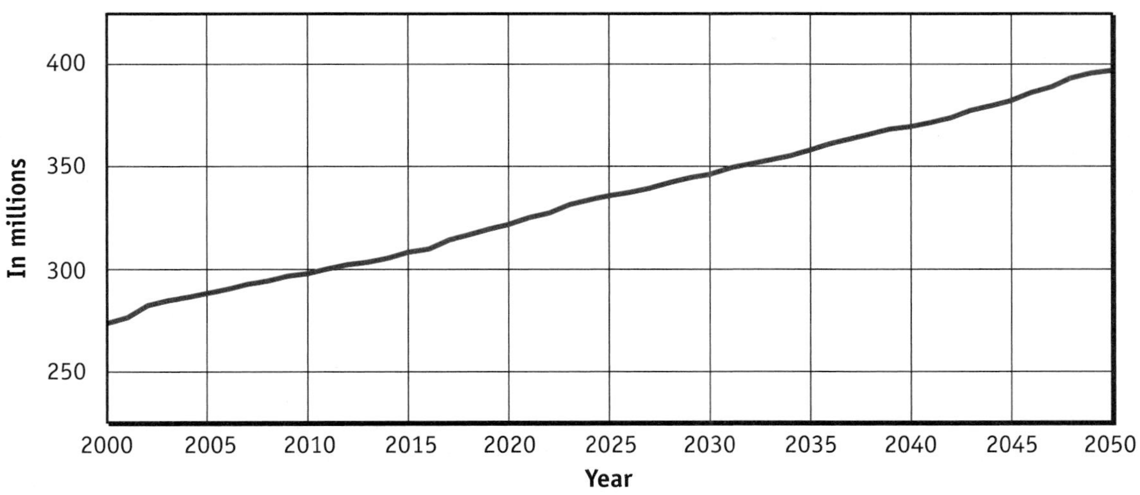


**Source:** U.S. Bureau of the Census

### Civilian Labor Force, 1950–2000

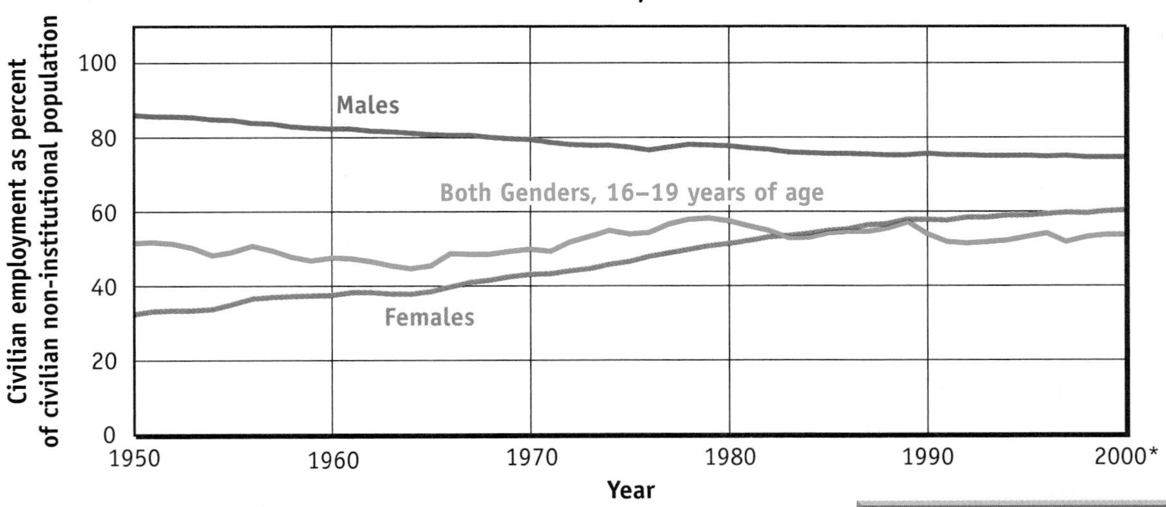


**Source:** Department of Labor, Bureau of Labor Statistics
*Estimate

**ECONOMICS Online**

Visit ett.glencoe.com and click on ***Textbook Updates—Databank*** for an update of the data.

STANDARD & POOR'S

## The American People

### Hours and Earnings in Private Industries, 1960–1999

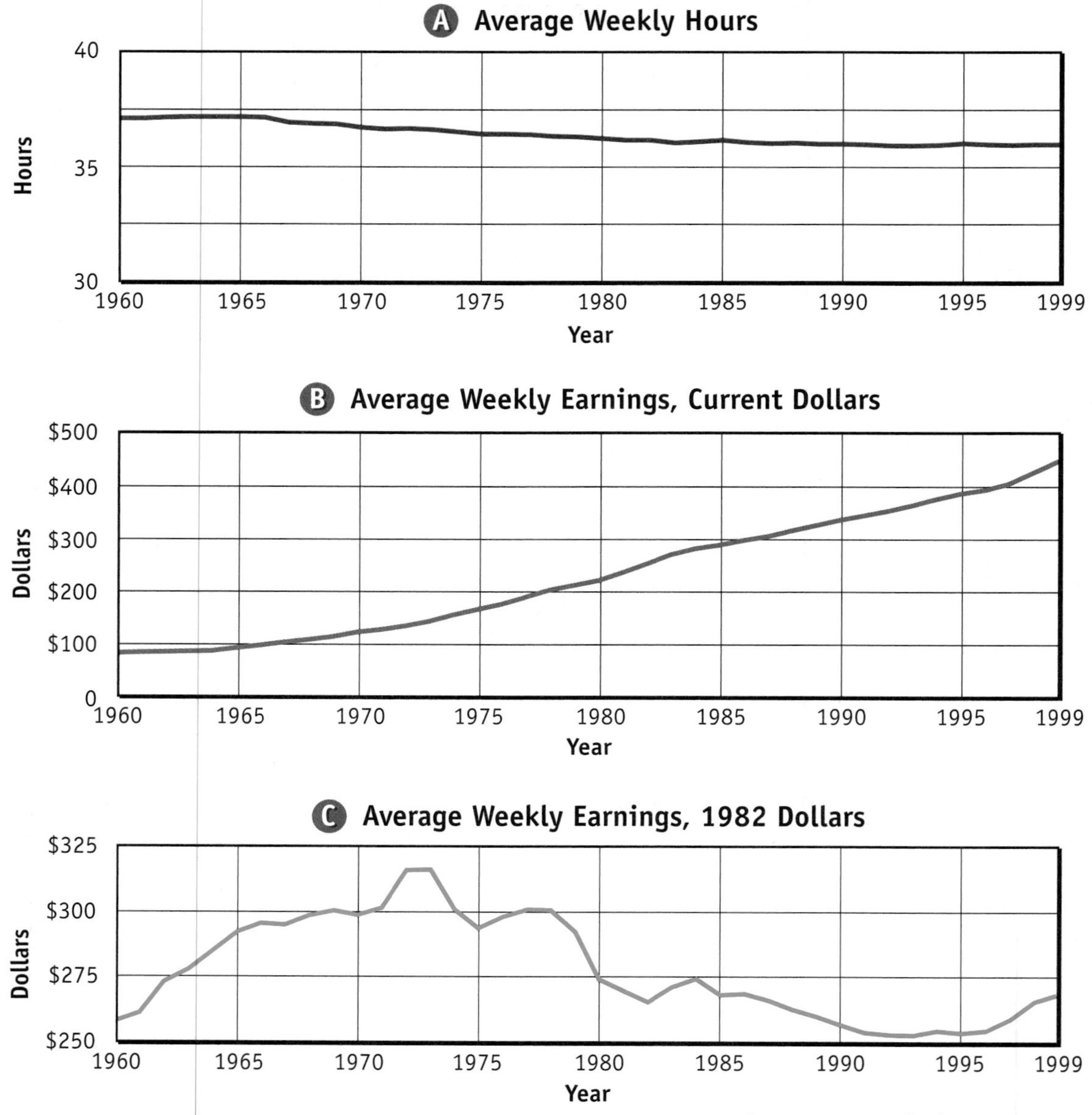

#### A Average Weekly Hours

Hours: 40, 35, 30
Year: 1960, 1965, 1970, 1975, 1980, 1985, 1990, 1995, 1999

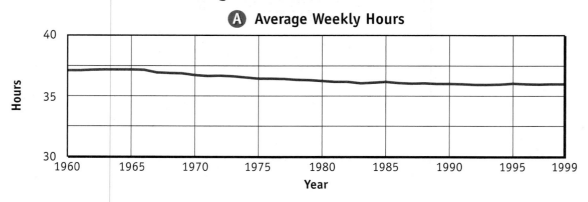

#### B Average Weekly Earnings, Current Dollars

Dollars: $500, $400, $300, $200, $100, 0
Year: 1960, 1965, 1970, 1975, 1980, 1985, 1990, 1995, 1999

#### C Average Weekly Earnings, 1982 Dollars

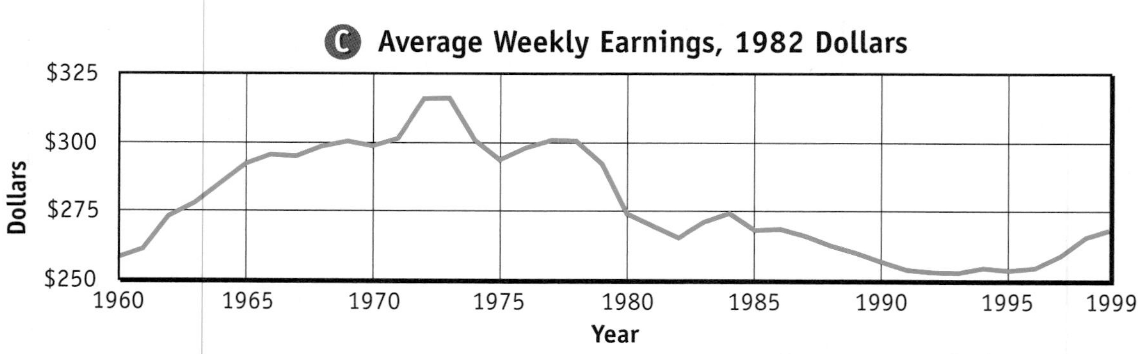


**Source:** Bureau of Labor Statistics

**ECONOMICS Online**

Visit ett.glencoe.com and click on *Textbook Updates—Databank* for an update of the data.

STANDARD & POOR'S

## The U.S. Economy

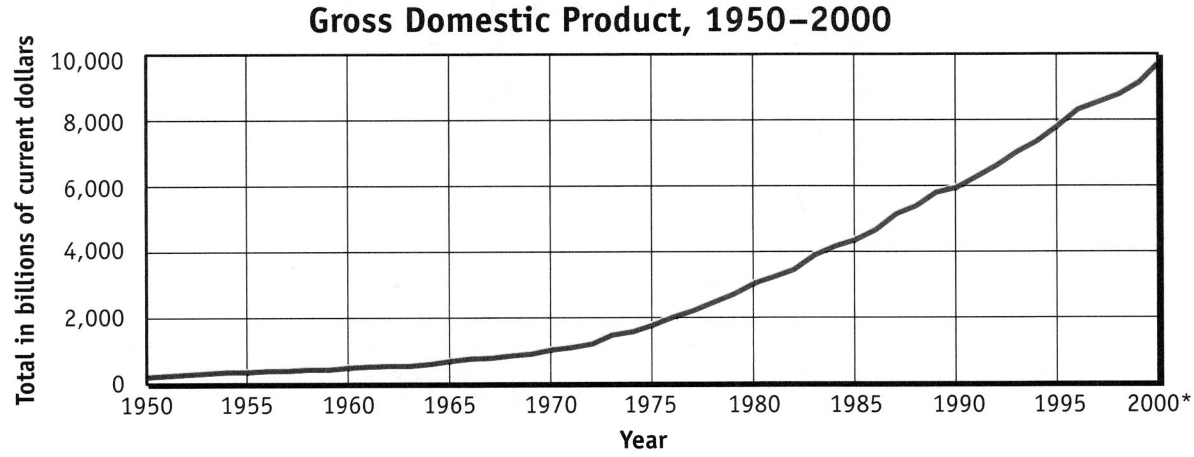


**Source:** U.S. Department of Commerce
*Estimate

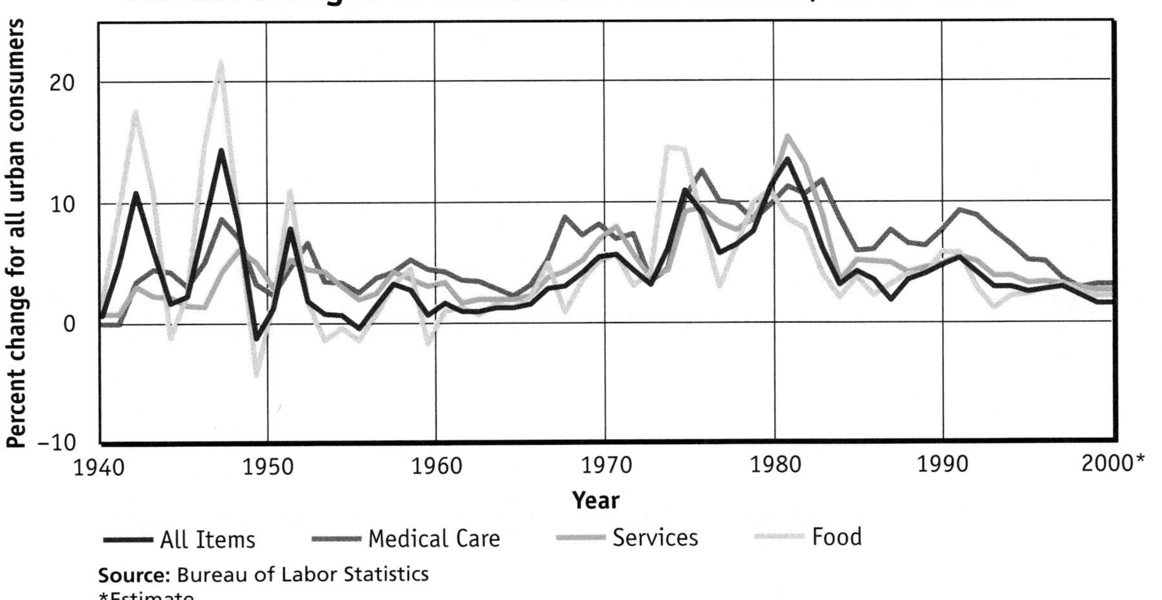


**Source:** Bureau of Labor Statistics
*Estimate

Visit ett.glencoe.com and click on ***Textbook Updates—Databank*** for an update of the data.

## The U.S. Economy

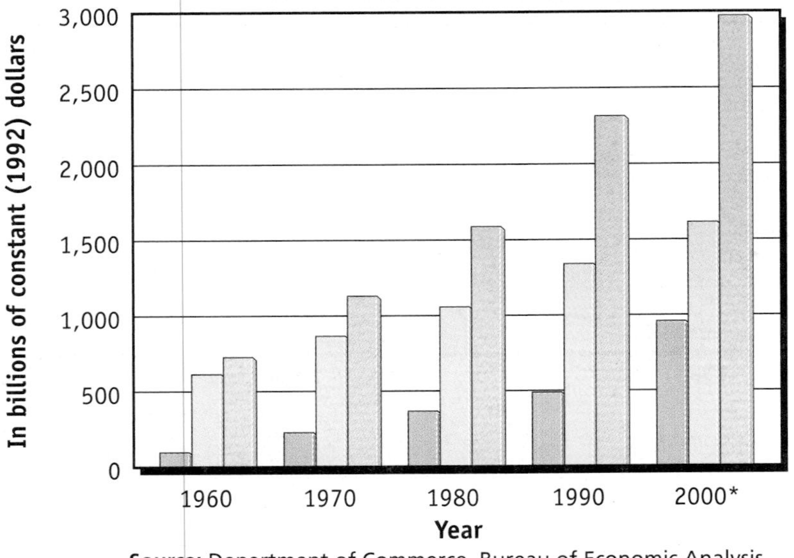


**Source:** Department of Commerce, Bureau of Economic Analysis

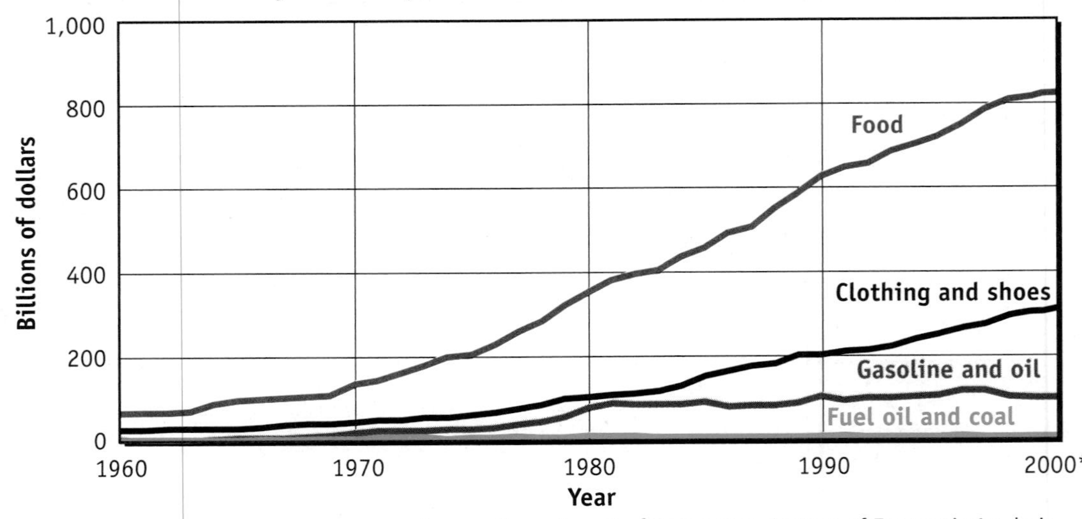


**Source:** Department of Commerce, Bureau of Economic Analysis
*Estimate

**ECONOMICS Online**

Visit ett.glencoe.com and click on ***Textbook Updates—Databank*** for an update of the data.

## The U.S. Economy

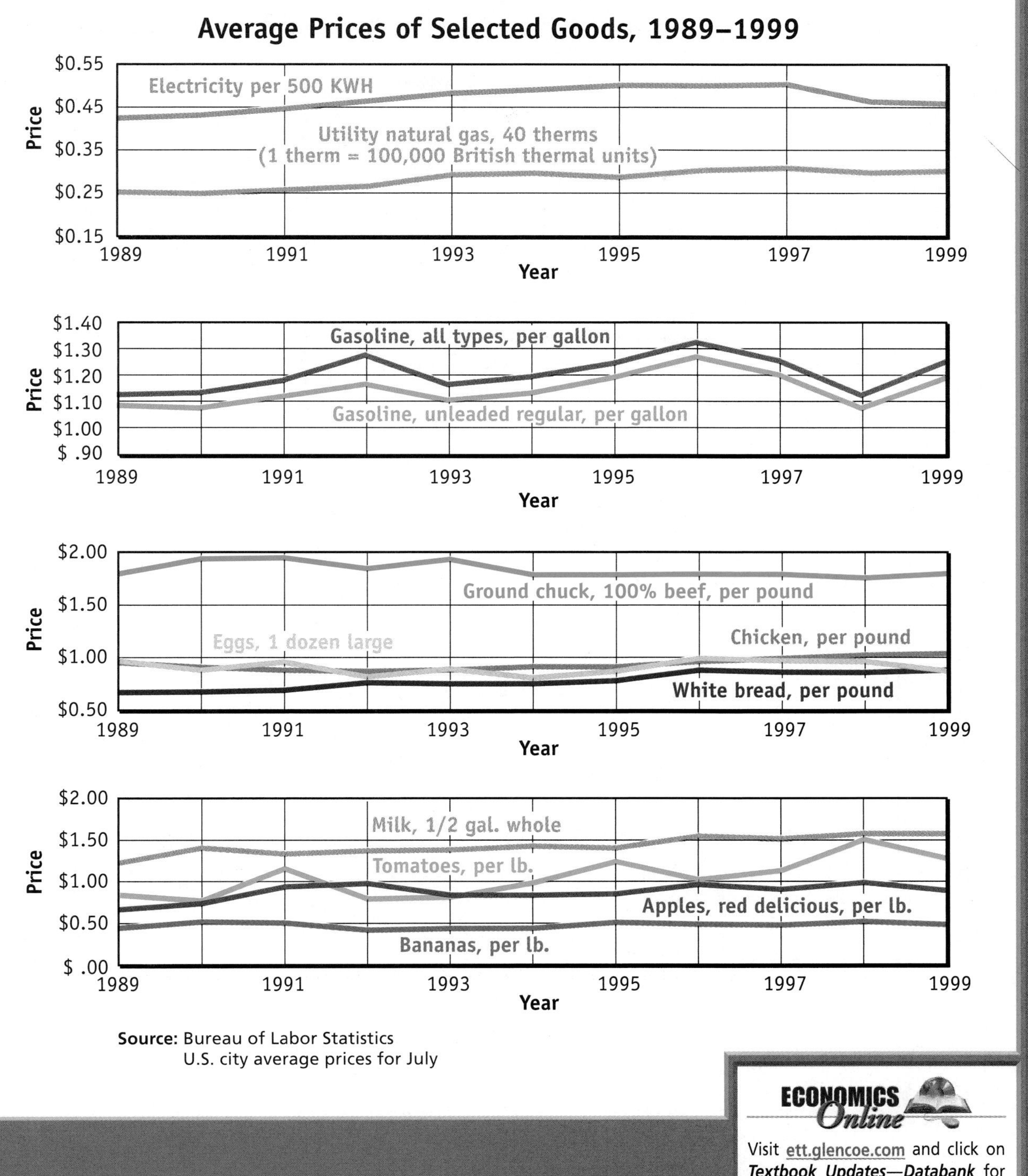


**Source:** Bureau of Labor Statistics
U.S. city average prices for July

**ECONOMICS Online**

Visit ett.glencoe.com and click on ***Textbook Updates—Databank*** for an update of the data.

STANDARD & POOR'S

## The U.S. Economy

### Business Sector: Changes in Productivity & Related Data, 1960–2000

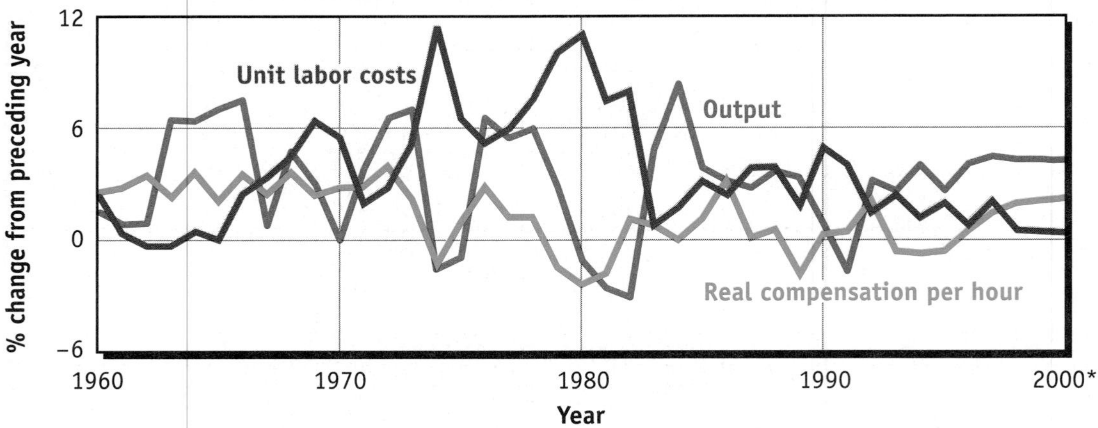


**Source:** Bureau of Labor Statistics
*Estimate

### Inflation in Consumer Prices, 1915–2000

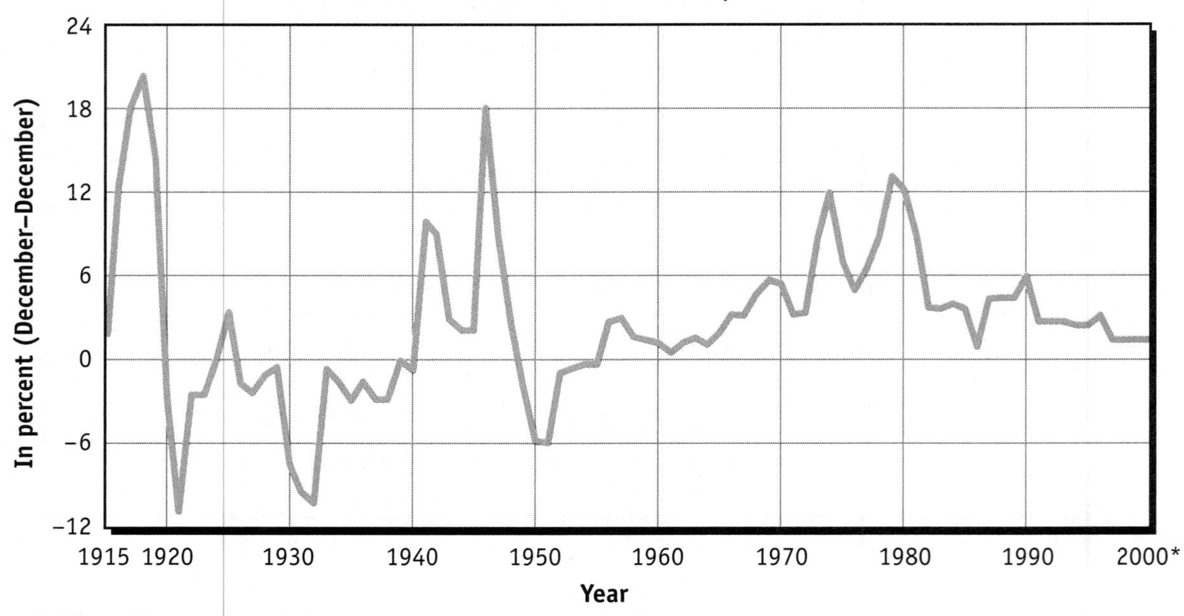


**Source:** Department of Commerce
*Estimate

**ECONOMICS Online**

Visit ett.glencoe.com and click on ***Textbook Updates—Databank*** for an update of the data.

# The Government Sector

## Federal Government Expenditures, 1949–1999

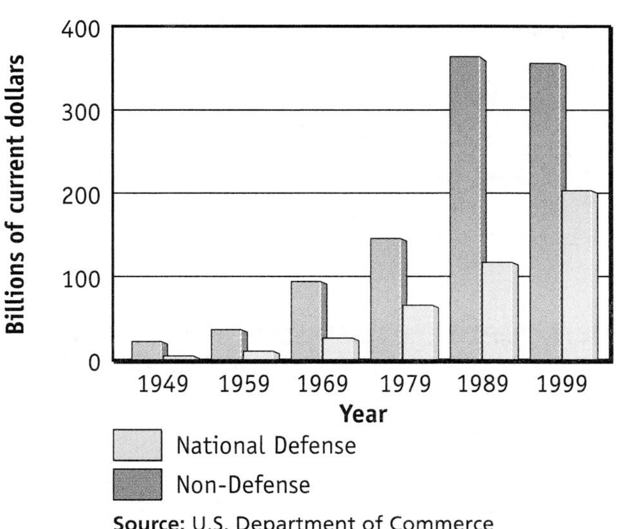


National Defense

Non-Defense

**Source:** U.S. Department of Commerce

## Total Government Expenditures, 1949–1999

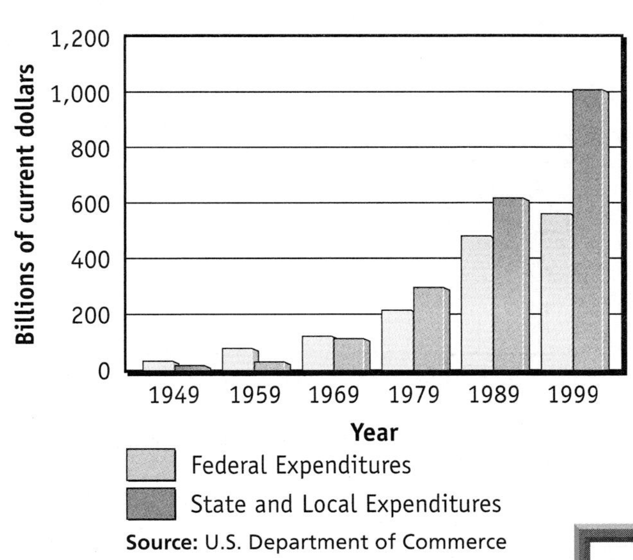


Federal Expenditures

State and Local Expenditures

**Source:** U.S. Department of Commerce

**ECONOMICS Online**

Visit ett.glencoe.com and click on ***Textbook Updates—Databank*** for an update of the data.

# The Government Sector

## Federal Government Net Receipts and Net Outlays, 1950–2000

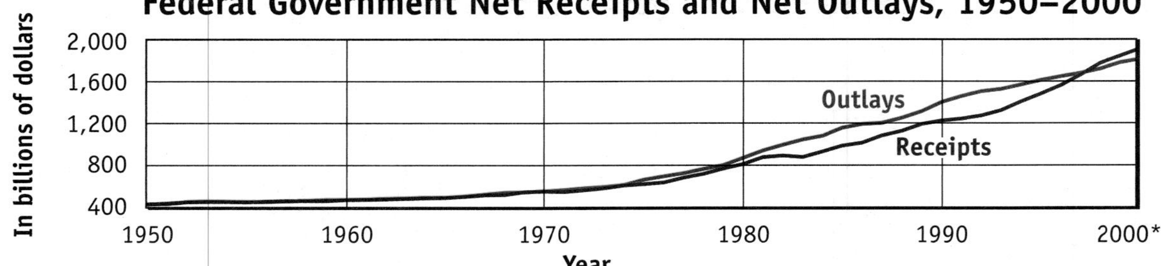


**Source:** *Economic Report of the President*, various editions
*Estimate

## Federal Debt, Total Outstanding, 1960–2000**

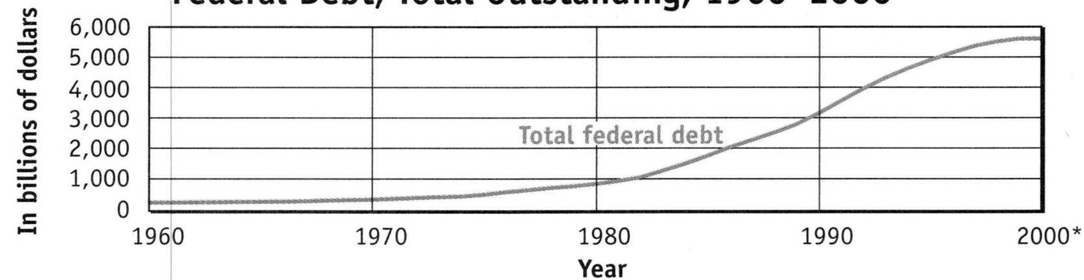


**Source:** U.S. Bureau of the Census
*Estimate
**Includes federal debt held by the public and by the federal government

## National Debt Per Capita, 1940–2000**

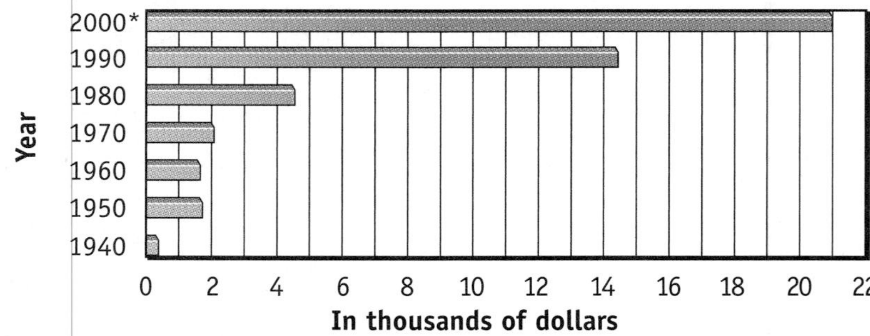


**Sources:** U.S. Bureau of the Census; U.S. Bureau of Public Debt
*Estimate
**Includes federal debt held by the public and by the federal government

**ECONOMICS Online**

Visit ett.glencoe.com and click on ***Textbook Updates—Databank*** for an update of the data.

## The Government Sector

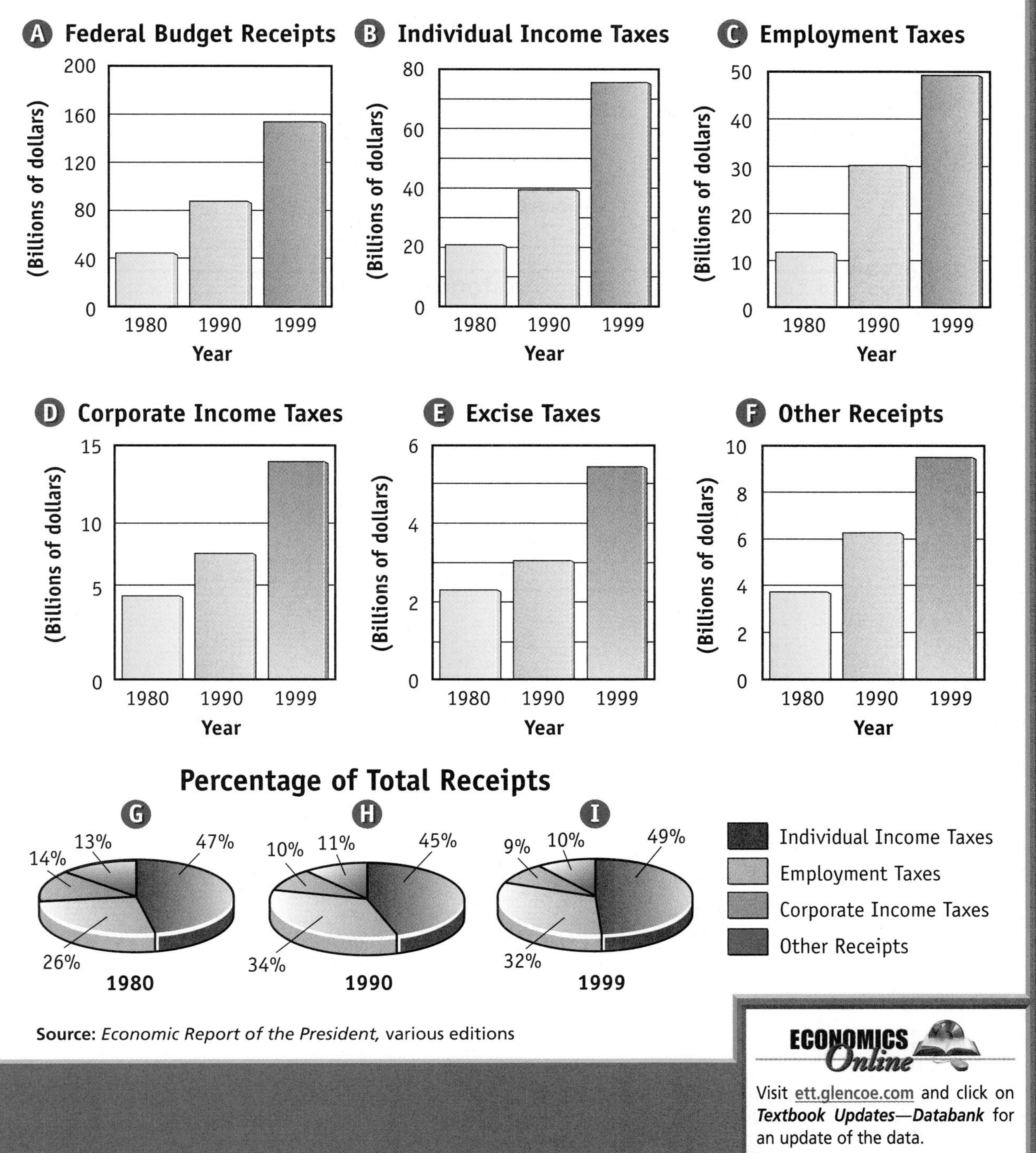


**Source:** *Economic Report of the President,* various editions

**ECONOMICS Online**

Visit ett.glencoe.com and click on ***Textbook Updates—Databank*** for an update of the data.

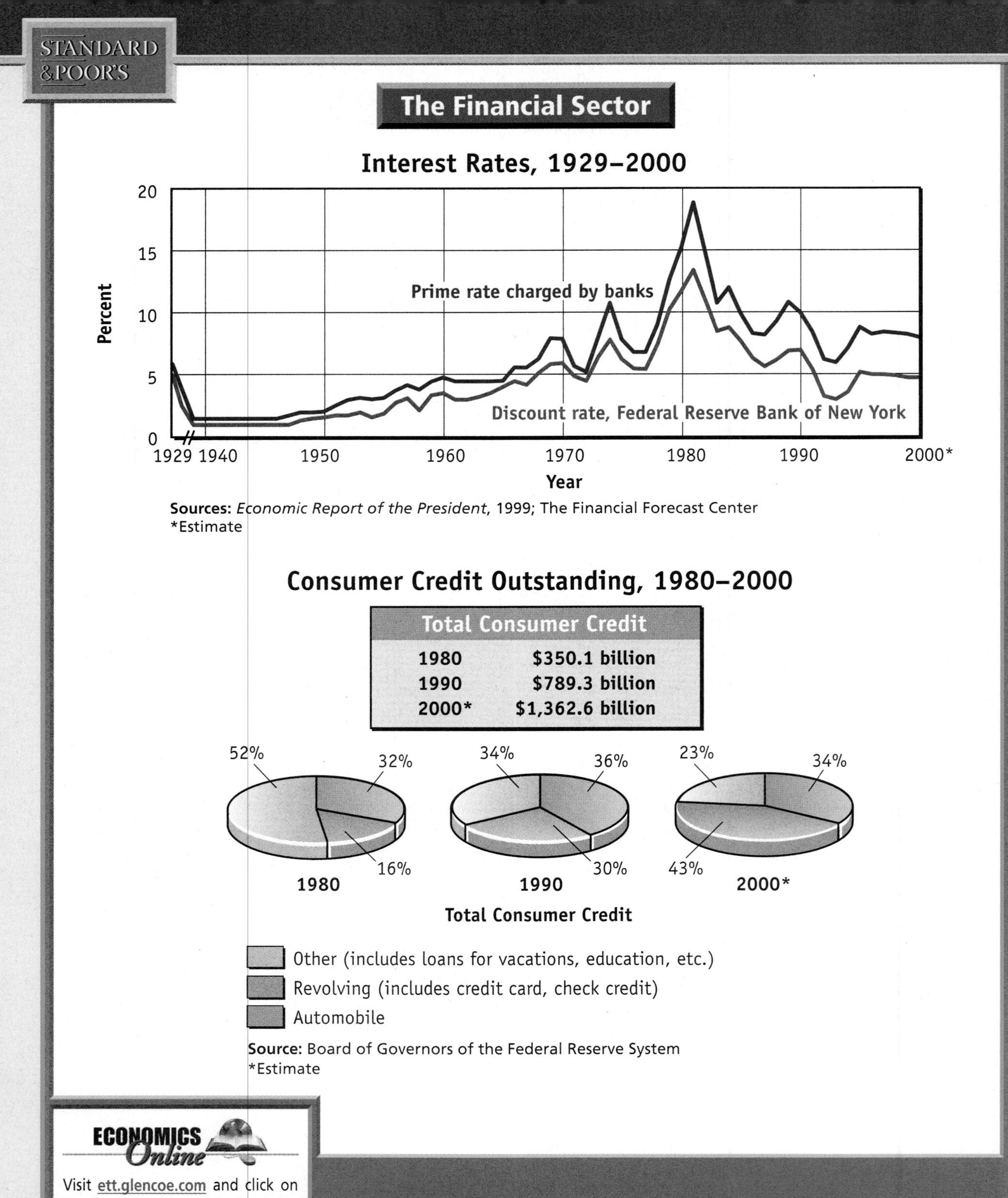


ECONOMICS Online

Visit ett.glencoe.com and click on *Textbook Updates—Databank* for an update of the data.

# The Financial Sector

## Personal Saving, 1960–2000

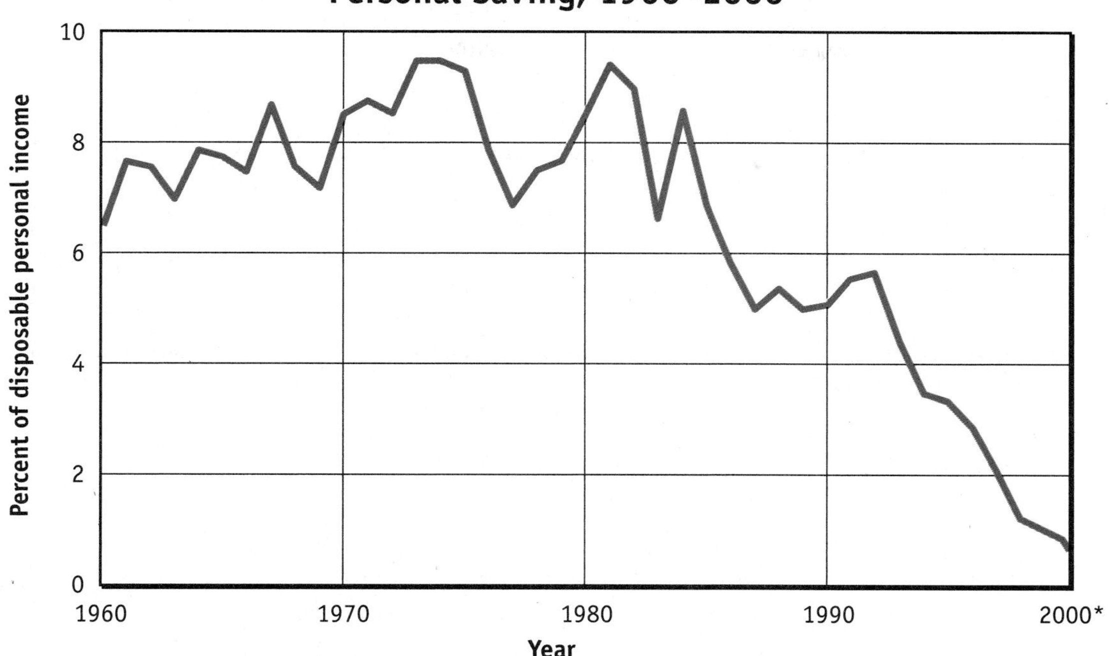


**Source:** U.S. Department of Commerce, Bureau of Economic Analysis
*Estimate

## Money Stock, 1970–2000

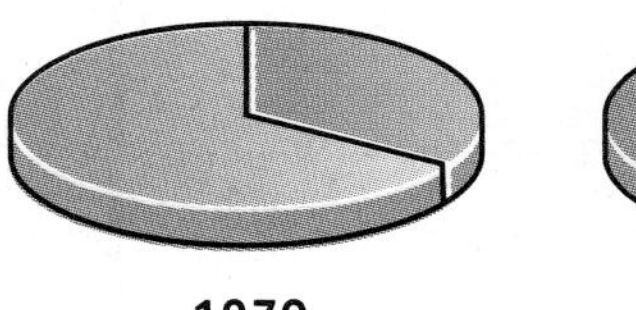

**1970**
M1 = $214.4
M2 = $626.5

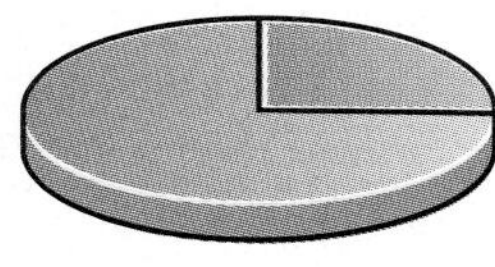

**1980**
M1 = $408.9
M2 = $1,601.1

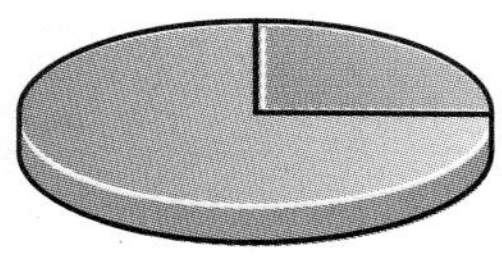

**1990**
M1 = $825.8
M2 = $3,279.6

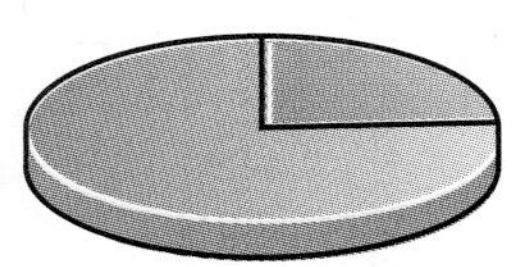

**2000***
M1 = $1,108.6
M2 = $4,627.7

**In billions of dollars**

**M1** consists of all currency and checkable deposits.

**M2** consists of M1 plus noncheckable savings accounts, money market deposit accounts, time deposits, and money market mutual funds.

**Source:** Board of Governors of the Federal Reserve System
*Estimate

Visit ett.glencoe.com and click on ***Textbook Updates—Databank*** for an update of the data.

STANDARD &POOR'S

## The Global Economy

### Economic Groups: Population, Exports, and GDP, 1998

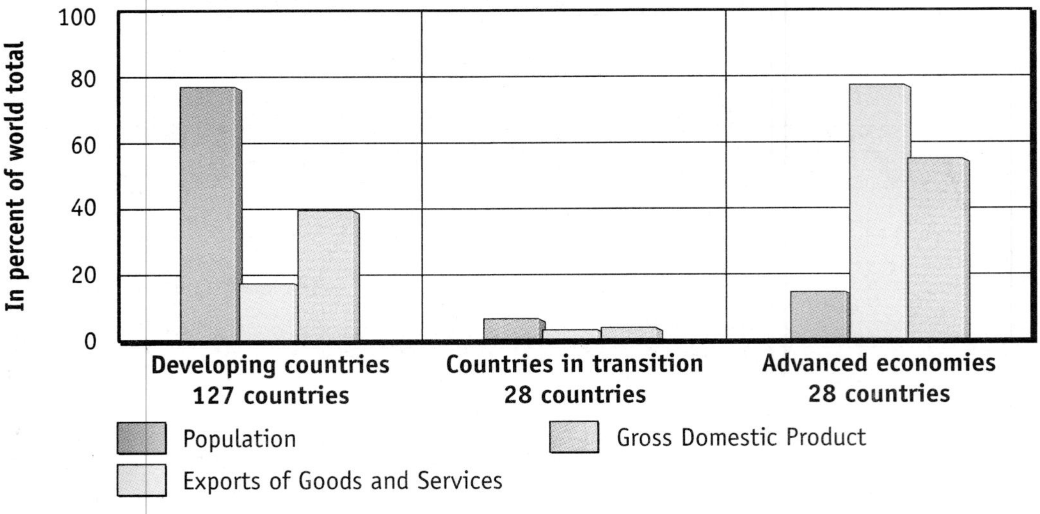


**Source:** International Monetary Fund

### Growth Rates in Real GDP, 1980–1998

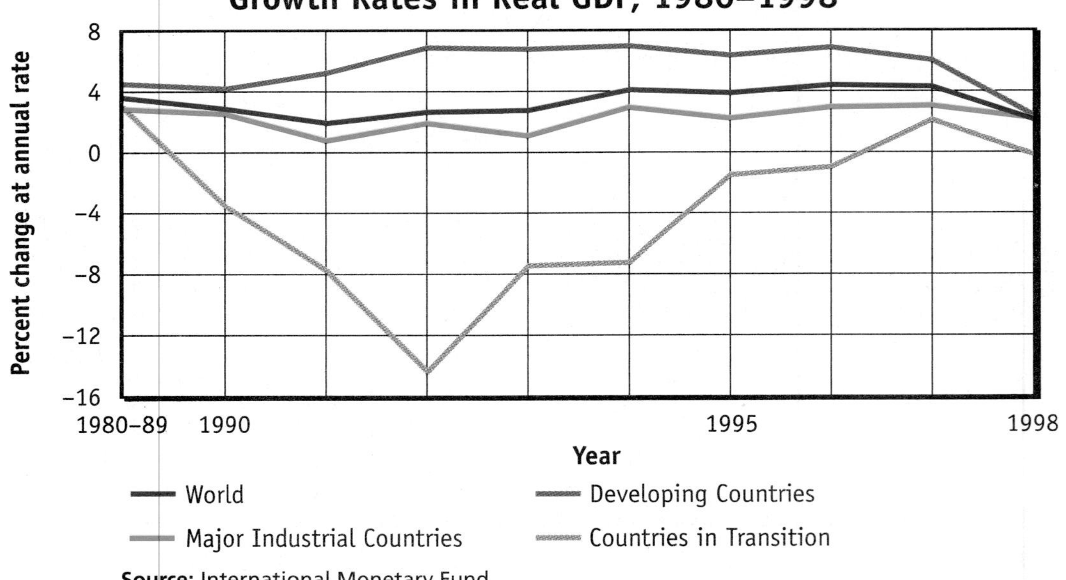


**Source:** International Monetary Fund

**ECONOMICS *Online***

Visit ett.glencoe.com and click on ***Textbook Updates—Databank*** for an update of the data.

STANDARD & POOR'S

## The Global Economy

### World Population by Age, 2000–2050

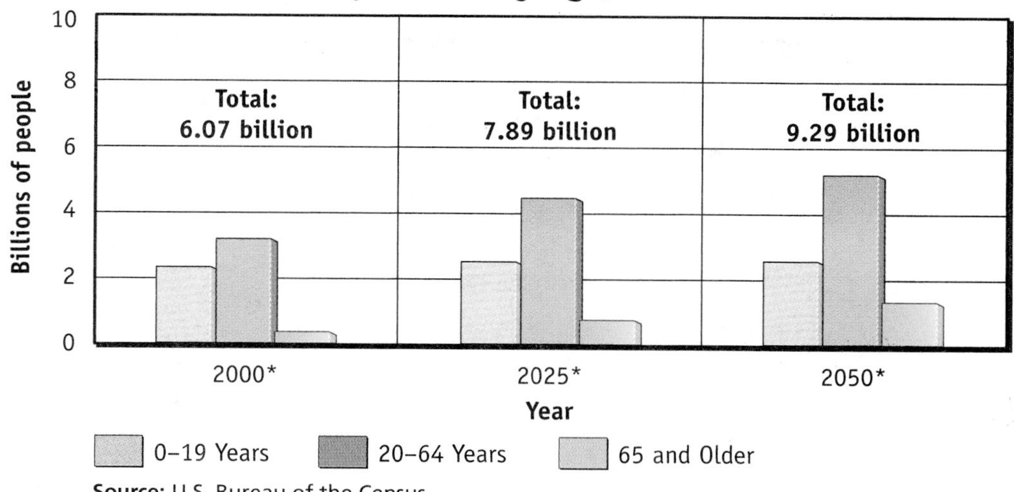


**Source:** U.S. Bureau of the Census
*Estimate

### Countries Ranked by Population, 2000 and 2050

| Country | Year 2000* Population (in millions) | Year 2000* Rank | Year 2050* Population (in millions) | Year 2050* Rank |
|---|---|---|---|---|
| China | 1,256 | 1 | 1,322 | (2) |
| India | 1,017 | 2 | 1,706 | (1) |
| United States | 274 | 3 | 394 | (3) |
| Indonesia | 219 | 4 | 330 | (5) |
| Brazil | 173 | 5 | 228 | (7) |
| Russia | 145 | 6 | 121 | (13) |
| Pakistan | 141 | 7 | 260 | (6) |
| Bangladesh | 129 | 8 | 211 | (8) |
| Japan | 126 | 9 | 101 | (18) |
| Nigeria | 117 | 10 | 337 | (4) |
| Mexico | 102 | 11 | 167 | (10) |

**Source:** U.S. Bureau of the Census
*Estimate

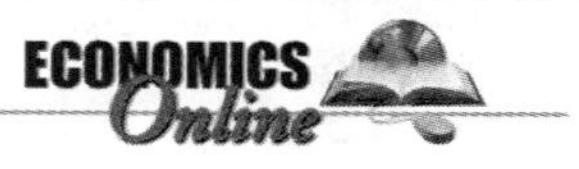


Visit ett.glencoe.com and click on *Textbook Updates—Databank* for an update of the data.

## The Global Economy

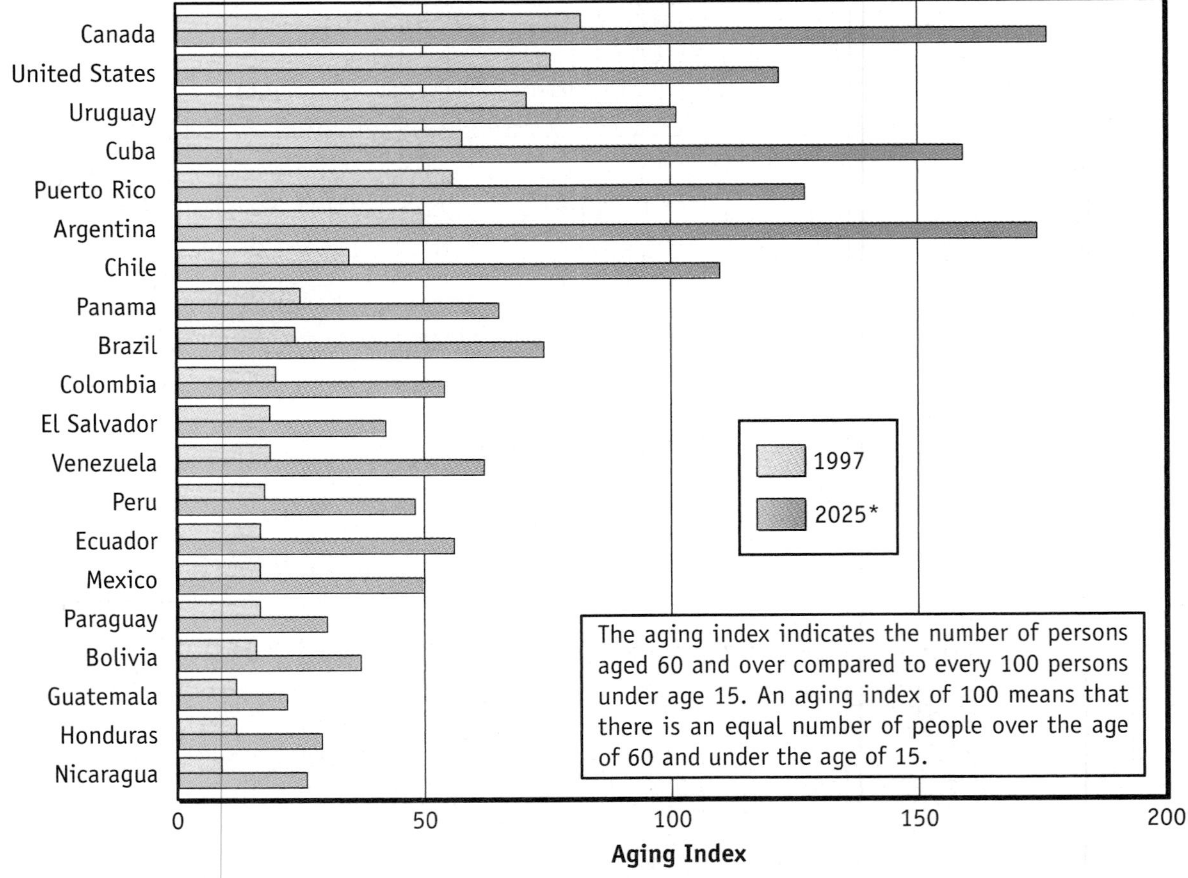


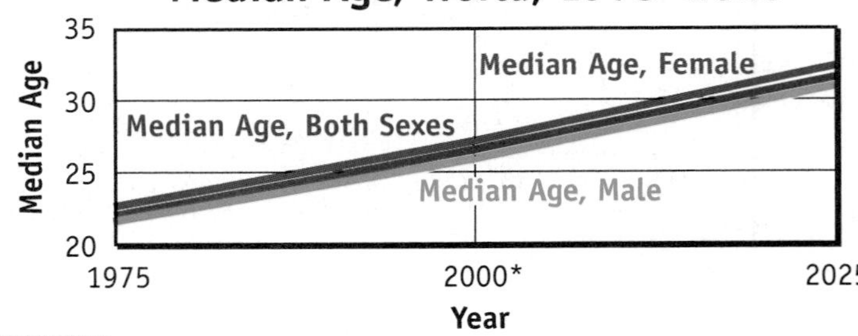


**Source:** U.S. Bureau of the Census
*Estimate

Visit ett.glencoe.com and click on ***Textbook Updates—Databank*** for an update of the data.

STANDARD & POOR'S

## The Global Economy

### U.S. Exports and Imports, 1950–2000

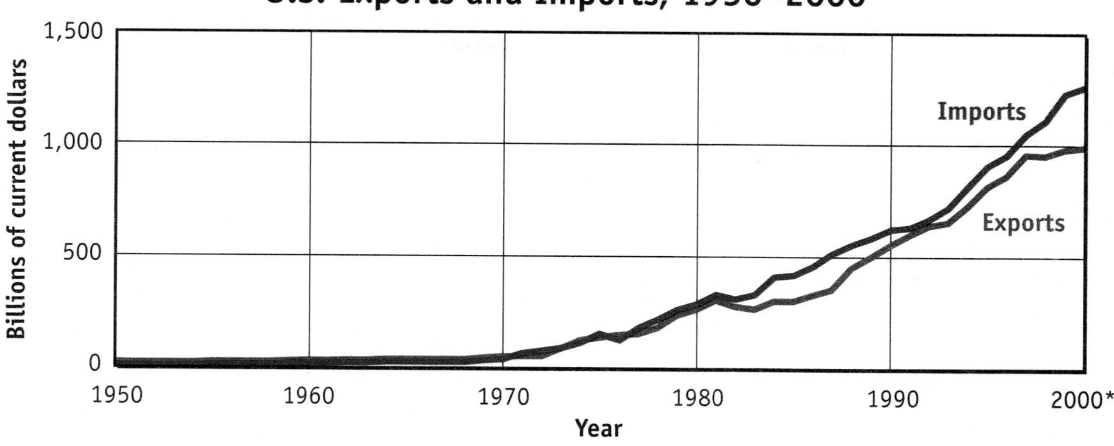


*Estimate

### Employment and Unemployment, Selected Economies

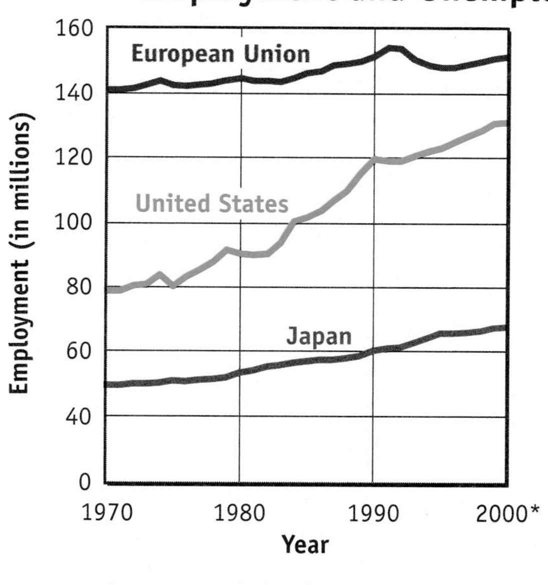


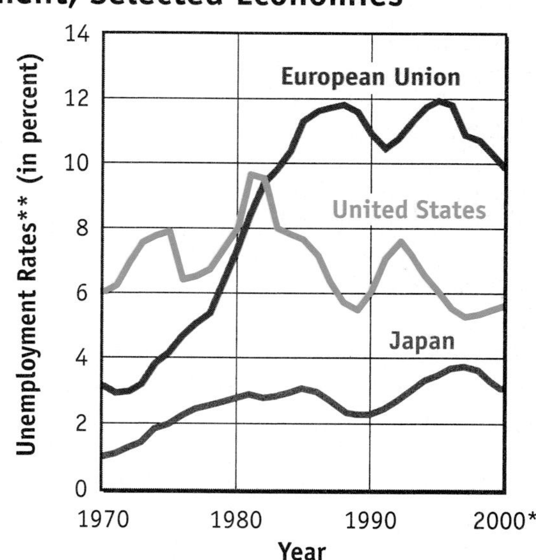


**Source:** International Monetary Fund
*Estimate
**Based on national definitions

Visit ett.glencoe.com and click on ***Textbook Updates—Databank*** for an update of the data.

## A

**ability-to-pay principle:** principle of taxation in which those with higher incomes pay more taxes than those with lower incomes, regardless of the number of government services they use (p. 442)

**absolute advantage:** ability of one country, using the same quantity of resources as another country, to produce a particular product at a lower absolute cost (p. 475)

**agency shop:** company in which employees are not required to join the union, but must pay union dues (p. 324)

**aggregate demand:** total quantity of goods and services in the entire economy that all citizens will demand at any single time (p. 356)

**aggregate demand curve:** a graphed line showing the relationship between the aggregate quantity demanded and the average of all prices as measured by the implicit GDP price deflator (p. 357)

**aggregates:** summation of all the individual parts in the economy (p. 356)

**aggregate supply:** real domestic output of producers based on the rise and fall of the price level (p. 358)

**aggregate supply curve:** a graphed line showing the relationship between the aggregate quantity supplied and the average of all prices as measured by the implicit GDP price deflator (p. 358)

**annual percentage rate (APR):** cost of credit expressed as a yearly percentage (p. 92)

**antitrust legislation:** laws passed by federal and state governments to prevent new monopolies from forming and to break up those that already exist (p. 249)

**arbitration:** stage of negotiation process in which union and management submit the issues they cannot agree on to a third party for a final decision (p. 329)

**articles of incorporation:** document listing basic information about a corporation that is filed with the state where the corporation will be headquartered (p. 221)

**assembly line:** production system in which the good being produced moves on a conveyor belt past workers who perform individual tasks in assembling it (p. 280)

**assets:** all items to which a business or household holds legal claim (p. 215)

**authoritarian socialism:** system that supports revolution as a means to overthrow capitalism and bring about socialist goals; the entire economy is controlled by a central government; also called *communism* (p. 500)

**automated teller machines (ATMs):** units that allow consumers to do their banking without the help of a teller (p. 385)

**automation:** production process in which machines do the work and people oversee them (p. 280)

## B

**bait and switch:** deceptive advertising practice that attracts consumers with a low-priced product, then tries to sell them a higher-priced product (p. 69)

**balance of trade:** difference between the value of a nation's exports and its imports (p. 483)

**bankruptcy:** the inability to pay debts based on the income received (p. 104)

**barriers to entry:** obstacles to competition that prevent others from entering a market (p. 240)

**barter:** exchange of goods and services for other goods and services (p. 376)

**base year:** year used as a point of comparison for other years in a series of statistics (p. 352)

**benefits-received principle:** system of taxation in which those who use a particular government service support it with taxes in proportion to the benefit they receive; those who do not use a service do not pay taxes for it (p. 440)

**black market:** "underground" or illegal market in which goods are traded at prices above their legal maximum prices or in which illegal goods are sold (p. 197)

**blue-collar workers:** category of workers employed in crafts, manufacturing, and nonfarm labor (p. 315)

**boom:** same as *peak* (p. 360)

**boycott:** economic pressure exerted by unions urging the public not to purchase the goods or services produced by a company (p. 331)

**brand name:** word, picture, or logo on a product that helps consumers distinguish it from similar products (p. 70)

**broker:** person who acts as a go-between for buyers and sellers of stocks and bonds (p. 149)

**budget deficit:** situation when the amount of government spending exceeds its receipts during the fiscal year (p. 438)

**budget surplus:** situation when the amount of government receipts is larger than its expenditures during the fiscal year (p. 439)



A30

**bureaucracies:** offices and agencies of the government that each deal with a specific area (p. 530)

**business cycle:** irregular changes in the level of total output measured by real GDP (p. 360)

**business fluctuations:** ups and downs in an economy (p. 360)

## C

**capital:** previously manufactured goods used to make other goods and services (p. 6)

**capital flight:** the legal or illegal export of currency or money capital from a nation by that nation's leaders (p. 530)

**capital gain:** increase in value of an asset from the time it was bought to the time it was sold (p. 147)

**capitalism:** economic system in which private individuals own the factors of production and decide how to use them within legislated limits (p. 41)

**capital loss:** decrease in value of an asset or bond from the time it was bought to the time it was sold (p. 147)

**cartel:** arrangement among groups of industrial businesses, often in different countries, to reduce international competition by controlling the price, production, and distribution of goods (p. 245)

**certificates of deposit:** time deposits that state the amount of the deposit, maturity, and rate of interest being paid (p. 143)

**channels of distribution:** routes by which goods are moved from producers to consumers (p. 302)

**charge account:** credit extended to a consumer allowing the consumer to buy goods or services from a particular company and to pay for them later (p. 90)

**checkable deposits:** money deposited in a bank that can be withdrawn at any time by presenting a check (p. 389)

**check clearing:** method by which a check that has been deposited in one institution is transferred to the issuer's depository institution (p. 405)

**checking account:** account in which deposited money can be withdrawn at any time by writing a check (p. 389)

**circular flow of economic activity:** economic model that pictures income as flowing continuously between businesses and consumers (p. 37)

**circular flow of income:** same as *circular flow of economic activity* (p. 458)

**civilian labor force:** total number of people 16 years old or older who are either employed or actively seeking work (p. 313)

**closed shop:** company in which only union members could be hired (p. 324)

**closing costs:** fees involved in arranging for a mortgage or in transferring ownership of property (p. 123)

**club warehouse store:** store that carries a limited number of large-quantity brands and items; less expensive than supermarkets (p. 112)

**coincident indicators:** economic indicators that usually change at the same time as changes in overall business activity (p. 367)

**collateral:** something of value that a borrower lets the lender claim if a loan is not repaid (p. 98)

**collective bargaining:** process by which unions and employers negotiate the conditions of employment (p. 328)

**command economy:** system in which the government controls the factors of production and makes all decisions about their use (p. 34)

**commercial bank:** bank whose main functions are to accept deposits, lend money, and transfer funds among banks, individuals, and businesses (p. 89)

**commodity money:** a medium of exchange such as cattle or gems that has value as a commodity or good aside from its value as money (p. 378)

**common stock:** shares of ownership in a corporation that give stockholders voting rights and a portion of future profits (after holders of preferred stock are paid) (p. 223)

**communism:** term used by Karl Marx for his ideal society in which no government is necessary (p. 500)

**comparative advantage:** ability of a country to produce a product at a lower opportunity cost than another country (p. 476)

**comparison shopping:** getting information on the types and prices of products available from different stores and companies before purchasing a product (p. 69)

**competition:** rivalry among producers or sellers of similar goods and services to win more business (p. 44)

**competitive advertising:** advertising that attempts to persuade consumers that a product is different from and superior to any other (p. 68)

**complementary good:** a product often used with another product; as the price of the second product decreases, the demand for the first product increases (p. 181)

**conglomerate:** large corporation made up of smaller corporations dealing in unrelated businesses (p. 250)

**consumer:** any person or group that buys or uses goods and services to satisfy personal needs and wants (p. 59)

**consumer-credit laws:** laws passed to protect consumers by giving them access to their credit records (p. 578)

**consumer goods:** goods produced for individuals and sold directly to the public to be used as they are (p. 277)

**consumerism:** movement to educate buyers about the purchases they make and to demand better and safer products from manufacturers (p. 72)

**consumer price index (CPI):** measure of the change in price over time of a specific group of goods and services used by the average household (p. 351)

**consumer sovereignty:** the role of the consumer as ruler of the market when determining the types of goods and services produced (p. 290)

**contraction:** part of the business cycle during which economic activity is slowing down, leading to a trough (p. 360)

**convenience store:** store open 16 to 24 hours a day, carrying a limited selection of relatively higher-priced items (p. 113)

**copyright:** government protection that gives an author or artist the exclusive right to sell, publish, or reproduce their works for a specified number of years (p. 241)

**corporate charter:** license to operate granted to a corporation by the state where it is established (p. 221)

**corporation:** type of business organization owned by many people but treated by law as though it were a person; it can own property, pay taxes, make contracts, and so on (p. 220)

**cost-benefit analysis:** a financial process in which a business estimates the cost of action and compares it with the benefits of that action (p. 265)

**cost-of-living adjustment (COLA):** union contract or other provision providing for an additional wage increase each year if the general level of prices in the economy rises beyond a certain level (p. 329)

**cost-push inflation:** theory that the wage demands of labor unions and the excessive profit motive of large corporations push up prices, resulting in stagflation (p. 455)

**craft union:** union made up of skilled workers in a specific trade or industry (p. 323)

**credit:** receipt of money either directly or indirectly to buy goods and services in the present with the promise to pay for them in the future (p. 83)

**credit bureau:** private business that investigates a person to determine the risk involved in lending money to that person (p. 96)

**credit card:** credit device that allows a person to make purchases at many kinds of stores, restaurants, and other businesses without paying cash (p. 91)

**credit check:** investigation of a person's income, current debts, personal life, and past history of borrowing and repaying debts (p. 96)

**credit rating:** rating of the risk involved in lending money to a specific person or business (p. 96)

**credit union:** depository institution owned and operated by its members to provide savings accounts and low-interest loans only to its members (p. 89)

**cybernomics:** an economic system driven by Internet commerce (p. 566)

## D

**day trading:** buying and selling securities directly over the Internet (p. 577)

**debit card:** device used to make cashless purchases; money is electronically withdrawn from the consumer's checkable account and transferred directly to the store's bank account (p. 389)

**debt financing:** raising money for a business through borrowing (p. 271)

**deficit financing:** government policy of spending more money than it is able to bring in through revenues (p. 439)

**deflation:** prolonged decline in the general price level of goods and services (p. 351)

**demand:** the amount of a good or service that consumers are able and willing to buy at various possible prices during a specified time period (p. 170)

**demand curve:** downward-sloping line that graphically shows the quantities demanded at each possible price (p. 179)

**demand-pull inflation:** theory that prices rise as the result of excessive business and consumer demand; demand increases faster than total supply, resulting in shortages that lead to higher prices (p. 454)

**demand schedule:** table showing quantities demanded at different possible prices (p. 178)

**democratic socialism:** system that works within the constitutional framework of a nation to elect socialists to office; the government usually controls only some areas of the economy (p. 500)

**depreciation:** loss of value because of wear and tear to durable goods and capital goods (p. 347); fall in the price of a currency through the action of supply and demand (p. 482)

**depression:** major slowdown of economic activity during which millions are out of work, many businesses fail, and the economy operates at far below capacity (p. 361)

**deregulation:** reduction of government regulation and control over business activity (p. 253)

**devaluation:** lowering a currency's value in relation to other currencies by government order (p. 481)

**developed nations:** nations with relatively high standards of living and economies based more on industry than on agriculture (p. 518)

**developing nations:** nations with little industrial development and low standards of living (p. 518)

**direct foreign investment (DFI):** the purchase by foreigners of real estate and businesses in another country (p. 549)

**direct-mail advertising:** type of promotion using a mailer that usually includes a letter describing the product or service and an order blank or application form (p. 299)

**discount rate:** interest rate that the Fed charges on loans to member banks (p. 414)

**discretionary income:** money income a person has left to spend on extras after necessities have been bought (p. 60)

**disposable income:** income remaining for a person to spend or save after all taxes have been paid (p. 60)

**disposable personal income (DI):** same as *disposable income* (p. 348)

**distance education:** education provided via telecommunications technology (p. 578)

**diversification:** spreading of investments among several different types of accounts to lower overall risk (p. 158)

**dividend:** portion of a corporation's profits paid to its stockholders (p. 223)

**division of labor:** breaking down of a job into small tasks performed by different workers (p. 280)

**durability:** ability of an item to last a long time (p. 118)

**durable goods:** manufactured items that have a life span longer than three years (p. 84)

## E

**e-commerce:** conducting business transactions over computer networks, in particular the World Wide Web (pp. 303, 567)

**economic assistance:** loans and outright grants of money or equipment to other nations to add to their capital resources (p. 525)

**economic efficiency:** wise use of available resources so that costs do not exceed benefits (p. 47)

**economic equity:** the attempt to balance an economic policy so that everyone benefits fairly (p. 47)

**economic growth:** expansion of the economy to produce more goods, jobs, and wealth (p. 48)

**economic indicators:** statistics that measure variables in the economy (p. 367)

**economic model:** a theory or simplified representation that helps explain and predict economic behavior in the real world (p. 19)

**economics:** the study of how individuals and societies make choices about ways to use scarce resources to fulfill their needs and wants (p. 3)

**economic system:** way in which a nation uses its resources to satisfy its people's needs and wants (p. 31)

**economies of scale:** decreases in long-run average costs of producing that result from the large size or scale of output (p. 241)

**economy:** the production and distribution of goods and services in a society (p. 19)

**elastic demand:** situation in which the rise or fall in a product's price greatly affects the amount that people are willing to buy (p. 184)

**elasticity:** economic concept dealing with consumers' responsiveness to an increase or decrease in price (p. 181)

**electronic funds transfer (EFT):** system of putting onto computers all the various banking functions that in the past were handled on paper (p. 384)

**embargo:** complete restriction on the import or export of a particular good (p. 487)

**entrepreneur:** person who organizes, manages, and assumes the risks of a business in order to gain profits (p. 208)

**entrepreneurship:** ability of risk-taking individuals to develop new products and start new businesses in order to make profits (p. 7)

**equilibrium price:** the price at which the amount producers are willing to supply is equal to the amount consumers are willing to buy (p. 195)

**ethical behavior:** acting in accordance with moral and ethical convictions about right and wrong (p. 75)

**European Union (EU):** organization of European nations whose goal is to encourage economic integration as a single market (p. 489)

**exchange rate:** the price of one nation's currency in terms of another nation's currency (p. 479)

**expansion:** part of the business cycle in which economic activity slowly increases (p. 361)

**exports:** goods sold to other countries (p. 474)

**externalities:** economic side effects or by-products that affect an uninvolved third party; can be negative or positive (p. 432)

## F

**factors of production:** resources of land, labor, capital, and entrepreneurship used to produce goods and services (p. 5)

**Fed:** the Federal Reserve System created by Congress in 1913 as the nation's central banking organization (p. 399)

**federal funds rate:** interest rate that banks charge each other on loans (usually overnight) (p. 415)

**Federal Open Market Committee:** 12-member committee in the Federal Reserve System that meets 8 times a year to decide the course of action that the Fed should take to control the money supply (p. 401)

**fiat money:** money that has value because a government fiat, or order, has established it as acceptable for payment of debts (p. 379)

**finance charge:** cost of credit expressed monthly in dollars and cents (p. 92)

**finance company:** company that takes over contracts for installment debts from stores and adds a fee for collecting the debt; consumer finance company makes loans directly to consumers at high rates of interest (p. 90)

**financing:** obtaining funds or money capital for business expansion (p. 263)

**fiscal policy:** federal government's use of taxation and spending policies to affect overall business activity (p. 457)

**fiscal year:** year by which accounts are kept; for the federal government, October 1 to September 30 of the next year (p. 437)

**five-year plans:** centralized planning system that was the basis for China's economic system; eventually was transformed to a regional planning system leading to limited free enterprise (p. 504)

**fixed rate of exchange:** system under which a national government sets the value of its currency in relation to a single standard (p. 480)

**flexible exchange rates:** arrangement in which the forces of supply and demand are allowed to set the price of various currencies (p. 482)

**foreign affiliates:** branches of multinational firms (p. 554)

**foreign aid:** money, goods, and services given by governments and private organizations to help other nations and their citizens (p. 525)

**foreign exchange markets:** markets dealing in buying and selling foreign currency for businesses that want to import goods from other countries (p. 480)

**fractional reserve banking:** system in which only a fraction of the deposits in a bank is kept on hand, or in reserve; the remainder is available to lend to borrowers or is otherwise invested (p. 408)

**franchise:** contract in which one business (the franchiser) sells to another business (the franchisee) the right to use the franchiser's name and sell its products (p. 224)

**free enterprise system:** economic system in which individuals own the factors of production and decide how to use them within legal limits; same as *capitalism* (p. 42)

**frequency marketing:** marketing directed by stored information about the frequency of a customer's use of a product (p. 568)

**full employment:** condition of the economy when the unemployment rate is lower than a certain percentage established by economists' studies (p. 453)

## G

**GDP:** see *gross domestic product (GDP)*

**GDP price deflator:** price index that removes the effect of inflation from GDP so that the overall economy in one year can be compared to another year (p. 353)

**General Agreement on Tariffs and Trade (GATT):** trade agreement under which countries met periodically to negotiate tariff reductions that were mutually advantageous to all members (p. 488)

**generic brand:** general name for a product rather than a specific brand name given by the manufacturer (p. 70)

**global integration:** interdependency among the countries of the world, especially within financial markets and telecommunications (p. 544)

**goods:** tangible objects that can satisfy people's wants (p. 6)

**gross domestic product (GDP):** total dollar value of all final goods and services produced in a nation in a single year (p. 344)

## H

**hypothesis:** an assumption involving two or more variables that must be tested for validity (p. 20)

## I

**import quota:** restriction imposed on the value of or on the number of units of a particular good that can be brought into the country (p. 487)

**imports:** goods bought from other countries for domestic use (p. 473)

**income redistribution:** government activity that takes income from some people through taxation and uses it to help citizens in need (p. 431)

**individual retirement account (IRA):** private retirement plan that allows individuals or married couples to save a certain amount of untaxed earnings per year with the interest being tax-deferred (p. 156)

**industrial union:** union made up of all the workers in an industry regardless of job or skill level (p. 324)

**inelastic demand:** situation in which a product's price change has little impact on the quantity demanded by consumers (p. 184)

**infant mortality rate:** death rate of infants who die during the first year of life (p. 520)

**inflation:** prolonged rise in the general price level of goods and services (p. 350)

**Information Age:** the period when telecommunications and computer technology gave information significant economic value (p. 571)

**informative advertising:** advertising that benefits consumers by giving information about a product (p. 68)

**injunction:** court order preventing some activity (p. 332)

**innovation(s):** development of new products, systems, or processes that have wide-ranging effects (pp. 365, 573)

**installment debt:** type of loan repaid with equal payments, or installments, over a specific period of time (p. 84)

**intellectual property:** creations of a person's intellect that are protected by copyright; for example, written works and music (p. 577)

**interest:** payment people receive when they lend money or allow someone else to use their money (pp. 84, 142)

**interlocking directorate:** a board of directors, the majority of whose members also serve as the board of directors of a competing corporation (p. 249)

**intermediate-term financing:** money borrowed by a business for 1 to 10 years (p. 272)

**International Monetary Fund (IMF):** agency whose member governments once were obligated to keep their foreign exchange rates more or less fixed; today it offers monetary advice and provides loans to developing nations (p. 481)

**Internet:** a worldwide system of interconnected computers that store, process, and share information (p. 566)

**inventory:** extra supply of the items used in a business, such as raw materials or goods for sale (p. 209)

## J

**joint venture:** partnership set up for a specific purpose just for a short period of time (p. 217)

## K

**Keogh Plan:** retirement plan that allows self-employed individuals to save a maximum of 15 percent of their income up to a specified amount each year, and to deduct that amount from their yearly taxable income (p. 156)

**knowledge economy:** economy in which information is the key to growth (p. 572)

## L

**labor:** human effort directed toward producing goods and services (p. 6)

**labor union:** association of workers organized to improve wages and working conditions for its members (p. 321)

**lagging indicators:** indicators that seem to lag behind changes in overall business activity (p. 367)

**laissez-faire:** economic system in which the government minimizes its interference with the economy (p. 41)

**land:** natural resources and surface land and water (p. 6)

**law of demand:** economic rule stating that the quantity demanded and price move in opposite directions (p. 171)

**law of diminishing marginal utility:** economic rule stating that the additional satisfaction a consumer gets from purchasing one more unit of a product will lessen with each additional unit purchased (p. 174)

**law of diminishing returns:** economic rule that says as more units of a factor of production (such as labor) are added to other factors of production (such as equipment), total output continues to increase but at a diminishing rate (p. 192)

**law of supply:** economic rule stating that price and quantity supplied move in the same direction (p. 187)

**leading indicators:** statistics that point to what will happen in the economy (p. 367)

**lease:** long-term agreement describing the terms under which property is rented (p. 124)

**legal tender:** money that by law must be accepted for payment of public and private debts (p. 379)

**liability insurance:** insurance that pays for bodily injury and property damage (p. 133)

**limited liability:** requirement in which an owner's responsibility for a company's debts is limited to the size of the owner's investment in the firm (p. 220)

**limited partnership:** special form of partnership in which one or more partners have limited liability but no voice in management (p. 217)

**local union:** members of a labor union in a particular factory, company, or geographic area (p. 324)

**lockout:** situation that occurs when management prevents workers from returning to work until they agree to a new contract (p. 331)

**long-term financing:** money borrowed by a business for a period of more than 10 years (p. 273)

**loose money policy:** monetary policy that makes credit inexpensive and abundant, possibly leading to inflation (p. 408)

## M

**M1:** narrowest definition of the money supply; consists of moneys that can be spent immediately and against which checks can be written (p. 391)

**M2:** broader definition of the money supply; includes all of M1, plus such near moneys as money market mutual fund balances, certificates of deposit, and Eurodollars (p. 391)

**macroeconomics:** the branch of economic theory dealing with the economy as a whole and decision making by large units such as governments (p. 18)

**marginal utility:** an additional amount of satisfaction (p. 174)

**market:** freely chosen activity between buyers and sellers of goods and services (pp. 36, 170)

**market basket:** representative group of goods and services used to compile the consumer price index (p. 352)

**market economy:** system in which individuals own the factors of production and make economic decisions through free interaction while looking out for their own and their families' best interests (p. 36)

**marketing:** all the activities needed to move goods and services from the producer to the consumer (p. 280)

**market research:** gathering, recording, and analyzing data about the types of goods and services that people want (p. 292)

**market structure:** the extent to which competition prevails in particular markets (p. 233)

**market survey:** survey in which researchers gather information about possible users of a product based on such characteristics as age, sex, income, education, and location (p. 293)

**maturity:** period of time at the end of which time deposits will pay a stated rate of interest (p. 143)

**mechanization:** combined labor of people and machines (p. 280)

**mediation:** stage in contract negotiations between union and management in which a neutral person steps in and tries to get both sides to reach an agreement (p. 329)

**Medicaid:** state and federal public-assistance program that provides free health care for low-income and disabled persons (p. 431)

**Medicare:** government program that provides health care for the aged (p. 426)

**medium of exchange:** use of money in exchange for goods or services (p. 376)

**merger:** a combined company that results when one corporation buys more than half the stock of another corporation and, thus, controls the second corporation (p. 249)

**microchip:** a tiny electronic circuit that processes and digitally transfers information (p. 565)



A36

**microeconomics:** the branch of economic theory that deals with behavior and decision making by small units such as individuals and firms (p. 18)

**military assistance:** economic or technical aid given to a nation's armed forces (p. 525)

**minimum wage law:** federal law that sets the lowest legal hourly wage rate that may be paid to certain types of workers (p. 319)

**mixed economy:** system combining characteristics of more than one type of economy (p. 38)

**monetarism:** theory that deals with the relationship between the amount of money the Fed places in circulation and the level of activity in the economy (p. 462)

**monetarists:** supporters of the theory of monetarism, often linked with Milton Friedman (p. 462)

**monetary policy:** policy that involves changing the rate of growth of the supply of money in circulation in order to affect the cost and availability of credit (p. 400)

**monetary rule:** monetarists' belief that the Fed should allow the money supply to grow at a smooth, consistent rate per year and not use monetary policy to stimulate or slow the economy (p. 463)

**money:** anything customarily used as a medium of exchange, a unit of accounting, and a store of value (p. 376)

**money market deposit account:** account that pays relatively high rates of interest, requires a minimum balance, and allows immediate access to money (p. 143)

**money market fund:** type of mutual fund that uses investors' money to make short-term loans to businesses and banks (p. 152)

**monopolistic competition:** market situation in which a large number of sellers offer similar but slightly different products and in which each has some control over price (p. 245)

**monopoly:** market situation in which a single supplier makes up an entire industry for a good or service that has no close substitutes (p. 240)

**mortgage:** installment debt owed on houses, buildings, or land (p. 85)

**multinationals:** firms that do business and have offices or factories in many countries (p. 553)

**mutual fund:** investment company that pools the money of many individuals to buy stocks, bonds, or other investments (p. 151)

## N

**national debt:** total amount of outstanding debt for the federal government (p. 439)

**national income (NI):** total income earned by everyone in the economy (p. 347)

**national income accounting:** measurement of the national economy's performance, dealing with the overall economy's output and income (p. 343)

**nationalization:** placement of railroads, businesses, or other industries under government ownership (p. 525)

**near moneys:** assets, such as savings accounts, that can be turned into money relatively easily and without the risk of loss of value (p. 390)

**net domestic product (NDP):** value of the nation's total output (GDP) minus the total value lost through depreciation on machines and equipment (p. 347)

**net exports:** difference between what the nation sells to other countries and what it buys from other countries (p. 346)

**North American Free Trade Agreement (NAFTA):** trade agreement designed to reduce tariff barriers between Mexico, Canada, and the United States (p. 489)

## O

**oligopoly:** industry dominated by a few suppliers who exercise some control over price (p. 243)

**open-market operations:** buying and selling of United States securities by the Fed to affect the money supply (p. 416)

**opportunity cost:** value of the next best alternative given up for the alternative that was chosen (p. 13)

**overdraft checking:** checking account that allows a customer to write a check for more money than exists in his or her account (p. 384)

**over-the-counter market:** electronic purchase and sale of stocks and bonds, often of smaller companies, which takes place outside the organized stock exchanges (p. 150)

## P

**partnership:** business that two or more individuals own and operate (p. 215)

**passbook savings account:** account for which a depositor receives a booklet in which deposits, withdrawals, and interest are recorded (p. 142)

**patent:** government protection that gives an inventor the exclusive right to make, use, or sell an invention for a specified number of years (p. 241)

**peak:** period of prosperity in a business cycle in which economic activity is at its highest point (p. 360)

**penetration pricing:** selling a new product at a low price to attract customers away from an established product (p. 298)

**pension plans:** company plans that provide retirement income for their workers (p. 155)

**perfect competition:** market situation in which there are numerous buyers and sellers, and no single buyer or seller can affect price (p. 234)

**personal income (PI):** total income that individuals receive before personal taxes are paid (p. 348)

**picketing:** activity in which striking workers walk up and down in front of a workplace carrying signs that state their disagreement with the company (p. 329)

**points:** fees paid to a lender and computed as percentage points of a loan (p. 123)

**preferred stock:** shares of ownership in a corporation that give stockholders a portion of future profits (before any profits go to holders of common stock), but no voting rights (p. 223)

**price ceiling:** a legal maximum price that may be charged for a particular good or service (p. 197)

**price elasticity of demand:** economic concept that deals with *how much* demand varies according to changes in price (p. 181)

**price floor:** a legal minimum price below which a good or service may not be sold (p. 198)

**price leadership:** practice of setting prices close to those charged by other companies selling similar products (p. 298)

**prime rate:** rate of interest that banks charge on loans to their best business customers (p. 414)

**principal:** amount of money originally borrowed in a loan (p. 84)

**private-labeled products:** lower-priced store-brand products carried by some supermarket chains and club wholesale chains (p. 113)

**private property:** whatever is owned by individuals rather than by government (p. 43)

**privatization:** change from state ownership of business, land, and buildings to private ownership (p. 509)

**producer price index (PPI):** measure of the change in price over time that United States producers charge for their goods and services (p. 353)

**product differentiation:** manufacturers' use of minor differences in quality and features to try to differentiate between similar goods and services (p. 244)

**production:** process of changing resources into goods that satisfy the needs and wants of individuals and businesses (p. 277)

**production possibilities curve:** graph showing the maximal combinations of goods and services that can be produced from a fixed amount of resources in a given period of time (p. 14)

**productivity:** the amount of output (goods and services) that results from a given level of inputs (land, labor, capital) (p. 7)

**product life cycle:** series of stages that a product goes through from first introduction to complete withdrawal from the market (p. 300)

**professionals:** highly educated individuals with college degrees and usually additional education or training (p. 316)

**profit:** money left after all the costs of production—wages, rents, interest, and taxes—have been paid (pp. 43, 265)

**profit incentive:** desire to make money that motivates people to produce and sell goods and services (p. 43)

**progressive tax:** tax that takes a larger percentage of higher incomes than lower incomes; justified on the basis of the ability-to-pay principle (p. 443)

**proletariat:** term used by Karl Marx referring to workers (p. 499)

**promotion:** use of advertising to inform consumers that a new or improved product or service is available and to persuade them to purchase it (p. 299)

**proportional tax:** tax that takes the same percentage of all incomes; as income rises, the amount of tax paid also rises (p. 443)

**proprietor:** owner of a business (p. 215)

**protectionists:** people who argue for trade restrictions to protect domestic industries (p. 487)

**protective tariff:** tax on imports used to raise the cost of imported goods and thereby protect domestic producers (p. 487)

**public-assistance programs:** government programs that make payments to citizens based on need (p. 431)

**public goods:** goods or services that government supplies to its citizens; can be used by many individuals at the same time without reducing the benefit each person receives (p. 430)

**public-works projects:** publicly used facilities, such as schools and highways, built by federal, state, or local governments with public money (p. 425)

**purchasing power:** the real goods and services that money can buy; determines the value of money (p. 351)

## Q

**quantity demanded:** the amount of a good or service that a consumer is willing and able to purchase at a specific price (p. 172)

**quantity supplied:** the amount of a good or service that a producer is willing and able to supply at a specific price (p. 187)

## R

**rational choice:** choosing the alternative that has the greatest value from among comparable-quality products (p. 62)

**rationing:** the distribution of goods and services based on something other than price (p. 197)

**real GDP:** GDP that has been adjusted for inflation by applying the price deflator (p. 353)

**real income effect:** economic rule stating that individuals cannot keep buying the same quantity of a product if its price rises while their income stays the same (p. 172)

**receipts:** income received from the sale of goods and/or services; also, slips of paper documenting a purchase (p. 209)

**recession:** part of the business cycle in which the nation's output (real GDP) does not grow for at least six months (p. 361)

**recovery:** same as *expansion* (p. 361)

**registration fee:** licensing fee, usually annual, paid to a state for the right to use a car (p. 130)

**regressive tax:** tax that takes a larger percentage of lower incomes than higher incomes (p. 443)

**representative money:** money that is backed by an item of value, such as gold or silver (p. 378)

**reserve requirements:** regulations set by the Fed requiring banks to keep a certain percentage of their deposits as cash in their own vaults or as deposits in their Federal Reserve district bank (p. 408)

**retailers:** businesses that sell consumer goods directly to the public (p. 303)

**revenues:** total income from sales of output (p. 265)

**revenue tariff:** tax on imports used primarily to raise income without restricting imports (p. 487)

**right-to-work laws:** state laws forbidding unions from forcing workers to join and pay union dues (p. 325)

**robotics:** sophisticated computer-controlled machinery that operates an assembly line (p. 281)

**Roth IRA:** private retirement plan that taxes income before it is saved, but which does not tax interest on that income when funds are used upon retirement (p. 156)

## S

**saving:** setting aside income for a period of time so that it can be used later (p. 141)

**savings and loan association (S&L):** depository institution that accepts deposits and lends money (p. 89)

**savings bank:** depository institution originally set up to serve small savers overlooked by commercial banks (p. 89)

**savings bonds:** bonds issued by the federal government as a way of borrowing money; they are purchased at half the face value and increase every 6 months until full face value is reached (p. 149)

**scarcity:** condition of not being able to have all of the goods and services one wants, because wants exceed what can be made from all available resources at any given time (p. 5)

**secured loan:** loan that is backed up by collateral (p. 98)

**security deposit:** money a renter lets an owner hold in case the rent is not paid or an apartment is damaged (p. 125)

**semiskilled workers:** people whose jobs require some training, often using modern technology (p. 316)

**service flow:** amount of use a person gets from an item over time and the value a person places on this use (p. 118)

**services:** actions that can satisfy people's wants (p. 6)

**service workers:** people who provide services directly to individuals (p. 315)

**shortage:** situation in which the quantity demanded is greater than the quantity supplied (p. 196)

**short-term financing:** money borrowed by a business for any period of time less than a year (p. 271)

**skilled workers:** people who have learned a trade or craft either through a vocational school or as an apprentice to an experienced worker (p. 316)

**small business incubator:** government-funded agency that assists new businesses by providing advice or low-rent buildings and supplies (p. 209)

**social insurance programs:** government programs that pay benefits to retired and disabled workers, their families, and the unemployed; financed by taxes paid into programs by workers and employers (p. 431)

**Social Security:** federal program that provides monthly payments to people who are retired or unable to work (p. 431)

**sole proprietorship:** business owned and operated by one person (p. 213)

**specialization:** concept that a nation should produce and export a limited assortment of goods for which it is particularly suited in order to remain profitable (p. 475)

**stabilization policies:** attempts by the federal government to keep the economy healthy; includes monetary and fiscal policies (p. 451)

**stagflation:** combination of inflation and low economic activity (p. 455)

**standard of living:** the material well-being of an individual, group, or nation measured by how well their necessities and luxuries are satisfied (p. 48)

**startup:** beginning business enterprise (p. 208)

**statement savings account:** account similar to a passbook savings account except that instead of a passbook, the depositor receives a monthly statement showing all transactions (p. 142)

**stock:** share of ownership in a corporation that entitles the buyer to a certain part of the future profits and assets of the corporation (p. 220)

**stockholders:** people who have invested in a corporation and own some of its stock (p. 147)

**store of value:** use of money to store purchasing power for later use (p. 377)

**strike:** deliberate work stoppage by workers to force an employer to give in to their demands (p. 323)

**subsistence agriculture:** growing of just enough food by a family to take care of its own needs; no crops are available for export or to feed an industrial workforce (p. 519)

**substitution effect:** economic rule stating that if two items satisfy the same need and the price of one rises, people will buy the other (p. 172)

**Supplemental Security Income:** federal programs that include food stamps, veterans' benefits, and payments to the aged, blind, and disabled (p. 431)

**supply:** the amount of a good or service that producers are able and willing to sell at various prices during a specified time period (p. 170)

**supply curve:** upward-sloping line that graphically shows the quantities supplied at each possible price (p. 189)

**supply schedule:** table showing quantities supplied at different possible prices (p. 188)

**surplus:** situation in which quantity supplied is greater than quantity demanded (p. 196)

**tariff:** tax placed on an imported product (p. 486)

**tax-exempt bonds:** bonds sold by local and state governments; interest paid on the bond is not taxed by the federal government (p. 148)

**technical assistance:** aid in the form of professionals such as engineers, teachers, and technicians; supplied by nations to teach skills to individuals in other nations (p. 525)

**technology:** advance in knowledge leading to new and improved goods and services and better ways of producing them (pp. 7, 190)

**telecommunications:** long-distance communication, usually electronic, using communications satellites and fiber-optic cables (pp. 544, 571)

**Temporary Assistance to Needy Families:** state-run public-assistance program that provides money to needy single parents raising young children (p. 431)

**test marketing:** offering a product for sale in a small area for a limited period of time to see how well it sells before offering it nationally (p. 293)

**thrift institutions:** mutual savings banks, S&Ls, and credit unions that offer many of the same services as commercial banks (p. 389)

**tight money policy:** monetary policy that makes credit expensive and in short supply in an effort to slow the economy (p. 408)

**time deposits:** savings plans that require savers to leave their money on deposit for certain periods of time (p. 143)

**time lags:** periods between the time fiscal policy is enacted and the time it becomes effective (p. 465)

**trade-off:** sacrificing one good or service to purchase or produce another (p. 12)

**traditional economy:** system in which economic decisions are based on customs and beliefs that have been handed down from generation to generation (p. 33)

**transfer payments:** welfare and other supplementary payments, such as unemployment compensation, Social Security, and Medicaid, that a state or the federal government makes to individuals (p. 348)

**Treasury bills:** certificates issued by the U.S. Treasury in exchange for a minimum amount of $10,000 and maturing in 3 months to 1 year (p. 149)

**Treasury bonds:** certificates issued by the U.S. Treasury in exchange for minimum amounts of $1,000 or $5,000 and maturing in 10 or more years (p. 149)

**Treasury notes:** certificates issued by the U.S. Treasury in exchange for minimum amounts of $1,000 or $5,000 and maturing in 2 to 10 years (p. 149)

**trough:** lowest part of the business cycle in which the downward spiral of the economy levels off (p. 361)

## U

**underground economy:** transactions by people who do not follow federal and state laws with respect to reporting earnings (p. 453)

**unemployment rate:** percentage of the civilian labor force that is unemployed but is actively looking for work (p. 452)

**union:** see *labor union*

**union shop:** company that requires new employees to join a union after a specific period of time (p. 324)

**unit of accounting:** use of money as a yardstick for comparing the values of goods and services in relation to one another (p. 376)

**unlimited liability:** requirement that an owner is personally and fully responsible for all losses and debts of a business (p. 215)

**unsecured loan:** loan guaranteed only by a promise to repay it (p. 98)

**unskilled workers:** people whose jobs require no specialized training (p. 316)

**usury law:** law restricting the amount of interest that can be charged for credit (p. 102)

**utility:** the ability of any good or service to satisfy consumer wants (p. 173); the amount of satisfaction one gets from a good or service (p. 290)

## V

**vicious cycle of poverty:** situation in which a less-developed country with low per capita incomes cannot save and invest enough to achieve acceptable rates of economic growth and thus is trapped (p. 536)

**voluntary exchange:** a transaction in which a buyer and a seller exercise their economic freedom by working out their own terms of exchange (p. 170)

## W

**warranty:** promise made by a manufacturer or a seller to repair or replace a product within a certain time period if it is found to be faulty (p. 70)

**Web sites:** electronic World Wide Web locations that store information to be viewed or downloaded (p. 566)

**weightless economy:** term coined to identify an economy based on products that are not tangible (p. 572)

**welfare:** same as *public-assistance programs* (p. 431)

**welfare state:** country that has a blend of capitalism and socialism, combining private ownership of the means of production and competitive allocation of resources with the goal of social equality for its citizens (p. 510)

**white-collar workers:** category of workers employed in offices, sales, or professional positions (p. 315)

**wholesalers:** businesses that purchase large quantities of goods from producers for resale to other businesses (p. 303)

**workers' compensation:** government program that extends payments for medical care to workers injured on the job (p. 431)

**World Trade Organization (WTO):** world's largest trade agreement currently among 134 nations (pp. 488, 506)

**World Wide Web:** part of the Internet, used for communications among consumers, business, governments, and other organizations (p. 566)

## A

**ability-to-pay principle/principio de la capacidad de pago:** principio de tributación que propone que los que tienen más ingresos deben pagar más impuestos que los que tienen menos, sin tomar en cuenta la cantidad de servicios gubernamentales que usan (p. 442)

**absolute advantage/ventaja absoluta:** capacidad de un país de producir un producto por menos dinero que otros países, usando la misma cantidad de recursos (p. 475)

**agency shop/fábrica con cuota por agencia sindical:** compañía en que los empleados no tienen que ser miembros del sindicato, pero sí tienen que pagar la misma cuota que los miembros (p. 324)

**aggregate demand/demanda agregada:** cantidad total de bienes y servicios de una economía entera que todos los habitantes demandan en un momento dado (p. 356)

**aggregate demand curve/curva de demanda agregada:** línea gráfica que muestra la relación entre la cantidad de demanda agregada y el promedio de todos los precios, medidos por el deflactor de precios del PIB implícito (p. 357)

**aggregates/agregado:** suma de todas las partes individuales de una economía (p. 356)

**aggregate supply/oferta agregada:** producción doméstica real, tomando en cuenta los aumentos y rebajas de los precios (p. 358)

**aggregate supply curve/curva de oferta agregada:** línea gráfica que muestra la relación entre la cantidad de oferta agregada y el promedio de todos los precios, medidos por el deflactor de precios del PIB implícito (p. 358)

**annual percentage rate (APR)/tasa de interés anual:** costo del crédito expresado como porcentaje anual (p. 92)

**antitrust legislation/legislación antimonopolista:** leyes aprobadas por los gobiernos federal y estatales para evitar que se formen nuevos monopolios o para deshacer los que ya existen (p. 249)

**arbitration/arbitraje:** etapa en el proceso de negociar un contrato en que el sindicato y los gerentes entregan los asuntos que no pueden resolver a un tercero para que tome una decisión final (p. 329)

**articles of incorporation/escritura de constitución:** documento que contiene información básica acerca de una sociedad anónima que se presenta al estado donde tendrá su oficina principal (p. 221)

**assembly line/línea de montaje:** sistema de producción en que el artículo producido es trasladado por una correa transportadora a distintos obreros que, por turnos, hacen labores particulares para ensamblarlo (p. 280)

**assets/activos:** todos los bienes que son la propiedad legal de un negocio o persona (p. 215)

**authoritarian socialism/socialismo autoritario:** sistema que apoya la revolución como modo de derrocar el capitalismo y realizar metas socialistas; la economía entera es controlada por el gobierno central; también se llama *comunismo* (p. 500)

**automated teller machines (ATMs)/cajero automático:** máquinas que le permiten a los consumidores hacer sus transacciones bancarias sin la ayuda de un cajero (p. 385)

**automation/automatización:** proceso de producción en que máquinas hacen el trabajo y personas las supervisan (p. 280)

## B

**bait and switch/engatusar:** práctica publicitaria engañosa que atrae a los consumidores con un producto a precio bajo para después tratar de venderles otro producto más caro (p. 69)

**balance of trade/balanza comercial:** diferencia entre el valor de las exportaciones e importaciones de una nación (p. 483)

**bankruptcy/bancarrota:** quiebra; no poder pagar las deudas con los ingresos que se reciben (p. 104)

**barriers to entry/barreras al mercado:** obstáculos que impiden que competidores entren en un mercado (p. 240)

**barter/trueque:** intercambio de bienes y servicios por otros bienes y servicios (p. 376)

**base year/año base:** año que se usa como punto de comparación con otros años en una series de estudios estadísticos (p. 352)

**benefits-received principle/principio de beneficio obtenido:** sistema de tributación en que los que usan un servicio gubernamental pagan impuestos por él en proporción al beneficio que reciben; los que no usan el servicio no pagan impuestos por él (p. 440)

**black market/mercado negro:** mercado ilegal en que se venden bienes a precios más altos de los que permite la ley o en que se venden productos ilegales (p. 197)

**blue-collar workers/obreros:** clasificación de trabajadores empleados en artesanías, manufactura y labores no agrícolas (p. 315)

**boom/auge:** véase *peak/auge* (p. 360)

**boycott/boicot:** presión económica que ejerce un sindicato, animando al público a que no compre los bienes o servicios producidos por una compañía (p. 331)

**brand name/marca de fábrica:** palabra, imagen o logotipo que lleva un producto para ayudar a los consumidores a distinguirlo de otros productos similares (p. 70)

**broker/corredor de bolsa:** persona que sirve de intermediario entre los vendedores y compradores de acciones y bonos (p. 149)

**budget deficit/déficit presupuestario:** situación en que la cantidad de dinero que el gobierno gasta es mayor que sus ingresos durante el año fiscal (p. 438)

**budget surplus/superávit presupuestario:** situación en que los ingresos del gobierno son mayores que los gastos durante el año fiscal (p. 439)

**bureaucracies/burocracias:** oficinas y agencias del gobierno que se ocupan de asuntos particulares (p. 530)

**business cycle/ciclo económico:** cambios irregulares en el nivel de producción total, medidos por el PIB real (p. 360)

**business fluctuations/fluctuaciones comerciales:** alzas y bajas en una economía (p. 360)

## C

**capital/capital:** bienes manufacturados que se usan para producir otros bienes y servicios; el dinero es capital financiero (p. 6)

**capital flight/fuga de capital al extranjero:** exportación legal o ilegal de divisas o del capital financiero de una nación por los líderes del mismo país (p. 530)

**capital gain/ganancia de capital:** aumento en el valor de un activo en el tiempo que transcurre entre su compra y su venta (p. 147)

**capitalism/capitalismo:** sistema económico en que individuos son dueños de los factores de producción y deciden cómo usarlos dentro de los límites de la ley (p. 41)

**capital loss/pérdida de capital:** disminución en el valor de un activo o bono entre el momento en que se compra y el momento en que se vende (p. 147)

**cartel/cártel:** arreglos entre grupos de negocios industriales, a menudo en distintos países, para controlar el precio, producción y distribución de bienes y así reducir la competencia internacional (p. 245)

**certificates of deposit/certificados de depósito:** depósitos a plazos que especifican la cantidad del depósito, la fecha de vencimiento y el tipo de interés que se paga (p. 143)

**channels of distribution/canales de distribución:** vías por las cuales se mueven los bienes de los fabricantes a los consumidores (p. 302)

**charge account/cuenta de crédito:** crédito que se le extiende a un consumidor, que le permite comprar bienes y servicios de una compañía en particular y pagar por ellos más adelante (p. 90)

**checkable deposits/depósitos a la vista:** dinero depositado en un banco que se puede sacar en cualquier momento con sólo presentar un cheque (p. 389)

**check clearing/compensación de cheques:** método de pagar y transferir cheques de la institución en que se depositan a la institución depositaria de la persona que los emite (p. 405)

**checking account/cuenta corriente:** cuenta de la cual se puede sacar dinero depositado por medio de un cheque (p. 389)

**circular flow of economic activity/flujo circular de actividad económica:** modelo económico que representa a los ingresos circulando continuamente entre negocios y consumidores (p. 37)

**circular flow of income/flujo circular de ingresos:** modelo económico que representa a los ingresos circulando continuamente entre negocios y consumidores (p. 458)

**civilian labor force/fuerza laboral civil:** número total de personas mayores de 16 años que tienen empleo o lo están buscando (p. 313)

**closed shop/fábrica cerrada:** compañía en que sólo se puede dar empleo a miembros del sindicato (p. 324)

**closing costs/costos de cierre:** cuotas que se pagan para obtener una hipoteca o transferir una propiedad a un dueño nuevo (p. 123)

**club warehouse store/club almacén:** tienda que tiene un surtido limitado de marcas y artículos que vende en grandes cantidades; es más barato que los supermercados (p. 112)

**coincident indicators/indicadores coincidentes:** indicadores económicos que cambian a la misma vez que la actividad comercial en general (p. 367)

**collateral/garantía:** algo de valor que el prestatario se compromete a darle al prestamista si no le devuelve el dinero (p. 98)

**collective bargaining/negociación colectiva:** proceso mediante el cual los sindicatos y gerentes acuerdan las condiciones de trabajo (p. 328)

**command economy/economía dirigida:** sistema en que el gobierno controla los factores de producción y toma todas las decisiones sobre su uso (p. 34)

**commercial bank/banco comercial:** banco cuyas funciones principales son aceptar depósitos, prestar dinero y transferir fondos entre bancos, individuos y negocios (p. 89)

**commodity money/dinero material:** medios de cambio, como el ganado o las joyas, que tienen valor propio como mercancías además de su valor como dinero (p. 378)

**common stock/acciones ordinarias:** tipo de participaciones en una sociedad anónima que da a los accionistas el derecho al voto y una porción de las futuras ganancias (después de que se haya pagado a los accionistas con acciones preferentes); también se llaman acciones comunes (p. 223)

**communism/comunismo:** término usado por Carlos Marx para referirse a la sociedad ideal en que no hace falta gobierno (p. 500)

**comparative advantage/ventaja comparativa:** capacidad de un país de producir un producto por un costo de oportunidad más bajo que otro país (p. 476)

**comparison shopping/comparar antes de comprar:** obtener información sobre los tipos de productos y los precios de éstos en distintas tiendas y compañías (p. 69)

**competition/competencia:** rivalidad entre los productores o vendedores de bienes y servicios semejantes para tener más clientes (p. 44)

**competitive advertising/publicidad competitiva:** anuncios que tratan de convencer al consumidor que un producto es distinto o mejor que los demás (p. 68)

**complementary goods/bienes complementarios:** productos que se usan en conjunto; al bajar el precio de uno, la demanda por el otro sube (p. 181)

**conglomerate/conglomerado:** gran corporación compuesta de empresas más pequeñas cuyos negocios no están relacionados (p. 250)

**consumer/consumidor:** cualquier persona o grupo que compra o utiliza bienes y servicios para satisfacer sus necesidades o deseos personales (p. 59)

**consumer-credit laws/leyes sobre el crédito al consumidor:** leyes que protegen al consumidor, dándole acceso a sus expedientes de crédito (p. 578)

**consumer goods/bienes de consumo:** bienes producidos para individuos y vendidos directamente al público para usarse tal y como son (p. 277)

**consumerism/protección al consumidor:** movimiento dedicado a informar al consumidor sobre las compras que hace y a exigirles productos mejores y más seguros a los fabricantes (p. 72)

**consumer price index (CPI)/índice de precios al consumidor:** medida del cambio de precio a través del tiempo de un grupo de bienes y servicios escogidos que se usan en un domicilio típico (p. 351)

**consumer sovereignty/soberanía del consumidor:** manera en que el consumidor gobierna el mercado cuando determina los tipos de bienes y servicios que se producen (p. 290)

**contraction/contracción:** parte del ciclo económico en que la actividad económica disminuye hasta llegar al nivel más bajo (p. 360)

**convenience store/tiendas de artículos de consumo frecuente:** tienda que se mantiene abierta de 16 a 24 horas al día con un surtido limitado de artículos a precios más altos (p. 113)

**copyright/copyright:** protección que el gobierno le da a un escritor o artista, dándole el derecho exclusivo de vender, publicar o reproducir sus obras por un determinado número de años; también se llama derechos de autor (p. 241)

**corporate charter/licencia para negociar:** permiso para operar una sociedad anónima que da el estado en que se establece una compañía (p. 221)

**corporation/sociedad anónima:** tipo de empresa de la cual muchas personas son dueñas, pero la ley la trata como si fuera una persona; puede tener propiedad, pagar impuestos, entrar en contratos, etc.; también se llama corporación (p. 220)

**cost-benefit analysis/análisis de coste-beneficios:** proceso financiero en que un negocio calcula el costo de emprender una actividad y lo compara con los beneficios de esa actividad (p. 265)

**cost-of-living adjustment (COLA)/ajuste por el costo de la vida:** contrato sindical u otra provisión que proporciona un aumento de sueldo adicional si el nivel general de los precios en la economía sube por encima de un nivel determinado (p. 329)

**cost-push inflation/inflación de costes:** teoría que las demandas salariales de los sindicatos y el afán de lucro excesivo de las grandes compañías fuerzan los precios hacia arriba, resultando en estagflación (p. 455)

**craft union/sindicato de artesanos:** asociación de trabajadores especializados en un oficio o industria en particular (p. 323)

**credit/crédito:** recibir dinero directa o indirectamente para comprar bienes y servicios en el presente bajo promesa de pagar por ellos en el futuro (p. 83)

**credit bureau/oficina de crédito:** negocio privado que investiga a individuos para determinar el riesgo de prestarles dinero (p. 96)

**credit card/tarjeta de crédito:** instrumento de crédito que le permite a una persona hacer compras en muchas clases distintas de tiendas, restaurantes y negocios sin tener que pagar con dinero en efectivo (p. 91)

**credit check/investigación de crédito:** investigación de los ingresos, deudas actuales, vida privada e historial de préstamos pedidos y deudas pagadas de una persona (p. 96)

**credit rating/clasificación de crédito:** evaluación del riesgo de prestarle dinero a una persona o negocio en particular (p. 96)

**credit union/cooperativa de crédito:** institución de depósitos que es propiedad de sus miembros, que es administrada por ellos y que proporciona cuentas de ahorro y préstamos a intereses bajos exclusivamente a sus miembros; también se llama unión crediticia (p. 89)

**cybernomics/economía ciberespacial:** sistema económico impulsado por el comercio que se lleva a cabo a través de Internet (p. 566)

## D

**day trading/operar por cuenta propia:** comprar y vender valores (acciones y bonos) directamente a través de Internet (p. 577)

**debit card/tarjeta de débito:** utensilio que se usa para hacer compras sin dinero en efectivo; el dinero se retira electrónicamente de la cuenta de cheques del comprador y se transfiere directamente a la cuenta de banco de la tienda (p. 389)

**debt financing/financiamiento mediante deudas:** recaudar dinero para un negocio por medio de préstamos (p. 271)

**deficit financing/financiamiento del déficit:** política gubernamental de gastar más dinero de los ingresos que tiene y obtener préstamos para cubrir los gastos adicionales (p. 439)

**deflation/deflación:** caída prolongada en el nivel general de los precios de bienes y servicios (p. 351)

**demand/demanda:** cantidad de un producto o servicio que los consumidores pueden o están dispuestos a comprar a varios precios posibles durante un período de tiempo determinado (p. 170)

**demand curve/curva de demanda:** línea descendiente en una gráfica cuya inclinación muestra la cantidad de demanda a cada precio posible (p. 179)

**demand-pull inflation/inflación de demanda:** teoría que los precios suben como consecuencia de la demanda excesiva de los negocios y consumidores; la demanda aumenta más rápido que la oferta total, ocasionando una escasez que conduce a precios más altos (p. 454)

**demand schedule/lista de demanda:** tabla que muestra la cantidad de demandada a distintos precios (p. 178)

**democratic socialism/socialismo democrático:** sistema que obra dentro del marco de la constitución de una nación para elegir socialistas a cargos públicos; el gobierno generalmente controla solamente algunos sectores de la economía (p. 500)

**depreciation/depreciación:** pérdida de valor de los bienes duraderos y bienes capitales por causa del uso constante (p. 13); rebaja en el valor de una moneda a través de la acción de la oferta y la demanda (p. 482)

**depression/depresión:** disminución tan significativa en la actividad económica que millones de personas pierden el trabajo, muchos negocios quiebran y la economía funciona muy por debajo de su capacidad (p. 361)

**deregulation/desregulación:** reducción en el número de regulaciones y controles gubernamentales sobre las actividades comerciales (p. 253)

**devaluation/devaluación:** rebajar el valor de una moneda con relación a otras divisas (monedas extranjeras) por orden gubernamental (p. 481)

**developed nations/naciones desarrolladas:** naciones con niveles de vida relativamente altos y economías basadas en la industria más que en la agricultura (p. 518)

**developing nations/naciones en vías de desarrollo:** naciones con poco desarrollo industrial y niveles de vida bajos (p. 518)

**direct foreign investment/inversión extranjera directa:** compra de bienes inmuebles (terrenos y edificios) y negocios en un país por extranjeros (p. 549)

**direct-mail advertising/publicidad por correo directo:** tipo de promoción por correo que generalmente incluye una carta describiendo el producto o servicio y un formulario para encargar o solicitarlo (p. 299)

**discount rate/tasa de descuento:** tipo de interés que el Sistema de Reserva Federal les cobra por préstamos a los bancos que son miembros (p. 414)

**discretionary income/ingresos discrecionales:** dinero que le queda a una persona de sus ingresos después de cubrir lo imprescindible (p. 60)

**disposable income/ingresos disponibles:** ingresos que le quedan a una persona para ahorrar o gastar después de pagar los impuestos; también se llama renta disponible (p. 60)

**disposal personal income/ingresos personales disponibles:** véase *disposable income/ingresos disponibles* (p. 348)

**distance education/educación a distancia:** enseñanza que se proporciona por medio de la tecnología de la telecomunicación (p. 578)

**diversification/diversificación:** invertir en varios tipos de cuentas distintas para disminuir el riesgo total (p. 158)

**dividend/dividendo:** porción de las ganancias de una sociedad anónima que se paga a los accionistas (p. 223)

**division of labor/división del trabajo:** separar un trabajo en pequeñas tareas desempeñadas por distintos obreros (p. 280)

**durability/durabilidad:** cualidad de poder aguantar mucho tiempo sin estropearse o romperse (p. 118)

**durable goods/bienes duraderos:** artículos manufacturados con una vida de más de tres años (p. 84)

## E

**e-commerce/comercio electrónico:** llevar a cabo transacciones de negocio a través de redes de computadoras, en particular World Wide Web (pp. 303, 567)

**economic assistance/asistencia económica:** préstamos y subsidios de dinero o maquinaria a otras naciones para aumentar sus recursos capitales (p. 525)

**economic efficiency/eficiencia económica:** buen uso de los recursos disponibles para que los costos no excedan los beneficios (p. 47)

**economic equity/equidad económica:** una política económica gubernamental que trata de lograr que todos se beneficien de manera justa (p. 47)

**economic growth/crecimiento económico:** expansión de la economía para producir más bienes, trabajos y riqueza (p. 48)

**economic indicators/indicadores económicos:** estadísticas que miden muchas variables en la economía (p. 367)

**economic model/modelo económico:** teoría o representación simplificada que ayuda a explicar y prever la conducta económica en el mundo real (p. 19)

**economics/economía:** estudio de cómo individuos y sociedades deciden cómo usar recursos limitados para satisfacer sus necesidades y deseos (p. 3)

**economic system/sistema económico:** manera en que una nación usa sus recursos para satisfacer las necesidades y deseos de su pueblo (p. 31)

**economies of scale/economías de escala:** rebaja en el costo promedio de producción a largo plazo que resulta de la producción en gran cantidad o escala (p. 241)

**economy/economía:** producción y distribución de bienes y servicios en una sociedad (p. 19)

**elastic demand/demanda elástica:** situación en que el aumento o rebaja del precio de un producto tiene gran efecto en la cantidad de ese producto que los consumidores están dispuestos a comprar (p. 184)

**elasticity/elasticidad:** concepto económico que se refiere a la reacción de los consumidores a los aumentos o rebajas en los precios (p. 181)

**electronic funds transfer (EFT)/transferencia electrónica de fondos:** sistema que utiliza computadoras para realizar todas las funciones bancarias que antes se hacían con papel y pluma (p. 384)

**embargo/embargo:** prohibición total de la importación o exportación de un producto (p. 487)

**entrepreneur/empresario:** persona que organiza, administra y acepta los riesgos de un negocio para sacarle ganancias (p. 208)

**entrepreneurship/espíritu empresarial:** capacidad de tomar riesgos al desarrollar nuevos productos y empezar nuevos negocios para sacarles ganancias (p. 7)

**equilibrium price/precio de equilibrio:** precio al que la cantidad de un producto que los fabricantes están dispuestos a ofrecer es igual a la cantidad que los consumidores están dispuestos a comprar (p. 195)

**ethical behavior/comportamiento ético:** actuar de acuerdo con convicciones morales y éticas acerca del bien y el mal (p. 75)

**European Union/Unión Europea:** organización de naciones europeas cuyo objetivo es promover su integración económica para formar un solo mercado (p. 489)

**exchange rate/tipo de cambio:** valor de la moneda de una nación comparado con la moneda de otra (p. 479)

**expansion/expansión:** parte del ciclo económico en que la actividad económica aumenta lentamente (p. 361)

**exports/exportaciones:** bienes que se venden a otros países (p. 474)

**externalities/factores externos:** consecuencias indirectas de actividades económicas que afectan a terceras personas que no tomaron parte en ellas; pueden ser negativas o positivas (p. 432)

## F

**factors of production/factores de producción:** recursos de tierra, trabajo, capital y espíritu empresarial que se usan para producir bienes y servicios (p. 5)

**Fed/Sistema de Reserva Federal:** sistema creado por el Congreso en 1913 para servir de organización bancaria central de la nación; conocido como "Fed" (p. 399)

**federal funds rate/tasa federal por fondos prestados:** tipo de interés que se cobran los bancos unos a otros (generalmente por menos de 1 día) (p. 415)

**Federal Open Market Committee/Comité Federal del Mercado Libre:** comisión de 12 personas, parte del Sistema de Reserva Federal, que se reúne 8 veces al año para determinar lo que debe hacer la Reserva Federal para controlar la oferta monetaria; también se llama Comité Controlador del Dinero (p. 401)

**fiat money/dinero fiduciario:** dinero que tiene valor porque un decreto gubernamental ha establecido que se puede aceptar como pago por deudas (p. 379)

**finance charge/cargo de financiamiento:** costo mensual del crédito expresado en dólares y centavos (p. 92)

**finance company/compañía financiera:** compañía que asume los contratos de deudas a plazos de tiendas y les añade una cuota por cobrar la deuda; las *compañías de financiamiento directo al consumidor* hacen préstamos directamente a los consumidores a intereses altos (p. 90)

**financing/financiamiento:** obtener fondos o capital financiero para la expansión de un negocio; también se llama financiación (p. 263)

**fiscal policy/política fiscal:** uso por el gobierno federal de tributación (impuestos) y gastos para afectar la actividad comercial general (p. 457)

**fiscal year/año fiscal:** período de un año en que se llevan las cuentas; para el gobierno federal, empieza octubre 1 y termina septiembre 30 del próximo año (p. 437)

**five-year plans/planes quinquenales:** sistema de planificación central que formaba la base del sistema económico chino; fue transformado en un sistema de planificación regional que ha conducido a la libre empresa limitada (p. 504)

**fixed rate of exchange/tipo de cambio fijo:** sistema bajo el cual un gobierno nacional establece el valor de su moneda en relación con un patrón único (p. 480)

**flexible exchange rates/tipos de cambio flexibles:** arreglo bajo el cual la oferta y la demanda determinan el valor de varias monedas (p. 482)

**foreign affiliates/sucursales extranjeras:** establecimientos que forman parte de empresas multinacionales (p. 554)

**foreign aid/ayuda al exterior:** dinero, bienes y servicios que gobiernos y organizaciones privadas donan para ayudar a otras naciones y sus ciudadanos (p. 525)

**foreign exchange markets/mercados de divisas:** mercados donde negocios que desean importar bienes de otros países compran y venden divisas (monedas extranjeras) (p. 480)

**fractional reserve banking/reserva bancaria parcial:** sistema que permite que los bancos tengan sólo un porcentaje de sus depósitos a mano o en reserva; el resto lo pueden usar para hacer préstamos o inversiones (p. 408)

**franchise/franquicia:** contrato mediante el cual un negocio vende a otro el derecho de usar su nombre y vender sus productos; también se llama licencia (p. 224)

**free enterprise system/sistema de libre empresa:** sistema económico en que los individuos son dueños de los factores de producción y deciden cómo los van a usar dentro de los límites legales; lo mismo que *capitalismo* (p. 42)

**frequency marketing/promoción según la frecuencia de uso:** mercadotecnia dirigida por información almacenada sobre la frecuencia con que el cliente utiliza el producto (p. 568)

**full employment/pleno empleo:** condición económica en que el índice de desempleo está por debajo de un porcentaje establecido por estudios económicos (p. 453)

## G

**GDP:** véase *gross domestic product (GDP)*

**GDP price deflator/deflactor de precios del PIB:** índice de precios que sustrae del PIB los efectos de la inflación para poder comparar el estado de la economía en un año con el estado económico en otro (p. 353)

**General Agreement on Tariffs and Trade/Acuerdo General sobre Aranceles Aduaneros y Comercio:** acuerdo comercial bajo el cual muchos países se reunían periódicamente para negociar rebajas en los aranceles que eran ventajosas para todos los participantes (p. 488)

**generic brand/nombre genérico:** nombre común de un producto en vez de la marca de fábrica que le da el fabricante (p. 70)

**global integration/integración global:** dependencia mutua entre los países del mundo, en especial con respecto a los mercados financieros y las telecomunicaciones; también se llama integración mundial (p. 544)

**goods/bienes:** objetos materiales que pueden satisfacer los deseos del público (p. 6)

**gross domestic product (GDP)/producto interior bruto (PIB):** valor total en dólares de todos los bienes y servicios producidos por una nación en un año (p. 344)

## H

**hypothesis/hipótesis:** suposición que tiene dos o más variables y que se tiene que comprobar para ver si es válida (p. 20)

## I

**import quota/cuota de importación:** restricción en el valor o número de unidades de un producto que se puede traer a un país (p. 487)

**imports/importaciones:** bienes traídos de otro país para el uso doméstico (p. 473)

**income redistribution/redistribución de rentas:** actividad gubernamental que toma los ingresos de algunas personas a través de impuestos y los usa para ayudar a otras personas necesitadas (p. 431)

**individual retirement account/cuentas de retiro individuales:** planes de jubilación privados que permiten que individuos o matrimonios ahorren cierta porción de sus ingresos anuales sin pagar impuestos y que posponen el impuesto sobre los intereses (p. 156)

**industrial union/sindicato industrial:** asociación de todos los obreros de una industria, que no toma en cuenta el tipo de trabajo ni el nivel de especialización (p. 324)

**inelastic demand/demanda inelástica:** situación en que el precio de un producto tiene poco efecto en la cantidad demandada por los consumidores (p. 184)

**infant mortality rate/índice de mortalidad infantil:** porcentaje de muertes de niños en el primer año de vida (p. 520)

**inflation/inflación:** aumento prolongado en el nivel general de los precios de bienes y servicios (p. 350)

**Information Age/Edad de la Información:** período en que las telecomunicaciones y la informática dieron a la información valor económico significativo (p. 571)

**informative advertising/publicidad informativa:** anuncios que benefician a los consumidores al darles información sobre un producto (p. 68)

**injunction/prohibición judicial:** orden de un juez que impide alguna actividad (p. 332)

**innovation(s)/innovación:** desarrollo de nuevos productos, sistemas o procesos que tienen efectos de gran alcance (pp. 365, 573)

**installment debt/deudas pagadas a plazos:** tipo de préstamo que se paga en cantidades iguales durante un período determinado de tiempo (p. 84)

**intellectual property/propiedad intelectual:** creaciones de la mente de una persona que están protegidas por copyright; por ejemplo, obras escritas y musicales (p. 577)

**interest/interés:** pago que alguien recibe cuando presta dinero o permite que otra persona use su dinero (pp. 84, 142)

**interlocking directorate/directorio entrelazado:** junta directiva de una compañía cuya mayoría también sirve en la junta directiva de otra sociedad anónima que compite en el mismo mercado (p. 249)

**intermediate-term financing/financiamiento a mediano plazo:** dinero prestado que un negocio tiene entre 1 y 10 años para pagar (p. 272)

**International Monetary Fund (IMF)/Fondo Monetario Internacional (FMI):** agencia que antes obligaba a los gobiernos de países miembros a mantener sus tipos de cambio más o menos fijos; hoy ofrece asesoramiento monetario y proporciona préstamos a países en desarrollo (p. 481)

**Internet/Internet:** sistema mundial de computadoras interconectadas que almacenan, procesan y comparten información (p. 566)

**inventory/inventario:** artículos que un negocio tiene almacenados, como materias primas o mercancía para vender (p. 209)

## J

**joint venture/negocio en participación:** sociedad establecida por un corto período de tiempo con un propósito determinado (p. 217)

## K

**Keogh Plan/Plan Keogh:** plan de jubilación que le permite al que trabaja por su cuenta ahorrar un máximo del 15 por ciento de sus ingresos anuales hasta llegar a una cantidad determinada y descontar la cantidad ahorrada de sus ingresos anuales gravables (p. 156)

**knowledge economy/economía basada en los conocimientos:** economía en la cual la información es la clave del crecimiento (p. 572)

## L

**labor/trabajo:** esfuerzo humano dirigido a la producción de bienes y servicios (p. 6)

**labor union/sindicato de obreros:** asociación de trabajadores organizados para mejorar los salarios y condiciones de trabajo de sus miembros; también se llama sindicato laboral y gremio de obreros (p. 321)

**lagging indicators/indicadores de rezaga:** indicadores que ocurren después de los cambios en las actividades comerciales (p. 367)

**laissez-faire/dejad hacer:** sistema económico en que el gobierno interfiere lo menos posible en la economía (p. 41)

**land/tierra:** recursos naturales, la superficie terrestre y el agua (p. 6)

**law of demand/ley de la demanda:** regla económica que dice que al cambiar el precio, la cantidad demandada cambia en sentido contrario (p. 171)

**law of diminishing marginal utility/ley de utilidad marginal decreciente:** regla económica que dice que el consumidor recibe menos satisfacción adicional cada vez que compra una unidad más de un producto (p. 174)

**law of diminishing returns/ley de los rendimientos decrecientes:** regla económica que dice que al añadir más unidades de un solo factor económico (como el trabajo) a los otros factores económicos (como máquinas), el aumento en la producción será menos y menos significativo (p. 192)

**law of supply/ley de la oferta:** regla económica que dice que al cambiar el precio, la cantidad ofrecida cambia en el mismo sentido (p. 187)

**leading indicators/indicadores anticipados:** estadísticas que pronostican lo que va a suceder en la economía (p. 367)

**lease/contrato de alquiler:** acuerdo a largo plazo que describe los términos bajo los cuales se alquila o arrienda una propiedad (p. 124)

**legal tender/medios de curso legal:** moneda que, por ley, se tiene que aceptar en pago de deudas públicas y privadas (p. 379)

**liability insurance/seguro de responsabilidad civil:** seguro que paga por lesiones corporales y daños a propiedad (p. 133)

**limited liability/responsabilidad limitada:** requisito que limita la responsabilidad de cada dueño por las deudas de una compañía al tamaño de su inversión en la firma (p. 220)

**limited partnership/sociedad limitada:** tipo de sociedad en que uno o más socios tienen responsabilidad limitada, pero no pueden participar en la administración del negocio (p. 217)

**local union/sección sindical:** agrupación de miembros de un sindicato de obreros en una fábrica, compañía o área geográfica en particular (p. 324)

**lockout/cierre patronal:** situación en que los gerentes impiden que los trabajadores regresen al trabajo hasta que acepten un nuevo contrato; también se llama paro forzoso o paro patronal (p. 331)

**long-term financing/financiamiento a largo plazo:** préstamo de dinero que un negocio tiene por más de 10 años (p. 273)

**loose money policy/política monetaria expansiva:** política monetaria que resulta en crédito barato y abundante; puede conducir a la inflación (p. 408)

## M

**M1/M1:** definición más estricta de la oferta monetaria; comprende el dinero que se puede gastar inmediatamente y contra el cual se pueden emitir cheques (p. 391)

**M2/M2:** definición más general de la oferta monetaria; incluye la M1 más cuasi-dinero como los balances de los fondos de mercado monetario, certificados de depósito y eurodólares (p. 391)

**macroeconomics/macroeconomía:** rama de la teoría económica que trata de la economía en su totalidad y de los modos en que grandes organismos, como los gobiernos, toman decisiones (p. 18)

**marginal utility/utilidad marginal:** una cantidad adicional de satisfacción o provecho (p. 174)

**market/mercado:** actividad libre entre compradores y vendedores de bienes y servicios (pp. 36, 170)

**market basket/canasta de compras:** grupo representativo de bienes y servicios usado para calcular el índice de precios al consumidor (p. 352)

**market economy/economía de mercado:** sistema en que particulares son los dueños de los factores de producción y toman decisiones económicas, relacionándose libremente con otros, para el mayor beneficio de sus familias y sí mismos (p. 36)

**marketing/mercadotecnia:** todas las actividades necesarias para mover bienes y servicios de los productores a los consumidores; también se llama marketing (p. 280)

**market research/investigación de mercados:** reunir, anotar y analizar datos acerca de los tipos de bienes y servicios que desea el público (p. 292)

**market structure/estructura del mercado:** punto hasta el cual la competencia predomina en un mercado (p. 233)

**market survey/estudio del mercado:** encuesta en que los investigadores reúnen información sobre los posibles usuarios de un producto, como su edad, sexo, ingresos, estudios y ubicación (p. 293)

**maturity/plazo de vencimiento:** período de tiempo al final del cual los depósitos a plazos pagan una tasa de interés establecida (p. 143)

**mechanization/mecanización:** esfuerzo combinado de personas y máquinas (p. 280)

**mediation/mediación:** etapa en la negociación de un contrato entre el sindicato y los gerentes en que una persona neutral trata de hacer que ambas partes lleguen a un acuerdo (p. 329)

**Medicaid/Medicaid:** programa de asistencia pública de los gobiernos estatales y federal que proporciona cuidado de la salud gratis a personas discapacitadas o con ingresos bajos (p. 431)

**Medicare/Medicare:** programa gubernamental que proporciona cuidado de la salud para personas de la tercera edad (p. 426)

**medium of exchange/medio de cambio:** uso del dinero a cambio de bienes y servicios (p. 376)

**merger/corporación:** fusión de compañías en una sola que resulta cuando una sociedad anónima compra más de la mitad de las acciones de otra sociedad anónima y así controla la segunda empresa (p. 249)

**microchip/chip:** circuito electrónico diminuto que procesa y transfiere información digital (p. 565)

**microeconomics/microeconomía:** rama de la teoría económica que estudia la conducta y modos de tomar decisiones de unidades pequeñas, como individuos y empresas (p. 18)

**military assistance/asistencia militar:** ayuda económica o técnica dada a las fuerzas armadas de una nación (p. 525)

**minimum wage law/ley del salario mínimo:** ley federal que establece el sueldo por hora más bajo que se puede pagar legalmente a ciertos tipos de trabajadores (p. 319)

**mixed economy/economía mixta:** sistema que combina las características de más de un tipo de economía (p. 38)

**monetarism/monetarismo:** teoría que relaciona la cantidad de dinero que el Sistema de Reserva Federal pone en circulación con el nivel de actividad en la economía (p. 462)

**monetarists/monetaristas:** partidarios de la teoría del monetarismo, a menudo conectada con Milton Friedman (p. 462)

**monetary policy/política monetaria:** política que controla el crecimiento de la cantidad de dinero en circulación para afectar el costo y la facilidad de obtener crédito (p. 400)

**monetary rule/norma monetaria:** creencia de los monetaristas que el Sistema de Reserva Federal debe permitir que la oferta monetaria crezca a un ritmo anual constante y no usar la política monetaria para estimular o reducir la actividad económica (p. 463)

**money/moneda:** cualquier cosa que se acostumbra usar como medio de cambio, unidad de contabilidad y reserva de valor; también se llama dinero (p. 376)

**money market deposit account/cuenta de depósito de mercado monetario:** cuentas que pagan intereses relativamente altos, requieren saldos mínimos y mantienen el dinero disponible en cualquier momento (p. 143)

**money market fund/fondo de mercado monetario:** tipo de fondo mutualista que utiliza el dinero de los inversionistas para hacer préstamos a corto plazo a empresas y bancos (p. 152)

**monopolistic competition/competencia monopolística:** mercado en que un gran número de vendedores ofrecen productos parecidos aunque algo distintos y en que cada vendedor tiene algún control sobre el precio (p. 245)

**monopoly/monopolio:** mercado en que hay sólo un proveedor que comprende la industria entera de un producto o servicio sin verdaderos sustitutos (p. 240)

**mortgage/hipoteca:** tipo de deuda pagada a plazos por casas, edificios o terrenos (p. 85)

**multinationals/corporaciones multinacionales:** firmas que hacen negocio y tienen oficinas y fábricas en muchos países; también se llaman empresas transnacionales o internacionales (p. 553)

**mutual fund/fondo mutualista:** compañía inversionista que reúne el dinero de muchos individuos para comprar acciones, bonos y otros tipos de inversiones (p. 151)

## N

**national debt/deuda pública:** cantidad de deuda que tiene el gobierno federal (p. 439)

**national income/renta nacional:** ingresos totales de todas las personas que forman parte de una economía (p. 347)

**national income accounting/cálculo de la renta nacional:** medida del rendimiento económico de una nación, tomando en cuenta la producción y los ingresos totales (p. 343)

**nationalization/nacionalización:** toma de ferrocarriles, negocios y otras industrias por el gobierno como propiedad pública (p. 525)

**near moneys/cuasi-dinero:** activos, como las cuentas de ahorro, que se pueden convertir en dinero con bastante facilidad sin correr el riesgo de que pierdan valor (p. 390)

**net domestic product/producto interior neto:** valor de la producción total de un país (PIB) menos el valor total perdido por la depreciación de las máquinas y equipos (p. 347)

**net exports/exportaciones netas:** diferencia entre lo que una nación le vende a otros países y lo que compra de ellos (p. 346)

**North American Free Trade Agreement/Tratado de Libre Comercio Norteamericano:** acuerdo comercial diseñado para disminuir las barreras arancelarias entre México, Canadá y Estados Unidos (p. 489)

## O

**oligopoly/oligopolio:** industria dominada por pocos proveedores que ejercen algún control sobre los precios (p. 243)

**open-market operations/operaciones del mercado abierto:** compra y venta de valores de los Estados Unidos por el Sistema de Reserva Federal para afectar la oferta monetaria (p. 416)

**opportunity cost/costo de oportunidad:** valor de la mejor opción a la que se renuncia al escoger otra opción (p. 13)

**overdraft checking/cuenta corriente con descubierto:** cuenta corriente que le permite al cliente escribir cheques por más dinero del que tiene en la cuenta; también se llama cuenta corriente con sobregiro (p. 384)

**over-the-counter market/mercado extrabursátil:** compra y venta electrónica de acciones y bonos, a menudo de compañías pequeñas, que se realiza fuera de las bolsas de valores organizadas (p. 150)

## P

**partnership/sociedad:** negocio operado por dos o más individuos que son los dueños (p. 215)

**passbook savings account/cuenta de ahorro con libreta bancaria:** cuenta para la cual el ahorrador recibe una libreta en que se registran sus depósitos, retiros de fondos e intereses (p. 142)

**patent/patente:** protección del gobierno que da a un inventor el derecho exclusivo de fabricar, usar o vender su invento por un determinado número de años (p. 241)

**peak/auge:** período de prosperidad en el ciclo económico en que la actividad económica ha llegado a su nivel más alto (p. 360)

**penetration pricing/fijar un precio de penetración:** vender un producto nuevo a precio bajo para atraer a los compradores de un producto establecido (p. 298)

**pension plans/planes de pensiones:** planes que empresas tienen para proporcionar ingresos a sus trabajadores jubilados (p. 155)

**perfect competition/competencia perfecta:** mercado en que hay muchos vendedores y compradores y ninguno puede afectar el precio independientemente (p. 234)

**personal income/ingresos personales:** ingresos totales que recibe una persona antes de pagar sus impuestos personales; también se llama renta personal (p. 348)

**picketing/piquetear**: forma de protesta en que trabajadores en huelga se pasean delante del lugar de trabajo con letreros que declaran sus desacuerdos con la compañía (p. 329)

**points/puntos:** suma que se le paga a un prestamista y se calcula como puntos porcentuales del préstamo (p. 123)

**preferred stock/acciones preferentes:** participaciones en una sociedad anónima que dan a los accionistas una porción de las ganancias futuras (antes de pagar a dueños de acciones ordinarias), pero sin el derecho al voto; también se llaman acciones preferidas (p. 223)

**price ceiling/precio máximo:** precio más alto que la ley permite que se cobre por un producto o servicio en particular (p. 197)

**price elasticity of demand/efecto del precio en la elasticidad de la demanda:** concepto económico que trata de *cómo* la demanda varía de acuerdo con los cambios en el precio (p. 181)

**price floor/precio mínimo:** precio más bajo que la ley permite que se cobre por un producto o servicio (p. 198)

**price leadership/liderazgo en la fijación de precios:** práctica de seguir el ejemplo de una compañía que cambia el precio de un artículo por compañías que cobran aproximadamente el mismo precio por productos semejantes (p. 298)

**prime rate/tasa preferencial:** tipo de interés que los bancos cobran por préstamos a sus mejores clientes comerciales (p. 414)

**principal/principal:** cantidad de dinero prestado; también se llama capital (p. 84)

**private-labeled products/productos de marca privada:** productos a precios más bajos que llevan la marca de la tienda en que se venden y son vendidos por cadenas de supermercados y de clubes almacenes (p. 113)

**private property/propiedad privada:** todo lo que pertenece a particulares y no al gobierno (p. 43)

**privatization/privatización:** transferir al sector privado negocios, tierras y edificios que pertenecen al estado (p. 509)

**producer price index (PPI)/índice de precios de productores:** medida, a través del tiempo, de los cambios en los precios que los productores estadounidenses cobran a los mayoristas por sus bienes y servicios (p. 353)

**product differentiation/diferenciación de productos:** uso de pequeñas diferencias en calidad y características por parte de los fabricantes para tratar de diferenciar bienes y servicios parecidos (p. 244)

**production/producción:** proceso de convertir recursos en bienes que satisfacen las necesidades y deseos de individuos y negocios (p. 277)

**production possibilities curve/curva de posibilidades de producción:** gráfica que muestra la mayor combinación de bienes y servicios que se pueden producir con una cantidad fija de recursos en un período de tiempo determinado (p. 14)

**productivity/productividad:** producción final (cantidad de bienes y servicios) que rinde una cantidad determinada de insumos (tierra, trabajo y capital) (p. 7)

**product life cycle/ciclo de vida de un producto:** etapas por las que pasa un producto desde que se introduce hasta que se retira del mercado (p. 300)

**professionals/profesionales:** personas muy preparadas, que han cursado por lo menos cuatro años al nivel universitario y generalmente tienen educación o preparación adicional (p. 316)

**profit/ganancias:** dinero que queda después de pagar todos los costos de producción—incluyendo salarios, alquiler, intereses e impuestos; también se llama lucro, beneficios y utilidad (pp. 43, 265)

**profit incentive/ánimo de lucro:** deseo de ganar dinero que alienta a las personas a producir y vender bienes y servicios (p. 43)

**progressive tax/impuesto progresivo:** impuesto que grava un porcentaje mayor a los que tienen más ingresos y menor a los que tienen menos; se justifica con el principio de la capacidad de pago (p. 443)

**proletariat/proletariado:** término usado por Carlos Marx para referirse a los obreros (p. 499)

**promotion/promoción:** uso de la publicidad para informar a los consumidores que un producto o servicio nuevo o mejorado está en venta y para convencerlos a que lo compren (p. 299)

**proportional tax/impuesto proporcional:** impuesto que grava el mismo porcentaje a todos los ingresos; al subir los ingresos, la cantidad de impuestos que hay que pagar también sube (p. 443)

**proprietor/propietario:** dueño de un negocio (p. 215)

**protectionists/proteccionistas:** personas que abogan en favor de restricciones comerciales para proteger las industrias domésticas (p. 487)

**protective tariff/aranceles proteccionistas:** impuestos sobre las importaciones usados para subir el precio de bienes importados y proteger a los productores domésticos (p. 487)

**public-assistance programs/programas de asistencia pública:** programas gubernamentales que hacen pagos a personas necesitadas (p. 431)

**public goods/bienes públicos:** bienes y servicios que el gobierno proporciona al público; pueden ser usados por muchas personas a la misma vez sin reducir el beneficio que obtiene cada una (p. 430)

**public-works projects/proyectos de obras públicas:** edificaciones e instalaciones para el uso público, como escuelas y carreteras, construidas por el gobierno federal, estatal o local con dinero público (p. 425)

**purchasing power/poder adquisitivo:** cantidad real de bienes y servicios que se pueden comprar con el dinero; determina el valor del dinero (p. 351)

## Q

**quantity demanded/cantidad demandada:** cantidad de un producto o servicio que los consumidores están dispuestos y pueden comprar a un precio dado (p. 172)

**quantity supplied/cantidad ofrecida:** cantidad de un producto o servicio que un productor está dispuesto y puede ofrecer a un precio dado (p. 187)

## R

**rational choice/selección racional:** escoger la alternativa de mayor valor entre productos de la misma calidad (p. 62)

**rationing/racionamiento:** basar la distribución de bienes y servicios en razones que no incluyen el precio (p. 197)

**real GDP/PIB real:** PIB al que se le ha aplicado el deflactor de precios para corregir los efectos de la inflación (p. 353)

**real income effect/efecto de ingresos reales:** regla económica que dice que los consumidores no pueden continuar comprando la misma cantidad de un producto si el precio de éste sube mientras que sus ingresos se mantienen iguales (p. 172)

**receipts/entradas:** ingresos recibidos de la venta de bienes o servicios; recibos escritos que comprueban que se han hecho ciertas compras (p. 209)

**recession/recesión:** parte del ciclo económico en que el rendimiento nacional (PIB real) no aumenta por seis meses al menos (p. 361)

**recovery/recuperación:** lo mismo que *expansion/expansión* (p. 361)

**registration fee/cuota por la matrícula:** suma, generalmente anual, que se paga a un estado por el derecho de usar un automóvil (p. 130)

**regressive tax/impuesto regresivo:** impuesto que toma un mayor porcentaje de ingresos más bajos que de ingresos más altos (p. 443)

**representative money/dinero crediticio:** dinero que está respaldado por algo de valor, como el oro o la plata (p. 378)

**reserve requirements/reserva obligatoria:** regulación establecida por el Sistema de Reserva Federal que requiere que los bancos mantengan un porcentaje de sus depósitos en efectivo en sus propias bóvedas de seguridad o en el banco de la Reserva Federal de su distrito (p. 408)

**retailers/tiendas al por menor:** negocios que venden bienes directamente al consumidor (p. 303)

**revenues/entradas:** total de los ingresos provenientes de la venta de la producción de una compañía (p. 265)

**revenue tariff/derechos aduaneros:** impuesto sobre las importaciones usado principalmente para recaudar ingresos sin restringir las importaciones; también se llaman impuestos aduaneros o derechos arancelarios (p. 487)

**right-to-work laws/leyes de derecho al trabajo:** leyes estatales que prohiben que los sindicatos fuercen a los trabajadores a afiliarse y a pagar cuotas sindicales (p. 325)

**robotics/robótica:** maquinaria compleja, controlada por computadoras, que opera una línea de montaje (p. 281)

**Roth IRA/cuenta de retiro individual Roth:** plan de jubilación privado en que se gravan los ingresos antes de ser ahorrados, pero no se gravan los intereses por los ahorros cuando se usan esos fondos después de jubilarse (p. 156)

## S

**saving/ahorrar:** guardar ingresos por un período de tiempo para poder usarlos más adelante (p. 141)

**savings and loan association (S&L)/sociedad de ahorro y préstamos:** institución que acepta depósitos y presta dinero (p. 89)

**savings bank/banco de ahorro:** tipo de institución depositaria establecida originalmente para servir a personas que ahorraban pequeñas cantidades y eran ignorados por los bancos comerciales (p. 89)

**savings bonds/bonos de ahorro:** bonos emitidos por el gobierno federal para obtener dinero prestado; se compran a la mitad de su valor nominal, y cada 6 meses aumentan en valor hasta llegar al valor nominal completo (p. 149)

**scarcity/escasez:** condición de no poder tener todos los bienes y servicios que se desean porque los deseos exceden lo que se puede producir con los recursos que hay en un momento dado (p. 5)

**secured loan/préstamo garantizado:** préstamo que está asegurado por propiedad (p. 98)

**security deposit/depósito de garantía:** dinero que un inquilino pone en manos del dueño en caso de que no pague el alquiler o deje el apartamento dañado (p. 125)

**semiskilled workers/obreros semicalificados:** personas cuyos trabajos requieren un poco de preparación, a menudo en el uso de la tecnología moderna; también se llaman obreros semiespecializados (p. 316)

**service flow/servicio útil:** cantidad de uso que una persona le saca a un artículo a través del tiempo y el valor que le da a su uso (p. 118)

**services/servicios:** actividades económicas que satisfacen algún deseo del público (p. 6)

**service workers/trabajadores en el área de servicio:** personas que proporcionan servicios directamente al público (p. 315)

**shortage/escasez:** situación en que la cantidad demandada es mayor que la cantidad ofrecida; falta de un producto (p. 196)

**short-term financing/financiamiento a corto plazo:** préstamo de dinero que un negocio tiene que pagar en menos de un año (p. 271)

**skilled workers/obreros calificados:** personas que han aprendido un oficio o artesanía en una escuela de artes y oficios o como aprendices de obreros maestros; también se llaman obreros especializados (p. 316)

**small business incubator/incubadora de pequeños negocios:** agencia financiada por el gobierno que asiste a nuevos negocios, proporcionando asesoramiento, locales con alquileres bajos y artículos de uso diario (p. 209)

**social insurance programs/programas de seguridad social:** programas gubernamentales que pagan prestaciones a trabajadores retirados o inválidos, a sus familias y a los desempleados; son financiados con impuestos pagados para estos programas por trabajadores y empresas (p. 431)

**Social Security/Seguro Social:** programa federal que proporciona pagos mensuales a personas que están jubiladas o no pueden trabajar (p. 431)

**sole proprietorship/propiedad individual:** negocio operado por un solo dueño, el propietario único (p. 213)

**specialization/especialización:** concepto de que una nación debe limitarse a producir y exportar una selección de aquellos bienes que son más apropiados para ser producidos en ella, para sacar mayores ganancias (p. 475)

**stabilization policies/políticas de estabilización:** intentos por parte del gobierno federal de mantener sana la economía; incluyen las políticas monetaria y fiscal (p. 451)

**stagflation/estagflación:** combinación de inflación con poca actividad económica; también se llama estanflación (p. 455)

**standard of living/nivel de vida:** bienestar material de un individuo, grupo o nación, en forma de cálculo de lo bien que puede satisfacer sus necesidades y obtener lujos (p. 48)

**startup/negocio nuevo:** empresa nueva (p. 208)

**statement savings account/cuenta de ahorro con estado de cuenta:** cuenta similar a la cuenta de ahorro con libreta bancaria, pero en vez de tener una libreta, el ahorrador recibe un estado de cuenta mensual que enumera todas sus transacciones (p. 142)

**stock/acciones:** participaciones en una sociedad anónima que hacen al comprador uno de sus propietarios con derecho a recibir parte de las ganancias y activos de la sociedad (p. 220)

**stockholders/accionistas:** personas que han invertido en una sociedad anónima y son dueños de un número de acciones (p. 147)

**store of value/reserva de valor:** uso del dinero como almacén del poder adquisitivo que una persona recibe como pago, a cambio de su trabajo o de un artículo vendido, y que puede usar en el futuro (p. 377)

**strike/huelga:** paro de trabajo intencional por parte de los trabajadores para forzar a los patronos a que ceden a sus demandas (p. 323)

**subsistence agriculture/agricultura de subsistencia:** cultivar alimentos suficientes para satisfacer las necesidades de una familia solamente; la cosecha no alcanza para exportar o alimentar a la fuerza laboral industrial (p. 519)

**substitution effect/efecto de sustitución:** regla económica que dice que si dos artículos satisfacen la misma necesidad y el precio de uno sube, el público comprará el otro (p. 172)

**Supplemental Security Income/Ingresos Suplementarios de Seguridad:** programas federales que incluyen cupones para comprar alimentos y prestaciones a veteranos, ancianos, ciegos e inválidos (p. 431)

**supply/oferta:** cantidad de un producto o servicio que los productores pueden y están dispuestos a vender a varios precios durante un período de tiempo determinado (p. 170)

**supply curve/curva de oferta:** línea ascendiente en una gráfica cuya inclinación muestra la cantidad ofrecida a cada precio posible (p. 189)

**supply schedule/lista de oferta:** tabla que muestra las cantidades que se ofrecen a distintos precios (p. 188)

**surplus/superávit:** situación en que la cantidad ofrecida es mayor que la cantidad demandada (p. 196)

## T

**tariff/arancel:** impuesto que grava un producto importado (p. 486)

**tax-exempt bonds/bonos exentos de impuestos:** bonos emitidos por los gobiernos locales y estatales; los intereses que pagan no son gravados por el gobierno federal (p. 148)

**technical assistance/asistencia técnica:** ayuda que proporcionan profesionales como ingenieros, maestros y técnicos; proporcionada por naciones para enseñar técnicas a personas de otros países (p. 525)

**technology/tecnología:** avances en los conocimientos científicos que conducen a nuevos y mejorados bienes y servicios y a mejores maneras de producirlos (pp. 7, 190)

**telecommunications/telecomunicaciones:** comunicaciones a larga distancia, generalmente electrónicas, que usan satélites de comunicación y cables de fibra óptica (pp. 544, 571)

**Temporary Assistance to Needy Families/Asistencia Provisional a Familias Necesitadas:** programa de asistencia pública administrado por los estados que proporciona dinero a padres solteros necesitados que están criando niños pequeños (p. 431)

**test marketing/hacer una prueba de mercado:** poner un producto en venta en un área pequeña por un período de tiempo limitado para ver lo bien que se vende antes de ofrecerlo en todo el país (p. 293)

**thrift institutions/instituciones de ahorro:** bancos de ahorro mutuos, sociedades de ahorro y préstamos y cooperativas de crédito que ofrecen los mismos servicios que los bancos comerciales (p. 389)

**tight money policy/política monetaria restrictiva:** política monetaria que hace que el crédito sea caro y difícil de obtener para tratar de reducir la actividad económica (p. 408)

**time deposits/depósitos a plazos:** planes de ahorro que obligan al ahorrador a dejar su dinero en depósito por períodos de tiempo determinados (p. 143)

**time lags/demoras:** período entre el momento en que se aprueba una política fiscal y el momento en que entra en vigor (p. 465)

**trade-off/compensación:** renunciar a un producto o servicio para comprar o producir otro (p. 12)

**traditional economy/economía tradicional:** sistema en que las decisiones económicas se basan en las costumbres y creencias que se han pasado de generación en generación (p. 33)

**transfer payments/transferencias:** pagos de asistencia social y otros pagos suplementarios como los de seguros de desempleo, Seguro Social y Medicaid que el gobierno estatal o federal le hace a individuos (p. 348)

**Treasury bills/letras del Tesoro:** certificados emitidos por el Tesoro de los EE.UU. que requieren una inversión mínima de $10,000 y se vencen entre 3 meses y 1 año después (p. 149)

**Treasury bonds/bonos del Tesoro:** certificados emitidos por el Tesoro de los EE.UU. a cambio de inversiones mínimas de $1,000 ó $5,000 con fechas de vencimiento de 10 años o más en el futuro (p. 149)

**Treasury notes/pagarés del Tesoro:** certificados emitidos por el Tesoro de los EE.UU. a cambio de inversiones mínimas de $1,000 ó $5,000 con fechas de vencimiento de 2 a 10 años después (p. 149)

**trough/punto bajo:** parte del ciclo económico en que la actividad económica en disminución se nivela; también se llama depresión (p. 361)

## U

**underground economy/economía sumergida:** transacciones hechas por personas que no obedecen las leyes federales y estatales que requieren que se de parte al gobierno sobre los ingresos (p. 453)

**unemployment rate/índice de desempleo:** porcentaje de la fuerza laboral civil que no tiene empleo pero está buscando trabajo (p. 452)

**union/sindicato:** véase *labor union/sindicato de obreros*

**union shop/fábrica sindical:** compañía que obliga a nuevos empleados a hacerse miembros del sindicato después de un período de tiempo determinado (p. 324)

**unit of accounting/unidad de contabilidad:** uso del dinero como medida del valor de distintos bienes y servicios que se puede usar de criterio para compararlos (p. 376)

**unlimited liability/responsabilidad sin límite:** requisito que hace a un dueño total y personalmente responsable de todas las pérdidas y deudas de su negocio (p. 215)

**unsecured loan/préstamo no garantizado:** préstamo hecho sin obtener una garantía, sólo la promesa de devolver el dinero (p. 98)

**unskilled workers/trabajadores no calificados:** personas cuyos trabajos no requieren preparación especial (p. 316)

**usury law/ley contra la usura:** ley que limita la cantidad de interés que se puede cobrar por el crédito (p. 102)

**utility/utilidad:** capacidad de un producto o servicio de satisfacer los deseos de los consumidores (p. 173); cantidad de provecho que el consumidor recibe de un producto o servicio (p. 290)

## V

**vicious cycle of poverty/círculo vicioso de la pobreza:** situación en que un país poco desarrollado con ingresos *per capita* bajos no puede ahorrar e invertir dinero suficiente para alcanzar una tasa de crecimiento económico aceptable y queda estancado (p. 536)

**voluntary exchange/intercambio voluntario:** transacción en que el comprador y el vendedor ejercen su libertad económica al llegar a un acuerdo sobre las condiciones del intercambio (p. 170)

## W

**warranty/garantía:** promesa de un fabricante o vendedor de reparar o reemplazar un producto defectuoso dentro de un plazo de tiempo determinado (p. 70)

**Web sites/lugares de Web:** sitios en World Wide Web que almacenan información que se puede ver o trasladar a una computadora; también se llaman páginas de Web (p. 566)

**weightless economy/economía "sin peso":** frase inventada para identificar una economía basada en productos que no son materiales (p. 572)

**welfare/bienestar social:** lo mismo que *public-assistance programs/programas de asistencia pública* (p. 431)

**welfare state/estado de bienestar social:** país en que hay una mezcla de capitalismo y socialismo, combinando la propiedad privada de los medios de producción y la distribución competitiva de recursos con la meta de igualdad social para todos los habitantes (p. 510)

**white-collar workers/empleados en trabajos no manuales:** categoría de trabajadores empleados en oficinas, ventas o puestos profesionales (p. 315)

**wholesalers/mayoristas:** negocios que compran grandes cantidades de bienes de los fabricantes para vendérselas a otros negocios (p. 303)

**workers' compensation/compensación a trabajadores accidentados:** programas gubernamentales que hacen pagos para asistencia médica a trabajadores que se lesionan en el trabajo (p. 431)

**World Trade Organization/Organización Mundial del Comercio:** acuerdo comercial más extenso del mundo entre 134 naciones (pp. 488, 506)

**World Wide Web/World Wide Web:** parte de Internet usada para las comunicaciones entre consumidores, negocios, gobiernos y otras organizaciones (p. 566)

# CAPÍTULO 1 Resumen

## SECCIÓN 1 El problema fundamental en la economía

- La **economía** es el estudio de cómo individuos, familias, negocios y sociedades utilizan recursos limitados para satisfacer deseos sin límites.
- Los individuos escogen lo que prefieren para satisfacer sus deseos ilimitados en un mundo cuyos recursos son limitados.
- Es necesario escoger por causa de la **escasez,** el problema fundamental de la economía.
- Los recursos necesarios para producir bienes y servicios se llaman **factores de producción.**
- Los cuatro factores de producción son la **tierra,** o recursos naturales; el **trabajo,** también conocido como recursos humanos; el **capital,** o productos manufacturados que se usan para producir otros bienes y servicios; y el **espíritu empresarial,** o habilidad de empezar nuevos negocios y de introducir nuevos productos y procesos.
- Algunos economistas añaden la **tecnología** a la lista de factores de producción.

## SECCIÓN 2 La compensación

- Cada vez que utilizan sus recursos de una manera u otra, las personas aceptan su elección como **compensación** por las opciones que no escogieron.
- El **costo de oportunidad** es el valor de la mejor alternativa a la que se renuncia al escoger una opción en vez de otra.
- Una **curva de posibilidades de producción** es una gráfica que muestra la máxima combinación de bienes y servicios que se pueden producir con una cantidad fija de recursos en un período de tiempo determinado.
- El ejemplo clásico que se usa en la economía para explicar las posibilidades de producción es el modo en que se compensan las armas (defensa militar) y la mantequilla (bienes para los civiles).

## SECCIÓN 3 ¿Qué hacen los economistas?

- Los economistas estudian la **economía**—todas las actividades de una nación que afectan la producción, distribución y uso de bienes y servicios.
- Los economistas formulan teorías llamadas **modelos económicos,** que son representaciones simplificadas del mundo real.
- Los economistas ponen a prueba sus modelos de la misma manera que otros científicos comprueban sus **hipótesis** o suposiciones.
- Los economistas se fundan en los hechos, aunque sus opiniones personales pueden influir en sus teorías.
- Los economistas ofrecen soluciones a problemas económicos, pero no evalúan el mérito de las distintas soluciones.

# CAPÍTULO 2 Resumen

## SECCIÓN 1 Sistemas económicos

- Todo tipo de **sistema económico** tiene que responder a tres preguntas básicas: ¿Qué bienes y servicios se deben producir? ¿Cómo se deben producir? ¿Quién debe disfrutar de lo que se produce?
- Hay cuatro tipos de sistemas económicos: tradicional, dirigido, de mercado y mixto.
- En una **economía tradicional,** las decisiones económicas se basan en las costumbres y creencias que se han pasado de generación en generación.
- En una **economía dirigida,** los líderes del gobierno controlan los factores de producción y, por lo tanto, toman todas las decisiones sobre su uso.
- En una **economía de mercado,** cada cual toma sus propias decisiones económicas para el mayor beneficio de su familia y sí mismo.
- La mayoría de los países del mundo tienen una **economía mixta,** en que individuos tienen propiedad privada y toman sus propias decisiones y a la vez hay regulación gubernamental.

## SECCIÓN 2 Características de la economía de los Estados Unidos

- Un sistema de mercado puro tiene seis características principales: poco o ningún control gubernamental, libertad de empresa, libertad de elección, propiedad privada, ánimo de lucro y competencia.
- En Estados Unidos, se practica el **capitalismo** de manera que individuos son dueños de los factores de producción pero los usan dentro de los límites de la ley.
- El **ánimo de lucro** es el deseo que impulsa al empresario a establecer nuevos negocios, expandir los que ya existen y cambiar el tipo de bienes y productos que se producen.
- Una de las características más importantes del capitalismo es la existencia de la **propiedad privada.**
- La **competencia** conduce al uso eficiente de recursos, a bienes y servicios de mejor calidad y a precios más bajos para el consumidor.

## SECCIÓN 3 Las metas de la nación

- Los Estados Unidos tiene un sistema económico de **libre empresa** o capitalista.
- Entre las metas económicas de los estadounidenses están la libertad económica, **eficiencia económica, equidad económica,** seguridad económica, estabilidad económica y **crecimiento económico.**
- Para que un sistema de libre empresa funcione bien, los individuos tienen que aceptar ciertas responsabilidades económicas, entre ellas ser miembros productivos de la sociedad y elegir funcionarios del gobierno que sean responsables.

# CAPÍTULO 3 Resumen

## SECCIÓN 1 Consumo, ingresos y toma de decisiones

- Un **consumidor** es cualquier persona o grupo que compra o utiliza bienes y servicios para satisfacer sus deseos personales.
- Los ingresos pueden ser **disponibles** y **discrecionales.**
- La educación, ocupación, experiencia y salud influyen en lo que una persona puede ganar y, por lo tanto, en su capacidad para consumir.
- Las decisiones de consumo tienen tres partes: (1) decidir que uno va a gastar dinero; (2) determinar cuál es la mejor compra; (3) decidir cómo usar lo que se compra.
- Cuando uno toma decisiones de consumo basándose en el costo de oportunidad, hace una **selección racional.**

## SECCIÓN 2 Principios o estrategias de compra

- Tres principios de compra básicos que ayudan al comprador a obtener la mayor satisfacción de sus ingresos y tiempo limitados son reunir información, usar los anuncios con discreción y comparar antes de comprar.
- El valor del tiempo y el esfuerzo que el comprador emplea en obtener información no debe exceder el valor de la mejor selección.
- La mayoría de los anuncios caen en una de las dos siguientes categorías: **publicidad competitiva** o **publicidad informativa.** Hay que cuidarse de la publicidad engañosa, que incluye la práctica de **engatusar** al comprador.
- Para comparar eficientemente antes de comprar, se deben leer los anuncios de periódicos, hacer llamadas telefónicas, navegar por Internet y visitar distintas tiendas. También se deben considerar la garantía que ofrece el producto y las ventajas de las variedades genéricas y de marca.

## SECCIÓN 3 Protección al consumidor

- Existe un movimiento de **protección al consumidor** que tiene como fines informar al comprador acerca de las compras que hace y exigir productos mejores y más seguros de los fabricantes.
- Los defensores de los consumidores reclaman los siguientes derechos para ellos: el derecho a la seguridad, a ser informado, a seleccionar, a ser escuchado y a reparaciones.
- Entre los grupos privados que ayudan al consumidor están las agrupaciones cívicas de acción local y el "Better Business Bureau" (Agencia para el mejoramiento del comercio).
- Muchas agencias federales tienen programas que ayudan al consumidor, incluyendo la "Consumer Product Safety Commission" (Comisión de seguridad de productos) y la "Food and Drug Administration" (Administración de Alimentos y Drogas).
- Las responsabilidades del consumidor incluyen leer contratos y garantías, seguir las instrucciones para el uso correcto del producto, iniciar el proceso de resolver problemas y **comportarse éticamente.**

# CAPÍTULO 4 Resumen

## SECCIÓN 1 Los estadounidenses y el crédito

- El **crédito** es la aceptación de fondos directa o indirectamente para comprar bienes y servicios bajo promesa de pagar por ellos en el futuro.
- La cantidad que se debe—la deuda—equivale al **principal** más el **interés.**
- Muchas personas compran **bienes duraderos** y obtienen **hipotecas** en forma de **deudas pagadas a plazos.**
- Las personas asumen deudas porque no quieren esperar para comprar un artículo con dinero en efectivo y quieren extender el tiempo que tienen para hacer los pagos durante la vida útil del artículo.

## SECCIÓN 2 Fuentes de préstamos y crédito

- Las instituciones financieras principales que hacen préstamos a consumidores incluyen los **bancos comerciales, sociedades de ahorro y préstamos, cooperativas de crédito** y **compañías financieras.**
- Una **cuenta de crédito** le permite al cliente comprar bienes y servicios de una compañía en particular y pagárselos más adelante.
- Las **tarjetas de crédito** a menudo cobran intereses altos, pero se pueden usar en tiendas, restaurantes u otros negocios.
- Los **cargos de financiamiento** son el costo mensual del crédito en dólares y centavos.
- La **tasa de interés anual** es el costo anual del crédito expresado en porcentajes.

## SECCIÓN 3 Solicitar crédito

- Después de que una persona llena un formulario solicitando crédito, una **oficina de crédito** hace una **investigación de crédito** y determina la **clasificación de crédito** del solicitante.
- Antes de dar crédito, el acreedor evalúa la capacidad de pagar del solicitante, su carácter y cualquier **garantía** en forma de propiedad que tenga para asegurar que pagará.
- Las responsabilidades del prestatario incluyen pagar a tiempo, documentar todos los datos sobre la deuda y no gastar más de lo que puede devolver.

## SECCIÓN 4 Regulación del crédito por el gobierno

- La ley prohibe que los prestamistas se nieguen a dar crédito por razón de raza, religión, origen nacional, sexo, estado civil o edad del solicitante.
- Una **ley contra la usura** limita la cantidad de interés que se puede cobrar por el crédito, pero también conduce a la escasez de crédito disponible.
- Muchas personas que no pueden pagar sus deudas se tienen que declarar en **bancarrota.**

# Resumen

## SECCIÓN 1 Comprar alimentos

- Para comparar alimentos antes de comprarlos, hay que fijarse en las marcas, los tamaños y las tiendas.
- Un modo de comparar antes de comprar que a la vez ahorra tiempo y dinero es leer los anuncios y recortar los cupones de descuento.
- En general, los supermercados y los **clubes almacenes** tienen los precios más bajos, mientras que las pequeñas **tiendas de artículos de consumo frecuente** pueden ahorrarle tiempo al comprador.
- Los precios de productos por unidad hacen que sea más fácil comparar precios.
- Usando cupones, se puede ahorrar más del 10 por ciento del costo de los alimentos en un período de un año.

## SECCIÓN 2 La selección de ropa

- Los estadounidenses gastan unos 400 mil millones de dólares anualmente en ropa y otros productos personales.
- El valor de la ropa depende del precio, estilo, **durabilidad** y costo de mantenerla en buenas condiciones.
- Las prendas de vestir se compran por el **servicio útil** que dan.
- La cantidad de tiempo que hay que trabajar para comprar ropa se ha reducido en los últimos 100 años, pero el consumidor inteligente trata de comprar su ropa en rebaja.

## SECCIÓN 3 Alquilar o comprar

- Ambas opciones, alquilar y comprar una casa, tienen ventajas y desventajas económicas y psicológicas.
- Si una persona decide comprar casa, probablemente tendrá que conseguir una hipoteca, por la cual tendrá que pagar un adelanto en efectivo, mensualidades e intereses, además de **los costos de cierre** y **puntos.**
- Los inquilinos generalmente pagan un **depósito de garantía** y firman un **contrato de alquiler** que protege sus derechos y enumera sus responsabilidades.
- Las responsabilidades de los inquilinos incluyen pagar el alquiler a tiempo y cuidar la propiedad adecuadamente.

## SECCIÓN 4 Compra y manejo de un vehículo

- Algunas de las decisiones que tiene que tomar el comprador de un automóvil son si comprar un carro pequeño o uno grande, uno nuevo o de uso, con motor poderoso o que consuma poca gasolina.
- Los gastos de operar un automóvil incluyen la **cuota por la matrícula,** el mantenimiento normal, las reparaciones de mayor importancia, la depreciación y el **seguro de responsabilidad civil.**
- Una manera de evitar tener que pagar por reparos costosos es comprando una garantía a largo plazo.

# CAPÍTULO  Resumen

## SECCIÓN 1 ¿Por qué se ahorra?

- Los economistas explican que ***ahorrar*** es dejar de usar los ingresos por un período de tiempo para poder usarlos en el futuro.
- Los ahorros de un individuo son dinero que otros pueden invertir y que permite que los comercios crezcan.
- Los individuos pueden invertir su dinero de muchos modos distintos, como en **cuentas de ahorro** y **depósitos a plazos.**
- El ahorrador que tiene una **cuenta de ahorro con libreta bancaria** recibe una libreta en que se apuntan sus depósitos, retiros de dinero e intereses ganados.
- Una **cuenta de depósito del mercado monetario** paga intereses bastante altos y permite que el depositador tenga libre acceso a su dinero por medio de cheques. Pero estas cuentas requieren que se tenga un saldo mínimo de $1,000 a $2,500.
- Los depósitos a plazos, como los **certificados de depósito (CD),** pagan **intereses** más altos, pero hay que dejar los fondos depositados durante períodos de tiempo más largos.
- La Federal Deposit Insurance Corporation (Corporación Federal de Seguros de Depósitos) o FDIC asegura hasta $100,000 depositados en cuentas de bancos comerciales y bancos de ahorro.

## SECCIÓN 2 Las inversiones: correr riesgos con los ahorros

- El comprador de acciones tiene el derecho a recibir parte de las futuras ganancias y activos de la sociedad anónima que vende las acciones.
- Los **accionistas** hacen dinero de sus acciones por medio de dividendos y al vender las acciones por más de lo que pagaron por ellas.
- Muchas empresas y los tres niveles del gobierno emiten bonos para obtener dinero prestado. Los del gobierno incluyen **bonos exentos de impuestos; bonos de ahorro; letras, pagarés** y **bonos del Tesoro.**
- Se pueden comprar acciones por medio de **corredores de la bolsa** o por medio de Internet.
- Las acciones de las grandes sociedades anónimas se compran y venden en las bolsas de valores organizadas, mientras que las acciones de sociedades anónimas pequeñas y nuevas generalmente se venden en el **mercado extrabursátil.**
- Muchas personas invierten en la bolsa de valores por medio de **fondos mutualistas,** compañías inversionistas que reúnen el dinero de muchas personas para comprar acciones, bonos u otras inversiones.

## SECCIÓN 3 Metas y planes especiales de ahorro

- Cuando se jubilan, la mayoría de los estadounidenses necesitan ingresos adicionales a sus ahorros para vivir.
- Los **planes de pensiones,** el **Plan Keogh** y las **cuentas de retiro individuales (IRA)** son modos de aumentar la cantidad de dinero que uno tiene cuando se jubila.
- Otra manera de invertir para la jubilación es comprando bienes inmuebles, pero el riesgo es mucho más alto.
- Al decidir cuánto dinero invertir y en qué invertirlo, se debe considerar la **diversificación** para repartir y reducir los riesgos.

# CAPÍTULO 7 Resumen

## SECCIÓN 1 La demanda

- La **demanda** es la disposición y poder del consumidor para pagar por algo.
- La **ley de la demanda** dice que al subir el precio, la **cantidad demandada** baja. Al bajar el precio, la cantidad que se demanda sube.
- Los factores que explican la relación inversa entre la cantidad que se demanda y el precio incluyen el **efecto de ingresos reales,** el **efecto de sustitución** y la **utilidad marginal** decreciente—es decir, un producto proporciona menos provecho o satisfacción con la compra adicional de cada artículo semejante.

## SECCIÓN 2 La curva de demanda y la elasticidad de la demanda

- Una **curva de demanda** descendiente significa que al bajar el precio, la cantidad demandada aumenta.
- Los cambios en la población, ingresos, gustos y preferencias, y la existencia de sustitutos o de **bienes complementarios** afectan la demanda.
- El **efecto del precio en la elasticidad de la demanda** es una medida de cómo los consumidores responden a un cambio de precio.
- Si un cambio pequeño en el precio resulta en un gran cambio en la cantidad demandada, se dice que la demanda por ese producto es **elástica.**
- Si un cambio en el precio no resulta en un cambio importante en la cantidad demandada, la demanda se considera **inelástica.**

## SECCIÓN 3 La ley de la oferta y la curva de oferta

- La **ley de la oferta** dice que cuando aumenta el precio de un producto, la **cantidad ofrecida** también aumenta. Cuando el precio baja, la cantidad ofrecida también baja.
- La **curva de oferta** ascendente muestra la correspondencia que existe entre la cantidad ofrecida y el precio.
- Cuatro factores determinan la oferta en una economía de mercado. Estos son el precio de los insumos (bienes usados en la producción), el número de empresas en la industria, los impuestos y la **tecnología.**

## SECCIÓN 4 La relación entre la oferta y la demanda

- En un sistema de libre empresa, los precios les sirven de señales a los productores y consumidores.
- El punto en que la cantidad demandada y la cantidad ofrecida son iguales se llama el **precio de equilibrio.**
- La **escasez** o falta de un producto hace que suban los precios, señalando a los productores que deben producir más y a los consumidores que deben comprar menos.
- El **superávit** de bienes hace que bajen los precios, señalando a los productores que deben producir menos y a los consumidores que deben comprar más.
- Los **precios máximos** establecidos por ley no permiten que los precios suban más de una cantidad fija, pero a menudo hacen que escaseen los productos y conducen al **mercado negro.**
- Los **precios mínimos** evitan que ciertos precios, como el salario mínimo, bajen demasiado.

# CAPÍTULO 8 Resumen

## SECCIÓN 1 Empezar un negocio

- Las personas generalmente deciden empezar un negocio para obtener ganancias, hacer algo por cuenta propia o no tener que responder a un jefe.
- Los **empresarios** tienen que reunir los factores de producción necesarios y decidir qué tipo de organización sería mejor para el negocio que quieren establecer.
- Los que quieren empezar un negocio pequeño pueden obtener ayuda del gobierno o a través de Internet.
- Todo negocio tiene que ocuparse de cuatro elementos básicos: los gastos, la publicidad, la documentación de todas las transacciones (que incluye guardar **recibos**) y el riesgo.

## SECCIÓN 2 Propiedades individuales y sociedades

- El tipo de organización empresarial más básico es la **propiedad individual,** un negocio que es propiedad de una sola persona.
- Las mayores ventajas de la propiedad individual son que el propietario único puede sentirse orgulloso de su negocio y recibe todas las ganancias.
- La mayor desventaja es que el propietario único tiene **responsabilidad sin límite** y puede perder todos sus **activos,** incluyendo bienes personales junto con el negocio.
- Una **sociedad** es un tipo de empresa organizada por dos o más dueños.
- Un contrato de sociedad es un acuerdo legal que describe las responsabilidades de cada socio, cómo se dividirán las ganancias y cómo se distribuirán los activos si se disuelve la sociedad.
- En una **sociedad limitada,** un socio general asume responsabilidad por la administración y las deudas, mientras que los otros socios contribuyen dinero pero no tienen responsabilidad.

## SECCIÓN 3 Las sociedades anónimas y las franquicias

- Una **sociedad anónima** puede ser dueña de propiedades, pagar impuestos, entrar en contratos y tomar parte en pleitos judiciales.
- Una de las mayores ventajas de las sociedades anónimas es la **responsabilidad limitada.**
- Una desventaja importante es que las sociedades anónimas tienen que pagar impuestos más altos que otros tipos de empresas.
- Para formar una sociedad anónima, los fundadores tienen que inscribirse con el gobierno, vender **acciones** y elegir una junta de directores.
- Una **franquicia** es un contrato en que el franquiciador le vende a otro negocio el derecho de usar su nombre y vender sus productos.

# CAPÍTULO 9 Resumen

## SECCIÓN 1 La competencia perfecta

- En los Estados Unidos se encuentran cuatro clases de **estructuras de mercado** básicas: **monopolio, oligopolio, competencia monopolística** y **competencia perfecta.**
- La competencia perfecta se caracteriza por un gran número de compradores y vendedores, un producto idéntico, entrada fácil en el mercado, acceso libre a información sobre los precios y ningún control sobre los precios.
- El mercado de productos agrícolas a menudo se usa como ejemplo de la competencia perfecta porque los agricultores no tienen casi ningún control sobre el precio de sus productos en el mercado.
- Cuando existe la competencia perfecta, la sociedad se beneficia de la distribución eficiente de sus recursos productivos.

## SECCIÓN 2 Monopolio, oligopolio y competencia monopolística

- En un monopolio, un vendedor único controla la oferta de un producto o servicio y, por lo tanto, determina el precio.
- Los monopolios están protegidos por **barreras al mercado,** que pueden ser regulaciones gubernamentales, una inversión inicial muy grande o propiedad de las materias primas.
- Hay cuatro clases de monopolios: natural, geográfico, tecnológico y estatal.
- Los monopolios naturales a menudo son ventajosos porque les permiten a los fabricantes utilizar la **economía de escala**—es decir, por su gran tamaño, la empresa puede producir grandes cantidades al precio más bajo posible.
- Un oligopolio es una industria dominada por pocos productores que ejercen algún control sobre el precio.
- En los oligopolios y los mercados en que existe la competencia monopolística, los vendedores utilizan la **diferenciación de productos** para aumentar el valor de sus productos en los ojos del consumidor.
- La publicidad de las marcas de fábrica es sumamente importantes en los mercados que tienen competencia monopolística, en que muchos vendedores ofrecen productos muy parecidos con sólo detalles de diferencia.

## SECCIÓN 3 Política gubernamental hacia la competencia

- El gobierno ha aprobado **legislación antimonopolista** para impedir que se formen monopolios y deshacer los que ya existían.
- Dos leyes antimonopolistas importantes son la Sherman Antitrust Act (Ley Antimonopolista Sherman) y la Clayton Act (Ley Clayton).
- Se forman corporaciones mediante tres tipos de fusiones: horizontal, vertical y conglomerada.
- Hay agencias reguladoras federales que supervisan varias industrias para asegurar que los precios son razonables y los productos de buena calidad.
- La **desregulación** de algunas industrias en los 1980 y 1990 resultó en más competencia entre negocios.

# CAPÍTULO 10 Resumen

## SECCIÓN 1 La inversión en el sistema de libre empresa

- El **financiamiento** de las operaciones y del crecimiento de comercios son una parte integral de nuestro sistema de libre empresa. El dinero proviene de los depósitos de personas que ahorran su dinero en instituciones financieras.
- Las instituciones financieras ponen estos depósitos a la disposición de negocios que necesitan fondos para crecer y expandir.
- Los negocios generalmente hacen un **análisis de coste-beneficios** antes de decidir si deben obtener financiamiento para la expansión.
- Un análisis de coste-beneficios comprende estimar los costos, calcular las **entradas** anticipadas, calcular las **ganancias** anticipadas y calcular el costo de obtener los préstamos.

## SECCIÓN 2 Tipos de financiamiento para operaciones comerciales

- El **financiamiento mediante deudas,** o reunir dinero para un negocio a través de préstamos, se puede dividir en tres categorías basadas en la cantidad de tiempo que hay para pagarlos.
- Aquellos negocios que necesitan fondos para cubrir las alzas y bajas que ocurren mensualmente o por temporada obtienen **financiamiento a corto plazo.**
- Obtener préstamos por 1 a 10 años para comprar más terreno, edificios y maquinaria o materiales se considera **financiamiento a mediano plazo.**
- El **financiamiento a largo plazo,** como emitir acciones y vender bonos, se usa para la expansión comercial a gran escala.
- Los directores financieros tienen que examinar el tipo de interés que habrá que pagar, el clima comercial y la condición financiera de la compañía y tienen que informar a los dueños de acciones comunes antes de obtener financiación.

## SECCIÓN 3 El proceso de producción

- La **producción** es el proceso de convertir recursos en bienes que satisfacen las necesidades y deseos de individuos y otros negocios.
- La producción de **bienes de consumo** y bienes capitales requiere planificación, adquisición de materiales (compras), control de calidad y control del inventario.
- La planificación incluye escoger un local para el negocio y preparar un programa de producción.
- Las personas encargadas de compras tienen que determinar qué bienes comprar, de cuál proveedor obtenerlos y a qué precio comprarlos.
- Cinco avances importantes en la tecnología—la **mecanización,** la **línea de montaje,** la **división del trabajo,** la **automatización** y la **robótica**—han afectado drásticamente los métodos y costos de producción.

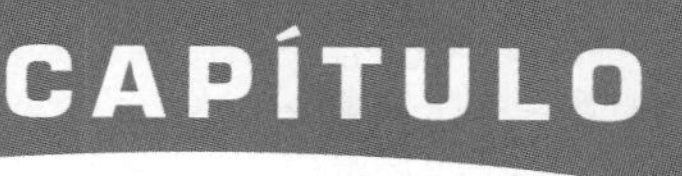

# CAPÍTULO 11 Resumen

## SECCIÓN 1 Los cambios en la mercadotecnia

- La **mercadotecnia** comprende todas las actividades necesarias para mover bienes y servicios del productor al consumidor.
- En la economía de hoy, el único objetivo de la mercadotecnia es convencer a los consumidores que recibirán mayor **utilidad** de un producto o servicio en particular.
- La utilidad es la capacidad de un producto o servicio de satisfacer los deseos de los consumidores. Hay cuatro clases de utilidad: utilidad por la forma que tiene, utilidad por el lugar donde se encuentra, utilidad por el tiempo en que es disponible y utilidad por la facilidad con que se puede transferir la propiedad.
- Por medio de la **investigación de mercados,** las compañías reúnen, anotan y analizan datos sobre los tipos de bienes y servicios que el público quiere.
- El primer paso en la investigación de un mercado es hacer un **estudio del mercado.**
- Antes de ofrecer un producto para distribución nacional, los investigadores del mercado a menudo **hacen una prueba de mercado.**

## SECCIÓN 2 Los componentes de la mercadotecnia

- Un plan del mercado tiene cuatro componentes: producto, precio, lugar y promoción.
- "Producto" significa que hay que hay que determinar cuáles servicios ofrecer con el producto, cómo empaquetarlo y qué identidad darle para que sea fácil de reconocer.
- Para establecer el precio de venta, una compañía tiene que tomar en consideración los costos de producción, de publicidad, de venta, de distribución y la cantidad de ganancias que quiere sacar.
- "Lugar" significa dónde se debe vender un producto.
- La **promoción** es el uso de anuncios y otras técnicas para informar a los consumidores que hay un nuevo producto en el mercado y para convencerlos a que lo compren.

## SECCIÓN 3 Canales de distribución

- Determinar cuáles **canales de distribución** usar es otra función de la mercadotecnia.
- Los negocios que compran grandes cantidades de productos de los fabricantes para vendérselos a otros negocios se llaman **mayoristas,** o comercios al por mayor.
- Los negocios que venden bienes de consumo directamente al público son **tiendas al por menor.**
- En los últimos 10 a 15 años, los canales de distribución se han aumentado gracias a la expansión de los clubes almacenes, las compras por catálogo y el **comercio electrónico.**

# CAPÍTULO 12 Resumen

## SECCIÓN 1 Los estadounidenses y el trabajo

- La **fuerza laboral civil** es el número total de personas mayores de 16 años que tienen empleo o lo están buscando.
- Los trabajadores en los Estados Unidos están clasificados de acuerdo con el tipo de trabajo que hacen—**obreros, empleados en trabajos no manuales** y **trabajadores en el área de servicio.**
- Otro modo de clasificar a los trabajadores es de acuerdo con las habilidades especiales que hacen falta para hacer sus trabajos—trabajadores **no calificados, semicalificados, calificados** o **profesionales.**
- Hay tres factores principales—calificación, tipo de empleo y localidad—que afectan como la oferta y la demanda determinan los precios, en este caso los sueldos, en el mercado laboral.
- Dos factores que limitan la influencia de la oferta y la demanda sobre los sueldos son las **leyes de salario mínimo** y los sindicatos laborales.

## SECCIÓN 2 Los sindicatos laborales

- Un **sindicato de obreros** es una asociación de trabajadores organizada para mejorar los sueldos y las condiciones de trabajo de sus miembros.
- Los sindicatos se formaron para obligar a los dueños a mejorar las condiciones de trabajo, reducir las horas de trabajo y poner fin al trabajo de menores.
- Durante gran parte de su historia los sindicatos en Estados Unidos han estado divididos en dos grupos: **sindicatos de artesanos** y **sindicatos industriales.**
- Los sindicatos laborales tienen tres niveles de operaciones: la **sección sindical** (local), el sindicato nacional o internacional y la federación.
- Cada sección sindical negocia para crear una **fábrica sindical** o **fábrica con cuota por agencia sindical.**

## SECCIÓN 3 Negociación colectiva

- La **negociación colectiva** es el proceso mediante el cual los sindicatos y los gerentes llegan a un acuerdo sobre las condiciones de trabajo.
- Los sindicatos y gerentes pueden negociar las horas de trabajo, los sueldos, beneficios adicionales y **ajustes por el costo de la vida.**
- Si las negociaciones se hacen hostiles o nadie está dispuesto a transigir, los sindicatos y los gerentes pueden probar la **mediación** o el **arbitraje.**
- Los sindicatos en huelga pueden **piquetear** u organizar un **boicot** para ejercer presión económica contra la compañía.
- Para contrarrestar una huelga, los gerentes pueden hacer un **cierre patronal** o pedir una **prohibición judicial** contra la huelga.
- El porcentaje de obreros que se hicieron miembros de sindicatos fue más alto en los 1940 y ha estado en descenso desde entonces.

# CAPÍTULO 13 Resumen

## SECCIÓN 1 Cálculo de la renta nacional

- El **cálculo de la renta nacional** es una medida de lo que rinde la economía de la nación en su totalidad e incluye cinco estudios estadísticos.
- El **producto interior bruto (PIB)** es el valor total en dólares de todos los bienes y servicios finales producidos en una nación durante un año.
- Cuando se resta la **depreciación** del PIB, se obtiene una estadística llamada **producto interior neto.**
- Tres medidas adicionales—la **renta nacional,** los **ingresos personales** y los **ingresos disponibles**—analizan cuánto dinero tienen para gastar individuos y negocios en todo el país.

## SECCIÓN 2 Tomar en cuenta la inflación

- Cuando hay **inflación,** el **poder adquisitivo** del dólar baja.
- La inflación sesga el PIB, haciendo parecer que ha subido la producción cuando, en realidad, sólo han subido los precios de bienes y servicios.
- Para calcular el **PIB real,** el gobierno mide el efecto de la inflación en el PIB actual.
- Tres medidas comunes de la inflación son el **índice de precios al consumidor,** el **índice de precios de productores** y el **deflactor de precios del PIB.**

## SECCIÓN 3 La oferta y demanda agregadas

- La **oferta agregada** y la **demanda agregada** relacionan la cantidad total de bienes y servicios en la economía entera con los precios.
- El nivel de producción nacional y el nivel de los precios están en equilibrio donde la **curva de oferta agregada** y la **curva de demanda agregada** se cruzan, indicando que no hay ni inflación ni **deflación.**

## SECCIÓN 4 Fluctuaciones comerciales

- La economía sufre alzas y bajas llamadas **fluctuaciones comerciales.**
- El **ciclo económico** comienza con un período de **auge,** entonces se **contrae** hasta llegar a una **recesión** (posiblemente una **depresión**). La actividad comercial disminuye hasta llegar a su **punto bajo** y luego empieza a aumentar de nuevo en una **expansión** o **recuperación.**
- La Gran Depresión fue la peor crisis económica en la historia de los Estados Unidos.

## SECCIÓN 5 Causas e indicadores de fluctuaciones comerciales

- Los economistas conectan las fluctuaciones comerciales con cuatro fuerzas principales: las inversiones comerciales, la actividad gubernamental, factores externos y factores psicológicos.
- Para ayudar a los líderes comerciales y gubernamentales a tomar decisiones económicas para el futuro, los economistas crean y revisan **indicadores económicos.**

# CAPÍTULO 14 Resumen

## SECCIÓN 1 Las funciones y características de la moneda

- La **moneda** tiene tres funciones. Se puede usar como **medio de cambio, unidad de contabilidad** y **reserva de valor.**
- Cualquier objeto que se use como moneda tiene que ser duradero, portátil, divisible, de valor estable, escaso y aceptado como medio de cambio para pagar deudas.
- La moneda que también tiene uso como mercancía—por ejemplo, el ganado, las joyas y el tabaco—se considera **dinero material.**
- La moneda que está respaldada o se puede cambiar por oro o plata se conoce como **dinero crediticio.**
- Hoy en día, toda la moneda de los Estados Unidos es **dinero fiduciario** o **medios de curso legal** cuyo valor lo establece el gobierno.

## SECCIÓN 2 Historia de la moneda y banca de Estados Unidos

- En el transcurso de la historia de Estados Unidos, la gente ha usado dinero material, monedas europeas, notas bancarias privadas y muchas otras clases de notas.
- La Constitución de los Estados Unidos le dio al Congreso el poder de imprimir monedas metálicas. No fue hasta la Guerra civil que el gobierno estableció una moneda segura y uniforme.
- Para controlar la cantidad de moneda en circulación, el Congreso estableció el Sistema de Reserva Federal en 1913. Éste sirve de banco central de la nación. En 1914, comenzó a emitir papel moneda llamado notas de la Reserva Federal, que pronto se convirtieron en el tipo de dinero más usado.
- En 1934, la nación cambio del patrón oro al patrón fiduciario (dinero fiduciario).
- La **transferencia electrónica de fondos** ha cambiado totalmente la industria bancaria, con el uso de **cajeros automáticos** y hasta Internet para hacer operaciones bancarias.

## SECCIÓN 3 Tipos de moneda en los Estados Unidos

- Hoy en día, la moneda comprende más que el dinero fiduciario emitido por el gobierno. También incluye depósitos en las **cuentas corrientes,** las **tarjetas de débito** y el **cuasi-dinero.**
- Los economistas determinan la cantidad de dinero en la economía calculando la **M1**—dinero fiduciario, **depósitos a la vista** y cheques de viajero. Entonces calculan la **M2**—toda la moneda en la M1 más los depósitos en cuentas de ahorro, depósitos a plazos, certificados de depósito en pequeñas denominaciones y saldos de otros tipos de cuentas.

# CAPÍTULO 15 Resumen

## SECCIÓN 1 Organización y función del Sistema de Reserva Federal

- El Congreso creó el **Sistema de Reserva Federal** (llamado Fed, en inglés) en 1913 como la organización bancaria central de los Estados Unidos.
- El Sistema de Reserva Federal esta compuesto de una Junta de Gobernadores, asistida por el Consejo Consultivo Federal (Federal Advisory Council), el **Comité Federal del Mercado Libre,** 12 bancos de distritos, 25 sucursales y miles de bancos miembros del sistema.
- Las funciones del Sistema de Reserva Federal incluyen **compensar cheques,** actuar como agente fiscal del gobierno federal, supervisar a los bancos estatales que son miembros, guardar reservas, suministrar papel moneda y llevar a cabo la **política monetaria.**

## SECCIÓN 2 La oferta monetaria y la economía

- La función más importante del Sistema de Reserva Federal es realizar la política monetaria, o controlar el aumento en la oferta monetaria.
- Cuando hay una **política monetaria expansiva,** el crédito es abundante y los préstamos son baratos. Cuando hay una **política monetaria restrictiva** el crédito escasea y es caro pedir dinero prestado.
- El sistema bancario está basado en la **reserva bancaria parcial,** en que los bancos mantienen un porcentaje fijo de sus depósitos totales en efectivo en sus propias bóvedas de seguridad o depositado en los bancos del Sistema de Reserva Federal.
- Una vez que los bancos tengan su **reserva obligatoria** separada, pueden prestar el resto del dinero y, de esta manera, crear dinero nuevo.

## SECCIÓN 3 Regulación de la oferta monetaria

- El Sistema de Reserva Federal puede controlar la oferta monetaria cambiando la reserva obligatoria que tienen que mantener las instituciones financieras. Al bajar la cantidad que tienen que tener en reserva, los bancos pueden prestar más dinero, así aumentando la oferta monetaria.
- Otra estrategia que puede usar el Sistema de Reserva Federal es cambiar la **tasa de descuento** y la **tasa federal por fondos prestados,** que también afectan la **tasa preferencial.** Al subir el costo del crédito, los bancos y consumidores tienden a gastar menos, lo que frena el crecimiento de la oferta monetaria.
- La estrategia principal que usa el Sistema de Reserva Federal son las **operaciones del mercado abierto**—la compra y venta de valores del gobierno. Cuando deposita dinero en el sistema bancario (al comprar valores), la oferta monetaria crece. Cuando retira dinero del sistema bancario (al vender valores), la oferta monetaria disminuye.

# CAPÍTULO 16 Resumen

## SECCIÓN 1 El crecimiento en el tamaño del gobierno

- Todos los niveles de gobierno—local, estatal y federal—toman parte en casi todos los aspectos de la economía de los Estados Unidos.
- Juntos, todos los niveles del gobierno emplean unos 20 millones de trabajadores civiles.
- El gobierno paga por carreteras, escuelas y otros **proyectos de obras públicas.** También regula la seguridad de productos y trabajadores.
- Los desembolsos o gastos gubernamentales totales, incluyendo compras actuales y prestaciones sociales (asistencia pública), exceden una tercera parte del PIB.

## SECCIÓN 2 Las funciones del gobierno

- Una función del gobierno es proporcionar **bienes públicos,** como parques nacionales y defensa nacional.
- Otra función del gobierno es promover el bienestar público por medio de **programas de seguridad social**—como el **Seguro Social, Medicare** y la **compensación a trabajadores accidentados**—y **programas de asistencia pública**—como los **Ingresos Suplementarios de Seguridad** y **Medicaid.**
- La tercera función del gobierno es regular los **factores externos** negativos del proceso de producción.
- La cuarta función del gobierno es asegurar la estabilidad económica, que significa disminuir las alzas y bajas en la actividad comercial de la nación.

## SECCIÓN 3 El presupuesto federal y la deuda pública

- Los gastos principales del gobierno federal son el Seguro Social, Medicare y los ingresos de seguridad; la defensa nacional; los intereses por la deuda pública y la salud.
- Las ramas ejecutiva y legislativa preparan un presupuesto federal para cada **año fiscal.**
- Cuando el gobierno gasta más dinero del que recauda en un año fiscal, el resultado es un **déficit presupuestario.**
- La suma de todos los déficits presupuestarios equivale a la **deuda pública.**

## SECCIÓN 4 La tributación

- De acuerdo con el **principio de beneficio obtenido,** las personas que utilizan un servicio gubernamental en particular lo deben apoyar con sus impuestos en proporción al beneficio que reciben.
- De acuerdo con el **principio de la capacidad de pago,** los que tienen más ingresos deben pagar más impuestos y los que tienen menos ingresos deben pagar menos impuestos, sin tenerse en cuenta la cantidad de servicios gubernamentales que usen.
- Los impuestos principales incluyen los que se pagan por ingresos personales, para la seguridad social, por ingresos empresariales, sobre las ventas y sobre los bienes inmuebles.
- Los impuestos se clasifican de acuerdo con el efecto que tienen en las personas que los tienen que pagar. Se consideran **proporcionales, progresivos** o **regresivos.**

# CAPÍTULO 17 Resumen

## SECCIÓN 1 El desempleo y la inflación

- Dos de las amenazas más importantes para la estabilidad económica de la nación son el desempleo y la inflación.
- El mantenimiento de un **índice de desempleo** bajo es una meta de las **políticas de estabilización.**
- Los cuatro tipos de desempleo son cíclico, estructural, temporal y friccional.
- De acuerdo con la teoría de la **inflación de demanda,** los precios suben cuando la demanda excesiva de los negocios y consumidores sube más rápido que la oferta total.
- La teoría de la **inflación de costes** dice que la demanda por sueldos más altos de los sindicatos y el ánimo de lucro excesivo de las grandes compañías hacen que aumenten los precios.

## SECCIÓN 2 La política fiscal y la estabilización

- Algunos economistas creen que la estabilización económica se puede lograr por medio de la **política fiscal**—el uso consciente de los impuestos y gastos por el gobierno federal para afectar la actividad comercial general.
- John Maynard Keynes desarrolló sus teorías acerca de la política fiscal durante la Gran Depresión.
- La teoría keynesiana dice que el retiro e inyección de dinero en el **flujo circular de ingresos** afectan la demanda agregada y que el gobierno debe contrarrestar los efectos por medio de sus políticas de tributación y gastos.
- Para disminuir el desempleo, los economistas keynesianos apoyan la formación de programas de trabajo subvencionados por el gobierno y la rebaja de impuestos federales.

## SECCIÓN 3 El monetarismo y la economía

- Los **monetaristas** creen que se debe manipular el ritmo con que crece la oferta monetaria para estabilizar la economía.
- La teoría del **monetarismo** a menudo es relacionada con Milton Friedman.
- Friedman y sus partidarios creen que el Sistema de Reserva Federal debe seguir la **norma monetaria,** es decir, debe aumentar la oferta monetaria por el mismo porcentaje todos los años.
- Los monetaristas critican la política fiscal porque se efectúa en el ruedo político y porque las **demoras** que se producen entre el momento en que se promulga y el momento en que se implementa pueden empeorar la situación.

# CAPÍTULO 18 Resumen

## SECCIÓN 1 Los beneficios del comercio mundial

- El comercio es importante porque las **importaciones** nos abastecen de muchos bienes y recursos naturales y muchos trabajadores en Estados Unidos están empleados en industrias que **exportan** productos al extranjero.
- La **ventaja absoluta** es la capacidad de un país de producir un producto en particular por un costo menor que otro país, usando la misma cantidad de recursos.
- La **ventaja comparativa** es la capacidad de un país de producir un producto por un costo de oportunidad más bajo que otro país.
- A la larga, las exportaciones pagan por las importaciones.

## SECCIÓN 2 El financiamiento del comercio mundial

- Los **mercados de divisas** les permiten a empresas alrededor del mundo cambiar su moneda por la de otros países. Las monedas de otros países se llaman divisas.
- Cuando se usaba el **tipo de cambio fijo,** el valor de la moneda de una nación se establecía de acuerdo con un patrón determinado—generalmente la cantidad de oro que esa nación tenía en reserva.
- Hoy en día se usa el **tipo de cambio flexible,** en que la oferta y la demanda determinan el precio de las divisas.
- La rapidez con que se intercambia la moneda de un país puede afectar su **balanza comercial.**
- Si la moneda de una nación es **depreciada,** esa nación probablemente exportará más. Si la moneda sube en valor, probablemente exporte menos.

## SECCIÓN 3 Restricciones al comercio mundial

- Tres barreras importantes al comercio mundial son los **aranceles,** las **cuotas de importación** y los **embargos.**
- Los **proteccionistas** están a favor de las restricciones comerciales para proteger los trabajos, la seguridad nacional y las industrias nacientes de los Estados Unidos.
- Los partidarios del libre comercio creen que la competencia resulta en mejores productos a precios más bajos y que restringir importaciones perjudica a las industrias de exportación.
- Varios acuerdos recientes han tratado de reducir las barreras comerciales, entre ellos la **Organización Mundial del Comercio,** el **Tratado de Libre Comercio Norteamericano** (NAFTA) y la **Unión Europea.**

# CAPÍTULO 19 Resumen

## SECCIÓN 1 Comparación entre el capitalismo y el socialismo

- El capitalismo puro opera a base de precios, ganancias y propiedad privada.
- El socialismo puro es un sistema económico en que hay poca propiedad privada y el estado es dueño de prácticamente todos los factores de producción.
- Carlos Marx predijo que habría una lucha entre los capitalistas y el **proletariado** que resultaría en un sistema llamado **comunismo.**
- En el **socialismo democrático,** el gobierno generalmente controla sólo algunas áreas de la economía.
- Los **socialistas autoritarios** creen que se debe usar la revolución para derrocar el capitalismo y realizar las metas socialistas.

## SECCIÓN 2 Cambios en el socialismo autoritario: el caso de la China

- La República Popular de China es la nación más grande que todavía tiene un tipo de socialismo dirigido.
- Después de la Segunda Guerra Mundial, el gobierno chino comenzó a basar su economía centralizada en **planes quinquenales.**
- Las reformas de los 1970 y 1980 dieron a individuos más poder para tomar decisiones y para vender personalmente parte de los bienes y servicios que producen para sacarles ganancias.
- El derecho incompleto a la propiedad privada, la falta de imperio de la ley y la resultante corrupción son problemas que la China enfrenta hoy.
- El ingreso en la **Organización Mundial del Comercio** ha abierto la economía china al resto del mundo.

## SECCIÓN 3 Las naciones adoptan el sistema de mercado

- Cuando Rusia comenzó la **privatización** de la economía, muchos trabajadores perdieron sus trabajos, los precios aumentaron vertiginosamente y la economía rusa se fue en declive.
- El pueblo ruso tiene que enfrentar muchas dificultades durante la transición a la libre empresa.
- Como **estado de bienestar social,** Suecia tiene impuestos muy altos para proporcionar asistencia pública a sus habitantes desde que nacen hasta que mueren.
- Recientemente, Suecia ha iniciado cambios en su sistema económico que combina capitalismo con socialismo.
- Muchos países de América Latina han privatizado sus industrias del transporte y la energía.

# Resumen

## SECCIÓN 1 Características de las naciones en desarrollo

- Las **naciones en vías de desarrollo** tienen poco desarrollo industrial y un nivel de vida relativamente bajo.
- Cinco características de las naciones en vías de desarrollo son un PIB bajo, una economía **agrícola de subsistencia,** malas condiciones de salud (incluyendo un **índice de mortalidad infantil** alto), un nivel bajo de alfabetización y un aumento rápido en la población.
- Muchas naciones en desarrollo no tienen gobiernos que apoyan un sistema sólido que garantice los derechos a la propiedad privada.

## SECCIÓN 2 El proceso de desarrollo económico

- Las tres etapas de desarrollo económico son la etapa agrícola, la etapa de manufactura y la etapa del sector de servicios.
- Un problema fundamental de las naciones en desarrollo es cómo financiar la maquinaria y enseñanza necesarias para mejorar su nivel de vida.
- Las naciones en vías de desarrollo reciben financiamiento por medio de inversiones del exterior y de ayuda del exterior.
- La **ayuda al exterior** puede darse en forma de **asistencia económica, asistencia técnica** y **asistencia militar.**
- Agencias internacionales como el Banco Mundial y el Fondo Monetario Internacional dirigen el dinero a las naciones en desarrollo.
- Los países desarrollados proporcionan ayuda al exterior por razones humanitarias, económicas, políticas y militares.

## SECCIÓN 3 Obstáculos al crecimiento en las naciones en desarrollo

- Cuatro obstáculos impiden el crecimiento económico en las naciones en desarrollo: creencias y actitudes tradicionales, el crecimiento continuo y rápido de la población, el mal uso de los recursos (incluyendo la **fuga de capital al extranjero**) y restricciones comerciales.
- El fracaso económico de Indonesia demuestra algunos de los problemas asociados con el crecimiento económico rápido: la falta de identidad nacional, un gobierno con **burocracias** enormes y extensa corrupción, dependencia en un producto único y la interferencia del gobierno en el comercio.

## SECCIÓN 4 La industrialización y el futuro

- La industrialización rápida presenta cuatro problemas: las malas inversiones, la falta de tiempo para adaptarse a nuevos modos de vida y trabajo, el uso de tecnología inapropiada y la falta de tiempo para atravesar las etapas de desarrollo.
- Los factores que fomentan el crecimiento económico incluyen el comercio con otros países, un sistema apropiado de incentivos (como impuestos relativamente bajos), un sistema político que favorece la libre empresa, recursos naturales y una rebaja en el crecimiento de la población.
- Los países en vías de desarrollo pueden escapar el **círculo vicioso de la pobreza** si sus sistemas políticos permiten que prosperen los empresarios y establecen el derecho a la propiedad privada.

# CAPÍTULO 21 Resumen

## SECCIÓN 1 Causas y resultados de la integración global

- La **integración global** ha aumentado de manera espectacular durante las últimas décadas, principalmente a causa de los avances en las **telecomunicaciones.**
- El aumento en comunicaciones ha fomentado cambios en las costumbres culturales y los hábitos de compras de personas en otros países, que afectan las exportaciones y el idioma.
- El mundo ha formado un solo mercado financiero, en el cual se compran y venden valores gubernamentales, divisas y acciones 24 horas al día.
- El mercado financiero globalizado hace que se sientan alrededor del mundo los efectos de un pánico financiero.

## SECCIÓN 2 La inversión extranjera directa

- Los Estados Unidos tiene una larga historia de inversión extranjera.
- La **inversión extranjera directa** en los Estados Unidos ha aumentado al punto que algunos estadounidenses quieren restringirla.
- Muchas personas están en contra de que extranjeros sean dueños de compañías estadounidenses porque temen el control extranjero de la economía o gobierno de los Estados Unidos.
- Los economistas creen que los extranjeros compran activos en Estados Unidos para maximizar sus ganancias.
- Los inversionistas extranjeros son dueños de un 6 por ciento de las acciones de industrias estadounidenses.
- La participación de los Estados Unidos en la inversión extranjera directa mundial es más del 40 por ciento.

## SECCIÓN 3 Las corporaciones multinacionales y la competencia económica

- Gran parte de las inversiones internacionales las llevan a cabo las **corporaciones multinacionales.**
- A fines de los 1990, había unas 37,000 corporaciones multinacionales con unas 200,000 **sucursales extranjeras.**
- Las 100 corporaciones multinacionales principales tienen el 15 por ciento de los activos productivos del mundo.
- La mayoría de las corporaciones multinacionales invierten en regiones cercanas a la oficina central.
- Las corporaciones multinacionales a menudo forman negocios en participación o por licencia.
- Un resultado de la globalización del mundo es el aumento en la inmigración y la diversidad, lo cual significa que la tolerancia e imparcialidad son más necesarias hoy que nunca.

# CAPÍTULO 22 Resumen

## SECCIÓN 1 El crecimiento del comercio electrónico

- Los números, que también se llaman dígitos, son tan imprescindibles para la vida moderna que nuestra época se ha llamado "la edad digital."
- Los **chips** en una red de computadoras interconectadas están cambiando la manera en que la gente se comunica, produce, consume, aprende y se entretiene.
- Algunos economistas creen que hemos entrado en la edad de la **economía ciberespacial**—una economía impulsada por un enorme aparato digital, **Internet.**
- Los **lugares de Web** conectan a negocios, organizaciones privadas, oficinas gubernamentales e instituciones educacionales y hacen que sea extraordinariamente fácil localizar información y comunicarse con otras partes del mundo. Internet le proporciona a empresas la oportunidad de ponerse en contacto directo con abastecedores y consumidores.
- El **comercio electrónico** se está expandiendo rápidamente, afectando las relaciones entre negocios y con los consumidores.
- En la economía ciberespacial, el consumidor es soberano. Si un vendedor no puede proporcionar un producto superior a un precio competitivo con rapidez, otro vendedor lo hará.
- Los vendedores pueden llevar cuenta de las compras electrónicamente y organizar comunidades ciberespaciales de sus clientes.

## SECCIÓN 2 ¿Una nueva economía?

- La **Edad de la Información** puede llegar a tener efectos tan significantes en la vida humana como la Revolución Industrial.
- La **economía basada en los conocimientos** incluye la tecnología de comunicaciones, la propiedad intelectual y los datos almacenados.
- Algunos economistas creen que nuevos conceptos son necesarios para explicar como la economía basada en los conocimientos se diferencia de conceptos y principios económicos anteriores.
- La mayoría de los economistas consideran que la **innovación** afecta los ciclos de crecimiento económicos.

## SECCIÓN 3 Cuestiones de la economía ciberespacial

- La economía ciberespacial ha planteado varios asuntos importantes. Las decisiones que hoy toman las personas encargadas de formular la política que la gobierna determinará el futuro económico.
- Entre las cuestiones importantes de hoy están garantizar la seguridad del comercio por Internet, asegurar los derechos a la **propiedad intelectual,** proteger la privacidad del consumidor y ayudar a las naciones en vías de desarrollo a tomar parte en la cambiante economía global.
- La tecnología de comunicación da acceso a los conocimientos y a la **educación a distancia,** pero hay que tomar buenas decisiones para crear un futuro económico mejor.

The following abbreviations are used in the index: *crt* = cartoon; *fig* = figure, chart, graph; *m* = map; *p* = photograph; *q* = quote

## A



## B

# INDEX

# INDEX

Graphic elements for unit and chapter openers and People & Perspectives pages, icon images for section openers, figure and summary numbers, Case Studies, Global Economy, Careers, Technology Activity and Skills features, and icons for Critical Thinking, Technology, and Study & Writing Skills: PhotoDisc, Inc.

Type design element for Study & Writing Skills pages: Tony Cordoza/Photonica.

Gear design element for Critical Thinking Skills pages: Allen Wallace/Photonica.

**Cover i** (l)Index Stock Photography, (r)Antonio Rosario/The Image Bank

**vi** Geoff Butler; **vii** (t)KS Studio, (b)Aaron Haupt; **viii** (tl)Russ Einhorn/Liaison Agency, (tc)CORBIS/Bettmann, (bl) Matt Mendelsohn/CORBIS, (bc)Jonathan Kirn/Liaison Agency, (br)Mark Scott/FPG; **ix** Illustration by Guy Crittendon; **x** (l)Doug Martin, (c)CORBIS, (r)Hulton-Getty Picture Collection/Liaison Agency; **xiv through xxiii** Illustration by Guy Crittendon; **xxiv** StudiOhio; **xxviii–1** Firefly Productions/The Stock Market; **2** Geoff Butler; **3** Jose Caruci/AP/Wide World Photos; **4** (t)Ross Harrison Koty/Tony Stone Images, (b)Charlyn Zlotnik/Woodfin Camp & Assoc.; **6** (l)Mark E. Gibson, (r)Jacques Chemet/Woodfin Camp & Assoc.; **7** (l)Adam Lubroth/Tony Stone Images, (r)Aaron Haupt. Location: Terra Cotta, Columbus OH; **10** Aaron Haupt; **10–11** Tim Flach/Tony Stone Images; **12** Aaron Haupt; **13** Mark Burnett; **14** Aaron Haupt; **14–15** Mark Burnett; **16** Aaron Haupt; **17** Paul L. Ruben; **18** Robert Brenner/PhotoEdit; **19** Aaron Haupt; **22** Mark Burnett; **24** Bernard Gotfryd/Woodfin Camp & Assoc.; **28** (l)Paul Souders/Liaison Agency, (r)Geoff Butler; **28–29** Geoff Butler; **29** Aaron Haupt; **30** Geoff Butler; **31** Jerry Alexander/Tony Stone Images; **32** (t)Richard Laird/FPG, (c)James Westwater, (b)Doug Martin; **34–35** A. Ramey/PhotoEdit; **35** (t)David McIntyre/Black Star, (b)Craig J. Brown/Liaison Agency; **40** Geoff Butler; **41** (l)Roger K. Burnard, (r)Mark Richards/PhotoEdit; **42** Mark Steinmetz; **43** Geoff Butler; **45** CORBIS/Bettmann; **46** Mark Burnett; **47** (t)Spencer Grant/Stock Boston, (b)Michael Newman/PhotoEdit; **49** Rob Gage/FPG; **50** (t)Johnny Johnson, (b)John Cancalosi/Stock Boston; **54** Matt Meadows; **55** (t)Geoff Butler; (others) Matt Meadows; **56–57 58** Geoff Butler; **59** Joe McBride/Tony Stone Images; **61** (t)Tom & DeeAnn McCarthy/The Stock Market, (b)Aaron Haupt; **63** Martucci Studio; **64** Aaron Haupt; **66** Skip Comer; **67** (l)Doug Martin, (r)Chris Mooney/FPG; **68** Mark Steinmetz; **71** (t)Daniel A. Erickson, (b)Ken Frick; **72** Mark Burnett; **73** Mark Steinmetz; **74** Martucci Studio; **76** Russ Einhorn/Liaison Agency; **80** (l)Pam Francis/Liaison Agency, (r)Mark Steinmetz; **80–81** Diamond; **81** Mark Steinmetz; **82** Geoff Butler; **83** Jessica Wecker/Photo Researchers; **85** (t)David Frazier, (b)Paul Markow/FPG; **86** Bob Daemmrich/Stock Boston; **87 88** Doug Martin; **89** (t)Toby Talbot/AP/Wide World Photos, (others)Mark Burnett; **91** (t)Willie L. Hill, Jr./Stock Boston; (b)Geoff Butler; **93 96 96–97** Doug Martin; **97** (tr)Aaron Haupt, (c)Jeff Greenberg/PhotoEdit, (br)Gianni Dagli Orti/CORBIS; **98** Geoff Butler; **100** (l)Doug Martin, (tr)Geoff Butler, (br)Ron Chapple/FPG; **103** Doug Martin; **104** Arthur Tilley/FPG; **106** J. Chiasson/Liaison Agency; **109** Geoff Butler; **110** (t)Tina Frissora, (c)StudiOhio, (b)Aaron Haupt; **111** Skip Comer; **112** Doug Martin; **113** Martucci Studio; **114 115** Doug Martin; **116** Courtesy Maytag Corporation; **117** Geoff Butler; **118** (tl)Peter M. Fisher/The Stock Market, (bl)Stewart Cohen/Tony Stone Images, (r)Tom & Deeann McCarthy/The Stock Market; **119** (t)Doug Martin, (b)Jeff Greenberg/Stock Boston; **120 121** Doug Martin; **122** (t)Joseph DiChello, (bl)Aaron Haupt, (br)Tim Courlas; **124** KS Studio; **125** Aaron Haupt; **126** KS Studios; **129** Michael Rosenfeld/Tony Stone Images; **130** (t)Volkswagen of America, (b)courtesy Chrysler Corporation; **131 132** KS Studio; **134** (l)Kazuaki Iwasaki/The Stock Market, (r)Myrleen Ferguson/PhotoEdit; **138** Robert Frerck/Tony Stone Images; **138–139** Tim Flach/Tony Stone Images; **139** Liaison Agency; **140** Llewellyn/Uniphoto; **141** Mark Steinmetz; **142** (t)Aaron Haupt, (b)Doug Martin; **143 144** KS Studio; **146** Aaron Haupt; **147** Mark Steinmetz; **148** Geoff Butler; **149** Aaron Haupt; **150** VCG/FPG; **150–151** Geoff Butler; **154** Courtesy Aerial Capital Management, Inc.; **155** Geoff Butler; **157** Eunice Harris/Photo Researchers; **158** Peter Christopher/Masterfile; **159** Martucci Studio; **160** (l)KS Studio, (r)David Young-Wolff/PhotoEdit; **164** (t)KS Studio, (b)Doug Martin; **165** Chuck Keeler/Tony Stone Images; **166–167** Geoff Butler; **168** Ken Reid/FPG; **169** Aaron Haupt; **170** Geoff Butler; **170–171** (t)Geoff Butler, (b)Mark Burnett; **171** (l)Aaron Haupt, (r)Geoff Butler; **173** Aaron Haupt; **174** (t)Bruce Kluckhohn/Liaison Agency, (b)Doug Martin; **176** (l)Aaron Haupt, (tr)Geoff Butler, (br)William Mercer McLeod; **177** Gerard Photography; **181** Mark Steinmetz; **182** Eric Pearle/FPG; **183** (t)Aaron Haupt, (c)Glencoe photo, (b)Mark Burnett; **184** (l)Geoff Butler, (r)Aaron Haupt; **186 186–187** Aaron Haupt; **188–189** KS Studio; **191** (tl, br)Geoff Butler; (tr)Matt Meadows, (bl)Doug Martin; **192** Courtesy Ford Motor Company; **194** Matt Meadows; **196–197** Aaron Haupt; **197** (l)Steven Frame/Stock Boston, (r)Picture Research Consultants; **199** Rat-Rossi/Liaison Agency; **200** Stock Montage; **204** Jim Olive/Uniphoto; **204–205** Tim Flach/Tony Stone Images; **206** Geoff Butler; **207** Susan Van Etten/PhotoEdit; **208** Geoff Butler; **210** (l)Martucci Studios, (tr)Geoff Butler, (others)Mark Burnett; **212** Geoff Butler; **213** Doug Martin; **214 216** Mark Burnett; **218** Jonathan Kirn/Liaison Agency; **219** Uli Degwert/International Stock Photography; **222** Mark Burnett; **225** Mitch Kezar/Tony Stone Images; **226** (t, c)Geoff Butler; (b)Burger King Corporation; **230** Tim Courlas; **231** (tl)courtesy Denny C. Jackson and students, (others)Geoff Butler; **232** Joe Towers/The Stock Market; **233** Don Spiro/Tony Stone Images; **234–235** Roger Ball/The Stock Market; **235** Mark Steinmetz; **236** (t)Aaron Haupt, (b)Hans Wolf/The Image Bank; **237** (t)Steve Proehl/The Image Bank, (b)James Carmichael/The Image Bank; **239** Geoff Butler; **240** M.L. Sinabaldi/The Stock Market; **241** (t)John Olson/The Stock Market, (b)Richard Burda/FPG; **242** (tl)Phil McCarten/PhotoEdit, (tr)Geoff Butler, (bl)Baron Wolman/Tony Stone Images, (br)Tom Bean/The Stock Market; **246** (l)Doug Martin, (r)Geoff Butler; **247** Mario Andretti Petroleum LP; **248** CORBIS/Bettmann; **250** Aaron Haupt;

# ACKNOWLEDGMENTS

**252** (t)file photo, (bl, r) Geoff Butler; **254** Mitchell Gerber/CORBIS; **258** John Chiasson/Liaison Agency; **258–259** Bob Daemmrich/ Stock Boston; **259** Doug Martin; **260–261 262** Geoff Butler; **263** (currency)Peter Gridley/FPG, (computer) Mark Burnett; **266** Robert Brenner/PhotoEdit; **267** (t)PhotoDisc, Inc., (b)Susan Van Etten; **270** Doug Martin; **271 272 273** KS Studio; **275** Mark Scott/FPG; **276** Terry Ashe/Liaison Agency; **277** Ray Soto/The Stock Market; **278 278–279** Geoff Butler; **279** (t)Schneps/The Image Bank, (b)Aaron Haupt; **280** Tony Page/Tony Stone Images; **282** (l)KS Studio, (r)Cindy Charles/PhotoEdit; **286** Paul Stuart: Eye Ubiquitous/CORBIS; **286–287** Tim Flach/Tony Stone Images; **288** Geoff Butler; **290** (l)Doug Martin, (r)CORBIS/Bettmann; **291** (l)Gaslight Advertising Archives, (c)Hulton-Getty Picture Library/Liaison Agency, (r)Geoff Butler; **292** Bob Daemmrich/Tony Stone Images; **293** Spencer Grant/ PhotoEdit; **295** (t)Brian Bailey/Tony Stone Images, (bl, r)Aaron Haupt; **296** Doug Martin; **297** (c)Geoff Butler, (others)KS Studio; **301** James D. Wilson/Liaison Agency; **302** Aaron Haupt; **304** (background)Tony Freeman/PhotoEdit, (foreground)Mark E. Gibson; **306 310** Aaron Haupt, **311** (t)Geoff Butler, (b)Doug Martin; **312 313** Geoff Butler; **315** (tl)Doug Martin, (bl)Llewellyn/Uniphoto, (r)Jeff Bates Photography; **316** Lawrence Migdale/Stock Boston; **318** (l)Ted Horowitz/ The Stock Market, (r)Richard Drew/AP/Wide World Photos; **320** (t)Geoff Butler, (b)Mark Richards/PhotoEdit; **321** CORBIS; **323** CORBIS/ Bettmann; **325** Reuters/ CORBIS; **327** CORBIS; **328** Skip Comer; **330** (t)Geoff Butler, (b)Steve Skjold/PhotoEdit; **331** (l)H. Armstrong Roberts, (r)Viviane Moos/The Stock Market; **334** file photo; **338** (t)KS Studios, (b)James D. Wilson/Liaison Agency; **339** KS Studios; **340–341** Comstock; **342 343** Geoff Butler; **345** Aaron Haupt; **346** Geoff Butler; **346–347** (l)Mark Steinmetz, (r)Fotosmith; **350** Telegraph Colour Library/FPG; **351** Swarthout & Assoc./The Stock Market; **353** Martucci Studio; **355** (l)Aaron Haupt, (r)Geoff Butler; **356** FBM Photography/CORBIS; **358** Rob Lewine/The Stock Market; **360** Aaron Haupt; **363** (l)National Archives, (c)Hulton-Getty Picture Library/Liaison Agency, (r)FPG; **364** NASA/Mark Marten/Photo Researchers; **365** Reuters/CORBIS; **366** Geoff Butler; **368** Mark Reinstein/Uniphoto; **372** file photo; **373** (t)Aaron Haupt, (b)Geoff Butler; **374** Stephen Grohe/The Stock Market; **375** Bridgeman Art Library, London/New York; **376** Martucci Studio; **377 378** Geoff Butler; **382** Library of Congress; **382–383** Martucci Studio; **386** (l)Aaron Haupt, (r)Geoff Butler; **387** (l)Liaison Agency; (r)Pat Vasquez-Cunningham/Wide World Photos; **391** Aaron Haupt; **392** Bert Van Den Broucke/PNS/Liaison Agency; **396–397** Tim Flach/Tony Stone Images; **397** (tl, bl)By courtesy of The Trustees of The British Museum, (tr)Bridgeman Art Library, London, New York, (br)Chris Hellier/CORBIS; **398** Skip Comer; **399** Geoff Butler; **402** Bob Daemmrich; **404** Martucci Studio; **409** Geoff Butler; **411** (l)Peter Beck/Uniphoto, (r)Dennis Brack/Black Star; **418** Matt Mendelsohn/CORBIS; **422** Geoff Butler; **423** Aaron Haupt; **424** (t)Rob Crandall/ Stock Boston, (b)Aaron Haupt; **425** (l)Aaron Haupt, (c)Craig Aurness/CORBIS, (r)David Frazier; **428** Hulton-Getty Picture Library/Liaison Agency; **429** Geoff Butler; **430** (l)Paul Conklin/ PhotoEdit, (r)Phyllis Picardi/Stock Boston; **434** (l)Peter L. Chapman/Stock Boston, (tr)Ron Chapple/ FPG, (br)Aaron Haupt; **435** Geoff Butler; **440** Painting by Don Troiani, photo courtesy Historic Art Prints, Ltd.; **441** Martucci Studio; **448** Bassignac/Stevens/Liaison Agency; **448–449** Aaron Haupt; **449** Judy Gelles/ Stock Boston; **450** Ed Elberfeld/Uniphoto; **451** Aaron Haupt; **453** Geoff Butler; **456** (l)Aaron Haupt, (tr)Mark Joseph/Tony Stone Images, (br)Jon Feingersh/ The Stock Market; **457** Geoff Butler; **460** (l)CORBIS, (r)Hulton-Getty Picture Library/Liaison Agency; **462** Geoff Butler; **466** Rose/ Liaison Agency; **470–471** Geoff Butler; **472** Uniphoto; **473** Geoff Butler; **474** (t)Geoff Butler, (b)Chad Slattery/Tony Stone Images; **476** Mark Burnett; **477** (t)Mark Burnett, (b)Gilmore J. Dufresne/Uniphoto; **478** Mark Burnett, **479** Llewellyn/ Uniphoto; **480** Mark Harwood/Tony Stone Images; **485** Charles Steiner/Corbis Sygma; **486** Photomorgana/ The Stock Market; **488** Kent Knudson/Uniphoto; **490** (l)Zigy Kaluzny/Tony Stone Images, (tr)Glencoe photo, (br)Viviane Moos/The Stock Market; **494** Andreas Rudolf/Tony Stone Images; **494–495** Tim Flach/Tony Stone Images; **496** Geoff Butler; **497** Peter Turnley/ CORBIS; **498** Geoff Butler; **499** Detail of a painting of Lenin during the October Revolution by Vassilji Chvostenko. Erich Lessing/ Art Resource; **502** CORBIS/ Archivo Iconografico, SA; **503** Nik Wheeler/CORBIS; **504** Tom Nebbia/CORBIS; **505** Forrest Anderson/Liaison Agency; **507** (l)Forrest Anderson/Liaison Agency, (r)Paul Lau/Liaison Agency; **508** Alexis Duclos/Liaison Agency; **509** Steven Weinberg/Tony Stone Images; **510** (t)PhotoLink/ PhotoDisc, Inc., (b)Dave Bartruff/CORBIS; **516** Geoff Butler; **517** Mark Steinmetz; **518** (l)Robert Frerck/ Woodfin Camp & Assoc., (r)Thomas Mayer/Black Star; **522** Hulton-Getty Picture Library/Liaison Agency; **523** Jeffrey Markowitz/Corbis Sygma; **524** Paul Conklin/ PhotoEdit; **525** Ray Cranbourne/Black Star; **528** Mark Peters/Liaison Agency; **529** Piero Guerrini/Liaison Agency; **531** (t)Tom McHugh/ Photo Researchers, (bl) Archive Photos, (br)CORBIS/ AFP; **533** (l)Peter Turnley/ Black Star, (r)Andres Hernandez/Liaison Agency; **534** Per-Anders Pettersson/ Black Star; **535** David Kampfer/Liaison Agency; **536** (t)Mike Yamashita/ Woodfin Camp & Assoc., (c)Mike Wilbur/Black Star, (b)Eric Lara Bakke/Black Star; **542** Phil Banko/Tony Stone Images; **543** Geoff Butler; **545** Richard Bickel/ CORBIS; **547** Chiaki Tsukumo/AP/Wide World Photos; **548** Michael S. Yamashita/CORBIS **551 553** Geoff Butler; **555** Martucci Studio; **556** Robert Holmes/ CORBIS; **558** Jeffrey Markowitz/Corbis Sygma; **562** (l)Geoff Butler, (r)Roger Ball/The Stock Market; **563** Geoff Butler; **564** Salem Krieger/The Image Bank; **565** Geoff Butler; **566** John Madere/The Stock Market; **570** (t)Aaron Haupt, (b) Chuck Savage/The Stock Market; **571** Geoff Butler; **573** Firefly Productions/The Stock Market; **579** (l)Charles Gupton/The Stock Market; **579** (r)Michael Newman/ PhotoEdit; **580** Eric Robert/ Corbis Sygma; **584** Frank Trapper/Corbis Sygma; **585** (t)Patrick Aventurier/Liaison Agency, (b)Stan Godlewski/ Liaison Agency.